TEXAS EDITION

# SOUTH-WESTERN CENTURY 21 ACCOUNTING

## MULTICOLUMN JOURNAL

**Kenton E. Ross, CPA**
Professor Emeritus of Accounting
Texas A&M University–Commerce
Commerce, Texas

**Mark W. Lehman, CPA**
Associate Professor
School of Accountancy
Mississippi State University
Starkville, Mississippi

**Claudia Bienias Gilbertson, CPA**
Teaching Professor
North Hennepin Community College
Brooklyn Park, Minnesota

**Robert D. Hanson**
Late Associate Dean
College of Business Administration
Central Michigan University
Mount Pleasant, Michigan

With Peachtree®

CENTURY 21 ACCOUNTING
100 YEARS OF EXCELLENCE

THOMSON
SOUTH-WESTERN

Australia · Canada · Mexico · Singapore · Spain · United Kingdom · United States

THOMSON
SOUTH-WESTERN

**Century 21 Accounting, Multicolumn Journal, Texas Edition**
by Kenton E. Ross, Claudia Bienias Gilbertson, Mark W. Lehman, and Robert D. Hanson

**Vice President/ Executive Publisher**
Dave Shaut
**Team Leader**
Karen Schmohe
**Acquisitions Editor**
Marilyn Hornsby
**Project Manager**
Carol Sturzenberger
**Sr. Marketing Manager**
Nancy A. Long
**Marketing Coordinator**
Yvonne Patton-Beard
**Production Manager**
Patricia Matthews Boies
**Manufacturing Coordinator**
Kevin Kluck
**Production Editor**
Todd McCoy
**Design Coordinator**
Tippy McIntosh
**Cycle Opener Artwork**
Marti Shohet
**Cover Design**
Tom Nikosey
**Composition/Prepress**
Better Graphics
**Printer**
Courier Kendallville



ISBN: 0-538-43731-6
**Printed in the United States of America**

**2 3 4 5 6 7 D 07 06 05 04**



For more information, contact South-Western, 5191 Natorp Boulevard, Mason, OH 45040; or find us on the World Wide Web at http://www.swep.com

*About the Authors*
**Kenton E. Ross,** Ed.D., C.P.A., is Professor Emeritus, Department of Accounting, at Texas A&M University—Commerce. He formerly served as Dean of the College of Business and Technology; Director of Business and Economic Research; and Head, Department of Accounting.

**Claudia Bienias Gilbertson,** M.B.A., C.P.A., is an experienced high school and community college instructor. She is currently a teaching professor at North Hennepin Community College.

**Mark W. Lehman,** Ph.D., C.P.A., is an Associate Professor in the School of Accountancy at Mississippi State University, where he teaches in the areas of microcomputers, accounting systems, and auditing. He regularly teaches continuing education classes on microcomputers and internal control.

The late **Robert D. Hanson**, Ph.D., was Professor of Business Education and Associate Dean of the College of Business Administration at Central Michigan University.

# REVIEWERS

**Bruce J. (Ike) Bergeron**
Business Instructor, Southeastern Vermont Career Education Center
Brattleboro Union High School
Brattleboro, Vermont

**Judith K. Berry**
Business Services and Technology Consultant
Michigan Department of Education
East Lansing, Michigan

**Margaret Chester**
Instructor, Business Technology Department
Biloxi High School
Biloxi, Mississippi

**Debbie Davidson**
Accounting Instructor, Business Department
Ben Davis High School
Indianapolis, Indiana

**Maurice Ellington**
Chairperson, Business Education Department
John Marshall Metropolitan High School
Chicago, Illinois

**Mary A. Gonzalez**
Business Education Instructor
Weslaco High School
Weslaco, Texas

**Cynthia A. Greene**
Chairperson, Career Technology Department
Centennial High School
Fulton County Schools
Roswell, Georgia

**James L. Knutson**
Finance Director
City of Anoka
Anoka, Minnesota

**Mary A. Lively**
Business Technology Instructor
Great Oaks Institute of Technology and Career Development
Cincinnati, Ohio

**Maria Medina-Perez**
Chairperson, Business Technology Education
Miami Palmetto Senior High School
Miami, Florida

**Kelvin Meeks**
Teacher, Business and Technology Department
Raleigh-Egypt High School
Memphis, Tennessee

**Lisa Olson**
Chairperson, Business Education Department
Hartford Union High School
Hartford, Wisconsin

**Ronald Romano**
Chairperson, Business Education Department
Ogdensburg Free Academy
Ogdensburg, New York

**Judith P. Sams**
Chairperson, Business Department
Fuqua School
Farmville, Virginia

**Patricia Samuels**
Director, Academy of Finance
Withrow High School
Cincinnati, Ohio

**William Sinai**
Chairperson, Computerized Accounting
West Valley Occupational Center
Woodland, California

**LInda L. White**
Chairperson, Business Education Department
Accounting Teacher
Waynesboro Area Senior High School
Waynesboro, Pennsylvania

**Vera M. White**
Chairperson, Vocational Technology
Hallandale High School
Hallandale, Florida

# SOUTH-WESTERN CENTURY 21 ACCOUNTING

## TEXAS EDITION


Family of Products .................................. v
Table of Contents .................................. vi
Instructional Strategies .................................. xii
Features .................................. xiv
Careers in Accounting .................................. xv

**CYCLE 1** **Accounting for a Service Business Organized as a Proprietorship** ............ **2**

**CYCLE 2** **Accounting for a Merchandising Business Organized as a Partnership** ..... **224**

**CYCLE 3** **Accounting for a Merchandising Business Organized as a Corporation** ..... **450**

Appendix A ............ A-1
Appendix B ............ B-1
Appendix C ............ C-1
Appendix D ............ D-1
Glossary ............ G-1
Index ............ I-1
Photo Credits ....... P-1


CENTURY 21 ACCOUNTING
100 YEARS OF EXCELLENCE

## CENTURY 21 ACCOUNTING

# FAMILY OF PRODUCTS

**South-Western Educational Publishing provides everything you and your students need to have a successful accounting classroom.**

***Wraparound Teacher's Edition*** provides

✷ **OVERVIEW** of each accounting cycle and each chapter within a cycle.

✷ **TEACHING STRATEGIES** loaded with hints, tips, and suggestions for reaching students with different learning styles—plus, a variety of instructional methods, such as cooperative learning, different media options, and more.

✷ **CHAPTER INTERLEAF CHARTS** that present concepts and skills covered in a chapter. Instructors can determine what will be new for students and what concepts and skills need reinforcement and emphasis. Also included is information about special features, technology and media, teaching strategies, and practice and assessment.

✷ **EFFECTIVE TEACHING MODEL LESSON PLANS** that provide step-by-step instructional support for every lesson. Each Lesson Plan includes the headings Motivate, Explain, Demonstrate, Guided Practice, Independent Practice, Reteach, Enrich, and Close.

✷ **CHECK FIGURES** that can be provided to students as guideposts as students complete their work or that can be used by instructors for quick and easy grading.

***Working Papers*** contain accounting forms and rulings for completing chapter problems and Reinforcement Activities. The *Working Papers* are carefully laid out so that forms for the next problem are available while the previous problem is being graded. Plenty of extra forms are provided for any necessary rework. The Teacher's Editions of the *Working Papers* provide solutions to the problems. A separate *Study Guide and Recycling Problem Working Papers* book is also available.

### *Transparency Packages*

An extensive array of **transparency packages** includes full-color teaching transparencies, blank accounting rulings to be used for guided practice and demonstrations, and transparencies of the solutions in the Teacher's Edition of the *Working Papers*.

### *Simulations*

A **new simulation** is available for each accounting cycle in both manual and automated versions.

- ❑ *FOREIGN EXCHANGE TRANSLATION SERVICE* is a language translation service business organized as a sole proprietorship.
- ❑ *FITNESS JUNCTION* is an exercise equipment merchandising business organized as a partnership.
- ❑ *PUTTING GREEN GOLF SUPPLY* is a golf equipment and supply merchandising business organized as a corporation.

### *Technology*

✷ **TEMPLATE DISKS** are available for use with *Automated Accounting Windows* and *Automated Accounting Macintosh.* Template files are available for many problems in the textbook, the comprehensive Reinforcement Activities in each cycle, plus the three simulations. *Electronic Auditors* are also available.

✷ **SPREADSHEET TEMPLATE DISKS** correspond to selected textbook problems.

Various end-of-chapter problems in the textbook, marked with a Peachtree sumbol, can be worked with *South-Western Accounting with Peachtree.*

***Assessment Binder Package*** Includes two separate versions of printed chapter and cycle tests, containing both objective questions and problems and a computerized testing program.

***Other items available include***

- ❑ **English and Spanish Dictionary**
- ❑ **Teacher's Resource Guide** in three-ring binder
- ❑ **Videotapes**
- ❑ **Multimedia CD-ROM**

# CYCLE 1 ACCOUNTING FOR A SERVICE BUSINESS ORGANIZED AS A PROPRIETORSHIP


## CHAPTER 1

**STARTING A PROPRIETORSHIP** 4

ACCOUNTING IN YOUR CAREER 5

*1-1* The Accounting Equation 6

*1-2* How Business Activities Change the Accounting Equation 9

*1-3* Reporting Financial Information on a Balance Sheet 13

*PROFESSIONAL BUSINESS ETHICS* 7

*CULTURAL DIVERSITY* 13

AUTOMATED ACCOUNTING 22

## CHAPTER 2

**STARTING A PROPRIETORSHIP: CHANGES THAT AFFECT OWNER'S EQUITY** 24

ACCOUNTING IN YOUR CAREER 25

*2-1* How Transactions Change Owner's Equity in an Accounting Equation 26

*2-2* Reporting a Changed Accounting Equation on a Balance Sheet 30

*CULTURAL DIVERSITY* 27

AUTOMATED ACCOUNTING 38

## CHAPTER 3

**ANALYZING TRANSACTIONS INTO DEBIT AND CREDIT PARTS** 40

ACCOUNTING IN YOUR CAREER 41

*3-1* Using T Accounts 42

*3-2* Analyzing How Transactions Affect Accounts 45

*3-3* Analyzing How Transactions Affect Owner's Equity Accounts 51

*TECHNOLOGY FOR BUSINESS* 43

*CULTURAL DIVERSITY* 54

AUTOMATED ACCOUNTING 63

## CHAPTER 4

**JOURNALIZING TRANSACTIONS** 64

ACCOUNTING IN YOUR CAREER 65

*4-1* Journals, Source Documents, and Recording Entries in a Journal 66

*4-2* Journalizing Buying Insurance, Buying on Account, and Paying on Account 72

*4-3* Journalizing Transactions That Affect Owner's Equity and Receiving Cash on Account 76

*4-4* Proving and Ruling a Journal 82

*ACCOUNTING AT WORK* 74

*LEGAL ISSUES IN ACCOUNTING* 80

*GLOBAL PERSPECTIVE* 82

*SMALL BUSINESS SPOTLIGHT* 83

AUTOMATED ACCOUNTING 94

## CHAPTER 5

**POSTING TO A GENERAL LEDGER** 96

ACCOUNTING IN YOUR CAREER 97

*5-1* Preparing a Chart of Accounts 98

*5-2* Posting Separate Amounts from a Journal to a General Ledger 103

*5-3* Posting Column Totals from a Journal to a General Ledger 107

*5-4* Completed Accounting Forms and Making Correcting Entries 112

*PROFESSIONAL BUSINESS ETHICS* 101

*CULTURAL DIVERSITY* 105

AUTOMATED ACCOUNTING 122

## CHAPTER 6

**CASH CONTROL SYSTEMS** 124

ACCOUNTING IN YOUR CAREER 125

*6-1* Checking Accounts 126

*6-2* Bank Reconciliation 131

*6-3* Dishonored Checks and Electronic Banking 136

*6-4* Petty Cash 141

*SMALL BUSINESS SPOTLIGHT* 134

*TECHNOLOGY FOR BUSINESS* 142

AUTOMATED ACCOUNTING 149

# Contents


## CHAPTER 7

**WORK SHEET FOR A SERVICE BUSINESS** 154

ACCOUNTING IN YOUR CAREER 155

*7-1* Creating a Work Sheet 156

*7-2* Planning Adjusting Entries on a Work Sheet 160

*7-3* Extending Financial Statement Information on a Work Sheet 165

*7-4* Finding and Correcting Errors on the Work Sheet 170

*GLOBAL PERSPECTIVE* 163

*ACCOUNTING AT WORK* 168

AUTOMATED ACCOUNTING 179

## CHAPTER 8

**FINANCIAL STATEMENTS FOR A PROPRIETORSHIP** 180

ACCOUNTING IN YOUR CAREER 181

*8-1* Preparing an Income Statement 182

*8-2* Balance Sheet Information on a Work Sheet 187

*CULTURAL DIVERSITY* 188

AUTOMATED ACCOUNTING 196

## CHAPTER 9

**RECORDING ADJUSTING AND CLOSING ENTRIES FOR A SERVICE BUSINESS** 198

ACCOUNTING IN YOUR CAREER 199

*9-1* Recording Adjusting Entries 200

*9-2* Recording Closing Entries 203

*9-3* Preparing a Post-Closing Trial Balance 210

*PROFESSIONAL BUSINESS ETHICS* 201

AUTOMATED ACCOUNTING 221

## FEATURES IN EVERY CHAPTER

***Explore Accounting***
16, 32, 57, 88, 118, 145, 174, 192, 216

***Internet Activity***
21, 37, 62, 93, 121, 148, 178, 195, 220

***Applied Communication***
21, 37, 62, 93, 121, 148, 178, 195, 220

***Cases for Critical Thinking***
21, 37, 62, 93, 121, 148, 178, 195, 220

## LESSON REVIEW AND PRACTICE

***Terms Review***
8, 12, 15, 29, 44, 50, 71, 87, 102, 106, 117, 130, 135, 140, 144, 158, 164, 169, 186, 202, 209, 215

***Audit Your Understanding***
8, 12, 15, 29, 31, 44, 50, 56, 71, 75, 81, 87, 102, 106, 111, 117, 130, 135, 140, 144, 158, 164, 169, 173, 186, 191, 202, 209, 215

***Work Together***
8, 12, 15, 29, 31, 44, 50, 56, 71, 75, 81, 87, 102, 106, 111, 117, 130, 135, 140, 144, 158, 164, 169, 173, 186, 191, 202, 209, 215

***On Your Own***
8, 12, 15, 29, 31, 44, 50, 56, 71, 75, 81, 87, 102, 106, 111, 117, 130, 135, 140, 144, 159, 164, 169, 173, 186, 191, 202, 209, 215

## CHAPTER REVIEW AND PRACTICE

***Chapter Summary***
16, 32, 57, 88, 118, 145, 174, 192, 216

***Application Problems***
17, 33, 58, 89, 119, 146, 175, 193, 217

***Mastery Problem***
19, 35, 60, 91, 120, 147, 176, 194, 218

***Challenge Problem***
20, 36, 61, 92, 120, 148, 177, 194, 219

## CYCLE REVIEW AND PRACTICE

***Reinforcement Activities***
151, 222

# CYCLE 2 Accounting for a Merchandising Business Organized as a Partnership


## CHAPTER 10

**JOURNALIZING PURCHASES AND CASH PAYMENTS** 226

Accounting in Your Career 227

*10-1* Journalizing Purchases of Merchandise for Cash 228

*10-2* Journalizing Puchases of Merchandise on Account and Buying Supplies 233

*10-3* Journalizing Cash Payments and Other Transactions 238

*Accounting at Work* 230

*Small Business Spotlight* 239

*Global Perspective* 242

AUTOMATED ACCOUNTING 249

## CHAPTER 11

**JOURNALIZING SALES AND CASH RECEIPTS** 252

Accounting in Your Career 253

*11-1* Journalizing Sales and Cash Receipts from Sales 254

*11-2* Proving and Ruling an Expanded Journal 260

*Legal Issues in Accounting* 254

*Professional Business Ethics* 263

AUTOMATED ACCOUNTING 272

## CHAPTER 12

**POSTING TO GENERAL AND SUBSIDIARY LEDGERS** 274

Accounting in Your Career 275

*12-1* Posting to a General Ledger 276

*12-2* Posting to an Accounts Payable Ledger 280

*12-3* Posting to an Accounts Receivable Ledger 286

*12-4* Accuracy of Accounting Records 292

*Global Perspective* 281

*Small Business Spotlight* 286

*Technology for Business* 293

AUTOMATED ACCOUNTING 301

## CHAPTER 13

**PREPARING PAYROLL RECORDS** 302

Accounting in Your Career 303

*13-1* Preparing Payroll Time Cards 304

*13-2* Determining Payroll Tax Withholding 308

*13-3* Preparing Payroll Records 314

*13-4* Preparing Payroll Checks 319

*Legal Issues in Accounting* 308

AUTOMATED ACCOUNTING 328

## CHAPTER 14

**PAYROLL ACCOUNTING, TAXES, AND REPORTS** 330

Accounting in Your Career 331

*14-1* Recording a Payroll 332

*14-2* Recording Employer Payroll Taxes 336

*14-3* Reporting Withholding and Payroll Taxes 341

*14-4* Paying Withholding and Payroll Taxes 346

*Technology for Business* 332

*Global Perspective* 344

AUTOMATED ACCOUNTING 358

## CHAPTER 15

**WORK SHEET FOR A MERCHANDISING BUSINESS** 364

Accounting in Your Career 365

*15-1* Beginning an 8-Column Work Sheet for a Merchandising Business 366

*15-2* Analyzing and Recording Work Sheet Adjustments 373

*15-3* Completing Work Sheets 378

*Legal Issues in Accounting* 364

*Accounting at Work* 376

AUTOMATED ACCOUNTING 389

# Contents


## CHAPTER 16

**FINANCIAL STATEMENTS FOR A PARTNERSHIP** 390
**ACCOUNTING IN YOUR CAREER** 391
*16-1* Income Statement 392
*16-2* Component Percentages 397
*16-3* Distribution of Net Income and Owners' Equity Statements 402
*16-4* Balance Sheet 408
***CULTURAL DIVERSITY*** 403
***PROFESSIONAL BUSINESS ETHICS*** 411
**AUTOMATED ACCOUNTING** 418

## CHAPTER 17

**RECORDING ADJUSTING AND CLOSING ENTRIES FOR A PARTNERSHIP** 420
**ACCOUNTING IN YOUR CAREER** 421
*17-1* Recording Adjusting Entries 422
*17-2* Recording Closing Entries for Income Statement Accounts 426
*17-3* Recording Additional Closing Entries 431
*17-4* Preparing a Post-Closing Trial Balance 435
***GLOBAL PERSPECTIVE*** 420
***SMALL BUSINESS SPOTLIGHT*** 424
**AUTOMATED ACCOUNTING** 447

## FEATURES IN EVERY CHAPTER

***Explore Accounting***
244, 267, 295, 322, 352, 385, 413, 440
***Internet Activity***
248, 271, 299, 327, 357, 388, 417, 446
***Applied Communication***
248, 271, 299, 327, 357, 388, 417, 446
***Cases for Critical Thinking***
248, 271, 300, 327, 357, 388, 417, 446

## LESSON REVIEW AND PRACTICE

***Terms Review***
232, 237, 259, 279, 294, 307, 313, 318, 340, 371, 396, 407, 412
***Audit Your Understanding***
232, 237, 243, 259, 266, 279, 285, 291, 294, 307, 313, 318, 321, 335, 340, 345, 351, 371, 377, 384, 396, 401, 407, 412, 425, 430, 434, 439
***Work Together***
232, 237, 243, 259, 266, 279, 285, 291, 294, 307, 313, 318, 321, 335, 340, 345, 351, 371, 377, 384, 396, 401, 407, 412, 425, 430, 434, 439
***On Your Own***
232, 237, 243, 259, 266, 279, 285, 291, 294, 307, 313, 318, 321, 335, 340, 345, 351, 372, 377, 384, 396, 401, 407, 412, 425, 430, 434, 439

## CHAPTER REVIEW AND PRACTICE

***Chapter Summary***
244, 267, 295, 322, 352, 385, 413, 440
***Application Problems***
245, 268, 296, 323, 353, 386, 387, 414, 441
***Mastery Problem***
246, 269, 298, 325, 354, 387, 416, 444
***Challenge Problem***
247, 270, 298, 326, 355, 388, 417, 445

## CYCLE REVIEW AND PRACTICE

***Reinforcement Activities***
360, 448

# CYCLE 3 Accounting for a Merchandising Business Organized as a Corporation


## CHAPTER 18

**RECORDING PURCHASES AND CASH PAYMENTS USING SPECIAL JOURNALS** 452

*Accounting in Your Career* 453

**18-1** Recording Purchases on Account Using a Purchases Journal 454

**18-2** Recording Expenses and Purchases Using a Cash Payments Journal 460

**18-3** Journalizing Petty Cash and Posting Using a Cash Payments Journal 465

**18-4** Recording Transactions Using a General Journal 470

*Accounting at Work* 463

*Legal Issues in Accounting* 470

AUTOMATED ACCOUNTING 483

## CHAPTER 19

**RECORDING SALES AND CASH RECEIPTS USING SPECIAL JOURNALS** 486

*Accounting in Your Career* 487

**19-1** Recording Sales on Account Using a Sales Journal 488

**19-2** Recording Cash Receipts Using a Cash Receipts Journal 493

**19-3** Recording Transactions Using a General Journal 499

**19-4** Recording International Sales 504

*Professional Business Ethics* 490

*Technology for Business* 502

AUTOMATED ACCOUNTING 518

## CHAPTER 20

**ACCOUNTING FOR UNCOLLECTIBLE ACCOUNTS RECEIVABLE** 524

*Accounting in Your Career* 525

**20-1** Estimating and Recording Uncollectible Accounts Expense 526

**20-2** Writing Off and Collecting Uncollectible Accounts Receivable 531

*Accounting at Work* 527

*Legal Issues in Accounting* 534

AUTOMATED ACCOUNTING 542

## CHAPTER 21

**ACCOUNTING FOR PLANT ASSETS AND DEPRECIATION** 544

*Accounting in Your Career* 545

**21-1** Buying Plant Assets and Paying Property Tax 546

**21-2** Calculating Depreciation Expense 549

**21-3** Journalizing Depreciation Expense 553

**21-4** Disposing of Plant Assets 557

**21-5** Declining-Balance Method of Depreciation 562

*Cultural Diversity* 551

*Legal Issues in Accounting* 564

AUTOMATED ACCOUNTING 571

## CHAPTER 22

**ACCOUNTING FOR INVENTORY** 572

*Accounting in Your Career* 573

**22-1** Determining the Quantity of Merchandise Inventory 574

**22-2** Determining the Cost of Merchandise Inventory 578

**22-3** Estimating Inventory 583

*Small Business Spotlight* 572

*Technology for Business* 584

AUTOMATED ACCOUNTING 590

## CHAPTER 23

**ACCOUNTING FOR NOTES AND INTEREST** 592

*Accounting in Your Career* 593

**23-1** Promissory Notes 594

**23-2** Notes Payable 598

**23-3** Notes Receivable 603

*Accounting at Work* 601

AUTOMATED ACCOUNTING 612

# Contents


## CHAPTER 24

**ACCOUNTING FOR ACCRUED REVENUE AND EXPENSES** 614

ACCOUNTING IN YOUR CAREER 615
**24-1** Accrued Revenue 616
**24-2** Accrued Expenses 621
*ACCOUNTING AT WORK* 625

AUTOMATED ACCOUNTING 632

## CHAPTER 25

**DISTRIBUTING DIVIDENDS AND PREPARING A WORK SHEET** 634

ACCOUNTING IN YOUR CAREER 635
**25-1** Distributing Corporate Dividends to Stockholders 636
**25-2** Preparing a Work Sheet for a Corporation 640
**25-3** Calculating Federal Income Tax and Completing a Work Sheet 646
*SMALL BUSINESS SPOTLIGHT* 640
*TECHNOLOGY FOR BUSINESS* 646

AUTOMATED ACCOUNTING 658

## CHAPTER 26

**FINANCIAL STATEMENTS AND END-OF-FISCAL-PERIOD ENTRIES FOR A CORPORATION** 660

ACCOUNTING IN YOUR CAREER 661
**26-1** Preparing an Income Statement 662
**26-2** Preparing a Statement of Stockholders' Equity 666
**26-3** Preparing a Balance Sheet 669
**26-4** Adjusting, Closing, and Reversing Entries for a Corporation 675
*PROFESSIONAL BUSINESS ETHICS* 663

AUTOMATED ACCOUNTING 686

## FEATURES IN EVERY CHAPTER

***Explore Accounting***
476, 510, 537, 566, 586, 607, 627, 653, 682

***Internet Activity***
482, 517, 540, 570, 589, 611, 630, 656, 685

***Applied Communication***
482, 517, 540, 570, 589, 611, 630, 656, 685

***Cases for Critical Thinking***
482, 517, 541, 570, 589, 611, 631, 657, 685

## LESSON REVIEW AND PRACTICE

***Terms Review***
459, 464, 469, 475, 492, 498, 503, 509, 530, 536, 548, 552, 556, 561, 565, 577, 582, 585, 597, 602, 606, 620, 626, 639, 665, 668, 674

***Audit Your Understanding***
459, 464, 469, 475, 492, 498, 503, 509, 530, 536, 548, 552, 556, 561, 565, 577, 582, 585, 597, 602, 606, 620, 626, 639, 645, 652, 665, 668, 674, 681

***Work Together***
459, 464, 469, 475, 492, 498, 503, 509, 530, 536, 548, 552, 556, 561, 565, 577, 582, 585, 597, 602, 606, 620, 626, 639, 645, 652, 665, 668, 674, 681

***On Your Own***
459, 464, 469, 475, 492, 498, 503, 509, 530, 536, 548, 552, 556, 561, 565, 577, 582, 585, 597, 602, 606, 620, 626, 639, 645, 652, 665, 668, 674, 681

## CHAPTER REVIEW AND PRACTICE

***Chapter Summary***
476, 510, 537, 566, 586, 607, 627, 653, 682

***Application Problems***
477, 511, 538, 567, 587, 608, 628, 654, 683

***Mastery Problem***
480, 513, 539, 568, 588, 610, 629, 655, 684

***Challenge Problem***
481, 515, 540, 569, 588, 610, 630, 656, 685

## CYCLE REVIEW AND PRACTICE

***Reinforcement Activities***
520, 688

SOUTH-WESTERN CENTURY 21 ACCOUNTING

# INSTRUCTIONAL STRATEGIES

## COMPLETE ACCOUNTING COVERAGE

Century 21 Accounting continues to provide complete coverage of three types of business—**proprietorship**, **partnership**, and **corporation**. Each type of business is presented in a complete accounting cycle covering analyzing transactions, journalizing, posting, petty cash, financial statements, and adjusting and closing entries. Accounting concepts are introduced using a modern business with owners that students can relate to in each cycle. In Cycle 1, students study Encore Music, a business that provides music lessons. Cycle 2 features Omni Import, a retail merchandising business that purchases and sells imported gift items. In Cycle 3, Winning Edge, Inc., sells sports equipment to school districts, colleges, and businesses and is organized as a corporation. Each accounting cycle opens with a two-page illustration connected to the business in the cycle.

South-Western Educational Publishing provides **two different approaches** to the study of first-year accounting. In its traditional blue cover, the Multicolumn Journal Approach lets students focus on analyzing transactions, knowing that all transactions will be entered in the same journal. Special journals are introduced in Cycle 3. In its familiar green cover, the General Journal Approach introduces special journals in Cycle 2. The earlier focus on special journals mirrors college accounting and automated accounting approaches.

## COLORFUL, ATTRACTIVE PAGES

**Bright, interesting colors** throughout the text draw students in and get them excited about accounting! Imagine how eager students will be about reading a bright and colorful textbook.

Scattered throughout are **eye-catching photos** that represent the featured businesses. Encore Music in Cycle 1 is represented by photos of musical instruments such as drums, maracas, and a trumpet. Omni Import in Cycle 2 by photos of imported gift items such as an elephant bowl from Africa, a mask from Asia, a jaguar figurine from Latin America, and nesting dolls from Europe. Winning Edge, Inc., in Cycle 3 by photos of athletic equipment such as a soccer ball, ice skates, and a baseball glove.

## MANAGEABLE PEDAGOGY WITH SHORT, ACCESSIBLE LESSONS

Have you ever heard a student say, "Accounting is hard"? Century 21 Accounting, Texas Edition has the answer. Chapters are divided into **short, accessible lessons** that cover one or two concepts.

The Wraparound Teacher's Edition contains comprehensive lesson plans for each lesson to help you plan your instructional time more easily.

- **Chart of Accounts** used throughout the cycle is provided on the cycle opening pages for easy reference.
- **Terms Preview** displays all the key words introduced in the chapter.
- **Objectives** are listed at the beginning of each chapter to highlight lesson concepts and preview what students will learn.

**Illustrations are consistently placed** directly above the corresponding text. No more flipping pages back and forth to find an illustration that appears on a different page from the explanatory text! Plus, students can quickly find the illustration they are looking for when reviewing or working problems.

**Steps and call-outs** are completely integrated into the illustrations. This makes it easy to understand and then apply the procedure being taught. Clear, concise, step-by-step instructions are directly linked to the specific part of the illustration where the work is recorded.

The **concentrated supporting text** covers one specific topic and motivates students to read each page. Students are not intimidated by pages of text, but are encouraged to investigate the illustration and get further information by reading.

**Many students are visual learners.** First-year accounting emphasizes learning step-by-step procedures. With the combination of consistently placed, easy-to-locate illustrations, call-outs and instructions placed inside the illustrations, and step-by-step instructions, students can see how to complete accounting procedures and can refer to **easy-to-read steps** for reinforcement and clarification.

## LESSON PRACTICE

Each lesson ends with an activity page that provides immediate reinforcement of the lesson material. Instructors can use the end-of-lesson activities to make sure students fully understand all concepts and procedures before moving on to the next lesson.

- **Terms Review** lists all the important new words learned in the lesson in the order they appear in the text.
- **Audit Your Understanding** asks two or more conceptual questions about the material covered in the lesson. The answers appear in Appendix D so students can check their understanding.
- **Work Together** provides guided practice through the students' first hands-on application of chapter procedures and concepts. Forms to complete the exercise are given in the Working Papers. Performing this exercise together with the instructor gives students a basis for completing similar problems later.
- **On Your Own** mirrors and builds on the Work Together problem to give the student independent practice. Forms to complete the exercise are given in the Working Papers. Students work this problem to demonstrate proficiency, giving them a real sense of accomplishment. Instructors can informally assess whether students have mastered the basic concept covered in the lesson. Accounting isn't so hard after all!
- Students get further independent practice from an end-of-chapter **Application Problem** that mirrors the end-of-lesson problems.

## WORK SHEET OVERLAY

The Work Sheet Overlay is an excellent visual summary of the steps taken to prepare a work sheet. Students can see how a work sheet is prepared one section at a time, simplifying the process. The Work Sheet Overlay appears in Chapter 7: Work Sheet for a Service Business.

## CHAPTER PRACTICE

Century 21 Accounting, Texas Edition gives students **many short problems**. Students can now easily find and fix mistakes.

The **Summary** is a quick, short list of the topics covered in each lesson. Students can use the Summary to review their understanding of the material presented in the chapter. Instructors can ask questions based on the Summary as a fast way to verify student comprehension.

**End-of-chapter exercises** contain

- **Application problems** at least one for each lesson.
- **Mastery problems** that test overall comprehension of the entire chapter.
- **Challenge problems** that test overall comprehension of the entire chapter.

Many end-of-chapter problems can be completed using *Automated Accounting* and/or *Peachtree* software.

- **Reinforcement Activities** in each cycle.

***And something new,*** most chapters contain one problem using real-life transaction statements.

## APPENDICES

- **Appendix A: Accounting Concepts** Lists in one place all of the accounting concepts that students encounter throughout the text.
- **Appendix B: Using a Calculator and Computer Keypad** Provides important instruction in business calculator use and the ten-key touch system.
- **Appendix C: Recycling Problems** Offers additional opportunities for student practice. There is one recycling problem for each chapter, and these problems mirror the end-of-chapter mastery problems. Working papers are provided in the Study Guide and Recycling Problem Working Papers.
- **Appendix D: Answers to Audit Your Understanding** Contains brief answers to Audit Your Understanding questions that appear at the end of each lesson. Students can use the questions and answers for self study.

# FEATURES

***Special features provide context for accounting learning and real-life information about business. Features provide cross-curricular material for the accounting classroom.***

## LESSON FEATURES

❑ **Cultural Diversity** shows students that many different cultures around the world and throughout history have contributed to the development of accounting and financial record keeping.

❑ **Professional Business Ethics** presents dilemmas that can arise in day-to-day business operations.

❑ **Small Business Spotlight** features information about how to become a successful entrepreneur.

❑ **Accounting at Work** introduces real-life businesspeople who tell their stories about how accounting helps in their careers.

❑ **Technology for Business** covers the interplay between technology and business life. Topics covered include spreadsheets, the Internet, and commercial accounting software.

❑ **Global Perspective** provides insight into working with international suppliers and customers. Most students will have some global business experience in their careers. This feature introduces students to some of the issues involved in global business.

❑ **Legal Issues in Accounting** covers the legal issues involved in forming and dissolving the different forms of business organization and touches on other legal aspects of business life.

❑ **Applied Mathematics** boxes visually represent the intersection between accounting and mathematics and are strategically placed near relevant text to ensure optimum learning.

❑ **Remember** appears at the bottom of selected pages to reinforce critical accounting facts and procedures.

❑ **FYI** gives additional accounting and general business information related to the topics in a chapter.

## CHAPTER FEATURES

❑ **Accounting in Your Career** features appear at the beginning of each chapter and entice students by showing how accounting is part of everyone's life. These scenarios answer the question, "Why should I learn this?" The Accounting in Your Career feature focuses your students' attention on the topics to be studied in the chapter.

❑ **Critical Thinking Questions** for Accounting in Your Career energize students with class discussions about accounting-related issues. The Critical Thinking Questions can even be used as an informal pretest and posttest to demonstrate how much students have learned after studying a chapter. Suggested answers to each question are provided in the Wraparound Teacher's Edition.

❑ **Internet Activity** provides the Web address and instructions for accessing the Internet activity for each chapter.

❑ **Applied Communication** offers exercises for strengthening communication skills, a must for all students. Employers are expecting their business and accounting new hires to be able to communicate effectively, so get started here.

❑ **Cases for Critical Thinking** require students to carefully consider one or more questions, based on the accounting scenario being presented. An excellent opportunity for in-class discussion or group work!

❑ **Explore Accounting** includes opportunities for higher-level learning with Discussion, Research, and Required exercises directly related to the material presented in the feature. Topics include GAAP, fiscal periods, cash controls, and more.

## SOFTWARE

❑ **Automated Accounting** sections conclude every chapter and provide hands-on computer instruction with Automated Accounting.

❑ A **Peachtree** symbol denotes end-of-chapter problems that can be worked with *South-Western Accounting with Peachtree.*

# INTRODUCTION

## After studying this introduction, you will be able to:

1. Identify the many job opportunities available that require an accounting background.
2. Identify numerous careers in the accounting profession.
3. Identify the transferable skills an accounting class can strengthen.

On the first day of school, Kendra headed toward her fourth period class: accounting. She wondered what the class would be like. She had taken some other business classes, and enjoyed them. She was even thinking about pursuing a career in business. Last year, one of her teachers recommended that she take accounting. She hoped she would like it.

When she arrived at the classroom, Kendra was happy to find her friend Rob already there. "Hey, Rob, what are you doing here? I didn't know you were interested in business courses."

"Well, this is the first one I've taken. I really don't know what I want to do when I graduate in a couple of years, so I thought I should check out accounting. I'm really not sure it's for me, though."

The bell rang and the teacher came into the room. Everyone took a seat to get ready for class. Kendra sat next to Rob.

"Hi, everybody. I'm Mr. Perez, your accounting teacher for this year. And your first assignment is to come to the cafeteria with me."

Rob and Kendra looked at each other and at several of the other students. What was this?

Everyone followed Mr. Perez through the halls to the cafeteria. On the way there, Mr. Perez said, "I've assembled lots of people in the cafeteria. Professionals in all kinds of jobs. Feel free to talk to them about accounting fields, job opportunities, and more. You might be surprised at what you find out."

When they arrived at the cafeteria, they found a dozen people waiting to talk to them. They were from many companies, including accounting firms, entrepreneurial businesses, and governmental agencies. The class broke into smaller groups, and Rob and Kendra decided to walk around together. They chose to talk to an accountant first, because

**When they arrived at the cafeteria, they found a dozen people waiting to talk to them. They were from many companies, including accounting firms, entrepreneurial businesses, and governmental agencies.**

**"I have a friend who has started her own floral shop, and she tells me she is very glad to have knowlege of accounting. It has really helped her ensure that the business succeeds."**

Kendra wanted to find out more about the different fields in accounting.

"Why, there are many different specialized jobs accountants can do," said Ms. Ikeda, an employee for a large accounting firm in town. "I am a financial accountant, which means I record a business's financial activities and prepare the financial reports for my business. What I do helps creditors, investors, bankers, and auditors know the financial stability of my firm.

"The managerial accountants I work with take the financial accounting information I prepare and then analyze, measure, and interpret the information for internal use. Managers then use these interpretations to help them make the right business decisions.

"Cost accountants analyze and control the costs of an organization. They provide information that aids in decision making concerning the costs of operating the business and the costs of manufacturing goods or services.

"And, of course, there are tax accountants. They prepare tax returns and also perform tax planning responsibilities. They must stay up-to-date with changes in the law to ensure a business complies with the law.

"Systems accountants design and adapt the accounting systems that create financial, managerial, cost, and tax information reports for an organization. They also work hard to make these systems more efficient.

"An auditor's job is to review the reliability of a business's accounting records, and issue an opinion based on the information analyzed. An auditor's opinion enables those outside the business to feel confident about the stability of the business.

"Lastly, some accountants decide to become personal financial planners. They help individuals manage their personal investments, and they make suggestions about when and where money should be invested."

Rob and Kendra thanked Ms. Ikeda and then went to speak to some of the other professionals in the cafeteria. They found out about different types of employment opportunities available to people who have accounting backgrounds. Private accountants work for only one business; they may do all of the required summarizing, analyzing, and reporting, or they may specialize in one specific field of accounting. Public accountants can work independently or as a member of a public accounting firm, selling services such as preparing accounting reports or completing the tax forms for a business. Governmental/not-for-profit agencies also seem to have many opportunities for accountants. The Internal Revenue Service, hospitals, and churches all have needs for people to perform accounting duties.

Kendra thought all of the things she was learning were interesting. But Rob wasn't as excited as Kendra about possibly becoming an accountant. It just didn't seem to be for him, and he told Kendra he might decide to take a different class. He walked over to Mr. Perez and said, "Mr. Perez, maybe I shouldn't be taking this class. I don't think I want to be an accountant."

Mr. Perez smiled. "You don't have to want to be an accountant to benefit from taking this class. I'm not an accountant, but I have to know accounting to be your teacher. There are also many other accounting-related occupations that may interest you—travel agent, law clerk, manager, nurse, veterinarian. For these jobs, you'll need an understanding of accounting to make the right business decisions. I have a friend who has started her own floral shop, and she tells me she is very glad she has a knowledge of accounting. It has really helped her ensure that the business succeeds.

"Also, lots of small businesses need people to perform general accounting tasks. Businesses look for employees who can handle billing and collections, and payroll. But this is only part of the employee's job. They may also answer the phone, communicate with clients, and prepare annual reports or other documentation.

"What's more, there are many skills you will learn and strengthen by taking this class—skills that will help you regardless of what you decide you want to do. One of the most important skills you'll learn is how to communicate well, both when you write and when you speak. Accountants need to be able to communicate well because they often must relay information to people who have little or no accounting knowledge. But, being a good communicator is an invaluable tool for everyone to learn. Taking an accounting course will also help you learn to pay attention to details, improve your problem solving abilities, evaluate your own work, listen well, and interpret data. Those are all skills that will help you with any occupation you choose."

"Thanks Mr. Perez. I never realized I could learn so many important things by taking accounting," Rob said.

After finding out they could use accounting knowledge in so many different ways, Kendra, Rob, and all the other students were looking forward to studying accounting for the rest of the term.

**Mr. Perez smiled. "You don't have to be an accountant to benefit from taking this class. I'm not an accountant, but I have to know accounting to be your teacher."**

# Accounting for a Service Business

## CYCLE 1

1 Starting a Proprietorship

2 Starting a Proprietorship: Changes that Affect Owner's Equity

3 Analyzing Transactions into Debit and Credit Parts

4 Journalizing Transactions

5 Posting to a General Ledger

6 Cash Control Systems

7 Work Sheet for a Service Business

8 Financial Statements for a Proprietorship

9 Recording Adjusting and Closing Entries for a Service Business

# Organized as a Proprietorship

## ENCORE MUSIC CHART OF ACCOUNTS

### General Ledger

**Balance Sheet Accounts**

(100) ASSETS
110 Cash
120 Petty Cash
130 Accounts Receivable—Kids Time
140 Accounts Receivable—Learn N Play
150 Supplies
160 Prepaid Insurance

(200) LIABILITIES
210 Accounts Payable—Ling Music Supplies
220 Accounts Payable—Sullivan Office Supplies

(300) OWNER'S EQUITY
310 Barbara Treviño, Capital
320 Barbara Treviño, Drawing
330 Income Summary

**Income Statement Accounts**

(400) REVENUE
410 Sales

(500) EXPENSES
510 Advertising Expense
520 Insurance Expense
530 Miscellaneous Expense
540 Rent Expense
550 Supplies Expense
560 Utilities Expense

*The chart of accounts for Encore Music is illustrated above for ready reference as you study Cycle 1 of this textbook.*

# 1 Starting a Proprietorship

**AFTER STUDYING CHAPTER 1, YOU WILL BE ABLE TO:**

1. Define accounting terms related to starting a service business organized as a proprietorship.
2. Identify accounting concepts and practices related to starting a service business organized as a proprietorship.
3. Classify accounts as assets, liabilities, or owner's equity and demonstrate their relationships in the accounting equation.
4. Analyze how transactions related to starting a service business organized as a proprietorship affect accounts in an accounting equation.
5. Prepare a balance sheet for a service business organized as a proprietorship from information in an accounting equation.

**TERMS PREVIEW**

accounting
accounting system
accounting records
service business
proprietorship
asset
equities
liability
owner's equity
accounting equation
transaction
account
account title
account balance
capital
balance sheet

## WHAT IS ACCOUNTING?

Planning, recording, analyzing, and interpreting financial information is called **accounting.** A planned process for providing financial information that will be useful to management is called an **accounting system.** Organized summaries of a business's financial activities are called **accounting records.**

Accounting is the language of business. Many individuals in a business complete accounting forms and prepare accounting reports. Owners, managers, and accounting personnel use their knowledge of accounting to understand the information provided in the accounting reports. Regardless of their responsibilities within an organization, individuals can perform their jobs more efficiently if they know the language of business—accounting.

Inaccurate accounting records often contribute to business failure and bankruptcy. Failure to understand accounting information can result in poor business decisions for both businesses and nonprofit organizations. Understanding accounting helps managers and owners make better business decisions.

In addition, nearly everyone in the United States earns money and must submit income tax reports to the federal and state governments. Everyone, personally or for a business, must plan ways to keep spending within available income.

# ACCOUNTING IN YOUR CAREER

## THE JOB INTERVIEW

Robert Walker had a job interview today. He has just finished his first year of college but is undecided about what he should major in for the rest of his program. He cannot depend on his family to finance his college education, so he is prepared to continue his education as a part-time student and get a full-time job to pay tuition. He has been considering majoring in business, maybe even accounting, but he knows very little about the realities of the business world. Although he knows that completing college as a part-time student will take longer, he feels comfortable with his decision because of the practical experience he will gain from working.

Robert is looking for an office job as an administrative assistant. He can key 60 words per minute and has taken courses in word processing and spreadsheets.

Robert was interviewed by Paula Humphries, who operates a plumbing contractor business in town. At the end of the interview she said to Robert:

> Robert, you've got a good academic record. My company is growing rapidly, and I need people I can count on to help it grow. You don't have enough experience to be an administrative assistant, but I would like to start you as a general office assistant, which is an entry-level position. You would do some typing of bids, invoices, purchase orders, and correspondence, set appointments, file, and manage the telephones. You would be required to take an accounting course, which the company will pay for, but you will have to do it on your own time and get a good grade. I am offering you an opportunity to grow with my company. With a good performance record and the additional education, it wouldn't be too long before I could consider promoting you to administrative assistant.

**Critical Thinking:**

1. Why would Ms. Humphries want Robert to take an accounting course?
2. Should Robert reject this offer and hold out for an administrative assistant position?

# 1-1 The Accounting Equation

*In 1989, Barbara Treviño started Encore Music. After several years of teaching at a local university, Barbara decided to start her own business so that she could have a more flexible schedule. After only two months, she had made all the arrangements and scheduled her first lessons. She has never looked back.*

*Barbara gets tremendous satisfaction from teaching music. Nothing matches the thrill of hearing a student master an instrument. She also really enjoys being her own boss. She gets a different kind of satisfaction from keeping her own accounting records and seeing that she is making money every month.*

## THE BUSINESS—ENCORE MUSIC

A business that performs an activity for a fee is called a **service business.** Barbara Treviño decided to start her own business, giving music lessons. A business owned by one person is called a **proprietorship.** A proprietorship is also referred to as a sole proprietorship. Ms. Treviño named her new proprietorship *Encore Music*. Encore Music will rent office space and the instruments used to teach music lessons.

Since Encore Music is a new business, Ms. Treviño must design the accounting system that will be used to keep Encore Music's accounting records. Ms. Treviño must be careful to keep Encore Music's accounting records separate from her own personal financial records. For example, Ms. Treviño owns a house and a personal car. Encore Music's financial records must *not* include information about Ms. Treviño's house, car, or other personal belongings. Ms. Treviño must use one checking account for her personal expenses and another checking account for Encore Music. The accounting concept, *Business Entity*, is applied when a business's financial information is recorded and reported separately from the owner's personal financial information. (*CONCEPT: Business Entity*)

Accounting concepts are described throughout this textbook when an application of a concept first occurs. When additional applications occur, a concept reference, such as (*CONCEPT: Business Entity*), indicates an application of a specific accounting concept. A brief description of each accounting concept used in this text is also provided in Appendix A.

# THE ACCOUNTING EQUATION

| Assets | = | Liabilities + Owner's Equity |
|---|---|---|
| Left side amount | | Right side amounts |
| $0 | = | $0 + $0 |

Encore Music will own items such as cash and supplies that will be used to conduct daily operations. Anything of value that is owned is called an **asset.** Assets have value because they can be used to acquire other assets or be used to operate a business. For example, Encore Music will use cash to buy supplies for the business. Encore Music will then use the asset, supplies, in the operation of the music lesson business.

Financial rights to the assets of a business are called **equities.** A business has two types of equities. (1) Equity of those to whom money is owed. For example, Encore Music may buy some supplies and agree to pay for the supplies at a later date. The business from whom supplies are bought will have a right to some of Encore Music's assets until Encore Music pays for the supplies. An amount owed by a business is called a **liability.** (2) Equity of the owner. Ms. Treviño will own Encore Music and invest in the assets of the business. Therefore, she will have a right to decide how the assets will be used. The amount remaining after the value of all liabilities is subtracted from the value of all assets is called **owner's equity.**

The relationship among assets, liabilities, and owner's equity can be written as an equation. An equation showing the relationship among assets, liabilities, and owner's equity is called the **accounting equation.** The accounting equation is most often stated as:

**Assets = Liabilities + Owner's Equity**

The accounting equation must be in balance to be correct. Thus, the total of the amounts on the left side of the equation must always equal the total of the amounts on the right side. Before Ms. Treviño actually starts the business, Encore Music's accounting equation would show all zeros.

## Introduction to Business Ethics

The principles of right and wrong that guide an individual in making decisions are called *ethics.* The use of personal ethics in making business decisions is called *business ethics.*

Throughout this textbook you will have the opportunity to analyze the ethics of common business situations by using the following three-step checklist as a guide in collecting relevant information regarding an action.

1. *Is the action illegal? Does the action violate any laws?* Obeying the law is in your best interest and the best interest of your business.
2. *Does the action violate company or professional standards?* Public laws often set only minimum standards of behavior. Many businesses and professions set even higher standards of behavior. Thus, an action may be legal, yet still violate standards of the business or profession. Violating these standards may affect your job security and professional certification.
3. *Who is affected, and how, by the action?* If an action is legal and complies with business and professional standards, you must rely on your principles of right and wrong to determine if the action is ethical. Determining how the action affects individuals and groups—including business employees and owners, customers, the local community, and society—will help you decide if an action is ethical.

**Professional Business Ethics**

## TERMS REVIEW

| | |
|---|---|
| accounting | asset |
| accounting system | equities |
| accounting records | liability |
| service business | owner's equity |
| proprietorship | accounting equation |

## AUDIT YOUR UNDERSTANDING

1. What is accounting?
2. Give two examples of service businesses.
3. What is a proprietorship?
4. State the accounting equation.

## WORK TOGETHER

**Completing the accounting equation**

Write the answers to the following problem in the *Working Papers*. Your instructor will guide you through the following example.

5. For each line, fill in the missing amount to complete the accounting equation:

| Assets | = | Liabilities | + | Owner's Equity |
|---|---|---|---|---|
| ? | | 3,000 | | 8,000 |
| 10,000 | | ? | | 6,000 |
| 63,000 | | 35,000 | | ? |

## ON YOUR OWN

**Completing the accounting equation**

Write the answers to the following problem in the *Working Papers*. Work this problem independently.

6. For each line, fill in the missing amount to complete the accounting equation:

| Assets | = | Liabilities | + | Owner's Equity |
|---|---|---|---|---|
| 23,000 | | ? | | 13,000 |
| ? | | 70,000 | | 30,000 |
| 48,000 | | 25,000 | | ? |

# 1-2 How Business Activities Change the Accounting Equation

## RECEIVING CASH

| | Assets | = | Liabilities | + | Owner's Equity |
|---|---|---|---|---|---|
| | Cash | = | | | Barbara Treviño, Capital |
| Beginning Balances | $0 | | $0 | | $0 |
| Received cash from owner as an investment | +10,000 | | | | +10,000 |
| New Balances | $10,000 | | $0 | | $10,000 |

Business activities change the amounts in the accounting equation. A business activity that changes assets, liabilities, or owner's equity is called a **transaction.** For example, a business that pays cash for supplies is engaging in a transaction. After each transaction, the accounting equation must remain in balance.

The accounting concept, *Unit of Measurement*, is applied when business transactions are stated in numbers that have common values; that is, using a common unit of measurement. (*CONCEPT: Unit of Measurement*) For example, in the United States, business transactions are recorded in dollars. In Ghana, business transactions are recorded in *cedis*. The unit of measurement concept is followed so that the financial reports of businesses can be clearly stated and understood in numbers that have comparable values.

### Received Cash from Owner as an Investment

Ms. Treviño uses $10,000.00 of her own money to invest in Encore Music. Encore Music should only be concerned with the effect of this transaction on Encore Music's records. The business should not be concerned about Ms. Treviño's personal records. (*CONCEPT: Business Entity*)

Transaction 1 ***August 1. Received cash from owner as an investment, $10,000.00.***

A record summarizing all the information pertaining to a single item in the accounting equation is called an **account.** The name given to an account is called an **account title.** Each part of the accounting equation consists of one or more accounts. For example, one of the asset accounts is titled Cash. The cash account is used to summarize information about the amount of money the business has available.

In the accounting equation shown above, the asset account, Cash, is increased by $10,000.00, the amount of cash received by the business. This increase is on the left side of the accounting equation. The amount in an account is called the **account balance.** Before the owner's investment, the account balance of Cash was zero. After the owner's investment, the account balance of Cash is $10,000.00.

The account used to summarize the owner's equity in a business is called **capital.** The capital account is an owner's equity account. Encore Music's capital account is titled Barbara Treviño, Capital. In the accounting equation shown above, the owner's equity account, Barbara Treviño, Capital, is increased by $10,000.00. This increase is on the right side of the accounting equation. Before the owner's investment, the account balance of Barbara Treviño, Capital was zero. After the owner's investment, the account balance of Barbara Treviño, Capital is $10,000.00.

The accounting equation has changed as a result of the receipt of cash as the owner's investment. However, both sides of the equation are changed by the same amount, $10,000.00. The $10,000.00 increase on the left side of the equation equals the $10,000.00 increase on the right side of the equation. Therefore, the accounting equation is still in balance.

## PAYING CASH

| | Assets | | | = Liabilities | + Owner's Equity |
|---|---|---|---|---|---|
| | Cash | + Supplies | + Prepaid Insurance | = | Barbara Treviño, Capital |
| Balances | $10,000 | $0 | $0 | $0 | $10,000 |
| Paid cash for supplies | −1,577 | +1,577 | | | |
| Balances | $8,423 | $1,577 | $0 | $0 | $10,000 |
| Paid cash for insurance | −1,200 | | +1,200 | | |
| New Balances | $7,223 | $1,577 | $1,200 | $0 | $10,000 |

Encore Music pays cash for supplies and insurance.

### Paid Cash for Supplies

Encore Music needs supplies to operate the business. Barbara Treviño uses some of Encore Music's cash to buy supplies.

**Transaction 2** ***August 3. Paid cash for supplies, $1,577.00.***

In this transaction, two asset accounts are changed. One asset, cash, has been exchanged for another asset, supplies. The asset account, Cash, is decreased by $1,577.00, the amount of cash paid out. This decrease is on the left side of the accounting equation. The asset account, Supplies, is increased by $1,577.00, the amount of supplies bought. This increase is also on the left side of the accounting equation.

For this transaction, two assets are changed. Therefore, the two changes are both on the left side of the accounting equation. When changes are made on only one side of the accounting equation, the equation must still be in balance. Therefore, if one account is increased, another account on the same side of the equation must be decreased. After this transaction, the new account balance of Cash is $8,423.00. The new account balance of Supplies is $1,577.00. The sum of the amounts on the left side is $10,000.00 (Cash, $8,423.00 + Supplies, $1,577.00). The amount on the right side is also $10,000.00. Therefore, the accounting equation is still in balance.

### Paid Cash for Insurance

Insurance premiums must be paid in advance. For example, Encore Music pays a $1,200.00 insurance premium for future insurance coverage.

**Transaction 3** ***August 4. Paid cash for insurance, $1,200.00.***

In return for this payment, Encore Music is entitled to insurance coverage for the length of the policy. The insurance coverage is something of value owned by Encore Music. Therefore, the insurance coverage is an asset. Because insurance premiums are paid in advance, or *prepaid*, the premiums are recorded in an asset account titled Prepaid Insurance.

In this transaction, two assets are changed. One asset, cash, has been exchanged for another asset, prepaid insurance. The asset account, Cash, is decreased by $1,200.00, the amount of cash paid out. The asset account, Prepaid Insurance, is increased by $1,200.00, the amount of insurance bought.

After this transaction, the new account balance of Cash is $7,223.00. The new account balance of Prepaid Insurance is $1,200.00. The sum of the amounts on the left side is $10,000.00 (Cash, $7,223.00 + Supplies, $1,577.00 + Prepaid Insurance, $1,200.00). The amount on the right side is also $10,000.00. Therefore, the accounting equation is still in balance.

## TRANSACTIONS ON ACCOUNT

| | Assets | | | = Liabilities | + Owner's Equity |
|---|---|---|---|---|---|
| | Cash | + Supplies | + Prepaid Insurance | = Accts. Pay.—Ling Music Supplies | + Barbara Treviño, Capital |
| Balances | $7,223 | $1,577 | $1,200 | $0 | $10,000 |
| Bought supplies on account | | +2,720 | | +2,720 | |
| New Balances | $7,223 | $4,297 | $1,200 | $2,720 | $10,000 |
| Paid cash on account | −1,360 | | | −1,360 | |
| New Balances | $5,863 | $4,297 | $1,200 | $1,360 | $10,000 |

### Bought Supplies on Account

Encore Music needs to buy additional supplies. The supplies are obtained from Ling Music Supplies, which is located in a different city. It is a common business practice to buy items and pay for them at a future date. Another way to state this activity is to say that these items are bought *on account*.

**Transaction 4** ***August 7. Bought supplies on account from Ling Music Supplies, $2,720.00.***

In this transaction, one asset and one liability are changed. The asset account, Supplies, is increased by $2,720.00, the amount of supplies bought. Ling Music Supplies will have a claim against some of Encore Music's assets until Encore Music pays for the supplies bought. Therefore, Accounts Payable—Ling Music Supplies is a liability account. The liability account, Accounts Payable—Ling Music Supplies, is increased by $2,720.00, the amount owed for the supplies.

After this transaction, the new account balance of Supplies is $4,297.00. The new account balance of Accounts Payable—Ling Music Supplies is $2,720.00. The sum of the amounts on the left side is $12,720.00 (Cash, $7,223.00 + Supplies, $4,297.00 + Prepaid Insurance, $1,200.00). The sum of the amounts on the right side is also $12,720.00 (Accounts Payable—Ling Music Supplies, $2,720.00 + Barbara Treviño, Capital, $10,000.00). Therefore, the accounting equation is still in balance.

### Paid Cash on Account

Since Encore Music is a new business, Ling Music Supplies has not done business with Encore Music before. Ling Music Supplies allows Encore Music to buy supplies on account but requires Encore Music to send a check for one half of the amount immediately. Encore Music will pay the remaining liability at a later date.

**Transaction 5** ***August 11. Paid cash on account to Ling Music Supplies, $1,360.00.***

In this transaction, one asset and one liability are changed. The asset account, Cash, is decreased by $1,360.00, the amount of cash paid out. After this payment, Encore Music owes less money to Ling Music Supplies. Therefore, the liability account, Accounts Payable—Ling Music Supplies, is decreased by $1,360.00, the amount paid on account.

After this transaction, the new account balance of Cash is $5,863.00. The new account balance of Accounts Payable—Ling Music Supplies is $1,360.00. The sum of the amounts on the left side is $11,360.00 (Cash, $5,863.00 + Supplies, $4,297.00 + Prepaid Insurance, $1,200.00). The sum of the amounts on the right side is also $11,360.00 (Accounts Payable—Ling Music Supplies, $1,360.00 + Barbara Treviño, Capital, $10,000.00). Therefore, the accounting equation is still in balance.

**REMEMBER**

The left side of the accounting equation must always equal the right side.

## TERMS REVIEW

transaction
account
account title
account balance
capital

## AUDIT YOUR UNDERSTANDING

1. What must be done if a transaction increases the left side of the accounting equation?
2. How can a transaction affect only one side of the accounting equation?
3. To what does the phrase *on account* refer?

## WORK TOGETHER

### Determining how transactions change an accounting equation

Write the answers to the following problem in the *Working Papers*. Your instructor will guide you through the following example.

| Trans. No. | Assets | = Liabilities | + Owner's Equity |
|---|---|---|---|
| 1. | | | |

4. For each transaction, place a plus (+) in the appropriate column if the classification is increased. Place a minus (−) in the appropriate column if the classification is decreased.

***Transactions:***

1. Bought supplies on account.
2. Received cash from owner as an investment.
3. Paid cash for insurance.
4. Paid cash on account.

## ON YOUR OWN

### Determining how transactions change an accounting equation

Write the answers to the following problem in the *Working Papers*. Work this problem independently.

| Trans. No. | Assets | = Liabilities | + Owner's Equity |
|---|---|---|---|
| 1. | | | |

5. For each transaction, place a plus (+) in the appropriate column if the classification is increased. Place a minus (−) in the appropriate column if the classification is decreased.

***Transactions:***

1. Received cash from owner as investment.
2. Paid cash for supplies.
3. Paid cash for insurance.
4. Bought supplies on account.
5. Paid cash on account.

# 1-3 Reporting Financial Information on a Balance Sheet

## BALANCE SHEET

Periodically a business reports details about its assets, liabilities, and owner's equity. The financial details about assets, liabilities, and owner's equity could be found on the last line of the accounting equation. However, most businesses prepare more formal financial statements that may be copied and sent to interested persons. A financial statement that reports assets, liabilities, and owner's equity on a specific date is called a **balance sheet.**

When a business is started, it is expected that the business will continue to operate indefinitely. For example, Barbara Treviño assumes that she will own and operate Encore Music for many years. When she retires, she expects to sell Encore Music to someone else who will continue its operation. The accounting concept, *Going Concern*, is applied when financial statements are prepared with the expectation that a business will remain in operation indefinitely. (*CONCEPT: Going Concern*)

### Body of a Balance Sheet

A balance sheet has three major sections. (1) *Assets* are on the left side of the accounting equation. Therefore, Encore Music lists its assets on the left side of the balance sheet. (2) *Liabilities* are on the right side of the accounting equation. Therefore, Encore Music lists its liabilities on the right side of the balance sheet. (3) *Owner's equity* is also on the right side of the accounting equation. Therefore, Encore Music lists its owner's equity on the right side of the balance sheet.

CULTURAL DIVERSITY

### PROFESSIONAL ORGANIZATIONS

Professional organizations provide important social and economic benefits to their members. For example, the National Association of Black Accountants is a professional organization. Members of this association are CPAs, accountants, and accounting students. The organizational purpose is to unite accountants and accounting students who have similar interests and ideals. Members must be committed to professional and academic excellence. They must possess a sense of professional and civic responsibility. They must also be concerned with enhancing opportunities for minorities in the accounting profession.

Activities of the National Association of Black Accountants are diverse. They include free income tax preparation, student scholarships, high school and university career seminars, regional student conferences, and technical seminars and lectures. Other services of the organization include a speakers' bureau, a placement service, and publications of a journal and newsletter.

# PREPARING A BALANCE SHEET

| | Assets | | | = | Liabilities | + | Owner's Equity |
|---|---|---|---|---|---|---|---|
| | Cash | + Supplies | + Prepaid Insurance | = | Accts. Pay.— Ling Music Supplies | + | Barbara Treviño, Capital |
| Balances | $5,863 | $4,297 | $1,200 | | $1,360 | | $10,000 |

**1.** Write the heading.

**2.** Prepare the assets section.

**3.** Prepare the liabilities section.

**4.** Prepare the owner's equity section.

**5.** Add amounts and compare the totals.

**6.** Rule single lines.

**7.** Write the totals.

**8.** Rule double lines.

*Encore Music*
*Balance Sheet*
*August 11, 20--*

| *Assets* | | *Liabilities* | |
|---|---|---|---|
| *Cash* | 5 863 00 | *A/P—Ling Music Supplies* | 1 360 00 |
| *Supplies* | 4 297 00 | *Owner's Equity* | |
| *Prepaid Insurance* | 1 200 00 | *Barbara Treviño, Capital* | 10 000 00 |
| *Total Assets* | 11 360 00 | *Total Liab. and Owner's Eq.* | 11 360 00 |

## STEPS Preparing a balance sheet

1. Write the *heading* centered on three lines at the top of the balance sheet: the name of the business, the name of the report, and the date of the report.
2. Because assets are on the LEFT side of the accounting equation, prepare the *assets section* on the LEFT side. Center the word *Assets* on the first line of the wide column. Under this heading, write each asset account title and amount.
3. Because liabilities are on the RIGHT side of the accounting equation, prepare the *liabilities section* on the RIGHT side. Center the word *Liabilities* on the first line of the wide column. Under this heading, write each liability account title and amount.
4. Because owner's equity is also on the RIGHT side of the accounting equation, prepare the *owner's equity section* on the RIGHT side. Center the words *Owner's Equity* on the next blank line. Under this heading, write the owner's equity account title and amount.
5. Add all the asset amounts. Add the liabilities and owner's equity amounts. If the totals equal, the balance sheet is *in balance*. If the totals do not equal, find the errors before completing any more work. Prepare a new balance sheet without errors.
6. Rule a single line across each amount column. A single line means that amounts are to be added or subtracted.
7. On the next line on the left side, write *Total Assets* and write the total asset amount under the single rule. On the right side, write *Total Liabilities and Owner's Equity* and write the total liabilities and owner's equity amount under the single rule.
8. Rule double lines below the amount column totals. Double rules mean that the totals have been verified as correct.

## TERM REVIEW

balance sheet

## AUDIT YOUR UNDERSTANDING

1. List the three sections of a balance sheet.
2. What kinds of accounts are listed on the left side of a balance sheet?
3. What kinds of accounts are listed on the right side of a balance sheet?
4. What should be done if a balance sheet is not in balance?

## WORK TOGETHER

**Preparing a balance sheet from information in an accounting equation**

Write the answers to the following problem in the *Working Papers*. Your instructor will guide you through the following example.

On October 31 the Hess Company's accounting equation indicated the following account balances.

| Trans. No. | Assets | | | | | = | Liabilities | + | Owner's Equity |
|---|---|---|---|---|---|---|---|---|---|
| | Cash | + | Supplies | + | Prepaid Insurance | = | Accts. Pay.—Hulett Company | + | Jim Hess, Capital |
| New Bal. | 2,400 | | 300 | | 600 | | 250 | | 3,050 |

5. Using the October 31 balances in the accounting equation, prepare a balance sheet for the Hess Company.

## ON YOUR OWN

**Preparing a balance sheet from information in an accounting equation**

Write the answers to the following problem in the *Working Papers*. Work this problem independently.

On July 31 the Goldstein Company's accounting equation indicated the following account balances.

| Trans. No. | Assets | | | | | = | Liabilities | + | Owner's Equity |
|---|---|---|---|---|---|---|---|---|---|
| | Cash | + | Supplies | + | Prepaid Insurance | = | Accts. Pay.—Heino Company | + | Mary Goldstein, Capital |
| New Bal. | 2,500 | | 800 | | 1,200 | | 500 | | 4,000 |

6. Using the July 31 balances in the accounting equation, prepare a balance sheet for the Goldstein Company.

# CHAPTER 1 SUMMARY

*Enrichment Activity*

**Purpose of Accounting**

*Accounting is defined on page 4. Use the definition as the basis of explaining the purpose of accounting in your own words.*

After completing this chapter, you can

1. Define important accounting terms related to starting a service business organized as a proprietorship.
2. Identify accounting concepts and practices related to starting a service business organized as a proprietorship.
3. Classify accounts as assets, liabilities, or owner's equity and demonstrate their relationships in the accounting equation.
4. Analyze how transactions related to starting a service business organized as a proprietorship affect accounts in an accounting equation.
5. Prepare a balance sheet for a service business organized as a proprietorship from information in an accounting equation.

## EXPLORE ACCOUNTING

### WHAT IS GAAP?

The standards and rules that accountants follow while recording and reporting financial activities are commonly referred to as generally accepted accounting principles, or GAAP. These rules have not been developed by any one group of rule makers, but have instead evolved over time and from many sources.

By law, the Securities and Exchange Commission (SEC) has the authority to establish GAAP. The SEC, however, has allowed a series of private organizations to determine GAAP. Currently the organization that has the authority to set accounting standards is the Financial Accounting Standards Board (FASB), which was established in 1973.

The standard-setting process includes getting input and feedback from many sources. FASB listens to this feedback and considers all sides of each issue.

### WHY IS GAAP NECESSARY?

Users of financial statements rely on the information those statements contain. If the preparers of financial statements were allowed to follow *any* measurement, recording, and reporting rules, the users of the statements would have no way to determine if the financial statements present fairly the financial position of the business.

By requiring the financial statement preparers to follow consistently certain standards and rules—such as GAAP—the users are able to compare the financial statements of several companies and to track the results of one company over several time periods.

**Discussion:** Why would a group of people disagree with a proposed accounting standard?

**Research:** Using your local library or the Internet, find additional information about the FASB. Write a one-page report on your findings.

## 1-1 APPLICATION PROBLEM
### Completing the accounting equation

***Instructions:***
For each line, fill in the missing amount to complete the accounting equation, using your *Working Papers*.

| Assets | = | Liabilities | + | Owner's Equity |
|---|---|---|---|---|
| 90,000 | | 49,000 | | ? |
| ? | | 68,000 | | 30,000 |
| 3,000 | | ? | | 2,000 |
| 108,000 | | 60,000 | | ? |
| 19,000 | | ? | | 11,000 |
| ? | | 4,000 | | 12,000 |
| 25,000 | | 13,000 | | ? |
| ? | | 113,000 | | 49,000 |
| 4,000 | | ? | | 2,000 |
| 86,000 | | 48,000 | | ? |
| 12,000 | | ? | | 7,000 |
| ? | | 5,000 | | 14,000 |
| 47,000 | | 24,000 | | ? |
| ? | | 29,000 | | 13,000 |
| 38,000 | | ? | | 21,000 |
| 125,000 | | 69,000 | | ? |
| 11,000 | | ? | | 6,000 |
| ? | | 1,000 | | 3,000 |

## 1-2 APPLICATION PROBLEM
### Determining how transactions change an accounting equation

Frank Mori is starting Mori Repair Shop, a small service business. Mori Repair Shop uses the accounts shown in the following accounting equation. Use the form in your *Working Papers* to complete this problem.

| | Assets | | | = | Liabilities | | + | Owner's Equity |
|---|---|---|---|---|---|---|---|---|
| Trans. No. | Cash + | Supplies + | Prepaid Insurance | = | Accts. Pay.— Swan's Supply Company + | Accts. Pay.— York Company | + | Frank Mori, Capital |
| Beg. Bal.<br>1. | 0<br>+2,000 | 0 | 0 | | 0 | 0 | | 0<br>+2,000 |
| New Bal.<br>2. | 2,000 | 0 | 0 | | 0 | 0 | | 2,000 |

***Transactions:***
1. Received cash from owner as an investment, $2,000.00.
2. Paid cash for insurance, $600.00.
3. Bought supplies on account from Swan's Supply Company, $100.00.
4. Bought supplies on account from York Company, $500.00.
5. Paid cash on account to Swan's Supply Company, $100.00.

6. Paid cash on account to York Company, $300.00.
7. Paid cash for supplies, $500.00.
8. Received cash from owner as an investment, $500.00.

***Instructions:***

For each transaction, complete the following. Transaction 1 is given as an example.

a. Analyze the transaction to determine which accounts in the accounting equation are affected.
b. Write the amount in the appropriate columns using a plus (+) if the account increases or a minus (−) if the account decreases.
c. Calculate the new balance for each account in the accounting equation.
d. Before going on to the next transaction, determine that the accounting equation is still in balance.

## 1-3 APPLICATION PROBLEM

### Determining how transactions change an accounting equation

Ellie VonSpreecken is starting Ellie's Computer Repair, a small service business. Ellie's Computer Repair uses the accounts shown in the following accounting equation. Use the form in your *Working Papers* to complete this problem.

| Trans. No. | Assets | | | = Liabilities | | + Owner's Equity |
|---|---|---|---|---|---|---|
| | Cash + | Supplies + | Prepaid Insurance | = Accts. Pay.—Seiler Supply | + Accts. Pay.—Miles Company | + Ellie Von Spreecken, Capital |
| Beg. Bal. | 0 | 0 | 0 | 0 | 0 | 0 |
| 1. | *+3,000* | | | | | *+3,000* |
| New Bal. | *3,000* | *0* | *0* | *0* | *0* | *3,000* |
| 2. | | | | | | |

***Transactions:***

1. The owner invested $3,000.00 cash in the business.
2. Paid $1,200.00 for insurance for the next year.
3. Purchased supplies from Seiler Supply for $800.00 on account.
4. Purchased $500.00 of supplies from Miles Company. Agreed to pay Miles next month for these supplies.
5. Paid $400.00 to Seiler Supply on account.
6. Ellie VonSpreecken invested an additional $1,000.00 in the business.

***Instructions:***

For each transaction, complete the following. Transaction 1 is given as an example.

a. Analyze the transaction to determine which accounts in the accounting equation are affected.
b. Write the amount in the appropriate columns using a plus (+) if the account increases or a minus (−) if the account decreases.
c. Calculate the new balance for each account in the accounting equation.
d. Before going on to the next transaction, determine that the accounting equation is still in balance.

## 1-4 APPLICATION PROBLEM
### Determining where items are listed on a balance sheet

Use the form in your *Working Papers* to complete this problem.

| 1 | 2 | 3 |
|---|---|---|
| Items | Balance Sheet | |
| | Left Side | Right Side |
| 1. Cash | *Asset* | |

***Instructions:***
Classify each item as an asset, liability, or owner's equity. Write the classification in Column 2 or 3 to show where each item is listed on a balance sheet. Item 1 is given as an example.

1. Cash
2. Michelle Sullivan, Capital
3. Supplies
4. Prepaid Insurance
5. Accounts Payable—Action Laundry
6. Anything owned
7. Any amount owed
8. Owner's capital account

## 1-5 APPLICATION PROBLEM
### Preparing a balance sheet from information in an accounting equation

On September 30 the Steffens Company's accounting equation indicated the following account balances.

| Trans. No. | Assets | | | | | | = | Liabilities | + | Owner's Equity |
|---|---|---|---|---|---|---|---|---|---|---|
| | Cash | + | Supplies | + | Prepaid Insurance | | = | Accts. Pay.—Morton Company | + | Steven Steffens, Capital |
| New Bal. (Sept. 30) | 1,200 | | 150 | | 300 | | | 250 | | 1,400 |

***Instructions:***
Using the September 30 balance in the accounting equation, prepare a balance sheet for the Steffens Company. A form is given in the *Working Papers*.

## 1-6 MASTERY PROBLEM
### Determining how transactions change an accounting equation and preparing a balance sheet

Nancy Dirks is starting Dirks Company, a small service business. Dirks Company uses the accounts shown in the following accounting equation. Use the form in your *Working Papers* to complete this problem.

| Trans. No. | Assets Cash | + Supplies | + Prepaid Insurance | = Liabilities Accts. Pay.— Helfrey Company | + Owner's Equity Nancy Dirks, Capital |
|---|---|---|---|---|---|
| New Bal.<br>1. | 0<br>+350 | 0 | 0 | 0 | 0<br>+350 |
| New Bal.<br>2. | *350* | *0* | *0* | *0* | *350* |

***Transactions:***

1. Received cash from owner as an investment, $350.00.
2. Bought supplies on account from Helfrey Company, $100.00.
3. Paid cash for insurance, $150.00.
4. Paid cash for supplies, $50.00.
5. Received cash from owner as an investment, $300.00.
6. Paid cash on account to Helfrey Company, $75.00.

***Instructions:***

1. For each transaction, complete the following. Transaction 1 is given as an example.
   a. Analyze the transaction to determine which accounts in the accounting equation are affected.
   b. Write the amount in the appropriate columns, using a plus (+) if the account increases or a minus (−) if the account decreases.
   c. Calculate the new balance for each account in the accounting equation.
   d. Before going on to the next transaction, determine that the accounting equation is still in balance.
2. Using the final balances in the accounting equation, prepare a balance sheet for Dirks Company. Use July 31 of the current year as the date of the balance sheet.

## 1-7 CHALLENGE PROBLEM

### Applying accounting concepts to determine how transactions change the accounting equation

Morgan Delivery Service, a new business owned by Gregory Morgan, uses the accounts shown in the following accounting equation. Use the form in your *Working Papers* to complete this problem.

| Trans. No. | Assets Cash | + Supplies | + Prepaid Insurance | = Liabilities Accts. Pay.— Mutual Savings Bank | + Accts. Pay.— Nelson Supply Co. | + Owner's Equity Gregory Morgan, Capital |
|---|---|---|---|---|---|---|
| Beg. Bal.<br>1. | 0<br>+1,500 | 0 | 0 | 0 | 0 | 0<br>+1,500 |
| New Bal.<br>2. | *1,500* | *0* | *0* | *0* | *0* | *1,500* |

***Transactions:***

1. Owner invested cash, $1,500.00.
2. Bought supplies for cash, $400.00.

## 2-3 APPLICATION PROBLEM
### Preparing a balance sheet

On June 30, the Heil Company's accounting equation indicated the following account balances.

| | Assets | | | | = | Liabilities | + Owner's Equity |
|---|---|---|---|---|---|---|---|
| | Cash | + Accts. Rec.— Jana Friestad | + Supplies | + Prepaid Insurance | = | Accts. Pay.— Franco Supplies | + Kevin Heil, Capital |
| Balance | 8,655 | 942 | 475 | 750 | | 665 | 10,157 |

Using the June 30 balances in the accounting equation, prepare a balance sheet for the Heil Company. Use the form in the *Working Papers* to complete this problem.

## 2-4 MASTERY PROBLEM
### Determining how transactions change an accounting equation and preparing a balance sheet

Mikaela Mundt operates a service business called Mundt Company. Mundt Company uses the accounts shown in the following accounting equation. Use the form in your *Working Papers* to complete this problem.

| Trans. No. | Assets | | | | = | Liabilities | + Owner's Equity |
|---|---|---|---|---|---|---|---|
| | Cash | + Accts. Rec.— Dorothy Romano | + Supplies | + Prepaid Insurance | = | Accts. Pay.— Sickle Co. | + Mikaela Mundt, Capital |
| Beg. Bal.<br>1. | 1,400<br>*−100* | —0— | 300 | 400 | | 1,500 | 600<br>*−100 (expense)* |
| New Bal.<br>2. | *1,300* | *—0—* | *300* | *400* | | *1,500* | *500* |

***Transactions:***

1. Paid cash for telephone bill, $100.00.
2. Received cash from owner as an investment, $200.00.
3. Paid cash for rent, $500.00.
4. Received cash from sales, $895.00.
5. Bought supplies on account from Sickle Company, $600.00.
6. Sold services on account to Dorothy Romano, $920.00.
7. Paid cash for supplies, $400.00.
8. Paid cash for advertising, $250.00.
9. Received cash on account from Dorothy Romano, $800.00.
10. Paid cash on account to Sickle Company, $1,500.00.
11. Paid cash for one month of insurance, $250.00.
12. Received cash from sales, $1,960.00.
13. Paid cash to owner for personal use, $1,000.00.

***Instructions:***

1. For each transaction, complete the following. Transaction 1 is given as an example.
   a. Analyze the transaction to determine which accounts in the accounting equation are affected.
   b. Write the amount in the appropriate columns, using a plus (+) if the account increases or a minus (−) if the account decreases.
   c. For transactions that change owner's equity, write in parentheses a description of the transaction to the right of the amount.
   d. Calculate the new balance for each account in the accounting equation.
   e. Before going on to the next transaction, determine that the accounting equation is still in balance.
2. Using the final balances in the accounting equation, prepare a balance sheet for Mundt Company. Use the date April 30 of the current year.

## 2-5 CHALLENGE PROBLEM

### Determining how transactions change an accounting equation

Zachary Martin owns Zachary's Repair Shop. On February 1, Zachary's Repair Shop's accounting equation indicated the following account balances. Use the form in your *Working Papers* to complete this problem.

| | Assets | | | | = Liabilities | + Owner's Equity |
|---|---|---|---|---|---|---|
| Trans. No. | Cash | + Accts. Rec.—Mary Lou Pier | + Supplies | + Prepaid Insurance | = Accts. Pay.—Kollasch Co. | + Zachary Martin, Capital |
| Beg. Bal. | 8,552 | 1,748 | 1,485 | 615 | 3,145 | 9,255 |
| 1. | | | | | | |

***Transactions:***

1. Took $400.00 of supplies for personal use.
2. Had equipment repaired at Kollasch Company and agreed to pay Kollasch Company at a later date, $250.00.
3. Mr. Martin had some personal property which he sold for $500.00 cash.
4. Paid Kollasch Company $120.00 on account.

***Instructions:***

1. For each transaction, complete the following.
   a. Analyze the transaction to determine which accounts in the accounting equation are affected.
   b. Write the amount in the appropriate columns, using a plus (+) if the account increases or a minus (−) if the account decreases.
   c. For transactions that change owner's equity, write in parentheses a description of the transaction to the right of the amount.
   d. Calculate the new balance for each account in the accounting equation.
   e. Before going on to the next transaction, determine that the accounting equation is still in balance.
2. Answer the following questions:
   a. Why can the owner of a business withdraw assets from that business for personal use?
   b. Why would the owner withdraw assets other than cash?

**INTERNET ACTIVITY**

Point your browser to

**http://accounting.swpco.com**

Choose **First-Year Course**, choose **Activities**, and complete the activity for Chapter 2.

## Applied Communication

A resume provides a statement of your education, experience, and qualifications for a prospective employer. Your resume should be accurate, honest, and perfect in every respect. It should include all work experience along with the companies and dates of employment. Education, activities, and interests are all important items that should be covered.

**Instructions:** Go to the library and research how to prepare an appropriate resume. Then prepare one that you could send to a prospective employer.

# Cases for Critical Thinking

**Case 1** Garcia Books received an investment from its owner, Ms. Juanita Garcia. This transaction is recorded in the following accounting equation. Is the analysis correct? Explain.

| Assets | | | | | | = Liabilities | | + Owner's Equity |
|---|---|---|---|---|---|---|---|---|
| Cash | + | Supplies | + | Prepaid Insurance | = | Accts. Pay.— Panther Supply Company | + | Juanita Garcia, Capital |
| $1,000 | | $3,000 | | $2,000 | | $2,500 | | $3,500 |
| +750 | | | | | | | | |
| $1,750 | | $3,000 | | $2,000 | | $2,500 | | $3,500 |

**Case 2** The manager of Phillip's Department Store prepares a balance sheet at the end of each business day. Is this a satisfactory procedure?

**Case 3** The supervisor of cash management at Joe's Consulting Agency wants to see how much cash was received from cash sales and sales on account. Which of the following transactions would be included in determining this amount? How do you know your analysis is correct? Explain.

***Transactions:***

1. Received cash from sales.
2. Sold services on account to Johnson Company.
3. Paid cash for advertising.
4. Paid cash to owner for personal use.
5. Received cash on account from Laundry Services.

# AUTOMATED ACCOUNTING

## LANGUAGE AND SKILLS FOR AUTOMATED ACCOUNTING

Using computer software to process accounting data can be an efficient and effective way to control the financial information of a business. In order to use the software, it is important to have a general understanding of computer and software terminology. Keyboarding skills are also essential for entering data. The more skilled you are and the greater your understanding, the better able you will be to accurately process financial information.

### Automated Accounting Software

*Automated Accounting 7.0* or higher software is used to teach students about computerized accounting principles. Accounting software is a set of instructions that operate the computer and enable the user to enter financial information and create reports, spreadsheets, and graphs. Specifically, *Automated Accounting* can process transactions for

- the purchase of assets, supplies, services, and the related payments.
- recording investments in the business.
- sales, cash receipts, and noncash transactions.

There are many other types of transactions that can be entered into an automated accounting system. Many of the various types of transactions will be studied in this class.

### Automated Accounting versus Manual Accounting

Most students learn accounting by first processing transactions manually (by hand). It is important to learn the methods of recording transactions by hand before entering this information into an automated accounting system. Learning the principles of accounting is necessary in order to analyze how to process transactions. Once you learn accounting principles, you will be better able to understand the functions of an automated system.

Understanding automated accounting will help you in the workplace. Many businesses use computers to enter accounting data to process information more efficiently. After learning automated accounting, you will be able to more easily follow trails of information to analyze and correct errors.

### Menu Bar and Drop-Down Lists versus Toolbar

The menu bar and drop-down lists enable you to communicate with the software. When a menu title is selected, a drop-down menu list appears. This drop-down list presents additional options to perform specific actions. Toolbar buttons can also be selected without using the drop-down list. Each toolbar button has a unique function that is similar to an item found on a drop-down list. The illustration shows the menu bar titles and the toolbar. *Automated Accounting 8.0* has additional menu

**Menu Bar—** Lists the menu titles.

**Current File Name and User Name—** Displays file and user name when a file is opened and loaded into memory.

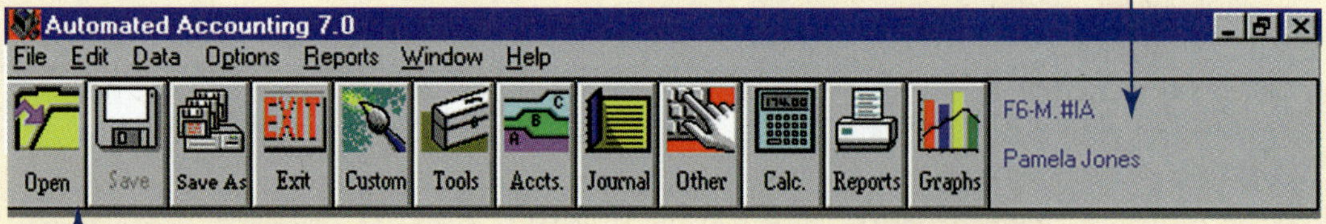


**Toolbar—**Provides a shortcut method of accessing the most commonly used menu items by clicking a button.

# Automated Accounting

options and toolbar buttons.

The following terms are elements of the *Automated Accounting 7.0* menu bar. Most of the terms will be studied again in later chapters.

**File** is a menu title that includes options to create a new document, open an existing document, save new or existing documents, and print. The Exit menu item is also listed under the File menu title.

**Edit** is a menu title that includes options to cut, copy, and paste text to separate spreadsheet and word processing documents. When processing information in the Journal Entries window, Find and Find Next can be used to locate data you wish to find.

**Data** is a menu title that includes options to customize accounting elements, select planning tools, maintain accounts, and create journal entries. The Other Activities option leads you to special activities such as Bank Reconciliation.

**Options** is a menu title that includes choices to generate depreciation adjusting entries, current payroll journal entries, employer's payroll taxes, and closing journal entries. Options also includes a calculator.

**Reports** is a menu title that includes options for report selection and graph selection. An important element of Reports is the run date because a report consists of accounting data up to and including the run date.

The run date is printed on reports prepared by the software. The run date can be changed on the report selection screen by changing the numbers in the Run Date field or using the calendar. If the run date is not manually changed, the run date will be the date of the last transaction entered in any of the journals.

**Window** is a menu title that includes an option to close all windows.

**Help** includes options to search and view help contents, problem instructions, and information about *Automated Accounting.*

*Automated Accounting 8.0* has an additional menu item, Internet for accessing the Web Browser.

## Selecting and Opening Files

When selecting and opening files, it is important to open the appropriate directory/folder in order to select the desired file. Also, it is best to save your files promptly upon completion of a problem before properly exiting the *Automated Accounting* system.

## Changing Directories/Folders

When changing directories/folders, choose the disk drive that contains the file you want to open. The desired file may not always be in the folder shown when the Open command is selected. Your instructor may tell you to change folders. After selecting the directory/folder that includes the file you need, highlight the file you wish to choose and click OK.

## Saving Files

Choose the Save menu item from the File menu or click on the Save toolbar button. Before using the Save menu item, be sure to check the upper right corner of the screen for the file name to which you want to save. (This information displays in the title bar in *Automated Accounting 8.0.*) The opening balance file, also called a template, includes a database of information about a particular business and can be used more than once.

Specifically, the opening balance file includes general information about the business, a chart of accounts, and account balances. If the file name has not been changed from the original opening balance file name, you must use the Save As menu item first. *Automated Accounting* will not allow you to save to the opening balance file.

## Exit

After you have completed your session and saved your file, click on the Exit toolbar button to exit *Automated Accounting.*

# 3 Analyzing Transactions into Debit and Credit Parts

**AFTER STUDYING CHAPTER 3, YOU WILL BE ABLE TO:**

1. Define accounting terms related to analyzing transactions into debit and credit parts.
2. Identify accounting practices related to analyzing transactions into debit and credit parts.
3. Use T accounts to analyze transactions showing which accounts are debited or credited for each transaction.
4. Analyze how transactions to set up a business affect accounts.
5. Analyze how transactions affect owner's equity accounts.

**TERMS PREVIEW**

T account

debit

credit

normal balance

chart of accounts

## ANALYZING THE ACCOUNTING EQUATION

Even though the effects of transactions *can* be recorded in an accounting equation, the procedure is not practical in an actual accounting system. The number of accounts used by most businesses would make the accounting equation cumbersome to use as a major financial record. Therefore, a separate record is commonly used for each account. The accounting equation can be represented as a T, as shown.

| Assets | = Liabilities + Owner's Equity |
|---|---|
| Left side | Right side |

The values of all things owned (assets) are on the left side of the accounting equation. The values of all equities or claims against the assets (liabilities and owner's equity) are on the right side of the accounting equation. The total of amounts on the left side of the accounting equation must always equal the total of amounts on the right side. Therefore, the total of all assets on the left side of the accounting equation must always equal the total of all liabilities and owner's equity on the right side.

# ACCOUNTING IN YOUR CAREER

## ADDING ACCOUNTS

John Robbin, the owner of Robbin's Auto Service, has requested a meeting with Diane Endo, his accounting assistant, to discuss changes in the business.

**Diane Endo:** You asked to see me, John. What's up?

**John Robbin:** Diane, you've been my accounting assistant for nine months, and I've been impressed with what you've learned and how well you journalize all the company's transactions.

**Diane Endo:** Thanks, John. It's been fun to learn and I enjoy working for this company.

**John Robbin:** Now I need your creative thinking. More and more people are servicing their own cars, so I've been thinking about branching out to sell auto parts.

**Diane Endo:** Sounds like a good idea. What do you want me to do?

**John Robbin:** I'd like you to recommend changes to the chart of accounts.

**Diane Endo:** I've got some thoughts already. What do you want to accomplish?

**John Robbin:** I want to be able to break sales and expenses down by departments. In addition to our existing repair business, the new department would be parts. I will also need to rent additional space next door to create a showroom area to merchandise the auto parts.

**Diane Endo:** When do you need this information?

**John Robbin:** Well, today is Monday. Can you have it ready by Wednesday? I want to move fast on this.

***Critical Thinking:***

1. What kinds of new accounts should Diane Endo recommend?
2. Should she recommend any changes to the numbering system of the chart of accounts?

# 3-1 Using T Accounts

## ACCOUNTS

| Assets | = Liabilities + Owner's Equity |
|---|---|
| Left side | Right side |

| T Account | |
|---|---|
| Left side<br>**DEBIT SIDE** | Right side<br>**CREDIT SIDE** |

A record summarizing all the information pertaining to a single item in the accounting equation is known as an account. Transactions change the balances of accounts in the accounting equation. Accounting transactions must be analyzed to determine how account balances are changed. An accounting device used to analyze transactions is called a **T account.**

There are special names for amounts recorded on the left and right sides of a T account. An amount recorded on the left side is called a **debit.** An amount recorded on the right side is called a **credit.** The words *debit* and *credit* come from the Latin and Italian words *debere* and *credere.* Common abbreviations are *dr.* for debit and *cr.* for credit.

## ACCOUNT BALANCES

Assets = Liabilities + Owner's Equity

| Any Asset | |
|---|---|
| Debit<br>**NORMAL BALANCE** | Credit |

| Any Liability | |
|---|---|
| Debit | Credit<br>**NORMAL BALANCE** |

| Owner's Capital Account | |
|---|---|
| Debit | Credit<br>**NORMAL BALANCE** |

The side of the account that is increased is called the **normal balance.** The process of increasing or decreasing account balances is discussed on the next page. Assets are on the left side of the accounting equation, and asset accounts have normal debit balances (left side).

Liabilities are on the right side of the accounting equation, and liability accounts have normal credit balances (right side). The owner's capital account is on the right side of the accounting equation and has a normal credit balance (right side).

## INCREASES AND DECREASES IN ACCOUNTS

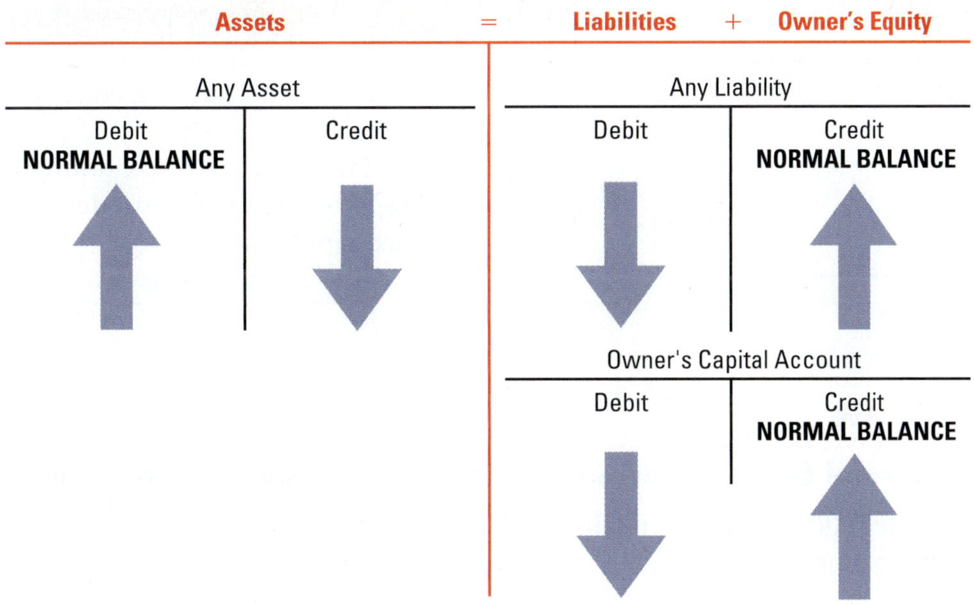


The sides of a T account are used to show increases and decreases in account balances.

Two basic accounting rules regulate increases and decreases of account balances. (1) Account balances increase on the normal balance side of an account. (2) Account balances decrease on the side opposite the normal balance side of an account.

Asset accounts have normal debit balances; therefore, asset accounts increase on the debit side and decrease on the credit side. Liability accounts have normal credit balances; therefore, liability accounts increase on the credit side and decrease on the debit side. The owner's capital account has a normal credit balance; therefore, the capital account increases on the credit side and decreases on the debit side.

### Dining Out with Computers

**TECHNOLOGY FOR BUSINESS**

Next time you order a taco—think technology. That's right, technology is changing the way restaurants do business. Computers are widely used to enter orders, generate guest checks, and print receipts. Computers also track the menu items that diners order—how many of each item is served each day, what time of day it is ordered, and what other items are ordered along with it.

The technology makes it possible for restaurant managers to predict how much of each food item to order, how much to prepare on a given day, and when to start cooking. Computer software programs also help managers plan their staffing needs based on trends developed from historical data.

Hand-held computers are used by servers in some restaurants to transmit information to the kitchen, where it is printed for the chef. This technology can reduce the time diners sit at a table. That translates into more diners served and more revenue for the restaurant.

Remember, technology is all around, even when you order that taco.

## TERMS REVIEW

T account

debit

credit

normal balance

## AUDIT YOUR UNDERSTANDING

1. Draw the accounting equation on a T account.
2. What are the two accounting rules that regulate increases and decreases of account balances?

## WORK TOGETHER

**Determining the normal balance, increase, and decrease sides for accounts**

Write the answers to the following problems in the *Working Papers.* Your instructor will guide you through the following examples.

Cash
Accounts Receivable—Christine Kelly
Supplies
Prepaid Insurance
Accounts Payable—Miller Supplies
Accounts Payable—Wayne Office Supplies
Jeff Dixon, Capital

For each of the accounts, complete the following:

3. Prepare a T account.
4. Label the debit and credit sides.
5. Label each side of the T account using the following labels:
   a. Normal balance
   b. Increase side
   c. Decrease side

## ON YOUR OWN

**Determining the normal balance, increase, and decrease sides for accounts**

Write the answers to the following problems in the *Working Papers.* Work these problems independently.

Cash
Accounts Receivable—Brian Lee
Supplies
Prepaid Insurance
Accounts Payable—Golf Tees
Vickie Haskins, Capital

For each of the accounts, complete the following:

6. Prepare a T account.
7. Label the debit and credit sides.
8. Label each side of the T account using the following labels:
   a. Normal balance
   b. Increase side
   c. Decrease side

# 3-2 Analyzing How Transactions Affect Accounts

## RECEIVED CASH FROM OWNER AS AN INVESTMENT

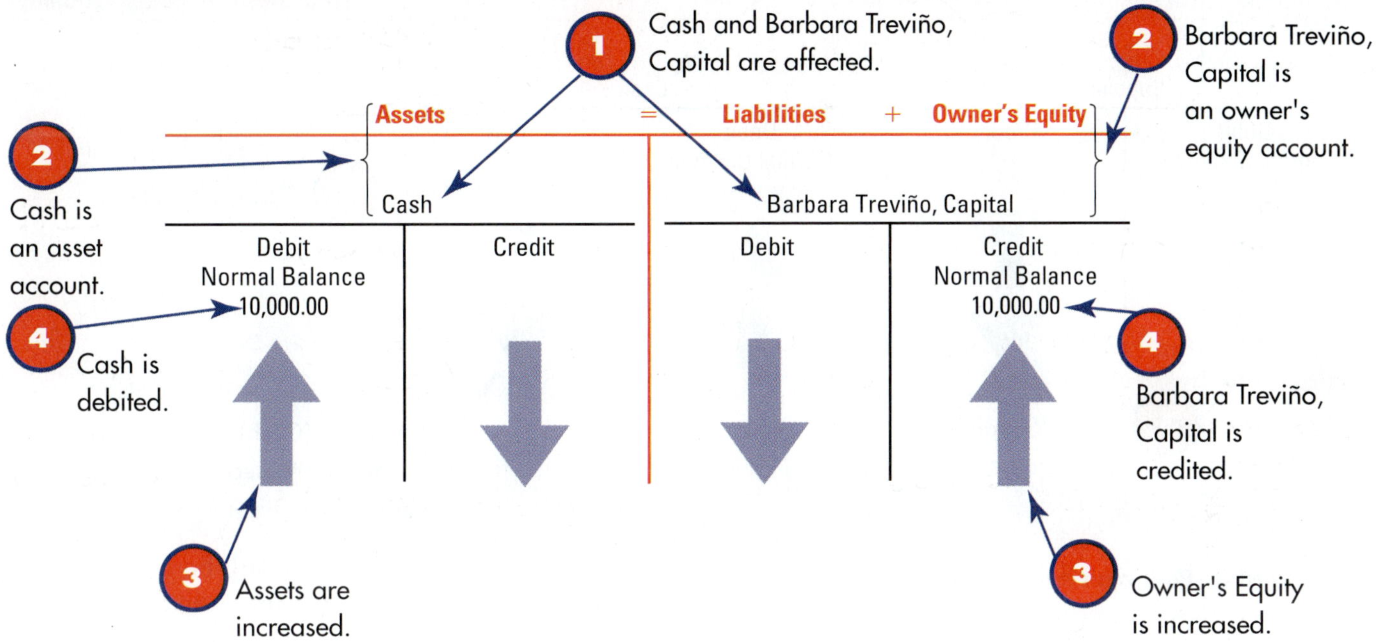


***August 1. Received cash from owner as an investment, $10,000.00.***

The effect of this transaction is shown in the illustration. Before a transaction is recorded in the records of a business, the information is analyzed to determine which accounts are changed and how. Each transaction changes the balances of at least two accounts. A list of accounts used by a business is called a **chart of accounts.** The chart of accounts for Encore Music is found on page 3.

Four questions are used in analyzing a transaction into its debit and credit parts. Debits equal credits for each transaction. In addition, after a transaction is recorded, total debits must equal total credits.

**STEPS**

**Questions for analyzing a transaction into its debit and credit parts**

1. Which accounts are affected?
   *Cash* and *Barbara Treviño, Capital*
2. How is each account classified?
   *Cash* is an asset account. *Barbara Treviño, Capital* is an owner's equity account.
3. How is each classification changed?
   Assets are increased. Owner's equity is increased.
4. How is each amount entered in the accounts?
   Assets increase on the debit side. Therefore, the asset account, *Cash,* is debited. Owner's equity accounts increase on the credit side. Therefore, the owner's equity account, *Barbara Treviño, Capital,* is credited.

## PAID CASH FOR SUPPLIES

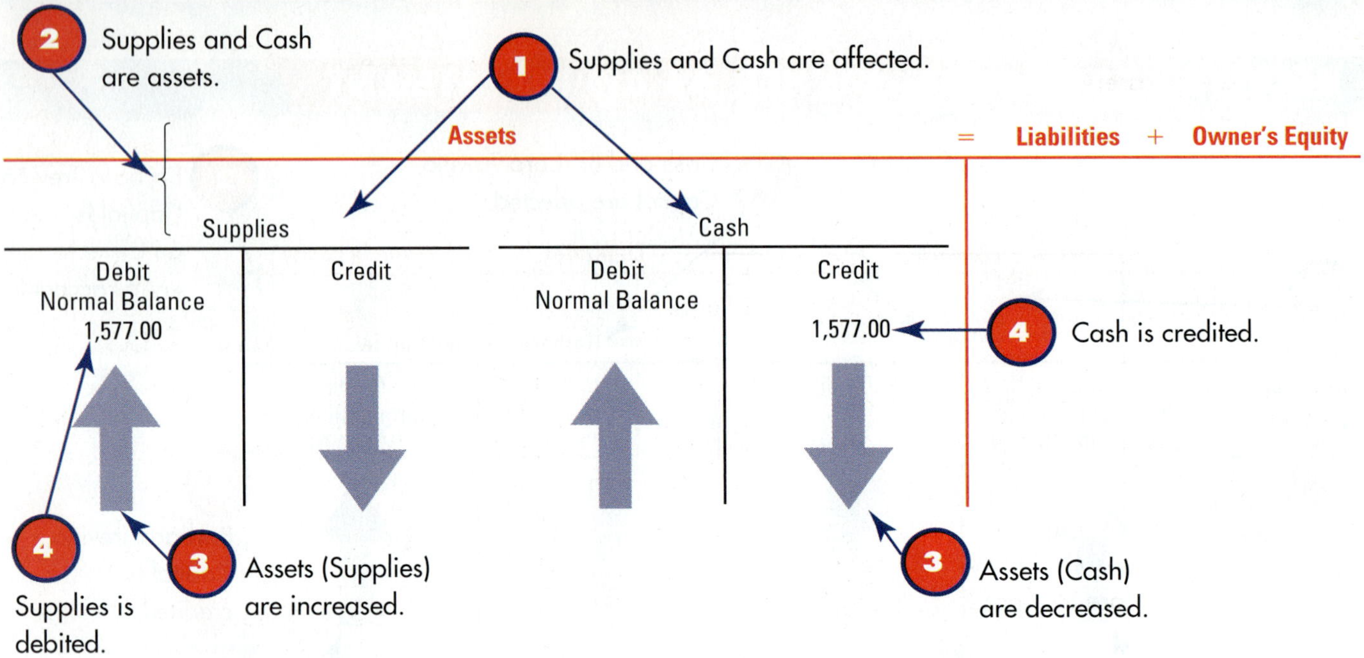


***August 3. Paid cash for supplies, $1,577.00.***

The effect of this transaction on the accounting equation is shown in the illustration. In this transaction, two asset accounts are changed. One asset, cash, has been exchanged for another asset, supplies. The asset account, Cash, is decreased by $1,577.00, the amount of cash paid out. This decrease is on the left side of the accounting equation. The asset account, Supplies, is increased by $1,577.00, the amount of supplies bought. This increase is also on the left side of the accounting equation.

The two changes are both on the left side of the accounting equation. When changes are made on only one side of the accounting equation, the equation must still be in balance. Therefore, if one account is increased, another account on the same side of the equation must be decreased.

As you have seen, transactions must be carefully analyzed. It must be determined if a transaction affects accounts from both sides of the accounting equation. Or a transaction may affect accounts that are on the same side of the accounting equation, as is true in this example. A common error is to assume that every transaction must affect accounts from both sides of the accounting equation.

The same four questions are used every time a transaction is analyzed.

**STEPS**

**Questions for analyzing a transaction into its debit and credit parts**

1. Which accounts are affected?
   *Supplies* and *Cash*
2. How is each account classified?
   *Supplies* is an asset account. *Cash* is an asset account.
3. How is each classification changed?
   Assets *(Supplies)* are increased and assets *(Cash)* are decreased.
4. How is each amount entered in the accounts?
   Assets increase on the debit side. Therefore, the asset account, *Supplies,* is debited. Assets decrease on the credit side. Therefore, the asset account, *Cash,* is credited.

## PAID CASH FOR INSURANCE

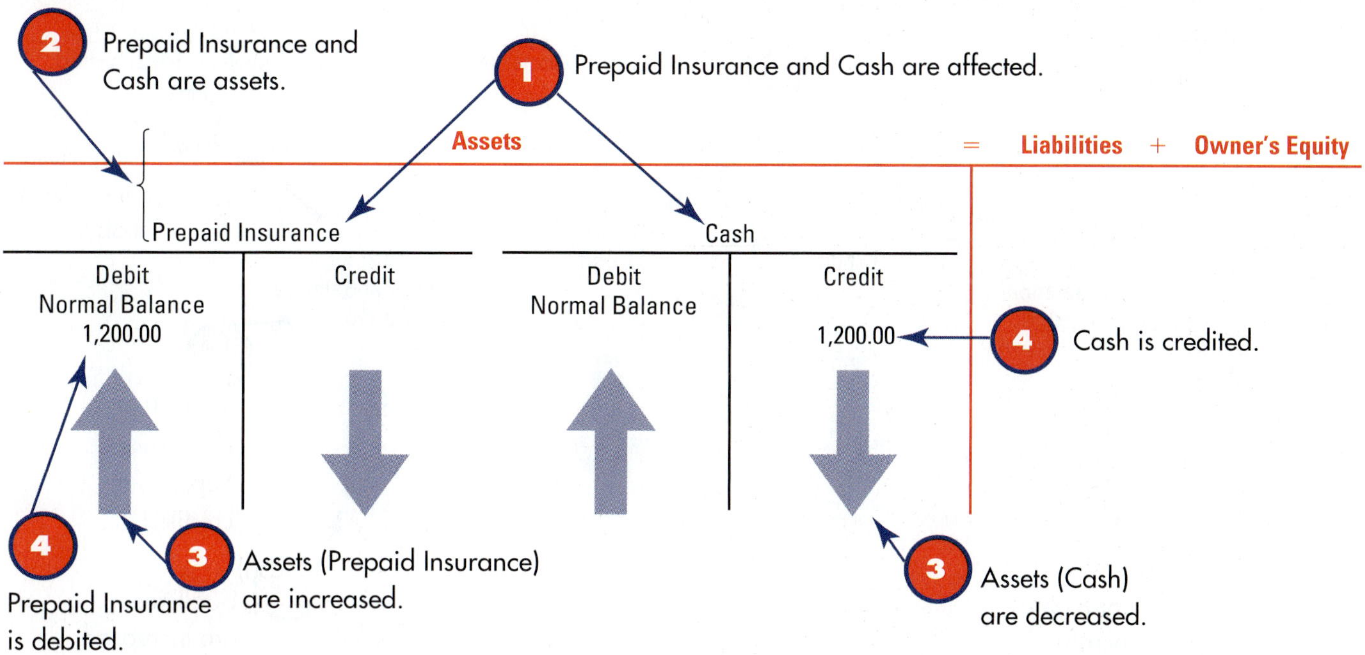


***August 4. Paid cash for insurance, $1,200.00.***

Paying cash for insurance is very similar to paying cash for supplies. One asset is increased and one asset is decreased.

The effect of this transaction on the accounting equation is shown in the illustration. In this transaction, two assets are changed. One asset, cash, has been exchanged for another asset, prepaid insurance. The asset account, Cash, is decreased by $1,200.00, the amount of cash paid out. This decrease is on the left side of the accounting equation. The asset account, Prepaid Insurance, is increased by $1,200.00, the amount of insurance bought. This increase is also on the left side of the accounting equation.

**FYI**

*T accounts get their names from the arrangement of the lines making up the account. The horizontal line on top of the centered vertical line together look like a capital T.*

**STEPS**

**Questions for analyzing a transaction into its debit and credit parts**

1. Which accounts are affected?
   *Prepaid Insurance* and *Cash*
2. How is each account classified?
   *Prepaid Insurance* is an asset account. *Cash* is an asset account.
3. How is each classification changed?
   Assets *(Prepaid Insurance)* are increased and assets *(Cash)* are decreased.
4. How is each amount entered in the accounts?
   Assets increase on the debit side. Therefore, the asset account, *Prepaid Insurance,* is debited. Assets decrease on the credit side. Therefore, the asset account, *Cash,* is credited.

**FYI**

*Paying cash for insurance and buying supplies for cash are examples of transactions that affect only one side of the accounting equation. All the accounts involved in these transactions are assets.*

## BOUGHT SUPPLIES ON ACCOUNT

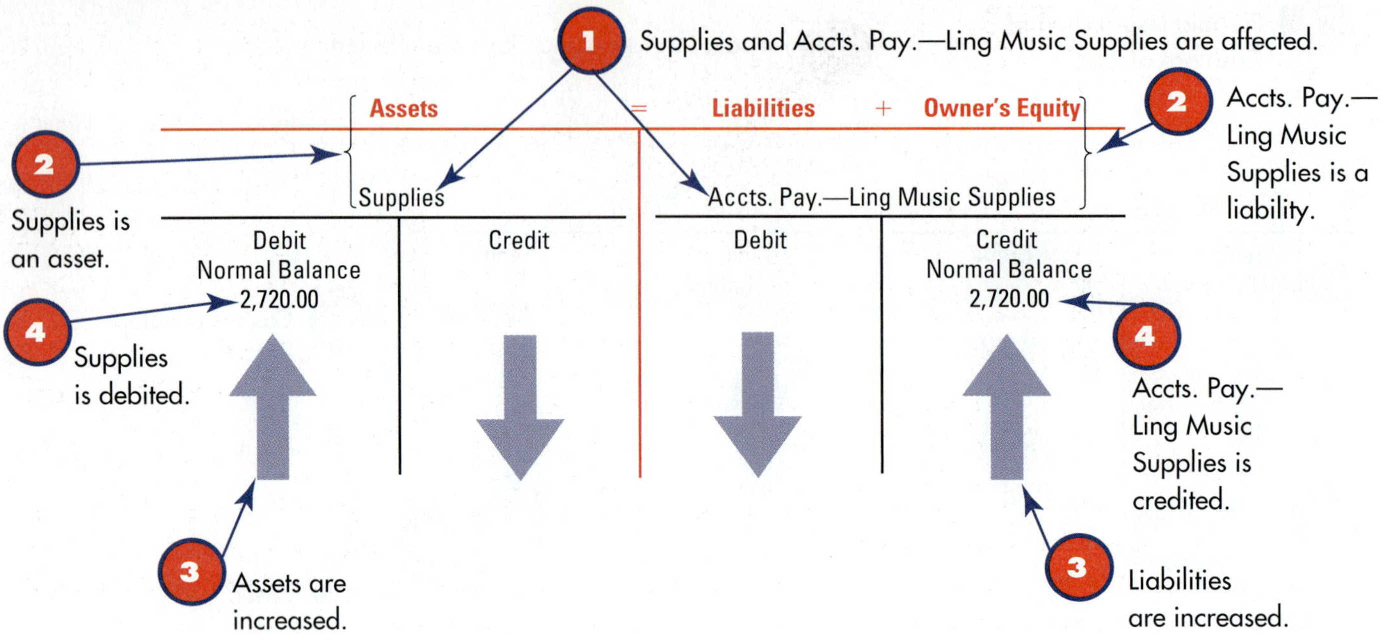


***August 7. Bought supplies on account from Ling Music Supplies, $2,720.00.***

The effect of this transaction on the accounting equation is shown in the illustration. In this transaction, one asset and one liability are changed. The asset account, Supplies, is increased by $2,720.00, the amount of supplies bought. This increase is on the left side of the accounting equation. Ling Music Supplies will have a claim against some of Encore Music's assets until Encore Music pays for the supplies bought. Therefore, Accounts Payable—Ling Music Supplies is a liability account. The liability account, Accounts Payable—Ling Music Supplies, is increased by $2,720.00, the amount owed for the supplies. This increase is on the right side of the accounting equation.

**STEPS**

### Questions for analyzing a transaction into its debit and credit parts

1. Which accounts are affected?
   *Supplies* and *Accounts Payable—Ling Music Supplies*
2. How is each account classified?
   *Supplies* is an asset account. *Accounts Payable—Ling Music Supplies* is a liability account.
3. How is each classification changed?
   Assets are increased. Liabilities are increased.
4. How is each amount entered in the accounts?
   Assets increase on the debit side. Therefore, the asset account, *Supplies,* is debited. Liabilities increase on the credit side. Therefore, the liability account, *Accounts Payable—Ling Music Supplies,* is credited.

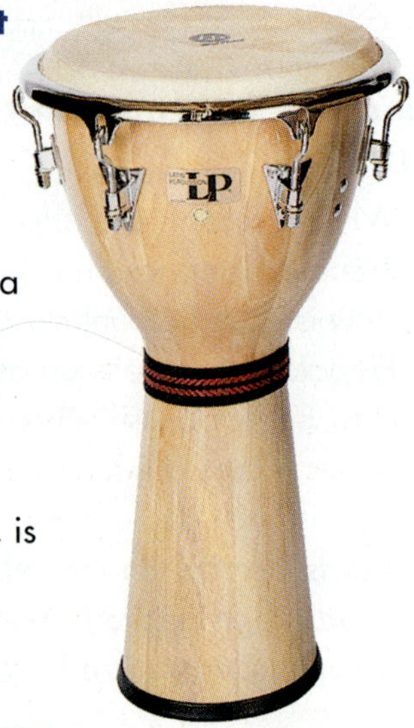

## PAID CASH ON ACCOUNT

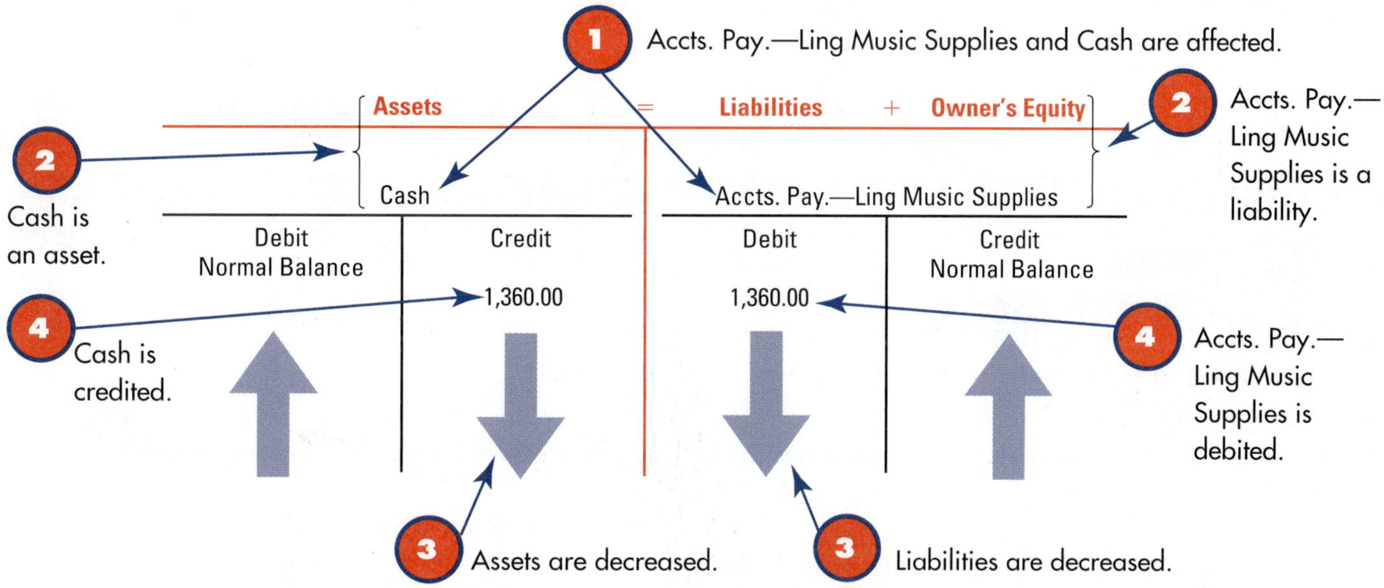


***August 11. Paid cash on account to Ling Music Supplies, $1,360.00.***

The effect of this transaction on the accounting equation is shown in the illustration. In this transaction, one asset and one liability are changed. The asset account, Cash, is decreased by $1,360.00, the amount of cash paid out. This decrease is on the left side of the accounting equation. After this payment, Encore Music owes less money to Ling Music Supplies. Therefore, the liability account, Accounts Payable—Ling Music Supplies, is decreased by $1,360.00, the amount paid on account. The decrease is on the right side of the accounting equation.

### STEPS: Questions for analyzing a transaction into its debit and credit parts

1. Which accounts are affected?
   *Accounts Payable—Ling Music Supplies* and *Cash*
2. How is each account classified?
   *Accounts Payable—Ling Music Supplies* is a liability account. *Cash* is an asset account.
3. How is each classification changed?
   Liabilities are decreased. Assets are decreased.
4. How is each amount entered in the accounts?
   Liabilities decrease on the debit side. Therefore, the liability account, *Accounts Payable—Ling Music Supplies,* is debited. Assets decrease on the credit side. Therefore, the asset account, *Cash,* is credited.

**FYI**

*A chart of accounts is sometimes referred to by its initials COA. Many accounting terms are often abbreviated or referred to by initials. For example, accounts payable is sometimes referred to as A/P.*

**REMEMBER**

When you decrease an account balance, record the decrease on the side opposite the normal balance side of the account. The side opposite the normal balance side can be on the left or the right depending on the type of account.

## TERM REVIEW

chart of accounts

## AUDIT YOUR UNDERSTANDING

1. State the four questions used to analyze a transaction.
2. What two accounts are affected when a business pays cash for supplies?

## WORK TOGETHER

**Analyzing a transaction into its debit and credit parts**

T accounts are given in the *Working Papers.* Your instructor will guide you through the following examples. Kathy Bergum owns Bergum Services. Bergum Services uses the following accounts. Some of the accounts will be explained in Lesson 3-3.

| | | | |
|---|---|---|---|
| Cash | Supplies | Kathy Bergum, Drawing | Rent Expense |
| Accts. Rec.—Sam Erickson | Prepaid Insurance | Sales | |
| Accts. Pay.—Bales Supplies | Kathy Bergum, Capital | Advertising Expense | |

***Transactions:*** Apr.
1. Received cash from owner as an investment, $5,000.00.
2. Paid cash for supplies, $50.00.
5. Paid cash for insurance, $75.00.
6. Bought supplies on account from Bales Supplies, $100.00.
9. Paid cash on account to Bales Supplies, $50.00.

3. For each transaction write on T accounts the account titles of the two accounts affected.
4. Write the debit or credit amount in each T account to show the transaction's effect.

## ON YOUR OWN

**Analyzing a transaction into its debit and credit parts**

T accounts are given in the *Working Papers.* Work these problems independently. Jens Puckett owns Jens Accounting Service. Jens Accounting Service uses the following accounts. Some of the accounts will be explained in Lesson 3-3.

| | | | |
|---|---|---|---|
| Cash | Supplies | Jens Puckett, Drawing | Utilities Expense |
| Accts. Rec.—King Company | Prepaid Insurance | Sales | |
| Accts. Pay.—Computer Supply | Jens Puckett, Capital | Miscellaneous Expense | |

***Transactions:*** Sept.
1. Received cash from owner as an investment, $3,000.00.
4. Paid cash for insurance, $100.00.
5. Paid cash for supplies, $90.00.
6. Bought supplies on account from Computer Supply, $200.00.
11. Paid cash on account to Computer Supply, $150.00.

5. For each transaction write on T accounts the account titles of the two accounts affected.
6. Write the debit or credit amount in each T account to show the transaction's effect.

# 3-3 Analyzing How Transactions Affect Owner's Equity Accounts

## RECEIVED CASH FROM SALES

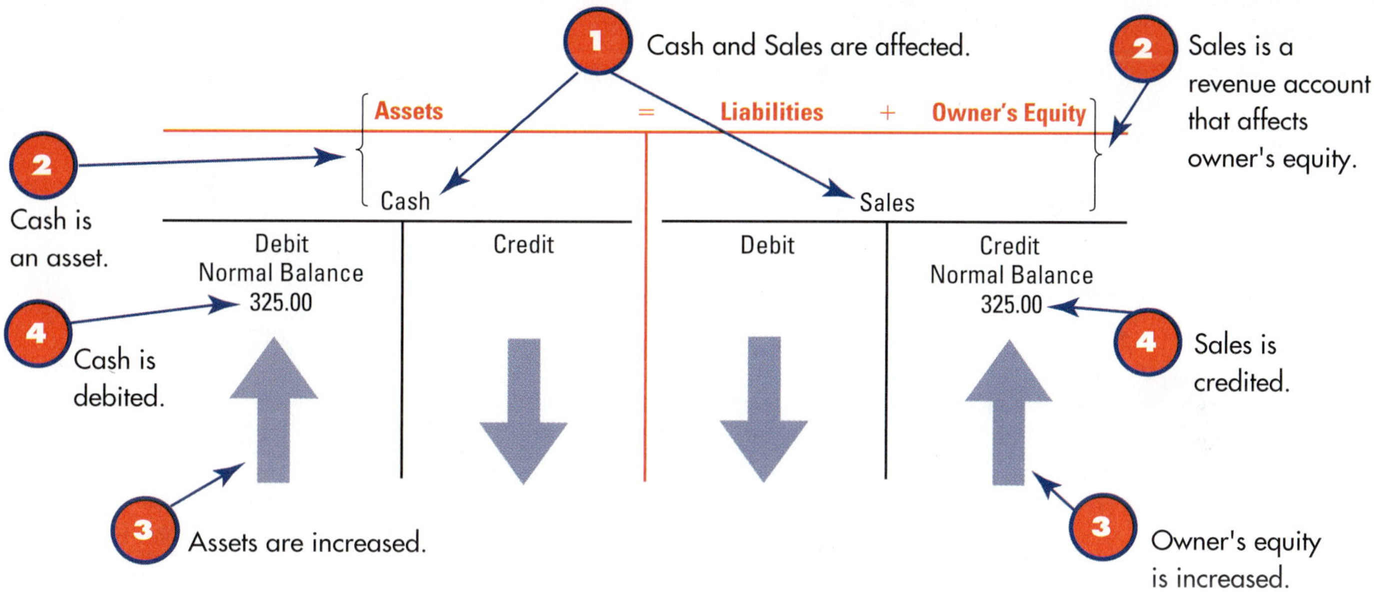


***August 12. Received cash from sales, $325.00.***

Revenue increases owner's equity. The increases from revenue could be recorded directly in the owner's capital account. However, to avoid a capital account with a large number of entries and to summarize revenue information separately from the other records, Encore Music uses a separate revenue account titled Sales.

The owner's capital account has a normal credit balance. Increases in the owner's capital account are shown as credits. Because revenue increases owner's equity, increases in revenue are recorded as credits. A revenue account has a normal credit balance.

**FYI**

*The Small Business Administration (SBA) offers two major types of loans to small businesses. One type of loan is made by private lending institutions. Another type of loan is made directly by the SBA.*

**STEPS**

### Questions for analyzing a transaction into its debit and credit parts

1. Which accounts are affected?
   *Cash* and *Sales*
2. How is each account classified?
   *Cash* is an asset account. *Sales* is a revenue account that affects owner's equity.
3. How is each classification changed?
   Assets are increased. Owner's equity is increased.
4. How is each amount entered in the accounts?
   Assets increase on the debit side. Therefore, the asset account, *Cash*, is debited. Owner's equity accounts increase on the credit side. Revenue increases owner's equity. Therefore, the revenue account, *Sales,* is credited.

## SOLD SERVICES ON ACCOUNT

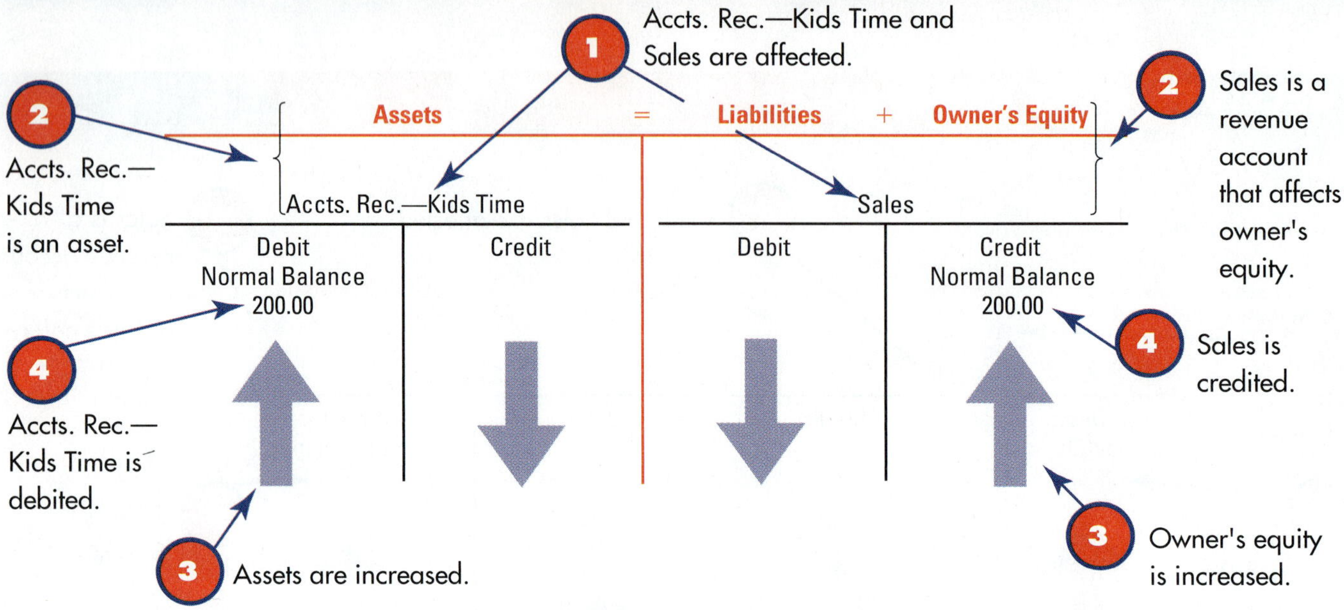


***August 12. Sold services on account to Kids Time, $200.00.***

The analysis for selling services on account is similar to that for selling services for cash. The only difference is that cash is not received at this time; therefore, the cash account is not affected by the transaction. Instead, this transaction increases an accounts receivable account. The same four questions are used to analyze this transaction into its debit and credit parts.

### STEPS: Questions for analyzing a transaction into its debit and credit parts

1. Which accounts are affected?
   *Accounts Receivable—Kids Time* and *Sales*
2. How is each account classified?
   *Accounts Receivable—Kids Time* is an asset account. *Sales* is a revenue account that affects owner's equity.
3. How is each classification changed?
   Assets are increased. Owner's equity is increased.
4. How is each amount entered in the accounts?
   Assets increase on the debit side. Therefore, the asset account, *Accounts Receivable—Kids Time,* is debited. Owner's equity accounts increase on the credit side. Revenue increases owner's equity. Therefore, the revenue account, *Sales,* is credited.

### REMEMBER

Owner's equity is recorded on the right side of the accounting equation. The right side of a T account is the credit side. Therefore, owner's equity has a normal credit balance.

## PAID CASH FOR AN EXPENSE

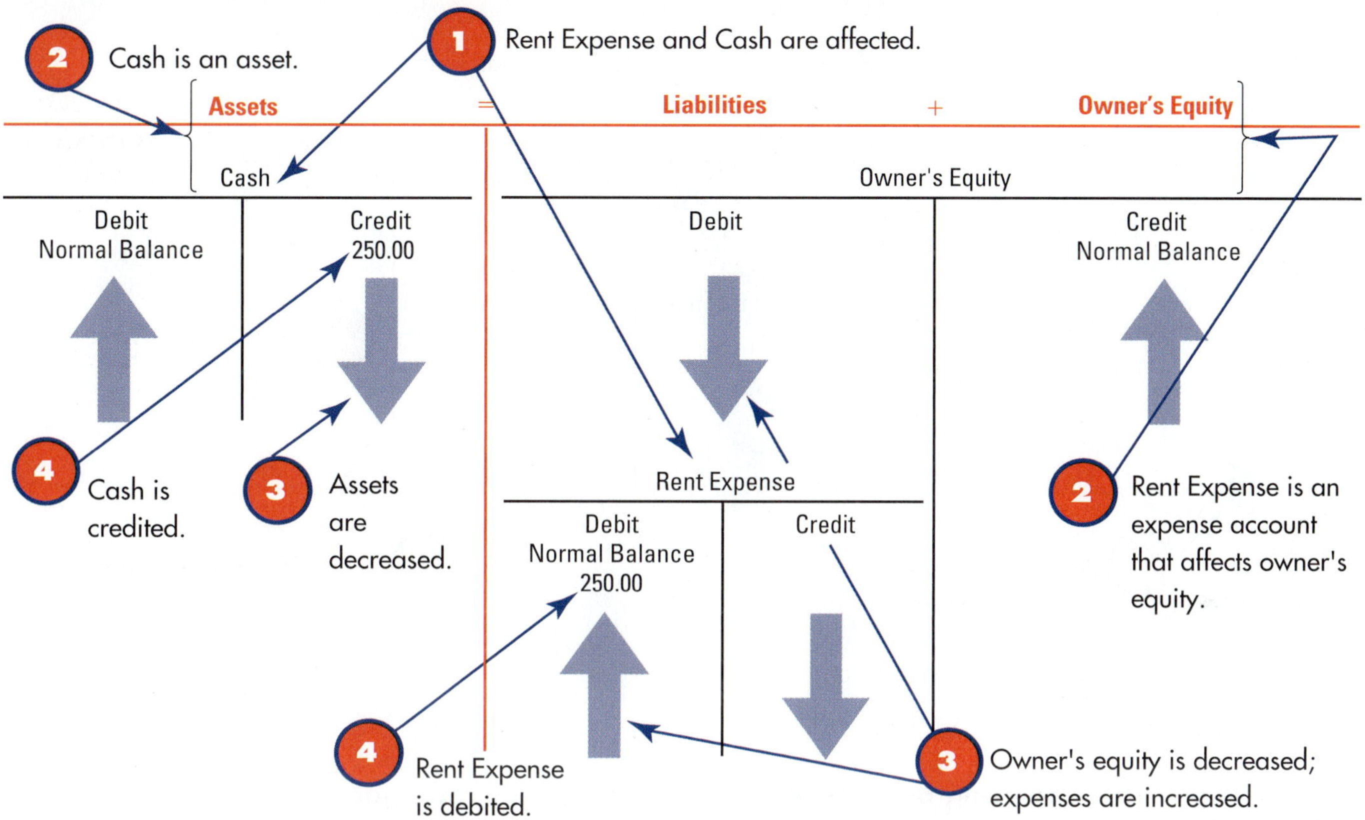


***August 12. Paid cash for rent, $250.00.***

Expenses decrease owner's equity. The decreases from expenses could be recorded directly in the owner's capital account. However, to avoid a capital account with a large number of entries and to summarize expense information separately from the other records, Encore Music uses separate expense accounts.

The titles of Encore Music's expense accounts are shown on its chart of accounts. The expense account, Rent Expense, is used to record all payments for rent.

The owner's capital account has a normal credit balance. Decreases in the owner's capital account are shown as debits. Therefore, an expense account has a normal debit balance. Because expenses decrease owner's equity, increases in expenses are recorded as debits.

All expense transactions are recorded in a similar manner.

### STEPS Questions for analyzing a transaction into its debit and credit parts

1. Which accounts are affected?
   *Rent Expense* and *Cash*
2. How is each account classified?
   *Rent Expense* is an expense account that affects owner's equity. *Cash* is an asset account.
3. How is each classification changed?
   Owner's equity is decreased by an increase in expenses. Assets are decreased.
4. How is each amount entered in the accounts?
   Owner's equity accounts decrease on the debit side. An increase in expenses decreases owner's equity. Expense accounts have normal debit balances. Therefore, the expense account, *Rent Expense,* is debited. Assets decrease on the credit side. Therefore, the asset account, *Cash,* is credited.

## RECEIVED CASH ON ACCOUNT

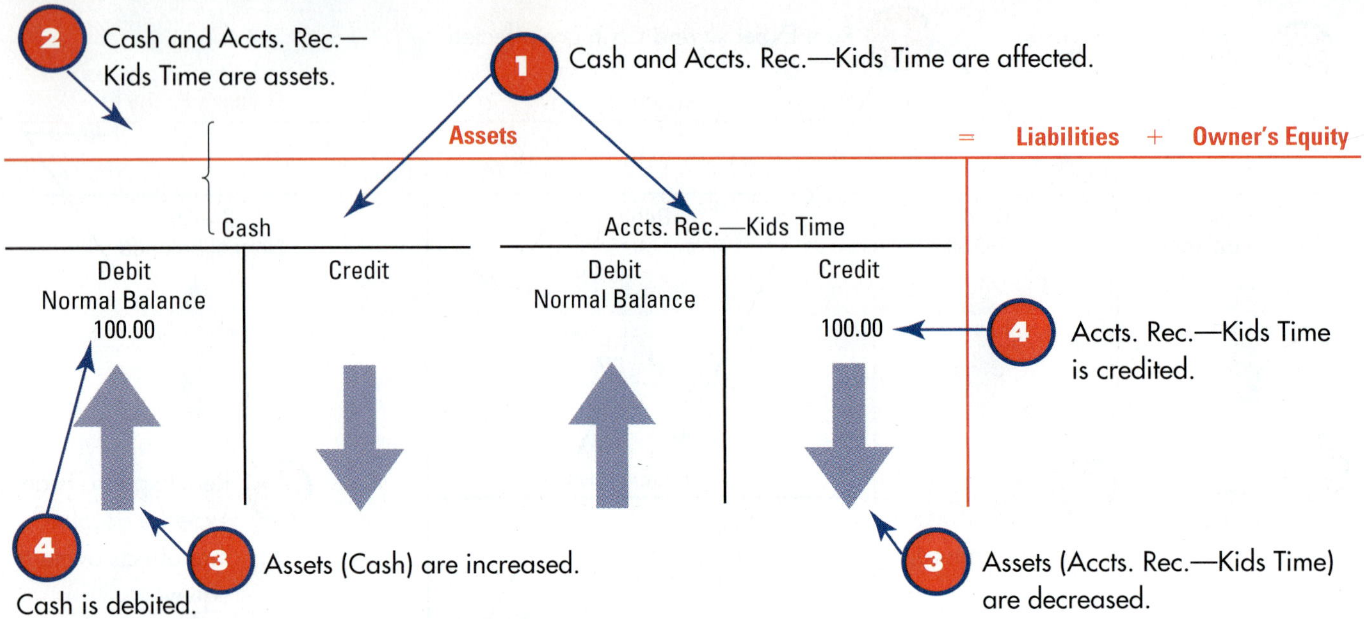


***August 12. Received cash on account from Kids Time, $100.00.***

### STEPS Questions for analyzing a transaction into its debit and credit parts

1. Which accounts are affected?
   *Cash* and *Accounts Receivable—Kids Time*
2. How is each account classified?
   *Cash* is an asset account. *Accounts Receivable—Kids Time* is an asset account.
3. How is each classification changed?
   Assets *(Cash)* are increased and assets *(Accounts Receivable—Kids Time)* are decreased.
4. How is each amount entered in the accounts?
   Assets increase on the debit side. Therefore, the asset account, *Cash,* is debited. Assets decrease on the credit side. Therefore, the asset account, *Accounts Receivable—Kids Time,* is credited.

### CULTURAL DIVERSITY

#### ANCIENT CHINA

By approximately 1000 B.C. the Chinese had developed one of the most sophisticated accounting systems in the world. The Chao Dynasty ruled China from 1122 to 256 B.C. During this time the dynasty oversaw territorial expansion and a Golden Age in literature and philosophy. The famous philosopher Confucius lived during this dynasty. Confucius was said to have been a government recordkeeper.

During the Chao Dynasty, the Chinese used a system of currency and had a central bank. The Office of the Superintendent of Records furnished compilations of receipts and payments. It also kept maps and records of production tools used. Many of the accounting and record keeping tasks that affect businesses and governments today can be traced back to systems established in ancient China.

## PAID CASH TO OWNER FOR PERSONAL USE

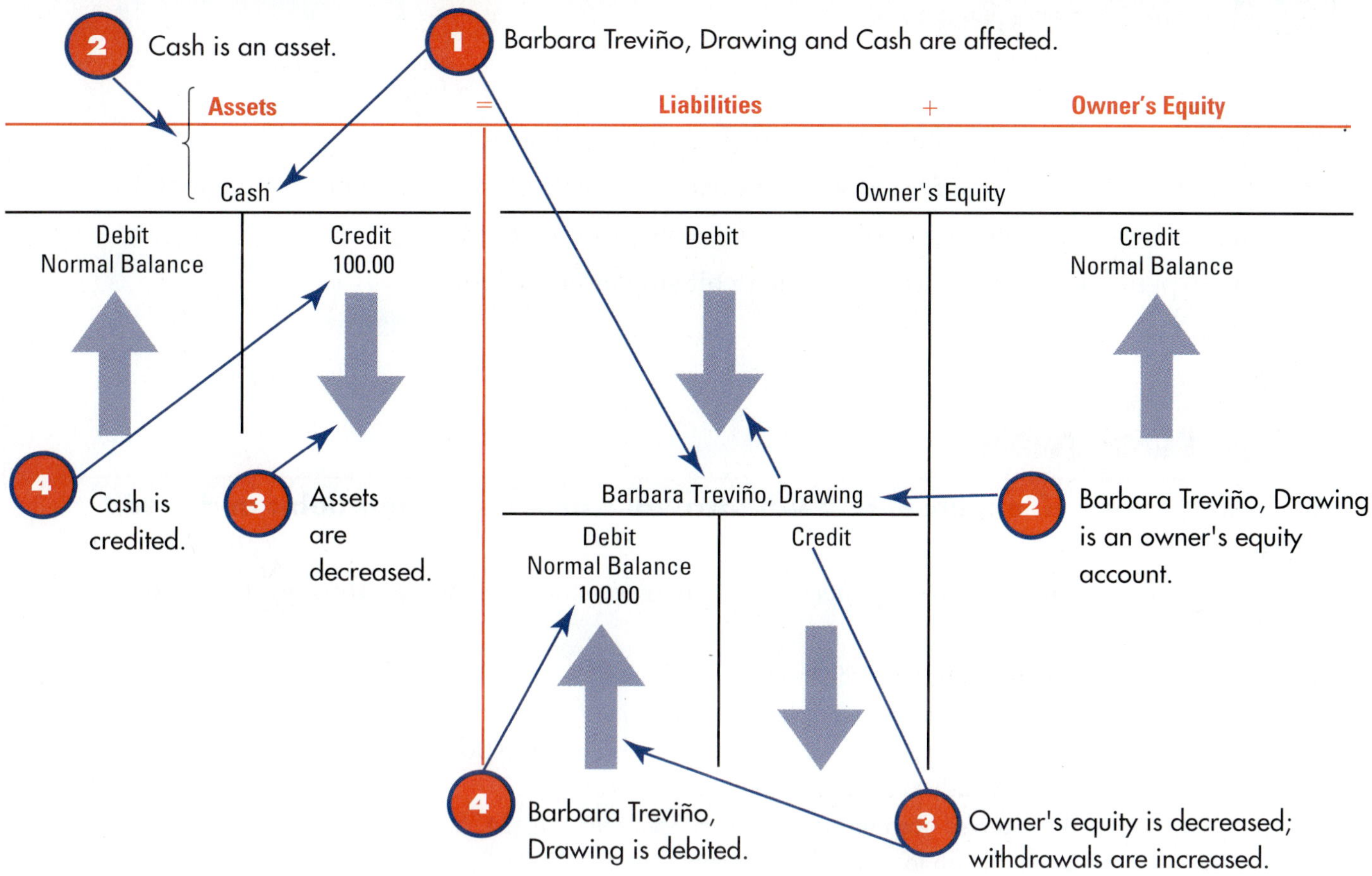


***August 12. Paid cash to owner for personal use, $100.00.***

Withdrawals decrease owner's equity. Withdrawals could be recorded directly in the owner's capital account. However, to avoid a capital account with a large number of entries and to summarize withdrawal information separately from the other records, Encore Music uses a separate withdrawal account titled Barbara Treviño, Drawing.

### STEPS Questions for analyzing a transaction into its debit and credit parts

1. Which accounts are affected?
   *Barbara Treviño, Drawing,* and *Cash*
2. How is each account classified?
   *Barbara Treviño, Drawing* is an owner's equity account. *Cash* is an asset account.
3. How is each classification changed?
   Owner's equity is decreased by an increase in withdrawals. Assets are decreased.
4. How is each amount entered in the accounts?
   Owner's equity accounts decrease on the debit side. An increase in withdrawals decreases owner's equity. Withdrawal accounts have normal debit balances. Therefore, the owner's equity account, *Barbara Treviño, Drawing,* is debited. Assets decrease on the credit side. Therefore, the asset account, *Cash,* is credited.

**FYI**

*When drawing T accounts to analyze transactions, stack the accounts instead of writing them horizontally. Stacking the accounts will make it easier to recognize debits and credits.*

## AUDIT YOUR UNDERSTANDING

1. What two accounts are affected when a business receives cash from sales?
2. What two accounts are affected when services are sold on account?
3. What two accounts are affected when a business pays cash to the owner for personal use?
4. Are revenue accounts increased on the debit side or credit side?
5. Are expense accounts increased on the debit side or credit side?

## WORK TOGETHER

**Analyzing revenue, expense, and withdrawal transactions into debit and credit parts**

T accounts are given in the *Working Papers*. Your instructor will guide you through the following examples.

Use the chart of accounts for Bergum Services on page 50.

***Transactions:*** Apr. 10. Received cash from sales, $600.00.
11. Sold services on account to Sam Erickson, $850.00.
14. Paid cash for rent, $250.00.
18. Received cash on account from Sam Erickson, $425.00.
20. Paid cash to owner for personal use, $300.00.

6. Prepare two T accounts for each transaction. On each T account, write the account title of one of the accounts affected by the transaction.
7. Write the debit or credit amount in each T account to show the transaction's effect.

## ON YOUR OWN

**Analyzing revenue, expense, and withdrawal transactions into debit and credit parts**

T accounts are given in the *Working Papers*. Work these problems independently.

Use the chart of accounts for Jens Accounting Service on page 50.

***Transactions:*** Sept. 13. Received cash from sales, $1,000.00.
15. Sold services on account to King Company, $1,500.00.
16. Paid cash for utilities, $500.00.
18. Received cash on account from King Company, $750.00.
21. Paid cash to owner for personal use, $650.00.

8. Prepare two T accounts for each transaction. On each T account, write the account title of one of the accounts affected by the transaction.
9. Write the debit or credit amount in each T account to show the transaction's effect.

# CHAPTER 3 SUMMARY

*Enrichment Activity*

**Accounting Careers**

*Many accounting careers have different levels of competence. Different levels might be indicated with descriptions such as "junior," "assistant," or "senior." Use a job search site on the Internet, such as monster.com, and search for accounting positions. Find three that indicate different levels of competence. Describe the experience level required for each of the three.*

After completing this chapter, you can

1. Define important accounting terms related to analyzing transactions into debit and credit parts.
2. Identify accounting practices related to analyzing transactions into debit and credit parts.
3. Use T accounts to analyze transactions showing which accounts are debited or credited for each transaction.
4. Analyze how transactions to set up a business affect accounts.
5. Analyze how transactions affect owner's equity accounts.

## EXPLORE ACCOUNTING

### OWNER WITHDRAWALS

Employee salaries are considered an expense that reduces the net income of a company. When the owner withdraws cash from the company, this withdrawal is *not* considered an expense. The income of a business is calculated by subtracting total expenses from total revenue. Since withdrawals are not considered to be an expense, they do not affect the business's income.

A business owned by one person is called a proprietorship. The Internal Revenue Service does not require the proprietorship, itself, to pay taxes. However, the owner of the proprietorship must include the net income of the proprietorship in his or her own taxable income.

Because the net income of a proprietorship is not affected by owner withdrawals, the income tax paid by the owner is not affected by how much cash the owner withdraws from the business. If Wang Accounting Services has revenues of $2,500.00 and expenses of $1,100.00, its net income is $1,400.00 ($2,500.00 – $1,100.00). Wang Accounting Services will have net income of $1,100.00 regardless of whether the owner withdraws $100.00 or $1,000.00 from the business during that period.

**Discussion:**

1. Ed Westing owns ESW Party Service. He is considering giving his employees a raise that would increase salaries by $15,000.00 per year. What effect would this raise have on Mr. Westing's income tax?
2. Mr. Westing is also considering withdrawing $5,000.00 from ESW Party Service for his personal use. What effect would this withdrawal have on the income tax Mr. Westing must pay this year?

## 3-1 APPLICATION PROBLEM
### Determining the normal balance, increase, and decrease sides for accounts

Write the answers for the following problem in the *Working Papers.*

Cash
Accounts Receivable—Laurie Menz
Supplies
Prepaid Insurance
Accounts Payable—Gerald B's
Accounts Payable—VanDyke Company
Vivian Marx, Capital

| 1 | 2 | 3 | 4 | 5 | 6 | 7 | 8 |
|---|---|---|---|---|---|---|---|
| Account | Account Classification | Account's Normal Balance | | Increase Side | | Decrease Side | |
| | | Debit | Credit | Debit | Credit | Debit | Credit |
| *Cash* | *Asset* | √ | | √ | | | √ |

***Instructions:***

Do the following for each account. The cash account is given as an example.

1. Write the account title in Column 1.
2. Write the account classification in Column 2.
3. Place a check mark in either Column 3 or 4 to indicate the normal balance of the account.
4. Place a check mark in either Column 5 or 6 to indicate the increase side of the account.
5. Place a check mark in either Column 7 or 8 to indicate the decrease side of the account.

## 3-2 APPLICATION PROBLEM
### Analyzing transactions into debit and credit parts

John Burke owns John's Marketing Services, which uses the following accounts:

Cash
Supplies
Prepaid Insurance
Accounts Receivable—Orv Grant
Accounts Payable—D & S Company
John Burke, Capital
John Burke, Drawing
Sales
Advertising Expense
Rent Expense

***Transactions:***

Mar. 1. Received cash from owner as an investment, $1,500.00.
1. Paid cash for insurance, $600.00.
3. Bought supplies on account from D & S Company, $800.00
5. Paid cash for supplies, $200.00.
8. Paid cash on account to D & S Company, $400.00.

***Instructions:***

1. Prepare two T accounts for each transaction. On each T account, write the account title of one of the accounts affected by the transaction. Use the forms in your *Working Papers.*

2. Write the debit or credit amount in each T account to show how the transaction affected that account. T accounts for the first transaction are given as an example.

**MARCH 1.**

| Cash | |
|---:|---|
| 1,500.00 | |

| John Burke, Capital | |
|---|---:|
| | 1,500.00 |

## 3-3 APPLICATION PROBLEM

### Analyzing revenue, expense, and withdrawal transactions into debit and credit parts

Use the chart of accounts for John's Marketing Services given in Application Problem 3-2.

***Transactions:***

Mar. 11. Received cash from sales, $2,200.00.
 12. Paid cash for advertising, $150.00.
 14. Sold services on account to Orv Grant, $1,700.00.
 18. Paid cash to owner for personal use, $500.00.
 19. Received cash on account from Orv Grant, $1,000.00.

***Instructions:***

1. Prepare two T accounts for each transaction. On each T account, write the account title of one of the accounts affected by the transaction. Use the forms in your *Working Papers.*
2. Write the debit or credit amount in each T account to show how the transaction affected that account.

## 3-4 APPLICATION PROBLEM

### Analyzing revenue, expense, and withdrawal transactions into debit and credit parts

Use the chart of accounts for John's Marketing Services given in Application Problem 3-2.

***Transactions:***

Mar. 25. Sold services for cash, $900.00.
 26. Performed $750.00 of services for Orv Grant on account.
 27. Ran an ad in the local newspaper. Paid $25.00 cash.
 28. John Burke withdrew $450.00 for his personal use.
 29. Received a $375.00 check from Orv Grant on account.

***Instructions:***

1. Prepare two T accounts for each transaction. On each T account, write the account title of one of the accounts affected by the transaction. Use the forms in your *Working Papers.*
2. Write the debit or credit amount in each T account to show how the transaction affected that account.

## 3-5 MASTERY PROBLEM
### Analyzing transactions into debit and credit parts

Mark Lands owns a business called LandScape. LandScape uses the following accounts.

| | |
|---|---|
| Cash | Mark Lands, Drawing |
| Accounts Receivable—Joseph Corbett | Sales |
| Accounts Receivable—Vera Rice | Advertising Expense |
| Supplies | Miscellaneous Expense |
| Prepaid Insurance | Rent Expense |
| Accounts Payable—Derner Office Supplies | Repair Expense |
| Accounts Payable—Janitor Supplies | Utilities Expense |
| Mark Lands, Capital | |

***Instructions:***

1. Prepare a T account for each account. Use the forms in your *Working Papers.*
2. Analyze each transaction into its debit and credit parts. Write the debit and credit amounts in the proper T accounts to show how each transaction changes account balances. Write the date of the transaction in parentheses before each amount.

***Transactions:***

June 1. Received cash from owner as an investment, $3,000.00.
2. Paid cash for supplies, $60.00.
4. Paid cash for rent, $200.00.
4. Received cash from sales, $350.00.
5. Paid cash for repairs, $10.00.
8. Sold services on account to Joseph Corbett, $200.00.
9. Bought supplies on account from Janitor Supplies, $500.00.
10. Paid cash for insurance, $100.00.
11. Received cash from owner as an investment, $900.00.
11. Received cash from sales, $300.00.
12. Bought supplies on account from Derner Office Supplies, $50.00.
13. Received cash on account from Joseph Corbett, $125.00.
15. Paid cash for miscellaneous expense, $5.00.
16. Paid cash on account to Janitor Supplies, $50.00.
22. Paid cash for electric bill (utilities expense), $35.00.
23. Paid cash for advertising, $30.00.
25. Sold services on account to Vera Rice, $220.00.
26. Paid cash to owner for personal use, $600.00.
30. Received cash on account from Vera Rice, $100.00.

## 3-6 CHALLENGE PROBLEM
### Analyzing transactions recorded in T accounts

Carol Burns owns a business for which the following T accounts show the current financial situation. Write the answers for the following problem in the *Working Papers.*

**Cash**

| | Debit | | Credit |
|---|---|---|---|
| (1) | 5,000.00 | (2) | 80.00 |
| (6) | 475.00 | (4) | 15.00 |
| (8) | 350.00 | (5) | 16.00 |
| (9) | 400.00 | (7) | 900.00 |
| | | (10) | 150.00 |
| | | (11) | 95.00 |
| | | (12) | 50.00 |

**Sales**

| | Debit | | Credit |
|---|---|---|---|
| | | (6) | 475.00 |
| | | (8) | 350.00 |
| | | (9) | 400.00 |
| | | (13) | 225.00 |

**Accts. Rec.—David Gotch**

| | Debit | | Credit |
|---|---|---|---|
| (13) | 225.00 | | |

**Advertising Expense**

| | Debit | | Credit |
|---|---|---|---|
| (5) | 16.00 | | |

**Supplies**

| | Debit | | Credit |
|---|---|---|---|
| (3) | 300.00 | | |
| (11) | 95.00 | | |

**Miscellaneous Expense**

| | Debit | | Credit |
|---|---|---|---|
| (4) | 15.00 | | |

**Accts. Pay.—Midwest Supplies**

| | Debit | | Credit |
|---|---|---|---|
| (10) | 150.00 | (3) | 300.00 |

**Rent Expense**

| | Debit | | Credit |
|---|---|---|---|
| (7) | 900.00 | | |

**Carol Burns, Capital**

| | Debit | | Credit |
|---|---|---|---|
| | | (1) | 5,000.00 |

**Utilities Expense**

| | Debit | | Credit |
|---|---|---|---|
| (12) | 50.00 | | |

**Carol Burns, Drawing**

| | Debit | | Credit |
|---|---|---|---|
| (2) | 80.00 | | |

| 1 | 2 | 3 | 4 | 5 | 6 |
|---|---|---|---|---|---|
| Trans. No. | Accounts Affected | Account Classification | Entered in Account as a | | Description of Transaction |
| | | | Debit | Credit | |
| 1. | *Cash*<br>*Carol Burns, Capital* | *Asset*<br>*Owner's Equity* | √ | <br>√ | *Received cash from owner as an investment* |

***Instructions:***

1. Analyze each numbered transaction in the T accounts. Write the titles of accounts affected in Column 2. For each account, write the classification of the account in Column 3.
2. For each account, place a check mark in either Column 4 or 5 to indicate if the account is affected by a debit or a credit.
3. For each transaction, write a brief statement in Column 6 describing the transaction. Information for Transaction 1 is given as an example.

INTERNET ACTIVITY

Point your browser to

**http://accounting.swpco.com**

Choose **First-Year Course**, choose **Activities**, and complete the activity for Chapter 3.

## Applied Communication

An entrepreneur is a person who attempts to earn a profit by taking the risk of operating a business. You have expressed an interest in starting your own business after graduation. Your family has agreed to help finance your new business if you can convince them that you would be successful.

**Instructions:** Develop a plan outlining the details of the business you would operate. Describe the type of business, the equipment or resources needed, and financial information, such as start-up costs and expenses. Write clear and persuasive sentences.

## Cases for Critical Thinking

**Case 1** Sharon Morris records all cash receipts as revenue and all cash payments as expenses. Is Ms. Morris recording her cash receipts and cash payments correctly? Explain your answer.

**Case 2** Thomas Bueler records all investments, revenue, expenses, and withdrawals in his capital account. At the end of each month, Mr. Bueler sorts the information to prepare a summary of what has caused the changes in his capital account balance. To help Mr. Bueler prepare this summary in the future, what changes would you suggest he make in his records?

# AUTOMATED ACCOUNTING

## SETTING UP THE AUTOMATED ACCOUNTING SOFTWARE DATABASE

The *Automated Accounting* software includes company information, a classification of all the accounts to be used, and required accounts necessary for a business. Also, a general ledger database needs to be created containing a chart of accounts that will be used to enter all transactions.

### General Ledger Database

The General Ledger Database consists of a collection of accounts and the related account numbers needed to prepare financial statements. The general ledger specifically lists accounts for assets, liabilities, owner's equity, expenses, and revenue.

#### Database

A prearranged file in which data can be entered and retrieved is a database. An example of a database in Automated Accounting is the general ledger. It contains general information about the business, a chart of accounts, and a list of the financial activities for each account. The database is designed so that when you enter information it updates the account balances and also stores data in a designated area for creating reports. The general ledger databases to be used for various problems are stored as templates.

#### Ledger and General Ledger

A *ledger* is a group of accounts. A ledger that contains all accounts needed to prepare financial statements is called a *general ledger*. The name given to an account is known as an account title.

### Chart of Accounts Numbering System

A chart of accounts numbering system includes the account numbers that will be used to process transactions for various accounts. This numbering system is generally the same for manual and automated systems. There are procedures designed to set up the chart of accounts. The process includes arranging accounts in the general ledger, assigning the numbers, and keeping records current. This is called *file maintenance*.

#### Account Number

The number assigned to an account is called an *account number*. The first digit of an account number describes the account type. The number of digits in an account number can vary. This book presents three- or four-digit account numbers.

#### File Maintenance

File maintenance includes adding and changing accounts in the chart of accounts. The process of file maintenance can be done in three steps:

1. Create an account number or modify an existing number.
2. Enter the account number in the chart of accounts.
3. Check for accuracy by creating a revised chart of accounts list.

#### Adding an Account Within a Ledger

Adding a new account within a ledger may be necessary when an asset is purchased, a liability is incurred, and for additional expense categories. When adding an account within a ledger, an unused middle number is used. The new account number for Insurance Expense is 525.

520 Gasoline Expense
525 Insurance Expense
530 Supplies Expense

#### Adding an Account at the End of a Ledger

The new account number is the next sequence of 10 from the last account number used so that new numbers can be added easily. There are nine unused numbers between each account when initially set up. New numbers can be assigned between existing account numbers without renumbering all existing accounts.

# 4 Journalizing Transactions

**AFTER STUDYING CHAPTER 4, YOU WILL BE ABLE TO:**

1. Define accounting terms related to journalizing transactions.
2. Identify accounting concepts and practices related to journalizing transactions.
3. Record in a five-column journal transactions to set up a business.
4. Record in a five-column journal transactions to buy insurance for cash and supplies on account.
5. Record in a five-column journal transactions that affect owner's equity and receiving cash on account.
6. Prove and rule a five-column journal and prove cash.

**TERMS PREVIEW**

journal
journalizing
special amount column
general amount column
entry
double-entry accounting
source document
check
invoice
sales invoice
receipt
memorandum
proving cash

## JOURNALS AND JOURNALIZING

As described in Chapter 3, transactions are analyzed into debit and credit parts before information is recorded. A form for recording transactions in chronological order is called a **journal.** Recording transactions in a journal is called **journalizing.**

Transactions could be recorded in the accounting equation. However, most companies wish to create a more permanent record by recording transactions in a journal.

Each business uses the kind of journal that best fits the needs of that business. The nature of a business and the number of transactions to be recorded determine the kind of journal to be used.

The word *journal* comes from the Latin *diurnalis,* meaning daily. Most businesses conduct transactions every day. To keep from getting overloaded, the businesses will make entries in their accounting journals every day.

**FYI**

*The Small Business Administration (SBA) has programs that offer free management and accounting advice to small business owners. The SBA sponsors various workshops and publishes a variety of booklets for small business owners.*

# ACCOUNTING IN YOUR CAREER

## HIGH STANDARDS FOR JOURNALIZING

Sandra Huffman has worked for Marquesa Advertising for 30 days as an accounting clerk, a position for which the company owner, Ramona Marquesa, hired her. She journalizes all transactions, about 50 per day, handles all incoming and outgoing mail, prepares and files all source documents, and performs other duties as assigned.

One day Ramona asked to see the journal. Sandra handed the journal to Ramona, who scanned a few pages while Sandra fidgeted in her chair. Sandra didn't know exactly what to expect, but she knew she had not done as good a job with journalizing transactions as she should have.

Ramona then sighed and said, "I'm concerned about this journal, Sandra. You have recorded all transactions in pencil, and I notice numerous erasures. I don't know if the debits equal the credits, but I can see right away that this one transaction for $20,000 should have been for $2,000. Some of the dates are missing and some are out of order. What do you suggest we do to turn this situation around?"

After apologizing, Sandra thanked Ramona for giving her the chance to improve her work. She explained that she realized she had not been giving the journal the priority it required and went on to describe how she would improve her performance in the future.

***Critical Thinking:***

1. What do you think Sandra should say about the journal to demonstrate that she knows it is important?
2. What specific improvements do you think Sandra should make?

# 4-1 Journals, Source Documents, and Recording Entries in a Journal

## A FIVE-COLUMN JOURNAL

JOURNAL PAGE

| | DATE | ACCOUNT TITLE | DOC. NO. | POST. REF. | 1 GENERAL DEBIT | 2 GENERAL CREDIT | 3 SALES CREDIT | 4 CASH DEBIT | 5 CASH CREDIT | |
|---|---|---|---|---|---|---|---|---|---|---|
| 1 | | | | | | | | | | 1 |
| 2 | | | | | | | | | | 2 |
| 3 | | | | | | | | | | 3 |

### Using a Journal

Encore Music uses a journal that has five amount columns: General Debit, General Credit, Sales Credit, Cash Debit, and Cash Credit. A journal amount column headed with an account title is called a **special amount column.** These columns are used for frequently occurring transactions. For example, most of Encore Music's transactions involve receipt or payment of cash. A large number of the transactions involve receipt of cash from sales. Therefore, Encore Music uses three special amount columns in its journal: Sales Credit, Cash Debit, and Cash Credit. Using special amount columns eliminates writing an account title in the Account Title column and saves time.

A journal amount column that is not headed with an account title is called a **general amount column.** In Encore Music's journal, the General Debit and General Credit columns are general amount columns.

### Accuracy

Information recorded in a journal includes the debit and credit parts of each transaction recorded in one place. The information can be verified by comparing the data in the journal with the transaction data.

### Chronological Record

Transactions are recorded in a journal in order by date. All information about a transaction is recorded in one place, making the information for a specific transaction easy to locate.

### Double-Entry Accounting

Information for each transaction recorded in a journal is called an **entry.** The recording of debit and credit parts of a transaction is called **double-entry accounting.** In double-entry accounting, each transaction affects at least two accounts. Both the debit and the credit parts are recorded, reflecting the dual effect of each transaction on the business's records. Double-entry accounting assures that debits equal credits.

### Source Documents

A business paper from which information is obtained for a journal entry is called a **source document.** Each transaction is described by a source document that proves that the transaction did occur. For example, Encore Music prepares a check stub for each cash payment made. The check stub describes information about the cash payment transaction for which the check is prepared. The accounting concept, *Objective Evidence,* is applied when a source document is prepared for each transaction. *(CONCEPT: Objective Evidence)*

A transaction should be journalized only if it actually occurs. The amounts recorded must be accurate and true. Nearly all transactions result in the preparation of a source document. Encore Music uses five source documents: checks, sales invoices, receipts, calculator tapes, and memorandums.

## CHECKS

NO. 1 $1,577.00
Date August 3, 20--
To Quick Clean Supplies Co.
For Supplies

| | | |
|---|---|---|
| BAL. BRO'T. FOR'D. | 0 | 00 |
| AMT. DEPOSITED 8/1/-- (Date) | 10,000 | 00 |
| SUBTOTAL | 10,000 | 00 |
| OTHER: | | |
| SUBTOTAL | 10,000 | 00 |
| AMT. THIS CHECK | 1,577 | 00 |
| BAL. CAR'D. FOR'D. | 8,423 | 00 |

Encore Music
530 Anoka Avenue
Tampa, FL 33601

NO. 1 63-109/631

August 3, 20--

PAY TO THE ORDER OF Quick Clean Supplies Co. $1,577.00

One thousand five hundred seventy-seven and no/100 DOLLARS

For Classroom Use Only

Peoples national bank
Tampa, FL 33602

FOR Supplies Barbara Treviño

⑆063101098⑆ 43⑈4521191⑈

A business form ordering a bank to pay cash from a bank account is called a **check.** The source document for cash payments is a check. Encore Music makes all cash payments by check. The checks are prenumbered to help Encore Music account for all checks. Encore Music's record of information on a check is the check stub prepared at the same time as the check. A check and check stub prepared by Encore Music are shown in the illustration above.

Procedures for preparing checks and check stubs are described in Chapter 6.

## SALES INVOICES

Encore Music
530 Anoka Avenue
Tampa, FL 33601

Sold to: Kids Time
405 Michigan Avenue
Tampa, FL 33619

No. 1
Date 8/12/--
Terms 30 days

| Description | Amount |
|---|---|
| Individual lessons on Aug. 12 | $200.00 |
| | |
| Total | $200.00 |

When services are sold on account, the seller prepares a form showing information about the sale. A form describing the goods or services sold, the quantity, and the price is called an **invoice.** An invoice used as a source document for recording a sale on account is called a **sales invoice.** A sales invoice is also referred to as a sales ticket or a sales slip.

A sales invoice is prepared in duplicate. The original copy is given to the customer. The copy is used as the source document for the sale on account transaction. *(CONCEPT: Objective Evidence)* Sales invoices are numbered in sequence.

No. **1**
Date *August 1,* 20 --
From *Barbara Treviño*
For *Investment*

$ *10,000 | 00*

Receipt No. **1**
*August 1,* 20 --
Rec'd from *Barbara Treviño*
For *Investment*
*Ten thousand and no/100* ——— Dollars
Amount $ *10,000 | 00*

Encore Music
530 Anoka Avenue
Tampa, FL 33601

*Barbara Treviño*
Received By

### Receipts

A business form giving written acknowledgement for cash received is called a **receipt.** When cash is received from sources other than sales, Encore Music prepares a receipt. The receipts are prenumbered to help account for all of the receipts. A receipt is the source document for cash received from transactions other than sales. *(CONCEPT: Objective Evidence)*

**MEMORANDUM**

Encore Music
530 Anoka Avenue
Tampa, FL 33601

No. **1**

*Bought supplies on account from Ling Music Supplies, $2,720.00*

Signed: *Barbara Treviño* Date: *August 7, 20--*

### Memorandums

A form on which a brief message is written describing a transaction is called a **memorandum.** When no other source document is prepared for a transaction, or when an additional explanation is needed about a transaction, Encore Music prepares a memorandum. *(CONCEPT: Objective Evidence)* Encore Music's memorandums are prenumbered to help account for all of the memorandums. A brief note is written on the memorandum to describe the transaction.

### Calculator Tapes

Encore Music collects cash at the time services are rendered to customers. At the end of each day, Encore Music uses a printing electronic calculator to total the amount of cash received from sales for that day. By totaling all the individual sales, a single source document is produced for the total sales of the day. Thus, time and space are saved by recording only one entry for all of a day's sales. The calculator tape is the source document for daily sales. *(CONCEPT: Objective Evidence)* A calculator tape used as a source document is shown.

```
          0•00 *
Aug. 12, 20--
T12     150•00 +
         65•00 +
        110•00 +
        325•00 *
```

Encore Music dates and numbers each calculator tape. For example, in the illustration, the number, *T12,* indicates that the tape is for the twelfth day of the month.

## RECEIVED CASH FROM OWNER AS AN INVESTMENT

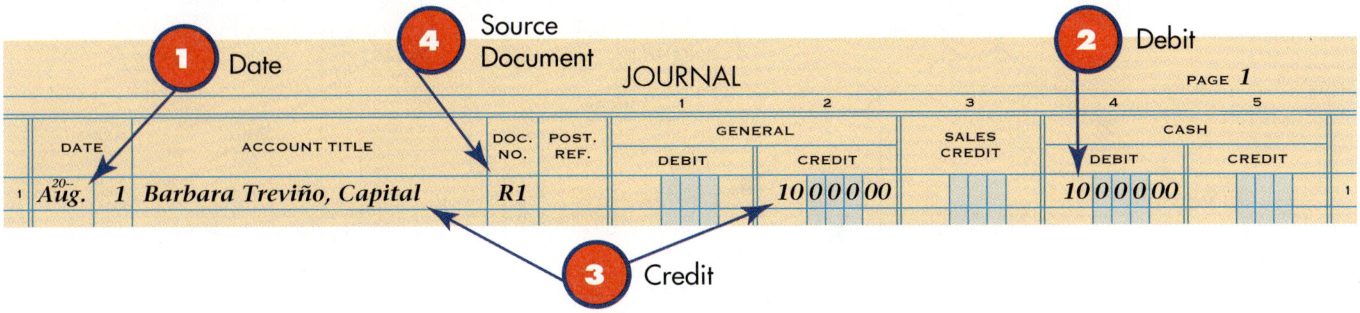


Information for each transaction recorded in a journal is known as an entry. An entry consists of four parts: (1) date, (2) debit, (3) credit, and (4) source document. Before a transaction is recorded in a journal, the transaction is analyzed into its debit and credit parts.

***August 1. Received cash from owner as an investment, $10,000.00. Receipt No. 1.***

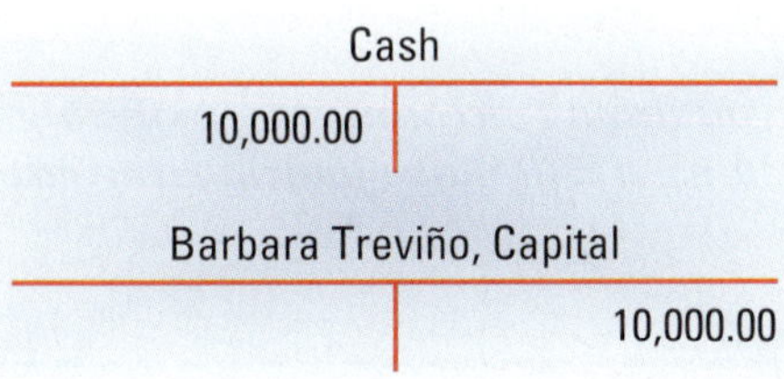


The source document for this transaction is Receipt No. 1. *(CONCEPT: Objective Evidence)* The analysis of this transaction is shown in the T accounts.

The asset account, Cash, is increased by a debit, $10,000.00. The owner's capital account, Barbara Treviño, Capital, is increased by a credit, $10,000.00.

**FYI** *Dollars and cents signs and decimal points are not used when writing amounts on ruled accounting paper. Sometimes a color tint or a heavy vertical rule is used on printed accounting paper to separate the dollars and cents columns.*

### STEPS: Journalizing cash received from owner as an investment

1. **Date.** Write the date, *20—, Aug. 1*, in the Date column. This entry is the first one on this journal page. Therefore, the year and month are both written for this entry. Neither the year nor the month are written again on the same page.
2. **Debit.** The journal has a special amount column for debits to Cash. Write the debit amount, *$10,000.00*, in the Cash Debit column. The title of the account is in the column heading. Therefore, the account title does not need to be written in the Account Title column.
3. **Credit.** There is no special amount column with the title of the account credited, Barbara Treviño, Capital, in its heading. Therefore, the credit amount, *$10,000.00*, is recorded in the General Credit column. In order to indicate what account is to be credited for this amount, write the title of the account, *Barbara Treviño, Capital,* in the Account Title column. (All amounts recorded in the General Debit or General Credit amount columns must have an account title written in the Account Title column.)
4. **Source document.** Write the source document number, *R1*, in the Doc. No. column. The source document number, R1, indicates that this is Receipt No. 1. (The source document number is a cross reference from the journal to the source document. If more details are needed about this transaction, a person can refer to Receipt No. 1.)

## PAID CASH FOR SUPPLIES

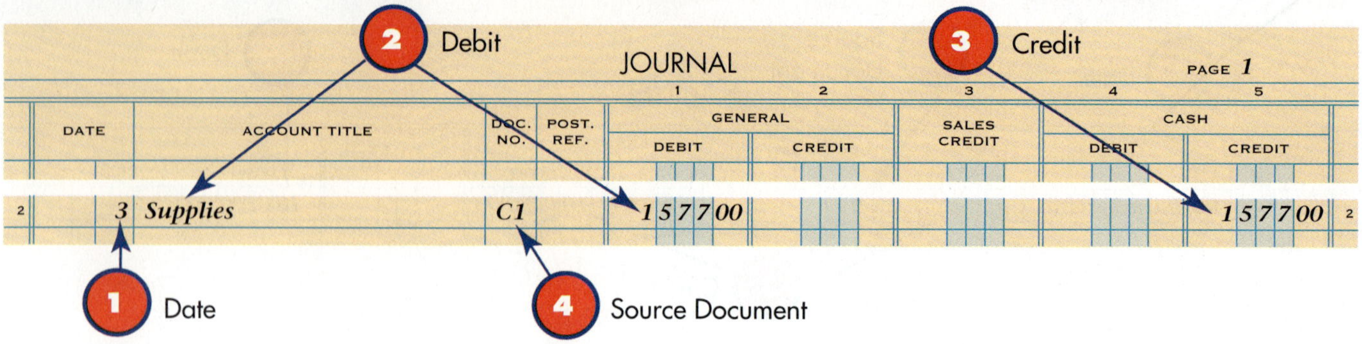


***August 3. Paid cash for supplies, $1,577.00. Check No. 1.***

Supplies

| Debit | Credit |
|---|---|
| 1,577.00 | |

Cash

| Debit | Credit |
|---|---|
| | 1,577.00 |

The source document for this transaction is Check No. 1. *(CONCEPT: Objective Evidence)* The analysis of this transaction is shown in the T accounts.

The asset account, Supplies, is increased by a debit, $1,577.00. The asset account, Cash, is decreased by a credit, $1,577.00.

**FYI**

*If you draw T accounts for analyzing transactions, it will make journalizing easier.*

**STEPS**

### Journalizing cash paid for supplies

1. **Date.** Write the date, *3*, in the Date column. This is not the first entry on the journal page. Therefore, the year and month are not written for this entry.
2. **Debit.** There is no special amount column with the title of the account debited, Supplies, in its heading. Therefore, the debit amount, *$1,577.00*, is recorded in the General Debit column. In order to indicate what account is to be debited for this amount, write the title of the account, *Supplies*, in the Account Title column.
3. **Credit.** The journal has a special amount column for credits to Cash. Write the credit amount, *$1,577.00*, in the Cash Credit column. The title of the account is in the column heading. Therefore, the account title does not need to be written in the Account Title column.
4. **Source document.** Write the source document number, *C1*, in the Doc. No. column. The source document number, C1, indicates that this is Check No. 1.

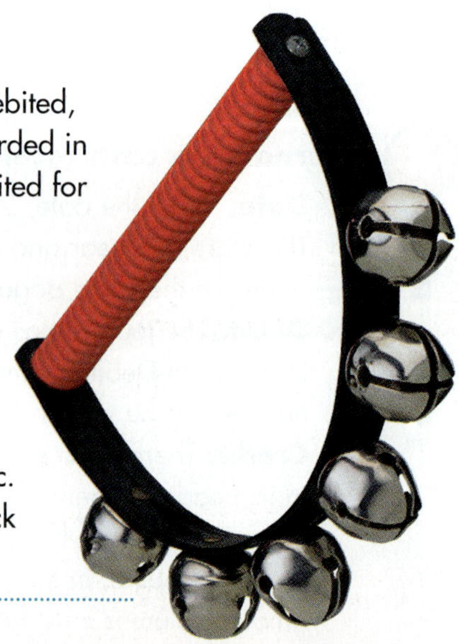

**REMEMBER**

When an account such as Cash is used frequently, it can be time-consuming to write the account title over and over. Using a special amount column for a frequently used account saves time.

## Terms Review

journal
journalizing
special amount column
general amount column
entry
double-entry accounting
source document
check
invoice
sales invoice
receipt
memorandum

## Audit Your Understanding

1. In what order are transactions recorded in a journal?
2. Why are source documents important?
3. List the four parts of a journal entry.

## Work Together

**Journalizing entries into a five-column journal**

A journal is given in the *Working Papers.* Your instructor will guide you through the following example.

Ruth Muldoon owns Muldoon Copy Center, which uses the following accounts:

| | | | |
|---|---|---|---|
| Cash | Prepaid Insurance | Ruth Muldoon, Drawing | Rent Expense |
| Accts. Rec.—Lester Dodge | Accts. Pay.—Ron's Supplies | Sales | Utilities Expense |
| Supplies | Ruth Muldoon, Capital | Miscellaneous Expense | |

***Transactions:*** Apr. 1. Received cash from owner as an investment, $7,000.00. R1.
2. Paid cash for supplies, $425.00. C1.

**4.** Journalize each transaction completed during April of the current year. Use page 1 of the journal. Source documents are abbreviated as follows: check, C; memorandum, M; receipt, R; sales invoice, S; calculator tape, T. Save your work to complete Work Together on page 75.

## On Your Own

**Journalizing entries into a five-column journal**

A journal is given in the *Working Papers.* Work this problem independently.

Gale Klein owns Klein's Service Center, which uses the following accounts:

| | | | |
|---|---|---|---|
| Cash | Prepaid Insurance | Gale Klein, Drawing | Miscellaneous Expense |
| Accts. Rec.—Connie Vaughn | Accts. Pay.—Osamu Supply Co. | Sales | Rent Expense |
| Supplies | Gale Klein, Capital | Advertising Expense | |

***Transactions:*** June 2 Received cash from owner as an investment, $1,500.00. R1.
3. Paid cash for supplies, $35.00. C1.

**5.** Jounalize each transaction completed during June of the current year. Use page 1 of the journal. Source documents are abbreviated as follows: check, C; memorandum, M; receipt, R; sales invoice, S; calculator tape, T. Save your work to complete On Your Own on page 75.

# 4-2 Journalizing Buying Insurance, Buying on Account, and Paying on Account

## PAID CASH FOR INSURANCE

JOURNAL PAGE *1*

| | DATE | | ACCOUNT TITLE | DOC. NO. | POST. REF. | 1 GENERAL DEBIT | 2 GENERAL CREDIT | 3 SALES CREDIT | 4 CASH DEBIT | 5 CASH CREDIT | |
|---|---|---|---|---|---|---|---|---|---|---|---|
| 3 | | 4 | *Prepaid Insurance* | *C2* | | *1 200 00* | | | | *1 200 00* | 3 |

1 Date
2 Debit
3 Credit
4 Source Document

***August 4. Paid cash for insurance, $1,200.00. Check No. 2.***

| Prepaid Insurance | |
|---|---|
| 1,200.00 | |

| Cash | |
|---|---|
| | 1,200.00 |

The source document for this transaction is Check No. 2. *(CONCEPT: Objective Evidence)* The analysis of this transaction is shown in the T accounts.

The asset account, Prepaid Insurance, is increased by a debit, $1,200.00. The asset account, Cash, is decreased by a credit, $1,200.00.

### STEPS Journalizing cash paid for insurance

1. **Date.** Write the date, *4*, in the Date column.
2. **Debit.** There is no special amount column with the title of the account debited, Prepaid Insurance, in its heading. Therefore, the debit amount, *$1,200.00*, is recorded in the General Debit column. In order to indicate what account is to be debited for this amount, write the title of the account, *Prepaid Insurance*, in the Account Title column.
3. **Credit.** The journal has a special amount column for credits to Cash. Write the credit amount, *$1,200.00*, in the Cash Credit column. The title of the account is in the column heading. Therefore, the account title does not need to be written in the Account Title column.
4. **Source document.** Write the source document number, *C2*, in the Doc. No. column.

**REMEMBER**

All amounts recorded in the General Debit or General Credit amount columns must have an account title written in the Account Title column.

# BOUGHT SUPPLIES ON ACCOUNT

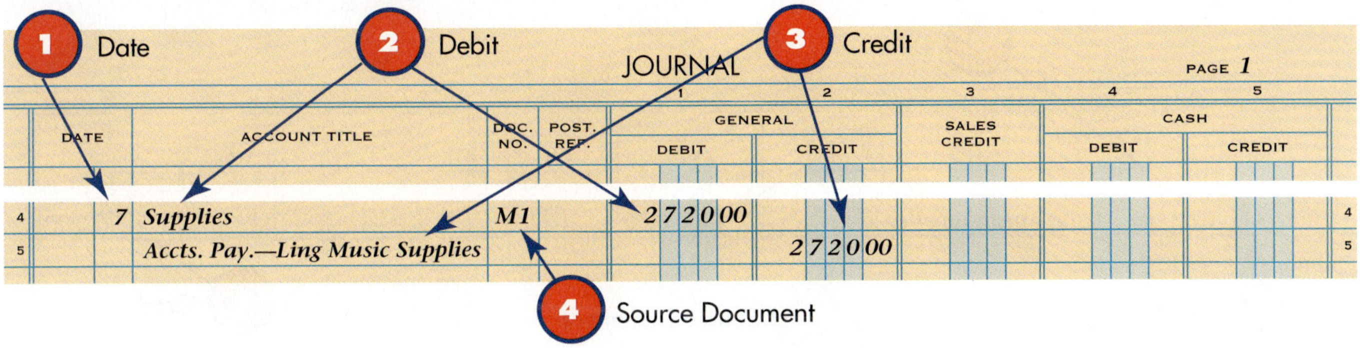


***August 7. Bought supplies on account from Ling Music Supplies, $2,720.00. Memorandum No. 1.***

| Supplies | |
|---|---|
| 2,720.00 | |

| Accts. Pay.—Ling Music Supplies | |
|---|---|
| | 2,720.00 |

Encore Music ordered these supplies by telephone. Encore Music wishes to record this transaction immediately. Therefore, a memorandum is prepared that shows supplies received on account.

The source document for this transaction is Memorandum No. 1. *(CONCEPT: Objective Evidence)* The analysis of this transaction is shown in the T accounts.

The asset account, Supplies, is increased by a debit, $2,720.00. The liability account, Accounts Payable—Ling Music Supplies, is increased by a credit, $2,720.00

**FYI**

*Of all service businesses in the United States, only 4 percent employ 50 or more people and 80 percent have fewer than 10 employees.*

**STEPS**

### Journalizing supplies bought on account

1. **Date.** Write the date, *7*, in the Date column.
2. **Debit.** There is no special amount column with the title of the account debited, Supplies, in its heading. Therefore, the debit amount, *$2,720.00*, is recorded in the General Debit column. In order to indicate what account is to be debited for this amount, write the title of the account, *Supplies*, in the Account Title column.
3. **Credit.** Again, there is no special amount column with the title of the account credited, Accounts Payable—Ling Music Supplies, in its heading. Therefore, the credit amount, *$2,720.00*, is recorded on the next journal line in the General Credit column. In order to indicate what account is to be credited for this amount, write the title of the account, *Accounts Payable—Ling Music Supplies*, in the Account Title column on the same line as the credit amount.

   This entry requires two lines in the journal because account titles for both the debit and credit amounts must be written in the Account Title column.
4. **Source document.** Write the source document number, *M1*, in the Doc. No. column on the first line of the entry.

JOURNAL — PAGE 1

| | DATE | | ACCOUNT TITLE | DOC. NO. | POST. REF. | GENERAL DEBIT (1) | GENERAL CREDIT (2) | SALES CREDIT (3) | CASH DEBIT (4) | CASH CREDIT (5) | |
|---|---|---|---|---|---|---|---|---|---|---|---|
| 6 | | 11 | *Accts. Pay.—Ling Music Supplies* | *C3* | | *1 360 00* | | | | *1 360 00* | 6 |

1 Date

2 Debit

3 Credit

4 Source Document

***August 11. Paid cash on account to Ling Music Supplies, $1,360.00. Check No. 3.***

| Accts. Pay.—Ling Music Supplies | |
|---|---|
| 1,360.00 | |

| Cash | |
|---|---|
| | 1,360.00 |

The source document for this transaction is Check No. 3. *(CONCEPT: Objective Evidence)* The analysis of this transaction is shown in the T accounts.

The liability account, Accounts Payable—Ling Music Supplies, is decreased by a debit, $1,360.00. The asset account, Cash, is decreased by a credit, $1,360.00.

## ACCOUNTING AT WORK

### MARY WITHERSPOON

In high school, Mary M. Witherspoon considered pursuing a degree in accounting. Her career choice was confirmed by ACCUMATION, a career education program for high school students sponsored by the Dallas Chapter of the Texas Society of CPAs. Students participate in this week-long summer program, which includes visits to an international accounting firm and the chance to sit in on university accounting classes.

Mary graduated with a BBA in Accounting and works for Oryx Energy Company, a large independent producer of oil and gas in Dallas. Currently in gas balancing accounting, she reconciles records of jointly owned properties to ensure Oryx receives their entitled gas volumes. Working in the corporate environment has allowed Mary to change job responsibilities over her career to gain additional experience.

Mary believes that exceptional people skills coupled with technical experience is the formula for business success. People skills include written and verbal communication, respecting diversity, and the ability to work in teams.

Mary also serves as a district vice-president of the American Business Women's Association (ABWA). ABWA promotes the advancement of women in business by sponsoring continuing education, providing leadership training, and offering encouragement.

"High school students can contact their state or local society of certified public accountants for accounting career information," says Mary. "We CPAs support programs to encourage student interest in our field."

## AUDIT YOUR UNDERSTANDING

1. Which journal columns are used to record paying cash for insurance?
2. Which journal columns are used to record buying supplies on account?
3. Which journal columns are used to record paying cash on account?

## WORK TOGETHER

### Journalizing entries into a five-column journal

Use the journal that you started for Work Together on page 71. Your instructor will guide you through the following example.

Ruth Muldoon owns Muldoon Copy Center, which uses the following accounts:

| | | | |
|---|---|---|---|
| Cash | Prepaid Insurance | Ruth Muldoon, Drawing | Rent Expense |
| Accts. Rec.—Lester Dodge | Accts. Pay.—Ron's Supplies | Sales | Utilities Expense |
| Supplies | Ruth Muldoon, Capital | Miscellaneous Expense | |

***Transactions:*** Apr. 5. Bought supplies on account from Ron's Supplies, $300.00. M1.
7. Paid cash for insurance, $600.00. C2.
9. Paid cash on account to Ron's Supplies, $300.00. C3.

4. Journalize the transactions continuing on the next blank line of page 1 of the journal. Save your work to complete Work Together on page 81.

## ON YOUR OWN

### Journalizing entries into a five-column journal

Use the chart of accounts above and the journal that you started for On Your Own on page 71. Work this problem independently.

Gale Klein owns Klein's Service Center, which uses the following accounts:

| | | | |
|---|---|---|---|
| Cash | Prepaid Insurance | Gale Klein, Drawing | Miscellaneous Expense |
| Accts. Rec.—Connie Vaughn | Accts. Pay.—Osamu Supply Co. | Sales | Rent Expense |
| Supplies | Gale Klein, Capital | Advertising Expense | |

***Transactions:*** June 5. Paid cash for insurance, $100.00. C2.
9. Bought supplies on account from Osamu Supply Co., $155.00. M1.
10. Paid cash on account to Osamu Supply Co., $155.00. C3.

5. Journalize the transactions continuing on the next blank line of page 1 of the journal. Save your work to complete On Your Own on page 81.

# 4-3 Journalizing Transactions That Affect Owner's Equity and Receiving Cash on Account

## RECEIVED CASH FROM SALES

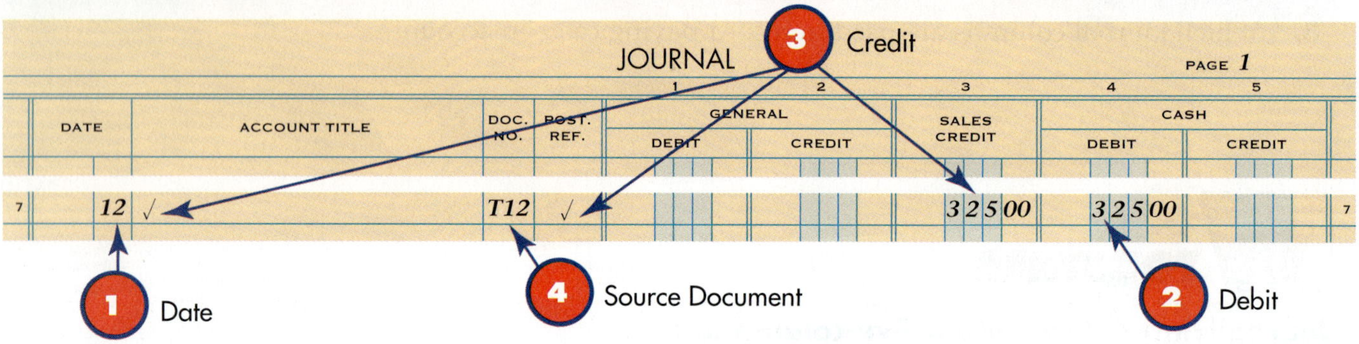


***August 12. Received cash from sales, $325.00. Tape No. 12.***

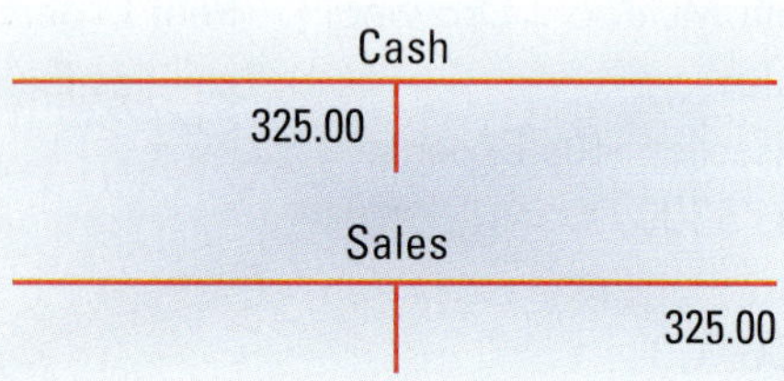


The source document for this transaction is Calculator Tape No. 12. *(CONCEPT: Objective Evidence)* The analysis of this transaction is shown in the T accounts.

The asset account, Cash, is increased by a debit, $325.00. The revenue account, Sales, is increased by a credit, $325.00.

The reason that Sales is increased by a credit is discussed in the previous chapter. The owner's capital account has a normal credit balance. Increases in the owner's capital account are shown as credits. Because revenue increases owner's equity, increases in revenue are recorded as credits. A revenue account, therefore, has a normal credit balance.

**STEPS**

### Journalizing cash received from sales

1. **Date.** Write the date, *12*, in the Date column.
2. **Debit.** The journal has a special amount column for debits to Cash. Write the debit amount, *$325.00*, in the Cash Debit column. The title of the account is in the column heading. Therefore, the account title does not need to be written in the Account Title column.
3. **Credit.** The journal also has a special amount column for credits to Sales. Write the credit amount, *$325.00*, in the Sales Credit column. The title of the account is in the column heading. Therefore, the account title does not need to be written in the Account Title column.

   Because both amounts for this entry are recorded in special amount columns, no account titles are written in the Account Title column. Therefore, a check mark is placed in the Account Title column to show that no account titles need to be written for this transaction. A check mark is also placed in the Post. Ref. column. The use of the Post. Ref. column is described in Chapter 5.
4. **Source document.** Write the source document number, *T12*, in the Doc. No. column.

## REMEMBER

In double-entry accounting, each transaction affects at least two accounts. At least one account will be debited and at least one account will be credited.

# SOLD SERVICES ON ACCOUNT

JOURNAL — PAGE 1

| | DATE | ACCOUNT TITLE | DOC. NO. | POST. REF. | GENERAL DEBIT (1) | GENERAL CREDIT (2) | SALES CREDIT (3) | CASH DEBIT (4) | CASH CREDIT (5) | |
|---|---|---|---|---|---|---|---|---|---|---|
| 8 | 12 | *Accts. Rec.—Kids Time* | *S1* | | *200 00* | | *200 00* | | | 8 |

1 Date
2 Debit
3 Credit
4 Source Document

***August 12. Sold services on account to Kids Time, $200.00. Sales Invoice No. 1.***

Accts. Rec.—Kids Time

| Debit | Credit |
|---|---|
| 200.00 | |

Sales

| Debit | Credit |
|---|---|
| | 200.00 |

The source document for this transaction is Sales Invoice No. 1. *(CONCEPT: Objective Evidence)* The analysis of this transaction is shown in the T accounts.

The asset account, Accounts Receivable—Kids Time, is increased by a debit, $200.00. The revenue account, Sales, is increased by a credit, $200.00.

STEPS

### Journalizing services sold on account

1. **Date.** Write the date, *12*, in the Date column.
2. **Debit.** There is no special amount column with the title of the account debited, Accounts Receivable—Kids Time, in its heading. Therefore, the debit amount, *$200.00*, is recorded in the General Debit column. In order to indicate what account is to be debited for this amount, write the title of the account, *Accounts Receivable—Kids Time*, in the Account Title column.
3. **Credit.** The journal has a special amount column for credits to Sales. Write the credit amount, *$200.00*, in the Sales Credit column. The title of the account is in the column heading. Therefore, the account title does not need to be written in the Account Title column.
4. **Source document.** Write the source document number, *S1*, in the Doc. No. column.

**FYI**

*Accounting is not just for accountants. For example, a performing artist earns revenue from providing a service. Financial decisions must be made such as the cost of doing a performance, the percentage of revenue paid to a manager, travel expenses, and the cost of rehearsal space.*

# PAID CASH FOR AN EXPENSE

2 Debit

JOURNAL PAGE 1

| | DATE | ACCOUNT TITLE | DOC. NO. | POST. REF. | 1 GENERAL DEBIT | 2 GENERAL CREDIT | 3 SALES CREDIT | 4 CASH DEBIT | 5 CASH CREDIT | |
|---|---|---|---|---|---|---|---|---|---|---|
| 9 | 12 | Rent Expense | C4 | | 250 00 | | | | 250 00 | 9 |
| 10 | 12 | Utilities Expense | C5 | | 45 00 | | | | 45 00 | 10 |

1 Date 4 Source Document 3 Credit

***August 12. Paid cash for rent, $250.00. Check No. 4.***

| Rent Expense | |
|---|---|
| 250.00 | |

| Cash | |
|---|---|
| | 250.00 |

The source document for this transaction is Check No. 4. *(CONCEPT: Objective Evidence)* The analysis of this transaction is shown in the T accounts.

The expense account, Rent Expense, is increased by a debit, $250.00. The asset account, Cash, is decreased by a credit, $250.00.

The reason that Rent Expense is increased by a debit is discussed in the previous chapter. The owner's capital account has a normal credit balance. Decreases in the owner's capital account are shown as debits.

Because expenses decrease owner's equity, increases in expenses are recorded as debits. An expense account, therefore, has a normal debit balance.

**FYI**

*Source documents can be critically important in tracking down errors. Businesses file their source documents so they can be referred to if it is necessary to verify information entered into their journals.*

**STEPS**

## Journalizing cash paid for an expense

1. **Date.** Write the date, *12*, in the Date column.
2. **Debit.** There is no special amount column with the title of the account debited, Rent Expense, in its heading. Therefore, the debit amount, *$250.00*, is recorded in the General Debit column. In order to indicate what account is to be debited for this amount, write the title of the account, *Rent Expense*, in the Account Title column.
3. **Credit.** The journal has a special amount column for credits to Cash. Write the credit amount, *$250.00*, in the Cash Credit column. The title of the account is in the column heading. Therefore, the account title does not need to be written in the Account Title column.
4. **Source document.** Write the source document number, *C4*, in the Doc. No. column.

Whenever cash is paid for an expense, the journal entry is similar to the entry discussed above. Therefore, the journal entry to record paying cash for utilities is also illustrated.

## RECEIVED CASH ON ACCOUNT

1 Date — 4 Source Document

JOURNAL PAGE *1*

| | | | | 1 | 2 | 3 | 4 | 5 |
|---|---|---|---|---|---|---|---|---|
| DATE | ACCOUNT TITLE | DOC. NO. | POST. REF. | GENERAL DEBIT | GENERAL CREDIT | SALES CREDIT | CASH DEBIT | CASH CREDIT |
| 12 | *Accts. Rec.—Kids Time* | *R2* | | | *100 00* | | *100 00* | |

3 Credit — 2 Debit

***August 12. Received cash on account from Kids Time, $100.00. Receipt No. 2.***

| Cash | |
|---|---|
| 100.00 | |

| Accts. Rec.—Kids Time | |
|---|---|
| | 100.00 |

The source document for this transaction is Receipt No. 2. *(CONCEPT: Objective Evidence)* The analysis of this transaction is shown in the T accounts.

The asset account, Cash, is increased by a debit, $100.00. The asset account, Accounts Receivable—Kids Time, is decreased by a credit, $100.00.

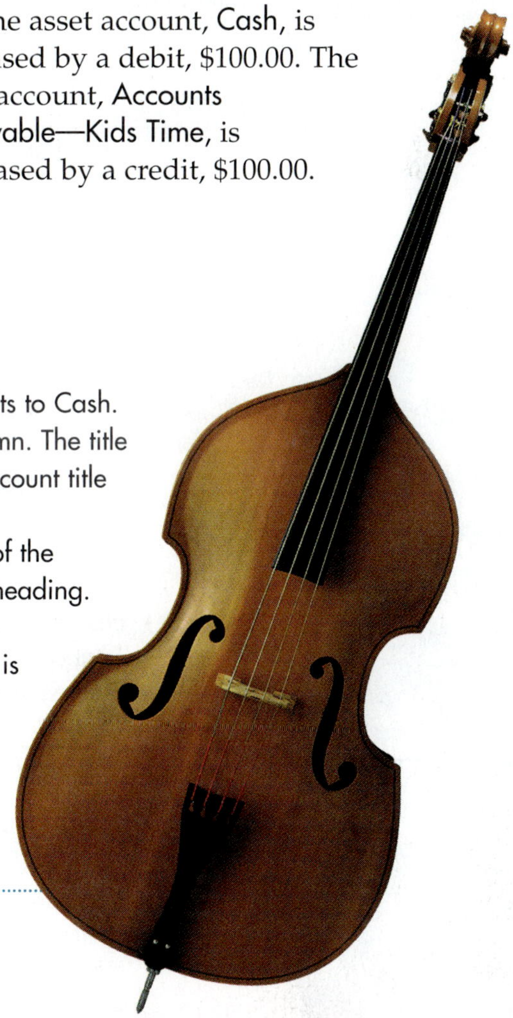

### STEPS Journalizing cash received on account

1. **Date.** Write the date, *12,* in the Date column.
2. **Debit.** The journal has a special amount column for debits to Cash. Write the debit amount, *$100.00,* in the Cash Debit column. The title of the account is in the column heading. Therefore, the account title does not need to be written in the Account Title column.
3. **Credit.** There is no special amount column with the title of the account credited, Accounts Receivable—Kids Time, in its heading. Therefore, the credit amount, *$100.00,* is recorded in the General Credit column. In order to indicate what account is to be credited for this amount, write the title of the account, *Accounts Receivable—Kids Time,* in the Account Title column.
4. **Source document.** Write the source document number, *R2,* in the Doc. No. column.

## REMEMBER

If you misspell words in your written communications, people may mistrust the quality of your accounting skills. Note that in the word receipt the "e" comes before the "i" and there is a silent "p" before the "t" at the end of the word.

# PAID CASH TO OWNER FOR PERSONAL USE

JOURNAL PAGE 1

| | DATE | ACCOUNT TITLE | DOC. NO. | POST. REF. | 1 GENERAL DEBIT | 2 GENERAL CREDIT | 3 SALES CREDIT | 4 CASH DEBIT | 5 CASH CREDIT | |
|---|---|---|---|---|---|---|---|---|---|---|
| 12 | 12 | *Barbara Treviño, Drawing* | *C6* | | *100 00* | | | | *100 00* | 12 |

1 Date
2 Debit
3 Credit
4 Source Document

***August 12. Paid cash to owner for personal use, $100.00. Check No. 6.***

| Barbara Treviño, Drawing | |
|---|---|
| 100.00 | |

| Cash | |
|---|---|
| | 100.00 |

The source document for this transaction is Check No. 6. *(CONCEPT: Objective Evidence)* The analysis of this transaction is shown in the T accounts.

The reason that Barbara Treviño, Drawing is increased by a debit is discussed in the previous chapter. Decreases in the owner's capital account are shown as debits. Because withdrawals decrease owner's equity, increases in withdrawals are recorded as debits. A withdrawal account, therefore, has a normal debit balance.

## LEGAL ISSUES IN ACCOUNTING

### FORMING AND DISSOLVING A PROPRIETORSHIP

A proprietorship is a business owned and controlled by one person. The advantages of a proprietorship include:

- Ease of formation.
- Total control by the owner.
- Profits that are not shared.

However, there are some disadvantages of organizing a proprietorship:

- Limited resources. The owner is the only person who can invest cash and other assets in the business.
- Unlimited liability. The owner is totally responsible for the liabilities of the business. Personal assets, such as a car, can be claimed by creditors to pay the business's liabilities.
- Limited expertise. Limited time, energy, and experience can be put into the business by the owner.
- Limited life. A proprietorship must be dissolved when the owner dies or decides to stop doing business.

The owner is required to follow the laws of both the federal government and the state and city in which the business is formed. Most cities and states have few, if any, legal procedures to follow. Once any legal requirements are met, the proprietorship can begin business.

Should the owner decide to dissolve the proprietorship, he or she merely needs to stop doing business. Noncash assets can be sold, with the cash used to pay any creditors.

## AUDIT YOUR UNDERSTANDING

1. Which journal columns are used to record receiving cash from sales?
2. Which journal columns are used to record sales on account?
3. Which journal columns are used to record paying cash for an expense?
4. Which journal columns are used to record receiving cash on account?
5. Which journal columns are used to record paying cash to owner for personal use?

## WORK TOGETHER

**Journalizing transactions that affect owner's equity into a five-column journal**

Use the chart of accounts and journal from Work Together on page 75. Your instructor will guide you through the following example.

***Transactions:*** Apr.
12. Paid cash for rent, $950.00. C4.
13. Received cash from sales, $2,200.00. T13.
14. Sold services on account to Lester Dodge, $625.00. S1.
19. Paid cash for electric bill, $157.00. C5.
20. Received cash on account from Lester Dodge, $300.00. R2.
21. Paid cash to owner for personal use, $1,400.00. C6.

6. Journalize the transactions continuing on the next blank line of page 1 of the journal. Save your work to complete Work Together on page 87.

## ON YOUR OWN

**Journalizing transactions that affect owner's equity into a five-column journal**

Use the chart of accounts and journal from On Your Own on page 75. Work this problem independently.

***Transactions:*** June
11. Paid cash for rent, $200.00. C4.
12. Sold services on account to Connie Vaughn, $200.00. S1.
16. Received cash from sales, $1,050.00. T16.
17. Paid cash for postage (Miscellaneous Expense), $32.00. C5.
19. Received cash on account from Connie Vaughn, $100.00. R2.
20. Paid cash to owner for personal use, $250.00. C6.

7. Journalize the transactions continuing on the next blank line of page 1 of the journal. Save your work to complete On Your Own on page 87.

# 4-4 Proving and Ruling a Journal

## PROVING A JOURNAL PAGE

1 Add each amount column

2 Add debit totals and credit totals

| Column | Debit Column Totals | Credit Column Totals |
|---|---|---|
| General | $ 7,960.00 | $12,840.00 |
| Sales | | 2,439.00 |
| Cash | 12,319.00 | 5,000.00 |
| Totals | $20,279.00 | $20,279.00 |

3 Totals equal

After Encore Music uses all but the last line on a journal page, columns are proved and ruled before totals are carried forward to the next page.

To prove a journal page, Encore Music verifies that the total debits on the page equal the total credits. Three steps are followed in proving a journal page.

If the total debits do not equal the total credits, the errors must be found and corrected before any more work is completed.

STEPS

### Proving a journal page

1. Add each of the amount columns. Use a calculator if one is available.
2. Add the debit column totals, and then add the credit column totals as shown.
3. Verify that the total debits and total credits are equal. Because the total debits equal the total credits, page 1 of Encore Music's journal is proved.

GLOBAL PERSPECTIVE

### FOREIGN CURRENCY

As our world becomes smaller and global trade increases, U.S. businesses become more involved in transactions with foreign businesses. These transactions can be stated in terms of U.S. dollars or in the currency of the other country. If the transaction involves foreign currency, a U.S. business must convert the foreign currency into U.S. dollars before the transaction can be recorded. *(CONCEPT: Unit of Measurement)*

The value of foreign currency may change daily. In the United States, the *exchange rate* is the value of foreign currency in relation to the U.S. dollar. Current exchange rates can be found in many daily newspapers, on-line services, or banks.

The exchange rate is stated in terms of one unit of foreign currency. Using Germany as an example, presume that one German *mark* is worth 0.5789 U.S. dollars (or about 58 U.S. cents). This rate would be used when exchanging German marks for U.S. dollars.

A *conversion formula* can be used to find out how many foreign currency units can be purchased with one U.S. dollar. The formula is:

1/exchange rate = foreign currency per U.S. dollar

1 dollar/0.5789 = 1.7272 marks per dollar

## RULING A JOURNAL PAGE

JOURNAL — PAGE 1

| | DATE | | ACCOUNT TITLE | DOC. NO. | POST. REF. | 1 GENERAL DEBIT | 2 GENERAL CREDIT | 3 SALES CREDIT | 4 CASH DEBIT | 5 CASH CREDIT | |
|---|---|---|---|---|---|---|---|---|---|---|---|
| 1 | 20-- Aug. | 1 | Barbara Treviño, Capital | R1 | | | 10000 00 | | 10000 00 | | 1 |
| 2 | | 3 | Supplies | C1 | | 1577 00 | | | | 1577 00 | 2 |
| 3 | | 4 | Prepaid Insurance | C2 | | 1200 00 | | | | 1200 00 | 3 |
| 23 | | 20 | Supplies | M2 | | 20 00 | | | | | 23 |
| 24 | | | Accts. Pay.—Sullivan Office Supplies | | | | 20 00 | | | | 24 |
| 25 | | 20 | Carried Forward | | ✓ | 7960 00 | 12840 00 | 2439 00 | 12319 00 | 5000 00 | 25 |

1 Single Rule

2 Date

3 Carried Forward

4 Column Totals

5 Double Rule

After a journal page is proved, it is ruled. Five steps are followed in ruling a journal page.

### STEPS: Ruling a journal page

1. Rule a single line across all amount columns directly below the last entry.
2. On the next line, write the date, *20*, in the Date column.
3. Write the words *Carried Forward* in the Account Title column. A check mark is also placed in the Post. Ref. column. The use of the Post. Ref. column is described in Chapter 5.
4. Write each column total below the single line.
5. Rule double lines below the column totals across all amount columns.

**SMALL BUSINESS SPOTLIGHT**

Successful small business owners typically have the following characteristics: confidence to make decisions, determination to keep trying during hard times for the business, willingness to take risks, creativity to surpass the competition, and an inner need to achieve.

## STARTING A NEW JOURNAL PAGE

JOURNAL PAGE 2

| | DATE | | ACCOUNT TITLE | DOC. NO. | POST. REF. | 1 GENERAL DEBIT | 2 GENERAL CREDIT | 3 SALES CREDIT | 4 CASH DEBIT | 5 CASH CREDIT | |
|---|---|---|---|---|---|---|---|---|---|---|---|
| 1 | 20-- Aug. | 20 | *Brought Forward* | | ✓ | 7 9 6 0 00 | 12 8 4 0 00 | 2 4 3 9 00 | 12 3 1 9 00 | 5 0 0 0 00 | 1 |
| 2 | | | | | | | | | | | 2 |

1 Page
2 Date
3 *Brought Forward*
4 Column Totals

The column totals from the previous page are carried forward to a new page. The totals are recorded on the first line of the new page, using the following four steps.

### STEPS: Starting a new journal page

1. Write the page number, *2*, at the top of the journal.
2. Write the date, *20—, Aug. 20*, in the Date column. Because this is the first time that a date is written on page 2, the year, month, and day are all written in the Date column.
3. Write *Brought Forward* in the Account Title column. A check mark is also placed in the Post. Ref. column.
4. Record the column totals brought forward from the previous page.

## PROVING AND RULING A JOURNAL AT THE END OF A MONTH

JOURNAL PAGE 2

| | DATE | | ACCOUNT TITLE | DOC. NO. | POST. REF. | 1 GENERAL DEBIT | 2 GENERAL CREDIT | 3 SALES CREDIT | 4 CASH DEBIT | 5 CASH CREDIT | |
|---|---|---|---|---|---|---|---|---|---|---|---|
| 1 | 20-- Aug. | 20 | *Brought Forward* | | ✓ | 7 9 6 0 00 | 12 8 4 0 00 | 2 4 3 9 00 | 12 3 1 9 00 | 5 0 0 0 00 | 1 |
| 2 | | 21 | ✓ | T21 | ✓ | | | 2 7 0 00 | 2 7 0 00 | | 2 |
| 13 | | 31 | ✓ | T31 | ✓ | | | 2 9 0 00 | 2 9 0 00 | | 13 |
| 14 | | 31 | *Miscellaneous Expense* | M3 | | 3 00 | | | | 3 00 | 14 |
| 15 | | 31 | *Totals* | | | 8 9 7 9 00 | 12 8 4 0 00 | 4 4 1 1 00 | 14 2 9 1 00 | 6 0 1 9 00 | 15 |

1 Single Rule
2 Date
3 Totals
4 Column Totals
5 Double Rule

Encore Music always proves and rules a journal at the end of each month even if the last page for the month is not full.

The last page of a journal for a month is proved using the same steps previously described. Then, cash is proved and the journal is ruled. The proof of page 2 of Encore Music's journal is completed as shown. Proving cash is discussed on the next page.

Page 2 of Encore Music's journal is proved because the total debits are equal to the total credits, $23,270.00.

| Column | Debit Column Totals | Credit Column Totals |
|---|---|---|
| General | $ 8,979.00 | $12,840.00 |
| Sales | | 4,411.00 |
| Cash | 14,291.00 | 6,019.00 |
| Totals | $23,270.00 | $23,270.00 |

## Proving Cash

Determining that the amount of cash agrees with the accounting records is called **proving cash.** Cash can be proved at any time Encore Music wishes to verify the accuracy of the cash records. However, Encore Music *always* proves cash at the end of a month when the journal is proved. Encore Music uses two steps to prove cash.

**1.** Calculate the cash balance.

| | |
|---|---:|
| Cash on hand at the beginning of the month | $ 0.00 |
| Encore Music began the month with no cash balance. Ms. Treviño invested the initial cash on August 1. | |
| *Plus* total cash received during the month | +14,291.00 |
| This amount is the total of the journal's Cash Debit column. | |
| *Equals* total | $14,291.00 |
| *Less* total cash paid during the month | − 6,019.00 |
| This amount is the total of the journal's Cash Credit column. | |
| *Equals* cash balance at the end of the month | $ 8,272.00 |
| Checkbook balance on the next unused check stub | $ 8,272.00 |

**2.** Verify that the cash balance equals the checkbook balance on the next unused check stub in the checkbook. Because the cash balance calculated using the journal and the checkbook balance are the same, $8,272.00, cash is proved.

## Ruling a Journal at the End of a Month

A journal is ruled at the end of each month even if the last journal page is not full. The procedures for ruling a journal at the end of a month are similar to those for ruling a journal page to carry the totals forward.

Encore Music uses five steps in ruling a journal at the end of each month, as shown on the previous page.

**STEPS**

### Ruling a journal at the end of a month (these steps illustrated on the previous page)

1. Rule a single line across all amount columns directly below the last entry to indicate that the columns are to be added.
2. On the next line, write the date, *31*, in the Date column.
3. Write the word *Totals* in the Account Title column.
   A check mark is not placed in the Post. Ref. column for this line. More information about the Totals line will be provided in Chapter 5.
4. Write each column total below the single line.
5. Rule double lines below the column totals across all amount columns. The double lines mean that the totals have been verified as correct.

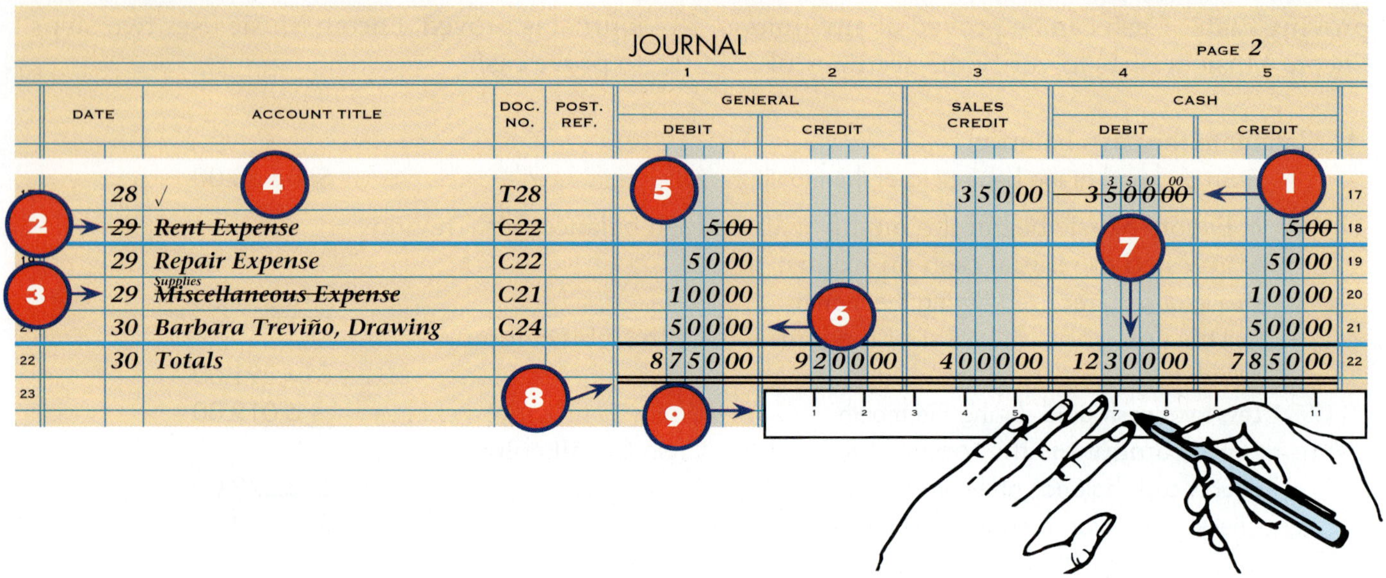

JOURNAL PAGE 2

| | DATE | ACCOUNT TITLE | DOC. NO. | POST. REF. | GENERAL DEBIT (1) | GENERAL CREDIT (2) | SALES CREDIT (3) | CASH DEBIT (4) | CASH CREDIT (5) | |
|---|---|---|---|---|---|---|---|---|---|---|
| 17 | 28 | √ | T28 | | | | 350 00 | 350 00 ~~3500 00~~ | | 17 |
| 18 | ~~29~~ | ~~Rent Expense~~ | ~~C22~~ | | ~~5 00~~ | | | | ~~5 00~~ | 18 |
| 19 | 29 | Repair Expense | C22 | | 50 00 | | | | 50 00 | 19 |
| 20 | 29 | Supplies ~~Miscellaneous Expense~~ | C21 | | 100 00 | | | | 100 00 | 20 |
| 21 | 30 | Barbara Treviño, Drawing | C24 | | 500 00 | | | | 500 00 | 21 |
| 22 | 30 | Totals | | | 8750 00 | 9200 00 | 4000 00 | 12300 00 | 7850 00 | 22 |
| 23 | | | | | | | | | | |

In completing accounting work, Encore Music follows standard accounting practices. These practices include procedures for error corrections, abbreviating words, writing dollar and cents signs, and rulings.

1. Errors are corrected in a way that does not cause doubts about what the correct information is. If an error is recorded, cancel the error by neatly drawing a line through the incorrect item. Write the correct item immediately above the canceled item.
2. Sometimes an entire entry is incorrect and is discovered before the next entry is journalized. Draw neat lines through all parts of the incorrect entry. Journalize the entry correctly on the next blank line.
3. Sometimes several correct entries are recorded after an incorrect entry is made. The next blank lines are several entries later. Draw neat lines through all incorrect parts of the entry. Record the correct items on the same lines as the incorrect items, directly above the canceled parts.
4. Words in accounting records are written in full when space permits. Words may be abbreviated only when space is limited. All items are written legibly.
5. Dollars and cents signs and decimal points are not used when writing amounts on ruled accounting paper. Sometimes a color tint or a heavy vertical rule is used on printed accounting paper to separate the dollars and cents columns.
6. Two zeros are written in the cents column when an amount is in even dollars, such as $500.00. If the cents column is left blank, doubts may arise later about the correct amount.
7. A single line is ruled across amount columns to indicate addition or subtraction.
8. A double line is ruled across amount columns to indicate that the totals have been verified as correct.
9. Neatness is very important in accounting records so that there is never any doubt about what information has been recorded. A ruler is used to make single and double lines.

**REMEMBER**

Double lines ruled below totals mean the totals have been verified as correct.

## TERM REVIEW

proving cash

## AUDIT YOUR UNDERSTANDING

1. List the three steps for proving a journal.
2. State the formula for proving cash.
3. List the five steps to rule a journal at the end of a month.

## WORK TOGETHER

**Proving and ruling a journal**

Use the journal from Work Together on page 81. Your instructor will guide you through the following examples.

***Transactions:*** Apr. 23. Sold services on account to Lester Dodge, $317.00. S2.
27. Paid cash to owner for personal use, $750.00. C7.
29. Received cash on account from Lester Dodge, $75.00. R3.
30. Received cash from sales, $743.00. T30.

4. Journalize the transactions for April 23 and 27.
5. Prove and rule page 1 of the journal. Carry the column totals forward to page 2 of the journal.
6. Use page 2 of the journal to journalize the rest of the transactions for April.
7. Prove page 2 of the journal.
8. Prove cash. The beginning cash balance on April 1 is zero. The balance on the next unused check stub is $5,736.00.
9. Rule page 2 of the journal.

## ON YOUR OWN

**Proving and ruling a journal.**

Use the journal from On Your Own on page 81. Work these problems independently.

***Transactions:*** June 23. Sold services on account to Connie Vaughn, $135.00. S2.
26. Paid cash for delivery charges (Miscellaneous Expense), $17.00. C7.
27. Received cash on account from Connie Vaughn, $100.00. R3.
30. Received cash from sales, $235.00. T30.

10. Journalize the transactions for June 23 and 26.
11. Prove and rule page 1 of the journal. Carry the column totals forward to page 2 of the journal.
12. Use page 2 of the journal to journalize the rest of the transactions for June.
13. Prove page 2 of the journal.
14. Prove cash. The beginning cash balance on June 1 is zero. The balance on the next unused check stub is $2,196.00.
15. Rule page 2 of the journal.

# CHAPTER 4 SUMMARY

*Enrichment Activity*

**Types of Businesses**

*Proprietorships are the most common form of business organization in the United States with over 17 million proprietorships filing tax returns. Review the advantages and disadvantages of proprietorships on page 80 and write a paragraph describing why you think proprietorships are the most common form of business organization.*

After completing this chapter, you can

1. Define important accounting terms related to journalizing transactions.
2. Identify accounting concepts and practices related to journalizing transactions.
3. Record in a five-column journal transactions to set up a business.
4. Record in a five-column journal transactions to buy insurance for cash and supplies on account.
5. Record in a five-column journal transactions that affect owner's equity and receiving cash on account.
6. Prove and rule a five-column journal and prove cash.

## EXPLORE ACCOUNTING

### PRENUMBERED DOCUMENTS

As one way to control the operations of the business, a company often will use prenumbered documents. Such a document is one that has the form number printed on it in advance. The most common example in everyday life is the personal check.

Businesses use several prenumbered documents. Examples include business checks, sales invoices, purchase orders, receipts, and memorandums.

The use of prenumbered documents allows a simple way to ensure that all documents are recorded. For example, when a business records the checks written during a period of time, all check numbers should be accounted for in numeric order. The person recording the checks must watch to see that no numbers are skipped. In this way, the business is more confident that all checks are recorded.

By using several types of prenumbered documents, the business helps ensure that all transactions are properly recorded.

Another way a business tries to control operations is through the use of batch totals. When many (sometimes hundreds) of documents are being recorded, the total amount can be used to help ensure that all documents are recorded.

For example, when sales invoices are recorded, the total of all the invoices is calculated prior to the invoices being recorded. Once all invoices are recorded, another total can be calculated. If the two totals are equal, it can be assumed that all invoices have been recorded. If the totals *do not equal*, it may indicate that a document was skipped.

**Research:** Contact a local business and ask what prenumbered documents are used there. Determine how the business uses the documents to ensure that all documents are recorded properly.

## 4-1 APPLICATION PROBLEM

### Journalizing transactions into a five-column journal

Dennis Gilbert owns a service business called D & G Company, which uses the following accounts:

| | | |
|---|---|---|
| Cash | Accts. Pay.—Ronken Supplies | Miscellaneous Expense |
| Accts. Rec.—Hetland Company | Dennis Gilbert, Capital | Rent Expense |
| Supplies | Dennis Gilbert, Drawing | Utilities Expense |
| Prepaid Insurance | Sales | |

***Transactions:***

Feb. 1. Received cash from owner as an investment, $10,000.00. R1.
4. Paid cash for supplies, $1,000.00. C1.
5. Paid cash for supplies, $50.00. C2.

***Instructions:***

Journalize the transactions completed during February of the current year. Use page 1 of the journal given in the *Working Papers*. Source documents are abbreviated as follows: check, C; memorandum, M; receipt, R; sales invoice, S; calculator tape, T.

Save your work to complete Application Problem 4-2.

## 4-2 APPLICATION PROBLEM

### Journalizing buying insurance, buying on account, and paying on account into a five-column journal

Use the chart of accounts and journal from Application Problem 4-1.

***Transactions:***

Feb. 6. Paid cash for insurance, $1,200.00. C3.
7. Bought supplies on account from Ronken Supplies, $1,400.00 M1.
8. Paid cash on account to Ronken Supplies, $700.00. C4.
12. Paid cash on account to Ronken Supplies, $700.00. C5.

***Instructions:***

Journalize the transactions. Source documents use the same abbreviations as stated in Application Problem 4-1. Save your work to complete Application Problem 4-3.

## 4-3 APPLICATION PROBLEM

### Journalizing transactions that affect owner's equity and receiving cash on account into a five-column journal

Use the chart of accounts given in Application Problem 4-1 and the journal from Application Problem 4-2.

***Transactions:***

Feb. 12. Paid cash for rent, $600.00. C6.
13. Received cash from sales, $500.00. T13.
14. Sold services on account to Hetland Company, $450.00. S1.
15. Paid cash for telephone bill, $225.00. C7.
15. Paid cash to owner for personal use, $1,800.00. C8.

Feb. 18. Received cash from sales, $278.00. T18.
19. Paid cash for postage (Miscellaneous Expense), $64.00. C9.
21. Received cash an account from Hetland Company, $250.00. R2.
22. Received cash from sales, $342.00. T22.
22. Paid cash for heating fuel bill, $329.00. C10.
25. Bought supplies on account from Ronken Supplies, $76.00. M2.

***Instructions:***

Journalize the transactions. Source documents use the same abbreviations as stated in Application Problem 4-1. Save your work to complete Application Problem 4-4.

## 4-4 APPLICATION PROBLEM
### Proving and ruling a journal

Use the chart of accounts given in Application Problem 4-1 and the journal from Application Problem 4-3.

***Transactions:***

Feb. 25. Received cash on account from Hetland Company, $200.00. R3.
25. Paid cash for a delivery (Miscellaneous Expense), $18.00. C11.
26. Sold services on account to Hetland Company, $136.00. S2.
26. Paid cash for supplies, $44.00. C12.
27. Paid cash for rent, $600.00. C13.
27. Paid cash for postage (Miscellaneous Expense), $10.00. C14.
28. Received cash from sales, $1,365.00. T28.
28. Paid cash to owner for personal use, $1,000.00. C15.

***Instructions:***

1. Journalize the transactions for February 25 and 26. Source documents use the same abbreviations as stated in Application Problem 4-1.
2. Prove and rule page 1 of the journal. Carry the column totals forward to page 2 of the journal.
3. Use page 2 of the journal to journalize the transactions for February 27 and 28.
4. Prove page 2 of the journal.
5. Prove cash. The beginning cash balance on February 1 is zero. The balance on the next unused check stub is $4,595.00.
6. Rule page 2 of the journal.

## 4-5 APPLICATION PROBLEM
### Journalizing transactions

Nick Bonnocotti owns a service business called The Lawn Doctor, which uses the following accounts:

| | | |
|---|---|---|
| Cash | Accts. Pay.—Western Supplies | Advertising Expense |
| Accts. Rec.—Leon Quarve | Nick Bonnocotti, Capital | Utilities Expense |
| Supplies | Nick Bonnocotti, Drawing | |
| Prepaid Insurance | Sales | |

***Transactions:***

Apr. 1. Nick Bonnocotti invested $2,000.00 of his own money in the business. Receipt No. 1.
3. Used business cash to purchase supplies costing $37.00. Wrote Check No. 1.

Apr. 4. Wrote Check No. 2 for insurance, $120.00.
5. Purchased supplies for $50.00 over the phone from Western Supplies, promising to send the check next week. Memo. No. 1.
11. Sent Check No. 3 to Western Supplies, $50.00.
12. Sent a check for the electricity bill, $65.00. Check No. 4.
15. Wrote a $850.00 check to Mr. Bonnocotti for personal use. Used Check No. 5.
16. Sold services for $259.00 to Leon Quarve, who agreed to pay for them within 10 days. Sales Invoice No. 1.
17. Recorded cash sales of $1,668.00.
18. Paid $50.00 for advertising. Wrote Check No. 6.
25. Received $259.00 from Leon Quarve for the services performed last week. Wrote Receipt No. 2.

***Instructions:***

Journalize the transactions completed during April of the current year. Use page 1 of the journal given in the *Working Papers*. Remember to enter source document numbers as necessary.

## 4-6 MASTERY PROBLEM

### Journalizing transactions and proving and ruling a journal

Jill Statsholt owns a service business called Jill's Car Wash, which uses the following accounts:

Cash
Accts. Rec.—David's Limos
Supplies
Prepaid Insurance
Accts. Pay.—Akita Supplies
Accts. Pay.—Long Supplies
Jill Statsholt, Capital
Jill Statsholt, Drawing
Sales
Advertising Expense
Miscellaneous Expense
Rent Expense
Repair Expense
Utilities Expense

***Transactions:***

June 1. Received cash from owner as an investment, $17,500.00. R1.
2. Paid cash for rent, $400.00. C1.
3. Paid cash for supplies, $1,200.00. C2.
4. Bought supplies on account from Akita Supplies, $2,000.00. M1.
5. Paid cash for insurance, $4,500.00. C3.
8. Paid cash on account to Akita Supplies, $1,500.00. C4.
8. Received cash from sales, $750.00. T8.
8. Sold services on account to David's Limos, $200.00. S1.
9. Paid cash for electric bill, $75.00. C5.
10. Paid cash for miscellaneous expense, $7.00. C6.
10. Received cash from sales, $750.00. T10.
11. Paid cash for repairs, $100.00. C7.
11. Received cash from sales, $850.00. T11.
12. Received cash from sales, $700.00. T12.
15. Paid cash to owner for personal use, $350.00. C8.
15. Received cash from sales, $750.00. T15.
16. Paid cash for supplies, $1,500.00. C9.
17. Received cash on account from David's Limos, $200.00. R2.
17. Bought supplies on account from Long Supplies, $750.00. M2.

June 17. Received cash from sales, $600.00. T17.
18. Received cash from sales, $800.00. T18.
19. Received cash from sales, $750.00. T19.
22. Bought supplies on account from Long Supplies, $80.00. M3.
22. Received cash from sales, $700.00. T22.
23. Paid cash for advertising, $130.00. C10.
23. Sold services on account to David's Limos, $650.00. S2.
24. Paid cash for telephone bill, $60.00. C11.
24. Received cash from sales, $600.00. T24.
25. Received cash from sales, $550.00. T25.
26. Paid cash for supplies, $70.00. C12.
26. Received cash from sales, $600.00. T26.
29. Received cash on account from David's Limos, $650.00. R3.
30. Paid cash to owner for personal use, $375.00. C13.
30. Received cash from sales, $800.00. T30.

***Instructions:***

1. The journals for Jill's Car Wash are given in the *Working Papers*. Use page 1 of the journal to journalize the transactions for June 1 through June 19. Source documents are abbreviated as follows: check, C; memorandum, M; receipt, R; sales invoice, S; calculator tape, T.
2. Prove and rule page 1 of the journal. Carry the column totals forward to page 2 of the journal.
3. Use page 2 of the journal to journalize the transactions for the remainder of June.
4. Prove page 2 of the journal.
5. Prove cash. The beginning cash balance on June 1 is zero. The balance on the next unused check stub is $17,283.00.
6. Rule page 2 of the journal.

## 4-7 CHALLENGE PROBLEM
### Journalizing transactions using a variation of the five-column journal

Tony Wirth owns a service business called Wirth's Tailors, which uses the following accounts:

Cash
Accts. Rec.—Amy's Uniforms
Supplies
Prepaid Insurance
Accts. Pay.—Marker Supplies
Tony Wirth, Capital
Tony Wirth, Drawing
Sales
Rent Expense
Utilities Expense

***Transactions:***

June 1. Received cash from owner as an investment, $17,000.00. R1.
2. Paid cash for insurance, $3,000.00. C1.
3. Bought supplies on account from Marker Supplies, $2,500.00. M1.
4. Paid cash for supplies, $1,400.00. C2.
8. Paid cash on account to Marker Supplies, $1,300.00. C3.
9. Paid cash for rent, $800.00. C4.
12. Received cash from sales, $550.00. T12.
15. Sold services on account to Amy's Uniforms, $300.00. S1.
16. Paid cash for telephone bill, $70.00. C5.
22. Received cash on account from Amy's Uniforms, $300.00. R2.
25. Paid cash to owner for personal use, $900.00. C6.

***Instructions:***

The journal for Wirth's Tailors is given in the *Working Papers*. Wirth's Tailors uses a journal that is slightly different from the journal used in this chapter. Use page 1 of the journal to journalize the transactions. Source documents are abbreviated as follows: check, C; memorandum, M; receipt, R; sales invoice, S; calculator tape, T.

**INTERNET ACTIVITY**

Point your browser to

**http://accounting.swpco.com**

Choose **First-Year Course**, choose **Activities**, and complete the activity for Chapter 4.

## Applied Communication

Careful research about careers will help prepare you for making career choices. There are several U.S. government publications that provide detailed descriptions of many job titles. Two that are available in most public libraries are the *Dictionary of Occupational Titles (DOT)* and the *Occupational Outlook Handbook*.

**Instructions:** Go to the library and, using one of the two publications listed or any other appropriate resource, find the description for any accounting-related job. Record information you find, such as qualifications needed, job outlook, and earnings. Write one paragraph describing the pros and cons of working in such a job. Be sure to write a topic sentence and a conclusion.

## Cases for Critical Thinking

**Case 1** During the summer, Willard Kelly does odd jobs to earn money. Mr. Kelly keeps all his money in a single checking account. He writes checks to pay for personal items and for business expenses. These payments include personal clothing, school supplies, gasoline for his car, and recreation. Mr. Kelly uses his check stubs as his accounting records. Are Mr. Kelly's accounting procedures and records correct? Explain your answer.

**Case 2** In his business, Michael Rock uses a journal with the following columns: Date, Account Title, Check No., Cash Debit, and Cash Credit. Mr. Rock's wife, Jennifer, suggests that he needs three additional amount columns: General Debit, General Credit, and Sales Credit. Mr. Rock states that all his business transactions are for cash, and he never buys on account. Therefore, he doesn't see the need for more than the Cash Debit and Cash Credit special amount columns. Who is correct, Mr. or Mrs. Rock? Explain your answer.

# AUTOMATED ACCOUNTING

## RECORDING TRANSACTIONS

### General Journal

A journal with two amount columns in which all kinds of entries can be recorded is called a *general journal.* General journal entries are entered in the automated accounting system through the General Journal tab. In a later chapter, special journals will be discussed to instruct you on how to use the other journals on the Journal Entries screen for specific types of transactions. The other tabs on the Journal Entries screen are used for entering purchases, cash payments, cash receipts, and sales.

In an automated accounting system, the transactions that are entered and posted in the general journal update ledger account balances immediately. For verification purposes, a general ledger report can be displayed or printed to prove account balances.

### Recording Transactions in the General Journal Screen

Entering general journal entries can be done in five steps.

1. Enter the date of the transaction, then press the Tab key.
2. Enter the source document number in the Reference column, then press the Tab key.
3. Enter the account number to be debited, then press the Tab key. The account title will be displayed at the bottom of the general journal, just above the command buttons. (In *Automated Accounting 8.0,* the account title is displayed next to the account number after tabbing to the next column.
4. Enter the debit amount, then press the Tab key twice. The cursor will automaticaly position itself in the Account Number field on the next line of the journal. Enter the account number to be credited, press the Tab key twice, then enter the credit amount.

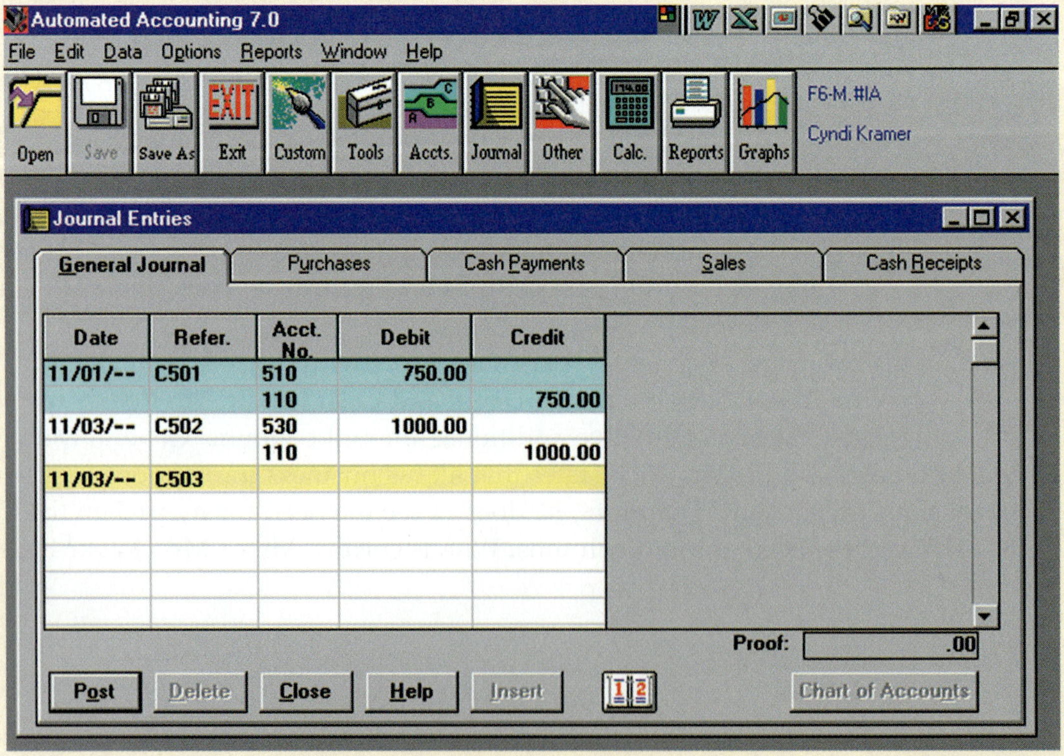

# AUTOMATED ACCOUNTING

5. When the transaction is complete, click the Post button. Posting will be discussed in Chapter 5.

## General Journal Transaction Additions, Changes, and Deletions

If you wish to add a part of a transaction, select the journal entry transaction to which you want to add a debit or credit. Click on the Insert button. When the blank line appears, enter the additional transaction debit or credit and click the Post button.

When changing or deleting general journal transactions, you need to select any portion of the desired transaction. Make corrections to the entry, then click the Post button. If you wish to delete the transaction, click the Delete button.

## General Journal Report

In this section you will learn how to generate journal reports and specify which journal entries are to appear in the journal report. The general journal report will display or print the general journal entries that were posted for a specified period. Reports are useful in detecting errors and verifying that debits and credits are equal.

A general journal report can be generated in three steps:

1. Choose the Report Selection menu item from the Reports menu or click the Reports toolbar button.
2. When the Report Selection window appears, choose the Journals option. To change the run date, shown in the upper right corner of the screen, enter the desired date or use the + key to increase and the − key to decrease the date. You may also click on the calendar.
3. Select the General Journal report, then click the OK button. You can choose to include all general journal entries or to customize your report.

## AUTOMATING APPLICATION PROBLEM 4-5: Journalizing transactions

**Instructions:**

1. Load *Automated Accounting 7.0* or higher software.
2. Select database F04-1 from the appropriate directory/folder.
3. Select File from the menu bar and choose the Save As menu command. Key the path to the drive and directory that contains your data files. Save the database with a file name of XXX041 (where XXX are your initials). (*Automated Accounting 8.0* allows long file names. Your instructor may direct you to use your full name when saving your files.)
4. Access Problem Instructions through the Help menu. Read the Problem Instructions screen. (In *Automated Accounting 8.0*, Problem Instructions are accessed by clicking the Browser toolbar button.)
5. Key the transactions listed on pages 90–91.
6. Exit the *Automated Accounting* software.

## AUTOMATING MASTERY PROBLEM 4-6: Journalizing transactions and proving and ruling a journal

**Instructions:**

1. Load *Automated Accounting 7.0* or higher software.
2. Select database F04-2 from the appropriate directory/folder.
3. Select File from the menu bar and choose the Save As menu command. Key the path to the drive and directory that contains your data files. Save the database with a file name of XXX042 (where XXX are your initials). (*Automated Accounting 8.0* allows long file names. Your instructor may direct you to use your full name when saving your files.)
4. Access Problem Instructions through the Help menu. Read the Problem Instructions screen. (In *Automated Accounting 8.0*, Problem Instructions are accessed by clicking the Browser toolbar button.)
5. Key the transactions listed on pages 91–92.
6. Exit the *Automated Accounting* software.

# 5 Posting to a General Ledger

**AFTER STUDYING CHAPTER 5, YOU WILL BE ABLE TO:**

1. Define accounting terms related to posting from a journal to a general ledger.
2. Identify accounting concepts and practices related to posting from a journal to a general ledger.
3. Prepare a chart of accounts for a service business organized as a proprietorship.
4. Post separate amounts from a journal to a general ledger.
5. Post column totals from a journal to a general ledger.
6. Analyze and journalize correcting entries.

**TERMS PREVIEW**

ledger

general ledger

account number

file maintenance

opening an account

posting

correcting entry

## ACCOUNT FORM

Encore Music records transactions in a journal as described in Chapter 4. A journal is a permanent record of the debit and credit parts of each transaction with transactions recorded in chronological order. A journal does not show, in one place, all the changes in a single account.

If only a journal is used, a business must search through all journal pages to find items affecting a single account balance. For this reason, a form is used to summarize in one place all the changes to a single account. A separate form is used for each account.

# ACCOUNTING IN YOUR CAREER

## TIME FOR POSTING

Shayla Graham is the bookkeeper at Hammonds Marketing Services. Tony Hammonds, who started the business, hired her to take full charge of accounting, but has never shown a great deal of interest in her daily work. Tony is now talking with Shayla to discuss ways to free up some time for her to take on additional responsibilities in the rapidly growing business.

Tony begins, "Shayla, you've done a great job with the accounting system here at Hammonds Marketing. I have come to rely on you totally for everything related to accounts. But now I need to see if we can find some ways for you to do your work in less time so you can help me with some other projects."

"Thank you for the vote of confidence, Tony," Shayla says, "I'd be happy to work with you on other projects if we can find a way for me to do so."

"Well, it looks like there's a lot of duplication in your work. You look at all the documents and then prepare some additional ones. Then you record them in the journal, and then you record them all again when you post them. You're doing the same thing three times."

"Tony," Shayla replies, "I promise you I am not creating unnecessary work. Each one of these steps is an important part of what we call the accounting cycle. And the accounting firm that audits our books has assured both you and me that I am following the correct procedures. Let me explain why each of these steps is important."

**Critical Thinking:**

1. How should Shayla explain the care she takes examining and preparing source documents?
2. What would be a good way to explain why both journalizing and posting are important?

# 5-1 Preparing a Chart of Accounts

## RELATIONSHIP OF A T ACCOUNT TO AN ACCOUNT FORM

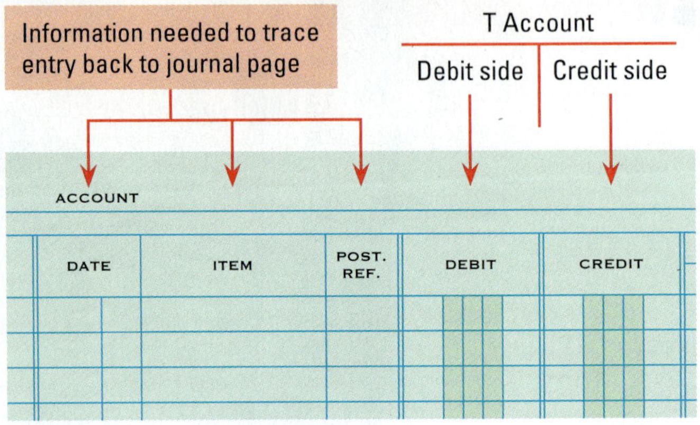


An account form is based on and includes the debit and credit sides of a T account. In addition to debit and credit columns, space is provided in the account form for recording the transaction date and journal page number. This information can be used to trace a specific entry back to where a transaction is recorded in a journal.

The major disadvantage of the account form shown is that no current, up-to-date account balance is shown. If this form is used, an up-to-date balance must be calculated each time the account is examined. When an account has a large number of entries, the balance is difficult and time consuming to calculate. Therefore, a more commonly used account form has Debit and Credit Balance columns as shown below.

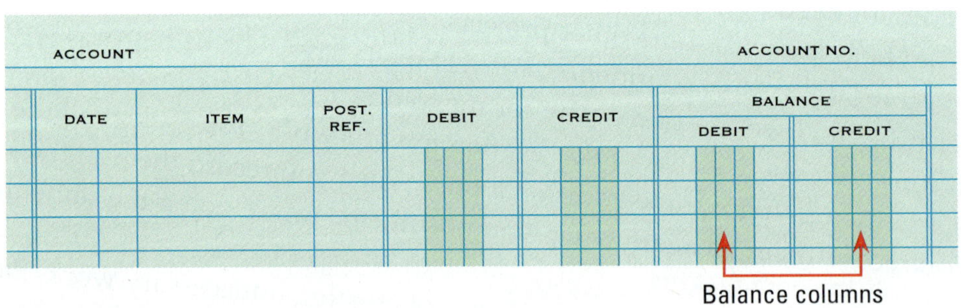


Because the form has columns for the debit and credit balance, it is often referred to as the balance-ruled account form.

The account balance is calculated and recorded as each entry is recorded in the account. Recording information in an account is described later in this chapter. The T account is a useful device for analyzing transactions into debit and credit parts. However, the balance-ruled account form is more useful as a permanent record of changes to account balances than is the T account. Encore Music uses the balance-ruled account form.

## CHART OF ACCOUNTS

**Encore Music**

**CHART OF ACCOUNTS**

| Balance Sheet Accounts | | Income Statement Accounts | |
|---|---|---|---|
| | (100) ASSETS | | (400) REVENUE |
| 110 | Cash | 410 | Sales |
| 120 | Petty Cash | | (500) EXPENSES |
| 130 | Accounts Receivable—Kids Time | 510 | Advertising Expense |
| 140 | Accounts Receivable—Learn N Play | 520 | Insurance Expense |
| 150 | Supplies | 530 | Miscellaneous Expense |
| 160 | Prepaid Insurance | 540 | Rent Expense |
| | (200) LIABILITIES | 550 | Supplies Expense |
| 210 | Accounts Payable—Ling Music Supplies | 560 | Utilities Expense |
| 220 | Accounts Payable—Sullivan Office Supplies | | |
| | (300) OWNER'S EQUITY | | |
| 310 | Barbara Treviño, Capital | | |
| 320 | Barbara Treviño, Drawing | | |
| 330 | Income Summary | | |

A group of accounts is called a **ledger.** A ledger that contains all accounts needed to prepare financial statements is called a **general ledger.** The name given to an account is known as an account title. The number assigned to an account is called an **account number.**

### Preparing a Chart of Accounts

A list of account titles and numbers showing the location of each account in a ledger is known as a chart of accounts. Encore Music's chart of accounts is shown above.

For ease of use while studying Cycle 1, Encore Music's chart of accounts is also shown on page 3.

Accounts in a general ledger are arranged in the same order as they appear on financial statements. Encore Music's chart of accounts shows five general ledger divisions: (1) Assets, (2) Liabilities, (3) Owner's Equity, (4) Revenue, and (5) Expenses.

## ACCOUNT NUMBERS

1 5 0 **Supplies**

General ledger division — Location within general ledger division

Encore Music assigns a three-digit account number to each account. For example, Supplies is assigned the number 150, as shown.

The first digit of each account number shows the general ledger division in which the account is located. For example, the asset division accounts are numbered in the 100s. Therefore, the number for the asset account, Supplies, begins with a 1.

The second two digits indicate the location of each account within a general ledger division. The 50 in the account number for Supplies indicates that the account is located between account number 140 and account number 160.

Encore Music initially assigns account numbers by 10s so that new accounts can be added easily. Nine numbers are unused between each account on Encore Music's chart of accounts. For example, numbers 111 to 119 are unused between accounts numbered 110 and 120. New numbers can be assigned between existing account numbers without renumbering all existing accounts. The procedure for arranging accounts in a general ledger, assigning account numbers, and keeping records current is called **file maintenance.**

Unused account numbers are assigned to new accounts. Encore Music records payments for gasoline in Miscellaneous Expense. If Ms. Treviño found that the amount paid each month for gasoline had become a major expense, she might decide to use a separate account. The account might be titled Gasoline Expense. Encore Music arranges expense accounts in alphabetic order in its general ledger. Therefore, the new account would be inserted between Advertising Expense and Insurance Expense.

| | | |
|---|---|---|
| 510 | Advertising Expense | (Existing account) |
| | **Gasoline Expense** | **(New Account)** |
| 520 | Insurance Expense | (Existing account) |

The number selected for the new account should leave some unused numbers on either side of it for other accounts that might need to be added. The middle, unused account number between existing numbers 510 and 520 is 515. Therefore, 515 is assigned as the account number for the new account.

| | | |
|---|---|---|
| 510 | Advertising Expense | (Existing account) |
| **515** | **Gasoline Expense** | **(New Account)** |
| 520 | Insurance Expense | (Existing account) |

When an account is no longer needed, it is removed from the general ledger and the chart of accounts. For example, if Encore Music were to buy its own equipment and building, there would be no need for the rent expense account. The account numbered 540 would be removed, and that number would become unused and available to assign to another account if the need should arise.

When a new account is added at the end of a ledger division, the next number in a sequence of 10s is used. For example, suppose Encore Music needs to add another expense account, Water Expense, to show more detail about one of the utility expenses. The expense accounts are arranged in alphabetic order. Therefore, the new account would be added at the end of the expense section of the chart of accounts. The last used expense account number is 560, as shown on the chart of accounts. The next number in the sequence of 10s is 570, which is assigned as the number of the new account.

| | | |
|---|---|---|
| 550 | Supplies Expense | (Existing account) |
| 560 | Utilities Expense | (Existing account) |
| **570** | **Water Expense** | **(New Account)** |

Encore Music has relatively few accounts in its general ledger and does not anticipate adding many new accounts in the future. Therefore, a three-digit account number adequately provides for the few account numbers that might be added. However, as the number of general ledger accounts increases, a business may change to four or more digits.

Charts of accounts with more than three digits are described in later chapters.

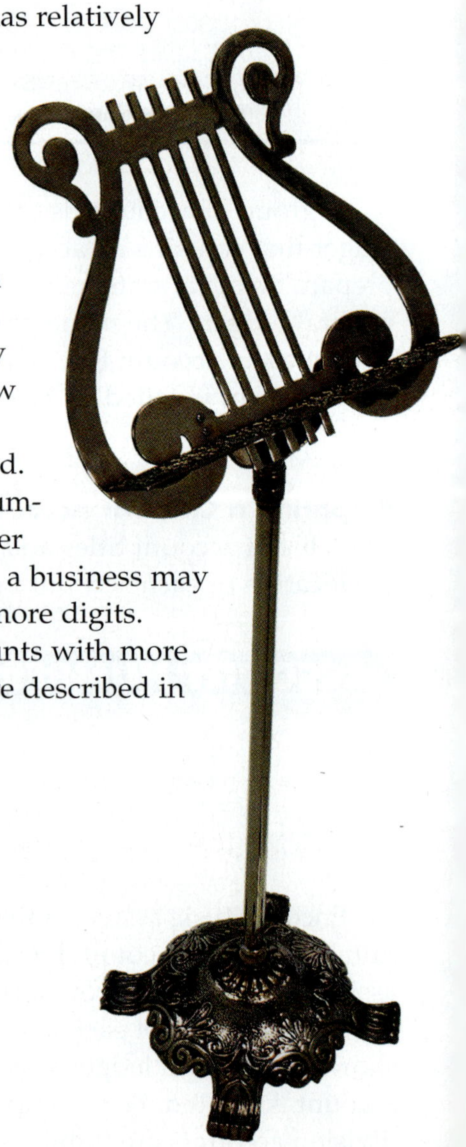

## OPENING AN ACCOUNT IN A GENERAL LEDGER

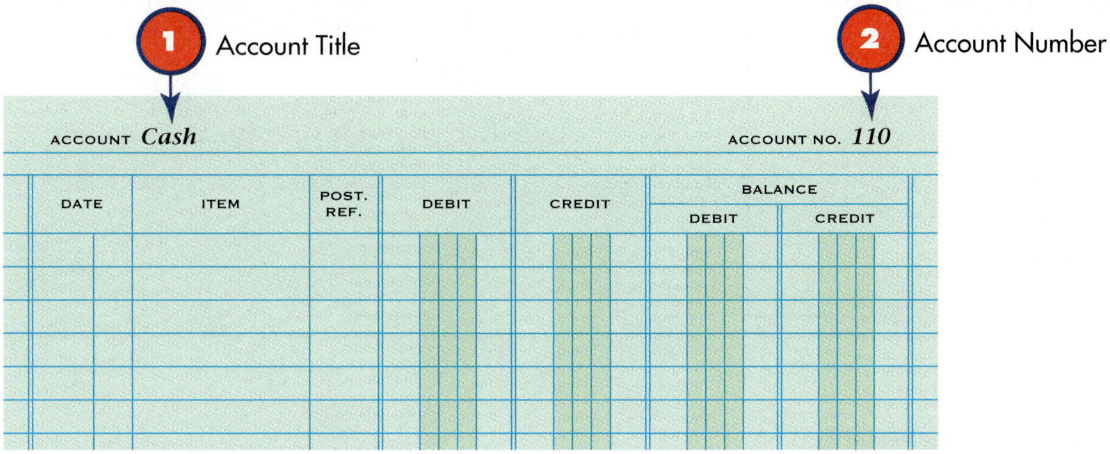


Writing an account title and number on the heading of an account is called **opening an account.** A general ledger account is opened for each account listed on a chart of accounts. Accounts are opened and arranged in a general ledger in the same order as on the chart of accounts.

Cash, account number 110, is the first account on Encore Music's chart of accounts. The cash account is opened using the following steps.

The same procedure is used to open all accounts listed on Encore Music's chart of accounts.

### STEPS: Opening an account in a general ledger

1. Write the account title, *Cash*, after the word *Account* in the heading.
2. Write the account number, *110*, after the words *Account No.* in the heading.

## PROFESSIONAL BUSINESS ETHICS

### CAN I SAY THIS ON MY RESUME?

Kendra Wheeler applied for a payroll clerk job with the Hampton Group, a market research firm. To improve her chances, she exaggerated her work experience on her resume.

Based on this resume, Kendra was hired. After one year, she received above-average ratings during her annual review. Shortly thereafter, her boss met Kendra's former supervisor and learned the truth.

**Instructions**

Use the three-step checklist to help determine whether or not each action demonstrated ethical behavior. (Suggested answers are provided for this case.)

1. *Is the action illegal?* No. Overstating qualifications is not illegal, but the employer could terminate your employment.
2. *Does the action violate company or professional standards?* No. Kendra was neither an employee of the company nor a member of any profession.
3. *Who is affected, and how, by the action?* Kendra: She obtained employment, but now she could be terminated. If retained, she could have difficulty being promoted. Other applicants: More highly qualified applicants lost an opportunity for employment. The Hampton Group: Managers may lose trust in employees.

Based on the above analysis, Kendra's actions were unethical.

## Terms Review

ledger
general ledger
account number
file maintenance
opening an account

## Audit Your Understanding

1. Describe the two parts of an account number.
2. List the two steps for opening an account.

## Work Together

### Preparing a chart of accounts and opening an account

Forms are given in the *Working Papers.* Your instructor will guide you through the following examples.

Clara Roseman owns a service business called Roseman's Services, which uses these accounts:

| | | | |
|---|---|---|---|
| Accts. Pay.—Kammerer Supplies | Miscellaneous Expense | Cash | Automobile Expense |
| Accts. Rec.—Tyler Cobb | Insurance Expense | Sales | Accts. Pay.—Campbell Office Supplies |
| Prepaid Insurance | Rent Expense | Supplies | Accts. Rec.—Amber Jorgenson |
| Clara Roseman, Drawing | Clara Roseman, Capital | | |

3. Prepare a chart of accounts. Arrange expense accounts in alphabetical order. Use 3-digit account numbers and number the accounts within a division by 10s.
4. Two new accounts, Gasoline Expense and Utilities Expense, are to be added to the chart of accounts prepared in Instruction 3. Assign account numbers to the two new accounts.
5. Using the account form in the *Working Papers,* open Cash.

## On Your Own

### Preparing a chart of accounts and opening an account

Forms are given in the *Working Papers.* Work these problems independently.

Eric Yunger owns a service business called Yunger's Hair Care, which uses these accounts:

| | | | |
|---|---|---|---|
| Accts. Pay.—Otgen Company | Supplies Expense | Cash | Delivery Expense |
| Accts. Rec.—Sarych Supplies | Insurance Expense | Sales | Accts. Pay.—North Star |
| Prepaid Insurance | Telephone Expense | Supplies | Accts. Rec.—Jaeson Keene |
| Eric Yunger, Drawing | Eric Yunger, Capital | | |

6. Prepare a chart of accounts. Arrange expense accounts in alphabetical order. Use 3-digit account numbers and number the accounts within a division by 10s.
7. Two new accounts, Rent Expense and Water Expense, are to be added to the chart of accounts prepared in Instruction 6. Assign account numbers to the two new accounts.
8. Using the account form in the *Working Papers,* open Delivery Expense.

# 5-2 Posting Separate Amounts from a Journal to a General Ledger

## POSTING AN AMOUNT FROM A GENERAL DEBIT COLUMN

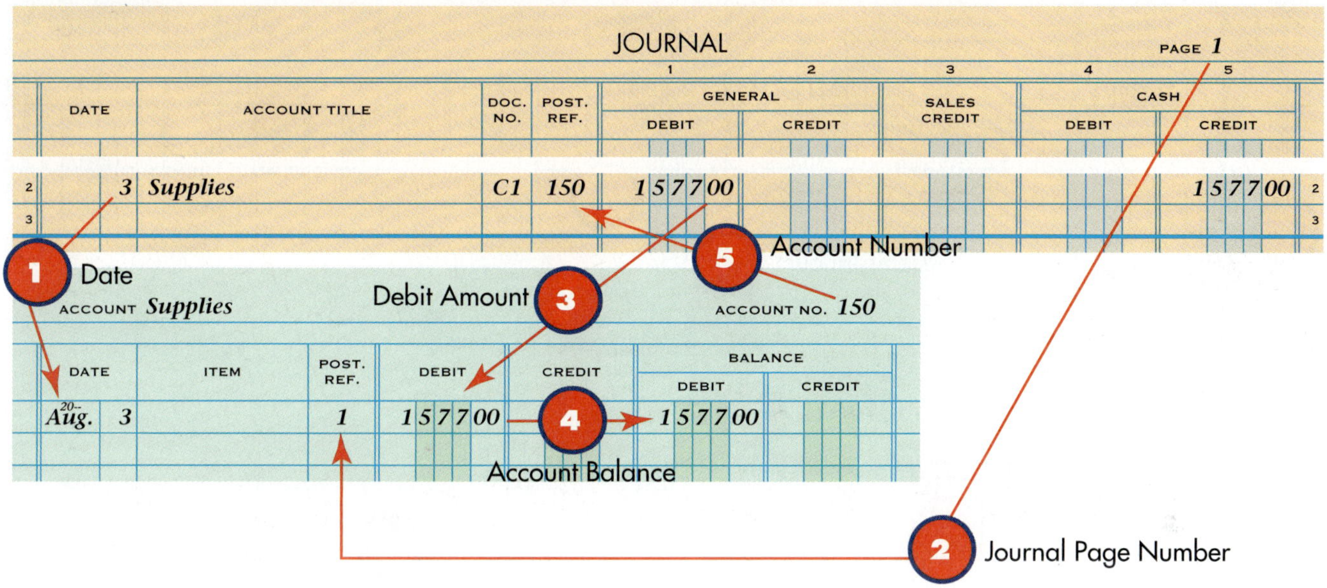


Transferring information from a journal entry to a ledger account is called **posting.** Posting sorts journal entries so that all debits and credits affecting each account are brought together. For example, all changes to Cash are brought together in the cash account.

Amounts in journal entries are recorded in either general amount columns or special amount columns. There are two rules for posting amounts from a journal. (1) Separate amounts in a journal's general amount columns are posted individually to the account written in the Account Title column. (2) Separate amounts in a journal's special amount columns are not posted individually. Instead, the special amount column totals are posted to the account named in the heading of the special amount column.

### Posting a Separate Amount from a General Debit Column

For most journal entries, at least one separate amount is posted individually to a general ledger account. When an entry in a journal includes an amount in a general amount column, the amount is posted individually.

Each separate amount in the General Debit and General Credit columns of a journal is posted to the account written in the Account Title column.

### STEPS: Posting an amount from a General Debit column

1. Write the date, *20—, Aug. 3,* in the Date column of the account, *Supplies.*
2. Write the journal page number, *1,* in the Post. Ref. column of the account. Post. Ref. is an abbreviation for Posting Reference.
3. Write the debit amount, *$1,577.00,* in the Debit amount column.
4. Write the new account balance, *$1,577.00,* in the Balance Debit column. Because this entry is the first in the Supplies account, the previous balance is zero.

| Previous Balance | + | Debit Column Amount | = | New Debit Balance |
|---|---|---|---|---|
| $0.00 | + | $1,577.00 | = | $1,577.00 |

5. Return to the journal and write the account number, *150,* in the Post. Ref. column of the journal.

## POSTING A SECOND AMOUNT TO AN ACCOUNT

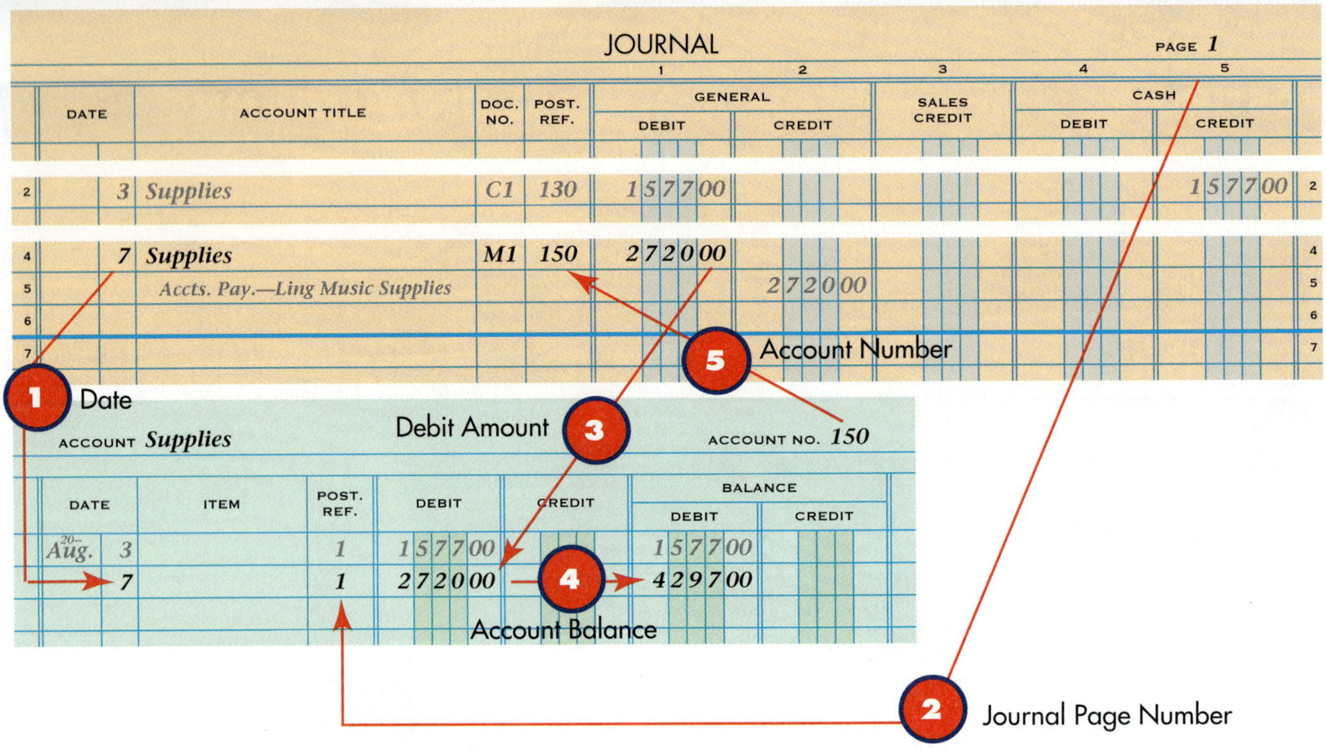


The numbers in the Post. Ref. columns of the general ledger account and the journal serve three purposes. (1) An entry in an account can be traced to its source in a journal. (2) An entry in a journal can be traced to where it was posted in an account. (3) If posting is interrupted, the accounting personnel can easily see which entries in the journal still need to be posted. A blank in the Post. Ref. column of the journal indicates that posting for that line still needs to be completed. *Therefore, the posting reference is always recorded in the journal as the last step in the posting procedure.*

The same five steps are followed when a second amount is posted to an account.

### STEPS: Posting a second amount to an account

1. Write the date, *7*, in the Date column of the account. The month and year are written only once on a page of a ledger account unless the month or year changes.
2. Write the journal page number, *1*, in the Post. Ref. column of the account.
3. Write the debit amount, *$2,720.00*, in the Debit amount column.
4. Write the new account balance, *$4,297.00*, in the Balance Debit column.
5. Return to the journal and write the account number, *150*, in the Post. Ref. column of the journal.

| Previous Debit Balance | + | Debit Column Amount | = | New Debit Balance |
|---|---|---|---|---|
| $1,577.00 | + | $2,720.00 | = | $4,297.00 |

### REMEMBER

Each separate amount in the General Debit and Credit columns of a journal is posted individually. The totals of these columns are not posted.

## POSTING AN AMOUNT FROM A GENERAL CREDIT COLUMN

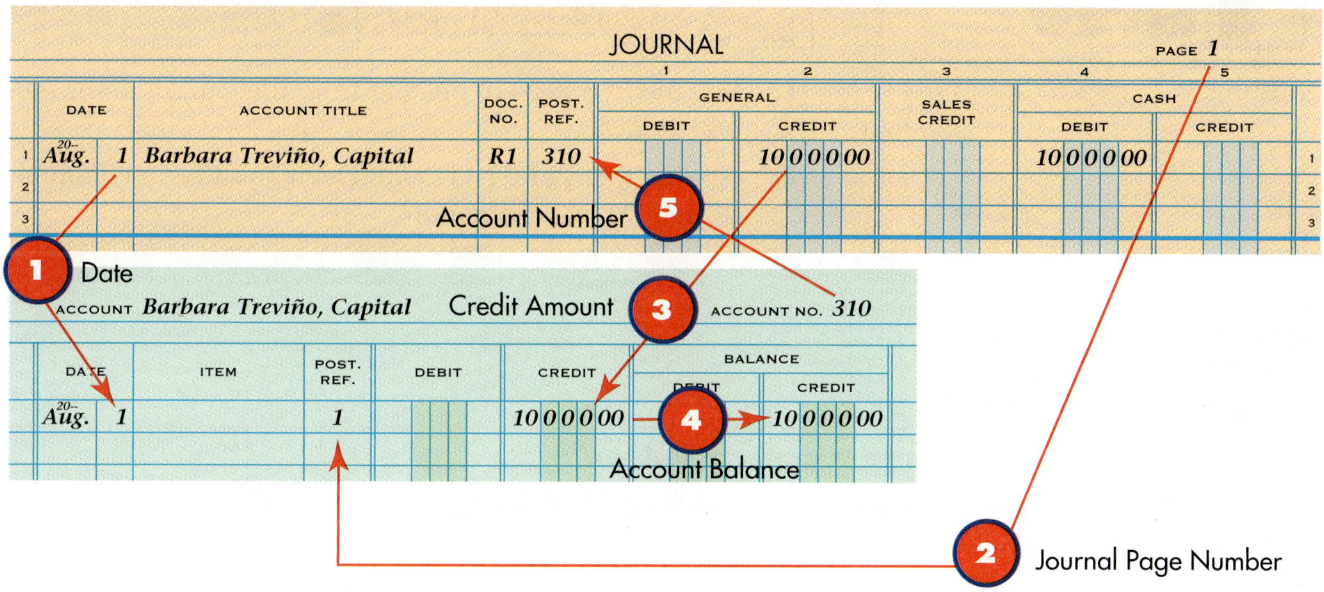


An amount in the General Credit column is posted separately. Five steps are followed when posting an amount from the General Credit column.

### STEPS: Posting an amount from a General Credit column

1. Write the date, *20—, Aug. 1*, in the Date column of the account.
2. Write the journal page number, *1*, in the Post. Ref. column of the account.
3. Write the credit amount, *$10,000.00*, in the Credit amount column.
4. Write the new account balance, *$10,000.00*, in the Balance Credit column.
5. Return to the journal and write the account number, *310*, in the Post. Ref. column of the journal.

| Previous Balance | + | Credit Column Amount | = | New Credit Balance |
|---|---|---|---|---|
| $0.00 | + | $10,000.00 | = | $10,000.00 |

### CULTURAL DIVERSITY

#### ACCOUNTING IN ANCIENT CIVILIZATIONS

In the ancient civilizations of Asia Minor and northern Africa, most citizens were illiterate. The scribe, who could read and write, became a very important person in the society. Of ancient Hebrew origin, the scribe has been called the forerunner of today's accountant.

Public scribes often recorded transactions as citizens arrived to do business. Most scribes recorded transactions on moist clay tablets that were then dried in the sun. Therefore, permanent records of transactions were not possible until there was someone able to write them down—the scribe—and a medium on which to record them—clay tablets.

Another important contribution to accounting was made by the Greeks around 630 B.C. The Greeks invented coined money, which facilitated assigning values to transactions.

The Babylonians in Asia Minor used an early form of banking. They transferred funds with a system resembling our modern-day checking accounts. This is believed to be one of the first uses of business documents.

These early practices provided the foundation for today's financial system and recordkeeping methods.

## TERM REVIEW

posting

## AUDIT YOUR UNDERSTANDING

1. List the five steps of posting from the journal to the general ledger.
2. Are the totals of the General Debit and Credit columns posted? Why or why not?

## WORK TOGETHER

### Posting separate amounts to a general ledger

A completed journal and general ledger accounts are given in the *Working Papers.* Your instructor will guide you through the following example.

Leonard Witkowski owns a service business that uses the following accounts:

**Assets**
- 110 Cash
- 120 Accounts Receivable—Danielle Braastad
- 130 Supplies
- 140 Prepaid Insurance

**Liabilities**
- 210 Accounts Payable—Joshua's Supplies

**Owner's Equity**
- 310 Leonard Witkowski, Capital
- 320 Leonard Witkowski, Drawing

**Revenue**
- 410 Sales

**Expenses**
- 510 Rent Expense

3. Post the separate amounts on each line of the journal that need to be posted individually. Save your work to complete Work Together on page 111.

## ON YOUR OWN

### Posting separate amounts to a general ledger

A completed journal and general ledger accounts are given in the *Working Papers.* Work this problem independently.

Melanie Komoko owns a service business which uses the following accounts:

**Assets**
- 110 Cash
- 120 Accounts Receivable—Brenden Otto
- 130 Supplies
- 140 Prepaid Insurance

**Liabilities**
- 210 Accounts Payable—Signs Plus

**Owner's Equity**
- 310 Melanie Komoko, Capital
- 320 Melanie Komoko, Drawing

**Revenue**
- 410 Sales

**Expenses**
- 510 Utilities Expense

4. Post the separate amounts on each line of the journal that need to be posted individually. Save your work to complete On Your Own on page 111.

# 5-3 Posting Column Totals from a Journal to a General Ledger

## CHECK MARKS SHOW THAT AMOUNTS ARE NOT POSTED

JOURNAL — PAGE 2

| | DATE | | ACCOUNT TITLE | DOC. NO. | POST. REF. | 1 GENERAL DEBIT | 2 GENERAL CREDIT | 3 SALES CREDIT | 4 CASH DEBIT | 5 CASH CREDIT | |
|---|---|---|---|---|---|---|---|---|---|---|---|
| 1 | 20-- Aug. | 20 | Brought Forward | | ✓ | 7,960 00 | 12,840 00 | 2,439 00 | 12,319 00 | 5,000 00 | 1 |
| 13 | | 31 | ✓ | T31 | ✓ | | | 290 00 | 290 00 | | 13 |
| 14 | | 31 | Miscellaneous Expense | M3 | | 3 00 | | | | 3 00 | 14 |
| 15 | | 31 | Totals | | | 8,979 00 | 12,840 00 | 4,411 00 | 14,291 00 | 6,019 00 | 15 |
| 16 | | | | | | (✓) | (✓) | | | | 16 |
| 17 | | | | | | | | | | | 17 |

Check mark indicates that amounts ARE NOT posted individually.

Check marks indicate that general amount column totals ARE NOT posted.

### Journal Entries That Are Not Posted Individually

Several lines in Encore Music's journal contain amounts that are not to be posted individually. These include forwarding totals and amounts recorded in special amount columns.

The totals brought forward from page 1 are shown on line 1 of the journal. None of these separate total amounts on line 1 are posted individually to general ledger accounts. To assure that no postings are overlooked, no blank posting reference spaces should be left in the Post. Ref. column of the journal. Therefore, when the totals were forwarded to page 2 of the journal, a check mark was placed in the Post. Ref. column of line 1 to show that no separate amounts are posted individually.

Separate amounts in the special amount columns, Sales Credit, Cash Debit, and Cash Credit, are not posted individually. For example, on line 13 of the journal, two separate $290.00 amounts are recorded in two special amount columns, Sales Credit and Cash Debit.

A check mark was placed in the Post. Ref. column on line 13 when the entry was journalized. The check mark indicates that no separate amounts are posted individually from this line. Instead, the totals of the special amount columns are posted.

### Totals of General Debit and General Credit Amount Columns

The General Debit and General Credit columns are not special amount columns because the column headings do not contain the name of an account. All of the separate amounts in the General Debit and General Credit amount columns are posted individually.

Therefore, the column totals *are not* posted. A check mark in parentheses is placed below each general amount column total as shown. The check mark indicates that the total of the General Debit column is not posted.

A check mark in the Post. Ref. column indicates that *no amounts on that line* are posted individually. On the totals line, the amounts in the special amount columns *are* posted. Therefore, a check mark is *not* placed in the Post. Ref. column for the totals line.

## POSTING THE TOTAL OF THE SALES CREDIT COLUMN

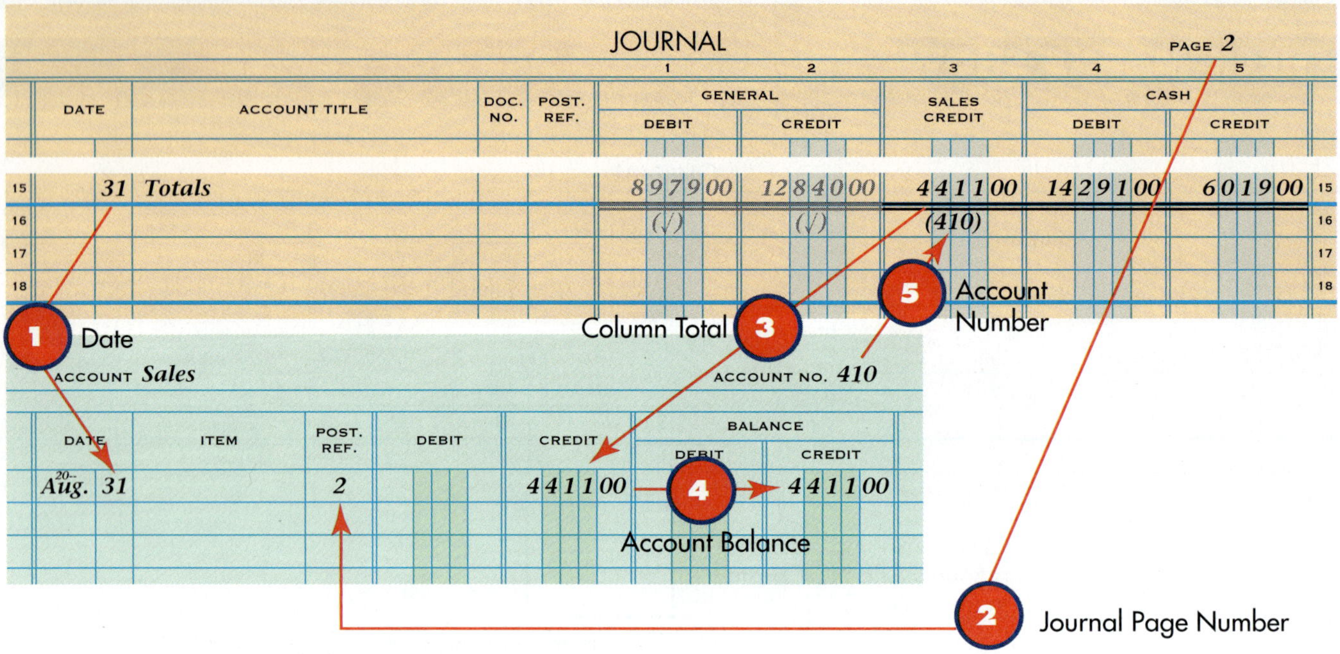


Separate amounts in special amount columns *are not* posted individually. The separate amounts are part of the special amount column totals. Only the *totals* of special amount columns are posted.

Encore Music's journal has three special amount columns for which only totals are posted: Sales Credit, Cash Debit, and Cash Credit.

The Sales Credit column of a journal is a special amount column with the account title Sales in the heading. Each separate amount in a special amount column could be posted individually. However, all of the separate amounts are debits or credits to the same account. Therefore, an advantage of a special amount column is that only the *column total* needs to be posted. For example, 14 separate sales transactions are recorded in the Sales Credit column of Encore Music's August journal. Instead of making 14 separate credit postings to Sales, only the column total is posted. As a result, only one posting is needed, which saves 13 postings. The smaller number of postings means 13 fewer opportunities to make a posting error. Posting special amount column totals saves time and results in greater accuracy.

The total of Encore Music's Sales Credit column is posted as shown.

### STEPS: Posting the total of the Sales Credit column

1. Write the date, *20—, Aug. 31*, in the Date column of the account, Sales.
2. Write the journal page number, *2*, in the Post. Ref. column of the account.
3. Write the column total, *$4,411.00*, in the Credit amount column.
4. Write the new account balance, *$4,411.00*, in the Balance Credit column.
5. Return to the journal and write the account number in parentheses, *(410)*, below the Sales Credit column total.

| Previous Balance | + | Credit Column Amount | = | New Credit Balance |
|---|---|---|---|---|
| $0.00 | + | $4,411.00 | = | $4,411.00 |

## POSTING THE TOTAL OF THE CASH DEBIT COLUMN

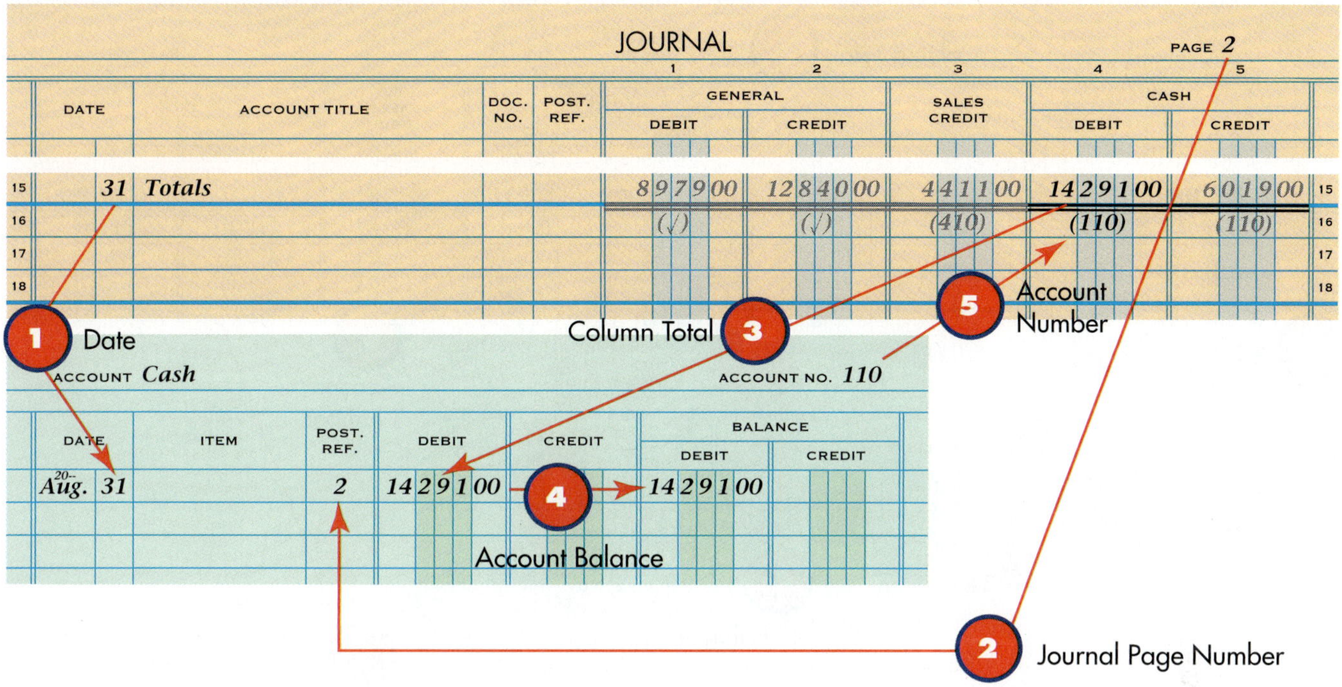


The Cash Debit column of a journal is a special amount column with the account title Cash in the heading. The Cash Debit column is posted using the following steps.

### STEPS: Posting the total of the Cash Debit column

1. Write the date, *20—, Aug. 31*, in the Date column of the account, Cash.
2. Write the journal page number, *2*, in the Post. Ref. column of the account.
3. Write the column total, *$14,291.00*, in the Debit amount column.
4. Write the new account balance, *$14,291.00*, in the Balance Debit column.

| Previous Balance | + | Debit Column Amount | = | New Debit Balance |
|---|---|---|---|---|
| $0.00 | + | $14,291.00 | = | $14,291.00 |

5. Return to the journal and write the account number in parentheses, *(110)*, below the Cash Debit column total.

## REMEMBER

Errors are corrected in a way that does not cause doubts about what the correct information is. If an error is recorded, cancel the error by neatly drawing a line through the incorrect item. Write the correct items immediately above the canceled item.

## POSTING THE TOTAL OF THE CASH CREDIT COLUMN

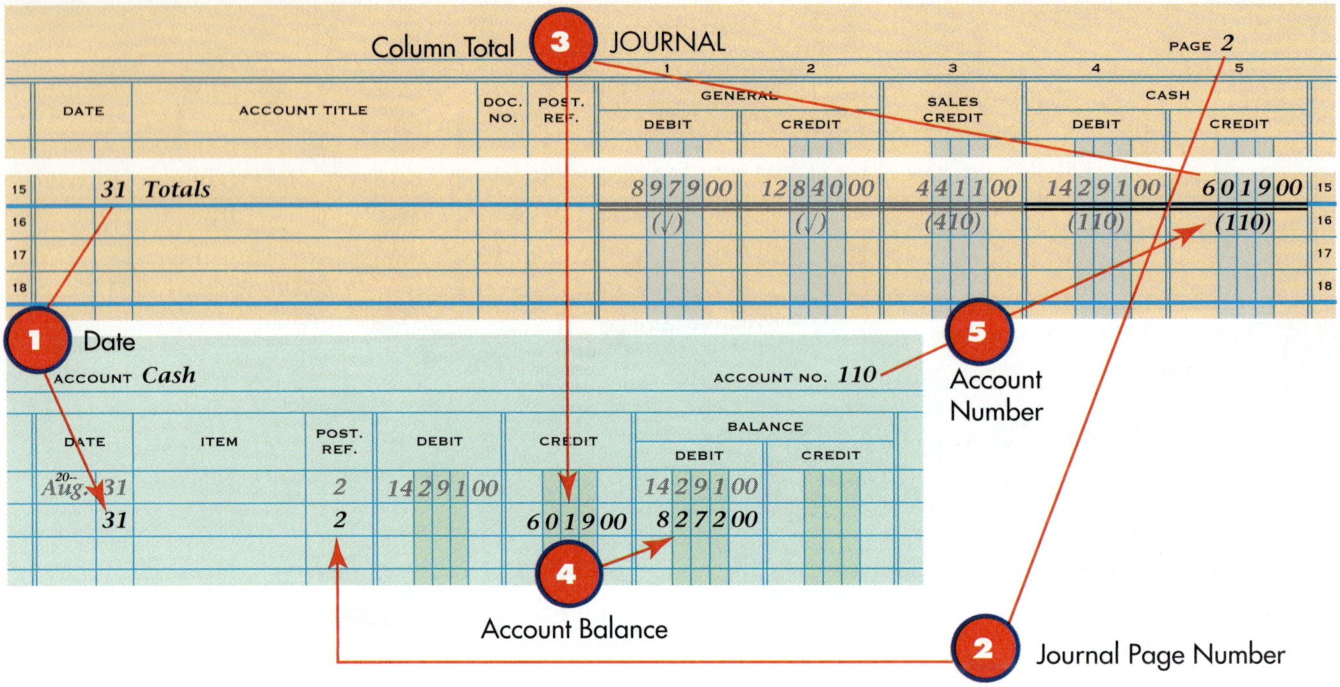


The Cash Credit column of a journal is a special amount column with the account title Cash in the heading. The Cash Credit column is posted using the following steps.

### STEPS: Posting the total of the Cash Credit column

1. Write the date, *31*, in the Date column of the account, Cash.
2. Write the journal page number, *2*, in the Post. Ref. column of the account.
3. Write the column total, *$6,019.00*, in the Credit amount column.
4. Write the new account balance, *$8,272.00*, in the Balance Debit column.

| Previous Debit Balance | – | Credit Column Amount | = | New Debit Balance |
|---|---|---|---|---|
| $14,291.00 | – | $6,019.00 | = | $8,272.00 |

5. Return to the journal and write the account number in parentheses, *(110)*, below the Cash Credit column total.

### REMEMBER

Whenever the debits in an account exceed the credits, the account balance is a debit. Whenever the credits in an account exceed the debits, the account balance is a credit.

## AUDIT YOUR UNDERSTANDING

1. Which column totals of a journal are posted?
2. Under what conditions will an account balance be a debit?
3. Under what conditions will an account balance be a credit?

## WORK TOGETHER

### Posting column totals to a general ledger

Use the journal and general ledger accounts from Work Together on page 106. Your instructor will guide you through the following example.

Leonard Witkowski owns a service business that uses the following accounts:

**Assets**

110 Cash
120 Accounts Receivable—Danielle Braastad
130 Supplies
140 Prepaid Insurance

**Liabilities**

210 Accounts Payable—Joshua's Supplies

**Owner's Equity**

310 Leonard Witkowski, Capital
320 Leonard Witkowski, Drawing

**Revenue**

410 Sales

**Expenses**

510 Rent Expense

4. Post the journal's special amount column totals.

## ON YOUR OWN

### Posting column totals to a general ledger

Use the journal and general ledger accounts from On Your Own on page 106. Work this problem independently.

Melanie Komoko owns a service business that uses the following accounts:

**Assets**

110 Cash
120 Accounts Receivable—Brenden Otto
130 Supplies
140 Prepaid Insurance

**Liabilities**

210 Accounts Payable—Signs Plus

**Owner's Equity**

310 Melanie Komoko, Capital
320 Melanie Komoko, Drawing

**Revenue**

410 Sales

**Expenses**

510 Utilities Expense

5. Post the journal's special amount column totals.

# 5-4 Completed Accounting Forms and Making Correcting Entries

## JOURNAL PAGE WITH POSTING COMPLETED

JOURNAL — PAGE 2

| | DATE | | ACCOUNT TITLE | DOC. NO. | POST. REF. | 1 GENERAL DEBIT | 2 GENERAL CREDIT | 3 SALES CREDIT | 4 CASH DEBIT | 5 CASH CREDIT | |
|---|---|---|---|---|---|---|---|---|---|---|---|
| 1 | 20-- Aug. | 20 | Brought Forward | | √ | 7960 00 | 12840 00 | 2439 00 | 12319 00 | 5000 00 | 1 |
| 2 | | 21 | √ | T21 | √ | | | 270 00 | 270 00 | | 2 |
| 3 | | 24 | √ | T24 | √ | | | 300 00 | 300 00 | | 3 |
| 4 | | 25 | √ | T25 | √ | | | 310 00 | 310 00 | | 4 |
| 5 | | 26 | √ | T26 | √ | | | 245 00 | 245 00 | | 5 |
| 6 | | 27 | Utilities Expense | C10 | 560 | 70 00 | | | | 70 00 | 6 |
| 7 | | 27 | √ | T27 | √ | | | 290 00 | 290 00 | | 7 |
| 8 | | 28 | Supplies | C11 | 150 | 434 00 | | | | 434 00 | 8 |
| 9 | | 28 | √ | T28 | √ | | | 267 00 | 267 00 | | 9 |
| 10 | | 31 | Miscellaneous Expense | C12 | 530 | 7 00 | | | | 12 00 | 10 |
| 11 | | | Advertising Expense | | 510 | 5 00 | | | | | 11 |
| 12 | | 31 | Barbara Treviño, Drawing | C13 | 320 | 500 00 | | | | 500 00 | 12 |
| 13 | | 31 | √ | T31 | √ | | | 290 00 | 290 00 | | 13 |
| 14 | | 31 | Miscellaneous Expense | M3 | 530 | 3 00 | | | | 3 00 | 14 |
| 15 | | 31 | Totals | | | 8979 00 | 12840 00 | 4411 00 | 14291 00 | 6019 00 | 15 |
| 16 | | | | | | (√) | (√) | (410) | (110) | (110) | 16 |
| 17 | | | | | | | | | | | 17 |

Page 2 of Encore Music's August journal is shown after all posting has been completed. With the exception of the Totals line, notice that the Post Ref. column is completely filled in with either an account number or a check mark.

## GENERAL LEDGER WITH POSTING COMPLETED

ACCOUNT *Cash* — ACCOUNT NO. *110*

| DATE | | ITEM | POST. REF. | DEBIT | CREDIT | BALANCE DEBIT | BALANCE CREDIT |
|---|---|---|---|---|---|---|---|
| 20-- Aug. | 31 | | 2 | 14291 00 | | 14291 00 | |
| | 31 | | 2 | | 6019 00 | 8272 00 | |

After all posting from the August journal is completed, Encore Music's general ledger is shown here and on the next several pages.

The use of the accounts Income Summary, Insurance Expense, and Supplies Expense is described in Chapter 7.

ACCOUNT *Petty Cash* ACCOUNT NO. *120*

| DATE | | ITEM | POST. REF. | DEBIT | CREDIT | BALANCE DEBIT | BALANCE CREDIT |
|---|---|---|---|---|---|---|---|
| 20-- Aug. | 17 | | 1 | 200 00 | | 200 00 | |

ACCOUNT *Accounts Receivable—Kids Time* ACCOUNT NO. *130*

| DATE | | ITEM | POST. REF. | DEBIT | CREDIT | BALANCE DEBIT | BALANCE CREDIT |
|---|---|---|---|---|---|---|---|
| 20-- Aug. | 12 | | 1 | 200 00 | | 200 00 | |
| | 12 | | 1 | | 100 00 | 100 00 | |

ACCOUNT *Accounts Receivable—Learn N Play* ACCOUNT NO. *140*

| DATE | | ITEM | POST. REF. | DEBIT | CREDIT | BALANCE DEBIT | BALANCE CREDIT |
|---|---|---|---|---|---|---|---|
| 20-- Aug. | 13 | | 1 | 20 00 | | 20 00 | |

ACCOUNT *Supplies* ACCOUNT NO. *150*

| DATE | | ITEM | POST. REF. | DEBIT | CREDIT | BALANCE DEBIT | BALANCE CREDIT |
|---|---|---|---|---|---|---|---|
| 20-- Aug. | 3 | | 1 | 1 577 00 | | 1 577 00 | |
| | 7 | | 1 | 2 720 00 | | 4 297 00 | |
| | 20 | | 1 | 20 00 | | 4 317 00 | |
| | 28 | | 2 | 434 00 | | 4 751 00 | |

ACCOUNT *Prepaid Insurance* ACCOUNT NO. *160*

| DATE | | ITEM | POST. REF. | DEBIT | CREDIT | BALANCE DEBIT | BALANCE CREDIT |
|---|---|---|---|---|---|---|---|
| 20-- Aug. | 4 | | 1 | 1 200 00 | | 1 200 00 | |

ACCOUNT *Accounts Payable—Ling Music Supplies* ACCOUNT NO. *210*

| DATE | | ITEM | POST. REF. | DEBIT | CREDIT | BALANCE DEBIT | BALANCE CREDIT |
|---|---|---|---|---|---|---|---|
| 20-- Aug. | 7 | | 1 | | 2 720 00 | | 2 720 00 |
| | 11 | | 1 | 1 360 00 | | | 1 360 00 |

ACCOUNT *Accounts Payable—Sullivan Office Supplies* ACCOUNT NO. *220*

| DATE | | ITEM | POST. REF. | DEBIT | CREDIT | BALANCE DEBIT | BALANCE CREDIT |
|---|---|---|---|---|---|---|---|
| 20-- Aug. | 20 | | 1 | | 20 00 | | 20 00 |

A General Ledger after Posting Has Been Completed *(continued)*

**ACCOUNT** *Barbara Treviño, Capital* **ACCOUNT NO.** *310*

| DATE | | ITEM | POST. REF. | DEBIT | CREDIT | BALANCE DEBIT | BALANCE CREDIT |
|---|---|---|---|---|---|---|---|
| 20-- Aug. | 1 | | 1 | | 10000 00 | | 10000 00 |

**ACCOUNT** *Barbara Treviño, Drawing* **ACCOUNT NO.** *320*

| DATE | | ITEM | POST. REF. | DEBIT | CREDIT | BALANCE DEBIT | BALANCE CREDIT |
|---|---|---|---|---|---|---|---|
| 20-- Aug. | 12 | | 1 | 100 00 | | 100 00 | |
| | 31 | | 2 | 500 00 | | 600 00 | |

**ACCOUNT** *Income Summary* **ACCOUNT NO.** *330*

| DATE | | ITEM | POST. REF. | DEBIT | CREDIT | BALANCE DEBIT | BALANCE CREDIT |
|---|---|---|---|---|---|---|---|
| | | | | | | | |

**ACCOUNT** *Sales* **ACCOUNT NO.** *410*

| DATE | | ITEM | POST. REF. | DEBIT | CREDIT | BALANCE DEBIT | BALANCE CREDIT |
|---|---|---|---|---|---|---|---|
| 20-- Aug. | 31 | | 2 | | 4411 00 | | 4411 00 |

**ACCOUNT** *Advertising Expense* **ACCOUNT NO.** *510*

| DATE | | ITEM | POST. REF. | DEBIT | CREDIT | BALANCE DEBIT | BALANCE CREDIT |
|---|---|---|---|---|---|---|---|
| 20-- Aug. | 14 | | 1 | 68 00 | | 68 00 | |
| | 18 | | 1 | 200 00 | | 268 00 | |
| | 31 | | 2 | 5 00 | | 273 00 | |

A General Ledger after Posting Has Been Completed *(continued)*

ACCOUNT *Insurance Expense* ACCOUNT NO. *520*

| DATE | | ITEM | POST. REF. | DEBIT | CREDIT | BALANCE DEBIT | BALANCE CREDIT |
|---|---|---|---|---|---|---|---|
| | | | | | | | |

ACCOUNT *Miscellaneous Expense* ACCOUNT NO. *530*

| DATE | | ITEM | POST. REF. | DEBIT | CREDIT | BALANCE DEBIT | BALANCE CREDIT |
|---|---|---|---|---|---|---|---|
| 20-- Aug. | 31 | | 2 | 7 00 | | 7 00 | |
| | 31 | | 2 | 3 00 | | 10 00 | |

ACCOUNT *Rent Expense* ACCOUNT NO. *540*

| DATE | | ITEM | POST. REF. | DEBIT | CREDIT | BALANCE DEBIT | BALANCE CREDIT |
|---|---|---|---|---|---|---|---|
| 20-- Aug. | 12 | | 1 | 250 00 | | 250 00 | |

ACCOUNT *Supplies Expense* ACCOUNT NO. *550*

| DATE | | ITEM | POST. REF. | DEBIT | CREDIT | BALANCE DEBIT | BALANCE CREDIT |
|---|---|---|---|---|---|---|---|
| | | | | | | | |

ACCOUNT *Utilities Expense* ACCOUNT NO. *560*

| DATE | | ITEM | POST. REF. | DEBIT | CREDIT | BALANCE DEBIT | BALANCE CREDIT |
|---|---|---|---|---|---|---|---|
| 20-- Aug. | 12 | | 1 | 45 00 | | 45 00 | |
| | 27 | | 2 | 70 00 | | 115 00 | |

A General Ledger after Posting Has Been Completed *(concluded)*

## MEMORANDUM FOR A CORRECTING ENTRY

**MEMORANDUM**

Encore Music
530 Anoka Avenue
Tampa, FL 33601

No. **45**

*A cash payment of $120.00 for advertising, October 30, 20--, was debited in error to Miscellaneous Expense.*

Signed: *Barbara Treviño* Date: *November 13, 20--*

Simple errors may be corrected by ruling through the item, as described in Chapter 4. However, a transaction may have been improperly journalized and posted to the ledger. In such a case, the incorrect journal entry should be corrected with an additional journal entry, called a **correcting entry.**

If an accounting error is discovered, a memorandum is prepared as the source document describing the the correction to be made.

## JOURNAL ENTRY TO RECORD A CORRECTING ENTRY

1 Date
2 Debit
3 Credit
4 Source Document

JOURNAL — PAGE 7

| | DATE | | ACCOUNT TITLE | DOC. NO. | POST. REF. | 1 GENERAL DEBIT | 2 GENERAL CREDIT | 3 SALES CREDIT | 4 CASH DEBIT | 5 CASH CREDIT | |
|---|---|---|---|---|---|---|---|---|---|---|---|
| 22 | | 13 | Advertising Expense | M45 | | 120 00 | | | | | 22 |
| 23 | | | Miscellaneous Expense | | | | 120 00 | | | | 23 |
| 24 | | | | | | | | | | | 24 |

***November 13. Discovered that a payment of cash for advertising in October was journalized and posted in error as a debit to Miscellaneous Expense instead of Advertising Expense, $120.00. Memorandum No. 45.***

| Advertising Expense | |
|---|---|
| 120.00 | |

| Miscellaneous Expense | |
|---|---|
| | 120.00 |

To correct the error, an entry is made to add $120.00 to the advertising expense account. The entry must also deduct $120.00 from the miscellaneous expense account.

Because the advertising expense account has a normal debit balance, Advertising Expense is debited for $120.00 to show the increase in this expense account. The miscellaneous expense account also has a normal debit balance. Therefore, Miscellaneous Expense is credited for $120.00 to show the decrease in this expense account.

## TERM REVIEW

correcting entry

## AUDIT YOUR UNDERSTANDING

1. What is a correcting entry?
2. When is a correcting entry necessary?
3. When an amount is journalized and posted as a debit to an incorrect expense account, why is the amount of the correcting entry debited to the correct expense account?
4. When an amount is journalized and posted as a debit to an incorrect expense account, why is the amount of the correcting entry credited to the incorrect expense account?

## WORK TOGETHER

### Journalizing correcting entries

A journal is given in the *Working Papers*. Your instructor will guide you through the following example.

***Transactions:*** Nov. 1. Discovered that a transaction for office supplies bought last month was journalized and posted in error as a debit to Prepaid Insurance instead of Supplies, $60.00. M15.

1. Discovered that a transaction for rent expense for last month was journalized and posted in error as a debit to Repair Expense instead of Rent Expense, $550.00. M16.

5. Journalize each correcting entry discovered during November of the current year. Use page 21 of the journal.

## ON YOUR OWN

### Journalizing correcting entries

A journal is given in the *Working Papers.* Work this problem independently.

***Transactions:*** June 1. Discovered that a transaction for office supplies bought last month was journalized and posted in error as a debit to Supplies—Store instead of Supplies—Office, $45.00. M23.

1. Discovered that a transaction for utilities expense for last month was journalized and posted in error as a debit to Miscellaneous Expense instead of Utilities Expense, $550.00. M24.

6. Journalize each correcting entry discovered during June of the current year. Use page 11 of the journal.

# CHAPTER 5 SUMMARY

*Enrichment Activity*

**Time Management**

*Often people work faster and more efficiently when they have a deadline to meet. Problem 5-5 has 17 transactions to journalize. Set a time deadline for completing the entire problem. Try to beat your self-set deadline. Did setting a deadline help you work the problem faster?*

After completing this chapter, you can

1. Define important accounting terms related to posting from a journal to a general ledger.
2. Identify accounting concepts and practices related to posting from a journal to a general ledger.
3. Prepare a chart of accounts for a service business organized as a proprietorship.
4. Post separate amounts from a journal to a general ledger.
5. Post column totals from a journal to a general ledger.
6. Analyze and journalize correcting entries.

## EXPLORE ACCOUNTING

Each company designs its chart of accounts to meet the needs of that company. Encore Music, the company described in this section of the textbook, has a relatively simple chart of accounts, with a small number of accounts. Therefore, Encore Music can use a three-digit account number for each account. A company with more accounts may need to use a four- or five-digit account number for each account. The numbering system used by the company should ensure that each account can be assigned a unique number.

When setting up a chart of accounts, a company does not have to use a straight series of numbers. If a company has several departments, it may choose to use account numbers such as 12-150. The first two digits (12) can be used to designate a specific department. The last three digits (150) identify a unique account within that department. If this company has many departments or many accounts within each department, it may have to increase the number of digits in the account, such as 123-4567.

A large corporation made up of smaller companies may have one chart of accounts for the entire corporation. If the managers of the corporation also want to be able to separate out the accounts for each company, they may choose to set up the account numbers in an xx-yyy-zzzz format. The first two digits (xx) would be a unique number for each company, the second set of numbers (yyy) refer to a department number, and the third set of numbers (zzzz) is a unique account.

Another example would be a company that manufactures goods for its customers. Such a company may want to include the job order number in each account number, so that it can easily trace the cost of each job.

As you can see, there is an infinite number of possible systems that can be followed when assigning account numbers. A company should consider future growth when first setting up a system so that it can avoid having to renumber accounts at a later date.

**Group Activity:**

Develop a chart of accounts for an imaginary business. Write a detailed description of the company and a rationale for the account numbering system you have developed.

## 5-1 APPLICATION PROBLEM
### Preparing a chart of accounts and opening an account

Lillian Deters owns a service business called Deters Duplicating, which uses the following accounts:

| | | | |
|---|---|---|---|
| Accounts Receivable—Teegan Walters | Lillian Deters, Capital | Postage Expense | Supplies |
| Accounts Receivable—Austin Kirnyczuk | Lillian Deters, Drawing | Charitable Expense | Sales |
| Accounts Payable—Dakota Company | Prepaid Insurance | Rent Expense | Cash |
| Accounts Payable—Falls Supply | Advertising Expense | | |

***Instructions:***

1. Prepare a chart of accounts similar to the one described in this chapter. Arrange expense accounts in alphabetical order. Use 3-digit account numbers and number the accounts within a division by 10s.
2. Two new accounts, Delivery Expense and Telephone Expense, are to be added to the chart of accounts prepared in Instruction 1. Assign account numbers to the two new accounts.
3. Using the forms in the *Working Papers*, open the Prepaid Insurance and the Postage Expense accounts.

## 5-2 APPLICATION PROBLEM
### Posting separate amounts to a general ledger

A completed journal and general ledger accounts are given in the *Working Papers*.
Michael Byrum owns a service business which uses the accounts given in the *Working Papers*.

***Instructions:***

Post the separate amounts on each line of the journal that need to be posted individually. Save your work to complete Application Problem 5-3.

## 5-3 APPLICATION PROBLEM
### Posting column totals to a general ledger

Use the journal and general ledger from Application Problem 5-2.

***Instructions:***

Post the journal's special amount column totals.

## 5-4 APPLICATION PROBLEM
### Journalizing correcting entries

The following errors were discovered after the incorrect entries were already journalized and posted.

***Transactions:***

Feb. 1. Discovered that a transaction for advertising expense was journalized and posted in error as a debit to Miscellaneous Expense instead of Advertising Expense, $135.00. M87.

5. Discovered that a cash withdrawal by Gregg Moen, owner, was journalized and posted in error as a credit to Sales instead of Cash, $550.00. M88.

***Instructions:***

Journalize each correcting entry discovered during February of the current year. Use page 3 of the journal given in the *Working Papers*.

## 5-5 MASTERY PROBLEM

### Journalizing transactions and posting to a general ledger

Allan Derner owns a service business called Derner Cleaning. Derner Cleaning's general ledger accounts are given in the *Working Papers*.

***Transactions:***

Nov. 1. Received cash from owner as an investment, $7,000.00. R1.
3. Paid cash for rent, $300.00. C1.
5. Sold services on account to Alphonse Gutenberg, $180.00. S1.
6. Received cash from sales, $750.00. T6.
9. Paid cash for miscellaneous expense, $5.00. C2.
11. Paid cash for supplies, $500.00. C3.
13. Bought supplies on account from Major Supplies, $600.00. M1.
13. Received cash from sales, $700.00. T13.
16. Paid cash for electric bill, $40.00. C4.
18. Paid cash on account to Major Supplies, $300.00. C5.
20. Paid cash for advertising, $30.00. C6.
20. Received cash on account from Alphonse Gutenberg, $90.00. R2.
25. Paid cash for supplies, $150.00. C7.
27. Paid cash for supplies, $100.00. C8.
27. Received cash from sales, $1,800.00. T27.
30. Paid cash to owner for personal use, $300.00. C9.
30. Received cash from sales, $410.00. T30.

***Instructions:***

1. Open an account for Utilities Expense. Use the 3-digit numbering system described in the chapter.
2. Journalize the transactions completed during November of the current year. Use page 1 of a journal. Source documents are abbreviated as follows: check, C; memorandum, M; receipt, R; sales invoice, S; calculator tape, T.
3. Prove the journal.
4. Prove cash. The beginning cash balance on November 1 is zero. The balance on the next unused check stub is $9,025.00.
5. Rule the journal.
6. Post from the journal to the general ledger.

## 5-6 CHALLENGE PROBLEM

### Posting using a variation of the five-column journal

Nathan Jackson owns a service business called HouseCare. HouseCare uses a five-column journal that is different from the journal used in this chapter. HouseCare's March journal and general ledger accounts (before posting) are given in the *Working Papers*.

***Instructions:***

1. Post the separate amounts on each line of the journal that need to be posted individually.
2. Post the journal's special amount column totals.

# AUTOMATED ACCOUNTING

ledger report with the posting completed.

### AUTOMATING APPLICATION PROBLEM 5-1: Preparing a chart of accounts and opening an account

**Instructions:**

1. Load *Automated Accounting 7.0* or higher software.
2. Select database F05-1 from the appropriate directory/folder.
3. Select File from the menu bar and choose the Save As menu command. Key the path to the drive and directory that contains your data files. Save the database with a file name of XXX051 (where XXX are your initials).
4. Access Problem Instructions through the Help menu. Read the Problem Instructions screen.
5. Refer to page 119 for data used in this problem.
6. Exit the *Automated Accounting* software.

### AUTOMATING MASTERY PROBLEM 5-5: Journalizing transactions and posting to a general ledger

**Instructions:**

1. Load *Automated Accounting 7.0* or higher software.
2. Select database F05-2 from the appropriate directory/folder.
3. Select File from the menu bar and choose the Save As menu command. Key the path to the drive and directory that contains your data files. Save the database with a file name of XXX052 (where XXX are your initials).
4. Access Problem Instructions through the Help menu. Read the Problem Instructions screen.
5. Key the transactions listed on page 120.
6. Exit the *Automated Accounting* software.

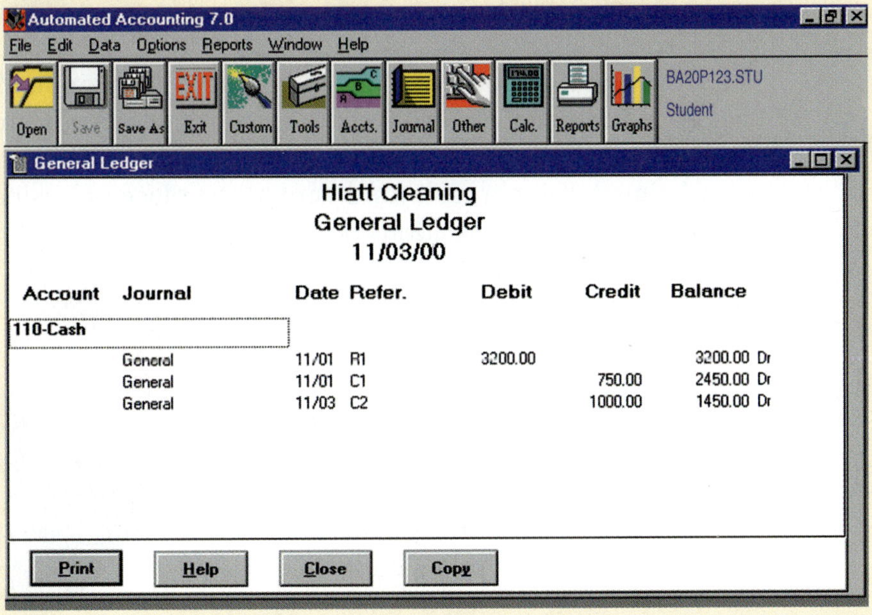

# 6 Cash Control Systems

**AFTER STUDYING CHAPTER 6, YOU WILL BE ABLE TO:**

1. Define accounting terms related to using a checking account and a petty cash fund.
2. Identify accounting concepts and practices related to using a checking account.
3. Prepare business papers related to using a checking account.
4. Reconcile a bank statement.
5. Journalize dishonored checks and electronic banking transactions.
6. Establish and replenish a petty cash fund.

**TERMS PREVIEW**

- checking account
- endorsement
- blank endorsement
- special endorsement
- restrictive endorsement
- postdated check
- bank statement
- dishonored check
- electronic funds transfer
- debit card
- petty cash
- petty cash slip

## HOW BUSINESSES USE CASH

In accounting, money is usually referred to as cash. Most businesses make major cash payments by check. However, small cash payments for items such as postage and some supplies may be made from a cash fund kept at the place of business.

Because cash transactions occur more frequently than other types of transactions, more chances occur to make recording errors affecting cash. Cash can be transferred from one person to another without any question about ownership. Also, cash may be lost as it is moved from one place to another.

As a safety measure, Encore Music keeps most of its cash in a bank. Because all cash receipts are placed in a bank, Encore Music has written evidence to support its accounting records. Encore Music can compare its record of checks written with the bank's record of checks paid. Greater control of Encore Music's cash and greater accuracy of its cash records result from these procedures.

# ACCOUNTING IN YOUR CAREER

## MANAGING CASH AND THE CHECKING ACCOUNT

Raymond Gutierrez owns Gutierrez Employment Agency. Raymond started this business a year ago and operated it alone until two months ago. He hired Shanelle Gibson as an administrative assistant to handle the accounting for the business and to assist him in other responsibilities when needed. Shanelle has reorganized the record keeping for the agency, and by filling in on other tasks has freed Raymond to spend more time building contacts with employers and placing clients. The business is growing rapidly.

In their regular weekly meeting to review their goals, Shanelle says, "Raymond, I enjoy working here, and I think I have really helped you be more successful. I'd like to make two proposals that will give you more time to devote to your activities." Shanelle proceeds to outline the proposals.

She recommends establishing a petty cash fund for making small cash payments, such as urgent office supplies and postage and delivery fees. She has already arranged to have overnight delivery services billed to the firm, so only small delivery fees will be paid from petty cash. She thinks $100.00 would be a sufficient balance to avoid replenishing petty cash too frequently.

Her second recommendation is to take over writing and signing all checks, receiving and depositing all cash receipts, and reconciling the bank statement—tasks that Raymond currently performs.

Raymond tells Shanelle that he will consider her proposals and that he appreciates her good work and concern for making the business more efficient.

***Critical Thinking:***

1. Is the proposal to establish a petty cash fund a good idea?
2. What is your opinion of Shanelle's proposal to take over managing cash and the checking account?

# 6-1 Checking Accounts

## DEPOSITING CASH

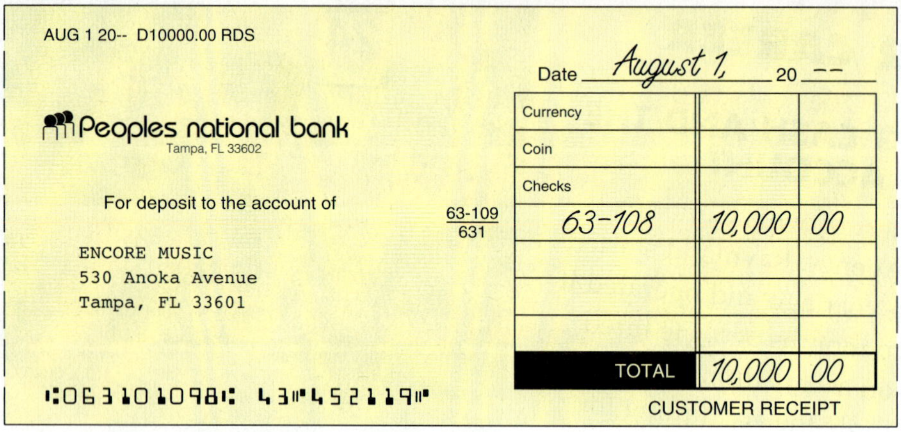
AUG 1 20-- D10000.00 RDS

Peoples national bank
Tampa, FL 33602

For deposit to the account of

ENCORE MUSIC
530 Anoka Avenue
Tampa, FL 33601

63-109
631

Date *August 1,* 20 --

| | | |
|---|---|---|
| Currency | | |
| Coin | | |
| Checks | | |
| *63-108* | *10,000* | *00* |
| | | |
| | | |
| | | |
| TOTAL | *10,000* | *00* |

CUSTOMER RECEIPT

A business form ordering a bank to pay cash from a bank account is known as a check. A bank account from which payments can be ordered by a depositor is called a **checking account.**

When a checking account is opened, the bank customer must provide a signature on a signature card for the bank records. If several persons are authorized to sign checks, each person's signature must be on the signature card.

A bank customer prepares a deposit slip each time cash or checks are placed in a bank account. Deposit slips may differ slightly from one bank to another. Each bank designs its own deposit slips to fit the bank's recording machines. However, all deposit slips contain the same basic information.

Checks are listed on a deposit slip according to the bank number on each check. For example, the number *63-108* identifies the bank on which the $10,000.00 check is written.

When a deposit is made, a bank gives the depositor a receipt. Many banks use a copy of the deposit slip with a printed or stamped verification as the receipt. The printed verification, *Aug 1 20— D10000.00 RDS,* is printed along the top left edge of the deposit slip. This printed verification means that a total of $10,000.00 was deposited on August 1. The initials *RDS* next to the amount are those of the bank employee who accepted the deposit.

## DEPOSIT RECORDED ON A CHECK STUB

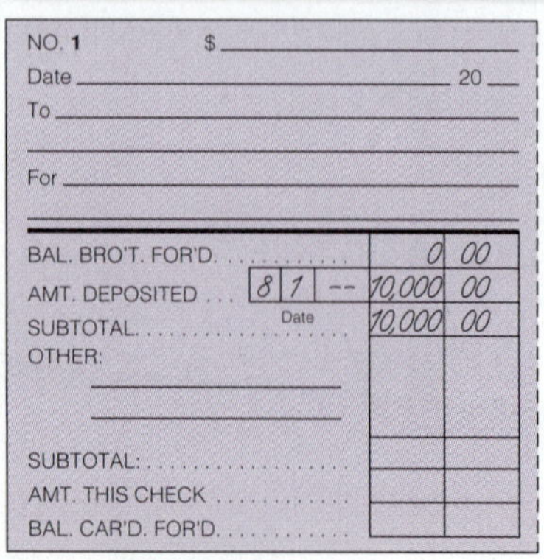
NO. 1 $
Date 20
To
For

| | | |
|---|---|---|
| BAL. BRO'T. FOR'D. | *0* | *00* |
| AMT. DEPOSITED *8/1/--* (Date) | *10,000* | *00* |
| SUBTOTAL | *10,000* | *00* |
| OTHER: | | |
| SUBTOTAL: | | |
| AMT. THIS CHECK | | |
| BAL. CAR'D. FOR'D. | | |

After the deposit is recorded on the check stub, a checkbook subtotal is calculated. The balance brought forward on Check Stub No. 1 is zero. The previous balance, $0.00, *plus* the deposit, $10,000.00, *equals* the subtotal, $10,000.00.

Cash receipts are journalized at the time cash is received. Later, the cash receipts are deposited in the checking account. Therefore, no journal entry is needed for deposits because the cash receipts have already been journalized.

## BLANK ENDORSEMENT, SPECIAL ENDORSEMENT, AND RESTRICTIVE ENDORSEMENT

**[Blank Endorsement]**

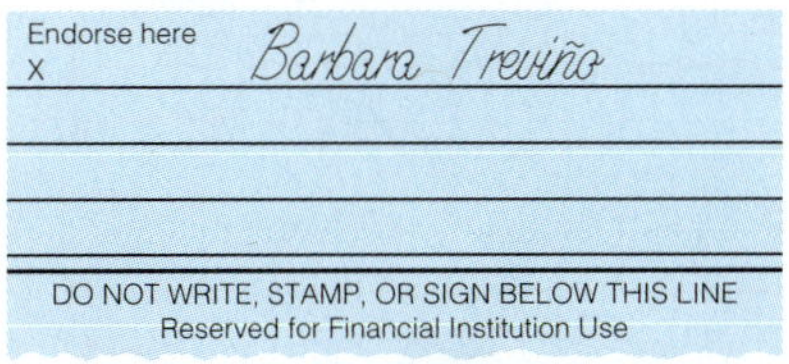


**[Special Endorsement]**

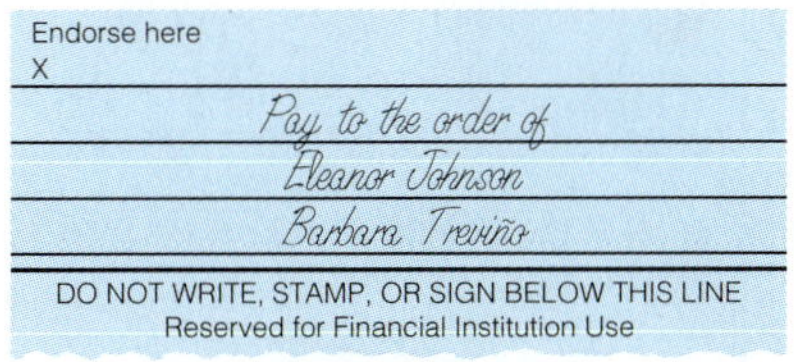


**[Restrictive Endorsement]**

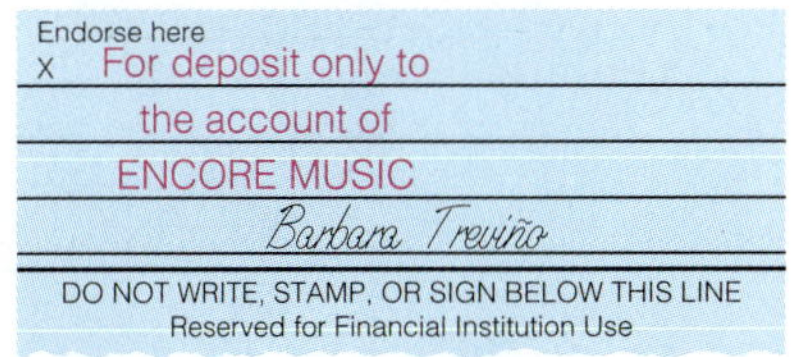


Ownership of a check can be transferred. The name of the first owner is stated on a check following the words *Pay to the order of.* Therefore, the person to whom payment is to be made must indicate that ownership of the check is being transferred. One person transfers ownership to another person by signing on the back of a check. A signature or stamp on the back of a check transferring ownership is called an **endorsement.** Federal regulations require that an endorsement be confined to a limited amount of space that is indicated on the back of a check.

An endorsement should be signed exactly as the person's name appears on the front of the check. For example, a check made payable to B. A. Treviño is endorsed on the back as *B. A. Treviño.* Immediately below that endorsement, Ms. Treviño writes her official signature, *Barbara Treviño.*

Ownership of a check might be transferred several times, resulting in several endorsements. Each endorser guarantees payment of the check. If a bank does not receive payment from the person who signed the check, each endorser is individually liable for payment.

Three types of endorsements are commonly used, each having a specific use in transferring ownership.

### Blank Endorsement

An endorsement consisting only of the endorser's signature is called a **blank endorsement.** A blank endorsement indicates that the subsequent owner is whoever has the check.

If a check with a blank endorsement is lost or stolen, the check can be cashed by anyone who has possession of it. Ownership may be transferred without further endorsement. A blank endorsement should be used *only* when a person is at the bank ready to cash or deposit a check.

### Special Endorsement

An endorsement indicating a new owner of a check is called a **special endorsement.** Special endorsements are sometimes known as endorsements in full.

Special endorsements include the words *Pay to the order of* and the name of the new check owner. Only the person or business named in a special endorsement can cash, deposit, or further transfer ownership of the check.

### Restrictive Endorsement

An endorsement restricting further transfer of a check's ownership is called a **restrictive endorsement.** A restrictive endorsement limits use of the check to whatever purpose is stated in the endorsement.

Many businesses have a stamp prepared with a restrictive endorsement. When a check is received, it is immediately stamped with the restrictive endorsement. This prevents unauthorized persons from cashing the check if it is lost or stolen.

**FYI**

*The Federal Deposit Insurance Corporation (FDIC) protects depositors from banks that fail. Bank deposits are generally covered up to $100,000 per depositor.*

## COMPLETED CHECK STUB AND CHECK

Encore Music uses printed checks with check stubs attached. Consecutive numbers are preprinted on Encore Music's checks. Consecutive numbers on checks provide an easy way of identifying each check. Also, the numbers help keep track of all checks to assure that none are lost or misplaced.

A check stub is a business's record of each check written for a cash payment transaction. *(CONCEPT: Objective Evidence)* To avoid forgetting to prepare a check stub, the check stub is prepared before the check is written.

After the check stub is completed, the check is written.

STEPS

### Preparing check stubs

1. Write the amount of the check, *$1,577.00*, in the space after the dollar sign at the top of the stub.
2. Write the date of the check, *August 3, 20—*, on the Date line at the top of the stub.
3. Write to whom the check is to be paid, *Quick Clean Supplies Co.*, on the To line at the top of the stub.
4. Record the purpose of the check, *Supplies*, on the For line.
5. Write the amount of the check, *$1,577.00*, in the amount column at the bottom of the stub on the line with the words *Amt. This Check*.
6. Calculate the new checking account balance, *$8,423.00*, and record the new balance in the amount column on the last line of the stub. The new balance is calculated as shown below.

| Subtotal | – | Amount of This Check | = | New Balance |
|---|---|---|---|---|
| $10,000.00 | – | $1,577.00 | = | $8,423.00 |

### Preparing checks

7. Write the date, *August 3, 20—*, in the space provided. The date should be the month, day, and year on which the check is issued. A check with a future date on it is called a **postdated check.** Most banks will not accept postdated checks because money cannot be withdrawn from a depositor's account until the date on the check.
8. Write to whom the check is to be paid, *Quick Clean Supplies Co.*, following the words *Pay to the order of.* If the person to whom a check is to be paid is a business, use the business's name rather than the owner's name. (*CONCEPT: Business Entity*) If the person to whom the check is to be paid is an individual, use that person's name.
9. Write the amount in figures, *$1,577.00*, following the dollar sign. Write the figures close to the printed dollar sign. This practice prevents anyone from writing another digit in front of the amount to change the amount of the check.

10. Write the amount in words, *One thousand five hundred seventy-seven and no/100*, on the line with the word *Dollars*. This written amount verifies the amount written in figures after the dollar sign. Begin the words at the extreme left. Draw a line through the unused space up to the word *Dollars*. This line prevents anyone from writing in additional words to change the amount. If the amounts in words and in figures are not the same, a bank may pay only the amount in words. Often, when the amounts do not agree, a bank will refuse to pay the check.
11. Write the purpose of the check, *Supplies*, on the line labeled For. (On some checks this space is labeled Memo.) Some checks do not have a line for writing the purpose of the check.
12. Sign the check. A check should not be signed until each item on the check and its stub has been verified for accuracy.

## RECORDING A VOIDED CHECK

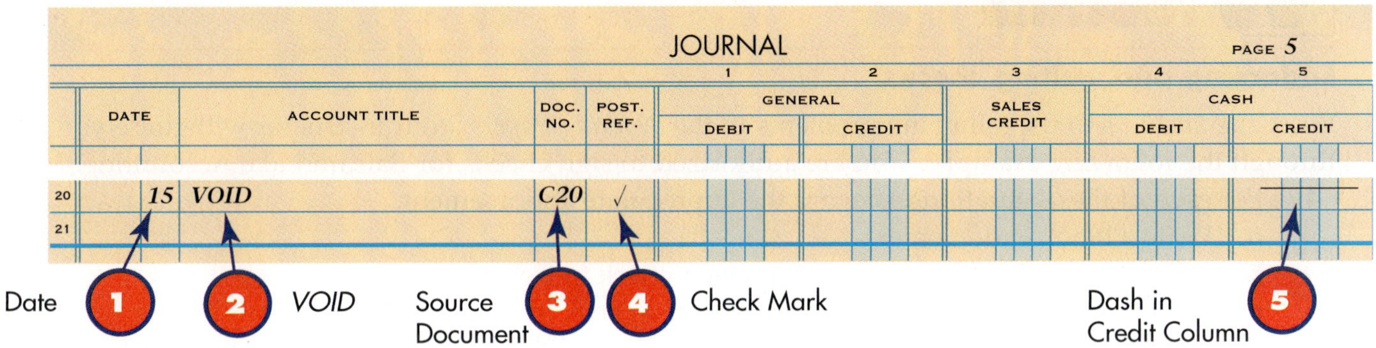


Banks usually refuse to accept altered checks. If any kind of error is made in preparing a check, a new check should be prepared. Because checks are prenumbered, all checks not used should be retained for the records. This practice helps account for all checks and assures that no checks have been lost or stolen.

A check that contains errors must be marked so that others will know that it is not to be used. The word *VOID* is written in large letters across both the check and its stub.

When Encore Music records a check in its journal, the check number is placed in the journal's Doc. No. column. If a check number is missing from the Doc. No. column, there is a question whether all checks have been journalized. To assure that all check numbers are listed in the journal, Encore Music records voided checks in the journal.

STEPS

### Recording a voided check in the journal

1. Record the date, *15*, in the Date column.
2. Write the word *VOID* in the Account Title column.
3. Write the check number, *C20*, in the Doc. No. column.
4. Place a check mark in the Post. Ref. column.
5. Place a dash in the Cash Credit column.

### REMEMBER

Always complete the check stub before writing the check. Otherwise you may forget to record the amount of the check on the check stub.

## TERMS REVIEW

- checking account
- endorsement
- blank endorsement
- special endorsement
- restrictive endorsement
- postdated check

## AUDIT YOUR UNDERSTANDING

1. List the three types of endorsements.
2. List the steps for preparing a check stub.
3. List the steps for preparing a check.

## WORK TOGETHER

### Endorsing and writing checks

Write the answers to the following problems in the *Working Papers.* Your instructor will guide you through the following examples. You are authorized to sign checks for Balsam Lake Accounting.

4. For each of these situations, prepare the appropriate endorsement.
   a. Write a blank endorsement.
   b. Write a special endorsement to transfer a check to Kelsey Sather.
   c. Write a restrictive endorsement to deposit a check in the account of Balsam Lake Accounting.
5. Record the balance brought forward on Check Stub No. 78, $1,805.75.
6. Record a deposit of $489.00 made on October 30 of the current year on Check Stub No. 78.
7. Prepare check stubs and write the following checks. Use October 30 of the current year as the date.
   a. Check No. 78 to Corner Garage for repairs, $162.00.
   b. Check No. 79 to St. Croix Supply for supplies, $92.00.

## ON YOUR OWN

### Endorsing and writing checks

Write the answers to the following problems in the *Working Papers.* Work these problems independently. You are authorized to sign checks for Dresser Hair Care.

8. For each of these situations, prepare the appropriate endorsement.
   a. Write a special endorsement to transfer a check to Kent Benson.
   b. Write a restrictive endorsement to deposit a check in the account of Dresser Hair Care.
9. Record the balance brought forward on Check Stub No. 345, $3,054.55.
10. Record a deposit of $587.00 made on May 31 of the current year on Check Stub No. 345.
11. Prepare check stubs and write the following checks. Use May 31 of the current year as the date.
    a. Check No. 345 to Uniforms Plus for uniform rental, $275.00.
    b. Check No. 346 to HairWorld for supplies, $593.00.

# 6-2 Bank Reconciliation

## BANK STATEMENT

**Peoples national bank**
Tampa, FL 33602

| STATEMENT OF ACCOUNT FOR | ACCOUNT NUMBER |
|---|---|
| ENCORE MUSIC<br>530 Anoka Avenue<br>Tampa, FL 33601 | 43-452-119 |
| | STATEMENT DATE: August 30, 20-- |

| BALANCE FROM PREVIOUS STATEMENT | NO. OF CHECKS | AMOUNT OF CHECKS | NO. OF DEPOSITS | AMOUNT OF DEPOSITS | SERVICE CHARGES | STATEMENT BALANCE |
|---|---|---|---|---|---|---|
| 0.00 | 11 | 5,504.00 | 14 | 14,001.00 | 3.00 | 8,494.00 |

| DATE | CHECK | AMOUNT | CHECK | AMOUNT | DEPOSIT | BALANCE |
|---|---|---|---|---|---|---|
| 08/01/-- | | | | | | 0.00 |
| 08/01/-- | | | | | 10,000.00 | 10,000.00 |
| 08/04/-- | 1 | 1,577.00 | | | | 8,423.00 |
| 08/07/-- | 2 | 1,200.00 | | | | 7,223.00 |
| 08/12/-- | | | | | 425.00 | 7,648.00 |
| 08/13/-- | 4 | 250.00 | 6 | 100.00 | | 7,298.00 |
| 08/14/-- | 3 | 1,360.00 | | | | 5,938.00 |
| 08/15/-- | | | | | 120.00 | 6,058.00 |
| 08/16/-- | | | | | 416.00 | 6,474.00 |
| 08/17/-- | 5 | 45.00 | | | 409.00 | 6,838.00 |
| 08/18/-- | 7 | 68.00 | | | 295.00 | 7,065.00 |
| 08/19/-- | 8 | 200.00 | | | 354.00 | 7,219.00 |
| 08/20/-- | 9 | 200.00 | | | 300.00 | 7,319.00 |
| 08/21/-- | | | | | 270.00 | 7,589.00 |
| 08/24/-- | | | | | 300.00 | 7,889.00 |
| 08/25/-- | | | | | 310.00 | 8,199.00 |
| 08/26/-- | | | | | 245.00 | 8,444.00 |
| 08/27/-- | | | | | 290.00 | 8,734.00 |
| 08/28/-- | | | | | 267.00 | 9,001.00 |
| 08/29/-- | 10 | 70.00 | | | | 8,931.00 |
| 08/30/-- | 11 | 434.00 | | | | 8,497.00 |
| | SC | 3.00 | | | | 8,494.00 |

**PLEASE EXAMINE AT ONCE** - IF NO ERRORS ARE REPORTED WITHIN 10 DAYS THE ACCOUNT WILL BE CONSIDERED CORRECT. REFER ANY DISCREPANCY TO OUR ACCOUNTING DEPARTMENT IMMEDIATELY.

A report of deposits, withdrawals, and bank balances sent to a depositor by a bank is called a **bank statement.**

When a bank receives checks, the amount of each check is deducted from the depositor's account. The bank stamps the checks to indicate that the checks are canceled and are not to be transferred further. Canceled checks are returned to a depositor with a bank statement. Outstanding checks are those checks issued by a depositor but not yet reported on a bank statement. Outstanding deposits are those deposits made at a bank but not yet shown on a bank statement. Account service charges are also listed on a bank statement.

Although banks seldom make mistakes, occasionally a check or deposit might be recorded in a wrong account. When a bank statement is received, a depositor should verify its accuracy. If errors are discovered, the bank should be notified at once. However, a bank's records and a depositor's records may differ while the bank's records are still correct. The difference may exist for several reasons.

1. A service charge may not have been recorded in the depositor's business records.
2. Outstanding deposits may be recorded in the depositor's records but not on a bank statement.
3. Outstanding checks may be recorded in the depositor's records but not on a bank statement.
4. A depositor may have made math or recording errors.

## BANK STATEMENT RECONCILIATION

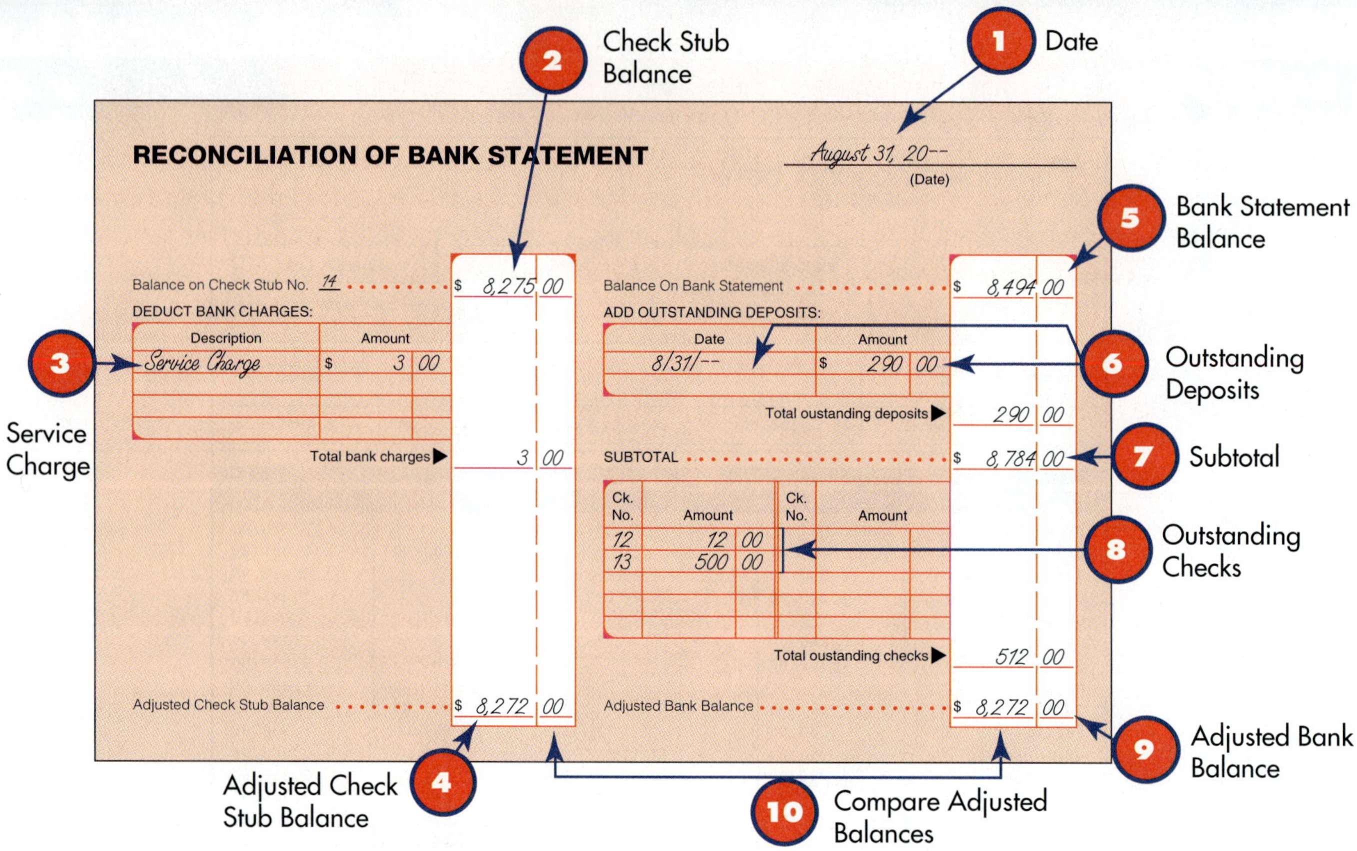


A bank statement is reconciled by verifying that information on a bank statement and a checkbook are in agreement. Reconciling immediately is an important aspect of cash control.

Encore Music's canceled checks are received with the bank statement. The returned checks are arranged in numeric order. For each canceled check, a check mark is placed on the corresponding check stub. A check stub with no check mark indicates an outstanding check.

Encore Music receives a bank statement dated August 30 on August 31. Encore Music uses a reconciliation form printed on the back of the bank statement.

### STEPS Reconciling a bank statement

1. Write the date on which the reconciliation is prepared, *August 31, 20—*.
2. In the left amount column, list the balance brought forward on Check Stub No. 14, the next unused check stub, *$8,275.00*.
3. In the space for bank charges, list any charges. The only such charge for Encore Music is the bank service charge, *$3.00*. The bank service charge is labeled *SC* on the bank statement.
4. Write the adjusted check stub balance, *$8,272.00*, in the space provided at the bottom of the left amount column. The balance on the check stub, $8,275.00, *minus* the bank's service charge, $3.00, *equals* the adjusted check stub balance, $8,272.00.
5. Write the ending balance shown on the bank statement, *$8,494.00*, in the right amount column.
6. Write the date, *8/31/—*, and the amount, *$290.00*, of any outstanding deposits in the space provided. Add the outstanding deposits. Write the total outstanding deposits, *$290.00*, in the right amount column.
7. Add the ending bank statement balance to the total outstanding deposits. Write the total, *$8,784.00*, in the space for the Subtotal.

8. List the outstanding checks, Nos. *12* and *13*, and their amounts, *$12.00* and *$500.00*, in the space provided. Add the amounts of the outstanding checks, and write the total, *$512.00*, in the right amount column.
9. Calculate the adjusted bank balance, and write the amount, *$8,272.00*, in the space provided at the bottom of the right amount column. The subtotal, $8,784.00, *minus* the total outstanding checks, $512.00, *equals* the adjusted bank balance, $8,272.00.
10. Compare adjusted balances. The adjusted balances must be the same. The adjusted check stub balance is the same as the adjusted bank balance. Because the two amounts are the same, the bank statement is reconciled. The completed reconciliation form is filed for future reference. If the two adjusted balances are not the same, the error must be found and corrected before any more work is done.

## RECORDING A BANK SERVICE CHARGE ON A CHECK STUB

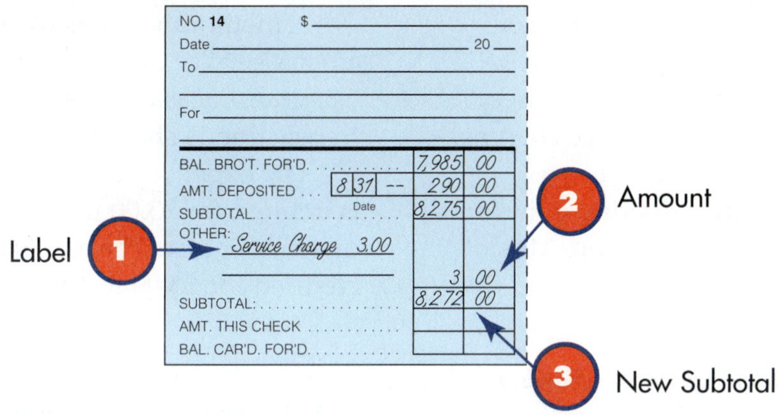


The bank deducts the service charge from Encore Music's checking account each month. Although Encore Music did not write a check for the bank service charge, this cash payment must be recorded in Encore Music's accounting records as a cash payment. First, Encore Music makes a record of a bank service charge on a check stub.

### STEPS: Recording a bank service charge on a check stub

1. Write *Service Charge $3.00* on the check stub under the heading Other.
2. Write the amount of the service charge, *$3.00*, in the amount column.
3. Calculate and record the new subtotal, *$8,272.00*, on the Subtotal line. A new Balance Carried Forward is not calculated until after Check No. 14 is written.

# JOURNALIZING A BANK SERVICE CHARGE

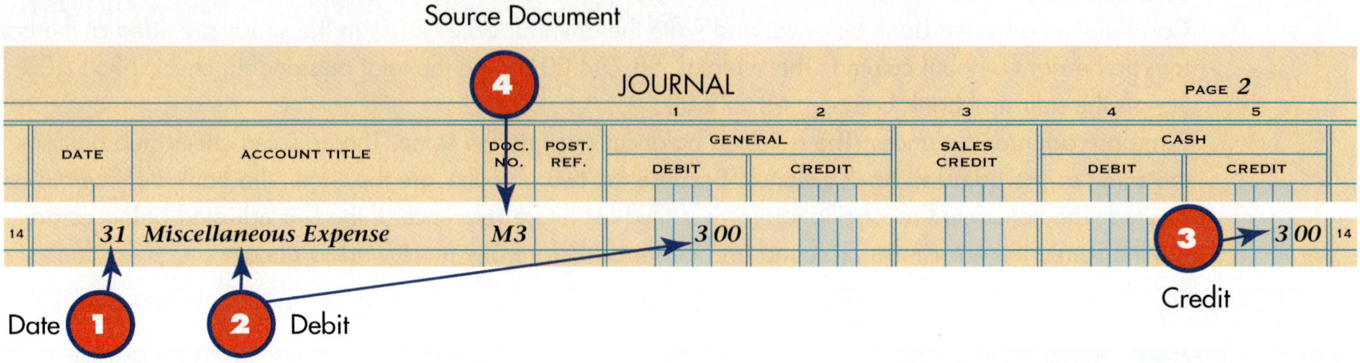


Because the bank service charge is a cash payment for which no check is written, Encore Music prepares a memorandum as the source document. Encore Music's bank service charges are relatively small and occur only once a month. Therefore, a separate ledger account for the expense is not used. Instead, Encore Music records the bank service charge as a miscellaneous expense.

***August 31. Received bank statement showing August bank service charge, $3.00. Memorandum No. 3.***

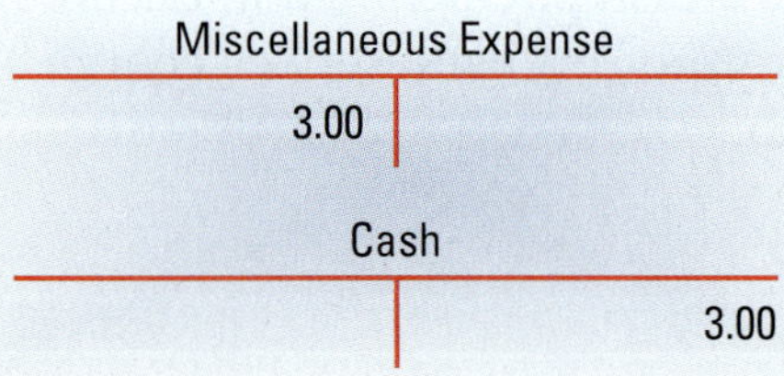


A memorandum is the source document for a bank service charge transaction. *(CONCEPT: Objective Evidence)* The analysis of this transaction is shown in the T accounts.

The expense account, Miscellaneous Expense, is debited for $3.00 to show the decrease in owner's equity. The asset account, Cash, is credited for $3.00 to show the decrease in assets.

**STEPS**

### Journalizing a bank service charge

1. **Date.** Write the date, *31*, in the Date column.
2. **Debit.** Write the title of the account to be debited, *Miscellaneous Expense,* in the Account Title column. Record the amount debited, *$3.00*, in the General Debit column.
3. **Credit.** Record the amount credited, *$3.00*, in the Cash Credit column.
4. **Source document.** Write the source document number, *M3*, in the Doc. No. column.

**SMALL BUSINESS SPOTLIGHT**

Three factors generally motivate people to start a new business: the desire to control their own destinies, the desire to work more closely with customers, and the desire to achieve substantial profits.

## TERM REVIEW

bank statement

## AUDIT YOUR UNDERSTANDING

1. List four reasons why a depositor's records and a bank's records may differ.
2. If a check mark is placed on the check stub of each canceled check, what does a check stub with no check mark indicate?

## WORK TOGETHER

**Reconciling a bank statement and recording a bank service charge**

Forms are given in the *Working Papers.* Your instructor will guide you through the following examples.

On July 29 of the current year, DeepClean received a bank statement dated July 28. The following information is obtained from the bank statement and from the records of the business.

| | | | |
|---|---|---|---|
| Bank statement balance | $1,528.00 | Outstanding checks: | |
| Bank service charge | 2.00 | No. 103 | $ 70.00 |
| Outstanding deposit, July 28 | 150.00 | No. 105 | 35.00 |
| | | Checkbook balance on Check Stub No. 106 | 1,575.00 |

3. Prepare a bank statement reconciliation. Use July 29 of the current year as the date.
4. Record the service charge on Check Stub No. 106.
5. Record the service charge on journal page 14. Use Memo. No. 44 as the source document.

## ON YOUR OWN

**Reconciling a bank statement and recording a bank service charge**

Forms are given in the *Working Papers.* Work these problems independently.

On Sept. 30 of the current year, Ajax Service Co. received a bank statement dated Sept. 29. The following information is obtained from the bank statement and from the records of the business.

| | | | |
|---|---|---|---|
| Bank statement balance | $3,208.00 | Outstanding checks: | |
| Bank service charge | 5.00 | No. 214 | $ 90.00 |
| Outstanding deposits: | | No. 215 | 135.00 |
| September 29 | 310.00 | No. 217 | 50.00 |
| September 30 | 330.00 | Checkbook balance on Check Stub No. 218 | 3,578.00 |

6. Prepare a bank statement reconciliation. Use Sept. 30 of the current year as the date.
7. Record the service charge on Check Stub No. 218.
8. Record the service charge on journal page 28. Use Memo. No. 74 as the source document.

# 6-3 Dishonored Checks and Electronic Banking

## RECORDING A DISHONORED CHECK ON A CHECK STUB

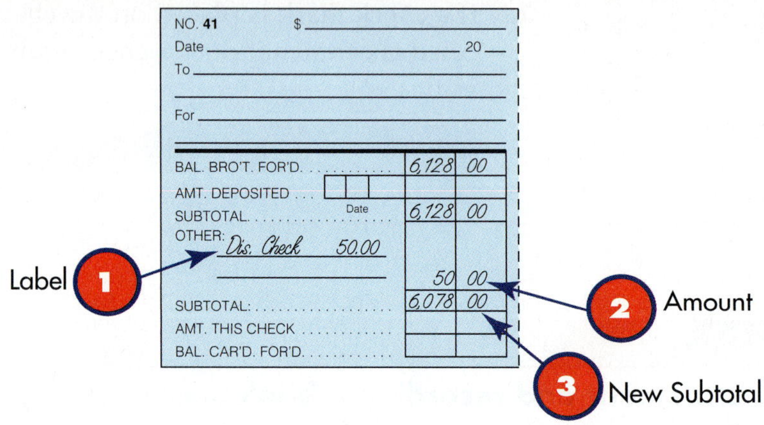


A check that a bank refuses to pay is called a **dishonored check.** Banks may dishonor a check for a number of reasons. (1) The check appears to be altered. (2) The signature of the person who signed the check does not match the one on the signature card at the bank. (3) The amounts written in figures and in words do not agree. (4) The check is postdated. (5) The person who wrote the check has stopped payment on the check. (6) The account of the person who wrote the check has insufficient funds to pay the check.

Issuing a check on an account with insufficient funds is illegal in most states. Altering or forging a check is illegal in all states. A dishonored check may affect the credit rating of the person or business who issued the check. Checking accounts and records should be maintained in such a way that all checks will be honored when presented to the bank.

Sometimes money for a dishonored check can be collected directly from the person or business who wrote the check. Often, however, the value of a dishonored check cannot be recovered and becomes an expense to the business.

Most banks charge a fee for handling dishonored checks that have been previously accepted for deposit. This fee is an expense of the business receiving a dishonored check. Encore Music's bank charges a $15.00 fee for handling dishonored checks. Encore Music attempts to collect the $15.00 fee in addition to the amount of the dishonored check.

When Encore Music receives a check, it records the check as a cash debit and deposits the check in the bank. When a check is dishonored, the bank deducts the amount of the check plus the fee, $15.00, from Encore Music's checking account. Therefore, Encore Music records a dishonored check as a cash payment transaction.

### STEPS: Recording a dishonored check on a check stub

1. Write *Dishonored check $50.00* on the line under the heading Other. The amount is the total of the dishonored check, $35.00, *plus* the service fee of $15.00.
2. Write the total of the dishonored check, *$50.00,* in the amount column.
3. Calculate and record the new subtotal, *$6,078.00,* on the Subtotal line. A new Balance Carried Forward is not calculated until after Check No. 41 is written.

## JOURNALIZING A DISHONORED CHECK

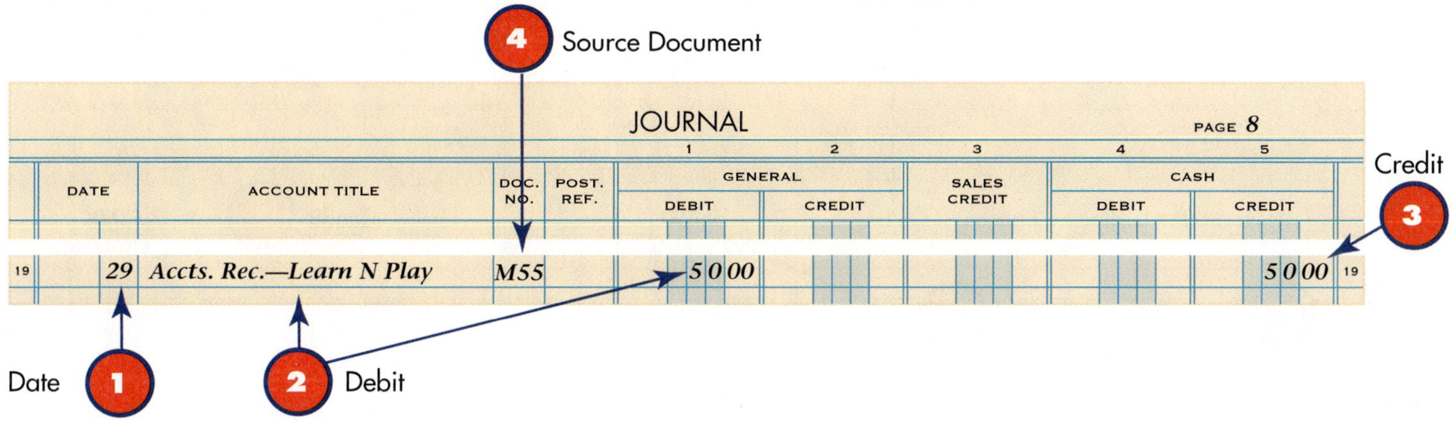


During August, Encore Music received no checks that were subsequently dishonored. However, in November Encore Music did receive a check from Learn N Play that was eventually dishonored.

***November 29. Received notice from the bank of a dishonored check from Learn N Play, \$35.00, plus \$15.00 fee; total, \$50.00. Memorandum No. 55.***

Accounts Receivable—Learn N Play

| Debit | Credit |
|---|---|
| 50.00 | |

Cash

| Debit | Credit |
|---|---|
| | 50.00 |

Because Encore Music did not write a check for this payment, a memorandum is prepared as the source document. *(CONCEPT: Objective Evidence)* The analysis of this transaction is shown in the T accounts.

All checks received are deposited in Encore Music's checking account. The entry for each cash receipts transaction includes a debit to Cash. If a check is subsequently returned as dishonored, the previous cash debit for the amount of the check must be offset by a cash credit. The asset account, Cash, is credited for \$50.00 to show the decrease in assets.

When Encore Music originally received the check from Learn N Play, Accounts Receivable—Learn N Play was credited to reduce the balance of the account. When Encore Music finds out that the check was not accepted by the bank, the account, Accounts Receivable—Learn N Play, must be increased to show that this amount, plus the bank charge, is still owed to Encore Music. The asset account, Accounts Receivable—Learn N Play, is debited for \$50.00 to show the increase in assets.

### STEPS: Journalizing a dishonored check

1. **Date.** Write the date, *29,* in the Date column.
2. **Debit.** Write the title of the account to be debited, *Accounts Receivable—Learn N Play,* in the Account Title column. Record the amount debited, *\$50.00,* in the General Debit column.
3. **Credit.** Write the amount credited, *\$50.00,* in the Cash Credit column.
4. **Source document.** Write the source document number, *M55,* in the Doc. No. column.

### REMEMBER

Checking accounts and records should be maintained in such a way that all checks will be honored when presented to the bank.

## JOURNALIZING AN ELECTRONIC FUNDS TRANSFER

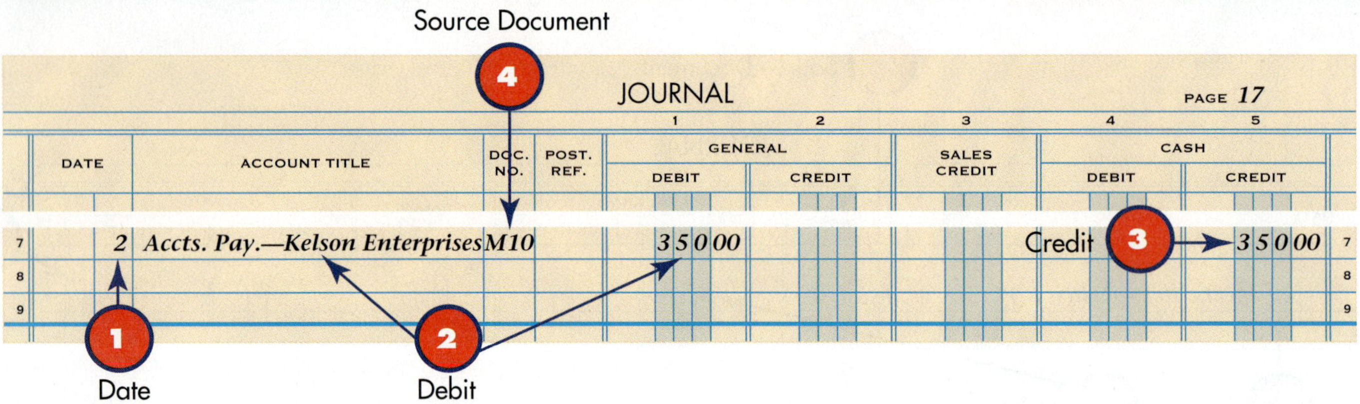


A computerized cash payments system that uses electronic impulses to transfer funds is called **electronic funds transfer.** Many businesses use electronic funds transfer (EFT) to pay vendors. To use EFT, a business makes arrangements with its bank to process EFT transactions. Arrangements are also made with vendors to accept EFT payments on account. After arranging for EFT payments on account, a telephone call is all that is needed to transfer funds from the business's account to the vendor's account.

To control cash payments through EFT, the person responsible for requesting transfers should be given a password. The bank should not accept EFT requests from any person unable to provide an established password.

Superior Cleaning Service uses electronic funds transfer to make payments on account to vendors. The journal entry for making payments on account through EFT is the same as when a check is written. The only change is the source document used to prove that the transaction did occur. Superior Cleaning Service uses a memorandum as the source document for an EFT. A note is written on the memorandum to describe the transaction.

***September 2. Paid cash on account to Kelson Enterprises, $350.00, using EFT. Memorandum No. 10.***

| Accounts Payable—Kelson Enterprises | |
|---|---|
| 350.00 | |

| Cash | |
|---|---|
| | 350.00 |

The source document for this transaction is Memorandum No. 10. (*CONCEPT: Objective Evidence*) The analysis of this transaction is shown in the T accounts.

The liability account, Accounts Payable—Kelson Enterprises, is decreased by a debit, $350.00. The asset account, Cash, is decreased by a credit, $350.00.

A cash payment made by EFT is recorded on the check stub as Other. This procedure keeps the checkbook in balance during the time lag from when the EFT is made until receipt of the bank statement. The EFT payments are verified as part of the regular bank statement reconciliation process. EFT payments are identified in the Check column of the bank statement by the notation EFT, rather than by a check number.

### STEPS: Journalizing an electronic funds transfer

1. **Date.** Write the date, *2,* in the Date column.
2. **Debit.** Write the title of the account to be debited, *Accounts Payable—Kelson Enterprises,* in the Account Title column. Record the amount debited, *$350.00,* in the General Debit column.
3. **Credit.** Record the amount credited, *$350.00,* in the Cash Credit column.
4. **Source document.** Write the source document number, *M10,* in the Doc. No. column.

# JOURNALIZING A DEBIT CARD TRANSACTION

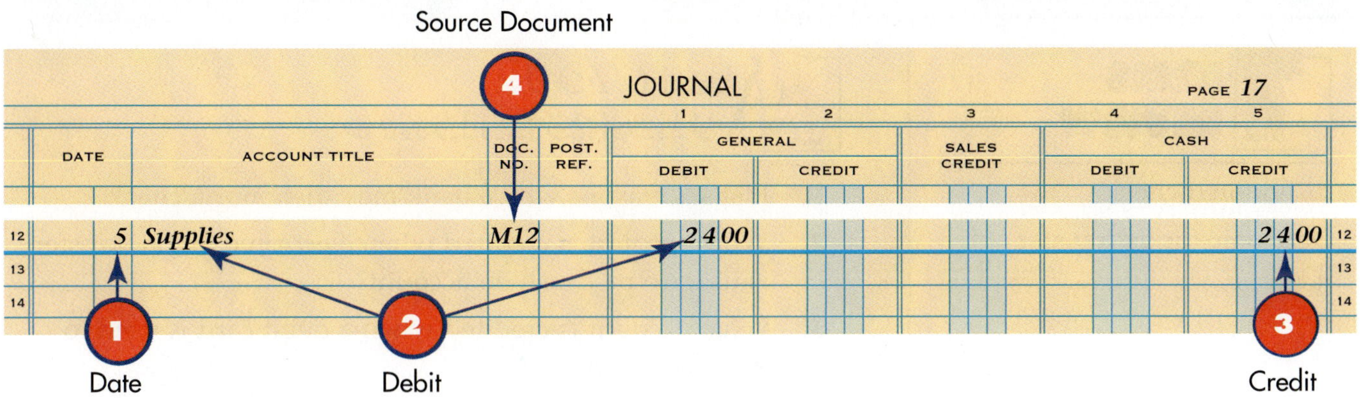


A bank card that, when making purchases, automatically deducts the amount of the purchase from the checking account of the cardholder is called a **debit card.** There is one major difference between a debit card and a credit card. When a purchase is made with a debit card, the amount of the purchase is automatically withdrawn from the checking account of the cardholder. A debit card eliminates the need to actually write out a check for the purchase. However, the effect is the same. The checking account balance is reduced by the amount of the purchase. A debit card also eliminates the need to carry a checkbook.

When using a debit card, it is important to remember to record all withdrawals to avoid errors in the checking account.

Superior Cleaning Service uses a debit card to make some purchases. Recording a cash payment made by a debit card is similar to recording a cash payment made by electronic funds transfer.

Superior Cleaning Service uses a memorandum as the source document for a debit card purchase. A note is written on the memorandum to describe the transaction.

***September 5. Purchased supplies, $24.00, using debit card. Memorandum No. 12.***

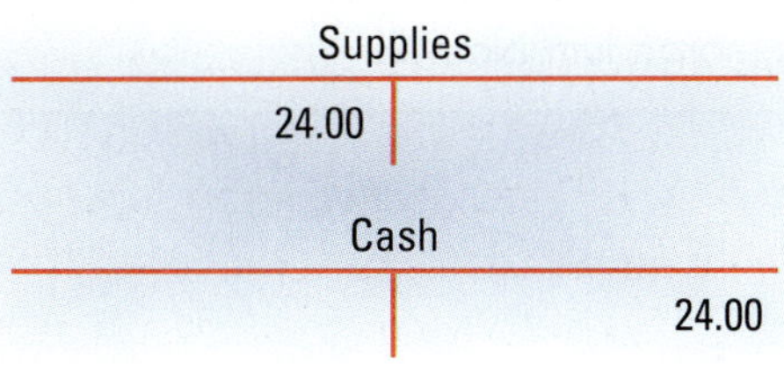


The source document for this transaction is Memorandum No. 12. *(CONCEPT: Objective Evidence)* The analysis of this transaction is shown in the T accounts.

The asset account, Supplies, is increased by a debit, $24.00. The asset account, Cash, is decreased by a credit, $24.00.

A cash payment made with a debit card is recorded on the check stub as Other. This procedure keeps the checkbook in balance during the time lag from when the debit card payment is made until receipt of the bank statement. The debit card payments are verified as part of the regular bank statement reconciliation process. Debit card payments are identified as a Purchase on the bank statement, with the date, time, location, and the amount of the debit card transaction stated.

**STEPS**

### Journalizing a debit card purchase

1. **Date.** Write the date, *5,* in the Date column.
2. **Debit.** Write the title of the account to be debited, *Supplies,* in the Account Title column. Record the amount debited, *$24.00,* in the General Debit column.
3. **Credit.** Record the amount credited, *$24.00,* in the Cash Credit column.
4. **Source document.** Write the source document number, *M12,* in the Doc. No. column.

## Terms Review

dishonored check

electronic funds transfer

debit card

## Audit Your Understanding

1. List six reasons why a bank may dishonor a check.
2. What account is credited when electronic funds transfer is used to pay cash on account?
3. What account is credited when a debit card is used to purchase supplies?

## Work Together

**Recording dishonored checks, electronic funds transfers, and debit card purchases**

Write the answers to this problem in the *Working Papers*. Your instructor will guide you through the following example.

**4.** Enter the following transactions on page 6 of a journal.

***Transactions:***

March 15. Received notice from the bank of a dishonored check from Christopher Ikola, $63.00, plus $10.00 fee; total, $73.00. Memorandum No. 121.

16. Paid cash on account to Laura Spinoza, $135.00, using EFT. Memorandum No. 122.

17. Purchased supplies, $31.00, using debit card. Memorandum No. 123.

## On Your Own

**Recording dishonored checks, electronic funds transfers, and debit card purchases**

Write the answers to this problem in the *Working Papers*. Work this problem independently.

**5.** Enter the following transactions on page 12 of a journal.

***Transactions:***

June 12. Received notice from the bank of a dishonored check from Tina Horasky, $55.00, plus $15.00 fee; total, $70.00. Memorandum No. 76.

13. Paid cash on account to Paul Mancini, $112.00, using EFT. Memorandum No. 77.

14. Purchased supplies, $79.00, using debit card. Memorandum No. 78.

# 6-4 Petty Cash

## ESTABLISHING A PETTY CASH FUND

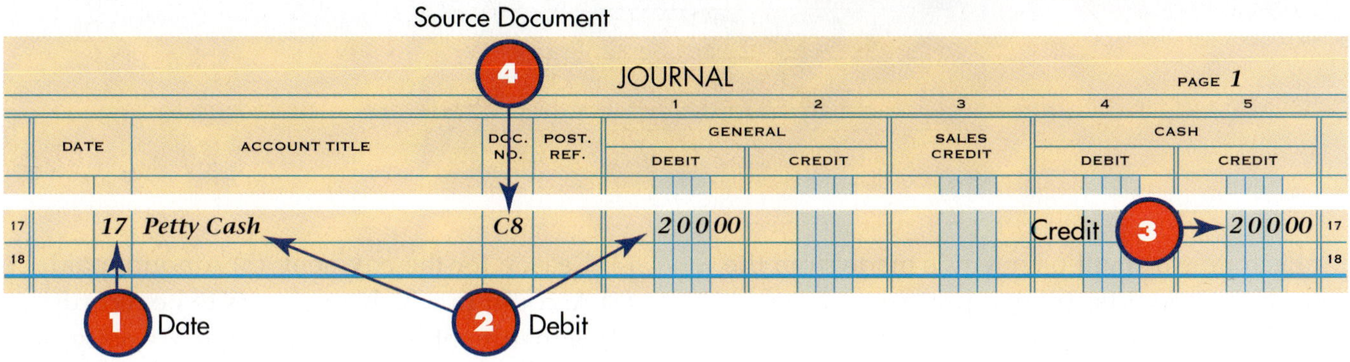


An amount of cash kept on hand and used for making small payments is called **petty cash.** A business usually has some small payments for which writing a check is not time or cost effective. Therefore, a business may maintain a separate cash fund for making small cash payments. The actual dollar amount considered to be a small payment differs from one business to another. Ms. Treviño has set $20.00 as the maximum amount to be paid at any one time from the petty cash fund.

The petty cash account is an asset with a normal debit balance. The balance of the petty cash account increases on the debit side and decreases on the credit side.

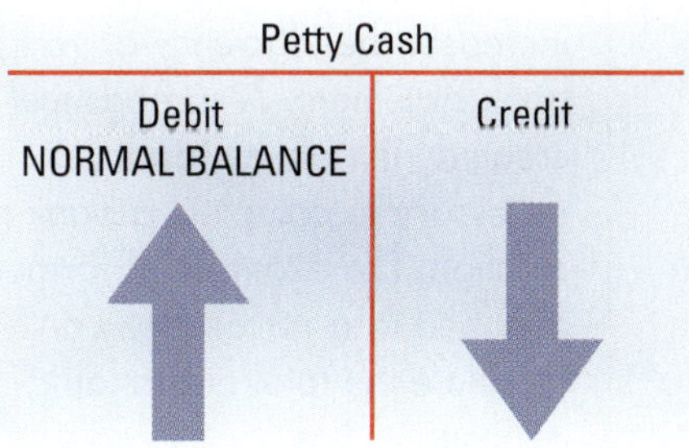


On August 17, Ms. Treviño decided that Encore Music needed a petty cash fund of $200.00. This amount should provide for small cash payments during a month.

***August 17. Paid cash to establish a petty cash fund, $200.00. Check No. 8.***

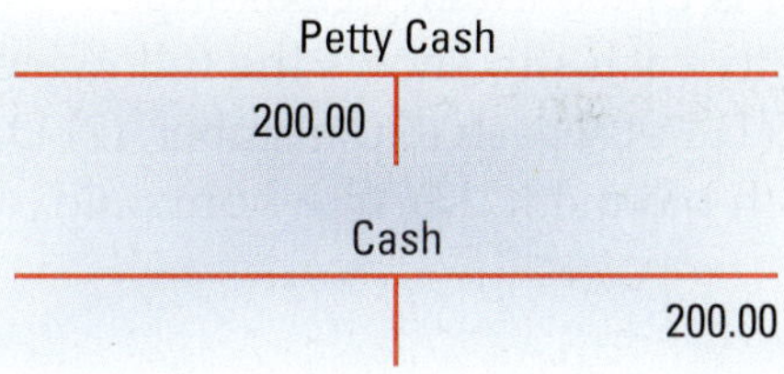


The source document for this transaction is Check No. 8. *(CONCEPT: Objective Evidence)* The analysis is shown in the T accounts. Petty Cash is debited for $200.00 to show the increase in this asset account balance. Cash is credited for $200.00 to show the decrease in this asset account balance.

Ms. Treviño cashed the check and placed the $200.00 in a locked petty cash box at her place of business. Only she is authorized to make these payments.

**STEPS**

### Establishing a petty cash fund

1. **Date.** Write the date, *17,* in the Date column.
2. **Debit.** Write the title of the account to be debited, *Petty Cash,* in the Account Title column. Record the amount debited, *$200.00,* in the General Debit column.
3. **Credit.** Record the amount credited, *$200.00,* in the Cash Credit column.
4. **Source document.** Write the source document number, *C8,* in the Doc. No. column.

# MAKING PAYMENTS FROM A PETTY CASH FUND WITH A PETTY CASH SLIP

**PETTY CASH SLIP** **No. 1**

Date: *August 18, 20--*

Paid to: *Tribune*

For: *Newspaper Ad* $ *5.00*

Account: *Advertising Expense*

Approved: *Barbara Treviño*

Each time a small payment is made from the petty cash fund, Ms. Treviño prepares a form showing the purpose and amount of the payment. A form showing proof of a petty cash payment is called a **petty cash slip.**

A petty cash slip shows the following information. (1) Petty cash slip number. (2) Date of petty cash payment. (3) To whom paid. (4) Reason for the payment. (5) Amount paid. (6) Account in which amount is to be recorded. (7) Signature of person approving the petty cash payment.

The petty cash slips are kept in the petty cash box until the fund is replenished. No entries are made in the journal for the individual petty cash payments.

## TECHNOLOGY FOR BUSINESS

### ELECTRONIC SPREADSHEETS AND BANK RECONCILIATION

Businesses often use forms to prepare accounting reports. Electronic spreadsheet software is a useful tool for preparing such accounting reports. Unlike paper forms, however, electronic spreadsheets contain formulas that automatically perform calculations.

An *electronic spreadsheet* displayed on a computer monitor consists of a group of rows and columns. Such spreadsheets can be extremely large, having hundreds of columns and thousands of rows. The space where a column intersects with a row is a *cell*. For example, cell A17 is located at the intersection of column A and row 17. This is known as the *cell address.*

The power of an electronic spreadsheet comes from the ability to let the software make calculations. This is accomplished by attaching formulas to different cells.

A bank reconciliation form increases the efficiency of verifying a bank statement. A spreadsheet can be created with all the formulas necessary to complete a bank reconciliation. For example, a formula attached to a certain cell can calculate the total outstanding deposits.

After the bank reconciliation is printed, the same spreadsheet can be used to reconcile other bank statements. Preparing a bank reconciliation using an electronic spreadsheet can help assure that the calculations are accurate.

## REPLENISHING PETTY CASH

1 Date — 4 Source Document

JOURNAL — PAGE 2

| | DATE | ACCOUNT TITLE | DOC. NO. | POST. REF. | GENERAL DEBIT (1) | GENERAL CREDIT (2) | SALES CREDIT (3) | CASH DEBIT (4) | CASH CREDIT (5) | |
|---|---|---|---|---|---|---|---|---|---|---|
| 10 | 31 | *Miscellaneous Expense* | *C12* | | *7 00* | | | | *12 00* | 10 |
| 11 | | *Advertising Expense* | | | *5 00* | | | | | 11 |

2 Debit — 3 Credit

As petty cash is paid out, the amount in the petty cash box decreases. Eventually, the petty cash fund must be replenished and the petty cash payments recorded. Encore Music replenishes its petty cash fund whenever the amount on hand is reduced to $75.00. Also, the petty cash fund is always replenished at the end of each month so that all of the expenses are recorded in the month they are incurred.

Before petty cash is replenished, a proof of the fund must be completed.

| | |
|---|---|
| Petty cash remaining in the petty cash fund | $188.00 |
| *Plus* total of petty cash slips | + 12.00 |
| *Equals* petty cash fund | $200.00 |

The last line of the proof must show the same total as the original balance of the petty cash fund, $200.00. If petty cash does not prove, the errors must be found and corrected before any more work is done.

The proof shows that a total of $12.00 has been paid out of petty cash. An inspection of the petty cash slips shows that $7.00 has been paid for miscellaneous expenses and $5.00 has been paid for advertising. Therefore, an additional $12.00 must be placed in the fund. Encore Music will write a check to replenish the fund.

***August 31. Paid cash to replenish the petty cash fund, $12.00: miscellaneous expense, $7.00; advertising, $5.00. Check No. 12.***

Unless the petty cash fund is permanently increased or decreased, the balance of the account is always the original amount of the fund. The check issued to replenish petty cash is a credit to Cash and does not affect Petty Cash. When the check is cashed, the money is placed in the petty cash box. The amount in the petty cash box changes as shown below.

| | |
|---|---|
| Amount in petty cash box before fund is replenished | $188.00 |
| Amount from check issued to replenish petty cash | + 12.00 |
| Amount in petty cash box after fund is replenished | $200.00 |

The total amount in the petty cash box, $200.00, is again the same as the balance of the petty cash account.

### STEPS: Journalizing the entry to replenish petty cash

1. **Date.** Write the date, *31*, in the Date column.
2. **Debit.** Write the title of the first account to be debited, *Miscellaneous Expense*, in the Account Title column. Write the amount to be debited to Miscellaneous Expense, *$7.00*, in the General Debit column on the same line as the account title. Write the title of the second account to be debited, *Advertising Expense*, on the next line in the Account Title column. Record the amount to be debited to Advertising Expense, *$5.00*, in the General Debit column on the same line as the account title.
3. **Credit.** Record the amount to be credited, *$12.00*, in the Cash Credit column on the first line of this entry.
4. **Source document.** Write the source document number, *C12*, in the Doc. No. column on the first line of the entry.

## TERMS REVIEW

petty cash

petty cash slip

## AUDIT YOUR UNDERSTANDING

1. Why do businesses use petty cash funds?
2. Why is Cash and not Petty Cash credited when a petty cash fund is replenished?

## WORK TOGETHER

**Establishing and replenishing a petty cash fund**

Write the answers to this problem in the *Working Papers.* Your instructor will guide you through the following example.

3. Journalize the following transactions completed during July of the current year. Use page 13 of a journal. The abbreviation for check is C.

***Transactions:***

July 3. Paid cash to establish a petty cash fund, $250.00. C57.

31. Paid cash to replenish the petty cash fund, $78.00: supplies, $25.00; miscellaneous expense, $8.00; repairs, $45.00. C97.

## ON YOUR OWN

**Establishing and replenishing a petty cash fund**

Write the answers to this problem in the *Working Papers.* Work this problem independently.

4. Journalize the following transactions completed during August of the current year. Use page 14 of a journal. The abbreviation for check is C.

***Transactions:***

Aug. 1. Paid cash to establish a petty cash fund, $500.00. C145.

31. Paid cash to replenish the petty cash fund, $134.00: supplies, $33.00; miscellaneous expense, $70.00; advertising, $31.00. C177.

# CHAPTER 6 SUMMARY

*Enrichment Activity*

**Accounting Careers**

*The U.S. Bureau of Labor Statistics publishes a reference titled* Occupational Outlook Handbook. *Either locate this book in the library or on the Internet and look up the title of an accounting occupation you might be interested in. Describe the outlook for this occupation.*

After completing this chapter, you can

1. Define accounting terms related to using a checking account and a petty cash fund.
2. Identify accounting concepts and practices related to using a checking account.
3. Prepare business papers related to using a checking account.
4. Reconcile a bank statement.
5. Journalize dishonored checks and electronic banking transactions.
6. Establish and replenish a petty cash fund.

## EXPLORE ACCOUNTING

### CASH CONTROLS

Cash transactions occur more frequently than other types of transactions. Because cash is easily transferred from one person to another, a business must try to safeguard its cash to protect it and other assets from errors.

An unintentional error occurs when someone mistakenly records an incorrect amount or forgets to record a transaction. An intentional error occurs when someone intentionally records an incorrect amount or purposely forgets to record a transaction in order to cover up fraud or theft. Good cash control procedures should guard against both types of errors.

One common method of controlling cash is to insist that all cash payments over a certain amount be paid by check. In addition, checks should be prenumbered so that it is easy to account for each check. The document number column of a journal can be used to ensure that all checks issued are recorded in the journal. Other cash controls are to have one person responsible for authorizing all checks, and requiring a source document in support of each cash payment.

One of the best ways to safeguard assets is to separate duties so that one employee does not have total control of an entire set of processes. For example, one employee could receive and record the receipt of cash on account; a second employee could make and record deposits; and a third employee could reconcile the bank statement. By separating the duties, it is less likely that errors will be made.

A company that does not have enough employees to institute the separation of duties concept may hire a certified public accountant (CPA) to perform some of these duties on a regular basis.

**Research Assignment:** Talk to a business person to determine what kind of controls are in place to safeguard cash. Schools, hospitals, charitable organizations, and government offices as well as retail, wholesale, and service businesses should have established controls that are being followed. Summarize and present your findings to your class.

## 6-1 APPLICATION PROBLEM
### Endorsing and writing checks

You are authorized to sign checks for Accounting Tutors. Forms are given in the *Working Papers*.

***Instructions:***

1. For each of the following situations, prepare the appropriate endorsement.
   a. Write a blank endorsement.
   b. Write a special endorsement to transfer a check to Bryan Astrup.
   c. Write a restrictive endorsement to deposit a check in the account of Accounting Tutors.
2. Record the balance brought forward on Check Stub No. 608, $9,811.71.
3. Record a deposit of $1,359.00 made on September 30 of the current year on Check Stub No. 608.
4. Prepare check stubs and write the following checks. Use September 30 of the current year as the date.
   a. Check No. 608 to Oak Street Supplies for supplies, $1,050.00.
   b. Check No. 609 to Blaine Tribune for advertising, $92.00.
   c. Check No. 610 to Bryce Kassola for rent, $750.00.

## 6-2 APPLICATION PROBLEM
### Reconciling a bank statement and recording a bank service charge

Forms are given in the *Working Papers*. On May 31 of the current year, Parties Plus received a bank statement dated May 30. The following information is obtained from the bank statement and from the records of the business.

| | |
|---|---:|
| Bank statement balance | $2,482.00 |
| Bank service charge | 10.00 |
| Outstanding deposit, May 30 | 756.25 |
| Outstanding checks: | |
| No. 310 | 421.76 |
| No. 311 | 150.50 |
| Checkbook balance on Check Stub No. 312 | 2,675.99 |

***Instructions:***

1. Prepare a statement reconciliation. Use May 31 of the current year as the date.
2. Record the service charge on Check Stub No. 312.
3. Record the service charge on journal page 10. Use Memorandum No. 58 as the source document.

## 6-3 APPLICATION PROBLEM
### Recording dishonored checks, electronic funds transfers, and debit card purchases

Enter the following transactions on page 3 of the journal given in the *Working Papers*.

***Transactions:***

Feb. 15. Received notice from the bank of a dishonored check from Patricia Dubay, $125.00, plus $20.00 fee; total, $145.00. Memorandum No. 217.

16. Paid cash on account to Alec Hongo, $354.00, using EFT. Memorandum No. 218.

17. Purchased supplies, $89.00, using debit card. Memorandum No. 219.

## 6-4 APPLICATION PROBLEM
### Establishing and replenishing a petty cash fund

Journalize the following transactions completed during November of the current year. Use page 22 of the journal given in the *Working Papers*. The abbreviation for check is C.

***Transactions:***

Nov. 5. Paid cash to establish a petty cash fund, $300.00. C527.

30. Paid cash to replenish the petty cash fund, $165.00: supplies, $57.00; miscellaneous expense, $58.00; repairs, $40.00; postage (Postage Expense), $10.00. C555.

## 6-5 MASTERY PROBLEM
### Reconciling a bank statement; journalizing a bank service charge, a dishonored check, and petty cash transactions

Joseph Cruz owns a business called LawnMow. Selected general ledger accounts are given below.

| | | |
|---|---|---|
| 110 Cash | 140 Prepaid Insurance | 535 Repair Expense |
| 115 Petty Cash | 320 Joseph Cruz, Drawing | 540 Supplies Expense |
| 120 Accts. Rec.—Stacey Griffith | 520 Miscellaneous Expense | 550 Utilities Expense |
| 130 Supplies | 530 Rent Expense | |

***Instructions:***

1. Journalize the following transactions completed during August of the current year. Use page 20 of the journal given in the *Working Papers*. Source documents are abbreviated as follows: check, C; memorandum, M.

***Transactions:***

Aug. 21. Paid cash to establish a petty cash fund, $200.00. C61.

24. Paid cash for repairs, $235.00. C62.

26. Paid cash for supplies, $40.00. C63.

27. Received notice from the bank of a dishonored check from Stacey Griffith, $35.00, plus $15.00 fee; total, $50.00. M22.

28. Paid cash for miscellaneous expense, $12.00. C64.

31. Paid cash to owner for personal use, $300.00. C65.

31. Paid cash to replenish the petty cash fund, $55.00: supplies, $35.00; miscellaneous expense, $20.00. C66.

2. On August 31 of the current year, LawnMow received a bank statement dated August 30. Prepare a bank statement reconciliation. Use August 31 of the current year as the date. The following information is obtained from the August 30 bank statement and from the records of the business.

| | |
|---|---|
| Bank statement balance | $1,521.00 |
| Bank service charge | 5.00 |
| Outstanding deposit, August 31 | 430.00 |
| Outstanding checks, Nos. 65 and 66 | |
| Checkbook balance on Check Stub No. 67 | 1,601.00 |

3. Continue using the journal and journalize the following transaction.

***Transaction:***

Aug. 31. Received bank statement showing August bank service charge, $5.00. M23.

## 6-6 CHALLENGE PROBLEM
### Reconciling a bank statement and recording a bank service charge

Use the bank statement, canceled checks, and check stubs given in the *Working Papers.*

***Instructions:***

1. Compare the canceled checks with the check stubs. For each canceled check, place a check mark next to the appropriate check stub number. For each deposit shown on the bank statement, place a check mark next to the deposit amount on the appropriate check stub.
2. Prepare a bank statement reconciliation. Use August 29 of the current year as the date.
3. Record the following transactions on page 8 of a journal. The abbreviation for memorandum is M.

***Transactions:***

Sept. 1. Received bank statement showing August bank service charge, $5.00. M25.

1. Received notice from the bank of a dishonored check from Sheldon Martindale, $170.00, plus $5.00 fee; total, $175.00. M26.

4. Record the bank service charge and dishonored check on Check Stub No. 165.

**INTERNET ACTIVITY**

Point your browser to

**http://accounting.swpco.com**

Choose **First-Year Course**, choose **Activities**, and complete the activity for Chapter 6.

### Applied Communication

All businesses are affected to some degree by issues and events that occur in the areas in which the businesses are located. For example, a city may gain an industry that will employ many people for a long time. Or, a town might build new roads or schools.

**Instructions:** Collect three to five newspaper or magazine articles about issues in your area that you think will affect local businesses. For each article, prepare a written list of consequences that a business might encounter.

## Cases for Critical Thinking

**Case 1** Iris Velez has a personal checking account for which she receives a bank statement every three months. She does not prepare a reconciliation. Sueanne Merker also has a personal checking account for which she receives bank statements once a month. She prepares a bank statement reconciliation for each bank statement received. Is Ms. Velez or Ms. Merker following the better procedure? Explain.

**Case 2** Dorset Company decides to establish a petty cash fund. The owner, Edna Dorset, wants to establish a $100.00 petty cash fund and limit payments to $20.00 or less. The manager, Roy Evans, suggests a petty cash fund of $3,000.00 limited to payments of $50.00 or less. Mr. Evans claims this limit will help him avoid writing so many checks. Do you agree with Ms. Dorset or Mr. Evans? Explain.

| | |
|---|---|
| Bank statement balance | $15,227.00 |
| Bank service charge | 13.00 |
| Outstanding deposit, May 28 | 275.00 |
| Outstanding checks: | |
| No. 14 | 50.00 |
| No. 15 | 25.00 |
| No. 16 | 210.00 |
| Checkbook balance on Check Stub No. 17 | 15,230.00 |

6. Continue using page 2 of the journal, and journalize the following transactions.

May 29. Received bank statement showing May bank service charge, $13.00. M3.
29. Paid cash for supplies, $60.00. C17.
29. Received cash from sales, $740.00. T29.
31. Paid cash to replenish the petty cash fund, $17.00: miscellaneous expense, $10.00; repairs, $7.00. C18.
31. Paid cash to owner for personal use, $250.00. C19.
31. Received cash from sales, $780.00. T31.

7. Prove page 2 of the journal.

8. Prove cash. The beginning cash balance on May 1 is zero. The balance on the next unused check stub is $16,410.00.

9. Rule page 2 of the journal.

10. Post the separate amounts on each line of page 2 of the journal that need to be posted individually.

11. Post the column totals on page 2 of the journal.

**The general ledger prepared in Reinforcement Activity 1—Part A is needed to complete Reinforcement Activity 1—Part B.**

# 7 Work Sheet for a Service Business

**AFTER STUDYING CHAPTER 7, YOU WILL BE ABLE TO:**

1. Define accounting terms related to a work sheet for a service business organized as a proprietorship.
2. Identify accounting concepts and practices related to a work sheet for a service business organized as a proprietorship.
3. Prepare a heading and a trial balance on a work sheet.
4. Plan adjustments for supplies and prepaid insurance.
5. Complete a work sheet for a service business organized as a proprietorship.
6. Identify selected procedures for finding and correcting errors in accounting records.

**TERMS PREVIEW**

fiscal period
work sheet
trial balance
adjustments
income statement
net income
net loss

## CONSISTENT REPORTING

General ledger accounts contain information needed by managers and owners. Before the information can be used, however, it must be analyzed, summarized, and reported in a meaningful way. The accounting concept, *Consistent Reporting,* is applied when the same accounting procedures are followed in the same way in each accounting period. *(CONCEPT: Consistent Reporting)* For example, in one year a delivery business might report the number of deliveries made. The next year the same business reports the amount of revenue received for the deliveries made. The information for the two years cannot be compared because the business has not been consistent in reporting information about deliveries.

A summary of preparing a work sheet is shown on the Work Sheet Overlay within this chapter.

# ACCOUNTING IN YOUR CAREER

## NETWORKING ON WORK SHEETS

Darnell Gleason, an administrative assistant at Micelli Tailoring, has been having a good time at the five-year reunion of his high school class. He has caught up with old friends and is surprised to find some familiar careers represented at the reunion today. He has been talking with Rebecca Fong, an employee at Watson Associates, a small marketing consulting company in town. Charles King, accounting assistant with Kovell Advertising, joins them.

Darnell tells Charles that he and Rebecca have been discussing their accounting procedures and had just started talking about preparing work sheets. He says that he does a standard work sheet on 8-column paper with columns for trial balance, adjustments, income statement, and balance sheet. Rebecca immediately says, "Darnell, you still use paper and pencil? I've designed a computer spreadsheet so that whenever I want to do a work sheet, all I have to do is plug in the numbers and all the calculations are done automatically. And if I change one of the numbers, the calculations are updated immediately."

Charles smiles and says, "My company has only one adjustment to make each month, so I don't do a work sheet at all. I run a trial balance, calculate my new adjustment, journalize it and post it, then do another trial balance just to be sure the debits and credits are still equal. Then I'm ready to do the financial statements."

Darnell has never considered other ways of preparing a work sheet. "You two have given me some ideas I think I can use," he tells Rebecca and Charles. "I guess we're networking. What would you think about getting together regularly to share ideas?"

### Critical Thinking:

1. Is it ethical for employees to share information about their companies this way?
2. What are the advantages and disadvantages of using a computer to perform accounting procedures?

# 7-1 Creating a Work Sheet

## FISCAL PERIODS

The length of time for which a business summarizes and reports financial information is called a **fiscal period** (also known as an accounting period). Businesses usually select a period of time for which to summarize and report financial information. The accounting concept, *Accounting Period Cycle,* is applied when changes in financial information are reported for a specific period of time in the form of financial statements. *(CONCEPT: Accounting Period Cycle)* Each business chooses a fiscal period length that meets its needs. Because federal and state tax reports are based on one year, most businesses use a one-year fiscal period. However, because Encore Music is a new business, Ms. Treviño wishes to have financial information reported frequently to help her make decisions. For this reason, Encore Music uses a one-month fiscal period.

A fiscal period can begin on any date. However, most businesses begin their fiscal periods on the first day of a month. Encore Music started business on August 1. Therefore, Encore Music's monthly fiscal period is for the period from August 1 through August 31, inclusive. Businesses often choose a one-year fiscal period that ends during a period of low business activity. In this way, the end-of-year accounting work comes at a time when other business activities are the lightest.

Financial information may be analyzed, summarized, and reported on any date a business needs the information. However, financial information is always summarized and reported at the end of a fiscal period.

## WORK SHEET

A columnar accounting form used to summarize the general ledger information needed to prepare financial statements is called a **work sheet.**

Accountants use a work sheet for four reasons. (1) To summarize general ledger account balances to prove that debits equal credits. (2) To plan needed changes to general ledger accounts to bring account balances up to date. (3) To separate general ledger account balances according to the financial statements to be prepared. (4) To calculate the amount of net income or net loss for a fiscal period.

Journals and ledgers are permanent records of a business and are usually prepared in ink or printed by a computer. However, a work sheet is a planning tool and is not considered a permanent accounting record. Therefore, a work sheet is prepared in pencil.

## PREPARING THE HEADING OF A WORK SHEET

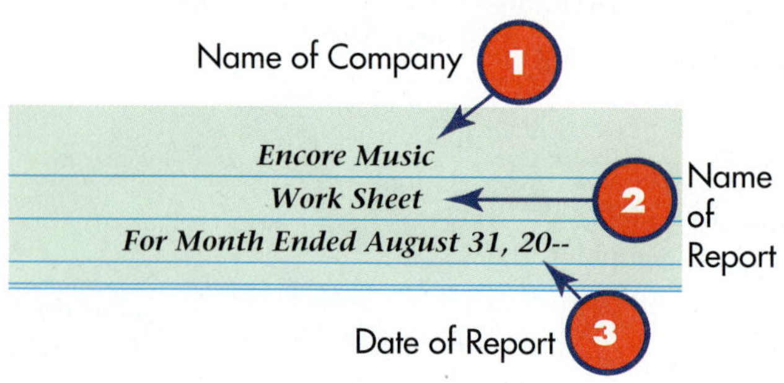


The heading on a work sheet consists of three lines and contains the name of the business, the name of the report, and the date of the report.

The date on Encore Music's work sheet indicates that the work sheet covers the 31 days from August 1 through and including August 31. If a work sheet were for a calendar year fiscal period, it might have a date stated as *For Year Ended December 31, 20—.*

## PREPARING A TRIAL BALANCE ON A WORK SHEET

Encore Music
Work Sheet
For Month Ended August 31, 20--

| | ACCOUNT TITLE | TRIAL BALANCE 1 DEBIT | TRIAL BALANCE 2 CREDIT |
|---|---|---|---|
| 1 | *Cash* | 8272 00 | |
| 2 | *Petty Cash* | 200 00 | |
| 3 | *Accounts Receivable—Kids Time* | 100 00 | |
| 4 | *Accounts Receivable—Learn N Play* | 20 00 | |
| 5 | *Supplies* | 4751 00 | |
| 6 | *Prepaid Insurance* | 1200 00 | |
| 7 | *Accounts Payable—Ling Music Supplies* | | 1360 00 |
| 8 | *Accounts Payable—Sullivan Office Supplies* | | 20 00 |
| 9 | *Barbara Treviño, Capital* | | 10000 00 |
| 10 | *Barbara Treviño, Drawing* | 600 00 | |
| 11 | *Income Summary* | | |
| 12 | *Sales* | | 4411 00 |
| 13 | *Advertising Expense* | 273 00 | |
| 14 | *Insurance Expense* | | |
| 15 | *Miscellaneous Expense* | 10 00 | |
| 16 | *Rent Expense* | 250 00 | |
| 17 | *Supplies Expense* | | |
| 18 | *Utilities Expense* | 115 00 | |
| 19 | Add Totals | 15791 00 | 15791 00 |
| 20 | | | |

1 Account Titles
2 Account Balances
3 Single Rule
4 Add Totals
5 Write Totals
6 Double Rule

The total of all debit account balances must equal the total of all credit account balances. A proof of the equality of debits and credits in a general ledger is called a **trial balance.**

Information for the trial balance is taken from the general ledger. General ledger account titles are listed on a trial balance in the same order as listed on the chart of accounts. All the account titles are listed, even if some accounts do not have balances.

### STEPS: Preparing a trial balance on a work sheet

1. Write the general ledger account titles in the work sheet's Account Title column.
2. Write the general ledger debit account balances in the Trial Balance Debit column. Write the general ledger credit account balances in the Trial Balance Credit column. If an account does not have a balance, the space in the Trial Balance columns is left blank.
3. Rule a single line across the two Trial Balance columns below the last line on which an account title is written. This single line shows that each column is to be added.
4. Add both the Trial Balance Debit and Credit columns. Use a calculator if one is available. If the two column totals are the same, then debits equal credits in the general ledger accounts. If the two column totals are not the same, recheck the Trial Balance columns to find the error. Other parts of a work sheet are not completed until the Trial Balance columns are proved. Suggestions for locating errors are described later in this chapter.
5. Write each column's total below the single line.
6. Rule double lines across both Trial Balance columns. The double lines mean that the Trial Balance column totals have been verified as correct.

## TERMS REVIEW

fiscal period

work sheet

trial balance

## AUDIT YOUR UNDERSTANDING

1. What is written on the three-line heading on a work sheet?
2. What general ledger accounts are listed in the Trial Balance columns of a work sheet?

## WORK TOGETHER

**Recording the trial balance on a work sheet**

Use the work sheet given in the *Working Papers.* Your instructor will guide you through the following example.

On February 28 of the current year, Golden Tan has the following general ledger accounts and balances. The business uses a monthly fiscal period.

| Account Titles | Account Balances | |
|---|---|---|
| | Debit | Credit |
| Cash | $9,800.00 | |
| Petty Cash | 150.00 | |
| Accounts Receivable—Ruby Prince | 2,795.00 | |
| Supplies | 456.00 | |
| Prepaid Insurance | 750.00 | |
| Accounts Payable—Richard Navarro | | $ 555.00 |
| Gary Baldwin, Capital | | 14,885.00 |
| Gary Baldwin, Drawing | 3,400.00 | |
| Income Summary | — | — |
| Sales | | 4,320.00 |
| Advertising Expense | 931.00 | |
| Insurance Expense | — | |
| Miscellaneous Expense | 378.00 | |
| Supplies Expense | — | |
| Utilities Expense | 1,100.00 | |

3. Prepare the heading and trial balance on a work sheet. Total and rule the Trial Balance columns. Save your work to complete Work Together on page 164.

## ON YOUR OWN

### Recording the trial balance on a work sheet

Use the work sheet given in the *Working Papers.* Work this problem independently.

On December 31 of the current year, Cragan's Copies has the following general ledger accounts and balances. The business uses a monthly fiscal period.

| Account Titles | Account Balances | |
|---|---|---|
| | Debit | Credit |
| Cash | $6,900.00 | |
| Petty Cash | 75.00 | |
| Accounts Receivable—Ross Kim | 1,398.00 | |
| Supplies | 228.00 | |
| Prepaid Insurance | 375.00 | |
| Accounts Payable—Renee Elk | | $ 278.00 |
| Lana Arola, Capital | | 7,443.00 |
| Lana Arola, Drawing | 1,700.00 | |
| Income Summary | — | — |
| Sales | | 4,160.00 |
| Advertising Expense | 466.00 | |
| Insurance Expense | — | |
| Miscellaneous Expense | 189.00 | |
| Supplies Expense | — | |
| Utilities Expense | 550.00 | |

**4.** Prepare the heading and trial balance on a work sheet. Total and rule the Trial Balance columns. Save your work to complete On Your Own on page 164.

# 7-2 Planning Adjusting Entries on a Work Sheet

## PLANNING ADJUSTMENTS ON A WORK SHEET

Sometimes a business will pay cash for an expense in one fiscal period, but the expense is not used until a later period. The expense should be reported in the same fiscal period that it is used to produce revenue. The accounting concept, *Matching Expenses with Revenue,* is applied when revenue from business activities and expenses associated with earning that revenue are recorded in the same accounting period. For example, Encore Music buys supplies in quantity in August, but some of the supplies are not used until September. Only the value of the supplies used in August should be reported as expenses in August. In this way, August revenue and the supplies expense associated with earning the August revenue are recorded in the same accounting period. *(CONCEPT: Matching Expenses with Revenue)*

In order to give accurate information on financial statements, some general ledger accounts must be brought up to date at the end of a fiscal period. For example, Encore Music debits an asset account, Supplies, each time supplies are bought. Supplies on hand are items of value owned by a business until the supplies are used. The value of supplies that are used becomes an expense to the business. However, recording an expense each time an individual supply, such as a pencil, is used would be impractical. Therefore, on August 31 the balance of the asset account, Supplies, is the value of all supplies bought rather than the value of only the supplies that have not yet been used. The amount of supplies that have been used must be deducted from the asset account, Supplies, and recorded in the expense account, Supplies Expense.

Likewise, the amount of insurance that has been used during the fiscal period is also an expense of the business. When the insurance premium for a year of insurance coverage is paid, the entire amount is debited to an asset account, Prepaid Insurance. Recording each day's amount of insurance used during August is impractical. Therefore, at the end of a fiscal period, the amount of the insurance coverage used must be deducted from the asset account, Prepaid Insurance, and recorded in the expense account, Insurance Expense.

Changes recorded on a work sheet to update general ledger accounts at the end of a fiscal period are called **adjustments.** The assets of a business, such as supplies and prepaid insurance, are used to earn revenue. The portions of the assets consumed in order to earn revenue become expenses of the business. The portions consumed are no longer assets but are now expenses. Therefore, adjustments must be made to both the asset and expense accounts for supplies and insurance. After the adjustments are made, the expenses incurred to earn revenue are reported in the same fiscal period as the revenue is earned and reported. *(CONCEPT: Matching Expenses with Revenue)*

A work sheet is used to plan adjustments. Changes are not made in general ledger accounts until adjustments are journalized and posted. The accuracy of the planning for adjustments is checked on a work sheet before adjustments are actually journalized.

Procedures for journalizing Encore Music's adjustments are described in Chapter 9.

**REMEMBER**

The ending balance of the asset account, Supplies, should represent the amount of supplies remaining on hand at the end of the fiscal period. The amount of supplies used during the period should be recorded in the expense account, Supplies Expense.

## SUMMARY OF PREPARATION OF A WORK SHEET FOR A SERVICE BUSINESS

The following overlay summarizes the preparation of a work sheet. Follow the directions below in using the overlay.

1. Before using the overlay, be sure the pages and transparent overlays are arranged correctly. The correct arrangement is shown below.

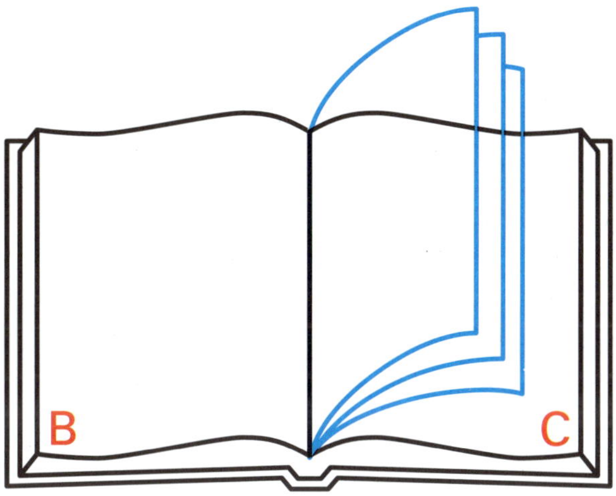


2. Place your book in a horizontal position. Study the steps on page C in preparing the work sheet. You will be able to read the text through the transparent overlays. When directed, carefully lift the transparent overlays and lay them over the work sheet as shown below.

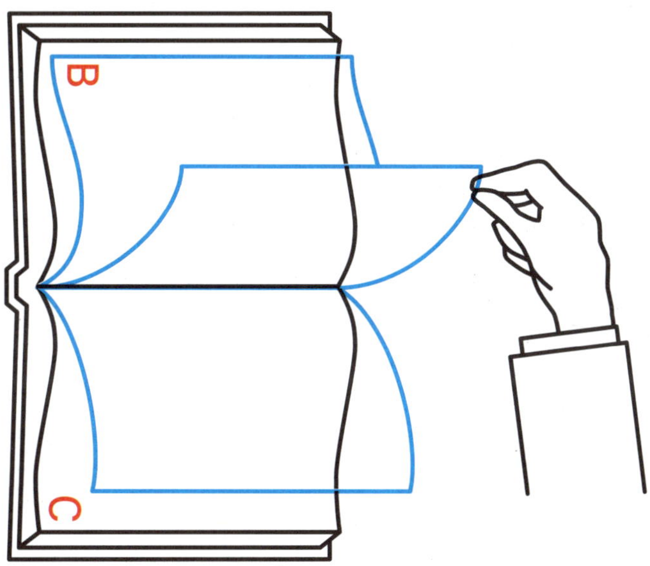

## PREPARING A WORK SHEET

To correctly use the insert, read the steps on page C. Apply the transparent overlays when directed to do so in the steps.

**Encore Music**
**Work Sheet**
**For Month Ended August 31, 20--**

(1) → heading; (2) → Account Title

| | ACCOUNT TITLE | 1 TRIAL BALANCE DEBIT | 2 TRIAL BALANCE CREDIT | 3 ADJUSTMENTS DEBIT | 4 ADJUSTMENTS CREDIT | 5 INCOME STATEMENT DEBIT | 6 INCOME STATEMENT CREDIT | 7 BALANCE SHEET DEBIT | 8 BALANCE SHEET CREDIT | |
|---|---|---|---|---|---|---|---|---|---|---|
| 1 | Cash | 8,272 00 | | | | | | | | 1 |
| 2 | Petty Cash | 200 00 | | | | | | | | 2 |
| 3 | Accounts Receivable—Kids Time | 100 00 | | | | | | | | 3 |
| 4 | Accounts Receivable—Learn N Play | 20 00 | | | | | | | | 4 |
| 5 | Supplies | 4,751 00 | | | | | | | | 5 |
| 6 | Prepaid Insurance | 1,200 00 | | | | | | | | 6 |
| 7 | Accounts Payable—Ling Music Supplies | | 1,360 00 | | | | | | | 7 |
| 8 | Accounts Payable—Sullivan Office Supplies | | 20 00 | | | | | | | 8 |
| 9 | Barbara Treviño, Capital | | 10,000 00 | | | | | | | 9 |
| 10 | Barbara Treviño, Drawing | 600 00 | | | | | | | | 10 |
| 11 | Income Summary | | | | | | | | | 11 |
| 12 | Sales | | 4,411 00 | | | | | | | 12 |
| 13 | Advertising Expense | 273 00 | | | | | | | | 13 |
| 14 | Insurance Expense | | | | | | | | | 14 |
| 15 | Miscellaneous Expense | 10 00 | | | | | | | | 15 |
| 16 | Rent Expense | 250 00 | | | | | | | | 16 |
| 17 | Supplies Expense | | | | | | | | | 17 |
| 18 | Utilities Expense | 115 00 | | | | | | | | 18 |
| 19 | | 15,791 00 | 15,791 00 | | | | | | | 19 |
| 20 | | | | | | | | | | 20 |
| 21 | | | | | | | | | | 21 |
| 22 | | | | | | | | | | 22 |
| 23 | | | | | | | | | | 23 |
| 24 | | | | | | | | | | 24 |
| 25 | | | | | | | | | | 25 |

# PREPARING A WORK SHEET

1. Write the heading.

2. Record the trial balance.
   - Write the general ledger account titles in the Account Title column.
   - Write the account balances in either the Trial Balance Debit or Credit column.
   - Rule a single line across the Trial Balance columns.
   - Add the Trial Balance columns and compare the totals.
   - Rule double lines across both Trial Balance columns.
   - *Carefully apply the first overlay.*

3. Record the supplies adjustment.
   - Write the debit amount in the Adjustments Debit column on the line with the account title Supplies Expense.
   - Write the credit amount in the Adjustments Credit column on the line with the account title Supplies.
   - Label this adjustment *(a)*.

4. Record the prepaid insurance adjustment.
   - Write the debit amount in the Adjustments Debit column on the line with the account title Insurance Expense.
   - Write the credit amount in the Adjustments Credit column on the line with the account title Prepaid Insurance.
   - Label this adjustment *(b)*.

5. Prove the Adjustments columns.
   - Rule a single line across the Adjustments columns.
   - Add the Adjustments columns and compare the totals to ensure that they are equal.
   - Write the proving totals below the single line.
   - Rule double lines across both Adjustments columns.
   - *Carefully apply the second overlay.*

6. Extend all balance sheet account balances.
   - Extend the up-to-date asset account balances to the Balance Sheet Debit column.
   - Extend the up-to-date liability account balances to the Balance Sheet Credit column.
   - Extend the owner's capital and drawing account balances to the Balance Sheet columns.

7. Extend all income statement account balances.
   - Extend the up-to-date revenue account balance to the Income Statement Credit column.
   - Extend the up-to-date expense account balances to the Income Statement Debit column.
   - *Carefully apply the third overlay.*

8. Calculate and record the net income (or net loss).
   - Rule a single line across the Income Statement and Balance Sheet columns.
   - Add the columns and write the totals below the single line.
   - Calculate the net income or net loss amount.
   - Write the amount of net income (or net loss) below the smaller of the two Income Statement column totals. Write the words *Net Income* or *Net Loss* in the Account Title column.
   - Extend the amount of net income (or net loss) to the Balance Sheet columns. Write the amount under the smaller of the two column totals. Write the amount on the same line as the words *Net Income* (or *Net Loss*).

9. Total and rule the Income Statement and Balance Sheet columns.
   - Rule a single line across the Income Statement and Balance Sheet columns immediately below the net income (or net loss) amounts.
   - Add the net income (or net loss) to the previous column totals. Compare the column totals to ensure that totals for each pair of columns are in balance.
   - Write the proving totals for each column below the single line.
   - Rule double lines across the Income Statement and Balance Sheet columns immediately below the proving totals.

## Legal Issues in Accounting

### Malpractice Liability of Accountants

Accountants are subject to the legal consequences of malpractice. They can be held financially liable for misconduct or improper practice in their profession.

Most lawsuits against public accountants involve audits of financial statements. Consider the following example. Best & Farrish, CPAs, audited the financial statements of Richmond, Inc. Relying on these statements, American Bank loaned $1,000,000 to Richmond. Unknown to the accountants, however, Richmond's president was involved in a scheme to steal cash. Richmond experienced financial difficulties and was unable to repay the loan to American Bank. The bank sued Best & Farrish for $1,000,000, claiming it was negligent for not detecting the president's fraud.

Should Best & Farrish be required to pay $1,000,000 to American Bank? Over many years the courts have established four guidelines for determining whether accountants are liable for the financial losses of third parties.

1. *Financial loss.* Did the third party incur a financial loss? Answering this question is typically an easy task. American Bank lost $1,000,000 when Richmond did not repay its loan.
2. *Reliance on financial statements.* Did the third party actually rely on the financial statements for making its decision? Accountants should not be held liable unless the third party used the financial statements in making its decision. If American Bank received a copy of the financial statements but relied solely on other information obtained from Richmond's managers, then Best & Farrish should not be held liable for American Bank's loss.
3. *Level of negligence.* Accountants who fail to exhibit a reasonable level of care are guilty of ordinary negligence. Gross negligence occurs when an accountant's actions represent a flagrant violation of professional standards.

   Professional standards recognize that accountants are not able to detect all frauds. Whether Best & Farrish were negligent in not detecting the president's fraud would depend on the facts of the case.
4. *Accountant-third party relationship.* Accountants have a contract with their clients; a client can sue the accountant for breach of contract. However, third parties do not have a contract with the accountant. Whether a third party can sue the accountant depends on whether the accountant specifically knew the third party intended to use the financial statements.

   If Best & Farrish knew American Bank would use the audited financial statements to grant a loan, then American Bank could sue Best & Farrish for ordinary negligence. However, if Best & Farrish did not know Richmond even intended to obtain a bank loan, then gross negligence or fraud would need to be proven for American Bank to win its case.

Accountants must take great care in performing their professional services. Accountants who can prove the audit was performed in accordance with professional accounting standards will prevail against negligence lawsuits.

## SUPPLIES ADJUSTMENT ON A WORK SHEET

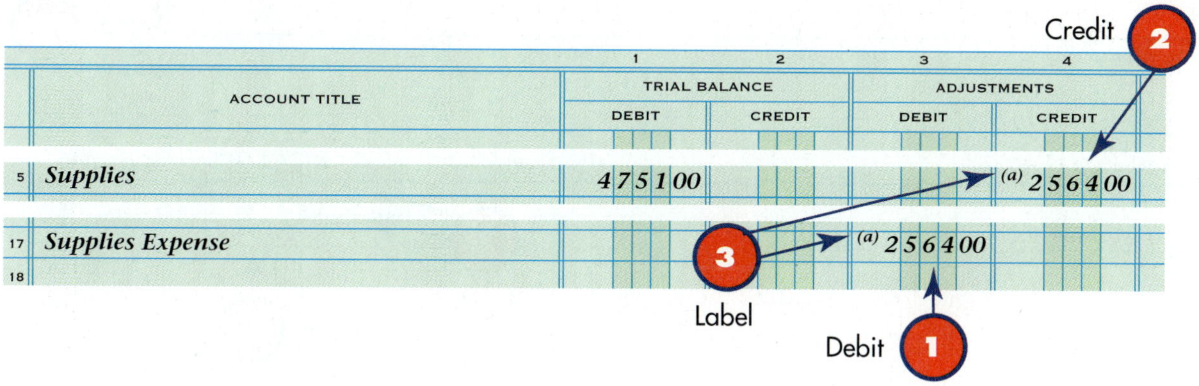


On August 31, before adjustments, the balance of Supplies is $4,751.00, and the balance of Supplies Expense is zero, as shown in the T accounts.

**BEFORE ADJUSTMENT**

Supplies Expense

| | |
|---|---|
| | |

Supplies

| | |
|---|---|
| Aug. 31 Bal. 4,751.00 | |

On August 31, Ms. Treviño counted the supplies on hand and found that the value of supplies still unused on that date was $2,187.00. The value of the supplies used is calculated as follows.

| Supplies Account Balance, August 31 | – | Supplies on Hand, August 31 | = | Supplies Used During August |
|---|---|---|---|---|
| $4,751.00 | – | $2,187.00 | = | $2,564.00 |

Four questions are asked in analyzing the adjustment for the asset account, Supplies.

1. **What is the balance of** Supplies**?** *$4,751.00*
2. **What should the balance be for this account?** *$2,187.00*
3. **What must be done to correct the account balance?** *Decrease $2,564.00*
4. **What adjustment is made?**
   *Debit* Supplies Expense, *$2,564.00*
   *Credit* Supplies, *$2,564.00*

The expense account, Supplies Expense, is increased by a debit, $2,564.00, the value of supplies used. The balance of Supplies Expense, $2,564.00, is the value of supplies used during the fiscal period from August 1 to August 31. *(CONCEPT: Matching Expenses with Revenue)*

**AFTER ADJUSTMENT**

Supplies Expense

| | |
|---|---|
| Adj. (a) 2,564.00 | |

Supplies

| | |
|---|---|
| Aug. 31 Bal. 4,751.00<br>*(New Bal. 2,187.00)* | Adj. (a) 2,564.00 |

The asset account, Supplies, is decreased by a credit, $2,564.00, the value of supplies used. The debit balance, $4,751.00, *less* the credit adjustment, $2,564.00, *equals* the new balance, $2,187.00. The new balance of Supplies is the same as the value of supplies on hand on August 31.

### STEPS: Recording the supplies adjustment on a work sheet

1. Write the debit amount, *$2,564.00,* in the work sheet's Adjustments Debit column on the line with the account title Supplies Expense.
2. Write the credit amount, *$2,564.00,* in the Adjustments Credit column on the line with the account title Supplies.
3. Label the two parts of this adjustment with a small letter *a* in parentheses, *(a)*. The letter *a* identifies the debit and credit amounts as part of the same adjustment.

# PREPAID INSURANCE ADJUSTMENT ON A WORK SHEET

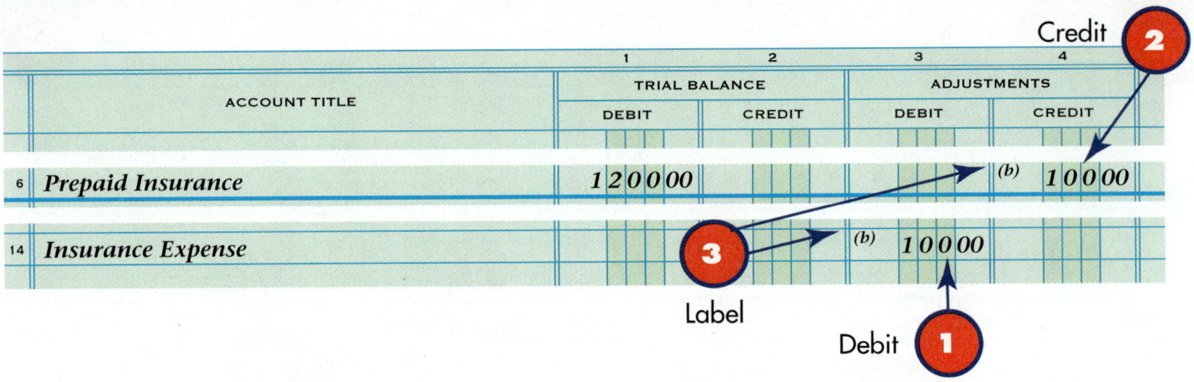


On August 31, before adjustments, the balance of Prepaid Insurance is $1,200.00 and the balance of Insurance Expense is zero.

**BEFORE ADJUSTMENT**

Insurance Expense

| | |
|---|---|
| | |

Prepaid Insurance

| | |
|---|---|
| Aug. 31 Bal. 1,200.00 | |

On August 31, Ms. Treviño checked the insurance records and found that the value of insurance coverage remaining was $1,100.00. The value of the insurance coverage used during the fiscal period is calculated as follows.

| Prepaid Insurance Balance, August 31 | – | Insurance Coverage Remaining Unused, August 31 | = | Insurance Coverage Used During August |
|---|---|---|---|---|
| $1,200.00 | – | $1,100.00 | = | $100.00 |

Four questions are asked in analyzing the adjustment for the asset account, Prepaid Insurance.

1. **What is the balance of** Prepaid Insurance? *$1,200.00*
2. **What should the balance be for this account?** *$1,100.00*
3. **What must be done to correct the account balance?** *Decrease $100.00*
4. **What adjustment is made?**
   *Debit* Insurance Expense, *$100.00*
   *Credit* Prepaid Insurance, *$100.00*

The expense account, Insurance Expense, is increased by a debit, $100.00, the value of insurance used. The balance of Insurance Expense, $100.00, is the value of insurance coverage used from August 1 to August 31. *(CONCEPT: Matching Expenses with Revenue)*

**AFTER ADJUSTMENT**

Insurance Expense

| | |
|---|---|
| Adj. (b) 100.00 | |

Prepaid Insurance

| | |
|---|---|
| Aug. 31 Bal. 1,200.00 | Adj. (b) 100.00 |
| *(New Bal. 1,100.00)* | |

The asset account, Prepaid Insurance, is decreased by a credit, $100.00, the value of insurance used. The debit balance, $1,200.00, *less* the credit adjustment, $100.00, *equals* the new balance, $1,100.00. The new balance of Prepaid Insurance is the same as the amount of insurance coverage unused on August 31.

**STEPS**

### Recording the prepaid insurance adjustment on a work sheet

1. Write the debit amount, *$100.00,* in the work sheet's Adjustments Debit column on the line with the account title Insurance Expense.
2. Write the credit amount, *$100.00,* in the Adjustments Credit column on the line with the account title Prepaid Insurance.
3. Label the two parts of this adjustment with a small letter *b* in parentheses, *(b).* The letter *b* identifies the debit and credit amounts as part of the same adjustment.

## PROVING THE ADJUSTMENTS COLUMNS OF A WORK SHEET

*Encore Music*
*Work Sheet*
*For Month Ended August 31, 20--*

| | ACCOUNT TITLE | 1 TRIAL BALANCE DEBIT | 2 TRIAL BALANCE CREDIT | 3 ADJUSTMENTS DEBIT | 4 ADJUSTMENTS CREDIT |
|---|---|---|---|---|---|
| 5 | *Supplies* | 4,751.00 | | | (a) 2,564.00 |
| 6 | *Prepaid Insurance* | 1,200.00 | | | (b) 100.00 |
| 14 | *Insurance Expense* | | | (b) 100.00 | |
| 15 | *Miscellaneous Expense* | 10.00 | | | |
| 16 | *Rent Expense* | 250.00 | | | |
| 17 | *Supplies Expense* | | | (a) 2,564.00 | |
| 18 | *Utilities Expense* | 115.00 | | | |
| 19 | | 15,791.00 | 15,791.00 | 2,664.00 | 2,664.00 |

1 Single Rule
2 Totals
3 Double Rule

After all adjustments are recorded in a work sheet's Adjustments columns, the equality of debits and credits for the two columns is proved by totaling and ruling the two columns.

### STEPS: Proving the Adjustments columns of a work sheet

1. Rule a single line across the two Adjustments columns on the same line as the single line for the Trial Balance columns.
2. Add both the Adjustments Debit and Credit columns. If the two column totals are the same, then debits equal credits for these two columns, and the work sheet's Adjustments columns are in balance. Write each column's total below the single line. If the two Adjustments column totals are not the same, the Adjustments columns are rechecked and errors corrected before completing the work sheet.
3. Rule double lines across both Adjustments columns. The double lines mean that the totals have been verified as correct.

### GLOBAL PERSPECTIVE

#### INTERNATIONAL WEIGHTS AND MEASURES

The primary system of measurement in the United States is the *customary system.* Among the units of measurement in the customary system are inches, feet, and quarts. The United States is one of the few major industrial countries that does not use the *metric system* exclusively. Among the units of measurement in the metric system are centimeters, meters, and liters. The metric system is based on a decimal system—like our currency. Some U.S. industries have converted to the metric system. Others specify measurements in both customary and metric systems.

To conduct international business, the U.S. has recognized the need to convert customary units to the metric system. For example, beverages are routinely packaged in liter containers. Automobile mechanics frequently need two sets of socket wrenches—one in the customary system and an additional set in the metric system. Although the U.S. is a global business leader, it has had to adjust to meet the needs of the rest of the world.

## TERMS REVIEW

adjustments

## AUDIT YOUR UNDERSTANDING

1. Explain how the concept of Matching Expenses with Revenue relates to adjustments.
2. List the four questions asked in analyzing an adjustment on a work sheet.

## WORK TOGETHER

**Planning adjustments on a work sheet**

Use the work sheet from Work Together on page 158. Your instructor will guide you through the following examples.

3. Analyze the following adjustment information into debit and credit parts. Record the adjustments on the work sheet.

| Adjustment Information, February 28 | |
|---|---|
| Supplies on hand | $325.00 |
| Value of prepaid insurance | 500.00 |

4. Total and rule the Adjustments columns. Save your work sheet to complete Work Together on page 169.

## ON YOUR OWN

**Planning adjustments on a work sheet**

Use the work sheet from On Your Own on page 159. Work these problems independently.

5. Analyze the following adjustment information into debit and credit parts. Record the adjustments on the work sheet.

| Adjustment Information, December 31 | |
|---|---|
| Supplies on hand | $130.00 |
| Value of prepaid insurance | 250.00 |

6. Total and rule the Adjustments columns. Save your work sheet to complete On Your Own on page 169.

# 7-3 Extending Financial Statement Information on a Work Sheet

## EXTENDING BALANCE SHEET ACCOUNT BALANCES ON A WORK SHEET

*Encore Music*
*Work Sheet*
*For Month Ended August 31, 20--*

| | | 1 | 2 | 3 | 4 | 5 | 6 | 7 | 8 | |
|---|---|---|---|---|---|---|---|---|---|---|
| | ACCOUNT TITLE | TRIAL BALANCE | | ADJUSTMENTS | | INCOME STATEMENT | | BALANCE SHEET | | |
| | | DEBIT | CREDIT | DEBIT | CREDIT | DEBIT | CREDIT | DEBIT | CREDIT | |
| 1 | *Cash* | 8272 00 | | | | | | 8272 00 | | 1 |
| 2 | *Petty Cash* | 200 00 | | | | | | 200 00 | | 2 |
| 3 | *Accts. Rec.—Kids Time* | 100 00 | | | | | | 100 00 | | 3 |
| 4 | *Accts. Rec.—Learn N Play* | 20 00 | | | | | | 20 00 | | 4 |
| 5 | *Supplies* | 4751 00 | | | (a) 2564 00 | | | 2187 00 | | 5 |
| 6 | *Prepaid Insurance* | 1200 00 | | | (b) 100 00 | | | 1100 00 | | 6 |
| 7 | *Accts. Pay.—Ling Music Sup.* | | 1360 00 | | | | | | 1360 00 | 7 |
| 8 | *Accts. Pay.—Sullivan Off. Sup.* | | 20 00 | | | | | | 20 00 | 8 |
| 9 | *Barbara Treviño, Capital* | | 10000 00 | | | | | | 10000 00 | 9 |
| 10 | *Barbara Treviño, Drawing* | 600 00 | | | | | | 600 00 | | 10 |

1 Debit Balances without Adjustments

2 Debit Balances with Adjustments

3 Credit Balances without Adjustments

At the end of each fiscal period, Encore Music prepares two financial statements from information on a work sheet. *(CONCEPT: Accounting Period Cycle)* The up-to-date account balances on a work sheet are extended to columns for the two financial statements.

A financial statement that reports assets, liabilities, and owner's equity on a specific date is known as a balance sheet. The balance sheet accounts are the asset, liability, and owner's equity accounts. Up-to-date balance sheet account balances are extended to the Balance Sheet Debit and Credit columns of the work sheet.

### STEPS Extending balance sheet account balances on a work sheet

1. Extend the balance of Cash, *$8,272.00,* to the Balance Sheet Debit column. The balance of Cash in the Trial Balance Debit column is up to date because no adjustment affects this account. Extend to the Balance Sheet Debit column the balances of all accounts with debit balances, which are not affected by adjustments.
2. Calculate the up-to-date adjusted balance of Supplies. The balance of Supplies in the Trial Balance Debit column is not up to date because it is affected by an adjustment. The debit balance, $4,751.00, *minus* the credit adjustment, $2,564.00, *equals* the up-to-date adjusted balance, $2,187.00. Extend the up-to-date balance, *$2,187.00,* to the Balance Sheet Debit column. Using the same procedure, calculate and extend the up-to-date adjusted balance of the other asset account affected by an adjustment, Prepaid Insurance.
3. Extend the up-to-date balance of Accounts Payable—Ling Music Supplies, *$1,360.00,* to the Balance Sheet Credit column. The balance of Accounts Payable—Ling Music Supplies in the Trial Balance Credit column is up to date because no adjustment affects this account. Extend to the Balance Sheet Credit column the balances of all accounts with credit balances, which are not affected by adjustments.

# EXTENDING INCOME STATEMENT ACCOUNT BALANCES ON A WORK SHEET

Expense Balances without Adjustments **2**

**1** Sales Balance

*Encore Music*
*Work Sheet*
*For Month Ended August 31, 20--*

| | ACCOUNT TITLE | 1<br>TRIAL BALANCE<br>DEBIT | 2<br>TRIAL BALANCE<br>CREDIT | 3<br>ADJUSTMENTS<br>DEBIT | 4<br>ADJUSTMENTS<br>CREDIT | 5<br>INCOME STATEMENT<br>DEBIT | 6<br>INCOME STATEMENT<br>CREDIT | 7<br>BALANCE SHEET<br>DEBIT | 8<br>BALANCE SHEET<br>CREDIT | |
|---|---|---|---|---|---|---|---|---|---|---|
| 11 | *Income Summary* | | | | | | | | | 11 |
| 12 | *Sales* | | 4411 00 | | | | 4411 00 | | | 12 |
| 13 | *Advertising Expense* | 273 00 | | | | 273 00 | | | | 13 |
| 14 | *Insurance Expense* | | | (b) 100 00 | | 100 00 | | | | 14 |
| 15 | *Miscellaneous Expense* | 10 00 | | | | 10 00 | | | | 15 |
| 16 | *Rent Expense* | 250 00 | | | | 250 00 | | | | 16 |
| 17 | *Supplies Expense* | | | (a) 2564 00 | | 2564 00 | | | | 17 |
| 18 | *Utilities Expense* | 115 00 | | | | 115 00 | | | | 18 |
| 19 | | 15791 00 | 15791 00 | 2664 00 | 2664 00 | | | | | 19 |
| 20 | | | | | | | | | | 20 |

Expense Balances with Adjustments **3**

A financial statement showing the revenue and expenses for a fiscal period is called an **income statement.** Encore Music's income statement accounts are the revenue and expense accounts. Up-to-date income statement account balances are extended to the Income Statement Debit and Credit columns of the work sheet.

**FYI**

*Use a ruler when extending amounts on a work sheet to keep track of the line you are on.*

**STEPS**

## Extending income statement account balances on a work sheet

1. Extend the balance of Sales, *$4,411.00,* to the Income Statement Credit column. The balance of Sales in the Trial Balance Credit column is up to date because no adjustment affects this account.
2. Extend the balance of Advertising Expense, *$273.00,* to the Income Statement Debit column. The balance of Advertising Expense is up to date because no adjustment affects this account. Extend the balances of all expense accounts not affected by adjustments to the Income Statement Debit column.
3. Calculate the up-to-date adjusted balance of Insurance Expense. The balance of Insurance Expense in the Trial Balance Debit column is zero. This zero balance is not up to date because this account is affected by an adjustment. The debit balance, $0.00, *plus* the debit adjustment, $100.00, *equals* the adjusted balance, $100.00. Extend the up-to-date adjusted debit balance, *$100.00,* to the Income Statement Debit column. Using the same procedure, calculate and extend the up-to-date adjusted balance of each expense account affected by an adjustment.

**FYI**

*A work sheet is prepared in manual accounting to adjust the accounts and sort amounts needed to prepare financial statements. However, in automated accounting, adjustments are prepared from the trial balance and the software automatically generates the financial statements with no need for a work sheet.*

## RECORDING NET INCOME, AND TOTALING AND RULING A WORK SHEET

**Encore Music**
**Work Sheet**
**For Month Ended August 31, 20--**

| | ACCOUNT TITLE | 1 TRIAL BALANCE DEBIT | 2 TRIAL BALANCE CREDIT | 3 ADJUSTMENTS DEBIT | 4 ADJUSTMENTS CREDIT | 5 INCOME STATEMENT DEBIT | 6 INCOME STATEMENT CREDIT | 7 BALANCE SHEET DEBIT | 8 BALANCE SHEET CREDIT | |
|---|---|---|---|---|---|---|---|---|---|---|
| 1 | Cash | 8272 00 | | | | | | 8272 00 | | 1 |
| 2 | Petty Cash | 200 00 | | | | | | 200 00 | | 2 |
| 3 | Accts. Rec.—Kids Time | 100 00 | | | | | | 100 00 | | 3 |
| 4 | Accts. Rec.—Learn N Play | 20 00 | | | | | | 20 00 | | 4 |
| 5 | Supplies | 4751 00 | | | (a) 2564 00 | | | 2187 00 | | 5 |
| 6 | Prepaid Insurance | 1200 00 | | | (b) 100 00 | | | 1100 00 | | 6 |
| 7 | Accts. Pay.—Ling Music Sup. | | 1360 00 | | | | | | 1360 00 | 7 |
| 8 | Accts. Pay.—Sullivan Off. Sup. | | 20 00 | | | | | | 20 00 | 8 |
| 9 | Barbara Treviño, Capital | | 10000 00 | | | | | | 10000 00 | 9 |
| 10 | Barbara Treviño, Drawing | 600 00 | | | | | | 600 00 | | 10 |
| 11 | Income Summary | | | | | | | | | 11 |
| 12 | Sales | | 4411 00 | | | | 4411 00 | | | 12 |
| 13 | Advertising Expense | 273 00 | | | | 273 00 | | | | 13 |
| 14 | Insurance Expense | | | (b) 100 00 | | 100 00 | | | | 14 |
| 15 | Miscellaneous Expense | 10 00 | | | | 10 00 | | | | 15 |
| 16 | Rent Expense | 250 00 | | | | 250 00 | | | | 16 |
| 17 | Supplies Expense | | | (a) 2564 00 | | 2564 00 | | | | 17 |
| 18 | Utilities Expense | 115 00 | | | | 115 00 | | | | 18 |
| 19 | | 15791 00 | 15791 00 | 2664 00 | 2664 00 | 3312 00 | 4411 00 | 12479 00 | 11380 00 | |
| 20 | Net Income | | | | | 1099 00 | | | 1099 00 | 20 |
| 21 | | | | | | 4411 00 | 4411 00 | 12479 00 | 12479 00 | |

1 Single Rule
2 Totals
3 Net Income
4 Extend Net Income
5 Single Rule
6 Totals
7 Double Rule

The difference between total revenue and total expenses when total revenue is greater is called **net income.** Before the work sheet is complete, net income must be calculated and the work sheet must be totaled and ruled. A summary of preparing a work sheet is shown on the Work Sheet Overlay.

### STEPS: Calculating and recording net income on a work sheet; totaling and ruling a work sheet

1. Rule a single line across the four Income Statement and Balance Sheet columns.
2. Add both the Income Statement and Balance Sheet columns. Write the totals below the single line.
3. Calculate the net income. The Income Statement Credit column total, $4,411.00, *minus* the Income Statement Debit column total, $3,312.00, *equals* net income, $1,099.00. Write the amount of net income, *$1,099.00,* below the Income Statement Debit column total. Write the words *Net Income* on the same line in the Account Title column.
4. Extend the amount of net income, *$1,099.00,* to the Balance Sheet Credit column on the same line as the words *Net Income.* The owner's equity account, Barbara Treviño, Capital, is increased by a credit. Therefore, the net income amount is extended to the Balance Sheet Credit column.
5. Rule a single line across the four Income Statement and Balance Sheet columns just below the net income amounts.
6. Add the subtotal and net income amount for each column to get proving totals for the Income Statement and Balance Sheet columns. Write the proving totals below the single line. Check the equality of the proving totals for each pair of columns.
7. Rule double lines across the Income Statement and Balance Sheet columns. The double lines mean that the totals have been verified as correct.

## CALCULATING AND RECORDING A NET LOSS ON A WORK SHEET

| | Account Title | 5 Income Statement Debit | 6 Income Statement Credit | 7 Balance Sheet Debit | 8 Balance Sheet Credit |
|---|---|---|---|---|---|
| 19 | | 2 200 00 | 1 800 00 | 5 100 00 | 5 500 00 |
| 20 | *Net Loss* | | 400 00 | 400 00 | |
| 21 | | 2 200 00 | 2 200 00 | 5 500 00 | 5 500 00 |
| 22 | | | | | |
| 23 | | | | | |

1 Single Rule; 2 Totals; 3 Net Loss; 4 Extend Net Loss

Encore Music's completed work sheet shows a net income. However, a business might have a net loss to report. The difference between total revenue and total expenses when total expenses is greater is called a **net loss.**

### S T E P S Calculating and recording a net loss on a work sheet

1. Rule a single line across the four Income Statement and Balance Sheet columns.
2. Add both the Income Statement and Balance Sheet columns. Write the totals below the single line.
3. Calculate the net loss. The Income Statement Debit column total, $2,200.00, *minus* the Income Statement Credit column total, $1,800.00, *equals* net loss, $400.00. The Income Statement Debit column total (expenses) is greater than the Income Statement Credit column total (revenue). Therefore, because expenses exceed revenue, there is a net loss. Write the amount of net loss, *$400.00,* below the Income Statement Credit column total. Write the words *Net Loss* on the same line in the Account Title column.
4. Extend the amount of net loss, *$400.00,* to the Balance Sheet Debit column on the same line as the words *Net Loss.* The owner's equity account, Barbara Treviño, Capital, is decreased by a debit. Therefore, a net loss is extended to the Balance Sheet Debit column.

## ACCOUNTING AT WORK

### DARYL STANTON

Daryl Stanton works for John Hancock Mutual Life Insurance Company as a Senior Financial Accountant and highly recommends accounting as a field full of opportunities for those who are dedicated to their work.

Daryl studied accounting in high school and later graduated from Suffolk University with a BSBA, majoring in accounting. At Suffolk, Daryl participated in an internship program, during which he interned at John Hancock. Each year he had a different set of responsibilities. This internship confirmed for Daryl that accounting was the career he wanted.

Daryl highly recommends seeking out an internship program in accounting. He says that it is the best way to discover what working in the accounting field is really like and whether you want to pursue it as a career. An internship program can also help you get your foot in the door of a particular company. In addition to acquiring accounting knowledge and skills, Daryl believes in the importance of developing strong communication skills so you can present yourself and your ideas well.

## TERMS REVIEW

income statement

net income

net loss

## AUDIT YOUR UNDERSTANDING

1. Which accounts are extended into the Balance Sheet columns of the work sheet?
2. Which accounts are extended into the Income Statement columns of the work sheet?
3. In which Balance Sheet column do you record net income on the work sheet?
4. In which Balance Sheet column do you record net loss on the work sheet?

## WORK TOGETHER

**Completing a work sheet**

Use the work sheet from Work Together on page 164. Your instructor will guide you through the following examples.

5. Extend the up-to-date balances to the Balance Sheet and Income Statement columns.
6. Rule a single line across the Income Statement and Balance Sheet columns. Total each column. Calculate and record the net income or net loss. Label the amount in the Account Title column.
7. Total and rule the Income Statement and Balance Sheet columns.

## ON YOUR OWN

**Completing a work sheet**

Use the work sheet from On Your Own on page 164. Work these problems independently.

8. Extend the up-to-date balances to the Balance Sheet or Income Statement columns.
9. Rule a single line across the Income Statement and Balance Sheet columns. Total each column. Calculate and record the net income or net loss. Label the amount in the Account Title column.
10. Total and rule the Income Statement and Balance Sheet columns.

# 7-4 Finding and Correcting Errors on the Work Sheet

## CORRECTING ACCOUNTING ERRORS ON THE WORK SHEET

Some errors in accounting records are not discovered until a work sheet is prepared. For example, a debit to Supplies may not have been posted from a journal to the general ledger supplies account. The omission may not be discovered until the work sheet's trial balance does not balance. Also, information may be transferred incorrectly from general ledger accounts to the work sheet's trial balance. Additional errors may be made, such as recording adjustment information incorrectly or adding columns incorrectly. In addition, errors may be made in extending amounts to the Income Statement and Balance Sheet columns.

Any errors found on a work sheet must be corrected before any further work is completed. If an incorrect amount is found on a work sheet, erase the error and replace it with the correct amount. If an amount is written in an incorrect column, erase the amount and record it in the correct column.

## CHECKING FOR TYPICAL CALCULATION ERRORS

When two column totals are not in balance, subtract the smaller total from the larger total to find the difference. Check the difference between the two amounts against the following guides.

1. **The difference is 1, such as $.01, $.10, $1.00, or $10.00.** For example, if the totals of the two columns are Debit, $14,657.00, and Credit, $14,658.00, the difference between the two columns is $1.00. The error is most likely in addition. Add the columns again.
2. **The difference can be divided evenly by 2.** For example, the difference between two column totals is $48.00, which can be divided by 2 with no remainder. Look for a $24.00 amount in the Trial Balance columns of the work sheet. If the amount is found, check to make sure it has been recorded in the correct Debit or Credit column. A $24.00 debit amount recorded in a credit column results in a difference between column totals of $48.00. If the error is not found on the work sheet, check the general ledger accounts and journal entries. An entry for $24.00 may have been recorded in an incorrect column in the journal or in an account.
3. **The difference can be divided evenly by 9.** For example, the difference between two columns is $45.00, which can be divided by 9 with no remainder. When the difference can be divided equally by 9, look for transposed numbers such as 54 written as 45 or 19 written as 91. Also, check for a "slide." A "slide" occurs when numbers are moved to the right or left in an amount column. For example, $12.00 is recorded as $120.00 or $350.00 is recorded as $35.00.
4. **The difference is an omitted amount.** Look for an amount equal to the difference. If the difference is $50.00, look for an account balance of $50.00 that has not been extended. Look for any $50.00 amount on the work sheet and determine if it has been handled correctly. Look in the accounts and journals for a $50.00 amount, and check if that amount has been handled correctly. Failure to record a $50.00 account balance will make a work sheet's column totals differ by $50.00.

## CHECKING FOR ERRORS IN THE WORK SHEET

### Check for Errors in the Trial Balance Column

1. Have all general ledger account balances been copied in the Trial Balance column correctly?
2. Have all general ledger account balances been recorded in the correct Trial Balance column?

### Check for Errors in the Adjustments Columns

1. Do the debits equal the credits for each adjustment? Use the small letters that label each part of an adjustment to help check accuracy and equality of debits and credits.
2. Is the amount for each adjustment correct?

### Check for Errors in the Income Statement and Balance Sheet Columns

1. Has each amount been copied correctly when extended to the Income Statement or Balance Sheet column?
2. Has each account balance been extended to the correct Income Statement or Balance Sheet column?
3. Has the net income or net loss been calculated correctly?
4. Has the net income or net loss been recorded in the correct Income Statement or Balance Sheet column?

For all three of these cases, correct any errors found and add the columns again.

## CORRECTING AN ERROR IN POSTING TO THE WRONG ACCOUNT

ACCOUNT *Supplies* ACCOUNT NO. *130*

| DATE | | ITEM | POST. REF. | DEBIT | CREDIT | BALANCE DEBIT | BALANCE CREDIT |
|---|---|---|---|---|---|---|---|
| 20-- Feb. | 1 | | 1 | 400 00 | | 400 00 | |
| | 25 | | 2 | 90 00 | | 490 00 | |
| | 12 | | 1 | 50 00 | | 540 00 | |

Correct Entry 2

ACCOUNT *Prepaid Insurance* ACCOUNT NO. *140*

| DATE | | ITEM | POST. REF. | DEBIT | CREDIT | BALANCE DEBIT | BALANCE CREDIT |
|---|---|---|---|---|---|---|---|
| 20-- Feb. | 9 | | 1 | 600 00 | | 600 00 | |
| | ~~12~~ | | ~~1~~ | ~~50 00~~ | | ~~650 00~~ | |

Incorrect Entry 1

If a pair of work sheet columns do not balance and an error cannot be found on the work sheet, look for an error in posting from the journal to the general ledger accounts.

As each item in an account or a journal entry is verified, a check mark should be placed next to it. The check mark indicates that the item has been checked for accuracy.

1. Have all amounts that need to be posted actually been posted from the journal? To correct, complete the posting to the correct account. When posting is corrected, recalculate the account balance and correct it on the work sheet.
2. Have all amounts been posted to the correct accounts? To correct, follow these steps.

### STEPS: Correcting an error in posting to the wrong account

1. Draw a line through the entire incorrect entry. Recalculate the account balance and correct the work sheet.
2. Record the posting in the correct account. Recalculate the account balance, and correct the work sheet.

## CORRECTING AN INCORRECT AMOUNT AND AN AMOUNT POSTED TO THE WRONG COLUMN

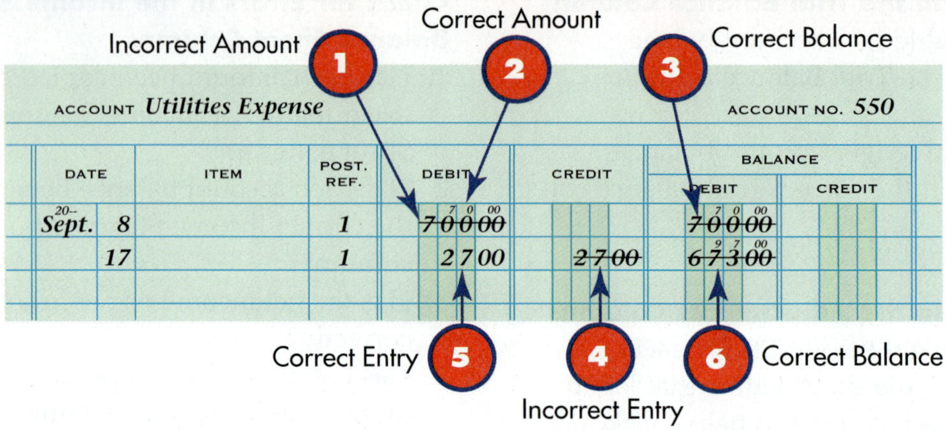


Errors may be made in writing amounts in general ledger accounts. Errors in permanent records should *never* be erased. Erasures in permanent records raise questions about whether important financial information has been altered.

**STEPS**

**Correcting an incorrect amount**

1. Draw a line through the incorrect amount.
2. Write the correct amount just above the correction in the same space.
3. Recalculate the account balance, and correct the account balance on the work sheet.

**Correcting an amount posted to the wrong column**

4. Draw a line through the incorrect item in the account.
5. Record the posting in the correct amount column.
6. Recalculate the account balance, and correct the work sheet.

## CHECKING FOR ERRORS IN JOURNAL ENTRIES

1. Do debits equal credits in each journal entry?
2. Is each journal entry amount recorded in the correct journal column?
3. Is information in the Account Title column correct for each journal entry?
4. Are all of the journal amount column totals correct?
5. Does the sum of debit column totals equal the sum of credit column totals in the journal?
6. Have all transactions been recorded?

Some suggestions for correcting errors in journal entries are described in Chapter 4.

## PREVENTING ERRORS

The best way to prevent errors is to work carefully. Check the work at each step in an accounting procedure. Most errors occur in doing arithmetic, especially in adding columns. When possible, use a calculator. When an error is discovered, do no more work until the cause of the error is found and corrections are made.

## AUDIT YOUR UNDERSTANDING

1. What is the first step in checking for arithmetic errors when two column totals are not in balance?
2. What is one way to check for an error caused by transposed numbers?
3. What term is used to describe an error that occurs when numbers are moved to the right or left in an amount column?

## WORK TOGETHER

**Finding and correcting errors in accounting records**

Paul Coty has completed the September monthly work sheet for his business, LeafyLift. The work sheet and general ledger accounts are given in the *Working Papers.* Mr. Coty believes that he has made one or more errors in preparing the work sheet. He asks you to help him verify the work sheet. Your instructor will guide you through the following examples.

4. Examine the work sheet and the general ledger accounts. Make a list of the errors you find.
5. Correct any errors you find in the general ledger accounts.
6. Prepare a corrected work sheet.

## ON YOUR OWN

**Finding and correcting errors in accounting records**

Marlene Lewis has completed the November monthly work sheet for her business, Internet Access. The work sheet and general ledger accounts are given in the *Working Papers.* Ms. Lewis believes that she has made one or more errors in preparing the work sheet. She asks you to help her verify the work sheet. Work these problems independently.

7. Examine the work sheet and the general ledger accounts. Make a list of the errors you find.
8. Correct any errors you find in the general ledger accounts.
9. Prepare a corrected work sheet.

# CHAPTER 7 SUMMARY

*Enrichment Activity*

**Time Management**

*Many people manage their time by creating a to-do list for each day. The to-do list shows everything that must be done in that day, both in work or school and personal activities. As tasks are completed, they are checked off as complete. Tasks left undone are transferred to the next day's to-do list. Create a to-do list of your activities for tomorrow.*

After completing this chapter, you can

1. Define important accounting terms related to a work sheet for a service business organized as a proprietorship.
2. Identify accounting concepts and practices related to a work sheet for a service business organized as a proprietorship.
3. Prepare a heading and a trial balance on a work sheet.
4. Plan adjustments for supplies and prepaid insurance.
5. Complete a work sheet for a service business organized as a proprietorship.
6. Identify selected procedures for finding and correcting errors in accounting records.

## EXPLORE ACCOUNTING

### FISCAL PERIODS

A fiscal period is the length of time for which a business summarizes and reports financial information. Since many companies are required to publish yearly annual reports, these companies choose a year for the fiscal period. In such a case, a company will prepare financial statements every year.

A fiscal year can be any consecutive 12-month period. The Internal Revenue Service (IRS) requires many companies to report taxable income for the fiscal year January 1 through December 31. A fiscal year beginning January 1 can also be called a *calendar year.* Because they use a calendar year for reporting taxable income, many companies choose to use the calendar year for issuing financial statements also.

However, there is no requirement to begin a fiscal year on January 1. Companies often choose a fiscal year that ends during a period of low business activity. Twelve consecutive months which end when business activities have reached the lowest point in their annual cycle are called a *natural business year.*

The following survey conducted on 600 businesses shows the number of companies that chose a fiscal year ending at the end of a specific month.

| Fiscal Year End | No. of Companies |
|---|---|
| January | 23 |
| February | 11 |
| March | 15 |
| April | 8 |
| May | 16 |
| June | 58 |
| July | 14 |
| August | 15 |
| September | 35 |
| October | 23 |
| November | 17 |
| December | 365 |

**Activity:** Assume you work for a company that makes snowmobiles. You must determine what fiscal year should be used. Make a written recommendation to the owner. Explain why your recommendation is preferable.

Source: *Accounting Trends and Techniques,* 1996, published by the American Institute of Certified Public Accountants.

## 7-1 APPLICATION PROBLEM
### Recording the trial balance on a work sheet

Use the work sheet given in the *Working Papers*. On June 30 of the current year, Renville Rental has the following general ledger accounts and balances. The business uses a monthly fiscal period.

| Account Titles | Account Balances | |
|---|---|---|
| | Debit | Credit |
| Cash | $10,610.00 | |
| Petty Cash | 100.00 | |
| Accounts Receivable—Noah Felsen | 805.00 | |
| Supplies | 750.00 | |
| Prepaid Insurance | 800.00 | |
| Accounts Payable—Faith Meltman | | $ 555.00 |
| Rebecca Chin, Capital | | 11,926.00 |
| Rebecca Chin, Drawing | 700.00 | |
| Income Summary | — | — |
| Sales | | 2,220.00 |
| Advertising Expense | 480.00 | |
| Insurance Expense | — | |
| Miscellaneous Expense | 144.00 | |
| Supplies Expense | — | |
| Utilities Expense | 312.00 | |

***Instructions:***

Prepare the heading and trial balance on a work sheet. Total and rule the Trial Balance columns. Save your work to complete Application Problem 7-2.

## 7-2 APPLICATION PROBLEM
### Planning adjustments on a work sheet

Use the work sheet from Application Problem 7-1.

***Instructions:***

1. Analyze the following adjustment information into debit and credit parts. Record the adjustments on the work sheet.

| Adjustment Information, June 30 | |
|---|---|
| Supplies on hand | $600.00 |
| Value of prepaid insurance | 700.00 |

2. Total and rule the Adjustments columns. Save your work to complete Application Problem 7-3.

## 7-3 APPLICATION PROBLEM
### Completing a work sheet

Use the work sheet from Application Problem 7-2.

***Instructions:***

1. Extend the up-to-date balances to the Balance Sheet or Income Statement columns.
2. Rule a single line across the Income Statement and Balance Sheet columns. Total each column. Calculate and record the net income or net loss. Label the amount in the Account Title column.
3. Total and rule the Income Statement and Balance Sheet columns.

## 7-4 APPLICATION PROBLEM

### Finding and correcting errors in accounting records

Ervin Watkins has completed the April monthly work sheet for his business, EverClean. The work sheet and general ledger accounts are given in the *Working Papers.* Mr. Watkins believes that he has made one or more errors in preparing the work sheet. He asks you to help him verify the work sheet.

***Instructions:***

1. Examine the work sheet and the general ledger accounts. Make a list of the errors you find.
2. Correct any errors you find in the general ledger accounts.
3. Prepare a corrected work sheet.

## 7-5 MASTERY PROBLEM

### Completing a work sheet

On April 30 of the current year, EasyGlo has the following general ledger accounts and balances. The business uses a monthly fiscal period. A work sheet is given in the *Working Papers.*

| Account Titles | Account Balances Debit | Account Balances Credit |
|---|---|---|
| Cash | $1,729.00 | |
| Petty Cash | 200.00 | |
| Accounts Receivable—Lois Mabry | 561.00 | |
| Supplies | 895.00 | |
| Prepaid Insurance | 1,000.00 | |
| Accounts Payable—Amery Supplies | | $ 500.00 |
| Natasha Kabila, Capital | | 3,500.00 |
| Natasha Kabila, Drawing | 400.00 | |
| Income Summary | — | — |
| Sales | | 2,300.00 |
| Advertising Expense | 425.00 | |
| Insurance Expense | — | |
| Miscellaneous Expense | 240.00 | |
| Rent Expense | 400.00 | |
| Supplies Expense | — | |
| Utilities Expense | 450.00 | |

***Instructions:***

1. Prepare the heading and trial balance on a work sheet. Total and rule the Trial Balance columns.
2. Analyze the following adjustment information into debit and credit parts. Record the adjustments on the work sheet.

| Adjustment Information, April 30 | |
|---|---|
| Supplies inventory | $200.00 |
| Value of prepaid insurance | 750.00 |

3. Total and rule the Adjustments columns.
4. Extend the up-to-date balances to the Balance Sheet or Income Statement columns.
5. Rule a single line across the Income Statement and Balance Sheet columns. Total each column. Calculate and record the net income or net loss. Label the amount in the Account Title column.
6. Total and rule the Income Statement and Balance Sheet columns.

## 7-6 CHALLENGE PROBLEM
### Completing a work sheet

Green Grass Company had a small fire in its office. The fire destroyed some of the accounting records. On November 30 of the current year, the end of a monthly fiscal period, the following information was constructed from the remaining records and other sources. A work sheet is given in the *Working Papers.*

Remains of the general ledger:

| Account Titles | Account Balances |
|---|---|
| Accounts Receivable—J. Kjeseth | $ 350.00 |
| Supplies | 1,700.00 |
| Donna Arnold, Drawing | 170.00 |
| Sales | 4,200.00 |
| Advertising Expense | 400.00 |
| Rent Expense | 700.00 |
| Utilities Expense | 490.00 |

Information from the business's checkbook:

| | |
|---|---|
| Cash balance on last unused check stub | $3,400.00 |
| Total payments for miscellaneous expense | 60.00 |
| Total payments for insurance | 325.00 |

Information obtained through inquiries to other businesses:

| | |
|---|---|
| Owed to Outdoor Supplies | $1,800.00 |
| Value of prepaid insurance, November 30 | 225.00 |

Information obtained by counting supplies on hand after the fire:

| | |
|---|---|
| Supplies on hand | $1,100.00 |

***Instructions:***

1. From the information given, prepare a heading and reconstruct a trial balance on a work sheet. The owner's capital account balance is the difference between the total of all debit account balances minus the total of all credit account balances.
2. Complete the work sheet.

INTERNET ACTIVITY

Point your browser to

**http://accounting.swpco.com**

Choose **First-Year Course**, choose **Activities**, and complete the activity for Chapter 7.

## Applied Communication

Accounting information is used by managers to make business decisions. But exactly what kind of decisions does the owner of a local business make? How does accounting information enable the manager to make better decisions?

**Instructions:** Identify a local business of personal interest to you. Write five questions you would ask the manager to learn how that person uses accounting information to make decisions. Interview the manager and write a one- or two-page summary of the interview.

## Cases for Critical Thinking

**Case 1** Peter Dowther owns a small business. At the end of a fiscal period, he does not make an adjustment for supplies. Are Mr. Dowther's accounting procedures correct? What effect will Mr. Dowther's procedures have on the business's financial reporting? Explain your answer.

**Case 2** When posting amounts from a journal to general ledger accounts, a $10.00 debit to Supplies is mistakenly posted as a credit to Utilities Expense. Will this error be discovered when the work sheet is prepared? Explain.

**Case 3** Accuracy is of critical importance in accounting. Most employees who are responsible for maintaining accounting records value accuracy and completeness. Accounting employees work very hard to avoid errors and to correct any errors that do get made. Other employees within a business and other people who have contact with a business also value accurate accounting records. Other than accounting employees, who are some of the other people who expect and require accurate accounting records? Why is accounting accuracy important to these people? How tolerant should people be of mistakes? Are a small number of mistakes acceptable? Are mistakes involving small amounts—for example, just a few cents—acceptable? Or should it be expected that accounting records are completely accurate?

# AUTOMATED ACCOUNTING

## MANUAL ACCOUNTING CYCLE VS. AUTOMATED ACCOUNTING CYCLE

The series of accounting activities included in recording financial information for a fiscal period is called an *accounting cycle*. Large businesses prepare financial statements each month and therefore complete the accounting cycle each month. Smaller businesses without a full-time accounting staff may complete the accounting cycle only quarterly, or annually when the year-end tax returns are due. Regardless of the size of the business, the steps in the accounting cycle are generally the same:

1. Source documents are checked for accuracy, and transactions are analyzed into debit and credit parts.
2. Transactions are recorded in a journal.
3. Journal entries are posted to the general ledger, and a trial balance is prepared.
4. Adjusting entries are journalized and posted.
5. Financial statements are prepared.
6. Closing entries are journalized and posted, and a post-closing trial balance is prepared.

### Manual Accounting

In a manual accounting system, all the steps are completed by hand, and a work sheet may be used to summarize information about the adjusting and closing entries and to complete the trial balance. Many of the steps are repetitive and time-consuming, particularly posting and the preparation of the various trial balances. However, all of the steps are important to ensure that accurate financial statements are available to management at the end of each period. Managers use these financial statements to make decisions, and must be able to rely on them.

### Automated Accounting

In automated accounting, the emphasis is on the analysis of the source documents and the preparation of timely and accurate journal entries and adjusting entries. These are the parts of the accounting cycle that require accounting personnel to apply the matching concept to ensure that revenues and expenses are recorded in the proper periods. The automated accounting system is programmed to post journal entries and to prepare trial balances, closing entries, and financial statements as needed. The accounting staff is freed from the more repetitive tasks associated with the accounting cycle and can concentrate on the analysis functions.

Automated accounting software may include additional features to integrate applications within the accounting cycle. Options within the software may aid in the reconciliation of bank accounts and in the processing of accounts payable and accounts receivable. Automated accounting may be used to track inventory and plant assets, and to process sales orders and payroll. Budgeting, graphing, and printing capabilities are also included in automated accounting systems. Advanced accounting systems also have options that allow the user to import or export data to and from spreadsheet and word processing software.

Since control over assets and transactions is one of the most important parts of any accounting system, automated systems include controls such as passwords and audit trails to ensure the integrity of the financial statements. Using the computer as a tool to process accounting data allows accountants and managers to work together to plan, operate, and control the business.

# 8 Financial Statements for a Proprietorship

**AFTER STUDYING CHAPTER 8, YOU WILL BE ABLE TO:**

1. Define an accounting term related to financial statements for a service business organized as a proprietorship.
2. Identify accounting concepts and practices related to preparation of financial statements for a service business organized as a proprietorship.
3. Prepare an income statement for a service business organized as a proprietorship and analyze an income statement using component percentages.
4. Prepare a balance sheet for a service business organized as a proprietorship.

**TERM PREVIEW**

component percentage

## REPORTING FINANCIAL INFORMATION

The financial information needed by managers and owners to make good business decisions can be found in the general ledger accounts. However, the information in the general ledger is very detailed. Therefore, to make this general ledger information more usable, the information is summarized, organized, and reported to the owners and managers.

Also, *all* financial information *must* be reported if good business decisions are to be made. A financial statement with incomplete information is similar to a book with missing pages. The complete story is not told. If a business has both rent and utilities expenses but reports only the rent expense, managers will have incomplete information on which to base decisions. The accounting concept, *Adequate Disclosure,* is applied when financial statements contain all information necessary to understand a business's financial condition. *(CONCEPT: Adequate Disclosure)*

Encore Music prepares two financial statements: an income statement and a balance sheet. Encore Music always prepares financial statements at the end of each monthly fiscal period. *(CONCEPT: Accounting Period Cycle)*

# ACCOUNTING IN YOUR CAREER

## ENHANCING FINANCIAL REPORTING

Tanya Allen works for Marci Stettner, who owns and operates Marci's Delivery Service, a proprietorship. Tanya is the office manager and does most of the clerical work, accounting, and appointment scheduling for the business. At the end of each month, Tanya prepares an income statement and a balance sheet for the business. Marci reviews the statements briefly and then files them away for future reference. In actual practice, Marci rarely looks at the statements again. The company's fiscal year ends on December 31. On December 31, Tanya prepares an income statement for the entire fiscal year, but not one for the month of December.

Tanya has not received much training in the preparation of financial statements. Each month she spends a number of hours keying each statement from scratch and arranging the columns in an attractive layout. Sometimes the appearance of the statements is inconsistent from that of the previous month.

Recently Marci has realized that the business is in trouble. She has been finding it difficult to pay the company's bills and also withdraw sufficient cash for her personal living expenses. Because she doesn't truly understand the financial statements, she spends little time reviewing them.

The company rarely shows more than $500.00 in cash on the balance sheet; total liabilities and owner's equity averages $25,000.00, but the owner's equity is usually around $5,000.00. The income statement rarely shows more than $1,000.00 in net income each month.

**Critical Thinking:**

1. What is your opinion of the financial condition of Marci's Delivery Service?
2. What recommendations would you make to Tanya Allen about her method of preparing the financial statements?

# 8-1 Preparing an Income Statement

## INCOME STATEMENT INFORMATION ON A WORK SHEET

| | ACCOUNT TITLE | 5 INCOME STATEMENT DEBIT | 6 INCOME STATEMENT CREDIT | 7 BALANCE SHEET DEBIT | 8 BALANCE SHEET CREDIT | |
|---|---|---|---|---|---|---|
| 12 | *Sales* | | 4411 00 | | | 12 |
| 13 | *Advertising Expense* | 273 00 | | | | 13 |
| 14 | *Insurance Expense* | 100 00 | | | | 14 |
| 15 | *Miscellaneous Expense* | 10 00 | | | | 15 |
| 16 | *Rent Expense* | 250 00 | | | | 16 |
| 17 | *Supplies Expense* | 2564 00 | | | | 17 |
| 18 | *Utilities Expense* | 115 00 | | | | 18 |
| 19 | | 3312 00 | 4411 00 | | | 19 |
| 20 | *Net Income* | 1099 00 | | | | 20 |
| 21 | | 4411 00 | 4411 00 | | | 21 |
| 22 | | | | | | 22 |

An income statement reports financial information over a *specific period of time,* indicating the financial *progress* of a business in earning a net income or a net loss.

Revenue is the earnings of a business from business activities. Expenses are the amounts a business pays to operate the business and earn the revenue. The revenue earned and the expenses incurred to earn that revenue are reported in the same fiscal period. *(CONCEPT: Matching Expenses with Revenue)*

Information needed to prepare financial statements could be obtained from the general ledger accounts. However, a work sheet is prepared to assist in planning the financial statements.

Information needed to prepare Encore Music's income statement is obtained from two places on the work sheet. Account titles are obtained from the work sheet's Account Title column. Account balances are obtained from the work sheet's Income Statement columns.

The income statement for a service business has four sections: (1) heading, (2) revenue, (3) expenses, and (4) net income or net loss.

## HEADING OF AN INCOME STATEMENT

*Encore Music* (1)
*Income Statement* (2)
*For Month Ended August 31, 20--* (3)

**1.** Name of Company
**2.** Name of Report
**3.** Date of Report

The income statement's date shows that this income statement reports information for the one-month period from August 1 through August 31.

**STEPS: Preparing the heading of an income statement**

1. Center the name of the company, *Encore Music,* on the first line.
2. Center the name of the report, *Income Statement,* on the second line.
3. Center the date of the report, *For Month Ended August 31, 20—,* on the third line.

## REVENUE, EXPENSES, AND NET INCOME SECTIONS OF AN INCOME STATEMENT

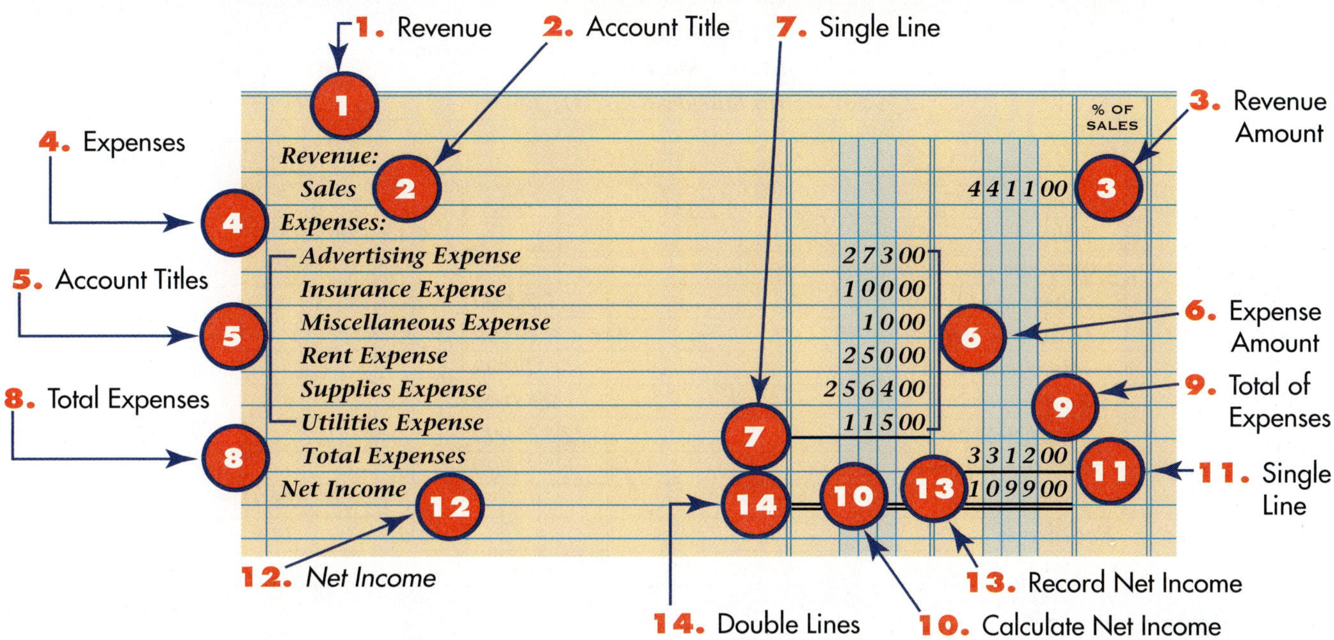


Information from the work sheet's Account Title column and Income Statement Credit column is used to prepare the revenue section.

Information from the work sheet's Account Title column and Income Statement Debit column is used to prepare the expenses section.

### STEPS: Preparing the revenue, expenses, and net income sections of an income statement

1. Write the name of the first section, *Revenue:*, at the extreme left of the wide column on the first line.
2. Write the title of the revenue account, *Sales,* on the next line, indented about one centimeter.
3. Record the balance of the account, *$4,411.00,* on the same line in the second amount column.
4. Write the name of the second section, *Expenses:*, on the next line at the extreme left of the wide column.
5. Write the title of each expense account in the wide column, indented about one centimeter.
6. Record the balance of each expense account in the first amount column on the same line as the account title.
7. Rule a single line across the first amount column under the last expense account balance to indicate addition.
8. Write the words *Total Expenses* on the next blank line in the wide column, indented about one centimeter.
9. Record the amount of total expenses, *$3,312.00,* on the same line in the second amount column.
10. Calculate and verify the amount of net income using two methods:
    a. Calculate net income from information on the income statement, as shown.

| Total Revenue | − | Total Expenses | = | Net Income |
|---|---|---|---|---|
| $4,411.00 | − | $3,312.00 | = | $1,099.00 |

    b. Compare the amount of net income, *$1,099.00,* with the net income shown on the work sheet. The two net income amounts must be the same. (If the two amounts are not the same, an error has been made.)
11. Rule a single line across the second amount column just below the amount of total expenses.
12. Write the words *Net Income* on the next line at the extreme left of the wide column.
13. On the same line, record the amount of net income, *$1,099.00,* in the second amount column.
14. Rule double lines across both amount columns below the amount of net income to show that the amount has been verified as correct.

# COMPONENT PERCENTAGE ANALYSIS OF AN INCOME STATEMENT

| *Encore Music* | | | |
|---|---|---|---|
| *Income Statement* | | | |
| *For Month Ended August 31, 20--* | | | |
| | | | % OF SALES |
| *Revenue:* | | | |
| *Sales* | | 4411 00 | 100.0 |
| *Expenses:* | | | |
| *Advertising Expense* | 273 00 | | |
| *Insurance Expense* | 100 00 | | |
| *Miscellaneous Expense* | 10 00 | | |
| *Rent Expense* | 250 00 | | |
| *Supplies Expense* | 2564 00 | | |
| *Utilities Expense* | 115 00 | | |
| *Total Expenses* | | 3312 00 | 75.1 |
| *Net Income* | | 1099 00 | 24.9 |

For a service business, the revenue reported on an income statement includes two components: (1) total expenses and (2) net income. To make decisions about future operations, a manager analyzes relationships between these two income statement components and the total sales. The percentage relationship between one financial statement item and the total that includes that item is called a **component percentage.** On an income statement, component percentages are calculated by dividing the amount of each component by the total amount of sales. Encore Music calculates a component percentage for total expenses and net income. The relationship between each component and total sales is shown in a separate column on the income statement at the right of the amount columns.

## Acceptable Component Percentages

For a component percentage to be useful, Ms. Treviño needs to know what component percentages are acceptable for businesses similar to Encore Music. Various industry organizations publish average percentages for similar businesses. In the future, Ms. Treviño could also compare Encore Music's component percentages from one fiscal period with the percentages of previous fiscal periods.

## Total Expenses Component Percentage

The total expenses component percentage, based on information from the August income statement, is calculated as shown. For businesses similar to Encore Music, an acceptable total expenses component percentage is not more than 80.0%. Therefore, Encore Music's percentage, 75.1%, is less than 80.0% and is acceptable.

| Total Expenses | ÷ | Total Sales | = | Total Expenses Component Percentage |
|---|---|---|---|---|
| \$3,312.00 | ÷ | \$4,411.00 | = | 75.1% |

## Net Income Component Percentage

The net income component percentage, based on information from the August income statement, is calculated as shown. For businesses similar to Encore Music, an acceptable net income component percentage is not less than 20.0%. Therefore Encore Music's percentage, 24.9%, is greater than 20.0% and is acceptable.

| Net Income | ÷ | Total Sales | = | Net Income Component Percentage |
|---|---|---|---|---|
| \$1,099.00 | ÷ | \$4,411.00 | = | 24.9% |

# INCOME STATEMENT WITH TWO SOURCES OF REVENUE AND A NET LOSS

**5.** *Total Sales*

**1.** Revenue

**2.** Account Titles

**3.** Revenue Amounts

**4.** Total of Sales

**6.** *Net Loss*

**7.** Record *Net Loss*

| *HighNote* | | | |
|---|---|---|---|
| *Income Statement* | | | |
| *For Month Ended August 31, 20--* | | | |
| | | | % OF SALES |
| *Revenue:* | | | |
| *Sales—Lessons* | 2,360.00 | | |
| *Sales—Repairs* | 1,250.00 | | |
| *Total Revenue* | | 3,610.00 | 100.0 |
| *Expenses:* | | | |
| *Advertising Expense* | 1,100.00 | | |
| *Insurance Expense* | 341.00 | | |
| *Rent Expense* | 1,450.00 | | |
| *Supplies Expense* | 1,575.00 | | |
| *Total Expenses* | | 4,466.00 | 123.7 |
| *Net Loss* | | (856.00) | (23.7) |

Encore Music receives revenue from only one source, the sale of services for music lessons. HighNote receives revenue from two sources, the sale of services for music lessons and the sale of services to repair musical instruments. The business's owner wants to know how much revenue is earned from each source. Therefore, the business uses two revenue accounts: Sales—Lessons and Sales—Repairs.

When an income statement is prepared for HighNote, both revenue accounts are listed. The revenue section of HighNote differs from the income statement prepared by Encore Music.

If total expenses exceed total revenue, a net loss is reported on an income statement. HighNote reported a net loss on its August income statement.

**STEPS**

**Preparing the revenue section of an income statement with two sources of revenue**

1. Write the section heading, *Revenue:*, at the left of the wide column.
2. Write the titles of both revenue accounts in the wide column, indented about one centimeter.
3. Record the balance of each account in the first amount column on the same line as the account title.
4. Total the two revenue account balances. Write the total amount on the next line in the second amount column.
5. Write the words *Total Revenue* in the wide column, indented about one centimeter on the same line as the total revenue amount.

**Preparing the net loss section of an income statement**

6. Write the words *Net Loss* at the extreme left of the wide column.
7. Subtract the total expenses from the revenue to calculate the net loss. Record the amount of net loss in the second amount column in parentheses. An amount written in parentheses on a financial statement indicates a negative amount.

## TERM REVIEW

component percentage

## AUDIT YOUR UNDERSTANDING

1. List the four sections of an income statement.
2. What is the formula for calculating the total expenses component percentage?
3. What is the formula for calculating the net income component percentage?

## WORK TOGETHER

**Preparing an income statement**

A partial work sheet of Darlene's Delivery Service for the month ended July 31 of the current year is given in the *Working Papers*. Also given is a blank form for completing an income statement. Your instructor will guide you through the following example.

4. Prepare an income statement for the month ended July 31 of the current year. Calculate and record the component percentages for total expenses and net income. Round percentage calculations to the nearest 0.1%.

## ON YOUR OWN

**Preparing an income statement**

A partial work sheet of Keith's Copies for the month ended February 28 of the current year is given in the *Working Papers*. Also given is a blank form for completing an income statement. Work this problem independently.

5. Prepare an income statement for the month ended February 28 of the current year. Calculate and record the component percentages for total expenses and net income. Round percentage calculations to the nearest 0.1%.

# 8-2 Balance Sheet Information on a Work Sheet

## BALANCE SHEET

| | ACCOUNT TITLE | 7<br>BALANCE SHEET<br>DEBIT | 8<br>BALANCE SHEET<br>CREDIT | |
|---|---|---|---|---|
| 1 | *Cash* | 8272 00 | | 1 |
| 2 | *Petty Cash* | 200 00 | | 2 |
| 3 | *Accounts Receivable—Kids Time* | 100 00 | | 3 |
| 4 | *Accounts Receivable—Learn N Play* | 20 00 | | 4 |
| 5 | *Supplies* | 2187 00 | | 5 |
| 6 | *Prepaid Insurance* | 1100 00 | | 6 |
| 7 | *Accounts Payable—Ling Music Supplies* | | 1360 00 | 7 |
| 8 | *Accounts Payable—Sullivan Office Supplies* | | 20 00 | 8 |
| 9 | *Barbara Treviño, Capital* | | 10000 00 | 9 |
| 10 | *Barbara Treviño, Drawing* | 600 00 | | 10 |
| 19 | | 12479 00 | 11380 00 | 19 |
| 20 | *Net Income* | | 1099 00 | 20 |
| 21 | | 12479 00 | 12479 00 | 21 |

A balance sheet reports financial information on a *specific date,* indicating the financial *condition* of a business. The financial condition of a business refers to its financial strength. If a business has adequate available assets and few liabilities, that business is financially strong. If the business's financial condition is not strong, adverse changes in the economy might cause the business to fail.

Information about assets, liabilities, and owner's equity might be obtained from the general ledger accounts or from a work sheet. However, the information is easier to use if reported in an organized manner such as on a balance sheet.

Information needed to prepare Encore Music's balance sheet is obtained from two places on the work sheet. Account titles are obtained from the work sheet's Account Title column. Account balances are obtained from the work sheet's Balance Sheet columns.

A balance sheet has four sections: (1) heading, (2) assets, (3) liabilities, and (4) owner's equity.

## HEADING OF A BALANCE SHEET

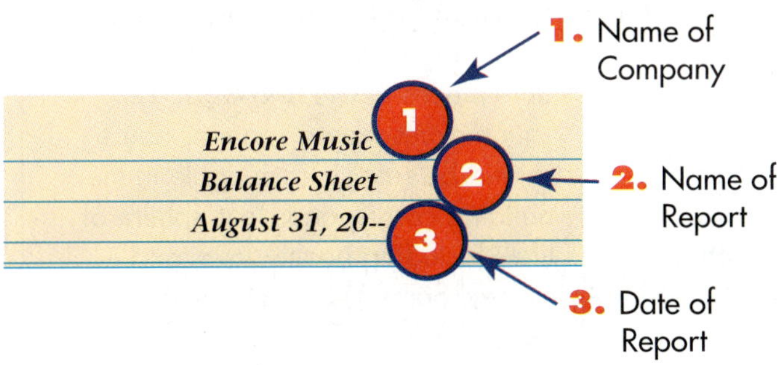


### STEPS: Preparing the heading of a balance sheet

1. Center the name of the company, *Encore Music,* on the first line.
2. Center the name of the report, *Balance Sheet,* on the second line.
3. Center the date of the report, *August 31, 20—,* on the third line.

## ASSETS AND LIABILITIES SECTIONS OF A BALANCE SHEET

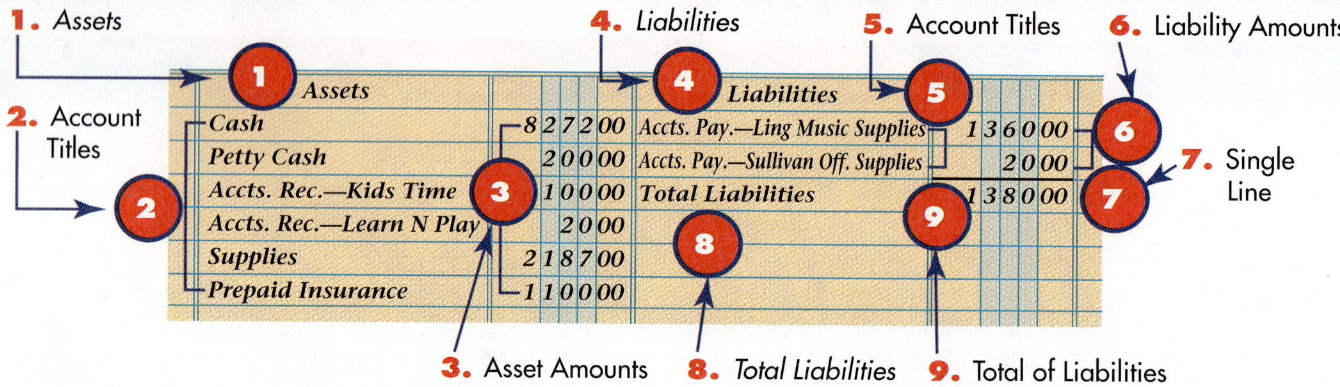


A balance sheet reports information about the elements of the accounting equation.

**Assets = Liabilities + Owner's Equity**

The assets are on the LEFT side of the accounting equation and on the LEFT side of Encore Music's balance sheet.

Two kinds of equities are reported on a balance sheet: (1) liabilities and (2) owner's equity. Liabilities and owner's equity are on the RIGHT side of the accounting equation and on the RIGHT side of Encore Music's balance sheet.

The information needed to prepare the assets section is obtained from the work sheet's Account Title column and the Balance Sheet Debit column. The information needed to prepare the liabilities section is obtained from the work sheet's Account Title column and the Balance Sheet Credit column.

### STEPS: Preparing the assets and liabilities sections of a balance sheet

1. Write the title of the first section, *Assets,* in the middle of the left wide column.
2. Write the titles of all asset accounts under the heading.
3. Record the balance of each asset account in the left amount column on the same line as the account title.
4. Write the title of the next section, *Liabilities,* in the middle of the right wide column.
5. Write the titles of all liability accounts under the heading.
6. Record the balance of each liability account in the right amount column on the same line as the account title.
7. Rule a single line across the right amount column under the last amount, to indicate addition.
8. Write the words *Total Liabilities* in the right wide column on the next blank line, indented about 1 centimeter.
9. Record the total of all liabilities, *$1,380.00,* in the right amount column.

### CULTURAL DIVERSITY

#### Feng Shui

In the U.S., culture has been influenced by the cultures of its foreign business partners. For example, the Chinese philosophy of *feng shui* (pronounced "fung shway") is having an influence on the design of homes and office buildings in America.

This philosophy reflects Chinese beliefs in luck. The goal is to maintain a flow of positive energies throughout a building and to find the most favorable places to live and work. *Feng shui* dictates how a room or house should be set up. Each angle in the building corresponds to a sphere of life—including health, love, and money. Some U.S. companies are using the *feng shui* philosophy in designing their facilities.

## OWNER'S EQUITY SECTION OF A BALANCE SHEET

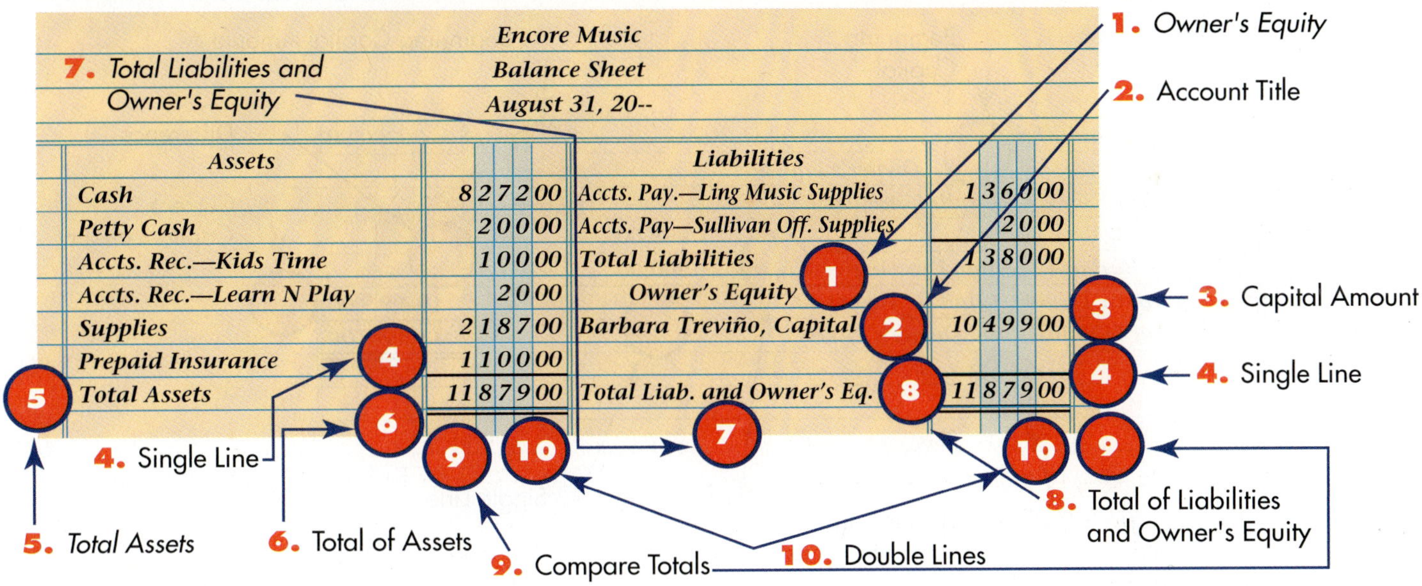


Only the amount of current capital is reported on Encore Music's balance sheet. The amounts needed to calculate the current capital are found in the work sheet's Balance Sheet Debit and Credit columns. The amount of current capital is calculated as shown.

| Capital Account Balance | + | Net Income | − | Drawing Account Balance | = | Current Capital |
|---|---|---|---|---|---|---|
| $10,000.00 | + | $1,099.00 | − | $600.00 | = | $10,499.00 |

The title of the owner's capital account is obtained from the work sheet's Account Title column. Encore Music's balance sheet prepared on August 31 is shown in the illustration.

When a business has a net loss, current capital is calculated as shown. The current capital is reported on the balance sheet in the same way as when the business has a net income.

| Capital Account Balance | − | Net Loss | − | Drawing Account Balance | = | Current Capital |
|---|---|---|---|---|---|---|
| $12,000.00 | − | $200.00 | − | $500.00 | = | $11,300.00 |

### STEPS: Preparing the owner's equity section of a balance sheet

1. Write the title of the section, *Owner's Equity,* in the middle of the right wide column on the next line below Total Liabilities.
2. Write the title of the owner's capital account, *Barbara Treviño, Capital,* on the next line.
3. Record the current amount of owner's equity, *$10,499.00,* in the right amount column.
4. Determine which amount column is longer. For Encore Music, the longer column is the left amount column. Rule a single line under the last amount in the left amount column: Prepaid Insurance, $1,100.00. Rule a single line in the right amount column on the same line as in the left amount column.
5. Write the words *Total Assets* on the next line, in the left wide column.
6. Record the amount of total assets, *$11,879.00,* in the left amount column.
7. Write the words *Total Liab. and Owner's Eq.* in the right wide column on the same line as *Total Assets.*
8. Record the amount of total liabilities and owner's equity, *$11,879.00,* in the right amount column.
9. Compare the totals of the two amount columns. Because the totals are the same on both sides of Encore Music's balance sheet, $11,879.00, the balance sheet is in balance.
10. Rule double lines across both the left and right amount columns just below the column totals to show that the totals have been verified as correct.

# OWNER'S EQUITY REPORTED IN DETAIL ON A BALANCE SHEET

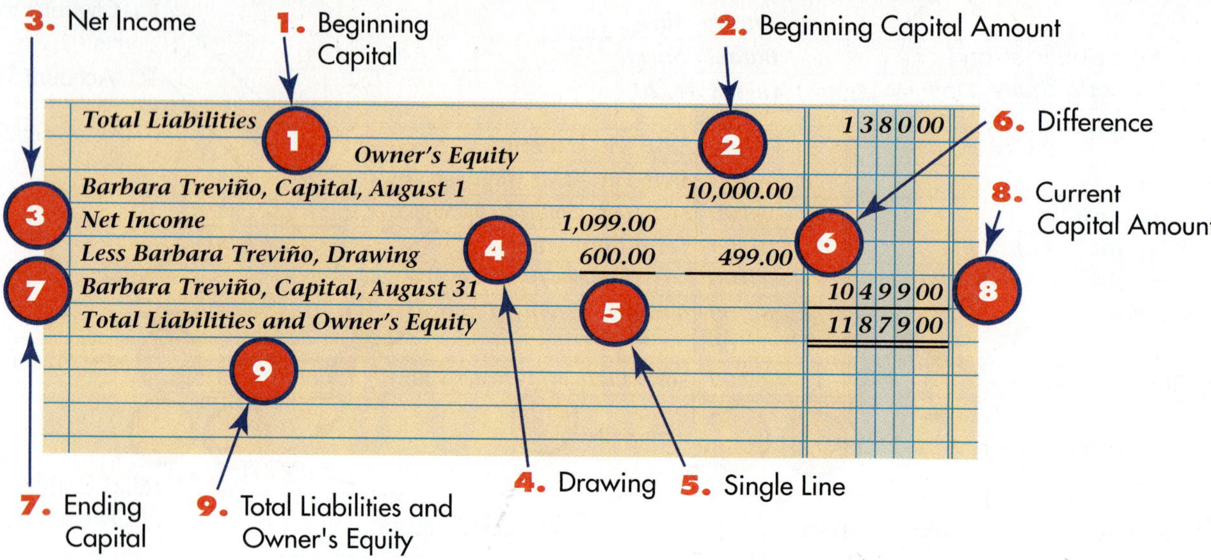


Encore Music's balance sheet reports the current capital on August 31 but does not show how this amount was calculated. Encore Music is a small business with relatively few changes in owner's equity to report. Therefore, Barbara Treviño decided that the business does not need to report all the details in the owner's equity section. However, some businesses prefer to report the details about how owner's equity is calculated.

If Encore Music were to report details about owner's equity, the owner's equity section of the balance sheet would be prepared as shown in the illustration.

## STEPS: Preparing the owner's equity section reported in detail on a balance sheet

1. Write the words *Barbara Treviño, Capital, August 1* on the first line under the words *Owner's Equity.*
2. Record the owner's capital account balance on August 1, *$10,000.00,* in the wide column.
3. Write the words *Net Income* on the next line. Record the net income, *$1,099.00,* in the wide column to the left of the capital account balance.
4. Write the words *Less Barbara Treviño, Drawing* on the next line. Record the balance of the drawing account, *$600.00,* in the wide column.
5. Rule a single line under the amount.
6. Subtract the balance of the drawing account from the net income. Record the difference, *$499.00,* in the wide column to the right of the drawing account balance.
7. Write the words *Barbara Treviño, Capital, August 31* on the next line.
8. Add the August 1 capital amount, *$10,000.00,* and the difference between the net income and the drawing account, *$499.00.* Record the sum, *$10,499.00,* in the right amount column.
9. Write the words *Total Liabilities and Owner's Equity* on the next line. Record the amount of total liabilities and owner's equity, *$11,879.00,* in the right amount column.

## REMEMBER

Capital is not copied from the work sheet to the balance sheet. Capital is calculated using beginning capital, plus net income or minus net loss, minus drawing.

## AUDIT YOUR UNDERSTANDING

1. List the four sections on a balance sheet.
2. What is the formula for calculating current capital?

## WORK TOGETHER

### Preparing a balance sheet

A partial work sheet of Ken's Carpet Cleaning for the month ended April 30 of the current year is given in the *Working Papers*. Also given is a blank form for completing a balance sheet. Your instructor will guide you through the following example.

3. Prepare a balance sheet for April 30 of the current year.

## ON YOUR OWN

### Preparing a balance sheet

A partial work sheet of Jane's Sewing Machine Repair for the month ended October 31 of the current year is given in the *Working Papers*. Also given is a blank form for completing a balance sheet. Work this problem independently.

4. Prepare a balance sheet for October 31 of the current year.

# CHAPTER 8 SUMMARY

*Enrichment Activity*

**Types of Businesses**

*Examine the financial statements illustrated in this chapter. Which parts of which statements do you think would be different if this business were not organized as a proprietorship?*

After completing this chapter, you can

1. Define an important accounting term related to financial statements for a service business organized as a proprietorship.
2. Identify accounting concepts and practices related to preparation of financial statements for a service business organized as a proprietorship.
3. Prepare an income statement for a service business organized as a proprietorship and analyze an income statement using component percentages.
4. Prepare a balance sheet for a service business organized as a proprietorship.

## EXPLORE ACCOUNTING

### COMPARATIVE AND INTERIM FINANCIAL STATEMENTS

A corporation that trades its stock on a U.S. stock exchange must submit an annual report to the Securities and Exchange Commission (SEC). The SEC has specific requirements as to what must be included in the financial statements.

One requirement is that the financial statements included in the annual report must show amounts for more than one year. The balance sheet must show ending balances for the current and the previous year. The income statement and statement of stockholder's equity must show amounts for the current year and the two previous years. Financial statements providing information for multiple fiscal periods are called *comparative financial statements.*

These statements make it possible for a user to compare performance from year to year. For example, the net income for the current year can be compared to the net income for the two previous years. In this way, the user can determine if there is a positive or negative trend occuring in net income. On the balance sheet, the ending cash balance for the current year can be compared to the ending cash balance from the previous year to determine if the amount of cash on hand is increasing or decreasing.

Businesses that are required to submit an annual report to the SEC must also submit a quarterly report. This report is not as detailed as the annual report, but it must include the financial statements for the quarter. Financial statements providing information for a time period shorter than the fiscal year are called *interim financial statements.* Users of financial information are able to evaluate the progress of the firm every three months rather than waiting an entire year. The importance of interim financial statements can be verified by the fact that the results reported in these statements are often summarized and reported in financial news sources, such as the *Wall Street Journal* and CNBC.

**Activity:** Contact a corporation near you. Ask if the business prepares interim financial statements and, if it does, find out how often these statements are prepared.

## 8-1 APPLICATION PROBLEM
### Preparing an income statement

A form is given in the *Working Papers*. The following information is obtained from the work sheet of Robbie's Rugcare for the month ended August 31 of the current year.

| | Account Title | 5 Income Statement Debit | 6 Income Statement Credit | 7 Balance Sheet Debit | 8 Balance Sheet Credit | |
|---|---|---|---|---|---|---|
| 11 | *Sales* | | 5,707 00 | | | 11 |
| 12 | *Advertising Expense* | 900 00 | | | | 12 |
| 13 | *Insurance Expense* | 20 00 | | | | 13 |
| 14 | *Miscellaneous Expense* | 267 00 | | | | 14 |
| 15 | *Supplies Expense* | 500 00 | | | | 15 |
| 16 | *Utilities Expense* | 1,542 00 | | | | 16 |
| 17 | | 3,229 00 | 5,707 00 | 11,547 00 | 9,069 00 | 17 |
| 18 | *Net Income* | 2,478 00 | | | 2,478 00 | 18 |
| 19 | | 5,707 00 | 5,707 00 | 11,547 00 | 11,547 00 | 19 |
| 20 | | | | | | 20 |

***Instructions:***

1. Prepare an income statement for the month ended August 31 of the current year.
2. Calculate and record the component percentages for total expenses and net income. Round percentage calculations to the nearest 0.1%.

## 8-2 APPLICATION PROBLEM
### Preparing a balance sheet

A form is given in the *Working Papers*. The following information is obtained from the work sheet of Robbie's Rugcare for the month ended August 31 of the current year.

| | Account Title | 7 Balance Sheet Debit | 8 Balance Sheet Credit | |
|---|---|---|---|---|
| 1 | *Cash* | 8,752 00 | | 1 |
| 2 | *Accts. Rec.—Crystal Thompson* | 200 00 | | 2 |
| 3 | *Accts. Rec.—Robert Boje* | 175 00 | | 3 |
| 4 | *Supplies* | 400 00 | | 4 |
| 5 | *Prepaid Insurance* | 220 00 | | 5 |
| 6 | *Accts. Pay.—Daniel Supplies* | | 442 00 | 6 |
| 7 | *Accts. Pay.—Irene's Irons* | | 676 00 | 7 |
| 8 | *Roberta Greenstein, Capital* | | 7,951 00 | 8 |
| 9 | *Roberta Greenstein, Drawing* | 1,800 00 | | 9 |
| 10 | *Income Summary* | | | 10 |
| 17 | | 11,547 00 | 9,069 00 | 17 |
| 18 | *Net Income* | | 2,478 00 | 18 |
| 19 | | 11,547 00 | 11,547 00 | 19 |
| 20 | | | | 20 |

***Instructions:***

Prepare a balance sheet for August 31 of the current year.

# 8-3 MASTERY PROBLEM
## Preparing financial statements with a net loss

Forms are given in the *Working Papers*. The following information is obtained from the work sheet of Mancini Hair Care for the month ended September 30 of the current year.

| | ACCOUNT TITLE | 5 INCOME STATEMENT DEBIT | 6 INCOME STATEMENT CREDIT | 7 BALANCE SHEET DEBIT | 8 BALANCE SHEET CREDIT | |
|---|---|---|---|---|---|---|
| 1 | Cash | | | 7678 00 | | 1 |
| 2 | Petty Cash | | | 100 00 | | 2 |
| 3 | Accts. Rec.—Jennifer Balsa | | | 164 00 | | 3 |
| 4 | Supplies | | | 690 00 | | 4 |
| 5 | Prepaid Insurance | | | 700 00 | | 5 |
| 6 | Accts. Pay.—Alto Supplies | | | | 733 00 | 6 |
| 7 | Jon Mancini, Capital | | | | 9500 00 | 7 |
| 8 | Jon Mancini, Drawing | | | 500 00 | | 8 |
| 9 | Income Summary | | | | | 9 |
| 10 | Sales | | 4596 00 | | | 10 |
| 11 | Advertising Expense | 550 00 | | | | 11 |
| 12 | Insurance Expense | 175 00 | | | | 12 |
| 13 | Miscellaneous Expense | 58 00 | | | | 13 |
| 14 | Supplies Expense | 1500 00 | | | | 14 |
| 15 | Utilities Expense | 2714 00 | | | | 15 |
| 16 | | 4997 00 | 4596 00 | 9832 00 | 10233 00 | 16 |
| 17 | Net Loss | | 401 00 | 401 00 | | 17 |
| 18 | | 4997 00 | 4997 00 | 10233 00 | 10233 00 | 18 |
| 19 | | | | | | 19 |
| 20 | | | | | | 20 |

***Instructions:***

1. Prepare an income statement for the month ended September 30 of the current year.
2. Calculate and record the component percentages for total expenses and net loss. Place the percentage for net loss in parentheses to show that it is for a net loss. Round percentage calculations to the nearest 0.1%.
3. Prepare a balance sheet for September 30 of the current year.

# 8-4 CHALLENGE PROBLEM
## Preparing financial statements with two sources of revenue and a net loss

Forms are given in the *Working Papers*. The information on the next page is obtained from the work sheet of LawnMow for the month ended October 31 of the current year.

***Instructions:***

1. Prepare an income statement for the month ended October 31 of the current year.
2. Calculate and record the component percentages for total expenses and net loss. Place the percentage for net loss in parentheses to show that it is for a net loss. Round percentage calculations to the nearest 0.1%.
3. Prepare a balance sheet for October 31 of the current year.

| | ACCOUNT TITLE | 5 INCOME STATEMENT DEBIT | 6 INCOME STATEMENT CREDIT | 7 BALANCE SHEET DEBIT | 8 BALANCE SHEET CREDIT | |
|---|---|---|---|---|---|---|
| 1 | *Cash* | | | 1898 00 | | 1 |
| 2 | *Accts. Rec.—Sandra Rohe* | | | 95 00 | | 2 |
| 3 | *Supplies* | | | 650 00 | | 3 |
| 4 | *Prepaid Insurance* | | | 1200 00 | | 4 |
| 5 | *Accts. Pay.—Corner Garage* | | | | 58 00 | 5 |
| 6 | *Accts. Pay.—Broadway Gas* | | | | 110 00 | 6 |
| 7 | *Accts. Pay.—Esko Repair* | | | | 215 00 | 7 |
| 8 | *Ryo Morrison, Capital* | | | | 4000 00 | 8 |
| 9 | *Ryo Morrison, Drawing* | | | 100 00 | | 9 |
| 10 | *Income Summary* | | | | | 10 |
| 11 | *Sales—Lawn Care* | | 4900 00 | | | 11 |
| 12 | *Sales—Shrub Care* | | 2500 00 | | | 12 |
| 13 | *Advertising Expense* | 390 00 | | | | 13 |
| 14 | *Insurance Expense* | 400 00 | | | | 14 |
| 15 | *Miscellaneous Expense* | 550 00 | | | | 15 |
| 16 | *Rent Expense* | 3300 00 | | | | 16 |
| 17 | *Supplies Expense* | 3200 00 | | | | 17 |
| 18 | | 7840 00 | 7400 00 | 3943 00 | 4383 00 | 18 |
| 19 | *Net Loss* | | 440 00 | 440 00 | | 19 |
| 20 | | 7840 00 | 7840 00 | 4383 00 | 4383 00 | 20 |
| 21 | | | | | | 21 |

## INTERNET ACTIVITY

Point your browser to
**http://accounting.swpco.com**
Choose **First-Year Course**, choose **Activities**, and complete the activity for Chapter 8.

## Applied Communication

Assume that you are the owner of a proprietorship, and you have just hired a new assistant. In the past, your assistants have had difficulty understanding the importance of financial statements to your business.

**Instructions:** Write down what you would say to your assistant about the importance of income statements and balance sheets in making financial decisions. Your statements should be no longer than one or two paragraphs.

# Cases for Critical Thinking

**Case 1** Romelle Woods and Ahti Indihar each own small businesses. Ms. Woods prepares an income statement and balance sheet at the end of each day for her business, in order to make business decisions. Mr. Indihar prepares an income statement and balance sheet for his business only at the end of each one-year fiscal period, when preparing tax reports. Which owner is using the better procedure? Explain your answer.

# AUTOMATED ACCOUNTING

## FINANCIAL STATEMENTS GENERATED FROM AUTOMATED ACCOUNTING

Financial information needed by managers and owners of a business to make decisions is recorded in the journals and the ledgers. While this information may be helpful in analyzing the activity in a particular account, it is too detailed to be useful in decision making. When information from the ledgers is summarized and organized, the reports that are prepared are referred to as *financial statements*. The most commonly presented financial statements for a business organized as a sole proprietorship are the balance sheet and the income statement.

To display financial statements:

1. Click the Reports toolbar button, or choose the Report Selection menu item from the Report menu.
2. When the Report Selection dialog appears, choose the Financial Statements option from the Select a Report Group list.
3. Choose the financial statement report you would like to display from the Choose a Report to Display list.
4. Click the OK button.

The up-to-date account balances stored by the software are used to calculate and display the current financial statements.

### Income Statement

An income statement shows the revenue and expenses for a fiscal period. Revenues are the amounts earned from business activities. Expenses are the amounts paid to operate a business. The software will display net income or loss (the difference between revenues earned and expenses incurred) in one of two formats:

1. *Report by Fiscal Period:* This format shows the profitability of the business from the beginning of the fiscal year to the date the income statement is displayed.
2. *Report by Month and Year:* This format includes columns for the current month and for the year to date.

A component percentage is included for each dollar amount. A component percentage shows the percentage relationship between one financial statement item and the total that includes that item. Component percentages calculated on the income statement show the relationship of items to total sales.

### Balance Sheet

The balance sheet is the financial statement that reports assets, liabilities, and owner's equity on a specific date, usually the end of the fiscal period. It is used to help evaluate the financial strength of the business. Additional information about owner's equity is shown on the Statement of Owner's Equity. This statement shows changes to the capital account during the period.

### AUTOMATING MASTERY PROBLEM 8-3: Preparing financial statements with a net loss

**Instructions:**

1. Load *Automated Accounting 7.0* or higher software.

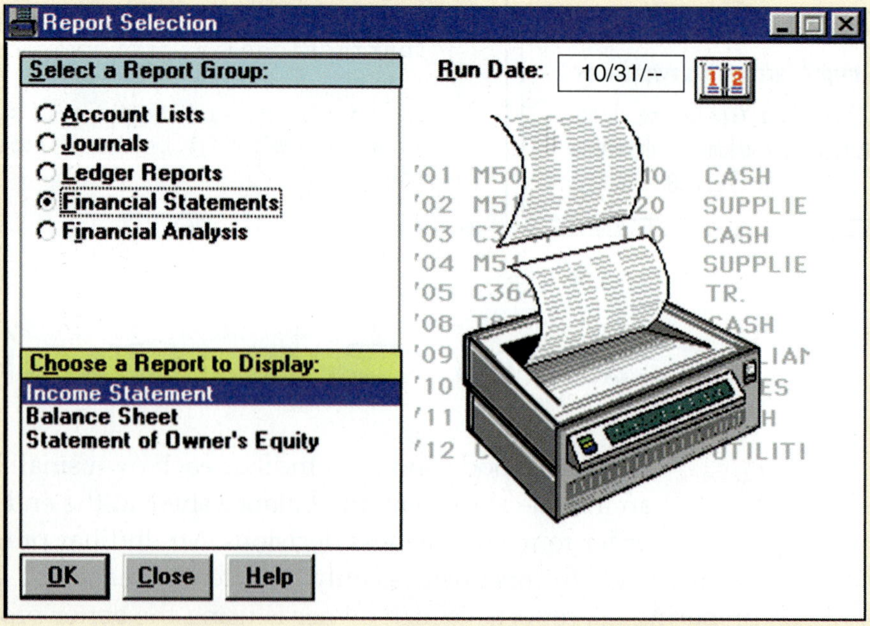

## ADJUSTING ENTRY FOR PREPAID INSURANCE

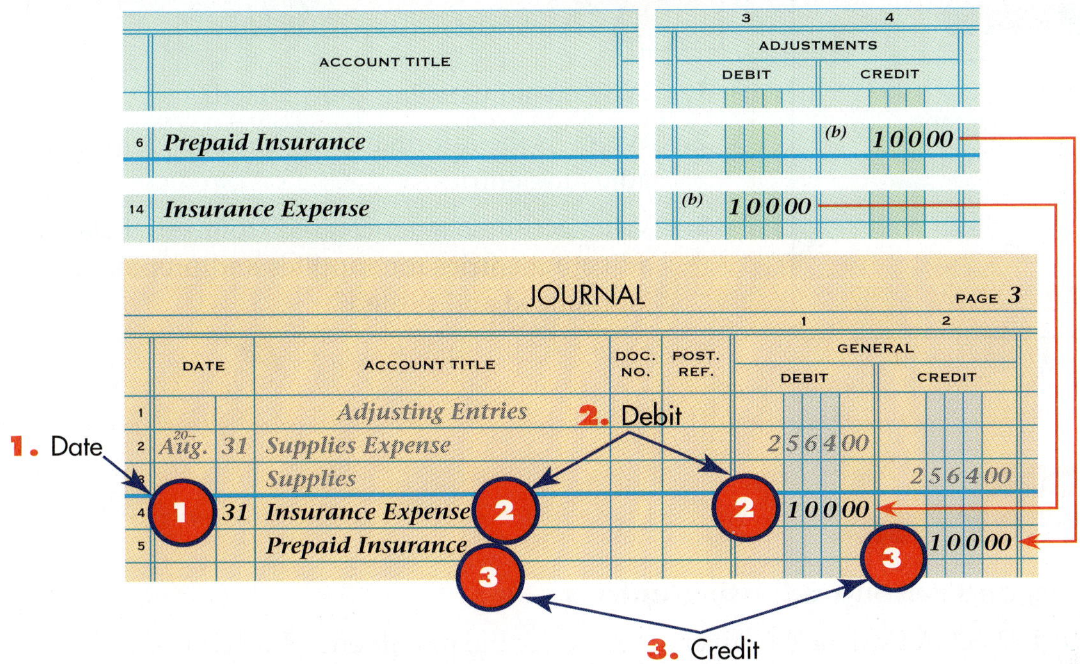


The information needed to journalize the adjusting entry for prepaid insurance is obtained from lines 6 and 14 of the work sheet. The entry must be recorded in a journal and posted to the general ledger accounts affected by the entry.

The effect of posting the adjusting entry for prepaid insurance to the general ledger accounts is shown in the T accounts.

**Insurance Expense**

| Debit | | Credit | |
|---|---|---|---|
| Adj. (b) | 100.00 | | |

**Prepaid Insurance**

| Debit | | Credit | |
|---|---|---|---|
| Bal. | 1,200.00 | Adj. (b) | 100.00 |
| *(New Bal.* | *1,100.00)* | | |

## PROFESSIONAL BUSINESS ETHICS

### Is It Discrimination or Poor Judgment?

CyberMarket provides market research for companies that sell products and services on the Internet.

**Instructions**

Use the three-step checklist to help determine whether or not the following situation demonstrates ethical behavior.

Your group at CyberMarket has an opening for a research analyst. You are on the search committee to pick candidates to be interviewed.

Committee members give the following reasons for wanting to eliminate various candidates.

a. "She graduated from college before I was born. She can't possibly know anything about our business."

b. "The ad said two to five years of experience, but we really need someone with more than two years of experience."

c. "This guy went to the same college I did. Let's give him a shot."

## Term Review

adjusting entries

## Audit Your Understanding

1. Why are adjustments journalized?
2. Where is the information obtained to journalize adjusting entries?
3. What accounts are increased from zero balances after adjusting entries for supplies and prepaid insurance are journalized and posted?

## Work Together

### Journalizing and posting adjusting entries

A partial work sheet of Darlene's Delivery Service for the month ended July 31 of the current year is given in the *Working Papers*. Also given are a journal and general ledger accounts. The general ledger accounts do not show all details for the fiscal period. The Balance shown in each account is the account's balance before adjusting entries are posted. Your instructor will guide you through the following example.

4. Use page 4 of a journal. Journalize and post the adjusting entries. Save your work to complete Work Together on page 209.

## On Your Own

### Journalizing and posting adjusting entries

A partial work sheet of Keith's Copies for the month ended February 28 of the current year is given in the *Working Papers*. Also given are a journal and general ledger accounts. The general ledger accounts do not show all details for the fiscal period. The Balance shown in each account is the account's balance before adjusting entries are posted. Work this problem independently.

5. Use page 8 of a journal. Journalize and post the adjusting entries. Save your work to complete On Your Own on page 209.

# 9-2 Recording Closing Entries

## NEED FOR PERMANENT AND TEMPORARY ACCOUNTS

Accounts used to accumulate information from one fiscal period to the next are called **permanent accounts.** Permanent accounts are also referred to as real accounts. Permanent accounts include the asset and liability accounts and the owner's capital account. The ending account balances of permanent accounts for one fiscal period are the beginning account balances for the next fiscal period.

Accounts used to accumulate information until it is transferred to the owner's capital account are called **temporary accounts.** Temporary accounts are also referred to as nominal accounts. Temporary accounts include the revenue, expense, and owner's drawing accounts plus the income summary account. Temporary accounts show changes in the owner's capital for a single fiscal period. Therefore, at the end of a fiscal period, the balances of temporary accounts are summarized and transferred to the owner's capital account. The temporary accounts begin a new fiscal period with zero balances.

## NEED FOR CLOSING TEMPORARY ACCOUNTS

Journal entries used to prepare temporary accounts for a new fiscal period are called **closing entries.** The temporary account balances must be reduced to zero at the end of each fiscal period. This procedure prepares the temporary accounts for recording information about the next fiscal period. Otherwise, the amounts for the next fiscal period would be added to amounts for previous fiscal periods. *(CONCEPT: Matching Expenses with Revenue)* The net income for the next fiscal period would be difficult to calculate because amounts from several fiscal periods remain in the accounts. Therefore, the temporary accounts must start each new fiscal period with zero balances.

To close a temporary account, an amount equal to its balance is recorded in the account on the side opposite to its balance. For example, if an account has a credit balance of $4,411.00, a debit of $4,411.00 is recorded to close the account.

## NEED FOR THE INCOME SUMMARY ACCOUNT

Whenever a temporary account is closed, the closing entry must have equal debits and credits. If an account is debited for $3,000.00 to close the account, some other account must be credited for the same amount. A temporary account titled Income Summary is used to summarize the closing entries for the revenue and expense accounts.

The income summary account is unique because it does not have a normal balance side. The balance of this account is determined by the amounts posted to the account at the end of a fiscal period. When revenue is greater than total expenses, resulting in a net income, the income summary account has a credit balance, as shown in the T account.

Income Summary

| Debit | Credit |
|---|---|
| Total expenses | Revenue (greater than expenses)<br>(Credit balance is the net income.) |

When total expenses are greater than revenue, resulting in a net loss, the income summary account has a debit balance, as shown in the T account.

Income Summary

| Debit | Credit |
|---|---|
| Total expenses (greater than revenue)<br>(Debit balance is the net loss.) | Revenue |

Thus, whether the balance of the income summary account is a credit or a debit depends upon whether the business earns a net income or incurs a net loss. Because Income Summary is a temporary account, the account is also closed at the end of a fiscal period when the net income or net loss is recorded.

Encore Music records four closing entries: (1) an entry to close income statement accounts with credit balances; (2) an entry to close income statement accounts with debit balances; (3) an entry to record net income or net loss and close Income Summary; and (4) an entry to close the owner's drawing account.

Information needed to record the four closing entries is found in the Income Statement and Balance Sheet columns of the work sheet.

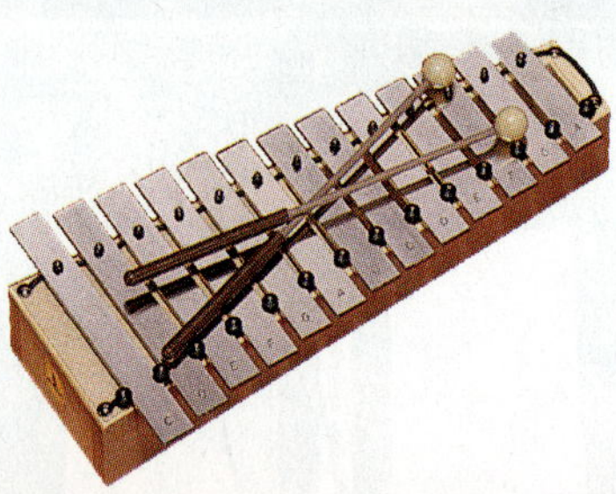

**FYI**

*Most small businesses use the calendar year as their fiscal year because it matches the way in which the owners have to file their personal income tax returns.*

**REMEMBER**

Encore Music makes four closing entries: (1) Close income statement accounts with credit balances. (2) Close income statement accounts with debit balances. (3) Record net income or loss in the owner's capital account and close Income Summary. (4) Close the owner's drawing account.

# CLOSING ENTRY FOR AN INCOME STATEMENT ACCOUNT WITH A CREDIT BALANCE

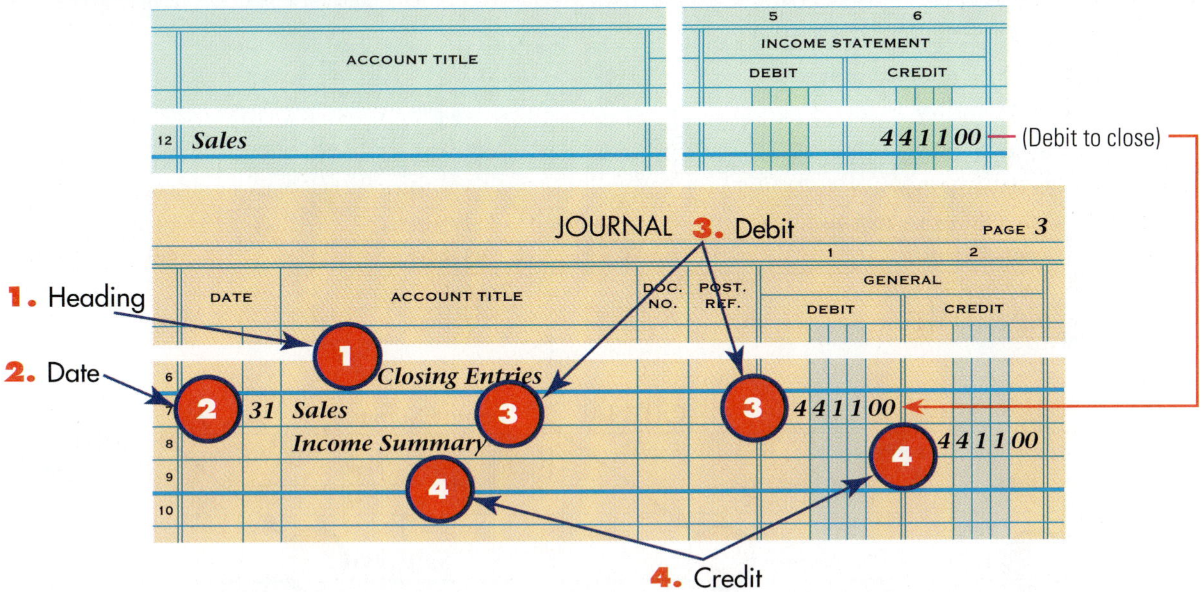


Encore Music has one income statement account with a credit balance, Sales. This credit balance must be reduced to zero to prepare the account for the next fiscal period. To reduce the balance to zero, Sales is debited for the amount of the balance. Because debits must equal credits for each journal entry, some other account must be credited. The account used for the credit part of this closing entry is Income Summary.

The effect of this closing entry on the general ledger accounts is shown in the T accounts.

**Sales**

| | | | |
|---|---|---|---|
| Closing | 4,411.00 | Bal. | 4,411.00 |
| | | *(New Bal. zero)* | |

**Income Summary**

| | | | |
|---|---|---|---|
| | | Closing (revenue) | 4,411.00 |

The balance of Sales is now zero, and the account is ready for the next fiscal period. The credit balance of Sales is transferred to Income Summary.

## STEPS: Closing entry for an income statement account with a credit balance

1. Write the heading, *Closing Entries,* in the middle of the Account Title column of the journal. For Encore Music, this heading is placed in the journal on the first blank line after the last adjusting entry.
2. Write the date, *31,* on the next line in the Date column.
3. Write the title of the account debited, *Sales,* in the Account Title column. Record the debit amount, *$4,411.00,* in the General Debit column on the same line as the account title.
4. Write the title of the account credited, *Income Summary,* on the next line in the Account Title column. Record the credit amount, *$4,411.00,* in the General Credit column on the same line as the account title.

**FYI**

*The reasons for recording closing entries can be compared to a trip odometer. Closing entries are recorded to prepare the temporary accounts for the next fiscal period by reducing their balances to zero. Likewise, a trip odometer must be reset to zero to begin recording the miles for the next trip.*

# CLOSING ENTRY FOR INCOME STATEMENT ACCOUNTS WITH DEBIT BALANCES

| | ACCOUNT TITLE | 5 INCOME STATEMENT DEBIT | 6 INCOME STATEMENT CREDIT |
|---|---|---|---|
| 13 | *Advertising Expense* | 273 00 | |
| 14 | *Insurance Expense* | 100 00 | |
| 15 | *Miscellaneous Expense* | 10 00 | |
| 16 | *Rent Expense* | 250 00 | |
| 17 | *Supplies Expense* | 2 564 00 | |
| 18 | *Utilities Expense* | 115 00 | |

(Credit to close)

JOURNAL **2.** Income Summary PAGE *3*

| | DATE | ACCOUNT TITLE | DOC. NO. | POST. REF. | 1 GENERAL DEBIT | 2 GENERAL CREDIT |
|---|---|---|---|---|---|---|
| 9 | 31 | *Income Summary* | | | 3 312 00 | |
| 10 | | *Advertising Expense* | | | | 273 00 |
| 11 | | *Insurance Expense* | | | | 100 00 |
| 12 | | *Miscellaneous Expense* | | | | 10 00 |
| 13 | | *Rent Expense* | | | | 250 00 |
| 14 | | *Supplies Expense* | | | | 2 564 00 |
| 15 | | *Utilities Expense* | | | | 115 00 |

**1.** Date
**2.** Income Summary
**3.** Credit
**4.** Debit Amount

Encore Music has six income statement accounts with debit balances. The six expense accounts have normal debit balances at the end of a fiscal period. The balances of the expense accounts must be reduced to zero to prepare the accounts for the next fiscal period. Each expense account is credited for an amount equal to its balance. Income Summary is debited for the total of all the expense account balances. The amount debited to Income Summary is not entered in the amount column until all expenses have been journalized and the total amount calculated.

The effect of this closing entry on the general ledger accounts is shown in the T accounts. The balance of each expense account is returned to zero, and the accounts are ready for the next fiscal period. The balance of Income Summary is the net income for the fiscal period, $1,099.00.

**Income Summary**

| | | | |
|---|---|---|---|
| Closing (expenses) | 3,312.00 | Closing (revenue) | 4,411.00 |
| | | *(New Bal.* | *1,099.00)* |

**Advertising Expense**

| | | | |
|---|---|---|---|
| Bal. | 273.00 | Closing | 273.00 |
| *(New Bal. zero)* | | | |

**Rent Expense**

| | | | |
|---|---|---|---|
| Bal. | 250.00 | Closing | 250.00 |
| *(New Bal. zero)* | | | |

**Insurance Expense**

| | | | |
|---|---|---|---|
| Bal. | 100.00 | Closing | 100.00 |
| *(New Bal. zero)* | | | |

**Supplies Expense**

| | | | |
|---|---|---|---|
| Bal. | 2,564.00 | Closing | 2,564.00 |
| *(New Bal. zero)* | | | |

**Miscellaneous Expense**

| | | | |
|---|---|---|---|
| Bal. | 10.00 | Closing | 10.00 |
| *(New Bal. zero)* | | | |

**Utilities Expense**

| | | | |
|---|---|---|---|
| Bal. | 115.00 | Closing | 115.00 |
| *(New Bal. zero)* | | | |

# CLOSING ENTRY TO RECORD NET INCOME OR LOSS AND CLOSE THE INCOME SUMMARY ACCOUNT

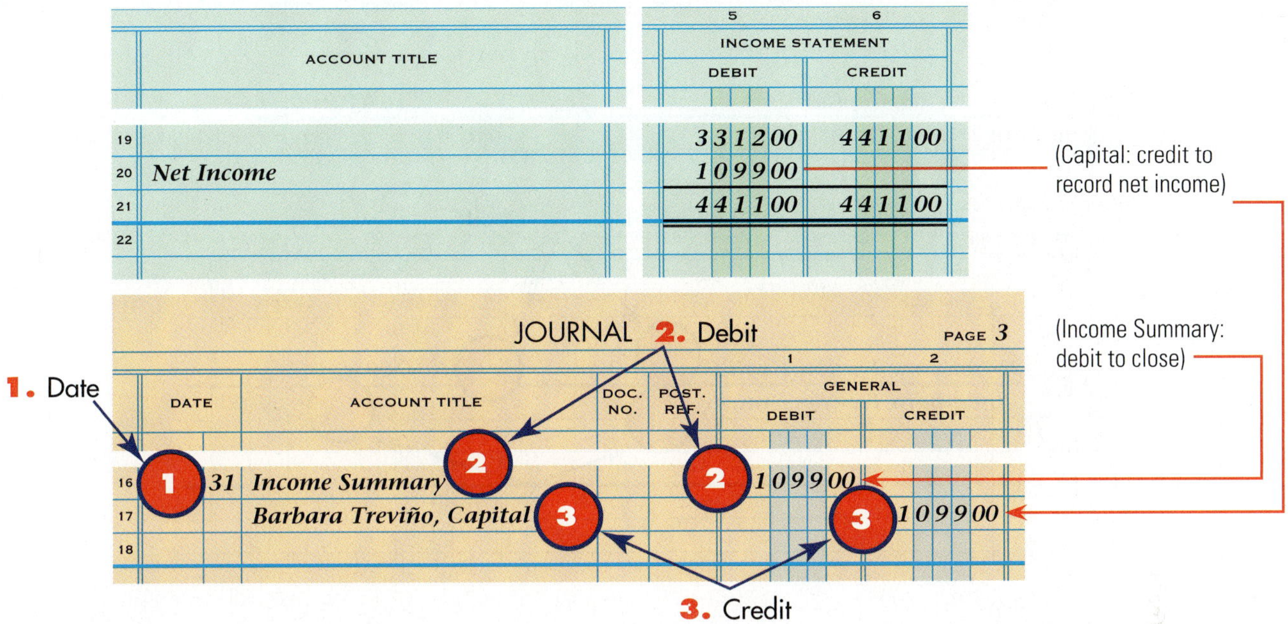


Encore Music's net income appears on line 20 of the work sheet. The amount of net income increases the owner's capital and, therefore, must be credited to the owner's capital account. The balance of the temporary account, Income Summary, must be reduced to zero to prepare the account for the next fiscal period.

The effect of this closing entry on the general ledger accounts is shown in the T accounts.

The debit to the income summary account, $1,099.00, reduces the account balance to zero and prepares the account for the next fiscal period. The credit, $1,099.00, increases the balance of the owner's capital account, Barbara Treviño, Capital.

**Income Summary**

| Debit | | Credit | |
|---|---|---|---|
| Closing (expenses) | 3,312.00 | Closing (revenue) | 4,411.00 |
| Closing | 1,099.00 | *(New Bal. zero)* | |

**Barbara Treviño, Capital**

| Debit | | Credit | |
|---|---|---|---|
| | | Bal. | 10,000.00 |
| | | Closing (net inc.) | 1,099.00 |
| | | *(New Bal.* | *11,099.00)* |

If a business incurs a net loss, the closing entry is a debit to the owner's capital account and a credit to the income summary account.

### STEPS: Closing entry to record net income or loss and close the income summary account

1. Write the date, *31*, on the next line in the Date column.
2. Write the title of the account debited, *Income Summary,* in the Account Title column. Record the debit amount, *$1,099.00,* in the General Debit column on the same line as the account title.
3. Write the title of the account credited, *Barbara Treviño, Capital,* on the next line in the Account Title column. Record the credit amount, *$1,099.00,* in the General Credit column on the same line as the account title.

**REMEMBER**

Amounts for closing entries are taken from the Income Statement and Balance Sheet columns of the work sheet.

# CLOSING ENTRY FOR THE OWNER'S DRAWING ACCOUNT

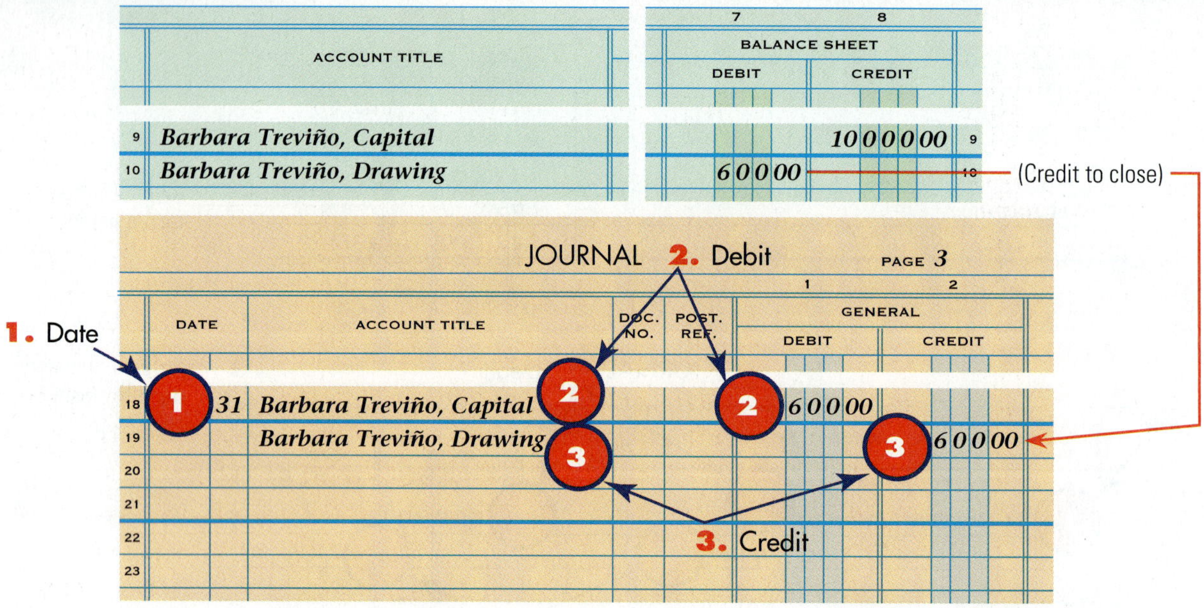


Withdrawals are assets that the owner takes out of a business and which decrease the amount of the owner's equity. The drawing account is a temporary account that accumulates information separately for each fiscal period. Therefore, the drawing account balance is reduced to zero at the end of one fiscal period to prepare the account for the next fiscal period.

The drawing account is neither a revenue nor an expense account. Therefore, the drawing account is not closed through Income Summary. The drawing account balance is closed directly to the owner's capital account.

The effect of the entry to close the drawing account is shown in the T accounts.

The drawing account has a zero balance and is ready for the next fiscal period. The capital account's new balance, $10,499.00, is verified by comparing the balance to the amount of capital shown on the balance sheet prepared at the end of the fiscal period. The capital account balance shown on Encore Music's balance sheet in Chapter 8 is $10,499.00. The two amounts are the same, and the capital account balance is verified.

**Barbara Treviño, Capital**

| | | | |
|---|---|---|---|
| Closing (drawing) | 600.00 | Bal. | 10,000.00 |
| | | Net Income | 1,099.00 |
| | | *(New Bal.* | *10,499.00)* |

**Barbara Treviño, Drawing**

| | | | |
|---|---|---|---|
| Bal. | 600.00 | Closing | 600.00 |
| *(New Bal. zero)* | | | |

## STEPS: Closing entry for the owner's drawing account

1. Write the date, *31,* in the Date column.
2. Write the title of the account debited, *Barbara Treviño, Capital,* in the Account Title column. Record the debit amount, *$600.00,* in the General Debit column on the same line as the account title.
3. Write the title of the account credited, *Barbara Treviño, Drawing,* in the Account Title column. Record the credit amount, *$600.00,* in the General Credit column on the same line as the account title.

## TERMS REVIEW

permanent accounts
temporary accounts
closing entries

## AUDIT YOUR UNDERSTANDING

1. What do the ending balances of permanent accounts for one fiscal period represent at the beginning of the next fiscal period?
2. What do the balances of temporary accounts show?
3. List the four closing entries.

## WORK TOGETHER

**Journalizing and posting closing entries**

Use the journal and general ledger accounts from Work Together on page 202. A partial work sheet for the month ended July 31 of the current year is given in the *Working Papers*. Your instructor will guide you through the following example.

4. Continue on the same journal page. Journalize and post the closing entries. Save your work to complete Work Together on page 215.

## ON YOUR OWN

**Journalizing and posting closing entries**

Use the journal and general ledger accounts from On Your Own on page 202. A partial work sheet for the month ended February 28 of the current year is given in the *Working Papers*. Work this problem independently.

5. Continue on the same journal page. Journalize and post the closing entries. Save your work to complete On Your Own on page 215.

# 9-3 Preparing a Post-Closing Trial Balance

## GENERAL LEDGER ACCOUNTS AFTER ADJUSTING AND CLOSING ENTRIES ARE POSTED

ACCOUNT *Cash* ACCOUNT NO. *110*

| DATE | | ITEM | POST. REF. | DEBIT | CREDIT | BALANCE DEBIT | BALANCE CREDIT |
|---|---|---|---|---|---|---|---|
| 20-- Aug. | 31 | | 2 | 14,291.00 | | 14,291.00 | |
| | 31 | | 2 | | 6,019.00 | 8,272.00 | |

ACCOUNT *Petty Cash* ACCOUNT NO. *120*

| DATE | | ITEM | POST. REF. | DEBIT | CREDIT | BALANCE DEBIT | BALANCE CREDIT |
|---|---|---|---|---|---|---|---|
| 20-- Aug. | 17 | | 1 | 200.00 | | 200.00 | |

ACCOUNT *Accounts Receivable—Kids Time* ACCOUNT NO. *130*

| DATE | | ITEM | POST. REF. | DEBIT | CREDIT | BALANCE DEBIT | BALANCE CREDIT |
|---|---|---|---|---|---|---|---|
| 20-- Aug. | 12 | | 1 | 200.00 | | 200.00 | |
| | 12 | | 1 | | 100.00 | 100.00 | |

ACCOUNT *Accounts Receivable—Learn N Play* ACCOUNT NO. *140*

| DATE | | ITEM | POST. REF. | DEBIT | CREDIT | BALANCE DEBIT | BALANCE CREDIT |
|---|---|---|---|---|---|---|---|
| 20-- Aug. | 13 | | 1 | 20.00 | | 20.00 | |

ACCOUNT *Supplies* ACCOUNT NO. *150*

| DATE | | ITEM | POST. REF. | DEBIT | CREDIT | BALANCE DEBIT | BALANCE CREDIT |
|---|---|---|---|---|---|---|---|
| 20-- Aug. | 3 | | 1 | 1,577.00 | | 1,577.00 | |
| | 7 | | 1 | 2,720.00 | | 4,297.00 | |
| | 20 | | 1 | 20.00 | | 4,317.00 | |
| | 28 | | 2 | 434.00 | | 4,751.00 | |
| | 31 | | 3 | | 2,564.00 | 2,187.00 | |

Encore Music's general ledger, after the adjusting and closing entries are posted, is shown here and on the next several pages. When an account has a zero balance, lines are drawn in both the Balance Debit and Balance Credit columns. The lines assure a reader that a balance has not been omitted.

ACCOUNT *Prepaid Insurance* ACCOUNT NO. 160

| DATE | | ITEM | POST. REF. | DEBIT | CREDIT | BALANCE DEBIT | BALANCE CREDIT |
|---|---|---|---|---|---|---|---|
| 20-- Aug. | 4 | | 1 | 1,200.00 | | 1,200.00 | |
| | 31 | | 3 | | 100.00 | 1,100.00 | |

ACCOUNT *Accounts Payable—Ling Music Supplies* ACCOUNT NO. 210

| DATE | | ITEM | POST. REF. | DEBIT | CREDIT | BALANCE DEBIT | BALANCE CREDIT |
|---|---|---|---|---|---|---|---|
| 20-- Aug. | 7 | | 1 | | 2,720.00 | | 2,720.00 |
| | 11 | | 1 | 1,360.00 | | | 1,360.00 |

ACCOUNT *Accounts Payable—Sullivan Office Supplies* ACCOUNT NO. 220

| DATE | | ITEM | POST. REF. | DEBIT | CREDIT | BALANCE DEBIT | BALANCE CREDIT |
|---|---|---|---|---|---|---|---|
| 20-- Aug. | 20 | | 1 | | 20.00 | | 20.00 |

ACCOUNT *Barbara Treviño, Capital* ACCOUNT NO. 310

| DATE | | ITEM | POST. REF. | DEBIT | CREDIT | BALANCE DEBIT | BALANCE CREDIT |
|---|---|---|---|---|---|---|---|
| 20-- Aug. | 1 | | 1 | | 10,000.00 | | 10,000.00 |
| | 31 | | 3 | | 1,099.00 | | 11,099.00 |
| | 31 | | 3 | 600.00 | | | 10,499.00 |

ACCOUNT *Barbara Treviño, Drawing* ACCOUNT NO. 320

| DATE | | ITEM | POST. REF. | DEBIT | CREDIT | BALANCE DEBIT | BALANCE CREDIT |
|---|---|---|---|---|---|---|---|
| 20-- Aug. | 12 | | 1 | 100.00 | | 100.00 | |
| | 31 | | 2 | 500.00 | | 600.00 | |
| | 31 | | 3 | | 600.00 | — | — |

ACCOUNT *Income Summary* ACCOUNT NO. 330

| DATE | | ITEM | POST. REF. | DEBIT | CREDIT | BALANCE DEBIT | BALANCE CREDIT |
|---|---|---|---|---|---|---|---|
| 20-- Aug. | 31 | | 3 | | 4,411.00 | | 4,411.00 |
| | 31 | | 3 | 3,312.00 | | | 1,099.00 |
| | 31 | | 3 | 1,099.00 | | — | — |

ACCOUNT *Sales* ACCOUNT NO. 410

| DATE | | ITEM | POST. REF. | DEBIT | CREDIT | BALANCE DEBIT | BALANCE CREDIT |
|---|---|---|---|---|---|---|---|
| 20-- Aug. | 31 | | 2 | | 4,411.00 | | 4,411.00 |
| | 31 | | 3 | 4,411.00 | | — | — |

A General Ledger after Adjusting and Closing Entries Are Posted *(continued)*

ACCOUNT *Advertising Expense* ACCOUNT NO. *510*

| DATE | | ITEM | POST. REF. | DEBIT | CREDIT | BALANCE DEBIT | BALANCE CREDIT |
|---|---|---|---|---|---|---|---|
| 20-- Aug. | 14 | | 1 | 68 00 | | 68 00 | |
| | 18 | | 1 | 200 00 | | 268 00 | |
| | 31 | | 2 | 5 00 | | 273 00 | |
| | 31 | | 3 | | 273 00 | — | — |

ACCOUNT *Insurance Expense* ACCOUNT NO. *520*

| DATE | | ITEM | POST. REF. | DEBIT | CREDIT | BALANCE DEBIT | BALANCE CREDIT |
|---|---|---|---|---|---|---|---|
| 20-- Aug. | 31 | | 3 | 100 00 | | 100 00 | |
| | 31 | | 3 | | 100 00 | — | — |

ACCOUNT *Miscellaneous Expense* ACCOUNT NO. *530*

| DATE | | ITEM | POST. REF. | DEBIT | CREDIT | BALANCE DEBIT | BALANCE CREDIT |
|---|---|---|---|---|---|---|---|
| 20-- Aug. | 31 | | 2 | 7 00 | | 7 00 | |
| | 31 | | 2 | 3 00 | | 10 00 | |
| | 31 | | 3 | | 10 00 | — | — |

ACCOUNT *Rent Expense* ACCOUNT NO. *540*

| DATE | | ITEM | POST. REF. | DEBIT | CREDIT | BALANCE DEBIT | BALANCE CREDIT |
|---|---|---|---|---|---|---|---|
| 20-- Aug. | 12 | | 1 | 250 00 | | 250 00 | |
| | 31 | | 3 | | 250 00 | — | — |

ACCOUNT *Supplies Expense* ACCOUNT NO. *550*

| DATE | | ITEM | POST. REF. | DEBIT | CREDIT | BALANCE DEBIT | BALANCE CREDIT |
|---|---|---|---|---|---|---|---|
| 20-- Aug. | 31 | | 3 | 2564 00 | | 2564 00 | |
| | 31 | | 3 | | 2564 00 | — | — |

ACCOUNT *Utilities Expense* ACCOUNT NO. *560*

| DATE | | ITEM | POST. REF. | DEBIT | CREDIT | BALANCE DEBIT | BALANCE CREDIT |
|---|---|---|---|---|---|---|---|
| 20-- Aug. | 12 | | 1 | 45 00 | | 45 00 | |
| | 27 | | 2 | 70 00 | | 115 00 | |
| | 31 | | 3 | | 115 00 | — | — |

A General Ledger after Adjusting and Closing Entries Are Posted *(concluded)*

# POST-CLOSING TRIAL BALANCE

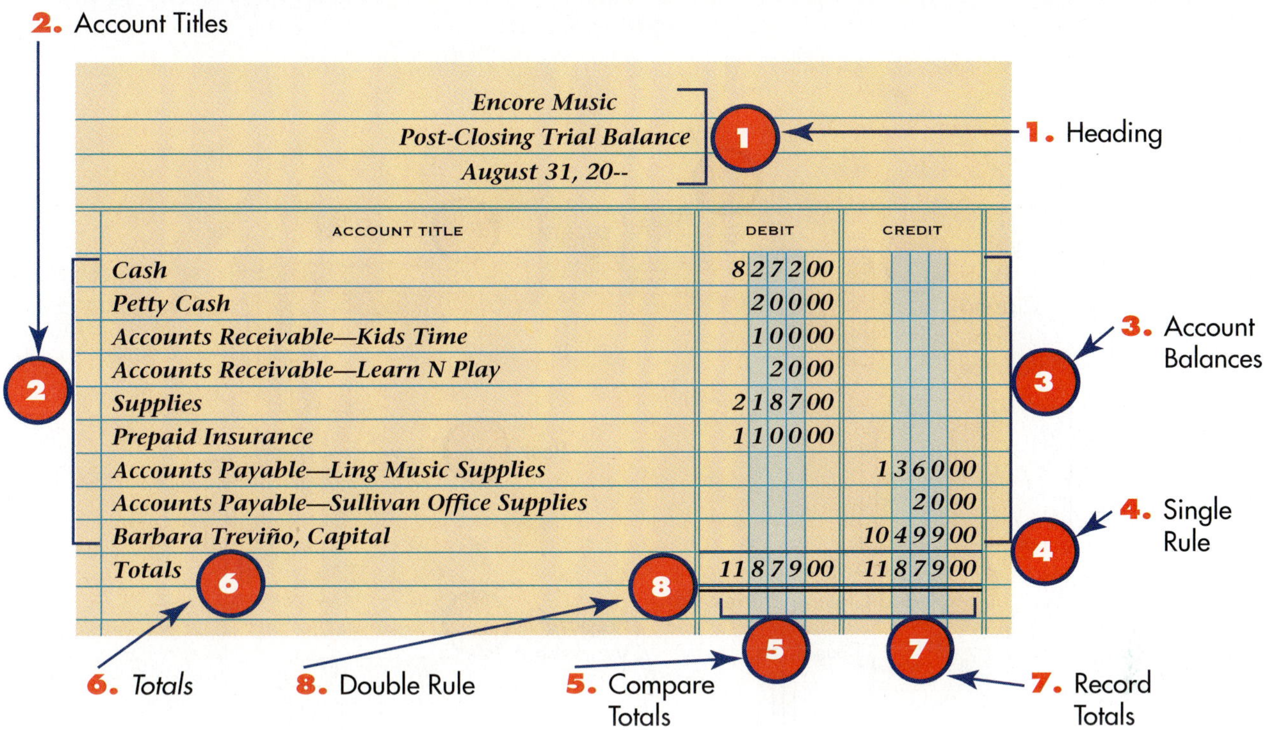

| Encore Music | | |
|---|---|---|
| Post-Closing Trial Balance | | |
| August 31, 20-- | | |
| ACCOUNT TITLE | DEBIT | CREDIT |
| Cash | 8272 00 | |
| Petty Cash | 200 00 | |
| Accounts Receivable—Kids Time | 100 00 | |
| Accounts Receivable—Learn N Play | 20 00 | |
| Supplies | 2187 00 | |
| Prepaid Insurance | 1100 00 | |
| Accounts Payable—Ling Music Supplies | | 1360 00 |
| Accounts Payable—Sullivan Office Supplies | | 20 00 |
| Barbara Treviño, Capital | | 10499 00 |
| Totals | 11879 00 | 11879 00 |



After the closing entries are posted, Encore Music verifies that debits equal credits in the general ledger accounts by preparing a trial balance. A trial balance prepared after the closing entries are posted is called a **post-closing trial balance.**

Only general ledger accounts with balances are included on a post-closing trial balance. The permanent accounts (assets, liabilities, and owner's capital) have balances and do appear on a post-closing trial balance. Because the temporary accounts (income summary, revenue, expense, and drawing) are closed and have zero balances, they do not appear on a post-closing trial balance.

The total of all debits must equal the total of all credits in a general ledger. The totals of both columns on Encore Music's post-closing trial balance are the same, $11,879.00. Encore Music's post-closing trial balance shows that the general ledger account balances are in balance and ready for the new fiscal period.

## STEPS: Preparing a post-closing trial balance

1. Write the heading on three lines.
2. Write the titles of all general ledger accounts with balances in the Account Title column.
3. On the same line with each account title, write each account's balance in either the Debit or Credit column.
4. Rule a single line across both amount columns below the last amount, and add each amount column.
5. Compare the two column totals. The two column totals must be the same. If the two column totals are not the same, the errors must be found and corrected before any more work is completed.
6. Write the word *Totals* on the line below the last account title.
7. Write the column totals, *$11,879.00,* below the single line.
8. Rule double lines across both amount columns to show that the totals have been verified as correct.

# ACCOUNTING CYCLE FOR A SERVICE BUSINESS

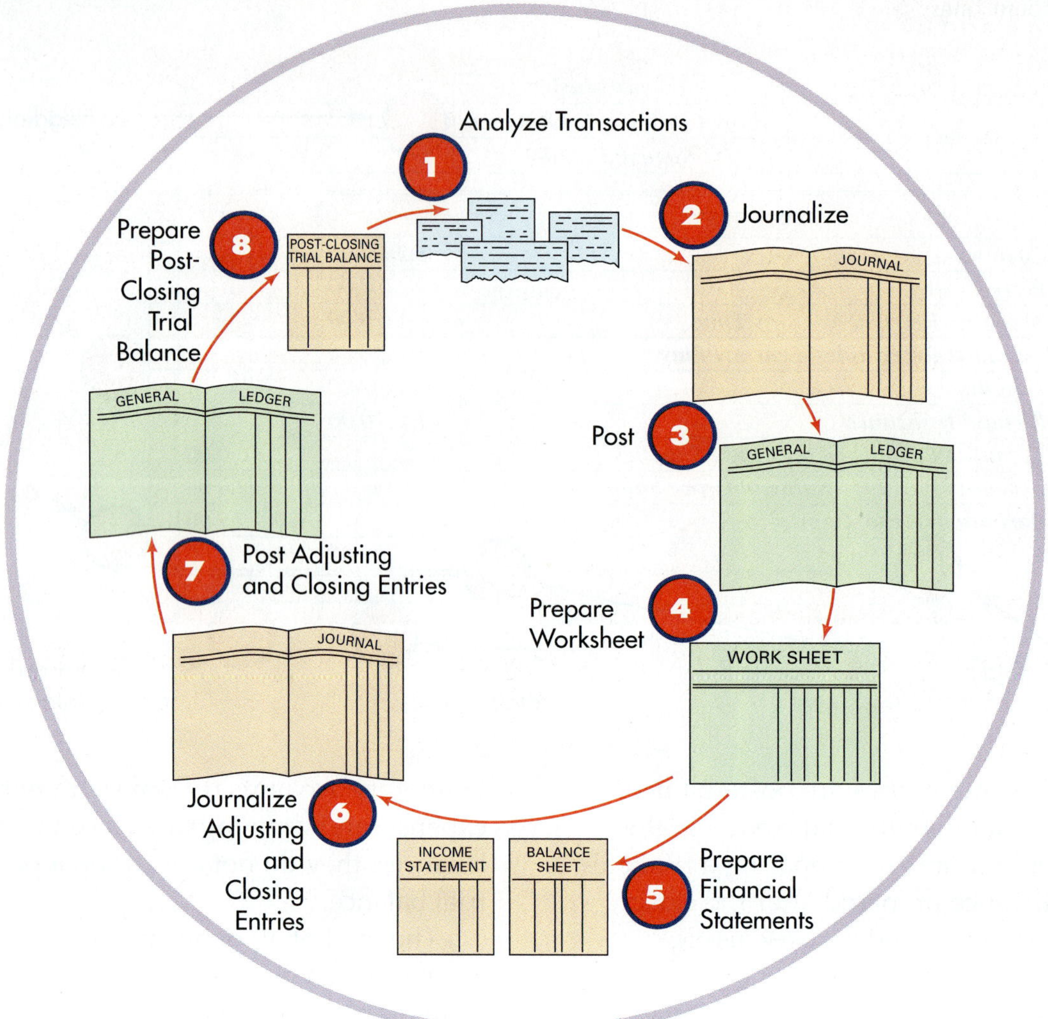


Chapters 1 through 9 describe Encore Music's accounting activities for a one-month fiscal period. The series of accounting activities included in recording financial information for a fiscal period is called an **accounting cycle.** *(CONCEPT: Accounting Period Cycle)*

For the next fiscal period, the cycle begins again at Step 1.

## STEPS: Steps in an accounting cycle

1. Source documents are checked for accuracy, and transactions are analyzed into debit and credit parts.
2. Transactions, from information on source documents, are recorded in a journal.
3. Journal entries are posted to the general ledger.
4. A work sheet, including a trial balance, is prepared from the general ledger.
5. Financial statements are prepared from the work sheet.
6. Adjusting and closing entries are journalized from the work sheet.
7. Adjusting and closing entries are posted to the general ledger.
8. A post-closing trial balance of the general ledger is prepared.

**FYI**

*The word* post *means* after. *The Post-Closing Trial Balance is prepared after closing entries.*

## TERMS REVIEW

post-closing trial balance

accounting cycle

## AUDIT YOUR UNDERSTANDING

1. Why are lines drawn in both the Balance Debit and Balance Credit columns when an account has a zero balance?
2. Which accounts go on the post-closing trial balance?
3. Why are temporary accounts omitted from a post-closing trial balance?

## WORK TOGETHER

**Preparing a post-closing trial balance**

Use the general ledger accounts from Work Together on page 209. Your instructor will guide you through the following example. A form to complete a post-closing trial balance is given in the *Working Papers.*

4. Prepare a post-closing trial balance for Darlene's Delivery Service on July 31 of the current year.

## ON YOUR OWN

**Preparing a post-closing trial balance**

Use the general ledger accounts from On Your Own on page 209. Work this problem independently. A form to complete a post-closing trial balance is given in the *Working Papers.*

5. Prepare a post-closing trial balance for Keith's Copies on February 28 of the current year.

# CHAPTER 9 SUMMARY

*Enrichment Activity*

**Accounting Careers**

*Integrity is a characteristic of the accounting profession. The AICPA Professional Code of Conduct states, "...an accountant shall not knowingly misrepresent facts." Why is integrity of accountants so important to financial statements?*

After completing this chapter, you can

1. Define accounting terms related to adjusting and closing entries for a service business organized as a proprietorship.
2. Identify accounting concepts and practices related to adjusting and closing entries for a service business organized as a proprietorship.
3. Record adjusting entries for a service business organized as a proprietorship.
4. Record closing entries for a service business organized as a proprietorship.
5. Prepare a post-closing trial balance for a service business organized as a proprietorship.

## EXPLORE ACCOUNTING

### PUBLIC ACCOUNTING FIRMS

A business that helps other businesses with accounting issues is known as a public accounting firm.

The independent reviewing and issuing of an opinion on the reliability of accounting records is known as *auditing*.

When performing an audit for a client, the accounting firm looks closely at the client's financial statements and the way the client records transactions. The auditor's job is to determine if the financial statements fairly present the financial position of the client. The auditor issues an opinion, which is a statement as to whether the financial statements follow standard accounting rules (GAAP). This "opinion" is used by bankers deciding to lend money to the company. It is also used by investors when making investment decisions.

Auditing, however, is just one of many services provided by public accounting firms. Other services include tax preparation, tax advice, payroll services, bookkeeping services, financial statement preparation, and consulting services. These other services often make up a higher percentage of business for the accounting firm than performing audits.

Many accounting firms report that they are getting more requests for consulting services than for other services they can provide. In many cases, consulting is also the area that produces the largest profit margin for the public accounting firm.

Therefore, some firms are actively advertising their ability to provide management consulting services for clients.

**Activity:** Contact a public accounting firm in your area. Research what services the firm provides and which service area (if any) is growing. Present your findings to your class.

# 9-1 APPLICATION PROBLEM
## Journalizing and posting adjusting entries

A journal and general ledger accounts are given in the *Working Papers.* A partial work sheet for the month ended April 30 of the current year is shown below.

| | ACCOUNT TITLE | 3 ADJUSTMENTS DEBIT | 4 ADJUSTMENTS CREDIT |
|---|---|---|---|
| 5 | *Supplies* | | (a) 180 00 |
| 6 | *Prepaid Insurance* | | (b) 160 00 |
| 14 | *Insurance Expense* | (b) 160 00 | |
| 15 | *Miscellaneous Expense* | | |
| 16 | *Supplies Expense* | (a) 180 00 | |

Use page 12 of a journal. Journalize and post the adjusting entries. Save your work to complete Application Problem 9-2.

# 9-2 APPLICATION PROBLEM
## Journalizing and posting closing entries

Use the journal and general ledger accounts from Application Problem 9-1. A partial work sheet for the month ended April 30 of the current year is shown below.

| | ACCOUNT TITLE | 5 INCOME STATEMENT DEBIT | 6 INCOME STATEMENT CREDIT | 7 BALANCE SHEET DEBIT | 8 BALANCE SHEET CREDIT | |
|---|---|---|---|---|---|---|
| 1 | *Cash* | | | 9500 00 | | 1 |
| 2 | *Petty Cash* | | | 100 00 | | 2 |
| 3 | *Accounts Receivable—Betsy Russell* | | | 1650 00 | | 3 |
| 4 | *Accounts Receivable—Charles Healy* | | | 1403 00 | | 4 |
| 5 | *Supplies* | | | 220 00 | | 5 |
| 6 | *Prepaid Insurance* | | | 640 00 | | 6 |
| 7 | *Accounts Payable—Lindgren Supply* | | | | 548 00 | 7 |
| 8 | *Accounts Payable—Taxes By Thomas* | | | | 111 00 | 8 |
| 9 | *Ken Cherniak, Capital* | | | | 11810 00 | 9 |
| 10 | *Ken Cherniak, Drawing* | | | 855 00 | | 10 |
| 11 | *Income Summary* | | | | | 11 |
| 12 | *Sales* | | 4400 00 | | | 12 |
| 13 | *Advertising Expense* | 800 00 | | | | 13 |
| 14 | *Insurance Expense* | 160 00 | | | | 14 |
| 15 | *Miscellaneous Expense* | 351 00 | | | | 15 |
| 16 | *Supplies Expense* | 180 00 | | | | 16 |
| 17 | *Utilities Expense* | 1010 00 | | | | 17 |
| 18 | | 2501 00 | 4400 00 | 14368 00 | 12469 00 | 18 |
| 19 | *Net Income* | 1899 00 | | | 1899 00 | 19 |
| 20 | | 4400 00 | 4400 00 | 14368 00 | 14368 00 | 20 |
| 21 | | | | | | 21 |

Continue on the same journal page. Journalize and post the closing entries. Save your work to complete Application Problem 9-3.

## 9-3 APPLICATION PROBLEM
### Preparing a post-closing trial balance

Use the general ledger accounts from Application Problem 9-2. A form to complete a post-closing trial balance is given in the *Working Papers*.

Prepare a post-closing trial balance for Ken's Carpet Cleaning on April 30 of the current year.

## 9-4 MASTERY PROBLEM
### Journalizing and posting adjusting and closing entries; preparing a post-closing trial balance

Jane's Sewing Machine Repair's partial work sheet for the month ended October 31 of the current year is given below. The general ledger accounts are given in the *Working Papers*. The general ledger accounts do not show all details for the fiscal period. The Balance shown in each account is the account's balance before adjusting and closing entries are posted.

| | ACCOUNT TITLE | 3 ADJUSTMENTS DEBIT | 4 ADJUSTMENTS CREDIT | 5 INCOME STATEMENT DEBIT | 6 INCOME STATEMENT CREDIT | 7 BALANCE SHEET DEBIT | 8 BALANCE SHEET CREDIT | |
|---|---|---|---|---|---|---|---|---|
| 1 | *Cash* | | | | | 6,400.00 | | 1 |
| 2 | *Petty Cash* | | | | | 100.00 | | 2 |
| 3 | *Accts. Rec.—Debbie McDonald* | | | | | 657.00 | | 3 |
| 4 | *Accts. Rec.—Howard Kikles* | | | | | 599.00 | | 4 |
| 5 | *Supplies* | | (a) 120.00 | | | 155.00 | | 5 |
| 6 | *Prepaid Insurance* | | (b) 150.00 | | | 300.00 | | 6 |
| 7 | *Accts. Pay.—Bailey's Supply* | | | | | | 187.00 | 7 |
| 8 | *Accts. Pay.—Freida's on Fulton* | | | | | | 126.00 | 8 |
| 9 | *Jane Wisen, Capital* | | | | | | 6,430.00 | 9 |
| 10 | *Jane Wisen, Drawing* | | | | | 1,500.00 | | 10 |
| 11 | *Income Summary* | | | | | | | 11 |
| 12 | *Sales* | | | | 4,238.00 | | | 12 |
| 13 | *Advertising Expense* | | | 382.00 | | | | 13 |
| 14 | *Insurance Expense* | (b) 150.00 | | 150.00 | | | | 14 |
| 15 | *Supplies Expense* | (a) 120.00 | | 120.00 | | | | 15 |
| 16 | *Utilities Expense* | | | 618.00 | | | | 16 |
| 17 | | 270.00 | 270.00 | 1,270.00 | 4,238.00 | 9,711.00 | 6,743.00 | 17 |
| 18 | *Net Income* | | | 2,968.00 | | | 2,968.00 | 18 |
| 19 | | | | 4,238.00 | 4,238.00 | 9,711.00 | 9,711.00 | 19 |
| 20 | | | | | | | | 20 |

***Instructions:***

1. Use page 20 of a journal. Journalize and post the adjusting entries.
2. Continue to use page 20 of the journal. Journalize and post the closing entries.
3. Prepare a post-closing trial balance.

## 9-5 CHALLENGE PROBLEM

### Journalizing and posting adjusting and closing entries with a net loss; preparing a post-closing trial balance

Mancini Hair Care's partial work sheet for the month ended September 30 of the current year is given below. The general ledger accounts are given in the *Working Papers.* The general ledger accounts do not show all details for the fiscal period. The Balance shown in each account is the account's balance before adjusting and closing entries are posted.

| | | 3 | 4 | 5 | 6 | 7 | 8 | |
|---|---|---|---|---|---|---|---|---|
| | | ADJUSTMENTS | | INCOME STATEMENT | | BALANCE SHEET | | |
| | ACCOUNT TITLE | DEBIT | CREDIT | DEBIT | CREDIT | DEBIT | CREDIT | |
| 1 | *Cash* | | | | | 7678 00 | | 1 |
| 2 | *Petty Cash* | | | | | 100 00 | | 2 |
| 3 | *Accts. Rec.—Jennifer Balsa* | | | | | 164 00 | | 3 |
| 4 | *Supplies* | | (a) 1500 00 | | | 690 00 | | 4 |
| 5 | *Prepaid Insurance* | | (b) 175 00 | | | 700 00 | | 5 |
| 6 | *Accts. Pay.—Alto Supplies* | | | | | | 733 00 | 6 |
| 7 | *Jon Mancini, Capital* | | | | | | 9500 00 | 7 |
| 8 | *Jon Mancini, Drawing* | | | | | 500 00 | | 8 |
| 9 | *Income Summary* | | | | | | | 9 |
| 10 | *Sales* | | | | 4596 00 | | | 10 |
| 11 | *Advertising Expense* | | | 550 00 | | | | 11 |
| 12 | *Insurance Expense* | (b) 175 00 | | 175 00 | | | | 12 |
| 13 | *Miscellaneous Expense* | | | 58 00 | | | | 13 |
| 14 | *Supplies Expense* | (a) 1500 00 | | 1500 00 | | | | 14 |
| 15 | *Utilities Expense* | | | 2714 00 | | | | 15 |
| 16 | | 1675 00 | 1675 00 | 4997 00 | 4596 00 | 9832 00 | 10233 00 | 16 |
| 17 | *Net Loss* | | | | 401 00 | 401 00 | | 17 |
| 18 | | | | 4997 00 | 4997 00 | 10233 00 | 10233 00 | 18 |

***Instructions:***

1. Use page 18 of a journal. Journalize and post the adjusting entries.
2. Continue to use page 18 of the journal. Journalize and post the closing entries.
3. Prepare a post-closing trial balance.
4. Jon Mancini, owner of Mancini Hair Care, is disappointed that his business incurred a net loss for September of the current year. Mr. Mancini would have preferred not to have to reduce his capital by \$401.00. He knows that you are studying accounting, so Mr. Mancini asks you to analyze his work sheet for September. Based on your analysis of the work sheet, what would you suggest may have caused the net loss for Mancini Hair Care? What steps would you suggest so that Mr. Mancini can avoid a net loss in future months?

## INTERNET ACTIVITY

Point your browser to

**http://accounting.swpco.com**

Choose **First-Year Course**, choose **Activities**, and complete the activity for Chapter 9.

## Applied Communication

Service businesses are the fastest growing part of our business world. Social and economic changes create needs for new and different kinds of service businesses to satisfy customer demands.

For example, the growing popularity of the World Wide Web led to the creation of service businesses that design Web pages. These businesses create text, graphics, animation, and links for business and private clients. Another example of a new type of service business is a personal services business that runs errands or stands in long lines for clients. As lifestyles become busier and busier, some people do not have the time to take care of all their personal errands. Service businesses have appeared to fill this need.

**Instructions:** Using library, online, or other information resources, write a one-page report on a new or unusual service business that you would be interested in working for or owning.

## Cases for Critical Thinking

**Case 1** Gretel Bakken forgot to journalize and post the adjusting entry for prepaid insurance at the end of the June fiscal period. What effect will this omission have on the records of Ms. Bakken's business as of June 30? Explain your answer.

**Case 2** Miles Reed states that his business is so small that he just records supplies and insurance as expenses when he pays for them. Thus, at the end of a fiscal period, Mr. Reed does not record adjusting and closing entries for his business. Do you agree with his accounting procedures? Explain your answer.

**Case 3** As you have learned, accounting procedures can be complicated and time-consuming. However, completing accounting work in a timely fashion is very important to business operations and decision making. Business owners rely upon accounting information in order to make good plans for the future. Knowing whether sales are increasing or decreasing or whether the business is earning net income or incurring a net loss is critical information for the owner and other people interested in the financial results of a business.

Completing a work sheet, preparing financial statements, and journalizing and posting adjusting and closing entries are sometimes referred to as end-of-fiscal-period activities. How important is it for end-of-fiscal-period activities to be completed soon after a fiscal period ends? Why do accounting employees often work long hours and weekends just before and just after a fiscal period ends? Explain your answers.

# AUTOMATED ACCOUNTING

## AUTOMATED ADJUSTING AND CLOSING ENTRIES FOR PROPRIETORSHIPS

During the fiscal period, numerous transactions are analyzed, journalized, and posted. When a transaction affects more than one accounting period, an adjusting entry may be needed to match revenues and expenses with the appropriate accounting period. To complete the accounting cycle, adjusting entries are recorded, entered into the computer, and verified for accuracy. The financial statements are generated, and then closing entries are generated and posted by the software.

### Adjusting Entries

After all the usual transactions of the business are entered as journal entries, a preliminary trial balance is generated. This trial balance and period-end adjustment data are used as the basis for the adjusting entries. Usually this will include entries for assets that have been consumed or sold during the period and have become expenses, such as supplies and insurance policies. For most asset accounts, such as Supplies and Insurance, the adjustment is made to the related expense account. The General Journal tab within the Journal Entries window is used to enter and post the adjusting entries. All of the adjusting entries are dated the last day of the fiscal period, and use Adj. Ent. as the reference.

### Period-End Closing for a Proprietorship

In an automated accounting system, closing entries are generated and posted by the software. The software automatically closes net income to the owner's capital account after closing the revenue and expense accounts. The drawing account is closed as well.

To perform a period-end closing:

1. Choose Generate Closing Journal Entries from the Options menu.
2. Click Yes to generate the closing entries.
3. The general journal will appear, containing the journal entries.
4. Click the Post button.

### AUTOMATING MASTERY PROBLEM 9-4: Journalizing and posting adjusting and closing entries; preparing a post-closing trial balance

**Instructions:**

1. Load *Automated Accounting 7.0* or higher software.
2. Select database F09-1 from the appropriate directory/folder.
3. Select File from the menu bar and choose the Save As menu command. Key the path to the drive and directory that contains your data files. Save the database with a file name of XXX091 (where XXX are your initials).
4. Access Problem Instructions through the Help menu (7.0) or Browser tool (8.0). Read the Problem Instructions screen.
5. Refer to page 212 for data used in this template.
6. Exit the *Automated Accounting* software.

### AUTOMATING CHALLENGE PROBLEM 9-5: Journalizing and posting adjusting and closing entries with a net loss; preparing a post-closing trial balance

**Instructions:**

1. Load *Automated Accounting 7.0* or higher software.
2. Select database F09-2 from the appropriate directory/folder.
3. Select File from the menu bar and choose the Save As menu command. Key the path to the drive and directory that contains your data files. Save the database with a file name of XXX092 (where XXX are your initials).
4. Access Problem Instructions through the Help menu (7.0) or Browser tool (8.0). Read the Problem Instructions screen.
5. Refer to page 213 for data used in this template.
6. Exit the *Automated Accounting* software.

## REINFORCEMENT ACTIVITY 1—PART B

# An Accounting Cycle for a Proprietorship: End-of-Fiscal-Period Work

The general ledger prepared in Reinforcement Activity 1—Part A is needed to complete Reinforcement Activity 1—Part B.

Reinforcement Activity 1—Part B includes end-of-fiscal-period activities studied in Chapters 7 through 9.

## WORK SHEET

***Instructions:***

12. Prepare a trial balance on the work sheet given in the *Working Papers*. Use a one-month fiscal period ended May 31 of the current year.
13. Analyze the following adjustment information into debit and credit parts. Record the adjustments on the work sheet.

**Adjustment Information, May 31**

| | |
|---|---|
| Supplies on hand | $520.00 |
| Value of prepaid insurance | 800.00 |

14. Total and rule the Adjustments columns.
15. Extend the up-to-date account balances to the Balance Sheet and Income Statement columns.
16. Complete the work sheet.

## FINANCIAL STATEMENTS

***Instructions:***

17. Prepare an income statement. Figure and record the component percentages for sales, total expenses, and net income. Round percentage calculations to the nearest 0.1%.
18. Prepare a balance sheet.

## ADJUSTING ENTRIES

***Instructions:***

19. Use page 3 of the journal. Journalize and post the adjusting entries.

## CLOSING ENTRIES

***Instructions:***

20. Continue using page 3 of the journal. Journalize and post the closing entries.

## POST-CLOSING TRIAL BALANCE

***Instructions:***

21. Prepare a post-closing trial balance.

# ACCOUNTING IN YOUR CAREER

## UNTANGLING CASH PAYMENTS

Denise Klein and Martin Nadler are partners in an office supply business called OfficeTown. Their store is located next to a complex of office towers, ensuring frequent purchases by nearby companies.

The partners are considering a major expansion to include more emphasis on computer supplies, both hardware and software, and they believe they can also profit from adding copying and packing and delivery services. They have just hired David Bradford as office manager because he has a degree in accounting and extensive experience with computers. David has discovered the following problems related to cash payments.

- Both partners withdraw a set amount of cash each month, paid by check. During the week, however, both Denise and Martin take cash from the cash register for their daily personal expenses.
- Both partners regularly take office and computer supplies home for personal use.
- Incidental small payments, such as delivery charges and postage stamps, are paid for by removing cash from the cash register.
- When office supplies are needed for the operation of the business, they are removed from the stock of the store. No journal entry is made.
- At the end of the day, the cash in the cash register is counted and the cash register tape shows the total sales for the day. The cash count is subtracted from the total of the beginning cash plus total sales, and the difference is posted as Miscellaneous Expense.

**Critical Thinking:**

1. How could each problem area be corrected and what journal entries should be recorded?
2. Describe for each of the five identified problems which accounts are affected and whether they will be overstated or understated on the financial statements.

# 10-1 Journalizing Purchases of Merchandise for Cash

*When Michelle Wu and Karl Koehn were exchange students in Thailand, they talked about someday going into business together. After each gained a variety of international business experience, Michelle and Karl started Omni Import five years ago. They both enjoy applying their knowledge about other countries and cultures to the operation of their business.*

*Michelle is especially good at traveling and finding merchandise that people want to buy. Karl has a knack for displaying the merchandise in the most attractive way. These compatible skills make Michelle and Karl more successful as partners than if each ran a business alone. Both partners are convinced, moreover, that keeping accurate and complete accounting records is essential to the success of their business.*

## THE BUSINESS—OMNI IMPORT

Encore Music, the business described in Cycle 1, sells services for a fee. A business that sells a service for a fee is known as a service business. However, many other businesses purchase goods to sell. A business that purchases and sells goods is called a **merchandising business.** A merchandising business that sells to those who use or consume the goods is called a **retail merchandising business.** Goods that a merchandising business purchases to sell are called **merchandise.** The selling of merchandise rather than a service is what makes the activities of a merchandising business different from those of a service business.

Omni Import, the business described in this cycle, is a retail merchandising business organized as a partnership. The business is owned by Michelle Wu and Karl Koehn. The business purchases and sells imported novelty and gift items such as Russian nesting dolls, African masks, and Irish woolens. Because of the complexities of importing merchandise from numerous foreign countries, Omni purchases its merchandise from other domestic businesses that import foreign merchandise and resell to other businesses. A business that buys and resells merchandise to retail merchandising businesses is called a **wholesale merchandising business.** Omni rents the building in which the business is located as well as the equipment used for operation. Omni expects to make money and continue in business indefinitely. *(CONCEPT: Going Concern)*

# EXPANDED JOURNAL

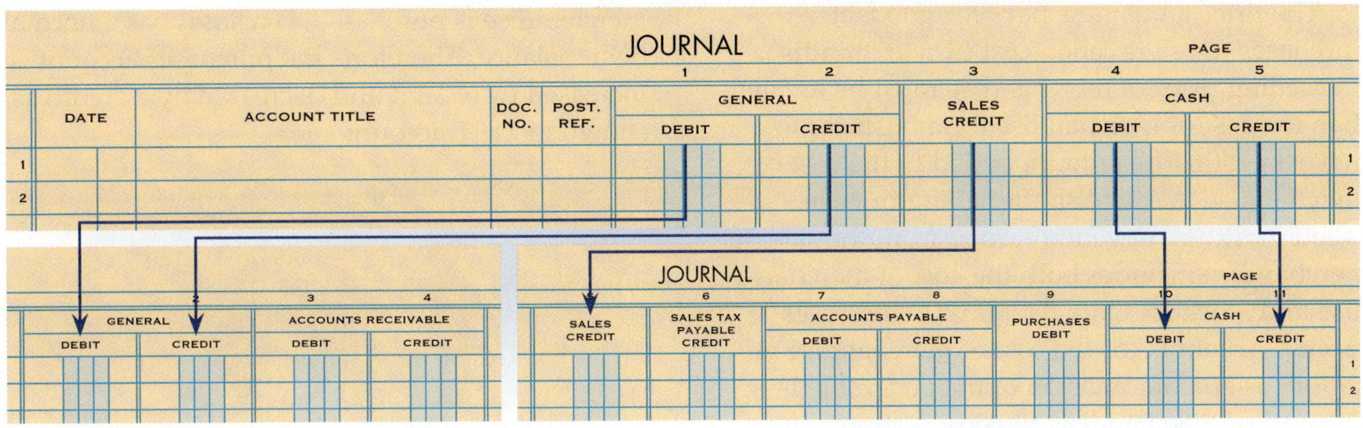


Omni Import, a merchandising business, has many noncash and other frequently occurring transactions that affect single accounts. Omni could use the 5-column journal used by Encore Music. However, without adding more special amount columns to the journal, the large number of transactions would require many entries in the General Debit and Credit columns.

To save time and space in journalizing transactions, Omni uses an expanded 11-column journal. The journal includes additional special amount columns for recording frequently occurring transactions that affect single accounts.

An expanded journal is commonly used by small merchandising businesses in which only one person records transactions. Karl Koehn records all transactions for Omni.

Omni's journal has special amount columns for the recording of frequently occurring transactions related to the purchasing and selling of merchandise. The columns are arranged to make accurate journalizing and posting easier. Debit and credit columns for cash, accounts receivable, and accounts payable are arranged in pairs. This arrangement helps avoid errors in recording amounts in the wrong columns. All columns are placed to the right of the Account Title column. The General Debit and Credit amount columns are placed first so that amounts in these columns will be close to the titles in the Account Title column.

**FYI**

*The number and arrangement of columns in a journal is determined by the type and frequency of transactions.*

## PURCHASING MERCHANDISE

The price a business pays for goods it purchases to sell is called **cost of merchandise.** The selling price of merchandise must be greater than the cost of merchandise for a business to make a profit. The amount added to the cost of merchandise to establish the selling price is called **markup.** Revenue earned from the sale of merchandise includes both the cost of merchandise and markup. Only the markup increases capital. Accounts for the cost of merchandise are kept in a separate division of the general ledger. The cost of merchandise division is shown in Omni's chart of accounts on page 225.

In addition to purchasing merchandise to sell, a merchandising business also buys supplies and other assets for use in the business. A business from which merchandise is purchased or supplies or other assets are bought is called a **vendor.**

The account used for recording the cost of merchandise is titled Purchases. Purchases is classified as a cost account because it is in the cost of merchandise division in the chart of accounts. Purchases is a temporary account. Because the cost of merchandise reduces capital when the merchandise is purchased, Purchases has a normal debit balance. Therefore, the purchases account is increased by a debit and decreased by a credit, as shown in the T account.

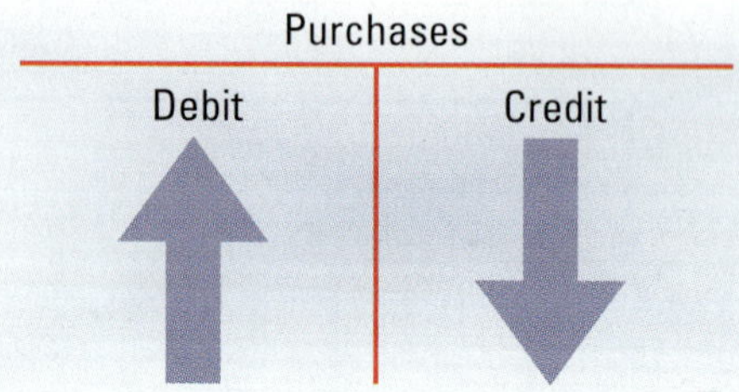


Purchases is used only to record the cost of merchandise purchased. Therefore, only purchases of merchandise are recorded in the Purchases Debit column of the journal. All other items bought, such as supplies, are recorded in the General Debit column of the journal. Merchandise and other items bought are recorded and reported at the price agreed upon at the time the transactions occur. The accounting concept, *Historical Cost,* is applied when the actual amount paid for merchandise or other items bought is recorded. *(CONCEPT: Historical Cost)*

### ACCOUNTING AT WORK

### JOHN CHUANG

With two partners, John Chuang started MacTemps, a temporary employment agency for workers skilled in using Macintosh computers. Today, John Chuang is the sole shareholder and chairman and chief executive officer. MacTemps has 2,300 temporary workers on assignment on an average day and more than 40 offices worldwide.

John earned his MBA from Harvard and says that his cost accounting course was one of the most useful. It is important to know what each division is earning and what it costs to earn it. "Cost accounting is critical to success," John says.

In the early years of MacTemps, cash flow was difficult to manage because temporary workers had to be paid weekly, but clients often didn't pay for 40 days. Managing cash is essential to the ongoing operations of any business enterprise.

Understanding an income statement and balance sheet are important skills for a business owner, too. John says, "It is surprising how many business owners make terrible decisions because they don't understand their financial statements. Accounting is like reading a box score at a baseball game. It is how we measure ourselves in business. It is the language of business. Furthermore, if you plan to invest, you will need to understand accounting to read an annual report intelligently."

In two years, his company's revenue doubled to $100 million. John Chuang knows what he's talking about.

# PURCHASING MERCHANDISE FOR CASH

**1.** Date **2.** Check Mark **3.** Check Number **4.** Check Mark **5.** Debit **6.** Credit

PAGE 21 — JOURNAL — PAGE 21

| | DATE | | ACCOUNT TITLE | DOC. NO. | POST. REF. | 9 PURCHASES DEBIT | 10 CASH DEBIT | 11 CASH CREDIT | |
|---|---|---|---|---|---|---|---|---|---|
| 1 | 20-- Nov. | 1 | √ | C290 | √ | 575 00 | | 575 00 | 1 |
| 2 | | | | | | | | | 2 |

***November 1. Purchased merchandise for cash, $575.00. Check No. 290.***

| Purchases | |
|---|---|
| 575.00 | |

| Cash | |
|---|---|
| | 575.00 |

Omni pays cash for some purchases. All cash payments are made by check.

A cash purchase transaction increases the purchases account balance and decreases the cash account balance.

Because the purchases account has a normal debit balance, Purchases is debited for $575.00 to show the increase in this cost account. The cash account also has a normal debit balance. Therefore, Cash is credited for $575.00 to show the decrease in this asset account.

## STEPS

### Journalizing a purchase of merchandise for cash

1. Write the date, *20—, Nov. 1,* in the Date column.
2. Place a check mark in the Account Title column to show that no account title needs to be written. Both the debit and credit amounts will be recorded in special amount columns.
3. Write the check number, *C290,* in the Doc. No. column.
4. Place a check mark in the Post. Ref. column to show that amounts on this line are not to be posted individually. Both the debit and credit amounts will be posted as part of special amount column totals.
5. Write the debit amount, *$575.00,* in the Purchases Debit column.
6. Write the credit amount, *$575.00,* in the Cash Credit column.

## REMEMBER

A check mark in the Account Title column means that all accounts in the transaction have their own special amount columns. A check mark in the Post. Ref. column means don't post.

## TERMS REVIEW

partnership
partner
merchandising business
retail merchandising business
merchandise
wholesale merchandising business
cost of merchandise
markup
vendor

## AUDIT YOUR UNDERSTANDING

1. Why would two or more persons want to own a single business?
2. What makes the activities of a merchandising business different from those of a service business?
3. What are the special amount columns of an expanded journal?

## WORK TOGETHER

**Journalizing purchases of merchandise for cash**

The journal for Elite Draperies is given in the *Working Papers.* Your instructor will guide you through the following example.

4. Using the current year, journalize the following transactions on page 10 of the journal. Save your work to complete On Your Own below. Source document for check, C.

***Transactions:***

Oct. 1. Purchased merchandise for cash, $810.00. C317.
2. Purchased merchandise for cash, $1,530.00. C318.

## ON YOUR OWN

**Journalizing purchases of merchandise for cash**

Use the journal for Elite Draperies you started above in Work Together. Work this problem independently.

5. Using the current year, journalize the following transactions, continuing on the next blank line of page 10 of the journal. Save your work to complete Work Together on page 237.

***Transactions:***

Oct. 3. Purchased merchandise for cash, $345.00. C319.
4. Purchased merchandise for cash, $295.00. C320.

# 10-2 Journalizing Purchases of Merchandise on Account and Buying Supplies

## PURCHASE INVOICE

Stamp date received and purchase invoice number. (1)

REC'D 11/02/-- P83

**Crown Ltd.**
2611 Industrial
Fremont, NH 03044-2672

TO: Omni Import
1374 Parklane
Ashton, RI 02805

DATE: 10/26/--
INV. NO.: 2389
TERMS: 30 days
ACCT. NO.: 260

| QUANTITY | CAT. NO. | DESCRIPTION | UNIT PRICE | TOTAL |
|---|---|---|---|---|
| 10 | 4422 | Wool Sweaters | 53.00 | 530.00✓ |
| 12 | 4424 | Wool Sweaters | 62.00 | 744.00✓ |
| 15 | 6620 | Wool Shirts | 36.00 | 540.00✓ |
| 15 | 7715 | Wool Scarves | 15.00 | 225.00✓ |
| | | Total | | 2,039.00 EDH |

(4) Review vendor's terms of sale.

(2) Place a check mark by each amount.

(3) Initials of person who checked invoice.

A transaction in which the merchandise purchased is to be paid for later is known as a purchase on account.

When a vendor sells merchandise to a buyer, the vendor prepares a form showing what has been sold. A form describing the goods sold, the quantity, and the price is known as an invoice. An invoice used as a source document for recording a purchase on account transaction is called a **purchase invoice.** *(CONCEPT: Objective Evidence)*

### STEPS: Receiving a purchase invoice

1. Stamp the date received, *11/02/—*, and Omni's purchase invoice number, *P83*, in the upper right corner. This date should not be confused with the vendor's date on the invoice, 10/26. Omni assigns numbers in sequence to easily identify all purchase invoices. The number stamped on the invoice, P83, is the number assigned by Omni to this purchase invoice. This number should not be confused with the invoice number, 2389, assigned by the vendor. Each vendor uses a different numbering system. Therefore, vendor invoice numbers could not be recorded in sequence, which would make it impossible to detect a missing invoice.
2. Place a check mark by each of the amounts in the Total column to show that the items have been received and that amounts have been checked and are correct.
3. The person who checked the invoice should initial below the total amount in the Total column.
4. Review the vendor's terms. An agreement between a buyer and a seller about payment for merchandise is called the **terms of sale.** The terms of sale on the invoice are 30 days. These terms mean that payment is due within 30 days from the vendor's date of the invoice. The invoice is dated October 26. Therefore, payment must be made by November 25.

# PURCHASING MERCHANDISE ON ACCOUNT

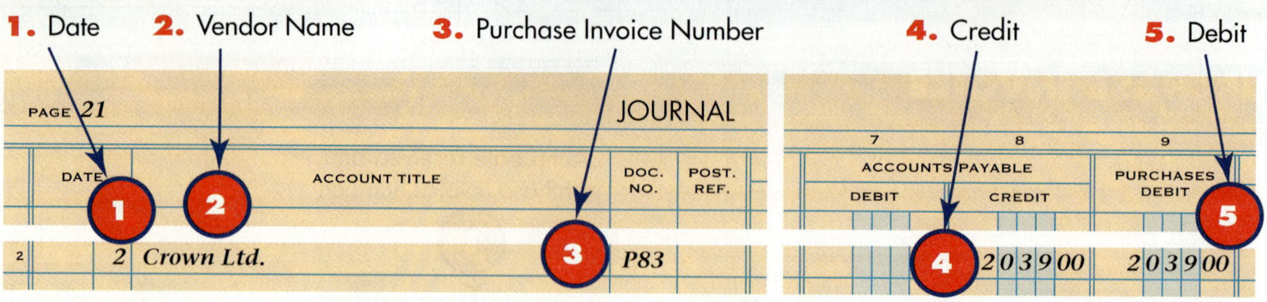


Some businesses that purchase on account from only a few vendors keep a separate general ledger account for each vendor to whom money is owed. Businesses that purchase on account from many vendors will have many accounts for vendors. To avoid a bulky general ledger, the total amount owed to all vendors can be summarized in a single general ledger account. A liability account that summarizes the amounts owed to all vendors is titled Accounts Payable. Omni uses an accounts payable account.

The liability account, Accounts Payable, has a normal credit balance. Therefore, the accounts payable account is increased by a credit and decreased by a debit, as shown in the T account.

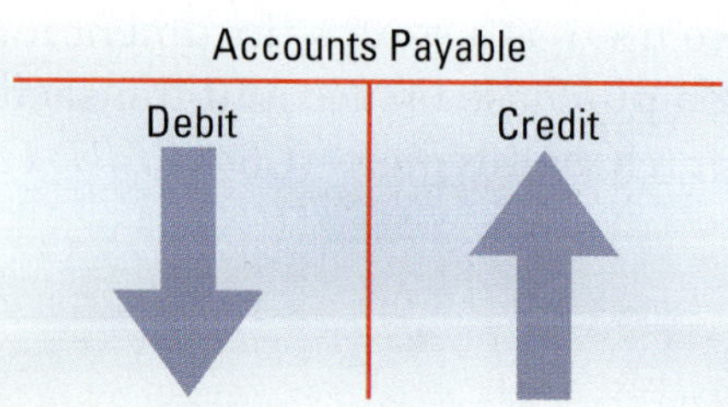


***November 2. Purchased merchandise on account from Crown Ltd., $2,039.00. Purchase Invoice No. 83.***

A purchase on account transaction increases the amount owed to a vendor. This transaction increases the purchases account balance and increases the accounts payable account balance.

Because the purchases account has a normal debit balance, Purchases is debited for $2,039.00 to show the increase in this cost account. The accounts payable account has a normal credit balance. Therefore, Accounts Payable is credited for $2,039.00 to show the increase in this liability account.

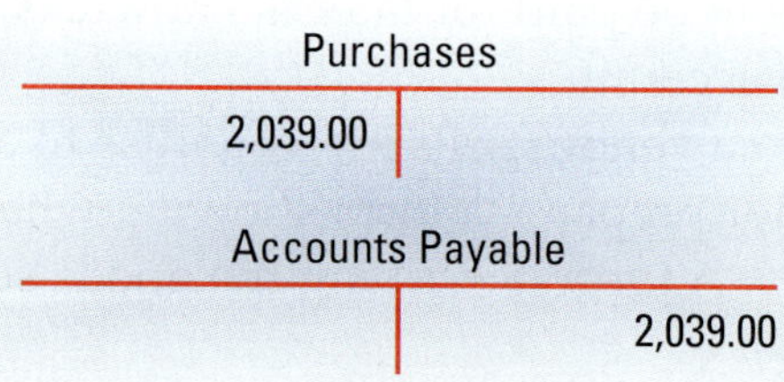


### STEPS: Journalizing a purchase of merchandise on account

1. Write the date, *2*, in the Date column.
2. Write the vendor name, *Crown Ltd.*, in the Account Title column. The debit to Purchases and the credit to Accounts Payable are recorded in special amount columns. Therefore, it is not necessary to write the title of either general ledger account in the Account Title column. However, the name of the vendor is written in the Account Title column to show to whom the amount is owed. The way Omni keeps records of the amount owed to each vendor is described in Chapter 12.
3. Write the purchase invoice number, *P83*, in the Doc. No. column.
4. Write the credit amount, *$2,039.00*, in the Accounts Payable Credit column.
5. Write the debit amount, *$2,039.00*, in the Purchases Debit column.

### REMEMBER

The cost account, Purchases, is used only to record the cost of merchandise purchased. All other items bought, such as supplies, are recorded in the appropriate asset account.

## BUYING SUPPLIES FOR CASH

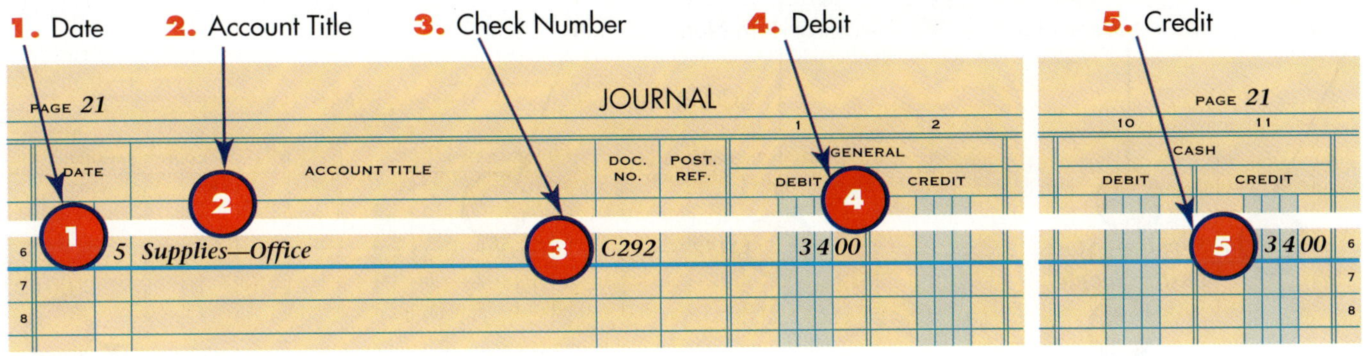


***November 5. Paid cash for office supplies, $34.00. Check No. 292.***

| Supplies—Office | |
|---|---|
| 34.00 | |

| Cash | |
|---|---|
| | 34.00 |

Omni buys supplies for use in the business. Supplies are not recorded in the purchases account because supplies are not intended for sale. Cash register tapes and price tags are examples of supplies used in a merchandising business. Omni buys most of its supplies for cash.

Because the office supplies account has a normal debit balance, Supplies—Office is debited for $34.00 to show the increase in this asset account. The cash account also has a normal debit balance. Therefore, Cash is credited for $34.00 to show the decrease in this asset account.

### STEPS: Journalizing buying supplies for cash

1. Write the date, *5*, in the Date column.
2. Write the account title, *Supplies—Office*, in the Account Title column.
3. Write the check number, *C292*, in the Doc. No. column.
4. Write the debit amount to Supplies—Office, *$34.00*, in the General Debit column.
5. Write the credit amount, *$34.00*, in the Cash Credit column.

## MEMORANDUM FOR BUYING SUPPLIES ON ACCOUNT

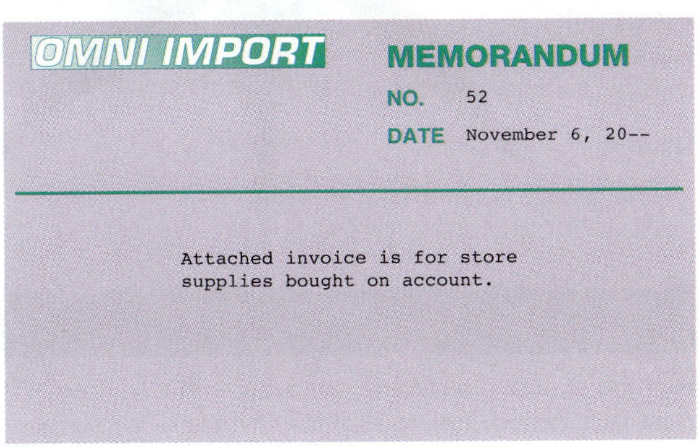
OMNI IMPORT
MEMORANDUM
NO. 52
DATE November 6, 20--

Attached invoice is for store supplies bought on account.

Omni usually buys supplies for cash. Occasionally, however, Omni buys some supplies on account.

When Omni buys supplies on account, an invoice is received from the vendor. This invoice is similar to the purchase invoice received when merchandise is purchased. To assure that no mistake is made, a memorandum is attached to the invoice, noting that the invoice is for supplies and not for purchases.

# BUYING SUPPLIES ON ACCOUNT

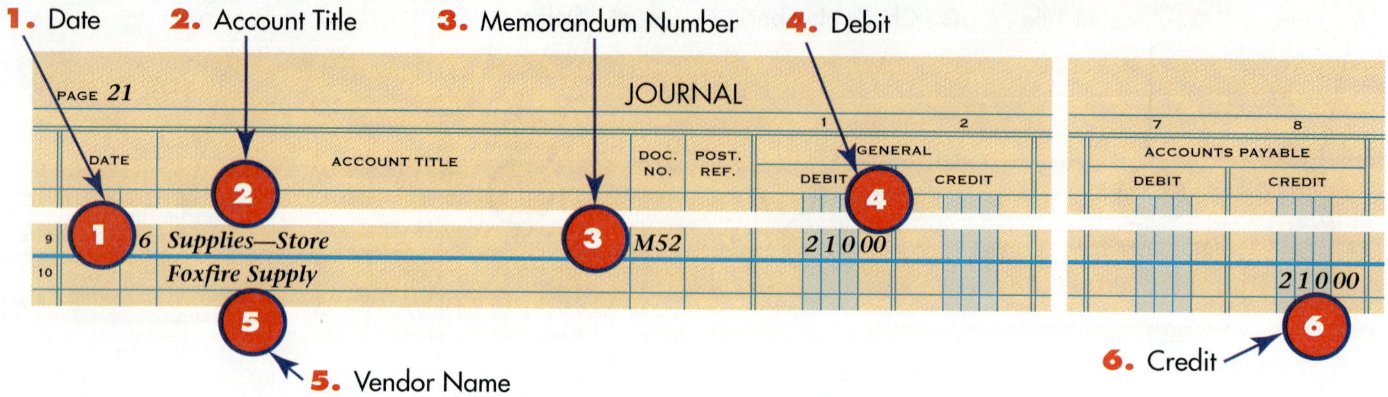


***November 6. Bought store supplies on account from Foxfire Supply, $210.00. Memorandum No. 52.***

| Supplies—Store | |
|---|---|
| 210.00 | |

| Accounts Payable | |
|---|---|
| | 210.00 |

This transaction increases the store supplies account balance and increases the accounts payable account balance.

Because the store supplies account has a normal debit balance, Supplies—Store is debited for $210.00 to show the increase in this asset account. The accounts payable account has a normal credit balance. Therefore, Accounts Payable is credited for $210.00 to show the increase in this liability account.

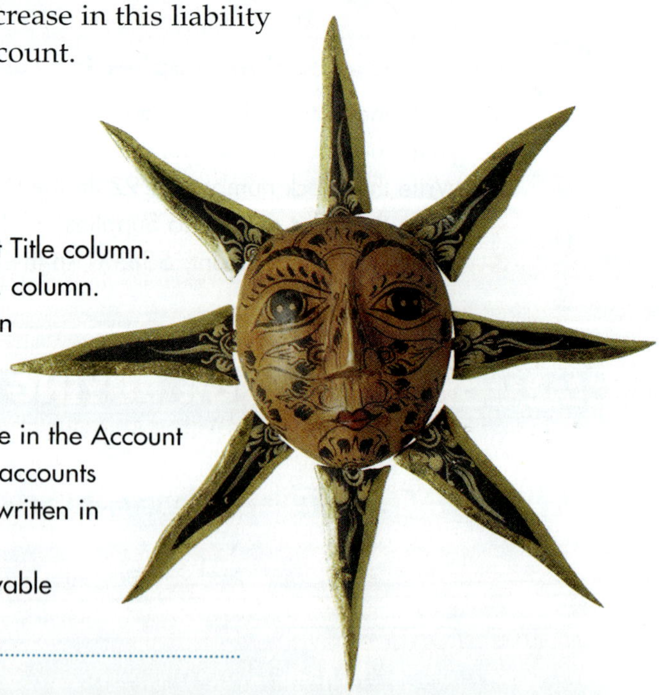

### STEPS Journalizing buying supplies on account

1. Write the date, *6,* in the Date column.
2. Write the account title, *Supplies—Store,* in the Account Title column.
3. Write the memorandum number, *M52,* in the Doc. No. column.
4. Write the debit amount to Supplies—Store, *$210.00,* in the General Debit column on the same line as the account title.
5. Write the vendor name, *Foxfire Supply,* on the next line in the Account Title column. A special amount column is provided for accounts payable. Therefore, this general ledger account is not written in the Account Title column.
6. Write the credit amount, *$210.00,* in the Accounts Payable Credit column.

## REMEMBER

When supplies are bought on account, an invoice is received from the vendor. To avoid confusion with purchase invoices received when merchandise is purchased, a memorandum is attached, noting that the invoice is for supplies and not for purchases.

## TERMS REVIEW

purchase invoice
terms of sale

## AUDIT YOUR UNDERSTANDING

1. In what amount columns would the debit amount and credit amount be written for a purchase of merchandise on account?
2. What account titles would be written in the Account Title column for buying supplies on account?

## WORK TOGETHER

**Journalizing purchases of merchandise on account and buying supplies**

Use the journal for Elite Draperies from On Your Own on page 232. Your instructor will guide you through the following example.

3. Using the current year, journalize the following transactions on page 10 of the journal. Source documents are abbreviated as follows: check, C; memorandum, M; purchase invoice, P. Save your work to complete On Your Own below.

***Transactions:***

Oct. 5. Purchased merchandise on account from Fabric Outlet, $1,230.00. P116.
6. Paid cash for office supplies, $52.00. C321.
7. Bought store supplies on account from Designer Supplies, $180.00. M62.

## ON YOUR OWN

**Journalizing purchases of merchandise on account and buying supplies**

Use the journal for Elite Draperies from Work Together above. Work this problem independently.

4. Using the current year, journalize the following transactions, continuing on the next blank line of page 10 of the journal. Source documents are abbreviated as follows: check, C; memorandum, M; purchase invoice, P. Save your work to complete Work Together on page 243.

***Transactions:***

Oct. 8. Purchased merchandise on account from Drapery Hardware, Inc., $480.00. P117.
10. Paid cash for store supplies, $76.00. C322.
11. Bought office supplies on account from Office Express, $240.00. M63.

# 10-3 Journalizing Cash Payments and Other Transactions

## CASH PAYMENT ON ACCOUNT

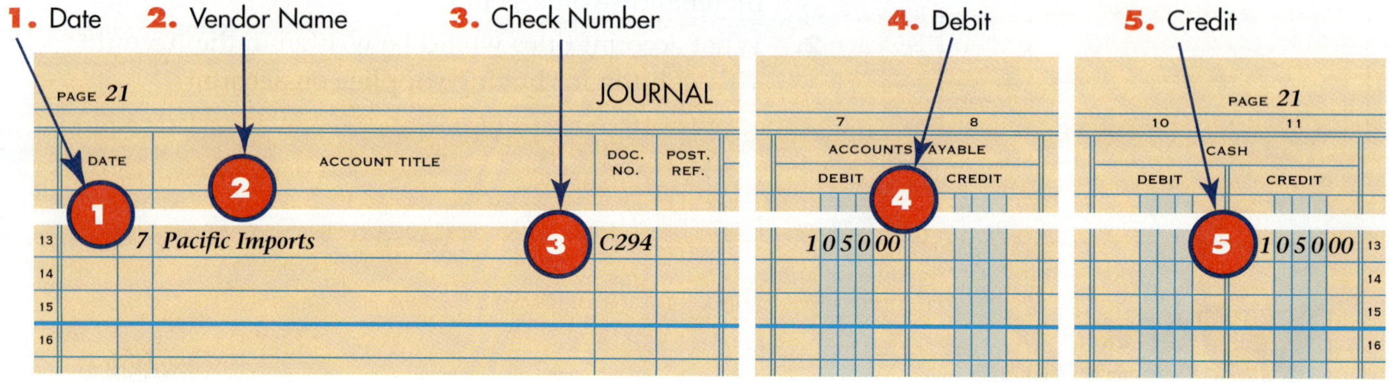


***November 7. Paid cash on account to Pacific Imports, $1,050.00, covering Purchase Invoice No. 81. Check No. 294.***

| Accounts Payable | |
|---|---|
| 1,050.00 | |

| Cash | |
|---|---|
| | 1,050.00 |

Payments to vendors are made according to the terms of sale on the purchase invoices. Payment for an expense is usually made at the time the expense occurs.

Omni pays by check for all cash purchases and for payments on account.

The cash payment on account transaction shown decreases the amount owed to a vendor. This transaction decreases the accounts payable account balance and decreases the cash account balance.

Because the accounts payable account has a normal credit balance, Accounts Payable is debited for $1,050.00 to show the decrease in this liability account. The cash account has a normal debit balance. Therefore, Cash is credited for $1,050.00 to show the decrease in this asset account.

**FYI**

*CFO stands for Chief Financial Officer.*

**STEPS**

### Journalizing a cash payment on account

1. Write the date, *7*, in the Date column.
2. Write the vendor name, *Pacific Imports*, in the Account Title column.
3. Write the check number, *C294*, in the Doc. No. column.
4. Write the debit amount, *$1,050.00*, in the Accounts Payable Debit column.
5. Write the credit amount, *$1,050.00*, in the Cash Credit column.

**REMEMBER**

The name of the vendor must be written in the Account Title column to show to whom the payment is made.

## CASH PAYMENT OF AN EXPENSE

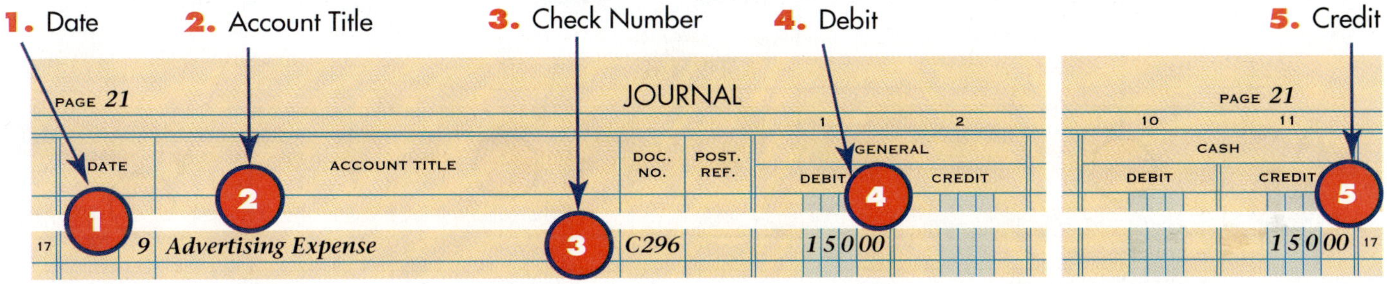


***November 9. Paid cash for advertising, $150.00. Check No. 296.***

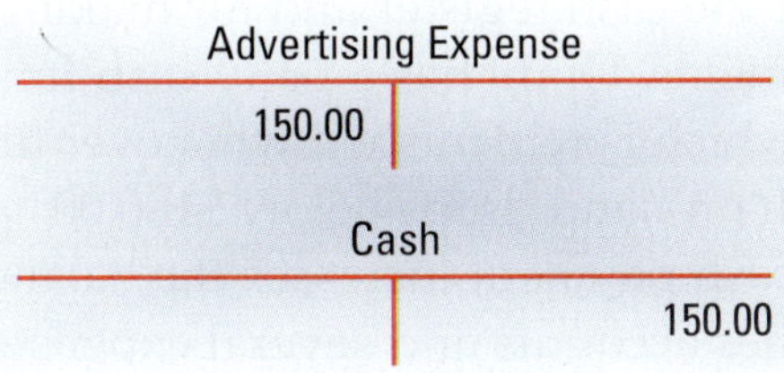


Omni usually pays for an expense at the time the transaction occurs.

This cash payment increases the advertising expense account balance and decreases the cash account balance. Because the advertising expense account has a normal debit balance, Advertising Expense is debited for $150.00 to show the increase in this expense account. The cash account also has a normal debit balance. Therefore, Cash is credited for $150.00 to show the decrease in this asset account.

### STEPS Journalizing a cash payment of an expense

1. Write the date, *9*, in the Date column.
2. Write the account title, *Advertising Expense*, in the Account Title column.
3. Write the check number, *C296*, in the Doc. No. column.
4. Write the debit amount to Advertising Expense, *$150.00*, in the General Debit column.
5. Write the credit amount, *$150.00*, in the Cash Credit column.

**FYI**

*Gross Domestic Product (GDP) is the total dollar value of all final goods and services produced by resources located in the United States (regardless of who owns the resources) during one year's time.*

**SMALL BUSINESS SPOTLIGHT**

A business plan is required by most banks before they will consider lending money to hopeful small business owners. A typical business plan includes goals and objectives, marketing plans, management and operations plans, estimated financial statements, and budgets.

## CASH PAYMENT TO REPLENISH PETTY CASH

**1.** Date **2.** Account Titles **3.** Check Number **4.** Debit **5.** Credit

JOURNAL PAGE 21

| | DATE | | ACCOUNT TITLE | DOC. NO. | POST. REF. | 1 GENERAL DEBIT | 2 GENERAL CREDIT | 10 CASH DEBIT | 11 CASH CREDIT | |
|---|---|---|---|---|---|---|---|---|---|---|
| 18 | | 9 | *Supplies—Office* | *C297* | | 35 00 | | | 205 00 | 18 |
| 19 | | | *Supplies—Store* | | | 47 00 | | | | 19 |
| 20 | | | *Advertising Expense* | | | 92 00 | | | | 20 |
| 21 | | | *Miscellaneous Expense* | | | 31 00 | | | | 21 |

***November 9. Paid cash to replenish the petty cash fund, $205.00: office supplies, $35.00; store supplies, $47.00; advertising, $92.00; miscellaneous, $31.00. Check No. 297.***

| Supplies—Office | |
|---|---|
| 35.00 | |

| Supplies—Store | |
|---|---|
| 47.00 | |

| Advertising Expense | |
|---|---|
| 92.00 | |

| Miscellaneous Expense | |
|---|---|
| 31.00 | |

| Cash | |
|---|---|
| | 205.00 |

Omni deposits all cash in a bank. Some cash, however, is kept in a petty cash fund for making change at the cash register and for making small cash payments. Omni has a petty cash fund of $300.00, which is replenished whenever the petty cash on hand drops below $100.00.

This cash payment increases the balances of the supplies accounts and several expense accounts and decreases the cash account balance.

The supplies accounts have normal debit balances. Therefore, Supplies—Office is debited for $35.00 and Supplies—Store is debited for $47.00 to show the increases in these two asset accounts. The expense accounts also have normal debit balances. Therefore, Advertising Expense is debited for $92.00 and Miscellaneous Expense is debited for $31.00 to show the increases in these expense accounts. The cash account has a normal debit balance. Therefore, Cash is credited for $205.00, the total amount needed to replenish the petty cash fund, to show the decrease in this asset account.

### STEPS Journalizing a cash payment to replenish petty cash

1. Write the date, *9*, in the Date column.
2. Write the titles of the accounts for which the petty cash fund was used on separate lines in the Account Title column since there are no special amount columns for these accounts.
3. Write the check number, *C297*, in the Doc. No. column.
4. Write the debit amounts for the various accounts in the General Debit column.
5. Write the credit amount, *$205.00*, in the Cash Credit column on the first line of the entry.

### REMEMBER

The account title Petty Cash is used only when establishing the petty cash account.

## CASH WITHDRAWALS BY PARTNERS

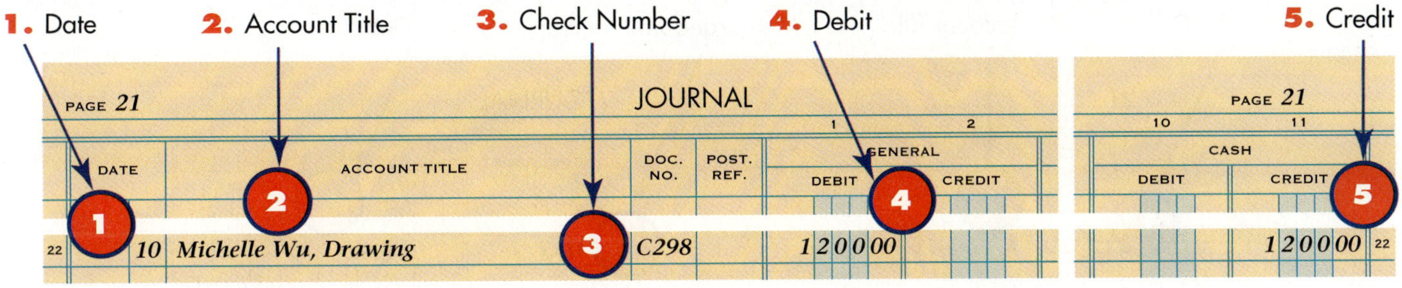


Assets taken out of a business for the personal use of an owner are known as withdrawals. The two assets generally taken out of a merchandising business are cash and merchandise. Withdrawals reduce the amount of a business's capital. The account titles of the partners' drawing accounts are Michelle Wu, Drawing and Karl Koehn, Drawing. Since capital accounts have credit balances, partners' drawing accounts have normal debit balances. Therefore, the drawing accounts are increased by a debit and decreased by a credit, as shown in the T accounts.

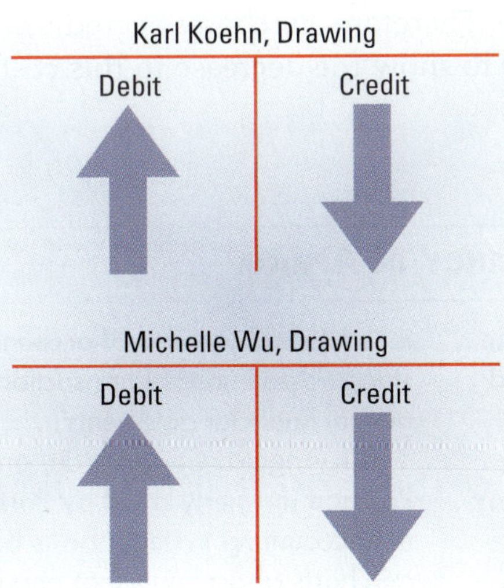


Withdrawals could be recorded as debits directly to the partners' capital accounts. However, withdrawals are normally recorded in separate accounts so that the total amounts are easily determined for each accounting period.

When either Michelle Wu or Karl Koehn withdraws cash from Omni, a check is written for the payment.

***November 10. Michelle Wu, partner, withdrew cash for personal use, $1,200.00. Check No. 298.***

This cash withdrawal increases Michelle Wu's drawing account balance and decreases the cash account balance.

Because the drawing account has a normal debit balance, Michelle Wu, Drawing is debited for $1,200.00 to show the increase in this account. The cash account also has a normal debit balance. Therefore, Cash is credited for $1,200.00 to show the decrease in this asset account.

| Michelle Wu, Drawing | |
|---|---|
| 1,200.00 | |

| Cash | |
|---|---|
| | 1,200.00 |

### STEPS: Journalizing cash withdrawals by partners

1. Write the date, *10,* in the Date column.
2. Write the account title, *Michelle Wu, Drawing,* in the Account Title column.
3. Write the check number, *C298,* in the Doc. No. column.
4. Write the debit amount to Michelle Wu, Drawing, *$1,200.00,* in the General Debit column.
5. Write the credit amount, *$1,200.00,* in the Cash Credit column.

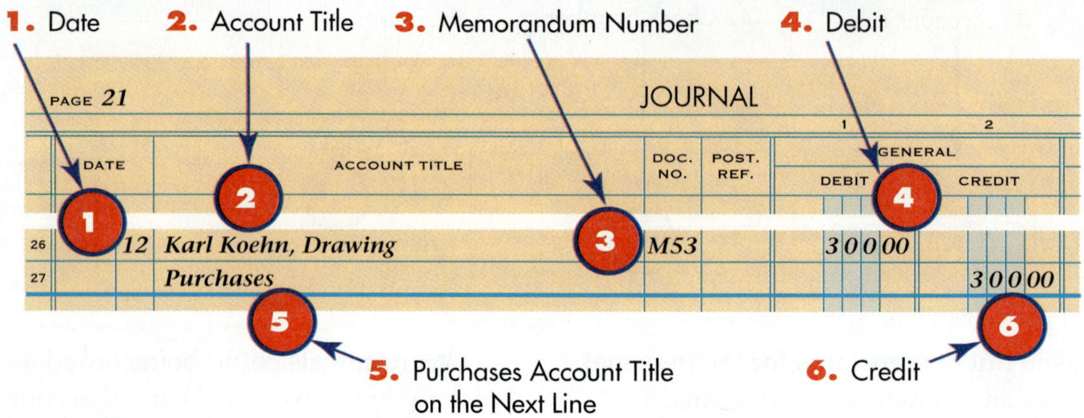


***November 12. Karl Koehn, partner, withdrew merchandise for personal use, $300.00. Memorandum No. 53.***

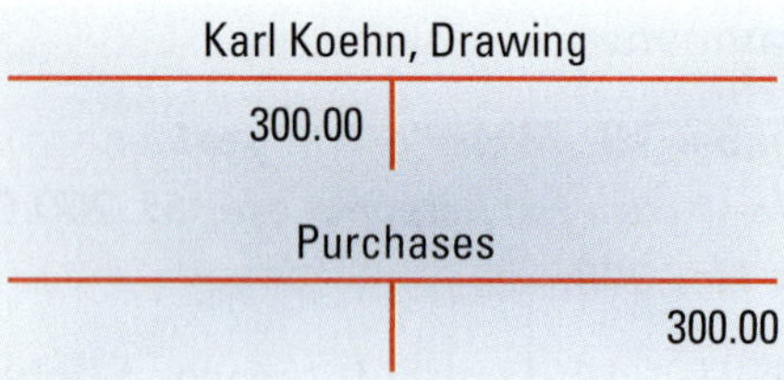


A partner usually withdraws cash for personal use. However, a partner may also withdraw merchandise for personal use.

This merchandise withdrawal increases Karl Koehn's drawing account balance and decreases the purchases account balance.

Because the drawing account has a normal debit balance, Karl Koehn, Drawing is debited for $300.00 to show the increase in this account. The purchases account also has a normal debit balance. Therefore, Purchases is credited for $300.00 to show the decrease in this cost account.

## Global Perspective

### Accountancy in Africa

The accounting profession in Africa has been influenced by the European colonial powers who formerly governed there. Most African nations gained independence in the mid-twentieth century.

In Nigeria, Kenya, Ghana, and Zimbabwe (formerly under British rule), accounting is seen as a tool for financial management and is oriented toward the needs of the enterprise. Tax authorities are concerned with account items that can be valued in different ways, like fixed assets, inventories, and depreciation.

In Togo, Rwanda, and Gambia (formerly ruled by France), accountancy is regulated by *charts of accounts* that standardize financial transactions and annual financial statements.

In Angola, Cape Verde, and Principe (formerly ruled by Portugal), the accounting system also is based on charts of accounts that provide rules and regulations for companies. There are no professional accounting organizations in these countries.

In the expanding economies of many developing African countries, the belief is that it is important to have well-qualified and experienced accountants and a sound accounting framework to sustain economic growth.

## AUDIT YOUR UNDERSTANDING

1. In what amount columns would the debit amount and credit amount be written for a cash payment on account?
2. What account title, if any, would be written in the Account Title column for paying cash for advertising expense?
3. What is the purpose of using a petty cash fund?
4. What account title would be written in the Account Title column for a partner's withdrawal of cash?
5. In what amount columns would the debit amount and credit amount be written for a partner's withdrawal of merchandise?

## WORK TOGETHER

### Journalizing cash payments and other transactions

Use the journal from On Your Own on page 237. Your instructor will guide you through the following example.

6. Using the current year, journalize the following transactions, continuing on the next blank line of page 10 of the journal. Save your work to complete On Your Own below.

*Transactions:*

Oct. 12. Paid cash on account to Design Fabrics, $563.00. C323.
13. Paid cash for telephone bill, $85.00. C324.
14. Paid cash to replenish petty cash fund, $309.00: office supplies, $82.00; store supplies, $43.00; advertising, $94.00; miscellaneous, $90.00. C325.
15. Steven Cafaro, partner, withdrew cash for personal use, $400.00. C326.
15. Consuela Martinez, partner, withdrew merchandise for personal use, $225.00. M66.

## ON YOUR OWN

### Journalizing cash payments and other transactions

Use the journal that you used above in Work Together. Work this problem independently.

7. Using the current year, journalize the following transactions, continuing on the next blank line of page 10 of the journal.

*Transactions:*

Oct. 16. Paid cash for advertising, $140.00. C327.
18. Paid cash on account to Fabric Outlet, $1,150.00. C328.
18. Steven Cafaro, partner, withdrew merchandise for personal use, $200.00. M69.
20. Paid cash to replenish petty cash fund, $305.00: office supplies, $62.00; store supplies, $116.00; advertising, $38.00; miscellaneous, $89.00. C329.
22. Consuela Martinez, partner, withdrew cash for personal use, $500.00. C330.

# CHAPTER 10 SUMMARY

*Enrichment Activity*

**Types of Businesses**

*How does a merchandising business differ from a service business? Give three examples of merchandising businesses with which you are familiar.*

After completing this chapter, you can

1. Define accounting terms related to purchases and cash payments for a merchandising business.
2. Identify accounting concepts and practices related to purchases and cash payments for a merchandising business.
3. Journalize purchases of merchandise for cash.
4. Journalize purchases of merchandise on account and buying supplies.
5. Journalize cash payments and other transactions.

## EXPLORE ACCOUNTING

### FREIGHT CHARGES

When a business purchases merchandise from a vendor, ordinarily a third-party freight company is used to deliver the merchandise from the seller (vendor) to the buyer (purchasing business). As part of the terms of sale, the buyer and seller must agree who is responsible for the freight charges. Those terms will be listed on the seller's sales invoice as either FOB shipping point or FOB destination. FOB is an abbreviation for the phrase "Free on Board." FOB shipping point means that the buyer is responsible for the freight charges. FOB destination means that the seller is responsible for the freight charges. Shipping point is the location where the freight company receives the merchandise from the seller. Destination refers to the receiving point of the buyer.

The accounting entries for freight charges can be complicated when one business is responsible for the freight charges according to the terms of sale, but the other business pays the freight company. For example, terms of sale may be FOB shipping point, meaning that the buyer is responsible for the freight charges. However, the freight company may require payment in advance. Therefore, the seller pays the freight company for the freight charges.

Four different situations may occur:

1. FOB shipping point, seller pays freight company.
2. FOB shipping point, buyer pays freight company.
3. FOB destination, seller pays freight company.
4. FOB destination, buyer pays freight company.

**Research:** Investigate this issue by reviewing collegiate Principles of Accounting or Intermediate Accounting textbooks. Also, you might interview a merchandising business manager to determine how the business accounts for freight charges.

After completing your research, write a report on the issue of freight charges that would clearly explain the correct accounting procedures to a new accounting department employee.

## 10-1 APPLICATION PROBLEM
### Journalizing purchases of merchandise for cash

Ralph Bridges and Olivia Herron, partners, own a small appliance store.

***Instructions:***

Journalize the following transactions completed during August of the current year. Use page 17 of the journal given in the *Working Papers*. Source documents are abbreviated as follows: check, C; memorandum, M; purchase invoice, P.

***Transactions:***

Aug. 1. Purchased merchandise for cash, $300.00. C210.
10. Purchased merchandise for cash, $817.00. C211.
22. Purchased merchandise for cash, $184.00. C212.

## 10-2 APPLICATION PROBLEM
### Journalizing purchases of merchandise on account and buying supplies

Ralph Benitez and Tina Chirfo, partners, own a small music store.

***Instructions:***

Journalize the following transactions completed during September of the current year. Use page 17 of the journal given in the *Working Papers*. Source documents are abbreviated as follows: check, C; memorandum, M; purchase invoice, P.

***Transactions:***

Sept. 4. Purchased merchandise on account from Woodland Music, $2,600.00. P54.
7. Paid cash for office supplies, $75.00. C211.
10. Purchased merchandise on account from Quality Wholesalers, $1,460.00. P55.
15. Bought store supplies on account from Displays Warehouse, $275.00. M39.

## 10-3 APPLICATION PROBLEM
### Journalizing cash payments and other transactions

Mary Caesar and Glen Kelly, partners, own an auto parts store.

***Instructions:***

Journalize the following transactions completed during October of the current year. Use page 19 of the journal given in the *Working Papers*. Source documents are abbreviated as follows: check, C; memorandum, M; purchase invoice, P.

***Transactions:***

Oct. 2. Paid cash for telephone bill, $96.00. C241.
6. Mary Caesar, partner, withdrew cash for personal use, $1,000.00. C242.
6. Glen Kelly, partner, withdrew cash for personal use, $1,200.00. C243.
12. Paid cash on account to East Gate Auto Parts, $1,250.00, covering P67. C244.
16. Paid cash for advertising, $75.00. C245.
24. Paid cash on account to Auto Center, $925.00, covering P68. C246.
26. Mary Caesar, partner, withdrew merchandise for personal use, $120.00. M51.
30. Paid cash to replenish the petty cash fund, $211.00: office supplies, $41.00; store supplies, $29.00; advertising, $63.00; miscellaneous, $78.00. C247.

## 10-4 APPLICATION PROBLEM
### Journalizing purchases, cash payments, and other transactions

Michael Deaton and Pamela Parks, partners, own a bridal shop.

***Instructions:***

Journalize the following transactions completed during November of the current year. Use page 22 of the journal given in the *Working Papers*. Source documents are abbreviated as follows: check, C; memorandum, M; purchase invoice, P.

***Transactions:***

Nov. 1. Purchased merchandise on account from Formal Wear, $1,850.00. P71.
5. Bought store supplies on account from Classic Fixtures, $180.00. M48.
10. Purchased merchandise for cash, $330.00. C240.
12. Paid cash for office supplies, $50.00. C241.
18. Purchased merchandise on account from Bridal Designs, $2,300.00. P72.
22. Paid cash on account to Formal Wear, $1,850.00, covering P71. C242.
25. Paid cash for advertising, $110.00. C243.
26. Michael Deaton, partner, withdrew merchandise for personal use, $140.00. M49.
29. Michael Deaton, partner, withdrew cash for personal use, $1,110.00. C244.
29. Pamela Parks, partner, withdrew cash for personal use, $1,250.00. C245.
30. Paid cash to replenish the petty cash fund, $261.00: office supplies, $52.00; store supplies, $40.00; advertising, $77.00; miscellaneous, $92.00. C246.

## 10-5 MASTERY PROBLEM
### Journalizing purchases, cash payments, and other transactions

Jimmie Chang and Susan Shirey, partners, own a gift shop.

***Instructions:***

Journalize the following transactions completed during October of the current year. Use page 19 of the journal given in the *Working Papers*. Source documents are abbreviated as follows: check, C; memorandum, M; purchase invoice, P.

***Transactions:***

Oct. 1. Paid cash for rent, $1,500.00. C361.
2. Purchased merchandise on account from Marion's Collectibles, $1,115.00. P108.
3. Paid cash for office supplies, $74.00. C362.
5. Paid cash on account to Gift Supplies, Inc., $548.00, covering P105. C363.
6. Purchased merchandise for cash, $155.00. C364.
9. Purchased merchandise on account from Jarvis Fabrics, $850.00. P109.
9. Bought store supplies on account from Creative Store Supplies, $150.00. M50.
10. Purchased merchandise for cash, $103.00. C365.
12. Paid cash on account to Contemporary Gifts, $885.00, covering P106. C366.
12. Bought office supplies on account from A to Z Supplies, $80.00. M51.
16. Jimmie Chang, partner, withdrew cash for personal use, $1,000.00. C367.
16. Susan Shirey, partner, withdrew cash for personal use, $1,000.00. C368.
17. Paid cash for advertising, $100.00. C369.
19. Paid cash on account to Classic Gifts, $490.00, covering P107. C370.
19. Purchased merchandise on account from Jarvis Fabrics, $625.00. P110.

Oct. 20. Susan Shirey, partner, withdrew merchandise for personal use, $120.00. M52.
22. Purchased merchandise for cash, $60.00. C371.
24. Paid cash on account to Marion's Collectibles, $1,115.00, covering P108. C372.
25. Jimmie Chang, partner, withdrew merchandise for personal use, $225.00. M53.
27. Paid cash for store supplies, $92.00. C373.
30. Paid cash to replenish the petty cash fund, $201.00: office supplies, $53.00; store supplies, $27.00; advertising, $100.00; miscellaneous, $21.00. C374.
30. Paid cash on account to Jarvis Fabrics, $850.00, covering P109. C375.

## 10-6 CHALLENGE PROBLEM
### Journalizing purchases, cash payments, and other transactions

Jack Armstrong and Barbara Kirk, partners, own an exercise equipment store.

***Instructions:***

1. Journalize the following transactions completed during November of the current year. Use page 26 of the journal given in the *Working Papers*. Record the appropriate source document for each transaction.

***Transactions:***

Nov. 1. Wrote Check No. 361 for the monthly rent of $1,300.00.
2. Wrote Checks No. 362 and 363 for $1,250.00 each to partners, Jack Armstrong and Barbara Kirk, for their personal use.
4. Paid $150.00 with Check No. 364 for merchandise.
6. Wrote Check No. 365 for $1,020.00 to Pacer Equipment for Purchase Invoice 82's payment on account.
9. Purchased $2,900.00 of merchandise on account from Trackmaster on Purchase Invoice 85.
10. Paid $52.00 for office supplies with Check No. 366.
12. Wrote Check No. 367 for $90.00 to pay the monthly insurance premium.
15. Bought $120.00 worth of store supplies on account from Mecca Store Supplies and recorded on Memo 43.
19. Jack Armstrong took $75.00 worth of merchandise for his personal use and recorded it on Memo 44.
24. Wrote Check No. 368 for $2,900.00 to pay Trackmaster amount owed on Purchase Invoice 85
30. Wrote Check No. 369 for $206.00 to the employee who maintains the petty cash fund for the purpose of replenishing the fund. Receipts were submitted for the following: office supplies, $48.00; store supplies $24.00; advertising, $68.00; and miscellaneous, $66.00.

2. Evaluate and then write a response to the following questions.
   a. The expanded journal used in this problem has nine special amount columns. Under what circumstances would you recommend additional special amount columns be added or existing amount columns be deleted from an expanded journal?
   b. Jack Armstrong has asked why he could not be paid a salary rather than making withdrawals from his ownership in the partnership. How would you respond to him?
   c. When insurance premiums are paid, should the debit entry be to the asset account, Prepaid Insurance, or to the expense account, Insurance Expense? Are there circumstances where either entry could be correct? Explain.

## INTERNET ACTIVITY

Point your browser to

**http://accounting.swpco.com**

Choose **First-Year Course**, choose **Activities**, and complete the activity for Chapter 10.

## Applied Communication

When you purchase merchandise for your business, you are considered a customer. Sometimes a customer might have a problem or complaint about the product. There are several ways to go about resolving the problem. One suggestion is to write to the person or company selling the product.

**Instructions:** Assume that you bought stereo speakers for your consumer electronics store last week. Write a business-like letter of complaint to the company selling the merchandise because the speakers make a strange static noise. Be specific about the problem and provide factual information about the purchase. Request a refund or a new set of speakers.

## Cases for Critical Thinking

**Case 1** Sophia Perez is a high school student who works part time in a local sports equipment store. As part of her duties, she records daily transactions in a journal. One day she asks the owner, "You use the purchase invoice as your source document for recording purchases of merchandise on account. You use a memorandum as your source document for recording the entry when supplies are bought on account. Why don't you use the invoice for both entries?" How would you respond to this question?

**Case 2** Charles Davis owns and operates an antique shop in a downtown shopping area. Because of a shopping mall that has opened in one of the suburbs, the antique shop's business has been declining. Mr. Davis has an opportunity to move the business to the shopping mall. Additional capital, however, is required to move and operate the business in a new location. The local bank has agreed to lend the money needed. The business hours would be extended at the new location. The business would also be open seven days a week. The extended hours plus the expected increase in business would require the hiring of one additional employee. Mr. Davis has been contacted by Kathryn Harless, a person with similar merchandising experience, who would like to become a partner. As an alternative to borrowing cash, Ms. Harless would provide the capital necessary to move the business to the new location. For the capital provided, Ms. Harless would share equally in the net income or loss of the business. Ms. Harless would also share equally in the operation of the business. Should Mr. Davis (1) borrow the money from the bank or (2) bring in a partner? Explain your answer.

# AUTOMATED ACCOUNTING

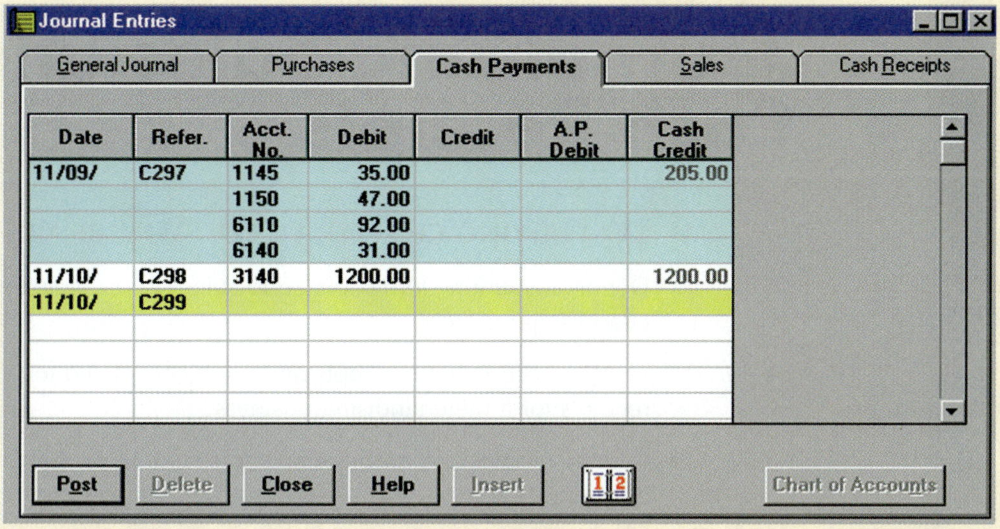


To record transactions in the cash payments journal:

1. Choose the Journal Entries menu item from the Data menu or click the Journal toolbar button.
2. Click the Cash Payments tab.
3. Enter the transaction date and press Tab.
4. Enter the check number in the Refer. column and press Tab.
5. If making a direct payment, enter the account number and amounts to debit or credit and press Tab. If more than one account is debited or credited in the transaction, enter the first account number and the corresponding debit or credit. Press Tab until the cursor appears in the Acct. No. column on the next line. Then enter the next account number and its corresponding debit or credit. Continue this procedure for all accounts involved in the transaction.The cash credit is automatically calculated and displayed by the computer.
6. If making a payment on account, enter the accounts payable debit amount and choose the vendor from the drop-down vendor list. The cash credit is automatically calculated and displayed by the computer.
7. If the transaction is correct, click the Post button.

## AUTOMATING MASTERY PROBLEM 10-5: Journalizing purchases, cash payments, and other transactions

**Instructions:**

1. Load *Automated Accounting 7.0* or higher software.
2. Select database F10-1 from the appropriate directory/folder.
3. Select File from the menu bar and choose the Save As menu command. Key the path to the drive and directory that contains your data files. Save the database with a file name of XXX101 (where XXX are your initials).
4. Access Problem Instructions through the Help menu. Read the Problem Instructions screen.
5. Key the data listed on page 246.
6. Exit the *Automated Accounting* software.

# 11 Journalizing Sales and Cash Receipts

**AFTER STUDYING CHAPTER 11, YOU WILL BE ABLE TO:**

1. Define accounting terms related to sales and cash receipts for a merchandising business.
2. Identify accounting concepts and practices related to sales and cash receipts for a merchandising business.
3. Journalize sales and cash receipts transactions for a merchandising business.
4. Prove and rule a journal.

**TERMS PREVIEW**

customer

sales tax

cash sale

credit card sale

## SALES TAX

Purchases and sales of merchandise are the two major activities of a merchandising business. A person or business to whom merchandise or services are sold is called a **customer.** Omni Import sells merchandise.

Laws of most states and some cities require that a tax be collected from customers for each sale made. A tax on a sale of merchandise or services is called a **sales tax.** Sales tax rates are usually stated as a percentage of sales. Regardless of the tax rates used, accounting procedures are the same.

Businesses must file reports with the proper government unit and pay the amount of sales tax collected. Every business collecting a sales tax needs accurate records of the amount of (1) total sales and (2) total sales tax collected. The amount of sales tax collected is a business liability until paid to the state government. Therefore, the sales tax amount is recorded in a separate liability account titled Sales Tax Payable, which has a normal credit balance.

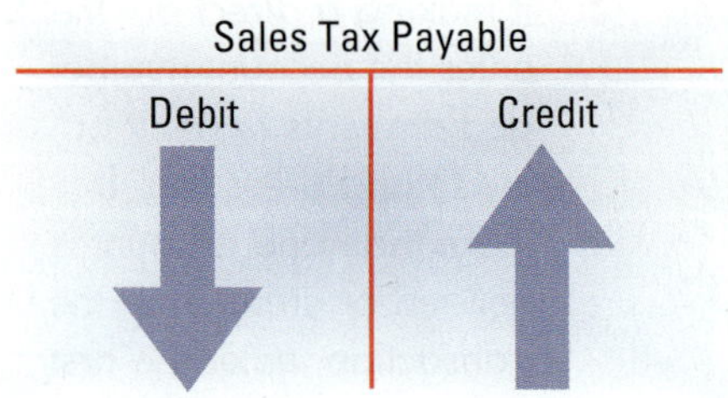


Omni operates in a state with a 6% sales tax rate. The total amount of a sale of merchandise priced at $300.00 is calculated as follows.

| Price of Goods | × | Sales Tax Rate | = | Sales Tax |
|---|---|---|---|---|
| $300.00 | × | 6% | = | $18.00 |
| **Price of Goods** | **+** | **Sales Tax** | **=** | **Total Amount Received** |
| $300.00 | + | $18.00 | = | $318.00 |

A customer must pay $318.00 for the merchandise. Omni records the price of goods sold, the sales tax, and the total amount received.

# ACCOUNTING IN YOUR CAREER

## GROWING THE BUSINESS

David Bradford, the office manager of OfficeTown, has been asked by the owners, Denise Klein and Martin Nadler, to help plan a business expansion into computer supplies and office services.

"David," says Denise, "Martin and I need to make this expansion. Our location is so good that if we don't do it, someone else will. We may not be able to survive with increased competition."

"Yes, that's true," adds Martin, "but I don't think we have the cash to make this expansion. The store is very successful, and we make a good living. But I don't know what happens to all the money we make. That's what we need your help with. Please investigate and give us some ideas."

David recognizes that this is a great opportunity to make a contribution to the business. He begins immediately and discovers:

- Twenty percent of the accounts receivable, including several with large outstanding balances, are over one month overdue.
- There is nearly a three-month supply of most inventory items.
- The partners do not withdraw extraordinary amounts of cash each month.
- The company has not borrowed from a bank in ten years, but has good credit.
- An investor with computer retailing experience is interested in joining the partnership.

### Critical Thinking:

1. What kinds of recommendations should David make regarding accounts receivable?
2. What are some possible solutions to the problem of overstocked inventory?
3. Besides generating more cash from the business, what are some other options for financing an expansion of the business? What are some advantages and disadvantages of these options?

# 11-1 Journalizing Sales and Cash Receipts from Sales

## SALES OF MERCHANDISE

A sale of merchandise may be (1) for cash or (2) on account. A sale of merchandise increases the revenue of a business. Regardless of when payment is made, revenue is recorded at the time of a sale, not on the date cash is received. *(CONCEPT: Realization of Revenue)* For example, on June 15 Omni sells merchandise on account to a customer. The customer pays Omni for the merchandise on July 12. Omni records the revenue on June 15, the date of the sale.

Omni sells most of its merchandise for cash. A sale in which cash is received for the total amount of the sale at the time of the transaction is called a **cash sale.** Omni also sells merchandise to customers who have a bank-approved credit card. A sale in which a credit card is used for the total amount of the sale at the time of the transaction is called a **credit card sale.** Major bank-approved credit cards include VISA, MasterCard, and Discover Card. Omni accepts all major bank-approved credit cards from customers. A customer who uses a credit card promises to pay the amount due for the credit card transaction to the bank issuing the credit card.

Omni prepares a credit card slip for each credit card sale. At the end of each week, these credit card slips are included with Omni's bank deposit. Omni's bank accepts the credit card slips the same way it accepts checks and cash for deposit. If a credit card was issued by another bank, Omni's bank sends the credit card slips to the issuing bank. The issuing bank then bills the customer and collects the amount owed. The bank that accepts and processes the credit card slips for a business charges a fee for this service. This fee is included on Omni's monthly bank statement.

**LEGAL ISSUES IN ACCOUNTING**

### FORMING A PARTNERSHIP

Two or more persons may form a partnership. This form of organization has several advantages:

- More assets such as cash that can be invested in the business.
- More time, energy, and experience brought to the new business.

However, there are also some disadvantages to a partnership:

- Shared decision making. Business decisions must be discussed and agreements reached by both partners. Disagreements among partners must be resolved.
- Unlimited liability. Each partner is responsible for the liabilities of the business, even those incurred by the other partner. Either partner's personal assets may be claimed by creditors to pay the partnership's liabilities.
- Shared profits. Any profits earned must be divided between the partners. Losses also must be shared.

In most states, the minimum legal requirement to form a partnership is to file a document to register the business name. A document called a *partnership agreement* also should be created by the partners. This is a written agreement setting forth the conditions under which the partnership is to operate. It includes the name and description of the business, capital investments of each partner, distribution of profits and losses, duties and responsibilities of each partner, and provisions for dissolving the partnership. A partnership agreement is not required by law, but it is in the best interest of both partners.

# CASH AND CREDIT CARD SALES

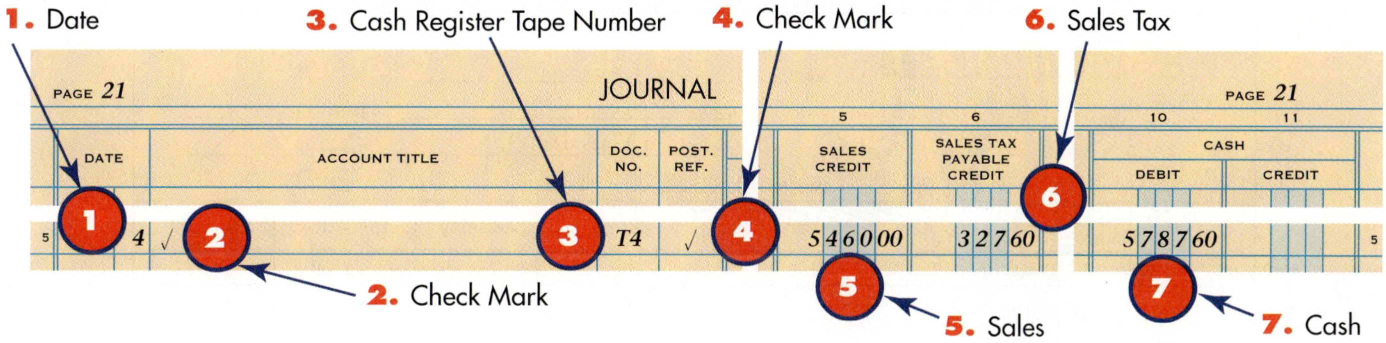


Omni's bank accepts credit card slips the same way it accepts cash. Therefore, Omni combines all cash and credit card sales and records the two revenue items as a single cash sales transaction.

***November 4. Recorded cash and credit card sales, $5,460.00, plus sales tax, $327.60; total, $5,787.60. Cash Register Tape No. 4.***

| Cash | |
|---|---|
| 5,787.60 | |

| Sales | |
|---|---|
| | 5,460.00 |

| Sales Tax Payable | |
|---|---|
| | 327.60 |

Omni uses a cash register to list all cash and credit card sales. When a transaction is entered on the cash register, a paper tape is printed as a receipt for the customer. The cash register also internally accumulates data about total cash and credit card sales.

At the end of each week, a cash register tape is printed showing total cash and credit card sales. The tape is removed from the cash register and marked with a T and the date (T4). The cash register tape is used by Omni as the source document for weekly cash and credit card sales transactions. *(CONCEPT: Objective Evidence)* Cash sales are also totaled at the end of each month so Omni can analyze monthly sales. Because October of the current year ended on Tuesday, the first weekend of November is November 4. Thus, there are only four days' sales recorded on this tape.

Because the asset account, Cash, has a normal debit balance, Cash is debited for the total sales and sales tax, $5,787.60, to show the increase in this asset account. The sales account has a normal credit balance. Therefore, Sales is credited for the total price of all goods sold, $5,460.00, to show the increase in this revenue account. The sales tax payable account also has a normal credit balance. Therefore, Sales Tax Payable is credited for the total sales tax, $327.60, to show the increase in this liability account.

## STEPS: Journalizing cash and credit card sales

1. Write the date, *4*, in the Date column.
2. Place a check mark in the Account Title column to show that no account title needs to be written. The debit and credit amounts will be recorded in special amount columns.
3. Write the cash register tape number, *T4*, in the Doc. No. column.
4. Place a check mark in the Post. Ref. column to show that amounts on this line are not to be posted individually.
5. Write the sales amount, *$5,460.00*, in the Sales Credit column.
6. Write the sales tax amount, *$327.60*, in the Sales Tax Payable Credit column.
7. Write the cash amount, *$5,787.60*, in the Cash Debit column.

## SALES INVOICE

**OMNI IMPORT**
1374 Parklane
Ashton, RI 02805

Sold to: Children's Paradise
430 Main Street
Alton, RI 02803-1163

Cust. No. 120

No. **76**
Date 11/3/--
Terms 30 days

| Stock No. | Description | Quantity | Unit Price | Amount |
|---|---|---|---|---|
| 4422 | African masks | 25 | 18.00 | 450.00 |
| 7710 | Russian nesting dolls | 30 | 12.20 | 366.00 |
| | | | | |
| | | | | |
| | | | | |
| | | | | |
| | | | Subtotal | 816.00 |
| Customer's Signature | *Max Schindler* | Salesclerk *S. A.* | Sales Tax | 48.96 |
| | | | Total | 864.96 |

A sale for which cash will be received at a later date is known as a sale on account. A sale on account is also referred to as a charge sale.

When merchandise is sold on account, the seller prepares a form showing what has been sold. A form describing the goods or services sold, the quantity, and the price is known as an invoice. An invoice used as a source document for recording a sale on account is known as a sales invoice. *(CONCEPT: Objective Evidence)* A sales invoice is also referred to as a sales ticket or a sales slip.

The seller considers an invoice for a sale on account to be a sales invoice. The same invoice is considered by the customer to be a purchase invoice.

Three copies of a sales invoice are prepared. The original copy is given to the customer. The second copy goes to Omni's shipping department. The third copy is used as the source document for the sale on account transaction. *(CONCEPT: Objective Evidence)* Sales invoices are numbered in sequence. The number 76 is the number of the sales invoice issued to Children's Paradise.

**FYI**

*The bank that accepts and processes credit card slips for a business charges a fee for this service. Businesses may choose not to accept credit cards in order to avoid such fees.*

## SALE ON ACCOUNT

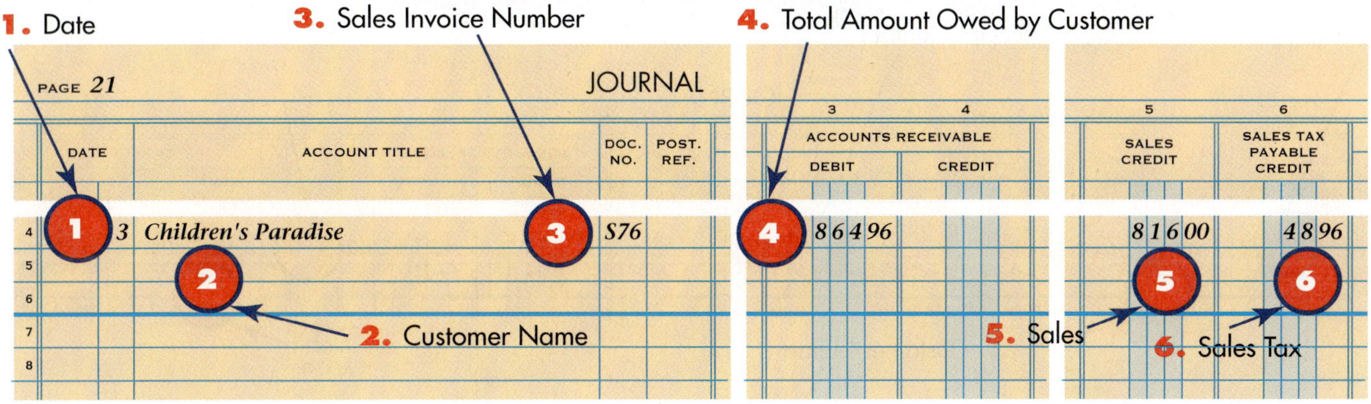


Omni sells on account only to businesses. Other customers must either pay cash or use a credit card.

Omni summarizes the total due from all charge customers in a general ledger account titled Accounts Receivable. Accounts Receivable is an asset account with a normal debit balance. Therefore, the accounts receivable account is increased by a debit and decreased by a credit.

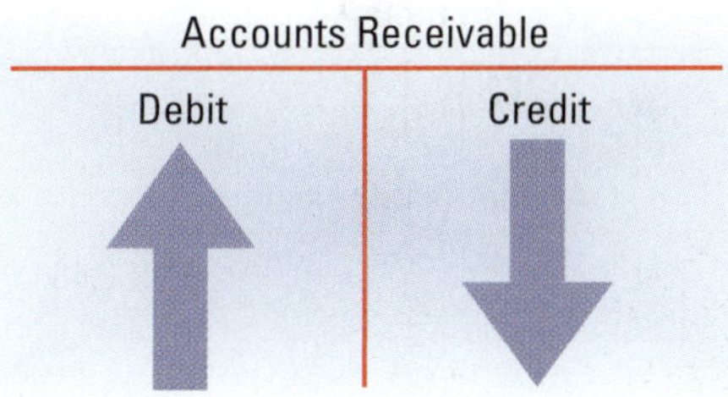


***November 3. Sold merchandise on account to Children's Paradise, $816.00, plus sales tax, $48.96; total, $864.96. Sales Invoice No. 76.***

A sale on account transaction increases the amount to be collected later from a customer. Payment for this sale will be received at a later date. However, the sale is recorded at the time the sale is made. *(CONCEPT: Realization of Revenue)*

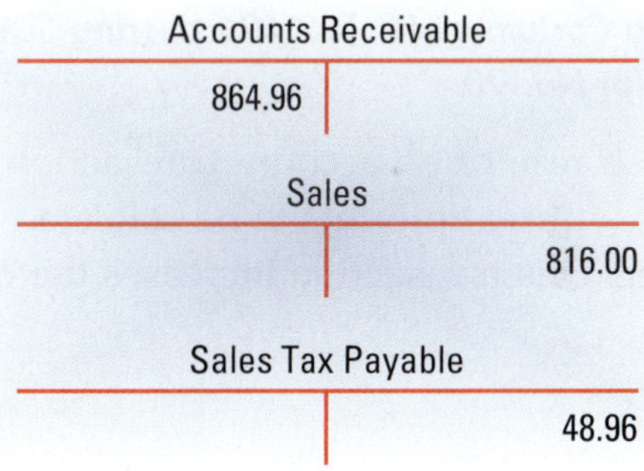


### STEPS: Journalizing a sale on account

1. Write the date, *3*, in the Date column.
2. Write the customer name, *Children's Paradise*, in the Account Title column. The debit and credit amounts are recorded in special amount columns. Therefore, writing the titles of the general ledger accounts in the Account Title column is not necessary. However, the name of the customer is written in the Account Title column to show from whom the amount is due. Omni's procedures for keeping records of the amounts to be collected from each customer are described in Chapter 12.
3. Write the sales invoice number, *S76*, in the Doc. No. column.
4. Write the total amount owed by the customer, *$864.96*, in the Accounts Receivable Debit column.
5. Write the sales amount, *$816.00*, in the Sales Credit column.
6. Write the sales tax amount, *$48.96*, in the Sales Tax Payable Credit column.

# CASH RECEIPTS ON ACCOUNT

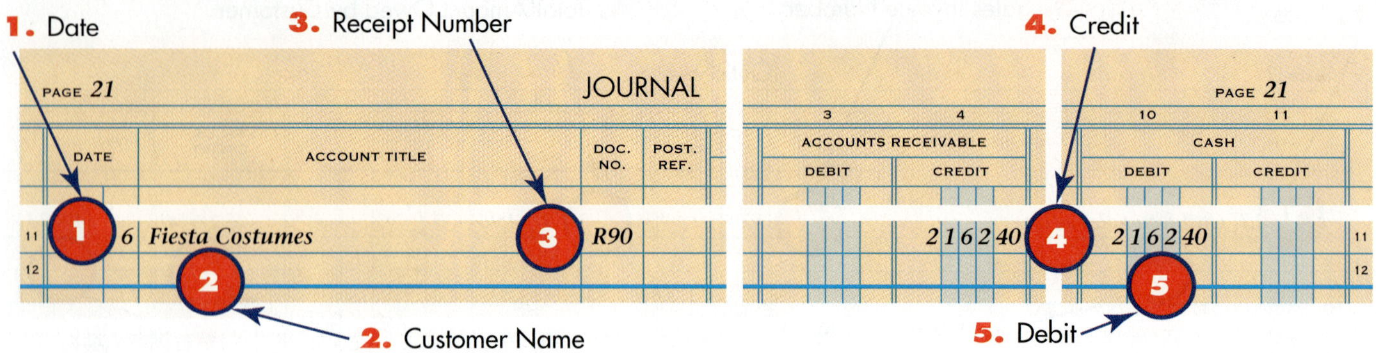


When cash is received on account from a customer, Omni prepares a receipt. The receipts are prenumbered so that all receipts can be accounted for. Receipts are prepared in duplicate. The original copy of the receipt is given to the customer. The copy of the receipt is used as the source document for the cash receipt on account transaction. *(CONCEPT: Objective Evidence)*

***November 6. Received cash on account from Fiesta Costumes, $2,162.40, covering S69. Receipt No. 90.***

A cash receipt on account transaction decreases future amounts to be collected from a customer. This transaction increases the cash account balance and decreases the accounts receivable account balance. Because the cash account has a normal debit balance, Cash is debited for the amount of cash received, $2,162.40, to show the increase in this asset account. The accounts receivable account also has a normal debit balance. Therefore, Accounts Receivable is credited for $2,162.40 to show the decrease in this asset account.

| Cash | |
|---|---|
| 2,162.40 | |

| Accounts Receivable | |
|---|---|
| | 2,162.40 |

### STEPS: Journalizing cash receipts on account

1. Write the date, *6*, in the Date column.
2. Write only the customer's name, *Fiesta Costumes*, in the Account Title column.
3. Write the receipt number, *R90*, in the Doc. No. column.
4. Write the credit amount, *$2,162.40*, in the Accounts Receivable Credit column.
5. Write the debit amount, *$2,162.40*, in the Cash Debit column.

## Terms Review

customer
sales tax
cash sale
credit card sale

## Audit Your Understanding

1. How do merchandising and service businesses differ?
2. How are sales tax rates usually stated?
3. Why is sales tax collected considered a liability?
4. Which accounting concept is being applied when revenue is recorded at the time a sale is made, regardless of when payment is made?
5. What is the title of the general ledger account used to summarize the total amount due from all charge customers?

## Work Together

### Journalizing sales and cash receipts

The journal for Distinctive Appliances is given in the *Working Papers*. Your instructor will guide you through the following example.

**6.** Using the current year, journalize the following transactions on page 9 of the journal. Source documents are abbreviated as follows: receipt, R; sales invoice; S; cash register tape, T. Save your work to complete On Your Own below.

***Transactions:***

Sept. 1. Sold merchandise on account to Adrian Makowski, $800.00, plus sales tax, $48.00; total, $848.00. S104.
4. Received cash on account from Jessica Oakley, $371.00, covering S96. R144.
6. Recorded cash and credit card sales, $5,840.00, plus sales tax, $350.40; total, $6,190.40. T6.

## On Your Own

### Journalizing sales and cash receipts

Use the journal for Distinctive Appliances you started above in Work Together. Work this problem independently.

**7.** Journalize the following transactions continuing on the next blank line of page 9 of the journal. Source documents are abbreviated as follows: receipt, R; sales invoice, S; cash register tape, T.

***Transactions:***

Sept. 8. Received cash on account from Marcia Hakala, $265.00, covering S98. R145.
10. Sold merchandise on account to Perry Rajan, $1,050.00, plus sales tax, $63.00; total, $1,113.00. S105.
13. Recorded cash and credit card sales, $6,200.00, plus sales tax, $372.00; total, $6,572.00. T13.

# 11-2 Proving and Ruling an Expanded Journal

## CARRYING TOTALS FORWARD ON THE LEFT PAGE

PAGE 21 JOURNAL

| | DATE | | ACCOUNT TITLE | DOC. NO. | POST. REF. | 1 GENERAL DEBIT | 2 GENERAL CREDIT | 3 ACCOUNTS RECEIVABLE DEBIT | 4 ACCOUNTS RECEIVABLE CREDIT | |
|---|---|---|---|---|---|---|---|---|---|---|
| 1 | 20-- Nov. | 1 | ✓ | C290 | ✓ | | | | | 1 |
| 2 | | 2 | Crown Ltd. | P83 | | | | | | 2 |
| 32 | | 15 | Ashton Jaycees | R93 | | | | | 381 60 | 32 |
| 33 | | 15 | ✓ | T15 | ✓ | | | | | 33 |
| 34 | | 15 | Carried Forward | | ✓ | 5 151 60 | 384 00 | 4 070 40 | 4 770 00 | 34 |

**2.** Write the date. **3.** Write the words *Carried Forward.* **4.** Place a check mark.

A journal is proved and ruled whenever a journal page is filled and always at the end of a month.

After all November 15 entries are recorded, page 21 of Omni's journal is filled. Page 21 is totaled and proved before column totals are forwarded to page 22. The proof that Omni's debit totals equal the credit totals on page 21 of the journal is shown below.

After a journal page has been proved, the journal must be prepared for forwarding.

| Col. No. | Column Title | Debit Totals | Credit Totals |
|---|---|---|---|
| 1 | General Debit | $ 5,151.60 | |
| 2 | General Credit | | $ 384.00 |
| 3 | Accounts Receivable Debit | 4,070.40 | |
| 4 | Accounts Receivable Credit | | 4,770.00 |
| 5 | Sales Credit | | 17,700.00 |
| 6 | Sales Tax Payable Credit | | 1,062.00 |
| 7 | Accounts Payable Debit | 6,432.00 | |
| 8 | Accounts Payable Credit | | 14,028.00 |
| 9 | Purchases Debit | 14,415.60 | |
| 10 | Cash Debit | 19,461.60 | |
| 11 | Cash Credit | | 11,587.20 |
| | Totals | $49,531.20 | $49,531.20 |

## CARRYING TOTALS FORWARD ON THE RIGHT PAGE

PAGE *21*

| | 5 | 6 | 7 | 8 | 9 | 10 | 11 | |
|---|---|---|---|---|---|---|---|---|
| | SALES CREDIT | SALES TAX PAYABLE CREDIT | ACCOUNTS PAYABLE | | PURCHASES DEBIT | CASH | | |
| | | | DEBIT | CREDIT | | DEBIT | CREDIT | |
| 1 | | | | | 575 00 | | 575 00 | 1 |
| 2 | | | | 2039 00 | 2039 00 | | | 2 |
| 32 | | | | | | 381 60 | | 32 |
| 33 | 6120 00 | 367 20 | | | | 6487 20 | | 33 |
| 34 | 17700 00 | 1062 00 | 6432 00 | 14028 00 | 14415 60 | 19461 60 | 11587 20 | 34 |

**1.** Rule a single line.

**5.** Write each column total.

**6.** Rule double lines.

### STEPS: Ruling an expanded journal to carry totals forward

1. Rule a single line across all amount columns directly below the last entry to indicate that all the columns are to be added. Be sure to rule the single line on both the left and right pages.
2. On the next line write the date, *15*, in the Date column.
3. Write the words *Carried Forward* in the Account Title column.
4. Place a check mark in the Post. Ref. column to show that nothing on this line needs to be posted.
5. For both the left and right pages, write each column total below the single line.
6. Rule double lines below the column totals across all amount columns to show that the totals have been verified as correct. Be sure to rule the double line on both the left and right pages.

**REMEMBER**

Double lines below totals show that the totals have been verified as correct.

## STARTING A NEW EXPANDED JOURNAL LEFT PAGE

**1.** Write journal page number.

PAGE 22

JOURNAL

| | DATE | | ACCOUNT TITLE | DOC. NO. | POST. REF. | 1 GENERAL DEBIT | 2 GENERAL CREDIT | 3 ACCOUNTS RECEIVABLE DEBIT | 4 ACCOUNTS RECEIVABLE CREDIT | |
|---|---|---|---|---|---|---|---|---|---|---|
| 1 | 20-- Nov. | 15 | Brought Forward | | ✓ | 5151 60 | 384 00 | 4070 40 | 4770 00 | 1 |
| 2 | | | | | | | | | | 2 |
| 3 | | | | | | | | | | 3 |
| 4 | | | | | | | | | | 4 |

**2.** Write the date. **3.** Write the words *Brought Forward.* **4.** Place check mark.

The totals from the previous journal page are carried forward to the next journal page. The totals are recorded on the first line of the new page.

### STEPS: Forwarding totals to a new journal page

1. Write the journal page number, *22,* at the top of the journal on both the left and right pages.
2. Write the date, *20—, Nov. 15,* in the Date column.
3. Write the words *Brought Forward* in the Account Title column.
4. Place a check mark in the Post. Ref. column to show that nothing on this line needs to be posted.
5. For both the left and right pages, record the column totals brought forward from page 21 of the journal.

## STARTING A NEW EXPANDED JOURNAL RIGHT PAGE

**1.** Write journal page number.

PAGE 22

| | 5 | 6 | 7 | 8 | 9 | 10 | 11 | |
|---|---|---|---|---|---|---|---|---|
| | SALES CREDIT | SALES TAX PAYABLE CREDIT | ACCOUNTS PAYABLE | | PURCHASES DEBIT | CASH | | |
| | | | DEBIT | CREDIT | | DEBIT | CREDIT | |
| 1 | 17 700 00 | 1 062 00 | 6 432 00 | 14 028 00 | 14 415 60 | 19 461 60 | 11 587 20 | 1 |
| 2 | | | | | | | | 2 |
| 3 | | | | | | | | 3 |
| 4 | | | | | | | | 4 |

**5.** Record column totals brought forward.

## Is Anyone Listening?

Riverside Payroll enjoys a reputation as a good place to work. The company strives to provide quality services for clients. In addition, Riverside is committed to a diverse workforce and is a drug-free workplace.

As an account manager, you are participating in a management retreat focused on ethics. During the retreat you are asked to analyze the situations described below.

**Instructions**

Use the three-step checklist to help determine whether or not each of the following situations demonstrates ethical behavior.

*Situation 1.* Seamus Ryan likes to be the first to know what is going on in the office. One of the reasons he is so well informed is that he looks through the papers on other employees' desks.

*Situation 2.* To improve customer service quality, employees' telephone calls are monitored. Monitoring is random, and employees do not know when a quality manager is listening to a call. Customer service representative Ricki Bassett made a personal phone call while Lillian Issacs was monitoring the line. During the call, Ricki made plans for her weekend activities.

*Situation 3.* Lynnette Tillar and Bob Rebold are co-workers and good friends. Their supervisor, George Parton, has previously reprimanded them for spending too much time chatting on the phone and visiting. George has decided to access their e-mail to see if they are wasting company time with personal online communications as well.

*Situation 4.* Ann Xiao used her office computer to prepare her resume and some cover letters. Ann worked on these documents after hours and provided her own paper for printing. She later learned that her supervisor knew about her job search. The supervisor, Kathy Martz, found the computer files while looking for a report that Ann prepared.

**Professional Business Ethics**

## PROVING AND RULING THE LEFT PAGE OF AN EXPANDED JOURNAL AT THE END OF THE MONTH

PAGE *23* — JOURNAL

| | DATE | | ACCOUNT TITLE | DOC. NO. | POST. REF. | 1 GENERAL DEBIT | 2 GENERAL CREDIT | 3 ACCOUNTS RECEIVABLE DEBIT | 4 ACCOUNTS RECEIVABLE CREDIT | |
|---|---|---|---|---|---|---|---|---|---|---|
| 15 | | *30* | ✓ | *T30* | ✓ | | | | | 15 |
| 16 | | *30* | *Totals* | | | *18823 54* | *2434 82* | *11066 40* | *9540 00* | 16 |
| 17 | | | | | | | | | | 17 |
| 18 | | | | | | | | | | 18 |
| 19 | | | | | | | | | | 19 |
| 20 | | | | | | | | | | 20 |

**2.** Write the date. **3.** Write the word *Totals*. **1.** Rule a single line.

Equality of debits and credits in a journal is proved at the end of each month. Compare the sum of the debit totals to the sum of the credit totals for Omni at the end of November. Use the same steps that were completed to prove a journal whenever a journal page is filled. The two totals, $99,270.34, are equal. Equality of debits and credits in Omni's journal for November is proved.

The accuracy of the cash account is also proved at the end of each month. Omni's cash proof at the end of November is shown below.

Since the balance on the next unused check stub is the same as the cash proof, cash is proved.

| | |
|---|---|
| Cash on hand at the beginning of the month ........ (November 1 balance of cash account in general ledger) | $17,647.44 |
| *Plus* total cash received during the month .......... (Cash Debit column total, line 16, Journal page 23) | 38,668.80 |
| *Equals* total .................................... | $56,316.24 |
| *Less* total cash paid during the month .............. (Cash Credit column total, line 16, Journal page 23) | 28,056.24 |
| *Equals* cash balance on hand at end of the month ... | $28,260.00 |
| Checkbook balance on the next unused check stub .. | $28,260.00 |

**REMEMBER**

When cash is proved, it must always equal the amount on the next unused check stub.

## PROVING AND RULING THE RIGHT PAGE OF AN EXPANDED JOURNAL AT THE END OF THE MONTH

PAGE *23*

| | 5 | 6 | 7 | 8 | 9 | 10 | 11 | |
|---|---|---|---|---|---|---|---|---|
| | SALES CREDIT | SALES TAX PAYABLE CREDIT | ACCOUNTS PAYABLE | | PURCHASES DEBIT | CASH | | |
| | | | DEBIT | CREDIT | | DEBIT | CREDIT | |
| 15 | 1380 00 | 82 80 | | | | 1462 80 | | 15 |
| 16 | 37920 00 | 2275 20 | 12984 00 | 19044 08 | 17727 60 | 38668 80 | 28056 24 | 16 |
| 17 | | | | | | | | 17 |
| 18 | | | | | | | | 18 |
| 19 | | | | | | | | 19 |
| 20 | | | | | | | | 20 |

**4.** Write each column total.

**5.** Rule double lines.

After Omni's journal and cash are proved at the end of the month, the journal is ruled.

Some of the column totals will be posted as described in Chapter 12. Therefore, a check mark is not placed in the Post. Ref. column for this line.

### STEPS: Ruling an expanded journal at the end of the month

1. Rule a single line across all amount columns directly below the last entry to indicate that all the columns are to be added. Be sure to rule the single line on both the left and right pages.
2. On the next line write the date, *30*, in the Date column.
3. Write the word *Totals* in the Account Title column.
4. For both the left and right pages, write each column total below the single line.
5. Rule double lines across all amount columns to show that the totals have been verified as correct. Be sure to rule the double line on both the left and right pages.

**FYI**

*To prove a journal page, use a calculator to verify that total debit amounts equal total credit amounts.*

## AUDIT YOUR UNDERSTANDING

1. What is the purpose of proving a journal?
2. How often should a journal be proved?
3. What is the purpose of ruling double lines below amount columns of a journal?
4. Describe how to prove cash.

## WORK TOGETHER

**Proving and ruling an expanded journal**

Partial journal pages 15 and 16 for Graphics Co. are given in the *Working Papers*. Your instructor will guide you through the following examples.

5. October 18 column totals to be carried forward have been entered on line 32 of journal page 15. Prove the equality of debits and credits and rule page 15 of the journal.
6. Record the totals brought forward from journal page 15 to line 1 of page 16 of the journal. Prove the equality of debits and credits again.
7. October 31 column totals have been entered on line 30 of journal page 16. Prove the equality of debits and credits of journal page 16.
8. Prove cash. The October 1 cash account balance in the general ledger was $11,764.96. On October 31 the balance on the next unused check stub was $18,840.00.
9. Rule page 16 of the journal.

## ON YOUR OWN

**Proving and ruling an expanded journal**

Partial journal pages 17 and 18 for Graphics Co. are given in the *Working Papers*. Work these problems independently.

10. November 16 column totals to be carried forward have been entered on line 32 of journal page 17. Prove the equality of debits and credits and rule page 17 of the journal.
11. Record the totals brought forward from journal page 17 to line 1 of page 18 of the journal. Prove the equality of debits and credits again.
12. November 30 column totals have been entered on line 28 of journal page 18. Prove the equality of debits and credits of journal page 18.
13. Prove cash. The November cash account balance in the general ledger was $18,840.00. On November 30 the balance on the next unused check stub was $26,799.42.
14. Rule page 18 of the journal.

# CHAPTER 11 SUMMARY

*Enrichment Activity*

**Types of Businesses**

*The advantages and disadvantages of a partnership are described on page 254. What are the advantages of a partnership over a proprietorship? What are the disadvantages of a partnership over a proprietorship?*

After completing this chapter, you can

1. Define accounting terms related to sales and cash receipts for a merchandising business.
2. Identify accounting concepts and practices related to sales and cash receipts for a merchandising business.
3. Journalize sales and cash receipts transactions for a merchandising business.
4. Prove and rule a journal.

## EXPLORE ACCOUNTING

### BUSINESS FORMS

Properly designed business forms can provide several important functions for a company. Business forms may (1) initiate action, (2) exercise control, (3) provide essential accounting information, and (4) provide information to multiple users.

Review Omni Import's sales invoice on page 256 to identify how these various functions have been or can be achieved.

1. *Initiate action.* The major action initiated is the collection of the amount owed by a customer for merchandise received. Information needed to accomplish this action is the customer's name and address; stock number, description, quantity, unit price, and total amounts owed for items purchased; Omni's name and address; date of the invoice; and terms of sale (due in 30 days).

2. *Exercise control.* Omni needs to insure that all merchandise shipped is properly invoiced to the customer and the information on the invoice is correct. Omni's invoices are sequentially numbered, which permits Omni to insure that all invoices are accounted for. The invoice date and terms permit Omni to file the invoice by the due date so that the company can follow up if payment is not received.

The sales clerk's initials show who made the sale so that person can be consulted if there are any questions. If the merchandise is delivered in person, the customer's signature confirms the delivery. If the merchandise is delivered by a freight company, the freight company normally requires a signature to verify delivery.

3. *Provide essential accounting information.* To account for the merchandise sold, the accounting department needs the description, unit price and total amounts of merchandise, name, address, customer number, and invoice date and terms of sale.

4. *Provide information to multiple users.* Several individuals or departments need some or all of the information on a business form. Omni has color-coded multiple copies of its sales invoice. The first copy (white) goes to the customer, Children's Paradise. The second copy (yellow) goes to Omni's shipping department. The third copy (salmon) goes to Omni's accounts receivable department. Although different businesses may use different colors, the use of color coding insures that the appropriate copy goes to the correct user.

**Required:** Visit a local business and request a copy of one of their business forms. Identify the items on the form that achieve the important functions for the company.

## 11-1 APPLICATION PROBLEM
### Journalizing sales and cash receipts

James Edwards and Mildred Edwards, partners, own a boot store.

***Instructions:***

Journalize the following transactions completed during August of the current year on page 15 of the expanded journal given in the *Working Papers*. Source documents are abbreviated as follows: receipt, R; sales invoice, S; cash register tape, T.

***Transactions:***

Aug. 1. Sold merchandise on account to Frieda Leno, $137.50, plus sales tax, $8.25; total, $145.75. S62.
4. Sold merchandise on account to Alfredo Guiterrez, $95.00, plus sales tax, $5.70; total, $100.70. S63.
5 Received cash on account from Dorothy Reader, $153.70, covering S57. R88.
6. Recorded cash and credit card sales, $2,596.00, plus sales tax, $155.76; total, $2,751.76. T6.
9. Received cash on account from Denise Thibodeau, $222.60, covering S58. R89.
11. Sold merchandise on account to Rick Wisener, $126.00, plus sales tax, $7.56; total, $133.56. S64.
13. Recorded cash and credit card sales, $3,180.00, plus sales tax, $190.80; total, $3,370.80. T13.

## 11-2 APPLICATION PROBLEM
### Journalizing sales and cash receipts

Susan Gaines and Lee Kemp, partners, own a camera and film shop.

***Instructions:***

Journalize the following transactions completed during September of the current year on page 16 of the expanded journal given in the *Working Papers*. Sales tax rate is 8%. Source documents are abbreviated as follows: receipt, R; sales invoice, S; cash register tape, T.

***Transactions:***

Sept. 2. We received a check from Charles Brittain for $111.30 as payment in full on his account covering S84. R115.
5. Jessica Gilcrease bought $126.00 worth of merchandise on account from us. Sales tax was $10.08 for a total of $136.08. S90.
7. Weekly cash and credit card sales were $3,372.00 plus sales tax of $269.76 for a total amount collected of $3,641.76. T7.
10. Sold $90.00 worth of merchandise on account to Penelope Horwitz. Sales tax was $7.20 for a total of $97.20. S91.
12. Sharon Kelly paid us $168.48 on her account covering S87. R116.
14. Weekly cash and credit card sales were $3,180.00 plus sales tax of $254.40 for a total collected of $3,434.40. T14.

## 11-3 APPLICATION PROBLEM
### Proving and ruling an expanded journal

John Nye and Donna Kirton, partners, own a novelty store.
Partial journal pages 13 and 14 for Novelties Galore are given in the *Working Papers.*

***Instructions:***

1. The July 20 column totals to be carried forward have been entered on line 32 of journal page 13. Prove the equality of debits and credits and rule the column totals of journal page 13.
2. Record the totals brought forward from journal page 13 to line 1 of page 14 of the journal. Prove the equality of debits and credits again.

## 11-4 APPLICATION PROBLEM
### Proving and ruling an expanded journal

Wanda Hagan and Art Kline, partners, own a trophies store.
A partial journal page 16 for Elegant Trophies is given in the *Working Papers.*

***Instructions:***

1. August 31 column totals have been entered on line 22 of journal page 16. Prove the equality of debits and credits of journal page 16.
2. Prove cash. The August 1 cash account balance in the general ledger was $7,346.50. On August 31 the balance on the next unused check stub was $18,218.86.
3. Rule page 16 of the journal.

## 11-5 MASTERY PROBLEM
### Journalizing sales and cash receipts transactions; proving and ruling a journal

Jose Manuel and Beth Rose, partners, own Neat Look, a clothing accessories boutique.
Partial journal pages 19 and 20 for Neat Look are given in the *Working Papers.*

***Instructions:***

1. October 24 column totals to be carried forward have been entered on line 32 of journal page 19. Prove the equality of debits and credits and rule the column totals of journal page 19.
2. Record the totals brought forward from journal page 19 to line 1 of page 20 of the journal. Prove the equality of debits and credits again.
3. Journalize the following transactions completed during the remainder of October on journal page 20. Sales tax rate is 4%. Source documents are abbreviated as follows: receipt, R; sales invoice, S; cash register tape, T.

***Transactions:***

Oct. 25. Received cash on account from Bertha Libby, $143.00, covering S77. R104.
26. Sold merchandise on account to Bertha Libby, $192.50, plus sales tax, $7.70; total, $200.20. S81.
27. Recorded cash and credit card sales, $2,915.00, plus sales tax, $116.60; total, $3,031.60. T27.
29. Received cash on account from Jack Olson, $97.24, covering S78. R105.
30. Sold merchandise on account to Lisa Gardiner, $104.50, plus sales tax, $4.18; total, $108.68. S82.
31. Recorded cash and credit card sales, $1,694.00, plus sales tax, $67.76; total, $1,761.76. T31.

4. Total the journal. Prove the equality of debits and credits.
5. Rule the journal.

## 11-6 CHALLENGE PROBLEM

### Journalizing transactions; proving and ruling a journal

Cynthia Lincoln and Mike McGinty, partners, own Always Green, a lawn and garden store.

***Instructions:***

1. Journalize the following transactions completed during May of the current year. Use page 19 of the journal given in the *Working Papers*. Sales tax rate is 8%. Compute and add the appropriate sales tax amount to each sale. Source documents are abbreviated as follows: check, C; memorandum, M; purchase invoice, P; receipt, R; sales invoice, S; cash register tape, T.

***Transactions:***

May 1. Paid cash for rent, $1,500.00. C224.
2. Cynthia Lincoln, partner, withdrew cash for personal use, $720.00. C225.
2. Mike McGinty, partner, withdrew cash for personal use, $720.00. C226.
3. Paid cash for electric bill, $156.00. C227.
3. Purchased merchandise on account from Accent Lawn Supplies, $2,730.00. P50.
4. Paid cash on account to Garden World, $1,632.00, covering P48. C228.
4. Sold merchandise on account to Colette Buckner, $1,356.00, plus sales tax. S57.
5. Bought office supplies for cash, $74.40. C229.
5. Paid cash for some merchandise, $198.00. C230.
5. Recorded cash and credit card sales, $7,020.00, plus sales tax. T5.
7. Charles Chuang bought merchandise on account, $430.00, plus sales tax. S58.
8. Felipe Garza paid cash on his account, $2,170.80, covering S53. R106.
9. Bought office supplies on account from Office Mart, $81.60. M41.
10. Purchased merchandise for cash, $216.00. C231.
10. Leonard Houston paid $1,218.24 on his account, covering S54. R107.
11. Paid cash on account to Magic Lawn and Garden, $1,638.00, covering P49. C232.
12. Mike McGinty, partner, withdrew merchandise for personal use with a cost of $462.00. M42.
12. Cash and credit card sales for the week were $3,216.00, plus sales tax. T12.
15. Cynthia Lincoln, partner, withdrew $720.00 cash for personal use. C233.
15. Mike McGinty, partner, withdrew $720.00 cash for personal use. C234.
16. Purchased merchandise on account from Lawn Doctor, $990.00. P51.
17. Paid $235.20 cash for some merchandise. C235.
17. Bought store supplies on account from McKinney Supply, $110.40. M43.
18. Paid cash on account to Office Mart, $81.60, covering M41. C236.
19. Cash and credit card sales for the week were $2,920.00, plus sales tax. T19.
21. Paid $52.80 cash for office supplies. C237.
21. Sheila Macy paid $771.12 cash on her account, covering S55. R108.
22. Nicole Oman bought merchandise on account for $390.00 plus sales tax. S59.

2. Prepare page 19 of the journal for forwarding. Total the amount columns. Prove the equality of debits and credits, and record the totals to be carried forward on line 32. Rule the column totals.
3. Record the totals brought forward on line 1 of page 20 of the journal. Prove the equality of debits and credits again.
4. Journalize the following transactions on page 20 of the journal.

***Transactions:***

May 23. Purchased merchandise on account from Lawn Scapes, Inc., $1,488.00. P52.
25. Paid $102.00 cash for advertising. C238.
26. Cash and credit card sales for the week were $3,216.00, plus sales tax. T26.
28. Jeffery Reagan paid $1,574.64 on his account, covering S56. R109.

May 29. Derek Sims bought merchandise on account for $174.00, plus sales tax. S60.

30. Paid cash to replenish the petty cash fund, $360.40: office supplies, $74.40; store supplies, $85.00; advertising, $105.00; miscellaneous, $96.00. C239.

30. Recorded cash and credit card sales, $768.00, plus sales tax. T30.

5. Total page 20 of the journal. Prove the equality of debits and credits.
6. Prove cash. The May 1 cash account balance in the general ledger was $7,314.50. On May 31 the balance on the next unused check stub was $22,434.10.
7. Rule page 20 of the journal.

## INTERNET ACTIVITY

Point your browser to

**http://accounting.swpco.com**

Choose **First-Year Course**, choose **Activities**, and complete the activity for Chapter 11.

## Applied Communication

The tendency for prices to increase over time is referred to as inflation. Increasing prices reduce what an individual or company can purchase with the same amount of money.

**Instructions:** The following table represents the prices for selected consumer goods in 1990. Copy the table and add a column for the current year and a column for the percent of change. Use the newspaper and identify current prices for the products listed. Determine the percentage change in the price of each item. If an item decreased in price, can you explain the reason for the decrease?

COMPARISON OF PRICES FOR SELECTED CONSUMER ITEMS

| Item | 1990 Price |
|---|---|
| 19-inch color television | $149.00 |
| Cassette tape | 13.50 |
| Milk (gallon) | 1.99 |
| Ground beef (pound) | 1.69 |
| Eggs, medium (dozen) | .99 |
| Raisin bran | 1.99 |
| Film, 24 exposures | 3.88 |
| Theater ticket | 6.50 |
| Motor oil (quart) | .84 |
| Refrigerator (19.1 cu. ft.) | 790.00 |

## Cases for Critical Thinking

**Case 1** Linda Tyner, an accountant for an office supplies store, has noted a major increase in overdue amounts from charge customers. All invoice amounts from sales on account are due within 30 days. The amounts due have reduced the amount of cash available for the day-to-day operation of the business. Ms. Tyner recommends that the business (1) stop all sales on account and (2) begin accepting bank credit cards. The owner is reluctant to accept the recommendations because the business might lose some reliable customers who do not have credit cards. Also, the business will have increased expenses because of the credit card fee. How would you respond to Ms. Tyner's recommendations? What alternatives might the owner consider?

# AUTOMATED ACCOUNTING

## AUTOMATED ENTRIES FOR SALES AND CASH RECEIPTS USING SPECIAL JOURNALS

A merchandising business is a business that purchases and resells goods. All transactions involving the receipt of cash are recorded in a special journal called the *Cash Receipts Journal*. The sale of merchandise on account is recorded in the *Sales Journal*.

A business or individual to whom merchandise or services are sold is called a *customer*. Businesses that have many customers maintain a separate customer file. The total owed by all customers maintained in a customer file is summarized in a single general ledger asset account called Accounts Receivable. Customer accounts may be added, changed, or deleted from the accounting system just as general ledger accounts are.

### Sales

A transaction in which merchandise or services are sold in exchange for another asset is called a *sales transaction*. A sales transaction may be on account or for cash. The sales journal is used to enter sales on account transactions. Sales transactions may be entered directly into the computer from the invoice (source document). When the credit portion of a sales transaction is entered, the computer will automatically make the debit to Accounts Receivable.

To record transactions in the sales journal:

1. Click the Journal toolbar button.
2. Click the Sales tab.
3. Enter the transaction date and press Tab.
4. Enter the invoice number in the Refer. column and press Tab.
5. Enter the amount of the invoice in the Sales Credit column and press Tab. The Accounts Receivable debit amount is calculated and displayed automatically.
6. If the transaction involves sales tax, enter the amount in the Sales Tax Credit column and press Tab. If there is no sales tax, press Tab to bypass the Sales Tax Credit column.
7. Press Tab as necessary to position the cursor in the Customer column. Choose a customer name from the Customer drop-down list.
8. Click the Post button.

### Cash Receipts

The cash receipts journal is used to enter all cash receipt transactions. The debit to cash is automatically calculated and displayed by the computer. There are two types of cash receipts:

1. *Cash and credit card sales* are cash receipts that *do not* affect Accounts Receivable.
2. *Receipts on account* are cash receipts that *do* affect Accounts Receivable.

To record transactions in the cash receipts journal:

1. Click the Journal toolbar button.
2. Click the Cash Receipts tab.
3. Enter the transaction date and press Tab.
4. Enter the transaction reference and press Tab.
5. Enter the account number to debit or credit.
6. If recording a cash or credit card sale, press Tab until the cursor appears in the Sales Credit column. Enter the sales amount of the merchandise sold and press Tab. Enter the amount of sales tax in the Sales Tax Payable Credit column. The debit to Cash is auto-

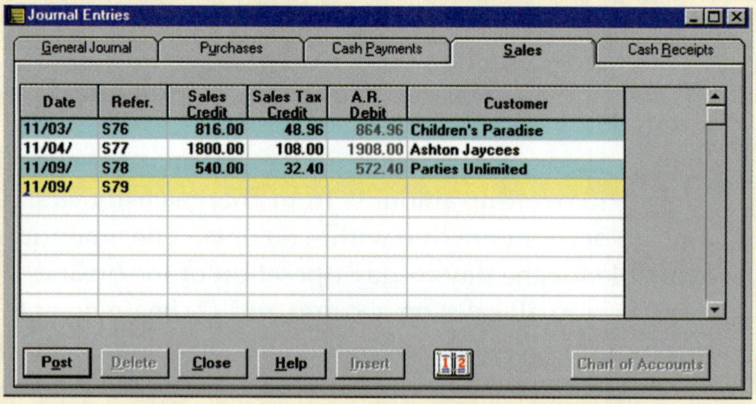

# AUTOMATED ACCOUNTING

matically calculated and displayed.

7. If recording a receipt on account, press Tab until the cursor appears in the A.R. Credit column. Enter the amount. The debit to Cash is automatically calculated and displayed. Press Tab until the cursor appears in the Customer column. Choose the customer from the Customer drop-down list.
8. Click the Post button.

## AUTOMATING MASTERY PROBLEM 11-5: Journalizing sales and cash receipts transactions; proving and ruling a journal

**Instructions:**

1. Load *Automated Accounting 7.0* or higher software.
2. Select database F11-1 from the appropriate directory/folder.
3. Select File from the menu bar and choose the Save As menu command. Key the path to the drive and directory that contains your data files. Save the database with a file name of XXX111 (where XXX are your initials).
4. Access Problem Instructions through the Help menu. Read the Problem Instructions screen.
5. Key the data listed on page 269.
6. Exit the *Automated Accounting* software.

## AUTOMATING CHALLENGE PROBLEM 11-6: Journalizing transactions; proving and ruling a journal

**Instructions:**

1. Load *Automated Accounting 7.0* or higher software.
2. Select database F11-2 from the appropriate directory/folder.
3. Select File from the menu bar and choose the Save As menu command. Key the path to the drive and directory that contains your data files. Save the database with a file name of XXX112 (where XXX are your initials).
4. Access Problem Instructions through the Help menu. Read the Problem Instructions screen.
5. Key the data listed on pages 270–271.
6. Exit the *Automated Accounting* software.

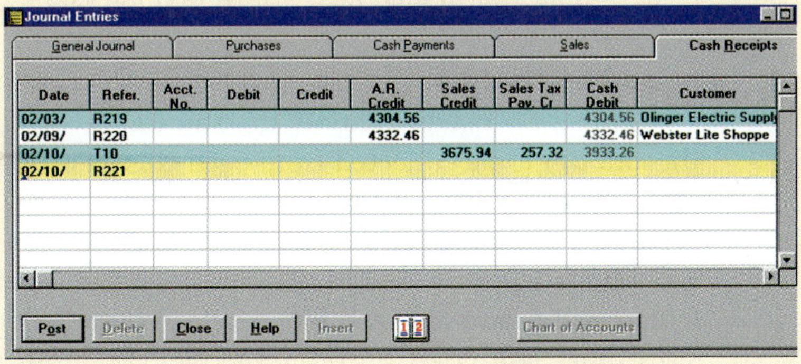

# 12 Posting to General and Subsidiary Ledgers

**AFTER STUDYING CHAPTER 12, YOU WILL BE ABLE TO:**

1. Define accounting terms related to posting to ledgers.
2. Identify accounting practices related to posting to ledgers.
3. Post to a general ledger from a journal.
4. Post to an accounts payable ledger.
5. Post to an accounts receivable ledger.
6. Verify the accuracy of accounting records.

**TERMS PREVIEW**

- subsidiary ledger
- accounts payable ledger
- accounts receivable ledger
- controlling account
- schedule of accounts payable
- schedule of accounts receivable

## LEDGERS AND CONTROLLING ACCOUNTS

A business's size, number of transactions, and type of transactions determine the number of ledgers used in an accounting system.

### General Ledger

Omni Import's general ledger chart of accounts is on page 225. However, because of the business's size and the number and type of transactions, Omni also uses additional ledgers in its accounting system.

### Subsidiary Ledgers

A business needs to know the amount owed each vendor as well as the amount to be collected from each charge customer. Therefore, a separate account is needed for each vendor and each customer. Omni keeps a separate ledger for vendors and a separate ledger for customers. Each separate ledger is summarized in a single general ledger account. A ledger that is summarized in a single general ledger account is called a **subsidiary ledger.** A subsidiary ledger containing only accounts for vendors from whom items are purchased or bought on account is called an **accounts payable ledger.** A subsidiary ledger containing only accounts for charge customers is called an **accounts receivable ledger.** Total amounts are summarized in single general ledger accounts: Accounts Payable for vendors and Accounts Receivable for charge customers. An account in a general ledger that summarizes all accounts in a subsidiary ledger is called a **controlling account.** The balance of a controlling account equals the total of all account balances in its related subsidiary ledger.

# ACCOUNTING IN YOUR CAREER

## HOW TO KEEP YOUR JOB

Ramon Suarez is the new manager of the accounting department at Toys-for-Kids, a retail toy shop with stores in 20 locations within the state. The business has grown rapidly over the last three years, and Ramon was hired because of his expertise in automated accounting systems.

Up to now, the accounting work has all been done manually. The accounting department has two accounting clerks, Celia Johnson and Thomas Vinton. Both employees have received good performance ratings and are valued employees. However, with the increase in the business, the increased number of accounting transactions can no longer be handled by two clerks efficiently. Ramon has announced that the accounting system will soon be automated.

Meeting privately, Ramon tells Celia that she will operate the new automated accounting system. "You have always done more than your job requires, and you have taken additional accounting and computer courses. I like that kind of initiative. You'll start training on the new system next week." He explains that Thomas will be reassigned to another department, where he will be responsible for maintaining inventory records.

"Ramon, from what I already know about automated accounting, I'm not ever going to have to post again, am I?" asks Celia.

"No, you're right about that," he says with a smile on his face. "The routine parts of the accounting cycle will be handled by the software. Of course, you'll still have to get the transactions analyzed and entered into the computer. But I'm looking at ways to automate some of that also."

**Critical Thinking:**

1. Celia will receive a new work assignment as a result of the new automated accounting system. What can employees do to increase their chances of receiving similar opportunities?
2. Ramon referred to automating some kinds of data entry in the accounting system. What are some of the kinds of data that can be entered automatically, and how can it be done?

# 12-1 Posting to a General Ledger

## POSTING A JOURNAL'S GENERAL AMOUNT COLUMNS

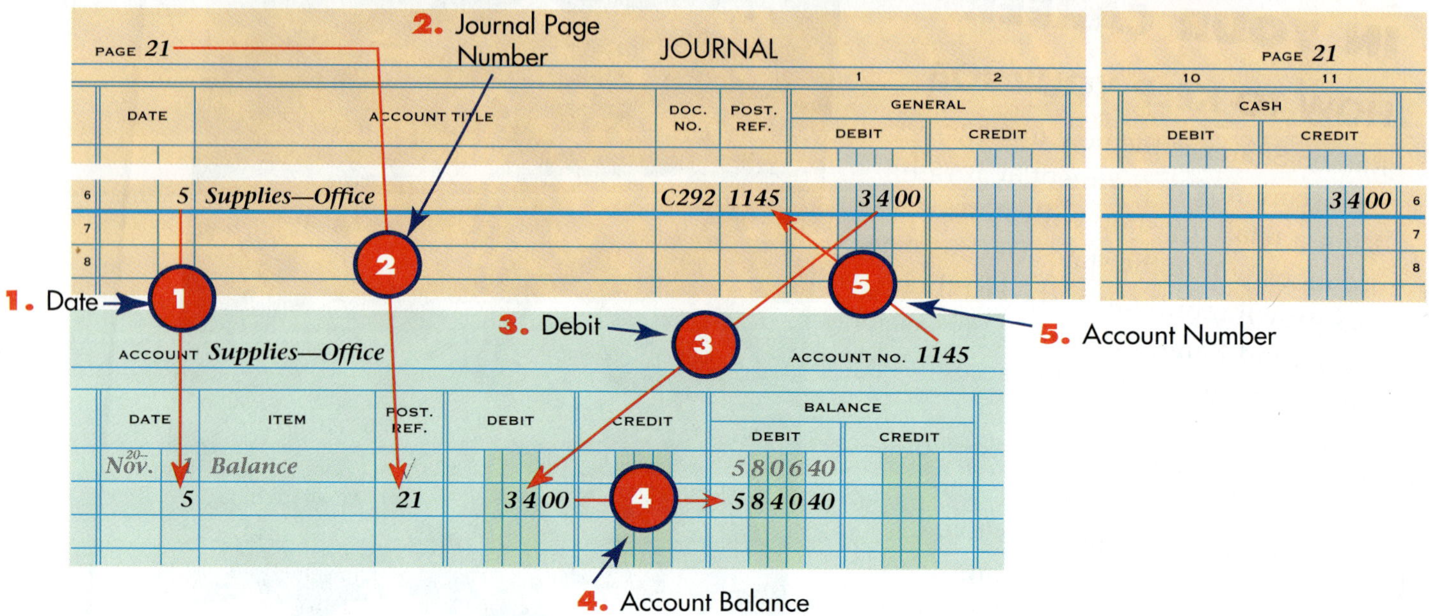


Daily general ledger account balances are usually not necessary. Balances of general ledger accounts are needed only when financial statements are prepared. Posting from a journal to a general ledger can be done periodically throughout a month. The number of transactions determines how often to post to a general ledger. A business with many transactions would normally post more often than a business with few transactions. Posting often helps keep the work load evenly distributed throughout a month. However, posting must always be done at the end of a month.

Amounts recorded in a journal's general amount columns are amounts for which no special amount columns are provided. Therefore, separate amounts in a journal's General Debit and General Credit columns *are* posted individually to the accounts written in the journal's Account Title column.

### STEPS: Posting a debit entry to the general ledger

1. Write the date, *5,* in the Date column of the account.
2. Write the journal page number, *21,* in the Post. Ref. column of the account.
3. Write the debit amount, *$34.00,* in the account's Debit amount column.
4. Add the amount in the Debit column to the previous balance in the Balance Debit column ($5,806.40 + $34.00 = $5,840.40). Write the new account balance, *$5,840.40,* in the Balance Debit column.
5. Write the general ledger account number, *1145,* in the Post. Ref. column of the journal.

**REMEMBER**

Separate amounts in a journal's general amount columns are posted individually.

# POSTING A JOURNAL'S SPECIAL AMOUNT COLUMNS

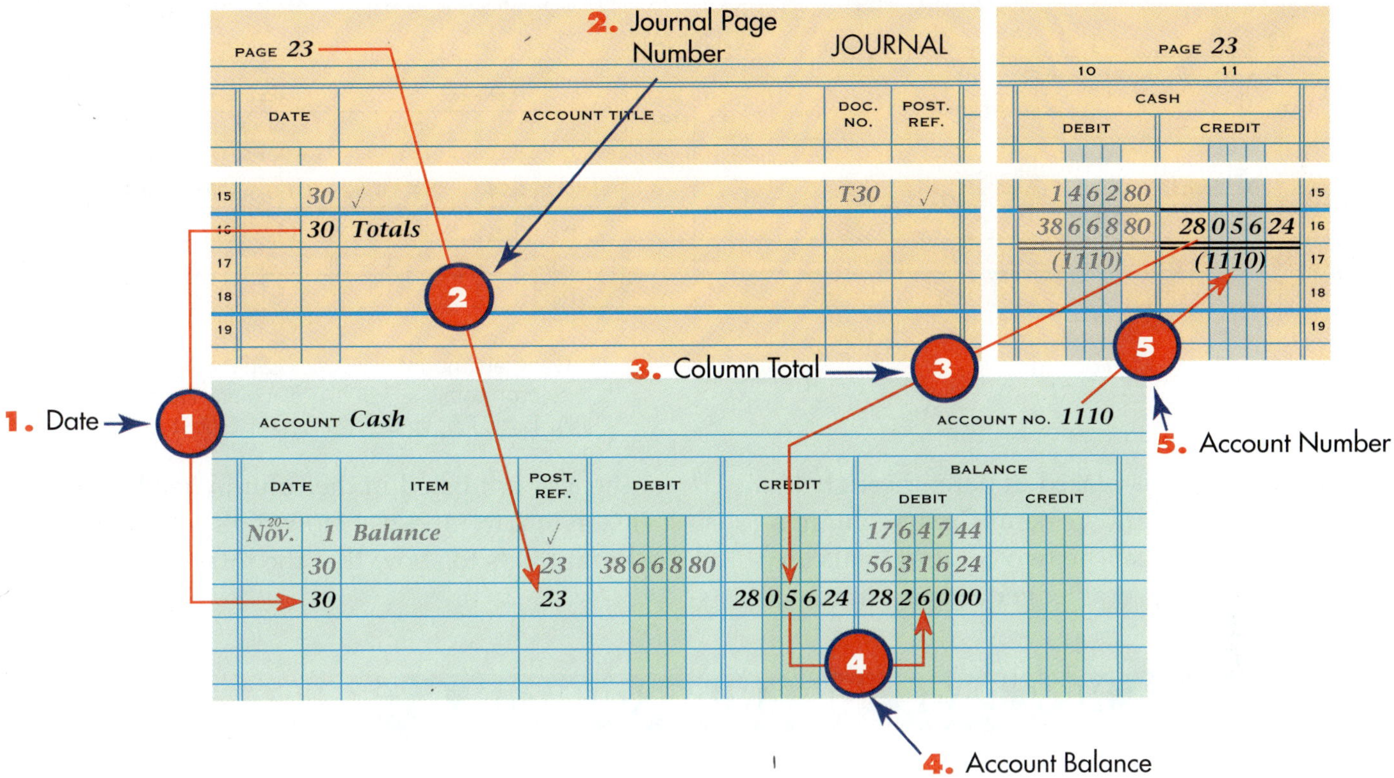


Omni's journal has nine special amount columns. Separate amounts written in these special amount columns are *not* posted individually to the general ledger. Separate amounts in a special amount column all affect the same general ledger account. Therefore, only the totals of special amount columns *are* posted to the general ledger. Each special amount column total is posted to the general ledger account listed in the column heading.

**STEPS**

### Posting the Cash Credit column total to the general ledger

1. Write the date, *30,* in the Date column of the account.
2. Write the journal page number, *23,* in the Post. Ref. column of the account.
3. Write the Cash Credit column total, *$28,056.24,* in the account's Credit column.
4. Subtract the amount in the Credit column from the previous balance in the Balance Debit column ($56,316.24 – $28,056.24 = $28,260.00). Write the new account balance, *$28,260.00,* in the Balance Debit column.
5. Return to the journal and write the general ledger account number, *1110,* in parentheses below the Cash Credit column total.

## RULES FOR POSTING A JOURNAL'S COLUMN TOTALS

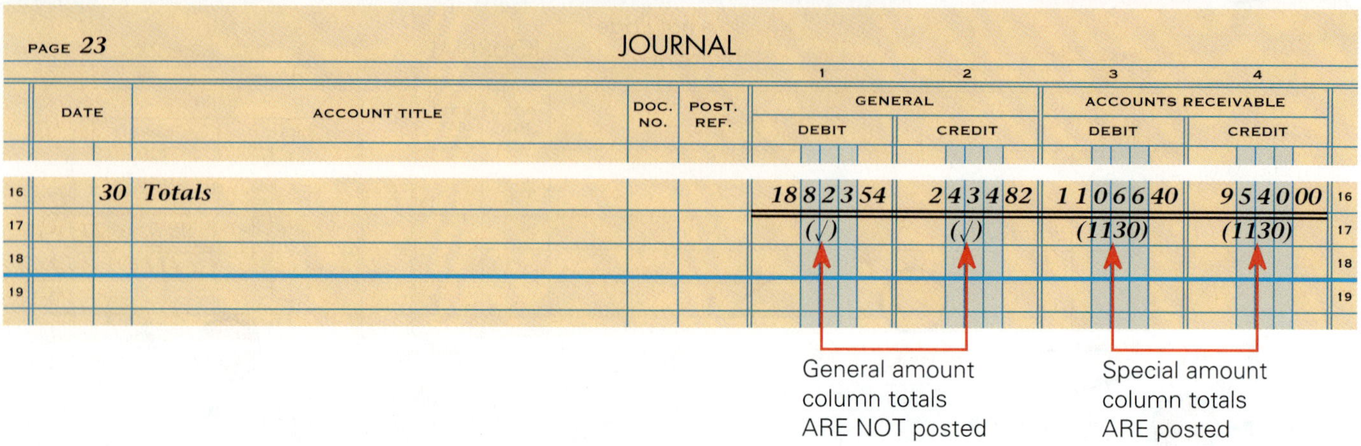


A check mark is placed in parentheses below the General Debit and General Credit column totals to indicate that the two column totals are *not* posted. The general ledger account number of the account listed in the column heading is written in parentheses below the special amount column totals to show that the totals *are* posted.

## STARTING A NEW PAGE FOR AN ACCOUNT IN A GENERAL LEDGER

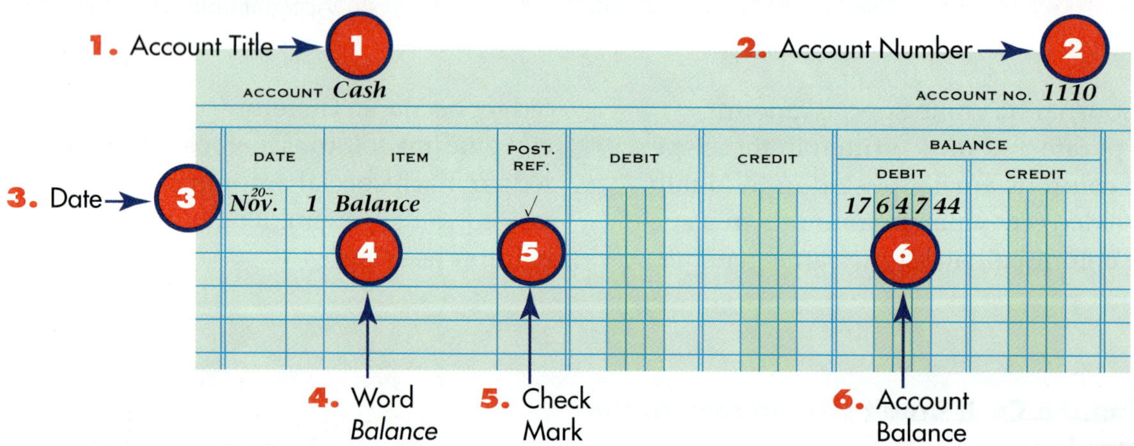


When all lines of a general ledger account form have been used, a new page is prepared.

On November 1 Omni prepared a new page for Cash in the general ledger because the existing page was full.

### STEPS: Starting a new page for a general ledger account

1. Write the account title, *Cash,* at the top of the page.
2. Write the account number, *1110,* at the top of the page.
3. Write the date, *20 —, Nov. 1,* in the Date column.
4. Write the word *Balance* in the Item column.
5. Place a check mark in the Post. Ref. column to show that the entry has been carried forward from a previous page rather than posted from a journal.
6. Write the account balance, *$17,647.44,* in the Balance Debit column.

## TERMS REVIEW

subsidiary ledger

accounts payable ledger

accounts receivable ledger

controlling account

## AUDIT YOUR UNDERSTANDING

1. What is a controlling account?
2. What is the relationship between a controlling account and a subsidiary ledger?
3. What are the four amount columns of the general ledger account form?
4. What are the rules for posting a journal's column totals?

## WORK TOGETHER

**Posting to a general ledger**

Partial journal page 16 for Graphics, Inc. is given in the *Working Papers*. Also given in the *Working Papers* are two general ledger account forms: one for Cash and a blank form. Your instructor will guide you through the following examples.

5. Start a new page for a general ledger account for Supplies—Office. The account number is 1145, and the balance for October 1 of the current year is $3,824.00.
6. Post the General Debit entry on line 2, page 16 of the journal to the Supplies—Office account.
7. Post the Cash Debit column total on line 30, page 16 of the journal to Cash.
8. Record the appropriate entry under the General Debit and Cash Debit column totals on line 31, page 16 of the journal. Save your work to complete Work Together on page 285.

## ON YOUR OWN

**Posting to a general ledger**

Partial journal page 18 for Graphics, Inc. is given in the *Working Papers*. Also given in the *Working Papers* are two general ledger account forms: one for Cash and a blank form. Work these problems independently.

9. Start a new page for a general ledger account for Supplies—Store. The account number is 1150, and the balance for November 1 of the current year is $4,302.00.
10. Post the General Debit entry on line 2, page 18 of the journal to the Supplies—Store account.
11. Post the Cash Credit column total on line 28, page 18 of the journal to Cash.
12. Record the appropriate entry under the General Debit and Cash Credit column totals on line 29, page 18 of the journal. Save your work to complete On Your Own on page 285.

# 12-2 Posting to an Accounts Payable Ledger

## ACCOUNTS PAYABLE LEDGER AND GENERAL LEDGER CONTROLLING ACCOUNT

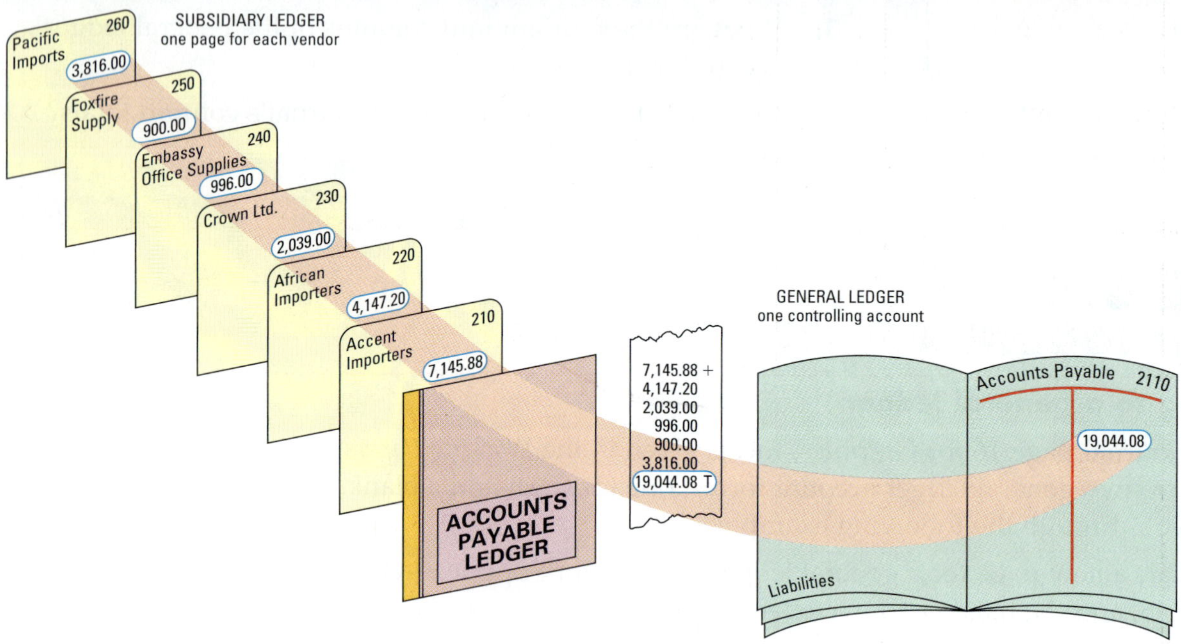


Omni assigns a vendor number to each account in the accounts payable ledger. A three-digit number is used. The first digit identifies the division in which the controlling account appears in the general ledger. The second two digits show each account's location within a subsidiary ledger. Accounts are assigned by 10s beginning with the second digit. Accounts in the subsidiary ledgers can be located by either number or name.

The vendor number for Accent Importers is 210. The first digit, *2,* shows that the controlling account is a liability, Accounts Payable. The second and third digits, *10,* show the vendor number assigned to Accent Importers.

The procedure for adding new accounts to subsidiary ledgers is the same as described for Encore Music's general ledger in Chapter 5. Accounts are arranged in alphabetical order within the subsidiary ledgers. New accounts are assigned the unused middle number. If the proper alphabetical order places a new account as the last account, the next number in the sequence of 10s is assigned. Omni's chart of accounts for the subsidiary ledgers is on page 225.

When the balance of a vendor account in an accounts payable ledger is changed, the balance of the controlling account, Accounts Payable, is also changed. The total of all vendor account balances in the accounts payable ledger equals the balance of the controlling account, Accounts Payable.

# OPENING ACCOUNTS PAYABLE LEDGER FORMS

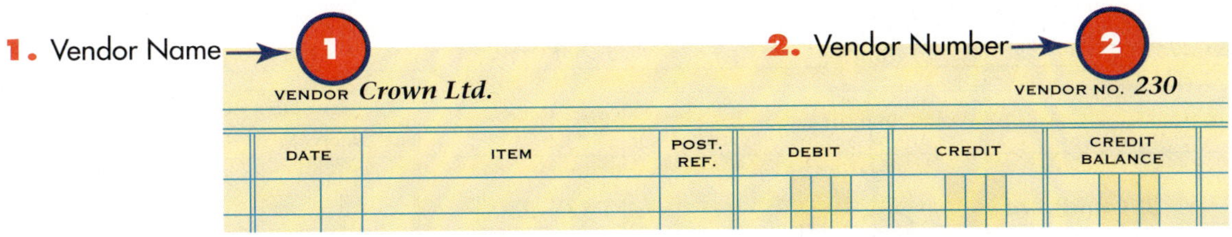


Omni Import uses a 3-column accounts payable subsidiary account form. Information to be recorded in the accounts payable ledger includes the date, posting reference, debit or credit amount, and new account balance. Accounts payable are liabilities, and liabilities have normal credit balances. Therefore, the Debit Balance column is usually not needed for the accounts payable ledger accounts.

Each new account is opened by:

1. Writing the vendor name on the heading of the ledger account.
2. Writing the vendor number on the heading of the ledger account.

The vendor name is obtained from the first purchase invoice received. The vendor number is assigned using the three-digit numbering system previously described. The correct alphabetical order for Crown Ltd. places the account as the third account in the accounts payable subsidiary ledger. Vendor number 230 is assigned to Crown Ltd.

Some businesses record both the vendor name and vendor address on the ledger form. However, the address information is usually kept in a separate name and address file. This practice eliminates having to record the vendor address on the ledger form each time a new ledger page is started or the address changes.

## THE INTERNATIONAL BUSINESS DAY

American business offices normally operate Monday through Friday, eight hours a day, with a 30- to 45-minute lunch break. This is not necessarily true in other countries, however. In the People's Republic of China, for example, employees usually work Monday through Saturday, eight hours a day, with lunch from 1:00 P.M. to 2:00 P.M.

When doing business internationally, both time zone differences and cultural factors affecting the business day must be taken into consideration. For example, in Spain, many businesses close at 2:00 P.M. so that employees may eat lunch with their families. The office reopens at 5:00 P.M. and stays open until about 8:00 P.M. Spain is in a time zone that is five hours ahead of *Eastern Standard Time (EST)*, the time zone along the eastern coast of the United States. If doing business with a company in Spain, it would not be a good idea to try to call at 9:00 A.M. EST because the business may just be closing for lunch. A better time to call Spain from the EST time zone would be between noon and 3:00 P.M.

**GLOBAL PERSPECTIVE**

## POSTING A CREDIT TO AN ACCOUNTS PAYABLE LEDGER

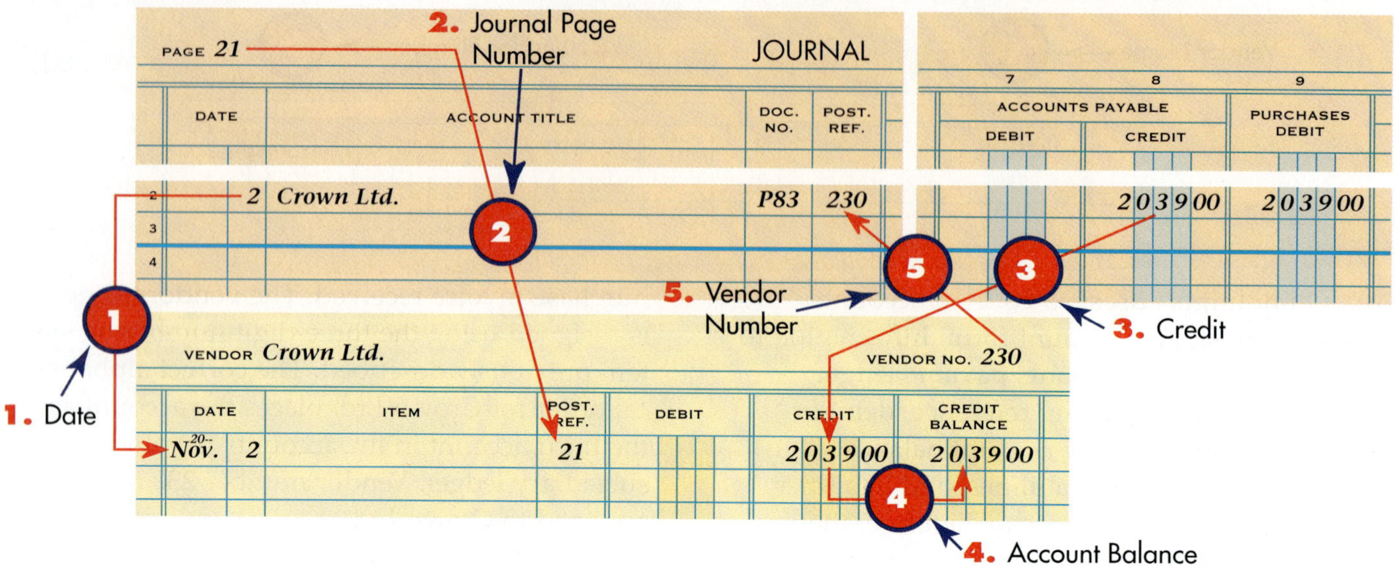


Each entry in the Accounts Payable columns of a journal affects the vendor named in the Account Title column. Omni posts each amount in these two columns often. Posting often keeps each vendor account balance up to date. Totals of Accounts Payable special amount columns are posted to the general ledger at the end of each month.

The controlling account in the general ledger, Accounts Payable, is also increased by this entry. At the end of the month, the journal's Accounts Payable Credit column total is posted to the controlling account, Accounts Payable.

**FYI**

*When an account that is no longer used is removed from the accounts payable ledger, that vendor number is available for assignment to a new vendor.*

**STEPS**

### Posting a credit entry to an accounts payable ledger

1. Write the current date, *20—, Nov. 2,* in the Date column of the account.
2. Write the journal page number, *21,* in the Post. Ref. column of the account.
3. Write the credit amount, *$2,039.00,* in the Credit column of the account for Crown Ltd.
4. Add the amount in the Credit column to the previous balance in the Credit Balance column. Crown Ltd. has no previous balance; therefore, $0 + $2,039.00 = $2,039.00. Write the new account balance, *$2,039.00,* in the Credit Balance column.
5. Write the vendor number, *230,* in the Post. Ref. column of the journal. The vendor number recorded in the journal shows that the posting for this entry is complete.

## POSTING A DEBIT TO AN ACCOUNTS PAYABLE LEDGER

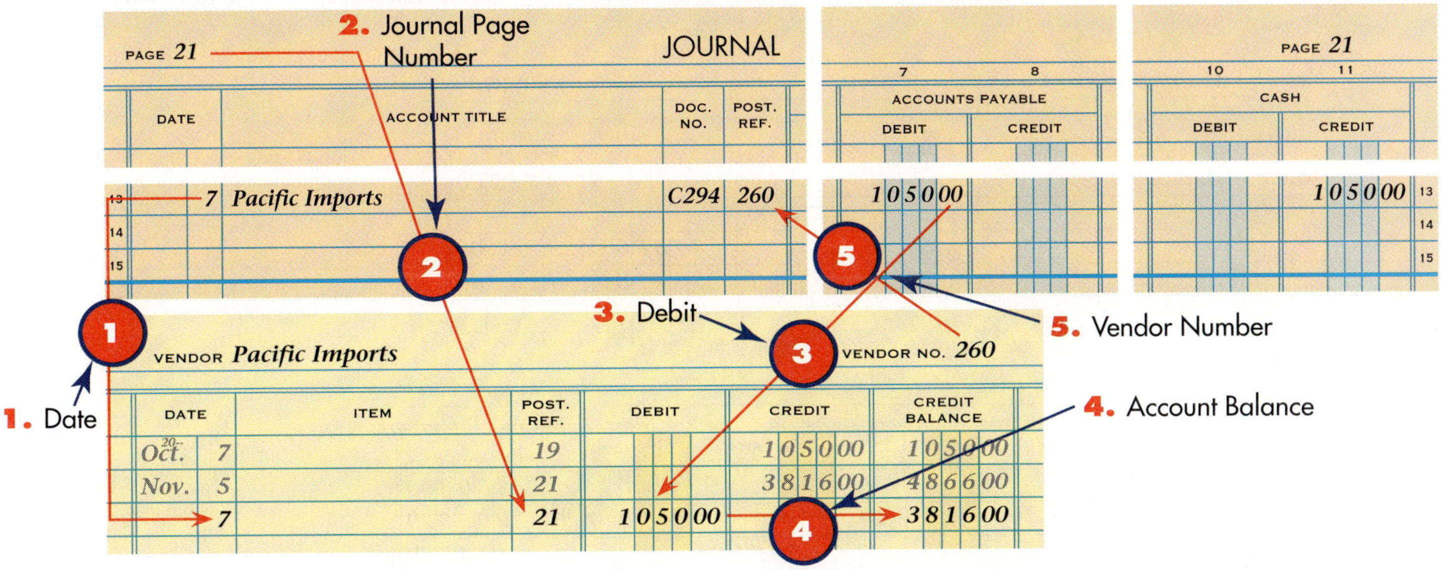


Similar steps are followed to post a debit to a vendor account as are used to post a credit. However, the debit amount is entered in the Debit column of the vendor account. The debit amount is subtracted from the previous credit balance. The controlling account in the general ledger, Accounts Payable, is decreased by this entry. At the end of the month, the journal's Accounts Payable Debit column total is posted to the controlling account, Accounts Payable.

## STARTING A NEW PAGE FOR A VENDOR IN AN ACCOUNTS PAYABLE LEDGER

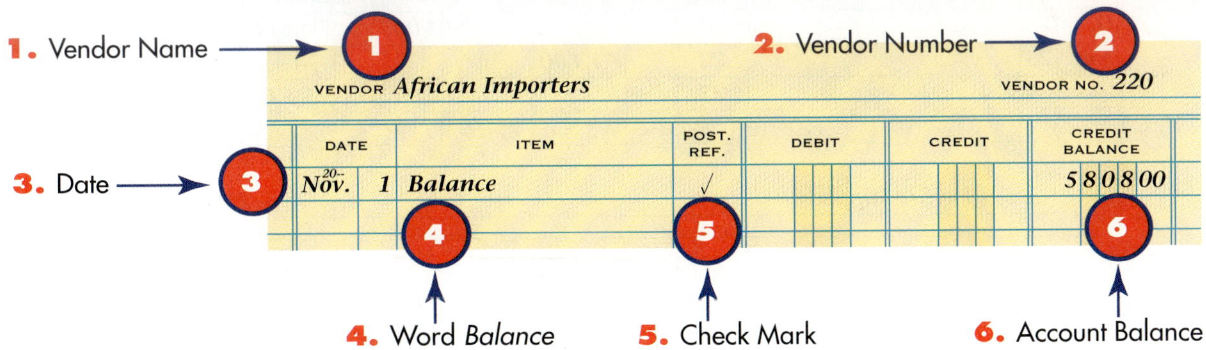


When all lines have been used, a new page is prepared. The vendor name, vendor number, and account balance are recorded on the new page.

**STEPS**

### Starting a new page in the accounts payable ledger

1. Write the vendor name, *African Importers,* on the Vendor line.
2. Write the vendor number, *220,* on the Vendor No. line.
3. Write the date, *20—, Nov. 1,* in the Date column.
4. Write the word *Balance* in the Item column.
5. Place a check mark in the Post. Ref. column to show that the amount has been carried forward from a previous page rather than posted from a journal.
6. Write the account balance, *$5,808.00,* in the Credit Balance column.

# COMPLETED ACCOUNTS PAYABLE LEDGER

VENDOR *Accent Importers* VENDOR NO. *210*

| DATE | | ITEM | POST. REF. | DEBIT | CREDIT | CREDIT BALANCE |
|---|---|---|---|---|---|---|
| 20-- Nov. | 1 | Balance | √ | | | 4,752.00 |
| | 6 | | 21 | 4,752.00 | | — |
| | 13 | | 21 | | 3,768.00 | 3,768.00 |
| | 20 | | 22 | | 3,377.88 | 7,145.88 |

VENDOR *African Importers* VENDOR NO. *220*

| DATE | | ITEM | POST. REF. | DEBIT | CREDIT | CREDIT BALANCE |
|---|---|---|---|---|---|---|
| 20-- Nov. | 1 | Balance | √ | | | 5,808.00 |
| | 5 | | 21 | | 4,147.20 | 9,955.20 |
| | 20 | | 22 | 5,808.00 | | 4,147.20 |

VENDOR *Crown Ltd.* VENDOR NO. *230*

| DATE | | ITEM | POST. REF. | DEBIT | CREDIT | CREDIT BALANCE |
|---|---|---|---|---|---|---|
| 20-- Nov. | 2 | | 21 | | 2,039.00 | 2,039.00 |

VENDOR *Embassy Office Supplies* VENDOR NO. *240*

| DATE | | ITEM | POST. REF. | DEBIT | CREDIT | CREDIT BALANCE |
|---|---|---|---|---|---|---|
| 20-- Oct. | 23 | | 20 | | 744.00 | 744.00 |
| Nov. | 23 | | 22 | 744.00 | | — |
| | 24 | | 22 | | 996.00 | 996.00 |

VENDOR *Foxfire Supply* VENDOR NO. *250*

| DATE | | ITEM | POST. REF. | DEBIT | CREDIT | CREDIT BALANCE |
|---|---|---|---|---|---|---|
| 20-- Oct. | 12 | | 19 | | 498.00 | 498.00 |
| Nov. | 6 | | 21 | | 210.00 | 708.00 |
| | 11 | | 21 | 498.00 | | 210.00 |
| | 23 | | 22 | | 690.00 | 900.00 |

VENDOR *Pacific Imports* VENDOR NO. *260*

| DATE | | ITEM | POST. REF. | DEBIT | CREDIT | CREDIT BALANCE |
|---|---|---|---|---|---|---|
| 20-- Oct. | 7 | | 19 | | 1,050.00 | 1,050.00 |
| Nov. | 5 | | 21 | | 3,816.00 | 4,866.00 |
| | 7 | | 21 | 1,050.00 | | 3,816.00 |

Omni's accounts payable ledger has been posted for the month of November.

## AUDIT YOUR UNDERSTANDING

1. What is the title of the balance amount column of the accounts payable ledger form? Why is that title used?
2. How is a new vendor account opened?
3. List the five steps for posting to an accounts payable ledger.

## WORK TOGETHER

**Posting to an accounts payable ledger**

Use the partial journal page 16 for Graphics, Inc. from Work Together on page 279. Also given in the *Working Papers* are two accounts payable ledger account forms: one for Electro-Graphic Supply and a blank form. Your instructor will guide you through the following examples.

4. Start a new page for an accounts payable ledger account for Regal Designs. The account number is 240, and the balance for October 1 of the current year is $877.00.
5. Post the Accounts Payable Credit entry on line 3, page 16 of the journal to the accounts payable account for Regal Designs.
6. Post the Accounts Payable Debit entry on line 4, page 16 of the journal to the accounts payable account for Electro-Graphic Supply. Save your work to complete Work Together on page 291.

## ON YOUR OWN

**Posting to an accounts payable ledger**

Use the partial journal page 18 for Graphics, Inc. from On Your Own on page 279. Also given in the *Working Papers* are two accounts payable ledger account forms: one for Art and Things and a blank form. Work these problems independently.

7. Start a new page for an accounts payable ledger account for Can Do Graphics. The account number is 220, and the balance for November 1 of the current year is $986.00.
8. Post the Accounts Payable Credit entry on line 3, page 18 of the journal to the accounts payable account for Can Do Graphics.
9. Post the Accounts Payable Debit entry on line 4, page 18 of the journal to the accounts payable account for Art and Things. Save your work to complete On Your Own on page 291.

# 12-3 Posting to an Accounts Receivable Ledger

## ACCOUNTS RECEIVABLE LEDGER AND GENERAL LEDGER CONTROLLING ACCOUNT

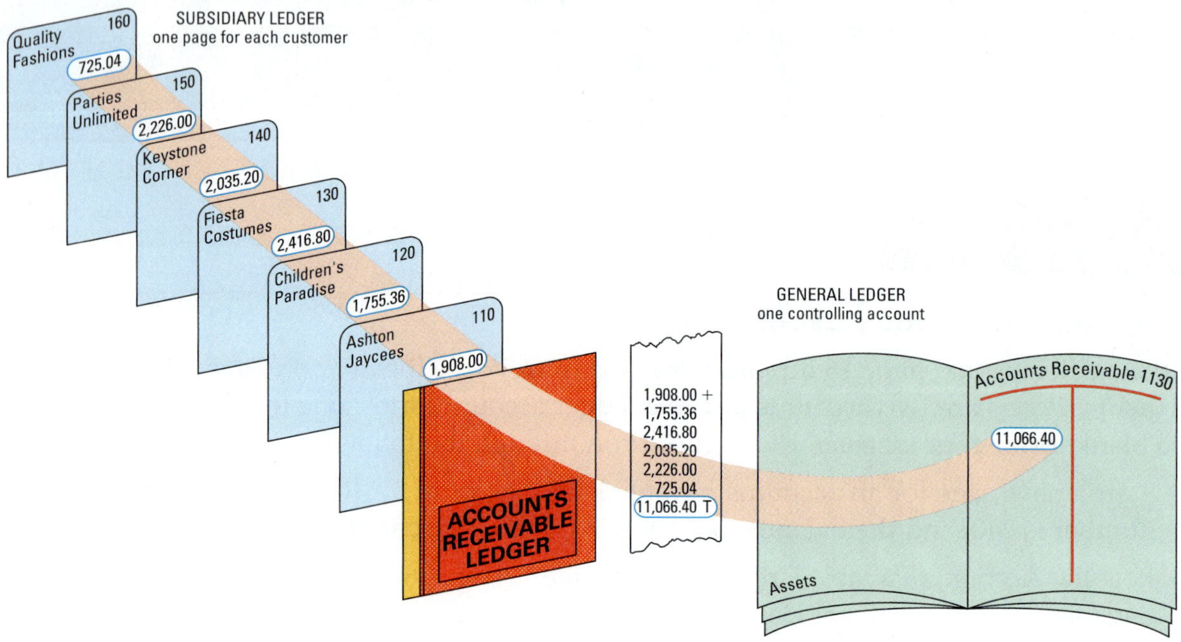


Omni assigns a customer number to each account in the accounts receivable ledger. A three-digit number is used.

The customer number for Ashton Jaycees is 110. The first digit, *1,* shows that the controlling account is an asset, Accounts Receivable. The second and third digits, *10,* show the customer number assigned to Ashton Jaycees.

When the balance of a customer account in an accounts receivable ledger is changed, the balance of the controlling account, Accounts Receivable, is also changed. The total of all customer account balances in the accounts receivable ledger equals the balance of the controlling account, Accounts Receivable.

**SMALL BUSINESS SPOTLIGHT**

The major ways of starting a new small business are:

1. Buy an existing business.
2. Buy a franchise.
3. Start a business from scratch.

## OPENING ACCOUNTS RECEIVABLE LEDGER FORMS

Omni Import uses a 3-column accounts receivable subsidiary account form. The accounts receivable account form is similar to the one used for the accounts payable ledger. Accounts receivable are assets, and assets have normal debit balances. Therefore, the form used in the accounts receivable ledger has a Debit Balance column instead of a Credit Balance column.

Procedures for opening customer accounts are similar to those used for opening vendor accounts. Each new account is opened by:

1. Writing the customer name on the heading of the ledger account.
2. Writing the customer number on the heading of the ledger account.

The customer name is obtained from the first sales invoice prepared for a customer. The customer number is assigned using the three-digit numbering system previously described.

Some businesses record both the customer name and customer address on the ledger form. However, the address information is usually kept in a separate name and address file. This practice eliminates having to record the customer address on the ledger form each time a new ledger page is started or the address changes.

**FYI**

*When an account that is no longer used is removed from the accounts receivable ledger, that customer number is available for assignment to a new customer.*

## POSTING A DEBIT TO AN ACCOUNTS RECEIVABLE LEDGER

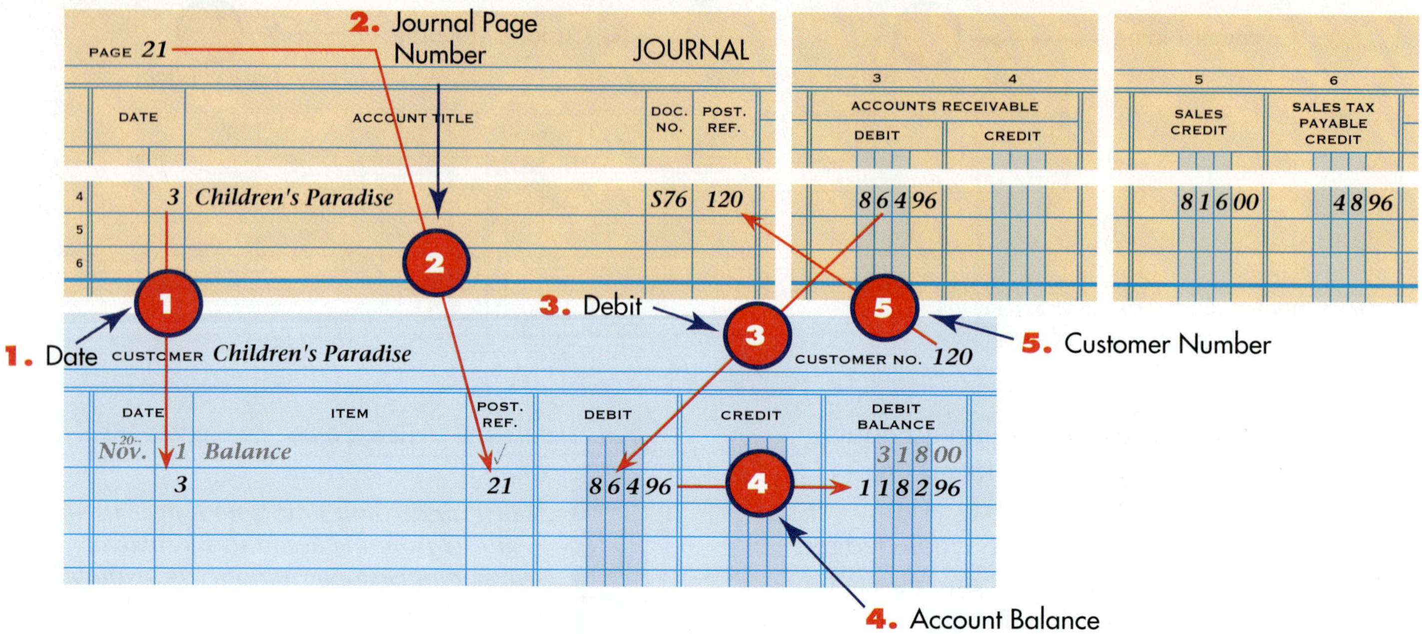


Each entry in the Accounts Receivable columns of a journal affects the customer named in the Account Title column. Each amount listed in these two columns is posted to a customer account in the accounts receivable ledger often. Posting often keeps each customer account balance up to date. Totals of Accounts Receivable special amount columns are posted to the general ledger at the end of each month.

The controlling account in the general ledger, Accounts Receivable, is also increased by this entry. At the end of the month, the journal's Accounts Receivable Debit column total is posted to the controlling account, Accounts Receivable.

### STEPS: Posting a debit entry to an accounts receivable ledger

1. Write the date, *3,* in the Date column of the account.
2. Write the journal page number, *21,* in the Post. Ref. column of the account.
3. Write the debit amount, *$864.96,* in the Debit column of the account for Children's Paradise.
4. Add the amount in the Debit column to the previous balance in the Debit Balance column ($318.00 + $864.96 = $1,182.96). Write the new account balance, *$1,182.96,* in the Debit Balance column.
5. Write the customer number, *120,* in the Post. Ref. column of the journal. The customer number shows that the posting for this entry is complete.

**FYI**

*An error in posting may cause a business to overcharge or undercharge its customers.*

## POSTING A CREDIT TO AN ACCOUNTS RECEIVABLE LEDGER

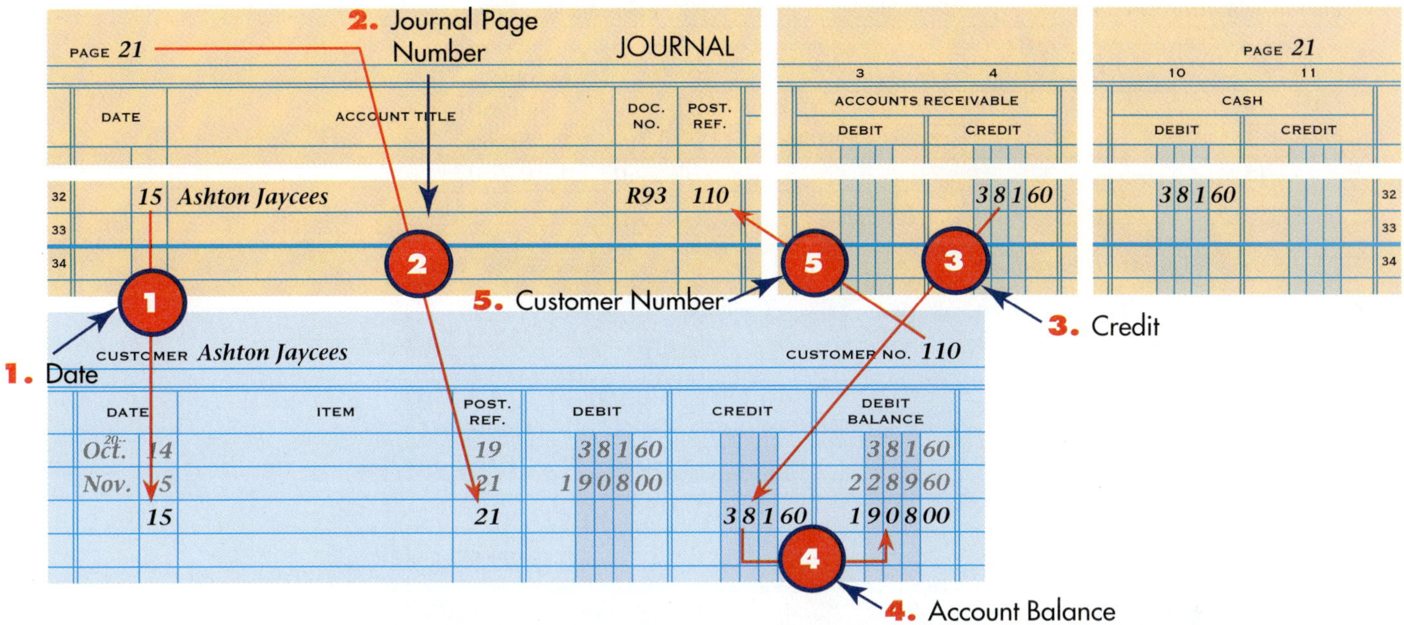


Similar steps are followed to post a credit to a customer account as are used to post a debit. However, the credit amount is written in the Credit column of the customer account. The credit amount is subtracted from the previous debit balance to determine the new balance. The new balance is written in the Debit Balance column.

The controlling account in the general ledger, Accounts Receivable, is decreased by this entry. However, the amount is not posted individually to the accounts receivable account. At the end of the month, the amount, $381.60, is posted as part of the special amount column total to Accounts Receivable.

## STARTING A NEW PAGE FOR A CUSTOMER IN AN ACCOUNTS RECEIVABLE LEDGER

Procedures for starting a new page in an accounts receivable ledger are similar to those used for starting new pages for vendor accounts.

The vendor name and number are written in the heading of the account. The date is written in the Date column. The word *Balance* is written in the Item column, and a check mark is placed in the Post. Ref. column. The balance is written in the Debit Balance column.

# COMPLETED ACCOUNTS RECEIVABLE LEDGER

CUSTOMER *Ashton Jaycees* CUSTOMER NO. *110*

| DATE | | ITEM | POST. REF. | DEBIT | CREDIT | DEBIT BALANCE |
|---|---|---|---|---|---|---|
| 20-- Oct. | 14 | | 19 | 381 60 | | 381 60 |
| Nov. | 5 | | 21 | 1908 00 | | 2289 60 |
| | 15 | | 21 | | 381 60 | 1908 00 |

CUSTOMER *Children' Paradise* CUSTOMER NO. *120*

| DATE | | ITEM | POST. REF. | DEBIT | CREDIT | DEBIT BALANCE |
|---|---|---|---|---|---|---|
| 20-- Nov. | 1 | Balance | ✓ | | | 318 00 |
| | 3 | | 21 | 864 96 | | 1182 96 |
| | 24 | | 22 | 890 40 | | 2073 36 |
| | 25 | | 22 | | 318 00 | 1755 36 |

CUSTOMER *Fiesta Costumes* CUSTOMER NO. *130*

| DATE | | ITEM | POST. REF. | DEBIT | CREDIT | DEBIT BALANCE |
|---|---|---|---|---|---|---|
| 20-- Nov. | 1 | Balance | ✓ | | | 2162 40 |
| | 6 | | 21 | | 2162 40 | — |
| | 18 | | 22 | 2416 80 | | 2416 80 |

CUSTOMER *Keystone Corner* CUSTOMER NO. *140*

| DATE | | ITEM | POST. REF. | DEBIT | CREDIT | DEBIT BALANCE |
|---|---|---|---|---|---|---|
| 20-- Oct. | 10 | | 19 | 1144 80 | | 1144 80 |
| Nov. | 10 | | 21 | | 1144 80 | — |
| | 24 | | 22 | 381 60 | | 381 60 |
| | 29 | | 22 | 1653 60 | | 2035 20 |

CUSTOMER *Parties Unlimited* CUSTOMER NO. *150*

| DATE | | ITEM | POST. REF. | DEBIT | CREDIT | DEBIT BALANCE |
|---|---|---|---|---|---|---|
| 20-- Nov. | 1 | Balance | ✓ | | | 2989 20 |
| | 9 | | 21 | 572 40 | | 3561 60 |
| | 16 | | 22 | 1653 60 | | 5215 20 |
| | 17 | | 22 | | 2989 20 | 2226 00 |

CUSTOMER *Quality Fashions* CUSTOMER NO. *160*

| DATE | | ITEM | POST. REF. | DEBIT | CREDIT | DEBIT BALANCE |
|---|---|---|---|---|---|---|
| 20-- Nov. | 1 | Balance | ✓ | | | 2544 00 |
| | 11 | | 21 | 725 04 | | 3269 04 |
| | 13 | | 21 | | 1081 20 | 2187 84 |
| | 20 | | 22 | | 1462 80 | 725 04 |

Omni Import's accounts receivable ledger has been posted for the month of November.

## AUDIT YOUR UNDERSTANDING

1. Why does the 3-column account form used in an accounts receivable ledger have a Debit Balance column?
2. List the five steps for posting to an accounts receivable ledger.

## WORK TOGETHER

### Posting to an accounts receivable ledger

Use the partial journal page 16 for Graphics, Inc., from Work Together on page 285. Also given in the *Working Papers* are two accounts receivable ledger account forms: one for Alfredo Lopez and a blank form. Your instructor will guide you through the following examples.

3. Start a new page for an accounts receivable ledger account for Maria Farrell. The account number is 120, and the balance for October 1 of the current year is $212.00.
4. Post the Accounts Receivable Debit entry on line 5, page 16 of the journal to the accounts receivable account for Maria Farrell.
5. Post the Accounts Receivable Credit entry on line 6, page 16 of the journal to the accounts receivable account for Alfredo Lopez.

## ON YOUR OWN

### Posting to an accounts receivable ledger

Use the partial journal page 18 for Graphics, Inc., from On Your Own on page 285. Also given in the *Working Papers* are two accounts receivable ledger account forms: one for Brandee Sparks and a blank form. Work these problems independently.

6. Start a new page for an accounts receivable ledger account for David Bishop. The account number is 110, and the balance for November 1 of the current year is $238.50.
7. Post the Accounts Receivable Debit entry on line 5, page 18 of the journal to the accounts receivable account for David Bishop.
8. Post the Accounts Receivable Credit entry on line 6, page 18 of the journal to the accounts receivable account for Brandee Sparks.

# 12-4 Accuracy of Accounting Records

## PROVING THE ACCURACY OF POSTING

A single error in posting to a ledger account may cause the trial balance to be out of balance. An error in posting may cause the cash account balance to disagree with the actual cash on hand. An error in posting may cause the income to be understated or overstated on an income statement. An error in posting may cause a business to overpay or underpay its vendors. Posting must be accurate to assure correct account balances. Therefore, to prove the accuracy of posting, three things are done. (1) Cash is proved. (2) Subsidiary schedules are prepared to prove that the total of the balances in the subsidiary ledgers equals the balance of the controlling account in the general ledger. (3) A trial balance is prepared to prove that debits equal credits in the general ledger.

Preparation of a trial balance is described in Chapter 15.

### Proving Cash

The method used to prove cash is described in Chapter 11. The cash proof total is compared with the balance on the next unused check stub in the checkbook.

## PROVING THE ACCOUNTS PAYABLE LEDGER

| *Omni Import*<br>*Schedule of Accounts Payable*<br>*November 30, 20--* | |
|---|---|
| *Accent Importers* | *7145.88* |
| *African Importers* | *4147.20* |
| *Crown Ltd.* | *2039.00* |
| *Embassy Office Supplies* | *996.00* |
| *Foxfire Supply* | *900.00* |
| *Pacific Imports* | *3816.00* |
| *Total Accounts Payable* | *19044.08* |

A controlling account balance in a general ledger must equal the sum of all account balances in a subsidiary ledger. Omni Import proves subsidiary ledgers at the end of each month.

A listing of vendor accounts, account balances, and total amount due all vendors is called a **schedule of accounts payable.** A schedule of accounts payable is prepared after all entries in a journal are posted. The balance of Accounts Payable in the general ledger is $19,044.08. The total of the schedule of accounts payable is $19,044.08. Because the two amounts are the same, the accounts payable ledger is proved.

# PROVING THE ACCOUNTS RECEIVABLE LEDGER

| *Omni Import* | | |
|---|---|---|
| *Schedule of Accounts Receivable* | | |
| *November 30, 20--* | | |
| *Ashton Jaycees* | 1908 | 00 |
| *Children's Paradise* | 1755 | 36 |
| *Fiesta Costumes* | 2416 | 80 |
| *Keystone Corner* | 2035 | 20 |
| *Parties Unlimited* | 2226 | 00 |
| *Quality Fashions* | 725 | 04 |
| *Total Accounts Receivable* | 11066 | 40 |

A listing of customer accounts, account balances, and total amount due from all customers is called a **schedule of accounts receivable.** A schedule of accounts receivable is prepared after all entries in a journal are posted. The balance of Accounts Receivable in the general ledger is $11,066.40. The total of the schedule of accounts receivable is $11,066.40. Because the two amounts are the same, the accounts receivable ledger is proved.

**TECHNOLOGY FOR BUSINESS**

### COMMUNICATION OVERLOAD

Electronic mail or *e-mail* is intended to make an employee's job easier. E-mail is a convenient way to communicate with other workers within a company. Through the use of the Internet, e-mail also provides a way to communicate with colleagues, suppliers, and clients in other locations.

The volume of e-mail is growing. In the past, more than 700 billion messages passed through U.S.-based computer networks. Currently, that number exceeds 6.6 trillion.

In the case of e-mail, is more better? Who sends all the messages? Who receives them? What do the messages say?

Some managers and executives may receive more than 200 messages per day. Many of these messages are *CCs*—copies of messages sent to others. (CC originally meant carbon copy.) This kind of e-mail overload eats into productivity as workers spend time reading and managing messages.

It's important to remember that e-mail is not a private communication. Some companies routinely review e-mail communications. Others check e-mail when they suspect a problem. Many companies back up their computer systems and save all data including e-mail files. You might have deleted an e-mail message from your computer, but there is a good chance it is still lurking somewhere in the system.

## TERMS REVIEW

schedule of accounts payable

schedule of accounts receivable

## AUDIT YOUR UNDERSTANDING

1. Why is accuracy in posting important?
2. How are subsidiary ledgers proved at the end of the month?
3. What accounts are listed on a schedule of accounts payable?
4. What does it mean when the total of the schedule of accounts receivable is the same as the balance of Accounts Receivable in the general ledger?

## WORK TOGETHER

**Proving an accounts payable ledger**

Given in the *Working Papers* is a blank form for preparation of a schedule of accounts payable. Your instructor will guide you through the following example.

5. One step in proving the accuracy of posting for Graphics, Inc., is proving accounts payable. Prepare a schedule of accounts payable for Graphics, Inc. on October 31 of the current year. October 31 balances are: Art and Things, $873.00; Can Do Graphics, $986.00; Electro-Graphic Supply, $2,544.00; and Regal Designs, $2,280.20. Accounts Payable balance in the general ledger on October 31 is $6,683.20.

## ON YOUR OWN

**Proving an accounts receivable ledger**

Given in the *Working Papers* is a blank form for preparation of a schedule of accounts receivable. Work this problem independently.

6. Prepare a schedule of accounts receivable for Graphics, Inc., on November 30 of the current year. November 30 balances are: David Bishop, $887.22; Maria Farrell, $788.64; Alfredo Lopez, $1,272.00; and Brandee Sparks, $1,431.00. Accounts Receivable balance in the general ledger on November 30 is $4,378.86.

# CHAPTER 12 SUMMARY

After completing this chapter, you can

1. Define important accounting terms related to posting to ledgers.
2. Identify accounting practices related to posting to ledgers.
3. Post to a general ledger from a journal.
4. Post to an accounts payable ledger.
5. Post to an accounts receivable ledger.
6. Verify the accuracy of accounting records.

### *Enrichment Activity*

**Time Management**

*A to-do list can be more valuable if items are prioritized. A to-do list could have columns labeled A, B, and C. A checkmark is then placed in one of the three columns for each item on the list to show whether it is of the highest priority (A), medium priority (B), or low priority (C). Create a form with three narrow columns labeled A, B, and C and a wider column for to-do items. Create a to-do list for tomorrow's activities in the wide column. Then put a checkmark in column A, B, or C to show each item's priority.*

## EXPLORE ACCOUNTING

### CATEGORIES OF INTERNAL CONTROL

Posting transactions from a journal to both the general ledger and subsidiary ledgers presents opportunities for errors. Omni Import is a small company with few employees. Generally, the same person at Omni posts to both the general ledger and subsidiary ledgers. Larger businesses with more employees generally split up duties among several employees to reduce the chances of error.

To avoid errors and their resulting losses, businesses should institute effective internal controls. Internal controls may be categorized in three phases: (1) preventive, (2) detective, and (3) corrective.

A preventive control prevents the individual from making the error. Establishing and following consistent procedures for posting transactions is a preventive control. A detective control detects or finds the error. Preparing a trial balance is a detective control. A corrective control restores the business back to normal if an error occurs. Insurance, such as a fidelity bond on a cashier, is a corrective control.

**Discussion:** Describe internal control procedures that you have observed either as an employee or as a customer. Identify each procedure as (1) preventive, (2) detective, or (3) corrective.

## 12-1 APPLICATION PROBLEM
### Posting to a general ledger

Selected entries from the journal for Healthy Nutrition, a health food store, are given in the *Working Papers*.

***Instructions:***

1. Start new pages for the following accounts in the general ledger. Record the balances as of August 1 of the current year.

**General Ledger**

| Account No. | Account Title | Balance |
|---|---|---|
| 1110 | Cash | $ 21,960.00 |
| 1150 | Supplies—Office | 4,416.00 |
| 1170 | Prepaid Insurance | 1,870.00 |
| 2120 | Sales Tax Payable | 1,778.00 |
| 4110 | Sales | 206,904.00 |
| 6110 | Advertising Expense | 2,230.00 |
| 6160 | Rent Expense | 8,400.00 |

2. Post the separate items recorded in the journal's General Debit column.
3. Post the totals of the special columns of the journal.

## 12-2 APPLICATION PROBLEM
### Posting to an accounts payable ledger

Selected entries from the journal for Healthy Nutrition, a health food store, are given in the *Working Papers*.

***Instructions:***

1. Start new pages for the following accounts in the general ledger. Record the balances as of September 1 of the current year.

**General Ledger**

| Account No. | Account Title | Balance |
|---|---|---|
| 1110 | Cash | $ 40,650.20 |
| 2110 | Accounts Payable | 12,666.00 |
| 5110 | Purchases | 115,800.00 |

2. Start new pages for the following vendor accounts in the accounts payable ledger. Record the balances as of September 1 of the current year.

| Vendor No. | Vendor Name | Account Balance |
|---|---|---|
| 210 | Cornucopia, Inc. | $3,090.00 |
| 220 | Healthy Foods | 5,064.00 |
| 230 | Nutrition Center | — |
| 240 | Sports Nutrition | 4,512.00 |

3. Post the separate items recorded in the Accounts Payable Debit and Credit columns of the journal.
4. Post the totals of the special columns of the journal. Save your work to complete Application Problem 12-4.

## 12-3 APPLICATION PROBLEM
### Posting to an accounts receivable ledger

Selected entries from the journal for Healthy Nutrition are given in the *Working Papers*.

***Instructions:***

1. Start new pages for the following accounts in the general ledger. Record the balances as of October 1 of the current year.

**General Ledger**

| Account No. | Account Title | Balance |
|---|---|---|
| 1110 | Cash | $ 18,300.00 |
| 1130 | Accounts Receivable | 10,164.00 |
| 2120 | Sales Tax Payable | 1,235.00 |
| 4110 | Sales | 172,420.00 |

2. Start new pages for the following customer accounts in the accounts receivable ledger. Record the balances as of October 1 of the current year.

| Customer No. | Customer Name | Account Balance |
|---|---|---|
| 110 | Children's Center | $4,416.00 |
| 120 | Eastman Sports Arena | 2,220.00 |
| 130 | Maple Tree Club | 3,528.00 |
| 140 | Southwest Community Club | — |

3. Post the separate items recorded in the Accounts Receivable Debit and Credit columns of the journal.
4. Post the totals of the special columns of the journal. Save your work to complete Application Problem 12-4.

## 12-4 APPLICATION PROBLEM
### Proving subsidiary ledgers

Use the general ledger and vendor accounts from Application Problem 12-2. Also use the general ledger and customer accounts from Application Problem 12-3. Blank forms for preparation of a schedule of accounts payable and a schedule of accounts receivable are given in the *Working Papers*.

***Instructions:***

1. Prepare a schedule of accounts payable as of September 30 of the current year. Compare the total of the schedule with the balance of the controlling account, Accounts Payable, in the general ledger. If the totals are not the same, find and correct the errors.
2. Prepare a schedule of accounts receivable as of October 31 of the current year. Compare the total of the schedule with the balance of the controlling account, Accounts Receivable, in the general ledger. If the totals are not the same, find and correct the errors.

## 12-5 MASTERY PROBLEM
### Posting to ledgers from a journal

The journal and ledgers for Aqua Pools, a swimming pool supply company, are given in the *Working Papers*.

***Instructions:***

1. Post the separate items recorded in the following columns of the journal. (a) General Debit and Credit. (b) Accounts Receivable Debit and Credit. (c) Accounts Payable Debit and Credit.
2. Post the totals of the special columns of the journal.
3. Using the current year, prepare a schedule of accounts payable and a schedule of accounts receivable. Prove the accuracy of the subsidiary ledgers by comparing the schedule totals with the balances of the controlling accounts in the general ledger. If the totals are not the same, find and correct the errors.

## 12-6 CHALLENGE PROBLEM
### Journalizing and posting business transactions

The general, accounts payable, and accounts receivable ledgers for Custom Golf Land are given in the *Working Papers*.

***Instructions:***

1. Journalize the following transactions completed during October of the current year. Use page 21 of a journal similar to the one described in this chapter. Add an 8% sales tax to all sales transactions. Source documents are abbreviated as follows: check, C; memorandum, M; purchase invoice, P; receipt, R; sales invoice, S; cash register tape, T.

***Transactions:***

Oct. 2. Wrote a check for rent, $1,150.00. C263.
3. Received an invoice from Vista Golf Co. for merchandise purchased on account, $1,950.00. P71.
4. Paid for merchandise, $142.80. C264.
6. A check was received in payment on account from Viola Davis, $829.44, covering S45. R43.
7. Eagle Golf Equipment was paid on account, $2,358.00, covering P67. C265.
7. Cash and credit card sales, $5,676.00. T7.
**Posting.** Post the items that are to be posted individually.
9. Julie Freed, partner, withdrew merchandise for personal use, $200.00. M33.
11. Merchandise was sold on account to Doris McCarley, $306.00. S49.
13. Store supplies were bought on account from Golf Source, $258.00. M34.
14. Cash and credit card sales, $5,808.00. T14.
**Posting.** Post the items that are to be posted individually.
16. Cash was withdrawn by Julie Freed, partner, for personal use, $1,500.00. C266.
16. Cash was withdrawn by Troy Nordstrom, partner, for personal use, $1,500.00. C267.
17. Wrote a check for electric bill, $220.20. C268.
20. Wrote a check to Vista Golf Co. on account, $3,216.00, covering P68. C269.
21. Recorded cash and credit card sales, $5,376.00. T21.
**Posting.** Post the items that are to be posted individually.
23. Design Golf was paid on account, $2,916.00, covering P69. C270.
24. Barry Fuller bought merchandise on account, $1,315.00. S50.
24. Received payment on account from Leona Silva, $285.12, covering S46. R44.

Oct. 25. Merchandise was purchased on account from Pro Golf Supply, $1,542.00. P72.
27. A check was received in payment on account from David Bench, $972.00, covering S47. R45.
28. Received an invoice on account from Design Golf for merchandise purchased on account, $2,790.00. P73.
28. Merchandise was sold on account to Leona Silva, $1,314.00. S51.
28. Recorded cash and credit card sales, $5,556.00. T28.
**Posting.** Post the items that are to be posted individually.
31. Replenish the petty cash fund, $251.00: office supplies, $40.00; store supplies, $51.00; advertising, $62.00; miscellaneous, $98.00. C271.
31. Recorded cash and credit card sales, $1,680.00. T31.
**Posting.** Post the items that are to be posted individually.

2. Total the journal. Prove the equality of debits and credits.
3. Prove cash. The balance on the next unused check stub is $35,076.24.
4. Rule the journal.
5. Post the totals of the special columns of the journal.
6. Prepare a schedule of accounts payable and a schedule of accounts receivable. Prove the accuracy of the subsidiary ledgers by comparing the schedule totals with the balances of the controlling accounts in the general ledger. If the totals are not the same, find and correct the errors.

In states that have sales taxes, businesses are required to collect taxes on their sales and submit the taxes to the state. This additional activity requires considerable extra effort: keeping a separate record of the taxes collected at the time of sale, maintaining a separate account for the sales taxes collected, Sales Taxes Payable, and recording the collection and payment of the sales taxes in the account. These additional activities place an additional administrative burden on businesses, especially small businesses with few employees.

Can you think of a procedure that would not require the separate record for collecting and accounting for sales taxes, yet comply with a state's requirement to collect and submit sales taxes based on sale of merchandise sold? Write a brief response, providing an alternative approach to collecting and paying sales taxes.

## INTERNET ACTIVITY

Point your browser to
**http://accounting.swpco.com**
Choose **First-Year Course**, choose **Activities**, and complete the activity for Chapter 12.

## Applied Communication

Write a letter to the Cute and Cuddly Corporation explaining you are returning an order of stuffed toys because of poor workmanship. You would like to receive a refund for the full amount of the order, $350.25. Explain that you are providing a copy of the invoice, and ask for written confirmation of the processing of the refund. Include information that will allow the Cute and Cuddly Corp. to comply with your request.

# Cases for Critical Thinking

**Case 1** Heritage House purchased merchandise on account six weeks ago for $600.00 from Pegasus Supply. A check for $600.00 was sent three weeks ago in payment of the account. Although no additional purchases have been made, Heritage House recently received a bill from Pegasus Supply that listed the balance due as $1,200.00. What probably caused this error? When would the error probably be discovered?

**Case 2** Larry Hayes observes his accountant at work and says, "You post each individual accounts receivable entry in the journal. Then you post the totals of the Accounts Receivable columns. You are posting these entries twice, which will make the records wrong." The accountant does not agree that the posting procedure is incorrect. Is Mr. Hayes or his accountant correct? Why?

**Case 3** The accounting method presented in this textbook is double-entry accounting. Each transaction has debit and credit parts. Each transaction affects at least two accounts. For example, paying the rent requires a debit to Rent Expense and a credit to Cash. The accounting equation remains in balance after each transaction is posted. Verifying that the accounting equation remains balanced is one way of ensuring accuracy in maintaining accounting records.

Increasingly used by many small businesses, some financial management software programs are based on a different accounting method. These programs use *single-entry accounting*. Debits and credits are not used. Many transactions are recorded to only one account. For example, paying the rent is accounted for by increasing the balance in Rent Expense. The software deducts the amount of the rent from the checkbook balance, but does not use a cash account. Accuracy is verified when financial statements are created. The amount of cash shown on the balance sheet should equal the checkbook balance.

Compared to double-entry accounting, what are the advantages of using a single-entry accounting system? Are there any disadvantages?

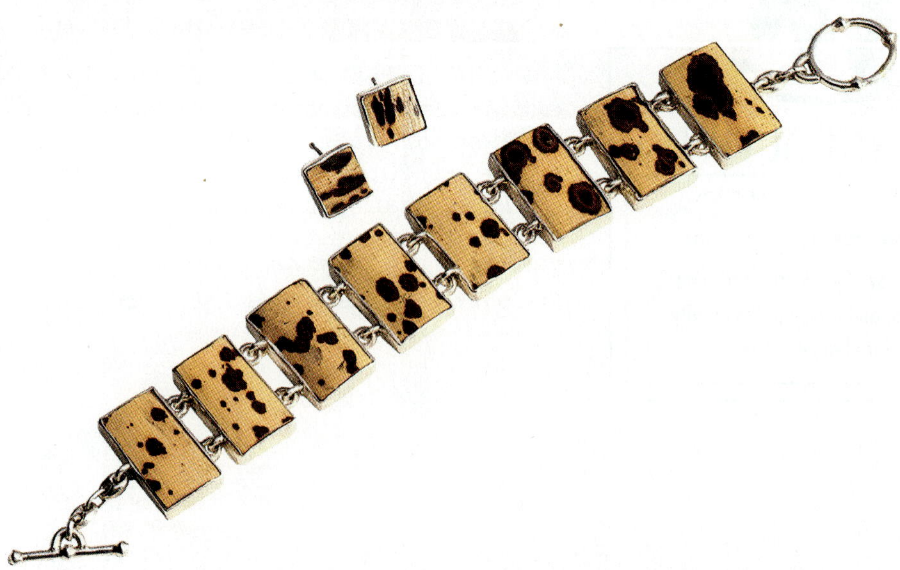

# AUTOMATED ACCOUNTING

## CORRECTION OF ERRORS

In manual accounting, errors can be made even though care is taken in recording transactions. Likewise in automated accounting, an incorrect entry can be journalized or posted. Account numbers or dollar amounts can be transposed, or the wrong customer, vendor, or general ledger account selected. If an error has been made, it is necessary to locate and correct the inaccurate journal entry.

Decision makers in business base their decisions on the various types of reports they receive. That is why it is important to detect incorrect entries early in order to eliminate reports that may be generated with incorrect amounts. Therefore, finding and correcting errors is very important in order to create accurate, reliable financial reports as well as to make decisions based on correct information.

The procedures for locating and correcting journal entries are identical for all journals.

### Finding a Journal Entry

1. Click the desired journal tab: General, Purchases, Sales, Cash Payments, or Cash Receipts.
2. Choose Find from the Edit menu bar.
3. Enter the date, reference, name, or amount you want to find in the Find What text box. Click OK.
4. If a matching transaction is found, it will be highlighted in the journal.

### Changing or Deleting Journal Transactions

1. Select (highlight) the specific transaction text box that you wish to change or delete.
2. To change the transaction, enter the correction and click the Post command button. To delete the entire transaction, choose the Delete command button.

### AUTOMATING CHALLENGE PROBLEM 12-6: Journalizing and posting business transactions

**Instructions:**

1. Load *Automated Accounting 7.0* or higher software.
2. Select database F12-1 from the appropriate directory/ folder.
3. Select File from the menu bar and choose the Save As menu command. Key the path to the drive and directory that contains your data files. Save the database with a file name of XXX121 (where XXX are your initials).
4. Access Problem Instructions through the Help menu. Read the Problem Instructions screen.
5. Refer to the data listed on pages 298–299.
6. Exit the *Automated Accounting* software.

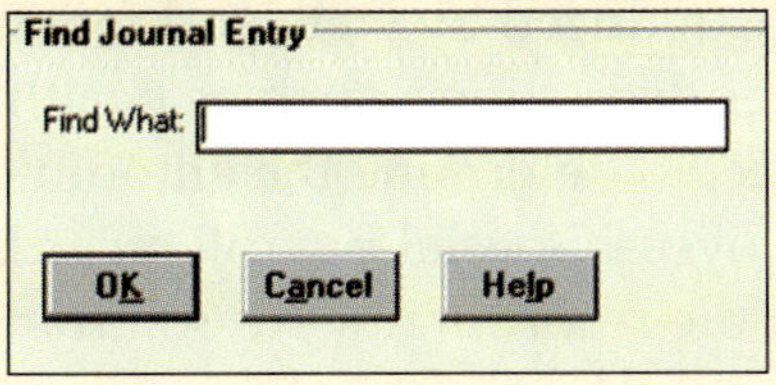

# 13 Preparing Payroll Records

**AFTER STUDYING CHAPTER 13, YOU WILL BE ABLE TO:**

1. Define accounting terms related to payroll records.
2. Identify accounting practices related to payroll records.
3. Complete a payroll time card.
4. Calculate payroll taxes.
5. Complete a payroll register and an employee earnings record.
6. Prepare payroll checks.

**TERMS PREVIEW**

salary
pay period
payroll
total earnings
payroll taxes
withholding allowance
social security tax
Medicare tax
tax base
payroll register
net pay
employee earnings record

## PAYING EMPLOYEES

Omni Import employs several people to work in the business. These employees record the time they work for Omni each day. Periodically Omni pays its employees for the number of hours each employee has worked. The money paid for employee services is called a **salary.** The period covered by a salary payment is called a **pay period.** A business may decide to pay employee salaries every week, every two weeks, twice a month, or once a month. Omni uses a semimonthly pay period. Employees are paid twice a month, on the 15th and last day of each month.

The total amount earned by all employees for a pay period is called a **payroll.** The payroll is reduced by state and federal taxes and other deductions, such as health insurance, to determine the amount paid to all employees. Special payroll records support the recording of payroll transactions in a journal. The business also uses these records to inform employees of their annual earnings and to prepare payroll reports for the government.

**FYI**

*Salaries are usually stated as a fixed amount on a weekly, biweekly, semimonthly, or monthly basis. Salaried workers do not normally receive overtime pay.*

# ACCOUNTING IN YOUR CAREER

## WHY COMPANIES OFFER BENEFITS

MaryAnn Spargo directs the recruiting program for Computex Publishing Company. The company has prospered by publishing books on computer topics. Computex needs to increase its editorial, marketing, and sales staff, and MaryAnn has been recruiting new employees at college campuses.

On her first day back from a three-week recruiting trip, she meets her friend Donald Hawkins, who works in the payroll department, for lunch in the cafeteria. "How was the trip, MaryAnn?" asks Donald. "Did you find us some new talent?"

"No, Don," replies MaryAnn. "I talked to over 50 candidates. Of course they weren't all qualified, but I offered positions to 15 of them and only one has accepted. I know unemployment is very low and so there are more jobs being offered than there are skilled workers to fill them. But what am I doing wrong?"

"I don't know, MaryAnn," says Don. "What kind of salaries are you offering?"

"Oh, Don, we've studied that. Our salaries are competitive with the other publishers in the market. I've thought about this a lot, and I wonder if it's our benefits program."

"That could be it, MaryAnn. You know, I belong to an accounting association, and I remember that there are surveys available on benefits packages. Would you like me to try to get that information for you?"

MaryAnn replies, "Yes, Don, that might help. If I can show management that our benefits need to be improved to attract skilled workers, it might help us all."

***Critical Thinking:***

1. Do you think most employees consider the benefits offered when they look for a job?
2. What are some kinds of benefits offered by companies today?
3. If Computex wanted to get creative with its benefit package to attract new employees, what kinds of benefits might they offer?

# 13-1 Preparing Payroll Time Cards

## ANALYZING A PAYROLL TIME CARD

**Omni Import**

**EMPLOYEE NO.** 3

**NAME** Rick E. Selby

**PAY PERIOD ENDED** December 15, 20--

| MORNING | | AFTERNOON | | OVERTIME | | HOURS | |
|---|---|---|---|---|---|---|---|
| IN | OUT | IN | OUT | IN | OUT | REG | OT |
| $7^{58}$ | $12^{02}$ | $12^{59}$ | $5^{06}$ | | | | |
| | | | | | | | |

A payroll system must include an accurate record of the time each employee has worked. Several methods are used for keeping time records. One of the more frequently used methods is a time card. Time cards are used as the basic source of information to prepare a payroll.

Some time cards require employees to record only the total hours worked each day. Employees who record the total hours worked each day usually complete time cards by hand.

A business may use a time card that requires employees to record their arrival and departure times. Omni uses a time clock to record the daily arrival and departure times of its employees.

The time card shown here is for Rick E. Selby. Mr. Selby's employee number is at the top of the card. Below the employee number are the employee name and the ending date of the pay period.

Omni's time cards have three sections (Morning, Afternoon, and Overtime), with In and Out columns under each section. When Mr. Selby reported for work on December 1, he inserted the card in the time clock. The clock recorded his time of arrival, 7:58, on the first line of the time card. The other entries on this line indicate that he left for lunch at 12:02. He returned at 12:59 and left for the day at 5:06.

Omni calculates overtime pay for each employee who works more than 8 hours in one day. No employee works more than 5 days in any one week.

**FYI**

*Using a time card system provides internal control for accurate reporting of time worked.*

## CALCULATING EMPLOYEE HOURS WORKED

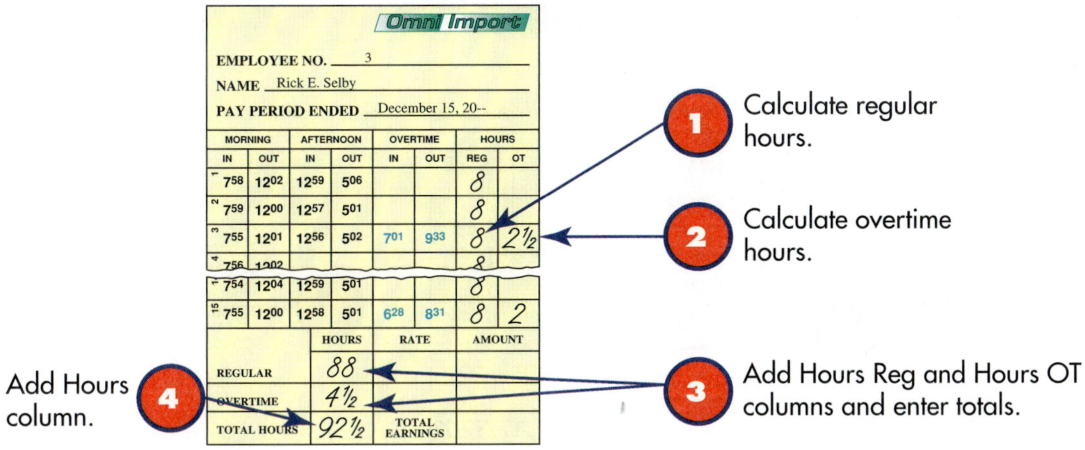


The first task in preparing a payroll is to calculate the number of hours worked by each employee.

### STEPS: Calculating employee hours worked

**1.** Calculate the number of regular hours for each day and enter the amounts in the Hours Reg column. Mr. Selby works 8 hours during a normal day. The hours worked on December 3, the third line of the time card, are calculated using the arrival and departure times imprinted on the time card. Times are rounded to the nearest quarter hour to calculate the hours worked.

The hours worked in the morning and afternoon are calculated separately. The morning departure time of 12:01 is rounded to the nearest quarter hour, 12:00. The rounded arrival time, 8:00, subtracted from the departure time, 12:00, equals the morning hours worked. Hours worked of 4:00 means that Mr. Selby worked 4 hours and no (00) minutes. The total regular hours worked, 8, is recorded in the Hours Reg column.

| | Departure Time | – | Arrival Time | = | Hours Worked |
|---|---|---|---|---|---|
| Morning: | | | | | |
| Time card | 12:01 | | 7:55 | | |
| Nearest quarter hour | 12:00 | – | 8:00 | = | 4:00 |
| Afternoon: | | | | | |
| Time card | 5:02 | | 12:56 | | |
| Nearest quarter hour | 5:00 | – | 1:00 | = | 4:00 |
| Total regular hours worked on December 3 | | | | | 8:00 |

**2.** Calculate the number of overtime hours for each day and enter the amounts in the Hours OT column. Overtime hours for December 3 are calculated using the same procedure as for regular hours.

| | Departure Time | – | Arrival Time | = | Hours Worked |
|---|---|---|---|---|---|
| Time card | 9:33 | | 7:01 | | |
| Nearest quarter hour | 9:30 | – | 7:00 | = | 2:30 |

The hours worked of 2:30 means that Mr. Selby worked 2 hours and 30 minutes ($\frac{1}{2}$ hour) of overtime.

**3.** Add the hours worked in the Hours Reg and Hours OT columns and enter the totals in the spaces provided at the bottom of the time card. Mr. Selby worked 88 regular hours (8 hours × 11 days) and $4\frac{1}{2}$ overtime hours during the semimonthly pay period.

**4.** Add the Hours column to calculate the total hours. Enter the total in the Hours column at the bottom of the time card. Mr. Selby worked 88 regular hours and $4\frac{1}{2}$ overtime hours for a total of $92\frac{1}{2}$ hours.

# CALCULATING EMPLOYEE TOTAL EARNINGS

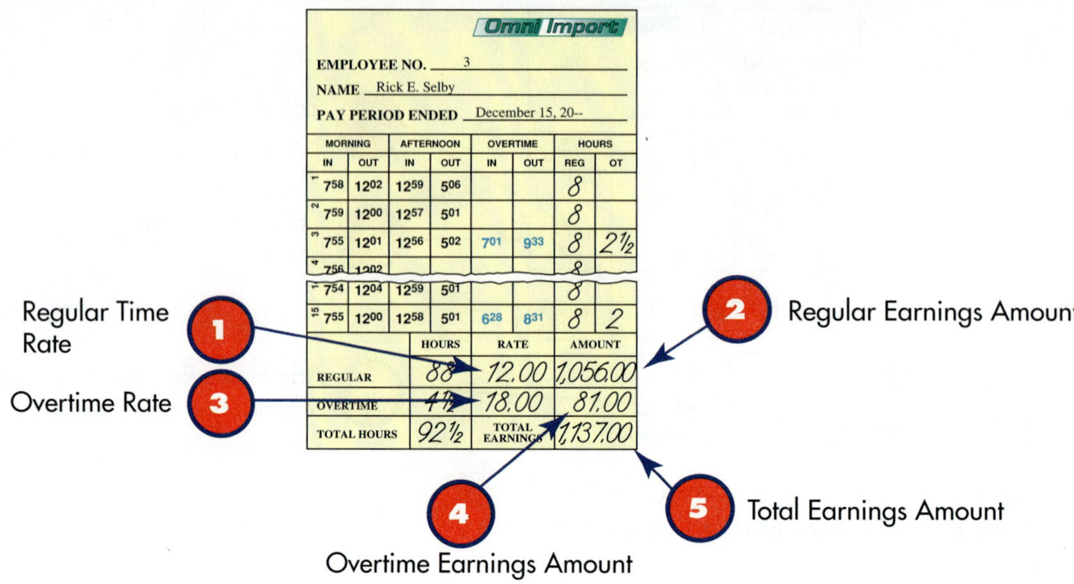


Once the total regular and overtime hours are determined, employee earnings can be calculated. The total pay due for a pay period before deductions is called **total earnings.** Total earnings are sometimes referred to as gross pay or gross earnings.

Omni owes Mr. Selby $1,137.00 for his work during the pay period ending December 15. However, taxes and other deductions must be subtracted from total earnings to determine the actual amount Omni will pay Mr. Selby.

### STEPS Calculating an employee's total earnings

1. Enter the rate for regular time in the Rate column. Mr. Selby's regular hourly rate is *$12.00.*
2. Calculate the regular earnings by multiplying regular hours times the regular rate. Enter the amount of regular earnings, *$1,056.00*, in the Regular Amount space.
3. Enter the rate for overtime, *$18.00*, in the Rate column. Mr. Selby is paid $1\frac{1}{2}$ times his regular rate for overtime work.
4. Calculate the overtime earnings by multiplying overtime hours times the overtime rate. Enter the amount of overtime earnings, *$81.00*, in the Overtime Amount space.
5. Add the Amount column to calculate the total earnings. Enter the amount of total earnings, *$1,137,00*, in the Total Earnings space.

| Regular Hours | × | Regular Rate | = | Regular Earnings |
|---|---|---|---|---|
| 88 | × | $12.00 | = | $1,056.00 |

| Regular Rate | × | $1\frac{1}{2}$ | = | Overtime Rate |
|---|---|---|---|---|
| $12.00 | × | $1\frac{1}{2}$ | = | $18.00 |

| Overtime Hours | × | Overtime Rate | = | Overtime Earnings |
|---|---|---|---|---|
| $4\frac{1}{2}$ | × | $18.00 | = | $81.00 |

## Terms Review

salary
pay period
payroll
total earnings

## Audit Your Understanding

1. What is a payroll?
2. How many hours were worked by an employee who arrived at 8:29 and departed at 12:02?
3. How does Omni calculate overtime earnings?
4. What are the total earnings of an employee who worked 40 hours and earned $11.00 per hour?

## Work Together

**Preparing payroll time cards**

Information taken from employee time cards is provided in the *Working Papers.* Your instructor will guide you through the following example.

5. For each employee, calculate the amount of regular, overtime, and total earnings. Overtime hours are paid at $1\frac{1}{2}$ times the regular rate.

## On Your Own

**Preparing payroll time cards**

Information taken from employee time cards is provided in the *Working Papers.* Work this problem independently.

6. For each employee, calculate the amount of regular, overtime, and total earnings. Overtime hours are paid at $1\frac{1}{2}$ times the regular rate.

# 13-2 Determining Payroll Tax Withholding

## PAYROLL TAXES

Taxes based on the payroll of a business are called **payroll taxes.** A business is required by law to withhold certain payroll taxes from employee salaries. All payroll taxes are based on employee total earnings. Therefore, accurate and detailed payroll records must be maintained. Errors in payroll records could cause incorrect payroll tax payments. Federal and state governments may charge a business a penalty for failure to pay correct payroll taxes when they are due. Payroll taxes withheld represent a liability for the employer until payment is made to the government.

### Employee Income Tax

A business must withhold federal income taxes from employee total earnings. Federal income taxes withheld must be forwarded periodically to the federal government. Federal income tax is withheld from employee earnings in all 50 states. Employers in many states also are required to withhold state, city, or county income taxes from employee earnings.

**FYI**

*Each employee must have a social security number. Current law ensures that most infants who are at least one year old by the end of a tax year will have a social security number. Therefore, most employees will have received their social security number as a child. Employees without social security numbers can apply for a number at the nearest Social Security office.*

**LEGAL ISSUES IN ACCOUNTING**

### DISSOLVING A PARTNERSHIP

Under the Uniform Partnership Act (UPA), any change in the membership of a partnership causes a *dissolution.* Members may decide to dissolve a partnership for several reasons: (1) One or more of the partners wants to discontinue doing business. (2) The partners need more capital and agree to admit an additional partner. (3) The partners may disagree on how to operate the business. (4) The partnership agreement may call for the partnership to be dissolved on a specific date.

When a partnership is dissolved, legal requirements must be met and correct accounting procedures followed. The terms of the dissolution may be set forth in the partnership agreement. Any such terms must be followed. If no partnership agreement was created, the UPA or laws of the state will govern its dissolution.

Noncash assets are usually sold, and the available cash is used to pay creditors. Any remaining cash is distributed to the partners. Each partner receives the balance of his or her capital account.

The UPA calls the process of finishing up the firm's business, paying off creditors, and dividing remaining assets *winding up* the partnership. When the winding up process has been completed, the partnership is *terminated.*

# EMPLOYEE'S WITHHOLDING ALLOWANCE CERTIFICATE

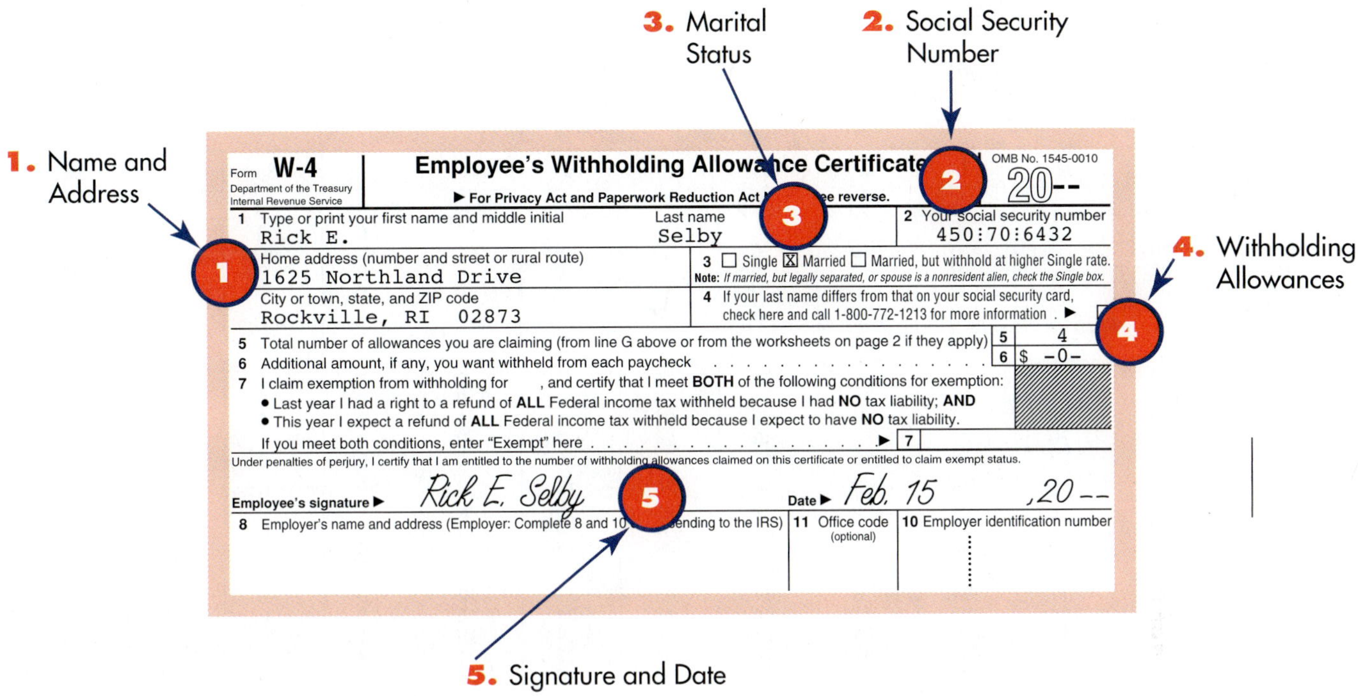


Form **W-4** Department of the Treasury Internal Revenue Service

**Employee's Withholding Allowance Certificate**

► For Privacy Act and Paperwork Reduction Act Notice, see reverse.

OMB No. 1545-0010 20--

1 Type or print your first name and middle initial: Rick E. Last name: Selby

2 Your social security number: 450:70:6432

Home address (number and street or rural route): 1625 Northland Drive

3 ☐ Single ☒ Married ☐ Married, but withhold at higher Single rate.
Note: If married, but legally separated, or spouse is a nonresident alien, check the Single box.

City or town, state, and ZIP code: Rockville, RI 02873

4 If your last name differs from that on your social security card, check here and call 1-800-772-1213 for more information ► ☐

5 Total number of allowances you are claiming (from line G above or from the worksheets on page 2 if they apply) 5 | 4

6 Additional amount, if any, you want withheld from each paycheck 6 | $ -0-

7 I claim exemption from withholding for , and certify that I meet **BOTH** of the following conditions for exemption:
- Last year I had a right to a refund of **ALL** Federal income tax withheld because I had **NO** tax liability; **AND**
- This year I expect a refund of **ALL** Federal income tax withheld because I expect to have **NO** tax liability.

If you meet both conditions, enter "Exempt" here ► 7

Under penalties of perjury, I certify that I am entitled to the number of withholding allowances claimed on this certificate or entitled to claim exempt status.

Employee's signature ► *Rick E. Selby* Date ► *Feb. 15* , 20--

8 Employer's name and address (Employer: Complete 8 and 10 only if sending to the IRS) | 11 Office code (optional) | 10 Employer identification number

The information used to determine the amount of income tax withheld is identified on Form W-4, Employee's Withholding Allowance Certificate. A deduction from total earnings for each person legally supported by a taxpayer, including the employee, is called a **withholding allowance.** Employers are required to have on file a current Form W-4 for all employees. The amount of income tax withheld is based on employee marital status and number of withholding allowances. A married employee will have less income tax withheld than a single employee with the same total earnings. The larger the number of withholding allowances claimed, the smaller the amount of income tax withheld.

Most employees are required to have federal income taxes withheld from their salaries. An exemption from withholding is available for certain low-income and part-time employees. The employee must meet the requirements listed in item 7 of the Form W-4. However, individuals cannot claim exemption from withholding if (1) their income exceeds $700 and includes unearned income such as interest and dividends and (2) another person can claim them as a dependent on their tax return.

The Form W-4 shown was the form in use when this textbook was prepared. Employers must be aware of changes in tax laws and forms. If Form W-4 is changed, an employer must obtain a new W-4 from each employee.

**STEPS**

**Preparing an Employee's Withholding Allowance Certificate**

1. Write the employee's name and address.
2. Write the employee's social security number.
3. Check appropriate marital status block. Mr. Selby checked the married box for item 3 of the Form W-4.
4. Write the total number of withholding allowances claimed. Mr. Selby claimed four withholding allowances, one each for himself, his wife, and his two children.
5. Employee signs and dates the Form W-4.

# EMPLOYEE'S INCOME TAX WITHHOLDING—SINGLE PERSONS

**SEMIMONTHLY PAYROLL PERIOD — SINGLE PERSONS**

| And the wages are– | | And the number of withholding allowances claimed is– | | | | | | | | | | |
|---|---|---|---|---|---|---|---|---|---|---|---|---|
| At least | But less than | 0 | 1 | 2 | 3 | 4 | 5 | 6 | 7 | 8 | 9 | 10 |
| | | The amount of income tax to be withheld shall be– | | | | | | | | | | |
| $0 | $115 | 0 | 0 | 0 | 0 | 0 | 0 | 0 | 0 | 0 | 0 | 0 |
| 115 | 120 | 1 | 0 | 0 | 0 | 0 | 0 | 0 | 0 | 0 | 0 | 0 |
| 120 | 125 | 2 | 0 | 0 | 0 | 0 | 0 | 0 | 0 | 0 | 0 | 0 |
| 125 | 130 | 3 | 0 | 0 | 0 | 0 | 0 | 0 | 0 | 0 | 0 | 0 |
| 130 | 135 | 3 | 0 | 0 | 0 | 0 | 0 | 0 | 0 | 0 | 0 | 0 |
| 640 | 660 | 81 | 64 | 48 | 31 | 15 | 0 | 0 | 0 | 0 | 0 | 0 |
| 660 | 680 | 84 | 67 | 51 | 34 | 18 | 1 | 0 | 0 | 0 | 0 | 0 |
| 680 | 700 | 87 | 70 | 54 | 37 | 21 | 4 | 0 | 0 | 0 | 0 | 0 |
| 700 | 720 | 90 | 73 | 57 | 40 | 24 | 7 | 0 | 0 | 0 | 0 | 0 |
| 720 | 740 | 93 | 76 | 60 | 43 | 27 | 10 | 0 | 0 | 0 | 0 | 0 |
| 740 | 760 | 96 | 79 | 63 | 46 | 30 | 13 | 0 | 0 | 0 | 0 | 0 |
| 760 | 780 | 99 | 82 | 66 | 49 | 33 | 16 | 0 | 0 | 0 | 0 | 0 |
| 780 | 800 | 102 | 85 | 69 | 52 | 36 | 19 | 3 | 0 | 0 | 0 | 0 |
| 800 | 820 | 106 | 88 | 72 | 55 | 39 | 22 | 6 | 0 | 0 | 0 | 0 |
| 820 | 840 | 108 | 91 | 75 | 58 | 42 | 25 | 9 | 0 | 0 | 0 | 0 |
| 840 | 860 | 111 | 94 | 78 | 61 | 45 | 28 | 12 | 0 | 0 | 0 | 0 |
| 860 | 880 | 114 | 97 | 81 | 64 | 48 | 31 | 15 | 0 | 0 | 0 | 0 |
| 880 | 900 | 117 | 100 | 84 | 67 | 51 | 34 | 18 | 1 | 0 | 0 | 0 |
| 900 | 920 | 120 | 103 | 87 | 70 | 54 | 37 | 21 | 4 | 0 | 0 | 0 |
| 920 | 940 | 123 | 106 | 90 | 73 | 57 | 40 | 24 | 7 | 0 | 0 | 0 |
| 940 | 960 | 126 | 109 | 93 | 76 | 60 | 43 | 27 | 10 | 0 | 0 | 0 |
| 960 | 980 | 129 | 112 | 96 | 79 | 63 | 46 | 30 | 13 | 0 | 0 | 0 |
| 980 | 1,000 | 132 | 115 | 99 | 82 | 66 | 49 | 33 | 16 | 0 | 0 | 0 |
| 1,000 | 1,020 | 135 | 118 | 102 | 85 | 69 | 52 | 36 | 19 | 2 | 0 | 0 |
| 1,020 | 1,040 | 138 | 121 | 105 | 88 | 72 | 55 | 39 | 22 | 5 | 0 | 0 |
| 1,040 | 1,060 | 141 | 124 | 108 | 91 | 75 | 58 | 42 | 25 | 8 | 0 | 0 |
| 1,060 | 1,080 | 144 | 127 | 111 | 94 | 78 | 61 | 45 | 28 | 11 | 0 | 0 |
| 1,080 | 1,100 | 147 | 130 | 114 | 97 | 81 | 64 | 48 | 31 | 14 | 0 | 0 |
| 1,100 | 1,120 | 153 | 133 | 117 | 100 | 84 | 67 | 51 | 34 | 17 | 1 | 0 |
| 1,120 | 1,140 | 158 | 136 | 120 | 103 | 87 | 70 | 54 | 37 | 20 | 4 | 0 |
| 1,140 | 1,160 | 164 | 139 | 123 | 106 | 90 | 73 | 57 | 40 | 23 | 7 | 0 |
| 1,160 | 1,180 | 169 | 142 | 126 | 109 | 93 | 76 | 60 | 43 | 26 | 10 | 0 |
| 1,180 | 1,200 | 175 | 145 | 129 | 112 | 96 | 79 | 63 | 46 | 29 | 13 | 0 |
| 1,200 | 1,220 | 181 | 150 | 132 | 115 | 99 | 82 | 66 | 49 | 32 | 16 | 0 |
| 1,220 | 1,240 | 186 | 155 | 135 | 118 | 102 | 85 | 69 | 52 | 35 | 19 | 2 |
| 1,240 | 1,260 | 192 | 161 | 138 | 121 | 105 | 88 | 72 | 55 | 38 | 22 | 5 |
| 1,260 | 1,280 | 197 | 166 | 141 | 124 | 108 | 91 | 75 | 58 | 41 | 25 | 8 |
| 1,280 | 1,300 | 203 | 172 | 144 | 127 | 111 | 94 | 78 | 61 | 44 | 28 | 11 |
| 1,300 | 1,320 | 209 | 178 | 147 | 130 | 114 | 97 | 81 | 64 | 47 | 31 | 14 |
| 1,320 | 1,340 | 214 | 183 | 152 | 133 | 117 | 100 | 84 | 67 | 50 | 34 | 17 |
| 1,340 | 1,360 | 220 | 189 | 158 | 136 | 120 | 103 | 87 | 70 | 53 | 37 | 20 |
| 1,360 | 1,380 | 225 | 194 | 164 | 139 | 123 | 106 | 90 | 73 | 56 | 40 | 23 |
| 1,380 | 1,400 | 231 | 200 | 169 | 142 | 126 | 109 | 93 | 76 | 59 | 43 | 26 |
| 1,400 | 1,420 | 237 | 206 | 175 | 145 | 129 | 112 | 96 | 79 | 62 | 46 | 29 |
| 1,420 | 1,440 | 242 | 211 | 180 | 149 | 132 | 115 | 99 | 82 | 65 | 49 | 32 |

The amount of federal income tax withheld from each employee's total earnings is determined from withholding tables prepared by the Internal Revenue Service. These withholding tables are revised each year and are available from the Internal Revenue Service in Circular E, Employer's Tax Guide. The withholding tables shown in this chapter are those available when this textbook was prepared.

Tables are prepared for various payroll periods—monthly, semimonthly, biweekly, weekly, and daily. Single persons are taxed at different levels of income than married persons. Therefore, one table is available for single persons and another table is available for married persons for each pay period.

Omni Import's pay period is semimonthly, so Omni uses the semimonthly witholding tables.

# EMPLOYEE'S INCOME TAX WITHHOLDING—MARRIED PERSONS

**1.** Select the appropriate table.

**SEMIMONTHLY PAYROLL PERIOD — MARRIED PERSONS**

(For Wages Paid in )

| And the wages are– | | And the number of withholding allowances claimed is– | | | | | | | | | | |
|---|---|---|---|---|---|---|---|---|---|---|---|---|
| At least | But less than | 0 | 1 | 2 | 3 | 4 | 5 | 6 | 7 | 8 | 9 | 10 |
| | | The amount of income tax to be withheld shall be– | | | | | | | | | | |
| 520 | 540 | 39 | 23 | 6 | 0 | 0 | 0 | 0 | 0 | 0 | 0 | 0 |
| 540 | 560 | 42 | 26 | 9 | 0 | 0 | 0 | 0 | 0 | 0 | 0 | 0 |
| 560 | 580 | 45 | 29 | 12 | 0 | 0 | 0 | 0 | 0 | 0 | 0 | 0 |
| 580 | 600 | 48 | 32 | 15 | 0 | 0 | 0 | 0 | 0 | 0 | 0 | 0 |
| 600 | 620 | 51 | 35 | 18 | 2 | 0 | 0 | 0 | 0 | 0 | 0 | 0 |
| 620 | 640 | 54 | 38 | 21 | 5 | 0 | 0 | 0 | 0 | 0 | 0 | 0 |
| 640 | 660 | 57 | 41 | 24 | 8 | 0 | 0 | 0 | 0 | 0 | 0 | 0 |
| 660 | 680 | 60 | 44 | 27 | 11 | 0 | 0 | 0 | 0 | 0 | 0 | 0 |
| 680 | 700 | 63 | 47 | 30 | 14 | 0 | 0 | 0 | 0 | 0 | 0 | 0 |
| 700 | 720 | 66 | 50 | 33 | 17 | 0 | 0 | 0 | 0 | 0 | 0 | 0 |
| 720 | 740 | 69 | 53 | 36 | 20 | 3 | 0 | 0 | 0 | 0 | 0 | 0 |
| 740 | 760 | 72 | 56 | 39 | 23 | 6 | 0 | 0 | 0 | 0 | 0 | 0 |
| 760 | 780 | 75 | 59 | 42 | 26 | 9 | 0 | 0 | 0 | 0 | 0 | 0 |
| 780 | 800 | 78 | 62 | 45 | 29 | 12 | 0 | 0 | 0 | 0 | 0 | 0 |
| 800 | 820 | 81 | 65 | 48 | 32 | 15 | 0 | 0 | 0 | 0 | 0 | 0 |
| 820 | 840 | 84 | 68 | 51 | 35 | 18 | 1 | 0 | 0 | 0 | 0 | 0 |
| 840 | 860 | 87 | 71 | 54 | 38 | 21 | 4 | 0 | 0 | 0 | 0 | 0 |
| 860 | 880 | 90 | 74 | 57 | 41 | 24 | 7 | 0 | 0 | 0 | 0 | 0 |
| 880 | 900 | 93 | 77 | 60 | 44 | 27 | 10 | 0 | 0 | 0 | 0 | 0 |
| 900 | 920 | 96 | 80 | 63 | 47 | 30 | 13 | 0 | 0 | 0 | 0 | 0 |
| 920 | 940 | 99 | 83 | 66 | 50 | 33 | 16 | 0 | 0 | 0 | 0 | 0 |
| 940 | 960 | 102 | 86 | 69 | 53 | 36 | 19 | 3 | 0 | 0 | 0 | 0 |
| 960 | 980 | 105 | 89 | 72 | 56 | 39 | 22 | 6 | 0 | 0 | 0 | 0 |
| 980 | 1,000 | 108 | 92 | 75 | 59 | 42 | 25 | 9 | 0 | 0 | 0 | 0 |
| 1,000 | 1,020 | 111 | 95 | 78 | 62 | 45 | 28 | 12 | 0 | 0 | 0 | 0 |
| 1,020 | 1,040 | 114 | 98 | 81 | 65 | 48 | 31 | 15 | 0 | 0 | 0 | 0 |
| 1,040 | 1,060 | 117 | 101 | 84 | 68 | 51 | 34 | 18 | 1 | 0 | 0 | 0 |
| 1,060 | 1,080 | 120 | 104 | 87 | 71 | 54 | 37 | 21 | 4 | 0 | 0 | 0 |
| 1,080 | 1,100 | 123 | 107 | 90 | 74 | 57 | 40 | 24 | 7 | 0 | 0 | 0 |
| 1,100 | 1,120 | 126 | 110 | 93 | 77 | 60 | 43 | 27 | 10 | 0 | 0 | 0 |
| 1,120 | 1,140 | 129 | 113 | 96 | 80 | 63 | 46 | 30 | 13 | 0 | 0 | 0 |
| 1,140 | 1,160 | 132 | 116 | 99 | 83 | 66 | 49 | 33 | 16 | 0 | 0 | 0 |
| 1,160 | 1,180 | 135 | 119 | 102 | 86 | 69 | 52 | 36 | 19 | 3 | 0 | 0 |
| 1,180 | 1,200 | 138 | 122 | 105 | 89 | 72 | 55 | 39 | 22 | 6 | 0 | 0 |
| 1,200 | 1,220 | 141 | 125 | 108 | 92 | 75 | 58 | 42 | 25 | 9 | 0 | 0 |
| 1,220 | 1,240 | 144 | 128 | 111 | 95 | 78 | 61 | 45 | 28 | 12 | 0 | 0 |
| 1,240 | 1,260 | 147 | 131 | 114 | 98 | 81 | 64 | 48 | 31 | 15 | 0 | 0 |
| 1,260 | 1,280 | 150 | 134 | 117 | 101 | 84 | 67 | 51 | 34 | 18 | 1 | 0 |
| 1,280 | 1,300 | 153 | 147 | 120 | 104 | 87 | 40 | 54 | 37 | 21 | 4 | 0 |
| 1,300 | 1,320 | 156 | 140 | 123 | 107 | 90 | 43 | 57 | 40 | 24 | 7 | 0 |
| 1,320 | 1,340 | 159 | 143 | 126 | 110 | 93 | 46 | 60 | 43 | 27 | 10 | 0 |
| 1,340 | 1,360 | 162 | 146 | 129 | 113 | 96 | 49 | 63 | 46 | 30 | 13 | 0 |
| 1,360 | 1,380 | 165 | 149 | 132 | 116 | 99 | 82 | 66 | 49 | 33 | 16 | 0 |
| 1,380 | 1,400 | 168 | 152 | 135 | 119 | 102 | 85 | 69 | 52 | 36 | 19 | 3 |
| 1,400 | 1,420 | 171 | 155 | 138 | 122 | 105 | 88 | 72 | 55 | 39 | 22 | 6 |
| 1,420 | 1,440 | 174 | 158 | 141 | 125 | 108 | 91 | 75 | 58 | 42 | 25 | 9 |
| 1,440 | 1,460 | 177 | 161 | 144 | 128 | 111 | 94 | 78 | 61 | 45 | 28 | 12 |
| 1,460 | 1,480 | 180 | 164 | 147 | 131 | 114 | 97 | 91 | 64 | 48 | 31 | 15 |
| 1,480 | 1,500 | 183 | 167 | 150 | 134 | 117 | 100 | 94 | 67 | 51 | 34 | 18 |
| 1,500 | 1,520 | 186 | 170 | 153 | 137 | 120 | 103 | 97 | 70 | 54 | 37 | 21 |
| 1,520 | 1,540 | 189 | 173 | 156 | 140 | 123 | 106 | 90 | 73 | 57 | 40 | 24 |
| 1,540 | 1,560 | 192 | 176 | 159 | 143 | 126 | 109 | 93 | 76 | 60 | 43 | 27 |
| 1,560 | 1,580 | 195 | 179 | 162 | 146 | 129 | 112 | 96 | 79 | 63 | 46 | 30 |
| 1,580 | 1,600 | 198 | 182 | 165 | 149 | 132 | 115 | 99 | 82 | 66 | 49 | 33 |
| 1,600 | 1,620 | 201 | 185 | 168 | 152 | 135 | 118 | 102 | 85 | 69 | 52 | 36 |

**2.** Locate employee's total earnings.

**3.** Follow selected wages line across to column headed by number of withholding allowances.

## STEPS

### Determining an employee's income tax withholding

**1.** Select the appropriate table. Semimonthly Payroll Period—Married Persons is selected to determine income tax withholding for employee Rick E. Selby.

**2.** Locate employee's total earnings between the appropriate lines of the At Least and But Less Than columns. Mr. Selby's total earnings for the pay period ended December 15, 20—, are $1,137.00. Locate the line At Least $1,120.00 But Less Than $1,140.00.

**3.** Follow the selected wages line across to the column headed by the employee's number of withholding allowances. The amount listed at the intersection of the wages line and number of withholding allowances is the employee's amount of income tax withholding. Mr. Selby's federal income tax withholding, with total earnings of $1,137.00 and withholding allowances of four, is $63.00 for the semimonthly pay period ended December 15, 20—.

## EMPLOYEE SOCIAL SECURITY AND MEDICARE TAX

The Federal Insurance Contributions Act (FICA) provides for a federal system of old-age, survivors, disability, and hospital insurance. A federal tax paid for old-age, survivors, and disability insurance is called **social security tax.** A federal tax paid for hospital insurance is called **Medicare tax.** Each of these taxes is accounted for and reported separately.

Social security and Medicare taxes are paid by both employees and employer. Employers are required to withhold and deposit employees' part of the taxes and pay a matching amount of these taxes.

Social security tax is calculated on employee earnings up to a maximum paid in a calendar year. The maximum amount of earnings on which a tax is calculated is called a **tax base.** Congress sets the tax base and the tax rates for social security tax. An act of Congress can change the tax base and tax rate at any time. The social security tax rate and base used in this text are 6.5% of earnings up to a maximum of $65,400.00 in each calendar year.

Between January 1 and December 15, Mr. Selby's earnings are less than the social security tax base. Therefore, Mr. Selby's social security tax deduction for the semimonthly pay period ended December 15, 20—, is calculated as shown.

| Total Earnings | × | Social Security Tax Rate | = | Social Security Tax Deduction |
|---|---|---|---|---|
| $1,137.00 | × | 6.5% | = | $73.91 |

Medicare does not have a tax base. Therefore, Medicare tax is calculated on total employee earnings. The Medicare tax rate used in this text is 1.5% of total employee earnings.

Rick E. Selby's Medicare tax deduction for the semimonthly pay period ended December 15, 20—, is calculated as shown.

| Total Earnings | × | Medicare Tax Rate | = | Medicare Tax Deduction |
|---|---|---|---|---|
| $1,137.00 | × | 1.5% | = | $17.06 |

**FYI**

*Accounting procedures are the same regardless of changes in the tax base and tax rate. The social security tax rate and the tax base shown above are assumed for all payroll calculations in this textbook.*

**REMEMBER**

When an employee's earnings exceed the tax base, no more social security tax is deducted.

## TERMS REVIEW

payroll taxes

withholding allowance

social security tax

Medicare tax

tax base

## AUDIT YOUR UNDERSTANDING

1. Where does an employer get the information used to determine the amount of federal income tax to withhold from employees' earnings?
2. Employee federal income tax withholdings are based on what two factors?
3. Does the employer or employee pay social security tax and Medicare tax?

## WORK TOGETHER

**Determining payroll tax withholding**

Information taken from a semimonthly payroll is given in the *Working Papers.* Your instructor will guide you through the following examples.

4. For each employee, determine the federal income tax that must be withheld. Use the tax withholding tables shown on pages 310–311.
5. Calculate the amount of social security tax and Medicare tax that must be withheld for each employee. Use a social security tax rate of 6.5% and a Medicare tax rate of 1.5%. None of the employees has accumulated earnings greater than the tax base.

## ON YOUR OWN

**Determining payroll tax withholding**

Information taken from a semimonthly payroll is given in the *Working Papers.* Work these problems independently.

6. For each employee, determine the federal income tax that must be withheld. Use the tax withholding tables on pages 310–311.
7. Calculate the amount of social security tax and Medicare tax that must be withheld for each employee. Use a social security tax rate of 6.5% and a Medicare tax rate of 1.5%. None of the employees has accumulated earnings greater than the tax base.

# 13-3 Preparing Payroll Records

## PAYROLL REGISTER

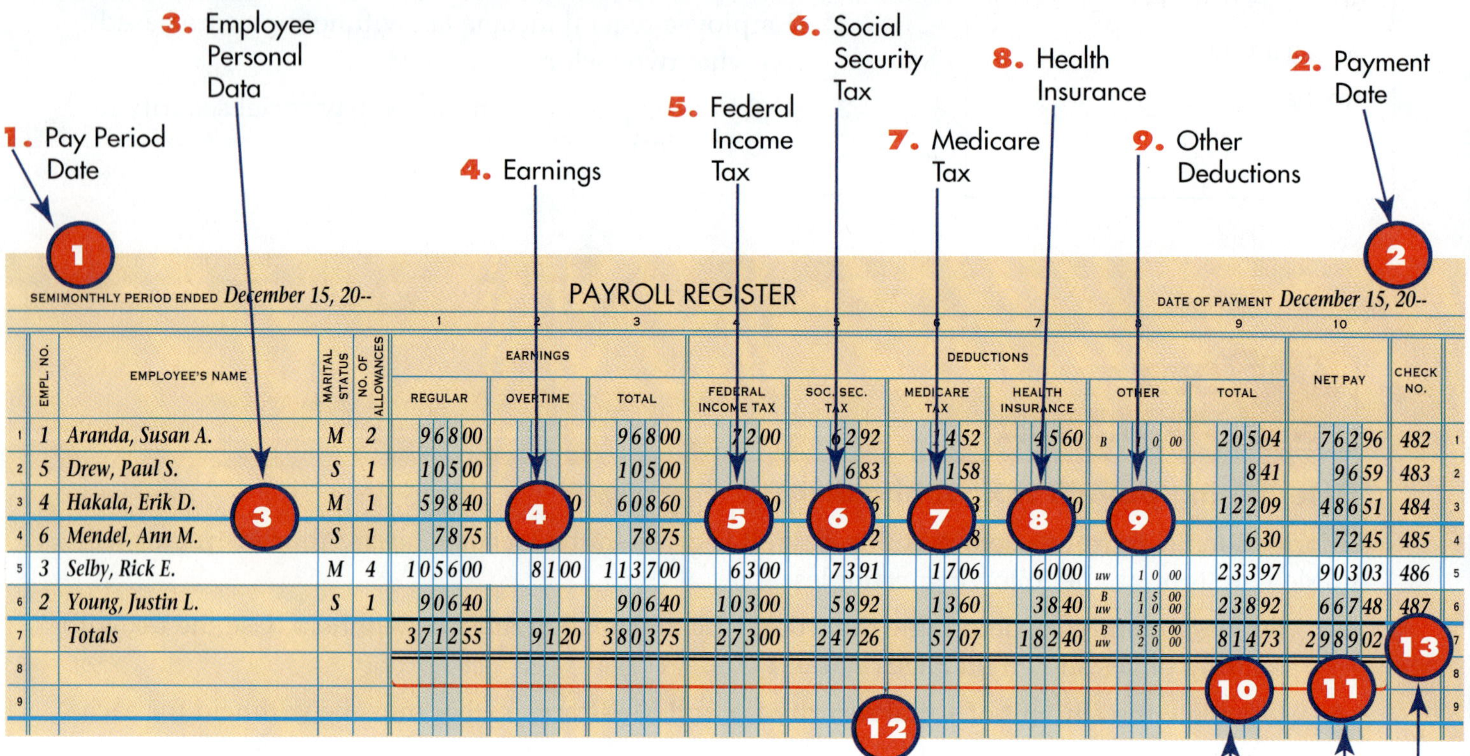


SEMIMONTHLY PERIOD ENDED *December 15, 20--* PAYROLL REGISTER DATE OF PAYMENT *December 15, 20--*

| | | | | | 1 | 2 | 3 | 4 | 5 | 6 | 7 | 8 | | 9 | 10 | | |
|---|---|---|---|---|---|---|---|---|---|---|---|---|---|---|---|---|---|
| | EMPL. NO. | EMPLOYEE'S NAME | MARITAL STATUS | NO. OF ALLOWANCES | EARNINGS | | | DEDUCTIONS | | | | | | | NET PAY | CHECK NO. | |
| | | | | | REGULAR | OVERTIME | TOTAL | FEDERAL INCOME TAX | SOC. SEC. TAX | MEDICARE TAX | HEALTH INSURANCE | OTHER | | TOTAL | | | |
| 1 | 1 | Aranda, Susan A. | M | 2 | 968 00 | | 968 00 | 72 00 | 62 92 | 14 52 | 45 60 | B | 10 00 | 205 04 | 762 96 | 482 | 1 |
| 2 | 5 | Drew, Paul S. | S | 1 | 105 00 | | 105 00 | | 6 83 | 1 58 | | | | 8 41 | 96 59 | 483 | 2 |
| 3 | 4 | Hakala, Erik D. | M | 1 | 598 40 | [illegible] | 608 60 | [illegible] | [illegible] | [illegible] | [illegible] | | | 122 09 | 486 51 | 484 | 3 |
| 4 | 6 | Mendel, Ann M. | S | 1 | 78 75 | | 78 75 | | [illegible] | [illegible] | | | | 6 30 | 72 45 | 485 | 4 |
| 5 | 3 | Selby, Rick E. | M | 4 | 1,056 00 | 81 00 | 1,137 00 | 63 00 | 73 91 | 17 06 | 60 00 | UW | 10 00 | 233 97 | 903 03 | 486 | 5 |
| 6 | 2 | Young, Justin L. | S | 1 | 906 40 | | 906 40 | 103 00 | 58 92 | 13 60 | 38 40 | B<br>UW | 15 00<br>10 00 | 238 92 | 667 48 | 487 | 6 |
| 7 | | Totals | | | 3,712 55 | 91 20 | 3,803 75 | 273 00 | 247 26 | 57 07 | 182 40 | B<br>UW | 35 00<br>20 00 | 814 73 | 2,989 02 | | 7 |
| 8 | | | | | | | | | | | | | | | | | 8 |
| 9 | | | | | | | | | | | | | | | | | 9 |

A business form used to record payroll information is called a **payroll register.** A payroll register summarizes the payroll for one pay period and shows total earnings, payroll withholdings, and net pay of all employees. Omni prepares a separate payroll register for each semimonthly payroll.

### STEPS Preparing a payroll register

1. Enter the last date of the semimonthly payroll period, *December 15, 20—*, at the top of the payroll register.
2. Enter the date of payment, *December 15, 20—*, also at the top of the payroll register.
3. For each employee, enter employee number, name, marital status, and number of allowances. This information is taken from personnel records. Entries for Rick E. Selby are on line 5 of the register.
4. Enter regular earnings, overtime earnings, and total earnings for each employee in columns 1, 2, and 3 of the payroll register. This information is taken from each employee's time card.
5. Enter in column 4 the federal income tax withheld from each employee. Mr. Selby's federal tax withholding is *$63.00.*

**6.** Enter in column 5 of the payroll register the social security tax withheld from each employee. Mr. Selby's social security tax deduction, *$73.91*, is recorded in column 5 of the payroll register. Mr. Selby's total earnings for the year have not exceeded the social security tax base, so his total earnings for the pay period are taxed.

**7.** Enter in column 6 the Medicare tax withheld from each employee. Mr. Selby's Medicare tax deduction is *$17.06*.

**8.** Enter in column 7 the health insurance premium deductions. Full-time employees of Omni Import participate in a group health insurance plan to take advantage of lower group rates. Mr. Selby's semimonthly health insurance premium is *$60.00*. Premiums are set by the insurance company and are usually based on the employee marital status and whether coverage is for an individual or a family. Some health insurance premiums may be based on the number of individuals covered.

**9.** Enter in column 8 all other employee payroll deductions. The Other column is used to record voluntary deductions requested by an employee. Entries are identified by code letters. Omni uses the letter *B* to identify amounts withheld for buying U.S. Savings Bonds. *UW* is used to identify amounts withheld for employee contributions to United Way. Mr. Selby has authorized Omni to withhold *$10.00* each pay period to buy U.S. Savings Bonds for him. Mr. Selby has also authorized that *$10.00* be withheld as a contribution to the United Way.

**10.** After all deductions are entered in the payroll register, add all the deduction amounts for each employee and enter the totals in column 9. Mr. Selby's total deductions, *$233.97*, are calculated as shown.

| Federal Income Tax | + | Social Security Tax | + | Medicare Tax | + | Health Insurance | + | Other | = | Total Deductions |
|---|---|---|---|---|---|---|---|---|---|---|
| $63.00 | + | $73.91 | + | $17.06 | + | $60.00 | + | $20.00 | = | $233.97 |

**11.** Determine the net pay for each employee. The total earnings paid to an employee after payroll taxes and other deductions is called **net pay.** Subtract the total deductions, column 9, from total earnings, column 3, to determine net pay. Enter net pay in column 10. Mr. Selby's net pay, *$903.03*, is calculated as shown.

| Total Earnings | – | Total Deductions | = | Net Pay |
|---|---|---|---|---|
| $1,137.00 | – | $233.97 | = | $903.03 |

**12.** Total, prove, and rule the payroll register. Total each amount column. Subtract the Total Deductions column from the Total Earnings column. The result should equal the total of the Net Pay column. If the totals do not agree, the errors must be found and corrected. Proving the accuracy of Omni's payroll register for pay period ended December 15, 20—, is shown.

| Total Earnings | – | Total Deductions | = | Net Pay |
|---|---|---|---|---|
| $3,803.75 | – | $814.73 | = | $2,989.02 |

The net pay, *$2,989.02*, is the same as the total of the Net Pay column. The payroll register is proved. After the payroll register is proved, rule double lines below all amount column totals to show the totals have been verified as correct.

**13.** Payroll checks are written after payroll calculations are verified and a partner approves the payroll. Write the payroll check numbers in the Check No. column.

# EMPLOYEE EARNINGS RECORDS

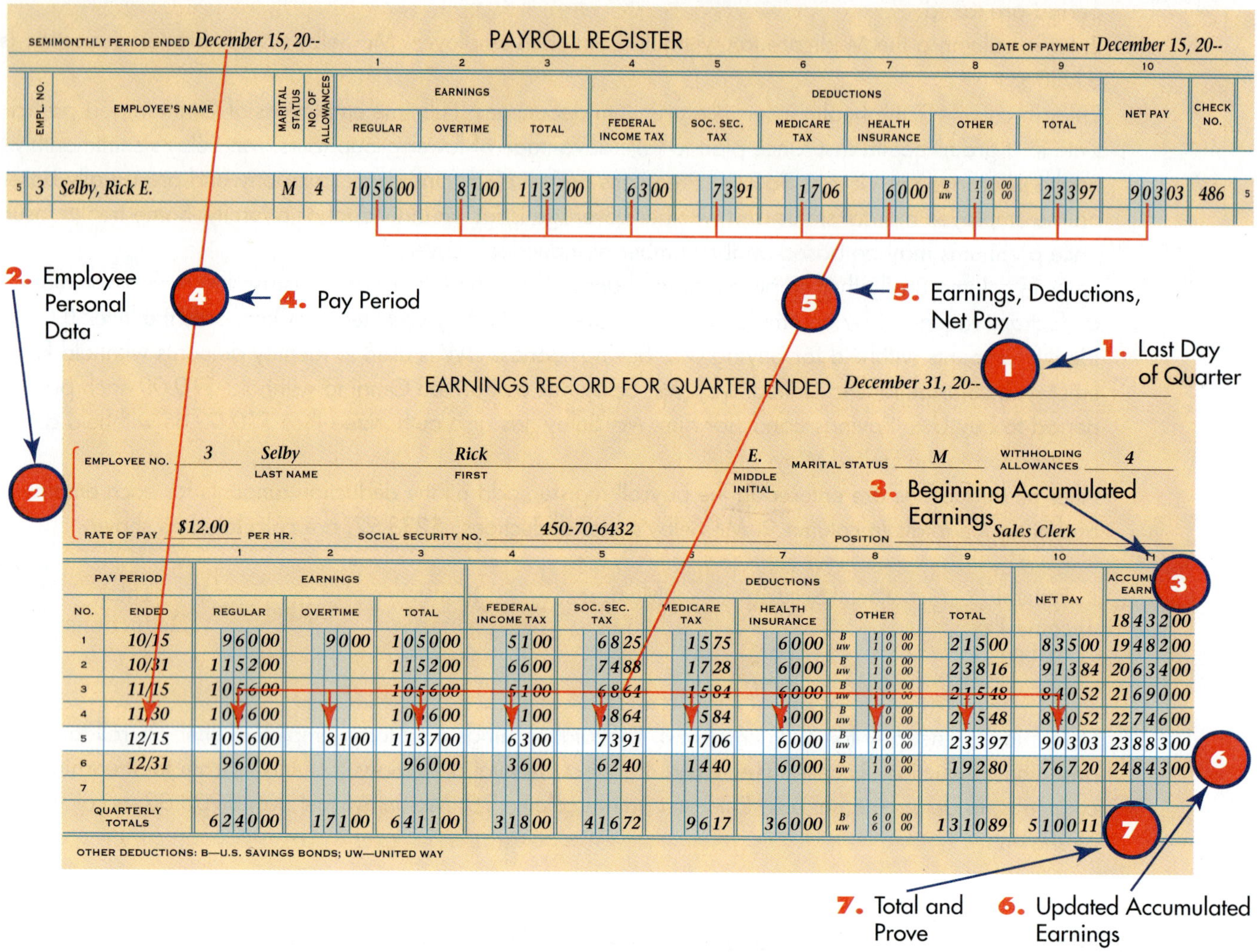

SEMIMONTHLY PERIOD ENDED *December 15, 20--* PAYROLL REGISTER DATE OF PAYMENT *December 15, 20--*

| | EMPL. NO. | EMPLOYEE'S NAME | MARITAL STATUS | NO. OF ALLOWANCES | EARNINGS 1 REGULAR | 2 OVERTIME | 3 TOTAL | DEDUCTIONS 4 FEDERAL INCOME TAX | 5 SOC. SEC. TAX | 6 MEDICARE TAX | 7 HEALTH INSURANCE | 8 OTHER | 9 TOTAL | 10 NET PAY | CHECK NO. | |
|---|---|---|---|---|---|---|---|---|---|---|---|---|---|---|---|---|
| 5 | 3 | Selby, Rick E. | M | 4 | 1056 00 | 81 00 | 1137 00 | 63 00 | 73 91 | 17 06 | 60 00 | B 10 00<br>UW 10 00 | 233 97 | 903 03 | 486 | 5 |

EARNINGS RECORD FOR QUARTER ENDED *December 31, 20--*

EMPLOYEE NO. *3* LAST NAME *Selby* FIRST *Rick* MIDDLE INITIAL *E.* MARITAL STATUS *M* WITHHOLDING ALLOWANCES *4*

RATE OF PAY *$12.00* PER HR. SOCIAL SECURITY NO. *450-70-6432* POSITION *Sales Clerk*

| PAY PERIOD NO. | ENDED | EARNINGS 1 REGULAR | 2 OVERTIME | 3 TOTAL | DEDUCTIONS 4 FEDERAL INCOME TAX | 5 SOC. SEC. TAX | 6 MEDICARE TAX | 7 HEALTH INSURANCE | 8 OTHER | 9 TOTAL | 10 NET PAY | 11 ACCUMULATED EARNINGS |
|---|---|---|---|---|---|---|---|---|---|---|---|---|
| | | | | | | | | | | | | 18432 00 |
| 1 | 10/15 | 960 00 | 90 00 | 1050 00 | 51 00 | 68 25 | 15 75 | 60 00 | B 10 00<br>UW 10 00 | 215 00 | 835 00 | 19482 00 |
| 2 | 10/31 | 1152 00 | | 1152 00 | 66 00 | 74 88 | 17 28 | 60 00 | B 10 00<br>UW 10 00 | 238 16 | 913 84 | 20634 00 |
| 3 | 11/15 | 1056 00 | | 1056 00 | 51 00 | 68 64 | 15 84 | 60 00 | B 10 00<br>UW 10 00 | 215 48 | 840 52 | 21690 00 |
| 4 | 11/30 | 1056 00 | | 1056 00 | 51 00 | 68 64 | 15 84 | 60 00 | B 10 00<br>UW 10 00 | 215 48 | 840 52 | 22746 00 |
| 5 | 12/15 | 1056 00 | 81 00 | 1137 00 | 63 00 | 73 91 | 17 06 | 60 00 | B 10 00<br>UW 10 00 | 233 97 | 903 03 | 23883 00 |
| 6 | 12/31 | 960 00 | | 960 00 | 36 00 | 62 40 | 14 40 | 60 00 | B 10 00<br>UW 10 00 | 192 80 | 767 20 | 24843 00 |
| 7 | | | | | | | | | | | | |
| QUARTERLY TOTALS | | 6240 00 | 171 00 | 6411 00 | 318 00 | 416 72 | 96 17 | 360 00 | B 60 00<br>UW 60 00 | 1310 89 | 5100 11 | |

OTHER DEDUCTIONS: B—U.S. SAVINGS BONDS; UW—UNITED WAY



A business must send a quarterly report to federal and state governments showing employee taxable earnings and taxes withheld from employee earnings. Detailed information about each employee's earnings is summarized in a single record for each employee. A business form used to record details affecting payments made to an employee is called an **employee earnings record.** An employee's earnings and deductions for each pay period are summarized on one line of the employee earnings record. A new earnings record is prepared for each employee each quarter. Rick E. Selby's earnings record for the fourth quarter is shown.

## Preparing an employee earnings record

STEPS

1. Enter the last day of the yearly quarter, *December 31, 20—*, at the top of the earnings record.
2. Enter the employee's number, name, marital status, withholding allowances, hourly rate, social security number, and position in the provided space. This information is taken from the employee's personnel records.
3. Enter the fiscal year's accumulated earnings for the beginning of the current quarter. This information is taken from the ending accumulated earnings for the previous quarter. Mr. Selby's accumulated earnings for the first three quarters ended September 30 are *$18,432.00*. The Accumulated Earnings column of the employee earnings record shows the accumulated earnings since the beginning of the fiscal year.
4. Enter the last date of the pay period being recorded.
5. Enter the earnings, deductions, and net pay in the columns of the employee earnings record. This information is taken from the current pay period's payroll register.
6. Add the current pay period's total earnings to the previous period's accumulated earnings. Mr. Selby's accumulated earnings as of December 15 are calculated as shown.

| Accumulated Earnings as of December 1 | + | Total Earnings for Pay Period Ended December 15 | = | Accumulated Earnings as of December 15 |
|---|---|---|---|---|
| $22,746.00 | + | $1,137.00 | = | $23,883.00 |

The Accumulated Earnings column shows the total earnings for Mr. Selby since the first of the year. The amounts in the Accumulated Earnings column supply an up-to-date reference for an employee's year-to-date earnings. When employee earnings reach the tax base, certain payroll taxes do not apply. For example, social security taxes are paid only on a specified amount of earnings.

7. At the end of each quarter, total and prove the earnings record for each employee. Calculate quarterly totals for each amount column. Subtract the Total Deductions column from the Total Earnings column. The result should equal the total of the Net Pay column. If the totals do not agree, the errors must be found and corrected. Proving the accuracy of Mr. Selby's fourth quarterly totals is shown.

| Total Earnings | – | Total Deductions | = | Net Pay |
|---|---|---|---|---|
| $6,411.00 | – | $1,310.89 | = | $5,100.11 |

The net pay, *$5,100.11*, is compared to the total of the Net Pay column. The earnings record is proved because these amounts are equal. These totals are needed to prepare required government reports.

**REMEMBER**

Total earnings, not net pay, are added to the previous accumulated earnings amount on the earnings record.

## TERMS REVIEW

payroll register
net pay
employee earnings record

## AUDIT YOUR UNDERSTANDING

1. What does the payroll register summarize?
2. How is net pay calculated?
3. Why do companies complete employee earnings records?

## WORK TOGETHER

### Preparing payroll records

Selected payroll data for Antique Shop are provided in a payroll register in the *Working Papers.* Your instructor will guide you through the following examples.

4. Complete the payroll register entries for Judy Hensley and Mike McCune for the semimonthly pay period ended July 15, 20—. Use the tax withholding tables shown on pages 310–311. The tax rate for social security tax is 6.5% and for Medicare tax, 1.5%. Neither employee has reached the tax base. For each employee, withhold $60.00 for health insurance and $15.00 for U.S. Savings bonds, per pay period.
5. Total all the amount columns of the payroll register. Prove the payroll register.
6. Prepare a quarterly earnings record for Ms. Hensley for the quarter ended September 30, 20—, and enter the July 15 payroll information. Ms. Hensley's employee number is 5; rate of pay is $13.00; social security number is 543-69-0123; position is sales clerk. Accumulated earnings at the end of the second quarter are $13,520.00. Save your work to complete Work Together on page 321.

## ON YOUR OWN

### Preparing payroll records

Selected payroll data for The Sign Store are provided in a payroll register in the *Working Papers.* Work these problems independently.

7. Complete the payroll register entries for Gary Eubanks and Ellen Park for the semimonthly pay period ended July 15, 20—. Use the tax withholding tables shown on page 310–311. The tax rate for social security tax is 6.5%, and for Medicare tax, 1.5%. For each employee, withhold $50.00 for health insurance and $10.00 for United Way, per pay period. For Mr. Eubanks also withhold $10.00 for U.S. Savings Bonds per pay period.
8. Total all the amount columns of the payroll register. Prove the payroll register.
9. Prepare a quarterly earnings record for Mr. Eubanks for the quarter ended September 30, 20—, and enter the July 15 payroll information. Mr. Eubanks's employee number is 8; rate of pay is $12.80; social security number is 345-68-9876; position is sales clerk. Accumulated earnings at the end of the second quarter are $13,312.00. Save your work to complete On Your Own on page 321.

# 13-4 Preparing Payroll Checks

## PAYROLL BANK ACCOUNT

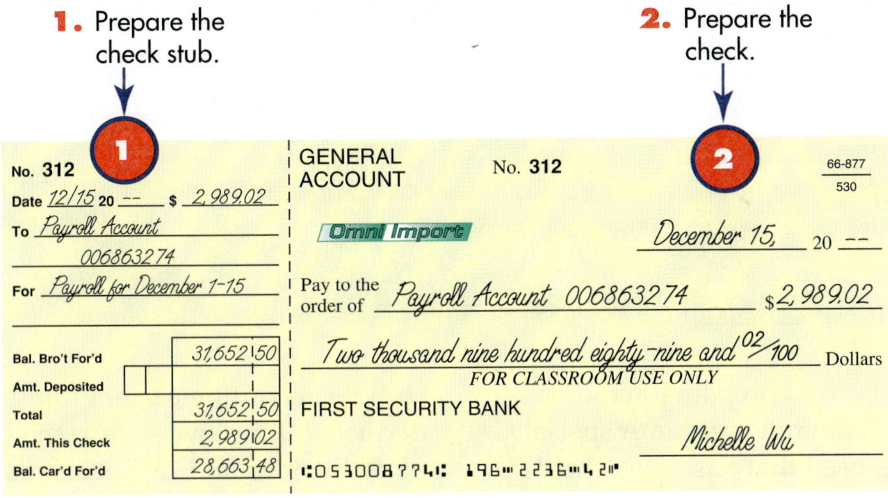


Omni Import pays its employees with checks written on a special payroll checking account. A check for the total net pay is written on Omni's general checking account. The check is deposited in the payroll checking account.

A separate checking account for payroll checks helps to protect and control payroll payments. The exact amount needed to pay the payroll is deposited in the special payroll checking account. If amounts on checks are altered or unauthorized payroll checks are prepared, the amount in the special payroll account would be insufficient to cover all the checks. Thus, the bank and Omni would be alerted quickly to an unauthorized payroll check. Also, since payroll checks are drawn on the separate account, any balance in this account will correspond to the sum of outstanding payroll checks.

**STEPS**

### Preparing a check for total net pay

1. Prepare the check stub. The date of the check is *12/15.* The amount, *$2,989.02,* is the total of the Net Pay column of the payroll register. The check is payable to *Payroll Account 006863274,* Omni's special payroll checking account. The payment is for the payroll period from December 1 to 15. Calculate and record the new general checking account balance.
2. Prepare the check from the information on the check stub. Omni's check is drawn on the company's general account and is signed by partner Michelle Wu.

**REMEMBER**

Using a separate checking account for payroll checks provides internal control and helps to prevent fraud.

## EMPLOYEE'S PAYROLL CHECK

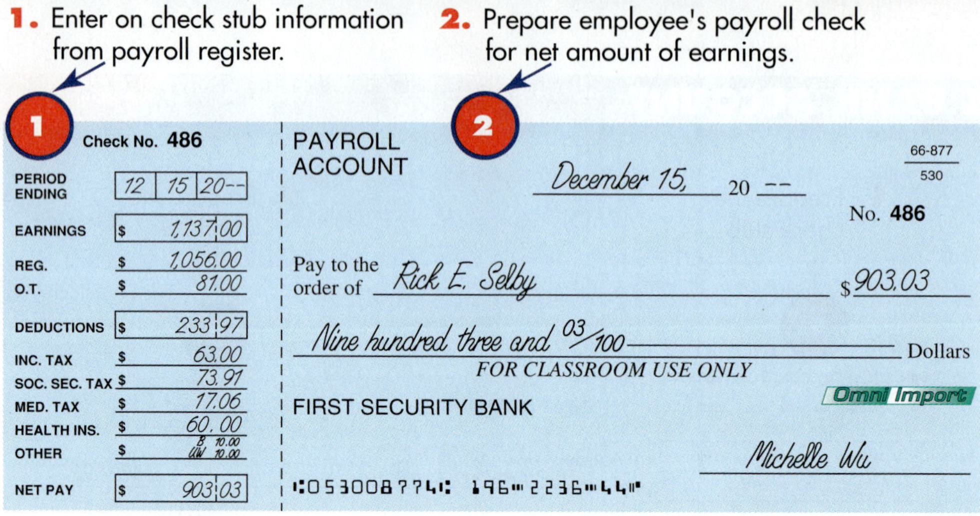


The information used to prepare payroll checks is taken from a payroll register. A special payroll check form is used that has a detachable stub for recording earnings and amounts deducted. Employees keep the stubs for a record of deductions and cash received.

### STEPS: Preparing an employee's payroll check

1. Prepare the check stub of each employee's payroll check. Enter information from the payroll register.
2. Prepare each employee's payroll check payable for the amount of net pay for the pay period. Rick E. Selby's net pay for the pay period ended December 15, 20—, is *$903.03*.

## ELECTRONIC FUNDS TRANSFER

A computerized cash payments system that uses electronic impulses to transfer funds is known as electronic funds transfer (EFT). Some businesses deposit employee net pay directly to each employee bank account by using EFT. When EFT is used, the bank's computer deducts the amount of net pay from the business's bank account and adds the amount to each employee bank account. The payroll must still be calculated, but individual checks are not written and do not have to be distributed. Under this system, each employee receives a statement of earnings and deductions similar to the detachable stub on a payroll check.

## AUDIT YOUR UNDERSTANDING

1. Why does Omni Import have a separate checking account for payroll checks?
2. What is the source of the information that is recorded on each employee's payroll check stub?
3. How do payroll procedures differ for an employee who requests that her pay be deposited through electronic funds transfer?

## WORK TOGETHER

### Preparing payroll checks

Use the payroll register from Work Together on page 318. In the *Working Papers* are three blank checks: one General Account check and two Payroll Account checks. Your instructor will guide you through the following examples.

4. Prepare Antique Shop's General Account check for the pay period ended July 15, 20—. The payment date is July 15. Balance brought forward from the previous check is $16,542.00. The Payroll Account number is 0639583. Sign your name as a partner of Antique Shop.
5. For the pay period ended July 15, 20—, prepare payroll checks for Judy Hensley and Mike McCune. The payment date is July 15. Sign your name as a partner of Antique Shop. Record the two payroll check numbers in the payroll register.

## ON YOUR OWN

### Preparing payroll checks

Use the payroll register from On Your Own on page 318. In the *Working Papers* are three blank checks: one General Account check and two Payroll Account checks. Work these problems independently.

6. Prepare The Sign Shop's General Account check for the pay period ended July 15, 20—. The payment date is July 15. Balance carried forward from the previous check is $13,597.00. The Payroll Account number is 983-5839. Sign your name as a partner of The Sign Shop.
7. For the pay period ended July 15, 20—, prepare payroll checks for Gary Eubanks and Ellen Park. The payment date is July 15. Sign your name as a partner of The Sign Shop. Record the two payroll checks in the payroll register.

# CHAPTER 13 SUMMARY

*Enrichment Activity*

**Technology**

*Many companies offer the option of direct deposit payroll checks. The company transmits payroll data directly to the employee's bank for direct deposit to the employee's bank account. Employees receive a report of their earnings and deductions. What advantages does this direct deposit of payroll have for employees?*

After completing this chapter, you can

1. Define important accounting terms related to payroll records.
2. Identify accounting practices related to payroll records.
3. Complete a payroll time card.
4. Calculate payroll taxes.
5. Complete a payroll register and an employee earnings record.
6. Prepare payroll checks.

## EXPLORE ACCOUNTING

### EMPLOYEE VS. INDEPENDENT CONTRACTOR

A business sometimes contracts with individuals to perform specified services for the business. Determining whether such an individual is an employee or a self-employed independent contractor is an important issue.

If the person is found to be an employee, the employer must withhold and submit employee income tax, social security tax, and Medicare tax to the Internal Revenue Service (IRS). The employer must pay an equal amount of social security and Medicare tax. Also, the employer will pay unemployment taxes (discussed in Chapter 14) and be subject to various employer reporting requirements.

A person who is found to be a self-employed independent contractor must pay an amount of social security and Medicare tax that is equivalent to both the employer and employee taxes.

If an employer incorrectly treats an employee as a self-employed independent contractor, the penalties can be severe. Therefore, it is important to a business to make an accurate determination of the status of all individuals performing work for the business.

The IRS has provided guidelines to help businesses make the distinction. Every individual who performs services subject to the will and control of an employer both as to what shall be done and how it shall be done, is considered an employee for withholding purposes. The major determining factor is whether the employer has the legal right to control both the method and result of the services. If the business has the right to control *only* the result of the service performed and *not* the means and methods of accomplishing the result, the individual is probably a self-employed independent contractor.

**Research:** Review federal tax publications or interview local businesses on the issues below. Then prepare a written or oral report to present to your class. (1) Why is it important to determine an individual's status? What is at stake for the individual, the employer, and the IRS? (2) What are the advantages and disadvantages of determining an individual to be an employee or independent contractor—to the individual? to the employer? to the IRS?

## 13-1 APPLICATION PROBLEM
### Preparing payroll time cards

Employee time cards are given in the *Working Papers.*

***Instructions:***

1. Calculate the regular, overtime, and total hours worked by each employee. Any hours over the regular 8-hour day are considered overtime. Record the hours on the time cards.
2. Determine the regular, overtime, and total earnings for each employee. The overtime rate is $1\frac{1}{2}$ times the regular rate. Complete the time cards.

## 13-2 APPLICATION PROBLEM
### Determining payroll tax withholding

Information taken from the semimonthly payroll register is given in the *Working Papers.*

***Instructions:***

1. Determine the federal income tax that must be withheld for each of the eight employees. Use the tax withholding tables shown on pages 310–311.
2. Calculate the amount of social security tax and Medicare tax that must be withheld for each employee using 6.5% and 1.5% tax rates, respectively. None of the eight employees has accumulated earnings greater than the tax base.

## 13-3 APPLICATION PROBLEM
### Preparing a payroll register

The information for the semimonthly pay period October 1–15 of the current year is given in the *Working Papers.*

***Instructions:***

Complete a payroll register. The date of payment is October 15. Use the tax withholding tables shown on pages 310–311 for the income tax withholding for each employee. Calculate social security and Medicare taxes withholding using 6.5% and 1.5% tax rates, respectively. None of the employee accumulated earnings has exceeded the social security tax base.

## 13-4 APPLICATION PROBLEM
### Preparing an employee earnings record

Grady R. Hurley's earnings for the six semimonthly pay periods in July, August, and September of the current year are given in the *Working Papers*. Deductions and net pay have been completed for July and August.

The following additional data about Grady R. Hurley are needed to complete the employee earnings record.

1. Employee number: 28
2. Marital status: married
3. Withholding allowances: 2
4. Rate of pay: regular, $15.00
5. Social security number: 462-81-5823
6. Position: service manager
7. Accumulated earnings for the end of second quarter: $15,750.00
8. Deductions from total earnings:
   a. Health insurance: $60.00 each semimonthly pay period
   b. U. S. Savings Bonds: $10.00 each semimonthly pay period
   c. Federal income tax: determined each pay period by using the withholding tables on pages 310–311.
   d. Social security taxes: 6.5% of total earnings each pay period
   e. Medicare taxes: 1.5% of total earnings each pay period

***Instructions:***

1. Calculate and record the accumulated earnings for the July and August pay periods.
2. Complete the earnings record for the pay periods ended September 15 and September 30.
3. Total all amount columns on the earnings record.
4. Verify the accuracy of the completed employee earnings record. The Quarter Total for Regular and Overtime Earnings should equal the Quarter Total for Net Pay plus Total Deductions. The Quarter Total for Total Earnings should equal the end-of-quarter Accumulated Earnings minus the beginning-of-quarter Accumulated Earnings.

## 13-5 APPLICATION PROBLEM
### Preparing payroll checks

Royal Appliances' net payroll for the semimonthly pay period ended May 15, 20—, is $7,498.80. Payroll checks are prepared May 15, 20—. Blank checks are provided in the *Working Papers*.

***Instructions:***

1. Prepare a General Account check for the total amount of the net pay. Make the check payable to Payroll Account 018-65-4237, and sign your name as partner of Royal Appliances. The beginning check stub balance is $10,138.95.
2. Prepare payroll checks for two employees of Royal Appliances. Payroll information for the two employees is as follows. Sign your name as a partner of Royal Appliances.
   a. Wanda M. Curtis
      Check No. 823
      Regular Earnings $740.00
      Overtime Earnings 40.00

Deductions:

Federal Income Tax $ 85.00

Social Security Tax 50.70

Medicare Tax 11.70

Net Pay 632.60

b. Kevin R. Hayes

Check No. 827

Regular Earnings $920.00

Overtime Earnings 30.00

Deductions:

Federal Income Tax $ 69.00

Social Security 61.75

Medicare Tax 14.25

Health Insurance 60.00

Net Pay 745.00

## 13-6 MASTERY PROBLEM

### Preparing a semimonthly payroll

The following information is for the semimonthly pay period May 1-15 of the current year. Forms are given in the *Working Papers*.

| EMPL. NO. | EMPLOYEE'S NAME | MARITAL STATUS | NO. OF ALLOWANCES | EARNINGS | | DEDUCTIONS | |
|---|---|---|---|---|---|---|---|
| | | | | REGULAR | OVERTIME | HEALTH INSURANCE | SAVINGS BONDS |
| 3 | Baird, Panette L. | M | 2 | 721 60 | 18 45 | 42 00 | 20 00 |
| 6 | Carmichael, Gary R. | S | 1 | 809 60 | 27 60 | | |
| 8 | Fields, Margo S. | M | 3 | 880 00 | 15 00 | 54 00 | 10 00 |
| 1 | Hahn, Todd M. | M | 2 | 792 00 | 47 25 | 42 00 | 10 00 |
| 5 | Liu, Jin C. | S | 1 | 941 60 | | | |
| 9 | Pruitt, Wilma C. | M | 2 | 862 40 | 102 90 | 42 00 | 20 00 |
| 10 | Roth, Thomas B. | S | 2 | 756 80 | 19 35 | 42 00 | 20 00 |
| 2 | Sevilla, Jose C. | M | 4 | 862 40 | | 62 00 | |
| 4 | Taylor, Cindy J. | S | 1 | 897 60 | 45 90 | | |
| 7 | Wylie, Howard K. | S | 1 | 660 00 | | | 30 00 |

***Instructions:***

1. Prepare a payroll register. The date of payment is May 15. Use the income tax withholding tables shown on pages 310–311 to find the income tax withholding for each employee. Calculate social security and Medicare tax withholdings using 6.5% and 1.5% tax rates, respectively. None of the employee accumulated earnings has exceeded the social security tax base.
2. Prepare a check for the total amount of the net pay. Make the check payable to Payroll Account 156-42-8796, and sign your name as a partner of Rainbo Company. The beginning check stub balance is $14,344.60.
3. Prepare payroll checks for Todd M. Hahn, Check No. 528, and Cindy J. Taylor, Check No. 533. Sign your name as a partner of Rainbo Company. Record the two payroll check numbers in the payroll register.

## 13-7 CHALLENGE PROBLEM
### Calculating piecework wages

Production workers in factories are frequently paid on the basis of the number of units they produce. This payroll method is referred to as the piecework incentive wage plan. Most piecework incentive wage plans include a guaranteed hourly rate to employees regardless of the number of units they produce. This guaranteed hourly rate is referred to as the base rate.

Time and motion study engineers usually determine the standard time required for producing a single unit. Assume, for example, that time studies determine that one-third of an hour is the standard time required to produce a unit. Then the standard rate for an 8-hour day would be 24 units (8 hours divided by $\frac{1}{3}$ hour = 24 units per day). If a worker's daily base pay is \$96.00, the incentive rate per unit is \$4.00 (\$96.00 divided by 24 units = \$4.00 per unit). Therefore, the worker who produces 24 or fewer units per day is paid the base pay, \$96.00. However, each worker is paid an additional \$4.00 for each unit over 24 produced each day.

Premier Woodworks Company has eight employees in production departments that are paid on a piecework incentive wage plan. The following standard and incentive wage rates are listed by department.

| Department | Standard Production per Employee | Incentive Rate per Unit |
|---|---|---|
| Cutting | 30 units per day | \$3.50 |
| Assembly | 20 units per day | \$6.20 |
| Finishing | 40 units per day | \$2.70 |

A payroll register is given in the *Working Papers*. Each employee worked eight hours a day during the semimonthly pay period, June 1–15. Payroll records for June 1–15 are summarized in the following table.

| Employee | | Marital Status | No. of Allow-ances | Guaranteed Daily Rate | Units Produced per Day Pay Period June 1–15 | | | | | | | | | |
|---|---|---|---|---|---|---|---|---|---|---|---|---|---|---|
| No. | Name | | | | 2 | 3 | 4 | 5 | 6 | 9 | 10 | 11 | 12 | 13 |
| | Cutting Department | | | | | | | | | | | | | |
| C2 | Martinez, Luis L. | S | 1 | \$105.00 | 29 | 32 | 31 | 34 | 28 | 27 | 30 | 32 | 36 | 26 |
| C4 | Price, Nancy C. | M | 1 | \$105.00 | 32 | 31 | 28 | 29 | 27 | 29 | 31 | 32 | 27 | 28 |
| C8 | King, Debra S. | M | 2 | \$105.00 | 31 | 28 | 27 | 24 | 31 | 33 | 32 | 29 | 30 | 29 |
| | Assembly Department | | | | | | | | | | | | | |
| A1 | Heath, Scott R. | S | 1 | \$124.00 | 20 | 21 | 19 | 19 | 18 | 18 | 19 | 21 | 20 | 21 |
| A6 | Nowlin, Daniel W. | M | 3 | \$124.00 | 25 | 21 | 17 | 18 | 19 | 21 | 20 | 20 | 21 | 18 |
| A7 | Scofield, Martha A. | S | 1 | \$124.00 | 22 | 24 | 25 | 21 | 20 | 19 | 23 | 21 | 18 | 17 |
| | Finishing Department | | | | | | | | | | | | | |
| F5 | Isaacs, Julie M. | M | 2 | \$108.00 | 41 | 40 | 38 | 39 | 42 | 43 | 41 | 40 | 38 | 37 |
| F3 | Stewart, Gary W. | M | 2 | \$108.00 | 37 | 37 | 38 | 38 | 39 | 38 | 40 | 41 | 41 | 42 |

***Instructions:***

Prepare a payroll register. The earnings column Incentive is used instead of Overtime. The date of payment is June 15. Use the income tax withholding tables shown on pages 310–311. Calculate the employee social security and Medicare tax withholdings using 6.5% and 1.5% tax rates, respectively. None of the employees has health insurance or other deductions.

## INTERNET ACTIVITY

Point your browser to

**http://accounting.swpco.com**

Choose **First-Year Course**, choose **Activities**, and complete the activity for Chapter 13.

## Applied Communication

The employees of Kaden Company currently use time cards and a time clock to record their arrival and departure times. Management plans to replace the time clock with a device that reads a magnetic strip on the back of each employee's name badge. The badge is scanned by a reader in the same manner that credit cards are scanned. Because the badge reader is connected to a computer, the information is recorded directly to a computer file. Thus, the new system will enable management to make daily analyses of employee hours and productivity. This information should allow managers to make more timely decisions and increase profits.

**Instructions:** Assume you work in the payroll department for Kaden Company. Write a memo to the employees informing them of the new system. Because some employees may not be happy with this new system, be sure to include reasons why the policy is being implemented.

## Cases for Critical Thinking

**Case 1** Sullivan Lumber currently requires each employee to inform the accounting clerk of the total hours worked each day during the pay period. The total number of hours worked by all employees has been steadily increasing during the prior pay periods. The new store manager has suggested that a time clock be installed to record arrival and departure times. The accounting clerk believes the current system is satisfactory. Do you agree with the new manager or the accounting clerk? Explain your response.

**Case 2** A banker has recommended that Mueller Construction Company open a second checking account. The company would write payroll checks on the new checking account. The company's 50 employees are currently paid with checks written on its general checking account. Do you agree with the banker's recommendation? Explain the reason for your decision.

# AUTOMATED ACCOUNTING

## AUTOMATED PAYROLL ACCOUNTING

In an automated payroll system, the computer is used to maintain the employee database, to record payroll transactions at the end of each pay period, to calculate withholding taxes, and to create all the related journal entries. The employee database identifies each employee by employee number. Other data required for each employee includes the employee's name, social security number, marital status, number of withholding allowances, pay rate, and voluntary deductions. Employee accounts may be added, changed, or deleted from the accounting system.

### Maintaining Employees

Since payroll data is used to calculate income taxes, the payroll system must contain accurate, up-to-date data for each employee. Maintenance is required to:

1. Add new employees.
2. Remove employees who no longer work for the company.
3. Record changes in employee information, including changes in marital status, number of withholding allowances, pay rate, and voluntary deductions.

To perform employee maintenance in *Automated Accounting 7.0* or higher:

1. Click the Accounts toolbar button.
2. Click the Employees tab.
3. To add a new employee:
   - Enter the sequential employee number.
   - Enter information in all the data fields, including name, address, social security number, and marital status.
   - Press Enter or click Add Employee.
4. To change or delete data for a current employee:
   - Select the employee by clicking the grid cell containing the data you wish to change.
   - Enter the correct data.
   - Click the Change Employee button, or click the Delete button to remove the employee from the database. (Employees with cumulative earnings may be deleted only after the end of the calendar year.)

### Entering Payroll Transactions

1. Click the Other toolbar button.
2. Click the Payroll tab.
3. Enter the date of the check.
4. Select the employee from the employee drop-down list.
5. Verify that the check number displayed is correct, or key the correct number.
6. For salaried employees, the salary amount will be automatically displayed. For hourly employees, enter the regular and overtime hours worked during the current payroll period.
7. Click the Calculate Taxes button to direct the software to calculate the employee taxes.
8. Enter the employee's voluntary deductions.
9. Click OK to generate and display the payroll check.
10. Click the Close button to dismiss the check and continue, or click Print to print the check.

### Automating Application Problem 13-5: Preparing payroll checks

**Instructions:**

1. Load *Automated Accounting 7.0* or higher software.
2. Select database F13-1 from the appropriate directory/folder.
3. Select File from the menu bar and choose the Save As menu command. Key the path to the drive and directory that contains your data files. Save the database with a file name of XXX131 (where XXX are your initials).
4. Access Problem Instructions through the Help menu. Read the Problem Instructions screen.
5. Key the data listed on pages 324–325.
6. Exit the *Automated Accounting* software.

# AUTOMATED ACCOUNTING

Other Activities

Reconciliation | Payroll

| Date | Employee Name | Check No. | Salary | Reg. Hours | O.T. Hours | Pieces | Comm. Sales | Federal Tax |
|---|---|---|---|---|---|---|---|---|
| 10/31/ | Chadwick, Carl | 447 | | 176.00 | | | | 159.71 |
| 10/31/ | Feng, Chan | 448 | 2270.00 | | | | | 164.56 |
| 10/31/ | Lienhardt, Jody | 449 | 2340.00 | | | | | 238.81 |
| 10/31/ | Salas, Luis | 450 | | 168.00 | | | | 252.83 |
| 11/30/ | Barnard, Melinda | 451 | | 176.00 | 2.50 | | | 272.34 |
| 11/30/ | Chadwick, Carl | 452 | | 176.00 | | | | 159.71 |
| 11/30/ | Feng, Chan | 453 | 2270.00 | | | | | 164.56 |
| 11/30/ | Lienhardt, Jody | 454 | 2340.00 | | | | | 238.81 |
| 11/30/ | Salas, Luis | 455 | | 160.00 | | | | 237.71 |
| 11/30/ | | 456 | | | | | | |

OK | Delete | Help | Close | Calculate Taxes | Gross:

ation | Payroll

| State Tax | City Tax | Social Security | Medicare | Health Insurance | Dental Insurance | Credit Union | Net Pay |
|---|---|---|---|---|---|---|---|
| 61.74 | 22.70 | 140.74 | 32.92 | 45.00 | 18.00 | 50.00 | 1734.34 |
| 70.38 | 23.40 | 145.08 | 33.93 | 45.00 | 28.00 | 75.00 | 1680.40 |
| 59.56 | 21.17 | 131.24 | 30.69 | 40.00 | 24.00 | 30.00 | 1527.31 |
| 65.87 | 22.47 | 139.31 | 32.58 | 40.00 | 24.00 | 25.00 | 1625.31 |
| 31.30 | 14.96 | 92.75 | 21.69 | 40.00 | 24.00 | 35.00 | 1076.59 |
| 61.74 | 22.70 | 140.74 | 32.92 | 45.00 | 18.00 | 50.00 | 1734.34 |
| 70.38 | 23.40 | 145.08 | 33.93 | 45.00 | 28.00 | 75.00 | 1680.40 |
| 54.68 | 20.16 | 124.99 | 29.23 | 40.00 | 24.00 | 30.00 | 1455.23 |
| | | | | | | | |
| | | | | | | | |

# 14 Payroll Accounting, Taxes, and Reports

**AFTER STUDYING CHAPTER 14, YOU WILL BE ABLE TO:**

1. Define accounting terms related to payroll accounting, taxes, and reports.
2. Identify accounting concepts and practices related to payroll accounting, taxes, and reports.
3. Analyze payroll transactions and record a payroll.
4. Record employer payroll taxes.
5. Prepare selected payroll tax reports.
6. Pay and record withholding and payroll taxes.

**TERMS PREVIEW**

federal unemployment tax

state unemployment tax

## DIFFERENT FORMS OF PAYROLL INFORMATION

Payroll information for each pay period is recorded in a payroll register. Each pay period the payroll information for each employee is also recorded on each employee earnings record. Separate payroll accounts for each employee are not kept in the general ledger. Instead, accounts are kept in the general ledger to summarize total earnings and deductions for all employees.

The payroll register and employee earnings records provide all the payroll information needed to prepare a payroll and payroll tax reports. Journal entries are made to record the payment of the payroll and the employer payroll taxes. In addition, various quarterly and annual payroll tax reports are required to report the payment of payroll taxes.

# ACCOUNTING IN YOUR CAREER

## HOW MUCH DO EMPLOYEES REALLY COST?

Walter Johnson, staff accountant for VideoPlus Company, is meeting with the two partners to discuss how they will begin making plans for next year's operations. Deborah Stricklin and Paul Kassem, partners, like to have their management strategy planned before meeting with the department managers to prepare the next year's budget.

Deborah begins the meeting with the statement, "Walter, we're about to plan the budget for next year, and we need your help."

"That's right, Walter," continues Paul. "You've been in these budget meetings before. Every time we ask for increases in sales, all the managers ask for more employees. That seems to be their answer to everything. They never talk about economizing on costs, or finding more efficient ways to operate. How can we get them to realize that new employees are not always the solution?"

"Deborah, Paul," answers Walter, "you're right. I've been in those meetings, and you've described what goes on pretty accurately. I wonder if it would help to show the managers how much a new employee really costs."

"I'm not sure I know what you're getting at, Walter," responds Paul.

"Well, I think most of the managers look only at salary costs. They forget all the other payroll costs, such as taxes and benefits, not to mention the cost of training a new employee."

Deborah and Paul like this analysis and ask Walter to work up some estimates and make a presentation at the first budget meeting next week.

**Critical Thinking:**

1. Where could Walter Johnson find a record of all salary and benefit costs paid for all employees in a year?
2. How could Walter quickly calculate the average annual salary of a VideoPlus employee?
3. How should Walter use the information in the ledger accounts for Employee Income Tax Payable, Social Security Tax Payable, and Medicare Tax Payable?

# 14-1 Recording a Payroll

## PAYROLL REGISTER

SEMIMONTHLY PERIOD ENDED *December 15, 20--* PAYROLL REGISTER DATE OF PAYMENT *December 15, 20--*

| | EMPL. NO. | EMPLOYEE'S NAME | MARITAL STATUS | NO. OF ALLOWANCES | 1 EARNINGS REGULAR | 2 EARNINGS OVERTIME | 3 EARNINGS TOTAL | 4 DEDUCTIONS FEDERAL INCOME TAX | 5 SOC. SEC. TAX | 6 MEDICARE TAX | 7 HEALTH INSURANCE | 8 OTHER | 9 TOTAL | 10 NET PAY | CHECK NO. | |
|---|---|---|---|---|---|---|---|---|---|---|---|---|---|---|---|---|
| 1 | 1 | Aranda, Susan A. | M | 2 | 968 00 | | 968 00 | 72 00 | 62 92 | 14 52 | 45 60 | B 10 00 | 205 04 | 762 96 | 482 | 1 |
| 2 | 5 | Drew, Paul S. | S | 1 | 105 00 | | 105 00 | | 6 83 | 1 58 | | | 8 41 | 96 59 | 483 | 2 |
| 3 | 4 | Hakala, Erik D. | M | 1 | 598 40 | 10 20 | 608 60 | 35 00 | 39 56 | 9 13 | 38 40 | | 122 09 | 486 51 | 484 | 3 |
| 4 | 6 | Mendel, Ann M. | S | 1 | 78 75 | | 78 75 | | 5 12 | 1 18 | | | 6 30 | 72 45 | 485 | 4 |
| 5 | 3 | Selby, Rick E. | M | 4 | 1,056 00 | 81 00 | 1,137 00 | 63 00 | 73 91 | 17 06 | 60 00 | B 10 00<br>uw 10 00 | 233 97 | 903 03 | 486 | 5 |
| 6 | 2 | Young, Justin L. | S | 1 | 906 40 | | 906 40 | 103 00 | 58 92 | 13 60 | 38 40 | B 15 00<br>uw 10 00 | 238 92 | 667 48 | 487 | 6 |
| 7 | | Totals | | | 3,712 55 | 91 20 | 3,803 75 | 273 00 | 247 26 | 57 07 | 182 40 | B 35 00<br>uw 20 00 | 814 73 | 2,989 02 | | 7 |
| 8 | | | | | | | | | | | | | | | | 8 |
| 9 | | | | | | | | | | | | | | | | 9 |

The column totals of a payroll register provide the debit and credit amounts needed to journalize a payroll.

As you will learn in this chapter, the payroll journal entry is based on the totals of the Earnings Total column, each deduction column, and the Net Pay column. The totals of the Earnings Regular, Earnings Overtime, and Deductions Total columns are not used to journalize the payroll.

**TECHNOLOGY FOR BUSINESS**

### HOW SMART ARE YOUR CARDS?

Americans use lots of cards—library cards, credit cards, ATM cards, insurance cards. When you use them, do you ever think that cards may be smart?

A *smart card* looks like a plastic credit card, but it has a microprocessor, or computer chip, planted inside. Depending on the intended use, these chip cards can be really smart.

One type of smart card is called a *stored value card.* Generally you purchase a stored value card through a vending machine. You insert cash, a credit card, or a debit card to buy the stored value card. Each time you use it, the card deducts the amount of your purchase from its stored value.

While smart cards are relatively new in the U. S., other countries are using them for more complex reasons. For example, Spain has issued 500,000 identification cards, with stored fingerprints for verification, that give access to medical benefits.

Just how smart do you think cards will be in the future?

# ANALYZING PAYMENT OF A PAYROLL

| Salary Expense | |
|---|---|
| Dec. 15 3,803.75 | |

=

| Employee Income Tax Payable | |
|---|---|
| | Dec. 15 273.00 |

| Social Security Tax Payable | |
|---|---|
| | Dec. 15 247.26 |

| Medicare Tax Payable | |
|---|---|
| | Dec. 15 57.07 |

| Health Insurance Premiums Payable | |
|---|---|
| | Dec. 15 182.40 |

| U. S. Savings Bonds Payable | |
|---|---|
| | Dec. 15 35.00 |

| United Way Donations Payable | |
|---|---|
| | Dec. 15 20.00 |

| Cash | |
|---|---|
| | Dec. 15 2,989.02 |

Data about Omni Import's semimonthly pay period ended December 15, obtained from the payroll register, is summarized in the T accounts.

The Total Earnings column total, $3,803.75, is the salary expense for the period. Salary Expense is debited for this amount.

The Federal Income Tax column total, $273.00, is the amount withheld from employee salaries for federal income tax. The amount withheld is a liability of the business until the taxes are sent to the federal government. Employee Income Tax Payable is credited for $273.00 to record this liability.

The Social Security Tax column total, $247.26, is the amount withheld for social security tax. The amount is a liability of the business until the tax is paid to the government. Social Security Tax Payable is credited for $247.26.

The Medicare Tax column total, $57.07, is the amount withheld for Medicare tax. The amount is a liability of the business until the tax is paid to the government. Medicare Tax Payable is credited for $57.07.

The Health Insurance column total, $182.40, is the amount withheld for health insurance premiums. The amount is a liability of the business until the premiums are paid to the insurance company. Health Insurance Premiums Payable is credited for $182.40 to record this liability.

Two types of Other deductions are recorded in Omni's payroll register. The $35.00 Other column total identified with the letter *B* is withheld to buy savings bonds for employees. The $20.00 total identified with the letters *UW* is withheld for employee United Way pledges. Until these amounts have been paid by the employer, they are liabilities of the business. U.S. Savings Bonds Payable is credited for $35.00. United Way Donations Payable is credited for $20.00.

The Net Pay column total, $2,989.02, is the net amount paid to employees. Cash is credited for $2,989.02. A check for the total net pay amount, $2,989.02, is written on Omni's general checking account and is deposited in a special payroll checking account. Individual payroll checks are then written on the special payroll checking account.

## JOURNALIZING PAYMENT OF A PAYROLL

**1.** Date **2.** Account Debited **3.** Check Number **4.** Amount Debited **5.** Amount Paid to Employees

PAGE 24 — JOURNAL — PAGE 24

| | DATE | | ACCOUNT TITLE | DOC. NO. | POST. REF. | GENERAL DEBIT (1) | GENERAL CREDIT (2) | CASH DEBIT (10) | CASH CREDIT (11) | |
|---|---|---|---|---|---|---|---|---|---|---|
| 21 | | 15 | *Salary Expense* | *C312* | | 3803 75 | | | 2989 02 | 21 |
| 22 | | | *Employee Income Tax Payable* | | | | 273 00 | | | 22 |
| 23 | | | *Social Security Tax Payable* | | | | 247 26 | | | 23 |
| 24 | | | *Medicare Tax Payable* | | | | 57 07 | | | 24 |
| 25 | | | *Health Insurance Prem. Payable* | | | | 182 40 | | | 25 |
| 26 | | | *U. S. Savings Bonds Payable* | | | | 35 00 | | | 26 |
| 27 | | | *United Way Donations Payable* | | | | 20 00 | | | 27 |

**6.** Accounts Credited **7.** Amounts Credited

Omni Import journalized the company's payroll for the semimonthly period ended December 15, 20—.

***December 15. Paid cash for semimonthly payroll, $2,989.02 (total payroll, $3,803.75, less deductions: employee income tax, $273.00; social security tax, $247.26; Medicare tax, $57.07; health insurance premiums, $182.40; U.S. Savings Bonds, $35.00; United Way donations, $20.00). Check No. 312.***

Amounts recorded in the General columns of a journal are posted individually to general ledger accounts. The credit to Cash, $2,989.02, is not posted separately to the cash account. The amount is included in the journal's Cash Credit column total that is posted at the end of the month. The same procedures are followed to post this journal entry to the appropriate accounts as were described in Chapter 12.

**STEPS**

### Journalizing payment of a payroll

1. Write the date, *15,* in the Date column.
2. Write the title of the account debited, *Salary Expense,* in the Account Title column.
3. Write the check number, *C312,* in the Doc. No. column.
4. Write the amount debited to Salary Expense, *$3,803.75,* in the General Debit column.
5. On the same line, write the total amount paid to employees, *$2,989.02,* in the Cash Credit column.
6. On the next six lines, write the titles of the accounts credited, *Employee Income Tax Payable, Social Security Tax Payable, Medicare Tax Payable, Health Insurance Premiums Payable, U.S. Savings Bonds Payable,* and *United Way Donations Payable,* in the Account Title column.
7. On the same six lines, write the amounts credited to the corresponding liability accounts, *$273.00, $247.26, $57.07, $182.40, $35.00,* and *$20.00,* in the General Credit column.

**REMEMBER**

Total Earnings is the debit amount for Salary Expense. Net Pay is the credit amount for cash.

## AUDIT YOUR UNDERSTANDING

1. What account title is used to journalize the Total Earnings column of the payroll register?
2. What account title is used to journalize the Federal Income Tax column of the payroll register?
3. What account title is used to journalize the Social Security Tax column of the payroll register?
4. What account title is used to journalize the Medicare Tax column of the payroll register?

## WORK TOGETHER

### Recording a payroll

Metro Company's payroll register has the following totals for the semimonthly pay period, July 1–15 of the current year.

T accounts and a journal page are provided in the *Working Papers*. Your instructor will guide you through the following examples.

| Total Earnings | Federal Income Tax Withheld | Social Security Tax Withheld | Medicare Tax Withheld |
|---|---|---|---|
| $12,600.00 | $1,386.00 | $819.00 | $189.00 |

5. Use the T accounts provided to analyze Metro's July 1–15 payroll.
6. Journalize the payment of Metro's July 1–15 payroll on page 15 of the journal. The payroll was paid by Check No. 455 on July 15 of the current year.

## ON YOUR OWN

### Recording a payroll

Metro Company's payroll register has the following totals for the semimonthly pay period, July 16–31 of the current year.

T accounts and a journal page are provided in the *Working Papers*. Work independently to complete these problems.

| Total Earnings | Federal Income Tax Withheld | Social Security Tax Withheld | Medicare Tax Withheld |
|---|---|---|---|
| $12,950.00 | $1,424.50 | $841.75 | $194.25 |

7. Use the T accounts provided to analyze Metro's July 16–31 payroll.
8. Journalize the payment of Metro's July 16–31 payroll on page 16 of a journal. The payroll was paid by Check No. 483 on July 31 of the current year.

# 14-2 Recording Employer Payroll Taxes

## CALCULATING EMPLOYER PAYROLL TAXES

Employers must pay to the government the taxes withheld from employee earnings. Omni Import has withheld federal income tax, social security tax, and Medicare tax from employee salaries. The amounts withheld are liabilities to the business until they are actually paid to the government. In addition, employers must pay several of their own payroll taxes. Employer payroll taxes are business expenses.

Most employers must pay four separate payroll taxes. These taxes are (1) employer social security tax, (2) Medicare tax, (3) federal unemployment tax, and (4) state unemployment tax. Employer payroll taxes expense is based on a percentage of employee earnings.

### Employer Social Security and Medicare Taxes

The social security and Medicare taxes are the only payroll taxes paid by *both* the employees and the employer. Omni withheld $247.26 in social security tax and $57.07 in Medicare tax from employee wages for the pay period ended December 15. Omni owes the same amount of social security and Medicare taxes as the amount withheld from employees. Therefore, Omni's social security and Medicare taxes for the pay period ended December 15 are also $247.26 and $57.07 respectively.

Congress sets the social security and Medicare tax rates for employees and employers. Periodically, Congress may change the tax rates and tax base. The social security tax rate and base used in this text are 6.5% of earnings up to a maximum of $65,400.00 in each calendar year. Medicare does not have a tax base. Therefore, Medicare tax is calculated on total employee earnings. The Medicare tax rate used in this text is 1.5% of total employee earnings.

**REMEMBER**

Employers must pay four taxes on employee earnings—social security tax, Medicare tax, federal unemployment tax, and state unemployment tax.

## UNEMPLOYMENT TAXABLE EARNINGS

| OMNI IMPORT<br>Taxable Earnings<br>for December 15, 20—, Pay Period | | | |
|---|---|---|---|
| | Accumulated Earnings as of Nov. 30, 20-- | Total Earnings for Dec. 15, 20-- Pay Period | Unemployment Taxable Earnings |
| Aranda, Susan A. ...... | $21,115.00 | $ 968.00 | — |
| Drew, Paul S. ......... | 2,595.25 | 105.00 | $105.00 |
| Hakala, Erik D. ...... | 13,518.00 | 608.60 | — |
| Mendel, Ann M. ...... | 2,030.00 | 78.75 | 78.75 |
| Selby, Rick E. ........ | 22,746.00 | 1,137.00 | — |
| Young, Justin L. ....... | 19,816.00 | 906.40 | — |
| | | | $183.75 |

**1.** Enter accumulated earnings and total earnings for each employee.

**2.** Enter unemployment taxable earnings.

**3.** Total the unemployment taxable earnings column.

Federal unemployment insurance laws require that employers pay taxes for unemployment compensation. These tax funds are used to pay workers benefits for limited periods of unemployment and to administer the unemployment compensation program.

The total earnings subject to unemployment tax is referred to as unemployment taxable earnings. The unemployment tax is applied to the first $7,000.00 earned by each employee for each calendar year. The amount of unemployment taxable earnings for Omni's pay period ended December 15, 20—, is shown in the illustration.

### STEPS: Calculating unemployment taxable earnings

**1.** For each employee, enter accumulated earnings as of November 30 and total earnings for the December 15 pay period. These amounts are taken from each employee earnings record. Rick E. Selby's accumulated earnings as of November 30, *$22,746.00,* are recorded in the first column. His total earnings for the December 15 pay period, *$1,137.00,* are recorded in the second column.

**2.** Enter unemployment taxable earnings for the pay period in the Unemployment Taxable Earnings column for employees whose accumulated earnings are less than $7,000.00. The November 30 accumulated earnings for Paul S. Drew, *$2,595.25,* are less than $7,000.00. Therefore, his total earnings for the December 15 pay period, *$105.00,* are subject to unemployment tax and are recorded in the Unemployment Taxable Earnings column. Since the accumulated earnings for Mr. Selby are greater than $7,000.00, none of his current earnings are subject to unemployment tax. Thus, the amount of unemployment taxable earnings recorded in the third column is zero, which is represented by a dash.

**3.** Total the Unemployment Taxable Earnings column. This total amount, *$183.75,* is used to calculate the unemployment tax.

# UNEMPLOYMENT TAXES

Omni Import pays two unemployment taxes, federal unemployment tax and state unemployment tax.

### Federal Unemployment Tax

A federal tax used for state and federal administrative expenses of the unemployment program is called **federal unemployment tax.** The federal unemployment tax is 6.2% of the first $7,000.00 earned by each employee. An employer generally can deduct from federal unemployment payments the amounts paid to state unemployment funds. This deduction cannot be more than 5.4% of taxable earnings. The effective federal unemployment tax rate in most states is, therefore, 0.8% on the first $7,000.00 earned by each employee. (Federal, 6.2% − deductible for state, 5.4% = 0.8%.) All of the unemployment tax on the first $7,000.00 of salary is paid by the employer.

Omni's federal unemployment tax for the pay period ended December 15, 20—, is calculated as shown.

| Unemployment Taxable Earnings | × | Federal Unemployment Tax Rate | = | Federal Unemployment Tax |
|---|---|---|---|---|
| $183.75 | × | 0.8% | = | $1.47 |

### State Unemployment Tax

A state tax used to pay benefits to unemployed workers is called **state unemployment tax.** The Social Security Act specifies certain standards for unemployment compensation laws. Therefore, a high degree of uniformity exists in state unemployment laws. However, details of state unemployment laws do differ. Because of these differences, employers must know the requirements of the states in which they operate.

Most states require that employers pay unemployment tax of 5.4% on the first $7,000.00 earned by each employee. The unemployment taxable earnings used to calculate the federal unemployment tax are also used to calculate the state unemployment tax. Omni's state unemployment tax for the pay period ended December 15, 20—, is calculated as shown.

| Unemployment Taxable Earnings | × | State Unemployment Tax Rate | = | State Unemployment Tax |
|---|---|---|---|---|
| $183.75 | × | 5.4% | = | $9.92 |

# JOURNALIZING EMPLOYER PAYROLL TAXES

1. Date 2. Account Debited 3. Memorandum Number 4. Amount Debited

PAGE 24 — JOURNAL — PAGE 24

| | DATE | ACCOUNT TITLE | DOC. NO. | POST. REF. | GENERAL (1) DEBIT | GENERAL (2) CREDIT | CASH (10) DEBIT | CASH (11) CREDIT | |
|---|---|---|---|---|---|---|---|---|---|
| 28 | 15 | *Payroll Taxes Expense* | *M63* | | *315 72* | | | | 28 |
| 29 | | *Social Security Tax Payable* | | | | *247 26* | | | 29 |
| 30 | | *Medicare Tax Payable* | | | | *57 07* | | | 30 |
| 31 | | *Unemployment Tax Payable—Federal* | | | | *1 47* | | | 31 |
| 32 | | *Unemployment Tax Payable—State* | | | | *9 92* | | | 32 |

5. Accounts Credited 6. Amounts Credited

Employer payroll taxes are paid to the government at a later date. However, the liability is incurred when salaries are paid. Therefore, the transaction to record employer payroll taxes expense is journalized on the same date the payroll is journalized. The salary expense and the employer payroll taxes expense are, therefore, both recorded in the same accounting period.

***December 15. Recorded employer payroll taxes expense, $315.72, for the semimonthly pay period ended December 15. Taxes owed are: social security tax, $247.26; Medicare tax, $57.07; federal unemployment tax, $1.47; state unemployment tax, $9.92. Memorandum No. 63.***

Payroll Taxes Expense is debited for $315.72 to show the increase in the balance of this expense account. Four liability accounts are credited to show the increase in payroll tax liabilities.

| Payroll Taxes Expense | |
|---|---|
| 315.72 | |

| Social Security Tax Payable | |
|---|---|
| | 247.26 |

| Medicare Tax Payable | |
|---|---|
| | 57.07 |

| Unemployment Tax Payable—Federal | |
|---|---|
| | 1.47 |

| Unemployment Tax Payable—State | |
|---|---|
| | 9.92 |

Amounts recorded in the General columns of the journal are posted individually to general ledger accounts. The same procedures are followed to post this journal entry to the appropriate accounts as were described in Chapter 12.

## STEPS: Journalizing employer payroll taxes

1. Write the date, *15,* in the Date column.
2. Write the title of the expense account debited, *Payroll Taxes Expense,* in the Account Title column.
3. Write the memorandum number, *M63,* in the Doc. No. column.
4. Write the debit amount, *$315.72,* in the General Debit column.
5. Write the titles of the liability accounts credited, *Social Security Tax Payable, Medicare Tax Payable, Unemployment Tax Payable—Federal,* and *Unemployment Tax Payable—State,* on the next four lines of the Account Title column.
6. Write the credit amounts, *$247.26, $57.07, $1.47,* and *$9.92,* respectively, in the General Credit column.

## TERMS REVIEW

federal unemployment tax

state unemployment tax

## AUDIT YOUR UNDERSTANDING

1. What is the tax rate Omni Import must pay on employees for each of the following taxes: social security, Medicare, federal unemployment, and state unemployment?
2. What is the amount of each employee's earnings that is subject to federal and state unemployment taxes at Omni Import?

## WORK TOGETHER

### Recording employer payroll taxes

Payroll information taken from employee earnings records is given below. A form and journal page are provided in the *Working Papers.* Your instructor will guide you through the following examples.

| Employee Name | Accumulated Earnings, April 30 | Total Earnings for May 1–15 Pay Period |
|---|---|---|
| Beltran, Tamela C. | $5,100.00 | $637.50 |
| Cintron, Irma V. | 7,350.00 | 920.00 |

3. Calculate the amount of earnings subject to unemployment taxes. Unemployment taxes are owed on the first $7,000.00 of earnings for each employee.
4. Calculate the amount of employer payroll taxes owed for the May 1–15 pay period. Use the employer payroll tax rates shown in this chapter.
5. Journalize the employer's payroll taxes for the May 1–15 pay period on May 15 of the current year. Use journal page 10 and Memorandum No. 46.

## ON YOUR OWN

### Recording employer payroll taxes

Payroll information taken from employee earnings records is given below. A form and journal page are provided in the *Working Papers.* Work independently to complete these problems.

| Employee Name | Accumulated Earnings, May 31 | Total Earnings for June 1–15 Pay Period |
|---|---|---|
| Cowaski, Renee Y. | $ 5,730.00 | $ 720.00 |
| LeCrone, Mark J. | 10,500.00 | 1,320.00 |

6. Calculate the amount of earnings subject to unemployment taxes. Unemployment taxes are owed on the first $7,000.00 of earnings for each employee.
7. Calculate the amount of employer payroll taxes owed for the June 1–15 pay period. Use the employer payroll tax rates shown in this chapter.
8. Journalize the employer's payroll taxes for the June 1–15 pay period on June 15 of the current year. Use journal page 12 and Memorandum No. 52.

# 14-3 Reporting Withholding and Payroll Taxes

## EMPLOYER ANNUAL REPORT TO EMPLOYEES OF TAXES WITHHELD

| a Control number | 22222 | Void ☐ | For Official Use Only ▶ OMB No. 1545-0008 |
|---|---|---|---|
| b Employer's identification number 31-0429632 | | 1 Wages, tips, other compensation 24,843.00 | 2 Federal income tax withheld 1,152.00 |
| c Employer's name, address, and ZIP code<br>Omni Import<br>1374 Parklane<br>Ashton, RI 02805 | | 3 Social security wages 24,843.00 | 4 Social security tax withheld 1,614.80 |
| | | 5 Medicare wages and tips 24,843.00 | 6 Medicare tax withheld 372.65 |
| | | 7 Social security tips | 8 Allocated tips |
| d Employee's social security number 450-70-6432 | | 9 Advanced EIC payment | 10 Dependent care benefits |
| e Employee's name (first, middle initial, last) Rick E. Selby | | 11 Nonqualified plans | 12 Benefits included in box 1 |
| 1625 Northland Drive<br>Ashton, RI 02805 | | 13 See Instrs. for box 13 | 14 Other |
| f Employee's address and ZIP code | | 15 Statutory employee ☐ Deceased ☐ Pension plan ☐ Legal rep. ☐ Hshld. emp. ☐ Subtotal ☐ Deferred compensation ☐ | |

| 16 State | Employer's state I.D. No. | 17 State wages, tips, etc. | 18 State income tax | 19 Locality name | 20 Local wages, tips, etc. | 21 Local income tax |
|---|---|---|---|---|---|---|
| | | | | | | |
| | | | | | | |

Form **W-2** Wage and Tax Statement **20—**

Copy A For Social Security Administration

39-1754529 Department of the Treasury—Internal Revenue Service
For Paperwork Reduction Act Notice, see separate instructions.

Each employer who withholds income tax, social security tax, and Medicare tax from employee earnings must furnish each employee with an annual report of these withholdings. The report shows total year's earnings and the amounts withheld for taxes for an employee. These amounts are obtained from the employee earnings records. The report is prepared on the Internal Revenue Service Form W-2, Wage and Tax Statement. The Form W-2 prepared by Omni Import for Rick E. Selby is shown.

Employers are required to furnish Form W-2 to each employee by January 31 of the next year. If an employee ends employment before December 31, Form W-2 must be furnished within 30 days of the last date of employment.

Four copies (A to D) of Form W-2 are prepared for each employee. Copies B and C are given to the employee. The employee attaches Copy B to a personal federal income tax return and keeps Copy C for a personal record. The employer sends Copy A to the Social Security Administration and keeps Copy D for the business's records.

Businesses in states with state income tax must prepare additional copies of Form W-2. The employee attaches the additional copy to the personal state income tax return.

# EMPLOYER'S QUARTERLY FEDERAL TAX RETURN

1. Heading

Form **941** (Rev. January 20--) Department of the Treasury Internal Revenue Service

4141

## Employer's Quarterly Federal Tax Return

► See separate instructions for information on completing this return.

Please type or print.

Enter state code for state in which deposits made . ► (see page 3 of instructions).

| Name (as distinguished from trade name) | Date quarter ended | OMB No. 1545-0029 Expires 5-31-93 |
|---|---|---|
| Omni Import | December 31, 20-- | T |
| Trade name, if any | Employer identification number | FF |
| | 31-0429632 | FD |
| Address (number and street) | City, state, and ZIP code | FP |
| 1374 Parklane | Ashton, RI 02805 | I |
| | | T |

If address is different from prior return, check here ► ☐

IRS Use

If you do not have to file returns in the future, check here . . . ► ☐ and enter date final wages paid. . . . ►

If you are a seasonal employer, see **Seasonal employers** on page 1 of the instructions and check here . . . ► ☐

| Line | Description | | Line | Amount |
|---|---|---|---|---|
| 1 | Number of employees (except household) employed in the pay period that includes March 12th | | 1 | 6 |
| 2 | Total wages and tips subject to withholding, plus other compensation | | 2 | $22,575 00 |
| 3 | Total income tax withheld from wages, tips, and sick pay | | 3 | 1,614 00 |
| 4 | Adjustment of withheld income tax for preceding quarters of calendar year | | 4 | -0- |
| 5 | Adjusted total of income tax withheld (line 3 as adjusted by line 4—see instructions) | | 5 | 1,614 00 |
| 6 | Taxable social security wages | 6a $ 22,575 00 × 13% (.13) = | 6b | 2,934 75 |
| | Taxable social security tips | 6c $ -0- × 13% (.13) = | 6d | -0- |
| 7 | Taxable Medicare wages and tips | 7a $ 22,575 00 × 3% (.03) = | 7b | 677 25 |
| 8 | Total social security and Medicare taxes (add lines 6b, 6d, and 7b). Check here if wages are not subject to social security and/or Medicare tax. ► ☐ | | 8 | 3,612 00 |
| 9 | Adjustment of social security and Medicare taxes (see instructions for required explanation) Sick Pay $ ____ ± Fractions of Cents $ ____ ± Other $ ____ = | | 9 | -0- |
| 10 | Adjusted total of social security and Medicare taxes (line 8 as adjusted by line 9—see instructions) | | 10 | 3,612 00 |
| 11 | **Total taxes** (add lines 5 and 10) | | 11 | 5,226 00 |
| 12 | Advance earned income credit (EIC) payments made to employees | | 12 | -0- |
| 13 | Net taxes (subtract line 12 from line 11). This should equal line 17, column (d) below (or line D of Schedule B (Form 941)) | | 13 | 5,226 00 |
| 14 | Total deposits for quarter, including overpayment applied from a prior quarter | | 14 | 5,226 00 |
| 15 | **Balance due** (subtract line 14 from 13). See instructions | | 15 | -0- |

16 **Overpayment,** if line 14 is more than 13, enter excess here ► $ ________

and check if to be: ☐ Applied to next return **OR** ☐ Refunded.

- **All filers:** If line 13 is less than $500. you need not complete line 17 or Schedule B.
- **Semiweekly schedule depositors:** Complete Schedule B and check here . . . ► ☐
- **Monthly schedule depositors:** Complete line 17, columns (a) through (d), and check here. . . . ► ☒

**17 Monthly Summary of Federal Tax Liability**

| (a) First month liability | (b) Second month liability | (c) Third month liability | (d) Total liability for quarter |
|---|---|---|---|
| $1,753.88 | $1,717.30 | $1,754.82 | $5,226.00 |

**Sign Here** Under penalties of perjury, I declare that I have examined this return, including accompanying schedules and statements, and to the best of my knowledge and belief, it is true, correct, and complete.

Signature ► *Karl Koehn* Print Your Name and Title ► Karl Koehn, Partner Date ► 1/24/--

For Paperwork Reduction Act Notice, see page 2. Cat. No. 17001Z Form 941

2. Number of Employees

3. Total Quarterly Earnings

4. Income Tax Withheld

5. Employee and Employer Social Security and Medicare Taxes

6. Social Security plus Medicare Taxes

7. Total Taxes

8. Total Taxes for Each Month

9. Total Taxes

## PREPARING EMPLOYER'S QUARTERLY FEDERAL TAX RETURN

Each employer is required by law to periodically report the payroll taxes withheld from employee salaries and the employer payroll taxes due the government. Some reports are submitted quarterly and others, annually.

Each employer must file a quarterly federal tax return showing the federal income tax, social security tax, and Medicare tax due the government. This information is submitted on Form 941, Employer's Quarterly Federal Tax Return. Form 941 is filed before the last day of the month following the end of a quarter. Omni Import's Form 941 for the quarter ended December 31 is shown on the previous page. The information needed to prepare Form 941 is obtained from employee earnings records.

### STEPS Preparing an employer's quarterly federal tax return

1. Enter company name, address, employer identification number, date quarter ended, and state code in the heading section of Form 941.
2. Enter number of employees, *6,* on line 1 of Form 941.
3. Enter total quarterly earnings, *$22,575.00,* on line 2. This amount is the sum of the fourth quarter total earnings of all employees. Total earnings, *$22,575.00,* is also recorded on lines 6a and 7a.
4. Enter the income tax withheld, *$1,614.00,* on line 3. The amount is the total of the fourth quarter federal income tax withheld from all employees. The same amount is entered on line 5.
5. Enter the quarterly employee and employer social security taxes, *$2,934.75,* and Medicare taxes, *$677.25,* on lines 6b and 7b, respectively. The taxes due are calculated as shown.

| | Total Earnings | × | Tax Rate | = | Tax |
|---|---|---|---|---|---|
| Social Security | $22,575.00 | × | 13% | = | $2,934.75 |
| Medicare | $22,575.00 | × | 3% | = | $ 677.25 |

The 13% tax rate is the sum of the *employee* 6.5% and the *employer* 6.5% social security tax rates. The 3% tax rate is the sum of the *employee* 1.5% and the *employer* 1.5% Medicare tax rates.

6. Enter the total social security tax plus Medicare tax, *$3,612.00* ($2,934.75 + $677.25 = $3,612.00), on line 8. Since Omni has no adjustment to its taxes, the total is also entered on line 10.
7. Enter the total taxes, *$5,226.00,* on lines 11 and 13. Omni is required to pay the federal government the sum of the social security tax, Medicare tax, and federal income tax withheld.
8. Enter on lines 17a, 17b, and 17c the total amounts of employee income tax withheld and employee and employer social security and Medicare taxes for each month of the quarter. For the month of December, the amount of taxes owed is calculated as shown and recorded on line 17c.

| | Federal Income Tax Withheld | + | Employee Social Security and Medicare Tax | + | Employer Social Security and Medicare Tax | = | Federal Tax Liability |
|---|---|---|---|---|---|---|---|
| Dec. 1–15 | $273.00 | + | $304.33 | + | $304.33 | = | $ 881.66 |
| Dec. 16–31 | $269.00 | + | $302.08 | + | $302.08 | = | $ 873.16 |
| Totals | $542.00 | + | $606.41 | + | $606.41 | = | $1,754.82 |

9. Enter the total quarterly withholding and payroll taxes, *$5,226.00,* on line 17d. This total is the sum of the three monthly totals reported on line 17 ($1,753.88 + $1,717.30 + $1,754.82 = $5,226.00).

DO NOT STAPLE

| a Control number | 33333 | For Official Use Only ► OMB No. 1545-0008 | |
|---|---|---|---|
| b Kind of Payer: 941 [X] Military [ ] 943 [ ] CT-1 [ ] Hshld. [ ] Medicare govt. emp. [ ] | | 1 Wages, tips, other compensation 89,400.00 | 2 Federal income tax withheld 6,416.00 |
| | | 3 Social security wages 89,400.00 | 4 Social security tax withheld 5,811.00 |
| c Total number of statements | d Establishment number | 5 Medicare wages and tips 89,400.00 | 6 Medicare tax withheld 1,341.00 |
| e Employer's identification number 31-0429632 | | 7 Social security tips | 8 Allocated tips |
| f Employer's name Omni Import | | 9 Advance EIC payments | 10 Dependent care benefits |
| 1374 Parklane Ashton, RI 02805 | | 11 Nonqualified plans | 12 Deferred compensation |
| | | 13 Adjusted total social security wages and tips 89,400.00 | |
| g Employer's address and ZIP code | | 14 Adjusted total Medicare wages and tips 89,400.00 | |
| h Other EIN used this year | | 15 Income tax withheld by third-party payer | |
| i Employer's state I.D. No. | | | |

Under penalties of perjury, I declare that I have examined this return and accompanying documents, and, to the best of my knowledge and belief, they are true, correct, and complete.

Signature ► *Karl Koehn* Title ► *Partner* Date ► 2/27/--

Telephone number (401) 555-9368

Form **W-3 Transmittal of Income and Tax Statements 20—** Department of the Treasury Internal Revenue Service

Form W-3, Transmittal of Wage and Tax Statements, is sent to the Social Security Administration by February 28 each year. Form W-3 reports the previous year's earnings and payroll taxes withheld for all employees. Attached to Form W-3 is Copy A of each employee Form W-2. Employers with more than 250 employees must send the information to the Internal Revenue Service in computer files rather than the actual Forms W-2 and W-3.

At the end of a calendar year, employers must also report to the federal and state governments a summary of all earnings paid to employees during the twelve months.

## Global Perspective

### International Quality Standards

The quality of products is a major concern for industry, especially when trading those products among nations. In order for some products to be used in other nations, they must be standardized. In this sense, a *standard* is a technical specification or other precise criteria used consistently in the production of a product.

Companies who intend to sell their products globally must produce them in compliance with the standards set for the industry. International standardization has been established for many fields, including information processing and communications, textiles, packaging, energy production, shipbuilding, and banking and financial services. Standardization will continue to grow in importance for all sectors of business activity.

## Audit Your Understanding

1. When must employers furnish a W-2 statement to their employees?
2. What taxes are included in the quarterly federal tax return filed by the employer?

## Work Together

### Reporting withholding and payroll taxes

A Form 941, Employer's Quarterly Federal Tax Return, is given in the *Working Papers.* Your instructor will guide you through the following example. The following data is for Digital Supplies.

| Date Paid | Total Earnings | Federal Income Tax Withheld | Employee Social Security Tax Withheld | Employee Medicare Tax Withheld |
|---|---|---|---|---|
| Jan. 31 | $10,440.00 | $1,148.00 | $678.60 | $156.60 |
| Feb. 28 | 10,950.00 | 1,204.00 | 711.75 | 164.25 |
| Mar. 31 | 12,600.00 | 1,386.00 | 819.00 | 189.00 |

- **a.** Company address: 625 Sandpiper Street, Ormond Beach, Florida 32074-4060
- **b.** Employer identification number: 70-7818356
- **c.** Number of employees: 6

3. Prepare a Form 941 for Digital Supplies for the first quarter of the current year. Use the preparation date of April 24. Sign your name as a partner of the company.

## On Your Own

### Reporting withholding and payroll taxes

A Form 941, Employer's Quarterly Federal Tax Return, is given in the *Working Papers.* Work independently to complete this problem. The following data is for Digital Supplies. Company address, employer identification number, and number of employees are the same as in Work Together.

| Date Paid | Total Earnings | Federal Income Tax Withheld | Employee Social Security Tax Withheld | Employee Medicare Tax Withheld |
|---|---|---|---|---|
| Apr. 30 | $11,600.00 | $1,276.00 | $754.00 | $174.00 |
| May 31 | 12,160.00 | 1,338.00 | 790.40 | 182.40 |
| June 30 | 13,986.00 | 1,538.00 | 909.09 | 209.79 |

4. Prepare a Form 941 for Digital Supplies for the second quarter of the current year. Use the preparation date of July 22. Sign your name as a partner of the company.

# 14-4 Paying Withholding and Payroll Taxes

## PAYING THE LIABILITY FOR EMPLOYEE INCOME TAX, SOCIAL SECURITY TAX, AND MEDICARE TAX

Employers must pay to the federal, state, and local governments all payroll taxes withheld from employee earnings as well as the employer payroll taxes. The frequency of payments is determined by the amount owed.

Frequency and method of payment of withheld employees' federal income tax, social security tax, and Medicare tax plus employer's social security tax and Medicare tax is determined by the total amount of tax paid each year. If the total amount paid in the previous four quarters is $50,000.00 or less, a business is classified as a monthly schedule depositor. A monthly schedule depositor must pay the total amount due to an authorized financial institution by the 15th day of the following month accompanied by Form 8109, Federal Tax Deposit Coupon. A semiweekly schedule depositor must deposit amounts accumulated on salary payments made on Saturday, Sunday, Monday, or Tuesday by the following Friday. For salary payments made on Wednesday, Thursday, or Friday, payment must be made by the following Wednesday. Payment must be made through an authorized agent to the Internal Revenue Service by Electronic Federal Tax Payment System (EFTPS).

There are two exceptions to the standard tax payment schedules: (1) If less than $500.00 tax liability is accumulated during a three-month quarter, the deposit may be paid at the end of the month following the end of the quarter. (2) If a tax liability of $100,000.00 or more is accumulated on any day, the amount must be deposited on the next banking day.

Omni Import is classified as a monthly depositor. So the payroll taxes are deposited with a local authorized financial institution by the 15th day of the following month accompanied by Form 8109.

**F.Y.I.**

*Methods of paying payroll taxes described in this chapter were in effect when this textbook was written. Businesses with payroll tax liabilities of more than $20,000.00 in 1997 were required to pay electronically using the Electronic Federal Tax Payment System by 1999. There will probably be a time when all businesses will be required to pay payroll taxes electronically.*

**REMEMBER**

For monthly schedule depositor businesses, a deposit coupon, Form 8109, must accompany payment of employee income tax, social security, and Medicare tax to the federal government. For semiweekly schedule depositor businesses, payment must be made electronically through an automated clearing agent.

## FORM 8109, FEDERAL DEPOSIT COUPON

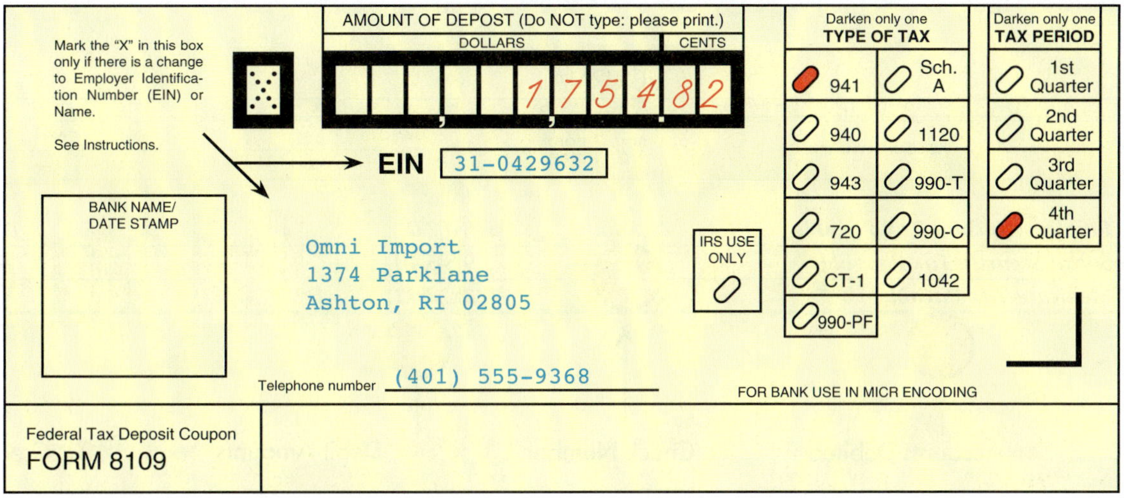
Mark the "X" in this box only if there is a change to Employer Identification Number (EIN) or Name.

See Instructions.

AMOUNT OF DEPOST (Do NOT type: please print.)

DOLLARS | CENTS

1,754.82

EIN 31-0429632

BANK NAME/ DATE STAMP

Omni Import
1374 Parklane
Ashton, RI 02805

IRS USE ONLY

Telephone number (401) 555-9368

Darken only one TYPE OF TAX

941 (marked), Sch. A, 940, 1120, 943, 990-T, 720, 990-C, CT-1, 1042, 990-PF

Darken only one TAX PERIOD

1st Quarter, 2nd Quarter, 3rd Quarter, 4th Quarter (marked)

FOR BANK USE IN MICR ENCODING

Federal Tax Deposit Coupon
FORM 8109

In December, Omni Import withheld $542.00 from employee salaries for federal income taxes. The December liability for social security tax is $985.40 and for Medicare tax is $227.42. These amounts include both the employer share and the amounts withheld from employees. Omni's federal tax payment, $1,754.82, is sent January 15 to an authorized bank with Form 8109 as shown.

The type of tax—federal income, social security, and Medicare taxes—is identified by marking the 941 circle. These taxes are reported to the government using Form 941. The calendar quarter is identified on the right side of the form.

**FYI**

*Tax rates change periodically. Always check the most current tax information before calculating an amount for any tax.*

**REMEMBER**

Social security tax and Medicare tax are the only payroll taxes paid by both the employer and employee. A business pays the same amount of social security tax and Medicare tax as the amount withheld from employees.

# JOURNALIZING PAYMENT OF LIABILITY FOR EMPLOYEE INCOME TAX, SOCIAL SECURITY TAX, AND MEDICARE TAX

JOURNAL — PAGE 27

| | DATE | ACCOUNT TITLE | DOC. NO. | POST. REF. | GENERAL DEBIT (1) | GENERAL CREDIT (2) | CASH DEBIT (10) | CASH CREDIT (11) | |
|---|---|---|---|---|---|---|---|---|---|
| 25 | 15 | Employee Income Tax Payable | C330 | | 542 00 | | | 1 754 82 | 25 |
| 26 | | Social Security Tax Payable | | | 985 40 | | | | 26 |
| 27 | | Medicare Tax Payable | | | 227 42 | | | | 27 |

**1.** Date **2.** Accounts Debited **3.** Check Number **4.** Debit Amounts **5.** Credit Amount

***January 15. Paid cash for liability for employee income tax, $542.00; social security tax, $985.40; and Medicare tax, $227.42; total, $1,754.82. Check No. 330.***

The balances of the liability accounts are reduced by this transaction. Therefore, Employee Income Tax Payable is debited for $542.00. Social Security Tax Payable is debited for $985.40. Medicare Tax Payable is debited for $227.42. The balance of Cash is decreased by a credit for the total payment, $1,754.82.

| Employee Income Tax Payable | |
|---|---|
| 542.00 | |

| Social Security Tax Payable | |
|---|---|
| 985.40 | |

| Medicare Tax Payable | |
|---|---|
| 227.42 | |

| Cash | |
|---|---|
| | 1,754.82 |

**FYI**

*Semimonthly pay periods are paid twice a month. Biweekly pay periods are paid every two weeks.*

**STEPS**

## Journalizing a payment of liability for employee income tax, social security tax, and Medicare tax

1. Write the date, *15,* in the Date column.
2. Write the titles of the three accounts debited, *Employee Income Tax Payable, Social Security Tax Payable,* and *Medicare Tax Payable,* in the Account Title column.
3. Write the check number, *C330,* in the Doc. No. column.
4. Write the three debit amounts, *$542.00, $985.40,* and *$227.42,* in the General Debit column.
5. Write the amount of the credit to Cash, *$1,754.82,* in the Cash Credit column.

## PAYING THE LIABILITY FOR FEDERAL UNEMPLOYMENT TAX

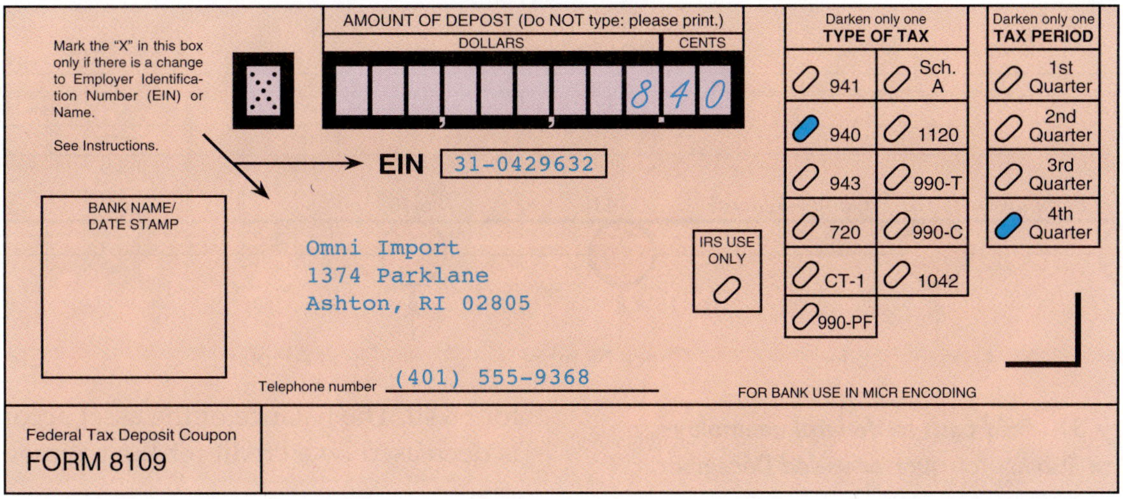
AMOUNT OF DEPOST (Do NOT type: please print.)

DOLLARS | CENTS

8 40

Mark the "X" in this box only if there is a change to Employer Identification Number (EIN) or Name.

See Instructions.

EIN 31-0429632

BANK NAME/ DATE STAMP

Omni Import
1374 Parklane
Ashton, RI 02805

Telephone number (401) 555-9368

IRS USE ONLY

Darken only one TYPE OF TAX

941 | Sch. A | 940 | 1120 | 943 | 990-T | 720 | 990-C | CT-1 | 1042 | 990-PF

Darken only one TAX PERIOD

1st Quarter | 2nd Quarter | 3rd Quarter | 4th Quarter

FOR BANK USE IN MICR ENCODING

Federal Tax Deposit Coupon
FORM 8109

Federal unemployment insurance is paid by the end of the month following each quarter if the liability amount is more than $100. However, all unemployment tax liabilities outstanding at the end of a calendar year should be paid. Federal unemployment tax is paid to the federal government by sending the check to an authorized bank. The payment for federal unemployment tax is similar to the one required for income tax, social security tax, and Medicare tax. Form 8109, Federal Tax Deposit Coupon accompanies the unemployment tax payment. A payment is made each quarter that the liability exceeds $100.00, but no report is due until the end of the year.

Omni's federal unemployment tax liability at the end of December 31 is $8.40. Omni's Form 8109 for the fourth quarter is shown.

The type of tax, federal unemployment tax, is identified by marking the 940 circle since this tax is reported to the government using Form 940. The calendar quarter is identified on the right side of the form.

## JOURNALIZING PAYMENT OF LIABILITY FOR FEDERAL UNEMPLOYMENT TAX

PAGE 28 — JOURNAL — PAGE 28

| | DATE | ACCOUNT TITLE | DOC. NO. | POST. REF. | GENERAL DEBIT (1) | GENERAL CREDIT (2) | CASH DEBIT (10) | CASH CREDIT (11) | |
|---|---|---|---|---|---|---|---|---|---|
| 27 | 31 | *Unemployment Tax Payable—Federal* | *C343* | | *8 40* | | | *8 40* | 27 |
| 28 | | | | | | | | | 28 |

**1.** Date **2.** Account Debited **3.** Check Number **4.** Debit Amount **5.** Credit Amount

***January 31. Paid cash for federal unemployment tax liability for quarter ended December 31, $8.40. Check No. 343.***

| Unemployment Tax Payable—Federal | |
|---|---|
| 8.40 | |

| Cash | |
|---|---|
| | 8.40 |

The balance of the liability account is reduced by this transaction. Therefore, Unemployment Tax Payable—Federal is debited for $8.40. The balance of the asset account, Cash, is decreased by a credit for the payment, $8.40.

### STEPS: Journalizing a payment of liability for federal unemployment tax

1. Write the date, *31,* in the Date column.
2. Write the title of the account debited, *Unemployment Tax Payable—Federal,* in the Account Title column.
3. Write the check number, *C343,* in the Doc. No. column.
4. Write the debit amount, *$8.40,* in the General Debit column.
5. Write the amount of the credit to Cash, *$8.40,* in the Cash Credit column.

## JOURNALIZING PAYMENT OF LIABILITY FOR STATE UNEMPLOYMENT TAX

PAGE 28 — JOURNAL — PAGE 28

| | DATE | ACCOUNT TITLE | DOC. NO. | POST. REF. | GENERAL DEBIT (1) | GENERAL CREDIT (2) | CASH DEBIT (10) | CASH CREDIT (11) | |
|---|---|---|---|---|---|---|---|---|---|
| 28 | 31 | *Unemployment Tax Payable—State* | *C344* | | *56 70* | | | *56 70* | 27 |
| 29 | | | | | | | | | 28 |

**1.** Date **2.** Account Debited **3.** Check Number **4.** Debit Amount **5.** Credit Amount

***January 31. Paid cash for state unemployment tax liability for quarter ended December 31, $56.70. Check No. 344.***

State requirements for reporting and paying state unemployment taxes vary. In general, employers are required to pay the state unemployment tax during the month following each calendar quarter.

## AUDIT YOUR UNDERSTANDING

1. For a monthly schedule depositor, when are payroll taxes paid to the federal government?
2. What are two different uses for Form 8109?

## WORK TOGETHER

### Paying withholding and payroll taxes

A journal page is provided in the *Working Papers.* Your instructor will guide you through the following examples. The following payroll data is for Digital Supplies for the monthly pay period ended March 31 of the current year.

| Date Paid | Federal Income Tax Withheld | Employee Social Security Tax Withheld | Employee Medicare Tax Withheld |
|---|---|---|---|
| Mar. 31 | $1,386.00 | $819.00 | $189.00 |

Credit balances on March 31 for the unemployment tax accounts for the first quarter are as follows: Unemployment Tax Payable—Federal, $100.80; Unemployment Tax Payable—State, $680.40. Digital Supplies pays both unemployment taxes each quarter, regardless of the amount owed.

3. Prepare a journal entry for payment of the withheld taxes. Digital Supplies is classified as a monthly schedule depositor. Date journal page 14 on the day taxes are due to the federal government. Check No. 383.
4. Prepare journal entries for payment of the federal and state unemployment taxes liability. State taxes are due on the same day as federal taxes. Check Nos. 401 and 402.

## ON YOUR OWN

### Paying withholding and payroll taxes

A journal page is provided in the *Working Papers.* Work independently to complete these problems. The following payroll data is for Digital Supplies for the monthly pay period ended June 30 of the current year.

| Date Paid | Federal Income Tax Withheld | Employee Social Security Tax Withheld | Employee Medicare Tax Withheld |
|---|---|---|---|
| June 30 | $1,538.00 | $909.09 | $209.79 |

Credit balances on June 30 for the unemployment tax accounts for the second quarter are as follows: Unemployment Tax Payable—Federal, $108.48; Unemployment Tax Payable—State, $732.24. Digital Supplies pays both unemployment taxes each quarter, regardless of the amount owed.

5. Prepare a journal entry for payment of the withheld taxes. Date journal page 18 on the day taxes are due to the federal government. Check No. 496.
6. Prepare journal entries for payment of the federal and state unemployment taxes liability. State taxes are due on the same day as federal taxes. Check Nos. 515 and 516.

# CHAPTER 14 SUMMARY

*Enrichment Activity*

**Accounting Careers**

*The Professional Code of Conduct of the AICPA forbids public accountants from disclosing any confidential information without the client's permission. There are exceptions to this rule, such as when replying to a subpoena. Why do you think this rule exists?*

After completing this chapter, you can

1. Define important accounting terms related to payroll accounting, taxes, and reports.
2. Identify accounting concepts and practices related to payroll accounting, taxes, and reports.
3. Analyze payroll transactions and record a payroll.
4. Record employer payroll taxes.
5. Prepare selected payroll tax reports.
6. Pay and record withholding and payroll taxes.

## EXPLORE ACCOUNTING

### NET INCOME VS. TAXABLE INCOME

Financial statements should provide important information that is accurate, reliable, comparable, and consistent. Over the years, a set of principles and concepts for maintaining accounting records and preparing financial statements has been developed. These guidelines are known as Generally Accepted Accounting Principles (GAAP). Most businesses use GAAP in preparing their financial statements and determining their net income.

The Internal Revenue Service (IRS) is responsible for collecting money to operate the federal government. Federal income taxes are calculated as a percentage of business or individual income. To accomplish its task, the IRS prepares Internal Revenue Service Regulations.

The objectives of the accounting profession and business community, however, are not necessarily the same as those of the federal government and the IRS. For example, a GAAP concept, Matching Expenses with Revenue, requires that the cost of business equipment be allocated over the usable life of the equipment. However, to encourage businesses to replace equipment more rapidly, IRS Regulations may permit the cost of equipment to be allocated more rapidly. Thus, in a certain year the expense for allocating cost would be greater for tax purposes than for financial reporting purposes. These types of differences create different amounts reported as net income for financial reporting purposes and for tax reporting purposes.

Thus, most businesses follow GAAP in preparing their financial statements but must follow IRS Regulations in preparing their tax returns. As a result, net income on financial statements generally differs from taxable income reported on tax returns.

**Research:** Examine several company annual reports. Study the financial statements and the notes connected with those statements. Is there any information indicating a difference between net income reported on the financial statements and taxable income for tax purposes? What are they, if any?

## 14-1 APPLICATION PROBLEM
### Recording a payroll

Dana's payroll register has the following totals for two semimonthly pay periods, July 1–15 and July 16–31 of the current year.

| Period | Total Earnings | Deductions | | | | | Net Pay |
|---|---|---|---|---|---|---|---|
| | | Federal Income Tax | Social Security Tax | Medicare Tax | Other | Total | |
| July 1–15 . . . . . . . . . . . . | $6,970.00 | $766.00 | $453.05 | $104.55 | B $180.00 | $1,503.60 | $5,466.40 |
| July 16–31 . . . . . . . . . . . | 6,040.00 | 664.00 | 392.60 | 90.60 | B 150.00 | 1,297.20 | 4,742.80 |
| Other Deductions: B—U.S. Savings Bonds | | | | | | | |

***Instructions:***
Journalize payment of the two payrolls on page 15 of the journal given in the *Working Papers*. The first payroll was paid by Check No. 547 on July 15 of the current year. The second payroll was paid by Check No. 568 on July 31 of the current year.

## 14-2 APPLICATION PROBLEM
### Recording employer payroll taxes

Malone's selected payroll information for the two semimonthly pay periods, April 1–15 and April 16–30 of the current year, are given. Forms and a journal are given in the *Working Papers*.

| Employee Name | Accumulated Earnings, March 31 | Total Earnings for April 1–15 Pay Period | Total Earnings for April 16–30 Pay Period |
|---|---|---|---|
| Bolser, Frank T. | $4,860.00 | $ 810.00 | $ 795.00 |
| Denham, Beth R. | 5,670.00 | 945.00 | 980.00 |
| Harjo, Teresa S. | 7,500.00 | 1,250.00 | 1,250.00 |
| Knutzen, John L. | 3,720.00 | 620.00 | 635.00 |
| Prescott, Laura F. | 4,560.00 | 760.00 | 740.00 |
| Schmidt, Ian T. | 6,900.00 | 1,150.00 | 1,125.00 |

Employer payroll tax rates are as follows: social security, 6.5%; Medicare, 1.5%; federal unemployment, 0.8%; state unemployment, 5.4%. Unemployment taxes are owed on the first $7,000.00 of earnings for each employee.

***Instructions:***
1. Calculate the amount of earnings subject to unemployment taxes for the April 1–15 pay period.
2. Calculate the employer payroll tax amounts for the April 1–15 pay period.
3. Journalize the employer payroll taxes on page 16 of a journal. Use the date of April 15 of the current year. The source document is Memorandum No. 69.
4. Calculate the employer payroll taxes for the April 16–30 pay period. Calculate April 15 accumulated earnings by adding total earnings for the April 1–15 pay period to the March 31 accumulated earnings.
5. Journalize the employer payroll taxes on page 16 of a journal. Use the date of April 30 of the current year. The source document is Memorandum No. 76.

## 14-3 APPLICATION PROBLEM
### Reporting withholding and payroll taxes

The following payroll data is for Eagle Toys for the second quarter of the current year.

| Date Paid | Total Earnings | Federal Income Tax Withheld | Employee Social Security Tax Withheld | Employee Medicare Tax Withheld |
|---|---|---|---|---|
| Apr. 30 | $ 9,166.00 | $1,008.00 | $595.79 | $137.49 |
| May 31 | 10,224.00 | 1,125.00 | 664.56 | 153.36 |
| June 30 | 9,872.00 | 1,086.00 | 641.68 | 148.08 |

Additional data:

1. Company address: 784 MacDonald Street, Mesa, AZ 85201
2. Employer identification number: 80-7818356
3. Number of employees: 5
4. Federal tax payments have been made on May 15, June 15, and July 15.

***Instructions:***

Prepare the Form 941, Employer's Quarterly Federal Tax Return, given in the *Working Papers*. Use the date July 21. Sign your name as a partner of the company.

## 14-4 APPLICATION PROBLEM
### Paying withholding and payroll taxes

The following payroll data is for Zimmerman Company for the first quarter of the current year.

| Period | Total Earnings | Federal Income Tax Withheld |
|---|---|---|
| March | $17,552.00 | $1,728.00 |
| First Quarter | $52,210.00 | — |

In addition, total earnings are subject to 6.5% employee and 6.5% employer social security tax, plus 1.5% employee and 1.5% employer Medicare tax. The federal unemployment tax rate is 0.8% and the state unemployment tax rate is 5.4% of total earnings. No total earnings have exceeded the tax base for calculating unemployment taxes.

***Instructions:***

1. Calculate the appropriate liability amount of social security and Medicare taxes for March. Journalize the payment of the withheld taxes on page 8 of the journal given in the *Working Papers*. The taxes were paid by Check No. 813 on April 15 of the current year.
2. Calculate the appropriate federal unemployment tax liability for the first quarter. Journalize payment of this liability in the journal. The tax was paid by Check No. 830 on April 30 of the current year.
3. Calculate the appropriate state unemployment tax liability for the first quarter. Journalize payment of this liability in the journal. The tax was paid by Check No. 831 on April 30 of the current year.

## 14-5 MASTERY PROBLEM
### Journalizing payroll transactions

Travis Athletics completed payroll transactions during the period April 1 to May 15 of the current year. Payroll tax rates are as follows: social security, 6.5%; Medicare, 1.5%; federal unemployment, 0.8%; state unemployment, 5.4%. The company buys savings bonds for employees as accumulated withholdings reach the necessary amount to purchase a bond. No total earnings have exceeded the tax base for calculating unemployment taxes.

***Instructions:***

1. Journalize the following transactions on page 12 of the journal given in the *Working Papers*. Source documents are abbreviated as follows: check, C, and memorandum, M.

***Transactions:***

Apr. 15. Paid cash for liability for employee income tax, $948.00; social security tax, $1,120.60; and Medicare tax, $258.60; total, $2,327.20. C331.

15. Paid cash for semimonthly payroll, $3,618.20 (total payroll, $4,560.00, less deductions: employee income tax, $502.00; social security tax, $296.40; Medicare tax, $68.40; U.S. Savings Bonds, $75.00). C332.

15. Recorded employer payroll taxes expense. M22.

15. Paid cash for U.S. Savings Bonds for employees, $375.00. C333.

30. Paid cash for semimonthly payroll, $3,733.84 (total payroll, $4,702.00, less deductions: employee income tax, $517.00; social security tax, $305.63; Medicare tax, $70.53; U.S. Savings Bonds, $75.00). C351.

30. Recorded employer payroll taxes expense. M26.

30. Paid cash for federal unemployment tax liability for quarter ended March 31, $214.89. C352.

30. Paid cash for state unemployment tax liability for quarter ended March 31, $1,450.51. C353.

2. Prove and rule journal page 12.
3. Journalize the following transactions on page 13 of the journal.

***Transactions:***

May 15. Paid cash for liability for employee income tax, $1,019.00; social security tax, $1,204.06; and Medicare tax, $277.86; total, $2,500.92. C380.

15. Paid cash for semimonthly payroll, $3,491.75 (total payroll, $4,403.00, less deductions: employee income tax, $484.00; social security tax, $286.20; Medicare tax, $66.05; U.S. Savings Bonds, $75.00). C381.

15. Recorded employer payroll taxes expense. M33.

4. Prove and rule journal page 13.

## 14-6 CHALLENGE PROBLEM

### Journalizing and posting payroll transactions

Dozier Spring Water completed payroll transactions during the period January 1 to April 30 of the current year. Payroll tax rates are as follows: social security, 6.5%; Medicare, 1.5%; federal unemployment, 0.8%; and state unemployment, 5.4%. The company buys savings bonds for employees as the accumulated withholdings reach the necessary amount to purchase a bond. No total earnings have exceeded the tax base for calculating unemployment taxes.

The balances in the general ledger as of January 1 of the current year are recorded in the *Working Papers.*

**Chart of Accounts**

| Account Number | Account Title |
|---|---|
| 2120 | Employee Income Tax Payable |
| 2130 | Social Security Tax Payable |
| 2140 | Medicare Tax Payable |

| Account Number | Account Title |
|---|---|
| 2150 | Unemployment Tax Payable—Federal |
| 2160 | Unemployment Tax Payable—State |
| 2180 | U.S. Savings Bonds Payable |
| 6150 | Payroll Taxes Expense |
| 6170 | Salary Expense |

***Instructions:***

1. Journalize the following transactions on page 1 of the journal given in the *Working Papers*. Source documents are abbreviated as follows: check, C, and memorandum, M.

***Transactions:***

Jan. 2. Wrote a check for 12 U.S. Savings Bonds at $25.00 each for employees. C163.

15. Paid the December liability for employee income tax, social security tax, and Medicare tax. C172.

31. Wrote a check for federal unemployment tax liability for quarter ended December 31. C178.

31. Wrote a check for state unemployment tax liability for quarter ended December 31. C179.

31. Paid January payroll, $9,524.44 (total payroll, $11,882.00, less deductions: employee income tax, $1,307.00; social security tax, $772.33; Medicare tax, $178.23; U.S. Savings Bonds, $100.00). C184.

31. Recorded employer payroll taxes expense. M98.

**Posting.** Post the items that are to be posted individually.

Feb. 15. Wrote a check for January liability for employee income tax and for social security tax and Medicare tax. C190.

28. Paid February payroll, $9,650.03 (total payroll, $12,037.00, less deductions: employee income tax, $1,324.00; social security tax, $782.41; Medicare tax, $180.56; U.S. Savings Bonds, $100.00). C200.

28. Recorded employer payroll taxes expense. M107.

**Posting.** Post the items that are to be posted individually.

2. Prove and rule journal page 1. Carry the column totals forward to page 2 of the journal.
3. Journalize the following transactions on page 2 of the journal.

***Transactions:***

Mar. 15. Wrote a check for February liability for employee income tax, social security tax, and Medicare tax. C205.

31. Paid March payroll, $10,138.80 (total payroll, $12,640.00, less deductions: employee income tax, $1,390.00; social security tax, $821.60; Medicare tax, $189.60; U.S. Savings Bonds, $100.00). C226.

31. Recorded employer payroll taxes expense. M116.

**Posting.** Post the items that are to be posted individually.

Apr. 1. Paid cash for 12 U.S. Savings Bonds at $25.00 each for employees. C227.

15. Wrote a check for March liability for employee income tax, social security tax, and Medicare tax. C238.

30. Wrote a check for federal unemployment tax liability for quarter ended March 31. C244.

30. Wrote a check for state unemployment tax liability for quarter ended March 31. C245.

**Posting.** Post the items that are to be posted individually.

4. Prove and rule journal page 2.

## INTERNET ACTIVITY

Point your browser to

**http://accounting.swpco.com**

Choose **First-Year Course**, choose **Activities**, and complete the activity for Chapter 14.

## Applied Communication

As a worker, you will receive a paycheck. In addition, you will be required to pay certain federal and state taxes, including social security tax and Medicare tax. These taxes will be withheld from your paycheck.

**Instructions:** Look up the Social Security Act in an encyclopedia or other reference work in your library or on the Internet. Find out why social security was created, who the U.S. president was at the time, and the purpose of social security. Write a one- or two-paragraph history of social security. Use clear, descriptive sentences.

## Cases for Critical Thinking

**Case 1** The partners of Myers and Woods have decided to hire a sales manager. They agree that the business can afford to pay the manager a salary of only $30,000.00. The accounting assistant informs the partners that hiring the manager will cost the business more than the $30,000.00 salary. Do you agree with the accounting assistant? Explain your response.

**Case 2** Penner Manufacturing had a total salary expense for the month of November of $60,000.00. Jerry Cruz, accounting clerk, calculated the November employer social security and Medicare taxes as $4,800.00 ($60,000.00 x 8%). Jean Edens, accountant, stated that the social security and Medicare taxes withheld from employee earnings were $4,275.00. What is the most likely reason for the difference between Mr. Cruz's and Ms. Edens's calculations for social security and Medicare taxes? Explain.

**Case 3** One of the unwritten rules of business is that payroll information is private and confidential. People usually do not want their coworkers to know how much they are paid. This common business practice presents a challenge for employees responsible for payroll accounting. Payroll workers handle many different types of data. The payroll department records personal information about employees, such as addresses and social security numbers, and verifies and totals time cards. In addition, each pay period payroll accountants calculate each employee's earnings, deductions, and net pay. Why is it important for payroll employees to be trustworthy and able to maintain confidentiality?

# AUTOMATED ACCOUNTING

## PAYROLL TAXES AND JOURNAL ENTRIES

In an automated payroll system, the computer is used to maintain the employee database, to record payroll transactions at the end of each pay period, and to display and print various payroll reports.

### Generating Payroll Journal Entries

*Automated Accounting 7.0* can generate the current payroll journal entry, including salary expenses; employee federal, state, and city taxes payable; social security and Medicare taxes payable; and all voluntary deductions.

1. Choose the Current Payroll Journal Entry menu item from the Options menu.
2. When the confirmation dialog box appears, click Yes.
3. Click the Post button.

### Generating the Employer's Payroll Taxes Journal Entries

The employer's payroll taxes journal entry includes social security, Medicare, federal unemployment, and state unemployment taxes.

1. Choose the Employer's Payroll Taxes menu item from the Options menu.
2. When the confirmation dialog box appears, click Yes.
3. Click the Post button.

### Generating Payroll Reports

1. Click the Reports toolbar button.
2. Choose the Payroll Reports option from the Select a Report Group list.

There are four types of payroll reports available:

1. *Employee List Report:* The report provides a complete listing of the employee payroll information.
2. *Payroll Report:* The report shows employee earnings and withholding information for the month, quarter, and year. Information is listed by employee and is summarized.
3. *Quarterly Report:* The report summarizes wages subject to social security and Medicare taxes. The information is listed by employee.
4. *W-2 Statements:* The report summarizes an employee's taxable wages and various withholdings for both the employee and the Internal Revenue Service.

**Current Payroll Journal Entries**

| Acct. # | Account Title | Debit | Credit |
|---|---|---|---|
| 6210 | Sales Salary Expense | 10522.03 | |
| 6170 | Office Salary Expense | 9320.88 | |
| 2140 | Emp. Fed. Inc. Tax Pay. | | 2102.62 |
| 2150 | Emp. State Inc. Tax Pay. | | 653.10 |
| 2160 | Social Security Tax Pay. | | 1230.27 |
| 2170 | Medicare Tax Payable | | 287.72 |
| 2155 | Emp. City Inc. Tax Pay. | | 198.43 |
| 2200 | Health Ins. Premiums Pay. | | 505.00 |
| 2210 | Dental Ins. Premiums Pay. | | 203.00 |
| 2220 | Credit Union Deduct. Pay. | | 1025.00 |
| 2130 | Salaries Payable | | 13637.77 |

Post Cancel Help

# AUTOMATED ACCOUNTING

After each payroll period, the appropriate reports may be generated as needed. The W-2 statement is generated only at the end of the calendar year.

## AUTOMATING MASTERY PROBLEM 14-5: Journalizing payroll transactions

**Instructions:**

1. Load *Automated Accounting 7.0* or higher software.
2. Select database F14-1 from the appropriate directory/folder.
3. Select File from the menu bar and choose the Save As menu command. Key the path to the drive and directory that contains your data files. Save the database with a file name of XXX141 (where XXX are your initials).
4. Access Problem Instructions through the Help menu. Read the Problem Instructions screen.
5. Key the data listed on page 355.
6. Exit the *Automated Accounting* software.

## AUTOMATING CHALLENGE PROBLEM 14-6: Journalizing and posting payroll transactions

**Instructions:**

1. Load *Automated Accounting 7.0* or higher software.
2. Select database F14-2 from the appropriate directory/folder.
3. Select File from the menu bar and choose the Save As menu command. Key the path to the drive and directory that contains your data files. Save the database with a file name of XXX142 (where XXX are your initials).
4. Access Problem Instructions through the Help menu. Read the Problem Instructions screen.
5. Key the data listed on page 356.
6. Exit the *Automated Accounting* software.

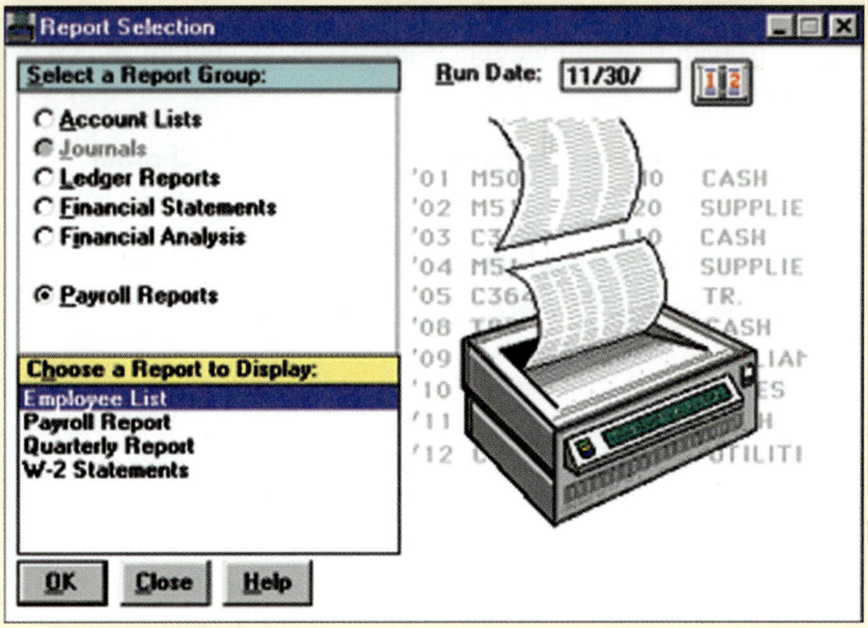

# REINFORCEMENT ACTIVITY 2—PART A

## An Accounting Cycle for a Partnership: Journalizing and Posting Transactions

Reinforcement Activity 2 reinforces learnings from Cycle 2, Chapters 10 through 17. Activities cover a complete accounting cycle for a merchandising business organized as a partnership. Reinforcement Activity 2 is a single problem divided into two parts. Part A includes learnings from Chapters 10 through 14. Part B includes learnings from Chapters 15 through 17.

The accounting work of a single merchandising business for the last month of a yearly fiscal period is used in this reinforcement activity. The records kept and reports prepared, however, illustrate the application of accounting concepts for all merchandising businesses.

### CLEARVIEW OPTICAL

Ester Burks and Juan Ortiz, partners, own and operate ClearView Optical, a merchandising business. The business sells a complete line of fashion, sun, and sport eyewear. ClearView is located in a downtown shopping area and is open for business Monday through Saturday. A monthly rent is paid for the building and fixtures. ClearView accepts credit cards from customers.

### CHART OF ACCOUNTS

ClearView Optical uses the chart of accounts shown on the next page.

### JOURNAL AND LEDGERS

The journal and ledgers used by ClearView Optical are listed below. Models of the journal and ledgers are shown in the textbook chapters indicated.

| Journal and Ledgers | Chapter |
|---|---|
| Expanded journal | 11 |
| Accounts payable ledger | 12 |
| Accounts receivable ledger | 12 |
| General ledger | 12 |

## CHART OF ACCOUNTS

**Balance Sheet Accounts**

(1000) ASSETS
1110 Cash
1120 Petty Cash
1130 Accounts Receivable
1140 Merchandise Inventory
1145 Supplies—Office
1150 Supplies—Store
1160 Prepaid Insurance

(2000) LIABILITIES
2110 Accounts Payable
2120 Employee Income Tax Payable
2130 Social Security Tax Payable
2135 Medicare Tax Payable
2140 Sales Tax Payable
2150 Unemployment Tax Payable—Federal
2160 Unemployment Tax Payable—State
2170 Health Insurance Premiums Payable
2180 U.S. Savings Bonds Payable
2190 United Way Donations Payable

(3000) OWNER'S EQUITY
3110 Ester Burks, Capital
3120 Ester Burks, Drawing
3130 Juan Ortiz, Capital
3140 Juan Ortiz, Drawing
3150 Income Summary

**Income Statement Accounts**

(4000) OPERATING REVENUE
4110 Sales

(5000) COST OF MERCHANDISE
5110 Purchases

(6000) OPERATING EXPENSES
6110 Advertising Expense
6120 Credit Card Fee Expense
6130 Insurance Expense
6140 Miscellaneous Expense
6150 Payroll Taxes Expense
6160 Rent Expense
6170 Salary Expense
6175 Supplies Expense—Office
6180 Supplies Expense—Store
6190 Utilities Expense

### SUBSIDIARY LEDGERS

**Accounts Receivable Ledger**

110 Doritha Busch
120 Linda Cortez
130 Dallas Giles
140 Kristin Jung
150 Jack O'Brien
160 Don Teal

**Accounts Payable Ledger**

210 ABC Optical Co.
220 Central Office Supply
230 Eyecare Optical
240 Optical Mart
250 Solar Optical
260 Zen Supply

## RECORDING TRANSACTIONS

The December 1 account balances for the general and subsidiary ledgers are given in the *Working Papers*.

***Instructions:***

**1.** Journalize the following transactions on page 23 of a journal. A 6% sales tax has been added to each sale. Source documents are abbreviated as follows: check, C; memorandum, M; purchase invoice, P; receipt, R; sales invoice, S; cash register tape, T.

Dec. 1. Paid cash for rent, $1,200.00. C372.
1. Ester Burks, partner, withdrew cash for personal use, $1,500.00. C373.
1. Juan Ortiz, partner, withdrew cash, for personal use, $1,500.00. C374.
2. Paid cash for electric bill, $346.20. C375.
2. Received cash on account from Linda Cortez, $413.40, covering S64. R92.
3. Paid cash for miscellaneous expense, $72.00. C376.
3. Paid cash on account to Solar Optical, $580.00, covering P73. C377.
4. Sold merchandise on account to Doritha Busch, $450.00, plus sales tax, $27.00; total, $477.00. S67.
5. Recorded cash and credit card sales, $5,796.00, plus sales tax, $347.76; total, $6,143.76. T5.

**Posting.** Post the items that are to be posted individually.

7. Sold merchandise on account to Dallas Giles, $462.00, plus sales tax, $27.72; total, $489.72. S68.
7. Received cash on account from Don Teal, $432.48, covering S65. R93.
8. Bought office supplies on account from Central Office Supply, $351.60. M43.
9. Purchased merchandise on account from Optical Mart, $1,350.00. P77.
9. Bought store supplies on account from Zen Supply, $330.00. M44.
10. Ester Burks, partner, withdrew merchandise for personal use, $300.00. M45.
10. Paid cash for office supplies, $174.00. C378.
11. Paid cash on account to Eyecare Optical, $1,170.00, covering P74. C379.
11. Purchased merchandise on account from Solar Optical, $1,032.00. P78.
12. Paid cash for store supplies, $264.00. C380.
12. Recorded cash and credit card sales, $7,125.00, plus sales tax, $427.50; total, $7,552.50. T12.

**Posting.** Post the items that are to be posted individually.

14. Juan Ortiz, partner, withdrew merchandise for personal use, $390.00. M46.
14. Purchased merchandise on account from Eyecare Optical, $3,276.00. P79.
14. Sold merchandise on account to Jack O'Brien, $170.00, plus sales tax, $10.20; total, $180.20. S69.
14. Paid cash for advertising, $415.00. C381.
15. Paid cash on account to ABC Optical Co., $1,272.00, covering P75. C382.
15. Received cash on account from Kristin Jung, $821.50, covering S66. R94.
15. Sold merchandise on account to Linda Cortez, $490.00, plus sales tax, $29.40; total, $519.40. S70.
15. Paid cash for liability for employee income tax, $342.00, social security tax, $767.00, and Medicare tax, $177.00; total, $1,286.00. C383.

**Posting.** Post the items that are to be posted individually.

**2.** Prove and rule page 23 of the journal.

**3.** Carry the column totals forward to page 24 of the journal.

**4.** Journalize the following transactions on page 24 of the journal.

Dec. 15. Paid cash for semimonthly payroll, $2,303.60 (total payroll, $2,930.00, less deductions: employee income tax, $162.00; social security tax, $190.45; Medicare tax, $43.95; health insurance, $170.00; U.S. Savings Bonds, $30.00; United Way donations, $30.00). C384.

15. Recorded employer payroll taxes, $259.20, for the semimonthly pay period ended December 15. Taxes owed are: social security tax, $190.45; Medicare tax, $43.95; federal unemployment tax, $3.20; and state unemployment tax, $21.60. M47.

19. Recorded cash and credit card sales, $6,925.00, plus sales tax, $415.50; total, $7,340.50. T19.

23. Paid cash on account to Optical Mart, $2,200.00, covering P76. C385.

26. Recorded cash and credit card sales, $6,980.00, plus sales tax, $418.80; total, $7,398.80. T26.

**Posting.** Post the items that are to be posted individually.

ClearView Optical's bank charges a fee for handling the collection of credit card sales deposited during the month. The credit card fee is deducted from ClearView Optical's bank account. The amount is then shown on the bank statement. The credit card fee is recorded in the journal as a reduction in cash.

Dec. 28. Recorded credit card fee expense, $342.00. M48. (Debit Credit Card Fee Expense; credit Cash.)

30. Purchased merchandise on account from ABC Optical Co., $1,940.00. P80.

31. Paid cash to replenish the petty cash fund, $364.00: office supplies, $75.00; store supplies, $70.00; advertising, $104.00; miscellaneous, $115.00. C386.

31. Paid cash for semimonthly payroll, $2,451.40 (total payroll, $3,120.00, less deductions: employee income tax, $189.00; social security tax, $202.80; Medicare tax, $46.80; health insurance, $170.00; U.S. Savings Bonds, $30.00; United Way donations, $30.00). C387.

31. Recorded employer payroll taxes, $274.40, for the semimonthly pay period ended December 31. Taxes owed are: social security tax, $202.80: Medicare tax, $46.80; federal unemployment tax, $3.20; and state unemployment tax, $21.60. M49.

31. Recorded cash and credit card sales, $3,890.00, plus sales tax, $233.40; total, $4,123.40. T31.

**Posting.** Post the items that are to be posted individually.

**5.** Total page 24 of the journal. Prove the equality of debits and credits.
**6.** Prove cash. The balance on the next unused check stub is $40,126.14.
**7.** Rule the journal.
**8.** Post the totals of the special columns of the journal.
**9.** Prepare a schedule of accounts payable and a schedule of accounts receivable. Prove the accuracy of the subsidiary ledgers by comparing the schedule totals with the balances of the controlling accounts in the general ledger. If the totals are not the same, find and correct the errors.

**The ledgers used in Reinforcement Activity 2—Part A are needed to complete Reinforcement Activity 2—Part B.**

# 15 Work Sheet for a Merchandising Business

**AFTER STUDYING CHAPTER 15, YOU WILL BE ABLE TO:**

1. Define accounting terms related to a work sheet for a merchandising business.
2. Identify accounting concepts and practices related to a work sheet for a merchandising business.
3. Begin a work sheet for a merchandising business.
4. Plan adjustments on a work sheet for a merchandising business.
5. Complete a work sheet for a merchandising business.

**TERMS PREVIEW**

inventory

merchandise inventory

## FINANCIAL INFORMATION

Management decisions about future business operations are often based on financial information. This information shows whether a profit is being made or a loss is being incurred. Profit or loss information helps an owner or manager determine future changes. Financial information is also needed to prepare required tax reports. A business summarizes financial information at least once each fiscal period. Omni Import uses a one-year fiscal period that begins on January 1 and ends on December 31. Therefore, Omni Import summarizes its financial information on December 31 of each year.

**LEGAL ISSUES IN ACCOUNTING**

### LIMITED LIABILITY PARTNERSHIPS

A new form of partnership in the U.S. is called a *limited liability partnership (LLP).* The LLP tries to combine the advantages of the partnership and the corporation, while avoiding their disadvantages. At least two members, or partners, are necessary.

The primary advantage of the LLP is that it does not pay separate income tax. LLP partners allocate profits and losses among themselves, according to the partnership agreement.

All members in the LLP have "limited" liability for the debts of the business. This means that none of the personal assets of the members are subject to the claims of business creditors.

The LLP follows partnership rules for dissolution. If one member drops out, all others must formally agree to continue the business.

Many major accounting firms have changed to the LLP form of business organization in an effort to limit the costs associated with malpractice liability.

# ACCOUNTING IN YOUR CAREER

## DISCOVERING THE TRUTH ABOUT WORK SHEETS

Cheryl Wendling is a junior accountant at a large accounting firm. She specializes in financial analysis, has recently passed the CPA examination, and is working toward becoming a full partner in the firm. The firm expects all its partners to participate in community service, so Cheryl volunteers her time talking with students enrolled in accounting courses at local high schools and colleges.

Cheryl recently admitted to one of her friends that at first she thought this volunteer work was just another hoop to jump through to earn her partnership. But after a few classroom visits, she discovered that she genuinely liked sharing her knowledge and experience, and she now believes she may have inspired a few students to pursue accounting careers.

Today Cheryl is visiting with Mr. Stern's Accounting I class at Lamont High School. The students have just finished a unit on work sheets for partnerships and are eager to discuss work sheets with her. Cheryl likes to begin with a dramatic statement that grabs the students' attention. So today she says, "I'm going to tell you three lies about work sheets. Then I want you to tell me what's wrong with my statements." She gives a big grin and then says, "If you get these three right, then I'll tell you how to succeed in the field of accounting."

**Critical Thinking:**

1. Cheryl's first statement is: *A 10-column work sheet is always better than an 8-column work sheet.* When might an 8-column work sheet be preferable to a 10-column work sheet?
2. The second statement is: *The trial balance totals prove that all the work in the general ledger is correct.* What kinds of errors are not detected by a trial balance?
3. The third statement is: *All the account balances in the Income Statement and Balance Sheet columns are the amounts that will appear on the income statement and balance sheet.* What account would be an exception to this statement and why?

# 15-1 Beginning an 8-Column Work Sheet for a Merchandising Business

## TRANSFERRING GENERAL LEDGER ACCOUNT BALANCES TO A WORK SHEET

ACCOUNT *Cash* ACCOUNT NO. *1110*

| DATE | | ITEM | POST. REF. | DEBIT | CREDIT | BALANCE DEBIT | BALANCE CREDIT |
|---|---|---|---|---|---|---|---|
| 20-- Dec. | 1 | Balance | ✓ | | | 28 260 00 | |
| | 31 | | 25 | 37 180 80 | | 65 440 80 | |
| | 31 | | 25 | | 36 360 52 | 29 080 28 | |

ACCOUNT *Sales* ACCOUNT NO. *4110*

| DATE | | ITEM | POST. REF. | DEBIT | CREDIT | BALANCE DEBIT | BALANCE CREDIT |
|---|---|---|---|---|---|---|---|
| 20-- Dec. | 1 | Balance | ✓ | | | | 387 919 20 |
| | 31 | | 25 | | 35 200 80 | | 423 120 00 |

A columnar accounting form on which the financial information needed to prepare financial statements is summarized is known as a work sheet. A work sheet is used to plan adjustments and sort financial statement information. A work sheet may be prepared whenever a business wishes to summarize and report financial information. A work sheet is always prepared at the end of each fiscal period because financial statements are prepared at the end of each fiscal period. *(CONCEPT: Accounting Period Cycle)* Omni Import prepares a work sheet and financial statements annually. To begin a work sheet, Omni completes the Trial Balance columns. Two selected general ledger accounts are shown in the illustration.

# RECORDING A TRIAL BALANCE ON A WORK SHEET

**Omni Import**
**Work Sheet**
**For Year Ended December 31, 20--**

| | ACCOUNT TITLE | TRIAL BALANCE 1 DEBIT | TRIAL BALANCE 2 CREDIT |
|---|---|---|---|
| 1 | Cash | 29 080 28 | |
| 2 | Petty Cash | 300 00 | |
| 3 | Accounts Receivable | 11 198 40 | |
| 4 | Merchandise Inventory | 270 480 00 | |
| 5 | Supplies—Office | 6 480 00 | |
| 6 | Supplies—Store | 6 944 00 | |
| 7 | Prepaid Insurance | 5 800 00 | |
| 8 | Accounts Payable | | 12 542 38 |
| 9 | Employee Income Tax Payable | | 542 00 |
| 10 | Social Security Tax Payable | | 985 40 |
| 11 | Medicare Tax Payable | | 227 42 |
| 12 | Sales Tax Payable | | 2 112 05 |
| 13 | Unemployment Tax Payable—Federal | | 8 40 |
| 14 | Unemployment Tax Payable—State | | 56 70 |
| 15 | Health Insurance Premiums Payable | | 1 008 00 |
| 16 | U.S. Savings Bonds Payable | | 60 00 |
| 17 | United Way Donations Payable | | 72 00 |
| 18 | Karl Koehn, Capital | | 136 750 00 |
| 19 | Karl Koehn, Drawing | 29 100 00 | |
| 20 | Michelle Wu, Capital | | 136 552 48 |
| 21 | Michelle Wu, Drawing | 28 800 00 | |
| 22 | Income Summary | | |
| 23 | Sales | | 423 120 00 |
| 24 | Purchases | 189 960 00 | |
| 25 | Advertising Expense | 6 600 00 | |
| 26 | Credit Card Fee Expense | 3 385 00 | |
| 27 | Insurance Expense | | |
| 28 | Miscellaneous Expense | 2 584 15 | |
| 29 | Payroll Taxes Expense | 9 105 00 | |
| 30 | Rent Expense | 21 000 00 | |
| 31 | Salary Expense | 89 400 00 | |
| 32 | Supplies Expense—Office | | |
| 33 | Supplies Expense—Store | | |
| 34 | Utilities Expense | 3 820 00 | |
| 35 | | 714 036 83 | 714 036 83 |

**1.** Account Titles

**2.** Account Balances

**3.** Total and rule the Debit and Credit columns.

## STEPS Recording a trial balance on a work sheet

1. Write the title of each general ledger account in the work sheet's Account Title column in the same order they appear in the general ledger. All accounts are listed regardless of whether there is a balance or not. Listing all accounts reduces the possibility of overlooking an account that needs to be brought up to date.
2. Write the balance of each account in the appropriate work sheet's Trial Balance Debit or Credit column. The amounts are taken from the general ledger accounts.
3. Total, prove, and rule the Trial Balance Debit and Credit columns of the work sheet.

After posting is completed at the end of a fiscal period, some general ledger accounts, such as the two supplies accounts and the prepaid insurance account, are not up to date. Adjustments for supplies and prepaid insurance are described in Chapter 7. In addition to supplies and prepaid insurance, Omni Import needs to adjust the merchandise inventory account. Changes recorded on a work sheet to update general ledger accounts at the end of a fiscal period are known as adjustments.

Adjustments are planned in the Adjustments columns of a work sheet. Adjustments recorded on a work sheet are for planning purposes only. The general ledger account balances are not changed until entries are journalized and posted. Journal entries made to bring general ledger accounts up to date are known as adjusting entries.

The amount of goods on hand is called an **inventory.** The amount of goods on hand for sale to customers is called **merchandise inventory.** The general ledger account in which merchandise inventory is recorded is titled Merchandise Inventory. Merchandise Inventory is an asset account with a normal debit balance.

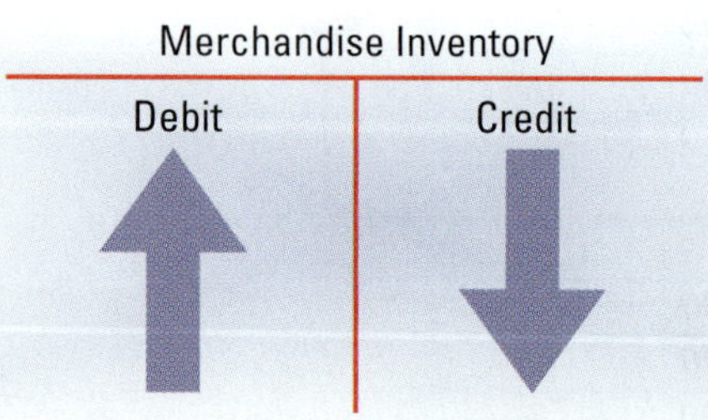


Omni Import's merchandise inventory account on January 1, the beginning of the fiscal year, has a debit balance of $270,480.00.

| Merchandise Inventory | | |
|---|---|---|
| Jan. 1 Bal. | 270,480.00 | |

The balance of the merchandise inventory account on December 31, the end of the fiscal year, is the same amount, $270,480.00. The January 1 and December 31 balances are the same because no entries have been made in the account during the fiscal year. The changes in inventory resulting from purchases and sales transactions have not been recorded in the merchandise inventory account.

During a fiscal period, the amount of merchandise on hand increases each time merchandise is purchased. However, all purchases are recorded in the purchases account. The amount of merchandise on hand decreases each time merchandise is sold. However, all sales are recorded in the sales account. This procedure makes it easier to determine the total purchases and sales during a fiscal period. The merchandise inventory account balance, therefore, must be adjusted to reflect the changes resulting from purchases and sales during a fiscal period.

## ANALYZING A MERCHANDISE INVENTORY ADJUSTMENT

The two accounts used to adjust the merchandise inventory are Merchandise Inventory and Income Summary. The T accounts show the merchandise inventory and income summary accounts before the merchandise inventory adjustment is made.

**BEFORE ADJUSTMENT**

Income Summary

| | | | |
|---|---|---|---|
| | | | |

Merchandise Inventory

| | | | |
|---|---|---|---|
| Jan. 1 Bal. | 270,480.00 | | |

Before the adjustment, the merchandise inventory account has a January 1 debit balance of $270,480.00. The merchandise inventory account balance, however, is not up to date. The actual count of merchandise on December 31 shows that the inventory is valued at $254,640.00. Therefore, the merchandise inventory account balance must be adjusted to show the current value of merchandise on hand.

Most accounts needing adjustment at the end of a fiscal period have a related temporary account. For example, when the account Supplies is adjusted, Supplies Expense is the related expense account, a temporary account. Merchandise Inventory, however, does not have a related expense account. Therefore, Income Summary, a temporary account, is used to adjust the merchandise inventory account at the end of a fiscal period.

Four questions are asked in analyzing the adjustment for merchandise inventory.

1. **What is the balance of** Merchandise Inventory**?** *$270,480.00*
2. **What should the balance be for this account?** *$254,640.00*
3. **What must be done to correct the account balance?** *Decrease $15,840.00*
4. **What adjustment is made?**
   *Debit* Income Summary, *$15,840.00*
   *Credit* Merchandise Inventory, *$15,840.00*

The merchandise inventory adjustment is shown in the T accounts.

**AFTER ADJUSTMENT**

Income Summary

| | | | |
|---|---|---|---|
| Adj. (a) | 15,840.00 | | |

Merchandise Inventory

| | | | |
|---|---|---|---|
| Jan. 1 Bal. | 270,480.00 | Adj. (a) | 15,840.00 |
| *(New Bal.* | *254,640.00)* | | |

Income Summary is debited and Merchandise Inventory is credited for $15,840.00. The beginning debit balance of Merchandise Inventory, $270,480.00, *minus* the adjustment credit amount, $15,840.00, *equals* the ending debit balance of Merchandise Inventory, $254,640.00.

### REMEMBER

When an account that requires adjusting does not have a related expense account, the temporary account Income Summary is used.

## RECORDING A MERCHANDISE INVENTORY ADJUSTMENT

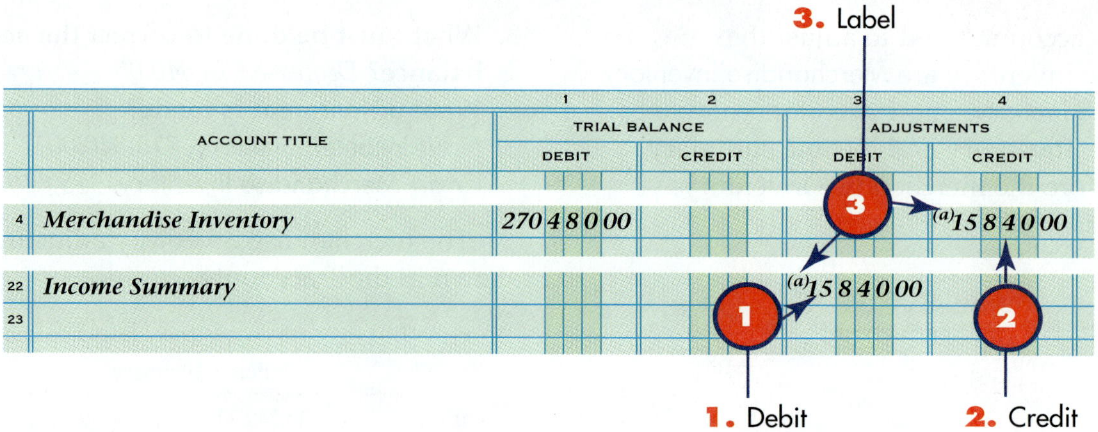


### STEPS: Recording a merchandise inventory adjustment on a work sheet

1. Write the debit amount, *$15,840.00,* in the Adjustments Debit column on the line with the account title Income Summary.
2. Write the credit amount, *$15,840.00,* in the Adjustments Credit column on the line with the account title Merchandise Inventory.
3. Label the two parts of this adjustment with the small letter *a* in parentheses, *(a).*

## ANALYZING AN ADJUSTMENT WHEN ENDING MERCHANDISE INVENTORY IS GREATER THAN BEGINNING MERCHANDISE INVENTORY

If the amount of merchandise inventory on hand is greater than the January 1 balance of Merchandise Inventory, opposite entries would be made—debit Merchandise Inventory and credit Income Summary. For example, Venable Company's merchandise inventory account on January 1 has a debit balance of $294,700.00. The count of merchandise on December 31 shows that the inventory is valued at $298,900.00. The merchandise on hand is $4,200.00 *greater* than the January 1 balance of Merchandise Inventory.

Four questions are asked in analyzing the adjustment for merchandise inventory.

1. **What is the balance of Merchandise Inventory?** *$294,700.00*
2. **What should the balance be for this account?** *$298,900.00*
3. **What must be done to correct the account balance?** *Increase $4,200.00*
4. **What adjustment is made?**

*Debit* Merchandise Inventory, *$4,200.00*
*Credit* Income Summary, *$4,200.00*

The merchandise inventory adjustment is shown in the T accounts.

AFTER ADJUSTMENT

Merchandise Inventory

| | | | |
|---|---|---|---|
| Jan. 1 Bal. | 294,700.00 | | |
| Adj. (a) | 4,200.00 | | |
| *(New Bal.* | *298,900.00)* | | |

Income Summary

| | | | |
|---|---|---|---|
| | | Adj. (a) | 4,200.00 |

Merchandise Inventory is debited and Income Summary is credited for $4,200.00. The beginning debit balance of Merchandise Inventory, $294,700.00, *plus* the adjustment debit amount, $4,200.00, *equals* the ending debit balance of Merchandise Inventory, $298,900.00.

## TERMS REVIEW

inventory

merchandise inventory

## AUDIT YOUR UNDERSTANDING

1. In what order should general ledger accounts be listed on a work sheet?
2. What accounts are used for the adjustment for merchandise inventory?

## WORK TOGETHER

**Beginning an 8-column work sheet for a merchandising business**

A work sheet for Paradise Company is given in the *Working Papers.* The company's general ledger account balances on December 31 of the current year, after all transactions have been posted, are listed below. Your instructor will guide you through the following examples.

| Account | Debit | Credit |
|---|---|---|
| Cash | $ 26,424.00 | |
| Petty Cash | 300.00 | |
| Accounts Receivable | 10,693.00 | |
| Merchandise Inventory | 254,244.00 | |
| Supplies—Office | 6,091.00 | |
| Supplies—Store | 6,516.00 | |
| Prepaid Insurance | 5,540.00 | |
| Accounts Payable | | $ 10,740.00 |
| Sales Tax Payable | | 1,985.00 |
| Jean Brower, Capital | | 117,875.00 |
| Jean Brower, Drawing | 20,530.00 | |
| Dale Edson, Capital | | 118,520.00 |
| Dale Edson, Drawing | 20,980.00 | |
| Income Summary | | |
| Sales | | 316,440.00 |
| Purchases | 178,560.00 | |
| Advertising Expense | 6,200.00 | |
| Credit Card Fee Expense | 3,264.00 | |
| Insurance Expense | | |
| Miscellaneous Expense | 2,470.00 | |
| Rent Expense | 20,160.00 | |
| Supplies Expense—Office | | |
| Supplies Expense—Store | | |
| Utilities Expense | 3,588.00 | |

3. Enter the trial balance on the work sheet.
4. Total, prove, and rule the trial balance.
5. From a physical count of merchandise inventory, the December 31 balance is determined to be $239,354.00. Analyze the merchandise inventory adjustment and enter the adjustment on the work sheet. Save your work to complete Work Together on page 377.

## ON YOUR OWN

### Beginning an 8-column work sheet for a merchandising business

A work sheet for Mueller Company is given in the *Working Papers.* The company's general ledger account balances on December 31 of the current year, after all transactions have been posted, are listed below. Work these problems independently.

| Account | Debit | Credit |
|---|---|---|
| Cash | $ 27,210.00 | |
| Petty Cash | 500.00 | |
| Accounts Receivable | 12,475.00 | |
| Merchandise Inventory | 296,620.00 | |
| Supplies—Office | 7,106.00 | |
| Supplies—Store | 7,602.00 | |
| Prepaid Insurance | 6,480.00 | |
| Accounts Payable | | $ 12,530.00 |
| Sales Tax Payable | | 2,315.00 |
| Harry Glover, Capital | | 134,550.00 |
| Harry Glover, Drawing | 23,950.00 | |
| Laura Montez, Capital | | 138,270.00 |
| Laura Montez, Drawing | 24,475.00 | |
| Income Summary | | |
| Sales | | 369,180.00 |
| Purchases | 208,320.00 | |
| Advertising Expense | 7,240.00 | |
| Credit Card Fee Expense | 3,808.00 | |
| Insurance Expense | | |
| Miscellaneous Expense | 2,873.00 | |
| Rent Expense | 24,000.00 | |
| Supplies Expense—Office | | |
| Supplies Expense—Store | | |
| Utilities Expense | 4,186.00 | |

6. Enter the trial balance on the work sheet.
7. Total, prove, and rule the trial balance.
8. From a physical count of merchandise inventory, the December 31 balance is determined to be $279,247.00. Analyze the merchandise inventory adjustment and enter the adjustment on the work sheet. Save your work to complete On Your Own on page 377.

# 15-2 Analyzing and Recording Work Sheet Adjustments

## ANALYZING A SUPPLIES ADJUSTMENT

Omni Import uses office and store supplies in the daily operation of the business. The amount of supplies *not used* during a fiscal period represents an asset. The amount of supplies *used* during a fiscal period represents an expense. Accurate financial reporting includes recording expenses in the fiscal period in which the expenses contribute to earning revenue. *(CONCEPT: Matching Expenses with Revenue)*

The account balance for Supplies—Office, $6,480.00, includes two items: (1) the account balance on January 1 and (2) the cost of office supplies bought during the year. The account balance does not reflect the value of any office supplies *used* during the year (an expense). Therefore, the office supplies account balance must be adjusted to show the value of office supplies on hand on December 31. The amount of supplies on hand on December 31 is determined by counting the supplies on hand and calculating the value.

The two accounts used to adjust office supplies are Supplies—Office and Supplies Expense—Office. Before the adjustment, the office supplies account has a December 31 debit balance of $6,480.00. However, office supplies have been used throughout the fiscal period. These changes in office supplies were not recorded in the office supplies account. Therefore, the office supplies account balance is not up to date.

BEFORE ADJUSTMENT

Supplies Expense—Office

| Debit | | Credit |
|---|---|---|
| | | |

Supplies—Office

| Debit | | Credit |
|---|---|---|
| Dec. 31 Bal. | 6,480.00 | |

The actual count of office supplies on December 31 shows that the value of the inventory is $1,750.00. The office supplies account balance must be adjusted to show the current value of the office supplies inventory.

Four questions are asked in analyzing the adjustment for office supplies inventory.

1. **What is the balance of Supplies—Office?** *$6,480.00*
2. **What should the balance be for this account?** *$1,750.00*
3. **What must be done to correct the account balance?** *Decrease $4,730.00*
4. **What adjustment is made?**
   *Debit* Supplies Expense—Office, *$4,730.00*
   *Credit* Supplies—Office, *$4,730.00*

The office supplies inventory adjustment is shown in the T accounts.

AFTER ADJUSTMENT

Supplies Expense—Office

| Debit | | Credit | |
|---|---|---|---|
| Adj. (b) | 4,730.00 | | |

Supplies—Office

| Debit | | Credit | |
|---|---|---|---|
| Dec. 31 Bal. | 6,480.00 | Adj. (b) | 4,730.00 |
| *(New Bal.* | *1,750.00)* | | |

Supplies Expense—Office is debited and Supplies—Office is credited for $4,730.00. The beginning debit balance of Supplies—Office, $6,480.00, *minus* the adjustment credit amount, $4,730.00, *equals* the ending debit balance of Supplies—Office, $1,750.00.

**FYI**

*In automated accounting, adjustments are prepared from the trial balance. The software automatically generates the financial statements with no need for a work sheet.*

# RECORDING SUPPLIES ADJUSTMENTS

3. Labels 2. Credits

| | ACCOUNT TITLE | 1 TRIAL BALANCE DEBIT | 2 TRIAL BALANCE CREDIT | 3 ADJUSTMENTS DEBIT | 4 ADJUSTMENTS CREDIT |
|---|---|---|---|---|---|
| 5 | *Supplies—Office* | 6 480 00 | | | (b) 4 730 00 |
| 6 | *Supplies—Store* | 6 944 00 | | | (c) 3 910 00 |
| 32 | *Supplies Expense—Office* | | | (b) 4 730 00 | |
| 33 | *Supplies Expense—Store* | | | (c) 3 910 00 | |
| 34 | | | | | |
| 35 | | | | | |
| 36 | | | | | |
| 37 | | | | | |
| 38 | | | | | |

1. Debits

Omni Import makes a similar adjustment for store supplies. The steps in recording the *two* supplies inventory adjustments are the same as those described for Encore Music in Chapter 7. The *two* supplies inventory adjustments are shown in the Adjustments columns of the work sheet above. The adjustment for Supplies—Office is labeled *(b)* and is shown on lines 5 and 32. The adjustment for Supplies—Store is labeled *(c)* and is shown on lines 6 and 33.

### STEPS: Recording supplies adjustments on a work sheet

1. Write the debit amounts in the Adjustments Debit column on the lines with the appropriate account titles: *$4,730.00* with Supplies Expense—Office and *$3,910.00* with Supplies Expense—Store.
2. Write the credit amounts in the Adjustments Credit column on the lines with the appropriate account titles: *$4,730.00* with Supplies—Office and *$3,910.00* with Supplies—Store.
3. Label the two parts of the Supplies—Office adjustment with a small letter *b* in parentheses, *(b)*. Label the two parts of the Supplies—Store adjustment with a small letter *c* in parentheses, *(c)*.

### REMEMBER

The adjustment for supplies is the amount of supplies used.

## ANALYZING A PREPAID INSURANCE ADJUSTMENT

Payment for insurance protection is paid in advance. The value of prepaid insurance *not expired* during a fiscal period is an asset. The value of prepaid insurance *expired* during a fiscal period is an expense.

The account balance for Prepaid Insurance, $5,800.00, includes two items: (1) the account balance on January 1 and (2) the cost of insurance premiums paid during the year. The account balance does not reflect the value of the insurance expired during the year (an expense). Therefore, the prepaid insurance account balance must be adjusted to bring the balance up to date. *(CONCEPT: Matching Expenses with Revenue)*

The two accounts used to adjust the prepaid insurance account are Prepaid Insurance and Insurance Expense. Before the adjustment, the prepaid insurance account has a December 31 debit balance of $5,800.00. The account balance, however, is not up to date. The value of the prepaid insurance *not expired* is determined to be $2,630.00. The prepaid insurance account balance must be adjusted to show its current value.

**BEFORE ADJUSTMENT**

Insurance Expense

| | | | |
|---|---|---|---|
| | | | |

Prepaid Insurance

| | | | |
|---|---|---|---|
| Dec. 31 Bal. | 5,800.00 | | |

Four questions are asked in analyzing the adjustment for prepaid insurance.

1. **What is the balance of** Prepaid Insurance**?** *$5,800.00*
2. **What should the balance be for this account?** *$2,630.00*
3. **What must be done to correct the account balance?** *Decrease $3,170.00*
4. **What adjustment is made?**
   *Debit* Insurance Expense, *$3,170.00*
   *Credit* Prepaid Insurance, *$3,170.00*

The prepaid insurance adjustment is shown in the T accounts.

**AFTER ADJUSTMENT**

Insurance Expense

| | | | |
|---|---|---|---|
| Adj. (d) | 3,170.00 | | |

Prepaid Insurance

| | | | |
|---|---|---|---|
| Dec. 31 Bal. | 5,800.00 | Adj. (d) | 3,170.00 |
| *(New Bal.* | *2,630.00)* | | |

Insurance Expense is debited and Prepaid Insurance is credited for $3,170.00. The beginning debit balance of Prepaid Insurance, $5,800.00, *minus* the adjustment credit amount, $3,170.00, *equals* the ending debit balance of Prepaid Insurance, $2,630.00.

**FYI** *Companies with more complicated businesses and charts of accounts will need to make more adjustments than companies with less complicated businesses and charts of accounts.*

# RECORDING A PREPAID INSURANCE ADJUSTMENT

2. Credit

3. Labels

1. Debit

| | ACCOUNT TITLE | TRIAL BALANCE DEBIT (1) | TRIAL BALANCE CREDIT (2) | ADJUSTMENTS DEBIT (3) | ADJUSTMENTS CREDIT (4) |
|---|---|---|---|---|---|
| 7 | *Prepaid Insurance* | 5 8 0 0 00 | | | (d) 3 1 7 0 00 |
| 27 | *Insurance Expense* | | | (d) 3 1 7 0 00 | |
| 28 | | | | | |
| 29 | | | | | |
| 30 | | | | | |

The steps in recording the prepaid insurance adjustment on a work sheet are the same as those followed by Encore Music in Chapter 7.

The adjustment for Prepaid Insurance is labeled *(d)* and is shown in the Adjustments columns on lines 7 and 27 of the work sheet above.

## ACCOUNTING AT WORK

### GLENDA COUSINS

Glenda Cousins is the branch manager of Star Bank's Over-the-Rhine branch in Cincinnati, Ohio. She began her career with Star Bank as a teller and worked her way through several different positions to reach her current job. She was first promoted from teller to loan and documentation processor. In this job she was responsible for inputting information about certificates of deposit (CDs) and commercial notes. She then worked as a customer service representative, selling new accounts and CDs.

As an assistant manager, she gained supervisory experience and took part in the management of a branch office. She also was the branch manager's backup. Then finally she had her own branch to manage. When asked how she was able to consistently rise in the organization, Glenda said, "It took hard work and a positive attitude. I had to remain positive even when others were promoted to positions I felt I deserved."

Glenda advises that "students who hope to enter the banking industry at the teller level need a customer service orientation. You will learn the bank's products and must be able to refer customers to the different services offered by the bank. Another good skill for a prospective teller is experience in dealing with cash. You can usually obtain this experience in a retail environment as a sales associate."

Glenda recommends that students determine one or two career fields and then focus on a career choice. This focus will guide your decisions about education and the courses you enroll in. She says that her two years of high school accounting well prepared her for her entry into banking. The knowledge of debits and credits gave her an understanding that other bank employees lacked.

## AUDIT YOUR UNDERSTANDING

1. What accounts are used for the adjustment to office supplies?
2. What accounts are used for the adjustment to prepaid insurance?

## WORK TOGETHER

**Analyzing and recording adjustments on a work sheet for a merchandising business**

Use the work sheet from Work Together on page 371. Your instructor will guide you through the following examples.

3. From a physical count of the following, December 31 balances are determined to be:

| | |
|---|---|
| Supplies—Office | $1,646.00 |
| Supplies—Store | 2,838.00 |
| Prepaid Insurance | 2,540.00 |

   Analyze adjustments that need to be made for the accounts above and enter the adjustments on the work sheet.

4. Total, prove, and rule the Adjustments columns. Save your work to complete Work Together on page 384.

## ON YOUR OWN

**Analyzing and recording adjustments on a work sheet for a merchandising business**

Use the work sheet from On Your Own on page 372. Work these problems independently.

5. From a physical count of the following, December 31 balances are determined to be:

| | |
|---|---|
| Supplies—Office | $1,920.00 |
| Supplies—Store | 3,310.00 |
| Prepaid Insurance | 2,940.00 |

   Analyze adjustments that need to be made for the accounts above and enter the adjustments on the work sheet.

6. Total, prove, and rule the Adjustments columns. Save your work to complete On Your Own on page 384.

## COMPLETING AN 8-COLUMN WORK SHEET

1. Extend balance sheet items to Balance Sheet columns.
2. Extend income statement items to Income Statement columns.
3. Total Income Statement and Balance Sheet columns.
4. Calculate net income or net loss.
5. Extend net income or net loss to Balance Sheet Debit or Credit column.
6. Total Income Statement and Balance Sheet columns.
7. Check that totals are in balance.

| | ACCOUNT TITLE | 1 TRIAL BALANCE DEBIT | 2 TRIAL BALANCE CREDIT | 3 ADJUSTMENTS DEBIT | 4 ADJUSTMENTS CREDIT | 5 INCOME STATEMENT DEBIT | 6 INCOME STATEMENT CREDIT | 7 BALANCE SHEET DEBIT | 8 BALANCE SHEET CREDIT | |
|---|---|---|---|---|---|---|---|---|---|---|
| 1 | Cash | 29 080 28 | | | | | | 29 080 28 | | 1 |
| 2 | Petty Cash | 300 00 | | | | | | 300 00 | | 2 |
| 3 | Accounts Receivable | 11 198 40 | | | | | | 11 198 40 | | 3 |
| 4 | Merchandise Inventory | 270 480 00 | | | (a) 15 840 00 | | | 254 640 00 | | 4 |
| 5 | Supplies—Office | 6 480 00 | | | (b) 4 730 00 | | | 1 750 00 | | 5 |
| 6 | Supplies—Store | 6 944 00 | | | (c) 3 910 00 | | | 3 034 00 | | 6 |
| 7 | Prepaid Insurance | 5 800 00 | | | (d) 3 170 00 | | | 2 630 00 | | 7 |
| 8 | Accounts Payable | | 12 542 38 | | | | | | 12 542 38 | 8 |
| 18 | Karl Koehn, Capital | | 136 750 00 | | | | | | 136 750 00 | 18 |
| 19 | Karl Koehn, Drawing | 29 100 00 | | | | | | 29 100 00 | | 19 |
| 20 | Michelle Wu, Capital | | 136 552 48 | | | | | | 136 552 48 | 20 |
| 21 | Michelle Wu, Drawing | 28 800 00 | | | | | | 28 800 00 | | 21 |
| 22 | Income Summary | | | (a) 15 840 00 | | 15 840 00 | | | | 22 |
| 23 | Sales | | 423 120 00 | | | | 423 120 00 | | | 23 |
| 24 | Purchases | 189 960 00 | | | | 189 960 00 | | | | 24 |
| 32 | Supplies Exp.—Office | | | (b) 4 730 00 | | 4 730 00 | | | | 32 |
| 33 | Supplies Exp.—Store | | | (c) 3 910 00 | | 3 910 00 | | | | 33 |
| 34 | Utilities Expense | 3 820 00 | | | | 3 820 00 | | | | 34 |
| 35 | | 714 036 83 | 714 036 83 | 27 650 00 | 27 650 00 | 353 504 15 | 423 120 00 | 360 532 68 | 290 916 83 | 35 |
| 36 | Net Income | | | | | 69 615 85 | | | 69 615 85 | 36 |
| 37 | | | | | | 423 120 00 | 423 120 00 | 360 532 68 | 360 532 68 | 37 |
| 38 | | | | | | | | | | 38 |

Omni Import follows the same procedures for completing a work sheet as described for Encore Music in Chapter 7, with the exception of the income summary account. Encore Music sells a service, not merchandise. Therefore, Encore Music has no amount recorded in the income summary account, a related account used to adjust Merchandise Inventory. Omni Import sells merchandise. Therefore, the income summary account is used as the related account to adjust Merchandise Inventory. The merchandise inventory adjustment reflects the increases and decreases in the amount of goods on hand resulting from purchases and sales. Therefore, the amount recorded in Income Summary is extended to the work sheet's Income Statement Debit or Credit column. An Income Summary debit amount is extended to the Income Statement Debit column. An Income Summary credit amount is extended to the Income Statement Credit column.

Omni Import's completed work sheet for the year ended December 31, 20—, is shown on the following two pages.

## STEPS Completing an 8-column work sheet for a merchandising business

1. Extend balance sheet items to the work sheet's Balance Sheet columns.
2. Extend income statement items, including Income Summary, to the work sheet's Income Statement columns.
3. Subtotal the Income Statement and Balance Sheet columns.
4. Calculate the net income or net loss. If the Income Statement Credit column total (revenue) is larger than the Debit column total (costs and expenses), a net income has occurred. If the Income Statement Debit column total (costs and expenses) is larger than the Credit column total (revenue), a net loss has occurred. Omni Import's net income is calculated as shown below.

| Income Statement Credit Column Total | – | Income Statement Debit Column Total | = | Net Income |
|---|---|---|---|---|
| $423,120.00 | – | $353,504.15 | = | $69,615.85 |

5. Extend the amount of net income or net loss to the Balance Sheet Debit or Credit column. When a net income occurs, the net income amount is extended to the Balance Sheet Credit amount column, as shown on line 36. When a net loss occurs, the net loss amount is extended to the Balance Sheet Debit amount column.
6. Total the four Income Statement and Balance Sheet amount columns.
7. Check that the totals for each pair of columns are in balance. As shown on line 37, the totals for the Income Statement columns, *$423,120.00*, are the same. The totals for the Balance Sheet columns, *$360,532.68*, are also the same. Omni Import's work sheet is in balance.

## A COMPLETED 8-COLUMN WORK SHEET FOR A MERCHANDISING BUSINESS

*Omni Import*
*Work Sheet*
*For Year Ended December 31, 20--*

| | | 1 | 2 | 3 | 4 | 5 | 6 | 7 | 8 | |
|---|---|---|---|---|---|---|---|---|---|---|
| | ACCOUNT TITLE | TRIAL BALANCE | | ADJUSTMENTS | | INCOME STATEMENT | | BALANCE SHEET | | |
| | | DEBIT | CREDIT | DEBIT | CREDIT | DEBIT | CREDIT | DEBIT | CREDIT | |
| 1 | *Cash* | 29080 28 | | | | | | 29080 28 | | 1 |
| 2 | *Petty Cash* | 300 00 | | | | | | 300 00 | | 2 |
| 3 | *Accounts Receivable* | 11198 40 | | | | | | 11198 40 | | 3 |
| 4 | *Merchandise Inventory* | 270480 00 | | | (a) 15840 00 | | | 254640 00 | | 4 |
| 5 | *Supplies—Office* | 6480 00 | | | (b) 4730 00 | | | 1750 00 | | 5 |
| 6 | *Supplies—Store* | 6944 00 | | | (c) 3910 00 | | | 3034 00 | | 6 |
| 7 | *Prepaid Insurance* | 5800 00 | | | (d) 3170 00 | | | 2630 00 | | 7 |
| 8 | *Accounts Payable* | | 12542 38 | | | | | | 12542 38 | 8 |
| 9 | *Employee Income Tax Payable* | | 542 00 | | | | | | 542 00 | 9 |
| 10 | *Social Security Tax Payable* | | 985 40 | | | | | | 985 40 | 10 |
| 11 | *Medicare Tax Payable* | | 227 42 | | | | | | 227 42 | 11 |
| 12 | *Sales Tax Payable* | | 2112 05 | | | | | | 2112 05 | 12 |
| 13 | *Unemployment Tax Payable—Federal* | | 8 40 | | | | | | 8 40 | 13 |
| 14 | *Unemployment Tax Payable—State* | | 56 70 | | | | | | 56 70 | 14 |
| 15 | *Health Insurance Premiums Payable* | | 1008 00 | | | | | | 1008 00 | 15 |
| 16 | *U.S. Savings Bonds Payable* | | 60 00 | | | | | | 60 00 | 16 |
| 17 | *United Way Donations Payable* | | 72 00 | | | | | | 72 00 | 17 |
| 18 | *Karl Koehn, Capital* | | 136750 00 | | | | | | 136750 00 | 18 |
| 19 | *Karl Koehn, Drawing* | 29100 00 | | | | | | 29100 00 | | 19 |
| 20 | *Michelle Wu, Capital* | | 136552 48 | | | | | | 136552 48 | 20 |
| 21 | *Michelle Wu, Drawing* | 28800 00 | | | | | | 28800 00 | | 21 |

| | Account Title | Trial Balance Debit | Trial Balance Credit | Adjustments Debit | Adjustments Credit | Income Statement Debit | Income Statement Credit | Balance Sheet Debit | Balance Sheet Credit | |
|---|---|---|---|---|---|---|---|---|---|---|
| 22 | *Income Summary* | | | (a) 15 840 00 | | 15 840 00 | | | | 22 |
| 23 | *Sales* | | 423 120 00 | | | | 423 120 00 | | | 23 |
| 24 | *Purchases* | 189 960 00 | | | | 189 960 00 | | | | 24 |
| 25 | *Advertising Expense* | 6 600 00 | | | | 6 600 00 | | | | 25 |
| 26 | *Credit Card Fee Expense* | 3 385 00 | | | | 3 385 00 | | | | 26 |
| 27 | *Insurance Expense* | | | (d) 3 170 00 | | 3 170 00 | | | | 27 |
| 28 | *Miscellaneous Expense* | 2 584 15 | | | | 2 584 15 | | | | 28 |
| 29 | *Payroll Taxes Expense* | 9 105 00 | | | | 9 105 00 | | | | 29 |
| 30 | *Rent Expense* | 21 000 00 | | | | 21 000 00 | | | | 30 |
| 31 | *Salary Expense* | 89 400 00 | | | | 89 400 00 | | | | 31 |
| 32 | *Supplies Expense—Office* | | | (b) 4 730 00 | | 4 730 00 | | | | 32 |
| 33 | *Supplies Expense—Store* | | | (c) 3 910 00 | | 3 910 00 | | | | 33 |
| 34 | *Utilities Expense* | 3 820 00 | | | | 3 820 00 | | | | 34 |
| 35 | | 714 036 83 | 714 036 83 | 27 650 00 | 27 650 00 | 353 504 15 | 423 120 00 | 360 532 68 | 290 916 83 | 35 |
| 36 | *Net Income* | | | | | 69 615 85 | | | 69 615 85 | 36 |
| 37 | | | | | | 423 120 00 | 423 120 00 | 360 532 68 | 360 532 68 | 37 |
| 38 | | | | | | | | | | 38 |
| 39 | | | | | | | | | | 39 |
| 40 | | | | | | | | | | 40 |
| 41 | | | | | | | | | | 41 |
| 42 | | | | | | | | | | 42 |
| 43 | | | | | | | | | | 43 |
| 44 | | | | | | | | | | 44 |
| 45 | | | | | | | | | | 45 |
| 46 | | | | | | | | | | 46 |
| 47 | | | | | | | | | | 47 |

# A 10-COLUMN WORK SHEET FOR A MERCHANDISING BUSINESS (LEFT PAGE)

**1.** Trial Balance **2.** Adjustments

*Omni Import*
*Work Sheet*
*For Year Ended December 31, 20--*

| | ACCOUNT TITLE | 1 TRIAL BALANCE DEBIT | 2 TRIAL BALANCE CREDIT | 3 ADJUSTMENTS DEBIT | 4 ADJUSTMENTS CREDIT | |
|---|---|---|---|---|---|---|
| 1 | *Cash* | 29 080 28 | | | | 1 |
| 2 | *Petty Cash* | 300 00 | | | | 2 |
| 3 | *Accounts Receivable* | 11 198 40 | | | | 3 |
| 4 | *Merchandise Inventory* | 270 480 00 | | | (a) 15 840 00 | 4 |
| 5 | *Supplies—Office* | 6 480 00 | | | (b) 4 730 00 | 5 |
| 6 | *Supplies—Store* | 6 944 00 | | | (c) 3 910 00 | 6 |
| 7 | *Prepaid Insurance* | 5 800 00 | | | (d) 3 170 00 | 7 |
| 8 | *Accounts Payable* | | 12 542 38 | | | 8 |
| 9 | *Employee Income Tax Payable* | | 542 00 | | | 9 |
| 29 | *Payroll Taxes Expense* | 9 105 00 | | | | 29 |
| 30 | *Rent Expense* | 21 000 00 | | | | 30 |
| 31 | *Salary Expense* | 89 400 00 | | | | 31 |
| 32 | *Supplies Expense—Office* | | | (b) 4 730 00 | | 32 |
| 33 | *Supplies Expense—Store* | | | (c) 3 910 00 | | 33 |
| 34 | *Utilities Expense* | 3 820 00 | | | | 34 |
| 35 | | 714 036 83 | 714 036 83 | 27 650 00 | 27 650 00 | 35 |
| 36 | *Net Income* | | | | | 36 |
| 37 | | | | | | 37 |
| 38 | | | | | | 38 |

Some large merchandising businesses *with many accounts to be adjusted* at the end of a fiscal period may use a 10-column work sheet. A 10-column work sheet includes an additional pair of amount columns titled Adjusted Trial Balance.

### STEPS: Completing a 10-column work sheet

1. Record the trial balance on the work sheet.
2. Plan the adjustments on the work sheet.
3. Extend the balances in the Trial Balance Debit and Credit columns to the Adjusted Trial Balance Debit and Credit columns. Calculate up-to-date adjusted balances for all accounts affected by adjustments.
4. Total, prove, and rule the Adjusted Trial Balance Debit and Credit columns.
5. Extend the amounts in the Adjusted Trial Balance Debit and Credit columns to the appropriate Income Statement and Balance Sheet columns.
6. Total, prove, and rule the Income Statement and Balance Sheet columns in the same way as on an 8-column work sheet.

# A 10-COLUMN WORK SHEET FOR A MERCHANDISING BUSINESS (RIGHT PAGE)

**3.** Adjusted Trial Balance

**5.** Extend Amounts

**4.** Total, Prove, and Rule

**6.** Total, Prove, and Rule

| | 5 | 6 | 7 | 8 | 9 | 10 | |
|---|---|---|---|---|---|---|---|
| | ADJUSTED TRIAL BALANCE | | INCOME STATEMENT | | BALANCE SHEET | | |
| | DEBIT | CREDIT | DEBIT | CREDIT | DEBIT | CREDIT | |
| 1 | 2908 28 | | | | 2908 28 | | 1 |
| 2 | 300 00 | | | | 300 00 | | 2 |
| 3 | 11198 40 | | | | 11198 40 | | 3 |
| 4 | 254640 00 | | | | 254640 00 | | 4 |
| 5 | 1750 00 | | | | 1750 00 | | 5 |
| 6 | 3034 00 | | | | 3034 00 | | 6 |
| 7 | 2630 00 | | | | 2630 00 | | 7 |
| 8 | | 12542 38 | | | | 12542 38 | 8 |
| 9 | | 542 00 | | | | 542 00 | 9 |
| 29 | 9105 00 | | 9105 00 | | | | 29 |
| 30 | 21000 00 | | 21000 00 | | | | 30 |
| 31 | 89400 00 | | 89400 00 | | | | 31 |
| 32 | 4730 00 | | 4730 00 | | | | 32 |
| 33 | 3910 00 | | 3910 00 | | | | 33 |
| 34 | 3820 00 | | 3820 00 | | | | 34 |
| 35 | 714036 83 | 714036 83 | 353504 15 | 423120 00 | 360532 68 | 290916 83 | 35 |
| 36 | | | 69615 85 | | | 69615 85 | 36 |
| 37 | | | 423120 00 | 423120 00 | 360532 68 | 360532 68 | 37 |
| 38 | | | | | | | 38 |

Any business with adjustments to make at the end of a fiscal period could use either an 8-column or a 10-column work sheet. However, completing two extra amount columns when most of the account balances *are not* adjusted requires extra time and work. Account balances not adjusted must be extended from the Trial Balance columns to the Adjusted Trial Balance columns; whereas, with an 8-column work sheet, account balances *not* adjusted are extended directly to the Balance Sheet or Income Statement columns. Omni Import prefers to use an 8-column work sheet because only four adjustments are needed at the end of each fiscal period.

**REMEMBER**

A 10-column work sheet is often used by large merchandising companies with many accounts to be adjusted.

## Audit Your Understanding

1. In what column is the Income Summary amount extended?
2. When does a net loss appear on a work sheet?
3. To which Balance Sheet column is a net loss amount extended?
4. What extra step is required when a 10-column work sheet is prepared instead of an 8-column work sheet?

## Work Together

**Completing an 8-column work sheet for a merchandising business**

Use the Paradise Company work sheet from Work Together on page 377. Your instructor will guide you through the following examples.

5. Extend balance sheet items to the work sheet's Balance Sheet columns.
6. Extend income statement items, including Income Summary, to the work sheet's Income Statement columns.
7. Subtotal the Income Statement and Balance Sheet columns.
8. Calculate the net income or net loss.
9. Extend the amount of net income or net loss to the Balance Sheet Debit or Credit column.
10. Total the four Income Statement and Balance Sheet amount columns.
11. Check that the totals for each pair of columns are in balance.

## On Your Own

**Completing an 8-column work sheet for a merchandising business**

Use the Mueller Company work sheet from On Your Own on page 377. Work these problems independently.

12. Extend balance sheet items to the work sheet's Balance Sheet columns.
13. Extend income statement items, including Income Summary, to the work sheet's Income Statement columns.
14. Subtotal the Income Statement and Balance Sheet columns.
15. Calculate the net income or net loss.
16. Extend the amount of net income or net loss to the Balance Sheet Debit or Credit column.
17. Total the four Income Statement and Balance Sheet amount columns.
18. Check that the totals for each pair of columns are in balance.

# CHAPTER 15 SUMMARY

*Enrichment Activity*

**Accounting Careers**

*Interview one or more accountants who work in a corporation, government, accounting firm, or private practice about career opportunities. Write a summary of the interview that emphasizes entry-level job requirements, career tracks, and projected trends for the future.*

After completing this chapter, you can

1. Define important accounting terms related to a work sheet for a merchandising business.
2. Identify accounting concepts and practices related to a work sheet for a merchandising business.
3. Begin a work sheet for a merchandising business.
4. Plan adjustments on a work sheet for a merchandising business.
5. Complete a work sheet for a merchandising business.

## EXPLORE ACCOUNTING

### ACCOUNTING SYSTEMS DESIGN

An important role of accountants is to prepare financial statements for businesses. In addition, many accountants design accounting systems used to prepare the various financial reports important to successful business operations.

An accounting system should be designed to meet the needs of the business it serves. Factors to consider are size of the company, number of facility locations, geographic area of operations (local, statewide, national, international), number of employees, and type of organization (service, merchandising, manufacturing). Also to be considered are the intended uses of the information: traditional financial statements (income statement, balance sheet, cash flow statement), income tax information, management decision information, management control information, and product pricing information.

An accounting system is built around a chart of accounts, which provides the organizational system around which information will be collected, filed, and made available for various types of financial reports.

A small business owned and operated by one person may not need detailed information. However, as a business grows in size and complexity, more detailed information is required. Large international businesses need very complex accounting systems with hundreds of accounts to furnish management with the information needed to make decisions and the data for various reports required by governments and other agencies. As businesses grow, accountants constantly look for ways to provide better information. Thus, accountants play a key role in the successful growth of a business.

**Activity:** Assume Omni Import has made the decision to change from a merchandising business to a manufacturing business. It will import fine yarns and cloth from Europe and Asia. From these imported materials, it will manufacture various items of clothing. As the accountant, how would you recommend the chart of accounts be modified to meet the changing needs of the company?

## 15-1 APPLICATION PROBLEM

### Beginning an 8-column work sheet for a merchandising business

A work sheet for Drake Park Supply Company is given in the *Working Papers*. The company's general ledger account balances on December 31 of the current year, after all transactions have been posted, are listed below.

| | | |
|---|---|---|
| Cash | $ 29,066.00 | |
| Petty Cash | 330.00 | |
| Accounts Receivable | 11,762.00 | |
| Merchandise Inventory | 279,668.00 | |
| Supplies—Office | 6,700.00 | |
| Supplies—Store | 7,168.00 | |
| Prepaid Insurance | 6,094.00 | |
| Accounts Payable | | $ 11,814.00 |
| Sales Tax Payable | | 2,184.00 |
| Tracey Johnson, Capital | | 129,663.00 |
| Tracey Johnson, Drawing | 22,583.00 | |
| Bill Fujiwara, Capital | | 130,394.00 |
| Bill Fujiwara, Drawing | 23,078.00 | |
| Income Summary | | |
| Sales | | 348,084.00 |
| Purchases | 196,416.00 | |
| Advertising Expense | 6,820.00 | |
| Credit Card Fee Expense | 3,590.00 | |
| Insurance Expense | | |
| Miscellaneous Expense | 2,717.00 | |
| Rent Expense | 22,200.00 | |
| Supplies Expense—Office | | |
| Supplies Expense—Store | | |
| Utilities Expense | 3,947.00 | |

***Instructions:***

1. Enter Drake Park Supply Company's general ledger accounts and balances in the appropriate columns of the work sheet.
2. Total, prove, and rule the trial balance.
3. From a physical count of merchandise inventory, the December 31 balance is determined to be $263,289.00. Analyze the merchandise inventory adjustment and enter the adjustment on the work sheet.

## 15-2 APPLICATION PROBLEM

### Analyzing and recording adjustments on a work sheet

The following chart contains adjustment information related to the preparation of work sheets for three businesses. A form for analyzing transactions is given in the *Working Papers*.

| Business | Account Title and Balance | | End-of-Fiscal-Period Information | |
|---|---|---|---|---|
| A | 1. Merchandise Inventory . . . . . . . | $177,600.00 | Merchandise inventory . . . . . . . | $160,800.00 |
| | 2. Supplies—Office . . . . . . . . . . . | 6,900.00 | Office supplies inventory . . . . . | 5,040.00 |
| | 3. Supplies—Store . . . . . . . . . . . . | 5,905.00 | Store supplies inventory . . . . . . | 4,610.00 |
| | 4. Prepaid Insurance . . . . . . . . . . . | 2,230.00 | Value of prepaid insurance . . . . | 1,490.00 |
| B | 1. Merchandise Inventory . . . . . . . | $218,400.00 | Merchandise inventory . . . . . . . | $199,200.00 |
| | 2. Supplies—Office . . . . . . . . . . . | 5,620.00 | Office supplies inventory . . . . . | 4,150.00 |
| | 3. Supplies—Store . . . . . . . . . . . . | 7,110.00 | Store supplies inventory . . . . . . | 5,185.00 |
| | 4. Prepaid Insurance . . . . . . . . . . . | 3,025.00 | Value of prepaid insurance . . . . | 1,510.00 |
| C | 1. Merchandise Inventory . . . . . . . | $199,800.00 | Merchandise inventory . . . . . . . | $213,600.00 |
| | 2. Supplies—Office . . . . . . . . . . . | 6,550.00 | Office supplies inventory . . . . . | 5,425.00 |
| | 3. Supplies—Store . . . . . . . . . . . . | 7,175.00 | Store supplies inventory . . . . . . | 5,950.00 |
| | 4. Prepaid Insurance . . . . . . . . . . . | 2,590.00 | Value of prepaid insurance . . . . | 1,295.00 |

***Instructions:***

For each business, analyze the adjustments for merchandise inventory, office supplies inventory, store supplies inventory, and prepaid insurance. List the accounts affected and the amounts for each of the adjustments. List the account titles in Column 3 and the amounts in either Column 4 or 5. Adjustment 1 for Business A is given as an example in the *Working Papers.*

## 15-3 APPLICATION PROBLEM

### Completing an 8-column work sheet for a merchandising business

Lotus Gallery's partially completed work sheet is given in the *Working Papers.*

***Instructions:***

1. Extend the balance sheet items to the Balance Sheet columns of the work sheet.
2. Extend the income statement items to the Income Statement columns of the work sheet.
3. Subtotal the Income Statement and Balance Sheet columns.
4. Calculate and record the net income or net loss.
5. Extend the amount of net income or net loss to the Balance Sheet Debit or Credit column.
6. Total and rule the Income Statement and Balance Sheet columns.

## 15-4 MASTERY PROBLEM

### Preparing an 8-column work sheet for a merchandising business

Seidler Supply's trial balance as of December 31 of the current year is recorded on a work sheet in the *Working Papers.*

***Instructions:***

1. Analyze the following adjustment information and record the adjustments on the work sheet.

| End-of-Fiscal-Period Information | |
|---|---|
| Merchandise inventory . . . . . . . . . . . . . . . . . . . . . | $250,320.00 |
| Office supplies inventory . . . . . . . . . . . . . . . . . . | 2,226.00 |
| Store supplies inventory . . . . . . . . . . . . . . . . . . . . | 2,825.00 |
| Value of prepaid insurance . . . . . . . . . . . . . . . . . | 1,890.00 |

2. Complete the work sheet.

## 15-5 CHALLENGE PROBLEM

### Preparing a 10-column work sheet for a merchandising business

K.B. Cycle Shop's trial balance as of December 31 of the current year is recorded on a work sheet in the *Working Papers*.

***Instructions:***

1. Use the following adjustment information. Complete the 10-column work sheet.

**End-of-Fiscal-Period Information**

| | |
|---|---|
| Merchandise inventory | $308,055.00 |
| Office supplies inventory | 3,240.00 |
| Store supplies inventory | 3,290.00 |
| Value of prepaid insurance | 1,980.00 |

2. Compare and contrast the advantages and disadvantages of 8-column and 10-column work sheets.

**INTERNET ACTIVITY**

Point your browser to

**http://accounting.swpco.com**

Choose **First-Year Course**, choose **Activities**, and complete the activity for Chapter 15.

## Applied Communication

Sometimes a credit customer does not pay off the amount due on an account receivable by the deadline specified in the terms of the sale on account. In this situation, a business wants to (1) receive the amount owed and (2) preserve a long-term relationship so there can be repeated sales to that customer.

**Instructions:** Write a first-notice letter to a customer who has not yet paid an amount due. Balance your business's need to receive payment with the desire to keep the customer's goodwill now and in the future. Use a supportive opening and closing.

## Cases for Critical Thinking

**Case 1** After completing a work sheet, Park's Boutique finds that garment bags still in boxes were overlooked in calculating the supplies inventory. The value of the garment bags overlooked is $60.00. Jerry Park suggests that the accountant not worry because the oversight does not have any effect on balancing the Income Statement and Balance Sheet columns of the work sheet. Mr. Park says that the oversight will be corrected when the store supplies are counted at the end of the next fiscal period. The accountant recommends that the work sheet be redone to reflect the recalculated supplies inventory. Do you agree with Mr. Park or the accountant? Explain your answer.

**Case 2** High Five Sports Equipment paid $1,800.00 for a one-year fire insurance policy. The company prepares an income statement and balance sheet every three months. However, the accountant prepares a prepaid insurance adjustment only at the end of the year. Wanda Fielder, one of the partners in the business, thinks the prepaid insurance should be adjusted every three months. Who is correct? Why?

# AUTOMATED ACCOUNTING

## UNDERSTANDING GRAPHS

Charts and graphs provide a picture of numeric data. Computer presentations and printed reports frequently include charts and graphs. Charts and graphs do not replace the numeric data, but they do help explain the data. To be effective, charts and graphs should be clearly labeled. Charts and graphs are commonly used to track sales goals, monitor expenses, identify trends, and make forecasts.

Graphs and charts effectively communicate summary data such as component percentages. Different styles of graphs are used to display different types of financial information. A pie graph is used to illustrate parts of a whole. For example, a pie graph could be used to show cost of goods sold, operating expenses, and net income as percentages of net sales. Bar graphs are used to show the relative size of related items, such as expenses. Line graphs are used to illustrate trends, such as net sales or net income over a period of years.

Many accounting software packages are capable of producing charts and graphs from data contained within their files. *Automated Accounting 7.0* can generate two- and three-dimensional pie and bar charts and line graphs from data found on the:

- Balance sheet.
- Income statement.
- Sales report.
- Expense distribution report.
- Actual versus budget comparison report.

To prepare a graph based on financial data:

1. Choose the Graph Selection menu item from the Reports menu or click the Graphs toolbar button.
2. When the Graph Selection dialog box appears, select an option from the Data to Graph list.
3. Select an option from the Type of Graph list. (Menu items may be unavailable for charts and graphs that are inappropriate for some reports.) (In *Automated Accounting 8.0*, graphs are selected from the Graph selection window. The types of graphs available depend on the types of company and available data.)
4. Click the OK button to produce the graph.

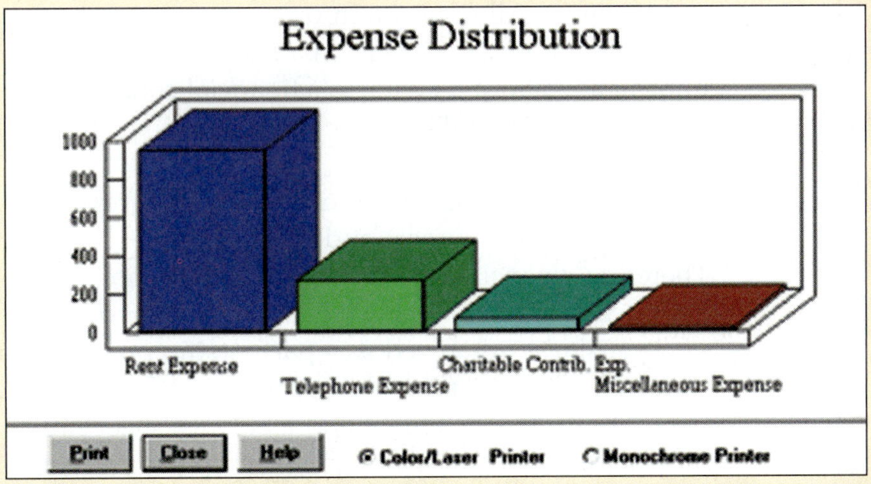

# 16 Financial Statements for a Partnership

**AFTER STUDYING CHAPTER 16, YOU WILL BE ABLE TO:**

1. Define accounting terms related to financial statements for a merchandising business organized as a partnership.
2. Identify accounting concepts and practices related to financial statements for a merchandising business organized as a partnership.
3. Prepare an income statement for a merchandising business organized as a partnership.
4. Analyze an income statement using component percentages for a merchandising business organized as a partnership.
5. Prepare a distribution of net income statement and an owners' equity statement for a merchandising business organized as a partnership.
6. Prepare a balance sheet for a merchandising business organized as a partnership.

**TERMS PREVIEW**

cost of merchandise sold

gross profit on sales

distribution of net income statement

owners' equity statement

supporting schedule

## USES OF FINANCIAL STATEMENTS

Financial statements provide the primary source of information needed by owners and managers to make decisions on the future activity of a business. All financial information must be reported in order to make sound business decisions. The financial statements should provide information about a business's financial condition, changes in this financial condition, and the progress of operations. *(CONCEPT: Adequate Disclosure)*

Comparing financial condition and progress for more than one fiscal period also helps owners and managers make sound business decisions. Therefore, financial information must be reported the same way from one fiscal period to the next. *(CONCEPT: Consistent Reporting)*

A business organized as a partnership prepares four financial statements to report financial progress and condition. A partnership prepares an income statement and a balance sheet similar to those used by a proprietorship. A partnership also prepares two additional financial statements. One statement reports the distribution of net income or net loss for each partner. The other statement reports the changes in owners' equity for the fiscal period.

# ACCOUNTING IN YOUR CAREER

## SUPERSTAR PARTNERSHIP

Huston's is a new restaurant in town, owned by Marcus Huston. Marcus has a degree in business but has opened his own restaurant to combine his culinary skills with his business training. The restaurant business is very competitive, and Marcus spends up to $5,000 per month on advertising and promotion costs to attract customers. Huston's is beginning to become a well-known downtown restaurant and Marcus is earning a good living, but he has the space and the ambition to make the restaurant even more successful. He's been looking for something dramatic to draw media attention to his restaurant.

Drew Taylor is a popular professional football player in town. He is a solid player on the championship team and is also well-liked and respected by people who live in the area. Drew has approached Marcus, an old college friend, with the idea of forming a partnership to run Huston's. Both Drew and Marcus believe that Drew's fame and popularity could be the dramatic turn that would make the business soar.

Marcus is tempted. So he consults with his accountant and attorney for advice.

### *Critical Thinking:*

1. The accountant advises against forming the partnership unless Drew Taylor invests a substantial amount of cash to buy his share of the business. What is the advantage of this plan?
2. The accountant suggests that there might be more advantages in just paying Drew for the use of his name for advertising purposes. Why would the accountant make this recommendation?
3. The accountant tells Marcus that if he pursues the partnership, he must be sure to have a written agreement that specifies the responsibilities of each partner and the distribution of earnings. Do you think this is necessary when friends go into business together?

# 16-1 Income Statement

## INCOME STATEMENT INFORMATION ON A WORK SHEET

**Omni Import**
**Work Sheet**
**For Year Ended December 31, 20--**

| | ACCOUNT TITLE | 1 TRIAL BALANCE DEBIT | 2 TRIAL BALANCE CREDIT | 3 ADJUSTMENTS DEBIT | 4 ADJUSTMENTS CREDIT | 5 INCOME STATEMENT DEBIT | 6 INCOME STATEMENT CREDIT | 7 BALANCE SHEET DEBIT | 8 BALANCE SHEET CREDIT | |
|---|---|---|---|---|---|---|---|---|---|---|
| 4 | Merchandise Inventory | 270,480.00 | | | (a) 15,840.00 | | | 254,640.00 | | 4 |
| 23 | Sales | | 423,120.00 | | | | 423,120.00 | | | 23 |
| 24 | Purchases | 189,960.00 | | | | 189,960.00 | | | | 24 |
| 25 | Advertising Expense | 6,600.00 | | | | 6,600.00 | | | | 25 |
| 26 | Credit Card Fee Expense | 3,385.00 | | | | 3,385.00 | | | | 26 |
| 27 | Insurance Expense | | | (d) 3,170.00 | | 3,170.00 | | | | 27 |
| 28 | Miscellaneous Expense | 2,584.15 | | | | 2,584.15 | | | | 28 |
| 29 | Payroll Taxes Expense | 9,105.00 | | | | 9,105.00 | | | | 29 |
| 30 | Rent Expense | 21,000.00 | | | | 21,000.00 | | | | 30 |
| 31 | Salary Expense | 89,400.00 | | | | 89,400.00 | | | | 31 |
| 32 | Supplies Expense—Office | | | (b) 4,730.00 | | 4,730.00 | | | | 32 |
| 33 | Supplies Expense—Store | | | (c) 3,910.00 | | 3,910.00 | | | | 33 |
| 34 | Utilities Expense | 3,820.00 | | | | 3,820.00 | | | | 34 |
| 35 | | 714,036.83 | 714,036.83 | 27,650.00 | 27,650.00 | 353,504.15 | 423,120.00 | 360,532.68 | 290,916.83 | 35 |
| 36 | Net Income | | | | | 69,615.85 | | | 69,615.85 | 36 |
| 37 | | | | | | 423,120.00 | 423,120.00 | 360,532.68 | 360,532.68 | 37 |
| 38 | | | | | | | | | | 38 |
| 39 | | | | | | | | | | 39 |
| 40 | | | | | | | | | | 40 |
| 41 | | | | | | | | | | 41 |
| 42 | | | | | | | | | | 42 |

An income statement is used to report a business's financial progress. Merchandising businesses report revenue, cost of merchandise sold, gross profit on sales, expenses, and net income or loss. Current and previous income statements can be compared to determine the reasons for increases or decreases in net income. This comparison is helpful in making management decisions about future operations.

Information from a completed work sheet is used to prepare an income statement.

The income statement of a merchandising business has three main sections: (1) revenue section, (2) cost of merchandise sold section, and (3) expenses section. The total original price of all merchandise sold during a fiscal period is called the **cost of merchandise sold.** *(CONCEPT: Historical Cost)* Cost of merchandise sold is sometimes known as cost of goods sold or cost of sales. Omni uses eight steps in preparing an income statement. The steps are described on the following three pages.

## FIRST TWO SECTIONS OF AN INCOME STATEMENT FOR A MERCHANDISING BUSINESS

1. Heading
2. Revenue Section
3. Cost of Merchandise Sold Section

*Omni Import*
*Income Statement*
*For Year Ended December 31, 20--*

| | | | % OF SALES |
|---|---|---|---|
| *Revenue:* | | | |
| *Sales* | | *423 1 2 0 00* | |
| *Cost of Merchandise Sold:* | | | |
| *Merchandise Inventory, January 1, 20--* | *270 4 8 0 00* | | |
| *Purchases* | *189 9 6 0 00* | | |
| *Total Cost of Mdse. Available for Sale* | *460 4 4 0 00* | | |
| *Less Mdse. Inventory, December 31, 20--* | *254 6 4 0 00* | | |
| *Cost of Merchandise Sold* | | *205 8 0 0 00* | |

### STEPS: Preparing an income statement

1. Write the income statement heading on three lines.
2. Prepare the revenue section. Use information from the Income Statement Credit column of the work sheet.
   a. Write the name of this section, *Revenue:*, at the extreme left of the wide column on the first line.
   b. Write the title of the revenue account, *Sales,* on the next line, indented about one centimeter.
   c. Write the balance of the sales account, *$423,120.00,* in the second amount column. For Omni Import, this amount is also the total of the revenue section.
3. Prepare the cost of merchandise sold section.
   a. Write the name of this section, *Cost of Merchandise Sold:*, at the extreme left of the wide column.
   b. Indent about one centimeter on the next line, and write the items needed to calculate cost of merchandise sold. Write the amount of each item in the first amount column.

| | |
|---|---|
| Beginning merchandise inventory, January 1 ...... (Debit balance of Merchandise Inventory in the Trial Balance Debit column of the work sheet.) | $ 270,480.00 |
| *Plus* purchases made during the fiscal period ...... (Debit balance of Purchases in the Income Statement Debit column of the work sheet.) | +189,960.00 |
| *Equals* total cost of merchandise available for sale during the fiscal period. ...................... | $ 460,440.00 |
| *Less* ending merchandise inventory, December 31 (Debit balance of Merchandise Inventory in the Balance Sheet Debit column of the work sheet.) | −254,640.00 |
| *Equals* cost of merchandise sold during the fiscal period .................................. | $ 205,800.00 |

   c. Indent about one centimeter on the next line, and write *Cost of Merchandise Sold.* Write the cost of merchandise sold amount, *$205,800.00,* in the second amount column.

# COMPLETING AN INCOME STATEMENT FOR A MERCHANDISING BUSINESS

8. Component Percentages

| Omni Import<br>Income Statement<br>For Year Ended December 31, 20-- | | | % OF SALES |
|---|---|---|---|
| *Revenue:* | | | |
| *Sales* | | 423120 00 | 100.0 |
| *Cost of Merchandise Sold:* | | | |
| *Merchandise Inventory, January 1, 20--* | 270480 00 | | |
| *Purchases* | 189960 00 | | |
| *Total Cost of Mdse. Available for Sale* | 460440 00 | | |
| *Less Mdse. Inventory, December 31, 20--* | 254640 00 | | |
| *Cost of Merchandise Sold* | | 205800 00 | 48.6 |
| ***Gross Profit on Sales*** | | 217320 00 | 51.4 |
| ***Expenses:*** | | | |
| ***Advertising Expense*** | 6600 00 | | |
| ***Credit Card Fee Expense*** | 3385 00 | | |
| ***Insurance Expense*** | 3170 00 | | |
| ***Miscellaneous Expense*** | 2584 15 | | |
| ***Payroll Taxes Expense*** | 9105 00 | | |
| ***Rent Expense*** | 21000 00 | | |
| ***Salary Expense*** | 89400 00 | | |
| ***Supplies Expense—Office*** | 4730 00 | | |
| ***Supplies Expense—Store*** | 3910 00 | | |
| ***Utilities Expense*** | 3820 00 | | |
| ***Total Expenses*** | | 147704 15 | 34.9 |
| ***Net Income*** | | 69615 85 | 16.5 |

4. Gross Profit on Sales

5. Expenses Section

6. Net Income

7. Double Lines

## STEPS

### Preparing an income statement *(continued)*

4. Calculate the gross profit on sales. The revenue remaining after cost of merchandise sold has been deducted is called **gross profit on sales.**
   a. Write *Gross Profit on Sales* on the next line at the extreme left of the wide column.
   b. Write the gross profit on sales amount, *$217,320.00*, in the second amount column. (Total revenue, $423,120.00, *less* cost of merchandise sold, $205,800.00, *equals* gross profit on sales, $217,320.00.)
5. Prepare the expenses section. Use the information from the Income Statement Debit column of the work sheet.
   a. Write the name of this section, *Expenses:*, at the extreme left of the wide column.
   b. On the next line, indented about one centimeter, list the expense account titles, one per line, in the order in which they appear on the work sheet.
   c. Write the amount of each expense account balance in the first amount column.

d. Indent about one centimeter, and write *Total Expenses* on the next line in the wide column below the last expense account title.

e. Total the individual expense amounts and write the total, *$147,704.15,* in the second amount column on the total line.

**6.** Calculate the net income.

a. Write *Net Income* on the next line at the extreme left of the wide column.

b. Write the net income amount, *$69,615.85,* in the second amount column on the net income line. (Gross profit on sales, $217,320.00, *less* total expenses, $147,704.15, *equals* net income, $69,615.85.)

c. Verify accuracy by comparing the amount of net income calculated on the income statement, $69,615.85, with the amount on the work sheet, $69,615.85. The two amounts must be the same.

**7.** Rule double lines across both amount columns to show that the income statement has been verified as correct.

**8.** Calculate the component percentages. The percentage relationship between one financial statement item and the total that includes that item is known as a component percentage. On the income statement, sales includes four components: cost of merchandise sold, gross profit on sales, total expenses, and net income.

a. Calculate the component percentages by dividing the amount of each component by the amount of sales.

| **Cost of Merchandise Sold** | **÷** | **Sales** | **=** | **Cost of Merchandise Sold Component Percentage** |
|---|---|---|---|---|
| $205,800.00 | ÷ | $423,120.00 | = | 48.6% |
| **Gross Profit on Sales** | **÷** | **Sales** | **=** | **Gross Profit on Sales Component Percentage** |
| $217,320.00 | ÷ | $423,120.00 | = | 51.4% |
| **Total Expenses** | **÷** | **Sales** | **=** | **Total Expenses Component Percentage** |
| $147,704.15 | ÷ | $423,120.00 | = | 34.9% |
| **Net Income** | **÷** | **Sales** | **=** | **Net Income Component Percentage** |
| $69,615.85 | ÷ | $423,120.00 | = | 16.5% |

b. Write each component percentage in the % of Sales column. The use of the component percentages is described later in this chapter.

## REMEMBER

Amounts are listed in the first amount column of the financial statement and totaled in the second column. These are amount columns, not debit and credit columns.

## TERMS REVIEW

cost of merchandise sold

gross profit on sales

## AUDIT YOUR UNDERSTANDING

1. What is the major difference between the income statement for a merchandising business and a service business?
2. How is the cost of merchandise sold calculated?
3. How can the amount of net income calculated on the income statement be verified?

## WORK TOGETHER

**Preparing an income statement for a merchandising business**

A to Z Auto Parts' work sheet for the year ended December 31 of the current year is given in the *Working Papers.* Your instructor will guide you through the following examples.

4. Prepare an income statement.
5. Calculate and record on the income statement the following component percentages: (a) cost of merchandise sold, (b) gross profit on sales, (c) total expenses, and (d) net income or loss. Round percentage calculations to the nearest 0.1%. Save your work to complete Work Together on page 401 and page 407.

## ON YOUR OWN

**Preparing an income statement for a merchandising business**

Electron Games' work sheet for the year ended December 31 of the current year is given in the *Working Papers.* Work independently to complete these problems.

6. Prepare an income statement.
7. Calculate and record on the income statement the following component percentages: (a) cost of merchandise sold, (b) gross profit on sales, (c) total expenses, and (d) net income or loss. Round percentage calculations to the nearest 0.1%. Save your work to complete On Your Own on page 401 and page 407.

# 16-2 Component Percentages

## ANALYZING AN INCOME STATEMENT SHOWING A NET INCOME

For Omni Import, a merchandising business, every sales dollar reported on the income statement includes four components: (1) cost of merchandise sold, (2) gross profit on sales, (3) total expenses, and (4) net income. To help make decisions about future operations, Omni analyzes relationships between these four income statement components and sales. Omni calculates a component percentage for each of the four components. The relationship between each component and sales is shown in a separate column on the income statement.

## ACCEPTABLE COMPONENT PERCENTAGES

| | Acceptable Industry Standards | Omni Import Component Percentages |
|---|---|---|
| Sales | 100% | 100.0% |
| Cost of merchandise sold | not more than 50.0% | 48.6% |
| Gross profit on sales | not less than 50.0% | 51.4% |
| Total expenses | not more than 35.0% | 34.9% |
| Net income | not less than 15.0% | 16.5% |

For a component percentage to be useful, a business must know acceptable percentages. This information is determined by making comparisons with prior fiscal periods as well as with industry standards that are published by industry organizations. Based on these sources, Omni Import determines acceptable component percentages. Each percentage represents the amount of each sales dollar that is considered acceptable. For example, Omni Import determines that no more than 50 cents, or 50.0%, of each sales dollar should be devoted to cost of merchandise sold.

**FYI**

*Unacceptable component percentages serve as a warning that management action is necessary. Calculating and reporting component percentages is an example of how accounting information can help management planning and decision making. Well-run businesses greatly value the information provided from account-*

## ANALYSIS OF COMPONENT PERCENTAGES

Omni compares four of its component percentages to its acceptable component percentages. The four component percentages are for cost of merchandise sold, gross profit on sales, total expenses, and net income.

### Cost of Merchandise Sold Component Percentage

The cost of merchandise sold is a major cost and must be kept as low as possible. Analysis of Omni Import's component percentages shows that the cost of merchandise sold is 48.6% of sales.

The component percentage for cost of merchandise sold, 48.6%, is *less than* the maximum acceptable percentage, 50.0%. Therefore, Omni Import's component percentage for cost of merchandise sold is considered acceptable.

### Gross Profit on Sales Component Percentage

Gross profit must be large enough to cover total expenses and the desired amount of net income. Acceptable industry standards show that at least 50 cents, or 50.0%, of each sales dollar should result in gross profit. Omni Import's component percentage for gross profit on sales is 51.4%.

The component percentage for gross profit on sales, 51.4%, is *not less than* the minimum acceptable percentage, 50.0%. Therefore, Omni Import's component percentage for gross profit on sales is considered acceptable.

### Total Expenses Component Percentage

Total expenses must be less than gross profit on sales to provide a desirable net income. Acceptable industry standards show that no more than 35 cents, or 35.0%, of each sales dollar should be devoted to total expenses. Omni Import's component percentage for total expenses is 34.9%.

The component percentage for total expenses, 34.9%, is *not more than* the maximum acceptable percentage, 35.0%. Therefore, Omni Import's component percentage for total expenses is considered acceptable.

### Net Income Component Percentage

The component percentage for net income shows the progress being made by a business. Acceptable industry standards show that at least 15 cents, or 15.0%, of each sales dollar should result in net income. Omni Import's component percentage for net income is 16.5%.

The component percentage for net income, 16.5%, is *not less than* the minimum acceptable percentage, 15.0%. Therefore, Omni Import's component percentage for net income is considered acceptable.

**FYI**

*A partnership is a traditional and very common form of business organization. The Revised Uniform Partnership Act is a law that governs partnerships in most states. Employees responsible for accounting records should be aware of the laws that apply to business operations.*

# ANALYZING AN INCOME STATEMENT SHOWING A NET LOSS

| Cloth Circuit<br>Income Statement<br>For Year Ended December 31, 20-- | | | % OF SALES |
|---|---|---|---|
| ***Revenue:*** | | | |
| *Sales* | | 270,480.00 | 100.0 |
| ***Cost of Merchandise Sold:*** | | | |
| *Merchandise Inventory, January 1, 20--* | 291,840.00 | | |
| *Purchases* | 166,680.00 | | |
| *Total Cost of Mdse. Available for Sale* | 458,520.00 | | |
| *Less Mdse. Inventory, December 31, 20--* | 310,910.00 | | |
| *Cost of Merchandise Sold* | | 147,610.00 | 54.6 |
| ***Gross Profit on Sales*** | | 122,870.00 | 45.4 |
| ***Expenses:*** | | | |
| *Advertising Expense* | 6,240.00 | | |
| *Credit Card Fee Expense* | 3,744.00 | | |
| *Insurance Expense* | 1,260.00 | | |
| *Miscellaneous Expense* | 2,868.00 | | |
| *Payroll Taxes Expense* | 7,615.00 | | |
| *Rent Expense* | 17,280.00 | | |
| *Salary Expense* | 74,770.00 | | |
| *Supplies Expense—Office* | 5,544.00 | | |
| *Supplies Expense—Store* | 5,136.00 | | |
| *Utilities Expense* | 4,093.00 | | |
| *Total Expenses* | | 128,550.00 | 47.5 |
| ***Net Loss*** | | (5,680.00) | (2.1) |

When a business's total expenses are greater than the gross profit on sales, the difference is known as a net loss. For example, the income statement above shows a net loss of $5,680.00 for the fiscal period.

Total expenses, $128,550.00, *less* gross profit on sales, $122,870.00, *equals* net loss, $5,680.00. The net loss amount, $5,680.00, is written in parentheses in the second amount column on the line with the words *Net Loss.* An amount written in parentheses on a financial statement indicates a negative amount.

Cloth Circuit uses the same acceptable component percentages as Omni Import. Analysis of the income statement indicates unacceptable component percentages: (1) The component percentage for cost of merchandise sold, 54.6%, is *more than* the maximum acceptable component percentage, 50.0%. (2) The component percentage for gross profit on sales, 45.4%, is *less than* the minimum acceptable component percentage, 50.0%. (3) The component percentage for total expenses, 47.5%, is *more than* the maximum acceptable component percentage, 35.0%. (4) Because a net loss occurred, the component percentage for net income, (2.1%), means that Cloth Circuit lost 2.1 cents on each sales dollar. The net loss amount, $5,680.00, is considered unacceptable.

## REMEMBER

Negative amounts are written in parentheses.

## ACTIONS TO CORRECT UNACCEPTABLE COMPONENT PERCENTAGES

The goal of any business is to earn an acceptable net income. When component percentages are not acceptable, regardless of whether a net income or net loss occurred, management action is necessary.

### Unacceptable Component Percentage for Gross Profit on Sales

The component percentage for gross profit on sales is directly related to sales revenue and cost of merchandise sold. An unacceptable component percentage for gross profit on sales requires one of three actions: (1) increase sales revenue, (2) decrease cost of merchandise sold, or (3) increase sales revenue and also decrease cost of merchandise sold.

Increasing sales revenue while keeping the cost of merchandise sold the same will increase gross profit on sales. To increase sales revenue, management may consider increasing the markup on merchandise purchased for sale. However, a business must be cautious on the amount of the markup increase. If the increase in markup is too large, a decrease in sales revenue could occur for two reasons: (1) the sales price is beyond what customers are willing to pay or (2) the sales price is higher than what competing businesses charge for the same merchandise.

Decreasing the cost of merchandise sold while keeping the sales revenue the same will also increase gross profit on sales. To decrease cost of merchandise sold, management should review purchasing practices. For example, would purchasing merchandise in larger quantities or from other vendors result in a lower cost?

Combining a small increase in sales revenue and a small decrease in the cost of merchandise sold may also result in an acceptable component percentage for gross profit on sales.

### Unacceptable Component Percentage for Total Expenses

Each expense account balance must be reviewed to determine if major increases have occurred. This review should include comparisons with prior fiscal periods as well as with industry standards. Actions must then be taken to reduce any expenses for which major increases have occurred or that are beyond industry standards.

### Unacceptable Component Percentage for Net Income

If the component percentages for cost of merchandise sold, gross profit on sales, and total expenses are brought within acceptable ranges, net income will also be acceptable.

## AUDIT YOUR UNDERSTANDING

1. For a merchandising business, every sales dollar includes what four components?
2. How does a company determine acceptable component percentages?
3. What is the result if total expenses are greater than gross profit on sales?

## WORK TOGETHER

### Analyzing component percentages

Use the income statement for A to Z Auto Parts from Work Together on page 396. A form for completing these problems is given in the *Working Papers.* Your instructor will guide you through the following examples.

4. A to Z Auto Parts determines that no more than 63 cents, or 63.0%, of each sales dollar should be devoted to cost of merchandise sold. Compare the actual component percentage for cost of merchandise sold to the acceptable percentage. Indicate if the actual component percentage is acceptable or unacceptable. If it is unacceptable, suggest an action that corrects it.
5. Acceptable auto parts industry standards show that at least 37 cents, or 37.0%, of each sales dollar should result in gross profit. For A to Z Auto Parts, compare the actual component percentage for gross profit on sales to the acceptable percentage. Indicate if the actual component percentage is acceptable or unacceptable. If it is unacceptable, suggest an action that corrects it.

## ON YOUR OWN

### Analyzing component percentages

Use the income statement for Electron Games from On Your Own on page 396. A form for completing these problems is given in the *Working Papers.* Work independently to complete these problems.

6. Acceptable game industry standards show that no more than 13 cents, or 13.0%, of each sales dollar should be devoted to total expenses. For Electron Games, compare the actual component percentage for total expenses to the acceptable percentage. Indicate if the actual component percentage is acceptable or unacceptable. If it is unacceptable, suggest an action that corrects it.
7. Acceptable game industry standards show that at least 25 cents, or 25.0%, of each sales dollar should result in net income. For Electron Games, compare the actual component percentage for net income to the acceptable percentage. Indicate if the actual component percentage is acceptable or unacceptable. If it is unacceptable, suggest an action that corrects it.

# 16-3 Distribution of Net Income and Owners' Equity Statements

## PREPARING A DISTRIBUTION OF NET INCOME STATEMENT

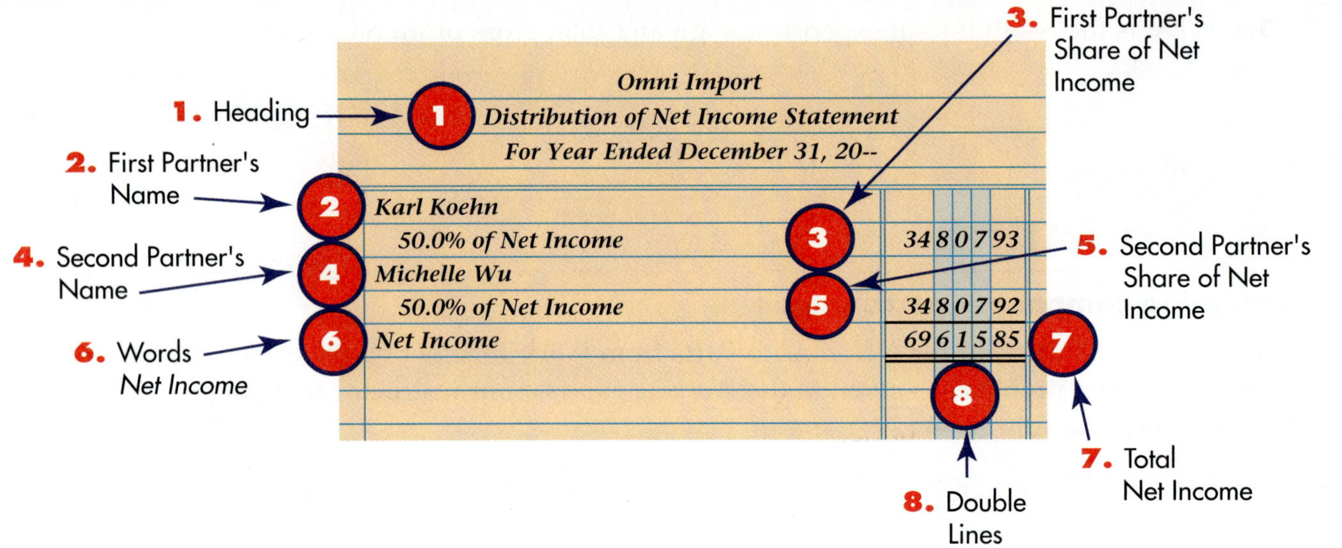


A partnership's net income or net loss may be divided in any way agreed upon by the partners in their partnership agreement. Karl Koehn and Michelle Wu, partners in Omni Import, agreed to share net income or net loss equally.

A partnership distribution of net income or net loss is usually shown on a separate financial statement. A partnership financial statement showing net income or loss distribution to partners is called a **distribution of net income statement.**

The net income, $69,615.85, from Omni Import's income statement is used to prepare the distribution of net income statement.

### STEPS Preparing a distribution of net income statement

1. Write the heading of the distribution of net income statement on three lines.
2. Write one partner's name, *Karl Koehn,* on the first line at the extreme left of the wide column.
3. Indent about one centimeter on the next line, and write Karl Koehn's share of net income as a percentage, *50.0% of Net Income.* Write Mr. Koehn's share of net income, *$34,807.93* (50.0% × $69,615.85), in the amount column on the same line. The last time net income was an odd number, Ms. Wu received the extra penny. For the current year, therefore, Mr. Koehn receives the extra penny.
4. Write the other partner's name, *Michelle Wu,* on the next line at the extreme left of the wide column.
5. Indent about one centimeter on the next line, and write Michelle Wu's share of net income as a percentage, *50.0% of Net Income.* Write Ms. Wu's share of net income, *$34,807.92* (50.0% × $69,615.85), in the amount column on the same line.
6. Write *Net Income* on the next line at the extreme left of the wide column.
7. Add the distribution of net income for Karl Koehn, *$34,807.93,* and for Michelle Wu, *$34,807.92.* Write the total amount, *$69,615.85,* in the amount column. Verify accuracy by comparing the total amount, $69,615.85, with the net income reported on the income statement, $69,615.85. The two amounts must be the same.
8. Rule double lines across the amount column to show that the distribution of net income statement has been verified as correct.

## DISTRIBUTION OF NET INCOME STATEMENT WITH UNEQUAL DISTRIBUTION OF EARNINGS

| *Custom Cabinets* | |
|---|---|
| ***Distribution of Net Income Statement*** | |
| ***For Year Ended December 31, 20--*** | |
| ***Beth Castillo*** | |
| *60.0% of Net Income* | *48,960.00* |
| ***Jana Kenyon*** | |
| *40.0% of Net Income* | *32,640.00* |
| ***Net Income*** | *81,600.00* |

Regardless of how earnings are shared, the steps in preparing a distribution of net income statement are the same. The only difference is the description of how the earnings are to be shared by the partners.

Beth Castillo and Jana Kenyon are partners in a business. Because Ms. Castillo spends more time in the business than Ms. Kenyon, the partners agree to share net income or loss unequally. Ms. Castillo gets 60.0% of net income or loss. Ms. Kenyon gets 40.0% of net income or loss. With a net income of $81,600.00, Ms. Castillo receives 60.0%, or $48,960.00. Ms. Kenyon receives 40.0%, or $32,640.00.

### CULTURAL DIVERSITY

### BUSINESS CULTURE AND ACCOUNTANCY IN RUSSIA

The changeover of Russia's economy from socialism to *free enterprise* is strongly influencing Russian business culture. Employees, who for generations have depended on the government to fulfill their needs, now have the opportunity to get ahead individually.

Russian business culture—the way Russians do business—is changing gradually. An example of this change can be seen in the accounting profession.

In the emerging Russian market economy, the person performing the role of accountant is called an "economist." These employees have a degree in "economics" and years of experience. Employees performing the role of "bookkeeper" have lower status and lower pay. The chief bookkeeper, however, has a prominent position because of his or her responsibility for the accuracy of financial statements.

The accounting profession in Russia is devising a regulatory framework based upon similar frameworks in existing market economies. Regulations are being written that include precise definitions for accounting terms. Regulations on the qualifications of auditors also are being developed.

## PARTNERS' CAPITAL AND DRAWING ACCOUNTS

ACCOUNT *Karl Koehn, Capital* ACCOUNT NO. *3110*

| DATE | | ITEM | POST. REF. | DEBIT | CREDIT | BALANCE DEBIT | BALANCE CREDIT |
|---|---|---|---|---|---|---|---|
| 20-- Jan. | 1 | Balance | ✓ | | | | 136 750 00 |

ACCOUNT *Karl Koehn, Drawing* ACCOUNT NO. *3120*

| DATE | | ITEM | POST. REF. | DEBIT | CREDIT | BALANCE DEBIT | BALANCE CREDIT |
|---|---|---|---|---|---|---|---|
| 20-- Dec. | 1 | Balance | ✓ | | | 26 700 00 | |
| | 5 | | 24 | 1 200 00 | | 27 900 00 | |
| | 20 | | 25 | 1 200 00 | | 29 100 00 | |

ACCOUNT *Michelle Wu, Capital* ACCOUNT NO. *3130*

| DATE | | ITEM | POST. REF. | DEBIT | CREDIT | BALANCE DEBIT | BALANCE CREDIT |
|---|---|---|---|---|---|---|---|
| 20-- Jan. | 1 | Balance | ✓ | | | | 136 552 48 |

ACCOUNT *Michelle Wu, Drawing* ACCOUNT NO. *3140*

| DATE | | ITEM | POST. REF. | DEBIT | CREDIT | BALANCE DEBIT | BALANCE CREDIT |
|---|---|---|---|---|---|---|---|
| 20-- Dec. | 1 | Balance | ✓ | | | 26 400 00 | |
| | 5 | | 24 | 1 200 00 | | 27 600 00 | |
| | 20 | | 25 | 1 200 00 | | 28 800 00 | |

The amount of net income earned is important to business owners. Owners are also interested in changes that occur in owners' equity during a fiscal period. A financial statement that summarizes the changes in owners' equity during a fiscal period is called an **owners' equity statement.** Business owners can review an owners' equity statement to determine if owners' equity is increasing or decreasing and what is causing the change. Three factors can change owners' equity: (1) additional investments, (2) withdrawals, and (3) net income or net loss.

An owners' equity statement shows information about changes during a fiscal period in each partner's capital. Information needed to prepare an owners' equity statement is obtained from the distribution of net income statement and the general ledger capital and drawing accounts. The distribution of net income statement shows each partner's share of net income or net loss. Three kinds of information are obtained from each partner's capital and drawing account: (1) beginning capital amount, (2) any additional investments made during the fiscal period, and (3) each partner's withdrawal of assets during the fiscal period.

# OWNERS' EQUITY STATEMENT

1. Heading
2. First Partner's Name
3. First Partner's Ending Capital
4. Second Partner's Name
5. Second Partner's Ending Capital
6. Total Owners' Equity
7. Double Lines

| *Omni Import* | | | |
|---|---|---|---|
| *Owners' Equity Statement* | | | |
| *For Year Ended December 31, 20--* | | | |
| *Karl Koehn* | | | |
| *Capital, January 1, 20--* | | 136,750.00 | |
| *Share of Net Income* | 34,807.93 | | |
| *Less Withdrawals* | 29,100.00 | | |
| *Net Increase in Capital* | | 5,707.93 | |
| *Capital, December 31, 20--* | | | 142,457.93 |
| *Michelle Wu* | | | |
| *Capital, January 1, 20--* | | 136,552.48 | |
| *Share of Net Income* | 34,807.92 | | |
| *Less Withdrawals* | 28,800.00 | | |
| *Net Increase in Capital* | | 6,007.92 | |
| *Capital, December 31, 20--* | | | 142,560.40 |
| *Total Owners' Equity, December 31, 20--* | | | 285,018.33 |

Neither Karl Koehn nor Michelle Wu invested any additional capital during the year ended December 31. The beginning and ending capital balances, therefore, are the same as recorded in the accounts on January 1. Both partners withdrew cash and merchandise during the year ended December 31. Some businesses include the owners' equity statement information as part of the balance sheet. An example of this method of reporting changes in owner's equity is shown in Chapter 8.

## STEPS: Preparing an owners' equity statement

1. Write the heading of the owners' equity statement on three lines.
2. Write the name *Karl Koehn* on the first line at the extreme left of the wide column.
3. Calculate the net increase in capital and ending capital amount for Karl Koehn.
   a. Indent about one centimeter on the next line, and write *Capital, January 1, 20—*. Write the amount *$136,750.00* in the second amount column. (This amount is obtained from the capital account.)
   b. Indent about one centimeter on the next line, and write *Share of Net Income*. Write the amount *$34,807.93* in the first amount column. (This amount is obtained from the distribution of net income statement.)
   c. Indent about one centimeter on the next line, and write *Less Withdrawals*. Write the amount *$29,100.00* in the first amount column. (This amount is obtained from the drawing account.)
   d. Indent about one centimeter on the next line, and write *Net Increase in Capital*. Write the amount *$5,707.93* in the second amount column. ($34,807.93 − $29,100.00 = $5,707.93.)
   e. Indent about one centimeter on the next line, and write *Capital, December 31, 20—*. Write the amount *$142,457.93* in the third amount column. ($136,750.00 + $5,707.93 = $142,457.93.)
4. Write the name *Michelle Wu* on the next line at the extreme left of the wide column.
5. Calculate the net increase in capital and ending capital amount for Michelle Wu. Follow Step 3.
6. Write *Total Owners' Equity, December 31, 20—* on the next line at the extreme left of the wide column. Write the amount *$285,018.33* in the third amount column.
7. Rule double lines across the three amount columns to show that the totals have been verified as correct.

## OWNERS' EQUITY STATEMENT WITH AN ADDITIONAL INVESTMENT AND A NET LOSS

| *Cloth Circuit*<br>*Owners' Equity Statement*<br>*For Year Ended December 31, 20--* | | | |
|---|---|---|---|
| *Mark Gavin* | | | |
| *Capital, January 1, 20--* | 125,200.00 | | |
| *Plus Additional Investment* | 12,000.00 | | |
| *Total* | | 137,200.00 | |
| *Share of Net Loss* | 2,840.00 | | |
| *Plus Withdrawals* | 17,760.00 | | |
| *Net Decrease in Capital* | | 20,600.00 | |
| *Capital, December 31, 20--* | | | 116,600.00 |
| *Judy Oliver* | | | |
| *Capital, January 1, 20--* | 123,400.00 | | |
| *Plus Additional Investment* | 12,000.00 | | |
| *Total* | | 135,400.00 | |
| *Share of Net Loss* | 2,840.00 | | |
| *Plus Withdrawals* | 18,120.00 | | |
| *Net Decrease in Capital* | | 20,960.00 | |
| *Capital, December 31, 20--* | | | 114,440.00 |
| *Total Owners' Equity, December 31, 20--* | | | 231,040.00 |

On December 31 the capital accounts of Mark Gavin and Judy Oliver showed additional investments of $12,000.00 each. Also, the income statement for their company, Cloth Circuit, showed a net loss of $5,680.00. The partners agreed to share net income or net loss equally. The owners' equity statement above shows the net loss as a deduction from the owners' capital.

**FYI**

*Partnerships must file tax returns with the IRS to report how income was divided among the partners.*

## TERMS REVIEW

distribution of net income statement

owners' equity statement

## AUDIT YOUR UNDERSTANDING

1. What information used to prepare an owners' equity statement is obtained from the distribution of net income statement?
2. What information used to prepare an owners' equity statement is obtained from the partners' capital and drawing accounts?
3. What is the procedure for calculating an owner's end-of-year capital?

## WORK TOGETHER

**Preparing distribution of net income and owners' equity statements**

Use the A to Z Auto Parts work sheet and income statement from Work Together on page 396. Forms for completing these problems are given in the *Working Papers.* Your instructor will guide you through the following examples.

4. Prepare a distribution of net income statement for A to Z Auto Parts. Net income or loss is to be shared equally.
5. Using the balances of the general ledger capital and drawing accounts from the work sheet, prepare an owners' equity statement for A to Z Auto Parts. No additional investments were made. Save your work to complete Work Together on page 412.

## ON YOUR OWN

**Preparing distribution of net income and owners' equity statements**

Use the Electron Games work sheet and income statement from On Your Own on page 396. Forms for completing these problems are given in the *Working Papers.* Work independently to complete these problems.

6. Prepare a distribution of net income statement for Electron Games. Net income or loss is to be shared equally.
7. Using the balances of the general ledger capital and drawing accounts from the work sheet, prepare an owners' equity statement for Electron Games. No additional investments were made. Save your work to complete On Your Own on page 412.

# 16-4 Balance Sheet

## BALANCE SHEET INFORMATION ON A WORK SHEET

**Omni Import**
**Work Sheet**
**For Year Ended December 31, 20--**

| | ACCOUNT TITLE | 1 TRIAL BALANCE DEBIT | 2 TRIAL BALANCE CREDIT | 3 ADJUSTMENTS DEBIT | 4 ADJUSTMENTS CREDIT | 5 INCOME STATEMENT DEBIT | 6 INCOME STATEMENT CREDIT | 7 BALANCE SHEET DEBIT | 8 BALANCE SHEET CREDIT | |
|---|---|---|---|---|---|---|---|---|---|---|
| 1 | *Cash* | 29 080 28 | | | | | | 29 080 28 | | 1 |
| 2 | *Petty Cash* | 300 00 | | | | | | 300 00 | | 2 |
| 3 | *Accounts Receivable* | 11 198 40 | | | | | | 11 198 40 | | 3 |
| 4 | *Merchandise Inventory* | 270 480 00 | | | (a) 15 840 00 | | | 254 640 00 | | 4 |
| 5 | *Supplies—Office* | 6 480 00 | | | (b) 4 730 00 | | | 1 750 00 | | 5 |
| 6 | *Supplies—Store* | 6 944 00 | | | (c) 3 910 00 | | | 3 034 00 | | 6 |
| 7 | *Prepaid Insurance* | 5 800 00 | | | (d) 3 170 00 | | | 2 630 00 | | 7 |
| 8 | *Accounts Payable* | | 12 542 38 | | | | | | 12 542 38 | 8 |
| 9 | *Employee Income Tax Pay.* | | 542 00 | | | | | | 542 00 | 9 |
| 10 | *Social Sec. Tax Payable* | | 985 40 | | | | | | 985 40 | 10 |
| 11 | *Medicare Tax Payable* | | 227 42 | | | | | | 227 42 | 11 |
| 12 | *Sales Tax Payable* | | 2 112 05 | | | | | | 2 112 05 | 12 |
| 13 | *Unemploy. Tax Pay.—Fed.* | | 8 40 | | | | | | 8 40 | 13 |
| 14 | *Unemploy. Tax Pay.—State* | | 56 70 | | | | | | 56 70 | 14 |
| 15 | *Health Ins. Premiums Pay.* | | 1 008 00 | | | | | | 1 008 00 | 15 |
| 16 | *U.S. Savings Bonds Pay.* | | 60 00 | | | | | | 60 00 | 16 |
| 17 | *United Way Donations Pay.* | | 72 00 | | | | | | 72 00 | 17 |

Some management decisions can best be made after owners have determined the amount of assets, liabilities, and owners' equity. Owners could obtain some of the information needed by inspecting general ledger accounts. The information needed might also be found on a work sheet. However, the information is easier to use when organized and reported on a balance sheet.

A balance sheet reports a business's financial condition on a specific date. A balance sheet may be prepared in account form or report form. As described in Chapter 8, Encore Music uses the account form. Omni Import uses the report form.

The information used to prepare a balance sheet is obtained from two sources: (1) the Balance Sheet columns of a work sheet and (2) the owners' equity statement.

### REMEMBER

A balance sheet reports a business's financial condition on a specific date.

## FIRST TWO SECTIONS OF A BALANCE SHEET FOR A MERCHANDISING BUSINESS

**1.** Heading

**2.** Assets Section

**3.** Liabilities Section

| Omni Import<br>Balance Sheet<br>December 31, 20-- | | |
|---|---|---|
| *Assets* | | |
| *Cash* | 29,080.28 | |
| *Petty Cash* | 300.00 | |
| *Accounts Receivable* | 11,198.40 | |
| *Merchandise Inventory* | 254,640.00 | |
| *Supplies—Office* | 1,750.00 | |
| *Supplies—Store* | 3,034.00 | |
| *Prepaid Insurance* | 2,630.00 | |
| *Total Assets* | | 302,632.68 |
| *Liabilities* | | |
| *Accounts Payable* | 12,542.38 | |
| *Employee Income Tax Payable* | 542.00 | |
| *Social Security Tax Payable* | 985.40 | |
| *Medicare Tax Payable* | 227.42 | |
| *Sales Tax Payable* | 2,112.05 | |
| *Unemployment Tax Payable—Federal* | 8.40 | |
| *Unemployment Tax Payable—State* | 56.70 | |
| *Health Insurance Premiums Payable* | 1,008.00 | |
| *U.S. Savings Bonds Payable* | 60.00 | |
| *United Way Donations Payable* | 72.00 | |
| *Total Liabilities* | | 17,614.35 |

Omni Import prepares a balance sheet for the end-of-fiscal date, December 31. Omni uses the seven steps described below and on the following page to prepare a balance sheet.

STEPS

### Preparing a balance sheet

**1.** Write the balance sheet heading on three lines.

**2.** Prepare the assets section of the balance sheet. Use information from the work sheet.
   a. Write the section title, *Assets,* on the first line in the middle of the wide column.
   b. Beginning on the next line, at the extreme left of the wide column, write the asset account titles in the order in which they appear on the work sheet.
   c. Write the balance of each asset account in the first amount column.
   d. Write *Total Assets* on the next line below the last asset account title.
   e. Write the amount of total assets, *$302,632.68,* on the same line in the second amount column.

**3.** Prepare the liabilities section of the balance sheet. Use information from the work sheet.
   a. Write the section title, *Liabilities,* on the next line in the middle of the wide column.
   b. Beginning on the next line, at the extreme left of the wide column, write the liability account titles in the order in which they appear on the work sheet.
   c. Write the balance of each liability account in the first amount column.
   d. Write *Total Liabilities* on the next line below the last liability account title.
   e. Write the total liabilities, *$17,614.35,* on the same line in the second amount column.

## COMPLETING A BALANCE SHEET FOR A MERCHANDISNG BUSINESS

| Omni Import<br>Balance Sheet<br>December 31, 20-- | | |
|---|---|---|
| **Assets** | | |
| Cash | 29,080.28 | |
| Petty Cash | 300.00 | |
| Accounts Receivable | 11,198.40 | |
| Merchandise Inventory | 254,640.00 | |
| Supplies—Office | 1,750.00 | |
| Supplies—Store | 3,034.00 | |
| Prepaid Insurance | 2,630.00 | |
| Total Assets | | 302,632.68 |
| **Liabilities** | | |
| Accounts Payable | 12,542.38 | |
| Employee Income Tax Payable | 542.00 | |
| Social Security Tax Payable | 985.40 | |
| Medicare Tax Payable | 227.42 | |
| Sales Tax Payable | 2,112.05 | |
| Unemployment Tax Payable—Federal | 8.40 | |
| Unemployment Tax Payable—State | 56.70 | |
| Health Insurance Premiums Payable | 1,008.00 | |
| U.S. Savings Bonds Payable | 60.00 | |
| United Way Donations Payable | 72.00 | |
| Total Liabilities | | 17,614.35 |
| **Owners' Equity** | | |
| Karl Koehn, Capital | 142,457.93 | |
| Michelle Wu, Capital | 142,560.40 | |
| Total Owners' Equity | | 285,018.33 |
| Total Liabilities and Owners' Equity | | 302,632.68 |

4. Owners' Equity Section 5. Total of Liabilities and Owners' Equity Sections 6. Verify Accuracy 7. Double Lines

**STEPS**

### Preparing a balance sheet *(continued)*

4. Prepare the owners' equity section of the balance sheet. Use information from the owners' equity statement.
   a. Write the section title, *Owners' Equity,* on the next line in the middle of the wide column.
   b. Write the account title, *Karl Koehn, Capital,* on the next line at the extreme left of the wide column.
   c. On the same line, write the amount of current capital, *$142,457.93,* in the first amount column.
   d. Write the account title, *Michelle Wu, Capital,* on the next line at the extreme left of the wide column.
   e. On the same line, write the amount of current capital, *$142,560.40,* in the first amount column.
   f. Write *Total Owners' Equity* on the next line at the extreme left of the wide column.
   g. Write the total amount, *$285,018.33,* on the same line in the second amount column.
5. Total the liabilities and owners' equity sections of the balance sheet.
   a. Write *Total Liabilities and Owners' Equity* on the next line at the extreme left of the wide column.
   b. Write the total amount, *$302,632.68,* on the same line in the second amount column.
6. Verify accuracy by comparing the total amount of assets and the total amount of liabilities and owners' equity. These two amounts must be the same. The two amounts, *$302,632.68,* are the same.
7. Rule double lines across both amount columns below Total Assets and below Total Liabilities and Owners' Equity. These two sets of double lines show that the amounts have been verified as correct.

## SUPPORTING SCHEDULES FOR A BALANCE SHEET

A report prepared to give details about an item on a principal financial statement is called a **supporting schedule.** A supporting schedule is sometimes referred to as a supplementary report or an exhibit.

Omni Import prepares two supporting schedules to accompany the balance sheet. The supporting schedules are a schedule of accounts payable and a schedule of accounts receivable. A balance sheet shows only the accounts payable total amount. The account balance for each vendor is not shown. When detailed information is needed, a supporting schedule of accounts payable is prepared showing the balance for each vendor. A balance sheet also shows only the accounts receivable total amount. When information about the account balance for each customer is needed, a supporting schedule of accounts receivable is prepared. Omni Import's supporting schedules on December 31 are similar to the supporting schedules for November 30 shown in Chapter 12.

**PROFESSIONAL BUSINESS ETHICS**

### TECHNOLOGY TEMPTATIONS

Along with many benefits, technology also presents us with new temptations. Technology allows us to access information for many legitimate reasons, but it can also create ethical dilemmas. What do you think about the situations presented below?

**Instructions**

Use the three-step checklist to help determine whether or not each of the following situations demonstrates ethical behavior.

*Situation 1.* Jack Azerrad collects overdue accounts for a large credit card company. He has access to records of all transactions for any customer. Jack sometimes looks up the records of famous people. He checks to see where they use their credit cards and how much money they spend. He sometimes tells his friends about the buying habits of entertainers and politicians.

*Situation 2.* Madilyn Hodges works for a not-for-profit organization. Recently, she found a list of computer passwords near a photocopier. She started using these passwords to look at other employees' e-mail files.

*Situation 3.* Elena Marquez is studying to be an accountant. While in college she works as a sales clerk in a bookstore. Occasionally, the scanner is unable to read a bar code on a customer's selection, and the clerk must enter the code using the keypad. Elena sometimes makes mistakes when she enters the code. As long as the customer does not object, Elena thinks it's unnecessary to correct her mistakes.

*Situation 4.* Andrew Kwan works for a mortgage company. As part of his job, he checks credit histories of loan applicants. He requests information from a company that specializes in providing credit checks. Mike Buckley, one of Andrew's friends, wanted to see what kind of information was included in his own credit history. He asked Andrew to request a credit check. Andrew made the request and passed the information on to Mike.

## TERM REVIEW

supporting schedule

## AUDIT YOUR UNDERSTANDING

1. What does a balance sheet report?
2. In what two forms may a balance sheet be prepared?
3. Where is the information found to prepare a balance sheet?
4. What are two supporting schedules that might accompany a balance sheet?

## WORK TOGETHER

### Preparing a balance sheet for a partnership

Use the A to Z Auto Parts work sheet from Work Together on page 407 and the owners' equity statement from Work Together on page 407. A form for completing this problem is given in the *Working Papers*. Your instructor will guide you through the following example.

5. Prepare a balance sheet in report form for A to Z Auto Parts.

## ON YOUR OWN

### Preparing a balance sheet for a partnership

Use the Electron Games work sheet from On Your Own on page 407 and the owners' equity statement from On Your Own on page 407. A form for completing this problem is given in the *Working Papers*. Work independently to complete this problem.

6. Prepare a balance sheet in report form for Electron Games.

# CHAPTER 16 SUMMARY

## *Enrichment Activity*

**Types of Businesses**

*Use the financial statements illustrated in this chapter to describe the major differences between the financial statements of a service business and a merchandising business.*

After completing this chapter, you can

1. Define accounting terms related to financial statements for a merchandising business organized as a partnership.
2. Identify accounting concepts and practices related to financial statements for a merchandising business organized as a partnership.
3. Prepare an income statement for a merchandising business organized as a partnership.
4. Analyze an income statement using component percentages for a merchandising business organized as a partnership.
5. Prepare a distribution of net income statement and an owners' equity statement for a merchandising business organized as a partnership.
6. Prepare a balance sheet for a merchandising business organized as a partnership.

## EXPLORE ACCOUNTING

### ALTERNATIVE FISCAL YEARS

Most small companies use a fiscal year that is the same as the calendar year, January 1 to December 31. However, there may be several reasons why a different fiscal period would be beneficial. If the calendar year end comes in the middle of a high sales period, a fiscal year ending at this time can be more difficult. All employees are extremely busy with sales and shipping. Because of this activity, accurately identifying sales, inventory, and accounts receivable is more difficult. If the calendar year end comes just before the high sales period begins, an analysis of the company's financial condition will not be as favorable. The company may have borrowed money to buy a high level of inventory, so the company has higher debt and high inventory levels. Therefore, some companies choose to use a *natural business year* as the fiscal year, as discussed in Chapter 7.

FanciFoods is a partnership that makes and sells decorative cakes, cookies, and candies. Approximately 90% of its sales are made between November 1 and February 15—or the three holidays of Thanksgiving, Christmas, and Valentine's Day. The company spends six months—May to November—preparing for its heavy sales period. The company has selected April 1 to March 31 as its fiscal year. By March 31, inventory is low, most accounts receivable have been collected, and the company has not yet replaced inventory to begin preparing for the next season. Thus, this is an ideal time to end the fiscal period. Inventory is easier to count, the level of accounts receivable is lower, and more employees are available to help with the closing activities.

**Research:** What other types of companies may find it beneficial to use a fiscal year different from the calendar year? What would be the ideal fiscal period for these companies? You may wish to find a local business that has a fiscal period different from the calendar year. If so, determine the reasons for selecting the fiscal period it now uses.

## 16-1 APPLICATION PROBLEM
### Preparing an income statement for a merchandising business

Flower Mart's partial work sheet for the year ended December 31 of the current year is given in the *Working Papers.*

***Instructions:***

1. Prepare an income statement.
2. Calculate and record on the income statement the following component percentages: (a) cost of merchandise sold, (b) gross profit on sales, (c) total expenses, and (d) net income or loss. Round percentage calculations to the nearest 0.1%.

## 16-2 APPLICATION PROBLEM
### Analyzing component percentages

The income statement for Carol and Teresa's Historic Door Supply Co. and a form for completing this problem are given in the *Working Papers.*

***Instructions:***

1. Carol and Teresa's Historic Door Supply determines that no more than 47.5 cents, or 47.5%, of each sales dollar should be devoted to cost of merchandise sold. Compare the actual component percentage for cost of merchandise sold to the acceptable percentage. Indicate if the actual component percentage is acceptable or unacceptable. If it is unacceptable, suggest a possible action to correct the unacceptable component percentage.
2. Acceptable door supply industry standards show that at least 52.5 cents, or 52.5%, of each sales dollar should result in gross profit. For Carol and Teresa's Historic Door Supply, compare the actual component percentage for gross profit on sales to the acceptable percentage. Indicate if the actual component percentage is acceptable or unacceptable. If it is unacceptable, suggest a possible action different from the suggestion in Instruction 1 to correct the unacceptable component percentage.
3. Acceptable door supply industry standards show that no more than 29 cents, or 29.0%, of each sales dollar should be devoted to total expenses. For Carol and Teresa's Historic Door Supply, compare the actual component percentage for total expenses to the acceptable percentage. Indicate if the actual component percentage is acceptable or unacceptable. If it is unacceptable, suggest a possible action to correct the unacceptable component percentage.
4. Acceptable door supply industry standards show that at least 23.5 cents, or 23.5%, of each sales dollar should result in net income. For Carol and Teresa's Historic Door Supply, compare the actual component percentage for net income to the acceptable percentage. Indicate if the actual component percentage is acceptable or unacceptable. If it is unacceptable, suggest a possible action different from any already suggested to correct the unacceptable component percentage.

## 16-3 APPLICATION PROBLEM
### Preparing distribution of net income and owners' equity statements (net income)

Janet Kelly and Paul Sharp are partners in a merchandising business, Kelly Appliances. Forms for completing this problem are given in the *Working Papers.* The following information was taken from the records on December 31 of the current year.

| Partner | Balance of Capital Account January 1 | Balance of Drawing Account | Distribution of Net Income |
|---|---|---|---|
| Kelly | $159,000.00 | $17,550.00 | 60.0% |
| Sharp | $142,600.00 | $18,800.00 | 40.0% |

***Instructions:***

1. On December 31, the partnership had a net income of $83,260.00. Prepare a distribution of net income statement for the partnership.
2. Prepare an owners' equity statement for Kelly Appliances. No additional investments were made.

## 16-4 APPLICATION PROBLEM
### Preparing an owners' equity statement (net loss)

Judy Fulton and Lee Terry are partners in a merchandising business, Elegant Cosmetics. Forms for completing this problem are given in the *Working Papers.* The following information was taken from the records on December 31 of the current year.

| Partner | Balance of Capital Account January 1 | Balance of Drawing Account | Distribution of Net Loss |
|---|---|---|---|
| Fulton | $124,300.00 | $13,950.00 | $3,750.00 |
| Terry | $118,000.00 | $14,900.00 | $3,750.00 |

***Instructions:***

Prepare an owners' equity statement for Elegant Cosmetics. Additional investments made during the year: Judy Fulton, $12,000.00; Lee Terry, $10,000.00.

## 16-5 APPLICATION PROBLEM
### Preparing a balance sheet for a partnership

Athletic Supply's partial work sheet for the year ended December 31 of the current year is given in the *Working Papers.* A form for completing this problem is also given in the *Working Papers.*

***Instructions:***

Prepare a balance sheet in report form. December 31 capital balances for partners are as follows: Glenda Tyler, $145,480.00; Ashley Winn, $144,260.00.

## 16-6 MASTERY PROBLEM

### Preparing financial statements

Central Electronics prepared the following work sheet for the year ended December 31 of the current year. Forms for completing this problem are given in the *Working Papers*.

*Central Electronics*
*Work Sheet*
*For Year Ended December 31, 20--*

| | ACCOUNT TITLE | 1 TRIAL BALANCE DEBIT | 2 TRIAL BALANCE CREDIT | 3 ADJUSTMENTS DEBIT | 4 ADJUSTMENTS CREDIT | 5 INCOME STATEMENT DEBIT | 6 INCOME STATEMENT CREDIT | 7 BALANCE SHEET DEBIT | 8 BALANCE SHEET CREDIT | |
|---|---|---|---|---|---|---|---|---|---|---|
| 1 | Cash | 33,110.00 | | | | | | 33,110.00 | | 1 |
| 2 | Petty Cash | 500.00 | | | | | | 500.00 | | 2 |
| 3 | Accounts Receivable | 14,760.00 | | | | | | 14,760.00 | | 3 |
| 4 | Merchandise Inventory | 334,190.00 | | | (a) 16,685.00 | | | 317,505.00 | | 4 |
| 5 | Supplies—Office | 6,180.00 | | | (b) 3,865.00 | | | 2,315.00 | | 5 |
| 6 | Supplies—Store | 6,720.00 | | | (c) 4,280.00 | | | 2,440.00 | | 6 |
| 7 | Prepaid Insurance | 5,920.00 | | | (d) 3,380.00 | | | 2,540.00 | | 7 |
| 8 | Accounts Payable | | 10,500.00 | | | | | | 10,500.00 | 8 |
| 9 | Sales Tax Payable | | 1,230.00 | | | | | | 1,230.00 | 9 |
| 10 | Irene Greer, Capital | | 164,400.00 | | | | | | 164,400.00 | 10 |
| 11 | Irene Greer, Drawing | 21,750.00 | | | | | | 21,750.00 | | 11 |
| 12 | Gayle Stewart, Capital | | 157,990.00 | | | | | | 157,990.00 | 12 |
| 13 | Gayle Stewart, Drawing | 21,100.00 | | | | | | 21,100.00 | | 13 |
| 14 | Income Summary | | | (a) 16,685.00 | | 16,685.00 | | | | 14 |
| 15 | Sales | | 295,900.00 | | | | 295,900.00 | | | 15 |
| 16 | Purchases | 148,670.00 | | | | 148,670.00 | | | | 16 |
| 17 | Advertising Expense | 6,420.00 | | | | 6,420.00 | | | | 17 |
| 18 | Credit Card Fee Expense | 2,715.00 | | | | 2,715.00 | | | | 18 |
| 19 | Insurance Expense | | | (d) 3,380.00 | | 3,380.00 | | | | 19 |
| 20 | Miscellaneous Expense | 3,040.00 | | | | 3,040.00 | | | | 20 |
| 21 | Rent Expense | 22,080.00 | | | | 22,080.00 | | | | 21 |
| 22 | Supplies Expense—Office | | | (b) 3,865.00 | | 3,865.00 | | | | 22 |
| 23 | Supplies Expense—Store | | | (c) 4,280.00 | | 4,280.00 | | | | 23 |
| 24 | Utilities Expense | 2,865.00 | | | | 2,865.00 | | | | 24 |
| 25 | | 630,020.00 | 630,020.00 | 28,210.00 | 28,210.00 | 214,000.00 | 295,900.00 | 416,020.00 | 334,120.00 | 25 |
| 26 | Net Income | | | | | 81,900.00 | | | 81,900.00 | 26 |
| 27 | | | | | | 295,900.00 | 295,900.00 | 416,020.00 | 416,020.00 | 27 |
| 28 | | | | | | | | | | 28 |

***Instructions:***

1. Prepare an income statement. Calculate and record the following component percentages: (a) cost of merchandise sold, (b) gross profit on sales, (c) total expenses, and (d) net income or loss. Round percentage calculations to the nearest 0.1%.
2. Prepare a distribution of net income statement. Net income or loss is to be shared equally.
3. Prepare an owners' equity statement. No additional investments were made.
4. Prepare a balance sheet in report form.

## 16-7 CHALLENGE PROBLEM

### Preparing financial statements (unequal distribution of net income; additional investment)

Central Electronics' work sheet is shown in Mastery Problem 16-6. Assume the facts given here for distribution of net income. Forms for completing this problem are given in the *Working Papers*.

***Instructions:***

1. Prepare a distribution of net income statement. The net income is to be shared as follows: Irene Greer, 8% of January 1 capital, $15,000.00 salary, 60% of remainder; Gayle Stewart, 8% of January 1 capital, $12,000.00 salary, 40% of remainder. Ms. Stewart made an additional investment during the year. Her January 1 capital was $139,990.00.
2. Prepare an owners' equity statement. Ms. Stewart made an additional investment of $18,000.00 during the year. She had January 1 capital of $139,990.00.

### INTERNET ACTIVITY

Point your browser to

**http://accounting.swpco.com**

Choose **First-Year Course**, choose **Activities**, and complete the activity for Chapter 16.

### Applied Communication

A long written report should contain numerous headings. A heading enables the reader to focus on the primary idea of the next section. An outline is a special document that lists only the headings of a report. By reviewing an outline before and after reading a report, the reader can gain a better understanding of the relationship among the topics being presented.

Each chapter of this textbook is similar to a long report. Headings are used to separate and emphasize major concepts.

**Instructions:** Prepare an outline of this chapter.

## Cases for Critical Thinking

### Case 1

Christy Burch and Myung Lim, partners, compared their current income statement with their income statement of a year ago. They noted that sales were 12.0% higher than a year ago. They also noted that the total expenses were 20.0% higher than a year ago. What type of analysis should be done to determine whether the increase in expenses is justified?

### Case 2

Rena Jacques and George Nadler are partners in a paint and decorating store. The store operates on a yearly fiscal period. At the end of each year, an accountant is hired to prepare financial statements. At the end of each month during the year, Ms. Jacques prepares a work sheet. The work sheet is prepared to determine if the business made or lost money that month. The accountant suggests that monthly financial statements also be prepared. Ms. Jacques believes, however, that the monthly work sheet is sufficient to determine how the business is doing. Do you agree with Ms. Jacques or the accountant? Why?

# AUTOMATED ACCOUNTING

## GENERATING AUTOMATED FINANCIAL STATEMENTS

Financial information needed by managers and owners of a business to make decisions is recorded in the journals and the ledgers. While this information may be helpful in analyzing the activity in a particular account, it is too detailed to be useful in decision making. When information from the ledgers is summarized and organized, the reports that are prepared are referred to as financial statements. The most commonly presented financial statements for a business organized as a partnership are the balance sheet and the income statement.

To display financial statements:

1. Click the Reports toolbar button, or choose the Report Selection menu item from the Reports menu.
2. When the Report Selection dialog appears, choose the Financial Statements option from the Select a Report Group list.
3. Choose the financial statement report you would like to display from the Choose a Report to Display list.
4. Click the OK button.

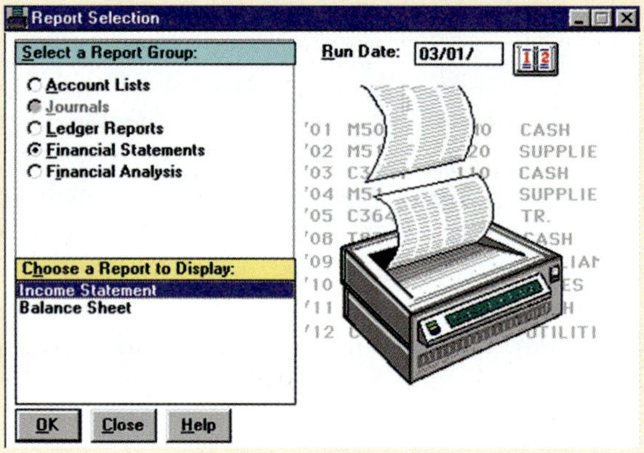


The up-to-date account balances stored by the software are used to calculate and display the current financial statements.

### Income Statement

An income statement shows the revenue and expenses for a fiscal period. Merchandising businesses report revenue, cost of merchandise sold, gross profit on sales, expenses, and net income or loss. The software will display net income or loss (the difference between revenues earned and expenses incurred) in one of two formats:

1. *Report by Fiscal Period:* This format shows the profitability of the business from the beginning of the fiscal year to the date the income statement is displayed.
2. *Report by Month and Year:* This format includes columns for the current month and for the year to date.

A component percentage is included for each dollar amount. A component percentage shows the percentage relationship between one financial statement item and the total that includes that item. Component percentages calculated on the income statement show the relationship of items to total sales.

### Balance Sheet

The balance sheet reports assets, liabilities, and owners' equity on a specific date, usually the end of the fiscal period. It is used to help evaluate the financial strength of the business. The owners' equity section of the balance sheet for a partnership shows the capital and drawing accounts for each partner. Net income is also included in the owners' equity section.

## PARTIAL WORK SHEET SHOWING ADJUSTMENTS

| | ACCOUNT TITLE | 1 TRIAL BALANCE DEBIT | 2 TRIAL BALANCE CREDIT | 3 ADJUSTMENTS DEBIT | 4 ADJUSTMENTS CREDIT |
|---|---|---|---|---|---|
| 4 | *Merchandise Inventory* | 270,480.00 | | | (a) 15,840.00 |
| 5 | *Supplies—Office* | 6,480.00 | | | (b) 4,730.00 |
| 6 | *Supplies—Store* | 6,944.00 | | | (c) 3,910.00 |
| 7 | *Prepaid Insurance* | 5,800.00 | | | (d) 3,170.00 |
| 22 | *Income Summary* | | | (a) 15,840.00 | |
| 27 | *Insurance Expense* | | | (d) 3,170.00 | |
| 32 | *Supplies Expense—Office* | | | (b) 4,730.00 | |
| 33 | *Supplies Expense—Store* | | | (c) 3,910.00 | |
| 34 | | | | | |

Information needed for journalizing the adjusting entries shown on the previous page is taken from the Adjustments columns of a work sheet.

## ADJUSTING ENTRY FOR MERCHANDISE INVENTORY

The debit and credit parts of the merchandise inventory adjustment are identified on the work sheet by the letter *(a)*. The merchandise inventory adjustment includes a debit to Income Summary and a credit to Merchandise Inventory of $15,840.00. Omni Import's adjusting entry for merchandise inventory is shown on lines 2 and 3 of the journal.

The effect of posting the adjusting entry for merchandise inventory is shown in the T accounts.

**Income Summary**

| | | | |
|---|---|---|---|
| Adj. (a) | 15,840.00 | | |

**Merchandise Inventory**

| | | | |
|---|---|---|---|
| Bal. | 270,480.00 | Adj. (a) | 15,840.00 |
| *(New Bal.* | *254,640.00)* | | |

**FYI**

*A document that describes a business idea and how the business will operate is known as a business plan. When creating a partnership, the partners should write a business plan to outline the purposes and goals of the business.*

## ADDITIONAL ADJUSTING ENTRIES

Omni Import also makes adjusting entries for office supplies, store supplies, and prepaid insurance.

### Adjusting Entry for Office Supplies Inventory

The debit and credit parts of the office supplies adjustment are identified on the work sheet by the letter *(b)*. The office supplies inventory adjustment includes a debit to Supplies Expense—Office and a credit to Supplies—Office of $4,730.00. Omni Import's adjusting entry for office supplies inventory is shown on lines 4 and 5 of the journal.

The effect of posting the adjusting entry for office supplies inventory is shown in the T accounts.

| Supplies Expense—Office | | | |
|---|---|---|---|
| Adj. (b) | 4,730.00 | | |

| Supplies—Office | | | |
|---|---|---|---|
| Bal. | 6,480.00 | Adj. (b) | 4,730.00 |
| *(New Bal.* | *1,750.00)* | | |

### Adjusting Entry for Store Supplies Inventory

The debit and credit parts of the store supplies adjustment are identified on the work sheet by the letter *(c)*. The store supplies inventory adjustment includes a debit to Supplies Expense—Store and a credit to Supplies—Store of $3,910.00. Omni Import's adjusting entry for store supplies inventory is shown on lines 6 and 7 of the journal.

The effect of posting the adjusting entry for store supplies inventory is shown in the T accounts.

| Supplies Expense—Store | | | |
|---|---|---|---|
| Adj. (c) | 3,910.00 | | |

| Supplies—Store | | | |
|---|---|---|---|
| Bal. | 6,944.00 | Adj. (c) | 3,910.00 |
| *(New Bal.* | *3,034.00)* | | |

### Adjusting Entry for Prepaid Insurance

The debit and credit parts of the prepaid insurance adjustment are identified on the work sheet by the letter *(d)*. The prepaid insurance adjustment includes a debit to Insurance Expense and a credit to Prepaid Insurance of $3,170.00. Omni Import's adjusting entry for prepaid insurance is shown on lines 8 and 9 of the journal.

The effect of posting the adjusting entry for prepaid insurance is shown in the T accounts.

| Insurance Expense | | | |
|---|---|---|---|
| Adj. (d) | 3,170.00 | | |

| Prepaid Insurance | | | |
|---|---|---|---|
| Bal. | 5,800.00 | Adj. (d) | 3,170.00 |
| *(New Bal.* | *2,630.00)* | | |

**SMALL BUSINESS SPOTLIGHT**

Buying a franchise is a popular way to start a small business. Franchises are particularly appealing to people with less experience because the failure rate is much lower than that of other new businesses. Advantages of purchasing a franchise include the franchise's proven reputation, established customers, and time-tested business procedures. Disadvantages include the franchisee's sometimes limited control over the new business and the relatively high initial fees attached to the purchase of a franchise.

## AUDIT YOUR UNDERSTANDING

1. What accounts are increased from zero balances after adjusting entries for prepaid insurance and merchandise inventory are journalized and posted?
2. When adjusting entries are journalized, why is no source document recorded?
3. What adjusting entry is recorded for a merchandising business that is not recorded for a service business?

## WORK TOGETHER

### Journalizing adjusting entries

The following information is related to adjustments needed at the end of a fiscal period for a partnership.

| Account Title | Work Sheet Trial Balance | Adjustment Information Ending Inventories | Ending Value |
|---|---|---|---|
| Merchandise Inventory | $446,200.00 | $419,750.00 | |
| Supplies—Office | 5,440.00 | 3,350.00 | |
| Supplies—Store | 6,020.00 | 3,990.00 | |
| Prepaid Insurance | 3,860.00 | | $970.00 |

Your instructor will guide you through the following example.

4. Record the appropriate adjusting entries on page 12 of a journal provided in the *Working Papers*. Use December 31 of the current year as the date.

## ON YOUR OWN

### Journalizing adjusting entries

The following information is related to adjustments needed at the end of a fiscal period for a partnership.

| Account Title | Work Sheet Trial Balance | Adjustment Information Ending Inventories | Ending Value |
|---|---|---|---|
| Merchandise Inventory | $328,800.00 | $343,200.00 | |
| Supplies—Office | 4,340.00 | 2,210.00 | |
| Supplies—Store | 4,740.00 | 2,530.00 | |
| Prepaid Insurance | 3,420.00 | | $680.00 |

Work independently to complete this problem.

5. Record the appropriate adjusting entries on page 15 of a journal provided in the *Working Papers*. Use December 31 of the current year as the date.

# 17-2 Recording Closing Entries for Income Statement Accounts

## THE INCOME SUMMARY ACCOUNT

At the end of a fiscal period, the temporary accounts are closed to prepare the general ledger for the next fiscal period. *(CONCEPT: Matching Expenses with Revenue)* To close a temporary account, an amount equal to its balance is recorded on the side opposite the balance. Omni Import records the four kinds of closing entries listed below. The first two kinds of closing entries are discussed in this lesson. The remaining two kinds of closing entries are discussed in the following lesson.

1. An entry to close income statement accounts with credit balances.
2. An entry to close income statement accounts with debit balances.
3. An entry to record net income or loss and close the income summary account.
4. Entries to close the partners' drawing accounts.

Amounts needed for the closing entries are obtained from the Income Statement and Balance Sheet columns of the work sheet and from the distribution of net income statement. Closing entries are recorded in the General Debit and Credit columns of a journal.

Chapter 9 discusses the difference between permanent accounts and temporary accounts. Permanent accounts, also referred to as real accounts, include the asset and liability accounts as well as the owners' capital accounts. The ending account balances of permanent accounts for one fiscal period are the beginning account balances for the next fiscal period. Temporary accounts, also referred to as nominal accounts, include the revenue, cost, expense, and owners' drawing accounts.

Another temporary account is used to summarize the closing entries for revenue, cost, and expenses. The account is titled Income Summary because it is used to summarize information about net income. Income Summary is used only at the end of a fiscal period to help prepare other accounts for a new fiscal period.

The income summary account is unique because it does not have a normal balance side. The balance of this account is determined by the amounts posted to the account at the end of a fiscal period. When revenue is greater than total expenses, resulting in a net income, the income summary account has a credit balance, as shown in the T account.

| Income Summary | |
|---|---|
| Debit<br>Total expenses | Credit<br>Revenue (greater than expenses)<br>(Credit balance is the net income.) |

**REMEMBER**

The income summary account is used only at the end of the fiscal period to help prepare other accounts for a new fiscal period.

## CLOSING ENTRY FOR AN INCOME STATEMENT ACCOUNT WITH A CREDIT BALANCE

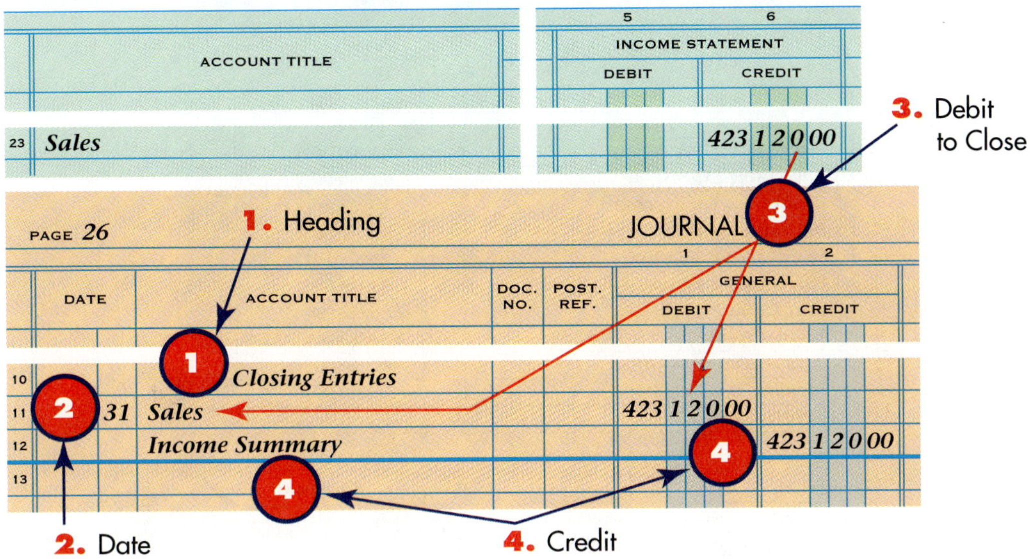


Omni Import's work sheet has one income statement account with a credit balance, Sales. This revenue account has a normal credit balance at the end of a fiscal period. This credit balance must be reduced to zero to prepare the account for the next fiscal period. *(CONCEPT: Matching Expenses with Revenue)*

To reduce the balance to zero, Sales is debited for the amount of the balance, $423,120.00. Income Summary is credited for $423,120.00 so that debits equal credits in this entry. The effect of this closing entry on the general ledger accounts is shown in the T accounts.

The balance of Sales is now zero, and the account is ready for the next fiscal period.

**Sales**

| | | | |
|---|---|---|---|
| Closing | 423,120.00 | Bal. | 423,120.00 |
| | | *(New Bal. zero)* | |

**Income Summary**

| | | | |
|---|---|---|---|
| Adj. (mdse. inv.) | 15,840.00 | Closing (revenue) | 423,120.00 |

**STEPS**

### Closing an income statement account with a credit balance

1. Write the heading, *Closing Entries,* in the middle of the journal's Account Title column following the last adjusting entry. This heading explains all of the closing entries that follow. Therefore, indicating a source document is unnecessary. The first closing entry is recorded on the first two lines below the heading.
2. Write the date, *31,* in the Date column.
3. Write the account debited, *Sales,* in the Account Title column. Write the account balance, *$423,120.00,* in the General Debit column.
4. Write the account credited, *Income Summary,* in the Account Title column. Write the amount, *$423,120.00,* in the General Credit column.

# CLOSING ENTRY FOR INCOME STATEMENT ACCOUNTS WITH DEBIT BALANCES

| | Account Title | 5 Income Statement Debit | 6 Income Statement Credit |
|---|---|---|---|
| 22 | Income Summary | 15,840.00 | |
| 23 | Sales | | 423,120.00 |
| 24 | Purchases | 189,960.00 | |
| 25 | Advertising Expense | 6,600.00 | |
| 26 | Credit Card Fee Expense | 3,385.00 | |
| 27 | Insurance Expense | 3,170.00 | |
| 28 | Miscellaneous Expense | 2,584.15 | |
| 29 | Payroll Taxes Expense | 9,105.00 | |
| 30 | Rent Expense | 21,000.00 | |
| 31 | Salary Expense | 89,400.00 | |
| 32 | Supplies Expense—Office | 4,730.00 | |
| 33 | Supplies Expense—Store | 3,910.00 | |
| 34 | Utilities Expense | 3,820.00 | |

1. Date
2. Account Debited
4. Debit Total
3. Credits to Close

JOURNAL PAGE 26

| | Date | Account Title | Doc. No. | Post. Ref. | 1 General Debit | 2 General Credit |
|---|---|---|---|---|---|---|
| 13 | 31 | Income Summary | | | 337,664.15 | |
| 14 | | Purchases | | | | 189,960.00 |
| 15 | | Advertising Expense | | | | 6,600.00 |
| 16 | | Credit Card Fee Expense | | | | 3,385.00 |
| 17 | | Insurance Expense | | | | 3,170.00 |
| 18 | | Miscellaneous Expense | | | | 2,584.15 |
| 19 | | Payroll Taxes Expense | | | | 9,105.00 |
| 20 | | Rent Expense | | | | 21,000.00 |
| 21 | | Salary Expense | | | | 89,400.00 |
| 22 | | Supplies Expense—Office | | | | 4,730.00 |
| 23 | | Supplies Expense—Store | | | | 3,910.00 |
| 24 | | Utilities Expense | | | | 3,820.00 |

Omni Import's work sheet has eleven income statement accounts with debit balances—the cost account, Purchases, and the ten expense accounts. These debit balances must be reduced to zero to prepare the accounts for the next fiscal period. *(CONCEPT: Matching Expenses with Revenue)* To reduce the balances to zero, the cost and expense accounts are credited for the amount of their balances. Income Summary is debited.

Income Summary has a debit balance shown on the work sheet. However, Income Summary is not closed as part of this closing entry. Instead, the account is closed with the third closing entry when net income is recorded.

## STEPS: Closing income statement accounts with debit balances

1. Write the date, *31*, in the Date column.
2. Write the title of the account debited, *Income Summary,* in the Account Title column. The debit to Income Summary is not entered in the amount column until all cost and expense balances have been journalized and the total amount calculated.
3. Write the account title of each cost and expense account in the Account Title column. Write the balance of each cost and expense account in the General Credit column.
4. Add the credit amounts for this entry. Write the total of the cost and expense accounts, *$337,664.15,* in the General Debit column on the same line as the account title Income Summary.

## SUMMARY OF CLOSING ENTRY FOR INCOME STATEMENT ACCOUNTS WITH DEBIT BALANCES

**Income Summary**

| Debit | | Credit | |
|---|---|---|---|
| Adj. (mdse. inv.) | 15,840.00 | Closing (revenue) | 423,120.00 |
| Closing (cost and expenses) | 337,664.15 | *(New Bal.* | *69,615.85)* |

**Purchases**

| Debit | | Credit | |
|---|---|---|---|
| Bal. | 189,960.00 | Closing | 189,960.00 |
| *(New Bal. zero)* | | | |

**Rent Expense**

| Debit | | Credit | |
|---|---|---|---|
| Bal. | 21,000.00 | Closing | 21,000.00 |
| *(New Bal. zero)* | | | |

**Advertising Expense**

| Debit | | Credit | |
|---|---|---|---|
| Bal. | 6,600.00 | Closing | 6,600.00 |
| *(New Bal. zero)* | | | |

**Salary Expense**

| Debit | | Credit | |
|---|---|---|---|
| Bal. | 89,400.00 | Closing | 89,400.00 |
| *(New Bal. zero)* | | | |

**Credit Card Fee Expense**

| Debit | | Credit | |
|---|---|---|---|
| Bal. | 3,385.00 | Closing | 3,385.00 |
| *(New Bal. zero)* | | | |

**Supplies Expense—Office**

| Debit | | Credit | |
|---|---|---|---|
| Bal. | 4,730.00 | Closing | 4,730.00 |
| *(New Bal. zero)* | | | |

**Insurance Expense**

| Debit | | Credit | |
|---|---|---|---|
| Bal. | 3,170.00 | Closing | 3,170.00 |
| *(New Bal. zero)* | | | |

**Supplies Expense—Store**

| Debit | | Credit | |
|---|---|---|---|
| Bal. | 3,910.00 | Closing | 3,910.00 |
| *(New Bal. zero)* | | | |

**Miscellaneous Expense**

| Debit | | Credit | |
|---|---|---|---|
| Bal. | 2,584.15 | Closing | 2,584.15 |
| *(New Bal. zero)* | | | |

**Utilities Expense**

| Debit | | Credit | |
|---|---|---|---|
| Bal. | 3,820.00 | Closing | 3,820.00 |
| *(New Bal. zero)* | | | |

**Payroll Taxes Expense**

| Debit | | Credit | |
|---|---|---|---|
| Bal. | 9,105.00 | Closing | 9,105.00 |
| *(New Bal. zero)* | | | |

The effect of this closing entry on the general ledger accounts is shown in the T accounts.

The cost account, **Purchases**, and the expense accounts are now closed and have zero balances. **Income Summary** has three amounts: (1) a debit of $15,840.00, the amount of the merchandise inventory adjustment; (2) a credit of $423,120.00, the amount of the entry to close the revenue account; and (3) a debit of $337,664.15, the total amount of the entry to close the cost and expense accounts. The balance of **Income Summary** is the net income for the fiscal period, $69,615.85.

## AUDIT YOUR UNDERSTANDING

1. Where is the information obtained for journalizing closing entries for revenue, cost, and expenses?
2. What is the name of the temporary account that is used to summarize the closing entries for revenue, cost, and expenses?

## WORK TOGETHER

**Journalizing closing entries for income statement accounts**

A partial work sheet of Fairbanks Auto Supply for the year ended December 31 of the current year is given in the *Working Papers*. Also given is a journal. Your instructor will guide you through the following example.

3. Record the following closing entries on page 12 of the journal. Save your work to complete Work Together on page 434.
   a. Close the income statement account with a credit balance.
   b. Close the income statement accounts with debit balances.

## ON YOUR OWN

**Journalizing closing entries for income statement accounts**

A partial work sheet of Custom Aquarium for the year ended December 31 of the current year is given in the *Working Papers*. Also given is a journal. Work this problem independently.

4. Record the following closing entries on page 15 of the journal. Save your work to complete On Your Own on page 434.
   a. Close the income statement account with a credit balance.
   b. Close the income statement accounts with debit balances.

# 17-3 Recording Additional Closing Entries

## CLOSING ENTRY TO RECORD NET INCOME OR LOSS AND CLOSE THE INCOME SUMMARY ACCOUNT

**Omni Import**
**Distribution of Net Income Statement**
**For Year Ended December 31, 20--**

| | |
|---|---|
| *Karl Koehn* | |
| *50% of Net Income* | 34 807 93 |
| *Michelle Wu* | |
| *50% of Net Income* | 34 807 92 |
| *Net Income* | 69 615 85 |

PAGE *26* JOURNAL

| DATE | | ACCOUNT TITLE | DOC. NO. | POST. REF. | GENERAL DEBIT | GENERAL CREDIT |
|---|---|---|---|---|---|---|
| 25 | 31 | *Income Summary* | | | 69 615 85 | |
| 26 | | *Karl Koehn, Capital* | | | | 34 807 93 |
| 27 | | *Michelle Wu, Capital* | | | | 34 807 92 |

**1.** Date
**2.** Account Debited
**3.** Debit to Close
**4.** Accounts Credited
**5.** Credits to Record Net Income

Net income increases the partners' equity and therefore must be credited to the partners' capital accounts. The share of the net income to be recorded for each partner is shown on the distribution of net income statement. The balance of the temporary account Income Summary must be reduced to zero to prepare the account for the next fiscal period. The effect of this closing entry on the general ledger accounts is shown in the T accounts.

If there is a net loss, partners' capital accounts are debited for their share of the net loss. Income Summary is credited for the total net loss.

**Income Summary**

| Debit | | Credit | |
|---|---|---|---|
| Adj. (mdse. inv.) | 15,840.00 | Closing (revenue) | 423,120.00 |
| Closing (cost and expenses) | 337,664.15 | | |
| Closing (net income) | 69,615.85 | *(New Bal. zero)* | |

**Karl Koehn, Capital**

| Debit | | Credit | |
|---|---|---|---|
| | | Bal. | 136,750.00 |
| | | Closing (net income) | 34,807.93 |

**Michelle Wu, Capital**

| Debit | | Credit | |
|---|---|---|---|
| | | Bal. | 136,552.48 |
| | | Closing (net income) | 34,807.92 |

**STEPS**

### Closing the income summary account to record net income or loss

1. Write the date, *31,* in the Date column.
2. Write the title of the account debited, *Income Summary,* in the Account Title column.
3. Write the debit amount, *$69,615.85,* in the General Debit column. This is the amount of net income.
4. Write the titles of the two partners' capital accounts on the next two lines in the Account Title column.
5. Write the credit amounts, *$34,807.93* and *$34,807.92,* in the General Credit column.

# CLOSING ENTRIES FOR THE PARTNERS' DRAWING ACCOUNTS

| | ACCOUNT TITLE | 7 BALANCE SHEET DEBIT | 8 BALANCE SHEET CREDIT | |
|---|---|---|---|---|
| 18 | *Karl Koehn, Capital* | | *136 750 00* | 18 |
| 19 | *Karl Koehn, Drawing* | *29 100 00* | | 19 |
| 20 | *Michelle Wu, Capital* | | *136 552 48* | 20 |
| 21 | *Michelle Wu, Drawing* | *28 800 00* | | 21 |

**1.** Date **2.** Account Debited **3.** Debit Amount **4.** Account Credited **5.** Credit to Close

JOURNAL PAGE *26*

| | DATE | ACCOUNT TITLE | DOC. NO. | POST. REF. | 1 GENERAL DEBIT | 2 GENERAL CREDIT |
|---|---|---|---|---|---|---|
| 28 | *31* | *Karl Koehn, Capital* | | | *29 100 00* | |
| 29 | | *Karl Koehn, Drawing* | | | | *29 100 00* |
| 30 | *31* | *Michelle Wu, Capital* | | | *28 800 00* | |
| 31 | | *Michelle Wu, Drawing* | | | | *28 800 00* |
| 32 | | | | | | |
| 33 | | | | | | |

As discussed in Chapter 9, the drawing accounts are not closed through Income Summary. The drawing account balances are closed directly to the partners' capital accounts.

The effect of these closing entries on the general ledger accounts is shown in the T accounts. After the closing entry for the partners' drawing accounts, the balances of the partners' capital accounts are the same as reported in the owners' equity section of the balance sheet.

**Karl Koehn, Capital**

| Debit | | Credit | |
|---|---|---|---|
| Closing (drawing) | 29,100.00 | Bal. | 136,750.00 |
| | | Closing (net income) | 34,807.93 |
| | | *(New Bal.* | *142,457.93)* |

**Michelle Wu, Capital**

| Debit | | Credit | |
|---|---|---|---|
| Closing (drawing) | 28,800.00 | Bal. | 136,552.48 |
| | | Closing (net income) | 34,807.92 |
| | | *(New Bal.* | *142,560.40)* |

**Karl Koehn, Drawing**

| Debit | | Credit | |
|---|---|---|---|
| Bal. | 29,100.00 | Closing | 29,100.00 |
| *(New Bal. zero)* | | | |

**Michelle Wu, Drawing**

| Debit | | Credit | |
|---|---|---|---|
| Bal. | 28,800.00 | Closing | 28,800.00 |
| *(New Bal. zero)* | | | |

STEPS

**Closing the partners' drawing accounts**

1. Write the date, *31*, in the Date column.
2. Write the title of the account debited, *Karl Koehn, Capital,* in the Account Title column.
3. Write the debit amount, *$29,100.00,* in the General Debit column.
4. Write the title of the account credited, *Karl Koehn, Drawing,* in the Account Title column.
5. Write the credit amount, *$29,100.00,* in the General Credit column.

Repeat Steps 1 through 5 to close the second partner's drawing account.

## COMPLETED CLOSING ENTRIES FOR A PARTNERSHIP RECORDED IN A JOURNAL

PAGE *26* JOURNAL

| | DATE | ACCOUNT TITLE | DOC. NO. | POST. REF. | 1 GENERAL DEBIT | 2 GENERAL CREDIT | 3 ACCOUNTS RECEIVABLE DEBIT | 4 ACCOUNTS RECEIVABLE CREDIT | |
|---|---|---|---|---|---|---|---|---|---|
| 10 | | *Closing Entries* | | | | | | | 10 |
| 11 | *31* | *Sales* | | | *423 120 00* | | | | 11 |
| 12 | | *Income Summary* | | | | *423 120 00* | | | 12 |
| 13 | *31* | *Income Summary* | | | *337 664 15* | | | | 13 |
| 14 | | *Purchases* | | | | *189 960 00* | | | 14 |
| 15 | | *Advertising Expense* | | | | *6 600 00* | | | 15 |
| 16 | | *Credit Card Fee Expense* | | | | *3 385 00* | | | 16 |
| 17 | | *Insurance Expense* | | | | *3 170 00* | | | 17 |
| 18 | | *Miscellaneous Expense* | | | | *2 584 15* | | | 18 |
| 19 | | *Payroll Taxes Expense* | | | | *9 105 00* | | | 19 |
| 20 | | *Rent Expense* | | | | *21 000 00* | | | 20 |
| 21 | | *Salary Expense* | | | | *89 400 00* | | | 21 |
| 22 | | *Supplies Expense—Office* | | | | *4 730 00* | | | 22 |
| 23 | | *Supplies Expense—Store* | | | | *3 910 00* | | | 23 |
| 24 | | *Utilities Expense* | | | | *3 820 00* | | | 24 |
| 25 | *31* | *Income Summary* | | | *69 615 85* | | | | 25 |
| 26 | | *Karl Koehn, Capital* | | | | *34 807 93* | | | 26 |
| 27 | | *Michelle Wu, Capital* | | | | *34 807 92* | | | 27 |
| 28 | *31* | *Karl Koehn, Capital* | | | *29 100 00* | | | | 28 |
| 29 | | *Karl Koehn, Drawing* | | | | *29 100 00* | | | 29 |
| 30 | *31* | *Michelle Wu, Capital* | | | *28 800 00* | | | | 30 |
| 31 | | *Michelle Wu, Drawing* | | | | *28 800 00* | | | 31 |

Omni Import's journal appears as shown above, after all closing entries have been recorded.

The next step would be to post the adjusting and closing entries to the general ledger.

## AUDIT YOUR UNDERSTANDING

1. Where is the information obtained for journalizing closing entries for net income or loss and partners' drawing accounts?
2. How is a temporary account closed?

## WORK TOGETHER

**Journalizing additional closing entries**

Use the journal from Work Together on page 430. Given in the *Working Papers* are a partial work sheet and a distribution of net income statement for the year ended December 31 of the current year. Your instructor will guide you through the following example.

3. Record the following closing entries on page 12 of the journal.
   - **a.** Close the income summary account and record the net income.
   - **b.** Close the partners' drawing accounts.

## ON YOUR OWN

**Journalizing additional closing entries**

Use the journal from On Your Own on page 430. Given in the *Working Papers* are a partial work sheet and a distribution of net income statement for the year ended December 31 of the current year. Work this problem independently.

4. Record the following closing entries on page 15 of the journal.
   - **a.** Close the income summary account and record the net income.
   - **b.** Close the partners' drawing accounts.

# 17-4 Preparing a Post-Closing Trial Balance

## COMPLETED GENERAL LEDGER AFTER ADJUSTING AND CLOSING ENTRIES ARE POSTED

ACCOUNT *Cash* — ACCOUNT NO. *1110*

| DATE | | ITEM | POST. REF. | DEBIT | CREDIT | BALANCE DEBIT | BALANCE CREDIT |
|---|---|---|---|---|---|---|---|
| 20-- Dec. | 31 | Balance | ✓ | | | 29080 28 | |

ACCOUNT *Petty Cash* — ACCOUNT NO. *1120*

| DATE | | ITEM | POST. REF. | DEBIT | CREDIT | BALANCE DEBIT | BALANCE CREDIT |
|---|---|---|---|---|---|---|---|
| 20-- Dec. | 31 | Balance | ✓ | | | 300 00 | |

ACCOUNT *Accounts Receivable* — ACCOUNT NO. *1130*

| DATE | | ITEM | POST. REF. | DEBIT | CREDIT | BALANCE DEBIT | BALANCE CREDIT |
|---|---|---|---|---|---|---|---|
| 20-- Dec. | 31 | Balance | ✓ | | | 11198 40 | |

ACCOUNT *Merchandise Inventory* — ACCOUNT NO. *1140*

| DATE | | ITEM | POST. REF. | DEBIT | CREDIT | BALANCE DEBIT | BALANCE CREDIT |
|---|---|---|---|---|---|---|---|
| 20-- Jan. | 1 | Balance | ✓ | | | 270480 00 | |
| Dec. | 31 | | 26 | | 15840 00 | 254640 00 | |

ACCOUNT *Supplies—Office* — ACCOUNT NO. *1145*

| DATE | | ITEM | POST. REF. | DEBIT | CREDIT | BALANCE DEBIT | BALANCE CREDIT |
|---|---|---|---|---|---|---|---|
| 20-- Dec. | 31 | Balance | ✓ | | | 6480 00 | |
| | 31 | | 26 | | 4730 00 | 1750 00 | |

ACCOUNT *Supplies—Store* — ACCOUNT NO. *1150*

| DATE | | ITEM | POST. REF. | DEBIT | CREDIT | BALANCE DEBIT | BALANCE CREDIT |
|---|---|---|---|---|---|---|---|
| 20-- Dec. | 31 | Balance | ✓ | | | 6944 00 | |
| | 31 | | 26 | | 3910 00 | 3034 00 | |

ACCOUNT *Prepaid Insurance* — ACCOUNT NO. *1160*

| DATE | | ITEM | POST. REF. | DEBIT | CREDIT | BALANCE DEBIT | BALANCE CREDIT |
|---|---|---|---|---|---|---|---|
| 20-- Dec. | 31 | Balance | ✓ | | | 5800 00 | |
| | 31 | | 26 | | 3170 00 | 2630 00 | |

ACCOUNT *Accounts Payable* — ACCOUNT NO. *2110*

| DATE | | ITEM | POST. REF. | DEBIT | CREDIT | BALANCE DEBIT | BALANCE CREDIT |
|---|---|---|---|---|---|---|---|
| 20-- Dec. | 31 | Balance | ✓ | | | | 12542 38 |

ACCOUNT *Employee Income Tax Payable* — ACCOUNT NO. *2120*

| DATE | | ITEM | POST. REF. | DEBIT | CREDIT | BALANCE DEBIT | BALANCE CREDIT |
|---|---|---|---|---|---|---|---|
| 20-- Dec. | 31 | Balance | ✓ | | | | 542 00 |

ACCOUNT *Social Security Tax Payable* — ACCOUNT NO. *2130*

| DATE | | ITEM | POST. REF. | DEBIT | CREDIT | BALANCE DEBIT | BALANCE CREDIT |
|---|---|---|---|---|---|---|---|
| 20-- Dec. | 31 | Balance | ✓ | | | | 985 40 |

ACCOUNT *Medicare Tax Payable* — ACCOUNT NO. *2135*

| DATE | | ITEM | POST. REF. | DEBIT | CREDIT | BALANCE DEBIT | BALANCE CREDIT |
|---|---|---|---|---|---|---|---|
| 20-- Dec. | 31 | | ✓ | | | | 227 42 |

ACCOUNT *Sales Tax Payable* — ACCOUNT NO. *2140*

| DATE | | ITEM | POST. REF. | DEBIT | CREDIT | BALANCE DEBIT | BALANCE CREDIT |
|---|---|---|---|---|---|---|---|
| 20-- Dec. | 31 | Balance | ✓ | | | | 2112 05 |

ACCOUNT *Unemployment Tax Payable—Federal* — ACCOUNT NO. *2150*

| DATE | | ITEM | POST. REF. | DEBIT | CREDIT | BALANCE DEBIT | BALANCE CREDIT |
|---|---|---|---|---|---|---|---|
| 20-- Dec. | 31 | Balance | ✓ | | | | 8 40 |

ACCOUNT *Unemployment Tax Payable—State* — ACCOUNT NO. *2160*

| DATE | | ITEM | POST. REF. | DEBIT | CREDIT | BALANCE DEBIT | BALANCE CREDIT |
|---|---|---|---|---|---|---|---|
| 20-- Dec. | 31 | Balance | ✓ | | | | 56 70 |

ACCOUNT *Health Insurance Premiums Payable* — ACCOUNT NO. *2170*

| DATE | | ITEM | POST. REF. | DEBIT | CREDIT | BALANCE DEBIT | BALANCE CREDIT |
|---|---|---|---|---|---|---|---|
| 20-- Dec. | 31 | Balance | ✓ | | | | 1008 00 |

ACCOUNT *U.S. Savings Bonds Payable* — ACCOUNT NO. *2180*

| DATE | | ITEM | POST. REF. | DEBIT | CREDIT | BALANCE DEBIT | BALANCE CREDIT |
|---|---|---|---|---|---|---|---|
| 20-- Dec. | 31 | Balance | ✓ | | | | 60 00 |

ACCOUNT *United Way Donations Payable* — ACCOUNT NO. *2190*

| DATE | | ITEM | POST. REF. | DEBIT | CREDIT | BALANCE DEBIT | BALANCE CREDIT |
|---|---|---|---|---|---|---|---|
| 20-- Dec. | 31 | Balance | ✓ | | | | 72 00 |

Omni Import's completed general ledger after adjusting and closing entries are posted is shown above and on the following page.

Balance sheet accounts (asset, liability, and capital accounts) have up-to-date balances to begin the new fiscal period.

Income statement accounts (revenue, cost, and expense accounts) have zero balances to begin the new fiscal period. *(CONCEPT: Matching Expenses with Revenue)*

**ACCOUNT** *Karl Koehn, Capital* — **ACCOUNT NO.** *3110*

| DATE | | ITEM | POST. REF. | DEBIT | CREDIT | BALANCE DEBIT | BALANCE CREDIT |
|---|---|---|---|---|---|---|---|
| 20-- Dec. | 31 | Balance | ✓ | | | | 136750 00 |
| | 31 | | 26 | | 34807 93 | | 171557 93 |
| | 31 | | 26 | 29100 00 | | | 142457 93 |

**ACCOUNT** *Karl Koehn, Drawing* — **ACCOUNT NO.** *3120*

| DATE | | ITEM | POST. REF. | DEBIT | CREDIT | BALANCE DEBIT | BALANCE CREDIT |
|---|---|---|---|---|---|---|---|
| 20-- Dec. | 31 | Balance | ✓ | | | 29100 00 | |
| | 31 | | 26 | | 29100 00 | — | — |

**ACCOUNT** *Michelle Wu, Capital* — **ACCOUNT NO.** *3130*

| DATE | | ITEM | POST. REF. | DEBIT | CREDIT | BALANCE DEBIT | BALANCE CREDIT |
|---|---|---|---|---|---|---|---|
| 20-- Dec. | 31 | Balance | ✓ | | | | 136552 48 |
| | 31 | | 26 | | 34807 92 | | 171360 40 |
| | 31 | | 26 | 28800 00 | | | 142560 40 |

**ACCOUNT** *Michelle Wu, Drawing* — **ACCOUNT NO.** *3140*

| DATE | | ITEM | POST. REF. | DEBIT | CREDIT | BALANCE DEBIT | BALANCE CREDIT |
|---|---|---|---|---|---|---|---|
| 20-- Dec. | 31 | Balance | ✓ | | | 28800 00 | |
| | 31 | | 26 | | 28800 00 | — | — |

**ACCOUNT** *Income Summary* — **ACCOUNT NO.** *3150*

| DATE | | ITEM | POST. REF. | DEBIT | CREDIT | BALANCE DEBIT | BALANCE CREDIT |
|---|---|---|---|---|---|---|---|
| 20-- Dec. | 31 | | 26 | 15840 00 | | 15840 00 | |
| | 31 | | 26 | | 423120 00 | | 407280 00 |
| | 31 | | 26 | 337664 15 | | | 69615 85 |
| | 31 | | 26 | 69615 85 | | — | — |

**ACCOUNT** *Sales* — **ACCOUNT NO.** *4110*

| DATE | | ITEM | POST. REF. | DEBIT | CREDIT | BALANCE DEBIT | BALANCE CREDIT |
|---|---|---|---|---|---|---|---|
| 20-- Dec. | 31 | Balance | ✓ | | | | 423120 00 |
| | 31 | | 26 | 423120 00 | | — | — |

**ACCOUNT** *Purchases* — **ACCOUNT NO.** *5110*

| DATE | | ITEM | POST. REF. | DEBIT | CREDIT | BALANCE DEBIT | BALANCE CREDIT |
|---|---|---|---|---|---|---|---|
| 20-- Dec. | 31 | Balance | ✓ | | | 189960 00 | |
| | 31 | | 26 | | 189960 00 | — | — |

**ACCOUNT** *Advertising Expense* — **ACCOUNT NO.** *6110*

| DATE | | ITEM | POST. REF. | DEBIT | CREDIT | BALANCE DEBIT | BALANCE CREDIT |
|---|---|---|---|---|---|---|---|
| 20-- Dec. | 31 | Balance | ✓ | | | 6600 00 | |
| | 31 | | 26 | | 6600 00 | — | — |

**ACCOUNT** *Credit Card Fee Expense* — **ACCOUNT NO.** *6120*

| DATE | | ITEM | POST. REF. | DEBIT | CREDIT | BALANCE DEBIT | BALANCE CREDIT |
|---|---|---|---|---|---|---|---|
| 20-- Dec. | 31 | Balance | ✓ | | | 3385 00 | |
| | 31 | | 26 | | 3385 00 | — | — |

**ACCOUNT** *Insurance Expense* — **ACCOUNT NO.** *6130*

| DATE | | ITEM | POST. REF. | DEBIT | CREDIT | BALANCE DEBIT | BALANCE CREDIT |
|---|---|---|---|---|---|---|---|
| 20-- Dec. | 31 | | 26 | 3170 00 | | 3170 00 | |
| | 31 | | 26 | | 3170 00 | — | — |

**ACCOUNT** *Miscellaneous Expense* — **ACCOUNT NO.** *6140*

| DATE | | ITEM | POST. REF. | DEBIT | CREDIT | BALANCE DEBIT | BALANCE CREDIT |
|---|---|---|---|---|---|---|---|
| 20-- Dec. | 31 | Balance | ✓ | | | 2584 15 | |
| | 31 | | 26 | | 2584 15 | — | — |

**ACCOUNT** *Payroll Taxes Expense* — **ACCOUNT NO.** *6150*

| DATE | | ITEM | POST. REF. | DEBIT | CREDIT | BALANCE DEBIT | BALANCE CREDIT |
|---|---|---|---|---|---|---|---|
| 20-- Dec. | 31 | Balance | ✓ | | | 9105 00 | |
| | 31 | | 26 | | 9105 00 | — | — |

**ACCOUNT** *Rent Expense* — **ACCOUNT NO.** *6160*

| DATE | | ITEM | POST. REF. | DEBIT | CREDIT | BALANCE DEBIT | BALANCE CREDIT |
|---|---|---|---|---|---|---|---|
| 20-- Dec. | 31 | Balance | ✓ | | | 21000 00 | |
| | 31 | | 26 | | 21000 00 | — | — |

**ACCOUNT** *Salary Expense* — **ACCOUNT NO.** *6170*

| DATE | | ITEM | POST. REF. | DEBIT | CREDIT | BALANCE DEBIT | BALANCE CREDIT |
|---|---|---|---|---|---|---|---|
| 20-- Dec. | 31 | Balance | ✓ | | | 89400 00 | |
| | 31 | | 26 | | 89400 00 | — | — |

**ACCOUNT** *Supplies Expense—Office* — **ACCOUNT NO.** *6175*

| DATE | | ITEM | POST. REF. | DEBIT | CREDIT | BALANCE DEBIT | BALANCE CREDIT |
|---|---|---|---|---|---|---|---|
| 20-- Dec. | 31 | | 26 | 4730 00 | | 4730 00 | |
| | 31 | | 26 | | 4730 00 | — | — |

**ACCOUNT** *Supplies Expense—Store* — **ACCOUNT NO.** *6180*

| DATE | | ITEM | POST. REF. | DEBIT | CREDIT | BALANCE DEBIT | BALANCE CREDIT |
|---|---|---|---|---|---|---|---|
| 20-- Dec. | 31 | | 26 | 3910 00 | | 3910 00 | |
| | 31 | | 26 | | 3910 00 | — | — |

**ACCOUNT** *Utilities Expense* — **ACCOUNT NO.** *6190*

| DATE | | ITEM | POST. REF. | DEBIT | CREDIT | BALANCE DEBIT | BALANCE CREDIT |
|---|---|---|---|---|---|---|---|
| 20-- Dec. | 31 | Balance | ✓ | | | 3820 00 | |
| | 31 | | 26 | | 3820 00 | — | — |

Completed General Ledger after Adjusting and Closing Entries Are Posted *(concluded)*

# POST-CLOSING TRIAL BALANCE

1. Heading
2. Accounts That Have Balances
3. Debit Balances
4. Credit Balances
5. Word *Totals*
6. Total Debits
7. Total Credits
8. Verify Equality of Totals
9. Double Lines

*Omni Import*
*Post-Closing Trial Balance*
*December 31, 20--*

| ACCOUNT TITLE | DEBIT | CREDIT |
|---|---|---|
| *Cash* | 29,080.28 | |
| *Petty Cash* | 300.00 | |
| *Accounts Receivable* | 11,198.40 | |
| *Merchandise Inventory* | 254,640.00 | |
| *Supplies—Office* | 1,750.00 | |
| *Supplies—Store* | 3,034.00 | |
| *Prepaid Insurance* | 2,630.00 | |
| *Accounts Payable* | | 12,542.38 |
| *Employee Income Tax Payable* | | 542.00 |
| *Social Security Tax Payable* | | 985.40 |
| *Medicare Tax Payable* | | 227.42 |
| *Sales Tax Payable* | | 2,112.05 |
| *Unemployment Tax Payable—Federal* | | 8.40 |
| *Unemployment Tax Payable—State* | | 56.70 |
| *Health Insurance Premiums Payable* | | 1,008.00 |
| *U.S. Savings Bonds Payable* | | 60.00 |
| *United Way Donations Payable* | | 72.00 |
| *Karl Koehn, Capital* | | 142,457.93 |
| *Michelle Wu, Capital* | | 142,560.40 |
| *Totals* | 302,632.68 | 302,632.68 |

A post-closing trial balance is prepared to prove the equality of debits and credits in the general ledger. Account balances on the post-closing trial balance agree with the balances on the balance sheet shown in Chapter 16. Because the post-closing trial balance debit and credit totals are the same, the equality of debits and credits in the general ledger is proved. The general ledger is ready for the next fiscal period. *(CONCEPT: Accounting Period Cycle)*

## STEPS: Preparing a post-closing trial balance

1. Write the post-closing trial balance heading on three lines.
2. List all general ledger accounts that have balances in the Account Title column. Accounts are listed in the same order as they appear in the general ledger. Accounts with zero balances are not listed.
3. Write the balance of each asset account in the Debit column.
4. Write the balance of each liability and capital account in the Credit column.
5. Write the word *Totals* on the next line below the last account title.
6. Total the amounts in the Debit column and write the amount, *$302,632.68,* on the Totals line.
7. Total the amounts in the Credit column and write the amount, *$302,632.68,* on the Totals line.
8. Verify equality by comparing the Debit column total with the Credit column total. The two amounts, $302,632.68, are the same. The equality of debits and credits is proved.
9. Rule double lines below both Debit and Credit total amounts.

# ACCOUNTING CYCLE FOR A MERCHANDISING BUSINESS ORGANIZED AS A PARTNERSHIP

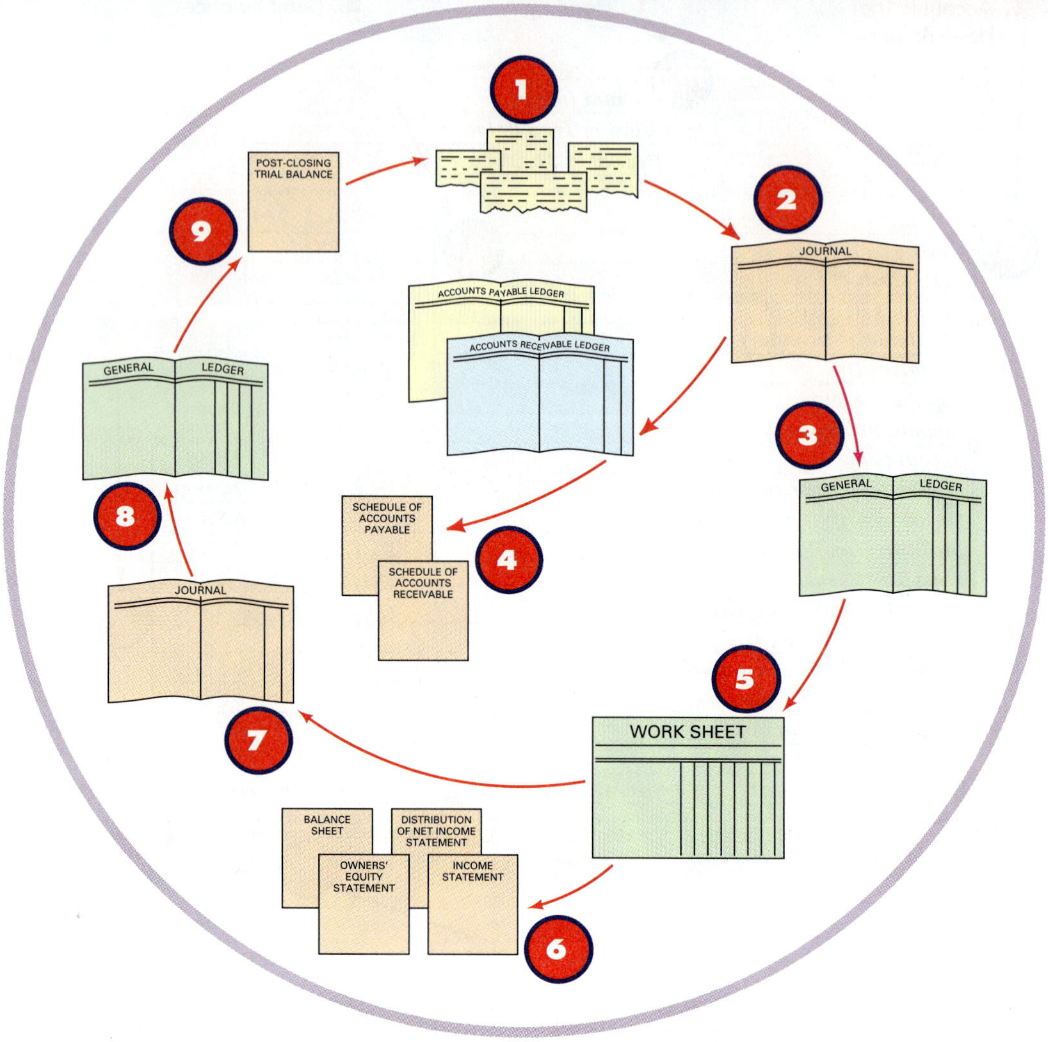


Service and merchandising businesses use a similar accounting cycle. The accounting cycles are also similar for a proprietorship and a partnership. Variations occur when subsidiary ledgers are used. Variations also occur in preparing financial statements.

**STEPS**

### Accounting cycle for a merchandising business

1. Source documents are checked for accuracy, and transactions are analyzed into debit and credit parts.
2. Transactions, from information on source documents, are recorded in a journal.
3. Journal entries are posted to the accounts payable ledger, the accounts receivable ledger, and the general ledger.
4. Schedules of accounts payable and accounts receivable are prepared from the subsidiary ledgers.
5. A work sheet, including a trial balance, is prepared from the general ledger.
6. Financial statements are prepared from the work sheet.
7. Adjusting and closing entries are journalized from the work sheet.
8. Adjusting and closing entries are posted to the general ledger.
9. A post-closing trial balance of the general ledger is prepared.

## AUDIT YOUR UNDERSTANDING

1. Which accounts are listed on a post-closing trial balance?
2. What is the purpose of preparing a post-closing trial balance?
3. In what order should accounts be listed on a post-closing trial balance?

## WORK TOGETHER

### Preparing a post-closing trial balance

For the current year, the December 31 balances for Visual Art Center's balance sheet accounts after adjusting and closing entries have been posted are given below.

| Account | Balance | Account | Balance |
|---|---|---|---|
| Cash | $ 21,810.20 | Accounts Payable | $ 11,676.50 |
| Petty Cash | 350.00 | Sales Tax Payable | 1,584.00 |
| Accounts Receivable | 8,398.80 | Jane Cole, Capital | 107,050.50 |
| Merchandise Inventory | 190,980.00 | Jane Cole, Drawing | — |
| Supplies—Office | 1,314.00 | Gary Klein, Capital | 106,790.00 |
| Supplies—Store | 2,268.00 | Gary Klein, Drawing | — |
| Prepaid Insurance | 1,980.00 | | |

Your instructor will guide you through the following example.

4. Prepare a post-closing trial balance on the form provided in the *Working Papers.*

## ON YOUR OWN

### Preparing a post-closing trial balance

For the current year, the December 31 balances for Jan's Pastry Boutique's balance sheet accounts after adjusting and closing entries have been posted are given below.

| Account | Balance | Account | Balance |
|---|---|---|---|
| Cash | $ 23,021.89 | Accounts Payable | $ 12,255.25 |
| Petty Cash | 300.00 | Sales Tax Payable | 1,672.00 |
| Accounts Receivable | 8,865.40 | Jan Dyer, Capital | 112,998.27 |
| Merchandise Inventory | 201,590.00 | Jan Dyer, Drawing | — |
| Supplies—Office | 1,387.00 | Becky Myers, Capital | 112,722.77 |
| Supplies—Store | 2,394.00 | Becky Myers, Drawing | — |
| Prepaid Insurance | 2,090.00 | | |

Work independently to complete this problem.

5. Prepare a post-closing trial balance on the form provided in the *Working Papers.*

# CHAPTER 17 SUMMARY

*Enrichment Activity*

**Types of Businesses**

*How do the financial statements and adjusting and closing entries for a partnership differ from those of a proprietorship? Could a proprietorship prepare an owner's equity statement?*

After completing this chapter, you can

1. Identify accounting concepts and practices related to adjusting and closing entries for a merchandising business organized as a partnership.
2. Record adjusting entries.
3. Record closing entries for income statement accounts.
4. Record closing entries for net income or loss and partners' drawing accounts.
5. Prepare a post-closing trial balance.

## EXPLORE ACCOUNTING

### THE PERPETUAL INVENTORY METHOD

Many companies use one of two merchandise inventory methods to account for their cost of merchandise sold. (Inventory counting methods are fully discussed in Chapter 22.) A merchandise inventory determined by counting, weighing, or measuring items of merchandise on hand is known as *periodic inventory.*

The disadvantage of this method is that the business does not know the cost of merchandise sold until the merchandise inventory has been counted at the end of the fiscal period and costs calculated.

An inventory method that provides more timely cost information is the *perpetual inventory method*, which is determined by keeping a continuous record of increases, decreases, and balance on hand. When perpetual inventory is used, both sales and cost of merchandise sold are recorded at the time of sale. Assume All Sports Shop purchases 10 soccer balls, Item 929, for $13.00 each. Further assume the store sells two of these soccer balls for $25.00 each. The journal entries for the purchase and sale are shown below.

When the perpetual inventory method is used, the purchases account is not used. When merchandise is purchased, it is added to the merchandise inventory account. Two entries are made each time a sale is made—one for the sale at the selling price and one for the cost at the cost of merchandise sold. An additional account is used, Cost of Merchandise Sold. The cost is recorded in this account at the time of the sale.

The advantage of this inventory method is that the cost of merchandise sold can be determined at any time by reviewing the cost of merchandise sold account. However, the disadvantage is that the number of entries is doubled and the information needed to keep current records of the merchandise inventory is much more complex.

**Activity:** All Sports Shop purchased 5 sets of golf clubs, Item No. 389, for $140.00 each. One set of clubs, Item No. 389, was sold for $250.00. Using the perpetual inventory method, prepare the journal entries to record the purchase of the clubs and to record the sale of one set of clubs.

| | | Debit | Credit |
|---|---|---|---|
| Purchase: | Merchandise Inventory (Item 929) (10 @ $13.00) | 130.00 | |
| | Cash | | 130.00 |
| Sale: | Cash (2 @ $25.00) | 50.00 | |
| | Sales | | 50.00 |
| | Cost of Merchandise Sold (2 @ $13.00) | 26.00 | |
| | Merchandise Inventory (Item 929) | | 26.00 |

## 17-1 APPLICATION PROBLEM
### Journalizing adjusting entries

The following information is related to adjustments needed at the end of a fiscal period for a partnership.

| Account Title | Work Sheet Trial Balance | Adjustment Information: Ending Inventories | Adjustment Information: Ending Value |
|---|---|---|---|
| Merchandise Inventory | $265,000.00 | $347,500.00 | |
| Supplies—Office | 5,600.00 | 2,810.00 | |
| Supplies—Store | 5,160.00 | 2,900.00 | |
| Prepaid Insurance | 4,000.00 | | $1,000.00 |

***Instructions:***

Record the appropriate adjusting entries on page 12 of the journal provided in the *Working Papers.* Use December 31 of the current year as the date.

## 17-2 APPLICATION PROBLEM
### Journalizing closing entries for income statement accounts

The following information is from the work sheet of Aladdin Cycle Shop for December 31 of the current year.

| | ACCOUNT TITLE | 5 INCOME STATEMENT DEBIT | 6 INCOME STATEMENT CREDIT |
|---|---|---|---|
| 15 | *Sales* | | 278500 00 |
| 16 | *Purchases* | 141600 00 | |
| 17 | *Advertising Expense* | 4880 00 | |
| 18 | *Credit Card Fee Expense* | 3200 00 | |
| 19 | *Insurance Expense* | 3780 00 | |
| 20 | *Miscellaneous Expense* | 2070 00 | |
| 21 | *Rent Expense* | 21600 00 | |
| 22 | *Supplies Expense—Office* | 4470 00 | |
| 23 | *Supplies Expense—Store* | 4680 00 | |
| 24 | *Utilities Expense* | 4410 00 | |

***Instructions:***

Prepare the following closing entries on page 14 of the journal provided in the *Working Papers.* Save your work to complete Application Problem 17-3.

1. Close the income statement account with a credit balance.
2. Close the income statement accounts with debit balances.

## 17-3 APPLICATION PROBLEM
### Journalizing additional closing entries

For Aladdin Cycle Shop on December 31 of the current year, the following information is from the work sheet and the distribution of net income statement. Use the journal from Application Problem 17-2.

| | ACCOUNT TITLE | 5 INCOME STATEMENT DEBIT | 6 INCOME STATEMENT CREDIT | 7 BALANCE SHEET DEBIT | 8 BALANCE SHEET CREDIT | |
|---|---|---|---|---|---|---|
| 10 | Sue Ogden, Capital | | | | 223 000 00 | 10 |
| 11 | Sue Ogden, Drawing | | | 26 500 00 | | 11 |
| 12 | Todd Marquez, Capital | | | | 231 000 00 | 12 |
| 13 | Todd Marquez, Drawing | | | 26 800 00 | | 13 |
| 14 | Income Summary | 18 000 00 | | | | 14 |

*Aladdin Cycle Shop*
*Distribution of Net Income Statement*
*For Year Ended December 31, 20--*

| | |
|---|---|
| *Sue Ogden* | |
| *50% of Net Income* | 34 905 00 |
| *Todd Marquez* | |
| *50% of Net Income* | 34 905 00 |
| *Net Income* | 69 810 00 |

***Instructions:***

Prepare the following closing entries on page 14 of the journal.

1. Close the income summary account and record the net income.
2. Close the partners' drawing accounts.

## 17-4 APPLICATION PROBLEM
### Preparing a post-closing trial balance

For the current year, the December 31 balances for Lawn and Garden Center's balance sheet accounts after adjusting and closing entries have been posted are given.

| Account | Balance | Account | Balance |
|---|---|---|---|
| Cash | $ 26,656.93 | Accounts Payable | $ 11,744.13 |
| Petty Cash | 500.00 | Sales Tax Payable | 1,936.00 |
| Accounts Receivable | 10,265.20 | Rob Gresham, Capital | 132,030.00 |
| Merchandise Inventory | 233,420.00 | Rob Gresham, Drawing | — |
| Supplies—Office | 1,606.00 | Jose Zavala, Capital | 131,710.00 |
| Supplies—Store | 2,552.00 | Jose Zavala, Drawing | — |
| Prepaid Insurance | 2,420.00 | | |

***Instructions:***

Prepare a post-closing trial balance on the form provided in the *Working Papers*.

## 17-5 APPLICATION PROBLEM

### Journalizing and posting adjusting and closing entries; preparing a post-closing trial balance

Use the following partial work sheet of Custom Marble Company for the year ended December 31 of the current year. The general ledger accounts and their balances as well as forms for completing this problem are in the *Working Papers.*

| | | 3 | 4 | 5 | 6 |
|---|---|---|---|---|---|
| | ACCOUNT TITLE | ADJUSTMENTS | | INCOME STATEMENT | |
| | | DEBIT | CREDIT | DEBIT | CREDIT |
| 4 | Merchandise Inventory | | (a) 15,600.00 | | |
| 5 | Supplies—Office | | (b) 2,568.00 | | |
| 6 | Supplies—Store | | (c) 2,940.00 | | |
| 7 | Prepaid Insurance | | (d) 3,168.00 | | |
| 22 | Income Summary | (a) 15,600.00 | | 15,600.00 | |
| 23 | Sales | | | | 275,060.00 |
| 24 | Purchases | | | 151,740.00 | |
| 25 | Advertising Expense | | | 5,664.00 | |
| 26 | Credit Card Fee Expense | | | 3,912.00 | |
| 27 | Insurance Expense | (d) 3,168.00 | | 3,168.00 | |
| 28 | Miscellaneous Expense | | | 2,316.00 | |
| 29 | Payroll Taxes Expense | | | 6,917.00 | |
| 30 | Rent Expense | | | 18,720.00 | |
| 31 | Salary Expense | | | 68,150.00 | |
| 32 | Supplies Expense—Office | (b) 2,568.00 | | 2,568.00 | |
| 33 | Supplies Expense—Store | (c) 2,940.00 | | 2,940.00 | |
| 34 | Utilities Expense | | | 3,528.00 | |
| 35 | | 24,276.00 | 24,276.00 | 285,223.00 | 275,060.00 |
| 36 | Net Loss | | | | 10,163.00 |
| 37 | | | | 285,223.00 | 285,223.00 |
| 38 | | | | | |

***Instructions:***

1. Use page 24 of a journal. Journalize the adjusting entries using information from the partial work sheet.
2. Post the adjusting entries.
3. Continue using page 24 of the journal. Journalize the closing entries using information from the work sheet. The distribution of net income statement shows equal distribution of the net loss. The partners' drawing accounts show the following debit balances in the work sheet's Balance Sheet Debit column: Emma Bose, Drawing, $18,225.00; Kris Manuel, Drawing, $18,400.00.
4. Post the closing entries.
5. Prepare a post-closing trial balance.

## 17-6 MASTERY PROBLEM

### Journalizing and posting adjusting and closing entries; preparing a post-closing trial balance

Use the following partial work sheet of Deco Paint Supplies for the year ended December 31 of the current year. The general ledger accounts and their balances as well as forms for completing this problem are in the *Working Papers*.

| | ACCOUNT TITLE | 3 ADJUSTMENTS DEBIT | 4 ADJUSTMENTS CREDIT | 5 INCOME STATEMENT DEBIT | 6 INCOME STATEMENT CREDIT |
|---|---|---|---|---|---|
| 4 | *Merchandise Inventory* | | (a) 15 000 00 | | |
| 5 | *Supplies—Office* | | (b) 2 916 00 | | |
| 6 | *Supplies—Store* | | (c) 2 724 00 | | |
| 7 | *Prepaid Insurance* | | (d) 2 736 00 | | |
| 22 | *Income Summary* | (a) 15 000 00 | | 15 000 00 | |
| 23 | *Sales* | | | | 374 500 00 |
| 24 | *Purchases* | | | 156 540 00 | |
| 25 | *Advertising Expense* | | | 6 216 00 | |
| 26 | *Credit Card Fee Expense* | | | 4 104 00 | |
| 27 | *Insurance Expense* | (d) 2 736 00 | | 2 736 00 | |
| 28 | *Miscellaneous Expense* | | | 2 472 00 | |
| 29 | *Payroll Taxes Expense* | | | 7 230 00 | |
| 30 | *Rent Expense* | | | 18 000 00 | |
| 31 | *Salary Expense* | | | 71 240 00 | |
| 32 | *Supplies Expense—Office* | (b) 2 916 00 | | 2 916 00 | |
| 33 | *Supplies Expense—Store* | (c) 2 724 00 | | 2 724 00 | |
| 34 | *Utilities Expense* | | | 3 456 00 | |
| 35 | | 23 376 00 | 23 376 00 | 292 634 00 | 374 500 00 |
| 36 | *Net Income* | | | 81 866 00 | |
| 37 | | | | 374 500 00 | 374 500 00 |
| 38 | | | | | |

***Instructions:***

1. Use page 25 of a journal. Journalize the adjusting entries using information from the partial work sheet.
2. Post the adjusting entries.
3. Continue using page 25 of the journal. Journalize the closing entries using information from the work sheet. The distribution of net income statement shows equal distribution of earnings. The partners' drawing accounts show the following debit balances in the work sheet's Balance Sheet Debit column: Anna Cao, Drawing, $22,800.00; Inez O'Neal, Drawing, $23,400.00.
4. Post the closing entries.
5. Prepare a post-closing trial balance.

## 17-7 CHALLENGE PROBLEM
### Completing end-of-fiscal-period work

Lighting Solutions' trial balance is recorded on a 10-column work sheet in the *Working Papers.* The general ledger accounts and their balances as well as forms for completing this problem are also given.

***Instructions:***

1. Use the following adjustment information. Complete the 10-column work sheet.

| **Adjustment Information, December 31** | |
|---|---|
| Merchandise inventory | $235,380.00 |
| Office supplies inventory | 3,030.00 |
| Store supplies inventory | 2,656.00 |
| Value of prepaid insurance | 2,530.00 |

2. Prepare an income statement from the information on the work sheet. Calculate and record the following component percentages: (a) cost of merchandise sold, (b) gross profit on sales, (c) total expenses, and (d) net income or loss. Round percentage calculations to the nearest 0.1%.
3. Prepare a distribution of net income statement. Net income or loss is to be shared equally.
4. Prepare an owners' equity statement. No additional investments were made.
5. Prepare a balance sheet in report form.
6. Use page 24 of a journal. Journalize the adjusting entries.
7. Post the adjusting entries.
8. Continue using page 24 of the journal. Journalize the closing entries.
9. Post the closing entries.
10. Prepare a post-closing trial balance.

### Inventory auditing challenges

For most businesses, merchandise inventory is a major portion of the business's assets. Therefore, reporting an accurate amount on the financial statements is important to accurate financial reporting. Whether a member of the business's accounting staff or an outside auditor audits the merchandise inventory of the business, determining an accurate count of the merchandise inventory is very important. Different types of merchandise present different kinds of challenges for the auditor.

a. **Actual count, common costs:** A sports store has 50 tennis rackets, all the same model. The rackets should be counted and multiplied times the cost per racket to determine the inventory value.

b. **Actual count, unique costs:** An automobile dealer has 60 new automobiles. Since each automobile probably has a unique and significant cost, the cost of each automobile should be totaled to determine the inventory value.

c. **Sampling:** A hardware store has many machine bolts. Since the value of each is low and there are many items, a small quantity may be counted or weighed. Then estimate the total cost based on the sample size or weight.

d. **Measuring/calculating:** An oil company stores crude oil in large tanks. The depth of the oil in the tank can be measured with a measuring rod, then the circumference of the tank can be measured. The total volume of crude oil can be calculated, then divided by the volume of one barrel of crude oil to determine the total barrels. This number can then be multiplied by the cost per barrel of crude oil.

*(Continued on next page)*

11. How would you determine the value of the following inventory items?
    a. Grain in a grain elevator.
    b. Lumber in a lumber yard.
    c. Diamond rings in a jewelry store.
    d. Nails in a home improvement store.

**INTERNET ACTIVITY**

Point your browser to

**http://accounting.swpco.com**

Choose **First-Year Course**, choose **Activities**, and complete the activity for Chapter 17.

## Applied Communication

Public speakers are judged by the ability of the audience to remember important points of their presentation. Effective public speakers use a variety of techniques to encourage the audience to listen to their message.

**Instructions:** Contact an instructor in your school or a local businessperson you have heard speak at school or community functions. Ask the person to describe the techniques used to help the audience listen and remember the message. Write a short report summarizing these techniques. Be prepared to present your report orally in class.

## Cases for Critical Thinking

**Case 1** Western Boot Warehouse's Trial Balance Debit column of the work sheet shows a debit balance of $3,000.00 for the office supplies account. The ending office supplies inventory is determined to be $2,200.00. The accounting clerk journalized the following adjusting entry: debit Supplies Expense—Office, $2,200.00; credit Supplies—Office, $2,200.00. Alice Hummell, partner, discussed the entry with the accounting clerk and suggested that the adjusting entry should have been for $800.00 instead of $2,200.00. The clerk indicated that there is no problem because the amounts will be adjusted again at the end of the next fiscal period. Do you agree with Ms. Hummell or the accounting clerk? Explain your answer.

**Case 2** Two businesses have been using different accounting practices. One business first closes the income summary account to record the net income in the capital accounts and then closes the drawing accounts. The other business first closes the drawing accounts and then closes the income summary account to record the net income in the capital accounts. Which practice is correct? Explain.

# AUTOMATED ACCOUNTING

## END-OF-FISCAL-PERIOD WORK FOR A PARTNERSHIP

When a transaction affects more than one accounting period, an adjusting entry may be needed to match revenues and expenses with the appropriate accounting period. To complete the accounting cycle, adjusting entries are recorded in the computer and verified for accuracy. The financial statements are generated, and then the software generates and posts the closing entries.

### Adjusting Entries

Changes in inventory resulting from purchases and sales transactions are not reflected in the merchandise inventory account. Therefore, this account balance must be adjusted to reflect the changes. Two accounts are used to adjust the merchandise inventory account balance: Merchandise Inventory and Income Summary. The asset account is increased (debited) or decreased (credited) to reflect the current balance, and the opposite entry is made in the income summary account. For other asset accounts, such as Supplies and Insurance, the adjustment is made to the related expense account.

### Closing Entries

In an automated accounting system, closing entries are generated and posted by the software. *Automated Accounting 7.0* automatically prepares all closing entries when income or loss is distributed equally among the partners.

If the partnership has an unequal distribution of income or loss, only the entries to close the revenue and expense accounts will be automatically prepared. Two additional closing entries must be manually entered: (1) To distribute the net income or loss. This entry transfers the balance in Income Summary to the partners' capital accounts using the distribution method defined in the partnership agreement. (2) To close the drawing accounts.

1. Choose Generate Closing Journal Entries from the Options menu.
2. Click Yes to generate the closing entries.
3. The general journal will appear, containing the journal entries.
4. Click the Post button.
5. Display a post-closing trial balance report.
   a. Click on the Reports toolbar button, or choose the Report Selection menu item from the Reports menu.
   b. Select the Ledger Reports option button from the Select a Report Group list.
   c. Choose Trial Balance from the Choose a Report to Display list.

### AUTOMATING APPLICATION PROBLEM 17-5: Journalizing and posting adjusting and closing entries; preparing a post-closing trial balance

**Instructions:**

1. Load *Automated Accounting 7.0* or higher software.
2. Select database F17-1 from the appropriate directory/folder.
3. Select File from the menu bar and choose the Save As menu command. Key the path to the drive and directory that contains your data files. Save the database with a file name of XXX171 (where XXX are your initials).
4. Access Problem Instructions through the Help menu. Read the Problem Instructions screen.
5. Key the adjusting entries from the work sheet on page 443.
6. Exit the *Automated Accounting* software.

### AUTOMATING MASTERY PROBLEM 17-6: Journalizing and posting adjusting and closing entries; preparing a post-closing trial balance

**Instructions:**

1. Load *Automated Accounting 7.0* or higher software.
2. Select database F17-2 from the appropriate directory/folder.
3. Select File from the menu bar and choose the Save As menu command. Key the path to the drive and directory that contains your data files. Save the database with a file name of XXX172 (where XXX are your initials).
4. Access Problem Instructions through the Help menu. Read the Problem Instructions screen.
5. Key the adjusting entries from the work sheet on page 444.
6. Exit the *Automated Accounting* software.

REINFORCEMENT ACTIVITY 2—PART B

# An Accounting Cycle for a Partnership: End-of-Fiscal-Period Work

The ledgers used in Reinforcement Activity 2—Part A are needed to complete Reinforcement Activity 2—Part B.

Reinforcement Activity 2—Part B includes those accounting activities needed to complete the accounting cycle of ClearView Optical.

## END-OF-FISCAL-PERIOD WORK

***Instructions:***

10. Prepare a trial balance on a work sheet. Use December 31 of the current year as the date.
11. Complete the work sheet using the following adjustment information:

**Adjustment Information, Account Balances on December 31**

| | |
|---|---:|
| Merchandise inventory | $243,800.00 |
| Office supplies inventory | 2,840.00 |
| Store supplies inventory | 3,890.00 |
| Value of prepaid insurance | 310.00 |

12. Prepare an income statement. Figure and record the following component percentages: (a) cost of merchandise sold, (b) gross profit on sales, (c) total expenses, and (d) net income or loss. Round percentage calculations to the nearest 0.1%
13. Prepare a distribution of net income statement. Net income or loss is to be shared equally.
14. Prepare an owners' equity statement. No additional investments were made.
15. Prepare a balance sheet in report form.
16. Use page 25 of a journal. Journalize and post the adjusting entries.
17. Continue using page 25 of the journal. Journalize and post the closing entries.
18. Prepare a post-closing trial balance.

# PURCHASES JOURNAL

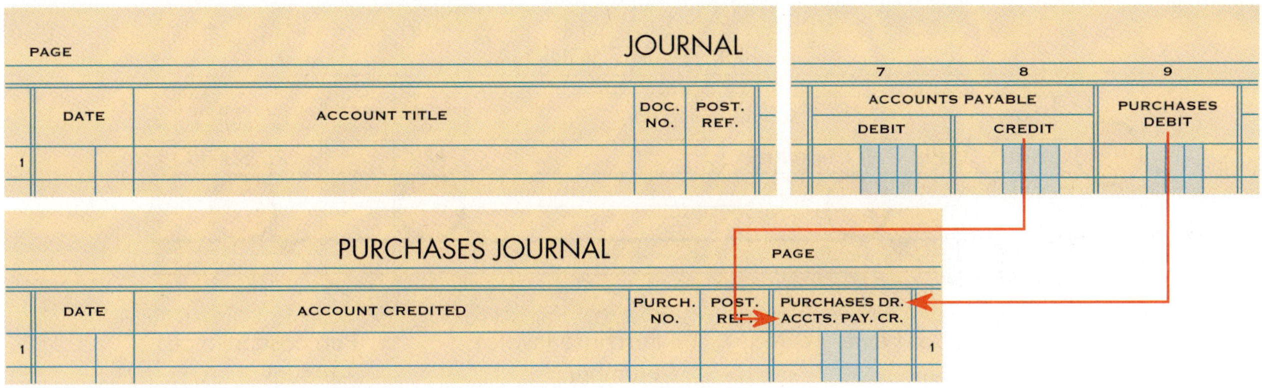


A business with few transactions may effectively record all its transactions in a single journal. In Cycle 1, Encore Music used a 5-column journal to record all transactions. In Cycle 2, Omni Import used an 11-column expanded journal to record all transactions. Larger businesses having many daily transactions use several different journals. A journal used to record only one kind of transaction is called a **special journal.** By recording similar transactions together, accounting personnel are able to record transactions with more efficiency and accuracy.

Winning Edge uses four special journals along with a general journal to record its transactions.

1. Purchases journal—for all purchases of merchandise on account
2. Cash payments journal—for all cash payments
3. Sales journal—for all sales of merchandise on account
4. Cash receipts journal—for all cash receipts

A general journal is used for all other transactions.

A special journal used to record *only* purchases of merchandise on account is called a **purchases journal.** The relationship between Winning Edge's purchases journal and the expanded journal described in Chapter 10 is shown.

A purchase on account transaction can be recorded on one line of a purchases journal. Each entry in the single special amount column is both a debit to Purchases and a credit to Accounts Payable. The titles of both general ledger accounts are listed in the special amount column heading. Since the debit and credit entries always affect the same two accounts, recording time is reduced by using only one amount column.

Notice the other similarities in the two journals. Both journals have a similar Date column and Post. Ref. column. The Doc. No. column is titled Purch. No. in the purchases journal because purchase invoices are the only kind of source document used to support entries in the purchases journal.

The Account Title column has been renamed. The new column title is Account Credited. The general ledger account Accounts Payable is credited in the entry for a purchase on account. The subsidiary ledger account affected is also credited in a purchase on account transaction. Therefore, the subsidiary ledger account title is recorded in the Account Credited column.

PURCHASES JOURNAL — PAGE 3

| | DATE | | ACCOUNT CREDITED | PURCH. NO. | POST. REF. | PURCHASES DR. ACCTS. PAY. CR. | |
|---|---|---|---|---|---|---|---|
| 1 | 20-- Mar. | 2 | Pro Golf Company | 179 | | 7 254 00 | 1 |
| 2 | | | | | | | 2 |
| 3 | | | | | | | 3 |
| 4 | | | | | | | 4 |

1. Date
2. Vendor Name
3. Purchase Invoice Number
4. Purchase Invoice Amount

When a purchase invoice is received from a vendor, Winning Edge's accounts payable clerk first verifies the mathematical accuracy of the purchase invoice. The date received and a number are then recorded on the purchase invoice. The purchase invoice is now ready to be recorded in the purchases journal.

***March 2. Purchased merchandise on account from Pro Golf Company, $7,254.00. Purchase Invoice No. 179.***

GENERAL LEDGER

Purchases

| | |
|---|---|
| 7,254.00 | |

Accounts Payable

| | |
|---|---|
| | 7,254.00 |

ACCOUNTS PAYABLE LEDGER

Pro Golf Company

| | |
|---|---|
| | 7,254.00 |

Purchases are recorded at their cost, including any related shipping costs and taxes. *(CONCEPT: Historical Cost)*

In Cycle 2, Omni Import used an abbreviation to indicate the type of source document in the Post. Ref. column of the expanded journal because all kinds of transactions are recorded in one journal. However, only purchase invoices are recorded in the purchases journal so the abbreviation *P* is not needed in the Purch. No. column. Instead, the number of the purchase invoice is entered as a reference.

**STEPS**

### Recording an entry in a purchases journal

1. Write the current year, *20—*, and the date, *Mar. 2,* in the Date column.
2. Write the vendor name, *Pro Golf Company,* in the Account Credited column.
3. Write the purchase invoice number recorded on the invoice, *179,* in the Purch. No. column.
4. Record the amount of the invoice, *$7,254.00,* in the amount column.

## REMEMBER

Only purchases of merchandise on account are journalized in the purchases journal. A business buys many other goods and services in the course of its operations. For example, a company may buy office suppplies on account. Office supplies are not merchandise for sale to customers, and therefore this transaction is not recorded in the purchases journal. A business may also purchase merchandise for cash. Because this is not an "on account" transaction, it is not recorded in the purchases journal.

## POSTING FROM A PURCHASES JOURNAL TO AN ACCOUNTS PAYABLE LEDGER

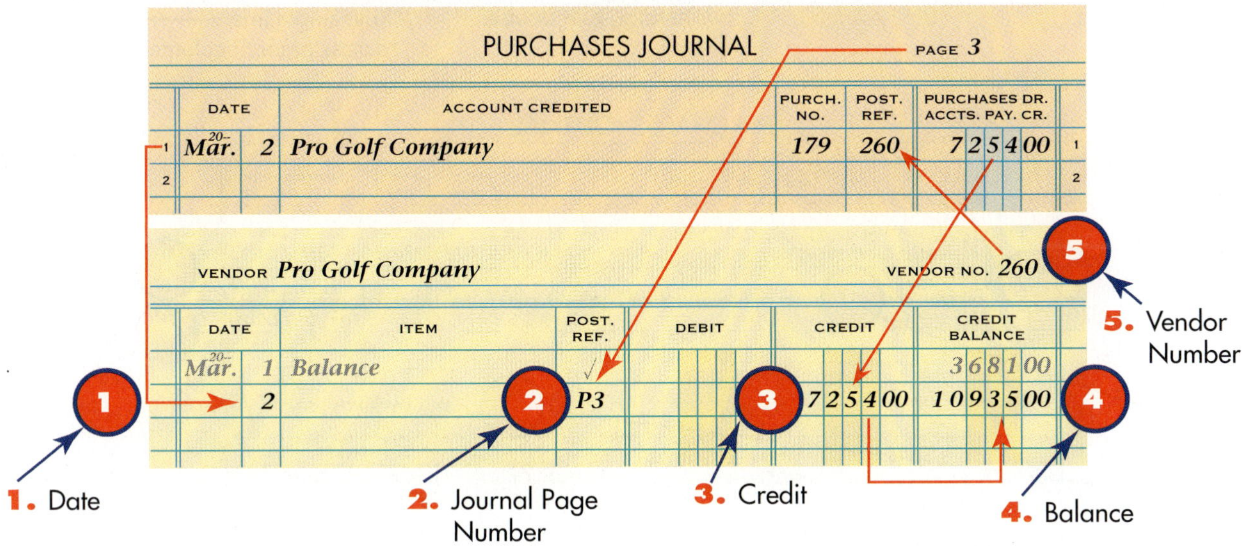


The amount on each line of a purchases journal is posted as a credit to the named vendor account in the accounts payable ledger. Winning Edge posts frequently to the accounts payable ledger. By posting frequently, each vendor account always shows an up-to-date balance.

When several journals are used, an abbreviation is used in the accounts payable subsidiary ledger to show the journal from which the posting is made. The abbreviation *P* is used for the purchases journal. The abbreviation *P3* means page 3 of the purchases journal.

Posting from a purchases journal to an accounts payable ledger is the same as posting from an expanded journal's Accounts Payable Credit column, as described in Chapter 12.

### STEPS: Posting from a purchases journal to an accounts payable ledger

1. Write the date, *2,* in the Date column of the vendor account.
2. Write *P* and the page number of the journal, *3,* in the Post. Ref. column of the account.
3. Write the amount, *$7,254.00,* in the Credit column of the vendor account.
4. Add the amount, $7,254.00, in the Credit column to the previous balance in the Credit Balance column, $3,681.00. Write the new account balance, *$10,935.00,* in the Credit Balance column.
5. Write the vendor number, *260,* in the Post. Ref. column of the purchases journal.

**FYI**

*Different vendors use different numbering schemes on their invoices. For example, one company may use 5-digit numbers. Another company may include the first initial of the customer's name as part of the invoice number. Because incoming invoices will have different kinds of numbers, Winning Edge stamps its own sequential number on purchase invoices. Because they are in sequence, it is easy to tell at a glance if one has not been recorded.*

## POSTING FROM A PURCHASES JOURNAL TO A GENERAL LEDGER

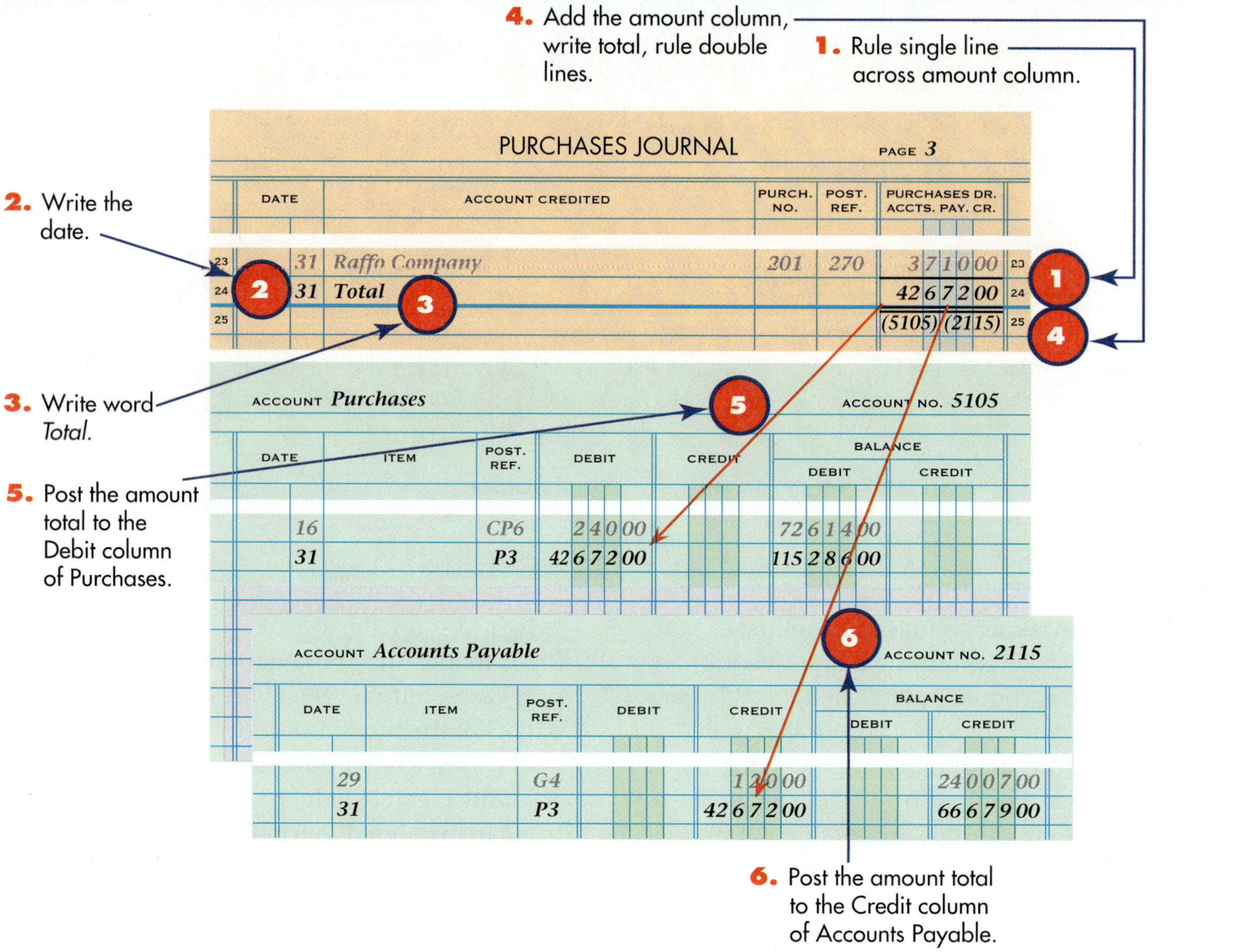


At the end of each month, a purchases journal is totaled and ruled. The total amount of the purchases journal is posted to the two general ledger accounts named in the amount column heading. The debit to Purchases increases the total of purchases during the year. The credit to Accounts Payable increases the current balance of this liability. The posting maintains the equality of debits and credits in the general ledger.

Both account numbers are written in parentheses on the purchases journal. This procedure is the same as posting totals of special amount columns in any journal.

### STEPS: Totaling, ruling, and posting from a purchases journal to the general ledger

1. Rule a single line across the amount column of the purchases journal under the last amount recorded.
2. Write the date of the last day of the month, *31*, in the Date column.
3. Write the word *Total* in the Account Credited column.
4. Add and verify the amount column; write the total, *$42,672.00*, directly below the single line; and rule double lines across the amount column.
5. Post the total of the purchases journal, *$42,672.00*, to the Debit column of Purchases. Use a *P* to show the posting is from a purchases journal.
6. Post the total of the purchases journal, *$42,672.00*, to the Credit column of Accounts Payable.

## TERMS REVIEW

corporation
share of stock
capital stock
special journal
purchases journal

## AUDIT YOUR UNDERSTANDING

1. What are some business transactions a corporation can conduct in its own name?
2. What is the principal difference between the accounting records of a corporation and those of a proprietorship or partnership?
3. What accounts are affected, and how, when the total amount of the purchases journal is posted?

## WORK TOGETHER

### Journalizing and posting purchase on account transactions

The general ledger and accounts payable ledger accounts for Magnolia Furniture are given in the *Working Papers*. Your instructor will guide you through the following examples.

4. Journalize the following purchases on account completed during April of the current year. Use page 4 of a purchases journal. The abbreviation for purchase invoice is P.

   ***Transactions:***

   April 2. Purchased merchandise on account from Farris, Inc., $1,700.00. P45.
   5. Purchased merchandise on account from Delta Manufacturing, $3,265.00. P46.
   8. Purchased merchandise on account from Williams Company, $780.00. P47.

5. Post each amount in the purchases journal to the accounts payable ledger.
6. Total and rule the purchases journal. Post the total.

## ON YOUR OWN

### Journalizing and posting purchase on account transactions

The general ledger and accounts payable ledger accounts for Adamson Luggage are given in the *Working Papers*. Work these problems independently.

7. Journalize the following purchases on account completed during March of the current year. Use page 3 of a purchases journal. The abbreviation for purchase invoice is P.

   ***Transactions:***

   March 1. Purchased merchandise on account from MJK, Inc., $3,200.00. P125.
   3. Purchased merchandise on account from Lambert Industries, $765.00. P126.
   6. Purchased merchandise on account from Taylor Imports, $1,964.00. P127.

8. Post each amount in the purchases journal to the accounts payable ledger.
9. Total and rule the purchases journal. Post the total.

# 18-2 Recording Expenses and Purchases Using a Cash Payments Journal

## JOURNALIZING CASH PAYMENTS FOR EXPENSES

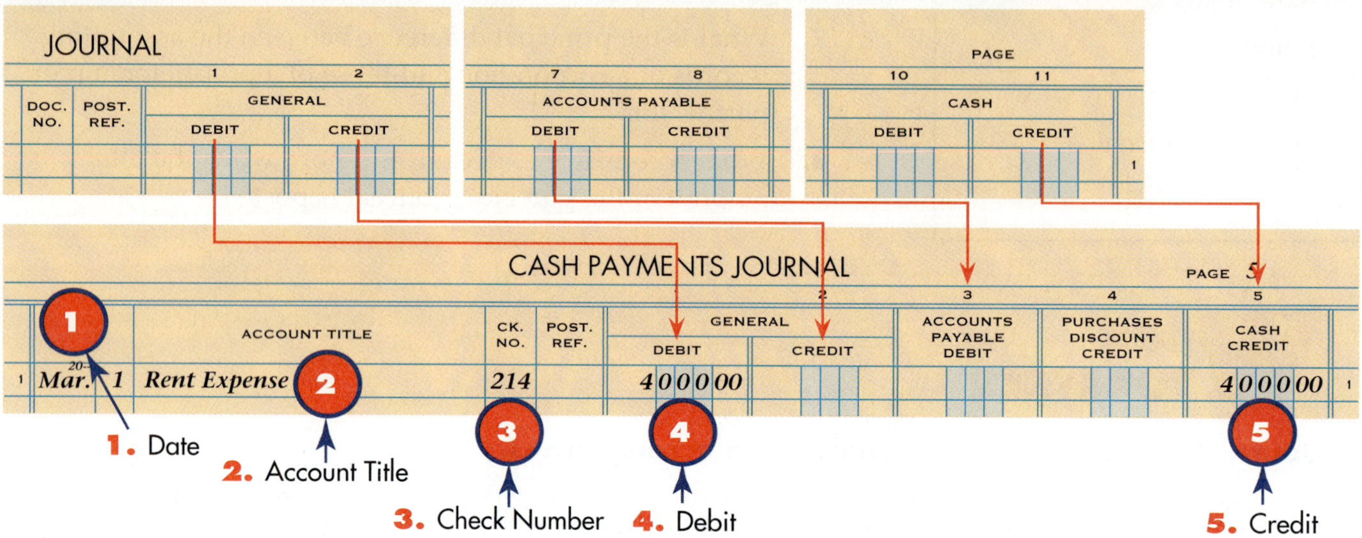


Winning Edge uses another special journal for recording only cash payments. A special journal used to record *only* cash payment transactions is called a **cash payments journal.** The relationship between a cash payments journal and the expanded journal described in Chapter 10 is shown.

Only those columns of an expanded journal needed to record cash payments are included in the cash payments journal. In addition, Winning Edge has many cash payment transactions that include a discount on the purchases. Therefore, a special amount column is provided in the cash payments journal to record this discount. Transactions that do not occur often, such as monthly rent, are recorded in the General columns because there are no special amount columns for the account debited.

All of Winning Edge's cash payments are recorded in a cash payments journal. A few payments, such as bank service charges, are made as direct withdrawals from the company's bank account. For these payments not using a check, the source document is a memorandum. Most cash payments are for (1) expenses, (2) cash purchases, and (3) payments to vendors.

***March 1. Paid cash for rent, $4,000.00. Check No. 214.***

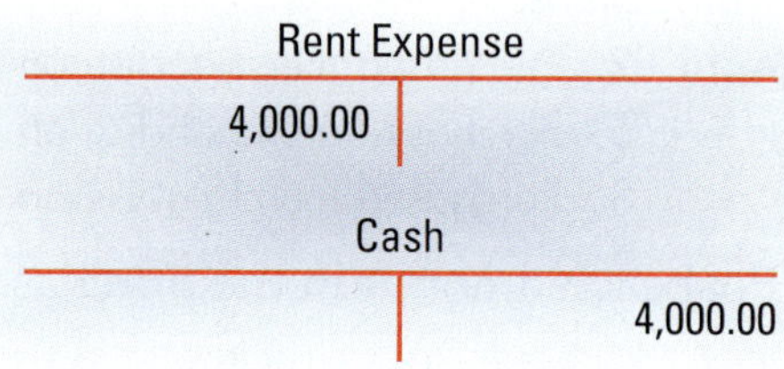


All cash payments are recorded in the Cash Credit column. Cash payments affecting accounts not named in special amount columns are recorded in the General Debit and Credit columns. Therefore, the debit amount for Rent Expense is recorded in the General Debit column.

### STEPS: Journalizing cash payments for expenses

1. Write the date, *20—, Mar. 1,* in the Date column.
2. Write the account title, *Rent Expense,* in the Account Title column.
3. Write the check number, *214,* in the Ck. No. column.
4. Write the amount of the expense, *$4,000.00,* in the General Debit column.
5. Write the amount, *$4,000.00,* in the Cash Credit column.

# JOURNALIZING CASH PAYMENTS FOR CASH PURCHASES

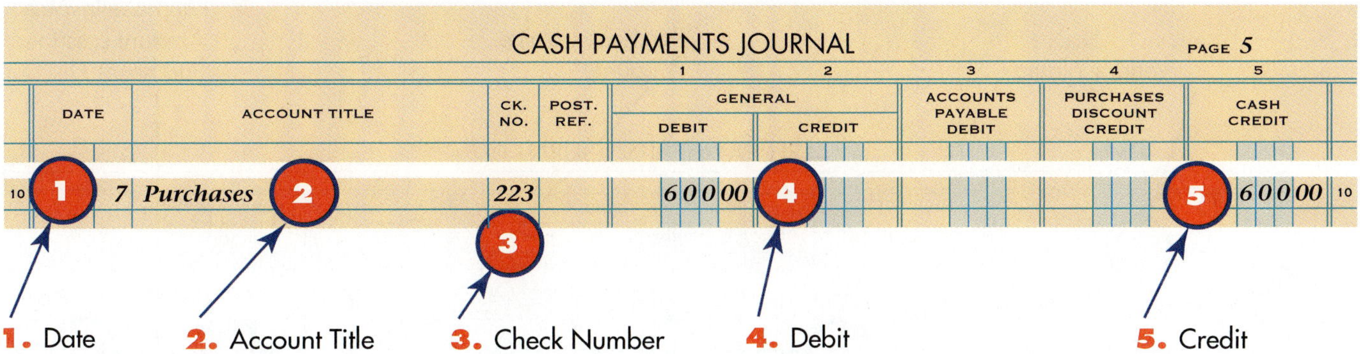


Businesses usually purchase merchandise on account. However, vendors may not extend credit to all of their customers. Thus, these businesses must give the vendor a check before the merchandise is either shipped or delivered.

### Trade Discount

Most manufacturers and wholesalers print price lists and catalogs to describe their products. Some businesses also make their products available in computer channels, such as Web sites on the Internet.

Generally, prices listed in catalogs are the manufacturers' suggested retail prices. A business's printed or catalog price is called a **list price.** When a merchandising business purchases a number of products from a manufacturer, the price frequently is quoted as "list price less trade discount." A reduction in the list price granted to customers is called a **trade discount.** Trade discounts are also used to quote different prices for different quantities purchased without changing catalog or list prices.

When a trade discount is granted, the seller's invoice shows the actual amount charged. This amount after the trade discount has been deducted from the list price is referred to as the invoice amount. Only the invoice amount is used in a journal entry. *(CONCEPT: Historical Cost)* No journal entry is made to show the amount of a trade discount.

### Cash Purchases

Winning Edge pays cash for 30 tennis rackets with an invoice amount of $600.00, the list price less a trade discount.

***March 7. Purchased merchandise for cash, $600.00. Check No. 223.***

| Purchases | |
|---|---|
| 600.00 | |

| Cash | |
|---|---|
| | 600.00 |

Winning Edge's list price for the 30 tennis rackets is $1,500.00, less 60% trade discount. The total invoice amount is calculated in two steps as follows.

**STEP 1:**

| Total List Price | × | Trade Discount Rate | = | Trade Discount |
|---|---|---|---|---|
| $1,500.00 | × | 60% | = | $900.00 |

**STEP 2:**

| Total List Price | – | Trade Discount | = | Invoice Amount |
|---|---|---|---|---|
| $1,500.00 | – | $900.00 | = | $600.00 |

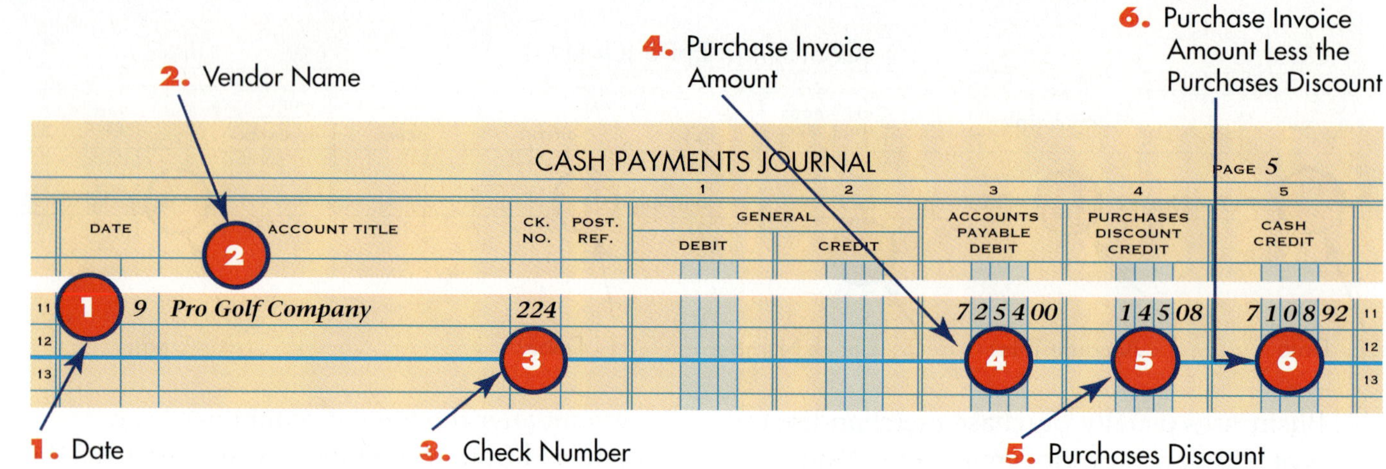


Normally, the total amount shown on a purchase invoice is the amount that a customer is expected to pay. To encourage early payment, a vendor may allow a deduction from the invoice amount. A deduction that a vendor allows on the invoice amount to encourage prompt payment is called a **cash discount.** A cash discount on purchases taken by a customer is called a **purchases discount.** When a purchases discount is taken, the customer pays less than the invoice amount previously recorded in the purchases account. Taking purchases discounts reduces the customer's cost of merchandise purchased.

A cash discount is stated as a percentage deducted from the invoice amount. For example, *2/10, n/30* is a common term of sale, which is read *two ten, net thirty. Two ten* means 2% of the invoice amount may be deducted if the invoice is paid within 10 days of the invoice date. *Net thirty* means that the total invoice amount must be paid within 30 days.

Purchases discounts are recorded in a general ledger account titled Purchases Discount. An account that reduces a related account on a financial statement is called a **contra account.** Purchases Discount is a contra account to Purchases and is included in the cost of merchandise division of the general ledger. On an income statement, Purchases Discount is deducted from the balance of its related account, Purchases.

Since contra accounts are deductions from their related accounts, contra account normal balances are opposite the normal balances of their related accounts. The normal balance for Purchases is a debit. Therefore, the normal balance for Purchases Discount, a contra account to Purchases, is a credit. Trade discounts are not recorded; however, cash discounts are recorded as purchases discounts because they decrease the recorded invoice amount.

***March 9. Paid cash on account to Pro Golf Company, $7,108.92, covering Purchase Invoice No. 179 for $7,254.00, less 2% discount, $145.08. Check No. 224.***

**STEP 1:**

| Purchase Invoice Amount (P179) | × | Purchases Discount Rate | = | Purchases Discount |
|---|---|---|---|---|
| $7,254.00 | × | 2% | = | $145.08 |

**STEP 2:**

| Purchase Invoice Amount (P179) | – | Purchases Discount | = | Cash Amount After Discount |
|---|---|---|---|---|
| $7,254.00 | – | $145.08 | = | $7,108.92 |

## JOURNALIZING CASH PAYMENTS ON ACCOUNT WITHOUT PURCHASES DISCOUNTS

CASH PAYMENTS JOURNAL — PAGE 5

| | DATE | ACCOUNT TITLE | CK. NO. | POST. REF. | 1 GENERAL DEBIT | 2 GENERAL CREDIT | 3 ACCOUNTS PAYABLE DEBIT | 4 PURCHASES DISCOUNT CREDIT | 5 CASH CREDIT | |
|---|---|---|---|---|---|---|---|---|---|---|
| 12 | 10 | Walter Manufacturing | 225 | | | | 2,650 00 | | 2,650 00 | 12 |
| 13 | | | | | | | | | | 13 |

1. Date
2. Vendor Name
3. Check Number
4. Total Purchase Invoice Amount
5. Total Purchase Invoice Amount

Some vendors do not offer purchases discounts. Sometimes a business does not have the cash available to take advantage of a purchases discount. In both cases, the full purchase invoice amount is paid.

Winning Edge purchased merchandise on account from Walter Manufacturing on February 25. Walter's credit terms are n/30. Therefore, Winning Edge will pay the full amount of the purchase invoice, \$2,650.00, within 30 days of the invoice date, February 25.

***March 10. Paid cash on account to Walter Manufacturing, \$2,650.00, covering Purchase Invoice No. 192. Check No. 225.***

### PAMELA AGUIRRE

Pamela Aguirre is the Chairman of the Board and CEO of Mexican Industries in Detroit. The company manufactures and assembles airbags, head and arm rests, consoles, leather steering wheels, cruise control assemblies, and other automotive assemblies. The company was started by Pamela's father, Detroit Tigers pitcher Hank Aguirre, in 1979. Today Mexican Industries employs 1,500 workers in eight plants and enjoys sales of over \$150 million.

Pamela once said, "My dad's dream was to give the Hispanic community the opportunity to help themselves." Of the 1,500 employees today, 86% are minorities. Most come to Mexican Industries from the inner city. The company provides a regular paycheck, benefits, training, and the life skills necessary to succeed in the working world.

Mexican Industries offers benefits such as health and life insurance and bonuses. But employees also enjoy company-paid college tuition, scholarships for children, English as a second language and G.E.D. classes, employee loans, and free cancer screening, among others.

Pamela says, "So many people in the world do not have the opportunity to learn and succeed. It hurts when I see students wasting the opportunities they are given today. They should work hard and take advantage of every educational opportunity that is offered because there might not be another chance later."

ACCOUNTING AT WORK

## TERMS REVIEW

cash payments journal
list price
trade discount
cash discount
purchases discount
contra account

## AUDIT YOUR UNDERSTANDING

1. Why would a vendor grant a cash discount to a customer?
2. What is meant by terms of sale 2/10, n/30?
3. What accounts are affected, and how, when a check is issued as payment on account for a purchase with a purchases discount?

## WORK TOGETHER

**Recording cash payments for expenses and purchases using a cash payments journal**

The cash payments journal for Preston Corporation is given in the *Working Papers*. Your instructor will guide you through the following example.

4. Record the following transactions completed during April of the current year. Use page 4 of a cash payments journal. The abbreviation for check is C.

***Transactions:***

April 4. Paid cash to Modern Radio for advertising, $275.00. C334.
5. Paid cash to Maken Industries for merchandise with a list price of $1,978.00. Maken offers its customers a 60% trade discount. C335.
16. Paid cash on account to Blanchard Company covering Purchase Invoice No. 156 for $4,346.00, less 2% discount. C336.

## ON YOUR OWN

**Recording cash payments for expenses and purchases using a cash payments journal**

The cash payments journal for BackDoor Music is given in the *Working Papers*. Work this problem independently.

5. Record the following transactions completed during June of the current year. Use page 6 of a cash payments journal. The abbreviation for check is C.

***Transactions:***

June 6. Paid cash to Lisle Management for rent, $2,000.00. C476.
9. Paid cash on account to MTX Company covering Purchase Invoice No. 267 for $1,709.60. MTX does not offer its customers a cash discount. C477.
21. Paid cash on account to Northeast Manufacturing covering Purchase Invoice No. 286 for $1,565.00, less 2% discount. C478.

# 18-3 Journalizing Petty Cash and Posting Using a Cash Payments Journal

## PETTY CASH REPORT

PETTY CASH REPORT

**Date:** February 28, 20-- **Custodian:** Janice Morgan

| Explanation | | Reconciliation | | Replenish Amount |
|---|---|---|---|---|
| Fund total | | | 250.00 | |
| Payments: | | | | |
| | **Supplies** | 45.34 | | |
| | **Advertising** | 25.00 | | |
| | **Miscellaneous** | 44.22 | | |
| *Less:* | Total payments | | 114.56 | → 114.56 |
| *Equals:* | Recorded amount on hand | | 135.44 | |
| *Less:* | Actual amount on hand | | 133.85 | |
| *Equals:* | Cash short (over) | | 1.59 | → 1.59 |
| **Amount to replenish** | | | | 116.15 |

1. Date and Custodian Name
2. Fund Total
3. Payments by General Ledger Account
4. Total Payments
5. Recorded Amount on Hand
6. Actual Cash on Hand
7. Subtract the actual cash on hand from the recorded amount on hand.
8. Amount to Replenish

A petty cash fund enables a business to pay cash for small expenses where it is not practical to write a check. Establishing and replenishing a petty cash fund is described in Chapter 6.

Regardless of the care taken by the custodian, or person who maintains the petty cash records, errors may be made when making payments from a petty cash fund. These errors cause a difference between actual cash on hand and the record of the amount of cash that should be on hand. A petty cash on hand amount that is less than a recorded amount is called **cash short.** A petty cash on hand amount that is more than a recorded amount is called **cash over.**

The custodian prepares a petty cash report when the petty cash fund is to be replenished. The report provides a logical method for determining the amount to be replenished.

### STEPS: Preparing a petty cash report

1. Write the date, *February 28, 20—,* and custodian name, *Janice Morgan,* in the report heading.
2. Write the fund total, *$250.00,* from the general ledger account.
3. Summarize petty cash payments by general ledger account and enter the totals for each account.
4. Calculate and write the total payments, *$114.56,* in the Reconciliation and Replenish Amount columns.
5. Calculate and write the recorded amount on hand, *$135.44* ($250.00 – $114.56).
6. Count the actual cash on hand and write the amount, *$133.85,* in the Reconciliation column.
7. Subtract the actual amount on hand, $133.85, from the recorded amount on hand, $135.44, and write the amount, *$1.59,* in the Reconciliation and Replenish Amount columns.
8. Add the amounts in the Replenish Amount column and write the total, *$116.15,* as the amount to replenish.

# JOURNALIZING CASH PAYMENTS TO REPLENISH A PETTY CASH FUND

PETTY CASH REPORT

**Date:** March 31, 20-- **Custodian:** Janice Morgan

| Explanation | | Reconciliation | | | Replenish Amount |
|---|---|---|---|---|---|
| Fund total | | | 250.00 | | |
| Payments: | | | | | |
| | **Supplies** | 32.33 | | | |
| | **Repair** | 40.00 | | | |
| | **Miscellaneous** | 28.50 | | | |
| *Less:* | Total payments | | 100.83 | → | 100.83 |
| *Equals:* | Recorded amount on hand | | 149.17 | | |
| *Less:* | Actual amount on hand | | 151.34 | | |
| *Equals:* | Cash short (over) | | (2.17) | → | (2.17) |
| **Amount to replenish** | | | | | 98.66 |

**4.** Expense Amounts

**6.** Total Cash Payment

CASH PAYMENTS JOURNAL PAGE 6

| | DATE | ACCOUNT TITLE | CK. NO. | POST. REF. | 1 GENERAL DEBIT | 2 GENERAL CREDIT | 3 ACCOUNTS PAYABLE DEBIT | 4 PURCHASES DISCOUNT CREDIT | 5 CASH CREDIT | |
|---|---|---|---|---|---|---|---|---|---|---|
| 19 | 31 | *Supplies* | 249 | | 32 33 | | | | 98 66 | 19 |
| 20 | | *Repair Expense* | | | 40 00 | | | | | 20 |
| 21 | | *Miscellaneous Expense* | | | 28 50 | | | | | 21 |
| 22 | | *Cash Short and Over* | | | | 2 17 | | | | 22 |

**1.** Date **2.** Account Titles **3.** Check Number **5.** Cash Short as a Debit, Cash Over as a Credit

Petty cash short and petty cash over are recorded in an account titled Cash Short and Over. The account is a temporary account. At the end of the fiscal year, the cash short and over account is closed to Income Summary.

The balance of Cash Short and Over can be either a debit or credit. However, the balance is usually a debit because the petty cash fund is more likely to be short than over. A cash shortage adds to the cost of operating a business. Thus, the account is classified as an operating expense.

| Cash Short and Over | |
|---|---|
| Debit<br>Increase cash short | Credit<br>Increase cash over |

***March 31. Paid cash to replenish the petty cash fund, \$98.66: supplies, \$32.33; repairs, \$40.00; miscellaneous, \$28.50; cash over, \$2.17. Check No. 249.***

The petty cash fund is replenished for the amount paid out, \$100.83, less cash over, \$2.17. This total amount, \$98.66, restores the fund's cash balance to its original amount, \$250.00 (\$100.83 − \$2.17 + \$151.34 cash on hand.)

## 18-1 APPLICATION PROBLEM
### Journalizing and posting purchase on account transactions

The general ledger and accounts payable ledger accounts for Wholesale Office Supply Company are given in the *Working Papers.* The balances are recorded as of June 1 of the current year.

***Instructions:***

1. Journalize the following purchases on account completed during June of the current year. Use page 6 of a purchases journal. The abbreviation for purchase invoice is P.

***Transactions:***

June 3. Purchased merchandise on account from Daniels Company, $276.00. P106.
6. Purchased merchandise on account from Perkins Supply, $1,693.00. P107.
12. Purchased merchandise on account from Tompson Mfg. Co., $870.00. P108.
14. Purchased merchandise on account from Perkins Supply, $4,691.00. P109.
21. Purchased merchandise on account from Tompson Mfg. Co., $713.00. P110.

2. Post each amount in the purchases journal to the accounts payable ledger.
3. Total and rule the purchases journal. Post the total.

## 18-2 APPLICATION PROBLEM
### Recording cash payments for expenses and purchases using a cash payments journal

The cash payments journal for HiTech Company is given in the *Working Papers.*

***Instructions:***

Journalize the following cash payments completed during November of the current year. Use page 21 of a cash payments journal. The abbreviation for check is C.

***Transactions:***

Nov. 1. Paid cash for rent, $800.00. C871.
8. Paid cash for supplies, $57.00. C872.
13. Paid cash to Opticon Industries for merchandise with a list price of $1,925.50. Opticon offers its customers a 42% trade discount. C873.
15. Paid cash on account to Miranda Company, $695.60, covering P706, no discount. C874.
18. Paid cash on account to AdTech Company covering P707 for $3,023.00, less 1% discount. C875.
22. Paid cash for repairs, $215.00. C876.
25. Paid cash to Bear Lake Industries for merchandise with a list price of $2,772.50. Bear Lake offers its customers a 45% trade discount. C877.
27. Paid cash on account to Technicraft Company covering P710 for $1,552.00, less 2% discount. C878.
28. Paid cash on account to Kasongo Company, $1,164.00, covering P705, no discount. C879.
30. Paid cash to replenish the petty cash fund: supplies, $37.00; advertising, $58.70; miscellaneous, $15.25; cash over, $1.22. C880.

## 18-3 APPLICATION PROBLEM
### Preparing a petty cash report

Kevin Tomlinson is the custodian of a $200.00 petty cash fund. On January 31 he had receipts for the following payments:

| Payee | Description | Amount |
|---|---|---|
| City Office Supply | Computer disks | $ 8.95 |
| KEWQ Radio | Voice fee for radio advertisement | 25.00 |
| Rocket Computers | Fix laser printer | 15.95 |
| Hooksville PTA | Advertisement in monthly newsletter | 10.00 |
| John Simmons | Pick up recyclable materials | 8.00 |
| Myers Hardware | Nails to repair outdoor sign | 2.50 |
| Books and More | Mouse pad | 3.15 |

***Instructions:***

1. Classify each expense into one of the general ledger accounts used by Winning Edge in this chapter.
2. Compute the total of expenses by account.
3. Prepare the petty cash report given in the *Working Papers.* A cash count shows $129.62 in the petty cash box.

## 18-4 APPLICATION PROBLEM
### Journalizing and posting cash payment transactions using a cash payments journal

The general ledger and accounts payable ledger accounts for Jenson Company are given in the *Working Papers*. The balances are recorded as of July 1 of the current year.

***Instructions:***

1. Journalize the following cash payments completed during July of the current year. Use page 7 of a cash payments journal. The abbreviation for check is C.

***Transactions:***

July 1. Paid cash for rent, $600.00. C216.
6. Paid cash on account to Argo Company covering P457 for $3,503.00, less 1% discount. C217.
8. Paid cash for supplies, $128.00. C218.
15. Paid cash on account to Catwell Company, $1,364.60, covering P463, no discount. C219.
22. Paid cash for miscellaneous expense, $250.00. C220.
25. Paid cash to Mober Industries for merchandise with a list price of $2,441.50. Mober offers its customers a 40% trade discount. C221.
31. Paid cash to replenish the petty cash fund: supplies, $42.00; advertising, $62.60; miscellaneous, $25.25; cash short, $1.30. C222.

2. Post accounts payable amounts to the appropriate accounts in the accounts payable ledger.
3. Post the amounts in the general columns to the appropriate general ledger accounts.
4. Prove and rule the cash payments journal. Post the totals of the special columns to the appropriate general ledger accounts.

## 18-5 APPLICATION PROBLEM
### Journalizing and posting transactions using a general journal

The general ledger and accounts payable ledger accounts for Kinard Company are given in the *Working Papers*. The balances are recorded as of August 1 of the current year.

***Instructions:***

1. Journalize the following transactions completed during August of the current year. Use page 8 of a general journal. Source documents are abbreviated as follows: memorandum, M; debit memorandum, DM.

***Transactions:***

Aug. 2. Bought supplies on account from Cantrell Company, $462.00. M69.
3. Returned merchandise to Flick, Inc., $128.00, from P434. DM26.
7. Bought store equipment on account from Office Solutions, $576.00. M70.
12. Returned merchandise to David Manufacturing, $93.00, from P428. DM27.
14. Bought office equipment on account from Office Solutions, $1,208.00. M71.
22. Bought supplies on account from Cantrell Company, $237.00. M72.

2. Post the general journal to the general and accounts payable ledgers.
3. Prepare a schedule of accounts payable similar to the one described in Chapter 12.

## 18-6 APPLICATION PROBLEM
### Journalizing and posting purchases transactions

The general ledger and accounts payable ledger accounts for Far East Company are given in the *Working Papers*. The balances are recorded as of September 1 of the current year.

***Instructions:***

1. Journalize the following transactions completed during September of the current year. Use page 9 of a purchases journal, page 17 of a cash payments journal, and page 9 of a general journal.

***Transactions:***

Sept. 3. Received an order of merchandise from Bell Supply costing $1,354.00 plus shipping charges of $45.00. Bell Supply offers its customers 2/10, n/30 credit terms. The purchase invoice number 252 was stamped on the vendor's invoice.
4. An order of merchandise from Brandon Company was received. The total cost was $2,354.00 plus $231.00 of shipping costs. Brandon offers 2/10, n/30 credit terms. The purchase invoice number 253 was stamped on the vendor's invoice.
6. One box of merchandise costing $275.00 from the Brandon Company order (P253) was found to be defective. The goods were returned to Brandon, with Brandon paying for the shipping charges. The accounting clerk sent a copy of debit memorandum 34 with the returned goods.
12. Issued check number 534 to pay for the Bell Supply shipment of September 3 (P252), taking advantage of the 2% discount.
14. Prepared and mailed check number 535 to pay the remaining payable resulting from the Brandon Company purchase on September 4. The check reflected a reduction for the 2% discount on the remaining account balance.

2. Total and post the journals to the general ledger and accounts payable ledger.

## 18-7 MASTERY PROBLEM
### Journalizing and posting purchases and cash payment transactions

The general ledger and accounts payable ledger accounts of City Plumbing Supply are given in the *Working Papers*. The balances are recorded as of November 1 of the current year. Use the following account titles.

**Partial General Ledger**
1105 Cash
1110 Petty Cash
1140 Supplies
2115 Accounts Payable
5105 Purchases
5110 Purchases Discount
5115 Purchases Returns and Allowances
6105 Advertising Expense
6110 Cash Short and Over
6135 Miscellaneous Expense
6145 Rent Expense

**Accounts Payable Ledger**
210 Bennett Supply
220 Black, Inc.
230 Ford Supply
240 Riddell Pipe Company
250 Wells Company

***Instructions:***

1. Journalize the following transactions affecting purchases and cash payments completed during November of the current year. Use page 11 of a purchases journal, page 21 of a cash payments journal, and page 11 of a general journal. Source documents are abbreviated as follows: check, C; debit memorandum, DM; memorandum, M; purchase invoice, P.

***Transactions:***

Nov. 1. Paid cash for rent, $500.00. C516.
2. Purchased merchandise on account from Black, Inc., $3,520.00. P135.
3. Paid cash on account to Bennett Supply covering P127 for $1,269.00, less 2% discount. C517.
5. Bought supplies on account from Ford Supply, $152.00. M235.
8. Purchased merchandise on account from Bennett Supply, $1,154.00. P136.
8. Paid cash on account to Wells Company covering P129 for $2,503.00, less 2% discount. C518.
9. Paid cash for supplies, $438.00. C519.
15. Purchased merchandise on account from Riddell Pipe Company, $362.00. P137.
15. Paid cash on account to Bennett Supply, covering P136, 2% discount. C520.
**Posting.** Post the items that are to be posted individually. Post from the journals in the following order: purchases, general, cash payments. Some transactions will not be in order by date in the accounts.
16. Returned merchandise to Black, Inc., $526.00, from P135. DM58.
17. Paid cash to Stafford Company for merchandise with a list price of $192.25. Stafford offers its customers a 60% trade discount. C521.
22. Purchased merchandise on account from Ford Supply, $378.00. P138.
23. Paid cash on account to Black, Inc., $2,994.00, covering P135, no discount. C522.
23. Paid cash for miscellaneous expense, $70.00. C523.
24. Bought supplies on account from Wells Company, $350.00. M236.
25. Returned merchandise to Riddell Pipe Company, $65.00, from P137. DM59.
29. Purchased merchandise on account from Wells Company, $763.00. P139.

Nov. 30. Purchased merchandise on account from Bennett Supply, $500.00. P140.

30. Paid cash to replenish the petty cash fund: supplies, $23.10; advertising, $42.20; miscellaneous, $16.75; cash short, $0.45. C524.

**Posting.** Post the items that are to be posted individually.

2. Total and rule the purchases journal. Post the total.
3. Prove and rule the cash payments journal. Post the totals of the special columns.
4. Prepare a schedule of accounts payable similar to the one described in Chapter 12. Compare the schedule total with the balance of the accounts payable account in the general ledger. The total and balance should be the same.

## 18-8 CHALLENGE PROBLEM
### Journalizing transactions in a combined purchases-cash payments journal

The accountant for City Plumbing Supply has suggested that time could be saved if the purchases journal and the cash payments journal were combined into one journal. The accountant suggests using a journal such as the following.

**Purchases—Cash Payments Journal**

| | | | | 1 | 2 | 3 | 4 | 5 | 6 | 7 |
|---|---|---|---|---|---|---|---|---|---|---|
| Date | Account Title | Doc. No. | Post. Ref. | General | | Purchases Debit | Accounts Payable | | Purchases Discount Credit | Cash Credit |
| | | | | Debit | Credit | | Debit | Credit | | |
| | | | | | | | | | | |

Christopher Howard, manager, has asked the accountant to show him how the journal would appear after transactions have been recorded. A purchases-cash payments journal and a general journal are given in the *Working Papers*.

***Instructions:***

1. Use page 21 of a purchases-cash payments journal and page 11 of a general journal. Journalize the transactions given in Mastery Problem 18-7. Do not post.
2. Prove and rule the combined purchases-cash payments journal.
3. Do you agree with the accountant that the combined purchases-cash payments journal used in this problem saves time in journalizing and posting? Why?

INTERNET ACTIVITY

Point your browser to

**http://accounting.swpco.com**

Choose **First-Year Course**, choose **Activities**, and complete the activity for Chapter 18.

## Applied Communication

The common stock of many corporations is traded on national stock exchanges. These corporations are required by the government to publish their financial statements in an annual report. The annual report also includes management's analysis of the year's operations and its projection of future financial activity. Annual reports are used by bankers, stockholders, and investment advisers for making business and investment decisions.

**Instructions:** Write a letter to a corporation requesting a copy of its annual report. Your letter should include your return address, inside address, and request for the report.

## Cases for Critical Thinking

**Case 1** Dessert Designs, Inc., has employed an accounting firm to install a new accounting system using special journals. You and two other accountants are designing the special journals. Patti Edwards, one of the accountants, recommends a cash payments journal with one special column—Cash Credit. Jose Ramundo, the other accountant, recommends a cash payments journal with three special columns—Accounts Payable Debit, Purchases Discount Credit, and Cash Credit. You have been asked to decide which cash payments journal should be used. Give your decision and the reason for that decision.

**Case 2** Ashford Company has established a $300.00 petty cash fund. During a routine review of the petty cash records, you discover that small shortages totaling $20.00 have occurred over the past four months. The fund custodian, Kim Benson, has not listed cash short or over on any of the reports prepared for replenishment. When asked about this practice, Ms. Benson said that she always waits until the amount of the shortage is significant—approximately $50.00. Then she requests replenishment for the amount of the shortage. What is your opinion of this practice? What action do you recommend?

# AUTOMATED ACCOUNTING

## AUTOMATED ENTRIES FOR PURCHASES AND CASH PAYMENTS USING SPECIAL JOURNALS FOR A CORPORATION

Corporations are owned by shareholders. These shareholders purchase interest in the corporation by buying shares of stock. The total of all shares held by shareholders is known as capital stock. Shareholders elect a board of directors to manage the corporation. The board of directors may declare a dividend that is paid from the earnings of the corporation. Because corporations are legal entities, they pay federal income taxes. The payment of dividends and federal income taxes will be discussed in a later chapter.

Corporations typically have thousands of purchases and cash payments transactions each month. Computerized accounting systems allow faster processing of these transactions. For example, when a cash payment is entered in the cash payments journal, a check for the payment can be automatically generated by the accounting software.

### Purchases of Merchandise

Merchandising businesses purchase the goods they sell to customers. All purchases of merchandise on account are recorded in the purchases journal. To record a purchase, enter the date, invoice number, debit to Purchases, and the name of the vendor. The credit to Accounts Payable will be automatically generated by the accounting system.

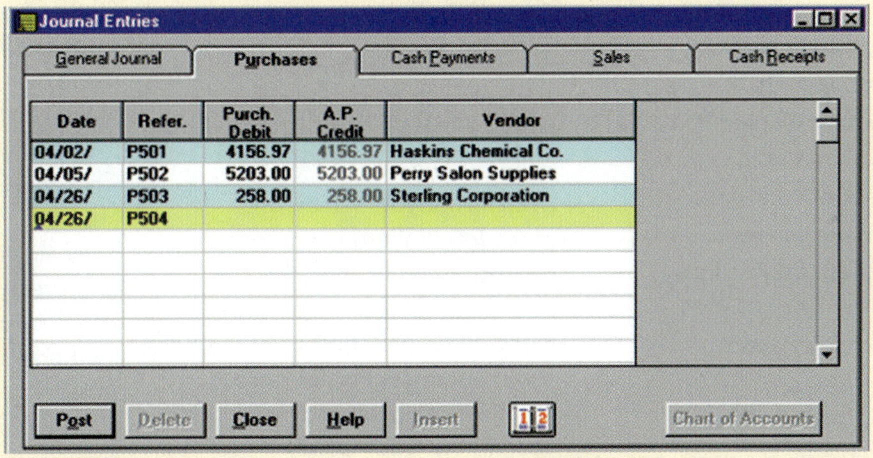


Merchandising businesses maintain a complete list of vendors. *Automated Accounting* maintains a vendor list using a procedure similar to maintaining the chart of accounts. To maintain the vendor list:

1. Click the Accounts toolbar button.
2. Click the Vendors tab.
3. Perform the maintenance:
   a. To add a vendor, enter the vendor name and click the Add Vendor button.
   b. To change an existing vendor, highlight the vendor's name, enter the correct name, and click the Change Vendor button.
   c. To delete a vendor, highlight the vendor's name and click the Delete button. (A vendor with a balance cannot be deleted.)
4. Click the Close button.

# AUTOMATED ACCOUNTING

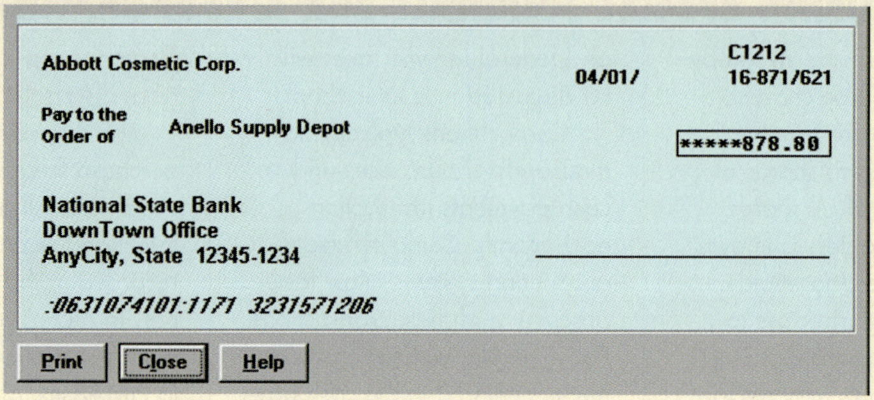


## Cash Payment for a Purchase

The cash payments journal is used to enter all cash payments transactions. All merchandise purchases made on account should be paid within the terms granted by the vendor. If a vendor name is entered in the Vendor column and the Computer Check option is turned on, a check will be displayed for these transactions.

To turn on the Computer check option in *Automated Accounting*:

1. Click the Custom toolbar button.
2. Click the Company Info. tab.
3. Click the Accounts Payable Checks check box.
4. Choose OK.

To process cash payments transactions for a purchase:

1. Choose the Journal Entries menu item from the Data menu or click the Journal toolbar button.
2. Click the Cash Payments tab.
3. Enter the transaction date and press Tab.
4. Enter the check number in the Refer. column and press Tab until the curser appears in the A.P. Debit column.
5. Enter the amount of the accounts payable debit and press Tab. If there is a purchases discount, enter the amount in the Purchase Discount Cr field and press Tab. The amount of the cash credit will appear automatically in the Cash Credit field.
6. Choose a vendor name from the Vendor drop-down list.
7. Click the Post button.

## Other Cash Payments

Businesses have many cash payments that do not involve the purchase of merchandise. Payments for such items as utilities, rent, office supplies, and dividends are also recorded in the cash payments journal. To record these cash payments:

1. Choose the Journal Entries menu item from the Data menu or click the Journal toolbar button.
2. Click the Cash Payments tab.
3. Enter the transaction date and press Tab.
4. Enter the check number in the Refer. column and press Tab.
5. Enter the account number of the account to be debited and press Tab.
6. Enter the amount of the debit in the Debit column. The amount of the cash credit will appear automatically in the Cash Credit field.
7. Click the Post button.

# AUTOMATED ACCOUNTING

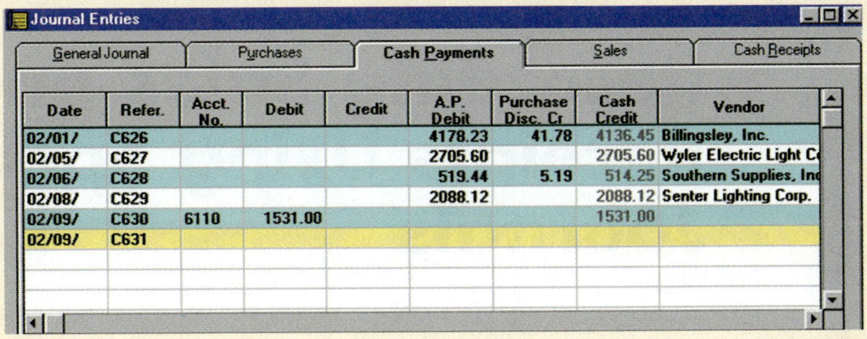

Journal Entries

General Journal | Purchases | Cash Payments | Sales | Cash Receipts

| Date | Refer. | Acct. No. | Debit | Credit | A.P. Debit | Purchase Disc. Cr | Cash Credit | Vendor |
|---|---|---|---|---|---|---|---|---|
| 02/01/ | C626 | | | | 4178.23 | 41.78 | 4136.45 | Billingsley, Inc. |
| 02/05/ | C627 | | | | 2705.60 | | 2705.60 | Wyler Electric Light C |
| 02/06/ | C628 | | | | 519.44 | 5.19 | 514.25 | Southern Supplies, Inc |
| 02/08/ | C629 | | | | 2088.12 | | 2088.12 | Senter Lighting Corp. |
| 02/09/ | C630 | 6110 | 1531.00 | | | | 1531.00 | |
| 02/09/ | C631 | | | | | | | |

## AUTOMATING APPLICATION PROBLEM 18-6: Journalizing and posting purchases transactions

**Instructions:**

1. Load *Automated Accounting 7.0* or higher software.
2. Select database F18-1 from the appropriate directory/folder.
3. Select File from the menu bar and choose the Save As menu command. Key the path to the drive and directory that contains your data files. Save the database with a file name of XXX181 (where XXX are your initials).
4. Access Problem Instructions through the Help menu. Read the Problem Instructions screen.
5. Key the data listed on page 479.
6. Exit the *Automated Accounting* software.

## AUTOMATING MASTERY PROBLEM 18-7: Journalizing and Posting purchases and cash payment transactions

**Instructions:**

1. Load *Automated Accounting 7.0* or higher software.
2. Select database F18-2 from the appropriate directory/folder.
3. Select File from the menu bar and choose the Save As menu command. Key the path to the drive and directory that contains your data files. Save the database with a file name of XXX182 (where XXX are your initials).
4. Access Problem Instructions through the Help menu. Read the Problem Instructions screen.
5. Key the data listed on pages 480–481.
6. Exit the *Automated Accounting* software.

# 19 Recording Sales and Cash Receipts Using Special Journals

**AFTER STUDYING CHAPTER 19, YOU WILL BE ABLE TO:**

1. Define accounting terms related to sales and cash receipts.
2. Identify accounting concepts and practices related to sales and cash receipts.
3. Record sales on account and post, using a sales journal.
4. Record cash receipts and post, using a cash receipts journal.
5. Record transactions and post, using a general journal.
6. Record transactions for international sales.

**TERMS PREVIEW**

- sales journal
- cash receipts journal
- sales discount
- sales return
- sales allowance
- credit memorandum
- exports
- imports
- contract of sale
- letter of credit
- bill of lading
- commercial invoice
- draft
- sight draft
- time draft
- trade acceptance

## SPECIAL JOURNALS IMPROVE EFFICIENCY

As the volume of business and the number of transactions increase for a business, efficiency of operation becomes more important in completing work accurately and on time. Winning Edge has sales of about $2,000,000.00 annually and has numerous transactions to record each day. Because of the size and the numerous transactions of the business, Winning Edge uses a system of special journals. Using special journals improves the efficiency of recording transactions and permits more than one accounting clerk to record transactions at the same time. Winning Edge uses four special journals and a general journal. A sales journal, a cash receipts journal, and selected uses of a general journal are described in this chapter. A purchases journal, a cash payments journal, and other selected uses of a general journal are described in Chapter 18.

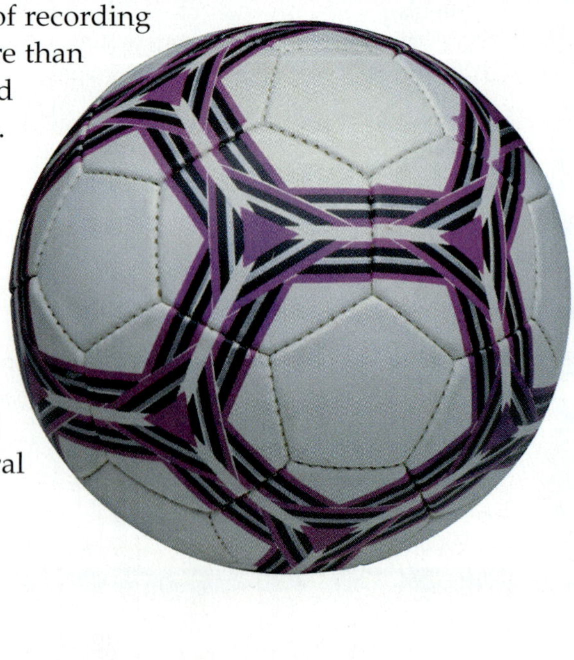

# ACCOUNTING IN YOUR CAREER

## 12 MONTHS SAME AS CASH

A-V Warehouse sells consumer audio and video equipment. The market is crowded with stores selling these same products. To compete effectively A-V Warehouse offers credit terms of no money down, 12 months same as cash.

The business is booming and is considering expanding by opening another store in the nearest large city. The morale among the sales associates is high, and they are making as much as 20% more than their regular salaries in commissions on the increased sales. However, the accounting department is having trouble managing the payment of vendors. To support the rapidly expanding sales, larger quantities of inventory are ordered. The commissions to sales associates are straining the payroll costs. Vendors have begun to refuse orders until payments are made for previous sales.

The bank has been lending money to meet immediate cash needs but has just denied the latest loan request. A-V Warehouse's board of directors has hired a consulting firm to analyze the problem and make recommendations. The preliminary report from Doris Jones, an experienced financial analyst with the consultants, makes the following points: (1) Accounts Receivable has become the largest asset on the balance sheet and is "non-productive." (2) The credit terms are the cause of the current cash crisis. (3) If vendor relationships are not quickly improved, there soon will not be enough cash to replenish the inventory.

**Critical Thinking:**

1. What does Doris Jones mean by referring to Accounts Receivable as "non-productive"?
2. How is it possible that sales are better than ever but the company does not have enough cash to pay its vendors?
3. How could the company begin to generate enough cash to meet current cash needs?

# 19-1 Recording Sales on Account Using a Sales Journal

## SALES JOURNAL

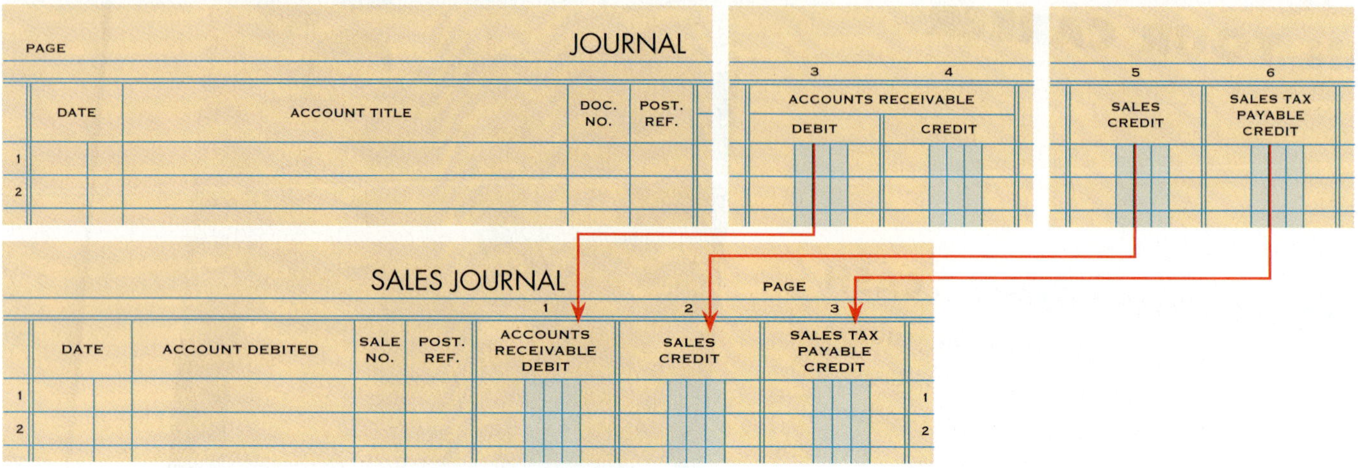


Winning Edge sells much of its merchandise for cash. However, to encourage additional sales, Winning Edge sells on account to customers with approved credit. Regardless of when cash is received, revenue should be recorded when merchandise is sold. *(CONCEPT: Realization of Revenue)* Since many sales are made on account, Winning Edge uses a special journal to record only sales of merchandise on account transactions. A special journal used to record *only* sales of merchandise on account is called a **sales journal.** The relationship between a sales journal and the expanded journal is shown in the illustration.

Those columns used in an expanded journal and needed to record only sales on account are included in a sales journal. These amount columns are Accounts Receivable Debit, Sales Credit, and Sales Tax Payable Credit. With these special amount columns, each sale on account transaction can be recorded on one line in a sales journal.

Sales tax rates vary from state to state and may even vary within a state. An 8% sales tax is collected on items sold at retail in the city in which Winning Edge is located. A retail business must collect the sales tax from customers and periodically send the sales tax collected to the state. Therefore, Winning Edge uses a sales journal with a Sales Tax Payable Credit column to keep a separate record of sales tax.

**FYI**

*Sales tax is a tax levied by most, but not all, states. Local governments in some states may have the option to impose additional sales tax. Retail customers pay the sales tax while the merchant acts only as a tax collector for the state. The merchant must keep careful records of sales and tax collected. Periodic reports and payments of the sales tax collected are made to the state. In some cases the state allows the merchant to keep part of the sales tax proceeds as a fee for collecting*

**REMEMBER**

The sales account is used only to record sales of merchandise. Occasionally a business may sell some other asset that is no longer needed, such as office equipment. The sales account is not used for this type of transaction.

## JOURNALIZING SALES ON ACCOUNT

**SALES JOURNAL** PAGE 7

| | DATE | | ACCOUNT DEBITED | SALE NO. | POST. REF. | 1 ACCOUNTS RECEIVABLE DEBIT | 2 SALES CREDIT | 3 SALES TAX PAYABLE CREDIT | |
|---|---|---|---|---|---|---|---|---|---|
| 1 | 20-- Mar. | 2 | Tennis Castle | 176 | | 1 944 00 | 1 800 00 | 144 00 | 1 |
| 2 | | | | | | | | | 2 |

**1.** Date
**2.** Customer Name
**3.** Sales Invoice Number
**4.** Sale Amount Plus Sales Tax
**5.** Sale Amount
**6.** Sales Tax Amount

Winning Edge prepares a sales invoice in duplicate for each sale on account. The original is given to the customer. The copy of the sales invoice is the source document for journalizing a sales on account transaction. *(CONCEPT: Objective Evidence)* Winning Edge's sales invoice is similar to the one described in Chapter 11.

Winning Edge owes the sales tax to the state government. Therefore, the amount of sales tax charged each customer is a liability.

Some states exempt schools and other organizations from paying sales tax. A sale to a tax-exempt organization would be recorded using the same amount in the Sales Credit and Accounts Receivable Debit columns. No amount would be entered in the Sales Tax Payable Credit column.

***March 2. Sold merchandise on account to Tennis Castle, $1,800.00, plus sales tax, $144.00; total, $1,944.00. Sales Invoice No. 176.***

GENERAL LEDGER

| Accounts Receivable | |
|---|---|
| 1,944.00 | |

| Sales | |
|---|---|
| | 1,800.00 |

| Sales Tax Payable | |
|---|---|
| | 144.00 |

ACCOUNTS RECEIVABLE LEDGER

| Tennis Castle | |
|---|---|
| 1,944.00 | |

(1) *Sales Tax:*

| Sales Invoice Amount | × | Sales Tax Rate | = | Sales Tax Payable |
|---|---|---|---|---|
| $1,800.00 | × | 8% | = | $144.00 |

(2) *Total Invoice:*

| Sales Invoice Amount | + | Sales Tax Payable | = | Total Invoice Amount |
|---|---|---|---|---|
| $1,800.00 | + | $144.00 | = | $1,944.00 |

### STEPS: Recording an entry in a sales journal

1. Write the date, *20—, Mar. 2,* in the Date column.
2. Write the customer name, *Tennis Castle,* in the Account Debited column.
3. Record the sales invoice number, *176,* in the Sale No. column.
4. Write the sale amount plus the sales tax, *$1,944.00,* in the Accounts Receivable Debit column.
5. Write the sale amount, *$1,800.00,* in the Sales Credit column.
6. Enter the sales tax amount, *$144.00,* in the Sales Tax Payable Credit column.

## POSTING FROM A SALES JOURNAL TO AN ACCOUNTS RECEIVABLE LEDGER

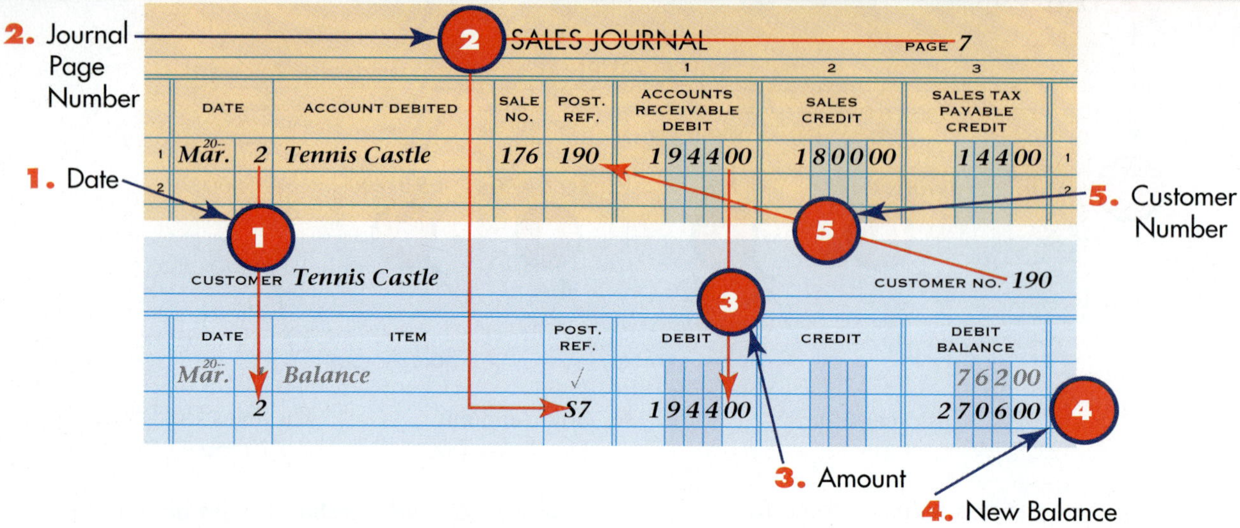


Each amount in a sales journal's Accounts Receivable Debit column is posted individually to the customer account in the accounts receivable ledger. Each amount is posted as a debit to the customer account listed in the Account Debited column. Winning Edge posts frequently to the accounts receivable ledger so that each customer account will show an up-to-date balance.

### STEPS: Posting from a sales journal to an accounts receivable ledger

1. Write the date, *2*, in the Date column of the account.
2. Write the abbreviation for the sales journal and the page number, *S7*, in the Post. Ref. column.
3. Enter the amount, *$1,944.00*, in the Debit column of the customer account.
4. Add the amount in the Debit column of the customer account to the previous balance and record the new balance, *$2,706.00*.
5. Record the customer number for Tennis Castle, *190*, in the Post. Ref. column of the journal.

### PROFESSIONAL BUSINESS ETHICS

### WHO OWNS MY TIME?

Employers and employees have a unique relationship. The employee agrees to provide the employer with a fair day's work. In return, the employer agrees to provide a fair day's wage.

**Instructions**

Use the three-step checklist to determine whether or not the following situations demonstrate ethical behavior.

*Situation 1.* Gabriel Peña is a receptionist for Traylor Technologies. After the company installed voice mail, Gabriel's workload became lighter, so his supervisor assigned additional responsibilities, including some accounting tasks. Even with these assignments, Gabriel is not always busy. To fill the time, he plays computer games.

*Situation 2.* At the Backyard Gourmet, most employees work less than 40 hours per week. However, only employees who work a minimum of 40 hours per week are eligible for health insurance.

# POSTING FROM A SALES JOURNAL TO A GENERAL LEDGER

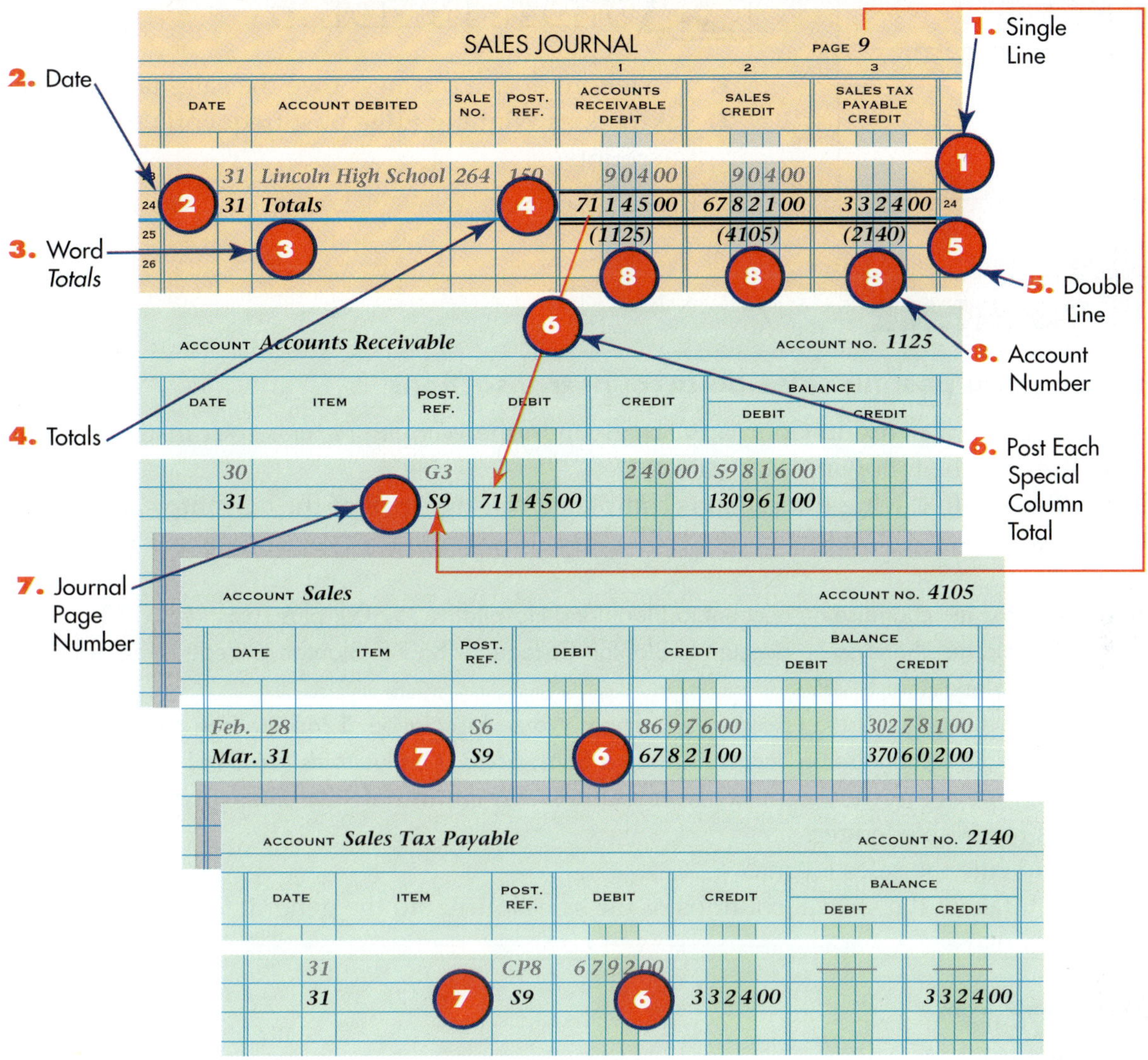


Equality of debits and credits is proved for a sales journal at the end of each month. The sales journal is then ruled, and the totals of special columns are posted.

**STEPS**

## Proving and ruling a sales journal and posting a sales journal to a general ledger

1. Rule a single line across the amount columns of the sales journal under the last amounts recorded.
2. Write the date of the last day of the month, *31*, in the Date column of the journal.
3. Write the word *Totals* in the Account Debited column.
4. To prove the journal, calculate the total of each column and record the totals below the single line. Determine that the totals of the debit and credit columns are equal.
5. Rule double lines across the amount columns under the totals.
6. Post the total of each special amount column by recording the date, amount, and new account balance in the related general ledger account.
7. Write the abbreviation for sales journal and the page number, *S9*, in the Post. Ref. column of each account.
8. Write each account number in parentheses under the amount column total in the sales journal.

## TERM REVIEW

sales journal

## AUDIT YOUR UNDERSTANDING

1. To whom does a business owe the sales taxes collected?
2. Why does Winning Edge post frequently to customer accounts?

## WORK TOGETHER

**Journalizing and posting sales on account transactions**

The ledger accounts for Nesbitt Company are given in the *Working Papers.* Your instructor will guide you through the following examples.

3. Journalize the following transactions completed during April of the current year. Use page 4 of a sales journal. The sales tax rate is 8%. The abbreviation for sales invoice is S.

   ***Transactions:***

   April 2. Sold merchandise on account to Northland Hospital, $352.00, plus sales tax. S138.
   4. Sold merchandise on account to Blanton College, $486.75. Blanton College is exempt from paying sales tax. S139.
   9. Sold merchandise on account to Belmont Water Association, $245.00, plus sales tax. S140.
   14. Sold merchandise on account to Tess & Sons, $623.00, plus sales tax. S141.

4. Post each amount in the Accounts Receivable Debit column of the sales journal to the accounts receivable ledger.
5. Prove and rule the sales journal.
6. Post the totals of the special columns of the sales journal to the general ledger.

## ON YOUR OWN

**Journalizing and posting sales on account transactions**

The ledger accounts for Jenson Industries are given in the *Working Papers.* Work these problems independently.

7. Journalize the following transactions completed during June of the current year. Use page 6 of a sales journal. The sales tax rate is 8%. The abbreviation for sales invoice is S.

   ***Transactions:***

   June 1. Sold merchandise on account to Lincoln Designs, $623.00, plus sales tax. S248.
   6. Sold merchandise on account to Gulf High School, $2,374.45. Gulf High School is exempt from paying sales tax. S249.
   12. Sold merchandise on account to King Services, $259.00, plus sales tax. S250.
   18. Sold merchandise on account to Lynch Interiors, $722.00, plus sales tax. S251.

8. Post each amount in the Accounts Receivable Debit column of the sales journal to the accounts receivable ledger.
9. Prove and rule the sales journal.
10. Post the totals of the special columns of the sales journal to the general ledger.

# 19-2 Recording Cash Receipts Using a Cash Receipts Journal

## JOURNALIZING CASH AND CREDIT CARD SALES

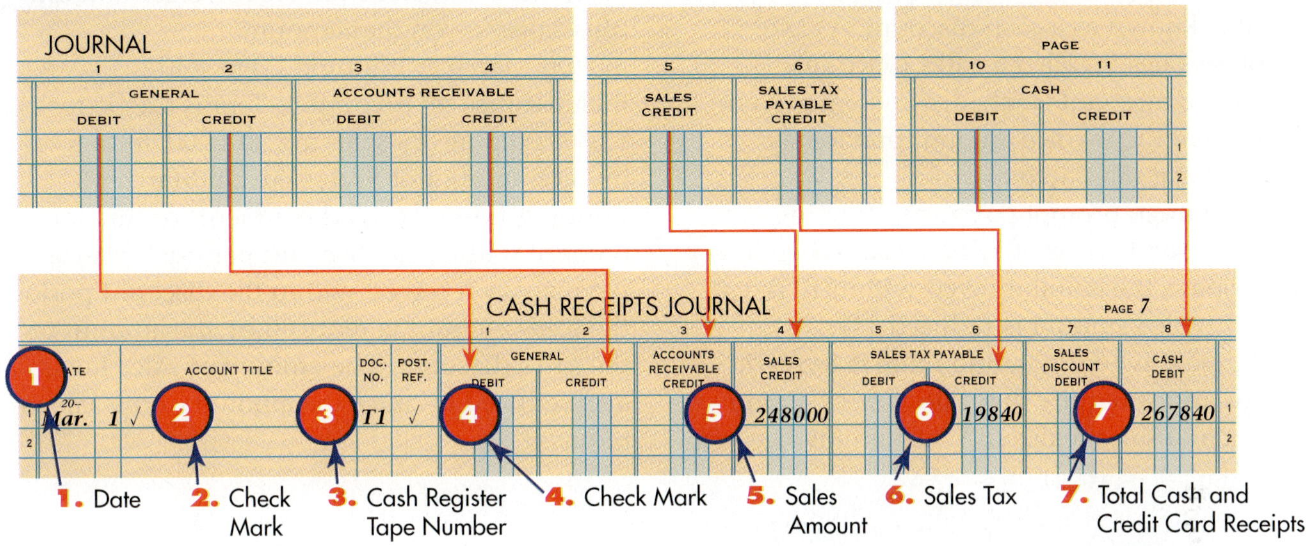


Winning Edge uses a special journal to record only cash receipt transactions. A special journal used to record *only* cash receipt transactions is called a **cash receipts journal.**

The relationship between a cash receipts journal and the expanded journal described in Chapter 10 is shown. Those columns used in an expanded journal and needed to record only cash receipts are included in a cash receipts journal. In addition, many transactions involve cash discounts. Two additional special amount columns, Sales Tax Payable Debit and Sales Discount Debit, are provided for recording cash received on account with a cash discount. Each cash receipt transaction can be recorded on one line in a cash receipts journal.

All cash receipts are recorded in a cash receipts journal. Most cash receipts are for (1) cash and credit card sales and (2) cash received from customers on account.

***March 1. Recorded cash and credit card sales, $2,480.00, plus sales tax, $198.40; total, $2,678.40. Cash Register Tape No. 1.***

| Cash | |
|---|---|
| 2,678.40 | |

| Sales | |
|---|---|
| | 2,480.00 |

| Sales Tax Payable | |
|---|---|
| | 198.40 |

### STEPS: Journalizing cash and credit card sales

1. Write the date, *20—, Mar. 1,* in the Date column.
2. Place a check mark in the Account Title column to show that no account title needs to be written.
3. Write the cash register tape number, *T1,* in the Doc. No. column.
4. Place a check mark in the Post. Ref. column to show that amounts on this line are not posted individually.
5. Write the amount credited to Sales, *$2,480.00,* in the Sales Credit column.
6. Write the amount credited to Sales Tax Payable, *$198.40,* in the Sales Tax Payable Credit column.
7. Write the amount of cash received, *$2,678.40,* in the Cash Debit column.

# CALCULATING CASH RECEIPTS ON ACCOUNT WITH SALES DISCOUNT

To encourage early payment for a sale on account, a deduction on the invoice amount may be allowed. A deduction that a vendor allows on the invoice amount to encourage prompt payment is known as a cash discount. A cash discount on sales is called a **sales discount.** When a sales discount is taken, a customer pays less cash than the invoice amount previously recorded in the sales account.

To encourage prompt payment, Winning Edge gives credit terms of 1/10, n/30. When a customer pays the amount owed within 10 days, the sales invoice amount is reduced 1%.

In the state where Winning Edge is located, state regulations require that sales taxes be paid only on actual sales realized. When an invoice for a sale on account is prepared, Winning Edge does not know whether the customer will pay within the sales discount period. Therefore, the customer is invoiced for the full sales amount plus sales tax on that amount.

On March 2, Winning Edge sold merchandise on account to Tennis Castle for $1,800.00 plus 8% sales tax, $144.00, for a total invoice amount of $1,944.00. On March 11, Winning Edge received payment for this sale on account within the discount period. Because the payment is received within the discount period, the sales amount is reduced by the amount of the sales discount. The amount of sales tax is also reduced because the amount of the sale is reduced.

(1) *Sales Discount:*

| Sales Invoice Amount | × | Sales Discount Rate | = | Sales Discount |
|---|---|---|---|---|
| $1,800.00 | × | 1% | = | $18.00 |

(2) *Sales Tax Reduction:*

| Sales Discount | × | Sales Tax Rate | = | Sales Tax Reduction |
|---|---|---|---|---|
| $18.00 | × | 8% | = | $1.44 |

(3) *Cash Received:*

| Total Invoiced Amount | − | Sales Discount | − | Sales Tax Reduction | = | Cash Received |
|---|---|---|---|---|---|---|
| $1,944.00 | − | $18.00 | − | $1.44 | = | $1,924.56 |

**FYI**

*In some states, sales taxes must be paid on the original invoice amount of sale. In these states a sales discount would not result in a reduction in the sales tax liability. It is critically important for accounting employees to be familiar with sales tax laws in the states in which their companies do business.*

# JOURNALIZING CASH RECEIPTS ON ACCOUNT WITH SALES DISCOUNTS

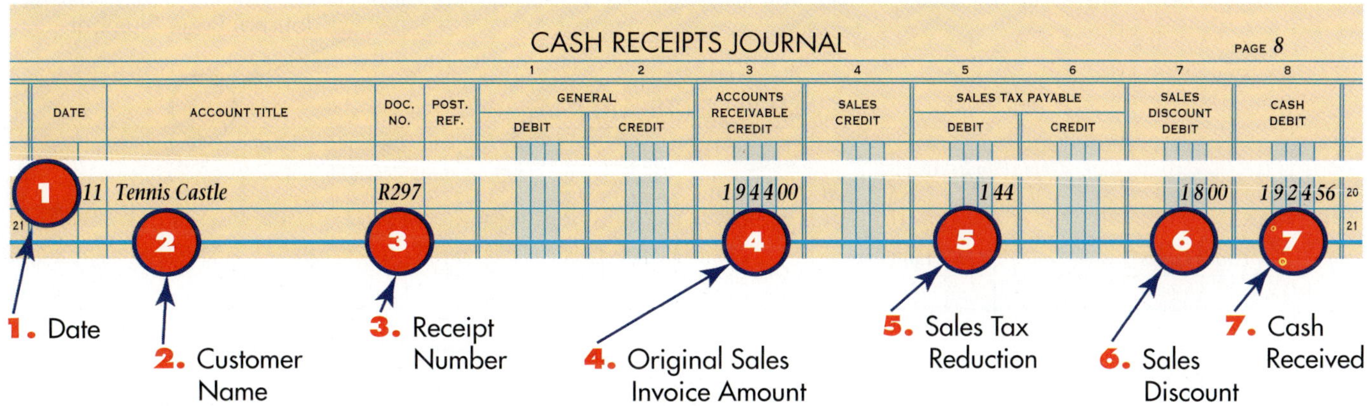


Sales discounts are recorded in a general ledger account titled Sales Discount. Since sales discounts decrease sales, the account Sales Discount is a contra account to Sales.

A business could debit Sales for the amount of the sales discount. However, better information is provided if these amounts are debited to Sales Discount. A separate account provides business managers with more information to evaluate whether a sales discount is a cost effective method of encouraging early payments of sales on account.

***March 11. Received cash on account from Tennis Castle, $1,924.56, covering Sales Invoice No. 176 for $1,944.00 ($1,800.00 plus sales tax, $144.00), less 1% discount, $18.00, and less sales tax, $1.44. Receipt No. 297.***

If a customer does not pay the amount owed within the sales discount period, the full invoice amount is due. If Tennis Castle had not taken the sales discount, the journal entry would be a debit to Cash, $1,944.00, and a credit to Accounts Receivable, $1,944.00. The same amount, $1,944.00, would also be credited to the account of Tennis Castle in the accounts receivable ledger.

**GENERAL LEDGER**

Cash

| | | | |
|---|---|---|---|
| Mar. 11 | 1,924.56 | | |

Sales Discount

| | | | |
|---|---|---|---|
| Mar. 11 | 18.00 | | |

Sales Tax Payable

| | | | |
|---|---|---|---|
| Mar. 11 | 1.44 | Mar. 2 | 144.00 |

Accounts Receivable

| | | | |
|---|---|---|---|
| Mar. 2 | 1,944.00 | Mar. 11 | 1,944.00 |

**ACCOUNTS RECEIVABLE LEDGER**

Tennis Castle

| | | | |
|---|---|---|---|
| Mar. 2 | 1,944.00 | Mar. 11 | 1,944.00 |

**STEPS**

### Journalizing cash receipts on account with sales discounts

1. Write the date, *11*, in the Date column.
2. Write the customer name, *Tennis Castle*, in the Account Title column.
3. Write the receipt number, *R297*, in the Doc. No. column.
4. Write the original invoice amount, *$1,944.00*, in the Accounts Receivable Credit column.
5. Write the reduction in sales tax, *$1.44*, in the Sales Tax Payable Debit column.
6. Write the amount of sales discount, *$18.00*, in the Sales Discount Debit column.
7. Write the debit to Cash, *$1,924.56*, in the Cash Debit column. The total of the three debits ($1.44 + $18.00 + $1,924.56) is $1,944.00 and is equal to the one credit of $1,944.00.

# POSTING FROM A CASH RECEIPTS JOURNAL TO AN ACCOUNTS RECEIVABLE LEDGER

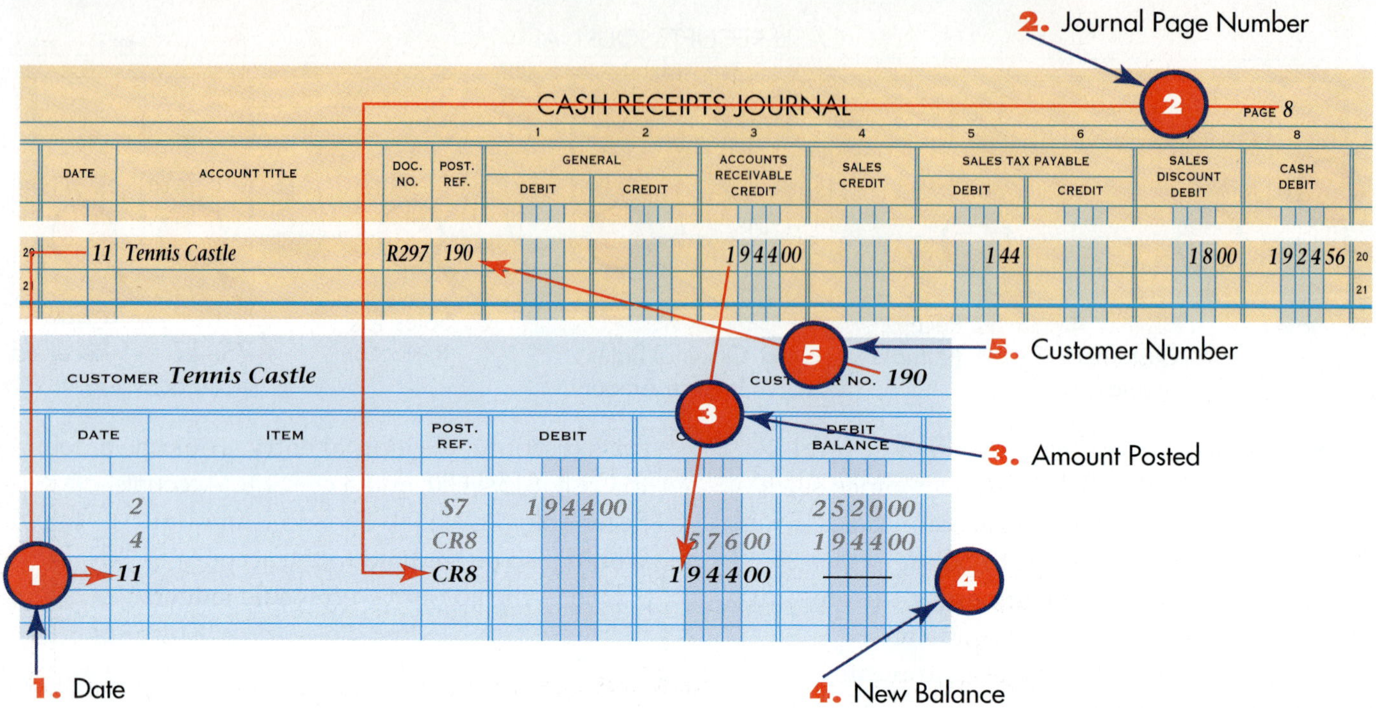


Each entry in the Accounts Receivable Credit column affects the account of the customer named in the Account Title column. Each amount listed in the Accounts Receivable Credit column is posted individually to the proper customer account in the accounts receivable ledger.

**STEPS**

### Posting from a cash receipts journal to an accounts receivable ledger

1. Write the date, *11,* in the Date column of the customer account.
2. Write the abbreviation and page number of the cash receipts journal, *CR8,* in the Post. Ref. column of the customer account.
3. Write the amount, *$1,944.00,* in the Credit column of the customer account.
4. Subtract the amount of $1,944.00 in the Credit column from the previous balance in the Debit Balance column. Write the amount or draw a horizontal line to indicate a new balance of zero.
5. Write the customer number for Tennis Castle, *190,* in the Post. Ref. column of the cash receipts journal.

**REMEMBER**

The abbreviation *CR* is used when posting from the cash receipts journal. The abbreviation provides a reference back to the cash receipts journal in case the original entry needs to be examined.

# POSTING TOTALS OF THE SPECIAL AMOUNT COLUMNS OF A CASH RECEIPTS JOURNAL TO A GENERAL LEDGER

**3.** Place a check mark.

CASH RECEIPTS JOURNAL — PAGE 9

| | DATE | ACCOUNT TITLE | DOC. NO. | POST. REF. | 1 GENERAL DEBIT | 2 GENERAL CREDIT | 3 ACCOUNTS RECEIVABLE CREDIT | 4 SALES CREDIT | 5 SALES TAX PAYABLE DEBIT | 6 SALES TAX PAYABLE CREDIT | 7 SALES DISCOUNT DEBIT | 8 CASH DEBIT | |
|---|---|---|---|---|---|---|---|---|---|---|---|---|---|
| 15 | 31 | √ | T31 | √ | | | | 1 795 00 | | 143 60 | | 1 938 60 | 15 |
| 16 | 31 | Totals | | | 300 00 | 7 130 00 | 69 948 00 | 56 275 00 | 46 40 | 3 970 00 | 580 00 | 136 396 60 | 16 |
| 17 | | | | | (√) | (√) | (1125) | (4105) | (2140) | (2140) | (4110) | (1105) | 17 |

ACCOUNT *Accounts Receivable* — ACCOUNT NO. *1125*

| DATE | ITEM | POST. REF. | DEBIT | CREDIT | BALANCE DEBIT | BALANCE CREDIT |
|---|---|---|---|---|---|---|
| 31 | | S9 | 71 145 00 | | 130 961 00 | |
| 31 | | CR9 | | 69 948 00 | 61 013 00 | |

ACCOUNT *Cash* — ACCOUNT NO. *1105*

| DATE | | ITEM | POST. REF. | DEBIT | CREDIT | BALANCE DEBIT | BALANCE CREDIT |
|---|---|---|---|---|---|---|---|
| 20--<br>Mar. | 1 | Balance | √ | | | 12 981 00 | |
| | 31 | | CR9 | 136 396 60 | | 149 377 60 | |
| | 31 | | CP6 | | 72 468 00 | 76 909 60 | |

**1.** Prove and rule the cash receipts journal.

**2.** Post each special column total; record account numbers.

At the end of each month, equality of debits and credits is proved for a cash receipts journal. The steps for proving and ruling the cash receipts journal are not shown in the illustration, but are similar to the steps described in Chapter 11 for proving and ruling an expanded journal.

The special column totals are posted to the general ledger, as shown in the illustration for two of the accounts. Each amount in the General columns is posted individually to the general ledger account named in the Account Title column. The totals of the General amount columns are not posted. To indicate that these totals are not posted, a check mark is placed in parentheses below each column total.

Each special amount column total is posted to the account named in the cash receipts journal column heading.

**STEPS**

### Posting from a cash receipts journal to a general ledger

1. Prove and rule the cash receipts journal.
2. Post the total of each special account column by recording the date, Post. Ref., amount, and new account balance in the related general ledger account. Write the account number in parentheses below the column total in the cash receipts journal.
3. Place a check mark in parentheses below each General column total.

## TERMS REVIEW

cash receipts journal

sales discount

## AUDIT YOUR UNDERSTANDING

1. Why do companies offer sales discounts?
2. What general ledger accounts are affected, and how, by a cash receipt from a customer on account when there is a sales discount and sales tax?

## WORK TOGETHER

### Journalizing and posting cash receipts transactions

The ledger accounts for Crawford Equipment Co. are given in the *Working Papers.* Your instructor will guide you through the following examples.

3. Using the current year, journalize the following transactions on page 5 of a cash receipts journal. Sales terms are 2/10, n/30. The sales tax rate is 8%. Source documents are abbreviated as follows: receipt, R; sales invoice, S; cash register tape, T.

   ***Transactions:***

   May 3. Recorded cash and credit card sales, $1,243.00, plus sales tax, $99.44, total, $1,342.44. T3.

   4. Received cash on account from Nelson Company, $542.43, covering S119 for $553.50 ($512.50 plus sales tax, $41.00), less discount and sales tax. R145.

   7. Received cash on account from Hawbecker Supply, $157.00, covering S103; no discount. R146.

4. Post each amount in the Accounts Receivable Credit column to the accounts receivable ledger.
5. Prove and rule the cash receipts journal.
6. Post the totals of the special columns of the cash receipts journal to the general ledger.

## ON YOUR OWN

### Journalizing and posting cash receipts transactions

The ledger accounts for Sunshine Flowers are given in the *Working Papers.* Work these problems independently.

7. Using the current year, journalize the following transactions on page 6 of a cash receipts journal. Sales terms are 2/10, n/30. The sales tax rate is 8%. Source documents are abbreviated as follows: receipt, R; sales invoice, S; cash register tape, T.

   ***Transactions:***

   June 3. Recorded cash and credit card sales, $2,526.00, plus sales tax, $202.08, total, $2,728.08. T3.

   5. Received cash on account from Pait Café, $264.60, covering S319 for $270.00 ($250.00 plus sales tax, $20.00), less discount and sales tax. R298.

   8. Received cash on account from Mason Insurance, $104.00, covering S302; no discount. R299.

8. Post each amount in the Accounts Receivable Credit column to the accounts receivable ledger.
9. Prove and rule the cash receipts journal.
10. Post the totals of the special columns of the cash receipts journal to the general ledger.

# 19-3 Recording Transactions Using a General Journal

## CREDIT MEMORANDUM FOR SALES RETURNS AND ALLOWANCES

CREDIT MEMORANDUM NO. 41

| DATE |
|---|
| March 11, 20-- |

Winning Edge
1420 College Plaza
Atlanta, GA 30337-1726

| TO |
|---|
| Parson Company<br>1151 Peach Lane<br>Atlanta, GA 30337 |

| ACCOUNT NO. |
|---|
| 160 |

*We have this day credited your account as follows:*

| Quantity | Units | Description | Price | Total |
|---|---|---|---|---|
| 3 | ea. | Stop watch, Model 15P6 | 19.50 | 58.50 |
| | | Sales tax | | 4.68 |
| | | Total | | 63.18 |

If the above is incorrect, please return stating difference.

Purchases-related transactions recorded in a general journal are described in Chapter 18. Winning Edge also records two sales-related transactions in a general journal. These two transactions are not sales of merchandise on account or cash receipts. Thus, they are not recorded in either the sales journal or the cash receipts journal. These two transactions are (1) sales returns and allowances and (2) correcting entries that affect customer accounts but not the controlling account.

### Sales Returns and Allowances

Most merchandising businesses expect to have some merchandise returned because a customer decides not to keep the merchandise. A customer may have received the wrong style, the wrong size, or damaged goods. A customer may return merchandise and ask for a credit on account or a cash refund. Credit allowed a customer for the sales price of returned merchandise, resulting in a decrease in the vendor's accounts receivable, is called a **sales return.**

Credit may be granted to a customer without requiring the return of merchandise. Credit also may be given because of a shortage in a shipment. Credit allowed a customer for part of the sales price of merchandise that is not returned, resulting in a decrease in the vendor's accounts receivable, is called a **sales allowance.**

A vendor usually informs a customer in writing when a sales return or a sales allowance is granted. A form prepared by the vendor showing the amount deducted for returns and allowances is called a **credit memorandum.** The form is called a credit memorandum because the vendor makes a credit to the customer account to show the decrease in Accounts Receivable.

The original copy of a credit memorandum is given to the customer. The second copy is used as the source document for sales returns and allowances. *(CONCEPT: Objective Evidence)*

Sales returns and sales allowances decrease the amount of sales. Therefore, the account Sales Returns and Allowances is a contra account to the revenue account Sales. Thus, the normal account balance of Sales Returns and Allowances is a debit, the opposite of the normal balance of Sales, a credit. The account is in the general ledger's operating revenue division.

Some businesses debit the sales account for the amount of a return or allowance. However, better information is provided if these amounts are debited to Sales Returns and Allowances.

## JOURNALIZING SALES RETURNS AND ALLOWANCES

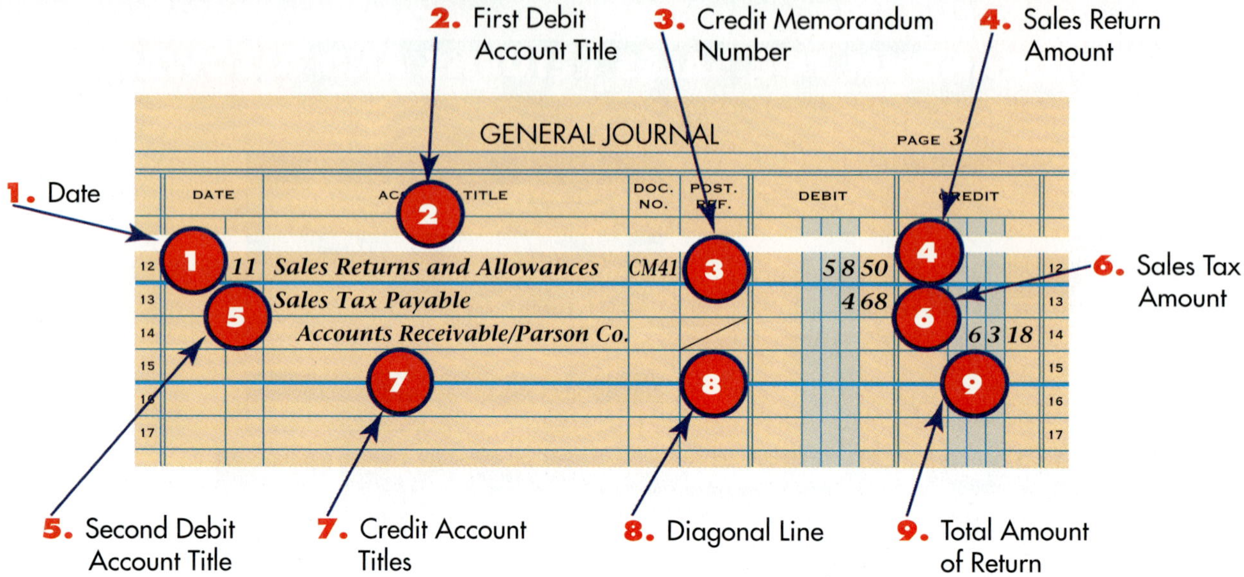


On March 8, Winning Edge sold merchandise on account to Parson Company for $475.00. Parson's account was debited for $513.00 ($475.00 sales and $38.00 sales tax). Later, Parson returned part of the merchandise. A customer is entitled to credit for the amount of a sales return or allowance. The credit must include the sales tax on the return or allowance.

***March 11. Granted credit to Parson Company for merchandise returned, $58.50, plus sales tax, $4.68, from S160; total, $63.18. Credit Memorandum No. 41.***

Parson is entitled to a $58.50 credit for the merchandise returned and a $4.68 credit for sales tax. Accounts Receivable is credited for the total amount of the return, $63.18. The same amount is also credited to Parson's account in the accounts receivable ledger.

GENERAL LEDGER

Sales Returns and Allowances

| | | | |
|---|---|---|---|
| Mar. 11 | 58.50 | | |

Sales Tax Payable

| | | | |
|---|---|---|---|
| Mar. 11 | 4.68 | Mar. 8 | 38.00 |

Accounts Receivable

| | | | |
|---|---|---|---|
| Mar. 8 | 513.00 | Mar. 11 | 63.18 |

ACCOUNTS RECEIVABLE LEDGER

Parson Company

| | | | |
|---|---|---|---|
| Mar. 8 | 513.00 | Mar. 11 | 63.18 |

### STEPS: Journalizing sales returns and allowances

1. Write the date, *11,* in the Date column.
2. Write *Sales Returns and Allowances* in the Account Title column.
3. Write *CM* and the credit memorandum number, *41,* in the Doc. No. column.
4. Write the amount of the sales return, *$58.50,* in the Debit column.
5. Write *Sales Tax Payable* on the next line in the Account Title column.
6. Write the sales tax amount, *$4.68,* in the Debit column.
7. Indent and write the accounts to be credited, *Accounts Receivable/Parson Company,* on the next line in the Account Title column.
8. Draw a diagonal line in the Post. Ref. column.
9. Write the total accounts receivable amount, *$63.18,* in the Credit column.

## JOURNALIZING CORRECTING ENTRIES AFFECTING CUSTOMER ACCOUNTS

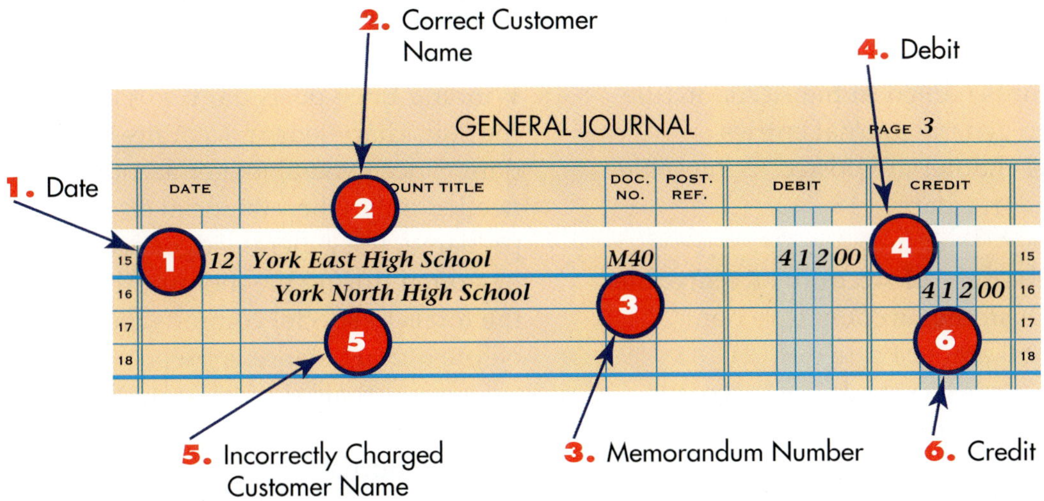


Errors may be made in recording amounts in subsidiary ledgers that do not affect the general ledger controlling account. For example, a sale on account may be recorded to the wrong customer in the sales journal. The column total posted from the sales journal to the general ledger is correct. The accounts receivable account shows the correct balance. However, two of the customer accounts in the accounts receivable ledger show incorrect balances. To correct this error, only the subsidiary ledger accounts need to be corrected.

***March 12. Discovered that a sale on account to York East High School on February 26, S133, was incorrectly charged to the account of York North High School, $412.00. Memorandum No. 40.***

On February 28, the total of the Accounts Receivable Debit column in the sales journal was posted correctly. Accounts Receivable was debited for the amount of the column total that included the $412.00 involved in this transaction. No correction is needed for this amount.

The account of York North High School was debited for $412.00 when the account of York East High School should have been debited. The correcting entry involves only subsidiary ledger accounts. York East High School's account is debited for $412.00 to record the charge sale in the correct account. York North High School's account is credited for $412.00 to cancel the incorrect entry.

**ACCOUNTS RECEIVABLE LEDGER**

York East High School

| Debit | | Credit | |
|---|---|---|---|
| Mar. 12 | 412.00 | | |

York North High School

| Debit | | Credit | |
|---|---|---|---|
| Feb. 26 | 412.00 | Mar. 12 | 412.00 |

### STEPS: Journalizing correcting entries affecting customer accounts

1. Write the date, *12*, in the Date column.
2. Write the name of the correct customer, *York East High School,* in the Account Title column.
3. Write *M* and the memorandum number, *40*, in the Doc. No. column.
4. Write the amount, *$412.00,* in the Debit column.
5. Indent and write the name of the incorrectly charged customer, *York North High School,* on the next line in the Account Title column.
6. Write the amount, *$412.00,* in the Credit column.

## SUMMARY OF POSTING

### Posting from a General Journal

Each amount in the Debit and Credit columns of a general journal is posted to the account or accounts named in the Account Title column. The two general journal entries discussed in this chapter are posted in the same way as described in Chapter 18.

### Preparing a Schedule of Accounts Receivable

A listing of customer accounts, account balances, and total amount due from all customers is known as a schedule of accounts receivable. A schedule of accounts receivable is prepared before financial statements are prepared to prove the accounts receivable ledger. If the total amount shown on a schedule of accounts receivable equals the accounts receivable controlling account balance in the general ledger, the accounts receivable ledger is proved. Preparation of a schedule of accounts receivable is described in Chapter 12.

### Order of Posting from Special Journals

Items affecting customer or vendor accounts are posted periodically during the month. Winning Edge posts daily so that the balances of the subsidiary ledger accounts will be up to date. Since general ledger account balances are needed only when financial statements are prepared, the general ledger accounts are posted less often during the month. All items, including the totals of special columns, must be posted before a trial balance is prepared.

The journals should be posted in the following order:

1. Sales journal.
2. Purchases journal.
3. General journal.
4. Cash receipts journal.
5. Cash payments journal.

This order of posting usually puts the debits and credits in the accounts in the order the transactions occurred.

**TECHNOLOGY FOR BUSINESS**

### COMPUTERIZED ACCOUNTING—NOT JUST FOR CORPORATIONS

For many years only large corporations could afford to computerize their accounting functions. Today a variety of computer software programs are available to handle the record keeping and accounting needs of small and not-so-small businesses. Examples include Peachtree, QuickBooks, and MYOB.

Depending on the needs of the business, there is a software program available to complete all or some accounting functions using a personal computer. These functions include the general ledger, accounts payable, accounts receivable, financial statements, and inventory. The software programs can print checks and maintain a check register, as well as reconcile bank statements. Some programs can help prepare payroll, calculate taxes, and prepare tax forms. Other programs allow transfer of data to payroll and tax preparation software.

Record keeping or accounting software provides significant benefits. The software allows a business to improve the accuracy and completeness of financial records. Safeguards within the software alert the user to mistakes, problems, and inconsistencies. In addition, the software can create graphs and charts to complement financial reports and statements. Organization of records is an added benefit.

## TERMS REVIEW

sales return

sales allowance

credit memorandum

## AUDIT YOUR UNDERSTANDING

1. What general ledger accounts are affected, and how, by a sales returns and allowances transaction?
2. What is the best order in which to post journals?

## WORK TOGETHER

### Journalizing and posting transactions using a general journal

The ledger accounts for Cline Interiors are given in the *Working Papers.* Your instructor will guide you through the following examples.

3. Using the current year, journalize the following transactions on page 6 of a general journal. Source documents: credit memorandum, CM; memorandum, M; sales invoice, S.

   ***Transactions:***

   June 3. Granted credit to Wilbanks and Associates for merchandise returned, $457.00, plus sales tax, $36.56, from S356; total, $493.56. CM41.

   6. Granted credit to Westfall High School for damaged merchandise, $67.00 (no sales tax), from S345. CM42.

   9. Discovered that a sale on account to D. Howell, MD, on May 25, S346, was incorrectly charged to the account of Howsley Dance Studio, $414.99 ($384.25 plus sales tax, $30.74). M17.

4. Post the items to the general and accounts receivable ledgers.
5. Prepare a schedule of accounts receivable as of June 30.

## ON YOUR OWN

### Journalizing and posting transactions using a general journal

The ledger accounts for Batson Hardware are given in the *Working Papers.* Work these problems independently.

6. Using the current year, journalize the following transactions on page 7 of a general journal. Source documents: credit memorandum, CM; memorandum, M; sales invoice, S.

   ***Transactions:***

   July 4. Granted credit to Ulman Builders for merchandise returned, $246.00, plus sales tax, $19.68, from S423; total, $265.68. CM54.

   8. Granted credit to Brooksville High School for damaged merchandise, $156.00 (no sales tax), from S426. CM55.

   12. Discovered that a sale on account to Naper Paper Co. on June 15, S435, was incorrectly charged to the account of Naper Glass Co., $372.60 ($345.00 plus sales tax, $27.60). M21.

7. Post the items to the general and accounts receivable ledgers.
8. Prepare a schedule of accounts receivable as of July 31.

# 19-4 Recording International Sales

## INTERNATIONAL SALES

Sales in the international market have become a major source of revenue for both small and large businesses. Businesses throughout the world are finding it necessary to buy and sell products and services from and to businesses in foreign countries.

Goods or services shipped out of a seller's home country to a foreign country are called **exports.** Goods or services bought from a foreign country and brought into a buyer's home country are called **imports.**

Businesses may be able to import materials or services that are not available or are less expensive than within their own country. Thus, many companies have entered into the export and import markets to maintain their competitiveness and provide the products and services to meet customer demand.

Selling merchandise to individuals or other businesses within one's own country, generally referred to as domestic sales, is much simpler than international sales.

Most domestic sales are sold for cash or on account after reviewing and approving a customer's credit. Because all transactions in the U. S. are covered by the same universal commercial laws and the same accounting standards, many transactions are based on trust. A customer with approved credit orders merchandise. The merchandise is shipped and an invoice is sent by the vendor. After receiving the merchandise and invoice, the customer pays the vendor.

However, because of the increased complexities of international sales, several issues must be considered. The lack of uniform commercial laws among countries makes settlement of disputes more difficult. Greater distances and sometimes more complex transportation methods increase the time to complete the transaction. The reduced ability to determine a customer's financial condition and ability to take legal action if a customer does not pay increases the risk of uncollected amounts. Unstable political conditions in some countries may affect the ability to receive payments from those countries. Therefore, most businesses dealing in exports and/or imports follow a general process in international trade that ensures the vendor receives payment for merchandise sold and the customer receives the merchandise ordered.

**FYI**

*The International Chamber of Commerce publishes Incoterms to attempt to coordinate international sales. This set of international rules interprets common sales terms used in foreign trade that are adopted by most international trade associations.*

## PROCESSING AN INTERNATIONAL SALE

A document that details all the terms agreed to by seller and buyer for a sales transaction is called a **contract of sale.** The contract includes a description and quantity of merchandise, price, point of delivery, packing and marking instructions, shipping information, insurance provisions, and method of payment.

Southwest Exports, Inc., located in San Diego, California, contracts to sell merchandise to Santiago Company in Mexico City, Mexico. The contract price is $25,000.00 in U.S. dollars, and merchandise is to be delivered to Mexico City. The Santiago Company is to pay transportation charges.

A letter issued by a bank guaranteeing that a named individual or business will be paid a specified amount provided stated conditions are met is called a **letter of credit.** The contract of sale specified a letter of credit as the method of payment.

Santiago prepared an application with its bank, Banco Nacional de Mexico, to issue a letter of credit. Banco Nacional de Mexico approved Santiago's application and issued the letter of credit. Banco Nacional de Mexico forwarded the letter of credit to Southwest's bank, First Bank in San Diego.

First Bank delivered the letter of credit to Southwest. Southwest reviewed the letter of credit to ensure that the provisions in the letter agreed with the contract of sale. Southwest then shipped the merchandise.

In order for Southwest to collect payment, three documents specified in the letter of credit must be submitted to First Bank: (1) a bill of lading, (2) a commercial invoice, and (3) a draft. A receipt signed by the authorized agent of a transportation company for merchandise received that also serves as a contract for the delivery of the merchandise is called a **bill of lading.** The transportation company sends the bill of lading to Southwest when the merchandise is shipped. Southwest then prepares the other two documents. A statement prepared by the seller of merchandise addressed to the buyer showing a detailed listing and description of merchandise sold, including prices and terms, is called a **commercial invoice.** A written, signed, and dated order from one party ordering another party, usually a bank, to pay money to a third party is called a **draft.** A draft is sometimes referred to as a bill of exchange. A draft payable on sight when the holder presents it for payment is called a **sight draft.**

First Bank examines the documents submitted by Southwest to ensure that all terms of sale are in compliance with the letter of credit. First Bank then forwards the documents to Santiago's bank, Banco Nacional de Mexico. Banco Nacional de Mexico examines the documents to ensure they are in compliance with the terms and conditions of the letter of credit. When Banco Nacional de Mexico determines all documents are in compliance, it deducts the amount of the sight draft from Santiago's account and sends that amount, $25,000.00, to Southwest's bank, First Bank.

Banco Nacional de Mexico then forwards the documents to Santiago Company. By presenting the bill of lading and letter of credit to the transportation company, Santiago can receive the merchandise.

**FYI**

*The United States federal government does not collect a sales tax. However, many countries of the world, including most of the major industrial powers, do collect what is referred to as a "value added tax" or VAT. A value added tax is basically a national sales tax.*

## JOURNALIZING AN INTERNATIONAL SALE

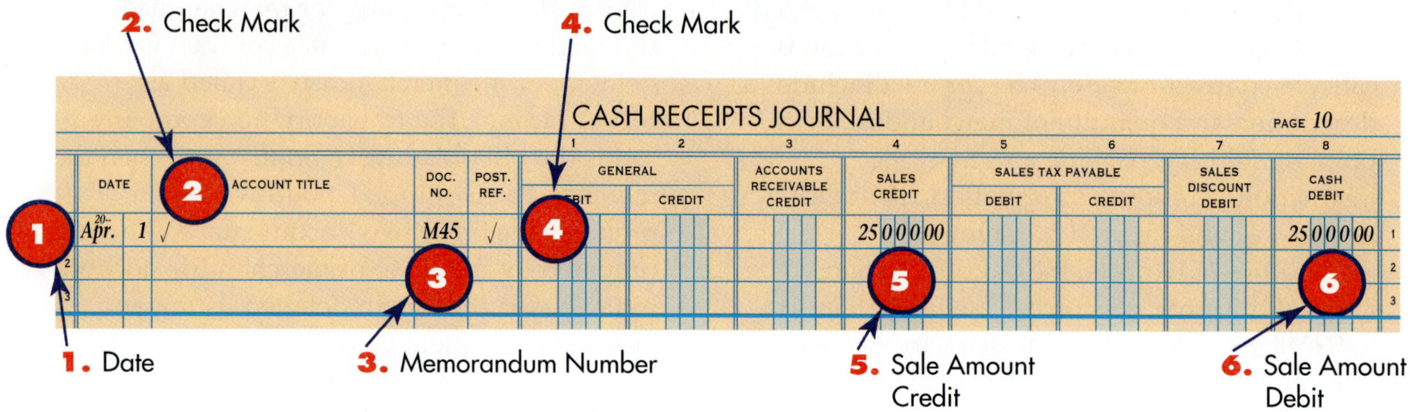


After receiving payment from Banco Nacional de Mexico, First Bank deposits the payment for the sale in Southwest's account and sends Southwest a deposit slip for the amount deposited. After receiving the deposit slip from First Bank, Southwest prepares a memorandum as a source document for the cash received. The sale is then recorded as a cash sale.

Sales taxes are normally paid only on sales to the final consumer. Southwest's sale is to Santiago Company, a manufacturing company. Therefore, sales tax is not collected.

The sales and collection process Southwest followed assured Southwest of receiving payment for its sale and Santiago Company of receiving the merchandise it ordered.

***April 1. Recorded international cash sale, $25,000.00. Memorandum 45.***

**Cash**

| Debit | | Credit | |
|---|---|---|---|
| Apr. 1 | 25,000.00 | | |

**Sales**

| Debit | | Credit | |
|---|---|---|---|
| | | Apr. 1 | 25,000.00 |

**FYI**

*Visitors to foreign countries with a value added tax (VAT) typically are required to pay the VAT. However, if items purchased exceed a specified amount, a refund of a portion of the VAT can be requested.*

**STEPS**

### Recording an entry for an international sale

1. Write the date, *20—, Apr. 1,* in the Date column.
2. Place a check mark in the Account Title column to indicate that no account title needs to be entered.
3. Write M and the memorandum number, *45,* in the Doc. No. column.
4. Place a check mark in the Post. Ref. column to indicate that the amounts on this line are not posted individually.
5. Write the sale amount, *$25,000.00,* in the Sales Credit column.
6. Write the sale amount, *$25,000.00,* in the Cash Debit column.

## Terms Review

- exports
- imports
- contract of sale
- letter of credit
- bill of lading
- commercial invoice
- draft
- sight draft
- time draft
- trade acceptance

## Audit Your Understanding

1. What are some of the issues that must be considered before making international sales?
2. What two purposes does a bill of lading serve?
3. How does a sight draft differ from a time draft?
4. Why do many companies dealing in international sales rely upon letters of credit from banks?
5. How does a trade acceptance differ from a draft?

## Work Together

### Journalizing international sales transactions

The cash receipts and general journals for Marlon Exports, Ltd. are given in the *Working Papers.* Your instructor will guide you through the following examples.

6. Using the current year, journalize the following international sales on page 9 of a cash receipts journal and page 5 of a general journal. Sales tax is not charged on these sales. Source documents are abbreviated as follows: memorandum, M; time draft, TD; receipt, R.

   May 1. Recorded an international cash sale, $14,000.00. M323.
   5. Received a 30-day time draft from Ying Shen for an international sale, $18,000.00. TD32.
   9. Received cash for the value of Time Draft No. 10, $21,000.00. R221.

7. Prove and rule the cash receipts journal.

## On Your Own

### Journalizing international sales transactions

The cash receipts and general journals for Kazsumori Gallery are given in the *Working Papers.* Work these problems independently.

8. Using the current year, journalize the following international sales on page 3 of a cash receipts journal and page 2 of a general journal. Sales tax is not charged on these sales. Source documents are abbreviated as follows: memorandum, M; time draft, TD; receipt, R.

   Feb. 1. Recorded an international cash sale, $12,000.00. M132.
   4. Received a 60-day time draft from Danjiro Mori for an international sale, $5,000.00. TD22.
   8. Received cash for the value of Time Draft No. 6, $13,500.00. R102.

9. Prove and rule the cash receipts journal.

# CHAPTER 19 SUMMARY

*Enrichment Activity*

**Types of Businesses**

*You have now been exposed to how three different types of businesses use three different types of journals for recording daily transactions. Describe how the type of business or business organization affects the types of journals used.*

After completing this chapter, you can

1. Define accounting terms related to sales and cash receipts.
2. Identify accounting concepts and practices related to sales and cash receipts.
3. Record sales on account and post, using a sales journal.
4. Record cash receipts and post, using a cash receipts journal.
5. Record transactions and post, using a general journal.
6. Record transactions for international sales.

## EXPLORE ACCOUNTING

### HOW CREDIT CARD SYSTEMS WORK

To promote sales, Chimes Music Store accepts major credit cards, such as VISA, MasterCard, American Express, and Discover. To process these sales, Chimes Music contracted with a processing center to install and maintain its credit card system.

When a customer presents Chimes with a credit card, the card is scanned and the amount of purchase is entered in a credit card reader. The reader uses phone lines to contact the processing center. If the processing center determines that the customer has an adequate amount of unused credit, the transaction is approved and a sales receipt is printed. At the same time, the transaction is added to daily totals maintained by the processing center. After the customer signs the credit card receipt, both the customer and business keep a copy.

At the end of the day, Chimes enters a command to instruct the system to close its account. The credit card reader prints a summary receipt that lists the total number and amount of sales by credit card company. The processing center notifies each credit card company of its daily total. The credit card companies then make electronic funds transfers to Chimes Music's bank account. This process often requires several days to complete.

Both the processing center and the credit card companies charge Chimes with a fee for processing credit card sales. These charges are accumulated and a monthly fee is charged directly to Chimes Music's bank account.

**Research:** Credit card processing companies can use different equipment and procedures to process credit card sales. Ask a local retailer to describe its credit card processing system. Prepare a report that describes the equipment and procedures used as well as the fees charged. Contrast the system you observed with Chimes Music's system. Which system is better? How could the system you researched be improved?

## 19-1 APPLICATION PROBLEM
### Journalizing and posting sales on account transactions

The general ledger and accounts receivable ledger accounts for Yasunari Company are given in the *Working Papers*. The balances are recorded as of March 1 of the current year.

***Instructions:***

1. Journalize the following sales on account transactions completed during March of the current year. Use page 3 of a sales journal. The sales tax rate is 8%. The abbreviation for sales invoice is S.

***Transactions:***

March 3. Sold merchandise on account to Maitland Supply, $523.00, plus sales tax. S78.
5. Sold merchandise on account to Hampton University, $745.40. Hampton University is exempt from paying sales tax. S79.
6. Sold merchandise on account to Cruz and Diaz, $1,635.00, plus sales tax. S80.
8. Sold merchandise on account to Valdez and Associates, $723.00, plus sales tax. S81.
12. Sold merchandise on account to Maitland Supply, $816.00, plus sales tax. S82.

2. Post each amount in the Accounts Receivable Debit column of the sales journal to the accounts receivable ledger.
3. Prove and rule the sales journal.
4. Post the totals of the special columns of the sales journal to the general ledger.

## 19-2 APPLICATION PROBLEM
### Journalizing and posting cash receipts transactions

The general ledger and accounts receivable ledger accounts for Gandy Stores are given in the *Working Papers*. The balances are recorded as of April 1 of the current year.

***Instructions:***

1. Journalize the following cash receipts transactions completed during April of the current year. Use page 5 of a cash receipts journal. Gandy Stores offers terms of 2/10, n/30. The sales tax rate is 8%. Source documents are abbreviated as follows: receipt, R; sales invoice, S; cash register tape, T.

***Transactions:***

April 4. Recorded cash and credit card sales, $3,623.00, plus sales tax, $289.84, total, $3,912.84. T4.
5. Received cash on account from Lambert Company, $489.51, covering S81 for $499.50 ($462.50 plus sales tax, $37.00), less discount and sales tax. R65.
7. Received cash on account from Fulton Supply, $315.00, covering S82; no discount. R66.
10. Recorded cash and credit card sales, $2,493.00, plus sales tax, $199.44, total, $2,692.44. T10.
14. Received cash on account from Westbrook Company, $723.00, covering S83; no discount. R67.
22. Received cash on account from Okora Industries, $449.82, covering S82 for $459.00 ($425.00 plus sales tax, $34.00), less discount and sales tax. R68.

2. Post each amount in the Accounts Receivable Credit column of the cash receipts journal to the accounts receivable ledger.
3. Prove and rule the cash receipts journal.
4. Post the totals of the special columns of the cash receipts journal to the general ledger.

## 19-3 APPLICATION PROBLEM

### Journalizing and posting transactions using a general journal

The general ledger and accounts receivable ledger accounts for VanHorn Designs are given in the *Working Papers*. The balances are recorded as of July 1 of the current year.

***Instructions:***

1. Journalize the following transactions affecting sales completed during July of the current year. Use page 7 of a general journal. Source documents are abbreviated as follows: credit memorandum, CM; memorandum, M; receipt, R; sales invoice, S.

***Transactions:***

July 2. Granted credit to Rhone Company for merchandise returned, $674.00, plus sales tax, $53.92, from S356; total, $727.92. CM141.

4. Granted credit to Summer & Moss for damaged merchandise, $126.00, plus sales tax, $10.08, from S345; total, $136.08. CM142.

7. Discovered that a sale on account to Norris Industries on May 25, S346, was incorrectly charged to the account of Farris Industries, $337.23 ($312.25 plus sales tax, $24.98). M67.

12. Granted credit to Osborne Middle School for damaged merchandise, $186.00, from S345. CM143.

19. Discovered that a sale on account to Pines Company on May 25, S346, was incorrectly charged to the account of Pineston, Inc., $153.36 ($142.00 plus sales tax, $11.36). M68.

23. Granted credit to Humber Crafts for merchandise returned, $345.00, plus sales tax, $27.60, from S356; total, $372.60. CM144.

2. Post the items to the general and accounts receivable ledgers.
3. Prepare a schedule of accounts receivable (similar to the one described in Chapter 12) as of July 31 of the current year. Compare the schedule total with the balance of the accounts receivable account in the general ledger. The total and balance should be the same.

## 19-4 APPLICATION PROBLEM

### Journalizing international sales transactions

The cash receipts and general journals for Parker Exports, Ltd. are given in the *Working Papers*.

***Instructions:***

1. Journalize the following international sales completed by Parker Exports, Ltd. during June of the current year. Use page 10 of a cash receipts journal and page 6 of a general journal. Sales tax is not charged on these sales. Source documents are abbreviated as follows: memorandum, M; time draft, TD; receipt, R.

***Transactions:***

June 1. Recorded an international cash sale, $12,000.00. M82.

5. Received a 30-day time draft from Bella Lamas for an international sale, $13,000.00. TD32.

9. Received cash for the value of Time Draft No. 24, $16,000.00. R116.

12. Received a 60-day time draft from Pablo Fuentes for an international sale, $8,000.00. TD33.

19. Received cash for the value of Time Draft No. 21, $22,000.00. R117.

21. Recorded an international cash sale, $17,500.00. M83.

25. Received a 30-day time draft from Rodrigo Soto for an international sale, $24,000.00. TD34.

2. Prove and rule the cash receipts journal.

## 19-5 APPLICATION PROBLEM
### Journalizing sales transactions

The sales, cash receipts, and general journals for Redmond Corporation are given in the *Working Papers.*

***Instructions:***

Journalize the following transactions affecting sales and cash receipts completed during February of the current year. Use page 2 of a sales journal, a general journal, and a cash receipts journal. Redmond Corporation offers terms of 2/10, n/30. The sales tax rate is 8%. Source documents are abbreviated as follows: credit memorandum, CM; memorandum, M; receipt, R; sales invoice, S; cash register tape, T.

***Transactions:***

Feb. 2. The total of cash and credit card sales recorded from the cash register is $2,843.00, plus sales tax. T2.

3. Pennington Industries purchased merchandise on account for $725.00, plus sales tax. S89.
5. Received a check for $3,373.65 from Partain Company covering S81 ($3,187.50, plus sales tax). Partain deducted the discount and related sales tax. R35.
7. Received a letter from Profitt and Spring stating that some of the merchandise received was damaged in transit. The merchandise has a sales price of $126.00, plus sales tax. CM18.
8. Received a letter from Pennington Industries questioning a $1,353.00 charge on their statement. The accounts receivable clerk determined that the sale should have been recorded to Pendley Company. M16.
9. Richmond College, a tax-exempt organization, purchased merchandise on account for $257.00. S90.
12. Received a check for $767.34 from Pennington Industries for the February 3 sale on S89. R36.
14. Boyles Company returned merchandise because it was the wrong color. The sales price of the merchandise was $189.00, plus sales tax. CM19.

## 19-6 MASTERY PROBLEM
### Journalizing and posting sales transactions

The general ledger and accounts receivable accounts for Bell Supply are given in the *Working Papers.* The balances are recorded as of February 1 of the current year. Use the following account titles.

**PARTIAL GENERAL LEDGER**

| **Account No.** | **Name** |
|---|---|
| 1105 | Cash |
| 1125 | Accounts Receivable |
| 1130 | Time Drafts Receivable |
| 2140 | Sales Tax Payable |
| 4105 | Sales |
| 4110 | Sales Discount |
| 4115 | Sales Returns and Allowances |

**ACCOUNTS RECEIVABLE LEDGER**

| **Account Title** | **Customer No.Customer** |
|---|---|
| 110 | Carol Box |
| 120 | Maxwell, Inc. |
| 130 | Platter Company |
| 140 | Josh Prescott |
| 150 | Howard Price |
| 160 | James Purden |
| 170 | Raulston, Inc. |
| 180 | Read Company |
| 190 | Reed, Inc. |

| 195 | Washington High School |
|---|---|

***Instructions:***

1. Journalize the following transactions affecting sales and cash receipts completed during February of the current year. Use page 2 of a sales journal, a general journal, and a cash receipts journal. Bell Supply offers terms of 2/10, n/30. The sales tax rate is 8%. Source documents are abbreviated as follows: credit memorandum, CM; memorandum, M; receipt, R; sales invoice, S; cash register tape, T; time draft, TD.

***Transactions:***

Feb. 1. Sold merchandise on account to Carol Box, $562.50, plus sales tax. S45.
2. Granted credit to Josh Prescott for merchandise returned, $38.00, plus sales tax. CM7.
4. Received cash on account from Platter Company, $423.36, covering S39 for $432.00 ($400.00 plus sales tax, $32.00), less discount and sales tax. R32.
5. Received a 30-day time draft from Akeo Doi for an international sale, $5,000.00. TD10.
5. Received cash on account from James Purden, $277.83, covering S41 for $283.50 ($262.50 plus sales tax, $21.00), less discount and less sales tax. R33.
6. Recorded cash and credit card sales, $2,642.00, plus sales tax, $211.36; total, $2,853.36. T6.
7. Sold merchandise on account to Raulston, Inc., $950.00, plus sales tax. S46.
10. Received cash on account from Carol Box, $595.35, covering S45; with discount. R34.
12. Granted credit to Howard Price for damaged merchandise, $112.50, plus sales tax, from S30. CM8.
12. Recorded international cash sale, $10,500.00. M8.
13. Recorded cash and credit card sales, $1,420.00, plus sales tax, $113.60; total, $1,533.60. T13.
14. Received cash for the value of Time Draft No. 4, $23,000.00. R35.
15. Discovered that a sale on account to Read Company on January 23, S28, was incorrectly charged to the account of Reed, Inc., $241.00. M9.

**Posting**. Post the items that are to be posted individually. Post from the journals in this order: sales journal, general journal, and cash receipts journal.

16. Sold merchandise on account to Maxwell, Inc., $487.50, plus sales tax. S47.
16. Received cash on account from Raulston, Inc., $1,005.48, covering S46; with discount. R36.
17. Granted credit to Washington High School for damaged merchandise, $89.00, from S25. CM9.
20. Recorded cash and credit card sales, $2,098.00, plus sales tax, $167.84; total, $2,265.84. T20.
21. Received cash for the value of Time Draft No. 4, $8,000.00. R37.
22. Sold merchandise on account to Washington High School, $645.50, no sales tax. S48.
22. Granted credit to Maxwell, Inc. for merchandise returned, $43.00, plus sales tax. CM10.
24. Received cash on account from Howard Price, $423.36, covering the unpaid portion of S30, no discount. R38.
27. Recorded cash and credit card sales, $3,254.00, plus sales tax, $260.32; total, $3,514.32. T27.
28. Received a 30-day time draft from Sachi Nozaki for international sale of merchandise, $6,000.00. TD11.

**Posting**. Post the items that are to be posted individually.

2. Prove and rule the sales journal.
3. Post the totals of the special columns of the sales journal.
4. Prove and rule the cash receipts journal.
5. Post the totals of the special columns of the cash receipts journal.
6. Prepare a schedule of accounts receivable as of February 28 of the current year. Compare the schedule total with the balance of the accounts receivable account in the general ledger. The total and

19-7

balance should be the same.

## CHALLENGE PROBLEM

### Journalizing and posting sales, purchases, cash receipts, and cash payments transactions

The general, accounts receivable, and accounts payable ledgers for Lewis Company are given in the *Working Papers*. The balances are recorded as of April 1 of the current year.

**PARTIAL GENERAL LEDGER**

| Account No. | Name |
|---|---|
| 1105 | Cash |
| 1110 | Petty Cash |
| 1125 | Accounts Receivable |
| 1140 | Supplies |
| 2115 | Accounts Payable |
| 2140 | Sales Tax Payable |
| 4105 | Sales |
| 4110 | Sales Discount |
| 4115 | Sales Returns and Allowances |
| 5105 | Purchases |
| 5110 | Purchases Discount |
| 5115 | Purchases Returns and Allowances |
| 6105 | Advertising Expense |
| 6110 | Cash Short and Over |
| 6130 | Miscellaneous Expense |
| 6140 | Rent Expense |

**ACCOUNTS RECEIVABLE LEDGER**

**Account TitleCustomer No. Customer**

| Customer No. | Customer |
|---|---|
| 110 | Altman & Baird |
| 120 | Bird Company |
| 130 | Hawbecker Company |
| 140 | Jenkins Co. |
| 150 | Parker Supply |

**ACCOUNTS PAYABLE LEDGER**

| Vendor No. | Vendor Name |
|---|---|
| 210 | Drake Supplies |
| 220 | Grath Electric Co. |
| 230 | Randle Company |
| 240 | Walters, Inc. |

***Instructions:***

1. Journalize the following transactions completed during April of the current year. Calculate and record sales tax on all sales and sales returns and allowances as described in this chapter. Use page 4 of a sales journal, a purchases journal, a general journal, a cash receipts journal, and a cash payments journal. Lewis Company offers its customers terms of 2/10, n/30. The sales tax rate is 8%. Source documents are abbreviated as follows: check, C; credit memorandum, CM; debit memorandum, DM; memorandum, M; purchase invoice, P; receipt, R; sales invoice, S; cash register tape, T.

***Transactions:***

Apr. 1. Wrote a check for April rent, $850.00. C124.

1. Wrote a check to pay on account to Randle Company, covering P74 for $366.00, less 1% discount. C125.
2. Cash was received on account from Jenkins Co., $635.04, covering S83 for $648.00 ($600.00 plus sales tax, $48.00), less discount and less sales tax on discount. R26.
2. Recorded cash and credit card sales, $1,926.00, plus sales tax. T2.
   **Posting**. Post the items that are to be posted individually. Post the journals in this order: sales journal, purchases journal, general journal, cash receipts journal, and cash payments journal.
5. Merchandise was returned to Walters, Inc., $468.32, from P175. DM9.
6. Bird Company bought merchandise on account, $347.00, plus sales tax. S85.
6. Wrote a check for money owed to Grath Electric Co., $1,945.00, covering P164; no discount. C126.

6. Received payment on account from Parker Supply, $291.60, covering S74; no discount. R27.
7. Bought supplies on credit from Drake Supplies, $537.00. M15.
9. Cash was received on account from Altman & Baird, $330.48, covering S61; no discount. R28.

Apr. 9. Recorded cash and credit card sales, $1,820.00, plus sales tax. T9.
**Posting**. Post the items that are to be posted individually.

12. Merchandise was purchased on account from Grath Electric Co., $1,675.00. P177.
13. Wrote a check for money owed to Walters, Inc., covering P175 for $3,010.00, less DM9, $468.32, and less 2% discount. C127.
14. Jenkins Co. bought merchandise on credit, $546.00, plus sales tax. S86.
14. Paid for advertising, $450.00. C128.
14. Issued a check on account to Drake Supplies, $1,413.00, covering M14; no discount. C129.
15. Bird Company returned merchandise for credit, $226.00, plus sales tax, from S85. CM18.
16. Sold merchandise on account to Altman & Baird, $642.00, plus sales tax. S87.
16. Received a check on account from Bird Company, $128.07, covering S85 for $374.76 ($347.00 plus sales tax, $27.76), less CM18 ($226.00 plus sales tax), less discount and less sales tax on discount. R29.
16. Recorded cash and credit card sales, $2,246.00, plus sales tax. T16.
**Posting**. Post the items that are to be posted individually.
19. Cash was received on account from Hawbecker Company, $697.40, covering S60; no discount. R30.
20. Merchandise was purchased on account from Randle Company, $216.00. P178.
21. Sold merchandise on credit to Parker Supply, $723.00, plus sales tax. S88.
23. Wrote a check for miscellaneous expense, $205.00. C130.
23. Received on account from Jenkins Co., $577.89, covering S86 for $589.68 ($546.00 plus sales tax, $43.68), less discount and less sales tax on discount. R31.
23. Recorded cash and credit card sales, $2,152.00, plus sales tax. T23.
**Posting**. Post the items that are to be posted individually.
26. Sold merchandise on account to Bird Company, $1,015.00, plus sales tax. S89.
26. Merchandise was purchased on account from Grath Electric Co., $1,975.00. P179.
29. Paid cash on account to Randle Company, covering P178 for $216.00, less 1% discount. C131.
29. Purchased merchandise on account from Walters, Inc., $985.00. P180.
30. Recorded cash and credit card sales, $1,847.00, plus sales tax. T30.
30. Issued a check to replenish the petty cash fund, $130.25: supplies, $45.15; advertising, $60.00; miscellaneous, $22.50; cash short, $2.60. C132.
**Posting**. Post the items that are to be posted individually.

2. Prove and rule the sales journal and post the totals of the special columns.
3. Total the purchases journal and post the column total.
4. Prove and rule the cash receipts journal and post the totals of the special columns.
5. Prove and rule the cash payments journal and post the totals of the special columns.
6. Prepare a schedule of accounts payable and a schedule of accounts receivable as of April 30 of the current year. Compare each schedule total with the balance of the controlling account in the general ledger. The total and balance should be the same.

## SUNSHINE GARDENS
## CHART OF ACCOUNTS

### Balance Sheet Accounts

(1000) ASSETS
1100 Current Assets
1105 Cash
1110 Petty Cash
1115 Notes Receivable
1120 Interest Receivable
1125 Accounts Receivable
1130 Allowance for Uncollectible Accounts
1135 Merchandise Inventory
1140 Supplies
1145 Prepaid Insurance
1200 Plant Assets
1205 Office Equipment
1210 Accumulated Depreciation—Office Equipment
1215 Store Equipment
1220 Accumulated Depreciation—Store Equipment

(2000) LIABILITIES
2100 Current Liabilities
2105 Notes Payable
2110 Interest Payable
2115 Accounts Payable
2120 Employee Income Tax Payable
2125 Federal Income Tax Payable
2130 Social Security Tax Payable
2135 Medicare Tax Payable
2140 Sales Tax Payable
2145 Unemployment Tax Payable—Federal
2150 Unemployment Tax Payable—State
2155 Health Insurance Premiums Payable
2160 Dividends Payable

(3000) STOCKHOLDERS' EQUITY
3105 Capital Stock
3110 Retained Earnings
3115 Dividends
3120 Income Summary

### Income Statement Accounts

(4000) OPERATING REVENUE
4105 Sales
4110 Sales Discount
4115 Sales Returns and Allowances

(5000) COST OF MERCHANDISE
5105 Purchases
5110 Purchases Discount
5115 Purchases Returns and Allowances

(6000) OPERATING EXPENSES
6105 Advertising Expense
6110 Cash Short and Over
6115 Credit Card Fee Expense
6120 Depreciation Expense—Office Equipment
6125 Depreciation Expense—Store Equipment
6130 Insurance Expense
6135 Miscellaneous Expense
6140 Payroll Taxes Expense
6145 Rent Expense
6150 Repair Expense
6155 Salary Expense
6160 Supplies Expense
6165 Uncollectible Accounts Expense
6170 Utilities Expense

(7000) OTHER REVENUE
7105 Gain on Plant Assets
7110 Interest Income

(8000) OTHER EXPENSES
8105 Interest Expense
8110 Loss on Plant Assets

(9000) INCOME TAX EXPENSE
9105 Federal Income Tax Expense

Dec. 1. Paid cash for rent, $1,750.00. C621.
1. Received cash on account from Jenni Baker, $1,336.50, covering S81 for $1,350.00 ($1,250.00 plus sales tax, $100.00), less discount and sales tax. R92.
2. Purchased merchandise on account from Glenson Company, $4,658.00. P125.
2. Granted credit to Patrick Felton for merchandise returned, $126.00, plus sales tax, from S73. CM18.
2. Received cash on account from Patrick Felton, $1,543.40 (covering S73 less CM18), no discount. R93.
2. Sold merchandise on account to Pam Ruocco, $2,475.00, plus sales tax. S86.
3. Paid cash on account to Buntin Supply Company covering P92 for $4,260.00, less 2% discount. C622.
3. Recorded cash and credit card sales, $8,364.30, plus sales tax, $669.14; total, $9,033.44. T3.

**Posting.** Post the items that are to be posted individually. Post the journals in this order: sales journal, purchases journal, general journal, cash receipts journal, and cash payments journal.

5. Returned merchandise to Glenson Company, $420.00, from P90. DM21.
5. Paid cash on account to SHF Corp., covering P93 for $4,255.80, less 2% discount. C623.
6. Received cash on account from Samuel Horton, $3,341.25, covering S82 for $3,375.00 ($3,125.00 plus sales tax, $250.00), less discount and sales tax. R94.
7. Purchased merchandise on account from Walbash Manufacturing, $6,230.00. P126.
8. Sold merchandise on account to Hilldale Middle School, $645.00, no sales tax. S87.
8. Paid cash on account to Walbash Manufacturing, covering P94 for $3,354.60, less 1% discount. C624.
9. Paid cash for liability for November health insurance premiums, $725.00. C625.
10. Recorded cash and credit card sales, $12,632.20, plus sales tax, $1,010.58; total, $13,642.78. T10.

**Posting.** Post the items that are to be posted individually.

12. Purchased merchandise on account from SHF Corp., $8,326.00. P127.
12. Paid cash for miscellaneous expense, $153.30. C626.
12. Received cash on account from Pam Ruocco, $2,646.27, covering S86 for $2,673.00 ($2,475.00 plus sales tax, $198.00), less discount and sales tax. R95.
13. Paid cash for supplies, $63.30. C627.
14. Sold merchandise on account to Camille Nelson for $2,875.00, plus sales tax. S88.
14. Paid cash for advertising, $634.30. C628.
15. Paid cash for semimonthly payroll, $3,319.00 (total payroll, $4,650.00, less deductions: employee income tax, $634.00; social security tax, $302.25; Medicare tax, $69.75; health insurance premiums, $325.00). C629.
15. Recorded employer payroll taxes expense, $426.65 (social security tax, $302.25; Medicare tax, $69.75; federal unemployment tax, $7.05; state unemployment tax, $47.60). M75.
15. Paid cash for liability for employee income tax, $2,125.00; social security tax, $1,150.00; Medicare tax, $265.40. C630.
15. Paid cash for quarterly estimated federal income tax, $3,000.00. C631. (Debit Federal Income Tax Expense; credit Cash.)
15. Paid cash to replenish the petty cash fund, $176.50: supplies, $25.75; advertising, $45.00; miscellaneous, $108.75; cash over, $3.00. C632.
16. Paid cash on account to Walbash Manufacturing, covering P126 for $6,230.00, less 1% discount. C633.
16. Received cash on account from Camille Nelson, $2,103.34, covering S83; no discount. R96.
16. Received cash on account from Hilldale Middle School, covering S87 for $645.00, less discount. R97.
17. Purchased merchandise for cash, $512.60. C634.
17. Paid cash for miscellaneous expense, $82.60. C635.
17. Recorded cash and credit card sales, $18,463.00, plus sales tax, $1,477.04; total, $19,940.04. T17.

**Posting.** Post the items that are to be posted individually.

2. Prove and rule page 23 of the cash payments journal.
3. Forward the totals from page 23 to page 24 of the cash payments journal.
4. Continue recording the following transactions.

Dec. 19. Sold merchandise on account to Patrick Felton for $1,850.00, plus sales tax. S89.
20. Paid cash on account to Glenson Company, $2,364.70, covering P90 for $2,784.70, less DM21, $420.00; no discount. C636.
21. Paid cash on account to Draper Company, $2,643.50, covering P91; no discount. C637.
22. Purchased merchandise on account from Buntin Supply Company, $7,165.00. P128.
22. Paid cash on account to SHF Corp. covering P127 for $8,326.00, less 2% discount. C638.
23. Sold merchandise on account to Samuel Horton for $672.00, plus sales tax. S90.
24. Recorded cash and credit card sales, $12,543.60, plus sales tax, $1,003.49; total, $13,547.09. T24.
**Posting.** Post the items that are to be posted individually.
26. Bought supplies on account from Hinsdale Supply Co., $533.00. M76.
27. Sold merchandise on account to Jenni Baker, $1,454.00, plus sales tax. S91.
27. Paid cash for repairs, $153.20. C639.
28. Purchased merchandise on account from Walbash Manufacturing, $12,734.00. P129.
28. Received cash on account from Patrick Felton, $1,978.02, covering S89 for $1,998.00 ($1,850.00 plus sales tax, $148.00), less discount and sales tax. R98.
29. Paid cash on account to Glenson Company, $4,658.00, covering P125; no discount. C640.
29. Sold merchandise on account to Pam Ruocco, $975.00, plus sales tax. S92.
30. Paid cash for liability for sales tax, $4,932.60. C641. (Debit Sales Tax Payable; credit Cash.)
31. Paid cash for semimonthly payroll, $3,284.00 (total payroll, $4,600.00, less deductions: employee income tax, $623.00; social security tax, $299.00; Medicare tax, $69.00; health insurance premiums, $325.00). C642.
31. Recorded employer payroll taxes expense, $421.50 (social security tax, $299.00; Medicare tax, $69.00; federal unemployment tax, $6.90; state unemployment tax, $46.60). M77.
31. Recorded credit card fee expense for December, $846.60. M78. (Debit Credit Card Fee Expense; credit Cash.)
31. Paid cash to replenish the petty cash fund, $109.20: supplies, $34.80; advertising, $22.00; miscellaneous, $46.40; cash short, $6.00. C643.
31. Recorded cash and credit card sales, $5,472.00, plus sales tax, $437.76; total, $5,909.76. T31.
**Posting.** Post the items that are to be posted individually.

5. Prove and rule the sales journal. Post the totals of the special columns.
6. Total and rule the purchases journal. Post the total.
7. Prove the equality of debits and credits for the cash receipts and cash payments journals.
8. Prove cash. The balance on the next unused check stub on December 31 is $21,796.26.
9. Rule the cash receipts journal. Post the totals of the special columns.
10. Rule the cash payments journal. Post the totals of the special columns.
11. Prepare a schedule of accounts receivable and a schedule of accounts payable. Compare each schedule total with the balance of the controlling account in the general ledger. The total and balance should be the same.

**The ledgers used in Reinforcement Activity 3—Part A are needed to complete Reinforcement Activity 3—Part B.**

# 20 Accounting for Uncollectible Accounts Receivable

**AFTER STUDYING CHAPTER 20, YOU WILL BE ABLE TO:**

1. Define accounting terms related to uncollectible accounts.
2. Identify accounting concepts and practices related to uncollectible accounts.
3. Calculate, journalize, and post estimated uncollectible accounts expense.
4. Journalize and post entries related to writing off and collecting uncollectible accounts receivable.

**TERMS PREVIEW**

- uncollectible accounts
- allowance method of recording losses from uncollectible accounts
- book value
- book value of accounts receivable
- writing off an account

## UNCOLLECTIBLE ACCOUNTS

A business sells on account to encourage sales. Customers may buy merchandise today even though they will not have the cash needed to pay the account until days or months later.

A business that sells on account expects full payment within the terms of sale. Before selling to customers on account, a business should thoroughly investigate customers' credit ratings to determine their ability to pay. Even with a thorough credit investigation, however, some accounts receivable will never be collected. Accounts receivable that cannot be collected are called **uncollectible accounts.**

If a business fails to collect from a customer, the business loses part of the asset Accounts Receivable. The amount of the accounts receivable not collected is recorded as an expense in an account titled Uncollectible Accounts Expense. An uncollectible amount does not decrease revenue. Instead, the loss is considered a regular expense of doing business. Revenue was earned when the sale was made. *(CONCEPT: Realization of Revenue)* Failing to collect an account does not cancel the sale. Therefore, the loss is treated as an expense.

**FYI**

*The term* bad debt *is also used to refer to uncollectible accounts. In this case, the title of the expense account would be Bad Debts Expense. Some companies use the term* doubtful accounts. *These companies use an expense account titled Doubtful Accounts Expense.*

# ACCOUNTING IN YOUR CAREER

## CREDIT PROBLEMS

Joffrey Kraft has worked for Technocraft, Inc., for ten years in the payroll department. In those years he has taken advantage of the company's tuition reimbursement program to study accounting at the city university. Last month he finished his bachelor's degree and plans to begin preparing for the CPA examination. In the meantime, though, he has been promoted to the new position of credit manager at Technocraft.

Technocraft sells expensive scientific instruments to research institutions across the country. The company does not maintain a retail outlet but sells directly to clients through a network of sales representatives. These representatives are compensated with a small base salary but also earn commissions on every item sold. They have a great deal of independence in their territories and use their own judgment in granting credit to new customers.

Joffrey is well aware of the compensation package for sales representatives because of his years in payroll. He has settled into his new position and has become aware of a growing problem. The economy is lagging, and some of the existing customers have begun to let their account balances grow. In addition, long-overdue accounts are increasing in number among the new customers. Management has asked Joffrey to analyze the problem with actual uncollectible accounts and make recommendations. At the risk of alienating the sales representatives and jeopardizing new customer growth, Joffrey recommends that all new accounts be approved by him.

***Critical Thinking:***

1. Why would sales representatives extend credit to customers who might not pay?
2. Does Joffrey's proposal to take responsibility for credit approvals appear justified?
3. What are some procedures that should be followed before extending credit to a new customer?

# 20-1 Estimating and Recording Uncollectible Accounts Expense

## ALLOWANCE METHOD OF RECORDING LOSSES FROM UNCOLLECTIBLE ACCOUNTS

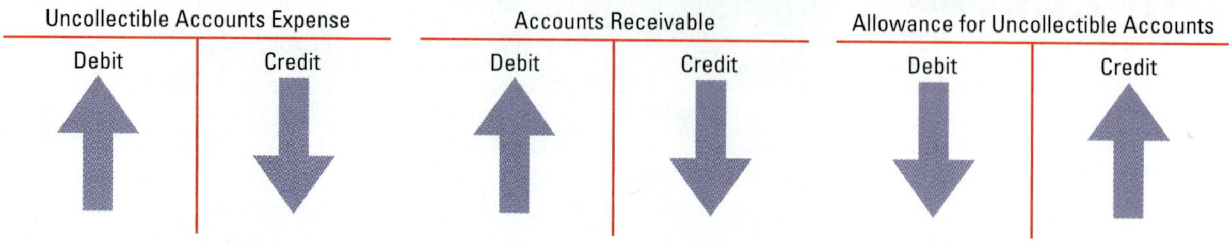


With each sale on account, a business takes a risk that customers will not pay their accounts. This risk is a cost of doing business that should be recorded as an expense in the same accounting period that the revenue is earned. Accurate financial reporting requires that expenses be recorded in the fiscal period in which the expenses contribute to earning revenue. *(CONCEPT: Matching Expenses with Revenue)*

At the end of a fiscal year, a business does not know which customer accounts will become uncollectible. If a business knew exactly which accounts would become uncollectible, it could credit Accounts Receivable and each customer account for the uncollectible amounts and debit Uncollectible Accounts Expense for the same amounts.

To solve this accounting problem, a business can calculate and record an *estimated* amount of uncollectible accounts expense. Estimating uncollectible accounts expense at the end of a fiscal period accomplishes two objectives:

(1) Reports a balance sheet amount for Accounts Receivable that reflects the amount the business expects to collect in the future.

(2) Recognizes the expense of uncollectible accounts in the same period in which the related revenue is recorded.

To record estimated uncollectible accounts, an adjusting entry is made affecting two accounts. The estimated amount of uncollectible accounts is debited to Uncollectible Accounts Expense and credited to an account titled Allowance for Uncollectible Accounts.

An account that reduces a related account is known as a contra account. Allowance for Uncollectible Accounts is a contra account to its related asset account, Accounts Receivable.

Crediting the estimated value of uncollectible accounts to a contra account is called the **allowance method of recording losses from uncollectible accounts.** The difference between an asset's account balance and its related contra account balance is called **book value.** The difference between the balance of Accounts Receivable and its contra account, Allowance for Uncollectible Accounts, is called the **book value of accounts receivable.** The book value of accounts receivable, reported on the balance sheet, represents the total amount of accounts receivable the business expects to collect in the future.

A contra account is usually assigned the next number of the account number sequence after its related account in the chart of accounts. Winning Edge's accounts receivable account is numbered 1125. Because Winning Edge numbers its accounts in sequences of five, Allowance for Uncollectible Accounts is numbered 1130.

**FYI**

*Allowance for Bad Debts and Allowance for Doubtful Accounts are account titles sometimes used instead of Allowance for Uncollectible Accounts.*

## ESTIMATING UNCOLLECTIBLE ACCOUNTS EXPENSE

| Total Sales on Account | × | Percentage | = | Estimated Uncollectible Accounts Expense |
|---|---|---|---|---|
| $982,800.00 | × | 1% | = | $9,828.00 |

Many businesses use a percentage of total sales on account to estimate uncollectible accounts expense. Each sale on account represents a risk of loss from an uncollectible account. Therefore, if the estimated percentage of loss is accurate, the amount of uncollectible accounts expense will be accurate regardless of when the actual losses occur.

Since a sale on account creates a risk of loss, estimating the percentage of uncollectible accounts expense for the same period matches sales revenue with the related uncollectible accounts expense. *(CONCEPT: Matching Expenses with Revenue)*

Winning Edge estimates uncollectible accounts expense by calculating a percentage of total sales on account. A review of Winning Edge's previous experience in collecting sales on account shows that actual uncollectible accounts expense has been about 1% of total sales on account. The company's total sales on account for the year is $982,800.00. Thus, Winning Edge estimates that $9,828.00 of the current fiscal period's sales on account will eventually be uncollectible.

## ACCOUNTING AT WORK

### TRACY STANHOFF

In 1988 Tracy Stanhoff founded AdPro, located in Huntington Beach, California, which offers full-service advertising and public relations. The company will perform any or all functions including marketing plans, display booths, advertising, graphic design, and in-house printing services.

Tracy holds a bachelor's degree in journalism, with minors in marketing, economics, and art. She also studied enough accounting to be able to read financial statements and understand the importance of accounting to a business.

As a member of the Potawatomi Tribe, Tracy was able to get some help from the National Center for American Indian Enterprise in locating clients for her new business. The Center helps connect new businesses with leading Fortune 500 companies and federal agencies. Today Tracy's company provides services for both small, start-up businesses and for multinational corporations.

She firmly believes in the value of a liberal education for providing a wide and varied background. Communication skills include speaking and writing clearly. "Listening skills," says Tracy, "are very important too—you have to hear what people are really saying."

# ANALYZING AND JOURNALIZING AN ADJUSTMENT FOR UNCOLLECTIBLE ACCOUNTS EXPENSE

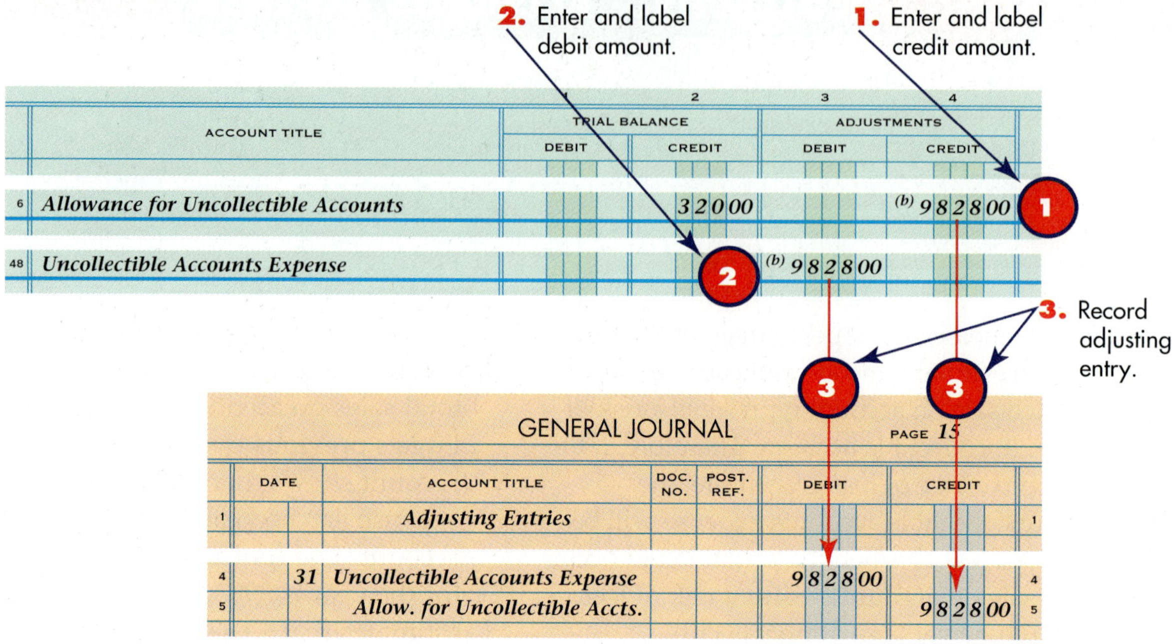


The percentage of total sales on account method of estimating uncollectible accounts expense assumes that a portion of every sale on account dollar will become uncollectible. Winning Edge has estimated that 1% of its $982,800.00 sales on account, or $9,828.00, will eventually become uncollectible.

At the end of a fiscal period, an adjustment for uncollectible accounts expense is planned on a work sheet.

The Allowance for Uncollectible Accounts balance in the Trial Balance Credit column, $320.00, is the allowance estimate from the previous fiscal period that has not yet been identified as uncollectible.

When the allowance account has a previous credit balance, the amount of the adjustment is added to the previous balance. This new balance of the allowance account is the estimated amount of accounts receivable that will eventually become uncollectible.

The adjustment planned on the work sheet must be recorded in a general journal and posted to the general ledger accounts.

**Uncollectible Accounts Expense**

| Debit | | Credit | |
|---|---|---|---|
| Dec. 31 Adj. | 9,828.00 | | |

**Allowance for Uncollectible Accounts**

| Debit | | Credit | |
|---|---|---|---|
| | | Bal. | 320.00 |
| | | Dec. 31 Adj. | 9,828.00 |
| | | *(New Bal.* | *10,148.00)* |

## STEPS: Analyzing and journalizing an adjustment for uncollectible accounts expense

1. Enter the estimated uncollectible amount, *$9,828.00,* in the Adjustments Credit column on the Allowance for Uncollectible Accounts line of the work sheet. Label the adjustment *(b)* with a small letter in parentheses.
2. Enter the same amount, *$9,828.00,* in the Adjustments Credit column on the Uncollectible Accounts Expense line of the work sheet. Label the adjustment using the same letter, *(b).*
3. Use the debit and credit amounts on the work sheet to record an adjusting entry in a general journal.

# POSTING AN ADJUSTING ENTRY FOR UNCOLLECTIBLE ACCOUNTS EXPENSE

GENERAL JOURNAL PAGE *15*

| | DATE | | ACCOUNT TITLE | DOC. NO. | POST. REF. | DEBIT | CREDIT | |
|---|---|---|---|---|---|---|---|---|
| 1 | | | *Adjusting Entries* | | | | | 1 |
| 4 | | *31* | *Uncollectible Accounts Expense* | | *6165* | *9 828 00* | | 4 |
| 5 | | | *Allow. for Uncollectible Accts.* | | *1130* | | *9 828 00* | 5 |

ACCOUNT *Accounts Receivable* ACCOUNT NO. *1125*

| DATE | | ITEM | POST. REF. | DEBIT | CREDIT | BALANCE DEBIT | BALANCE CREDIT |
|---|---|---|---|---|---|---|---|
| *Dec.* | *31* | | *S50* | *75 869 00* | | *135 174 00* | |
| | *31* | | *CR49* | | *62 716 00* | *72 458 00* | |

1. Debit

2. Credit

ACCOUNT *Allowance for Uncollectible Accounts* ACCOUNT NO. *1130*

| DATE | | ITEM | POST. REF. | DEBIT | CREDIT | BALANCE DEBIT | BALANCE CREDIT |
|---|---|---|---|---|---|---|---|
| *Dec.* | *27* | | *G14* | *420 00* | | | *320 00* |
| | *31* | | *G15* | | *9 828 00* | | *10 148 00* |

ACCOUNT *Uncollectible Accounts Expense* ACCOUNT NO. *6165*

| DATE | | ITEM | POST. REF. | DEBIT | CREDIT | BALANCE DEBIT | BALANCE CREDIT |
|---|---|---|---|---|---|---|---|
| 20-- *Dec.* | *31* | | *G15* | *9 828 00* | | *9 828 00* | |

The adjustment for uncollectible accounts expense planned on the work sheet is recorded as an adjusting entry in the general journal. The adjusting entry is then posted to the general ledger.

The adjusting entry impacts two of the three accounts related to accounts receivable. After the adjustment, Allowance for Uncollectible Accounts has a credit balance of $10,148.00. The balance of this contra account is an estimate of outstanding accounts receivable that will become uncollectible during the next fiscal period.

The debit balance of Uncollectible Accounts Expense, $9,828.00, is the estimated uncollectible accounts resulting from sales on account during the current fiscal year.

The adjusting entry does *not* impact the balance of Accounts Receivable. Accounts Receivable has a debit balance of $72,458.00 before and after the adjusting entry is posted.

The book value of accounts receivable on December 31, $62,310.00, is an estimate of the amount of accounts receivable Winning Edge expects to collect during the next fiscal year.

| Accounts Receivable | – | Balance of Allowance for Uncollectible Accounts | = | Book Value of Accounts Receivable |
|---|---|---|---|---|
| $72,458.00 | – | $10,148.00 | = | $62,310.00 |

## TERMS REVIEW

uncollectible accounts

allowance method of recording losses from uncollectible accounts

book value

book value of accounts receivable

## AUDIT YOUR UNDERSTANDING

1. Why is an uncollectible account recorded as an expense rather than a reduction in revenue?
2. When do businesses normally estimate the amount of their uncollectible accounts expense?
3. What two objectives will be accomplished by recording an estimated amount of uncollectible accounts expense?
4. Why is Allowance for Uncollectible Accounts called a contra account?
5. How is the book value of accounts receivable calculated?

## WORK TOGETHER

**Estimating and journalizing entries for uncollectible accounts expense**

A general journal, work sheet, and selected general ledger accounts for Velson Company are given in the *Working Papers.* Your instructor will guide you through the following examples.

6. Velson Company estimates uncollectible accounts expense as 0.3% of its total sales on account. During the current year, Velson had credit sales of $2,152,000.00. The balance in Allowance for Uncollectible Accounts before adjustment is a $853.00 credit. As of December 31, record the uncollectible accounts expense adjustment on a work sheet.
7. Journalize the adjusting entry on page 13 of a general journal.
8. Post the adjusting entry to the general ledger.

## ON YOUR OWN

**Estimating and journalizing entries for uncollectible accounts expense**

A general journal, work sheet, and selected general ledger accounts for McCain Company are given in the *Working Papers.* Work independently to complete these problems.

9. The McCain Company estimates uncollectible accounts expense as 0.8% of its total sales on account. During the current year, McCain had credit sales of $876,000.00. The balance in Allowance for Uncollectible Accounts before adjustment is a $145.00 credit. As of December 31, record the uncollectible accounts expense adjustment on a work sheet.
10. Journalize the adjusting entry on page 18 of a general journal.
11. Post the adjusting entry to the general ledger.

# 20-2 Writing Off and Collecting Uncollectible Accounts Receivable

## JOURNALIZING WRITING OFF AN UNCOLLECTIBLE ACCOUNT RECEIVABLE

1. Debit

GENERAL JOURNAL PAGE 18

| | DATE | | ACCOUNT TITLE | DOC. NO. | POST. REF. | DEBIT | CREDIT | |
|---|---|---|---|---|---|---|---|---|
| 8 | | 3 | Allow. for Uncollectible Accts. | M2 | | 462 00 | | 8 |
| 9 | | | Accts. Rec./Ryan Recreation | | | | 462 00 | 9 |
| 10 | | | | | | | | 10 |

2. Credit and Customer's Name

When a customer account is determined to be uncollectible, a journal entry is made to cancel the uncollectible account. This entry cancels the uncollectible amount from the general ledger account Accounts Receivable as well as the customer account in the accounts receivable subsidiary ledger. Canceling the balance of a customer account because the customer does not pay is called **writing off an account.**

After months of unsuccessful collection efforts, Winning Edge decides that the past-due account of Ryan Recreation is uncollectible.

***January 3. Wrote off Ryan Recreation's past-due account as uncollectible, $462.00. Memorandum No. 2.***

Because the account of Ryan Recreation has been determined to be uncollectible, the $462.00 is now an *actual* uncollectible amount. Therefore, the amount of the uncollectible account is deducted from the allowance account.

Accounts Receivable is credited to reduce the balance due from customers. Ryan Recreation's account is also credited to cancel the debit balance of the account. Ryan Recreation's account is written off.

The book value of accounts receivable is the same both before and after writing off an uncollectible account. This is true because the same amount is deducted from the accounts receivable and the allowance accounts.

GENERAL LEDGER

Allowance for Uncollectible Accounts

| | | | |
|---|---|---|---|
| Jan. 3 | 462.00 | Bal. | 10,148.00 |
| | | *(New Bal.* | *9,686.00)* |

Accounts Receivable

| | | | |
|---|---|---|---|
| Bal. | 72,458.00 | Jan. 3 | 462.00 |
| *(New Bal.* | *71,996.00)* | | |

ACCOUNTS RECEIVABLE LEDGER

Ryan Recreation

| | | | |
|---|---|---|---|
| Bal. | 462.00 | Jan. 3 | 462.00 |
| *(New Bal.* | *zero)* | | |

| | Before Account Written Off | After Account Written Off |
|---|---|---|
| Accounts Receivable | $ 72,458.00 | $ 71,996.00 |
| Allowance for Uncollectible Accounts | −10,148.00 | −9,686.00 |
| Book Value | $ 62,310.00 | $ 62,310.00 |

# POSTING AN ENTRY TO WRITE OFF AN UNCOLLECTIBLE ACCOUNT RECEIVABLE

GENERAL JOURNAL — PAGE 18

| | DATE | | ACCOUNT TITLE | DOC. NO. | POST. REF. | DEBIT | CREDIT | |
|---|---|---|---|---|---|---|---|---|
| 8 | | 3 | Allow. for Uncollectible Accts. | M2 | 1130 | 462 00 | | 8 |
| 9 | | | Accts. Rec./Ryan Recreation | | 1125/180 | | 462 00 | 9 |
| 10 | | | | | | | | 10 |

ACCOUNT Accounts Receivable — ACCOUNT NO. 1125

| DATE | | ITEM | POST. REF. | DEBIT | CREDIT | BALANCE DEBIT | BALANCE CREDIT |
|---|---|---|---|---|---|---|---|
| | 31 | | CR49 | | 62716 00 | 72458 00 | |
| 20X2 Jan. | 3 | | G18 | | 462 00 | 71996 00 | |

ACCOUNT Allowance for Uncollectible Accounts — ACCOUNT NO. 1130

| DATE | | ITEM | POST. REF. | DEBIT | CREDIT | BALANCE DEBIT | BALANCE CREDIT |
|---|---|---|---|---|---|---|---|
| | 31 | | G15 | | 9828 00 | | 10148 00 |
| 20X2 Jan. | 3 | | G18 | 462 00 | | | 9686 00 |

CUSTOMER Ryan Recreation — CUSTOMER NO. 180

| DATE | | ITEM | POST. REF. | DEBIT | CREDIT | DEBIT BALANCE |
|---|---|---|---|---|---|---|
| 20X1 Apr. | 6 | | S12 | 462 00 | | 462 00 |
| 20X2 Jan. | 3 | Written off | G18 | | 462 00 | — |

**1.** Post debit amount to general ledger.

**2.** Post credit amount to general ledger.

**3.** Post credit amount to customer account.

**4.** Write *Written off* in the customer account.

The journal entry to write off an uncollectible account affects the two general ledger accounts, Accounts Receivable and Allowance for Uncollectible Accounts, and the customer account. The words *Written off* are written in the Item column of the customer account to show the full credit history for the customer.

**STEPS**

**Posting an entry to write off an uncollectible account receivable**

1. Post the debit, *$462.00,* to Allowance for Uncollectible Accounts in the general ledger.
2. Post the credit, *$462.00,* to Accounts Receivable in the general ledger.
3. Post the credit, *$462.00,* to the customer account, Ryan Recreation, in the accounts receivable ledger.
4. Write the words *Written off* in the Item column of the customer account.

## REOPENING AN ACCOUNT PREVIOUSLY WRITTEN OFF

**1.** Debit and Customer's Name

GENERAL JOURNAL — PAGE 18

| | DATE | | ACCOUNT TITLE | DOC. NO. | POST. REF. | DEBIT | CREDIT | |
|---|---|---|---|---|---|---|---|---|
| 16 | | 29 | *Accts. Receivable/Ryan Recreation* | *M3* | / | *462 00* | | 16 |
| 17 | | | *Allow. for Uncollectible Accts.* | | | | *462 00* | 17 |
| 18 | | | | | | | | 18 |
| 19 | | | | | | | | 19 |
| 20 | | | | | | | | 20 |
| 21 | | | | | | | | 21 |
| 22 | | | | | | | | 22 |

**2.** Credit

A business writes off a specific account receivable after determining that the account probably will not be collected. Occasionally, after an account has been written off, the customer pays the delinquent account. Several accounts must be changed to recognize payment of a written-off account receivable.

***January 29. Received cash in full payment of Ryan Recreation's account, previously written off as uncollectible, $462.00. Memorandum No. 3 and Receipt No. 8.***

GENERAL LEDGER

Accounts Receivable

| | | | |
|---|---|---|---|
| Bal. | 72,458.00 | Jan. 3 | 462.00 |
| Jan. 29 | 462.00 | | |

Allowance for Uncollectible Accounts

| | | | |
|---|---|---|---|
| Jan. 3 | 462.00 | Bal. | 10,148.00 |
| | | Jan. 29 | 462.00 |

ACCOUNTS RECEIVABLE LEDGER

Ryan Recreation

| | | | |
|---|---|---|---|
| Bal. | 462.00 | Jan. 3 | 462.00 |
| Jan. 29 | 462.00 | | |
| *(New Bal.* | *462.00)* | | |

Several accounts must be changed to show that Ryan Recreation did pay its account. The accounts also should be changed to show a complete credit history of Ryan Recreation's dealings with Winning Edge.

Two journal entries are recorded for the collection of a written-off account receivable: (1) a general journal entry to reopen the customer account and (2) a cash receipts journal entry to record the cash received on account.

To show an accurate credit history, Ryan Recreation's account is reopened.

Accounts Receivable is debited for $462.00 to replace the amount previously written off in the general ledger account. Allowance for Uncollectible Accounts is credited for $462.00 to replace the amount that was removed when Ryan Recreation's account was previously written off. Also, Ryan Recreation's account in the accounts receivable ledger is debited for $462.00. This entry to reopen the account is the exact reverse of the entry to write off Ryan Recreation's account.

### STEPS: Reopening an account previously written off

1. Enter a debit, *$462.00,* to Accounts Receivable. Place a diagonal line after the account title and enter the customer's name, *Ryan Recreation.* Place a diagonal line in the Post. Ref. column.
2. Enter a credit, *$462.00,* to Allowance for Uncollectible Accounts.

## RECORDING CASH RECEIVED FOR AN ACCOUNT PREVIOUSLY WRITTEN OFF

**CASH RECEIPTS JOURNAL** PAGE 51

| | DATE | ACCOUNT TITLE | DOC. NO. | POST. REF. | 1 GENERAL DEBIT | 2 GENERAL CREDIT | 3 ACCOUNTS RECEIVABLE CREDIT | 4 SALES CREDIT | 5 SALES TAX PAYABLE DEBIT | 6 SALES TAX PAYABLE CREDIT | 7 SALES DISCOUNT DEBIT | 8 CASH DEBIT | |
|---|---|---|---|---|---|---|---|---|---|---|---|---|---|
| 21 | 29 | Ryan Recreation | R8 | | | | 462 00 | | | | | 462 00 | 21 |
| 22 | | | | | | | | | | | | | 22 |

After the entry to reopen Ryan Recreation's account is recorded, an entry is made to record the cash received on Ryan Recreation's account.

***January 29. Received cash in full payment of Ryan Recreation's account, previously written off as uncollectible, $462.00. Memorandum No. 3 and Receipt No. 8.***

The entry in the cash receipts journal is the same as for any other collection of accounts receivable.

**GENERAL LEDGER**

Cash

| | | | |
|---|---|---|---|
| Jan. 29 | 462.00 | | |

Accounts Receivable

| | | | |
|---|---|---|---|
| Bal. | 72,458.00 | Jan. 3 | 462.00 |
| Jan. 29 | 462.00 | Jan. 29 | 462.00 |

**ACCOUNTS RECEIVABLE LEDGER**

Ryan Recreation

| | | | |
|---|---|---|---|
| Bal. | 462.00 | Jan. 3 | 462.00 |
| Jan. 29 | 462.00 | Jan. 29 | 462.00 |
| | | *(New Bal.* | *zero)* |

**LEGAL ISSUES IN ACCOUNTING**

### FORMING A CORPORATION

A corporation is a business organization that has the legal rights of a person. A corporation's legal rights exist separately from the legal rights of its owners. A person becomes an owner of a corporation by purchasing shares of stock. Thus, owners of corporations are called *stockholders.*

The corporate form of business organization offers the following advantages: (1) *Expanded resources.* By selling stock, the corporation has access to more capital than as a proprietorship or partnership. (2) *Limited liability.* Stockholders will not be held personally responsible for the company's liabilities. (3) *Ease of ownership transfer.* Ownership is transferred when a share of stock is sold. Selling stock does not affect the continuation of the corporation. (4) *Legal rights.* Because a corporation has the legal rights of a person, the corporation may buy, own, and sell property in its corporate name.

The disadvantages of corporations include: (1) *High organization cost.* A corporation is the most complex and expensive form of business to establish. (2) *Extensive government regulation.* Corporations must comply with numerous government regulations. (3) *Double taxation.* As separate legal entities, the earnings of corporations are subject to taxation. The profits distributed to stockholders also are subject to taxation as stockholders' personal income.

# POSTING ENTRIES FOR COLLECTING A WRITTEN-OFF ACCOUNT RECEIVABLE

GENERAL JOURNAL PAGE 18

| | DATE | | ACCOUNT TITLE | DOC. NO. | POST. REF. | DEBIT | CREDIT | |
|---|---|---|---|---|---|---|---|---|
| 16 | | 29 | Accts. Receivable/Ryan Recreation | M3 | 1125/180 | 462 00 | | 16 |
| 17 | | | Allow. for Uncollectible Accts. | | 1130 | | 462 00 | 17 |

ACCOUNT Accounts Receivable ACCOUNT NO. 1125

| DATE | | ITEM | POST. REF. | DEBIT | CREDIT | BALANCE DEBIT | BALANCE CREDIT |
|---|---|---|---|---|---|---|---|
| | 31 | | CR49 | | 62,716 00 | 72,458 00 | |
| 20X2 Jan. | 3 | | G18 | | 462 00 | 71,996 00 | |
| | 29 | | G18 | 462 00 | | 72,458 00 | |

**1.** Post general journal entry to general ledger.

ACCOUNT Allowance for Uncollectible Accounts ACCOUNT NO. 1130

| DATE | | ITEM | POST. REF. | DEBIT | CREDIT | BALANCE DEBIT | BALANCE CREDIT |
|---|---|---|---|---|---|---|---|
| | 31 | | G15 | | 9,828 00 | | 10,148 00 |
| 20X2 Jan. | 3 | | G18 | 462 00 | | | 9,686 00 |
| | 29 | | G18 | | 462 00 | | 10,148 00 |

**2.** Post general journal entry to customer account.

**3.** Write *Reopen account* in customer account.

CUSTOMER Ryan Recreation CUSTOMER NO. 180

| DATE | | ITEM | POST. REF. | DEBIT | CREDIT | DEBIT BALANCE |
|---|---|---|---|---|---|---|
| 20X1 Apr. | 6 | | S12 | 462 00 | | 462 00 |
| 20X2 Jan. | 3 | Written off | G18 | | 462 00 | — |
| | 29 | Reopen account | G18 | 462 00 | | 462 00 |
| | 29 | | CR51 | | 462 00 | — |

**4.** Post cash receipts journal entry to customer account.

CASH RECEIPTS JOURNAL PAGE 51

| | DATE | | ACCOUNT TITLE | DOC. NO. | POST. REF. | 1 GENERAL DEBIT | 2 GENERAL CREDIT | 3 ACCOUNTS RECEIVABLE CREDIT | 4 SALES CREDIT | 5 SALES TAX PAYABLE DEBIT | 6 SALES TAX PAYABLE CREDIT | 7 SALES DISCOUNT DEBIT | 8 CASH DEBIT | |
|---|---|---|---|---|---|---|---|---|---|---|---|---|---|---|
| 21 | | 29 | Ryan Recreation | R8 | | | | 462 00 | | | | | 462 00 | 21 |

## STEPS: Posting entries for collecting a written-off account receivable

1. Post the general journal entry to the general ledger.
2. Post the debit portion of the general journal entry to the customer account.
3. Write the words *Reopen account* in the Item column of the customer account.
4. Post the cash receipts journal entry to the customer account.

## TERM REVIEW

writing off an account

## AUDIT YOUR UNDERSTANDING

1. Why is Allowance for Uncollectible Accounts debited when a customer account is written off?
2. Does the book value of accounts receivable differ before and after writing off an account? Explain.
3. Why is a customer account reopened when the account is paid after being previously written off?

## WORK TOGETHER

**Recording entries relating to uncollectible accounts receivable**

The journals and ledgers for Spartan Company are given in the *Working Papers.* Your instructor will guide you through the following examples.

4. The following transactions occurred during June of the current year. Journalize the transactions using page 6 of a general journal and page 9 of a cash receipts journal.

June 3. Wrote off Kelton Corporation's past-due account as uncollectible, $396.00. M14.
12. Wrote off Matlin Co.'s past-due account as uncollectible, $575.00. M18.
13. Received cash in full payment of Marris Inc.'s account, previously written off as uncollectible, $571.00. M19 and R134.
25. Wrote off Johnston, Inc.'s past-due account as uncollectible, $819.00. M23.
30. Received cash in full payment of Kelton Corporation's account, previously written off as uncollectible, $396.00. M27 and R152.

5. Post each entry to the customer accounts in the accounts receivable ledger.
6. Post general journal entries to the general ledger.

## ON YOUR OWN

**Recording entries relating to uncollectible accounts receivable**

The journals and ledgers for Potera Company are given in the *Working Papers.* Work independently to complete these problems.

7. The following transactions occurred during November of the current year. Journalize the transactions using page 11 of a general journal and page 15 of a cash receipts journal.

Nov. 5. Wrote off Angela White's past-due account as uncollectible, $159.00. M45.
8. Wrote off Peter Ewing's past-due account as uncollectible, $612.00. M47.
12. Received cash in full payment of Mike Novak's account, previously written off as uncollectible, $853.00. M51 and R313.
16. Wrote off Tim Haley's past-due account as uncollectible, $238.00. M58.
29. Received cash in full payment of Peter Ewing's account, previously written off as uncollectible, $612.00. M61 and R345.

8. Post each entry to the customer accounts in the accounts receivable ledger.
9. Post general journal entries to the general ledger.

# CHAPTER 20 SUMMARY

*Enrichment Activity*

**Types of Businesses**

*The advantages and disadvantages of a corporation are described on page 534. What are the advantages and disadvantages of the corporate form of business organization over partnerships and proprietorships?*

After completing this chapter, you can

1. Define accounting terms related to uncollectible accounts.
2. Identify accounting concepts and practices related to uncollectible accounts.
3. Calculate, journalize, and post estimated uncollectible accounts expense.
4. Journalize and post entries related to writing off and collecting uncollectible accounts receivable.

## EXPLORE ACCOUNTING

### ACCOUNTING ESTIMATES USE INTERESTING ASSUMPTIONS

Accountants use many accounting estimates to adjust the historical cost of certain transactions to better reflect the company's financial condition.

One of the most interesting accounting estimates concerns a payroll-related expense known as post retirement benefits other than pensions. Some companies offer their employees free services, such as health care, during their retirement. For many years companies have expensed these costs when the services were actually provided and paid for in cash. Accounting rules recently changed to require that these costs be recognized as an expense over the employee's years of work. The promise of free health care during retirement is part of the total benefits that the company provides an employee in exchange for the employee's services.

For example, Hass Industries has promised free health care to its retired employees and their family members under 21 years of age. Bob Atkinson is expected to work for Hass Industries for 30 years. Health care costs for Bob, his wife, and any future children during his retirement are currently estimated to be $30,000. Rather than expense the $30,000 when the bills are paid during Bob's retirement, the new accounting rule requires that the $30,000 be expensed over Bob's 30 years of service. Therefore, $1,000 will be expensed each year.

To estimate the projected benefit, assumptions must be made regarding the following items: (1) percentage annual growth rate in health care costs, (2) life expectancy, (3) retirement age, (4) number of children, and (5) interest costs.

Management's assumptions can dramatically impact accounting estimates. Companies that prepare public financial statements have independent auditors examine the assumptions used to compute accounting estimates to assure that these assumptions are reasonable.

**Research:** Research the annual growth rate of health care costs. Do you believe this growth rate will continue? Identify factors that might cause further increases or decreases in growth rate.

## 20-1 APPLICATION PROBLEM
### Estimating and journalizing entries for uncollectible accounts expense

A general journal, work sheet, and selected general ledger accounts for Kellogg, Inc., are given in the *Working Papers.*

***Instructions:***

1. Kellogg, Inc., estimates uncollectible accounts expense as 1.0% of its total sales on account. During the current year, Kellogg had credit sales of $3,426,000.00. The balance in Allowance for Uncollectible Accounts before adjustment is a $534.00 credit. Record the uncollectible accounts expense adjustment on a work sheet.
2. Journalize the adjusting entry on page 25 of a general journal.
3. Post the adjusting entry to the general ledger.

## 20-2 APPLICATION PROBLEM
### Recording entries related to uncollectible accounts receivable

The journals and ledgers for Waldron Company are given in the *Working Papers.*

***Instructions:***

1. The following transactions related to accounts receivable occurred during July of the current year. Journalize the transactions using page 7 of a general journal and page 9 of a cash receipts journal.

***Transactions:***

July 4. Wrote off Annie Jamison's past-due account as uncollectible, $102.00. M56.
6. Received cash in full payment of David Dowdle's account, previously written off as uncollectible, $157.00. M58 and R214.
13. Wrote off Jeanne Lewis's past-due account as uncollectible, $97.00. M61.
18. Wrote off Rebecca Snow's past-due account as uncollectible, $310.00. M67.
28. Received cash in full payment of Annie Jamison's account, previously written off as uncollectible, $102.00. M71 and R226.

2. Post each entry to the customer accounts in the accounts receivable ledger.
3. Post each entry in the general journal to the general ledger.

## 20-3 APPLICATION PROBLEM
### Recording entries related to uncollectible accounts receivable

The journals and ledgers for Wister Co. are given in the *Working Papers.*

***Instructions:***

1. The following transactions related to accounts receivable occurred during February of the current year. Journalize the transactions using page 4 of a general journal and page 2 of a cash receipts journal.

***Transactions:***

Feb. 3. Received a $1,458.00 check from Bearden Co. in full payment of its account. The account was written off in the previous month based on a newspaper story that indicated the company was about to close. M24 and R134.
7. Michelle Pearce, controller of Hampton Industries, just called stating that the company had serious cash flow problems and would not be able to pay its $2,584.00 account balance. M25.
10. Received a letter from Rankin Co.'s legal counsel stating that the company was in the process of filing bankruptcy. The letter gave little hope that Wister would collect Rankin's $948.00 account. M28.

Feb. 12. Received a check from Camden Enterprises in full payment of its $1,784.00 account. The account was written off in January after months of efforts to collect the account. M31 and R142.

21. A letter from Wilmont Co.'s receiving department supervisor stated that Wilmont refuses to pay for a prior year shipment of product for $548.00. The supervisor contends that the products were spoiled on arrival and were discarded. M34.

27. Received a letter and check in the mail from Michelle Pearce of Hampton Industries. Two weeks ago the company was purchased by another company and, therefore, has access to cash to pay its debt. M35 and R159.

2. Post each entry to the customer accounts in the accounts receivable ledger.
3. Post each entry in the general journal to the general ledger.

## 20-4 MASTERY PROBLEM
### Recording entries for uncollectible accounts

The accounts receivable and general ledger accounts for Lepanto Industries are given in the *Working Papers*. The following transactions relating to uncollectible accounts receivable occurred during the final quarter of the current fiscal year.

***Instructions:***

1. Journalize the following transactions completed during October using page 10 of a general journal. Post the transactions to the customer accounts and general ledger accounts.

***Transactions:***

Oct. 7. Wrote off Kingston Corporation's past-due account as uncollectible, $247.60. M202.

18. Wrote off Gentry Corporation's past-due account as uncollectible, $482.50. M206.

2. Journalize the following transactions completed during November using page 11 of a general journal and page 11 of a cash receipts journal. Prove the cash receipts journal. Post the transactions to the customer accounts and general ledger accounts.

***Transactions:***

Nov. 8. Wrote off Burrell Company's past-due account as uncollectible, $714.15. M219.

17. Received cash in full payment of Kingston Corporation's account, previously written off as uncollectible, $247.60. M223 and R461.

22. Received cash in full payment of Peterson, Inc.'s account, previously written off as uncollectible, $523.30. M225 and R476.

3. Journalize the following transactions for December. Use page 12 of a general journal and page 12 of a cash receipts journal. Prove the cash receipts journal. Post the transactions to the customer accounts and general ledger accounts.

***Transactions:***

Dec. 3. Wrote off Fiber-Tech's past-due account as uncollectible, $829.35. M226.

9. Received cash in full payment of Burrell Company's account, previously written off as uncollectible, $714.15. M229 and R514.

28. Received cash in full payment of Gentry Corporation's account, previou
uncollectible, $482.50. M235 and R547.

4. Journalize the December 31 adjusting entry for estimated uncollectible accoun
year. Use page 13 of the general journal. Uncollectible accounts expense is es
of total sales on account. Total sales on account for the year were $1,051,080
transaction to the general ledger accounts.

## 20-5 CHALLENGE PROBLEM
### Recording entries for uncollectible accounts

Information from the accounting records of Rosedale Company concerning uncollectible accounts during the past five years follows (presented in thousands of dollars).

| | 20X1 | 20X2 | 20X3 | 20X4 | 20X5 |
|---|---|---|---|---|---|
| Sales on account | $575 | $700 | $850 | $1,050 | $1,200 |
| Ending Accounts Receivable | 50 | 60 | 80 | 90 | 100 |
| Uncollectible Accounts Expense | 8 | 8 | 15 | 15 | 15 |
| Ending Allowance for Uncollectible Accounts | 5 | 1 | 4 | 3 | 1 |
| Accounts written off | 10 | 13 | 14 | 18 | 19 |
| Accounts collected after being written off | 1 | 1 | 2 | 2 | 2 |

The controller of the company has asked you to evaluate the prior annual adjustments to Allowance for Uncollectible Accounts. If the company expects to have sales of $1,400,000.00 next year, what amount would you suggest be expensed to Uncollectible Accounts Expense? Support your answer.

**INTERNET ACTIVITY**

Point your browser to

**http://accounting.swpco.com**

Choose **First-Year Course**, choose **Activities**, and complete the activity for Chapter 20.

## Applied Communication

For many years the accounting staff at St. Charles Furniture have written off uncollectible accounts receivable by debiting Uncollectible Accounts Expense and crediting Accounts Receivable. Despite relatively constant sales and collections on account, the annual amount of Uncollectible Accounts Expense has fluctuated between $5,000.00 and $90,000.00 during the past six years. Management admits that the amount of accounts written off depends largely on the time the managers have devoted to evaluating accounts receivable for possible collection problems.

**Instructions:** Prepare a memorandum to Duane Smith, president of St. Charles Furniture, explaining the correct way to account for uncollectible accounts receivable. The memorandum should persuade him to implement a change from the current accounting procedure.

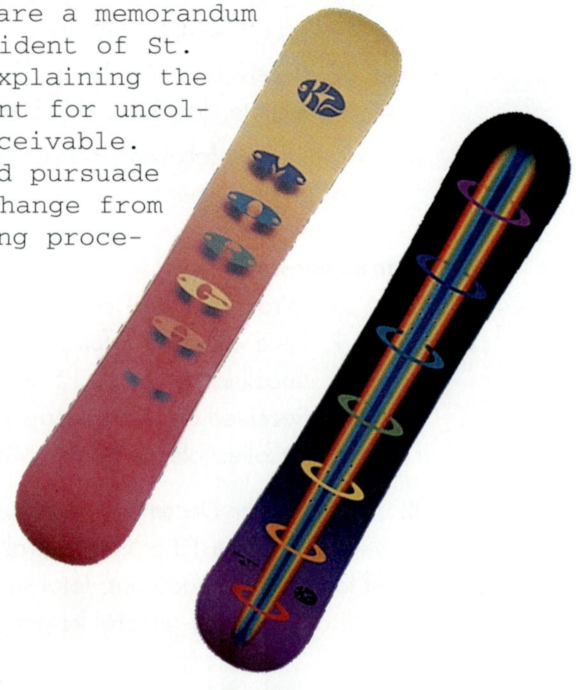

# Cases for Critical Thinking

**Case 1** Crain Corporation has always assumed that an account receivable is good until the account is proven to be uncollectible. When an account proves to be uncollectible, the credit manager notifies the accounting clerk to write off the account. The accounting clerk then debits Uncollectible Accounts Expense and credits Accounts Receivable. Recently the company's new accountant, Dawn Mitchner, suggested that the method be changed for recording uncollectible accounts expense. Ms. Mitchner recommended that the company estimate uncollectible accounts expense based on a percentage of total sales on account. Ms. Mitchner stated that the change would provide more accurate information on the income statement and balance sheet. Do you agree with Ms. Mitchner that her recommended method would provide more accurate information? Explain.

**Case 2** Tupelo Industries credits Accounts Receivable for the amount of estimated uncollectible accounts expense at the end of each fiscal period. Bluff Company credits Allowance for Uncollectible Accounts for the amount of estimated uncollectible accounts expense at the end of each fiscal period. Which company is using the better method? Why?

**Case 3** Some businesses have a policy of accepting only cash sales. Depending on economic conditions or the time of year, many potential customers may not be able to pay with currency, check, or debit card. Businesses with cash-only policies will lose those potential sales. As has been discussed in previous chapters, other businesses encourage more sales by selling on account to customers with approved credit. The key decision is defining what is *approved credit*. Employees responsible for meeting the sales goals of a business would have one set of standards for approving credit. Employees responsible for maintaining merchandise inventory and filling orders would have another set of standards for approving credit. What role, if any, do you believe that accounting employees should play in setting a company's standards for approving credit? What contributions can accounting employees make to discussions about credit standards?

# AUTOMATED ACCOUNTING

## AUTOMATED ENTRIES FOR UNCOLLECTIBLE ACCOUNTS AND WRITE-OFFS

Many businesses allow sales on account. Before granting credit, businesses investigate the creditworthiness of the customer. These investigations minimize the amount of losses from uncollectible accounts. Businesses maintain a separate customer file. The total owed by all customers maintained in a customer file is summarized in a single general ledger asset account called Accounts Receivable. If the business fails to collect from a customer, the business loses part of the asset Accounts Receivable. This loss is a regular expense of doing business.

### Recording Estimated Uncollectible Accounts

In order to properly match revenues with expenses at the end of the fiscal period, each business that sells on account must estimate the amount of current Accounts Receivable that will not be collected during the next period. A business may use a percentage of sales on account to make the estimate. The estimated amount is recorded in a contra asset account, Allowance for Uncollectible Accounts. An adjusting entry is made for the estimated amount.

To record the adjusting entry:

1. Click the Journal toolbar button.
2. Click the General Journal tab.
3. Enter the transaction date and press Tab.
4. Enter Adj. Ent. in the Refer. text box and press Tab.
5. Enter the account numbers for Uncollectible Account Expense and Allowance for Uncollectible Accounts, and the estimated amount of the loss. Press the Tab key as needed.
6. Click the Post button.

### Writing Off an Uncollectible Account Receivable

When a specific account is determined to be uncollectible, the balance of the account must be removed. The debit is made to Allowance for Uncollectible Accounts. The total of Accounts Receivable and the customer's account in the accounts receivable ledger are reduced by a credit.

1. Click the Journal toolbar button.
2. Click the General Journal tab.
3. Enter the transaction date and press Tab.
4. Enter the source document number in the Refer. text box and press Tab. A memorandum is generally prepared as the source document.
5. Enter the account number for Allowance for Uncollectible Accounts, and the debit amount.
6. Enter the account number for Accounts Receivable and the credit amount.
7. Tab to the Customer column and select the customer from the drop-down list.
8. Click the Post button.

### Collecting a Previously Written-Off Account Receivable

When a previously written-off account is collected, the customer account is first reinstated. Once the account is reinstated, the cash receipt is recorded in the cash receipts journal.

To reinstate the account:

1. Click the Journal toolbar button.
2. Click the General Journal tab.
3. Enter the transaction date and press Tab.
4. Enter the source document number in the Refer. text box and press Tab. A memorandum is generally prepared as the source document.
5. Enter the account number for Accounts Receivable and the debit amount.
6. Tab to the Customer column and select the customer from the drop-down list.
7. Tab to the next line and enter the account number for Allowance for Uncollectible Accounts and the credit amount.
8. Click the Post button.

# AUTOMATED ACCOUNTING

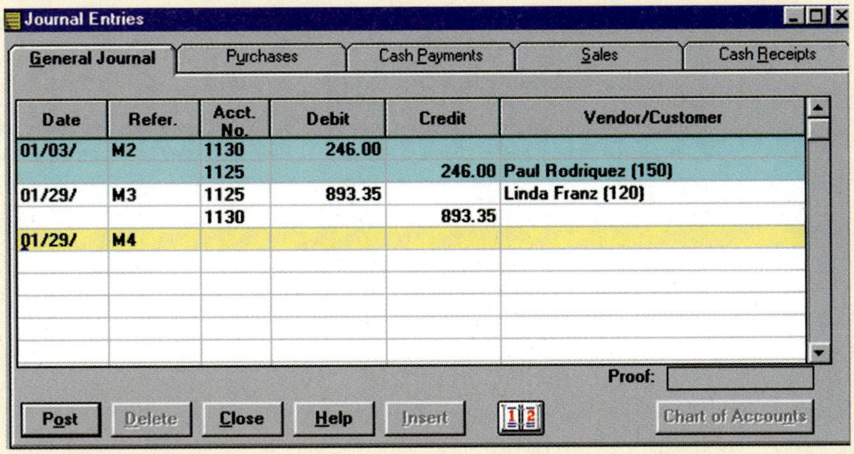


To record the cash receipt:

1. Click the Journal toolbar button.
2. Click the Cash Receipts tab.
3. Enter the transaction date and press Tab.
4. Enter the source document number in the Refer. text box and press Tab to move to the A.R. Credit text box.
5. Enter the Accounts Receivable credit amount. The debit to Cash will be automatically calculated. Press Tab to move to the Customer text box.
6. Choose the customer name from the Customer drop-down list.
7. Click the Post button.

**AUTOMATING APPLICATION PROBLEM 20-3: Recording entries related to uncollectible accounts expense**

**Instructions:**

1. Load *Automated Accounting 7.0* or higher software.
2. Select database F20-1 from the appropriate directory/folder.
3. Select File from the menu bar and choose the Save As menu command. Key the path to the drive and directory that contains your data files. Save the database with a file name of XXX201 (where XXX are your initials).
4. Access Problem Instructions through the Help menu. Read the Problem Instructions screen.
5. Key the data listed on pages 538–539.
6. Exit the *Automated Accounting* software.

**AUTOMATING MASTERY PROBLEM 20-4: Recording entries for uncollectible accounts**

**Instructions:**

1. Load *Automated Accounting 7.0* or higher software.
2. Select database F20-2 from the appropriate directory/folder.
3. Select File from the menu bar and choose the Save As menu command. Key the path to the drive and directory that contains your data files. Save the database with a file name of XXX202 (where XXX are your initials).
4. Access Problem Instructions through the Help menu. Read the Problem Instructions screen.
5. Key the data listed on page 539.
6. Exit the *Automated Accounting* software.

# 21 Accounting for Plant Assets and Depreciation

**TERMS PREVIEW**

current assets
plant assets
real property
personal property
assessed value
depreciation expense
estimated salvage value
straight-line method of depreciation
accumulated depreciation
book value of a plant asset
plant asset record
gain on plant assets
loss on plant assets
declining-balance method of depreciation

**AFTER STUDYING CHAPTER 21, YOU WILL BE ABLE TO:**

1. Define accounting terms related to plant assets, depreciation, and property tax expense.
2. Identify accounting concepts and practices related to accounting for plant assets, depreciation, and property tax expense.
3. Record the buying of a plant asset and the paying of property tax.
4. Calculate depreciation expense and book value using the straight-line method of depreciation.
5. Prepare plant asset records and journalize annual depreciation expense.
6. Record entries related to disposing of plant assets.
7. Calculate depreciation expense using the double declining-balance method of depreciation.

## CATEGORIES OF ASSETS

Most businesses use two broad categories of assets in their operations. Cash and other assets expected to be exchanged for cash or consumed within a year are called **current assets.** Assets that will be used for a number of years in the operation of a business are called **plant assets.** Some of the more significant current assets used by Winning Edge are cash, accounts receivable, merchandise inventory, supplies, and prepaid insurance. Some of Winning Edge's plant assets are computers, cash registers, sales display cases, and furniture. Winning Edge's complete list of current and plant assets is in the chart of accounts on page 451.

Businesses may have three major types of plant assets—equipment, buildings, and land. Winning Edge owns equipment that it uses to operate the business. However, the company rents the building and the land where the business is located. Therefore, Winning Edge has accounts for equipment, which is the only type of plant asset it owns. To provide more detailed financial information, Winning Edge records its equipment in two different equipment accounts—Office Equipment and Store Equipment. *(CONCEPT: Adequate Disclosure)*

# ACCOUNTING IN YOUR CAREER

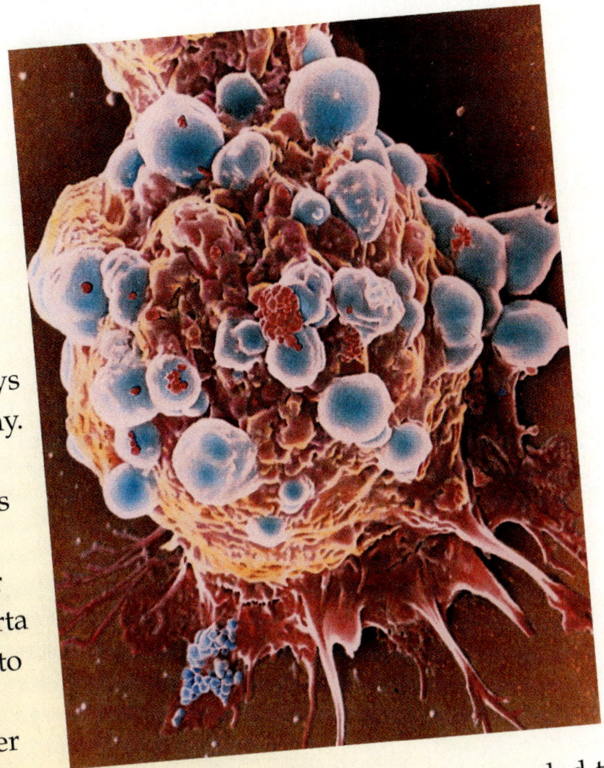

## SECRETS OF THE COMPETITION

Keith Birchhill is a senior accountant at GenSys Inc., a medical and scientific research company. Keith prepares the company's financial statements and federal tax returns, and supervises a team of accounting clerks. He is also well known in the company as an able researcher on the Internet. So it is not unusual that Marta Boswell, Chief Executive Officer, has asked to see him regarding a new research project.

Marta is interested in knowing whether any competing research firms have the electron microscopes and other expensive laboratory equipment that would be needed to pursue a new line of research on cancer treatment. She says that only the newest models of most lab equipment have the capacity needed for this research. At the end of her presentation, she emphasizes that only publicly available information should be used.

"Don't worry, Marta," Keith replies after some thought. "I think I can get the information right off the published financial statements. So you won't have to be concerned with ethical issues."

"That's amazing, Keith," Marta says. "Financial statements are included in annual reports that are public information. But I've read all those financial statements, and I don't remember seeing anything like what I'm asking you for."

"You just have to know where to look, Marta. That's what you pay me for."

### Critical Thinking:

1. The balance sheet of GenSys's major competitor, MedTech, Inc., shows: Laboratory Equipment, $5,500,000; Accumulated Depreciation—Laboratory Equipment, $4,000,000. GenSys's balance sheet reports: Laboratory Equipment, $7,500,000, and Accumulated Depreciation—Laboratory Equipment, $2,500,000. What percentage of lab equipment is undepreciated to date for the two companies? Notes to the financial statements report that the straight-line depreciation method is used for both companies.
2. What can Keith Birchhill conclude about the newness of the two companies' lab equipment?

# 21-1 Buying Plant Assets and Paying Property Tax

## RECORDING THE BUYING OF A PLANT ASSET

CASH PAYMENTS JOURNAL — PAGE 1

| | DATE | ACCOUNT TITLE | CK. NO. | POST. REF. | 1 GENERAL DEBIT | 2 GENERAL CREDIT | 3 ACCOUNTS PAYABLE DEBIT | 4 PURCHASES DISCOUNT CREDIT | 5 CASH CREDIT | |
|---|---|---|---|---|---|---|---|---|---|---|
| 4 | 2 | *Store Equipment* | 7 | 1215 | 1 250 00 | | | | 1 250 00 | 4 |
| 5 | | | | | | | | | | 5 |

1. Account Title
2. Cost of the Plant Asset
3. Cash Paid
4. Post

ACCOUNT *Store Equipment* — ACCOUNT NO. *1215*

| DATE | | ITEM | POST. REF. | DEBIT | CREDIT | BALANCE DEBIT | BALANCE CREDIT |
|---|---|---|---|---|---|---|---|
| 20-- Jan. | 1 | *Balance* | ✓ | | | 43 760 00 | |
| | 2 | | CP1 | 1 250 00 | | 45 010 00 | |

Procedures for recording the buying of a plant asset are similar to procedures for recording the buying of current assets such as supplies. The amount paid for a plant asset is debited to a plant asset account with a title such as Store Equipment. *(CONCEPT: Historical Cost)*

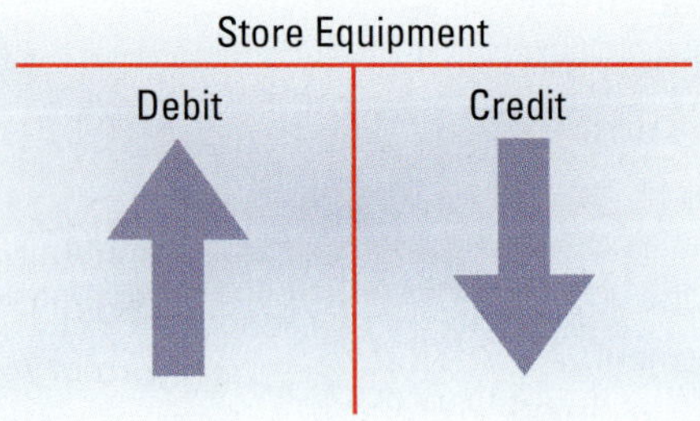


***January 2, 20X1. Paid cash for a display case, $1,250.00. Check No. 7.***

The entry in the General Debit column of the cash payments journal is posted individually to the account named in the Account Title column.

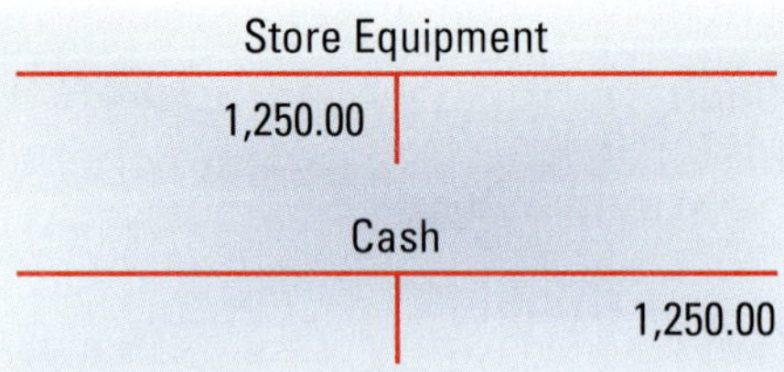


**STEPS**

### Journalizing and posting the buying of a plant asset

1. Write the plant asset account, *Store Equipment,* in the Account Title column of the cash payments journal.
2. Enter the cost of the plant asset, *$1,250.00,* in the General Debit column.
3. Enter the same amount, *$1,250.00,* in the Cash Credit column.
4. Post the entry in the General Debit column to the general ledger.

## CALCULATING AND PAYING PROPERTY TAX

CASH PAYMENTS JOURNAL — PAGE 3

| | DATE | | ACCOUNT TITLE | CK. NO. | POST. REF. | 1 GENERAL DEBIT | 2 GENERAL CREDIT | 3 ACCOUNTS PAYABLE DEBIT | 4 PURCHASES DISCOUNT CREDIT | 5 CASH CREDIT |
|---|---|---|---|---|---|---|---|---|---|---|
| 1 | 20-- Feb | 1 | Property Tax Expense | 187 | | 840 00 | | | | 840 00 |
| 2 | | | | | | | | | | |

For tax purposes, state and federal governments define two kinds of property—real and personal. Land and anything attached to the land is called **real property.** Real property is sometimes referred to as real estate. All property not classified as real property is called **personal property.** For tax purposes, these definitions apply whether the property is owned by a business or an individual.

The value of an asset determined by tax authorities for the purpose of calculating taxes is called the **assessed value.** Assessed value is usually based on the judgment of persons referred to as assessors. Assessors are elected by citizens or are specially trained employees of a governmental unit.

Most governmental units with taxing power have a tax based on the value of real property. The real property tax is used on buildings and land. Some governmental units also tax personal property such as cars, boats, trailers, and airplanes.

A governmental taxing unit determines a tax rate to use in calculating taxes. The tax rate is multiplied by an asset's *assessed value,* not the value recorded on a business's records.

Harrison Manufacturing's plant assets have been assessed for a total of $70,000.00. The city tax rate is 1.2%.

| Assessed Value | × | Tax Rate | = | Annual Property Tax |
|---|---|---|---|---|
| $70,000.00 | × | 1.2% | = | $840.00 |

### Paying Property Tax on Plant Assets

***February 1. Harrison Manufacturing paid cash for property tax, $840.00. Check No. 187.***

Payment of property taxes is necessary if a firm is to continue in business. Therefore, Harrison Manufacturing classifies property tax as an operating expense.

| Property Tax Expense | |
|---|---|
| 840.00 | |

| Cash | |
|---|---|
| | 840.00 |

**FYI**

*The assessed value of an asset may not be the same as the value on the business's or individual's records. The assessed value is assigned to an asset for tax purposes only. Often the assessed value is only a part of the true value of the asset.*

## TERMS REVIEW

current assets
plant assets
real property
personal property
assessed value

## AUDIT YOUR UNDERSTANDING

1. What are the two broad categories of assets used by most businesses in their operations?
2. What accounts are affected, and how, when cash is paid for office equipment?
3. What items are included in real property?
4. Who determines the assessed value of plant assets?

## WORK TOGETHER

### Journalizing buying plant assets and paying property tax

The cash payments journal and selected general ledger accounts for Bargain Center are given in the *Working Papers*. Your instructor will guide you through the following examples.

5. Journalize the following transactions completed during the current year. Use page 1 of a cash payments journal. The abbreviation for a check is C.

   ***Transactions:***

   Jan. 2. Paid cash for a computer printer, $900.00. C130.
   3. Paid cash for a cash register, $800.00. C132.
   Feb. 26. Paid property taxes on real property with an assessed value of $120,000.00. The tax rate in the city where the property is located is 1.5% of assessed value. C167.
   Apr. 2. Paid cash for a telephone system in the store, $1,500.00. C193.

6. Post the general columns of the cash payments journal.

## ON YOUR OWN

### Journalizing buying plant assets and paying property tax

The cash payments journal and selected general ledger accounts for Nelson Paint Store are given in the *Working Papers*. Work these problems independently.

7. Journalize the following transactions completed during the current year. Use page 1 of a cash payments journal. The abbreviation for a check is C.

   ***Transactions:***

   Jan. 3. Paid cash for a paint mixer, $500.00. C142.
   5. Paid cash for an office chair, $400.00. C145.
   Feb. 26. Paid property taxes on real property with an assessed value of $80,000.00. The tax rate in the city where the property is located is 3.0% of assessed value. C182.
   July 2. Paid cash for a filing cabinet, $260.00. C216.

8. Post the general columns of the cash payments journal.

# 21-2 Calculating Depreciation Expense

## DEPRECIATING PLANT ASSETS

A business buys plant assets to use in earning revenue. Winning Edge bought a new lighted display case to display sport watches. Winning Edge knows that the display case will be useful only for a limited period of time. After several years, most display cases become worn from use and no longer attractively display the products. Winning Edge replaces worn display cases with newer models. Thus, each display case has a limited useful life to the business.

In order to match revenue with the expenses used to earn the revenue, the cost of a plant asset should be expensed over the plant asset's useful life. A portion of a plant asset's cost is transferred to an expense account in each fiscal period that a plant asset is used to earn revenue. *(CONCEPT: Matching Expenses with Revenue)* The portion of a plant asset's cost that is transferred to an expense account in each fiscal period during a plant asset's useful life is called **depreciation expense.**

Three factors are considered in calculating the annual amount of depreciation expense for a plant asset.

1. *Original Cost.* The original cost of a plant asset includes all costs paid to make the asset usable to a business. These costs include the price of the asset, delivery costs, and any necessary installation costs.
2. *Estimated Salvage Value.* Generally, a business removes a plant asset from use and disposes of it when the asset is no longer usable. The amount that will be received for an asset at the time of its disposal is not known when the asset is bought. Thus, the amount that may be received at disposal must be estimated. The amount an owner expects to receive when a plant asset is removed from use is called **estimated salvage value.** Estimated salvage value may also be referred to as residual value or scrap value.
3. *Estimated Useful Life.* The total amount of depreciation expense is distributed over the estimated useful life of a plant asset. When a plant asset is bought, the exact length of useful life is impossible to predict. Therefore, the number of years of useful life must be estimated. Two factors affect the useful life of a plant asset: (1) physical depreciation and (2) functional depreciation. Physical depreciation is caused by wear from use and deterioration from aging and weathering. Functional depreciation occurs when a plant asset becomes inadequate or obsolete. An asset is inadequate when it can no longer satisfactorily perform the needed service. An asset is obsolete when a newer asset can operate more efficiently or produce better service.

Because of its permanent nature, land is generally not subject to depreciation. Buildings, after years of use, eventually become unusable. A building may be torn down and a new building constructed on the same land. Since land can be used indefinitely, it is considered permanent and is not depreciated.

The estimated useful life should be based on prior experience with similar assets and on available guidelines. Trade associations frequently publish guidelines for specialized plant assets. The Internal Revenue Service publishes depreciation guidelines for plant assets.

**FYI**

*Depreciation expense differs from many other business expenses in one significant way. For most business expenses, cash is paid out in the same fiscal period in which the expense is recorded. Cash is paid out in the fiscal period during which a plant asset is purchased, but the related depreciation expense is recorded over several years.*

## STRAIGHT-LINE DEPRECIATION

| Original Cost | − | Estimated Salvage Value | = | Estimated Total Depreciation Expense |
|---|---|---|---|---|
| $1,250.00 | − | $250.00 | = | 1 $1,000.00 |

| Estimated Total Depreciation Expense | ÷ | Years of Estimated Useful Life | = | Annual Depreciation Expense |
|---|---|---|---|---|
| $1,000.00 | ÷ | 5 | = | 2 $200.00 |

Charging an *equal* amount of depreciation expense for a plant asset in each year of useful life is called the **straight-line method of depreciation.**

On January 2, 20X1, Winning Edge bought a lighted display case for $1,250.00 with an estimated salvage value of $250.00 and an estimated useful life of 5 years.

Using the straight-line method of depreciation, the annual depreciation expense is the same for each full year in which the asset is used.

**STEPS**

**Calculating annual depreciation expense**

1. Subtract the asset's estimated salvage value from the asset's original cost. This difference is the estimated total depreciation expense for the asset's entire useful life.
2. Divide the estimated total depreciation expense by the years of estimated useful life. The result is the annual depreciation expense.

## CALCULATING DEPRECIATION EXPENSE FOR PART OF A YEAR

| Annual Depreciation Expense | ÷ | Months in a Year | = | Monthly Depreciation Expense |
|---|---|---|---|---|
| $900.00 | ÷ | 12 | = | 1 $75.00 |

| Monthly Depreciation Expense | × | Number of Months Asset Is Used | = | Partial Year's Depreciation Expense |
|---|---|---|---|---|
| $75.00 | × | 5 | = | 2 $375.00 |

A month is the smallest unit of time used to calculate depreciation. A plant asset may be placed in service at a date other than the first day of a fiscal period. In such cases, depreciation expense is calculated to the nearest first of a month.

Winning Edge bought a computer on August 2, 20X1. The annual straight-line depreciation expense is $900.00. The depreciation expense for the part of the year Winning Edge used the computer is $375.00.

**STEPS**

**Calculating partial year's depreciation expense**

1. Divide the annual depreciation expense by 12, the number of months in a year. The result is the monthly depreciation expense.
2. Multiply the monthly depreciation expense by the number of months the plant asset is used in a year. The result is the partial year's depreciation expense.

## CALCULATING ACCUMULATED DEPRECIATION AND BOOK VALUE

### Calculating Accumulated Depreciation

The total amount of depreciation expense that has been recorded since the purchase of a plant asset is called **accumulated depreciation.**

First, the depreciation expense that has accumulated over all prior years is determined. Second, the depreciation expense for the current year is calculated. Third, the prior accumulated depreciation and the current depreciation expense are added.

| 20X2 Accumulated Depreciation | + | 20X3 Depreciation Expense | = | 20X3 Accumulated Depreciation |
|---|---|---|---|---|
| $400.00 | + | $200.00 | = | $600.00 |

### Calculating Book Value

The original cost of a plant asset minus accumulated depreciation is called the **book value of a plant asset.** For the first year, the beginning book value is the original cost. Thereafter, the book value is calculated by subtracting the accumulated depreciation from the original cost of the asset. The ending book value is the beginning book value for the next year.

| Original Cost | – | Accumulated Depreciation | = | Ending Book Value |
|---|---|---|---|---|
| $1,250.00 | – | $600.00 | = | $650.00 |

The book value can also be calculated by subtracting the year's depreciation from that year's beginning book value. Either method of calculating a book value is acceptable because both methods calculate the same amount.

| Beginning Book Value | – | Annual Depreciation | = | Ending Book Value |
|---|---|---|---|---|
| $850.00 | – | $200.00 | = | $650.00 |

**CULTURAL DIVERSITY**

### VALUING DIVERSITY IN THE WORKPLACE

Employees in the U.S. have diverse cultural backgrounds. This diversity reflects the cultural differences in society.

All employees bring their cultural backgrounds and values with them to the workplace. In order to work effectively with people of other cultures, we need to understand each other.

Cultural differences do not exist only between people from different countries. They may arise with anyone in the workplace perceived to be different from the norm. Consider the differences in employees who are younger or older than average, who are physically handicapped, or who speak English as a second language.

Enlightened companies will encourage "valuing diversity" in the workplace. This means valuing the cultural backgrounds of each individual. It means respecting each person for what he or she can contribute to the goals of the organization.

## TERMS REVIEW

depreciation expense

estimated salvage value

straight-line method of depreciation

accumulated depreciation

book value of a plant asset

## AUDIT YOUR UNDERSTANDING

1. Which accounting concept is being applied when depreciation expense is recorded for plant assets?
2. What three factors are used to calculate a plant asset's annual depreciation expense?
3. Why is annual depreciation not recorded for land?

## WORK TOGETHER

### Calculating depreciation

Depreciation tables for Gabriel, Inc., are given in the *Working Papers.* Your instructor will guide you through the following example.

4. The following assets were bought during 20X1. Complete a depreciation table for each asset using the straight-line depreciation method. If the asset was not bought at the beginning of 20X1, calculate the depreciation expense for the part of 20X1 in which the company owned the asset. Save your work to complete Work Together on page 556.

***Transactions:***

Jan. 4. Bought a television costing $700.00 for use in a sales display; estimated salvage value, $100.00; estimated useful life, 3 years.

May 27. Bought an office desk, $920.00; estimated salvage value, $200.00; estimated useful life, 6 years.

## ON YOUR OWN

### Calculating depreciation

Depreciation tables for Yeatman Co. are given in the *Working Papers.* Work this problem independently.

5. The following assets were bought during 20X1. Complete a depreciation table for each asset using the straight-line depreciation method. If the asset was not bought at the beginning of 20X1, calculate the depreciation expense for the part of 20X1 in which the company owned the asset. Save your work to complete On Your Own on page 556.

***Transactions:***

Jan. 3. Bought a security camera costing $850.00; estimated salvage value, $250.00; estimated useful life, 5 years.

June 29. Bought a copy machine, $3,500.00; estimated salvage value, $500.00; estimated useful life, 4 years.

# 21-3 Journalizing Depreciation Expense

## PREPARING PLANT ASSET RECORDS

PLANT ASSET RECORD No. *123*

General Ledger Account No. *1215*

Description *Display Case* General Ledger Account *Store Equipment*

Date Bought *January 2, 20X1* Serial Number *B672981* Original Cost *$1,250.00* **1**

Estimated Useful Life *5 years* Estimated Salvage Value *$250.00* Depreciation Method *Straight-line*

Disposed of: Discarded ____ Sold ____ Traded ____ **2**

Date ____ Disposal Amount ____

| YEAR | ANNUAL DEPRECIATION EXPENSE | ACCUMULATED DEPRECIATION | ENDING BOOK VALUE |
|---|---|---|---|
| 20X1 | $200.00 | $ 200.00 | $1,050.00 |
| 20X2 | 200.00 | 400.00 | 850.00 |
| 20X3 | 200.00 | 600.00 | 650.00 |
| 20X4 | 200.00 | 800.00 | 450.00 |
| 20X5 | 200.00 | 1,000.00 | 250.00 |

**3**

Continue record on back of card

A separate record is kept for each plant asset. An accounting form on which a business records information about each plant asset is called a **plant asset record.**

Plant asset records may vary in arrangement for different businesses, but most records contain similar information. Winning Edge's plant asset record has three sections. Section 1 is prepared when a plant asset is bought. Section 2 provides space for recording the disposition of the plant asset. When the asset is disposed of, this information will be filled in. Section 3 provides space for recording annual depreciation expense and the changing book value of the asset each year it is used.

At the end of each fiscal period, Winning Edge brings each plant asset record up to date by recording three amounts: (1) annual depreciation expense, (2) accumulated depreciation, and (3) ending book value.

The amount recorded in the Annual Depreciation Expense column is the amount calculated for each year. These amounts may be different if the asset is bought or sold at a time other than near the fiscal year end.

Accumulated depreciation for the first year is the annual depreciation expense for the first year. In later years, accumulated depreciation is the depreciation expense that has accumulated over all prior years added to that year's annual depreciation expense.

The ending book value is the original cost less that year's accumulated depreciation.

STEPS

### Preparing a plant asset record

1. Write the information in Section 1 when the plant asset is purchased.
2. Do *not* write in Section 2 until the asset is disposed of.
3. Each year the asset is owned, record the year's annual depreciation expense in Section 3. Calculate and record accumulated depreciation and ending book value.

## JOURNALIZING ANNUAL DEPRECIATION EXPENSE

| | Account Title | 1 Trial Balance Debit | 2 Trial Balance Credit | 3 Adjustments Debit | 4 Adjustments Credit |
|---|---|---|---|---|---|
| 12 | *Store Equipment* | *52,781.00* | | | |
| 13 | *Accum. Depr.—Store Equipment* | | *7,054.00* | | *(g) 8,750.00* |
| 40 | *Depr. Exp.—Store Equipment* | | | *(g) 8,750.00* | |
| 41 | | | | | |

**1.** Depreciation Expense Debit

**2.** Accumulated Depreciation Credit

**GENERAL JOURNAL** PAGE *15*

| | Date | Account Title | Doc. No. | Post. Ref. | Debit | Credit | |
|---|---|---|---|---|---|---|---|
| 14 | *31* | *Depr. Exp.—Store Equipment* | | | *8,750.00* | | 14 |
| 15 | | *Accum. Depr.—Store Equipment* | | | | *8,750.00* | 15 |
| 16 | | | | | | | 16 |

**3.** Record Adjusting Entry

At the end of the fiscal year, Winning Edge calculates the depreciation expense for each plant asset. The depreciation expense for each asset is recorded on its plant asset record. Next, the total depreciation expense is calculated for all plant assets recorded in the same plant asset account.

Winning Edge determined that total depreciation expense for store equipment is $8,750.00. An adjustment is planned in the Adjustments columns of the work sheet. Using this information, an adjusting entry is then recorded in a general journal.

It is important to retain original cost information for plant assets. Rather than credit the plant asset account, depreciation is recorded to the contra asset account Accumulated Depreciation.

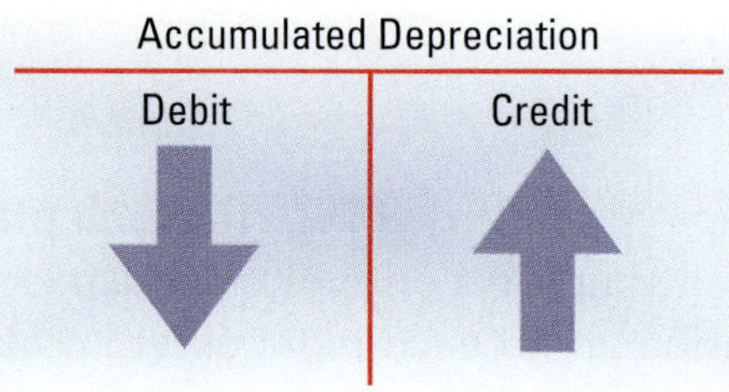


At any time, the book value of plant assets can be calculated by subtracting Accumulated Depreciation from the plant asset account.

**Store Equipment**

| Debit | | Credit |
|---|---|---|
| *Dec. 31 Bal.* | *52,781.00* | |

**Depreciation Expense—Store Equipment**

| Debit | | Credit |
|---|---|---|
| Dec. 31 Adj. | 8,750.00 | |

**Accumulated Depreciation—Store Equipment**

| Debit | Credit | |
|---|---|---|
| | Jan. 1 Bal. | 7,054.00 |
| | Dec. 31 Adj. | 8,750.00 |
| | *Dec. 31 Bal.* | *15,804.00* |

### STEPS: Analyzing and journalizing annual depreciation expense

1. Write the total annual depreciation expense, *$8,750.00,* in the Adjustments Debit column on the Depreciation Expense—Store Equipment line of the work sheet. Label the adjustment *(g),* with a small letter in parentheses.
2. Write the same amount, *$8,750.00,* in the Adjustments Credit column on the Accumulated Depreciation—Store Equipment line of the work sheet. Label the adjustment using the same letter, *(g).*
3. Use the debit and credit accounts on the work sheet to record an adjusting entry in a general journal.

## POSTING AN ADJUSTING ENTRY FOR DEPRECIATION EXPENSE

GENERAL JOURNAL — PAGE 15

| | DATE | | ACCOUNT TITLE | DOC. NO. | POST. REF. | DEBIT | CREDIT | |
|---|---|---|---|---|---|---|---|---|
| 14 | | 31 | Depr. Exp.—Store Equipment | | 6125 | 8 750 00 | | 14 |
| 15 | | | Accum. Depr.—Store Equipment | | 1220 | | 8 750 00 | 15 |
| 16 | | | | | | | | 16 |
| 17 | | | | | | | | 17 |

**1.** Debit Depreciation Expense

**2.** Credit Accumulated Depreciation

ACCOUNT Store Equipment — ACCOUNT NO. 1215

| DATE | | ITEM | POST. REF. | DEBIT | CREDIT | BALANCE DEBIT | BALANCE CREDIT |
|---|---|---|---|---|---|---|---|
| 20-- Jan. | 1 | Balance | ✓ | | | 52 781 00 | |

ACCOUNT Accumulated Depreciation—Store Equipment — ACCOUNT NO. 1220

| DATE | | ITEM | POST. REF. | DEBIT | CREDIT | BALANCE DEBIT | BALANCE CREDIT |
|---|---|---|---|---|---|---|---|
| 20-- Jan. | 1 | Balance | ✓ | | | | 7 054 00 |
| Dec. | 31 | | G15 | | 8 750 00 | | 15 804 00 |

ACCOUNT Depreciation Expense—Store Equipment — ACCOUNT NO. 6125

| DATE | | ITEM | POST. REF. | DEBIT | CREDIT | BALANCE DEBIT | BALANCE CREDIT |
|---|---|---|---|---|---|---|---|
| 20-- Dec. | 31 | | G15 | 8 750 00 | | 8 750 00 | |

The adjustment for depreciation expense planned on the work sheet is recorded as an adjusting entry in the general journal. The adjusting entry is then posted to the general ledger.

After posting, Store Equipment has a debit balance showing the original cost of all store equipment. The contra account Accumulated Depreciation—Store Equipment has a credit balance showing the accumulated depreciation recorded to date.

The debit balance of Depreciation Expense—Store Equipment is the portion of the cost of plant assets allocated to expense during the fiscal period.

**STEPS**

### Posting an adjusting entry for depreciation expense

1. Post the debit, *$8,750.00,* to the Depreciation Expense—Store Equipment account.
2. Post the credit, *$8,750.00,* to the Accumulated Depreciation—Store Equipment account.

**REMEMBER**

An adjusting entry is made to record the depreciation expense for each category of plant assets. Winning Edge also records an adjusting entry to Depreciation Expense—Office Equipment and Accumulated Depreciation—Office Equipment.

## TERM REVIEW

plant asset record

## AUDIT YOUR UNDERSTANDING

1. What method is used to record accumulated depreciation while also retaining original cost information for plant assets?
2. How does an adjusting entry for depreciation expense change the balance of the asset account?

## WORK TOGETHER

### Journalizing depreciation

Use the depreciation tables from Work Together on page 552. Additional forms are given in the *Working Papers*. Your instructor will guide you through the following examples.

3. Complete each plant asset record for the years 20X1 through 20X3. Use the following table:

| Description | General Ledger Account | Date Bought | Plant Asset Number | Serial Number |
|---|---|---|---|---|
| Television | 1215-Store Equipment | Jan. 4 | 134 | 15SG152 |
| Office Desk | 1205-Office Equipment | May 27 | 135 | GE572N |

4. On December 31, Gabriel, Inc., determined that total depreciation expense for office equipment was $3,120.00. Plan the work sheet adjustment and label the adjustment *(f)*. Record the adjusting entry on page 18 of a general journal and post the entry to the general ledger. Save your work to complete Work Together on page 561.

## ON YOUR OWN

### Journalizing depreciation

Use the depreciation tables from On Your Own on page 552. Additional forms are given in the *Working Papers*. Work these problems independently.

5. Complete each plant asset record from the years 20X1 through 20X3. Use the following table:

| Description | General Ledger Account | Date Bought | Plant Asset Number | Serial Number |
|---|---|---|---|---|
| Security Camera | 1215-Store Equipment | Jan. 3 | 253 | G1234MN2 |
| Copy Machine | 1205-Office Equipment | June 29 | 254 | 1776CM123 |

6. On December 31, Yeatman Co. determined that total depreciation expense for store equipment was $8,770.00. Plan the work sheet adjustment and label the adjustment *(g)*. Record the adjusting entry on page 13 of a general journal and post the entry to the general ledger. Save your work to complete On Your Own on page 561.

# 21-4 Disposing of Plant Assets

## SALE OF A PLANT ASSET FOR BOOK VALUE

CASH RECEIPTS JOURNAL — PAGE 1

| DATE | ACCOUNT TITLE | DOC. NO. | POST. REF. | 1 GENERAL DEBIT | 2 GENERAL CREDIT | 3 ACCOUNTS RECEIVABLE CREDIT | 4 SALES CREDIT | 5 SALES TAX PAYABLE DEBIT | 6 SALES TAX PAYABLE CREDIT | 7 SALES DISCOUNT DEBIT | 8 CASH DEBIT | |
|---|---|---|---|---|---|---|---|---|---|---|---|---|
| 5 | Accum. Depr.—Store Equipment | R4 | | 1 000 00 | | | | | | | 250 00 | 8 |
| | Store Equipment | | | | 1 250 00 | | | | | | | 9 |
| | | | | | | | | | | | | 10 |

**1.** Remove the original cost of the plant asset and its related accumulated depreciation. Record the cash received.

| Disposed of: | Discarded ______ | Sold ✓ | Traded ______ |
|---|---|---|---|
| Date | *January 5, 20X6* | Disposal Amount | *$250.00* |

**2.** Complete Section 2 of the plant asset record.

A plant asset may no longer be useful to a business for a number of reasons. When a plant asset is no longer useful to a business, the asset may be disposed of. The old plant asset may be sold, traded for a new asset, or discarded.

When a plant asset is disposed of, a journal entry is recorded that achieves the following:

1. Removes the original cost of the plant asset and its related accumulated depreciation.
2. Recognizes any cash or other asset received for the old plant asset.
3. Recognizes any gain or loss on the disposal.

After five years of use, Winning Edge sold a display case.

> ***January 5, 20X6. Received cash from sale of display case, $250.00: original cost, $1,250.00; total accumulated depreciation through December 31, 20X5, $1,000.00. Receipt No. 4.***

The amount of gain or loss, if any, is calculated by subtracting the book value from the cash received.

The display case was sold for its book value. Therefore, no gain or loss exists.

| | | |
|---|---|---|
| Cash received | | $250.00 |
| *Less:* Book value of asset sold: | | |
| Cost | $1,250.00 | |
| Accum. Depr. | 1,000.00 | 250.00 |
| Gain (loss) on sale of plant asset | | $ 0.00 |

**Cash**

| Debit | Credit |
|---|---|
| 250.00 | |

**Accumulated Depreciation—Store Equipment**

| Debit | Credit |
|---|---|
| 1,000.00 | Bal. 1,000.00 |

**Store Equipment**

| Debit | Credit |
|---|---|
| Bal. 1,250.00 | 1,250.00 |

### STEPS: Recording sale of a plant asset for book value

**1.** Record an entry in the cash receipts journal to remove the original cost, *$1,250.00,* from Store Equipment and *$1,000.00* from Accumulated Depreciation—Store Equipment. Record the cash received from the sale, *$250.00,* as a debit to Cash.

**2.** Check the type of disposal, *Sold,* and write the date, *January 5, 20X6,* and disposal amount, *$250.00,* in Section 2 of the plant asset record.

## RECORDING A PLANT ASSET'S DEPRECIATION EXPENSE FOR A PARTIAL YEAR

1. Debit the depreciation expense account.

GENERAL JOURNAL — PAGE 4

| | DATE | | ACCOUNT TITLE | DOC. NO. | POST. REF. | DEBIT | CREDIT | |
|---|---|---|---|---|---|---|---|---|
| 1 | 20X7 Apr. | 1 | Depr. Exp.—Store Equipment | M14 | | 30 00 | | 1 |
| 2 | | | Accum. Depr.—Store Equipment | | | | 30 00 | 2 |
| 3 | | | | | | | | 3 |

2. Credit the accumulated depreciation account.

3. Update Section 3 of the plant asset record.

| YEAR | ANNUAL DEPRECIATION EXPENSE | ACCUMULATED DEPRECIATION | ENDING BOOK VALUE |
|---|---|---|---|
| 20X5 | 120.00 | 450.00 | 250.00 |
| 20X6 | 120.00 | 570.00 | 130.00 |
| 20X7 | 30.00 | 600.00 | 100.00 |

A plant asset may be sold at any time during the asset's useful life. When a plant asset is sold, its depreciation from the beginning of the current fiscal year to the date of disposal is recorded.

On April 1, 20X7, Winning Edge intends to sell a cash register that was bought on August 1, 20X2. Annual depreciation expense for the cash register is $120.00. Depreciation recorded through December 31, 20X6, is $570.00.

The method to calculate a partial year's depreciation is the same as calculating depreciation when an asset is purchased during the fiscal year. The monthly depreciation expense is multiplied by the number of months the asset is used during the current fiscal year.

| Annual Depreciation Expense | ÷ | Months in a Year | = | Monthly Depreciation Expense |
|---|---|---|---|---|
| $120.00 | ÷ | 12 | = | $10.00 |

| Monthly Depreciation Expense | × | Number of Months Asset Is Used | = | Partial Year's Depreciation Expense |
|---|---|---|---|---|
| $10.00 | × | 3 | = | $30.00 |

***April 1, 20X7. Recorded a partial year's depreciation on cash register to be sold, $30.00. Memorandum No. 14.***

Depreciation Expense—Store Equipment

| Debit | Credit |
|---|---|
| Add. Depr. 30.00 | |

Accumulated Depreciation—Store Equipment

| Debit | Credit |
|---|---|
| | Bal. 570.00 |
| | Add. Depr. 30.00 |
| | *(New Bal. 600.00)* |

The depreciation is also recorded on the plant asset record for the cash register.

### STEPS: Recording a partial year's depreciation

1. Record a debit, *$30.00*, to Depreciation Expense—Store Equipment in the general journal.
2. Record a credit, *$30.00*, to Accumulated Depreciation—Store Equipment in the general journal.
3. Record the depreciation expense in Section 3 of the plant asset record for the cash register. Calculate and record accumulated depreciation and ending book value.

## SALE OF A PLANT ASSET FOR MORE THAN BOOK VALUE

CASH RECEIPTS JOURNAL — PAGE 10

| | DATE | ACCOUNT TITLE | DOC. NO. | POST. REF. | 1 GENERAL DEBIT | 2 GENERAL CREDIT | 3 ACCOUNTS RECEIVABLE CREDIT | 4 SALES CREDIT | 5 SALES TAX PAYABLE DEBIT | 6 SALES TAX PAYABLE CREDIT | 7 SALES DISCOUNT DEBIT | 8 CASH DEBIT | |
|---|---|---|---|---|---|---|---|---|---|---|---|---|---|
| 1 | 20X7 Apr. 1 | Accum. Depr.—Store Equipment | R39 | | 600 00 | | | | | | | 125 00 | 1 |
| 2 | | Store Equipment | | | | 700 00 | | | | | | | 2 |
| 3 | | Gain on Plant Assets | | | | 25 00 | | | | | | | 3 |

**1.** Record an entry to remove asset, record gain, and record cash.

| Disposed of: Discarded ______ | Sold ✓ | Traded ______ |
|---|---|---|
| Date April 1, 20X7 | Disposal Amount $125.00 | |

| YEAR | ANNUAL DEPRECIATION EXPENSE | ACCUMULATED DEPRECIATION | ENDING BOOK VALUE |
|---|---|---|---|

**2.** Complete Section 2 of the plant asset record.

Revenue that results when a plant asset is sold for more than book value is called **gain on plant assets.** Winning Edge is selling a cash register for $125.00. After the partial year's depreciation is recorded, a journal entry is made to record the sale of the cash register.

***April 1, 20X7. Received cash from sale of a cash register, $125.00: original cost, $700.00; accumulated depreciation through April 1, 20X7, $600.00. Receipt No. 39.***

The gain or loss on the sale of a plant asset is the book value subtracted from cash received.

| | | |
|---|---|---|
| Cash received | | $125.00 |
| *Less:* Book value of asset sold: | | |
| Cost | $700.00 | |
| Accum. Depr. | 600.00 | 100.00 |
| Gain (loss) on sale of plant asset | | $ 25.00 |

The gain realized on the disposal of a plant asset is credited to a revenue account titled Gain on Plant Assets.

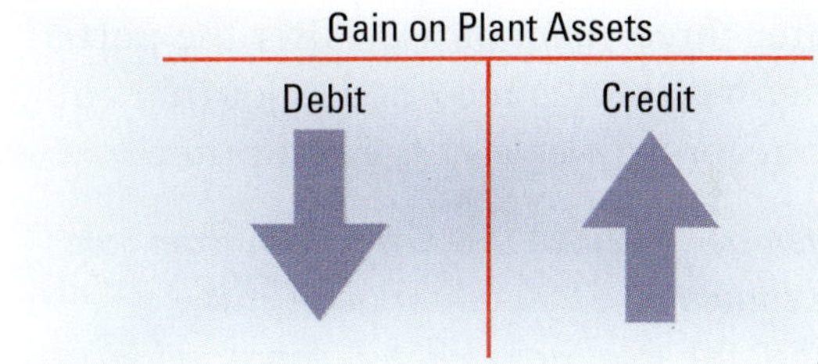


A gain from the sale of plant assets is not an operating revenue. Therefore, Gain on Plant Assets is listed in a classification titled Other Revenue in the chart of accounts.

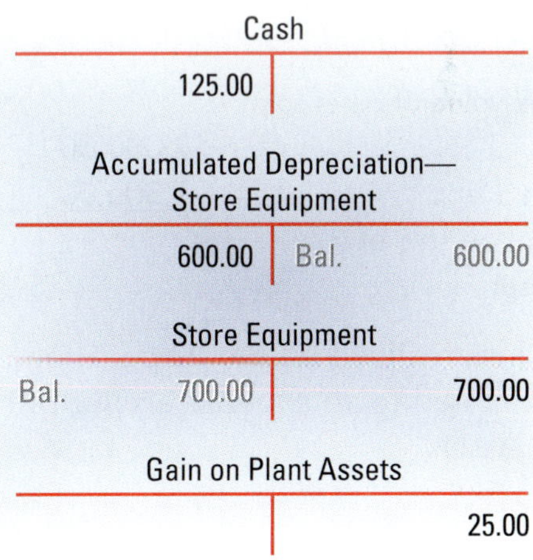


### STEPS: Recording sale of a plant asset for more than book value

1. Record an entry in the cash receipts journal to remove the original cost, *$700.00,* from Store Equipment and *$600.00* from Accumulated Depreciation—Store Equipment. Record the gain on sale, *$25.00,* as a credit to Gain on Plant Assets. Record the cash received from the sale, *$125.00,* as a debit to Cash.
2. Check the type of disposal, *Sold,* and write the date, *April 1, 20X7,* and disposal amount, *$125.00,* in Section 2 of the plant asset record for the cash register.

## SALE OF A PLANT ASSET FOR LESS THAN BOOK VALUE

| | DATE | | ACCOUNT TITLE | DOC. NO. | POST. REF. | GENERAL DEBIT | GENERAL CREDIT | ACCOUNTS RECEIVABLE CREDIT | SALES CREDIT | SALES TAX PAYABLE DEBIT | SALES TAX PAYABLE CREDIT | SALES DISCOUNT DEBIT | CASH DEBIT | |
|---|---|---|---|---|---|---|---|---|---|---|---|---|---|---|
| 1 | 20X7 Sept. | 1 | Accum. Depr.—Office Equipment | R281 | | 1 300 00 | | | | | | | 500 00 | 1 |
| 2 | | | Loss on Plant Assets | | | 200 00 | | | | | | | | 2 |
| 3 | | | Office Equipment | | | | 2 000 00 | | | | | | | 3 |

**1.** Record an entry to dispose of the asset, record a loss on plant assets, and record cash.

| Disposed of: | Discarded ______ | Sold ✓ | Traded ______ |
|---|---|---|---|
| Date | *September 1, 20X7* | Disposal Amount | *$500.00* |

**2.** Complete Section 2 of the plant asset record.

The loss that results when a plant asset is sold for less than book value is called **loss on plant assets.** Winning Edge sold a computer after three years of use. After the partial year's depreciation is recorded, a journal entry is made to record the sale of the computer.

***September 1, 20X7. Received cash from sale of a computer, $500.00: original cost, $2,000.00; total accumulated depreciation through September 1, 20X7, $1,300.00. Receipt No. 281.***

The gain or loss on the sale of a plant asset is the book value subtracted from cash received.

| | | |
|---|---|---|
| Cash received | | $ 500.00 |
| *Less:* Book value of asset sold: | | |
| Cost | $2,000.00 | |
| Accum. Depr. | 1,300.00 | 700.00 |
| Gain (loss) on sale of plant asset | | $ (200.00) |

The loss realized on the disposal of a plant asset is debited to an expense account titled Loss on Plant Assets.

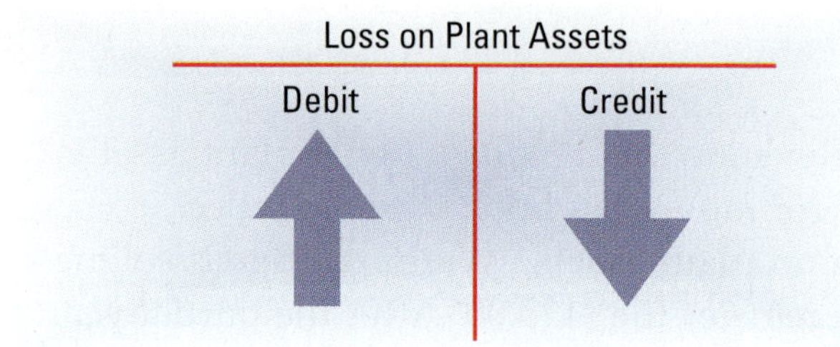


A loss from the sale of plant assets is not an operating expense. Therefore, Loss on Plant Assets is listed in a classification titled Other Expenses in the chart of accounts.

| Cash | |
|---|---|
| 500.00 | |

| Accumulated Depreciation—Office Equipment | |
|---|---|
| 1,300.00 | Bal. 1,300.00 |

| Loss on Plant Assets | |
|---|---|
| 200.00 | |

| Office Equipment | |
|---|---|
| Bal. 2,000.00 | 2,000.00 |

### STEPS: Recording sale of a plant asset for less than book value

**1.** Record an entry in the cash receipts journal to remove the original cost, *$2,000.00,* from Office Equipment and *$1,300.00* from Accumulated Depreciation—Office Equipment. Record the loss on sale, *$200.00,* as a debit to Loss on Plant Assets. Record the cash received from the sale, *$500.00,* as a debit to Cash.

**2.** Check the type of disposal, *Sold,* and write the date, *Sept. 1, 20X7,* and disposal amount, *$500.00,* in Section 2 of the plant asset record for the computer.

## TERMS REVIEW

gain on plant assets

loss on plant assets

## AUDIT YOUR UNDERSTANDING

1. What is recorded on plant asset records for plant assets that have been disposed of?
2. When an asset is disposed of after the beginning of the fiscal year, what entry may need to be recorded before an entry is made for the discarding of a plant asset?
3. What is the formula to compute the gain or loss on the sale of a plant asset?
4. In what account classification is Loss on Plant Assets listed?

## WORK TOGETHER

**Recording the disposal of plant assets**

Use the plant asset records from Work Together on page 556. Your instructor will guide you through the following examples.

5. For each of the following transactions completed in 20X4, journalize an entry for additional depreciation, if needed. Use page 3 of a general journal given in the *Working Papers*. Source documents are abbreviated as follows: check, C; memorandum, M; receipt, R.

   ***Transactions:***

   Jan. 3. Received cash for sale of a television, plant asset No.134, $100.00. R3.

   June 30. Received cash for sale of an office desk, plant asset No.135, $400.00. M25 and R45.

6. Use page 3 of a cash receipts journal to record the disposal of each plant asset.
7. Make appropriate notations in the plant asset records.

## ON YOUR OWN

**Recording the disposal of plant assets**

Use the plant asset records from On Your Own on page 556. Work these problems independently.

8. For each of the following transactions completed in 20X4, journalize an entry for additional depreciation, if needed. Use page 4 of a general journal given in the *Working Papers*. Source documents are abbreviated as follows: check, C; memorandum, M; receipt, R.

   ***Transactions:***

   Jan. 2. Received cash for sale of a copy machine, plant asset No. 254, $1,800.00. R8.

   Apr. 29. Received cash for sale of a security camera, plant asset No. 253, $450.00. M4 and R45.

9. Use page 1 of a cash receipts journal to record the disposal of each plant asset.
10. Make appropriate notations in the plant asset records.

# 21-5 Declining-Balance Method of Depreciation

## CALCULATING DEPRECIATION USING THE DOUBLE DECLINING-BALANCE METHOD

| Plant Asset: Truck<br>Depreciation Method: Declining-Balance | | Original Cost: $22,000.00<br>Estimated Salvage Value: $2,200.00<br>Estimated Useful Life: 5 years | | |
|---|---|---|---|---|
| **Year** | **Beginning Book Value** | **Declining-Balance Rate** | **Annual Depreciation** | **Ending Book Value** |
| 1 | $22,000.00 | 40% | $8,800.00 | $13,200.00 |
| 2 | 13,200.00 | 40% | 5,280.00 | 7,920.00 |

**4.** Transfer the book value to the following year.

**2.** Determine the annual depreciation expense.

**3.** Determine the ending book value.

The straight-line method of depreciation charges an equal amount of depreciation expense each year. However, not all assets depreciate the same amount each year. Many plant assets depreciate more in the early years of useful life than in later years. For example, a truck's value will decrease more in the first year of service than in later years. Therefore, charging more depreciation expense in the early years of a plant asset may be more accurate than charging the same amount each year. *(CONCEPT: Matching Expenses with Revenue)*

Multiplying the book value by a constant depreciation rate at the end of each fiscal period is called the **declining-balance method of depreciation.**

The declining-balance depreciation rate is a multiple of the straight-line rate. Many businesses use a declining-balance rate that is two times the straight-line rate. This method of depreciation is referred to as the double declining-balance method.

### STEPS: Calculating depreciation using the double declining-balance method

**1.** Calculate the double-declining balance rate. An example of a plant asset with a five-year life is shown.

| Estimated Depreciation Expense | ÷ | Years of Estimated Useful Life | = | Straight-Line Rate of Depreciation |
|---|---|---|---|---|
| 100% | ÷ | 5 | = | 20% |

| Straight-Line Rate of Depreciation | × | 2 | = | Double Declining-Balance Rate |
|---|---|---|---|---|
| 20% | × | 2 | = | 40% |

**2.** Multiply the double-declining balance rate by the beginning book value to determine the annual depreciation expense for a given year ($22,000.00 × 40% = $8,800.00).

**3.** Subtract the annual depreciation expense from the beginning book value to determine the ending book value ($22,000.00 − $8,800.00 = $13,200.00).

**4.** Transfer the ending book value to the beginning book value for the following year. Repeat this process for all remaining years except for the last year of useful life. Calculating the depreciation expense in the last year of an asset's life is covered on the next page.

## 21-1 APPLICATION PROBLEM
### Journalizing buying plant assets and paying property tax

The cash payments journal and selected general ledger accounts for Bates Grocery Stores are given in the *Working Papers.*

***Instructions:***

1. Journalize the following transactions completed during the current year. The abbreviation for a check is C.

***Transactions:***

Jan. 3. Paid cash for computer printer, $300.00. C126.
6. Paid cash for a freezer, $1,200.00. C130.
Feb. 27. Paid property taxes on real property with an assessed value of $180,000.00. The tax rate in the city where the property is located is 1.75% of assessed value. C214.
Apr. 5. Paid cash for a lobster tank, $850.00. C310.

2. Post the general columns of the cash payments journal.

## 21-2 APPLICATION PROBLEM
### Calculating depreciation

Planter Stores depreciates plant assets using the straight-line depreciation method. If the asset was not bought at the beginning of 20X1, calculate the depreciation expense for the part of 20X1 that the company owned the asset.

***Instructions:***

Prepare a depreciation table for each of the following plant assets bought by Planter Stores during 20X1. Depreciation tables are given in the *Working Papers.* Save your work to complete Application Problem 21-3.

***Transactions:***

Jan. 4. Bought a cooler costing $1,400.00; estimated salvage value, $350.00; estimated useful life, 7 years; plant asset No. 311; serial number, 47367BX34.
Mar. 30. Bought an office chair, $500.00; estimated salvage value, $50.00; estimated useful life, 5 years; plant asset No. 312; serial number, 1727X6B3.
Aug. 2. Bought a sale sign, $350.00; estimated salvage value, $50.00; estimated useful life, 5 years; plant asset No. 313; serial number, BC762761.

## 21-3 APPLICATION PROBLEM
### Preparing plant asset records

***Instructions:***

Using the depreciation tables prepared in Application Problem 21-2, prepare a plant asset record for each plant asset. Plant asset records are given in the *Working Papers.* Record the depreciation and book values for 20X1-20X4. Save the plant asset records for use in Application Problem 21-5.

## 21-4 APPLICATION PROBLEM
### Journalizing annual depreciation expense

***Instructions:***
On December 31, Baumann, Inc., determined that total depreciation expense for office equipment was $7,840.00. Plan the work sheet adjustment and label the adjustment *(f)*. Record the adjusting entry on page 13 of a general journal and post the transaction to the general ledger. Forms are given in the *Working Papers*.

## 21-5 APPLICATION PROBLEM
### Recording the disposal of plant assets

During 20X5, Planter Stores had the following transactions involving the sale of plant assets. Use the plant asset records completed in Application Problem 21-3. Journals are given in the *Working Papers*.

***Transactions:***

Jan. 6. Received cash for sale of an office chair, plant asset No. 312, $250.00. R4.
Mar. 29. Received cash for sale of a sale sign, plant asset No. 313, $130.00. M3 and R53.
July 8. Received cash for sale of a cooler, plant asset No. 311, $300.00. M34 and R125.

***Instructions:***

1. For each plant asset disposed of in 20X5, journalize an entry for additional depreciation, if needed. Use page 3 of a general journal. Source documents are abbreviated as follows: check, C; memorandum, M; receipt, R.
2. Use page 3 of a cash receipts journal to record the disposal of each plant asset.
3. Make appropriate notations in the plant asset records.

## 21-6 APPLICATION PROBLEM
### Calculating depreciation using the double declining-balance depreciation method

***Instructions:***
Depreciation tables are given in the *Working Papers*. Complete a depreciation table for each of the following plant assets purchased during the current year. Use the double declining-balance depreciation method. Round amounts to the nearest cent.

| Date | Description | Original Cost | Estimated Salvage Value | Estimated Useful Life |
|---|---|---|---|---|
| Jan. 3 | Computer Desk | $ 900.00 | $ 100.00 | 5 years |
| Jan. 5 | Truck | $45,000.00 | $5,000.00 | 4 years |
| Jan. 8 | Sound System | $ 2,400.00 | $ 250.00 | 8 years |

## 21-7 MASTERY PROBLEM
### Recording transactions for plant assets

Ocean View Apartments records plant assets in two accounts: Room Furnishings, Account No. 1205, and Equipment, Account No. 1215. Room furnishings are depreciated using the double declining-balance method. Equipment is depreciated using the straight-line method. Forms are given in the *Working Papers*.

***Instructions:***

1. Record the following transactions completed during 20X1 on page 1 of a cash payments journal.

***Transactions:***

Jan. 4. Bought an entertainment center for room 214: cost, $2,500.00; estimated salvage value, $300.00; estimated useful life, 5 years; plant asset No. 413; serial number, 16143G52. C125.

Feb. 27. Paid property taxes on plant assets assessed at $500,000.00. The tax rate is 1.2%. C167.

Mar. 2. Bought a vacuum cleaner: cost, $1,000.00; estimated salvage value, $100.00; estimated useful life, 5 years; plant asset No. 414; serial number, BD324RT23. C175.

2. Complete Section 1 of a plant asset record for each new plant asset.
3. Prepare a depreciation table for each new plant asset.
4. Complete Section 3 of the plant asset record for 20X1-20X4.
5. Record the following transactions completed during 20X5. Use page 2 of a cash receipts journal and page 2 of a general journal.

***Transactions:***

Jan. 3. Received cash for sale of an entertainment center, plant asset No. 413, $700.00. R3.

June 28. Received cash for sale of a vacuum cleaner, plant asset No. 414, $50.00. M29 and R67.

Dec. 31. Recorded the adjusting entry for depreciation expense—room furnishings. Total 20X5 depreciation expense of room furnishings was $42,534.00.

6. Complete the plant asset records for each plant asset sold during 20X5.

## 21-8 CHALLENGE PROBLEM
### Calculating a partial year's depreciation using the double declining-balance method

Blette and Associates uses the double declining-balance depreciation method for its office equipment. Because many purchases are made during the year, Blette must calculate a partial year's depreciation in the first year. Blette uses the same method to calculate a partial year's depreciation as was described for Winning Edge in this chapter. The annual depreciation expense is divided by 12 to calculate a monthly depreciation. The monthly depreciation is then multiplied by the number of months the plant asset was owned during the year. For subsequent years, the annual depreciation is calculated using the normal method—book value multiplied by the depreciation rate.

***Instructions:***

Depreciation tables are given in the *Working Papers*. Prepare depreciation tables for the following assets purchased in 20X1. Round to the nearest cent.

***Transactions:***

Mar. 29. Bought an office desk system, $2,600.00; estimated salvage value, $250.00; estimated useful life, 8 years.

June 1. Purchased an MICR scanner, $3,800.00; estimated salvage value, $300.00; estimated useful life, 5 years.

## INTERNET ACTIVITY

Point your browser to

**http://accounting.swpco.com**

Choose **First-Year Course**, choose **Activities**, and complete the activity for Chapter 21.

## Applied Communication

Public accountants often work with persons who do not understand the concept of depreciation. Although these individuals realize that equipment wears out and loses its value over time, they do not understand why depreciation is shown as an expense on the income statement.

Edward Dixon owns a business that manages several apartment buildings. The business had a net loss of $25,000.00 last year, largely because of $300,000.00 in building depreciation expense. The business also generated over $200,000.00 in cash. Mr. Dixon is confused by the financial statements and asks, "Did I make any money or not?"

**Instructions:** Write a letter to Mr. Dixon, explaining the concept of depreciation. Explain how his business can both "lose money" yet have a positive cash flow.

## Cases for Critical Thinking

**Case 1** Miguel Quintanilla, owner of a small business, does not record depreciation expense for the business's plant assets. Mr. Quintanilla says that he does not make actual cash payments for depreciation. Therefore, he records an expense for the use of plant assets only when cash is paid for a plant asset. Do you agree with Mr. Quintanilla's method? Explain.

**Case 2** TriState Company sold a payroll clock for $250.00 after using it for five years. TriState paid $800.00 for the payroll clock and at that time estimated the useful life to be five years with an estimated salvage value of $50.00. When the payroll clock was sold, a total of $250.00 accumulated depreciation had been recorded in its plant asset record. Jonathan Yancey, a new accounting clerk, recorded the sale as a $250.00 debit to Cash and a $250.00 credit to Gain on Plant Assets. When asked why he made that entry, Mr. Yancey said that since the payroll clock had been used for its full estimated useful life, he thought any amount realized from its sale should be recorded as a gain. Is Mr. Yancey correct? Explain.

# AUTOMATED ACCOUNTING

## AUTOMATED ACCOUNTING FOR DEPRECIATION

Plant assets are employed in the operation of a business and have a useful life of several years. A computerized system may be used to maintain accounting records for these assets. The information about plant assets is used to prepare depreciation schedules and to automatically prepare the adjusting entries for depreciation. The depreciation schedule information is used by the accounting system to prepare financial statements. The schedules also help managers make decisions about insurance coverage and trade-in values.

### Maintaining Plant Asset Data

In order for the accounting system to prepare depreciation schedules, complete information must be entered for each plant asset.

1. Click the Accounts toolbar button.
2. Click the Plant Assets tab.
3. To add a new asset:
   a. Enter the asset number.
   b. Complete the data fields in the text boxes—asset name, date acquired, useful life, original cost, and salvage value.
   c. Enter the appropriate accumulated depreciation and depreciation expense account numbers.
   d. Select the desired depreciation method from the drop-down list.
   e. Click Add Asset.
4. To change or delete data for an existing plant asset:
   a. Select the asset by clicking the text box containing the data you wish to change.
   b. Enter the correct data and click the Change Asset button, or click the Delete button to remove the asset from the database.

### Generating and Posting Depreciation Adjusting Entries

At the end of the fiscal period (month or year), the computerized accounting system will generate the adjusting entries from the information in the plant asset records. To generate and post the adjusting entries:

1. Choose Depreciation Adjusting Entries from the Options menu.
2. Click Yes to generate the depreciation adjusting entries.
3. Click the Post button. The general journal will appear, containing the posted journal entry. Verify the accuracy of the entry and click the Close button.

### AUTOMATING APPLICATION PROBLEM 21-2: Calculating depreciation

**Instructions:**

1. Load *Automated Accounting 7.0* or higher software.
2. Select database F21-1 from the appropriate directory/folder.
3. Select File from the menu bar and choose the Save As menu command. Key the path to the drive and directory that contains your data files. Save the database with a file name of XXX211 (where XXX are your initials).
4. Access Problem Instructions through the Help menu. Read the Problem Instructions screen.
5. Key the data listed on page 567.
6. Exit the *Automated Accounting* software.

### AUTOMATING MASTERY PROBLEM 21-7: Recording transactions for plant assets

**Instructions:**

1. Load *Automated Accounting 7.0* or higher software.
2. Select database F21-2 from the appropriate directory/folder.
3. Select File from the menu bar and choose the Save As menu command. Key the path to the drive and directory that contains your data files. Save the database with a file name of XXX212 (where XXX are your initials).
4. Access Problem Instructions through the Help menu. Read the Problem Instructions screen.
5. Key the data listed on pages 568–569.
6. Exit the *Automated Accounting* software.

# 22 Accounting for Inventory

**TERMS PREVIEW**

- periodic inventory
- perpetual inventory
- inventory record
- stock record
- stock ledger
- first-in, first-out inventory costing method
- last-in, first-out inventory costing method
- weighted-average inventory costing method
- gross profit method of estimating inventory

**AFTER STUDYING CHAPTER 22, YOU WILL BE ABLE TO:**

1. Define accounting terms related to inventory.
2. Identify accounting concepts and practices related to inventory.
3. Prepare a stock record.
4. Determine the cost of merchandise inventory using the fifo, lifo, and weighted-average inventory costing methods.
5. Estimate the cost of merchandise inventory using the gross profit method of estimating inventory.

## WHY MERCHANDISE INVENTORY IS IMPORTANT

Merchandise inventory on hand is typically the largest asset of a merchandising business. Successful businesses must have merchandise available for sale that customers want. A business therefore needs controls that assist managers in maintaining a merchandise inventory of sufficient quantity, variety, and price.

The cost of merchandise inventory is reported on both the balance sheet and the income statement. An accurate cost of merchandise inventory is required to correctly report current assets and retained earnings on the balance sheet. The accuracy of the inventory cost will also assure that gross profit and net income are reported correctly on the income statement. *(CONCEPT: Adequate Disclosure)*

**SMALL BUSINESS SPOTLIGHT**

Every state has a Small Business Development Center (SBDC) office, which provides a wide range of consulting services and seminars. Funded by state and federal governments, SBDCs are directed by the Small Business Administration and state university personnel.

# ACCOUNTING IN YOUR CAREER

## INVENTORY TIME

A group of employees gathered around the company bulletin board to read the announcement that the physical inventory would be taken the following week. It would begin on Monday after the store closed and continue to Wednesday morning. The store would be closed on Tuesday, but would reopen on Wednesday morning when the inventory was finished. All sales personnel were required to participate, working extra shifts to complete the count of the inventory.

The employees seemed unenthusiastic. Most liked working at Toy City, the largest toy store in the country, but taking inventory is long, hard work.

Chad Osborne, inventory specialist, conducted a meeting the following day to explain the inventory procedures. He thanked the employees in advance for the extra effort it would require. He then assigned teams and shifts. The morale improved somewhat when Chad announced that all teams would be paid overtime for the additional work. Then Chad asked the employees if they had questions.

One worker asked why inventory was being taken on January 23, 24, and 25; he thought it was an odd time to do so. Another asked why it was necessary to take inventory at all. After all, the inventory was completely automated, and the cash registers kept a constant count of what was sold through the bar code scanners. Chad answered these questions to the employees' satisfaction, and the meeting was adjourned.

**Critical Thinking:**

1. Why would a toy store schedule its physical inventory on January 23–25?
2. What do you think Chad's answer was to the question about the need to take an inventory?
3. If there are mistakes in the inventory, how would it affect the company's financial statements, and how many years would it affect?

# 22-1 Determining the Quantity of Merchandise Inventory

## THE MOST EFFICIENT QUANTITY OF INVENTORY

To determine the most efficient quantity of inventory, a business makes frequent analysis of purchases, sales, and inventory records. Many businesses fail because too much or too little merchandise inventory is kept on hand. A business that stocks merchandise that does not satisfy the demand of its customers is also likely to fail.

A merchandise inventory that is larger than needed may decrease the net income of a business for several reasons.

1. Excess inventory requires that a business spend money for expensive store and warehouse space.
2. Excess inventory uses capital that could be invested in other assets to earn a profit for the business.
3. Excess inventory requires that a business spend money for expenses, such as taxes and insurance premiums, that increase with the cost of the merchandise inventory.
4. Excess inventory may become obsolete and unsalable.

Merchandise inventory that is smaller than needed may also decrease the net income of a business for several reasons.

1. Sales may be lost to competitors if items wanted by customers are not on hand.
2. Sales may be lost to competitors if there is an insufficient variety of merchandise to satisfy customers.
3. When a business frequently orders small quantities of an item, the price paid is often more per unit than when merchandise is ordered in large quantities.

## METHODS USED TO DETERMINE THE QUANTITY OF MERCHANDISE INVENTORY

The quantity of items in inventory at the end of a fiscal period must be determined in order to calculate the cost of merchandise sold.

Two principal methods are used to determine the quantity of each item of merchandise on hand.

1. A merchandise inventory determined by counting, weighing, or measuring items of merchandise on hand is called a **periodic inventory.** A periodic inventory is also referred to as a physical inventory.
2. A merchandise inventory determined by keeping a continuous record of increases, decreases, and balance on hand is called a **perpetual inventory.** A perpetual inventory is also referred to as a book inventory.

Because controlling the quantity of merchandise inventory is so important to a business's success, many methods of keeping inventory records are used. Today, most companies use computers to keep track of the inventory on hand.

Keeping track of merchandise inventory also involves knowing the ideal quantity for each kind of merchandise in inventory. To ensure having the appropriate quantity, companies frequently establish an ideal minimum quantity and an ideal reorder quantity. When the minimum quantity is reached, new merchandise is ordered.

Minimum quantity levels must be established with consideration for how long it may take to receive new inventory. Otherwise, merchandise may not be available when a customer wants to buy it. Those who order new merchandise must also be aware of the ideal quantities to order to get the best prices and trade discounts.

# INVENTORY RECORD

**1.** Stock Number and Description

**2.** Actual Units on Hand

**3.** Unit Price and Total Cost

INVENTORY RECORD

DATE *December 31, 20--* ITEM *Tennis Rackets*

| 1 | 2 | 3 | 4 | 5 |
|---|---|---|---|---|
| STOCK NUMBER | DESCRIPTION | NO. OF UNITS ON HAND | UNIT PRICE | TOTAL COST |
| *T30* | *Grand Slam, 4 3/8" grip* | *16* | *26.00* | *416.00* |
| *T35* | *Grand Slam, 4 1/2" grip* | *27* | *9@27.00* | |
| | | | *18@28.00* | *747.00* |
| *T535* | *Grand Slam, special model* | *3* | *39.00* | *117.00* |
| | | | | |
| | *Total* | | | *4,588.00* |

Counting, weighing, or measuring merchandise on hand for a periodic inventory is commonly referred to as "taking an inventory." Employees count each item of inventory and record the quantities on special forms. To assure an accurate and complete count, a business will typically be closed during the periodic inventory.

Businesses frequently establish their fiscal period to end when inventory is at a minimum because it takes less time to count a smaller inventory. For example, a department store may take an inventory at the end of December. The amount of merchandise on hand is smaller because of holiday sales. Few purchases of additional merchandise are made in December after the holiday sales. All of these activities make the merchandise inventory smaller at the end of December.

A form used during a periodic inventory to record information about each item of merchandise on hand is called an **inventory record.** The inventory record has space to record the stock number, description, number of units on hand, unit price, and total cost of each item. Columns 1-3 are completed when the business is taking an inventory. Columns 4-5 are completed after the taking of inventory. The methods used to determine the unit prices are discussed later in this chapter.

**FYI**

*Taking an inventory is an involved and expensive task. An efficient inventory count requires extensive management planning and employee training. Some businesses hire independent companies that specialize in taking inventories to assist in planning for and counting the inventory.*

**STEPS**

### Preparing an inventory record

1. Write the stock number and description before the periodic inventory begins.
2. Write the actual count in the No. of Units on Hand column.
3. Write the unit price and calculate the total cost after the physical inventory is completed. These columns are usually completed by the accounting department.

## STOCK RECORD

STOCK RECORD

Description *Tennis Rackets* Stock No. *T35*

Reorder *18* Minimum *20* Location *Aisle C*

| INCREASES | | | DECREASES | | | BALANCE |
|---|---|---|---|---|---|---|
| DATE | PURCHASE INVOICE NO. | QUANTITY | DATE | SALES INVOICE NO. | QUANTITY | QUANTITY |
| | | | *Oct. 17* | | *4* | *19* |
| *Nov. 4* | *1672* | *18* | | | | *37* |
| | | | *Nov. 7* | *3276* | *3* | *34* |
| | | | *Nov. 21* | *3293* | *2* | *32* |
| | | | *Dec. 9* | *3381* | *5* | *27* |

**1.** Purchase Information **2.** Sales Information **3.** New Balance on Hand

Some businesses keep inventory records that show continuously the quantity on hand for each kind of merchandise. A form used to show the kind of merchandise, quantity received, quantity sold, and balance on hand is called a **stock record.** A separate stock record is prepared for each kind of merchandise on hand. A file of stock records for all merchandise on hand is called a **stock ledger.**

A perpetual inventory system provides day-to-day information about the quantity of merchandise on hand. The minimum balance allowed before a reorder must be placed is also shown on each stock record. The minimum balance is the quantity that will typically last until the ordered merchandise can be received from the vendors. When the quantity falls below the minimum, additional merchandise is ordered in the quantity shown on the reorder line of the stock record. A stock record shows the quantity but usually not the cost of the merchandise.

Purchase information is recorded in the Increases columns when additional merchandise is received. Sales information is recorded in the Decreases columns when merchandise is sold. The new balance on hand is recorded after each purchase and sale.

When a perpetual inventory is kept, errors may be made in recording or calculating amounts. Also, some stock records may be incorrect because merchandise is taken from stock and not recorded on stock records. A business should take a periodic inventory at least once a fiscal period. The perpetual records are corrected to reflect the actual quantity on hand as determined by the periodic inventory.

## PERPETUAL INVENTORY USING A COMPUTER

Many merchandising businesses use a computer to keep perpetual inventory records. The computer is connected to special cash registers known as point-of-sale terminals. The terminals read the Universal Product Codes (UPC) marked on products.

The stock ledger is stored in the computer. When a UPC is read at the terminal, the product description and the sales price are retrieved from the stock ledger and displayed on the terminal. The computer reduces the units on hand to reflect the item sold. The computer may also periodically check the quantities in the stock ledger and print a list of items that need to be reordered.

## TERMS REVIEW

periodic inventory
perpetual inventory
inventory record
stock record
stock ledger

## AUDIT YOUR UNDERSTANDING

1. Why do successful businesses need an effective inventory system?
2. Identify four reasons why a merchandise inventory that is larger than needed may decrease the net income of a business.
3. When are periodic inventories normally taken?
4. How do inventory levels affect the period a business selects for its fiscal year? Why?
5. How is the accuracy of a perpetual inventory checked?

## WORK TOGETHER

**Preparing a stock record**

A stock record for Riverville Electronics is given in the *Working Papers.* Your instructor will guide you through the following example.

6. Enter the following transactions on the stock record of Model No. XW142 cable adapter. Source documents are abbreviated as follows: purchase invoice, P; sales invoice, S.

***Transactions:***

Oct. 22. Received 9 XW142 cable adapters. P321
Nov. 12. Sold 6 XW142 cable adapters. S1816.
23. Sold 3 XW142 cable adapters. S1839.
Dec. 14. Sold 2 XW142 cable adapters. S1898.

## ON YOUR OWN

**Preparing a stock record**

A stock record for Fernandez Jewelry is given in the *Working Papers.* Work this problem independently.

7. Enter the following transactions on the stock record of Model No. C310 crystal biscuit barrel. Source documents are abbreviated as follows: purchase invoice, P; sales invoice, S.

***Transactions:***

Dec. 9. Received 20 C310 crystal biscuit barrels. P2076.
10. Sold 4 C310 crystal biscuit barrels. S6206.
13. Sold 1 C310 crystal biscuit barrels. S6271.
16. Sold 3 C310 crystal biscuit barrels. S6351.

# 22-2 Determining the Cost of Merchandise Inventory

## FIRST-IN, FIRST-OUT INVENTORY COSTING METHOD

| Purchase Dates | Units Purchased | Unit Price | Total Cost | FIFO Units on Hand | FIFO Cost |
|---|---|---|---|---|---|
| January 1, beginning inventory | 17 | $23.00 | $ 391.00 | | |
| March 17, purchases | 8 | 25.00 | 200.00 | | |
| June 29, purchases | 12 | 26.00 | 312.00 | | |
| August 25, purchases | 10 | 27.00 | 270.00 | 9 | $243.00 |
| November 4, purchases | 18 | 28.00 | 504.00 | 18 | 504.00 |
| Totals | 65 | | $1,677.00 | 27 | $747.00 |

1. Total Units on Hand
2. Units from the Most Recent Purchase
3. Units Needed to Equal the Total Units on Hand
4. Unit Price Times Fifo Units
5. Total Fifo Cost

Costs are not recorded on inventory records at the time a periodic inventory is taken. After the quantities of merchandise on hand are counted, purchase invoices are used to find merchandise unit prices. The total costs are then calculated using the quantities and unit prices recorded on the inventory records. Most businesses use one of three inventory costing methods: (1) first-in, first-out, (2) last-in, first-out, or (3) weighted-average.

Winning Edge uses the most recent invoices for purchases to determine the unit price of an item in inventory. The earliest invoices for purchases, therefore, are used to determine the cost of merchandise sold. Using the price of merchandise purchased first to calculate the cost of merchandise sold first is called the **first-in, first-out inventory costing method.** The first-in, first-out method is frequently abbreviated as *fifo*.

On December 31, a periodic inventory of Model No. T35 tennis racket showed 27 rackets on hand. Using the fifo method, the most recent purchase, November 4, is used to cost 18 of the 27 rackets in ending inventory. The remaining 9 rackets in ending inventory are costed using the next most recent purchase, August 25.

### STEPS: Costing inventory using the fifo method

1. Enter the total number of units on hand, *27*.
2. From the most recent purchase, November 4, enter the number of units purchased, *18*. In some cases, the number of units of the most recent purchase will be greater than or equal to the total number of units on hand. In such a case, enter the total number of units on hand and do not complete Step 3 below.
3. From the next most recent purchase, August 25, enter the number of units, *9*, needed for the fifo units to equal the total number on hand, 27. Sometimes the number of units from the two most recent purchases will not be greater than or equal to the total number of units on hand. In such a case, continue the process with the third most recent purchase and so on.
4. Multiply the unit price of each appropriate purchase times the fifo units on hand to determine the fifo cost.
5. Add the individual fifo costs to determine the fifo cost of the total number of units in ending inventory.

## LAST-IN, FIRST-OUT INVENTORY COSTING METHOD

| Purchase Dates | Units Purchased | Unit Price | Total Cost | LIFO Units On Hand | LIFO Cost |
|---|---|---|---|---|---|
| January 1, beginning inventory | 17 | $23.00 | $ 391.00 | 17 | $391.00 |
| March 17, purchases | 8 | 25.00 | 200.00 | 8 | 200.00 |
| June 29, purchases | 12 | 26.00 | 312.00 | 2 | 52.00 |
| August 25, purchases | 10 | 27.00 | 270.00 | | |
| November 4, purchases | 18 | 28.00 | 504.00 | | |
| Totals | 65 | | $1,677.00 | 27 | $643.00 |

**1.** Total Units on Hand
**2.** Beginning Inventory Units
**3.** Units from the Earliest Purchase
**4.** Units Needed to Equal the Total Units on Hand
**5.** Unit Price Times Lifo Units
**6.** Total Lifo Cost

Using the price of merchandise purchased last to calculate the cost of merchandise sold first is called the **last-in, first-out inventory costing method.** The last-in, first-out method is frequently abbreviated as *lifo.* This method is based on the idea that the most recent costs of merchandise should be charged against current revenue. *(CONCEPT: Matching Expenses with Revenue)*

Using the lifo method, each item on the inventory records is recorded at the earliest prices paid for the merchandise.

The earliest prices for the 27 tennis rackets would consist of the 17 units in the January 1 beginning inventory. The next earliest purchase, March 17, of 8 units is then used to cost 8 units in ending inventory. The remaining 2 units in ending inventory are costed using the next earliest purchase, June 29. On the inventory record, the 27 tennis rackets would show a total cost of $643.00.

### STEPS: Costing inventory using the lifo method

1. Enter the total number of units on hand, *27.*
2. Enter the number of units in beginning inventory, *17.* In some cases, the number of units of beginning inventory will be greater than or equal to the total number of units on hand. In such a case, enter the total number of units on hand and do not complete Steps 3 and 4 below.
3. From the earliest purchase, March 17, enter the number of units purchased, *8.*
4. From the next earliest purchase, June 29, enter the number of units, *2,* needed for the lifo units to equal the total number of units on hand, *27.*
5. Multiply the unit price of the beginning inventory times the lifo units on hand to determine the lifo cost for beginning inventory. Repeat this process for each appropriate purchase.
6. Add the lifo cost for the beginning inventory and each appropriate purchase to determine the lifo cost of the total number of units in ending inventory.

### REMEMBER

In the lifo method, the latest purchases are assumed to be sold first (first-out). Therefore, ending inventory consists of the units purchased the earliest, and the earliest purchase invoice costs are used to value the ending inventory.

# WEIGHTED-AVERAGE INVENTORY COSTING METHOD

| Purchases | | | Total |
|---|---|---|---|
| Date | Units | Unit Price | Cost |
| January 1, beginning inventory | 17 | $23.00 | $ 391.00 |
| March 17, purchases | 8 | 25.00 | 200.00 |
| June 29, purchases | 12 | 26.00 | 312.00 |
| August 25, purchases | 10 | 27.00 | 270.00 |
| November 4, purchases | 18 | 28.00 | 504.00 |
| Totals | 65 | | $1,677.00 |

**1.** Total Cost of Inventory Available

| Total of Beginning Inventory and Purchases | ÷ | Total Units | = | Weighted-Average Price per Unit |
|---|---|---|---|---|
| $1,677.00 | ÷ | 65 | = | $25.80 |

**2.** Weighted-Average Price per Unit

| Units in Ending Inventory | × | Weighted-Average Price per Unit | = | Cost of Ending Inventory |
|---|---|---|---|---|
| 27 | × | $25.80 | = | $696.60 |

**3.** Cost of Ending Inventory

Using the average cost of beginning inventory plus merchandise purchased during a fiscal period to calculate the cost of merchandise sold is called the **weighted-average inventory costing method.** The average unit price of the total inventory available is calculated. This average unit price is used to calculate both ending inventory and cost of merchandise sold. The average cost of merchandise is then charged against current revenue. *(CONCEPT: Matching Expenses with Revenue)*

Using the weighted-average method, the inventory is costed at the average price per unit of the beginning inventory plus the cost of all purchases during the fiscal year. On the inventory record, the 27 tennis rackets would show a total cost of $696.60.

## STEPS: Costing inventory using the weighted-average method

1. Calculate the total cost of beginning inventory and each purchase, *$1,677.00*, by multiplying the units by each unit price.
2. Calculate the weighted-average price per unit, *$25.80*, by dividing the total cost, *$1,677.00*, by the number of units available, *65*.
3. Calculate the cost of ending inventory, *$696.60*, by multiplying the weighted-average price per unit, *$25.80*, by the units in ending inventory, *27*.

### F.Y.I.

*A business usually determines the order in which products are sold based on the type of inventory. A grocery store, for example, must sell its earliest purchases first. A hardware store, however, could sell its most recent purchases first. The inventory costing method used to calculate the cost of merchandise sold should not, however, be determined by the order in which items are sold. A business should choose the inventory costing method that provides its managers with the best accounting information.*

## 22-1 APPLICATION PROBLEM
### Preparing a stock record

A stock record for Harrison Sound is given in the *Working Papers.*

***Instructions:***

Enter the following transactions on the stock record of Model No. BE211, speaker wire. Source documents are abbreviated as follows: purchase invoice, P; sales invoice, S.

***Transactions:***

Nov. 8. Received 88 BE211 speaker wire. P2960.
13. Sold 20 BE211 speaker wire. S3527.
30. Sold 30 BE211 speaker wire. S3698.
Dec. 5. Sold 15 BE211 speaker wire. S3729.

## 22-2 APPLICATION PROBLEM
### Determining the cost of inventory using the fifo, lifo, and weighted-average inventory costing methods

Forms for costing inventory for Harrison Sound are given in the *Working Papers.* There are 182 units in ending inventory.

| **Purchase Date** | **Quantity** | **Unit Price** |
|---|---|---|
| January 1, beginning inventory | 90 | $1.00 |
| March 29, purchases | 78 | 1.10 |
| May 6, purchases | 80 | 1.25 |
| August 28, purchases | 84 | 1.30 |
| November 8, purchases | 88 | 1.40 |

***Instructions:***

Calculate the cost of ending inventory using the fifo, lifo, and weighted-average methods.

## 22-3 APPLICATION PROBLEM
### Estimating ending inventory using the gross profit method

Use the following information obtained from the records and management of Cutshaw Company. A form for making inventory calculations and a form for completing an income statement are given in the *Working Papers.*

***Instructions:***

1. Estimate the cost of the ending inventory on August 31.

| | |
|---|---|
| Estimated beginning inventory, August 1 | $158,900.00 |
| Actual net purchases for August | $ 64,800.00 |
| Actual net sales for August | $254,800.00 |
| Estimated gross profit percentage | 30.0% |
| Actual operating expenses for August | $ 70,070.00 |

2. Prepare an income statement for the month ended August 31 of the current year.

## 22-4 MASTERY PROBLEM

### Determining the cost of inventory using the fifo, lifo, and weighted-average inventory costing methods

Chou Enterprises made the following purchases of a part during the fiscal year. There are 34 units in ending inventory. Forms are given in the *Working Papers.*

| Purchase Date | Quantity | Unit Price |
|---|---|---|
| January 1, beginning inventory | 6 | $25.30 |
| January 8, purchases | 25 | 26.00 |
| April 2, purchases | 25 | 26.00 |
| September 13, purchases | 25 | 27.00 |
| December 20, purchases | 25 | 27.50 |

***Instructions:***

1. Calculate the cost of ending inventory using the fifo, lifo, and weighted-average methods.
2. Which of the inventory costing methods resulted in the highest cost of merchandise sold?

## 22-5 CHALLENGE PROBLEM

### Determining the cost of merchandise inventory destroyed in a fire

A fire completely destroyed the warehouse of Wright Plumbing Company on the night of October 10 of the current year. The accounting records of the company and $3,500.00 of merchandise inventory remained safe in the company's showroom. The company does not maintain a perpetual inventory system. The insurance company therefore has requested an estimate of the merchandise inventory destroyed in the fire. Forms are given in the *Working Papers.*

The following income statement is for the previous fiscal year.

**Wright Plumbing Company**
**Income Statement**
**For Year Ended July 31, 20--**

| | | |
|---|---|---|
| Operating Revenue: | | |
| Net Sales | | $958,700.00 |
| Cost of Merchandise Sold: | | |
| Estimated Beginning Inventory, August 1 | $119,060.00 | |
| Net Purchases | 534,607.60 | |
| Merchandise Available for Sale | $653,667.60 | |
| Less Estimated Ending Inventory, July 31 | 128,300.00 | |
| Cost of Merchandise Sold | | 525,367.60 |
| Gross Profit on Operations | | $433,332.40 |
| Operating Expenses | | 325,180.00 |
| Net Income | | $108,152.40 |

The following additional financial information is obtained from the current year's accounting records.

| | |
|---|---|
| Net purchases, August 1 to October 10 | $ 57,800.00 |
| Net sales, August 1 to October 10 | 148,200.00 |
| Operating expenses, August 1 to October 10 | 48,390.00 |

***Instructions:***

1. Calculate the prior year's gross profit on operations as a percentage of net sales. Round the percentage calculation to the nearest whole percent.

2. Use the percentage calculated in Instruction 1 and the current year's financial information to calculate an estimate of the total merchandise inventory as of October 10.
3. To calculate the cost of the inventory destroyed in the fire, subtract the cost of the merchandise inventory that was not destroyed from the estimate of the total merchandise inventory as of October 10.
4. Prepare an income statement for the period August 1 to October 10.

The insurance company maintains that it is liable for paying only the book value of the inventory destroyed by fire. Wright Plumbing Company maintains that the insurance company should pay the replacement cost of the destroyed inventory.

***Instructions:***

5. What is meant by the book value and the replacement value of the inventory?
6. Wright Plumbing Company uses the fifo inventory costing method. How does that affect the difference between the book value and the replacement value of the destroyed inventory?
7. What should determine which value the insurance company uses?

**INTERNET ACTIVITY**

Point your browser to

**http://accounting.swpco.com**

Choose **First-Year Course**, choose **Activities**, and complete the activity for Chapter 22.

## Applied Communication

Arrange with your instructor to call the manager of a local merchandising company. Ask the manager questions concerning how the company maintains a count and cost of its merchandise inventory. Suggested questions include:

1. Does the company maintain a perpetual inventory system?
2. How often does the company take an inventory?
3. Who counts the inventory during a periodic inventory?
4. What method is used to cost the ending inventory?
5. If a perpetual inventory is used, how closely do the year-end quantities match the periodic counts?

## Cases for Critical Thinking

**Case 1**

Ballston Company uses the fifo method of costing its merchandise inventory. The manager is considering a change to the lifo method. Costs have increased steadily over the past three years. What effect will the change have on the following items? (1) The amount of net income on the income statement. (2) The amount of income taxes to be paid. (3) The quantity of each item of merchandise that must be kept in stock. Why?

**Case 2**

The Pet Center stocks many kinds of merchandise. The store has always taken a periodic inventory at the end of a fiscal year. The store has not kept a perpetual inventory because of the cost. However, the manager wants a reasonably accurate cost of merchandise inventory at the end of each month. The manager needs the amount to prepare monthly income statements and to help in making decisions about the business. What would you recommend?

# AUTOMATED ACCOUNTING

## AUTOMATED INVENTORY SYSTEMS

A merchandising business is a business that purchases and resells goods. Merchandise inventory may consist of thousands of different items. The total cost of the inventory consists of many different costs, including:

- The cost of purchasing the inventory.
- The cost of storing the inventory.
- The cost of record keeping.
- Taxes and insurance on the inventory.
- The cost of losses due to theft and damage.

A computerized inventory system allows business better access to accurate information about the inventory. Managers need information about which items are selling, the number of items currently in inventory, and when to reorder an item.

### Inventory Stock Maintenance

An inventory stock record is created for each item in inventory. The inventory stock record retains information such as stock number, description, unit of measure, reorder point, retail price, quantity sold, quantity ordered, quantity received, and purchase price. This data may be updated as often (daily, weekly, monthly) as necessary. All normal transactions related to inventory are entered into the system. Periodic inventory reports are generated.

To add or change inventory stock data:

1. Click the Accounts toolbar button.
2. Click the Inventory tab.
3. To add a new inventory stock item:
   a. Enter the stock number.
   b. Enter a short description for the item.
   c. Enter the unit of measure. Common units of measure are EA for Each, CS for Case, and BX for Box.
   d. Enter the reorder point. Merchandising businesses can sell only the goods they have in stock. The reorder point is set so that the item will not be out of stock.
   e. Enter the retail price, or the price the business charges its customers. (The cost of the item will be entered when each order is received.)
4. Click the Add Item button.
5. To change data for a current inventory stock item:
   a. Select the stock item by clicking the text cell containing the data you wish to change.
   b. Enter the correct data.
   c. Click the Change Item button, or click the Delete button to remove the item from the database. (Inventory items may be deleted only after current transaction data has been deleted or purged.)

### Inventory Transactions

All inventory transactions are recorded in the Other Activities Inventory window. These transactions include sales, purchases ordered, purchases received, and sales and purchases returns.

To enter inventory transactions:

1. Click the Other toolbar button.
2. Click the Inventory tab.
3. Enter the date of the inventory transaction.
4. Select the inventory item from the Inventory drop-down list.
5. Enter the transaction data in the appropriate text boxes.
6. Click OK.

To correct or delete an inventory transaction:

1. Select the transaction by clicking the text box containing the data you wish to correct.
2. Enter the correct data and click OK, or click the Delete button to remove the transaction.

*Automated Accounting 8.0* has a more complete inventory system:

1. When inventory items are ordered, a purchase order is recorded in the Purch. Order tab of the Other Activities window.
2. When an order is received, a purchase invoice is issued and recorded in the Purch. Invoice tab of the Other Activities window.
3. When merchandise is sold, the sales invoice is entered in

# Automated Accounting

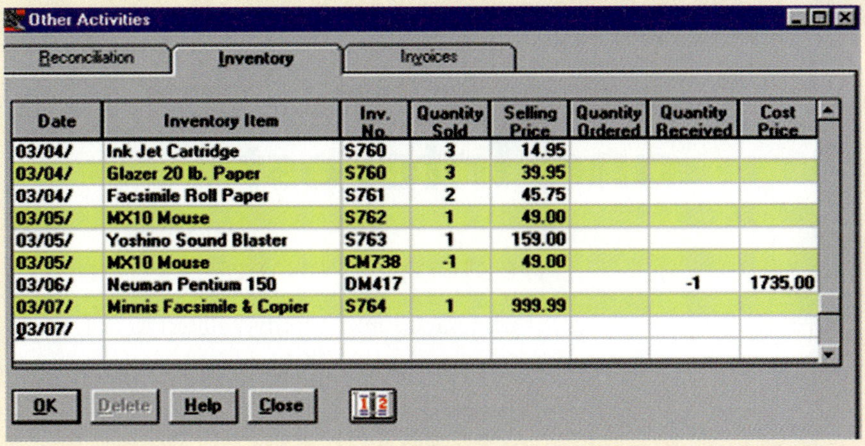


the Sales Invoice tab of the Other Activities window.

### Inventory Reports

Several inventory reports are available. Managers use these reports in planning and controlling inventory. To display inventory reports:

1. Click the Reports toolbar button, or choose the Reports Selection menu item from the Reports menu.
2. When the Report Selection dialog appears, choose the Inventory Reports option button from the Select a Report Group list.
3. Choose the inventory report you would like to display from the Choose a Report to Display list.
4. Click the OK button.

### AUTOMATING APPLICATION PROBLEM 22-1: Preparing a stock record

**Instructions:**

1. Load *Automated Accounting 7.0* or higher software.
2. Select database F22-1 from the appropriate directory/folder.
3. Select File from the menu bar and choose the Save As menu command. Key the path to the drive and directory that contains your data files. Save the database with a file name of XXX221 (where XXX are your initials).
4. Access Problem Instructions through the Help menu. Read the Problem Instructions screen.
5. Key the data listed on page 587.
6. Exit the *Automated Accounting* software.

### AUTOMATING MASTERY PROBLEM 22-4: Determining the cost of inventory using the fifo, lifo, and weighted-average inventory costing methods

**Instructions:**

1. Load *Automated Accounting 7.0* or higher software.
2. Select database F22-2 from the appropriate directory/folder.
3. Select File from the menu bar and choose the Save As menu command. Key the path to the drive and directory that contains your data files. Save the database with a file name of XXX222 (where XXX are your initials).
4. Access Problem Instructions through the Help menu. Read the Problem Instructions screen.
5. Key the data listed on page 588.
6. Exit the *Automated Accounting* software.

# 23 Accounting for Notes and Interest

**AFTER STUDYING CHAPTER 23, YOU WILL BE ABLE TO:**

1. Define accounting terms related to notes and interest.
2. Identify accounting concepts and practices related to notes and interest.
3. Calculate interest and maturity dates for notes.
4. Analyze and record transactions for notes payable.
5. Analyze and record transactions for notes receivable.

**TERMS PREVIEW**

number of a note
date of a note
payee of a note
time of a note
principal of a note
interest rate of a note
maturity date of a note
maker of a note
promissory note
creditor
notes payable
interest
maturity value
current liabilities
interest expense
notes receivable
interest income
dishonored note

## WHEN LENDING AND BORROWING ARE NECESSARY

Cash is the primary medium of exchange for business transactions. *(CONCEPT: Unit of Measurement)* Cash is used to purchase merchandise and to pay salaries and other expenses. In turn, businesses receive cash when they sell their products or services and collect payment. The cash received for products or services can be used to purchase more merchandise and continue to pay salaries and other expenses. Thus, the business cycle continues.

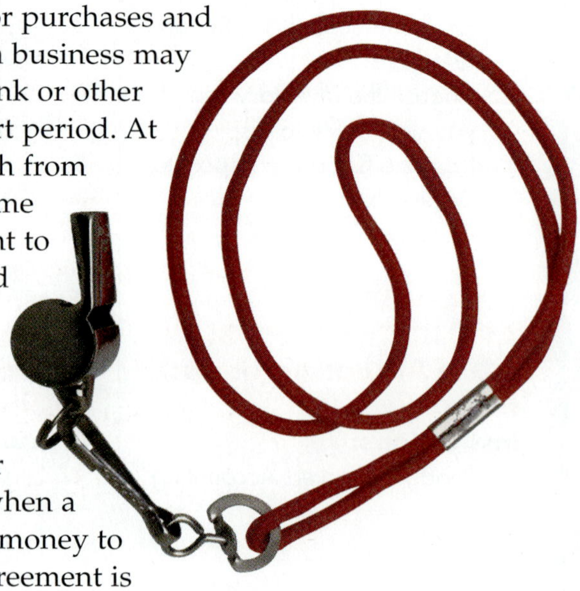

Sometimes a business receives more cash from sales than is needed to pay for purchases and expenses. When this occurs, a business may deposit the extra cash in a bank or other financial institution for a short period. At other times, the receipt of cash from sales does not occur at the same time and in amounts sufficient to pay for needed purchases and expenses. When this occurs, a business needs to borrow additional cash or make arrangements with its vendors to delay payment for a period of time. Generally, when a bank or other business lends money to another business, the loan agreement is made in writing.

# ACCOUNTING IN YOUR CAREER

## HOW TO CHOOSE A LOAN

Alisa Chavez is an experienced mechanical engineer and inventor who has financed the startup of a new company, Roboco, Inc. After two years of operations, the company is profitable, but most of the profits are reinvested in research. The research group has perfected a new kind of robotic arm that will allow manufacturers to produce their products faster and cheaper. It is expected that the sales of this new arm will dramatically increase revenues and profits for Roboco, Inc. However, new equipment costing $250,000 will be needed to produce these new arms.

Robert Greeley, accounting manager, has sought loans from the company's bankers to purchase this new equipment. One bank is offering a 10-year, 12% loan and another an 8-year, 11.5% loan. Both banks are also willing to finance the acquisition of the equipment with a 1-year, 9% loan. All the loans would require monthly payments of principal plus interest.

Robert explains to Alisa that it will take four months to acquire the equipment and get it set up to begin production. The first arms would be available for sale in about six months. Alisa does not like to carry much debt and has never borrowed on a long-term basis before. Therefore, she favors the 1-year loan. Robert says, "I recommend that we discuss this some more before making a decision. The 1-year loan might not be the best decision for the company right now."

**Critical Thinking:**

1. Why would banks require higher interest rates on longer-term loans?
2. The interest rate on the 1-year loan is clearly the lowest. Why would Robert suggest that the long-term loans might be better?

# 23-1 Promissory Notes

## USES OF PROMISSORY NOTES

**1. Number of a note.** The number assigned to identify a specific note.

**2. Date of a note.** The day a note is signed.

**3. Payee of a note.** The person or business to whom the amount of a note is payable.

**4. Time of a note.** The days, months, or years from the date of signing until a note is to be paid.

**5. Principal of a note.** The original amount of a note; sometimes referred to as face amount of a note.

**6. Interest rate of a note.** The percentage of the principal that is paid for use of the money.

**7. Maturity date of a note.** The date a note is due.

**8. Maker of a note.** The person or business who signs a note and thus promises to make payment.

**PROMISSORY NOTE**

NOTE NO. *1276* DATE: *January 12* 20*--*

NAME: *Winning Edge, Inc.*

For value received, I or We, the signers, promise to pay to the order of **Charter State Bank** of Atlanta, Georgia, *180* days from date, the principal sum of *$ 10,000.00*

*Ten thousand and xx/100* DOLLARS

with interest from date at the rate of *12* % per year, due on *July 11, 20--*.

*Cristina Stephens, President*

*Winning Edge, Inc.*

A written and signed promise to pay a sum of money at a specified time is called a **promissory note.** A person or organization to whom a liability is owed is called a **creditor.** Promissory notes signed by a business and given to a creditor are called **notes payable.** A note payable is frequently referred to as a note.

Promissory notes are used when money is borrowed for a period of time from a bank or other lending agency. Sometimes a business requests a note from a customer who wants credit beyond the usual time given for sales on account. Notes have an advantage over oral promises and accounts receivable or payable. Notes can be useful in a court of law as written evidence of a debt.

## INTEREST ON PROMISSORY NOTES

An amount paid for the use of money for a period of time is called **interest.** Banks and other lending institutions charge interest on money loaned to their customers. The interest rate is stated as a percentage of the principal. *Interest at 10% means that 10 cents will be paid for the use of each dollar borrowed for a full year.*

When businesses borrow money from banks, other lending institutions, or other businesses, promissory notes should be prepared to provide written evidence of the transaction.

Sometimes partial payments on a note are made each month. This arrangement is particularly true when an individual buys a car and signs a note for the amount owed. The monthly payment includes part of the principal and part of the interest to be paid.

To calculate interest for one year, the principal is multiplied by the interest rate. The interest on a $1,000.00, 12% note for one year is $120.00.

$$\text{Principal} \times \text{Interest Rate} \times \text{Time in Years} = \text{Interest for One Year}$$

$$\$1,000.00 \times 12\% \times 1 = \$120.00$$

The time of a note issued for less than one year is typically stated as a number of days, such as 30 days, 60 days, or 90 days. The time used in calculating interest is usually stated as a fraction of 360 days. The interest on a $1,000.00, 12% note for 60 days is $20.00.

$$\text{Principal} \times \text{Interest Rate} \times \text{Time as Fraction of Year} = \text{Interest for Fraction of Year}$$

$$\$1,000.00 \times 12\% \times \frac{60}{360} = \$20.00$$

The amount that is due on the maturity date of a note is called the **maturity value.** A 60-day note with a principal of $1,000.00 and interest rate of 12% will have a maturity value of $1,020.00.

$$\text{Principal} + \text{Interest} = \text{Maturity Value}$$

$$\$1,000.00 + \$20.00 = \$1,020.00$$

# MATURITY DATE OF PROMISSORY NOTES

**March 13, 90-Day Note**

| | |
|---|---|
| March 13-March 31 | 18 days |
| April | 30 days |
| May | 31 days |
| June 1-June 11 | 11 days |
| Total | 90 days |

**1.** Subtract the date of the note from the number of days in the first month.

**2.** Add 30 days for April.

**3.** Add 31 days for May.

**4.** Add only 11 days in June.

The time between the date a note is signed and the date a note is due is typically expressed in days. The maturity date is calculated by counting the exact number of days. The date the note is written is not counted, but the maturity date is counted. For example, a 90-day note dated March 13 is due on June 11.

## STEPS: Calculating the maturity date of a note

1. Calculate the number of days remaining in March, *18,* by subtracting the date of the note, *13,* from the number of days in March, *31.*
2. Calculate the number of days remaining in the term of the note, *72,* by subtracting the number of days in the previous month, *18,* from the term of the note, *90.* Because 72 is greater than the number of days in April, *30,* add all of the days in April.
3. Calculate the number of days remaining in the term of the note, *42,* by subtracting the number of days in the previous months, *48 (18 + 30),* from the term of the note, *90.* Because 42 is greater than the number of days in May, *31,* add all of the days in May.
4. Calculate the number of days remaining in the term of the note, *11,* by subtracting the number of days in the previous months, *79 (18 + 30 + 31),* from the term of the note, *90.* Because 11 is less than the number of days in June, 30, add only *11* days in June.

**FYI**

*Agencies of the federal government generally use a 365-day year when calculating interest. Consumer interest is also generally calculated on a 365-day year. However, many banks use a 360-day year when calculating interest. Therefore, the interest calculations in this textbook use a 360-day year.*

**FYI**

*An interest rate can be entered on a calculator or electronic spreadsheet either by using the Percent key (%) or the decimal equivalent of the interest rate. For example, 12% could be keyed as 0.12.*

## Terms Review

number of a note
date of a note
payee of a note
time of a note
principal of a note
interest rate of a note
maturity date of a note
maker of a note
promissory note
creditor
notes payable
interest
maturity value

## Audit Your Understanding

1. What conditions would cause a business to have extra cash to deposit in a bank, yet at another time of year need to borrow extra cash from a bank?
2. What is the advantage of a promissory note over an account receivable?
3. What does interest at 10% mean?
4. How is interest calculated for a fraction of a year?

## Work Together

**Calculating interest, maturity dates, and maturity values for promissory notes**

Write the answers to the following problem in the *Working Papers.* Your instructor will guide you through the following example.

5. For each of the following promissory notes, calculate (a) the interest on the note, (b) the maturity date of the note, and (c) the maturity value of the note. Save your work to complete Work Together on page 602.

| Date | Principal | Interest Rate | Time |
|---|---|---|---|
| March 3 | $6,000.00 | 12% | 90 days |
| March 18 | $2,000.00 | 18% | 60 days |

## On Your Own

**Calculating interest, maturity dates, and maturity values for promissory notes**

Write the answers to the following problem in the *Working Papers.* Work this problem independently.

6. For each of the following promissory notes, calculate (a) the interest on the note, (b) the maturity date of the note, and (c) the maturity value of the note. Save your work to complete On Your Own on page 602.

| Date | Principal | Interest Rate | Time |
|---|---|---|---|
| June 6 | $10,000.00 | 10% | 60 days |
| June 23 | $ 4,200.00 | 18% | 90 days |

# 23-2 Notes Payable

## SIGNING A NOTE PAYABLE

**1.** Date **2.** Account Title **3.** Receipt Number **4.** Principal Amount **5.** Cash Received

CASH RECEIPTS JOURNAL PAGE 8

| | | | | 1 | 2 | 3 | 4 | 5 | 6 | 7 | 8 | |
|---|---|---|---|---|---|---|---|---|---|---|---|---|
| | DATE | ACCOUNT TITLE | DOC. NO. | POST. REF. | GENERAL | | ACCOUNTS RECEIVABLE CREDIT | SALES CREDIT | SALES TAX PAYABLE | | SALES DISCOUNT DEBIT | CASH DEBIT | |
| | | | | | DEBIT | CREDIT | | | DEBIT | CREDIT | | | |
| | 13 | Notes Payable | R302 | | | 5 000 00 | | | | | | 5 000 00 | 21 |
| 22 | | | | | | | | | | | | | 22 |
| 23 | | | | | | | | | | | | | 23 |
| 24 | | | | | | | | | | | | | 24 |

Liabilities due within a short time, usually within a year, are called **current liabilities.** Because notes payable generally are paid within one year, they are classified as current liabilities.

When a business signs a note payable, the principal or face amount of the note is credited to a liability account titled Notes Payable.

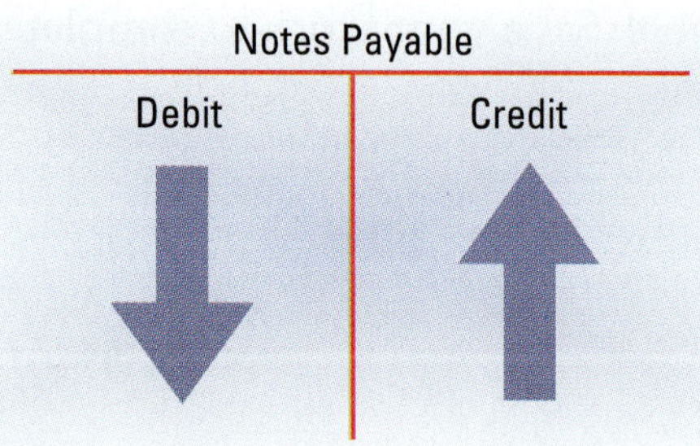


Winning Edge arranges to borrow money from its bank. A note payable is signed with the bank as evidence of the debt. The bank issues a check or deposits the principal amount of the note in Winning Edge's checking account.

***March 13. Signed a 90-day, 10% note, $5,000.00. Receipt No. 302.***

The bank retains the original of the note until Winning Edge pays the maturity value. A receipt is prepared to show the receipt of the principal amount of the note. *(CONCEPT: Objective Evidence)*

| Cash | |
|---|---|
| Mar. 13 5,000.00 | |

| Notes Payable | |
|---|---|
| | Mar. 13 5,000.00 |

No entry is made for interest until a later date when the interest is paid.

### STEPS Journalizing the receipt of cash from a note payable

1. Write the date, *13*, in the Date column of the cash receipts journal.
2. Write the account title, *Notes Payable*, in the Account Title column.
3. Write the receipt number, *R302*, in the Doc. No. column.
4. Write the principal amount, *$5,000.00*, in the General Credit column.
5. Write the same amount, *$5,000.00*, in the Cash Debit column.

# PAYING PRINCIPAL AND INTEREST ON A NOTE PAYABLE

**1.** Date **2.** First Account Title **3.** Check Number **4.** Principal Amount

CASH PAYMENTS JOURNAL — PAGE 11

| | DATE | | ACCOUNT TITLE | CK. NO. | POST. REF. | GENERAL DEBIT (1) | GENERAL CREDIT (2) | ACCOUNTS PAYABLE DEBIT (3) | PURCHASES DISCOUNT CREDIT (4) | CASH CREDIT (5) | |
|---|---|---|---|---|---|---|---|---|---|---|---|
| 15 | | 11 | *Notes Payable* | 627 | | 5 000 00 | | | | 5 125 00 | 15 |
| 16 | | | *Interest Expense* | | | 125 00 | | | | | 16 |

**5.** Second Account Title **6.** Interest Amount **7.** Maturity Value

When a note payable reaches its maturity date, the maker of the note pays the maturity value to the payee. The interest accrued on money borrowed is called **interest expense.** The interest accrued on a note payable is debited to an expense account titled Interest Expense.

| Interest Expense | |
|---|---|
| Debit ↑ | Credit ↓ |

Interest expense is a financial expense rather than an expense of the business's normal operations. Therefore, Interest Expense is listed in a classification titled Other Expenses in a chart of accounts.

Winning Edge paid the 90-day note payable it had signed on March 13.

***June 11. Paid cash for the maturity value of the March 13 note: principal, $5,000.00, plus interest, $125.00; total, $5,125.00. Check No. 627.***

| Notes Payable | | | |
|---|---|---|---|
| June 11 | 5,000.00 | Mar. 13 | 5,000.00 |

| Interest Expense | | | |
|---|---|---|---|
| June 11 | 125.00 | | |

| Cash | | | |
|---|---|---|---|
| | | June 11 | 5,125.00 |

| Principal | × | Interest Rate | × | Time as Fraction of Year | = | Interest for Fraction of Year |
|---|---|---|---|---|---|---|
| $5,000.00 | × | 10% | × | $\frac{90}{360}$ | = | $125.00 |

**STEPS**

### Journalizing a cash payment for the maturity value of a note payable

1. Write the date, *11,* in the Date column of the cash payments journal.
2. Write the account title, *Notes Payable,* in the Account Title column.
3. Write the check number, *627,* in the Ck. No. column.
4. Write the note's principal amount, *$5,000.00,* in the General Debit column.
5. Write the account title, *Interest Expense,* in the Account Title column on the next line.
6. Write the interest expense amount, *$125.00,* in the General Debit column.
7. Write the amount of cash paid, *$5,125.00,* in the Cash Credit column on the first line of the entry.

## SIGNING A NOTE PAYABLE FOR AN EXTENSION OF TIME

1. Debit to Accounts Payable

2. Credit to Notes Payable

GENERAL JOURNAL — PAGE 4

| | DATE | | ACCOUNT TITLE | DOC. NO. | POST. REF. | DEBIT | CREDIT | |
|---|---|---|---|---|---|---|---|---|
| 5 | | 5 | Accounts Payable/Pollard Supply | M47 | ✓ | 3 000 00 | | 5 |
| 6 | | | Notes Payable | | | | 3 000 00 | 6 |

A business may ask for an extension of time if it is unable to pay an account when due. The vendor may ask the business to sign a note payable. The note payable does not pay the amount owed to the vendor. However, the form of the liability is changed from an account payable to a note payable.

When this entry is posted, the balance of the accounts payable account for Pollard Supply will be zero. One liability, Accounts Payable, is replaced by another liability, Notes Payable.

***April 5. Winning Edge signed a 60-day, 18% note to Pollard Supply for an extension of time on its account payable, $3,000.00. Memorandum No. 47.***

GENERAL LEDGER

Accounts Payable

| | | | |
|---|---|---|---|
| Apr. 5 | 3,000.00 | Bal. | 3,000.00 |

Notes Payable

| | | | |
|---|---|---|---|
| | | Apr. 5 | 3,000.00 |

ACCOUNTS PAYABLE LEDGER

Pollard Supply

| | | | |
|---|---|---|---|
| Apr. 5 | 3,000.00 | Bal. | 3,000.00 |

**FYI**

*There are advantages to accepting a note from a customer for an extension of time. In addition to serving as legal evidence of the debt, accepting a note may avoid having an account become uncollectible if additional time is all the customer needs in order to pay the account eventually. The business accepting the note will also earn interest on the overdue account, usually at a relatively high interest rate. Also, in some industries, these notes can be sold for cash if the cash is needed to meet operating expenses.*

**STEPS**

### Journalizing signing a note payable for an extension of time

1. Record a debit, *$3,000.00,* to *Accounts Payable/Pollard Supply* in the general journal.
2. Record a credit, *$3,000.00,* to *Notes Payable.*

**REMEMBER**

When a note payable is signed for an extension of time on account, both the general ledger account, Accounts Payable, and the subsidiary ledger account are changed to a note payable. Therefore, both accounts must be debited to remove the amount from the accounts.

## PAYING A NOTE PAYABLE ISSUED FOR AN EXTENSION OF TIME

CASH PAYMENTS JOURNAL — PAGE 11

| | DATE | | ACCOUNT TITLE | CK. NO. | POST. REF. | 1 GENERAL DEBIT | 2 GENERAL CREDIT | 3 ACCOUNTS PAYABLE DEBIT | 4 PURCHASES DISCOUNT CREDIT | 5 CASH CREDIT | |
|---|---|---|---|---|---|---|---|---|---|---|---|
| 3 | | 4 | *Notes Payable* | 615 | | 3 000 00 | | | | 3 090 00 | 3 |
| 4 | | | *Interest Expense* | | | 90 00 | | | | | 4 |
| 5 | | | | | | | | | | | 5 |
| 6 | | | | | | | | | | | 6 |
| 7 | | | | | | | | | | | 7 |

The entry to record the cash payment at the maturity date of a note payable is the same regardless of the reason the note was signed.

***June 4. Paid cash for the maturity value of the note payable to Pollard Supply: principal, $3,000.00, plus interest, $90.00; total, $3,090.00. Check No. 615.***

Notes Payable

| | | | |
|---|---|---|---|
| June 4 | 3,000.00 | Apr. 5 | 3,000.00 |

Interest Expense

| | | | |
|---|---|---|---|
| June 4 | 90.00 | | |

Cash

| | | | |
|---|---|---|---|
| | | June 4 | 3,090.00 |

### ARTHUR R. VELASQUEZ

Arthur R. Velasquez and his family own Azteca Foods, one of the largest distributors of Mexican foods in the Midwest. Arthur and his wife, Joanne, started Azteca Foods in 1970 and built it into a successful company.

Azteca makes and distributes tortillas, tortilla chips, and salad shells throughout the Midwest and Southeast. Most of the business is retail, and the products can be found in more than 25,000 supermarkets in 35 states. Some products are also sold in Puerto Rico, Venezuela, and Europe, giving an international dimension to the enterprise.

Arthur holds B.S. and M.B.A. degrees. In his M.B.A. program, he was exposed to the subject of accounting, and he will talk at length about the importance of accounting to business success.

People who are not in business may believe that accounting is emphasized only in big businesses. But Arthur says, "An entrepreneur in a start-up business needs to follow standard accounting principles and practices. An entrepreneur is fulfilling a dream and wearing all the hats. But without a business plan based on sound accounting principles, proper accounting controls, and the analysis of an independent auditor, success is difficult."

Entrepreneurs in a start-up business may be immersed in the operations of the company. "But there is no substitute," says Arthur, "for timely and accurate reporting to keep a business running strongly, especially a start-up enterprise."

Arthur believes that it is important for students to develop a strong system of values and ethics. These are acquired in relating with family members, teachers, and the people you associate with. He says that the highest ideals should be practiced in your business life just as in your daily life.

### ACCOUNTING AT WORK

## TERMS REVIEW

current liabilities

interest expense

## AUDIT YOUR UNDERSTANDING

1. Why are notes payable generally classified as current liabilities?
2. What accounts are affected, and how, when a business signs a note payable for an extension of time on an account payable?

## WORK TOGETHER

**Journalizing notes payable transactions**

The journals for Landings, Inc., are provided in the *Working Papers*. Your instructor will guide you through the following examples.

3. Using the current year, journalize the following transactions. Use page 3 of a general journal and page 5 of a cash receipts journal. Source documents are abbreviated as follows: check, C; receipt, R; memorandum, M.

   Mar. 3. Signed a 90-day, 12% note, for $6,000.00 with First National Bank. R279.

   18. Signed a 60-day, 18% note with DryCreek Company for an extension of time on this account payable, $2,000.00. M288.

4. Journalize the following transactions on page 9 of a cash payments journal. Use the maturity dates and maturity values calculated in Work Together on page 597.

   Paid cash for the maturity value of the $2,000.00 note. C255.

   Paid cash for the maturity value of the $6,000.00 note. C263.

## ON YOUR OWN

**Journalizing notes payable transactions**

The journals for Modisto Corporation are provided in the *Working Papers*. Work these problems independently.

5. Using the current year, journalize the following transactions. Use page 10 of a general journal and page 20 of a cash receipts journal. Source documents are abbreviated as follows: check, C; receipt, R; memorandum, M.

   June 6. Signed a 60-day, 10% note, for $10,000.00 with National Bank of Industry. R244.

   23. Signed a 90-day, 18% note with Best Company for an extension of time on this account payable, $4,200.00. M180.

6. Journalize the following transactions on page 17 of a cash payments journal. Use the maturity dates and maturity values calculated in On Your Own on page 597.

   Paid cash for the maturity value of the $10,000.00 note. C155.

   Paid cash for the maturity value of the $4,200.00 note. C163.

# 23-3 Notes Receivable

## ACCEPTING A NOTE RECEIVABLE FROM A CUSTOMER

1. Debit to Notes Receivable

2. Credit to Accounts Receivable

GENERAL JOURNAL — PAGE 4

| | DATE | | ACCOUNT TITLE | DOC. NO. | POST. REF. | DEBIT | CREDIT | |
|---|---|---|---|---|---|---|---|---|
| 18 | | 22 | *Notes Receivable* | *NR7* | | *1 000 00* | | 18 |
| 19 | | | *Accounts Receivable/Peter Ange* | | / | | *1 000 00* | 19 |
| 20 | | | | | | | | 20 |

Promissory notes that a business accepts from customers are called **notes receivable.** Notes receivable are usually paid within one year. Therefore, they are classified as current assets.

A customer who is unable to pay an account on the due date may request additional time. The business should require the customer to sign a note. A note does not pay the amount the customer owes. However, the form of the asset is changed from an account receivable to a note receivable. The promissory note is a written confirmation of the amount owed, which provides the business with evidence of the debt in case legal action is required to collect.

When a customer signs a note, the principal amount of the note is debited to an asset account titled Notes Receivable. One asset, Accounts Receivable, is replaced by another asset, Notes Receivable.

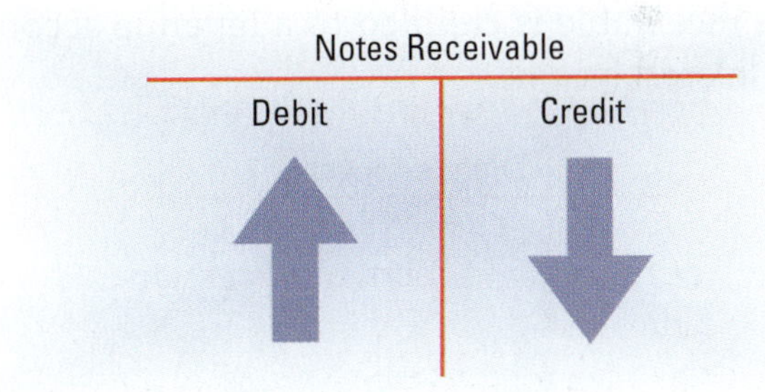


***April 22. Accepted a 90-day, 18% note from Peter Ange for an extension of time on his account, $1,000.00. Note Receivable No. 7.***

GENERAL LEDGER

Notes Receivable

| Debit | | Credit | |
|---|---|---|---|
| Apr. 22 | 1,000.00 | | |

Accounts Receivable

| Debit | | Credit | |
|---|---|---|---|
| Bal. | 1,000.00 | Apr. 22 | 1,000.00 |

ACCOUNTS RECEIVABLE LEDGER

Peter Ange

| Debit | | Credit | |
|---|---|---|---|
| Bal. | 1,000.00 | Apr. 22 | 1,000.00 |

When this entry is posted, the balance of the accounts receivable account for Mr. Ange is zero.

### STEPS: Journalizing accepting a note for an extension of time on an account receivable

1. Record a debit to *Notes Receivable* for the amount of the note, *$1,000.00,* in the general journal.
2. Record a credit to *Accounts Receivable/Peter Ange* for the same amount, *$1,000.00.*

## COLLECTING PRINCIPAL AND INTEREST ON A NOTE RECEIVABLE

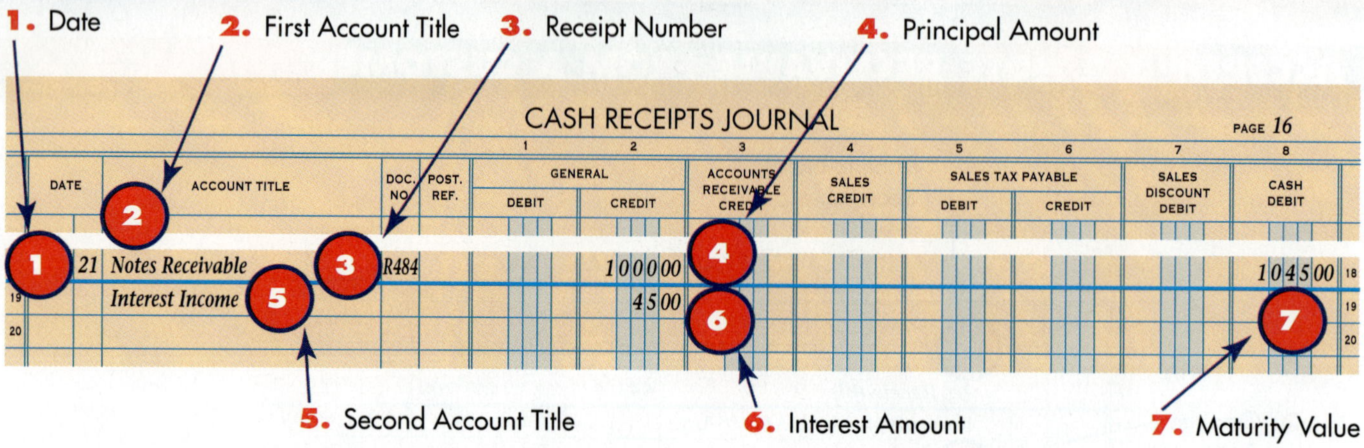


When a note receivable reaches its maturity date, the payee receives the maturity value from the maker. The interest earned on money loaned is called **interest income.** The interest earned on a note receivable is credited to a revenue account titled Interest Income.

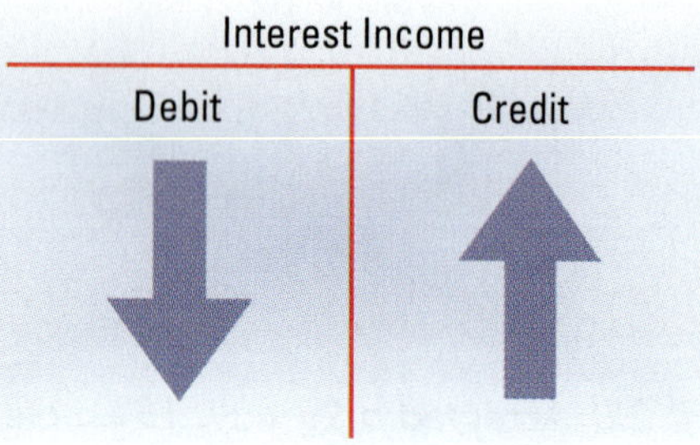


Interest income is investment revenue rather than revenue from normal operations. Therefore, Interest Income is listed in a classification titled Other Revenue in a chart of accounts.

Winning Edge received cash from Peter Ange for the principal and interest of the note signed by Mr. Ange on April 22.

***July 21. Received cash for the maturity value of Note Receivable No. 7, a 90-day, 18% note: principal, $1,000.00, plus interest, $45.00; total, $1,045.00. Receipt No. 484.***

**Cash**

| | | | |
|---|---|---|---|
| July 21 | 1,045.00 | | |

**Notes Receivable**

| | | | |
|---|---|---|---|
| Apr. 22 | 1,000.00 | July 21 | 1,000.00 |

**Interest Income**

| | | | |
|---|---|---|---|
| | | July 21 | 45.00 |

Interest income is calculated using the same method as used for notes payable. The principal is multiplied by the interest rate and the fraction of the year ($1,000.00 × 18% × 90/360) to calculate interest income, $45.00.

After the entry is recorded, the original of Note Receivable No. 7 is marked *Paid*. The original is given to Mr. Ange and a copy is kept by Winning Edge.

### STEPS: Journalizing cash received for maturity value of a note receivable

1. Write the date, *21*, in the Date column of the cash receipts journal.
2. Write the account title, *Notes Receivable*, in the Account Title column.
3. Write the receipt number, *R484*, in the Doc. No. column.
4. Write the principal amount, *$1,000.00*, in the General Credit column.
5. On the next line, write the account title, *Interest Income*, in the Account Title column.
6. Calculate and write the interest income amount, *$45.00*, in the General Credit column.
7. Write the maturity value, *$1,045.00*, in the Cash Debit column on the first line of the entry.

## RECORDING A DISHONORED NOTE RECEIVABLE

**1.** Debit to Accounts Receivable

GENERAL JOURNAL — PAGE 5

| | DATE | | ACCOUNT TITLE | DOC. NO. | POST. REF. | DEBIT | CREDIT | |
|---|---|---|---|---|---|---|---|---|
| 15 | | 15 | Accounts Receivable/Pam Carter | M85 | / | 418 00 | | 15 |
| 16 | | | Notes Receivable | | | | 400 00 | 16 |
| 17 | | | Interest Income | | | | 18 00 | 17 |
| 18 | | | | | | | | 18 |

**2.** Credit to Notes Receivable

**3.** Credit to Interest Income

A note that is not paid when due is called a **dishonored note.** The balance of the notes receivable account should show only the total amount of notes that probably will be collected. The amount of a dishonored note receivable should be removed from the notes receivable account.

The amount of the note plus interest income earned on the note is still owed by the customer. Therefore, the total amount owed should be debited to the accounts receivable account in the general ledger. The amount owed should also be debited to the customer account in the accounts receivable ledger. This information may be important if the customer requests credit in the future or if collection is achieved later.

***May 15. Pam Carter dishonored Note Receivable No. 9, a 90-day, 18% note, maturity value due today: principal, $400.00; interest, $18.00; total, $418.00. Memorandum No. 85.***

The interest income on the note has been earned as of the maturity date even though the note has not been paid. Pam Carter owes the principal amount of the note plus the interest earned. Therefore, the maturity value, $418.00, is debited to Accounts Receivable and to Pam Carter's account in the accounts receivable ledger. One asset, Notes Receivable, is replaced by another asset, Accounts Receivable.

GENERAL LEDGER

Accounts Receivable

| | | | |
|---|---|---|---|
| May 15 | 418.00 | | |

Notes Receivable

| | | | |
|---|---|---|---|
| Feb. 14 | 400.00 | May 15 | 400.00 |

Interest Income

| | | | |
|---|---|---|---|
| | | May 15 | 18.00 |

ACCOUNTS RECEIVABLE LEDGER

Pam Carter

| | | | |
|---|---|---|---|
| May 15 | 418.00 | | |

Winning Edge does not write off Ms. Carter's account when the note is dishonored. The company continues to try to collect the account.

Later Winning Edge may decide that the account cannot be collected. At that time the balance of the account will be written off as an uncollectible account. Allowance for Uncollectible Accounts will be debited, and Accounts Receivable and Pam Carter's account will be credited.

**STEPS**

### Journalizing a dishonored note receivable

1. Record a debit to *Accounts Receivable/Pam Carter* for the total maturity value of the note, *$418.00,* in the general journal.
2. Record a credit to *Notes Receivable* for the principal amount of the dishonored note, *$400.00.*
3. Record a credit to *Interest Income* for the interest earned on the note, *$18.00.*

## TERMS REVIEW

notes receivable

interest income

dishonored note

## AUDIT YOUR UNDERSTANDING

1. When a business asks a customer to sign a note receivable for an extension of time on the customer's account receivable, how does the amount and form of the business asset change?
2. Interest Income is listed in what chart of accounts classification?
3. What accounts are affected, and how, when a customer dishonors a note receivable?
4. Why is interest income recorded at the time a note is dishonored even though cash has not been received?

## WORK TOGETHER

**Journalizing notes receivable transactions**

The journals for Cruz Corporation are provided in the *Working Papers.* Your instructor will guide you through the following example.

5. Using the current year, journalize the following transactions. Use page 2 of a general journal and page 3 of a cash receipts journal. Source documents are abbreviated as follows: note receivable, NR; receipt, R; memorandum, M.

***Transactions:***

Feb. 2. Accepted a 90-day, 16% note from Paul Gary for an extension of time on his account, $1,800.00. NR17.

18. Received cash for the maturity value of NR14, a 60-day, 18% note for $500.00. R67.

27. Kirk Adams dishonored NR9, a 90-day, 18% note, for $400.00. M25.

## ON YOUR OWN

**Journalizing notes receivable transactions**

The journals for Reality, Inc. are provided in the *Working Papers.* Work this problem independently.

6. Using the current year, journalize the following transactions. Use page 3 of a general journal and page 5 of a cash receipts journal. Source documents are abbreviated as follows: note receivable, NR; receipt, R; memorandum, M.

***Transactions:***

Mar. 5. Accepted a 90-day, 18% note from Jan Paulson for an extension of time on her account, $1,500.00. NR22.

16. Received cash for the maturity value of NR16, a 60-day, 18% note for $800.00. R79.

21. Marshall Poe dishonored NR13, a 90-day, 15% note, for $2,600.00. M32.

# CHAPTER 23 SUMMARY

*Enrichment Activity*

**Time Management**

*Large tasks can be more manageable if broken into small parts. Consider a large personal or school project. Break the project down into the different tasks that must be done to complete the project. Write these tasks down. This list will be your to-do list for the project. Once you prioritize each item, you will have a plan of approach for the project.*

After completing this chapter, you can

1. Define accounting terms related to notes and interest.
2. Identify accounting concepts and practices related to notes and interest.
3. Calculate interest and maturity dates for notes.
4. Analyze and record transactions for notes payable.
5. Analyze and record transactions for notes receivable.

## EXPLORE ACCOUNTING

### LOW INTEREST OR CASH BACK?

"For a limited time, receive 1.9% financing or $2,000 cash back on your new car!" We often hear car dealers offer customers incentives of below-market financing or a cash refund. Each option provides the customer with a monetary value. The below-market financing spreads this value—a reduced monthly payment—over a period of time. The cash refund is received when the car is purchased.

Should the customer's choice have an impact on the way the sales transaction is recorded by the car dealer? Hammond Motors has two cars with sticker prices of $18,000.00. Donald Peters purchased one car, paying $3,000.00, down and financing the remaining $15,000.00 over 4 years at the 1.9% interest rate. Janice Edwards purchased the other car, paying only $1,000.00 down and using her $2,000.00 cash back option to reduce her 12% note to $15,000.00. Using this information, it appears that Hammond Auto sold Donald's car for $18,000.00 and Janice's car for $16,000.00. It also appears that both customers are responsible for $15,000.00 notes receivable.

However, accountants believe that, regardless of which sales incentive is offered, the value of the incentive should be deducted from the sales price. Accounting rules require that the recorded amount of below-market loans be reduced by the value of the incentive. This process, known as imputing interest, adjusts the note receivable to an amount that will yield a market rate of interest over the life of the note. Using the imputing interest rules, the below-market financing provided Donald Peters with a $2,000.00 benefit. Thus, Hammond Auto must record a $2,000.00 credit to Discount on Notes Receivable. The credit to Sales for Donald's car, therefore, is only $15,000.00.

**Required:** Identify a below-market financing or cash refund currently being offered by an auto dealer. If you were purchasing the car, which offer would you accept? Without knowing the accounting rules for imputing interest, how could you make an informed decision?

## 23-1 APPLICATION PROBLEM
### Calculating interest, maturity dates, and maturity values for promissory notes

Write the answers to the following problem in the *Working Papers.*

***Instructions:***

For each of the following promissory notes, calculate (a) the interest on the note, (b) the maturity date of the note, and (c) the maturity value of the note. Save your work to complete Application Problem 23-2.

| Date | Principal | Interest Rate | Time |
|---|---|---|---|
| April 2 | $10,000.00 | 12% | 180 days |
| April 8 | $ 600.00 | 18% | 60 days |
| April 15 | $ 5,000.00 | 14% | 90 days |
| April 18 | $ 1,200.00 | 18% | 60 days |

## 23-2 APPLICATION PROBLEM
### Journalizing notes payable transactions

The journals for Webster Company are provided in the *Working Papers.*

***Instructions:***

1. Using the current year, journalize each of the following transactions using page 4 of a general journal and page 6 of a cash receipts journal. Source documents are abbreviated as follows: receipt, R; memorandum, M.

***Transactions:***

Apr. 2. Signed a 180-day, 12% note, for $10,000.00 with First American Bank. R127.
8. Signed a 60-day, 18% note with Milligan Company for an extension of time on this account payable, $600.00. M32.
15. Signed a 90-day, 14% note, for $5,000.00 with First National Bank. R142.
18. Signed a 60-day, 18% note with Yeatman Industries for an extension of time on this account payable, $1,200.00. M42.

2. Journalize the following transactions on page 9 of a cash payments journal. Use the maturity dates and maturity values calculated in Application Problem 23-1. The abbreviation for a check is C.

***Transactions:***

Paid cash for the maturity value of the $600.00 note dated April 8. C310.
Paid cash for the maturity value of the $1,200.00 note dated April 18. C318.
Paid cash for the maturity value of the $5,000.00 note dated April 15. C456.
Paid cash for the maturity value of the $10,000.00 note dated April 2. C645.

## 23-3 APPLICATION PROBLEM
### Journalizing notes receivable transactions

The journals for Logistics Technical Corporation are provided in the *Working Papers.*

***Instructions:***

Using the current year, journalize the following transactions. Use page 12 of a general journal and page 8 of a cash receipts journal. Source documents are abbreviated as follows: notes receivable, NR; receipt, R; memorandum, M.

***Transactions:***

Aug. 6. Accepted a 90-day, 18% note from Len Lambert for an extension of time on his account, $2,000.00. NR32.

12. Received cash for the maturity value of NR21, a 60-day, 18% note for $600.00. R259.

16. Accepted a 90-day, 18% note from Ned Freeman for an extension of time on his account, $1,200.00. NR33.

22. Adam Richard dishonored NR25, a 90-day, 15% note, for $2,200.00. M53.

23. Received cash for the maturity value of NR26, a 90-day, 18% note for $800.00. R269.

28. Jamie Angle dishonored NR27, a 90-day, 15% note, for $2,500.00. M58.

## 23-4 APPLICATION PROBLEM
### Journalizing notes receivable transactions

Jack Farris, the credit manager of Jenkin Company, encourages customers of past-due accounts to sign notes receivable. Mr. Farris informs customers that future sales on account will be accepted only if the customers sign a note and subsequently pay the note with interest. Using this strategy, most of Jenkin's customers agree to sign notes. Jenkin Company requires all customers to sign 90-day, 18% notes.

***Instructions:***

Journalize the following transactions completed by Jenkin Company during the current year. The journals are provided in the *Working Papers*. Use page 18 of a general journal and page 11 of a cash receipts journal. Source documents are abbreviated as follows: notes receivable, NR; receipt, R; memorandum, M.

***Transactions:***

Nov. 3. Jack Farris visited the offices of AutoCare Industries. AutoCare's president agreed to sign a note for $3,000.00. NR63.

14. Received a check for $2,090.00 from Teltor Company. The payment covers a $2,000.00 note, number 52. R245.

28. A $4,000.00, 18%, 90-day note receivable from Sanford Company was due today, but no check has been received. Jack Farris attempted to call the company but discovered that its phone has been disconnected. M69.

## 23-5 MASTERY PROBLEM
### Journalizing notes payable and notes receivable transactions

The following transactions related to notes payable and notes receivable were completed by Amory Company during March of the current year. Journals are provided in the *Working Papers*.

***Transactions:***

Mar. 6. Signed a 90-day, 12% note, for $20,000.00 with First American Bank. R42.
8. Accepted a 90-day, 18% note from Patti Love for an extension of time on her account, $500.00. NR10.
10. Received cash for the maturity value of NR3, a 60-day, 18% note for $800.00. R52.
13. Accepted a 90-day, 18% note from Kelly Sullivan for an extension of time on her account, $1,400.00. NR11.
19. Received cash for the maturity value of NR4, a 60-day, 18% note for $600.00. R59.
21. Signed a 60-day, 15% note with Lawrence Supply for an extension of time on this account payable, $3,200.00. M34.
23. Jan Brothers dishonored NR5, a 90-day, 15% note, for $2,000.00. M35.
25. Signed a 180-day, 14% note, for $10,000.00 with First National Bank. R64.
28. Received cash for the maturity value of NR2, a 90-day, 18% note for $1,500.00. R69.

***Instructions:***

1. Journalize each transaction using page 3 of a general and page 6 of a cash receipts journal. Source documents are abbreviated as follows: check, C; receipt, R; memorandum, M; note receivable, NR.
2. Determine the maturity date and maturity value of each note signed by Amory Company.
3. Journalize the following transactions on page 9 of a cash payments journal. Use the maturity dates and maturity values calculated in previous steps.

***Transactions:***

Paid cash for the maturity value of the $3,200.00 note dated March 21. C231.
Paid cash for the maturity value of the $20,000.00 note dated March 6. C311.
Paid cash for the maturity value of the $10,000.00 note dated March 25. C467.

## 23-6 CHALLENGE PROBLEM
### Recording notes receivable stated in months

On June 18, James Whiley signed a $10,000.00 note payable with National Bank of Cressville. At his request, the bank drafted the note for a 3-month term, payable on September 18, with 15% interest. Mr. Whiley proudly stated, "Since my company began in 1972, we have never had to borrow money for more than 90 days." The loan officer, believing that Mr. Whiley did not fully understand the terms of the note, explained that the company would be responsible for interest for the number of days between June 18 and September 18. That number, he continued, would be slightly more than 90 days.

***Instructions:***

1. Use the forms given in the *Working Papers*. Determine the maturity value of the note on September 18. Use the actual number of days from June 18 in your calculation.
2. Mr. Whiley expected to pay only 90 days of interest on the note. Determine the maturity value of the note assuming interest is charged for only 90 days.
3. Assume the bank allows Mr. Whiley to pay only the interest amount computed in Instruction 2, even though the money will be borrowed for more than 90 days. Determine the actual interest rate of the note.
4. Should the bank allow Mr. Whiley to pay for only 90 days' interest?

INTERNET ACTIVITY

Point your browser to

**http://accounting.swpco.com**

Choose **First-Year Course**, choose **Activities**, and complete the activity for Chapter 23.

## Applied Communication

As an accountant for Hasler Corporation, you have been asked to assist the president in making a presentation to the board of directors. The president wants to report the 4-year growth in sales of four major products. The following table presents product sales (in thousands of dollars) from 20X1 to 20X4.

| | **20X1** | **20X2** | **20X3** | **20X4** |
|---|---|---|---|---|
| Lumber | $253 | $316 | $324 | $315 |
| Hardware | 166 | 182 | 169 | 175 |
| Carpet | 153 | 176 | 189 | 201 |
| Housewares | 122 | 112 | 114 | 103 |

**Instructions:** Prepare a graph depicting the data presented in the table. Determine what type of graph (pie, line, bar, stacked-bar) best communicates the sales trend of each product. If available, use the graph or chart feature of a spreadsheet program to create the

## Cases for Critical Thinking

**Case 1** Because of a temporary cash shortage, Balister Company requested an extension of time on its purchases on account. Balister's regular vendor, Custom Products, requires that a 12% note be signed for any extension of time over one month. Balister usually needs 90 days from time of purchase to time of payment. Because of the extra costs for interest expense, Balister has been exploring other vendor options. Another vendor, Nagano Supplies, will sell merchandise on account with credit terms of net due in 90 days. For the same quantity and brand of merchandise, Nagano Supplies charges 2.5% more than Custom Products. Since Nagano Supplies offers 90 days credit terms without any interest charges and the merchandise is only 2.5% higher than that from Custom Products, Balister's purchasing manager, Kelly Preston, has decided to buy the merchandise from Nagano. When asked why she is buying from the company with costs 2.5% higher, she said, "A 2.5% higher price is better than the 12% interest we would have to pay Custom Products." Do you agree with Ms. Preston? Explain.

**Case 2** Jim Johnson, a new accounting department employee, questions the practice of recording interest income when a note is dishonored. Instead, he believes that the interest earned on the note should be recorded only if and when the account is subsequently paid. Is this alternative method acceptable?

# AUTOMATED ACCOUNTING

## CALCULATING NOTES AND INTEREST USING PLANNING TOOLS

Planning tools function like specialized calculators. They are used to perform specific types of calculations. *Automated Accounting 7.0* includes several planning tools. These utilities quickly perform the calculations and display the results. A printing function also allows a report to be printed, showing the results of the planner's calculation. When a business uses notes receivable or notes payable to finance transactions, information about interest amounts, payment amounts, and due dates may be calculated using the Notes and Interest Planner.

### Notes and Interest Planner

The Notes and Interest Planner is used to calculate maturity date, amount of interest, and the maturity value of the note. A business can use the planner to calculate the total amount to be received or paid (maturity value) of its notes receivable or notes payable. The planner may also be used to determine the exact due date of a note when the term is stated as a number of days or months. To use the Notes and Interest Planner:

1. Click the Tools toolbar button.
2. Click the Notes and Interest tab.
3. In the Time Basis box, select one of the following: Number of Days based on 360 days, Number of Days based on 365 days, or the Number of Months, by clicking on the appropriate option button.
4. Enter the data and press the Tab key to move among the text boxes. The calculated results for Maturity Date of Note, Amount of Interest, and Maturity Value will appear at the bottom of the Planning dialog box.
5. Click on the Report button to produce a schedule of the results. Once displayed, the report may be printed or copied to the clipboard for pasting into a spreadsheet or word processor.
6. Click the Close button, or press ESC to exit the report and return to the planner.
7. Steps 3 through 5 may be repeated for different Calculate options, or for different data sets.
8. Click the Close button, or press ESC to exit the planner.

### Using Reports in Other Documents

Reports may be printed or copied to the clipboard for pasting into a spreadsheet or word

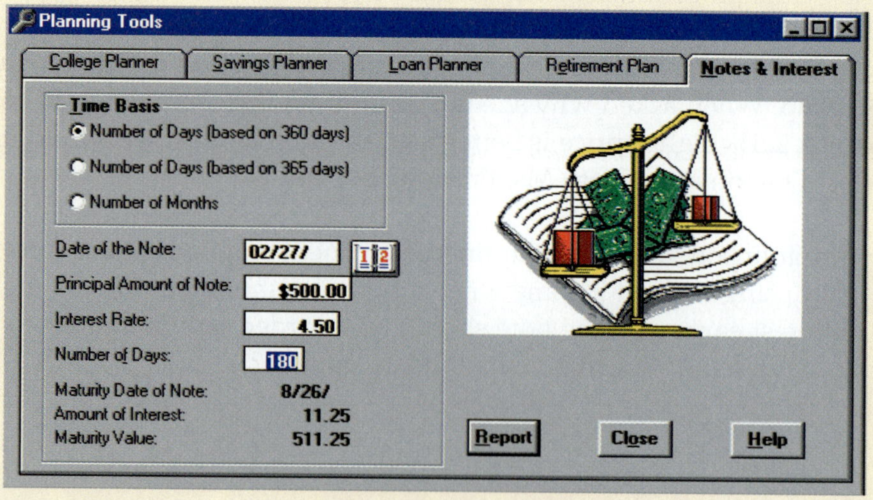

# AUTOMATED ACCOUNTING

processor. To print a report for use as a source document:

- Click on the Print command button.
- To select a printer or change printer options, choose Print Setup from the File menu.
- To change the font of the printed report, choose Change Printer Font from the File menu.

### Using Reports to Prepare Journal Entries

If recording a cash receipt for a note receivable:

1. Click the Journal toolbar button.
2. Click the Cash Receipts tab.
3. Enter the transaction date and press Tab.
4. Enter the source document number in the Refer. text box and press Tab as needed to move among text boxes.
5. Enter the account number for Notes Receivable, and the credit amount.
6. Choose the customer name from the Customer drop-down list, if appropriate.
7. Move to the next line of the journal.
8. Enter the account number for Interest Income and the credit amount. The interest amount is shown on the Notes & Interest Planner report. The Cash debit amount is automatically calculated and displayed by the computer.
9. Click the Post button.

### AUTOMATING APPLICATION PROBLEM 23-1: Calculating interest, maturity dates, and maturity values for promissory notes

**Instructions:**

1. Load *Automated Accounting 7.0* or higher software.
2. Select database F23-1 from the appropriate directory/folder.
3. Select File from the menu bar and choose the Save As menu command. Key the path to the drive and directory that contains your data files. Save the database with a file name of XXX231 (where XXX are your initials).
4. Access Problem Instructions through the Help menu. Read the Problem Instructions screen.
5. Key the data listed on page 608.
6. Exit the *Automated Accounting* software.

### AUTOMATING MASTERY PROBLEM 23-5: Journalizing notes payable and notes receivable transactions

**Instructions:**

1. Load *Automated Accounting 7.0* or higher software.
2. Select database F23-2 from the appropriate directory/folder.
3. Select File from the menu bar and choose the Save As menu command. Key the path to the drive and directory that contains your data files. Save the database with a file name of XXX232 (where XXX are your initials).
4. Access Problem Instructions through the Help menu. Read the Problem Instructions screen.
5. Key the data listed on page 610.
6. Exit the *Automated Accounting* software.

# 24 Accounting for Accrued Revenue and Expenses

**AFTER STUDYING CHAPTER 24, YOU WILL BE ABLE TO:**

1. Define accounting terms related to accrued revenue and accrued expenses.
2. Identify accounting concepts and practices related to accrued revenue and accrued expenses.
3. Record adjusting, closing, and reversing entries for accrued revenue.
4. Record adjusting, closing, and reversing entries for accrued expenses.

**TERMS PREVIEW**

- accrued revenue
- accrued interest income
- reversing entry
- accrued expenses
- accrued interest expense

## ACCOUNTING FOR INTEREST AT THE FISCAL YEAR END

Generally accepted accounting principles (GAAP) require that revenue and expenses be recorded in the accounting period in which revenue is earned and expenses are incurred. *(CONCEPT: Matching Expenses with Revenue)* Some revenues, however, are earned each day but are usually recorded only when cash is actually received. For example, interest is earned for each day a note receivable is held. However, the interest may not be received until the maturity date of the note. Likewise, some expenses may be incurred before they are actually paid. A note payable incurs interest expense each day the note is outstanding. Yet, the interest generally is not paid until the note's maturity date. At the end of the fiscal period, adjusting entries are recorded for these revenues and expenses.

Revenue earned in one fiscal period but not received until a later fiscal period is called **accrued revenue.** At the end of a fiscal period, accrued revenue is recorded by an adjusting entry. *(CONCEPT: Realization of Revenue)* The adjusting entry for accrued revenue increases a revenue account. The adjusting entry also increases a receivable account. The income statement will then report all revenue earned for the period even though some of the revenue has not yet been received. The balance sheet will report all the assets, including the accrued revenue receivable. *(CONCEPT: Adequate Disclosure)*

# ACCOUNTING IN YOUR CAREER

## NOTES PAYABLE SPREADSHEET

Boyce Anne Barnes is an assistant in the accounting department of General Cinema Corporation. She maintains a computerized spreadsheet of all the notes payable for the business. The spreadsheet includes columns for the date issued, length of note, interest rate, and due date. Boyce Anne sends a printout of the spreadsheet to the financial analyst at the end of each month.

Boyce Anne is very dedicated to the company. Interested in promotion to a higher position, she wants to understand how her work fits in with the rest of the company's procedures. At lunch in the cafeteria one day, she has the opportunity to sit with Eric Seng, the financial analyst. She asks him how he uses the notes payable report.

Eric explains that he uses the figures from the report to plan how much cash needs to be available to pay currently due notes and interest. Furthermore, he explains, at the end of each fiscal period he must calculate what portion of each month's interest is due at the end of the period, even though it does not yet have to be paid. "You see," he continues, "the amount that is owed but not yet due is an expense of the current fiscal period, and I have to report it as such." Boyce Anne thinks about this response for a bit and then asks Eric if it would help to build in another column for the amount of interest that is owed on December 31, the end of the fiscal period. "It certainly would," he replies. "Right now I calculate this by hand to get the figures I need. I've always meant to write a formula that would calculate this automatically but never seem to find time to do it."

"Let me give it a try," says Boyce Anne. "I think I can come up with something for you to look at."

***Critical Thinking:***

1. Why would Boyce Anne volunteer to take on an extra responsibility?
2. Suggest how Boyce Anne could write a formula to perform this calculation.

# 24-1 Accrued Revenue

## ANALYZING AN ADJUSTMENT FOR ACCRUED INTEREST INCOME

**1.** Debit Interest Receivable. **2.** Credit Interest Income.

*Winning Edge*
*Work Sheet*
*For Year Ended December 31, 20--*

| | Account Title | 1 Trial Balance Debit | 2 Trial Balance Credit | 3 Adjustments Debit | 4 Adjustments Credit | 5 Income Statement Debit | 6 Income Statement Credit | 7 Balance Sheet Debit | 8 Balance Sheet Credit | |
|---|---|---|---|---|---|---|---|---|---|---|
| 4 | *Interest Receivable* | | | (a) 20 00 | | | | 20 00 | | 4 |
| 51 | *Interest Income* | | 68 00 | | (a) 20 00 | | 88 00 | | | 51 |

**3.** Record the adjusting entry.

GENERAL JOURNAL PAGE *15*

| | Date | | Account Title | Doc. No. | Post. Ref. | Debit | Credit | |
|---|---|---|---|---|---|---|---|---|
| 1 | | | *Adjusting Entries* | | | | | 1 |
| 2 | 20-- Dec. | 31 | *Interest Receivable* | | | 20 00 | | 2 |
| 3 | | | *Interest Income* | | | | 20 00 | 3 |

At the end of each fiscal period, Winning Edge examines the notes receivable on hand. The amount of interest income earned but not yet collected is calculated. Interest earned but not yet received is called **accrued interest income.** On December 31, Winning Edge has one note receivable on hand, a 90-day, 12%, $1,000.00 note dated November 1. An adjusting entry must be made to record the amount of interest earned to date on this note.

The time period from November 1 to December 31 is 60 days. Therefore, the interest earned on the note is calculated for $\frac{60}{360}$ of a year.

| Principal | × | Interest Rate | × | Time as Fraction of Year | = | Accrued Interest Income |
|---|---|---|---|---|---|---|
| $1,000.00 | × | 12% | × | $\frac{60}{360}$ | = | $20.00 |

**Interest Receivable**

| Debit | | Credit | |
|---|---|---|---|
| Dec. 31 Adj. | 20.00 | | |

**Interest Income**

| Debit | | Credit | |
|---|---|---|---|
| | | Dec. 31 Bal. | 68.00 |
| | | Dec. 31 Adj. | 20.00 |
| | | *(New Bal.* | *88.00)* |

Interest Receivable is debited for $20.00 to show the interest income that has accrued at the end of the fiscal period. This revenue will not be collected until the next fiscal period.

The credit of $20.00 is added to the previous balance in Interest Income. The new account balance, $88.00, is the total amount of interest income earned during the fiscal period.

**STEPS**

### Recording an adjustment for accrued interest income

1. Write the accrued interest income amount, *$20.00,* in the Adjustments Debit column on the Interest Receivable line of the work sheet. Label the adjustment with a small letter *a* in parentheses, *(a).*
2. Write the same amount, *$20.00,* in the Adjustments Credit column on the Interest Income line of the work sheet. Label the adjustment using the same letter, *(a).*
3. Use the debit and credit amounts on the work sheet to record an adjusting entry in a general journal.

## POSTING AN ADJUSTING ENTRY FOR ACCRUED INTEREST INCOME

GENERAL JOURNAL — PAGE *15*

| | DATE | | ACCOUNT TITLE | DOC. NO. | POST. REF. | DEBIT | CREDIT | |
|---|---|---|---|---|---|---|---|---|
| 1 | | | *Adjusting Entries* | | | | | 1 |
| 2 | 20-- *Dec.* | *31* | *Interest Receivable* | | *1120* | *20 00* | | 2 |
| 3 | | | *Interest Income* | | *7110* | | *20 00* | 3 |
| 4 | | | | | | | | 4 |
| 5 | | | | | | | | 5 |

**1.** Post the debit. → 1

2 ← **2.** Post the credit.

ACCOUNT *Interest Receivable* — ACCOUNT NO. *1120*

| DATE | | ITEM | POST. REF. | DEBIT | CREDIT | BALANCE DEBIT | BALANCE CREDIT |
|---|---|---|---|---|---|---|---|
| 20-- *Dec.* | *31* | | *G15* | *20 00* | | *20 00* | |

ACCOUNT *Interest Income* — ACCOUNT NO. *7110*

| DATE | | ITEM | POST. REF. | DEBIT | CREDIT | BALANCE DEBIT | BALANCE CREDIT |
|---|---|---|---|---|---|---|---|
| *Dec.* | *29* | | *CR36* | | *12 00* | | *68 00* |
| | *31* | | *G15* | | *20 00* | | *88 00* |

The adjustment for accrued interest income planned on a work sheet is recorded as an adjusting entry in a general journal. The adjusting entry is then posted to the general ledger.

After posting, the interest receivable account has a debit balance of $20.00 and will appear on the balance sheet as a current asset. This debit balance is the accrued interest income earned but not yet collected at the end of the year. The interest income account has a credit balance of $88.00 and will appear on the income statement as other revenue. This amount is the total interest income for the year.

**STEPS**

### Posting an adjusting entry for accrued interest income

1. Post the debit, *$20.00,* to Interest Receivable.
2. Post the credit, *$20.00,* to Interest Income.

### REMEMBER

The interest receivable account appears in the Current Assets section of the balance sheet. The interest income account appears in the Other Revenue section of the income statement.

## REVERSING ENTRY FOR ACCRUED INTEREST INCOME

**1.** Write the heading.

**2.** Debit Interest Income.

GENERAL JOURNAL PAGE 17

| | DATE | | ACCOUNT TITLE | DOC. NO. | POST. REF. | DEBIT | CREDIT | |
|---|---|---|---|---|---|---|---|---|
| 1 | | | *Reversing Entries* | | | | | 1 |
| 2 | 20-- Jan. | 1 | *Interest Income* | | | 20 00 | | 2 |
| 3 | | | *Interest Receivable* | | | | 20 00 | 3 |
| 4 | | | | | | | | 4 |

**3.** Credit Interest Receivable.

On December 31, Interest Income is closed as part of the regular closing entry for income statement accounts with credit balances. Interest Income is debited for $88.00 to reduce the account balance to zero.

Adjusting entries for accrued revenues have an effect on transactions to be recorded in the following fiscal period. On the maturity date of the outstanding 90-day note receivable, Winning Edge will receive interest of $30.00.

However, an adjusting entry was made to record the amount of interest earned last year, $20.00. Thus, $20.00 of the $30.00 total interest income has already been recorded as revenue. The remaining $10.00 of the $30.00 total interest will be earned during the current fiscal period.

It is inconvenient to determine how much, if any, of cash received from notes receivable relates to interest accrued during the prior fiscal period. To avoid this inconvenience, an entry is made at the beginning of the new fiscal period to reverse the adjusting entry. An entry made at the beginning of one fiscal period to reverse an adjusting entry made in the previous fiscal period is called a **reversing entry.**

Interest Income

| | | | |
|---|---|---|---|
| Dec. 31 Closing | 88.00 | Dec. 31 Bal. | 68.00 |
| Jan. 1 Rev. | 20.00 | Dec. 31 Adj. | 20.00 |
| *(New Bal.* | *20.00)* | | |

Interest Receivable

| | | | |
|---|---|---|---|
| Dec. 31 Adj. | 20.00 | Jan. 1 Rev. | 20.00 |
| *(New Bal. zero)* | | | |

The reversing entry is the opposite of the adjusting entry. The entry creates a debit balance of $20.00 in Interest Income. A debit balance is the opposite of the normal balance of Interest Income. When the full amount of interest is received, the $30.00 will be credited to Interest Income, resulting in a $10.00 credit balance ($30.00 credit − $20.00 debit), the amount of interest earned in the new year.

The reversing entry reduced the balance in Interest Receivable to zero. When the interest is received, no entry will be made to Interest Receivable. Instead, the total amount of interest received will be credited to Interest Income.

### STEPS: Reversing an adjusting entry for accrued interest income

**1.** Write the heading *Reversing Entries* in the middle of the general journal's Account Title column. This heading explains all the reversing entries that follow. Therefore, indicating a source document is unnecessary.

**2.** Record a debit, *$20.00,* to Interest Income.

**3.** Record a credit, *$20.00,* to Interest Receivable.

## COLLECTING A NOTE RECEIVABLE ISSUED IN A PREVIOUS FISCAL PERIOD

**1.** Credit for Principal

**2.** Credit for Total Interest

**3.** Debit for Maturity Value

CASH RECEIPTS JOURNAL — PAGE 51

| | DATE | ACCOUNT TITLE | DOC. NO. | POST. REF. | 1 GENERAL DEBIT | 2 GENERAL CREDIT | 3 ACCOUNTS RECEIVABLE CREDIT | 4 SALES CREDIT | 5 SALES TAX PAYABLE DEBIT | 6 SALES TAX PAYABLE CREDIT | 7 SALES DISCOUNT DEBIT | 8 CASH DEBIT | |
|---|---|---|---|---|---|---|---|---|---|---|---|---|---|
| 22 | 30 | Notes Receivable | R9 | 1115 | | 1 000 00 | | | | | | 1 030 00 | 22 |
| 23 | | Interest Income | | 7110 | | 30 00 | | | | | | | 23 |
| 24 | | | | | | | | | | | | | 24 |

**4.** Post amounts in General columns.

ACCOUNT Notes Receivable — ACCOUNT NO. 1115

| DATE | | ITEM | POST. REF. | DEBIT | CREDIT | BALANCE DEBIT | BALANCE CREDIT |
|---|---|---|---|---|---|---|---|
| Nov. | 1 | | G11 | 1 000 00 | | 1 000 00 | |
| 20-- Jan. | 30 | | CR51 | | 1 000 00 | — | — |

ACCOUNT Interest Income — ACCOUNT NO. 7110

| DATE | | ITEM | POST. REF. | DEBIT | CREDIT | BALANCE DEBIT | BALANCE CREDIT |
|---|---|---|---|---|---|---|---|
| | 31 | | G15 | | 20 00 | | 88 00 |
| | 31 | | G16 | 88 00 | | — | — |
| 20-- Jan. | 1 | | G17 | 20 00 | | 20 00 | |
| | 30 | | CR51 | | 30 00 | | 10 00 |

On January 30, Winning Edge received the maturity value of the only note receivable on hand on December 31, the end of the previous fiscal year.

***January 30. Received cash for the maturity value of a 90-day, 12% note: principal, $1,000.00, plus interest, $30.00; total, $1,030.00. Receipt No. 9.***

**Cash**

| | | | |
|---|---|---|---|
| Jan. 30 Rec'd | 1,030.00 | | |

**Notes Receivable**

| | | | |
|---|---|---|---|
| Nov. 1 | 1,000.00 | Jan. 30 Rec'd | 1,000.00 |

**Interest Income**

| | | | |
|---|---|---|---|
| Dec. 31 Closing | 88.00 | Dec. 31 Bal. | 68.00 |
| Jan. 1 Rev. | 20.00 | Dec. 31 Adj. | 20.00 |
| | | Jan. 30 Rec'd | 30.00 |
| | | *(New Bal.* | *10.00)* |

The total interest, $30.00, was earned during two fiscal periods—$20.00 during the previous fiscal period and $10.00 during the current fiscal period. The reversing entry created a $20.00 debit balance in Interest Income. After the $30.00 credit is posted, Interest Income has a credit balance of $10.00, the amount of interest earned during the current fiscal period.

### STEPS: Collecting a note receivable issued in a previous fiscal period

1. Record a credit to Notes Receivable in the General Credit column of a cash receipts journal for the principal of the note, *$1,000.00.*
2. Record a credit to Interest Income in the General Credit column for the total interest, *$30.00.*
3. Record a debit in the Cash Debit column for the maturity value of the note, *$1,030.00.*
4. Post the amounts in the General columns of the cash receipts journal.

## TERMS REVIEW

accrued revenue

accrued interest income

reversing entry

## AUDIT YOUR UNDERSTANDING

1. Which accounting concept is being applied when an adjusting entry is made at the end of the fiscal period to record accrued revenue?
2. Why does a business use reversing entries as part of its procedures for accounting for accrued interest income?

## WORK TOGETHER

### Journalizing and posting entries for accrued revenue

The accounting forms for the following problems are in the *Working Papers*. Your instructor will guide you through the following examples. On December 31 of the current year, Wrenn Corporation has one note receivable outstanding, a 120-day, 18%, $3,000.00 note dated November 16.

3. Plan the adjustment on a work sheet. Label the adjustment *(a)*.
4. Journalize and post the adjusting entry for accrued interest income on December 31. Use page 14 of a general journal.
5. Journalize and post the closing entry for interest income using page 14 of a general journal.
6. Journalize and post the January 1 reversing entry for accrued interest income on page 15 of a general journal.
7. Journalize the receipt of cash for the maturity value of the note on March 16, Receipt No. 32. Use page 16 of a cash receipts journal. Post the amounts in the General columns.

## ON YOUR OWN

### Journalizing and posting entries for accrued revenue

The accounting forms for the following problems are in the *Working Papers*. Work these problems independently. On December 31 of the current year, Sierra, Inc., has one note receivable outstanding, a 90-day, 15%, $4,000.00 note dated December 1.

8. Plan the adjustment on a work sheet. Label the adjustment *(a)*.
9. Journalize and post the adjusting entry for accrued interest income on December 31. Use page 14 of a general journal.
10. Journalize and post the closing entry for interest income using page 14 of a general journal.
11. Journalize and post the January 1 reversing entry for accrued interest income on page 15 of a general journal.
12. Journalize the receipt of cash for the maturity value of the note on March 1, Receipt No. 65. Use page 19 of a cash receipts journal. Post the amounts in the General columns.

# 24-2 Accrued Expenses

## ANALYZING AN ADJUSTMENT FOR ACCRUED INTEREST EXPENSE

2. Credit Interest Payable.

**Winning Edge, Inc.**
**Work Sheet**
**For Year Ended December 31, 20--**

| | ACCOUNT TITLE | 1 TRIAL BALANCE DEBIT | 2 TRIAL BALANCE CREDIT | 3 ADJUSTMENTS DEBIT | 4 ADJUSTMENTS CREDIT | 5 INCOME STATEMENT DEBIT | 6 INCOME STATEMENT CREDIT | 7 BALANCE SHEET DEBIT | 8 BALANCE SHEET CREDIT | |
|---|---|---|---|---|---|---|---|---|---|---|
| 15 | Interest Payable | | | | (h) 200 00 | | | | 200 00 | 15 |
| 52 | Interest Expense | 1 143 00 | | (h) 200 00 | | 1 343 00 | | | | 52 |

1. Debit Interest Expense.

3. Record the adjusting entry.

**GENERAL JOURNAL** PAGE 15

| | DATE | ACCOUNT TITLE | DOC. NO. | POST. REF. | DEBIT | CREDIT | |
|---|---|---|---|---|---|---|---|
| 1 | | Adjusting Entries | | | | | 1 |
| 16 | 31 | Interest Expense | | | 200 00 | | 16 |
| 17 | | Interest Payable | | | | 200 00 | 17 |

Expenses incurred in one fiscal period but not paid until a later fiscal period are called **accrued expenses.** At the end of a fiscal period, accrued expense is recorded by an adjusting entry. *(CONCEPT: Matching Expenses with Revenue)* The adjusting entry increases an expense account. The adjusting entry also increases a payable account.

Interest incurred but not yet paid is called **accrued interest expense.** On December 31, Winning Edge has one note payable outstanding, a 180-day, 12%, $5,000.00 note dated September 2. Winning Edge owes $200.00 of interest for the 120 days from September 2 to December 31.

| Principal | × | Interest Rate | × | Time as Fraction of Year | = | Accrued Interest Expense |
|---|---|---|---|---|---|---|
| $5,000.00 | × | 12% | × | $\frac{120}{360}$ | = | $200.00 |

**Interest Expense**

| Debit | | Credit |
|---|---|---|
| Dec. 31 Bal. | 1,143.00 | |
| Dec. 31 Adj. | 200.00 | |
| *(New Bal.* | *1,343.00)* | |

**Interest Payable**

| Debit | Credit | |
|---|---|---|
| | Dec. 31 Adj. | 200.00 |

Interest Expense is debited for $200.00 to show the increase in the balance of this other expense account. The new balance of Interest Expense, $1,343.00, is the total amount of interest expense incurred during the fiscal period.

The credit to Interest Payable creates a $200.00 account balance that represents the interest owed on December 31 that will be paid in the next fiscal period.

# POSTING AN ADJUSTING ENTRY FOR ACCRUED INTEREST EXPENSE

GENERAL JOURNAL — PAGE 15

| | DATE | | ACCOUNT TITLE | DOC. NO. | POST. REF. | DEBIT | CREDIT | |
|---|---|---|---|---|---|---|---|---|
| 1 | | | Adjusting Entries | | | | | 1 |
| 16 | | 31 | Interest Expense | | 8105 | 200 00 | | 16 |
| 17 | | | Interest Payable | | 2110 | | 200 00 | 17 |
| 18 | | | | | | | | 18 |
| 19 | | | | | | | | 19 |
| 20 | | | | | | | | 20 |

**1.** Post the debit. → 1

2 ← **2.** Post the credit.

ACCOUNT Interest Payable — ACCOUNT NO. 2110

| DATE | | ITEM | POST. REF. | DEBIT | CREDIT | BALANCE DEBIT | BALANCE CREDIT |
|---|---|---|---|---|---|---|---|
| 20-- Dec. | 31 | | G15 | | 200 00 | | 200 00 |

ACCOUNT Interest Expense — ACCOUNT NO. 8105

| DATE | | ITEM | POST. REF. | DEBIT | CREDIT | BALANCE DEBIT | BALANCE CREDIT |
|---|---|---|---|---|---|---|---|
| Dec. | 21 | | CP36 | 75 00 | | 1 143 00 | |
| | 31 | | G15 | 200 00 | | 1 343 00 | |

The adjustment for accrued interest expense planned on a work sheet is recorded as an adjusting entry in a general journal. The adjusting entry is then posted to the general ledger.

After posting, the interest payable account has a credit balance of $200.00 and will appear on the December 31 balance sheet as a current liability. This credit balance is the accrued interest expense incurred but not yet paid at the end of the year.

The interest expense account has a debit balance of $1,343.00 and will appear on the income statement for the year ended December 31 as an other expense. This amount is the total interest expense for the year.

**STEPS — Posting an adjusting entry for accrued interest expense**

1. Post the debit, *$200.00,* to Interest Expense.
2. Post the credit, *$200.00,* to Interest Payable.

**REMEMBER**

The adjusting entry for accrued interest expense affects both the income statement and the balance sheet. The income statement will report all expenses for the period even though some of the expenses have not yet been paid. The balance sheet will report all liabilities, including the accrued expenses payable. *(CONCEPT: Adequate Disclosure)*

# REVERSING ENTRY FOR ACCRUED INTEREST EXPENSE

GENERAL JOURNAL — PAGE 17

| | DATE | | ACCOUNT TITLE | DOC. NO. | POST. REF. | DEBIT | CREDIT | |
|---|---|---|---|---|---|---|---|---|
| 1 | | | *Reversing Entries* | | | | | 1 |
| 4 | | 1 | *Interest Payable* | | | 200 00 | | 4 |
| 5 | | | *Interest Expense* | | | | 200 00 | 5 |
| 6 | | | | | | | | 6 |

**1.** Debit Interest Payable. **2.** Credit Interest Expense.

On December 31, Interest Expense is closed as part of the regular closing entries. Interest Expense is credited for $1,343.00 to reduce the account balance to zero. After the closing entry is posted, the interest expense account is closed.

Adjusting entries for accrued expenses have an effect on transactions to be recorded in the following fiscal period. For example, on the maturity date of the note payable on March 1, Winning Edge will pay the note's maturity value, including interest of $300.00.

| Principal | × | Interest Rate | × | Time as Fraction of Year | = | Interest Expense |
|---|---|---|---|---|---|---|
| $5,000.00 | × | 12% | × | $\frac{180}{360}$ | = | $300.00 |

However, an adjusting entry was made to record the amount of accrued interest expense last year, $200.00. Thus, $200.00 of the $300.00 total interest expense was incurred and recorded in the previous year. The remaining $100.00 was incurred during the current year.

Determining how much of the cash paid is for accrued interest expense and how much applies to the current year is an inconvenience. To avoid this inconvenience, a reversing entry is made at the beginning of the new fiscal period.

Interest Payable

| | Debit | | Credit |
|---|---|---|---|
| Jan. 1 Rev. | 200.00 | Dec. 31 Adj. | 200.00 |
| | | *(New Bal. zero)* | |

Interest Expense

| | Debit | | Credit |
|---|---|---|---|
| Dec. 31 Bal. | 1,143.00 | Dec. 31 Closing | 1,343.00 |
| Dec. 31 Adj. | 200.00 | Jan. 1 Rev. | 200.00 |
| *(New Bal.* | *1,343.00)* | *(New Bal.* | *200.00)* |

The reversing entry is the opposite of the adjusting entry. The entry creates a credit balance of $200.00 in Interest Expense. A credit balance is the opposite of the normal balance of the interest expense account. When the full amount of interest is paid, $300.00, this amount will be debited to Interest Expense. The account will then have a debit balance of $100.00 ($300.00 debit − $200.00 credit), the amount of interest expense incurred in the new year.

The reversing entry to Interest Payable reduces that account to a zero balance. Thus, when the interest is paid, no debit entry will be required to recognize payment of the balance of Interest Payable. The total amount of interest paid will be debited to Interest Expense.

STEPS

**Reversing an adjusting entry for accrued interest expense**

1. Record a debit, *$200.00*, to Interest Payable in the general journal.
2. Record a credit, *$200.00*, to Interest Expense.

# PAYING A NOTE PAYABLE SIGNED IN A PREVIOUS FISCAL PERIOD

1. Debit for Principal

CASH PAYMENTS JOURNAL — PAGE 55

| | DATE | ACCOUNT TITLE | CK. NO. | POST. REF. | 1 GENERAL DEBIT | 2 GENERAL CREDIT | 3 ACCOUNTS PAYABLE DEBIT | 4 PURCHASES DISCOUNT CREDIT | 5 CASH CREDIT | |
|---|---|---|---|---|---|---|---|---|---|---|
| 21 | 1 | Notes Payable | 916 | 2105 | 5 000 00 | | | | 5 300 00 | 21 |
| 22 | | Interest Expense | | 8105 | 300 00 | | | | | 22 |
| 23 | | | | | | | | | | 23 |

2. Debit for Total Interest

3. Credit for Maturity Value

ACCOUNT Notes Payable — ACCOUNT NO. 2105

| DATE | | ITEM | POST. REF. | DEBIT | CREDIT | BALANCE DEBIT | BALANCE CREDIT |
|---|---|---|---|---|---|---|---|
| Sept. | 2 | | CR28 | | 5 000 00 | | 5 000 00 |
| 20-- Mar. | 1 | | CP55 | 5 000 00 | | — | — |

4. Post amounts in General columns.

ACCOUNT Interest Expense — ACCOUNT NO. 8105

| DATE | | ITEM | POST. REF. | DEBIT | CREDIT | BALANCE DEBIT | BALANCE CREDIT |
|---|---|---|---|---|---|---|---|
| | 31 | | G15 | 200 00 | | 1 343 00 | |
| | 31 | | G16 | | 1 343 00 | — | — |
| 20-- Jan. | 1 | | G17 | | 200 00 | | 200 00 |
| Mar. | 1 | | CP55 | 300 00 | | 100 00 | |

On March 1, Winning Edge paid the maturity value of the only note payable on hand on December 31, the end of the previous fiscal year.

***March 1. Paid cash for the maturity value of the September 2 note: principal, $5,000.00, plus interest, $300.00; total, $5,300.00. Check No. 916.***

Notes Payable

| Debit | | Credit | |
|---|---|---|---|
| Mar. 1 Paid | 5,000.00 | Sept. 2 | 5,000.00 |

Interest Expense

| Debit | | Credit | |
|---|---|---|---|
| Dec. 31 Bal. | 1,143.00 | Dec. 31 Closing | 1,343.00 |
| Dec. 31 Adj. | 200.00 | Jan. 1 Rev. | 200.00 |
| Mar. 1 Paid | 300.00 | | |
| *(New Bal.* | *100.00)* | | |

Cash

| Debit | | Credit | |
|---|---|---|---|
| | | Mar. 1 Paid | 5,300.00 |

The total interest, $300.00, was incurred during two fiscal periods—$200.00 during the previous fiscal period and $100.00 during the current fiscal period. The reversing entry created a $200.00 credit balance in Interest Expense. After the $300.00 debit is recorded, Interest Expense has a debit balance of $100.00, the amount of interest expense incurred during the current fiscal period.

## STEPS: Paying a note payable signed in a previous fiscal period

1. Record a debit to Notes Payable in the General Debit column of a cash payments journal for the principal of the note, *$5,000.00.*
2. Record a debit to Interest Expense in the General Debit column for the total interest, *$300.00.*
3. Record a credit to Cash in the Cash Credit column for the maturity value of the note, *$5,300.00.*
4. Post the amounts in the General columns of the cash payments journal.

## EFFECT OF NOT USING REVERSING ENTRIES

If Winning Edge did not use a reversing entry for accrued interest expense, $200.00 of the interest would be reported twice. The $200.00 amount is recorded once as an adjusting entry in the last fiscal period. The amount is recorded a second time as part of the $300.00 debit in the current fiscal period when the note is paid.

The double charge might be avoided if accounting personnel are careful to divide the interest amount when the note is paid. The part of the interest chargeable to the previous fiscal period, $200.00, is recorded as a debit in Interest Payable. The part chargeable to the current fiscal period, $100.00, is recorded as a debit in Interest Expense.

Winning Edge prefers to use reversing entries. Winning Edge's accounting personnel do not have to remember to check an entry each time a note is paid to determine if interest should be divided. Winning Edge, like other companies that use reversing entries, records a reversing entry whenever an adjusting entry creates a balance in an asset or liability account that initially had a zero balance.

### ACCOUNTING AT WORK

### JAMES W. CRAWFORD, CPA

Jim Crawford started his CPA firm in Monroe, Louisiana, in 1972. He has a Bachelor of Science degree in business administration and has done some graduate studies toward an MBA degree. In his practice he offers the full spectrum of accounting services. His firm will do bookkeeping and financial statements, payroll reports, and all payroll functions. His firm will also train a client to do as many of the accounting functions in-house as the client wishes.

He also offers business consulting services. These services include writing business and marketing plans, administration and strategic planning, human resources, and finance, including procurement of working and expansion capital. He will provide productivity analysis, capacity planning, inventory management, and material requirements.

Jim prefers owning his own firm rather than working for a large accounting firm. He has the opportunity to see small businesses incubate and grow. He also has the satisfaction of being self-employed, with the professional respect that comes with it.

Jim has two suggestions for students: (1) Take an aptitude test to discover what kinds of work you might like to do. (2) Work hard in school to build your credentials and your ability to learn. He says, "In the modern world in which technology has taken over so much of the physical labor, you get paid more for what you know than for what you do."

## TERMS REVIEW

accrued expenses

accrued interest expense

## AUDIT YOUR UNDERSTANDING

1. Why should accrued expenses be recorded by an adjusting entry before financial statements are prepared at the end of a fiscal period?
2. What accounts are affected, and how, by the reversing entry for accrued interest expense?

## WORK TOGETHER

**Journalizing and posting entries for accrued expenses**

The accounting forms for the following problems are in the *Working Papers*. Your instructor will guide you through the following examples. On December 31 of the current year, Powers Corporation has one note payable outstanding, a 90-day, 18%, $2,000.00 note dated December 1.

3. Plan the adjustment on a work sheet. Label the adjustment *(h)*.
4. Journalize and post the adjusting entry for accrued interest expense on December 31. Use page 14 of a general journal.
5. Journalize and post the closing entry for interest expense using page 14 of a general journal.
6. Journalize and post the January 1 reversing entry for accrued interest expense on page 15 of a general journal.
7. Journalize the payment of cash for the maturity value of the note on March 1, Check No. 543. Use page 25 of a cash payments journal. Post the amounts in the General columns.

## ON YOUR OWN

**Journalizing and posting entries for accrued expenses**

The accounting forms for the following problems are in the *Working Papers*. Work these problems independently. On December 31 of the current year, Bartlett Industries has one note payable outstanding, a 180-day, 12%, $10,000.00 note dated September 2.

8. Plan the adjustment on a work sheet. Label the adjustment *(h)*.
9. Journalize and post the adjusting entry for accrued interest expense on December 31. Use page 14 of a general journal.
10. Journalize and post the closing entry for interest expense using page 14 of a general journal.
11. Journalize and post the January 1 reversing entry for accrued interest expense on page 15 of a general journal.
12. Journalize the payment of cash for the maturity value of the note on March 1, Check No. 845. Use page 29 of a cash payments journal. Post the amounts in the General columns.

# CHAPTER 24 SUMMARY

*Enrichment Activity*

**Types of Businesses**

*Not-for-profit organizations, such as governments and charitable organizations, use accounting systems and prepare financial statements similar to those used by for-profit businesses. Name three not-for-profit organizations and describe their sources of revenue.*

After completing this chapter, you can

1. Define accounting terms related to accrued revenue and accrued expenses.
2. Identify accounting concepts and practices related to accrued revenue and accrued expenses.
3. Record adjusting, closing, and reversing entries for accrued revenue.
4. Record adjusting, closing, and reversing entries for accrued expenses.

## EXPLORE ACCOUNTING

### ANNUAL REPORTS—FINANCIAL INFORMATION AND MORE

Corporations publish annual reports to communicate the results of operations to interested parties, such as stockholders, creditors, and government agencies. The typical annual report is a colorful, soft-cover brochure printed on $8\frac{1}{2}$-by-11-inch glossy paper and measuring 40 to 60 pages in length. The reports are grouped in two sections:

1. *Management's Analysis and Discussion.* This section provides management with an opportunity to promote the corporation. Through the use of pictures, graphs, and narrative, management can highlight the achievements of the past fiscal year and present its plans. Some corporations report on how the volunteer work of their employees is having a positive impact in their communities. Discussions of environmental and recycling programs could demonstrate how the corporation is socially responsible.

   The ultimate objective of any corporation is to increase the market price of its stock, thereby raising stockholders' investment. By "putting its best foot forward" in this section, management can increase the demand for the corporation's products and stock, thus increasing the stock's price.
2. *Financial Statements.* The financial statements section contains several items in addition to basic financial statements. Most of the additional items are required by GAAP or the Securities and Exchange Commission. As a result, these items are similar among corporations.
   (a) *Notes to the Financial Statements.* The notes contain additional, detailed information about items presented on the financial statements. For example, the note related to long-term debt would include the projected loan repayments for the next five years.
   (b) *Auditor's Report.* The report of the independent auditor states that a public accounting firm has tested the financial statements for accuracy and fair presentation. The report gives the reader confidence to use the financial statements to make business decisions.
   (c) *Financial Analysis.* Summary financial information, such as total assets, net income, and common financial ratios, are presented for several years.

**Required:** Obtain an annual report and prepare a detailed outline of its contents. Summarize the major topics in management's analysis and discussion. Did management do a good job of "putting its best foot forward"? Would you recommend that a friend purchase the corporation's stock? Support your answers.

## 24-1 APPLICATION PROBLEM
### Journalizing and posting entries for accrued revenue

The accounting forms for the following problem are in the *Working Papers*.

On December 31of the current year, Harris Lumber Company has one note receivable outstanding, a 90-day, 18%, $2,500.00 note dated November 1.

***Instructions:***

1. Plan the adjustment on a work sheet. Label the adjustment *(a)*.
2. Journalize and post the adjusting entry for accrued interest income on December 31. Use page 14 of a general journal.
3. Journalize and post the closing entry for interest income using page 14 of a general journal.
4. Journalize and post the January 1 reversing entry for accrued interest income on page 15 of a general journal.
5. Journalize the receipt of cash for the maturity value of the note on January 30, Receipt No. 624. Use page 19 of a cash receipts journal. Post the amounts in the General columns of the cash receipts journal.

## 24-2 APPLICATION PROBLEM
### Journalizing and posting entries for accrued expenses

The accounting forms for the following problem are in the *Working Papers*.

On December 31 of the current year, Delmar Plumbing Supply has one note payable outstanding, a 180-day, 10%, $12,000.00 note dated December 1.

***Instructions:***

1. Plan the adjustment on a work sheet. Label the adjustment *(h)*.
2. Journalize and post the adjusting entry for accrued interest expense on December 31. Use page 14 of a general journal.
3. Journalize and post the closing entry for interest expense using page 14 of a general journal.
4. Journalize and post the January 1 reversing entry for accrued interest expense on page 15 of a general journal.
5. Journalize the payment of cash for the maturity value of the note on May 30, Check No. 756. Use page 27 of a cash payments journal. Post the amounts in the General columns of the cash payments journal.

## 24-3 APPLICATION PROBLEM
### Journalizing and posting entries for accrued expenses

The accounting forms for the following problem are in the *Working Papers*.

On October 14 of the current year, Patti's Dress Shop signed a $10,000.00 note with National Bank of Columbus. The note term is 180 days at 12% interest.

***Instructions:***

1. Plan the adjustment on a work sheet for the fiscal year ended December 31.
2. Journalize and post the transactions to accrue, close, and reverse interest-related accounts at the fiscal year-end. Use page 16 of a general journal for December 31 transactions and page 17 for January 1 transactions.
3. Journalize the payment of cash for the maturity value of the note paid on April 12 with Check No. 377. Use page 23 of a cash payments journal. Post the amounts in the General columns of the cash payments journal.

## 24-4 MASTERY PROBLEM
### Journalizing and posting entries for accrued interest revenue and expense

The accounting forms for Farris Company are given in the *Working Papers*. The balances are recorded as of December 31 of the current year before adjusting entries.

Farris Company completed the following transactions related to notes receivable and notes payable during the current year and the following one year. The first two transactions have already been journalized and posted. One note receivable and one note payable are the only notes on hand at the end of the fiscal period. Source documents are abbreviated as follows: receipt, R; check, C; note receivable, NR.

***Transactions:***

**20X1**

Nov. 1. Accepted a 90-day, 18% note from James Donald for an extension of time on his account, $600.00. NR8.

Dec. 1. Signed a 120-day, 14% note, $2,400.00 with First National Bank. R453.

**20X2**

Jan. 30. Received cash for the maturity value of NR8. R207.

Mar. 31. Paid cash for the maturity value of the First National Bank note. C423.

***Instructions:***

1. Plan the adjustments on a work sheet.
2. Journalize and post the adjusting entries for accrued interest income and accrued interest expense on December 31. Use page 15 of a general journal.
3. Journalize and post the closing entries for interest income and interest expense. Continue to use page 15 of a general journal.
4. Journalize and post the reversing entries for accrued interest income and accrued interest expense. Use page 16 of a general journal.
5. Journalize the receipt of cash for the maturity value of NR8. Use page 13 of a cash receipts journal. Post the amounts in the General columns of the cash receipts journal.
6. Journalize the cash payment for the maturity value of the note payable. Use page 25 of a cash payments journal. Post the amounts in the General columns of the cash payments journal.

## 24-5 CHALLENGE PROBLEM
### Journalizing and posting entries for accrued interest revenue and expenses

The accounting forms for Blackwell Corporation are given in the *Working Papers*. The balances are recorded as of December 31 of the current year before adjusting entries.

Blackwell Corporation completed the following transactions related to notes receivable and notes payable during the current year and the following year. The first two transactions have already been journalized and posted. These notes are the only notes outstanding on December 31, 20X1, the fiscal year-end.

***Transactions:***

**20X1**

Dec. 8. Margaret Snider signed a 90-day, 18% note for an extension of time on her account, $900.00. NR56.

15. Signed a 180-day, 12% note with American National Bank, $10,000.00. R416.

**20X2**

Mar. 8. Margaret Snider dishonored NR56, maturity value due today. M98.

12. Paid off the American National Bank note ahead of the maturity date. American National charges interest only for the number of days the note is outstanding, with no early payment penalty. C645.

***Instructions:***

1. Plan the adjustments on a work sheet.
2. Journalize and post the transactions to accrue, close, and reverse interest-related accounts at the fiscal year-end. Use page 16 of a general journal for December 31 transactions and page 17 for January 1 transactions.
3. Journalize the 20X2 transactions using page 18 of a general journal and page 15 of a cash payments journal. Post the Credit column of the general journal and the amounts in the General columns of the cash payments journal.

### INTERNET ACTIVITY

Point your browser to

**http://accounting.swpco.com**

Choose **First-Year Course**, choose **Activities**, and complete the activity for Chapter 24.

## Applied Communication

Employers often screen prospective employees for written communication skills. As an applicant, you may be asked to write a short essay. Therefore, it is important for you to practice preparing documents that clearly communicate a message, demonstrate proper usage of grammar rules, and project a professional image.

**Instructions:** Write a one-page memo to Gerard Spikes, Controller of Jenkins Company, that gives your opinion on one of the following questions:

1. Why is a basic knowledge of accounting important for all employees of a company, even for those not directly involved in accounting?
2. Why should the company help its employees to continue their formal education by paying for one technical or college course each year?

# Cases for Critical Thinking

**Case 1** As a new accounting clerk at Sanders Appliance, you discover that $80.00 accrued interest income on notes receivable was not recorded at the end of the current fiscal period. Your manager says, "Don't worry about recording the interest income. It will be recorded when we collect the note and interest." Is this approach acceptable? Explain your answer. What effect will the omission of accrued interest income have on the current fiscal year's (a) income statement and (b) balance sheet?

**Case 2** At the end of each fiscal period, Kimura Corporation prepares adjusting entries to record accrued interest expense. However, the company does not record reversing entries for the accrued interest expense. At the end of the current fiscal year, Kimura had a $3,000.00, 90-day, 10% note payable outstanding, signed November 1. Kimura made the following journal entries related to the note.

| | | |
|---|---|---|
| *Signed Note Nov. 1* | | |
| Cash | $3,000.00 | |
| Notes Payable | | $3,000.00 |
| *Adj. Entry Dec. 31* | | |
| Interest Expense | 50.00 | |
| Interest Payable | | 50.00 |
| *Clos. Entry Dec. 31* | | |
| Income Summary | 50.00 | |
| Interest Expense | | 50.00 |
| *Paid Note Jan. 30* | | |
| Notes Payable | 3,000.00 | |
| Interest Payable | 50.00 | |
| Interest Expense | 25.00 | |
| Cash | | 3,075.00 |

Tonya Bean, an accounting supervisor, says that generally accepted accounting principles require that reversing entries be used in conjunction with adjusting entries for accrued expenses. Thus, Ms. Bean says Kimura must begin using reversing entries for all accrued expenses. Is Ms. Bean correct? Do the procedures Kimura has been using result in incorrect financial statements? Explain your answer.

# AUTOMATED ACCOUNTING

## AUTOMATED ADJUSTING AND CLOSING ENTRIES FOR ACCRUED REVENUES AND EXPENSES

During the fiscal period, numerous transactions are analyzed, journalized, and posted. When a transaction affects more than one accounting period, an adjusting entry may be needed to match revenues and expenses. To complete the accounting cycle, adjusting entries are entered into the computer and verified for accuracy. The financial statements are generated, and then closing entries are generated and posted by the software.

### Adjusting Entries

After all the usual transactions of the business are entered as journal entries, a preliminary trial balance is generated. This trial balance and period-end adjustment data are used as the basis for the adjusting entries. Adjusting entries are made for assets that have been consumed during the period and become expenses. In addition, adjusting entries are needed for accrued revenue and accrued expenses. Adjusting entries for accrued revenue recognize revenue that has been earned in the current fiscal period, but not yet received. Adjusting entries for accrued expenses recognize expenses incurred in the current fiscal period, but not actually paid until the next period.

To record adjusting entries:

1. Click the Journal toolbar button.
2. Click the General Journal tab.
3. Enter the transaction date and press Tab. All adjusting entries are made on the last day of the fiscal period.
4. Enter Adj. Ent. in the Refer. text box and press Tab.
5. Enter the account numbers and amounts for the adjusting entries. Press the Tab key to move among the text boxes.
6. Click the Post button.

### Closing Entries for Accrued Revenues and Expenses

Closing entries are made to close all temporary accounts at the end of the accounting period. *Automated Accounting 7.0* automatically prepares and posts closing entries.

To generate closing entries:

1. Choose Generate Closing Journal Entries from the Options menu.

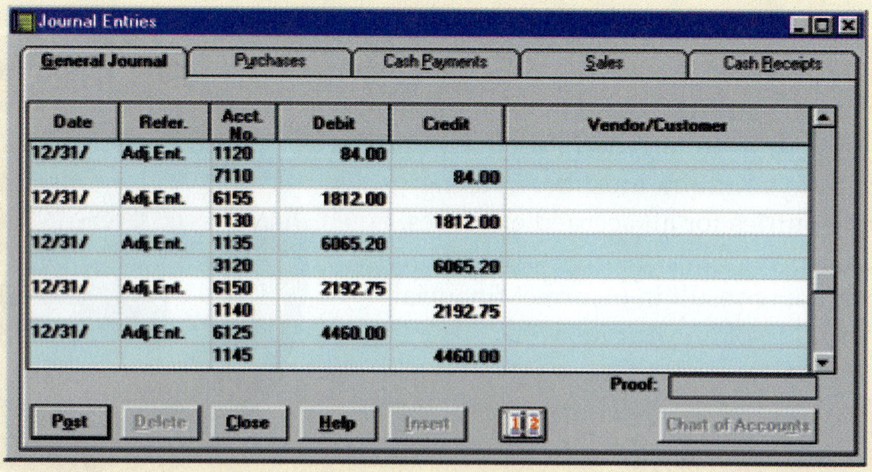

# AUTOMATED ACCOUNTING

2. Click Yes to generate the closing entries.

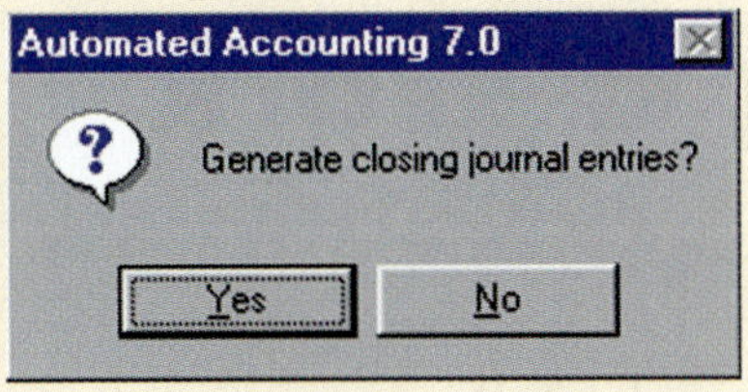


3. The general journal will appear, containing the journal entries.
4. Click the Post button.
5. To display a post-closing trial balance report:
   a. Click on the Reports toolbar button, or choose the Reports Selection menu item from the Reports menu.
   b. Select the Ledger Reports option button from the Report Selection dialog box.
   c. Choose Trial Balance report.

## AUTOMATING APPLICATION PROBLEM 24-2: Journalizing and posting entries for accrued expenses

**Instructions:**

1. Load *Automated Accounting 7.0* or higher software.
2. Select database F24-1 from the appropriate directory/folder.
3. Select File from the menu bar and choose the Save As menu command. Key the path to the drive and directory that contains your data files. Save the database with a file name of XXX241 (where XXX are your initials).
4. Access Problem Instructions through the Help menu. Read the Problem Instructions screen.
5. Refer to page 628 for data used in this template.
6. Exit the *Automated Accounting* software.

## AUTOMATING MASTERY PROBLEM 24-4: Journalizing and posting entries for accrued interest revenue and expense

**Instructions:**

1. Load *Automated Accounting 7.0* or higher software.
2. Select database F24-2 from the appropriate directory/folder.
3. Select File from the menu bar and choose the Save As menu command. Key the path to the drive and directory that contains your data files. Save the database with a file name of XXX242 (where XXX are your initials).
4. Access Problem Instructions through the Help menu. Read the Problem Instructions screen.
5. Refer to page 629 for data used in this template.
6. Exit the *Automated Accounting* software.

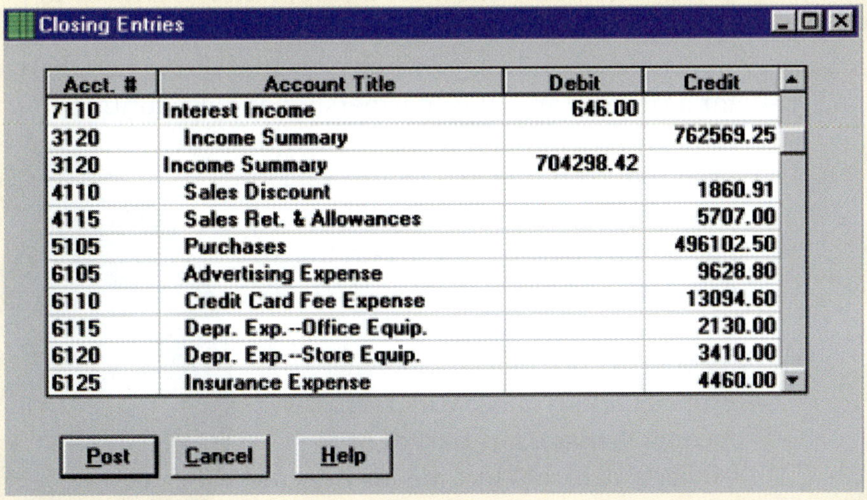


| Acct. # | Account Title | Debit | Credit |
|---|---|---|---|
| 7110 | Interest Income | 646.00 | |
| 3120 | Income Summary | | 762569.25 |
| 3120 | Income Summary | 704298.42 | |
| 4110 | Sales Discount | | 1860.91 |
| 4115 | Sales Ret. & Allowances | | 5707.00 |
| 5105 | Purchases | | 496102.50 |
| 6105 | Advertising Expense | | 9628.80 |
| 6110 | Credit Card Fee Expense | | 13094.60 |
| 6115 | Depr. Exp.--Office Equip. | | 2130.00 |
| 6120 | Depr. Exp.--Store Equip. | | 3410.00 |
| 6125 | Insurance Expense | | 4460.00 |

# 25 Distributing Dividends and Preparing a Work Sheet

**AFTER STUDYING CHAPTER 25, YOU WILL BE ABLE TO:**

1. Define accounting terms related to distributing dividends and preparing a work sheet for a merchandising business organized as a corporation.
2. Identify accounting concepts and practices related to distributing dividends and preparing a work sheet for a merchandising business organized as a corporation.
3. Journalize the declaration and payment of a dividend for a merchandising business organized as a corporation.
4. Plan end-of-fiscal-period adjustments for a merchandising business organized as a corporation.
5. Calculate federal income tax, plan an adjustment for federal income tax expense, and complete a work sheet.

**TERMS PREVIEW**

stockholder

retained earnings

dividends

board of directors

declaring a dividend

## ACCOUNTING FOR A CORPORATION

Many accounting procedures used for a corporation are similar to the procedures used for a proprietorship or a partnership. Consequently, preparing a work sheet for a corporation is similar to preparing a work sheet for a proprietorship or a partnership.

There are, however, three principal differences between accounting for a proprietorship or partnership and accounting for a corporation: (1) Different accounts are used to record owners' equity. (2) Different procedures are used to distribute income to owners. (3) Corporations calculate and pay federal income tax. Corporations must pay federal income tax on their net income. Proprietorship and partnership net income is treated as part of each owner's personal income for income tax purposes. Thus, federal income tax is not calculated for a proprietorship or partnership business.

# ACCOUNTING IN YOUR CAREER

## TAXES ON BUSINESSES

Jody Meehan has just lost her job in a corporate downsizing. Her company was generous, however, and Jody has a substantial amount of cash to invest in a new business. She is looking at a small local factory that she can buy and refit to produce car care chemicals, such as waxes and upholstery cleaners. She is uncertain about whether to organize her business as a proprietorship or a corporation. She knows some of the advantages and disadvantages of both forms of businesses, and she has decided to incorporate if the tax effect is equitable. She has hired Midori Tanaka, a tax accountant, to advise her on corporate income taxes.

At their first meeting, Jody explains what kind of business she is planning to start and the budget for the first year of operations. She also details what income she expects to make from the first year of operations. She forecasts net income of $100,000 during each of the first few years and wants to draw a salary of $35,000 each year.

Midori explains that both forms of business would be taxed on net income, the amount of revenue after expenses are deducted. But the salary is treated differently by the two forms of business. In a proprietorship, the business would not consider the $35,000 as a salary, and therefore the owner would pay tax on the entire net income of $100,000. In a corporation, the $35,000 salary would be deducted from the company's revenue as an expense. Jody would still have to pay personal income tax on the $35,000 salary, however.

Jody says, "Midori, I can't really understand the effect unless I do some calculations to compare the differences. Can you give me some tax rates to use?"

***Critical Thinking:***

1. In this scenario, what is the tax for the proprietorship using a personal income tax rate of 25% for this level of earnings?
2. How much tax does the corporation pay if corporate income tax rates are 15% on the first $50,000 plus 25% of the next $25,000? How much personal income tax will Jody pay on her salary using a 25% personal income tax rate?
3. Which form of business organization has the lower tax consequence in this scenario?

# 25-1 Distributing Corporate Dividends to Stockholders

## STOCKHOLDERS' EQUITY ACCOUNTS USED BY A CORPORATION

| (3000) STOCKHOLDERS' EQUITY | |
|---|---|
| 3105 | Capital Stock |
| 3110 | Retained Earnings |
| 3115 | Dividends |
| 3120 | Income Summary |

A corporation's ownership is divided into units. Each unit of ownership in a corporation is known as a share of stock. An owner of one or more shares of a corporation is called a **stockholder.** Each stockholder is an owner of a corporation.

A separate general ledger owner's equity account is maintained for each owner of a proprietorship or a partnership. However, a corporation may have many stockholders. Therefore, a separate owner's equity account is not maintained for each owner of a corporation. Instead, a single owners' equity account, titled Capital Stock, is used for the investment of all owners.

Owners' equity accounts for a corporation normally are listed under a major chart of accounts division titled Stockholders' Equity.

A second stockholders' equity account is used to record a corporation's earnings. Net income increases a corporation's total stockholders' equity. Some income may be retained by a corporation for business expansion. An amount earned by a corporation and not yet distributed to stockholders is called **retained earnings.** Retained Earnings is the title of the account used to record a corporation's earnings.

A third stockholders' equity account is used to record the distribution of a corporation's earnings to stockholders. Some income may be given to stockholders as a return on their investments. Earnings distributed to stockholders are called **dividends.** A corporation's dividend account is a temporary account similar to a proprietorship's or partnership's drawing account. Each time a dividend is declared, an account titled Dividends is debited. At the end of each fiscal period, the balance in the dividends account is closed to Retained Earnings.

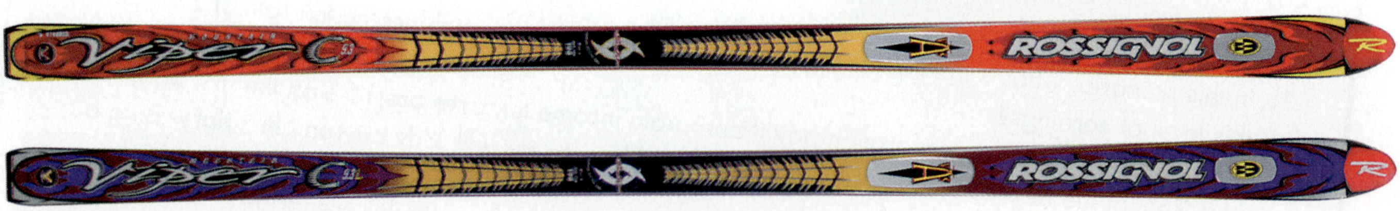


**REMEMBER**

Dividends is a temporary account that is closed to Retained Earnings at the end of the fiscal period.

## DECLARING A DIVIDEND

1. Debit Dividends

GENERAL JOURNAL — PAGE 14

| | DATE | | ACCOUNT TITLE | DOC. NO. | POST. REF. | DEBIT | CREDIT | |
|---|---|---|---|---|---|---|---|---|
| 1 | 20-- Dec. | 15 | Dividends | M189 | | 10 000 00 | | 1 |
| 2 | | | Dividends Payable | | | | 10 000 00 | 2 |

2. Credit Dividends Payable

A group of persons elected by the stockholders to manage a corporation is called a **board of directors.** Dividends can be distributed to stockholders only by formal action of a corporation's board of directors. *(CONCEPT: Business Entity)*

Action by a board of directors to distribute corporate earnings to stockholders is called **declaring a dividend.** Dividends normally are declared on one date and paid on a later date. A corporation's board of directors is not required to declare a dividend. In fact, declared dividends cannot exceed the balance of the retained earnings account. However, when a board of directors does declare a dividend, the corporation is then obligated to pay the dividend. The dividend is a liability that must be recorded in the corporation's accounts.

Winning Edge's board of directors declares a dividend every three months so that stockholders can share the corporation's earnings throughout the year. Winning Edge declares dividends each March 15, June 15, September 15, and December 15. The dividends are then paid on the 15th of the month following the declaration.

***December 15. Winning Edge's board of directors declared a quarterly dividend of $1.00 per share; capital stock issued is 10,000 shares; total dividend, $10,000.00. Date of payment is January 15. Memorandum No. 189.***

Dividends

| Debit | | Credit | |
|---|---|---|---|
| 3/15 Decl. | 10,000.00 | | |
| 6/15 Decl. | 10,000.00 | | |
| 9/15 Decl. | 10,000.00 | | |
| 12/15 Decl. | 10,000.00 | | |

Dividends Payable

| Debit | | Credit | |
|---|---|---|---|
| 4/15 Paid | 10,000.00 | 3/15 Decl. | 10,000.00 |
| 7/15 Paid | 10,000.00 | 6/15 Decl. | 10,000.00 |
| 10/15 Paid | 10,000.00 | 9/15 Decl. | 10,000.00 |
| | | 12/15 Decl. | 10,000.00 |

The stockholders' equity account, Dividends, has a normal debit balance and is increased by a $10,000.00 debit. Dividends Payable is credited for $10,000.00 to show the increase in this liability account.

| Number of Shares Outstanding | × | Quarterly Dividend per Share | = | Total Quarterly Dividend |
|---|---|---|---|---|
| 10,000 | × | $1.00 | = | $10,000.00 |

## PAYING A DIVIDEND

CASH PAYMENTS JOURNAL — PAGE 37

| | DATE | | ACCOUNT TITLE | CK. NO. | POST. REF. | 1 GENERAL DEBIT | 2 GENERAL CREDIT | 3 ACCOUNTS PAYABLE DEBIT | 4 PURCHASES DISCOUNT CREDIT | 5 CASH CREDIT | |
|---|---|---|---|---|---|---|---|---|---|---|---|
| 1 | 20-- Jan. | 15 | Dividends Payable | 879 | | 10 000 00 | | | | 10 000 00 | 1 |
| 2 | | | | | | | | | | | 2 |

1. Debit Dividends Payable

2. Credit Cash

Winning Edge issues one check for the amount of the total dividend to be paid. This check is deposited in a special dividend checking account. A separate check for each stockholder is drawn on this special account. The special account avoids a large number of cash payments journal entries and also reserves cash specifically for paying dividends.

A check is often made payable to an agent, such as a bank. The agent then handles the details of sending dividend checks to individual stockholders.

***January 15. Paid cash for quarterly dividend declared December 15, $10,000.00. Check No. 879.***

Dividends Payable

| | | | |
|---|---|---|---|
| 4/15 Paid | 10,000.00 | 3/15 Decl. | 10,000.00 |
| 7/15 Paid | 10,000.00 | 6/15 Decl. | 10,000.00 |
| 10/15 Paid | 10,000.00 | 9/15 Decl. | 10,000.00 |
| 1/15 Paid | 10,000.00 | 12/15 Decl. | 10,000.00 |

Cash

| | | | |
|---|---|---|---|
| | | 1/15 Paid | 10,000.00 |

### STEPS: Journalizing the payment of dividends

1. Record a debit for the total amount of dividends, *$10,000.00*, to Dividends Payable in the General Debit column of a cash payments journal.
2. Record a credit, *$10,000.00*, in the Cash Credit column.

When this entry is posted, the dividends payable account has a zero balance.

**FYI**

*Dividends are declared on one date and paid on a later date. Only stockholders owning the stock on the* date of record *specified by the board of directors receive the dividend. Stockholders owning the stock on the date of record receive the entire dividend, regardless of how long they have owned the stock.*

## TERMS REVIEW

stockholder
retained earnings
dividends
board of directors
declaring a dividend

## AUDIT YOUR UNDERSTANDING

1. How does accounting for a corporation differ from accounting for a proprietorship or partnership?
2. How many accounts are kept for the investment of all owners of a corporation?
3. What account does a corporation use to record earnings not yet distributed to stockholders?
4. What action is required before a corporation can distribute income to its stockholders?

## WORK TOGETHER

**Journalizing dividends**

Journals are given in the *Working Papers.* Your instructor will guide you through the following examples.

PTC Corporation completed the following transactions during December of the current year and January of the next year.

***Transactions:***

Dec. 15. The board of directors declared a dividend of $10.00 per share; capital stock issued is 2,500 shares. M212.

Jan. 15. Paid cash for dividend declared December 15. C543.

5. Use page 12 of a general journal. Journalize the dividend declared on December 15.
6. Use page 15 of a cash payments journal. Journalize payment of the dividend on January 15.

## ON YOUR OWN

**Journalizing dividends**

Journals are given in the *Working Papers.* Work these problems independently.

Lucita Manufacturing Corporation completed the following transactions during December of the current year and January of the next year.

***Transactions:***

Dec. 15. The board of directors declared a dividend of $3.50 per share; capital stock issued is 40,000 shares. M126.

Jan. 15. Paid cash for dividend declared December 15. C432.

7. Use page 24 of a general journal. Journalize the dividend declared on December 15.
8. Use page 18 of a cash payments journal. Journalize payment of the dividend.

# 25-2 Preparing a Work Sheet for a Corporation

## USE OF A WORK SHEET

Work sheets for proprietorships, partnerships, and corporations are similar. Businesses use work sheets to plan adjustments and provide information needed to prepare financial statements. Winning Edge may prepare a work sheet at any time financial statements are needed. However, Winning Edge always prepares a work sheet and financial statements at the end of a fiscal year. *(CONCEPT: Accounting Period Cycle)*

### Entering a Trial Balance on a Work Sheet

To prepare a work sheet, a trial balance is first entered in the Trial Balance columns. All general ledger accounts are listed in the same order as they appear in the general ledger. Trial Balance columns are totaled to prove equality of debits and credits.

On December 31, Winning Edge enters its trial balance on a work sheet. A corporation's accounts are similar to those of a proprietorship or partnership except for the capital stock, retained earnings, dividends, and federal income tax accounts.

### Planning Adjustments on a Work Sheet

Some general ledger accounts need to be brought up to date before financial statements are prepared. Accounts are brought up to date by planning and entering adjustments on a work sheet. Most adjustments on a corporation's work sheet are similar to those for proprietorships and partnerships.

The adjustments for merchandise inventory, supplies, and prepaid insurance are described in earlier chapters. Winning Edge makes nine adjustments: (1) Interest Income, (2) Uncollectible Accounts Expense, (3) Merchandise Inventory, (4) Supplies, (5) Prepaid Insurance, (6) Depreciation Expense—Office Equipment, (7) Depreciation Expense—Store Equipment, (8) Interest Expense, and (9) Federal Income Tax Expense.

Adjustments for depreciation expense, uncollectible accounts expense, interest income, and interest expense could also be made by proprietorships and partnerships. However, the adjustment for federal income tax is unique to corporations. This adjustment is not made for proprietorships and partnerships because taxes are paid by the owners, not the business. Adjustments generally are made in the order that accounts are listed on a work sheet.

**SMALL BUSINESS SPOTLIGHT**

Three to four million new small businesses form every year. Individuals are more willing to risk investing their time and money in small business ventures in a strong economy. However, about 60% of new small businesses will be out of business in five years.

## INTEREST INCOME ADJUSTMENT

1. Debit Interest Receivable

| | ACCOUNT TITLE | TRIAL BALANCE DEBIT | TRIAL BALANCE CREDIT | ADJUSTMENTS DEBIT | ADJUSTMENTS CREDIT |
|---|---|---|---|---|---|
| 4 | *Interest Receivable* | | | (a) 20 00 | |
| 51 | *Interest Income* | | 68 00 | | (a) 20 00 |

2. Credit Interest Income

Interest income earned during the current fiscal period but not yet received needs to be recorded. Two accounts are used for the adjustment for accrued interest income: Interest Receivable and Interest Income. An analysis of Winning Edge's adjustment for accrued interest income is described in Chapter 24.

### STEPS: Planning a work sheet adjustment for interest income

1. Enter the accrued interest income amount, *$20.00,* in the Adjustments Debit column on the Interest Receivable line of the work sheet. Label the adjustment *(a).*
2. Enter the same amount, *$20.00,* in the Adjustments Credit column on the Interest Income line. Label the adjustment *(a).*

## UNCOLLECTIBLE ACCOUNTS EXPENSE ADJUSTMENT

1. Credit Allowance for Uncollectible Accounts

| | ACCOUNT TITLE | TRIAL BALANCE DEBIT | TRIAL BALANCE CREDIT | ADJUSTMENTS DEBIT | ADJUSTMENTS CREDIT |
|---|---|---|---|---|---|
| 6 | *Allowance for Uncollectible Accounts* | | 320 00 | | (b) 9828 00 |
| 48 | *Uncollectible Accounts Expense* | | | (b) 9828 00 | |

2. Debit Uncollectible Accounts Expense

The estimated amount of uncollectible accounts expense for a fiscal period needs to be brought up to date. Two accounts are used for the adjustment for uncollectible accounts expense: Uncollectible Accounts Expense and Allowance for Uncollectible Accounts. An analysis of Winning Edge's uncollectible accounts expense adjustment is described in Chapter 20.

### STEPS: Planning a work sheet adjustment for uncollectible accounts expense

1. Enter the estimated uncollectible amount, *$9,828.00,* in the Adjustments Credit column on the Allowance for Uncollectible Accounts line of the work sheet. Label the adjustment *(b).*
2. Enter the same amount, *$9,828.00,* in the Adjustments Debit column on the Uncollectible Accounts Expense line. Label the adjustment *(b).*

# MERCHANDISE INVENTORY ADJUSTMENT

1. Debit Merchandise Inventory

| | ACCOUNT TITLE | TRIAL BALANCE DEBIT | TRIAL BALANCE CREDIT | ADJUSTMENTS DEBIT | ADJUSTMENTS CREDIT |
|---|---|---|---|---|---|
| 7 | *Merchandise Inventory* | 238 758 00 | | (c) 6 158 00 | |
| 29 | *Income Summary* | | | | (c) 6 158 00 |

2. Credit Income Summary

The merchandise inventory account balance in a trial balance is the beginning inventory for a fiscal period. The amount of the ending inventory is determined by counting the merchandise on hand at the end of the fiscal period. An adjusting entry is made to bring merchandise inventory up to date so that the end-of-fiscal-period balance will be shown in the merchandise inventory account. The procedure used to adjust Winning Edge's merchandise inventory account is the same as that described for a merchandising business organized as a partnership in Chapter 15.

Winning Edge's beginning merchandise inventory, $238,758.00, is shown on line 7 in the Trial Balance Debit column on the work sheet. Winning Edge's ending merchandise inventory on December 31 is counted and determined to be $244,916.00. To bring Winning Edge's merchandise inventory account up to date, the balance of Merchandise Inventory needs to be increased by $6,158.00. Merchandise Inventory is debited for the amount of the increase, $6,158.00. Income Summary is credited for the same amount.

| Ending Merchandise Inventory | – | Beginning Merchandise Inventory | = | Adjustment to Merchandise Inventory |
|---|---|---|---|---|
| $244,916.00 | – | $238,758.00 | = | $6,158.00 |

## STEPS: Planning a work sheet adjustment for merchandise inventory

1. Enter the increase in merchandise inventory, *$6,158.00,* in the Adjustments Debit column on the Merchandise Inventory line of the work sheet. Label the adjustment *(c).*
2. Enter the same amount, *$6,158.00,* in the Adjustments Credit column on the Income Summary line of the work sheet. Label the adjustment *(c).*

## REMEMBER

If the ending merchandise inventory is less than the beginning merchandise inventory, the difference (decrease) is debited to Income Summary and credited to Merchandise Inventory.

## SUPPLIES ADJUSTMENT

**1.** Credit Supplies

| | ACCOUNT TITLE | TRIAL BALANCE DEBIT | TRIAL BALANCE CREDIT | ADJUSTMENTS DEBIT | ADJUSTMENTS CREDIT |
|---|---|---|---|---|---|
| 8 | *Supplies* | 9158 00 | | | (d) 7472 00 |
| 47 | *Supplies Expense* | | | (d) 7472 00 | |

**2.** Debit Supplies Expense

The balance of Supplies in the trial balance, $9,158.00, is the cost of supplies on hand at the beginning of the year plus the supplies purchased during the year. The supplies on hand on December 31 are counted and determined to be $1,686.00. To bring the account up to date, the balance of Supplies needs to be decreased by $7,472.00 ($9,158.00 − $1,686.00), the cost of supplies used during the year. Supplies Expense is debited and Supplies is credited for the amount of the decrease.

**STEPS**

### Planning a work sheet adjustment for supplies

1. Enter the amount of supplies used, *$7,472.00,* in the Adjustments Credit column on the Supplies line of the work sheet. Label the adjustment *(d).*
2. Enter the same amount, *$7,472.00,* in the Adjustments Debit column on the Supplies Expense line of the work sheet. Label the adjustment *(d).*

## PREPAID INSURANCE ADJUSTMENT

**1.** Credit Prepaid Insurance

| | ACCOUNT TITLE | TRIAL BALANCE DEBIT | TRIAL BALANCE CREDIT | ADJUSTMENTS DEBIT | ADJUSTMENTS CREDIT |
|---|---|---|---|---|---|
| 9 | *Prepaid Insurance* | 12400 00 | | | (e) 9850 00 |
| 41 | *Insurance Expense* | | | (e) 9850 00 | |

**2.** Debit Insurance Expense

Insurance premiums are debited to a prepaid insurance account when paid. During the year, Winning Edge paid $12,400.00 of insurance premiums.

Winning Edge determined that the value of prepaid insurance on December 31 is $2,550.00. Therefore, the value of insurance used during the year is $9,850.00 ($12,400.00 − $2,550.00). Prepaid Insurance is credited and Insurance Expense is debited at the end of the fiscal period for the value of insurance used.

**STEPS**

### Planning a work sheet adjustment for prepaid insurance

1. Enter the amount of insurance used, *$9,850.00,* in the Adjustments Credit column on the Prepaid Insurance line of the work sheet. Label the adjustment *(e).*
2. Enter the same amount, *$9,850.00,* in the Adjustments Debit column on the Insurance Expense line of the work sheet. Label the adjustment *(e).*

## DEPRECIATION EXPENSE ADJUSTMENTS

**1.** Credit Accumulated Depreciation—Office Equipment

| | ACCOUNT TITLE | TRIAL BALANCE DEBIT | TRIAL BALANCE CREDIT | ADJUSTMENTS DEBIT | ADJUSTMENTS CREDIT |
|---|---|---|---|---|---|
| 11 | *Accumulated Depreciation—Office Equipment* | | 6173 00 | | (f) 4650 00 **1** |
| 13 | *Accumulated Depreciation—Store Equipment* | | 7054 00 | | (g) 8750 00 **3** |
| 39 | *Depreciation Expense—Office Equipment* | | | (f) 4650 00 **2** | |
| 40 | *Depreciation Expense—Store Equipment* | | | (g) 8750 00 **4** | |

**3.** Credit Accumulated Depreciation—Store Equipment

**2.** Debit Depreciation Expense—Office Equipment

**4.** Debit Depreciation Expense—Store Equipment

An analysis of Winning Edge's depreciation expense adjustments is described in Chapter 21. Winning Edge has two plant asset accounts: Office Equipment and Store Equipment. A separate adjustment is planned to record the depreciation for each type of equipment.

### STEPS Planning a work sheet adjustment for depreciation expense

1. Enter the office equipment depreciation amount, *$4,650.00,* in the Adjustments Credit column on the Accumulated Depreciation—Office Equipment line of the work sheet. Label the adjustment *(f).*
2. Enter the same amount, *$4,650.00,* in the Adjustments Debit column on the Depreciation Expense—Office Equipment line of the work sheet. Label the adjustment *(f).*
3. Enter the store equipment depreciation amount, *$8,750.00,* in the Adjustments Credit column on the Accumulated Depreciation—Store Equipment line of the work sheet. Label the adjustment *(g).*
4. Enter the same amount, *$8,750.00,* in the Adjustments Debit column on the Depreciation Expense—Store Equipment line of the work sheet. Label the adjustment *(g).*

## INTEREST EXPENSE ADJUSTMENT

**2.** Debit Interest Expense

**1.** Credit Interest Payable

| | ACCOUNT TITLE | TRIAL BALANCE DEBIT | TRIAL BALANCE CREDIT | ADJUSTMENTS DEBIT | ADJUSTMENTS CREDIT |
|---|---|---|---|---|---|
| 15 | *Interest Payable* | | | | (h) 200 00 **1** |
| 52 | *Interest Expense* | 1143 00 | | (h) 200 00 **2** | |

Interest expense incurred during the current fiscal period but not yet paid needs to be recorded. Two accounts are used for the adjustment for accrued interest expense: Interest Payable and Interest Expense. An analysis of Winning Edge's adjustment for accrued interest expense is described in Chapter 24.

## AUDIT YOUR UNDERSTANDING

1. What circumstances would require an adjustment that debits Merchandise Inventory?
2. What circumstances would require an adjustment that credits Merchandise Inventory?

## WORK TOGETHER

### Preparing a work sheet for a corporation

Webster Corporation's work sheet is given in the *Working Papers.* Your instructor will guide you through the following example.

3. For the current year ended December 31, record the adjustments on the work sheet using the following information. Do not total the Adjustments columns. Save your work to complete Work Together on page 652.

| | |
|---|---|
| Accrued interest income | $ 277.20 |
| Uncollectible accounts expense estimated as 1.5% of sales on account. Sales on account for year, $499,000.00. | |
| Merchandise inventory | 90,066.26 |
| Supplies inventory | 327.88 |
| Value of prepaid insurance | 3,023.60 |
| Annual depreciation expense—office equipment | 2,690.00 |
| Annual depreciation expense—store equipment | 1,607.60 |
| Accrued interest expense | 545.16 |

## ON YOUR OWN

### Preparing a work sheet for a corporation

Osborn Corporation's work sheet is given in the *Working Papers.* Work this problem independently.

4. For the current year ended December 31, record the adjustments on the work sheet using the following information. Do not total the Adjustments columns. Save your work to complete On Your Own on page 652.

| | |
|---|---|
| Accrued interest income | $ 543.20 |
| Uncollectible accounts expense estimated as 1.5% of sales on account. Sales on account for year, $869,000.00. | |
| Merchandise inventory | 106,597.06 |
| Supplies inventory | 896.53 |
| Value of prepaid insurance | 5,370.00 |
| Annual depreciation expense—office equipment | 5,480.00 |
| Annual depreciation expense—store equipment | 6,876.00 |
| Accrued interest expense | 523.25 |

# 25-3 Calculating Federal Income Tax and Completing a Work Sheet

## FEDERAL INCOME TAX EXPENSE ADJUSTMENT

Corporations anticipating annual federal income taxes of $500.00 or more are required to pay their estimated taxes each quarter. Estimated income tax is paid in quarterly installments in April, June, September, and December. However, the actual federal income tax owed is calculated at the end of a fiscal year. Based on the actual income tax owed for a year, a corporation must file an annual return. Any additional tax owed that was not paid in quarterly installments must be paid when the final return is sent.

Early in the current year, Winning Edge estimated $64,000.00 federal income tax for the year. Winning Edge paid $16,000.00 in each quarterly installment for a total of $64,000.00. Each tax payment is recorded as a debit to Federal Income Tax Expense and a credit to Cash.

Federal income tax is an expense of a corporation. However, the amount of tax depends on net income before the tax is recorded.

Federal Income Tax Expense is an expense account. The account appears under a major division titled Income Tax Expense in Winning Edge's chart of accounts. Federal Income Tax Payable, a liability account, appears under the heading Current Liabilities.

In order to make adjustments to federal income tax, you must first determine the net income before federal income tax expense. To calculate, follow these steps: (1) Complete all other adjustments on a work sheet. (2) Extend all amounts except Federal Income Tax Expense to the Income Statement or Balance Sheet columns. (3) On a separate sheet of paper, total the work sheet's Income Statement columns. Calculate the difference between the debit and credit totals. This difference becomes the net income before federal income tax expense.

| | |
|---|---|
| Total of Income Statement Credit column | $1,940,451.50 |
| *Less* total of Income Statement Debit column before federal income tax | −1,699,537.50 |
| *Equals* Net Income before Federal Income Tax | $ 240,914.00 |

### TECHNOLOGY FOR BUSINESS

#### SPENDING MORE THAN TIME ON THE WEB

The World Wide Web is changing and growing every day. While some companies target customers for on-line sales, others use the Web as a key part of their marketing strategy.

Every day thousands of companies invite consumers to visit company and product Web sites with the phrase "Visit our Web site" followed by the address. Web sites offer contests, discount offers, coupons, recipes, and product information. These sites feature more data than you get from a print ad or television commercial.

Business-to-business selling via the Web is growing, and it has a name—electronic commerce or E-commerce. Wal-Mart, General Motors, and Eastman Kodak are among the companies that pioneered E-commerce with their customers and suppliers. Advocates estimate that E-commerce could reduce the cost of handling a purchase order from more than $100 to about $25.

## CALCULATING FEDERAL INCOME TAX

15% of net income before taxes, zero to $50,000.00 (15% tax on the *first* $50,000.00 of net income)
*Plus* 25% of net income before taxes, $50,000.00 to $75,000.00 (25% tax on the *next* $25,000.00 of net income)
*Plus* 34% of net income before taxes, $75,000.00 to $100,000.00 (34% tax on the *next* $25,000.00 of net income)
*Plus* 39% of net income before taxes, $100,000.00 to $335,000.00 (39% tax on the *next* $225,000.00 of net income)
*Plus* 34% of net income before taxes over $335,000.00 (34% tax on net income *above* $335,000.00)

Step 1:

| **First Net Income Amount** | × | **First Tax Rate** | = | **Federal Income Tax on First $50,000.00 of Net Income** |
|---|---|---|---|---|
| $50,000.00 | × | 15% | = | $7,500.00 |

Step 2:

| **Second Net Income Amount** | × | **Second Tax Rate** | = | **Federal Income Tax on Next $25,000.00 of Net Income** |
|---|---|---|---|---|
| $25,000.00 | × | 25% | = | $6,250.00 |

Step 3:

| **Third Net Income Amount** | × | **Third Tax Rate** | = | **Federal Income Tax on Next $25,000.00 of Net Income** |
|---|---|---|---|---|
| $25,000.00 | × | 34% | = | $8,500.00 |

Step 4:

| **Total Net Income** | – | **Lowest Dollar Amount of Fourth Tax Range** | = | **Amount of Net Income to Which Fourth Tax Rate Is Applied** |
|---|---|---|---|---|
| $240,914.00 | – | $100,000.00 | = | $140,914.00 |

Step 5:

| **Fourth Net Income Amount** | × | **Fourth Tax Rate** | = | **Federal Income Tax on Next $140,914.00 of Net Income** |
|---|---|---|---|---|
| $140,914.00 | × | 39% | = | $54,956.46 |

Step 6:

| **First Federal Tax Amount** | + | **Second Federal Tax Amount** | + | **Third Federal Tax Amount** | + | **Fourth Federal Tax Amount** | = | **Total Federal Tax Amount** |
|---|---|---|---|---|---|---|---|---|
| $7,500.00 | + | $6,250.00 | + | $8,500.00 | + | $54,956.46 | = | $77,206.46 |

The amount of federal income tax expense a corporation must pay is calculated using a tax rate table furnished by the Internal Revenue Service. The federal income tax payable is based on the total net income of the corporation. However, different tax percentages are applied to different portions of the net income to determine the total federal income tax owed. Winning Edge's net income before federal income tax is $240,914.00. Corporation tax rates in effect when this text was written are used to calculate Winning Edge's federal income tax expense.

### STEPS: Calculating federal income tax

1. Multiply $50,000.00 by a tax rate of 15% to calculate the first federal income tax amount. This is the tax Winning Edge must pay on its first $50,000.00 of net income.
2. Multiply $25,000.00 by a tax rate of 25% to calculate the second federal income tax amount. This is the tax Winning Edge must pay on the next $25,000.00 of net income.
3. Multiply $25,000.00 by a tax rate of 34% to calculate the third federal income tax amount. This is the tax Winning Edge must pay on the next $25,000.00 of net income.
4. The tax rate of 39% applies to all net income that falls in the range of $100,000.00 to $335,000.00. Winning Edge's net income is $240,914.00. When the net income does not equal or exceed the highest dollar amount given in a range, the amount of net income to which the tax rate is applied is determined by subtracting the lowest dollar amount in the range from the total net income. ($240,914.00 – $100,000.00 = $140,914.00)
5. Multiply $140,914.00 by a tax rate of 39% to calculate the fourth federal income tax amount. This is the tax Winning Edge must pay on the remainder of its net income.
6. Add the four tax amounts together to determine the total federal income tax Winning Edge must pay.

# FEDERAL INCOME TAX ADJUSTMENT

| | Account Title | Trial Balance Debit (1) | Trial Balance Credit (2) | Adjustments Debit (3) | Adjustments Credit (4) | Income Statement Debit (5) | Income Statement Credit (6) | Balance Sheet Debit (7) | Balance Sheet Credit (8) | |
|---|---|---|---|---|---|---|---|---|---|---|
| 14 | Notes Payable | | 500000 | | | | | | 500000 | 14 |
| 15 | Interest Payable | | | | (h) 20000 | | | | 20000 | 15 |
| 16 | Accounts Payable | | 3145300 | | | | | | 3145300 | 16 |
| 17 | Employee Income Tax Payable | | 204900 | | | | | | 204900 | 17 |
| 18 | Federal Income Tax Payable | | | | (i) 1320646 | | | | 1320646 | 18 |
| 50 | Gain on Plant Assets | | 56000 | | | | 56000 | | | 50 |
| 51 | Interest Income | | 6800 | | (a) 2000 | | 8800 | | | 51 |
| 52 | Interest Expense | 114300 | | (h) 20000 | | 134300 | | | | 52 |
| 53 | Loss on Plant Assets | 120000 | | | | 120000 | | | | 53 |
| 54 | Federal Income Tax Expense | 6400000 | | (i) 1320646 | | 7720646 | | | | 54 |
| 55 | | 218615450 | 218615450 | 6013446 | 6013446 | | | | | 55 |
| 56 | | | | | | | | | | 56 |
| 57 | | | | | | | | | | 57 |
| 58 | | | | | | | | | | 58 |

**1.** Calculate and enter the federal income tax adjustment.

**2.** Total and rule the Adjustments columns.

**3.** Extend the account balances.

## STEPS

### Planning a work sheet adjustment for federal income tax expense

**1.** Calculate the amount of the federal income tax expense adjustment. The adjustment is the difference between the federal income tax for the year and the taxes paid during the year.

| | |
|---|---|
| Federal Income Tax | $77,206.46 |
| *Less* Total of Quarterly Installments | −64,000.00 |
| *Equals* Federal Income Tax Adjustment | $13,206.46 |

Enter the federal income tax expense adjustment, *$13,206.46,* in the Adjustments Credit column on the Federal Income Tax Payable line of the work sheet. Enter the same amount in the Adjustments Debit column of the Federal Income Tax Expense line of the work sheet. Label both parts of the adjustment *(i).*

**2.** Total and rule the Adjustments columns.

**3.** Extend the federal income tax expense account balance, *$77,206.46,* to the Income Statement Debit column. Extend the amount for Federal Income Tax Payable, *$13,206.46,* to the Balance Sheet Credit column.

**Federal Income Tax Expense**

| Debit | | Credit | |
|---|---|---|---|
| 4/15 | 16,000.00 | | |
| 6/15 | 16,000.00 | | |
| 9/15 | 16,000.00 | | |
| 12/15 | 16,000.00 | | |
| *(12/15 Bal.* | *64,000.00)* | | |
| 12/31 Adj. (i) | 13,206.46 | | |
| *(New Bal.* | *77,206.46)* | | |

**Federal Income Tax Payable**

| Debit | | Credit | |
|---|---|---|---|
| | | 12/31 Adj. (i) | 13,206.46 |

## COMPLETING A WORK SHEET

**1.** Total the income statement and balance sheet columns.

| | Account Title | 1 Trial Balance Debit | 2 Trial Balance Credit | 3 Adjustments Debit | 4 Adjustments Credit | 5 Income Statement Debit | 6 Income Statement Credit | 7 Balance Sheet Debit | 8 Balance Sheet Credit | |
|---|---|---|---|---|---|---|---|---|---|---|
| 14 | *Notes Payable* | | 5,000 00 | | | | | | 5,000 00 | 14 |
| 15 | *Interest Payable* | | | | (h) 200 00 | | | | 200 00 | 15 |
| 16 | *Accounts Payable* | | 31,453 00 | | | | | | 31,453 00 | 16 |
| 17 | *Employee Income Tax Payable* | | 2,049 00 | | | | | | 2,049 00 | 17 |
| 18 | *Federal Income Tax Payable* | | | | (i) 13,206 46 | | | | 13,206 46 | 18 |
| 50 | *Gain on Plant Assets* | | 560 00 | | | | 560 00 | | | 50 |
| 51 | *Interest Income* | | 68 00 | | (a) 20 00 | | 88 00 | | | 51 |
| 52 | *Interest Expense* | 1,143 00 | | (h) 200 00 | | 1,343 00 | | | | 52 |
| 53 | *Loss on Plant Assets* | 1,200 00 | | | | 1,200 00 | | | | 53 |
| 54 | *Federal Income Tax Expense* | 64,000 00 | | (i) 13,206 46 | | 77,206 46 | | | | 54 |
| 55 | | 2,186,154 50 | 2,186,154 50 | 60,134 46 | 60,134 46 | 1,776,743 96 | 1,940,451 50 | 452,223 00 | 288,515 46 | 55 |
| 56 | *Net Income after Federal Income Tax* | | | | | 163,707 54 | | | 163,707 54 | 56 |
| 57 | | | | | | 1,940,451 50 | 1,940,451 50 | 452,223 00 | 452,223 00 | 57 |
| 58 | | | | | | | | | | 58 |

**2.** Calculate and enter the net income after federal income tax.

**5.** Draw double lines.

**4.** Calculate the column totals.

**3.** Extend the net income amount.

After the adjustment for federal income tax expense has been recorded, the work sheet is ready to be completed. Income Statement column totals are used to calculate net income after federal income tax. Winning Edge's completed work sheet is shown on the following two pages.

### STEPS: Completing a work sheet

1. Total the Income Statement and Balance Sheet columns.
2. Write the words *Net Income after Federal Income Tax* on line 56 of the work sheet. Calculate and enter the net income after federal income tax, *$163,707.54,* in the Income Statement Debit column on this new line of the work sheet.

| | |
|---|---|
| Total of Income Statement Credit column . . . . . . . . . . . . . . . . | $1,940,451.50 |
| *Less* Total of Income Statement Debit column . . . . . . . . . . . . . | −1,776,743.96 |
| *Equals* Net Income after Federal Income Tax . . . . . . . . . . . . . . | $ 163,707.54 |

3. Extend the net income after federal income tax amount, *$163,707.54,* to the Balance Sheet Credit column.
4. Total the four Income Statement and Balance Sheet columns. Determine that the totals of each pair of columns are in balance.
5. Rule double lines across the Income Statement and Balance Sheet columns to show that the totals have been verified as correct.

## A COMPLETED 8-COLUMN WORK SHEET

**Winning Edge, Inc.**
**Work Sheet**
**For Year Ended December 31, 20--**

| | ACCOUNT TITLE | 1 TRIAL BALANCE DEBIT | 2 TRIAL BALANCE CREDIT | 3 ADJUSTMENTS DEBIT | 4 ADJUSTMENTS CREDIT | 5 INCOME STATEMENT DEBIT | 6 INCOME STATEMENT CREDIT | 7 BALANCE SHEET DEBIT | 8 BALANCE SHEET CREDIT | |
|---|---|---|---|---|---|---|---|---|---|---|
| 1 | Cash | 10,584.00 | | | | | | 10,584.00 | | 1 |
| 2 | Petty Cash | 250.00 | | | | | | 250.00 | | 2 |
| 3 | Notes Receivable | 1,000.00 | | | | | | 1,000.00 | | 3 |
| 4 | Interest Receivable | | | (a) 20.00 | | | | 20.00 | | 4 |
| 5 | Accounts Receivable | 72,458.00 | | | | | | 72,458.00 | | 5 |
| 6 | Allowance for Uncollectible Accounts | | 320.00 | | (b) 9,828.00 | | | | 10,148.00 | 6 |
| 7 | Merchandise Inventory | 238,758.00 | | (c) 6,158.00 | | | | 244,916.00 | | 7 |
| 8 | Supplies | 9,158.00 | | | (d) 7,472.00 | | | 1,686.00 | | 8 |
| 9 | Prepaid Insurance | 12,400.00 | | | (e) 9,850.00 | | | 2,550.00 | | 9 |
| 10 | Office Equipment | 25,978.00 | | | | | | 25,978.00 | | 10 |
| 11 | Accumulated Depreciation—Office Equip. | | 6,173.00 | | (f) 4,650.00 | | | | 10,823.00 | 11 |
| 12 | Store Equipment | 52,781.00 | | | | | | 52,781.00 | | 12 |
| 13 | Accumulated Depreciation—Store Equip. | | 7,054.00 | | (g) 8,750.00 | | | | 15,804.00 | 13 |
| 14 | Notes Payable | | 5,000.00 | | | | | | 5,000.00 | 14 |
| 15 | Interest Payable | | | | (h) 200.00 | | | | 200.00 | 15 |
| 16 | Accounts Payable | | 31,453.00 | | | | | | 31,453.00 | 16 |
| 17 | Employee Income Tax Payable | | 2,049.00 | | | | | | 2,049.00 | 17 |
| 18 | Federal Income Tax Payable | | | | (i) 13,206.46 | | | | 13,206.46 | 18 |
| 19 | Social Security Tax Payable | | 1,783.00 | | | | | | 1,783.00 | 19 |
| 20 | Medicare Tax Payable | | 412.00 | | | | | | 412.00 | 20 |
| 21 | Sales Tax Payable | | 10,482.00 | | | | | | 10,482.00 | 21 |
| 22 | Unemployment Tax Payable—Federal | | 38.00 | | | | | | 38.00 | 22 |
| 23 | Unemployment Tax Payable—State | | 244.00 | | | | | | 244.00 | 23 |
| 24 | Health Insurance Premiums Payable | | 498.00 | | | | | | 498.00 | 24 |
| 25 | Dividends Payable | | 10,000.00 | | | | | | 10,000.00 | 25 |
| 26 | Capital Stock | | 120,000.00 | | | | | | 120,000.00 | 26 |

| | Account Title | Trial Balance Debit | Trial Balance Credit | Adjustments Debit | Adjustments Credit | Income Statement Debit | Income Statement Credit | Balance Sheet Debit | Balance Sheet Credit | |
|---|---|---|---|---|---|---|---|---|---|---|
| 27 | Retained Earnings | | 56 375 00 | | | | | | 56 375 00 | 27 |
| 28 | Dividends | 40 000 00 | | | | | | 40 000 00 | | 28 |
| 29 | Income Summary | | | | (c) 6 158 00 | | 6 158 00 | | | 29 |
| 30 | Sales | | 1917 955 50 | | | | 1917 955 50 | | | 30 |
| 31 | Sales Discount | 7 584 00 | | | | 7 584 00 | | | | 31 |
| 32 | Sales Returns and Allowances | 21 486 00 | | | | 21 486 00 | | | | 32 |
| 33 | Purchases | 1045 832 00 | | | | 1045 832 00 | | | | 33 |
| 34 | Purchases Discount | | 10 548 00 | | | | 10 548 00 | | | 34 |
| 35 | Purchases Returns and Allowances | | 5 142 00 | | | | 5 142 00 | | | 35 |
| 36 | Advertising Expense | 28 472 00 | | | | 28 472 00 | | | | 36 |
| 37 | Cash Short and Over | 7 00 | | | | 7 00 | | | | 37 |
| 38 | Credit Card Fee Expense | 18 489 00 | | | | 18 489 00 | | | | 38 |
| 39 | Depr. Expense—Office Equipment | | | (f) 4 650 00 | | 4 650 00 | | | | 39 |
| 40 | Depr. Expense—Store Equipment | | | (g) 8 750 00 | | 8 750 00 | | | | 40 |
| 41 | Insurance Expense | | | (e) 9 850 00 | | 9 850 00 | | | | 41 |
| 42 | Miscellaneous Expense | 28 398 17 | | | | 28 398 17 | | | | 42 |
| 43 | Payroll Taxes Expense | 29 310 05 | | | | 29 310 05 | | | | 43 |
| 44 | Rent Expense | 60 000 00 | | | | 60 000 00 | | | | 44 |
| 45 | Repair Expense | 4 872 00 | | | | 4 872 00 | | | | 45 |
| 46 | Salary Expense | 393 844 28 | | | | 393 844 28 | | | | 46 |
| 47 | Supplies Expense | | | (d) 7 472 00 | | 7 472 00 | | | | 47 |
| 48 | Uncollectible Accounts Expense | | | (b) 9 828 00 | | 9 828 00 | | | | 48 |
| 49 | Utilities Expense | 18 150 00 | | | | 18 150 00 | | | | 49 |
| 50 | Gain on Plant Assets | | 560 00 | | | | 560 00 | | | 50 |
| 51 | Interest Income | | 68 00 | | (a) 20 00 | | 88 00 | | | 51 |
| 52 | Interest Expense | 1 143 00 | | (h) 200 00 | | 1 343 00 | | | | 52 |
| 53 | Loss on Plant Assets | 1 200 00 | | | | 1 200 00 | | | | 53 |
| 54 | Federal Income Tax Expense | 64 000 00 | | (i) 13 206 46 | | 77 206 46 | | | | 54 |
| 55 | | 2186 154 50 | 2186 154 50 | 60 134 46 | 60 134 46 | 1776 743 96 | 1940 451 50 | 452 223 00 | 288 515 46 | 55 |
| 56 | Net Income after Federal Income Tax | | | | | 163 707 54 | | | 163 707 54 | 56 |
| 57 | | | | | | 1940 451 50 | 1940 451 50 | 452 223 00 | 452 223 00 | 57 |

## AUDIT YOUR UNDERSTANDING

1. What must a corporation do if actual federal income tax owed is greater than estimated tax paid?
2. Why is federal income tax expense not calculated until all other adjustments have been planned on a work sheet?

## WORK TOGETHER

**Completing a work sheet for a corporation**

Use the work sheet from Work Together on page 645. Your instructor will guide you through the following examples.

3. Extend all amounts except Federal Income Tax Expense to the appropriate Income Statement or Balance Sheet columns. Do not total the columns.
4. On the form provided in the *Working Papers,* total the work sheet's Income Statement columns. Calculate the difference between the debit and credit totals. This difference becomes the net income before federal income tax expense.
5. Using the tax table shown in this chapter, calculate federal income tax expense and record the income tax adjustment on the work sheet. Complete the work sheet.

## ON YOUR OWN

**Completing a work sheet for a corporation**

Use the work sheet from On Your Own on page 645. Work these problems independently.

6. Extend all amounts except Federal Income Tax Expense to the appropriate Income Statement or Balance Sheet columns. Do not total the columns.
7. On the form provided in the *Working Papers,* total the work sheet's Income Statement columns. Calculate the difference between the debit and credit totals. This difference becomes the net income before federal income tax expense.
8. Using the tax table shown in this chapter, calculate federal income tax expense and record the income tax adjustment on the work sheet. Complete the work sheet.

# CHAPTER 25 SUMMARY

*Enrichment Activity*

**Types of Businesses**

*Compare how the owners of a proprietorship, a partnership, and a corporation receive the earnings of the business as their own personal income. Contrast who pays the taxes on the net income from a proprietorship, partnership, and corporation.*

After completing this chapter, you can

1. Define accounting terms related to distributing dividends and preparing a work sheet for a merchandising business organized as a corporation.
2. Identify accounting concepts and practices related to distributing dividends and preparing a work sheet for a merchandising business organized as a corporation.
3. Journalize the declaration and payment of a dividend for a merchandising business organized as a corporation.
4. Plan end-of-fiscal-period adjustments for a merchandising business organized as a corporation.
5. Calculate federal income tax, plan an adjustment for federal income tax expense, and complete a work sheet.

## EXPLORE ACCOUNTING

### AUDITS PROVIDE STOCKHOLDERS WITH POSITIVE ASSURANCE

Stockholders want assurance that the financial statements of their corporation accurately present its financial condition and results of operations. To provide this assurance, corporations hire independent public accountants to audit the financial statements. These accountants, referred to as auditors, provide a written opinion that informs stockholders whether the financial statements can be relied upon for making informed business decisions.

Auditors examine documents, journals, ledgers, and other accounting records to collect evidence that supports five declarations, or assertions, about each amount in the financial statements. Each assertion addresses a unique quality about the amount in the financial statements. These assertions are summarized as follows.

1. *Existence or Occurrence.* All assets and liabilities actually exist and all income statement transactions actually occurred during the period.
2. *Completeness.* All assets and liabilities that exist have been reported and all revenue and expense events have been recorded.
3. *Rights and Obligations.* All assets and liabilities are those of the corporation and not of its owners or another corporation.
4. *Valuation or Allocation.* Transactions are reported using amounts that correctly reflect the value of the item or event.
5. *Presentation and Disclosure.* Accounts are properly classified, described, and disclosed in conformity with generally accepted accounting principles.

**Required:** Create a table that shows how the five financial statement assertions relate to any one particular amount reported on the financial statements.

## 25-1 APPLICATION PROBLEM
### Journalizing dividends

Journals are given in the *Working Papers.* Lewis Corporation completed the following transactions during December of the current year and January of the next year.

***Transactions:***

Dec. 15. The board of directors declared a dividend of $0.06 per share; capital stock issued is 25,000 shares. M321.

Jan. 15. Paid cash for dividend declared December 15. C659.

***Instructions:***

1. Use page 18 of a general journal. Journalize the dividend declared on December 15.
2. Use page 24 of a cash payments journal. Journalize payment of the dividend on January 15.

## 25-2 APPLICATION PROBLEM
### Journalizing dividends

Journals are given in the *Working Papers.* Lynchburg Corporation's board of directors met on December 15 and raised the company's quarterly dividend to $6.50 per share. The company currently has 10,000 shares of stock outstanding. The dividends will be paid in one month.

***Instructions:***

1. Use page 12 of a general journal. Journalize the dividend declared using M177 as the source document.
2. Use page 18 of a cash payments journal to journalize the dividend payment using Check No. 865.

## 25-3 APPLICATION PROBLEM
### Preparing a work sheet for a corporation

***Instructions:***

Donovan Lumber Corporation's work sheet is given in the *Working Papers.* For the current year ended December 31, record the adjustments on the work sheet using the following information. Do not total the Adjustments columns. Save your work to complete Application Problem 25-4.

**Adjustment Information, December 31**

| | |
|---|---|
| Accrued interest income | $ 312.00 |
| Uncollectible accounts expense estimated as 1.0% of sales on account. Sales on account for year, $687,000.00. | |
| Merchandise inventory | 82,184.50 |
| Supplies inventory | 1,840.50 |
| Value of prepaid insurance | 4,200.00 |
| Annual depreciation expense—office equipment | 3,028.00 |
| Annual depreciation expense—store equipment | 3,489.00 |
| Accrued interest expense | 250.00 |

## 25-4 APPLICATION PROBLEM
### Completing a work sheet for a corporation

Use the work sheet from Application Problem 25-3 to complete this problem.

**Tax Table**

15% of net income before taxes, zero to $50,000.00
*Plus* 25% of net income before taxes, $50,000.00 to $75,000.00
*Plus* 34% of net income before taxes, $75,000.00 to $100,000.00
*Plus* 39% of net income before taxes, $100,000.00 to $335,000.00
*Plus* 34% of net income before taxes over $335,000.00

***Instructions:***

1. Extend all amounts except Federal Income Tax Expense to the appropriate Income Statement or Balance Sheet columns. Do not total the columns.
2. On the form provided in the *Working Papers,* total the work sheet's Income Statement columns. Calculate the difference between the debit and credit totals. This difference becomes the net income before federal income tax expense.
3. Using the tax table above, calculate federal income tax expense and record the income tax adjustment on the work sheet. Complete the work sheet.

## 25-5 MASTERY PROBLEM
### Journalizing dividends and preparing a work sheet for a corporation

Accounting forms are given in the *Working Papers*. Pennington Corporation completed the following transactions during December of the current year and January of the next year.

***Transactions:***

Dec. 15. The board of directors declared a dividend of $0.25 per share; capital stock issued is 40,000 shares. M327.

Jan. 15. Paid cash for dividend declared December 15. C983.

***Instructions:***

1. Use page 12 of a general journal. Journalize the dividend declared on December 15.
2. Use page 18 of a cash payments journal. Journalize payment of the dividend on January 15.
3. Prepare Pennington Corporation's work sheet for the current year ended December 31. Record the adjustments on the work sheet using the following information. Do not total the Adjustments columns.

**Adjustment Information, December 31**

| | |
|---|---|
| Accrued interest income | $ 684.00 |
| Uncollectible accounts expense estimated as 1.0% of sales on account. Sales on account for year, $956,000.00. | |
| Merchandise inventory | 218,687.20 |
| Supplies inventory | 332.40 |
| Value of prepaid insurance | 4,200.00 |
| Annual depreciation expense—office equipment | 5,847.00 |
| Annual depreciation expense—store equipment | 4,520.00 |
| Accrued interest expense | 300.00 |

4. Extend all amounts except Federal Income Tax Expense to the appropriate Income Statement or Balance Sheet columns. Do not total the columns.
5. On the form provided in the *Working Papers,* total the work sheet's Income Statement columns. Calculate the difference between the debit and credit totals. This difference becomes the net income before federal income tax expense.
6. Using the tax table in Application Problem 25-4, calculate federal income tax expense and record the income tax adjustment on the work sheet. Complete the work sheet.

## 25-6 CHALLENGE PROBLEM
### Completing a work sheet for a corporation

Matthew Williams, the accountant for Petal Corporation, has recorded all adjustments on the work sheet except for the income tax expense adjustment. Mr. Williams has written below the work sheet the column totals (excluding the $40,000.00 estimated tax payments in the income statement columns) before the income tax adjustment.

***Instructions:***

1. On the form provided in the *Working Papers,* record the totals of the work sheet's Income Statement columns. Calculate the difference between the debit and credit totals. This difference becomes the net income before federal income tax expense.
2. Using the tax table in Application Problem 25-4, calculate federal income tax expense and record the income tax adjustment on the work sheet. Complete the work sheet.
3. Proposals have been made to replace the corporate federal income tax with a national sales or consumption tax. How would such a change in taxes affect the way that businesses account for federal tax expense?

**INTERNET ACTIVITY**

Point your browser to
**http://accounting.swpco.com**
Choose **First-Year Course**, choose **Activities**, and complete the activity for Chapter 25.

## Applied Communication

Corporations maintain written documentation about their accounting procedures. The Securities and Exchange Commission requires regulated companies to maintain written documentation of their accounting systems. The documentation is also useful for auditors and employees to learn how the accounting system operates.

**Instructions:** Prepare the written procedures for completing a work sheet, assuming a company has a net loss. In this circumstance, the company would receive a refund for income taxes paid during the year. In addition, the company would be able to receive a refund of taxes paid in prior years, calculated using the tax rates applied to the net loss. For example, if a company with net income of $50,000.00 would pay income taxes of $7,500.00, a company with a net loss of $50,000.00 would receive a tax refund of $7,500.00.

# Cases for Critical Thinking

**Case 1** Harris Company's net income has been fluctuating between a small net income and a small net loss during the first four years of the corporation's existence, resulting in a retained earnings balance of $45,000.00. The company is hoping to earn $500,000.00 during its fifth year. Janet Crosland, newly appointed president of Harris Company, believes the corporation needs to take some positive action to regain the confidence of the stockholders. She suggests the corporation declare a $600,000.00 dividend December 15, to be paid February 1. Ms. Crosland also suggests that if the net income is not as high as expected, the board of directors can cancel the declared dividend before it is paid. Do you agree with Ms. Crosland's proposal? Explain.

**Case 2** At the beginning of the current year, Liang Company changed its organization from a partnership to a corporation. The president suggested that since the same six individuals owned the corporation as had owned the partnership, the same procedures should be used for paying income tax on the earnings of the business. The net income of the corporation would be treated as part of each corporation owner's personal income for income tax purposes. "If this procedure is followed," said the president, "the corporation will not need to pay any income tax." Do you agree with the president's suggestion? Explain.

**Case 3** The board of directors of Christina's Gift Shops, Inc., has not declared a dividend in any of the last five years. The net income from each year has been added to the corporation's retained earnings. Excess cash has been invested in opening new stores and upgrading store equipment in older stores. At the corporation's annual meeting last week, some stockholders supported the actions of the board of directors. Several other stockholders, however, disagreed strongly with the board's policy of not declaring dividends. These stockholders said that they invested in the corporation in the expectation of earning steady income from dividends. If you were the chairperson of the board of directors, how would you respond to the disagreement among the stockholders?

# AUTOMATED ACCOUNTING

## USING THE LOAN PLANNER

Planning tools function like specialized calculators. They are used to perform specific types of calculations. *Automated Accounting 7.0* includes several planning tools. These utilities quickly perform the calculations and display the results. A printing function also allows a report to be printed, showing the results of the planner's calculation.

### Loan Planner

The Loan Planner is used to calculate the amount of a loan, the loan payment amount, and the number of payments. A common application of this tool is to compute the monthly payment when a loan is made at a stated interest rate. The planner may then be used to generate an amortization table that will show the amount of principal and interest associated with each payment.

To use the Loan Planner:

1. Click the Tools toolbar button.
2. Click the Loan Planner tab.
3. Select the Loan Amount, Loan Payment Amount, or the Number of Payments option button in the Calculate option group.
4. Enter the data and press the Tab key. The unknown amount to be calculated will be dimmed, based on the options selected in Step 3. The calculated results will appear at the bottom of the Planning dialog box.
5. Click on the Report command button to produce a report schedule. Once

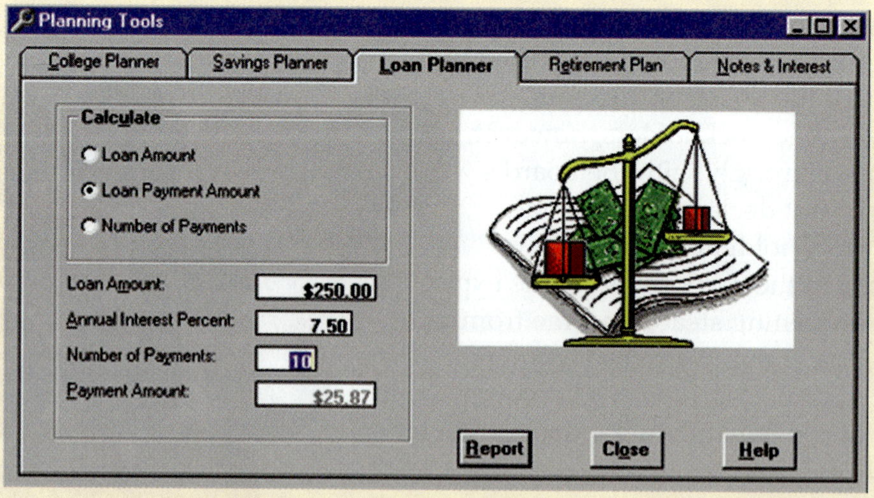

# AUTOMATED ACCOUNTING

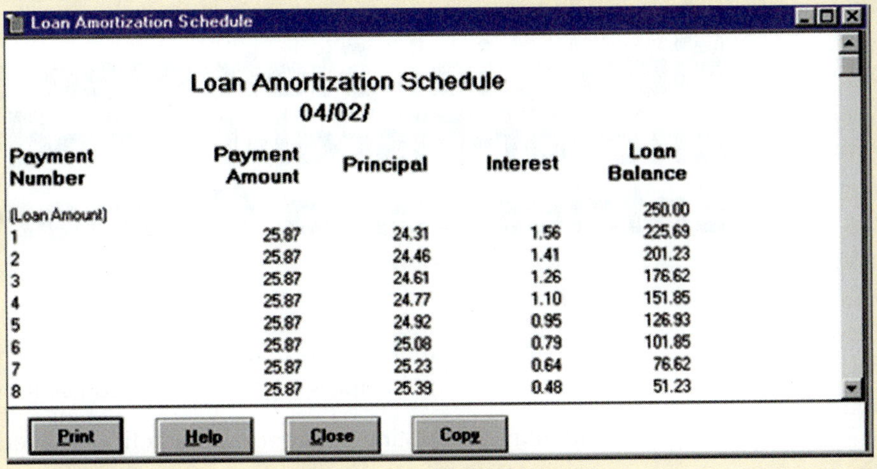

Loan Amortization Schedule

**Loan Amortization Schedule**
**04/02/**

| Payment Number | Payment Amount | Principal | Interest | Loan Balance |
|---|---|---|---|---|
| (Loan Amount) | | | | 250.00 |
| 1 | 25.87 | 24.31 | 1.56 | 225.69 |
| 2 | 25.87 | 24.46 | 1.41 | 201.23 |
| 3 | 25.87 | 24.61 | 1.26 | 176.62 |
| 4 | 25.87 | 24.77 | 1.10 | 151.85 |
| 5 | 25.87 | 24.92 | 0.95 | 126.93 |
| 6 | 25.87 | 25.08 | 0.79 | 101.85 |
| 7 | 25.87 | 25.23 | 0.64 | 76.62 |
| 8 | 25.87 | 25.39 | 0.48 | 51.23 |



displayed, the report may be printed or copied to the clipboard for pasting into a spreadsheet or word processor.

6. Click the Close button or press ESC to exit the report and return to the planner.
7. Steps 3 through 5 may then be repeated for different Calculate options or for different data sets.
8. Click the Close button or press ESC again to exit the planner.

## Using Reports in Other Documents

Reports may be printed or copied to the clipboard for pasting into a spreadsheet or word processor. To copy a report for use in another file:

1. Click on the Copy command button.
2. When the Copy Report to Clipboard dialog box appears, select the desired option button for spreadsheet or word processor.
3. Click on OK.
4. A message dialog box will appear, indicating the copy is complete. Click on OK.

## Using Special Tools—The Loan Planner

**Instructions:**

1. Load *Automated Accounting 7.0* or higher software.
2. Click on the Tools toolbar button.
3. Click on the Loan Planner tab. Select Loan Payment Amount from the Calculate box. Enter a loan amount of $800.00, an interest rate of 9.25, and 18 payments. The payment amount will be automatically calculated.
4. Click on the Report command button from within the Loan Planner tab. Print the report, or copy it to the clipboard for entering into a word processor or spreadsheet application.
5. Click Close to return to the Loan Planner. Steps 3 and 4 may then be repeated for different calculation options, or for different data sets.
6. Click Close to exit the planner. Upon exiting a planning tool, your data will not be saved. Be sure to print a report, or copy it to a word processor or spreadsheet and save it in that application.

# 26 Financial Statements and End-of-Fiscal-Period Entries for a Corporation

**AFTER STUDYING CHAPTER 26, YOU WILL BE ABLE TO:**

1. Define accounting terms related to financial statements for a merchandising business organized as a corporation.
2. Identify accounting concepts and practices related to financial statements and end-of-fiscal-period entries for a merchandising business organized as a corporation.
3. Prepare and analyze an income statement for a merchandising business organized as a corporation.
4. Prepare a statement of stockholders' equity for a merchandising business organized as a corporation.
5. Prepare and analyze a balance sheet for a merchandising business organized as a corporation.
6. Record adjusting, closing, and reversing entries for a merchandising business organized as a corporation.

**TERMS PREVIEW**

net sales
net purchases
statement of stockholders' equity
par value
long-term liabilities
working capital
ratio
current ratio

## FINANCIAL STATEMENTS FOR CORPORATIONS

Corporations prepare financial statements that provide financial information similar to that reported by proprietorships and partnerships. To furnish the corporation's managers and stockholders with information on how well the corporation is progressing, financial statements are prepared annually and sometimes monthly or quarterly. *(CONCEPT: Accounting Period Cycle)*

Financial statements are used to report a business's financial progress and condition as well as changes in the owners' equity. To report this information, Winning Edge prepares three financial statements: (1) income statement, (2) statement of stockholders' equity, and (3) balance sheet.

A corporation prepares an income statement and a balance sheet similar to those used by proprietorships and partnerships. However, a corporation reports changes in owners' equity differently. First, owners' equity for all owners is reported as a single amount rather than for each owner. Second, owners' equity is reported in two categories: (1) capital contributed by the owners and (2) capital earned by the corporation.

# ACCOUNTING IN YOUR CAREER

## TRYING ON A NEW ACCOUNTING SYSTEM

Eva Perez is anxious to get to the office today to do the end-of-fiscal-period work for the year just ended. She has been the accounting manager for GenTelsys, Inc., for five years and has done the year-end accounting work before. But this time it's different.

For the past three months, Eva and her assistant, Ed Duncan, have been using a new computerized accounting system. They have continued to keep all accounting records manually as well as enter all data into the new accounting system. For three months they have compared results from these two systems to be sure the computerized system was producing accurate results. So far everything has matched. But today they will close the year and get the final test before abandoning the manual system.

Eva rushes to a meeting while Ed keys the adjusting entries. The adjusted trial balance prints just as Eva returns from the meeting. A quick check confirms that it matches the manually-prepared trial balance. In a short while the financial statements are printed and they too match. Ed then selects the option for posting the closing entries and prints the post-closing trial balance. A quick comparison reveals that the computerized report shows a balance for Charitable Contributions Expense, a new account added in December, and for Loss on Plant Assets—accounts that should have been closed.

"Ed, that's not too bad," says Eva. "I think we can load the backup and fix this quickly. Everything should match then, and we can stop keeping both systems going at the same time. Then maybe things will get back to normal around here."

**Critical Thinking:**

1. What would explain why two accounts were not closed in the computerized closing entries?
2. Eva Perez referred to a backup. Once the system is permanently in place, would you recommend that the company continue to keep a backup of the accounting system?
3. Would your opinion about a backup be the same if the backup equipment and supplies were expensive and if considerable labor time was involved in each backup?

# 26-1 Preparing an Income Statement

## INCOME STATEMENT

**Winning Edge, Inc.**
**Income Statement**
**For Year Ended December 31, 20--**

| | | | | | % of Net Sales |
|---|---|---|---|---|---|
| Operating Revenue: | | | | | |
| Sales | | | $1,917,955.50 | | |
| Less: Sales Discount | | $ 7,584.00 | | | |
| Sales Ret. and Allow. | | 21,486.00 | 29,070.00 | | |
| Net Sales | | | | $1,888,885.50 | 100.0 |
| Cost of Merchandise Sold: | | | | | |
| Merchandise Inv., Jan. 1, 20-- | | | $ 238,758.00 | | |
| Purchases | | $1,045,832.00 | | | |
| Less: Purchases Discount | $10,548.00 | | | | |
| Purch. Ret. and Allow. | 5,142.00 | 15,690.00 | | | |
| Net Purchases | | | 1,030,142.00 | | |
| Total Cost of Mdse. Avail. for Sale | | | $1,268,900.00 | | |
| Less Mdse. Inventory, Dec. 31, 20-- | | | 244,916.00 | | |
| Cost of Merchandise Sold | | | | 1,023,984.00 | 54.2 |
| Gross Profit on Operations | | | | $ 864,901.50 | 45.8 |
| Operating Expenses: | | | | | |
| Advertising Expense | | | $ 28,472.00 | | |
| Cash Short and Over | | | 7.00 | | |
| Credit Card Fee Expense | | | 18,489.00 | | |
| Depreciation Exp.—Office Equip. | | | 4,650.00 | | |
| Depreciation Exp.—Store Equip. | | | 8,750.00 | | |
| Insurance Expense | | | 9,850.00 | | |
| Miscellaneous Expense | | | 28,398.17 | | |
| Payroll Taxes Expense | | | 29,310.05 | | |
| Rent Expense | | | 60,000.00 | | |
| Repair Expense | | | 4,872.00 | | |
| Salary Expense | | | 393,844.28 | | |
| Supplies Expense | | | 7,472.00 | | |
| Uncollectible Accounts Expense | | | 9,828.00 | | |
| Utilities Expense | | | 18,150.00 | | |
| Total Operating Expenses | | | | 622,092.50 | 32.9 |
| Income from Operations | | | | $ 242,809.00 | 12.9 |
| Other Revenue: | | | | | |
| Gain on Plant Assets | | $ 560.00 | | | |
| Interest Income | | 88.00 | | | |
| Total Other Revenue | | | $ 648.00 | | |
| Other Expenses: | | | | | |
| Interest Expense | | $ 1,343.00 | | | |
| Loss on Plant Assets | | 1,200.00 | | | |
| Total Other Expenses | | | 2,543.00 | | |
| Net Deduction | | | | 1,895.00 | 0.1 |
| Net Income before Fed. Inc. Tax | | | | $ 240,914.00 | 12.8 |
| Less Federal Income Tax Exp. | | | | 77,206.46 | |
| Net Income after Fed. Inc. Tax | | | | $ 163,707.54 | |

**1.** Net Sales

**2.** Net Purchases

**3.** Income from Operations

**4.** Net Income before and after Federal Income Tax

## USES OF AN INCOME STATEMENT

An income statement reports the financial progress of a business during a fiscal period. *(CONCEPT: Accounting Period Cycle)* Revenue, cost of merchandise sold, gross profit on operations, operating expenses, and net income or net loss are reported on an income statement. *(CONCEPT: Adequate Disclosure)* To help make decisions about current and future operations, Winning Edge also analyzes relationships between revenue and expense items. Based on this analysis, Winning Edge reports component percentages for all major income statement items.

Winning Edge's income statement differs from Omni Import's income statement shown in Cycle 2. Winning Edge has more accounts to report on the income statement. Because Winning Edge is a corporation, it must also report its federal income tax expense. As shown in the steps, there are four elements in the income statement of Winning Edge that do not appear in the income statement of Omni Import.

The work sheet Winning Edge used to prepare the financial statements in this chapter is shown in Chapter 25 on pages 650–651.

**STEPS**

### New elements in the income statement for Winning Edge

1. Subtract Sales Discount, *$7,584.00,* and Sales Returns and Allowances, *$21,486.00,* from Sales, *$1,917,955.50.* Total sales less sales discount and sales returns and allowances is called **net sales.**
2. Subtract Purchases Discount, *$10,548.00,* and Purchases Returns and Allowances, *$5,142.00,* from Purchases, *$1,045,832.00.* Total purchases less purchases discount and purchases returns and allowances is called **net purchases.**
3. Income from operations, *$242,809.00,* is reported separately from net income. Income from operations is the income earned only from normal business activities. Winning Edge's normal business activities are selling sports equipment. Other revenue and expenses, such as interest income, interest expense, and gains or losses on plant assets, are not normal business activities. Other revenue and expenses are not included in calculating income from operations.
4. Net income before federal income tax, *$240,914.00,* and net income after federal income tax, *$163,707.54,* are reported separately. Reporting net income before and after federal income tax is unique to corporation income statements.

### IS THIS REALLY A BUSINESS EXPENSE?

Cameron Duermit owns a computer consulting business. Each year he must report the amount of revenue and expenses involved in operating the firm. He must pay federal income tax on the amount by which revenues exceed expenses.

**Instructions**

Use the three-step checklist to help determine whether or not each of these actions demonstrates ethical behavior.

*Situation 1.* Mr. Duermit often makes personal long-distance phone calls from his office. He charges these calls to the business account.

*Situation 2.* Mr. Duermit hired his teenage son to work after school as an office assistant. Tyler comes in to the office every afternoon and earns $6.00 per hour. During this time he does homework and telephones friends. Mr. Duermit knows the business does not really need an assistant, but this is a good way for Tyler to earn spending money.

**PROFESSIONAL BUSINESS ETHICS**

| Income Statement Items | Acceptable Component Percentages | Actual Component Percentages |
|---|---|---|
| Net sales | 100.0% | 100.0% |
| Cost of merchandise sold | not more than 58.0% | 54.2% |
| Gross profit on operations | not less than 42.0% | 45.8% |
| Total operating expenses | not more than 35.0% | 32.9% |
| Income from operations | not less than 7.0% | 12.9% |
| Net deduction | not more than 0.1% | 0.1% |
| Net income before federal income tax | not less than 6.9% | 12.8% |

For a business to determine whether it is progressing satisfactorily, results of operations are compared with industry standards and/or previous fiscal periods. By analyzing revenues, costs, and expenses, management can gain information that it can use to improve future operations.

The percentage relationship between one financial statement item and the total that includes that item is known as a component percentage. Winning Edge prepares component percentages for six major items on its income statement, as shown in the illustration. Winning Edge uses net sales as the base for calculating component percentages.

The amount of each item on the income statement is divided by the amount of net sales. Thus, each component percentage shows the percentage that item is of net sales. For example, the cost of merchandise sold component percentage indicates that Winning Edge spent 54.2 cents out of each $1.00 of sales for the merchandise sold.

| Cost of Merchandise Sold | ÷ | Net Sales | = | Cost of Merchandise Sold Component Percentage |
|---|---|---|---|---|
| $1,023,984.00 | ÷ | $1,888,885.50 | = | 54.2% |

## Acceptable Component Percentages

Based on comparisons with industry standards as well as previous accounting periods, Winning Edge has determined acceptable component percentages for each major item of cost and expense on its income statement.

If the component percentage of any cost or expense item for a fiscal period exceeds the acceptable percentage, that cost or expense is reviewed further to determine the reason. After determining the reason why a cost or expense exceeded the acceptable percentage, ways are sought to bring the expense within acceptable limits.

**FYI**

*Component percentages are not calculated for federal income tax expense and net income after federal income tax. Corporations do not have much control over the amount of federal income taxes to be paid. Thus, the net income before federal income tax is the best measure the corporation has to assess its profitability.*

## TERMS REVIEW

net sales

net purchases

## AUDIT YOUR UNDERSTANDING

1. In what two ways does a corporation report changes in owners' equity differently from a proprietorship or partnership?
2. Why are other revenue and other expenses reported separately on the income statement from sales, cost of merchandise sold, and operating expenses?
3. What information is shown by component percentages on an income statement?

## WORK TOGETHER

### Preparing an income statement for a corporation

The completed work sheet for Webster Corporation and a blank income statement form are given in the *Working Papers.* Your instructor will guide you through the following examples.

4. Prepare an income statement for the current year. Calculate and record the following component percentages: (a) cost of merchandise sold; (b) gross profit on operations; (c) total operating expenses; (d) income from operations; (e) net addition or deduction resulting from other revenue and expenses; and (f) net income before federal income tax. Round percentage calculations to the nearest 0.1%.
5. The acceptable component percentages are given in the *Working Papers*. Analyze the income statement by determining if component percentages are within acceptable levels. If any component percentage is not within an acceptable level, suggest steps that the company should take. Save your work to complete Work Together on page 668.

## ON YOUR OWN

### Preparing an income statement for a corporation

The completed work sheet you completed for Osborn Corporation and a blank income statement form are given in the *Working Papers.* Work these problems independently.

6. Prepare an income statement for the current year. Calculate and record the following component percentages: (a) cost of merchandise sold; (b) gross profit on operations; (c) total operating expenses; (d) income from operations; (e) net addition or deduction resulting from other revenue and expenses; and (f) net income before federal income tax. Round percentage calculations to the nearest 0.1%.
7. The acceptable component percentages are given in the *Working Papers*. Analyze the income statement by determining if component percentages are within acceptable levels. If any component percentage is not within an acceptable level, suggest steps that the company should take. Save your work to complete On Your Own on page 668.

# 26-2 Preparing a Statement of Stockholders' Equity

## CAPITAL STOCK SECTION OF THE STATEMENT OF STOCKHOLDERS' EQUITY

**1.** Heading

**2.** Words *Capital Stock* and Par Value

**3.** Stock at Beginning of Year

**4.** Stock Issued during the Year

**5.** Total Stock Issued at End of Year

**Winning Edge, Inc.**
**Statement of Stockholders' Equity**
**For Year Ended December 31, 20--**

| | | |
|---|---|---|
| Capital Stock: | | |
| $10.00 Par Value | | |
| January 1, 20--, 10,000 Shares Issued | $100,000.00 | |
| Issued during Current Year 2,000 Shares | 20,000.00 | |
| Balance, December 31, 20--, 12,000 Shares Issued | | $120,000.00 |

A financial statement that shows changes in a corporation's ownership for a fiscal period is called a **statement of stockholders' equity.** A statement of stockholders' equity is similar to the owners' equity statement for a partnership.

A statement of stockholders' equity contains two major sections: (1) capital stock and (2) retained earnings.

The amount of capital stock issued as of the beginning of the year is the beginning balance of the capital stock account. Any additional stock transactions recorded in the general ledger during the fiscal year would be added up to calculate the amount of stock issued during the fiscal year. Thus, the amounts in the capital stock section of the income statement are obtained from the general ledger account, Capital Stock.

Each share of stock issued by a corporation has a monetary value. A value assigned to a share of stock and printed on the stock certificate is called **par value.**

### STEPS: Preparing the capital stock section of a statement of stockholders' equity

1. Write the heading: company name, *Winning Edge, Inc.;* statement name, *Statement of Stockholders' Equity;* and fiscal period, *For Year Ended December 31, 20—,* in the statement heading.
2. Write the the words *Capital Stock* and the par value of the stock, *$10.00 Par Value.*
3. Write the number of shares, *10,000,* and dollar amount, *$100,000.00,* of stock issued as of the beginning of the year.
4. Write the number of shares, *2,000,* and dollar amount, *$20,000.00,* of stock issued during the year.
5. Calculate the total dollar amount of stock issued as of the end of the fiscal year, *$120,000.00,* by adding the dollar amount of beginning stock, $100,000.00, and the dollar amount of shares issued during the year, $20,000.00.

# RETAINED EARNINGS SECTION OF THE STATEMENT OF STOCKHOLDERS' EQUITY

**Winning Edge, Inc.**
**Statement of Stockholders' Equity**
**For Year Ended December 31, 20--**

| | | | |
|---|---|---|---|
| Capital Stock: | | | |
| $10.00 Par Value | | | |
| January 1, 20--, 10,000 Shares Issued | | $100,000.00 | |
| Issued during Current Year, 2,000 Shares | | 20,000.00 | |
| Balance, December 31, 20--, 12,000 Shares Issued | | | $120,000.00 |
| (1) Retained Earnings: | | | |
| Balance, January 1, 20-- | | $ 56,375.00 (2) | |
| Net Income after Federal Income Tax for 20-- | (3) $163,707.54 | | |
| Less Dividends Declared during 20-- | (4) 40,000.00 | | |
| Net Increase during 20-- | | (5) 123,707.54 | |
| Balance, December 31, 20-- | | | (6) 180,082.54 |
| Total Stockholders' Equity, December 31, 20-- | | | $300,082.54 (7) |

1. Words *Retained Earnings*
2. Beginning Balance
3. Net Income after Federal Income Tax
4. Dividends Declared
5. Increase in Retained Earnings
6. Ending Balance
7. Total Stockholders' Equity

Net income increases a corporation's total capital. Some income may be retained by a corporation for business expansion. Some income may be distributed as dividends to provide stockholders with a return on their investments. During the year, Winning Edge's board of directors declared $40,000.00 in dividends.

Amounts used to prepare the statement of stockholders' equity are obtained from the income statement and balance sheet columns of the work sheet shown in Chapter 25.

## STEPS: Preparing the retained earnings section of a statement of stockholders' equity

1. Write the words *Retained Earnings.*
2. Write the beginning balance of retained earnings, *$56,375.00,* from the Balance Sheet Credit column.
3. Write the net income after federal income tax, *$163,707.54,* from the Income Statement Debit column.
4. Write the amount of dividends, *$40,000.00,* from the Balance Sheet Debit column.
5. Subtract dividends, $40,000.00, from net income after federal income tax, $163,707.54, to calculate the increase in retained earnings, *$123,707.54.*
6. Add the beginning balance of retained earnings, $56,375.00, and the increase in retained earnings, $123,707.54, to calculate the ending balance of retained earnings, *$180,082.54.*
7. Add the ending amounts of capital stock, $120,000.00, and retained earnings, $180,082.54, to calculate the total amount of stockholders' equity, *$300,082.54.*

## Terms Review

statement of stockholders' equity

par value

## Audit Your Understanding

1. What financial information does a statement of stockholders' equity report?
2. What are the two major sections of a statement of stockholders' equity?
3. Where is the information found to prepare the capital stock section of a statement of stockholders' equity?
4. Where is the beginning balance of retained earnings found?
5. How does a corporation distribute a portion of income to stockholders?
6. Where is the amount of dividends found?

## Work Together

**Preparing a statement of stockholders' equity for a corporation**

Use the work sheet and income statement for Webster Corporation from Work Together on page 665. A form for the statement of stockholders' equity is given in the *Working Papers*. Your instructor will guide you through the following example.

7. Prepare a statement of stockholders' equity for the current year. As of January 1, Webster Corporation had issued 9,000 shares of capital stock with a par value of $10.00 per share. During the fiscal year, the corporation issued 1,000 additional shares of capital stock. Save your work to complete Work Together on page 674.

## On Your Own

**Preparing a statement of stockholders' equity for a corporation**

Use the work sheet and income statement for Osborn Corporation from On Your Own on page 665. A form for the statement of stockholders' equity is given in the *Working Papers*. Work this problem independently.

8. Prepare a statement of stockholders' equity for the current year. As of January 1, Osborn Corporation had issued 75,000 shares of capital stock with a par value of $1.00 per share. During the fiscal year, the corporation issued 5,000 additional shares of stock. Save your work to complete On Your Own on page 674.

# 26-3 Preparing a Balance Sheet

## ASSETS SECTION OF A BALANCE SHEET

1. Heading *Current Assets*
3. Contra Account Balance
2. Account Balance
4. Book Value

**Winning Edge, Inc.**
**Balance Sheet**
**December 31, 20--**

| ASSETS | | | |
|---|---|---|---|
| Current Assets: | | | |
| Cash | | $ 10,584.00 | |
| Petty Cash | | 250.00 | |
| Notes Receivable | | 1,000.00 | |
| Interest Receivable | | 20.00 | |
| Accounts Receivable | $72,458.00 | | |
| Less Allowance for Uncollectible Accounts | 10,148.00 | 62,310.00 | |
| Merchandise Inventory | | 244,916.00 | |
| Supplies | | 1,686.00 | |
| Prepaid Insurance | | 2,550.00 | |
| Total Current Assets | | | $323,316.00 |
| Plant Assets: | | | |
| Office Equipment | $25,978.00 | | |
| Less Accumulated Depreciation—Office Equipment | 10,823.00 | $ 15,155.00 | |
| Store Equipment | $52,781.00 | | |
| Less Accumulated Depreciation—Store Equipment | 15,804.00 | 36,977.00 | |
| Total Plant Assets | | | 52,132.00 |
| Total Assets | | | $375,448.00 |

A corporation's balance sheet reports assets, liabilities, and stockholders' equity on a specific date. *(CONCEPT: Accounting Period Cycle)* A balance sheet is prepared from information found in the Balance Sheet columns of the work sheet and the statement of stockholders' equity.

Procedures for preparing Winning Edge's balance sheet are similar to those used by Omni Import in Cycle 2. However, Winning Edge must report the results of its accounting for accounts receivable and plant assets.

Winning Edge classifies its assets as current assets and plant assets. A business owning both current and plant assets usually lists them under separate headings on a balance sheet.

Some of Winning Edge's asset accounts have related contra accounts that reduce the related account on the balance sheet. The difference between an asset's account balance and its related contra account balance is known as book value. An asset's book value is reported on a balance sheet by listing three amounts: (1) the balance of the asset account, (2) the balance of the asset's contra account, and (3) book value.

### STEPS: Calculating the book value of accounts receivable

1. Write the heading *Current Assets.*
2. Write the total amount of accounts receivable, *$72,458.00,* in the first amount column.
3. Write the words *Less Allowance for Uncollectible Accounts* on the next line, indented about one centimeter, and the amount, *$10,148.00,* below the amount of accounts receivable, $72,458.00.
4. Subtract the allowance for uncollectible accounts, $10,148.00, from the total amount of accounts receivable, $72,458.00, to calculate the book value of accounts receivable, *$62,310.00.* Write the amount in the second amount column on the same line. Use the same procedure to report book values of the plant asset accounts.

## LIABILITIES SECTION OF A BALANCE SHEET

**1.** Heading *Current Liabilities*

| | | |
|---|---|---|
| Total Assets | | $375,448.00 |
| **LIABILITIES** | | |
| Current Liabilities: | | |
| Notes Payable | $ 5,000.00 | |
| Interest Payable | 200.00 | |
| Accounts Payable | 31,453.00 | |
| Employee Income Tax Payable | 2,049.00 | |
| Federal Income Tax Payable | 13,206.46 | |
| Social Security Tax Payable | 1,783.00 | |
| Medicare Tax Payable | 412.00 | |
| Sales Tax Payable | 10,482.00 | |
| Unemployment Tax Payable—Federal | 38.00 | |
| Unemployment Tax Payable—State | 244.00 | |
| Health Insurance Premiums Payable | 498.00 | |
| Dividends Payable | 10,000.00 | |
| Total Liabilities | | $ 75,365.46 |

**2.** Account Title and Amount of Each Current Liability

**3.** Total Liabilities

Liabilities are classified according to the length of time until they are due. Liabilities due within a short time, usually within a year, are known as current liabilities. All of Winning Edge's liabilities are current liabilities because they come due within a year.

Liabilities owed for more than a year are called **long-term liabilities.** An example of a long-term liability is Mortgage Payable. On December 31 of the current year, Winning Edge does not have any long-term liabilities.

### STEPS: Preparing the liabilities section of a balance sheet

1. Write the heading *Current Liabilities*.
2. Write the account title and amount of each current liability account.
3. Calculate and write the amount of total liabilities, *$75,365.46*.

**FYI**

*A company having both current liabilities and long-term liabilities would include headings and totals for each category. The process is similar to preparing the asset section of a balance sheet.*

## STOCKHOLDERS' EQUITY SECTION OF A BALANCE SHEET

| | | |
|---|---|---|
| Total Assets | | $375,448.00 |
| Total Liabilities | | $ 75,365.46 |
| **STOCKHOLDERS' EQUITY** ❶ | | |
| Capital Stock | ❷ $120,000.00 | |
| Retained Earnings | ❸ 180,082.54 | |
| Total Stockholders' Equity | | ❹ 300,082.54 |
| Total Liabilities and Stockholders' Equity | | $375,448.00 ❺ |

**1.** Heading *Stockholders' Equity*
**2.** Capital Stock
**3.** Retained Earnings
**4.** Total Stockholders' Equity
**5.** Total Liabilities and Stockholders' Equity

A major difference between corporation balance sheets and proprietorship or partnership balance sheets is the owners' equity section. The owners' equity section of Winning Edge's balance sheet is labeled Stockholders' Equity. Some corporations use the same label, Owners' Equity, as proprietorships and partnerships. Either label is acceptable.

The stockholders' equity section contains the total amounts of capital stock and retained earnings. These amounts are calculated and reported on the statement of stockholders' equity.

Winning Edge's completed balance sheet is shown on the following page.

### STEPS: Preparing the stockholders' equity section of a balance sheet

1. Write the heading *Stockholders' Equity.*
2. Write the amount of capital stock, *$120,000.00,* calculated on the statement of stockholders' equity.
3. Write the amount of retained earnings, *$180,082.54,* calculated on the statement of stockholders' equity.
4. Add the amount of capital stock, $120,000.00, and retained earnings, $180,082.54, to calculate the total of stockholders' equity, *$300,082.54.*
5. Add the amount of total liabilities, $75,365.46, and total stockholders' equity, $300,082.54, to calculate the total of liabilities and stockholders' equity, *$375,448.00.* Verify accuracy by comparing the total amount of assets and the total amount of liabilities and stockholders' equity. These two amounts must be the same.

### REMEMBER

Total assets must equal the total of liabilities and stockholders' equity. If these totals are not equal, identify the errors before preparing closing and reversing entries.

## COMPLETED BALANCE SHEET

**Winning Edge, Inc.**
**Balance Sheet**
**December 31, 20--**

| | | | |
|---|---|---|---|
| **ASSETS** | | | |
| Current Assets: | | | |
| Cash | | $ 10,584.00 | |
| Petty Cash | | 250.00 | |
| Notes Receivable | | 1,000.00 | |
| Interest Receivable | | 20.00 | |
| Accounts Receivable | $72,458.00 | | |
| Less Allowance for Uncollectible Accounts | 10,148.00 | 62,310.00 | |
| Merchandise Inventory | | 244,916.00 | |
| Supplies | | 1,686.00 | |
| Prepaid Insurance | | 2,550.00 | |
| Total Current Assets | | | $323,316.00 |
| Plant Assets: | | | |
| Office Equipment | $25,978.00 | | |
| Less Accumulated Depreciation—Office Equipment | 10,823.00 | $ 15,155.00 | |
| Store Equipment | $52,781.00 | | |
| Less Accumulated Depreciation—Store Equipment | 15,804.00 | 36,977.00 | |
| Total Plant Assets | | | 52,132.00 |
| Total Assets | | | $375,448.00 |
| **LIABILITIES** | | | |
| Current Liabilities: | | | |
| Notes Payable | | $ 5,000.00 | |
| Interest Payable | | 200.00 | |
| Accounts Payable | | 31,453.00 | |
| Employee Income Tax Payable | | 2,049.00 | |
| Federal Income Tax Payable | | 13,206.46 | |
| Social Security Tax Payable | | 1,783.00 | |
| Medicare Tax Payable | | 412.00 | |
| Sales Tax Payable | | 10,482.00 | |
| Unemployment Tax Payable—Federal | | 38.00 | |
| Unemployment Tax Payable—State | | 244.00 | |
| Health Insurance Premiums Payable | | 498.00 | |
| Dividends Payable | | 10,000.00 | |
| Total Liabilities | | | $ 75,365.46 |
| **STOCKHOLDERS' EQUITY** | | | |
| Capital Stock | | $120,000.00 | |
| Retained Earnings | | 180,082.54 | |
| Total Stockholders' Equity | | | 300,082.54 |
| Total Liabilities and Stockholders' Equity | | | $375,448.00 |

## ANALYZING A BALANCE SHEET

To continue operating successfully, a business must have adequate financial resources to buy additional merchandise, pay employee salaries, and pay for other operating expenses. Financial strength analysis measures the level of financial resources. The balance sheet is the primary source of data to determine the financial strength of a business.

Winning Edge analyzes its financial strength to assist the company in planning for future periods and to ensure that adequate resources are available to operate the business. Creditors and investors also use financial strength analysis to determine if the company is a good credit and investment risk. Before a creditor sells merchandise to a company on account, the creditor must believe that the company will later pay for the merchandise. A company that is considered to be a poor credit risk is usually a bad investment for an investor.

## WORKING CAPITAL

The amount of total current assets less total current liabilities is called **working capital.** The amount is stated in dollars. Working capital is a measure of the financial resources available for the daily operations of the business. For a company to operate efficiently, an adequate supply of resources must be available to purchase inventory, pay employee salaries, and pay for other operating expenses. Winning Edge's working capital is calculated as shown.

Working capital should not be confused with cash. Winning Edge does not have $247,950.54 of excess cash. However, Winning Edge does have $247,950.54 of financial resources that are available for use in daily operations at the beginning of the next fiscal year.

| Total Current Assets | – | Total Current Liabilities | = | Working Capital |
|---|---|---|---|---|
| $323,316.00 | – | $75,365.46 | = | $247,950.54 |

## CURRENT RATIO

Although working capital is a useful measure, working capital does not permit a business to compare itself to its industry or to provide a convenient relative measurement from year to year.

A more useful measure results from comparing the amount of total current assets to total current liabilities. A comparison between two numbers showing how many times one number exceeds the other is called a **ratio.** A ratio that shows the numeric relationship of current assets to current liabilities is called the **current ratio.** The current ratio is a measure of a company's ability to pay its current liabilities. Creditors use the ratio to determine if merchandise should be sold to a company on account. Winning Edge's current ratio is calculated as shown.

Winning Edge's current ratio is stated as 4.3 to 1, which means that total current assets are 4.3 times total current liabilities.

Based on previous experience, industry guidelines, and the need to maintain sufficient merchandise inventory, Winning Edge considers a current ratio between 3.0 to 1 and 4.5 to 1 to be acceptable. On December 31 of the current year, Winning Edge's current ratio, 4.3 to 1, is acceptable. This year's current ratio indicates a favorable condition of financial strength.

| Total Current Assets | ÷ | Total Current Liabilities | = | Current Ratio |
|---|---|---|---|---|
| $323,316.00 | ÷ | $75,365.46 | = | 4.3 to 1 |

## TERMS REVIEW

long-term liabilities

working capital

ratio

current ratio

## AUDIT YOUR UNDERSTANDING

1. How does Winning Edge classify its assets?
2. What three items are listed on the balance sheet for an account having a related contra asset account?
3. What is an example of a long-term liability?
4. Where are the amounts obtained for the stockholders' equity section of the balance sheet?
5. What is working capital?
6. Why is the current ratio a useful measure of financial strength?

## WORK TOGETHER

**Preparing and analyzing a balance sheet for a corporation**

Use the work sheet and statement of stockholders' equity from Work Together on page 668. A form for the balance sheet is given in the *Working Papers.* Your instructor will guide you through the following examples.

7. Prepare a balance sheet for the current year.
8. Calculate Webster Corporation's (a) working capital and (b) current ratio.
9. Determine if these items are within acceptable levels. The corporation considers working capital in excess of $150,000.00 and a current ratio between 2.0 to 1 and 3.0 to 1 to be acceptable indications of financial strength. Save your work to complete Work Together on page 681.

## ON YOUR OWN

**Preparing and analyzing a balance sheet for a corporation**

Use the work sheet and statement of stockholders' equity from On Your Own on page 668. A form for the balance sheet is given in the *Working Papers.* Work these problems independently.

10. Prepare a balance sheet for the current year.
11. Calculate Osborn Corporation's (a) working capital and (b) current ratio.
12. Determine if these items are within acceptable levels. The corporation considers working capital in excess of $100,000.00 and a current ratio between 2.0 to 1 and 3.0 to 1 to be acceptable indications of financial strength. Save your work to complete On Your Own on page 681.

# 26-4 Adjusting, Closing, and Reversing Entries for a Corporation

## ADJUSTING ENTRIES

GENERAL JOURNAL PAGE 15

| | DATE | | ACCOUNT TITLE | DOC. NO. | POST. REF. | DEBIT | CREDIT | |
|---|---|---|---|---|---|---|---|---|
| 1 | | | *Adjusting Entries* | | | | | 1 |
| 2 | 20-- Dec. | 31 | Interest Receivable | | | 20 00 | | 2 |
| 3 | | | Interest Income | | | | 20 00 | 3 |
| 4 | | 31 | Uncollectible Accounts Expense | | | 9828 00 | | 4 |
| 5 | | | Allowance for Uncoll. Accts. | | | | 9828 00 | 5 |
| 6 | | 31 | Merchandise Inventory | | | 6158 00 | | 6 |
| 7 | | | Income Summary | | | | 6158 00 | 7 |
| 8 | | 31 | Supplies Expense | | | 7472 00 | | 8 |
| 9 | | | Supplies | | | | 7472 00 | 9 |
| 10 | | 31 | Insurance Expense | | | 9850 00 | | 10 |
| 11 | | | Prepaid Insurance | | | | 9850 00 | 11 |
| 12 | | 31 | Depreciation Exp.—Office Equip. | | | 4650 00 | | 12 |
| 13 | | | Accum. Depr.—Office Equip. | | | | 4650 00 | 13 |
| 14 | | 31 | Depreciation Exp.—Store Equip. | | | 8750 00 | | 14 |
| 15 | | | Accum. Depr.—Store Equip. | | | | 8750 00 | 15 |
| 16 | | 31 | Interest Expense | | | 200 00 | | 16 |
| 17 | | | Interest Payable | | | | 200 00 | 17 |
| 18 | | 31 | Federal Income Tax Expense | | | 13206 46 | | 18 |
| 19 | | | Federal Income Tax Payable | | | | 13206 46 | 19 |
| 20 | | | | | | | | 20 |

The end-of-fiscal-period work of corporations is similar to the work of proprietorships and partnerships except for differences in the equity accounts. Because a corporation must pay federal income taxes, only a corporation will have an adjusting entry for federal income taxes payable.

After financial statements are prepared, adjusting and closing entries are journalized and posted. A post-closing trial balance is then prepared to prove the equality of debits and credits in the general ledger after adjusting and closing entries have been posted. The steps for preparing a post-closing trial balance are the same as discussed in Chapter 17. Finally, reversing entries are journalized and posted.

A corporation's adjusting entries are made from the Adjustments columns of a work sheet. To assure that each work sheet adjustment is journalized, record the entries in the order of the letters assigned to each adjustment on the work sheet.

Winning Edge's work sheet is shown in Chapter 25.

## CLOSING ENTRIES FOR A CORPORATION

Closing entries for a corporation are made from information in a work sheet. Closing entries for revenue and expense accounts are similar to those for proprietorships or partnerships. A corporation's closing entries to close net income and temporary equity accounts are similar to those for a partnership or proprietorship. However, these closing entries affect different accounts. A corporation records four closing entries:

1. Closing entry for income statement accounts with credit balances (revenue and contra cost accounts).
2. Closing entry for income statement accounts with debit balances (cost, contra revenue, and expense accounts).
3. Closing entry to record net income or net loss in the retained earnings account and close the income summary account.
4. Closing entry for the dividends account.

## CLOSING ENTRY FOR ACCOUNTS WITH CREDIT BALANCES

**1.** Enter the balance of accounts in the Income Statement credit column as a debit.

GENERAL JOURNAL — PAGE *16*

| | DATE | | ACCOUNT TITLE | DOC. NO. | POST. REF. | DEBIT | CREDIT | |
|---|---|---|---|---|---|---|---|---|
| 1 | | | *Closing Entries* | | | | | 1 |
| 2 | *20-- Dec.* | *31* | *Sales* | | | *1917955 50* | | 2 |
| 3 | | | *Purchases Discount* | | | *10548 00* | | 3 |
| 4 | | | *Purchases Returns and Allowances* | | | *5142 00* | | 4 |
| 5 | | | *Gain on Plant Assets* | | | *560 00* | | 5 |
| 6 | | | *Interest Income* | | | *88 00* | | 6 |
| 7 | | | *Income Summary* | | | | *1934293 50* | 7 |
| 8 | | | | | | | | 8 |
| 9 | | | | | | | | 9 |

**2.** Enter the total of debit entries as a credit to Income Summary.

Income statement credit balance accounts are the revenue (Sales, Gain on Plant Assets, and Interest Income) and the contra cost accounts (Purchases Discount and Purchases Returns and Allowances). Information needed for closing income statement credit balance accounts is obtained from the work sheet. Closing entries are recorded on a new page of the general journal.

**STEPS**

### Journalizing a closing entry for accounts with credit balances

**1.** Except for Income Summary, enter the balance of every account in the Income Statement credit column of the work sheet as a debit entry in a general journal.

**2.** Enter the total of the debit entries, *$1,934,293.50,* as a credit to Income Summary.

# CLOSING ENTRY FOR ACCOUNTS WITH DEBIT BALANCES

**1.** Enter Income Summary.

**3.** Enter the total as a debit to Income Summary.

GENERAL JOURNAL — PAGE *16*

| | DATE | | ACCOUNT TITLE | DOC. NO. | POST. REF. | DEBIT | CREDIT | |
|---|---|---|---|---|---|---|---|---|
| 8 | | *31* | *Income Summary* | | | *1776743 96* | | 8 |
| 9 | | | *Sales Discount* | | | | *7584 00* | 9 |
| 10 | | | *Sales Returns and Allowances* | | | | *21486 00* | 10 |
| 11 | | | *Purchases* | | | | *1045832 00* | 11 |
| 12 | | | *Advertising Expense* | | | | *28472 00* | 12 |
| 13 | | | *Cash Short and Over* | | | | *7 00* | 13 |
| 14 | | | *Credit Card Fee Expense* | | | | *18489 00* | 14 |
| 15 | | | *Depr. Expense—Off. Equip.* | | | | *4650 00* | 15 |
| 16 | | | *Depr. Expense—Store Equip.* | | | | *8750 00* | 16 |
| 17 | | | *Insurance Expense* | | | | *9850 00* | 17 |
| 18 | | | *Miscellaneous Expense* | | | | *28398 17* | 18 |
| 19 | | | *Payroll Taxes Expense* | | | | *29310 05* | 19 |
| 20 | | | *Rent Expense* | | | | *60000 00* | 20 |
| 21 | | | *Repair Expense* | | | | *4872 00* | 21 |
| 22 | | | *Salary Expense* | | | | *393844 28* | 22 |
| 23 | | | *Supplies Expense* | | | | *7472 00* | 23 |
| 24 | | | *Uncollectible Accounts Exp.* | | | | *9828 00* | 24 |
| 25 | | | *Utilities Expense* | | | | *18150 00* | 25 |
| 26 | | | *Interest Expense* | | | | *1343 00* | 26 |
| 27 | | | *Loss on Plant Assets* | | | | *1200 00* | 27 |
| 28 | | | *Federal Income Tax Expense* | | | | *77206 46* | 28 |

**2.** Enter the balance of every account in the Income Statement debit column as a credit.

Income statement debit balance accounts are the contra revenue accounts (Sales Discount and Sales Returns and Allowances) and the cost (Purchases) and expense accounts. Information needed for closing income statement debit balance accounts is obtained from the work sheet's Income Statement Debit column.

If Cash Short and Over has a credit balance, the account balance amount is closed to Income Summary with the credit balance accounts.

## STEPS

### Journalizing a closing entry for accounts with debit balances

1. Enter the account title *Income Summary.*
2. Enter the balance of every account in the Income Statement debit column of the work sheet as a credit entry in a general journal.
3. Enter the total of the credit entries, *$1,776,743.96,* as a debit on the line with the account title, Income Summary.

## CLOSING ENTRY TO RECORD NET INCOME

1. Debit Income Summary
2. Credit Retained Earnings

GENERAL JOURNAL PAGE 16

| | DATE | | ACCOUNT TITLE | DOC. NO. | POST. REF. | DEBIT | CREDIT | |
|---|---|---|---|---|---|---|---|---|
| 29 | | 31 | Income Summary | | | 163 707 54 | | 29 |
| 30 | | | Retained Earnings | | | | 163 707 54 | 30 |

After closing entries for the income statement accounts are posted, Income Summary has a credit balance of $163,707.54. This credit balance equals the net income calculated on the work sheet.

A corporation's net income should be recorded in the retained earnings account at the end of the fiscal year. After the closing entry is posted, Income Summary has a zero balance.

If a corporation has a net loss, Income Summary has a debit balance. Retained Earnings would then be debited and Income Summary credited for the net loss amount.

**STEPS Journalizing a closing entry for net income to retained earnings**

1. Record a debit to Income Summary for the amount of net income, *$163,707.54.*
2. Record a credit to Retained Earnings for the same amount, *$163,707.54.*

## CLOSING ENTRY FOR DIVIDENDS

1. Debit Retained Earnings
2. Credit Dividends

GENERAL JOURNAL PAGE 16

| | DATE | | ACCOUNT TITLE | DOC. NO. | POST. REF. | DEBIT | CREDIT | |
|---|---|---|---|---|---|---|---|---|
| 31 | | 31 | Retained Earnings | | | 40 000 00 | | 31 |
| 32 | | | Dividends | | | | 40 000 00 | 32 |
| 33 | | | | | | | | 33 |
| 34 | | | | | | | | 34 |

Because dividends decrease the earnings retained by a corporation, the dividends account is closed to Retained Earnings. After the closing entry for the dividends account is posted, Dividends has a zero balance. The amount of the dividends, $40,000.00, has reduced the balance of Retained Earnings.

**STEPS Journalizing a closing entry for dividends**

1. Record a debit to Retained Earnings for the amount of dividends, *$40,000.00.*
2. Record a credit to Dividends for the same amount, *$40,000.00.*

## REVERSING ENTRIES

GENERAL JOURNAL — PAGE 15

| | DATE | | ACCOUNT TITLE | DOC. NO. | POST. REF. | DEBIT | CREDIT | |
|---|---|---|---|---|---|---|---|---|
| 1 | | | *Adjusting Entries* | | | | | 1 |
| 2 | 20-- Dec. | 31 | Interest Receivable | | | 20 00 | | 2 |
| 3 | | | Interest Income | | | | 20 00 | 3 |
| 16 | | 31 | Interest Expense | | | 200 00 | | 16 |
| 17 | | | Interest Payable | | | | 200 00 | 17 |
| 18 | | 31 | Federal Income Tax Expense | | | 13 206 46 | | 18 |
| 19 | | | Federal Income Tax Payable | | | | 13 206 46 | 19 |
| 20 | | | | | | | | 20 |

**1.** Reverse the entry that created a balance in Interest Receivable.

GENERAL JOURNAL — PAGE 17

| | DATE | | ACCOUNT TITLE | DOC. NO. | POST. REF. | DEBIT | CREDIT | |
|---|---|---|---|---|---|---|---|---|
| 1 | | | *Reversing Entries* | | | | | 1 |
| 2 | 20-- Jan. | 1 | Interest Income | | | 20 00 | | 2 |
| 3 | | | Interest Receivable | | | | 20 00 | 3 |
| 4 | | 1 | Interest Payable | | | 200 00 | | 4 |
| 5 | | | Interest Expense | | | | 200 00 | 5 |
| 6 | | 1 | Federal Income Tax Payable | | | 13 206 46 | | 6 |
| 7 | | | Federal Income Tax Expense | | | | 13 206 46 | 7 |

**2.** Reverse the entry that created a balance in Interest Payable.

**3.** Reverse the entry that created a balance in Federal Income Tax Payable.

If an adjusting entry creates a balance in an asset or liability account, the adjusting entry should be reversed. A review of Winning Edge's adjusting entries shows that three adjusting entries created a balance in an asset or liability account.

1. The adjusting entry for accrued interest income created a balance in the interest receivable account.
2. The adjusting entry for accrued interest expense created a balance in the interest payable account.
3. The adjusting entry for federal income tax expense created a balance in the federal income tax payable account.

### STEPS: Journalizing reversing entries

1. Reverse the entry that created a balance in Interest Receivable.
2. Reverse the entry that created a balance in Interest Payable.
3. Reverse the entry that created a balance in Federal Income Tax Payable.

### REMEMBER

A post-closing trial balance is prepared to prove the equality of debits and credits in the general ledger after adjusting and closing entries have been posted.

## ACCOUNTING CYCLE FOR A MERCHANDISING BUSINESS ORGANIZED AS A CORPORATION

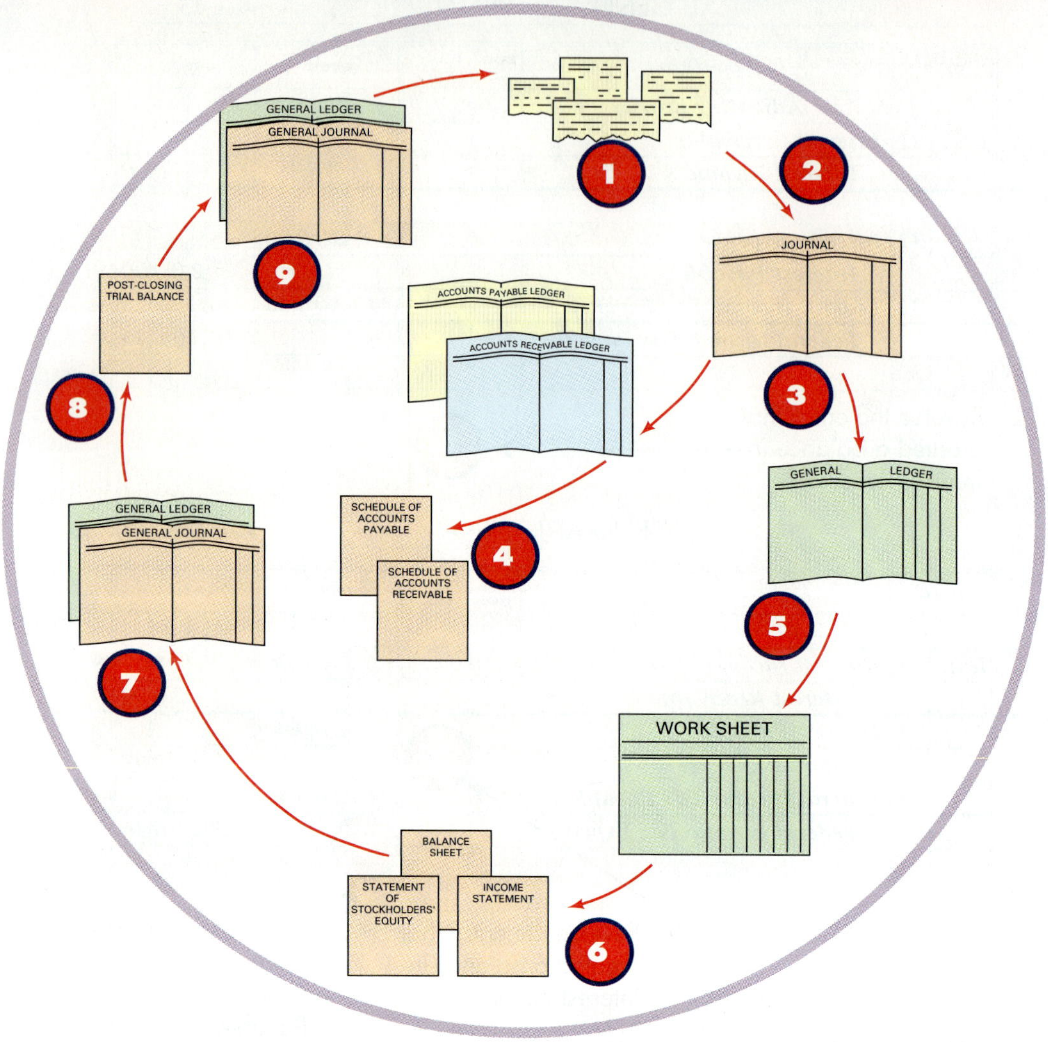


The accounting cycles are similar for merchandising businesses organized as either partnerships or corporations. Variations occur in preparing financial statements. Variations also occur when reversing entries are recorded.

**STEPS**

### Accounting cycle for a merchandising business organized as a corporation

1. Source documents are checked for accuracy, and transactions are analyzed into debit and credit parts.
2. Transactions, from information on source documents, are recorded in journals.
3. Journal entries are posted to the accounts payable, accounts receivable, and general ledgers.
4. Schedules of accounts payable and accounts receivable are prepared from the subsidiary ledgers.
5. A work sheet, including a trial balance and an adjustment for federal income tax expense, is prepared from the general ledger.
6. Financial statements are prepared from the work sheet.
7. Adjusting and closing entries are journalized from the work sheet and posted to the general ledger.
8. A post-closing trial balance of the general ledger is prepared.
9. Reversing entries are journalized and posted to the general ledger.

## AUDIT YOUR UNDERSTANDING

1. What adjusting entry is recorded only for a corporation?
2. What closing entry is recorded only for a corporation?
3. To what account is Dividends closed at the fiscal year end?

## WORK TOGETHER

**Journalizing adjusting, closing, and reversing entries for a corporation**

Use the work sheet and financial statements from Work Together on page 674. General journal pages are given in the *Working Papers*. Your instructor will guide you through the following examples.

4. For the current year, journalize the adjusting entries using page 15 of a general journal.
5. For the current year, journalize the closing entries using page 16 of a general journal.
6. For the following year, journalize the reversing entries using page 17 of a general journal.

## ON YOUR OWN

**Journalizing adjusting, closing, and reversing entries for a corporation**

Use the work sheet and financial statements from On Your Own on page 674. General journal pages are given in the *Working Papers*. Work these problems independently.

7. For the current year, journalize the adjusting entries using page 18 of a general journal.
8. For the current year, journalize the closing entries using page 19 of a general journal.
9. For the following year, journalize the reversing entries using page 20 of a general journal.

# CHAPTER 26 Summary

*Enrichment Activity*

**Types of Businesses**

*Compare the owner's equity section of the balance sheet of a proprietorship, partnership, and corporation.*

After completing this chapter, you can

1. Define accounting terms related to financial statements for a merchandising business organized as a corporation.
2. Identify accounting concepts and practices related to financial statements and end-of-fiscal-period entries for a merchandising business organized as a corporation.
3. Prepare and analyze an income statement for a merchandising business organized as a corporation.
4. Prepare a statement of stockholders' equity for a merchandising business organized as a corporation.
5. Prepare and analyze a balance sheet for a merchandising business organized as a corporation.
6. Record adjusting, closing, and reversing entries for a merchandising business organized as a corporation.

## EXPLORE ACCOUNTING

### STATEMENT OF CASH FLOWS

The income statement and balance sheet are prepared using the accrual basis of accounting. These accrual-basis financial statements do not, however, provide detailed information about the sources and uses of cash in a business. A financial statement that reports the cash flows of a business for a fiscal period is called a *statement of cash flows*.

A statement of cash flows is comprised of three primary sections. The first section, Cash Flows from Operating Activities, reports the amount of cash generated from the sale of goods and services. This section can be compared to an income statement, except that revenue, merchandise purchases, and expenses are reported on a cash basis. For example, a sale on account that remains unpaid at the fiscal year end does not result in an increase in cash. In addition, only expenses that are paid during the fiscal year result in a decrease in cash. For example, depreciation is an accrual-basis expense that requires no cash payment. Therefore, depreciation expense is not a use of cash as reported in this statement.

The section Cash Flows from Investing Activities reports the cash used to purchase plant assets and other long-term assets. The section Cash Flows from Financing Activities reports the cash generated by issuing long-term debt and capital stock. This section also reports the cash used to repay long-term debt and pay dividends.

The net change in cash, reported at the end of the statement, is an important measure of the financial strength of the company. A company must have an adequate supply of cash to finance its daily operations and long-term expansions.

**Required:** (1) Obtain the Statement of Cash Flows for a corporation. Identify the major sections of the statement. Did the corporation have an increase in cash from operations? What did the corporation do with this increase in cash? (2) Explain how a corporation could have net income yet have a decrease in cash. Does this situation indicate a positive or negative sign of financial strength?

## 26-1 APPLICATION PROBLEM
### Preparing an income statement for a corporation

Use the work sheet provided in the *Working Papers* to complete this problem.

***Instructions:***

1. Prepare an income statement for Donovan Lumber Corporation for the fiscal year ending December 31 of the current year.
2. Calculate and record the following component percentages: (a) cost of merchandise sold; (b) gross profit on operations; (c) total operating expenses; (d) income from operations; (e) net addition or deduction resulting from other revenue and expenses; and (f) net income before federal income tax. Round percentage calculations to the nearest 0.1%.
3. Analyze the corporation's income statement by determining if component percentages are within acceptable levels. If any component percentage is not within an acceptable level, suggest steps that the company should take. The corporation considers the following component percentages acceptable. Save your work to complete Application Problem 26-2.

| | |
|---|---|
| Cost of merchandise sold | Not more than 70.0% |
| Gross profit on operations | Not less than 30.0% |
| Total operating expenses | Not more than 25.0% |
| Income from operations | Not less than 5.0% |
| Net deduction from other revenue and expenses | Not more than 0.1% |
| Net income before federal income tax | Not less than 4.9% |

## 26-2 APPLICATION PROBLEM
### Preparing a statement of stockholders' equity for a corporation

Use the work sheet and income statement from Application Problem 26-1 to complete this problem.

***Instructions:***

Prepare a statement of stockholders' equity for Donovan Lumber Corporation for the fiscal year ended on December 31 of the current year. Use the following additional information. Save your work to complete Application Problem 26-3.

| | |
|---|---|
| January 1 balance of capital stock account . . . . . . . . . . . . . . . .<br>(8,000 shares issued for $5.00 per share) | $40,000.00 |
| Shares issued during the year . . . . . . . . . . . . . . . . . . . . . . . . . | 2,000 shares |

## 26-3 APPLICATION PROBLEM
### Preparing and analyzing a balance sheet for a corporation

Use the work sheet and financial statements from Application Problem 26-2 to complete this problem.

***Instructions:***

1. Prepare a balance sheet for Donovan Lumber Corporation as of December 31 of the current year.
2. Calculate the corporation's (a) working capital and (b) current ratio. Determine if these items are within acceptable levels. The corporation considers the following levels acceptable. Save your work to complete Application Problem 26-4.

| | |
|---|---|
| Working capital . . . . . . . . . . . . . . . . . . . . . . . . . . . . | Not less than $100,000.00 |
| Current ratio . . . . . . . . . . . . . . . . . . . . . . . . . . . . . | Between 3.0 to 1 and 3.5 to 1 |

## 26-4 APPLICATION PROBLEM

### Journalizing adjusting, closing, and reversing entries for a corporation

Use the work sheet and financial statements from Application Problem 26-3 to complete this problem.

***Instructions:***

1. For the current year, journalize the adjusting entries using page 15 of a general journal.
2. For the current year, journalize the closing entries using page 16 of a general journal.
3. For the following year, journalize the reversing entries using page 17 of a general journal.

## 26-5 MASTERY PROBLEM

### Preparing financial statements and end-of-fiscal-period entries for a corporation

Use the work sheet provided in the *Working Papers* for Pennington Corporation to prepare the financial statements and end-of-fiscal-period entries for the corporation for the current year.

***Instructions:***

1. Prepare an income statement. Calculate and record the following component percentages: (a) cost of merchandise sold; (b) gross profit on operations; (c) total operating expenses; (d) income from operations; (e) net addition or deduction resulting from other revenue and expenses; and (f) net income before federal income tax. Round percentage calculations to the nearest 0.1%.
2. Analyze the corporation's income statement by determining if component percentages are within acceptable levels. If any component percentage is not within an acceptable level, suggest steps that the company should take. The corporation considers the following component percentages acceptable.

| | |
|---|---|
| Cost of merchandise sold | Not more than 65.0% |
| Gross profit on operations | Not less than 35.0% |
| Total operating expenses | Not more than 16.0% |
| Income from operations | Not less than 19.0% |
| Net deduction from other revenue and expenses | Not more than 0.5% |
| Net income before federal income tax | Not less than 18.5% |

3. Prepare a statement of stockholders' equity. Use the following additional information.

| | |
|---|---|
| January 1 balance of capital stock account . . . . . . . . . . . .<br>(100,000 shares issued for $1.00 per share) | $100,000.00 |
| Shares issued during the year . . . . . . . . . . . . . . . . . . . . . . | None |

4. Prepare a balance sheet.
5. Calculate the corporation's (a) working capital and (b) current ratio. Determine if these items are within acceptable levels. The corporation considers the following levels acceptable.

| | |
|---|---|
| Working capital . . . . . . . . . . . . . . . . . . . . . . . . . . . . . . . | Not less than $150,000.00 |
| Current ratio . . . . . . . . . . . . . . . . . . . . . . . . . . . . . . . . | Between 3.0 to 1 and 4.0 to 1 |

6. Journalize the adjusting entries using page 15 of a general journal.
7. Journalize the closing entries using page 16 of a general journal.
8. Journalize the reversing entries using page 17 of a general journal.

## 26-6 CHALLENGE PROBLEM
### Analyzing financial strength

***Instructions:***

1. Obtain the financial statements of two corporations from two different industries. Calculate the amount of working capital and the current ratio of each corporation. Discuss the usefulness of each measure of financial strength between the companies in each industry and among the different industries.
2. The current ratio is often considered to be acceptable within a specified range. Investigate why a current ratio being too high might be undesirable.

**INTERNET ACTIVITY**

Point your browser to

**http://accounting.swpco.com**

Choose **First-Year Course**, choose **Activities**, and complete the activity for Chapter 26.

## Applied Communication

Congratulations on completing your study of accounting in this textbook. You have learned a wide variety of facts and concepts about accounting and the business world. Regardless of your future educational and career goals, this knowledge will provide you with a sound foundation to become a productive member of society.

**Instructions:** Prepare an essay to discuss how your knowledge of accounting will be useful to you in the future. How will accounting help you to complete your education, obtain a job, start a business, make personal investment decisions, and be successful in other facets of your life?

## Cases for Critical Thinking

**Case 1** The president of Wilson Company asked the accounting department to provide as much information as possible to help management improve the company's net income. Peter Lance, a new accountant, suggests that an income statement showing all the revenue and expense amounts should provide all the information management needs to analyze the company's results of operations. Do you agree with the accountant's suggestion? If not, what additional information do you recommend? Explain your answer.

**Case 2** LMP Company recently organized as a corporation with five stockholders. Tammy Kellogg, a CPA, is developing the accounting system. She suggested that although there are five stockholders, only one equity account be used. The account would be titled Corporation Capital. The president of Riverside questions the accountant's recommendation. Is this recommendation acceptable? If not, how should capital be recorded and reported? Explain your answer.

# AUTOMATED ACCOUNTING

## END-OF-FISCAL-PERIOD WORK FOR A CORPORATION

During the fiscal period, numerous transactions are analyzed, journalized, and posted. When a transaction affects more than one accounting period, an adjusting entry may be needed to match revenues and expenses with the appropriate accounting period. To complete the accounting cycle, adjusting entries are recorded in the computer and verified for accuracy. The financial statements are generated, and then closing entries are generated and posted by the software.

### Adjusting Entries

Adjusting entries are planned and recorded in the computerized accounting system. The general journal is used to record the adjusting entries. All adjusting entries are recorded on the last day of the accounting period. The entries are referenced by Adj. Ent. in the Refer. text box. Adjusting entries:

- Transfer to expenses the amounts of assets consumed (for example, office supplies and prepaid insurance).
- Update the merchandise inventory account.
- Recognize accrued revenues and accrued expenses.

### Financial Statements for a Corporation

The reports that summarize information from the ledgers are known as financial statements. The most common financial statements for a business organized as a corporation are the balance sheet and the income statement.

To display financial statements:

1. Click the Reports toolbar button, or choose the Reports Selection menu item from the Reports menu.
2. When the Report Selection dialog appears, choose the Financial Statements option button from the Select a Report Group list.
3. Choose the financial statement report you would like to display from the Choose a Report to Display list.
4. Click the OK button.

The up-to-date account balances stored by the software are used to calculate and display the current financial statements.

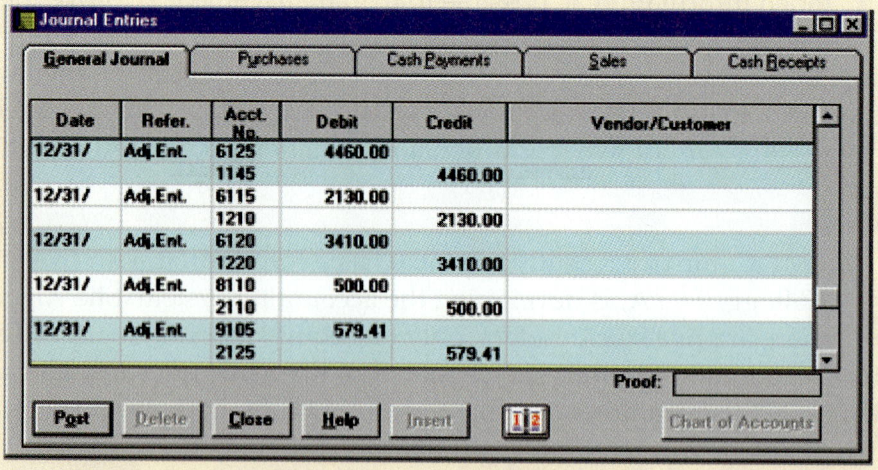


| Date | Refer. | Acct. No. | Debit | Credit | Vendor/Customer |
|---|---|---|---|---|---|
| 12/31/ | Adj.Ent. | 6125 | 4460.00 | | |
| | | 1145 | | 4460.00 | |
| 12/31/ | Adj.Ent. | 6115 | 2130.00 | | |
| | | 1210 | | 2130.00 | |
| 12/31/ | Adj.Ent. | 6120 | 3410.00 | | |
| | | 1220 | | 3410.00 | |
| 12/31/ | Adj.Ent. | 8110 | 500.00 | | |
| | | 2110 | | 500.00 | |
| 12/31/ | Adj.Ent. | 9105 | 579.41 | | |
| | | 2125 | | 579.41 | |

# Automated Accounting

## Closing Entries for a Corporation

In an automated accounting system, closing entries are generated and posted by the software. The software automatically closes net income to the retained earnings account after closing the revenue and expense accounts. The dividend account is closed as well.

1. Choose Generate Closing Journal Entries from the Options menu.
2. Click Yes to generate the closing entries.
3. The general journal will appear, containing the journal entries.
4. Click the Post button.

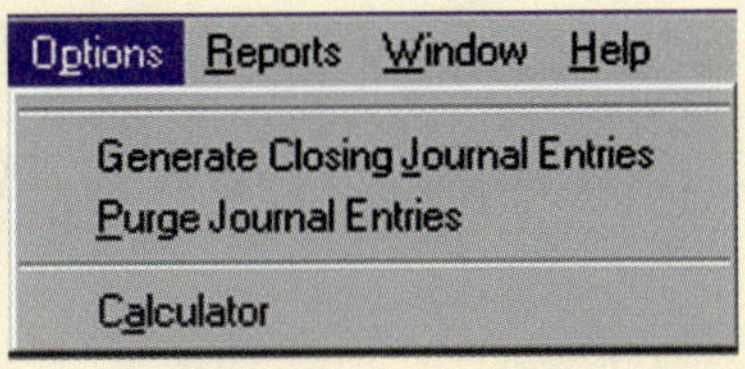


## AUTOMATING APPLICATION PROBLEM 26-1: Preparing an income statement for a corporation

**Instructions:**

1. Load *Automated Accounting 7.0* or higher software.
2. Select database F26-1 from the appropriate directory/folder.
3. Select File from the menu bar and choose the Save As menu command. Key the path to the drive and directory that contains your data files. Save the database with a file name of XXX261 (where XXX are your initials).
4. Access Problem Instructions through the Help menu. Read the Problem Instructions screen.
5. Refer to page 683 for data used in this template.
6. Exit the *Automated Accounting* software.

## AUTOMATING MASTERY PROBLEM 26-5: Preparing financial statements and end-of-fiscal-period entries for a corporation

**Instructions:**

1. Load *Automated Accounting 7.0* or higher software.
2. Select database F26-2 from the appropriate directory/folder.
3. Select File from the menu bar and choose the Save As menu command. Key the path to the drive and directory that contains your data files. Save the database with a file name of XXX262 (where XXX are your initials).
4. Access Problem Instructions through the Help menu. Read the Problem Instructions screen.
5. Refer to page 684 for data used in this template.
6. Exit the *Automated Accounting* software.

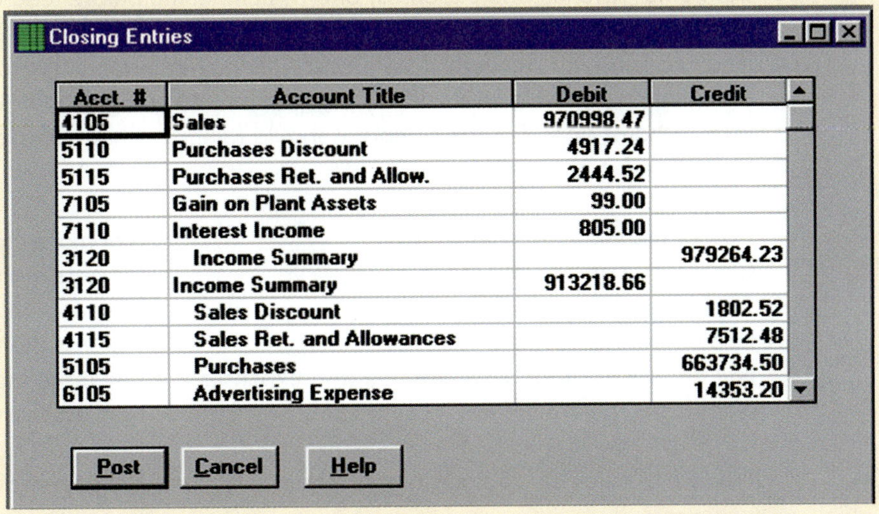

Closing Entries

| Acct. # | Account Title | Debit | Credit |
|---|---|---|---|
| 4105 | Sales | 970998.47 | |
| 5110 | Purchases Discount | 4917.24 | |
| 5115 | Purchases Ret. and Allow. | 2444.52 | |
| 7105 | Gain on Plant Assets | 99.00 | |
| 7110 | Interest Income | 805.00 | |
| 3120 | Income Summary | | 979264.23 |
| 3120 | Income Summary | 913218.66 | |
| 4110 | Sales Discount | | 1802.52 |
| 4115 | Sales Ret. and Allowances | | 7512.48 |
| 5105 | Purchases | | 663734.50 |
| 6105 | Advertising Expense | | 14353.20 |

## REINFORCEMENT ACTIVITY 3—PART B

# An Accounting Cycle for a Corporation: End-of-Fiscal-Period Work

The general ledger used in Reinforcement Activity 3—Part A is needed to complete Reinforcement Activity 3—Part B.

Reinforcement Activity 3—Part B includes those accounting activities needed to complete an accounting cycle for a corporation. In Part A, Sunshine Gardens' transactions were recorded for the last month of a fiscal year. In Part B, end-of-fiscal-period work is completed.

## END-OF-FISCAL-PERIOD WORK

***Instructions:***

12. Prepare a work sheet for the fiscal year ended December 31 of the current year. Use the following adjustment information.

**Adjustment Information, December 31**

| | |
|---|---|
| Accrued interest income | $ 54.00 |
| Uncollectible accounts expense is estimated as 0.5% of sales on account. Sales on account for the year, $84,000.00. | |
| Merchandise inventory | 84,969.00 |
| Supplies inventory | 660.00 |
| Value of prepaid insurance | 1,500.00 |
| Annual depreciation expense—office equipment | 5,480.00 |
| Annual depreciation expense—store equipment | 6,845.00 |
| Accrued interest expense | 200.00 |
| Federal income tax for the year | 13,981.59 |

13. Prepare an income statement. Calculate and record the following component percentages as a percent of net sales: (a) cost of merchandise sold; (b) gross profit on operations; (c) total operating expenses; (d) income from operations; (e) net additions/deductions from other revenue and expenses; and (f) net income before federal income tax. Round percentage calculations to the nearest 0.1%.
14. Analyze Sunshine Gardens' income statement by determining if component percentages are within acceptable levels. If any component percentage is not within an acceptable level, suggest steps that the company should take. Sunshine Gardens considers the following percentages acceptable.

| | |
|---|---|
| Cost of merchandise sold | Not more than 62.0% |
| Gross profit on operations | Not less than 38.0% |
| Total operating expenses | Not more than 25.0% |
| Income from operations | Not less than 13.0% |
| Net deductions from other revenue and expenses | Not more than 0.5% |
| Net income before federal income tax | Not less than 12.5% |

15. Prepare a statement of stockholders' equity. Use the following additional information.

| | |
|---|---|
| January 1 balance of capital stock account | $30,000.00 |
| (30,000 shares issued for $1.00 per share) | |
| January 1 balance of retained earnings account | 16,957.70 |

16. Prepare a balance sheet.
17. Calculate Sunshine Gardens' (a) working capital and (b) current ratio. Determine if these items are within acceptable levels. Sunshine Gardens considers the following amounts acceptable.

| | |
|---|---|
| Working capital | Not less than $50,000.00 |
| Current ratio | Between 2.0 to 1 and 3.0 to 1 |

18. Journalize the adjusting entries on page 13 of a general journal. Post the adjusting entries.
19. Journalize the closing entries on page 14 of a general journal. Post the closing entries.
20. Prepare a post-closing trial balance.
21. Journalize the reversing entries on page 15 of a general journal for the accrued interest income, accrued interest expense, and federal income tax expense adjusting entries. Post the reversing entries.

The activities included in the Putting Green simulation are:

1. Recording transactions in special journals from source documents.
2. Posting items to be posted individually to a general ledger and subsidiary ledger.
3. Posting column totals to a general ledger.
4. Preparing schedules of accounts receivable and accounts payable from subsidiary ledgers.
5. Preparing a trial balance on a work sheet.
6. Planning adjustments and completing a work sheet.
7. Preparing financial statements.
8. Journalizing and posting adjusting entries.
9. Journalizing and posting closing entries.
10. Preparing a post-closing trial balance.
11. Journalizing and posting reversing entries.

Putting Green Golf Supply is a merchandising business organized as a corporation. The company specializes in sales of everything golf-related: clubs, bags, umbrellas, shoes. You name it, they've got it. This simulation includes realistic transactions completed by Putting Green in the month of December, including end-of-fiscal-year activities. Source documents include transactions that are recorded in special journals and a general journal, similar to the ones used by Winning Edge, Inc., in Cycle 3.

The simulation is available in manual and in automated versions, for use with *Automated Accounting* software.

# ACCOUNTING CONCEPTS

The following accounting concepts and their definitions are provided in this appendix for ready reference.

## ACCOUNTING CONCEPTS

Accounting personnel are guided in their work by generally accepted accounting concepts. Ten commonly accepted accounting concepts are described in this appendix. Each concept is fully explained in the text the first time an application of the concept is described. Throughout the textbook, each time a concept application occurs, a concept reference is given, such as *(CONCEPT: Business Entity)*.

**1.** ACCOUNTING PERIOD CYCLE [Chapter 7]
Changes in financial information are reported for a specific period of time in the form of financial statements.

**2.** ADEQUATE DISCLOSURE [Chapter 8]
Financial statements contain all information necessary to understand a business's financial condition.

**3.** BUSINESS ENTITY [Chapter 1]
Financial information is recorded and reported separately from the owner's personal financial information.

**4.** CONSISTENT REPORTING [Chapter 7]
The same accounting procedures are followed in the same way in each accounting period.

**5.** GOING CONCERN [Chapter 1]
Financial statements are prepared with the expectation that a business will remain in operation indefinitely.

**6.** HISTORICAL COST [Chapter 10]
The actual amount paid for merchandise or other items bought is recorded.

**7.** MATCHING EXPENSES WITH REVENUE [Chapter 7]
Revenue from business activities and expenses associated with earning that revenue are recorded in the same accounting period.

**8.** OBJECTIVE EVIDENCE [Chapter 4]
A source document is prepared for each transaction.

**9.** REALIZATION OF REVENUE [Chapter 11]
Revenue is recorded at the time goods or services are sold.

**10.** UNIT OF MEASUREMENT [Chapter 1]
Business transactions are stated in numbers that have common values, that is, using a common unit of measurement.

# USING A CALCULATOR AND COMPUTER KEYPAD

## KINDS OF CALCULATORS

Many different models of calculators, both desktop and hand held, are available. All calculators have their own features and particular placement of operating keys. Therefore, it is necessary to refer to the operator's manual for specific instructions and locations of the operating keys for the calculator being used. A typical keyboard of a desktop calculator is shown in the illustration.

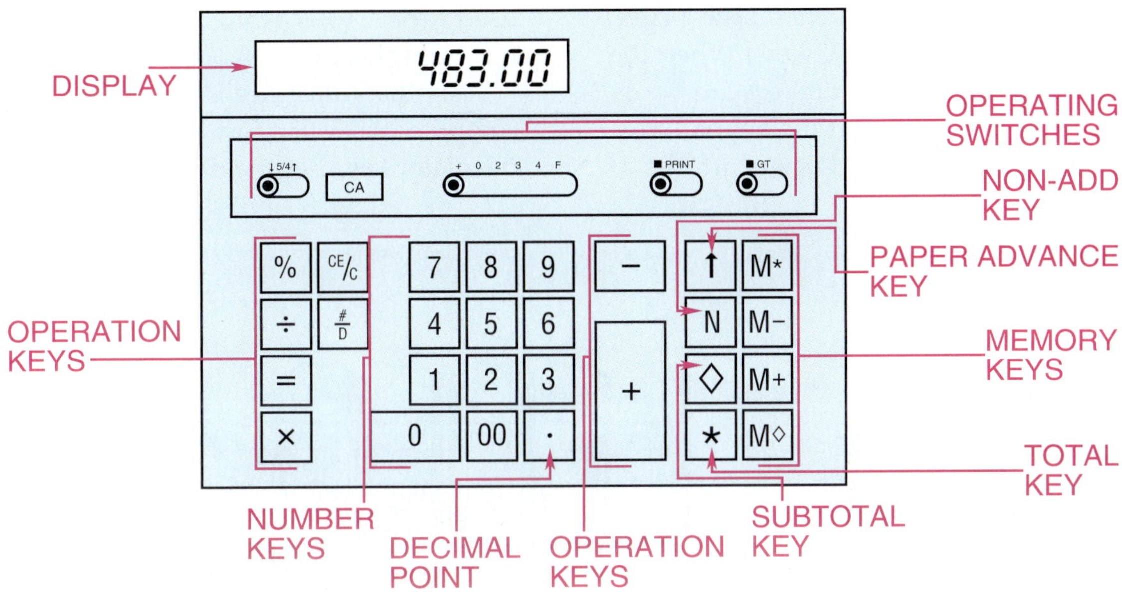


## DESKTOP CALCULATOR SETTINGS

Several operating switches on a desktop calculator must be engaged before the calculator will produce the desired results.

The *decimal selector* sets the appropriate decimal places necessary for the numbers that will be entered. For example, if the decimal selector is set at 2, both the numbers entered and the answer will have two decimal places. If the decimal selector is set at F, the calculator automatically sets the decimal places. The F setting allows the answer to be unrounded and carried out to the maximum number of decimal places possible.

The *decimal rounding selector* rounds the answers. The down arrow position will drop any digits beyond the last digit desired. The up arrow position will drop any digits beyond the last digit desired and round the last digit up. In the 5/4 position, the calculator rounds the last desired digit up only when the following digit is 5 or greater. If the following digit is less than 5, the last desired digit remains unchanged.

The *GT* or *grand total switch* in the on position accumulates totals.

## KINDS OF COMPUTER KEYBOARDS

The computer has a keypad on the right side of the keyboard called the *numeric keypad*. Even though several styles of keyboards for the IBM® and compatible computers are found, there are two basic layouts for the numeric keypad. The standard layout and enhanced layout are shown in the illustration. On the standard keyboard the directional arrow keys are found on the number keys. To use the numbers, press the key called *Num Lock*. (This key is found above the "7" key.) When the *Num Lock* is turned on, numbers are entered when the keys on the keypad are pressed. When the Num Lock is off, the arrow, Home, Page Up, Page Down, End, Insert, and Delete keys can be used.

The enhanced keyboards have the arrow keys and the other directional keys mentioned above to the left of the numeric keypad. When using the keypad on an enhanced keyboard, Num Lock can remain on.

The asterisk (*) performs a different function on the computer than the calculator. The asterisk on the calculator is used for the total while the computer uses it for multiplication.

Another difference is the division key. The computer key is the forward slash key (/). The calculator key uses the division key (÷).

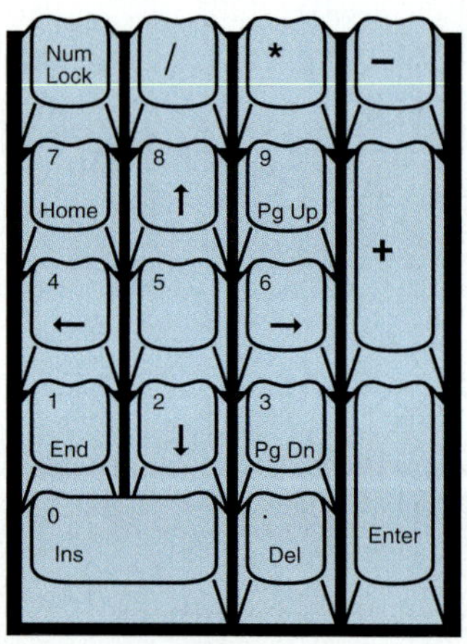


Standard Keyboard Layout

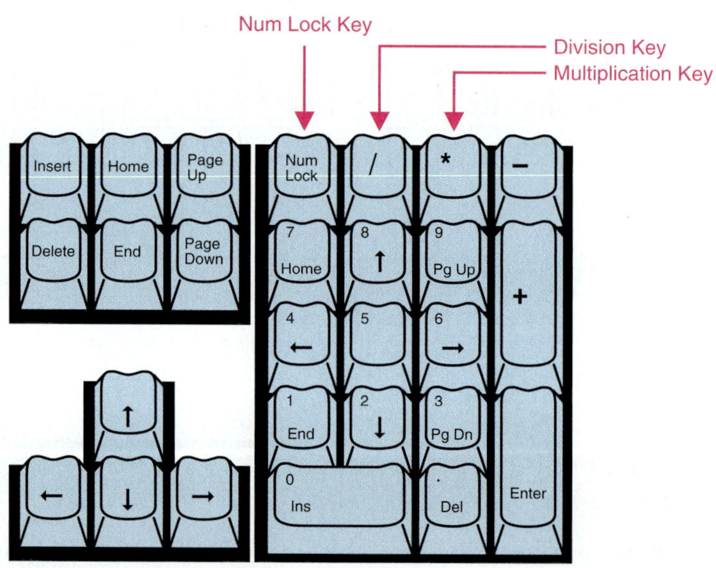


Enhanced Keyboard Layout

## TEN-KEY TOUCH SYSTEM

Striking the numbers 0 to 9 on a calculator or numeric keypad without looking at the keyboard is called the *touch system*. Using the touch system develops both speed and accuracy.

The 4, 5, and 6 keys are called the *home row*. If the right hand is used for the keyboard, the index finger is placed on the 4 key, the middle finger on the 5 key, and the ring finger on the 6 key. If the left hand is used, the ring finger is placed on the 4 key, the middle finger on the 5 key, and the index finger on the 6 key.

Place the fingers on the home row keys. Curve the fingers and keep the wrist straight. These keys may feel slightly concaved or the 5 key may have a raised dot. The differences in the home row allow the operator to recognize the home row by touch rather than by sight.

Maintain the position of the fingers on the home row. The finger used to strike the 4 key will also strike the 7 key and the 1 key. Stretch the finger up to reach the 7; then stretch the finger down to reach the 1 key. Visualize the position of these keys.

Again, place the fingers on the home row. Stretch the finger that strikes the 5 key up to reach the 8 key, then down to reach the 2 key. Likewise, stretch the finger that strikes the 6 key up to strike the 9 and down to strike the 3 key. This same finger will stretch down again to hit the decimal point.

If the right hand is used, the thumb will be used to strike the 0 and 00 keys and the little finger to strike the addition key. If the left hand is used, the little finger will be used to strike the 0 and 00 keys and the thumb to strike the addition key.

## HAND-HELD CALCULATORS

Hand-held calculators are slightly different from desktop calculators, not only in their size and features but also in their operation. Refer to the operator's manual for specific instructions for the calculator being used.

On a hand-held calculator, the numeric keys are usually very close together. In addition, the keys do not respond to touch as easily as on a desktop calculator. Therefore, the touch system is usually not used on a hand-held calculator.

## PERFORMING MATHEMATICAL OPERATIONS ON DESKTOP CALCULATORS

Mathematical operations can be performed on a calculator both quickly and efficiently. The basic operations of addition, subtraction, multiplication, and division are used frequently on a calculator.

### Addition

Each number to be added is called an *addend*. The answer to an addition problem is called the *sum*.

Addition is performed by entering an addend and striking the addition key (+). All numbers are entered on a calculator in the exact order they are given. To enter the number 4,455.65, strike the 4, 4, 5, 5, decimal, 6, and 5 keys in that order, and then strike the addition key. Commas are not entered. Continue in this manner until all addends have been entered. To obtain the sum, strike the total key on the calculator.

### Subtraction

The top number or first number of a subtraction problem is called the *minuend*. The number to be subtracted from the minuend is called the *subtrahend*. The answer to a subtraction problem is called the *difference*.

Subtraction is performed by first entering the minuend and striking the addition key (+). The subtrahend is then entered, followed by the minus key (−), followed by the total key.

### Multiplication

The number to be multiplied is called the *multiplicand*. The number of times the multiplicand will be multiplied is called the *multiplier*. The answer to a multiplication problem is called the *product*.

Multiplication is performed by entering

the multiplicand and striking the multiplication key (×). The multiplier is then entered, followed by the equals key (=). The calculator will automatically multiply and give the product.

### Division

The number to be divided is called the *dividend*. The number the dividend will be divided by is called the *divisor*. The answer to a division problem is called the *quotient*.

Division is performed by entering the dividend and striking the division key (÷). The divisor is then entered, followed by the equals key (=). The calculator will automatically divide and give the quotient.

### Correcting Errors

If an error is made while using a calculator, several methods of correction may be used. If an incorrect number has been entered and the addition key or equals key has not yet been struck, strike the clear entry (CE) key one time. This key will clear only the last number that was entered. However, if the clear entry key is depressed more than one time, the entire problem will be cleared on some calculators. If an incorrect number has been entered and the addition key has been struck, strike the minus key one time only. This will automatically subtract the last number added, thus removing it from the total.

## HAND-HELD CALCULATORS PERFORMING MATHEMATICAL OPERATIONS ON COMPUTERS

On a computer keypad or a hand-held calculator, addition is performed in much the same way as on a desktop calculator. However, after the + key is depressed, the display usually shows the accumulated total. Therefore, the total key is not found. Some computer programs will not calculate the total until Enter is pressed.

Subtraction is performed differently on many computer keypads and hand-held calculators. The minuend is usually entered, followed by the minus (−) key. Then the subtrahend is entered. Pressing either the + key or the = key will display the difference. Some computer programs will not calculate the difference until Enter is pressed.

Multiplication and division are performed the same way on a computer keypad and hand-held calculator as on a desktop calculator. Keep in mind that computers use the * for multiplication and / for division.

## SAFETY CONCERNS

Whenever electrical equipment such as a calculator or computer is being operated in a classroom or office, several safety rules apply. These rules protect the operator of the equipment, other persons in the environment, and the equipment itself.

1. Do not unplug equipment by pulling on the electrical cord. Instead, grasp the plug at the outlet and remove it.
2. Do not stretch electrical cords across an aisle where someone might trip over them.
3. Avoid food and beverages near the equipment where a spill might result in an electrical short.
4. Do not attempt to remove the cover of a calculator, computer, or keyboard for any reason while the power is turned on.
5. Do not attempt to repair equipment while it is plugged in.
6. Always turn the power off or unplug equipment when finished using it.

## CALCULATION DRILLS

### Instructions for Desktop Calculators

Complete each drill using the touch method. Set the decimal selector at the setting indicated in each drill. Compare the answer on the calculator to the answer in the book. If the two are the same, progress to the next problem. It is not necessary to enter 00 in the cents column if the decimal selector is set at 0-F. However, digits other than zeros in the cents column must be entered preceded by a decimal point.

### Instructions for Computer Keypads

Complete each drill using the touch method. There is no decimal selector on computer keypads. Set the number of decimal places as directed in the instructions for the computer program. In spreadsheets, for example, use the formatting options to set the number of decimal places. When the drill indicates "F" for floating, leave the computer application in its default format. Compare the answer on the computer monitor to the answer in the book. If the two are the same, progress to the next problem. It is not necessary to enter 00 in the cents column. However, digits other than zeros in the cents column must be entered preceded by a decimal point.

**DRILL D-1 Performing addition using the home row keys**
**Decimal Selector—2**

| | | | | |
|---:|---:|---:|---:|---:|
| 4.00 | 44.00 | 444.00 | 4,444.00 | 44,444.00 |
| 5.00 | 55.00 | 555.00 | 5,555.00 | 55,555.00 |
| 6.00 | 66.00 | 666.00 | 6,666.00 | 66,666.00 |
| 5.00 | 45.00 | 455.00 | 4,455.00 | 44,556.00 |
| 4.00 | 46.00 | 466.00 | 4,466.00 | 44,565.00 |
| 5.00 | 54.00 | 544.00 | 5,544.00 | 55,446.00 |
| 6.00 | 56.00 | 566.00 | 5,566.00 | 55,664.00 |
| 5.00 | 65.00 | 655.00 | 6,655.00 | 66,554.00 |
| 4.00 | 64.00 | 644.00 | 6,644.00 | 66,555.00 |
| 5.00 | 66.00 | 654.00 | 6,545.00 | 65,465.00 |
| 49.00 | 561.00 | 5,649.00 | 56,540.00 | 565,470.00 |

**DRILL D-2 Performing addition using the 0, 1, 4, and 7 keys**
**Decimal Selector—2**

| | | | | |
|---:|---:|---:|---:|---:|
| 4.00 | 11.00 | 444.00 | 4,440.00 | 44,000.00 |
| 7.00 | 44.00 | 777.00 | 7,770.00 | 77,000.00 |
| 4.00 | 74.00 | 111.00 | 1,110.00 | 11,000.00 |
| 1.00 | 71.00 | 741.00 | 4,400.00 | 41,000.00 |
| 4.00 | 70.00 | 740.00 | 1,100.00 | 71,000.00 |
| 7.00 | 10.00 | 101.00 | 4,007.00 | 10,000.00 |
| 4.00 | 14.00 | 140.00 | 7,001.00 | 10,100.00 |
| 1.00 | 17.00 | 701.00 | 1,007.00 | 40,100.00 |
| 4.00 | 40.00 | 700.00 | 1,004.00 | 70,100.00 |
| 7.00 | 77.00 | 407.00 | 7,700.00 | 74,100.00 |
| 43.00 | 428.00 | 4,862.00 | 39,539.00 | 448,400.00 |

**DRILL D-3 Performing addition using the 2, 5, and 8 keys**
**Decimal Selector—2**

| | | | | |
|---|---|---|---|---|
| 5.00 | 58.00 | 588.00 | 8,888.00 | 88,855.00 |
| 8.00 | 52.00 | 522.00 | 5,555.00 | 88,822.00 |
| 5.00 | 85.00 | 888.00 | 2,222.00 | 88,852.00 |
| 2.00 | 52.00 | 222.00 | 8,525.00 | 88,222.00 |
| 5.00 | 25.00 | 258.00 | 2,585.00 | 85,258.00 |
| 8.00 | 58.00 | 852.00 | 8,258.00 | 22,255.00 |
| 5.00 | 82.00 | 225.00 | 8,585.00 | 22,288.00 |
| 2.00 | 28.00 | 885.00 | 5,258.00 | 22,258.00 |
| 5.00 | 88.00 | 882.00 | 2,852.00 | 22,888.00 |
| 8.00 | 22.00 | 228.00 | 2,288.00 | 25,852.00 |
| 53.00 | 550.00 | 5,550.00 | 55,016.00 | 555,550.00 |

**DRILL D-4 Performing addition using the 3, 6, 9, and decimal point keys**
**Decimal Selector—2**

| | | | | |
|---|---|---|---|---|
| 6.00 | 66.66 | 666.66 | 6,666.99 | 66,699.33 |
| 9.00 | 99.99 | 999.99 | 9,999.66 | 99,966.66 |
| 6.00 | 33.33 | 333.33 | 3,333.99 | 33,366.33 |
| 3.00 | 33.66 | 666.99 | 3,366.99 | 36,963.36 |
| 6.36 | 33.99 | 999.66 | 6,699.33 | 69,636.36 |
| 3.36 | 99.66 | 333.66 | 9,966.33 | 33,333.66 |
| 9.36 | 99.33 | 696.36 | 9,636.69 | 66,666.99 |
| 9.63 | 33.36 | 369.63 | 3,696.36 | 99,999.33 |
| 6.33 | 33.69 | 336.69 | 6,963.99 | 96,369.63 |
| 9.93 | 69.63 | 963.36 | 6,699.33 | 36,963.36 |
| 68.97 | 603.30 | 6,366.33 | 67,029.66 | 639,965.01 |

**DRILL D-5 Performing subtraction using all number keys**
**Decimal Selector—F**

| | | | | |
|---|---|---|---|---|
| 456.73 | 789.01 | 741.00 | 852.55 | 987.98 |
| −123.21 | −456.00 | −258.10 | −369.88 | −102.55 |
| 333.52 | 333.01 | 482.90 | 482.67 | 885.43 |

**DRILL D-6 Performing multiplication using all number keys**
**Decimal Selector—F**

| | | | | |
|---|---|---|---|---|
| 654.05 | 975.01 | 487.10 | 123.56 | 803.75 |
| × 12.66 | × 27.19 | × 30.21 | × 50.09 | × 1.45 |
| 8,280.273 | 26,510.5219 | 14,715.291 | 6,189.1204 | 1,165.4375 |

## DRILL D-7 Performing division using all number keys Decimal Selector—F

| | | | | |
|---|---|---|---|---|
| 900.56 | ÷ | 450.28 | = | 2. |
| 500.25 | ÷ | 100.05 | = | 5. |
| 135.66 | ÷ | 6.65 | = | 20.4 |
| 269.155 | ÷ | 105.55 | = | 2.550023685* |
| 985.66 | ÷ | 22.66 | = | 43.49779346* |

*Number of decimal places may vary due to machine capacity.*

# RECYCLING PROBLEM 1-1

**Determining how transactions change an accounting equation and preparing a balance sheet**

Alston Eubanks is starting Reef Divers, a scuba diving service. Reef Divers uses the accounts shown in the following accounting equation. Use the form given in the *Recycling Problem Working Papers* to complete this problem.

| | Assets | | | | | = | Liabilities | + | Owner's Equity |
|---|---|---|---|---|---|---|---|---|---|
| **Trans. No.** | **Cash** | + | **Supplies** | + | **Prepaid Insurance** | = | **Accts. Pay.—Divers Supply** | + | **Alston Eubanks, Capital** |
| New Bal.<br>1. | 0<br>*+1,700* | | 0 | | 0 | | 0 | | 0<br>*+1,700* |
| New Bal.<br>2. | *1,700* | | *0* | | *0* | | *0* | | *1,700* |

***Transactions:***

1. Received cash from owner as an investment, $1,700.00.
2. Bought supplies on account from Divers Supply, $800.00.
3. Paid cash for insurance, $175.00.
4. Paid cash for supplies, $230.00.
5. Received cash from owner as an investment, $400.00.
6. Paid cash on account to Divers Supply, $500.00.

***Instructions:***

1. For each transaction, complete the following. Transaction 1 is given as an example.
   a. Analyze the transaction to determine which accounts in the accounting equation are affected.
   b. Write the amount in the appropriate columns, using a plus (+) if the account increases or a minus (−) if the account decreases.
   c. Calculate the new balance for each account in the accounting equation.
   d. Before going on to the next transaction, determine that the accounting equation is still in balance.
2. Using the final balances in the accounting equation, prepare a balance sheet for Reef Divers. Use November 30 of the current year as the date of the balance sheet.

# RECYCLING PROBLEM 2-1

**Determining how transactions change an accounting equation and preparing a balance sheet**

Alston Eubanks operates a scuba diving business called Reef Divers. Reef Divers uses the accounts shown in the following accounting equation. Use the form given in the *Recycling Problem Working Papers* to complete this problem.

| Trans. No. | Assets | | | | = | Liabilities | + | Owner's Equity |
|---|---|---|---|---|---|---|---|---|
| | Cash | + Accts. Rec.— Club Scuba | + Supplies | + Prepaid Insurance | = | Accts. Pay.— Divers Supply | + | Alston Eubanks, Capital |
| Beg. Bal.<br>1. | 1,195<br>*−150* | —0— | 1,030 | 175 | | 300 | | 2,100<br>*−150 (expense)* |
| New Bal.<br>2. | *1,045* | *—0—* | *1,030* | *175* | | *300* | | *1,950* |

***Transactions:***

1. Paid cash for telephone bill, $150.00.
2. Received cash from owner as an investment, $200.00.
3. Paid cash for rent, $400.00.
4. Received cash from sales, $550.00.
5. Bought supplies on account from Divers Supply, $220.00.
6. Sold services on account to Club Scuba, $300.00.
7. Paid cash for supplies, $300.00.
8. Paid cash for advertising, $550.00.
9. Received cash on account from Club Scuba, $200.00.
10. Paid cash on account to Divers Supply, $300.00.
11. Paid cash for insurance, $175.00.
12. Received cash from sales, $1,900.00.
13. Paid cash to owner for personal use, $1,000.00.

***Instructions:***

1. For each transaction, complete the following. Transaction 1 is given as an example.
   a. Analyze the transaction to determine which accounts in the accounting equation are affected.
   b. Write the amount in the appropriate columns, using a plus (+) if the account increases or a minus (−) if the account decreases.
   c. For transactions that change owner's equity, write in parentheses a description of the transaction to the right of the amount.
   d. Calculate the new balance for each account in the accounting equation.
   e. Before going on to the next transaction, determine that the accounting equation is still in balance.
2. Using the final balances in the accounting equation, prepare a balance sheet for Reef Divers. Use the date December 31 of the current year.

# RECYCLING PROBLEM 3-1

**Analyzing transactions into debit and credit parts**

Harrison Ennis owns a business called Cayman Copies. Cayman Copies uses the following accounts:

Cash
Accounts Receivable—Coral Supply Company
Accounts Receivable—Coconut Inn
Supplies
Prepaid Insurance
Accounts Payable—Palms Paper
Accounts Payable—Pappagallo Company
Harrison Ennis, Capital
Harrison Ennis, Drawing
Sales
Advertising Expense
Miscellaneous Expense
Rent Expense
Repair Expense
Utilities Expense

***Instructions:***
Use the forms given in the *Recycling Problem Working Papers.*

1. Prepare a T account for each account.
2. Analyze each transaction into its debit and credit parts. Write the debit and credit amounts in the proper T accounts to show how each transaction changes account balances. Write the date of the transaction in parentheses before each amount.

***Transactions:***

July 1. Received cash from owner as an investment, $6,000.00.
2. Paid cash for supplies, $120.00.
4. Paid cash for rent, $400.00.
4. Received cash from sales, $700.00.
5. Paid cash for repairs, $20.00.
8. Sold services on account to Coral Supply Co., $400.00.
9. Bought supplies on account from Pappagallo Co., $1,000.00.
10. Paid cash for insurance, $200.00.
11. Received cash from owner as an investment, $1,800.00.
11. Received cash from sales, $600.00.
12. Bought supplies on account from Palms Paper, $100.00.
13. Received cash on account from Coral Supply Co., $250.00.
15. Paid cash for miscellaneous expense, $10.00.
16. Paid cash on account to Pappagallo Co., $100.00.
22. Paid cash for electric bill (utilities expense), $70.00.
23. Paid cash for advertising, $60.00.
25. Sold services on account to Coconut Inn, $440.00.
26. Paid cash to owner for personal use, $1,200.00.
30. Received cash on account from Coconut Inn, $200.00.

# RECYCLING PROBLEM 4-1

**Journalizing transactions and proving and ruling a journal**

Merilda Bodden owns a service business called Bodden Express, which uses the following accounts:

| | | | |
|---|---|---|---|
| Cash | Accts. Pay.—Bahling Supplies | Sales | Repair Expense |
| Supplies | Accts. Pay.—Kirk Company | Advertising Expense | Utilities Expense |
| Prepaid Insurance | Merilda Bodden, Capital | Miscellaneous Expense | |
| Accts. Rec.—Leta Scott | Merilda Bodden, Drawing | Rent Expense | |

***Transactions:*** Aug.
1. Received cash from owner as an investment, $8,750.00. R1.
2. Paid cash for rent, $200.00. C1.
3. Paid cash for supplies, $600.00. C2.
4. Bought supplies on account from Bahling Supplies, $1,000.00. M1.
5. Paid cash for insurance, $2,250.00. C3.
8. Paid cash on account to Bahling Supplies, $750.00. C4.
8. Received cash from sales, $375.00. T8.
8. Sold services on account to Leta Scott, $100.00. S1.
9. Paid cash for electric bill, $30.00. C5.
10. Paid cash for miscellaneous expense, $9.00. C6.
10. Received cash from sales, $375.00. T10.
11. Paid cash for repairs, $50.00. C7.
11. Received cash from sales, $425.00. T11.
12. Received cash from sales, $350.00. T12.
15. Paid cash to owner for personal use, $175.00. C8.
15. Received cash from sales, $375.00. T15.
16. Paid cash for supplies, $750.00. C9.
17. Received cash on account from Leta Scott, $100.00. R2.
17. Bought supplies on account from Kirk Company, $375.00. M2.
17. Received cash from sales, $300.00. T17.
18. Received cash from sales, $400.00. T18.
19. Received cash from sales, $375.00. T19.
22. Bought supplies on account from Kirk Company, $40.00. M3.
22. Received cash from sales, $350.00. T22.
23. Paid cash for advertising, $65.00. C10.
23. Sold services on account to Leta Scott, $325.00. S2.
24. Paid cash for telephone bill, $30.00. C11.
24. Received cash from sales, $300.00. T24.
25. Received cash from sales, $275.00. T25.
26. Paid cash for supplies, $35.00. C12.
26. Received cash from sales, $300.00. T26.
29. Received cash on account from Leta Scott, $325.00. R3.
30. Paid cash to owner for personal use, $160.00. C13.
30. Received cash from sales, $400.00. T30.

***Instructions:***

1. Use page 1 of the journal given in the *Recycling Problem Working Papers*. Journalize the transactions for August 1 through August 19 of the current year. Source documents are abbreviated as follows: check, C; memorandum, M; receipt, R; sales invoice, S; calculator tape, T.
2. Prove and rule page 1 of the journal. Carry the column totals forward to page 2 of the journal.
3. Use page 2 of the journal to journalize the transactions for the remainder of August.
4. Prove page 2 of the journal.
5. Prove cash. The beginning cash balance on August 1 is zero. The balance on the next unused check stub is $8,671.00.
6. Rule page 2 of the journal.

# RECYCLING PROBLEM 5-1

**Journalizing transactions and posting to a general ledger**

Janet Porter owns a service business called Porter's Parties. Porter's Parties' general ledger accounts are given in the *Recycling Problem Working Papers.*

***Transactions:***

Aug. 1. Received cash from owner as an investment, $8,500.00. R1.
3. Paid cash for rent, $500.00. C1.
5. Sold services on account to Nicholas Calendo, $250.00. S1.
6. Received cash from sales, $830.00. T6.
9. Paid cash for miscellaneous expense, $15.00. C2.
11. Paid cash for supplies, $230.00. C3.
13. Bought supplies on account from Jordan Supplies, $700.00. M1.
13. Received cash from sales, $650.00. T13.
16. Paid cash for electric bill, $95.00. C4.
18. Paid cash on account to Jordan Supplies, $400.00. C5.
20. Paid cash for advertising, $55.00. C6.
20. Received cash on account from Nicholas Calendo, $150.00. R2.
25. Paid cash for supplies, $50.00. C7.
27. Paid cash for supplies, $75.00. C8.
27. Received cash from sales, $1,200.00. T27.
30. Paid cash to owner for personal use, $450.00. C9.
30. Received cash from sales, $780.00. T30.

***Instructions:***

1. Open an account for Utilities Expense. Use the 3-digit numbering system described in the chapter.
2. Journalize the transactions completed during August of the current year. Use page 1 of a journal. Source documents are abbreviated as follows: check, C; memorandum, M; receipt, R; sales invoice, S; calculator tape, T.
3. Prove the journal.
4. Prove cash. The beginning cash balance on August 1 is zero. The balance on the next unused check stub is $10,240.00.
5. Rule the journal.
6. Post from the journal to the general ledger.

# RECYCLING PROBLEM 6-1

**Reconciling a bank statement; journalizing a bank service charge, a dishonored check, and petty cash transactions**

Emil Ibraham owns a business called Fast Print. Selected general ledger accounts are given below. Forms are given in the *Recycling Problem Working Papers.*

110 Cash
115 Petty Cash
120 Accts. Rec.—Angus Restaurant
130 Supplies
140 Prepaid Insurance
320 Emil Ibraham, Drawing
520 Miscellaneous Expense
530 Rent Expense
535 Repair Expense
540 Supplies Expense
550 Utilities Expense

***Instructions:***

1. Journalize the following transactions completed during May of the current year. Use page 12 of a journal. Source documents are abbreviated as follows: check, C; memorandum, M.

***Transactions:***

May 21. Paid cash to establish a petty cash fund, $100.00. C61.
24. Paid cash for repairs, $115.00. C62.
26. Paid cash for supplies, $20.00. C63.
27. Received notice from the bank of a dishonored check from Angus Restaurant, $45.00, plus $20.00 fee; total, $65.00. M22.
28. Paid cash for miscellaneous expense, $24.00. C64.
31. Paid cash to owner for personal use, $200.00. C65.
31. Paid cash to replenish the petty cash fund, $65.00: supplies, $55.00; miscellaneous expense, $10.00. C66.

2. On May 31 of the current year, Fast Print received a bank statement dated May 30. Prepare a bank statement reconciliation. Use May 31 of the current year as the date. The following information is obtained from the May 30 bank statement and from the records of the business.

| | |
|---|---|
| Bank statement balance | $1,486.00 |
| Bank service charge | 25.00 |
| Outstanding deposit, May 31 | 340.00 |
| Outstanding checks, Nos. 65 and 66 | |
| Checkbook balance on Check Stub No. 67 | $1,586.00 |

3. Continue using the journal and journalize the following transaction.

***Transaction:***

May 31. Received bank statement showing May bank service charge, $25.00. M23.

# RECYCLING PROBLEM 7-1

**Completing a work sheet**

On February 28 of the current year, Chisholm Hair Care has the following general ledger accounts and balances. The business uses a monthly fiscal period.

| Account Titles | Account Balances Debit | Credit |
|---|---|---|
| Cash | $1,609.00 | |
| Petty Cash | 300.00 | |
| Accounts Receivable—Margo Angelo | 581.00 | |
| Supplies | 795.00 | |
| Prepaid Insurance | 1,100.00 | |
| Accounts Payable—Virginia Supplies | | $ 450.00 |
| Montana Freemantle, Capital | | 3,550.00 |
| Montana Freemantle, Drawing | 300.00 | |
| Income Summary | | |
| Sales | | 3,000.00 |
| Advertising Expense | 525.00 | |
| Insurance Expense | | |
| Miscellaneous Expense | 250.00 | |
| Rent Expense | 1,100.00 | |
| Supplies Expense | | |
| Utilities Expense | 440.00 | |

***Instructions:***

1. Prepare the heading and trial balance on the work sheet given in the *Recycling Problem Working Papers.* Total and rule the Trial Balance columns.
2. Analyze the following adjustment information into debit and credit parts. Record the adjustments on the work sheet.

| Adjustment Information, February 28 | |
|---|---|
| Supplies inventory | $ 250.00 |
| Value of prepaid insurance | 1,000.00 |

3. Total and rule the Adjustments columns.
4. Extend the up-to-date balances to the Balance Sheet or Income Statement columns.
5. Rule a single line across the Income Statement and Balance Sheet columns. Total each column. Calculate and record the net income or net loss. Label the amount in the Account Title column.
6. Total and rule the Income Statement and Balance Sheet columns.

# RECYCLING PROBLEM 8-1

**Preparing financial statements**

The following information is obtained from the work sheet of Robbie's Rugcare for the month ended August 31 of the current year. Forms are given in the *Recycling Problem Working Papers*.

| | ACCOUNT TITLE | 5 INCOME STATEMENT DEBIT | 6 INCOME STATEMENT CREDIT | 7 BALANCE SHEET DEBIT | 8 BALANCE SHEET CREDIT | |
|---|---|---|---|---|---|---|
| 1 | Cash | | | 8,752.00 | | 1 |
| 2 | Accounts Receivable—Crystal Thompson | | | 200.00 | | 2 |
| 3 | Accounts Receivable—Robert Boje | | | 175.00 | | 3 |
| 4 | Supplies | | | 400.00 | | 4 |
| 5 | Prepaid Insurance | | | 220.00 | | 5 |
| 6 | Accounts Payable—Daniel Supplies | | | | 442.00 | 6 |
| 7 | Accounts Payable—Irene's Irons | | | | 676.00 | 7 |
| 8 | Roberta Greenstein, Capital | | | | 7,951.00 | 8 |
| 9 | Roberta Greenstein, Drawing | | | 1,800.00 | | 9 |
| 10 | Income Summary | | | | | 10 |
| 11 | Sales | | 5,707.00 | | | 11 |
| 12 | Advertising Expense | 900.00 | | | | 12 |
| 13 | Insurance Expense | 20.00 | | | | 13 |
| 14 | Miscellaneous Expense | 267.00 | | | | 14 |
| 15 | Supplies Expense | 500.00 | | | | 15 |
| 16 | Utilities Expense | 1,542.00 | | | | 16 |
| 17 | | 3,229.00 | 5,707.00 | 11,547.00 | 9,069.00 | 17 |
| 18 | Net Income | 2,478.00 | | | 2,478.00 | 18 |
| 19 | | 5,707.00 | 5,707.00 | 11,547.00 | 11,547.00 | 19 |
| 20 | | | | | | 20 |

***Instructions:***

1. Prepare an income statement for the month ended August 31 of the current year.
2. Calculate and record the component percentages for total expenses and net income. Round percentage calculations to the nearest 0.1%.
3. Prepare a balance sheet for August 31 of the current year.

# RECYCLING PROBLEM 9-1

**Journalizing adjusting and closing entries**

The following information is obtained from the partial work sheet of Robbie's Rugcare for the month ended August 31 of the current year.

| | | 3 | 4 | 5 | 6 | 7 | 8 | |
|---|---|---|---|---|---|---|---|---|
| | | ADJUSTMENTS | | INCOME STATEMENT | | BALANCE SHEET | | |
| | ACCOUNT TITLE | DEBIT | CREDIT | DEBIT | CREDIT | DEBIT | CREDIT | |
| 1 | *Cash* | | | | | 8752 00 | | 1 |
| 2 | *Accts. Rec.—Crystal Thompson* | | | | | 200 00 | | 2 |
| 3 | *Accts. Rec.—Robert Boje* | | | | | 175 00 | | 3 |
| 4 | *Supplies* | | (a) 500 00 | | | 400 00 | | 4 |
| 5 | *Prepaid Insurance* | | (b) 20 00 | | | 220 00 | | 5 |
| 6 | *Accts. Pay.—Daniel Supplies* | | | | | | 442 00 | 6 |
| 7 | *Accts. Pay.—Irene's Irons* | | | | | | 676 00 | 7 |
| 8 | *Roberta Greenstein, Capital* | | | | | | 7951 00 | 8 |
| 9 | *Roberta Greenstein, Drawing* | | | | | 1800 00 | | 9 |
| 10 | *Income Summary* | | | | | | | 10 |
| 11 | *Sales* | | | | 5707 00 | | | 11 |
| 12 | *Advertising Expense* | | | 900 00 | | | | 12 |
| 13 | *Insurance Expense* | (b) 20 00 | | 20 00 | | | | 13 |
| 14 | *Miscellaneour Expense* | | | 267 00 | | | | 14 |
| 15 | *Supplies Expense* | (a) 500 00 | | 500 00 | | | | 15 |
| 16 | *Utilities Expense* | | | 1542 00 | | | | 16 |
| 17 | | 520 00 | 520 00 | 3229 00 | 5707 00 | 11547 00 | 9069 00 | 17 |
| 18 | *Net Income* | | | 2478 00 | | | 2478 00 | 18 |
| 19 | | | | 5707 00 | 5707 00 | 11547 00 | 11547 00 | 19 |
| 20 | | | | | | | | 20 |

***Instructions:***

1. Use page 16 of the journal given in the *Recycling Problem Working Papers.* Journalize the adjusting entries.
2. Continue to use page 16 of the journal. Journalize the closing entries.

# RECYCLING PROBLEM 10-1

**Journalizing purchases, cash payments, and other transactions**

Judy Daily and Donald Steele, partners, own a bookstore.

***Instructions:***
Journalize the following transactions completed during September of the current year. Use page 20 of the journal given in the *Recycling Problem Working Papers.* Source documents are abbreviated as follows: check, C; memorandum, M; purchase invoice, P.

***Transactions:***

Sept. 1. Paid cash for monthly rent, $800.00. C405.
2. Purchased merchandise for cash, $200.00. C406.
3. Purchased merchandise on account from Bookmaster, Inc., $900.00. P91.
6. Paid cash for office supplies, $75.00. C407.
7. Bought store supplies on account from Deluxe Display, $240.00. M53.
9. Paid cash on account to National Press, $600.00, covering P89. C408.
12. Purchased merchandise on account from Classic Books, $1,500.00. P92.
13. Paid cash for advertising, $75.00. C409.
18. Paid cash on account to Bookmaster, Inc., $900.00, covering P91. C410.
24. Donald Steele, partner, withdrew merchandise for personal use, $100.00. M54.
30. Judy Daily, partner, withdrew cash for personal use, $1,000.00. C411.
30. Donald Steele, partner, withdrew cash for personal use, $900.00. C412.
30. Paid cash to replenish the petty cash fund, $210.00: office supplies, $29.00; store supplies, $36.00; advertising, $90.00; miscellaneous, $55.00. C413.

# RECYCLING PROBLEM 11-1

**Journalizing sales and cash receipts transactions; proving and ruling a journal**

Olga Flores and James Lazarus, partners, own Outdoor Living, a hunting and fishing equipment store.

Partial journal page 17 and page 18 for Outdoor Living are given in the *Recycling Problem Working Papers.*

***Instructions:***

1. September 23 column totals to be carried forward have been entered on line 32 of journal page 17. Prove the equality of debits and credits and rule the column totals of journal page 17.
2. Record the totals brought forward from journal page 17 to line 1 of page 18 of the journal. Prove the equality of debits and credits again. Use the current year.
3. Journalize the following transactions completed during the remainder of September on journal page 18. Sales tax rate is 6%. Source documents are abbreviated as follows: receipt, R; sales invoice, S; cash register tape, T.

***Transactions:***

Sept. 23. Received cash on account from Timothy Cole, $82.68, covering S69. R100.
24. Sold merchandise on account to Doretha Hunt, $160.00, plus sales tax, $9.60; total, $169.60. S74.
25. Received cash on account from Valerie Seeley, $110.24, covering S70. R101.
26. Recorded cash and credit card sales, $3,372.00, plus sales tax, $202.32; total, $3,574.32. T26.
29. Sold merchandise on account to Anthony Zolte, $230.00, plus sales tax, $13.80; total, $243.80. S75.
30. Recorded cash and credit card sales, $1,387.00, plus sales tax, $83.22; total, $1,470.22. T30.

4. Total the journal. Prove the equality of debits and credits.
5. Rule the journal.

# RECYCLING PROBLEM 12-1

**Posting to ledgers from a journal**

The journal and ledgers for Custom Boots are given in the *Recycling Problem Working Papers.*

***Instructions:***

1. Post the separate items recorded in the following columns of the journal: (a) General Debit and Credit. (b) Accounts Receivable Debit and Credit. (c) Accounts Payable Debit and Credit.
2. Post the totals of the special columns of the journal.
3. Using the current year, prepare a schedule of accounts payable and a schedule of accounts receivable. Prove the accuracy of the subsidiary ledgers by comparing the schedule totals with the balances of the controlling accounts in the general ledger. If the totals are not the same, find and correct the errors.

# RECYCLING PROBLEM 13-1

### Preparing a semimonthly payroll

The following information is for the semimonthly pay period May 1–15 of the current year. Forms are given in the *Recycling Problem Working Papers.*

| EMPL. NO. | EMPLOYEE'S NAME | MARITAL STATUS | NO. OF ALLOWANCES | EARNINGS | | DEDUCTIONS |
|---|---|---|---|---|---|---|
| | | | | REGULAR | OVERTIME | HEALTH INSURANCE |
| 3 | *Boyd, Bruce E.* | *S* | *2* | 836 00 | 57 00 | 35 00 |
| 4 | *Gomez, Patti H.* | *M* | *3* | 739 20 | | 45 00 |
| 7 | *Logan, Curt M.* | *S* | *1* | 880 00 | | |
| 1 | *Payne, Myrna L.* | *S* | *1* | 774 40 | 13 20 | |
| 5 | *Sharp, Don E.* | *M* | *2* | 765 60 | | 35 00 |
| 6 | *Terry, Daphne I.* | *M* | *3* | 809 60 | | 45 00 |
| 8 | *Walsh, Linda P.* | *M* | *2* | 915 20 | 62 40 | 35 00 |

***Instructions:***

1. Prepare a payroll register. The date of payment is May 15. Use the federal income tax withholding tables shown on pages 310–311 to find the income tax withholding for each employee. Calculate social security and Medicare tax withholdings using 6.5% and 1.5% tax rates, respectively. None of the employee accumulated earnings has exceeded the social security tax base.
2. Prepare a check for the total amount of the net pay. Make the check payable to Payroll Account 982-561-4732, and sign your name as a partner of McKinley Company. The beginning check stub balance is $11,530.50.
3. Prepare payroll checks for Curt M. Logan, Check No. 286, and Daphne I. Terry, Check No. 289. Sign your name as a partner of McKinley Company. Record the two payroll check numbers in the payroll register.

# RECYCLING PROBLEM 14-1

**Journalizing payroll taxes**

Folger Manufacturing completed payroll transactions during the period January 31 to April 30 of the current year. Payroll tax rates are as follows: social security, 6.5%; Medicare, 1.5%; federal unemployment, 0.8%; and state unemployment, 5.4%. No total earnings have exceeded the tax base for calculating unemployment taxes.

***Instructions:***

1. Journalize the following transactions on page 3 of the journal given in the *Recycling Problem Working Papers*. Source documents are abbreviated as follows: check, C, and memorandum, M.

***Transactions:***

Jan. 31. Paid cash for monthly payroll, $4,876.40 (total payroll, $6,020.00, less deductions: employee income tax, $662.00; social security tax, $391.30; Medicare tax, $90.30). C217.

31. Recorded employer payroll taxes expense. M54.

Feb. 15. Paid cash for liability for employee income tax, $662.00; social security tax, $782.60; and Medicare tax, $180.60; total, $1,625.20. C242.

28. Paid cash for monthly payroll, $4,907.36 (total payroll, $6,058.00, less deductions: employee income tax, $666.00; social security tax, $393.77; Medicare tax, $90.87). C285.

28. Recorded employer payroll taxes expense. M59.

Mar. 15. Paid cash for liability for employee income tax, $666.00; social security tax, $787.54; and Medicare tax, $181.74; total, $1,635.28. C310.

31. Paid cash for monthly payroll, $5,171.28 (total payroll, $6,384.00, less deductions: employee income tax, $702.00; social security tax, $414.96; Medicare tax, $95.76). C330.

2. Prove and rule journal page 3. Carry the column totals forward to page 4 of the journal.
3. Journalize the following transactions on page 4 of the journal.

***Transactions:***

Mar. 31. Recorded employer payroll taxes expense. M64.

Apr. 15. Paid cash for liability for employee income tax, $702.00; social security tax, $829.92; and Medicare tax, $191.52; total, $1,723.44. C351.

30. Paid cash for federal unemployment tax liability for quarter ended March 31, $147.69. C372.

30. Paid cash for state unemployment tax liability for quarter ended March 31, $996.95. C373.

4. Prove and rule journal page 4.

# RECYCLING PROBLEM 15-1

**Preparing an 8-column work sheet for a merchandising business**

Jolson Music's trial balance as of December 31 of the current year is recorded on a work sheet in the *Recycling Problem Working Papers*.

***Instructions:***

1. Analyze the following adjustment information and record the adjustments on the work sheet.

***End-of-Fiscal-Period Information***

| | |
|---|---|
| Merchandise inventory | $262,520.00 |
| Office supplies inventory | 2,630.00 |
| Store supplies inventory | 2,645.00 |
| Value of prepaid insurance | 2,150.00 |

2. Complete the work sheet.

# RECYCLING PROBLEM 16-1

**Preparing financial statements**

Mat's Antiques prepared the following work sheet for the year ended December 31 of the current year. Forms are given in the *Recycling Problem Working Papers.*

*Mat's Antiques*
*Work Sheet*
*For Year Ended December 31, 20--*

| | ACCOUNT TITLE | 1 TRIAL BALANCE DEBIT | 2 TRIAL BALANCE CREDIT | 3 ADJUSTMENTS DEBIT | 4 ADJUSTMENTS CREDIT | 5 INCOME STATEMENT DEBIT | 6 INCOME STATEMENT CREDIT | 7 BALANCE SHEET DEBIT | 8 BALANCE SHEET CREDIT | |
|---|---|---|---|---|---|---|---|---|---|---|
| 1 | Cash | 22,300.00 | | | | | | 22,300.00 | | 1 |
| 2 | Petty Cash | 300.00 | | | | | | 300.00 | | 2 |
| 3 | Accounts Receivable | 10,270.00 | | | | | | 10,270.00 | | 3 |
| 4 | Merchandise Inventory | 295,780.00 | | | (a) 12,200.00 | | | 283,580.00 | | 4 |
| 5 | Supplies—Office | 5,890.00 | | | (b) 3,730.00 | | | 2,160.00 | | 5 |
| 6 | Supplies—Store | 5,610.00 | | | (c) 3,920.00 | | | 1,690.00 | | 6 |
| 7 | Prepaid Insurance | 5,550.00 | | | (d) 3,450.00 | | | 2,100.00 | | 7 |
| 8 | Accounts Payable | | 9,610.00 | | | | | | 9,610.00 | 8 |
| 9 | Sales Tax Payable | | 1,130.00 | | | | | | 1,130.00 | 9 |
| 10 | Mathew Logan, Capital | | 135,400.00 | | | | | | 135,400.00 | 10 |
| 11 | Mathew Logan, Drawing | 18,220.00 | | | | | | 18,220.00 | | 11 |
| 12 | Jerry Hill, Capital | | 133,270.00 | | | | | | 133,270.00 | 12 |
| 13 | Jerry Hill, Drawing | 18,320.00 | | | | | | 18,320.00 | | 13 |
| 14 | Income Summary | | | (a) 12,200.00 | | 12,200.00 | | | | 14 |
| 15 | Sales | | 270,800.00 | | | | 270,800.00 | | | 15 |
| 16 | Purchases | 132,440.00 | | | | 132,440.00 | | | | 16 |
| 17 | Advertising Expense | 6,210.00 | | | | 6,210.00 | | | | 17 |
| 18 | Credit Card Fee Expense | 2,660.00 | | | | 2,660.00 | | | | 18 |
| 19 | Insurance Expense | | | (d) 3,450.00 | | 3,450.00 | | | | 19 |
| 20 | Miscellaneous Expense | 2,860.00 | | | | 2,860.00 | | | | 20 |
| 21 | Rent Expense | 21,000.00 | | | | 21,000.00 | | | | 21 |
| 22 | Supplies Expense—Office | | | (b) 3,730.00 | | 3,730.00 | | | | 22 |
| 23 | Supplies Expense—Store | | | (c) 3,920.00 | | 3,920.00 | | | | 23 |
| 24 | Utilities Expense | 2,800.00 | | | | 2,800.00 | | | | 24 |
| 25 | | 550,210.00 | 550,210.00 | 23,300.00 | 23,300.00 | 191,270.00 | 270,800.00 | 358,940.00 | 279,410.00 | 25 |
| 26 | Net Income | | | | | 79,530.00 | | | 79,530.00 | 26 |
| 27 | | | | | | 270,800.00 | 270,800.00 | 358,940.00 | 358,940.00 | 27 |
| 28 | | | | | | | | | | 28 |

***Instructions:***

1. Prepare an income statement. Calculate and record the following component percentages: (a) cost of merchandise sold, (b) gross profit on sales, (c) total expenses, and (d) net income or loss. Round percentage calculations to the nearest 0.1%.
2. Prepare a distribution of net income statement. Net income or loss is to be shared equally.
3. Prepare an owners' equity statement. No additional investments were made.
4. Prepare a balance sheet in report form.

# RECYCLING PROBLEM 17-1

### Journalizing adjusting and closing entries

Use the following partial work sheet of Let's Go Camping for the year ended December 31 of the current year.

| | ACCOUNT TITLE | 3 ADJUSTMENTS DEBIT | 4 ADJUSTMENTS CREDIT | 5 INCOME STATEMENT DEBIT | 6 INCOME STATEMENT CREDIT |
|---|---|---|---|---|---|
| 4 | *Merchandise Inventory* | | (a) 11 810 00 | | |
| 5 | *Supplies—Office* | | (b) 3 012 00 | | |
| 6 | *Supplies—Store* | | (c) 3 156 00 | | |
| 7 | *Prepaid Insurance* | | (d) 3 096 00 | | |
| 22 | *Income Summary* | (a) 11 810 00 | | 11 810 00 | |
| 23 | *Sales* | | | | 357 600 00 |
| 24 | *Purchases* | | | 149 220 00 | |
| 25 | *Advertising Expense* | | | 5 736 00 | |
| 26 | *Credit Card Fee Expense* | | | 4 776 00 | |
| 27 | *Insurance Expense* | (d) 3 096 00 | | 3 096 00 | |
| 28 | *Miscellaneous Expense* | | | 2 568 00 | |
| 29 | *Payroll Taxes Expense* | | | 7 176 00 | |
| 30 | *Rent Expense* | | | 15 840 00 | |
| 31 | *Salary Expense* | | | 70 700 00 | |
| 32 | *Supplies Expense—Office* | (b) 3 012 00 | | 3 012 00 | |
| 33 | *Supplies Expense—Store* | (c) 3 156 00 | | 3 156 00 | |
| 34 | *Utilities Expense* | | | 3 310 00 | |
| 35 | | 21 074 00 | 21 074 00 | 280 400 00 | 357 600 00 |
| 36 | *Net Income* | | | 77 200 00 | |
| 37 | | | | 357 600 00 | 357 600 00 |
| 38 | | | | | |

***Instructions:***

1. Use page 25 of the journal given in the *Recycling Problem Working Papers*. Journalize the adjusting entries using information from the partial work sheet.
2. Continue using page 25 of the journal. Journalize the closing entries using information from the work sheet. The distribution of net income statement shows equal distribution of earnings. The partners' drawing accounts show the following debit balances in the work sheet's Balance Sheet Debit column: Tom Hill, Drawing, $22,170.00; Vern Teel, Drawing, $22,680.00.

# RECYCLING PROBLEM 18-1

**Journalizing and posting purchases and cash payment transactions**

The general ledger and accounts payable ledger accounts of Central Heating Supply are given in the *Recycling Problem Working Papers*. The balances are recorded as of July 1 of the current year. Use the following account titles.

**PARTIAL GENERAL LEDGER**
1105 Cash
1110 Petty Cash
1140 Supplies
2115 Accounts Payable
5105 Purchases
5110 Purchases Discount
5115 Purchases Returns and Allowances
6105 Advertising Expense
6110 Cash Short and Over
6135 Miscellaneous Expense
6145 Rent Expense

**ACCOUNTS PAYABLE LEDGER**
210 Carson Company
220 Delmar, Inc.
230 Garrison Supply
240 Macon Wire Company
250 Sanders Company

***Instructions:***

1. Journalize the following transactions affecting purchases and cash payments completed during July of the current year. Use page 7 of a purchases journal, page 11 of a cash payments journal, and page 7 of a general journal.

***Transactions:***

July 1. Paid cash for rent, $600.00. C461.
3. Purchased merchandise on account from Delmar, Inc., $3,250.00. P215.
4. Paid cash on account to Carson Company covering P210 for $1,364.00, less 2% discount. C462.
5. Bought supplies on account from Garrison Supply, $210.00. M235.
9. Purchased merchandise on account from Carson Company, $1,056.00. P216.
9. Paid cash on account to Sanders Company covering P211 for $2,480.00, less 2% discount. C463.
10. Paid cash for supplies, $536.00. C464.
12. Purchased merchandise on account from Macon Wire Company, $362.00. P217.
14. Paid cash on account to Carson Company, covering P216, less 2% discount. C465.
**Posting.** Post the items that are to be posted individually. Post from the journals in the following order: purchases, general, cash payments. Some transactions will not be in order by date in the accounts.
16. Returned merchandise to Delmar, Inc., $549.00, from P215. DM47.
18. Paid cash to Jackson Company for merchandise with a list price of $192.25. Jackson offers its customers a 60% trade discount. C466.
21. Purchased merchandise on account from Garrison Supply, $378.00. P218.
22. Paid cash on account to Delmar, Inc., $2,701.00, covering P215, no discount. C467.
23. Paid cash for miscellaneous expense, $90.00. C468.
24. Bought supplies on account from Sanders Company, $650.00. M242.
25. Returned merchandise to Macon Wire Company, $80.00, from P217. DM48.
29. Purchased merchandise on account from Carson Company, $700.00. P220.
31. Paid cash to replenish the petty cash fund: supplies, $26.40; advertising, $41.70; miscellaneous, $14.80; cash short, $0.60. C469.
**Posting.** Post the items that are to be posted individually.

2. Total and rule the purchases journal. Post the total.
3. Prove and rule the cash payments journal. Post the totals of the special columns.
4. Prepare a schedule of accounts payable. Compare the schedule total with the balance of the accounts payable account in the general ledger. The total and balance should be the same.

# RECYCLING PROBLEM 19-1

**Journalizing and posting sales transactions**

The general ledger and accounts receivable accounts for Kellogg Supply are given in the *Recycling Problem Working Papers*. The balances are recorded as of March 1 of the current year. Use the following account titles.

**PARTIAL GENERAL LEDGER**

| Account No. | Account Title |
|---|---|
| 1105 | Cash |
| 1125 | Accounts Receivable |
| 1130 | Time Drafts Receivable |
| 2140 | Sales Tax Payable |
| 4105 | Sales |
| 4110 | Sales Discount |
| 4115 | Sales Returns and Allowances |

**ACCOUNTS RECEIVABLE LEDGER**

| Customer No. | Customer Name |
|---|---|
| 110 | Sandy Acker |
| 120 | Clark, Inc. |
| 130 | Clayton Company |
| 140 | John Maxwell |
| 150 | Emily Parsons |
| 160 | Reston Company |
| 170 | Sawyer Supply |
| 180 | Valley High School |
| 190 | Walsh Associates |

***Instructions:***

1. Journalize the following transactions affecting sales and cash receipts completed during March of the current year. Use page 3 of a sales journal, a general journal, and a cash receipts journal. Kellogg Supply offers terms of 2/10, n/30. The sales tax rate is 8%. Source documents are abbreviated as follows: credit memorandum, CM; memorandum, M; receipt, R; sales invoice, S; cash register tape, T; time draft, TD.

***Transactions:***

Mar. 1. Sold merchandise on account to Sandy Acker, $725.00, plus sales tax. S63.

2. Granted credit to John Maxwell for merchandise returned, $60.00, plus sales tax. CM21.

3. Received a 30-day time draft from Alicia Alcon for international sale of merchandise, $4,300.00. TD10.

4. Received cash on account from Clayton Company, $444.53, covering S59 for $453.60 ($420.00 plus sales tax, $33.60), less discount and sales tax. R47.

5. Received cash on account from Reston Company, $555.66, covering S60 for $567.00 ($525.00 plus sales tax, $42.00), less discount and less sales tax. R48.

5. Recorded cash and credit card sales, $2,735.00, plus sales tax, $218.80; total, $2,953.80. T5.

7. Sold merchandise on account to Sawyer Supply, $840.00, plus sales tax. S64.

9. Recorded international cash sale, $6,500.00. M12.

12. Received cash on account from Sandy Acker, $783.00, covering S63; no discount. R49.

12. Granted credit to Emily Parsons for damaged merchandise, $128.00, plus sales tax, from S61. CM22.

12. Recorded cash and credit card sales, $2,534.00, plus sales tax, $202.72; total, $2,736.72. T12.

14. Received cash for the value of Time Draft No. 7, $8,500.00. R50.

15. Discovered that a sale on account to Clayton Company on February 16, S52, was incorrectly charged to the account of Clark, Inc., $352.00. M9.

**Posting.** Post the items that are to be posted individually. Post from the journals in this order: sales journal, general journal, and cash receipts journal.

16. Sold merchandise on account to Clark, Inc., $243.75, plus sales tax. S65.

18. Received cash on account from Sawyer Supply, $907.20, covering S64; no discount. R51.

19. Recorded cash and credit card sales, $2,184.00, plus sales tax, $174.72; total, $2,358.72. T19.

22. Granted credit to Walsh Associates for damaged merchandise, $26.00, plus sales tax, from S59. CM23.

23. Received cash for the value of Time Draft No. 8, $8,000.00. R52.

24. Sold merchandise on account to Valley High School, $645.50, no sales tax. S66.

25. Granted credit to Clark, Inc., for merchandise returned, $25.50, plus sales tax. CM24.

26. Recorded cash and credit card sales, $2,526.00, plus sales tax, $202.08; total, $2,728.08. T26.

30. Received cash on account from Emily Parsons, $125.00, covering the unpaid portion of S61; no discount. R53.

31. Received a 30-day time draft from Fernando Cortez for international sale of merchandise, $6,000.00. TD11.

**Posting.** Post the items that are to be posted individually.

*(continued on next page)*

2. Prove the sales journal.
3. Post the totals of the special columns of the sales journal.
4. Prove and rule the cash receipts journal.
5. Post the totals of the special columns of the cash receipts journal.
6. Prepare a schedule of accounts receivable as of March 31 of the current year. Compare the schedule total with the balance of the accounts receivable account in the general ledger. The total and balance should be the same.

## RECYCLING PROBLEM 20-1

**Recording entries for uncollectible accounts**

The accounts receivable and general ledger accounts for Fincher Industries are given in the *Recycling Problem Working Papers*. The following transactions relating to uncollectible accounts receivable occurred during the final quarter of the current fiscal year.

***Instructions:***

1. Journalize the transactions completed during October using page 10 of a general journal. Post the transactions to the customer accounts and general ledger accounts.

***Transactions:***

Oct. 6. Wrote off Chittenden Corporation's past-due account as uncollectible, $284.75. M216.
19. Wrote off Foster Corporation's past-due account as uncollectible, $574.10. M221.

2. Journalize the transactions completed during November using page 11 of a general journal and page 11 of a cash receipts journal. Prove the cash receipts journal. Post the transactions to the customer accounts and general ledger accounts.

***Transactions:***

Nov. 5. Wrote off Agnew Company's past-due account as uncollectible, $804.24. M236.
12. Received cash in full payment of Chittenden Corporation's account, previously written off as uncollectible, $284.75. M241 and R616.
17. Received cash in full payment of Dionne, Inc.'s account, previously written off as uncollectible, $468.30. M243 and R627.

3. Journalize the transactions for December. Use page 12 of a general journal and page 12 of a cash receipts journal. Prove the cash receipts journal. Post the transactions to the customer accounts and general ledger accounts.

***Transactions:***

Dec. 4. Wrote off Grant Company's past-due account as uncollectible, $705.18. M257.
10. Received cash in full payment of Agnew Company's account, previously written off as uncollectible, $804.24. M259 and R702.
21. Received cash in full payment of Foster Corporation's account, previously written off as uncollectible, $574.10. M265 and R729.

4. Journalize the December 31 adjusting entry for estimated uncollectible accounts expense for the year. Use page 13 of the general journal. Uncollectible accounts expense is estimated as 1.2% of total sales on account. Total sales on account for the year were $987,660.00. Post the transaction to the general ledger accounts.

# RECYCLING PROBLEM 21-1

**Recording transactions for plant assets**

Diamond Clothing records plant assets in two accounts: Store Equipment, Account No. 1215, and Office Equipment, Account No. 1205. Store equipment is depreciated using the straight-line method. Office equipment is depreciated using the double declining-balance method. Journals and plant asset records are given in the *Recycling Problem Working Papers*.

***Instructions:***

1. Record the following transactions completed during 20X1 on page 1 of a cash payments journal.

***Transactions:***

Jan. 3. Purchased a color printer: cost, $900.00; estimated salvage value, $100.00; estimated useful life, 4 years; plant asset No. 642; serial number, ZE532N34. C168.

Feb. 26. Paid property tax on plant assets assessed at $620,000.00. The tax rate is 1.4%. C216.

Apr. 3. Purchased a store display: cost, $3,000.00; estimated salvage value, $500.00; estimated useful life, 5 years; plant asset No. 643; serial number, 754NFE. C275.

2. Complete Section 1 of a plant asset record for each new plant asset.
3. Prepare a depreciation table for each new plant asset.
4. Complete Section 3 of the plant asset record for 20X1-20X4.
5. Record the following transactions completed during 20X5. Use page 2 of a cash receipts journal and page 2 of a general journal.

***Transactions:***

Jan. 3. Received cash for sale of a color printer, plant asset No. 642, $60.00. R7.

June 29. Received cash for sale of a store display, plant asset No. 643, $950.00. M69 and R171.

Dec. 31. Recorded the adjusting entry for depreciation expense—store equipment. Total 20X5 depreciation expense of store equipment was $17,765.00.

6. Complete the plant asset records for each plant asset sold during 20X5.

## RECYCLING PROBLEM 22-1

**Determining the cost of inventory using the fifo, lifo, and weighted-average inventory costing methods**

Stevens Company made the following purchases of a part during the fiscal year. There are 32 units in ending inventory. Forms for costing inventory are given in the *Recycling Problem Working Papers*.

| Purchase Date | Quantity | Unit Price |
|---|---|---|
| January 1, beginning inventory | 3 | $12.30 |
| January 3, purchases | 20 | 13.00 |
| March 29, purchases | 20 | 13.20 |
| August 15, purchases | 15 | 13.25 |
| November 13, purchases | 15 | 13.45 |

**Instructions:**

1. Calculate the cost of ending inventory using the fifo, lifo, and weighted-average methods.
2. Which of the inventory costing methods resulted in the highest cost of merchandise sold?

# RECYCLING PROBLEM 23-1

**Journalizing notes payable and notes receivable transactions**

The following transactions related to notes payable and notes receivable were completed by Miles Company during April of the current year. Journals are provided in the *Recycling Problem Working Papers.*

***Transactions:***

Apr. 5. Signed a 90-day, 10% note for $30,000.00 with First National Bank. R34.

9. Accepted a 90-day, 15% note from Phillip Majure for an extension of time on his account, $650.00. NR18.

12. Received cash for the maturity value of a 60-day, 18% note for $900.00. R67.

16. Accepted a 60-day, 14% note from Avery Harris for an extension of time on her account, $2,450.00. NR19.

19. Received cash for the maturity value of a 60-day, 18% note for $500.00. R74.

20. Signed a 90-day, 15% note with Rossman Supply for an extension of time on this account payable, $2,500.00. M49.

22. Patrick Isamen dishonored his 90-day, 15% note, for $3,000.00. M53.

27. Signed a 120-day, 12% note, for $20,000.00 with First Commerce Bank. R84.

29. Received cash for the maturity value of a 90-day, 18% note for $1,800.00. R89.

***Instructions:***

1. Journalize each transaction using page 3 of a general journal and page 6 of a cash receipts journal. Source documents are abbreviated as follows: check, C; receipt, R; memorandum, M; note receivable, NR.
2. Determine the maturity date and maturity value of each note signed by Miles Company.
3. Journalize the following transactions on page 10 of a cash payments journal. Use the maturity dates and maturity values calculated in the previous step.

***Transactions:***

Paid cash for the maturity value of the $30,000.00 note dated April 5. C452.
Paid cash for the maturity value of the $2,500.00 note dated April 20. C489.
Paid cash for the maturity value of the $20,000.00 note dated April 27. C672.

# RECYCLING PROBLEM 24-1

**Journalizing and posting entries for accrued interest revenue and expense**

The accounting forms for Rucker Company are given in the *Recycling Problem Working Papers*. The balances are recorded as of December 31 of the current year before adjusting entries.

Rucker Company completed the following transactions related to notes receivable and notes payable during the current year and the following year. The first two transactions have already been journalized and posted. One note receivable and one note payable are the only notes on hand at the end of the fiscal period. Source documents are abbreviated as follows: receipt, R; check, C; note receivable, NR.

***Transactions:***

**20X1**

Nov. 9. Accepted a 90-day, 18% note from Kayla Nelson for an extension of time on her account, $800.00. NR18.

Dec. 14. Signed a 120-day, 12% note, $4,800.00 with First National Bank. R364.

**20X2**

Feb. 7. Received cash for the maturity value of NR18. R132.

Apr. 13. Paid cash for the maturity value of the First National Bank note. C342.

***Instructions:***

1. Plan the adjustments on a work sheet.
2. Journalize and post the adjusting entries for accrued interest income and accrued interest expense on December 31. Use page 15 of a general journal.
3. Journalize and post the closing entries for interest income and interest expense. Continue to use page 15 of a general journal.
4. Journalize and post the reversing entries for accrued interest income and accrued interest expense. Use page 16 of a general journal.
5. Journalize the receipt of cash for the maturity value of NR18. Use page 13 of a cash receipts journal. Post the amounts in the General columns of the cash receipts journal.
6. Journalize the cash payment for the maturity value of the note payable. Use page 18 of a cash payments journal. Post the amounts in the General columns of the cash payments journal.

# RECYCLING PROBLEM 25-1

**Journalizing dividends and preparing a work sheet for a corporation**

Accounting forms are given in the *Recycling Problem Working Papers*. Dugan Corporation completed the following transactions during December of the current year and January of the next year.

***Transactions:***

Dec. 15. The board of directors declared a dividend of $0.20 per share; capital stock issued is 80,000 shares. M232.

Jan. 15. Paid cash for dividend declared December 15. C798.

***Instructions:***

1. Use page 12 of a general journal. Journalize the dividend declared on December 15.
2. Use page 18 of a cash payments journal. Journalize payment of the dividend on January 15.
3. Prepare Dugan Corporation's work sheet for the current year ended December 31. Record the adjustments on the work sheet using the following information. Do not total the Adjustments columns.

**Adjustment Information, December 31**

| | |
|---|---|
| Accrued interest income | $ 52.50 |
| Uncollectible accounts expense estimated as 1.0% of sales on account. Sales on account for year, $978,000.00. | |
| Merchandise inventory | 209,326.60 |
| Supplies inventory | 413.50 |
| Value of prepaid insurance | 3,200.00 |
| Annual depreciation expense—office equipment | 5,335.00 |
| Annual depreciation expense—store equipment | 4,210.00 |
| Accrued interest expense | 400.00 |

4. Extend all amounts except Federal Income Tax Expense to the appropriate Income Statement and Balance Sheet columns. Do not total the columns.
5. On the form provided in the *Recycling Problem Working Papers*, total the work sheet's Income Statement columns. Calculate the difference between the debit and credit totals. This difference becomes the net income before federal income tax expense.
6. Using the tax table on page 647, calculate the federal income tax expense and record the income tax adjustment on the work sheet. Complete the work sheet.

# RECYCLING PROBLEM 26-1

**Preparing financial statements and end-of-fiscal-period entries for a corporation**

Use the work sheet provided in the *Recycling Problem Working Papers* for Dugan Corporation to prepare the financial statements and end-of-fiscal-period entries for the corporation for the current year.

**Instructions:**

1. Prepare an income statement. Calculate and record the following component percentages. (a) cost of merchandise sold; (b) gross profit on operations; (c) total operating expenses; (d) income from operations; (e) net addition or deduction resulting from other revenue and expenses; and (f) net income before federal income tax. Round percentage calculations to the nearest 0.1%.
2. Analyze the corporation's income statement by determining if component percentages are within acceptable levels. If any component percentage is not within an acceptable level, suggest steps that the company should take. The corporation considers the following component percentages acceptable.

| | |
|---|---|
| Cost of merchandise sold | Not more than 64.0% |
| Gross profit on operations | Not less than 36.0% |
| Total operating expenses | Not more than 20.0% |
| Income from operations | Not less than 16.0% |
| Net deduction from other revenue and expenses | Not more than 1.0% |
| Net income before federal income tax | Not less than 15.0% |

3. Prepare a statement of stockholders' equity. Use the following additional information.

| | |
|---|---|
| January 1 balance of capital stock account . . . . . . . . . . | $80,000.00 |
| (80,000 shares issued for $1.00 per share) | |
| Shares issued during the year . . . . . . . . . . . . . . . . . . . | None |

4. Prepare a balance sheet.
5. Calculate the corporation's (a) working capital and (b) current ratio. Determine if these items are within acceptable levels. The corporation considers the following levels acceptable.

| | |
|---|---|
| Working capital . . . . . . . . . . . . . . . . . . . . . . . . . . . . . . | Not less than $200,000.00 |
| Current ratio . . . . . . . . . . . . . . . . . . . . . . . . . . . . . . . | Between 3.0 to 1 and 4.0 to 1 |

6. Journalize the adjusting entries using page 15 of a general journal.
7. Journalize the closing entries using page 16 of a general journal.
8. Journalize the reversing entries using page 17 of a general journal.

# ANSWERS TO AUDIT YOUR UNDERSTANDING

## Chapter 1, Page 8

**1.** Planning, recording, analyzing, and interpreting financial information.

**2.** Answers will vary but should involve businesses that perform activities for a fee.

**3.** A business owned by one person.

**4.** Assets = Liabilities + Owner's Equity.

## Chapter 1, Page 12

**1.** The right side must be increased.

**2.** If one account is increased, another account on the same side of the equation must be decreased by the same amount.

**3.** Buying items and paying for them at a future date.

## Chapter 1, Page 15

**1.** Assets, liabilities, and owner's equity.

**2.** Assets.

**3.** Liabilities and owner's equity.

**4.** Find the errors before completing any more work.

## Chapter 2, Page 29

**1.** Increased.

**2.** Increased

**3.** Decreased.

## Chapter 2, Page 31

**1.** The name of the business, the name of the report, and the date of the report.

**2.** Assets.

**3.** Liabilities and owner's equity.

## Chapter 3, Page 44

**1.** Assets 5 Liabilities 1 Owner's Equity

**2.** (1) Account balances increase on the normal balance side of an account. (2) Account balances decrease on the side opposite the normal balance side of an account.

## Chapter 3, Page 50

**1.** (1) Which accounts are affected?
(2) How is each account classified?
(3) How is each classification changed?
(4) How is each amount entered in the accounts?

**2.** Supplies and Cash.

## Chapter 3, Page 56

**1.** Cash and Sales.

**2.** Accounts Receivable and Sales.

**3.** Owner's drawing account and Cash.

**4.** Credit.

**5.** Debit.

## Chapter 4, Page 71

**1.** By date.

**2.** Source documents are one way to verify the accuracy of a specific journal entry.

**3.** Date, debit, credit, and source document.

## Chapter 4, Page 75

**1.** General Debit and Cash Credit.

**2.** General Debit and General Credit.

**3.** General Debit and Cash Credit.

## Chapter 4, Page 81

**1.** Cash Debit and Sales Credit.

**2.** General Debit and Sales Credit.

**3.** General Debit and Cash Credit.

**4.** Cash Debit and General Credit.

**5.** General Debit and Cash Credit.

## Chapter 4, Page 87

**1.** (1) Add each of the amount columns. (2) Add the debit column totals, and then add the credit column totals. (3) Verify that the total debits and total credits are equal.

**2.** Cash on hand at the beginning of the month, plus total cash received, less total cash paid.

**3.** (1) Rule a single line across all amount columns directly below the last entry to indicate that the columns are to be added. (2) On the next line, write the date in the Date column. (3) Write the word *Totals* in the Account Title column. (4) Write each column total below the single line. (5) Rule double lines below the column totals across all amount columns. The double lines mean that the totals have been verified as correct.

## Chapter 5, Page 102

**1.** The first digit indicates in which general ledger division the account is located. The second and third digits indicate the location of the account within that division.

**2.** (1) Write the account title in the heading. (2) Write the account number in the heading.

## Chapter 5, Page 106

**1.** (1) Write the date in the Date column of the account. (2) Write the journal page number in the Post. Ref. column of the account. (3) Write the amount in the Debit or Credit column. (4) Calculate and write the new account balance in the Balance Debit or Balance Credit column. (5) Write the account number in the Post. Ref. column of the journal.

**2.** No. Each separate amount in the General Debit and General Credit columns of a journal is posted to the account written in the Account Title column.

## Chapter 5, Page 111

**1.** Special amount columns.

**2.** Whenever the debits in an account exceed the credits.

**3.** Whenever the credits in an account exceed the debits.

## Chapter 5, Page 117

**1.** A journal entry made to correct an error in the ledger.

**2.** When a transaction has been improperly journalized and posted to the ledger.

**3.** To show the increase in this expense account.

**4.** To show the decrease in this expense account.

## Chapter 6, Page 130

**1.** Blank endorsement, special endorsement, and restrictive endorsement.

**2.** (1) Write the amount of the check after the dollar sign at the top of the stub. (2) Write the date of the check on the Date line. (3) Write to whom the check is to be paid on the To line. (4) Record the purpose of the check on the For line. (5) Write the amount of the check after the words *Amt. This Check*. (6) Calculate the new checking balance and record it in the amount column on the last line of the stub.

**3.** (1) Write the date. (2) Write to whom the check is to be paid following the words

*Pay to the order of*. (3) Write the amount in figures following the dollar sign. (4) Write the amount in words on the line with the word *Dollars*. (5) Write the purpose of the check on the line labeled For. (6) Sign the check.

### Chapter 6, Page 135

**1.** (1) A service charge may not have been recorded in the depositor's business records. (2) Outstanding deposits may be recorded in the depositor's records but not on a bank statement. (3) Outstanding checks may be recorded in the depositor's records but not on a bank statement. (4) A depositor may have made a math or recording error.

**2.** An outstanding check.

### Chapter 6, Page 140

**1.** (1) The check appears to be altered. (2) The signature on the check does not match the signature on the signature card. (3) The amounts written in figures and in words do not agree. (4) The check is postdated. (5) The person who wrote the check has stopped payment on it. (6) The account of the person who wrote the check has insufficient funds to pay the check.

**2.** Cash.

**3.** Cash.

### Chapter 6, Page 144

**1.** For making small cash payments.

**2.** The check issued to replenish petty cash is a credit to Cash and does not affect Petty Cash.

### Chapter 7, Page 158

**1.** Name of the business, name of report, and date of report.

**2.** All general ledger accounts are listed in the Trial Balance columns of a work sheet, even if some accounts do not have balances.

### Chapter 7, Page 164

**1.** An expense should be reported in the same fiscal period that it is used to produce revenue.

**2.** (1) What is the balance of the account? (2) What should the balance be for this account? (3) What must be done to correct the account balance? (4) What adjustment is made?

### Chapter 7, Page 169

**1.** Asset, liability, and owner's equity accounts.

**2.** Revenue and expense accounts.

**3.** Income Statement Debit and Balance Sheet Credit columns.

**4.** Income Statement Credit and Balance Sheet Debit columns.

### Chapter 7, Page 173

**1.** Subtract the smaller total from the larger total to find the difference.

**2.** The difference between two column totals can be divided evenly by 9.

**3.** A slide.

### Chapter 8, Page 186

**1.** Heading, revenue, expenses, and net income or net loss.

**2.** Total Expenses *divided by* Total Sales *equals* Total Expenses Component Percentage.

**3.** Net Income *divided by* Total Sales *equals* Net Income Component Percentage.

### Chapter 8, Page 191

**1.** Heading, assets, liabilities, and owner's equity.

**2.** Capital Account Balance *plus* Net Income

*minus* Drawing Account Balance *equals* Current Capital.

### Chapter 9, Page 202

1. To update general ledger accounts.
2. Adjustments column of the work sheet.
3. Supplies Expense and Insurance Expense.

### Chapter 9, Page 209

1. Beginning balances.
2. Changes in the owner's capital for a single fiscal period.
3. (1) An entry to close income statement accounts with credit balances. (2) An entry to close income statement accounts with debit balances. (3) An entry to record net income or net loss and close the income summary account. (4) An entry to close the owner's drawing account.

### Chapter 9, Page 215

1. To assure a reader that a balance has not been omitted.
2. Only those with balances (permanent accounts).
3. Because they are closed and have zero balances.

### Chapter 10, Page 232

1. Businesses often require the skills or capital of more than one person.
2. The selling of merchandise rather than a service.
3. Columns for the recording of frequently occurring transactions related to the purchasing and selling of merchandise.

### Chapter 10, Page 237

1. Purchases Debit column and Accounts Payable Credit column.
2. Supplies—Store and the vendor name.

### Chapter 10, Page 243

1. Accounts Payable Debit column and Cash Credit column.
2. Advertising Expense.
3. For making change at the cash register and for making small cash payments.
4. The partner's drawing account.
5. General Debit column and General Credit column.

### Chapter 11, Page 259

1. A merchandising business sells merchandise; a service business sells services.
2. As a percentage of sales.
3. The amount of sales tax collected is a business liability until paid to the government.
4. *Realization of Revenue.*
5. Accounts Receivable.

### Chapter 11, Page 266

1. To show the equality of debits and credits.
2. Whenever a journal page is filled and always at the end of a month.
3. To show that the totals have been verified as correct.
4. Cash on hand at the beginning of the month, *plus* total cash received during the month, *less* total cash paid during the month, *equals* cash balance on hand at the end of the month. Cash is proved if the balance on the next unused check stub is the same as the cash proof.

### Chapter 12, Page 279

1. An account in a general ledger that summarizes all accounts in a subsidiary ledger.
2. The balance of a controlling account

equals the total of all account balances in its related subsidiary ledger.

3. Debit, Credit, Balance Debit, and Balance Credit.

4. (1) A check mark is placed in parentheses below the General Debit and General Credit column totals to indicate that the two column totals are not posted. (2) The general ledger account number of the account listed in the column heading is written in parentheses below the special amount column totals to show that the totals are posted.

### Chapter 12, Page 285

1. Credit balance. Because accounts payable are liabilities and liabilities have normal credit balances.

2. By writing the vendor name and vendor number on the heading of the ledger account.

3. (1) Write the date in the Date column of the account. (2) Write the journal page number in the Post. Ref. column of the account. (3) Write the credit amount in the Credit column of the account. (4) Add the amount in the Credit column to the previous balance in the Credit Balance column. Write the new account balance in the Credit Balance column. (5) Write the vendor number in the Post. Ref. column of the journal. The vendor number shows that the posting for this entry is complete.

### Chapter 12, Page 291

1. Accounts receivable are assets, and assets have normal debit balances.

2. (1) Write the date in the Date column of the account. (2) Write the journal page number in the Post. Ref. column of the account. (3) Write the debit amount in the Debit column of the account. (4) Add the amount in the Debit column to the previous balance in the Debit Balance column. Write the new account balance in the Debit Balance column. (5) Write the vendor number in the Post. Ref. column of the journal. The vendor number shows that the posting for this entry is complete.

### Chapter 12, Page 294

1. Posting must be accurate to assure correct account balances.

2. A controlling account balance in a general ledger must equal the sum of all account balances in a subsidiary ledger.

3. Vendor accounts.

4. The accounts receivable ledger is proved.

### Chapter 13, Page 307

1. The total amount earned by all employees for a pay period.

2. $3\frac{1}{2}$ hours.

3. Overtime earnings × the overtime rate.

4. $440.00.

### Chapter 13, Page 313

1. Form W-4, Employee's Withholding Allowance Certificate.

2. Employee marital status and number of withholding allowances.

3. Both the employee and the employer.

### Chapter 13, Page 318

1. The payroll register summarizes the payroll for one pay period and shows total earnings, payroll withholdings, and net pay of all employees.

2. By subtracting total deductions from total earnings.

3. Because a business must send a quarterly report to federal and state governments showing employee taxable earnings and taxes withheld from employee earnings.

## Chapter 13, Page 321

1. To help protect and control payroll payments.
2. The payroll register.
3. Individual checks are not written and do not have to be distributed.

## Chapter 14, Page 335

1. Salary Expense.
2. Employee Income Tax Payable.
3. Social Security Tax Payable.
4. Medicare Tax Payable.

## Chapter 14, Page 340

1. Social security: 6.5% of earnings up to a maximum of $65,400.00 in each calendar year; Medicare: 1.5% of total employee earnings; federal unemployment: 0.8% of the first $7,000.00 earned by each employee; state unemployment: 5.4% on the first $7,000.00 earned by each employee.
2. The first $7,000.00.

## Chapter 14, Page 345

1. By January 31.
2. Federal income tax, social security tax, and Medicare tax.

## Chapter 14, Page 351

1. By the 15th day of the following month.
2. For paying payroll taxes and for paying federal unemployment tax.

## Chapter 15, Page 371

1. In the same order they appear in the general ledger.
2. Merchandise Inventory and Income Summary.

## Chapter 15, Page 377

1. Supplies—Office and Supplies Expense—Office.
2. Prepaid Insurance and Insurance Expense.

## Chapter 15, Page 384

1. Income Statement Debit or Credit column.
2. When the Income Statement Debit column total (costs and expenses) is larger than the Credit column total (revenue).
3. Balance Sheet Debit.
4. Trial balance amounts after adjustments are extended to the Adjusted Trial Balance columns, and the Adjusted Trial Balance columns are proved before extending amounts to the Income Statement and Balance Sheet columns.

## Chapter 16, Page 396

1. The cost of merchandise sold section.
2. Beginning merchandise inventory, *plus* purchases, *equals* total cost of merchandise available for sale, *less* ending merchandise inventory, *equals* cost of merchandise sold.
3. By comparing it with the amount calculated on the work sheet.

## Chapter 16, Page 401

1. (1) Cost of merchandise sold, (2) gross profit on sales, (3) total expenses, and (4) net income.
2. By making comparisons with prior fiscal periods as well as with industry standards that are published by industry organizations.
3. Net loss.

## Chapter 16, Page 407

1. Each partner's share of net income or loss.
2. (1) Beginning capital, (2) additional investments, and (3) each partner's withdrawal of assets.

3. The January 1 capital, *plus* the net increase in capital, *equals* the December 31 capital.

### Chapter 16, Page 412

1. A business's financial condition on a specific date.
2. In account form or report form.
3. The Balance Sheet columns of a work sheet and the owner's equity statement.
4. A schedule of accounts payable and a schedule of accounts receivable.

### Chapter 17, Page 425

1. Insurance Expense and Income Summary.
2. Because the explanation "Adjusting Entries" is recorded in the Account Title column to explain all of the adjusting entries that follow.
3. Adjusting entry for merchandising inventory.

### Chapter 17, Page 430

1. Income Statement and Balance Sheet columns of the work sheet and the distribution of net income statement.
2. Income Summary.

### Chapter 17, Page 434

1. The distribution of net income statement and the Balance Sheet columns of the work sheet.
2. An amount equal to its balance is recorded on the side opposite the balance.

### Chapter 17, Page 439

1. General ledger accounts with balances.
2. To prove the equality of debits and credits in the general ledger.
3. In the same order as they appear in the general ledger.

### Chapter 18, Page 459

1. A corporation can own property, incur liabilities, enter into contracts in its own name, and sell ownership in itself.
2. A corporation has separate capital accounts for the stock issued and for the earnings kept in the business.
3. The debit to Purchases increases the total of purchases during the year. The credit to Accounts Payable increases the current balance of this liability.

### Chapter 18, Page 464

1. To encourage early payment.
2. Two ten means 2% of the invoice amount may be deducted if the invoice is paid within 10 days of the invoice date. Net thirty means that the total invoice amount must be paid within 30 days.
3. Accounts Payable is debited, Purchases Discount is credited, and Cash is credited.

### Chapter 18, Page 469

1. The cash short and over account is closed to Income Summary.
2. Each amount in the General columns is posted individually to the general ledger account named in the Account Title Column.

### Chapter 18, Page 475

1. A business can track the amount of purchases returns and allowances in a fiscal period if a separate account is used.
2. The transaction can be recorded immediately without waiting for written confirmation from the vendor.
3. Supplies are not merchandise; only merchandise purchased on account is recorded in the purchases journal.

### Chapter 19, Page 492

1. The state government.

2. So that each customer account will show an up-to-date balance.

### Chapter 19, Page 498

1. To encourage early payment.

2. Cash, Sales Discount, and Sales Tax Payable are debited; Accounts Receivable is credited.

### Chapter 19, Page 503

1. Sales Returns and Allowances and Sales Tax Payable are debited; Accounts Receivable is credited.

2. Sales journal, purchases journal, general journal, cash receipts journal, and cash payments journal.

### Chapter 19, Page 509

1. (1) Settlement of disputes is more difficult; (2) transactions take more time to complete; (3) the risk of uncollected amounts is increased; (4) unstable political conditions may affect the ability to receive payments.

2. (1) A receipt signed by the authorized agent of a transportation company for merchandise received and (2) a contract for the delivery of the merchandise.

3. A sight draft is payable on sight when the holder presents it for payment. A time draft is payable at a fixed or determinable future time after it is accepted.

4. To assure receipt of payment for sales.

5. A draft is generally paid by a bank and a trade acceptance by the buyer.

### Chapter 20, Page 530

1. The loss is considered a regular expense of doing business. Revenue was earned when the sale was made. Failing to collect an account does not cancel the sale.

2. At the end of a fiscal period.

3. (1) Reports a balance sheet amount for Accounts Receivable that reflects the amount the business expects to collect in the future. (2) Recognizes the expense of uncollectible accounts in the same period in which the related revenue is recorded.

4. It reduces its related asset account, Accounts Receivable.

5. The difference between the balance of Accounts Receivable and its contra account, Allowance for Uncollectible Accounts.

### Chapter 20, Page 536

1. The balance of the customer account is an *actual* uncollectible amount and no longer an *estimate* of an uncollectible amount.

2. The book value is the same because the same amount is deducted from the accounts receivable and the allowance accounts.

3. To show an accurate credit history.

### Chapter 21, Page 548

1. Current assets and plant assets.

2. Office Equipment is debited; Cash is credited.

3. Land and anything attached to the land.

4. Tax authorities referred to as assessors.

### Chapter 21, Page 552

1. *Matching Expenses with Revenue.*

2. Original cost; estimated salvage value; estimated useful life.

3. Because of land's permanent nature. Land can be used indefinitely.

### Chapter 21, Page 556

1. Plant asset record.

2. The balance of the asset account is not changed by an adjusting entry for depreciation expense.

### Chapter 21, Page 561

1. Disposal date, disposal method, and disposal amount.
2. Partial year's depreciation.
3. Cash received less the book value of the asset sold.
4. Other Expenses.

### Chapter 21, Page 565

1. Depreciation rate.
2. Double declining-balance method.
3. It declines.
4. Its estimated salvage value.

### Chapter 22, Page 577

1. Successful business must have merchandise available for sale that customers want. A business needs controls that assist managers in maintaining a merchandise inventory of sufficient quantity, variety, and price.
2. (1) Excess inventory requires that a business spend money for expensive store and warehouse space. (2) Excess inventory uses capital that could be invested in other assets to earn a profit for the business. (3) Excess inventory requires that a business spend money for expenses, such as taxes and insurance premiums, that increase with the cost of the merchandise inventory. (4) Excess inventory may become obsolete and unsalable.
3. At the end of a fiscal period.
4. A business frequently establishes its fiscal period to end when inventory normally is at a minimum because it takes less time to count a smaller inventory.
5. A customary practice is to take a periodic inventory at least once a fiscal period. The periodic inventory is then compared with the perpetual inventory records.

### Chapter 22, Page 582

1. The most recent invoices for purchases are used in recording prices for each item on the inventory record.
2. The most recent costs of merchandise should be charged against current revenue.
3. Lifo.
4. Using the same inventory costing method for all fiscal periods provides financial statements that can be compared with other fiscal period statements. If a business changes inventory cost methods, part of the difference in gross profit and net income may be caused by the change in methods.

### Chapter 22, Page 585

1. By using the gross profit method of estimating inventory.
2. Actual net sales and net purchases amounts; the beginning inventory amount; and the gross profit percentage.
3. The beginning inventory for the month is the same as the ending inventory from the previous month.

### Chapter 23, Page 597

1. Sometimes a business receives more cash from sales than is needed to pay for purchases and expenses. When this occurs, a business may deposit the extra cash in a bank or other financial institution for a short period. At other times, the receipt of cash from sales does not occur at the same time and in sufficient amounts to pay for needed purchases and expenses. When this occurs, a business needs to borrow additional cash or make arrangements with its vendors to delay payment for a period of time.
2. A note can be useful in a court of law as written evidence of a debt.

3. Ten cents will be paid for the use of each dollar borrowed for a full year.

4. Multiply the principal times the interest rate times the time stated as a fraction of a year.

### Chapter 23, Page 602

1. Because notes payable generally are paid within one year.

2. Accounts Payable and the vendor are debited. Notes Payable is credited.

### Chapter 23, Page 606

1. A note receivable does not pay the amount the customer owes. Therefore, the amount of the asset does not change at the time the note is signed. The form of the asset does change from an account receivable to a note receivable. However, the asset will remain classified as a current asset.

2. Other Revenue.

3. Accounts Receivable and the customer account are each debited for the principal of the note and the interest. Notes Receivable is credited for the principal of the note. Interest Income is credited for the interest.

4. Because the interest has been earned.

### Chapter 24, Page 620

1. *Realization of Revenue.*

2. To avoid the inconvenience of determining how much, if any, of each cash receipt is for interest income earned and accrued during the previous year and how much is earned in the current year.

### Chapter 24, Page 626

1. So that the income statement will report all expenses for the period even though some of the expenses have not yet been paid. Also, so that the balance sheet will report all liabilities, including the accrued expenses payable.

2. Interest Payable is debited; Interest Expense is credited.

### Chapter 25, Page 639

1. (1) Different accounts are used to record owners' equity. (2) Different procedures are used to distribute income to owners. (3) Corporations calculate and pay federal income tax.

2. One capital stock account.

3. Retained Earnings.

4. When a corporation's board of directors declares a dividend, the liability for the dividend must be recorded in the accounts.

### Chapter 25, Page 645

1. If ending merchandise inventory is greater than beginning merchandise inventory.

2. If ending merchandise inventory is less than the beginning merchandise inventory.

### Chapter 25, Page 652

1. Any additional tax owed that was not paid in quarterly installments must be paid when the final return is sent.

2. Because you must first determine the net income before federal income tax expense.

### Chapter 26, Page 665

1. (1) Owners' equity for all owners is reported as a single amount rather than for each owner. (2) Owners' equity is reported in two categories: (a) capital contributed by the owners and (b) capital earned by the corporation.

2. Sales, cost of merchandise sold, and operating expenses are used to determine

income from operations. Other revenue and other expenses, such as interest income, interest expense, and gains or losses on plant assets, are not normal business activities. Therefore, they are not included in calculating income from operations and are reported separately.

3. Each component percentage shows the percentage that each item is of net sales.

### Chapter 26, Page 668

1. The changes in a corporation's ownership for a fiscal period.
2. Capital stock and retained earnings.
3. In the Capital Stock general ledger account.
4. In the Balance Sheet Credit column of a work sheet.
5. As a dividend.
6. In the Balance Sheet Debit column of a work sheet.

### Chapter 26, Page 674

1. Current and plant assets.
2. (1) The balance of the asset account, (2) the balance of the asset's contra account, and (3) book value.
3. Mortgage payable.
4. From the statement of stockholders' equity.
5. The amount of total current assets less total current liabilities.
6. The current ratio permits a business to compare itself to its industry or to provide a convenient relative measure from year to year.

### Chapter 26, Page 681

1. Federal income tax expense.
2. Closing entry for the dividends account.
3. Retained earnings.

## A

**Account** a record summarizing all the information pertaining to a single item in the accounting equation. (p. 9)

**Account balance** the amount in an account. (p. 9)

**Account number** the number assigned to an account. (p. 99)

**Account title** the name given to an account. (p. 9)

**Accounting** planning, recording, analyzing, and interpreting financial information. (p. 4)

**Accounting cycle** the series of accounting activities included in recording financial information for a fiscal period. (p. 214)

**Accounting equation** an equation showing the relationship among assets, liabilities, and owner's equity. (p. 7)

**Accounting period** see *fiscal period.*

**Accounting records** organized summaries of a business's financial activities. (p. 4)

**Accounting system** a planned process for providing financial information that will be useful to management. (p. 4)

**Accounts payable ledger** a subsidiary ledger containing only accounts for vendors from whom items are purchased or bought on account. (p. 274)

**Accounts receivable ledger** a subsidiary ledger containing only accounts for charge customers. (p. 274)

**Accrued expenses** expenses incurred in one fiscal period but not paid until a later fiscal period. (p. 621)

**Accrued interest expense** interest incurred but not yet paid. (p. 621)

**Accrued interest income** interest earned but not yet received. (p. 616)

**Accrued revenue** revenue earned in one fiscal period but not received until a later fiscal period. (p. 614)

**Accumulated depreciation** the total amount of depreciation expense that has been recorded since the purchase of a plant asset. (p. 551)

**Adjusting entries** journal entries recorded to update general ledger accounts at the end of a fiscal period. (p. 198)

**Adjustments** changes recorded on a work sheet to update general ledger accounts at the end of a fiscal period. (p. 160)

**Allowance method of recording losses from uncollectible accounts** crediting the estimated value of uncollectible accounts to a contra account. (p. 526)

**Assessed value** the value of an asset determined by tax authorities for the purpose of calculating taxes (p. 547)

**Asset** anything of value that is owned. (p. 7)

## B

**Bad debts** see *uncollectible accounts.*

**Balance sheet** a financial statement that reports assets, liabilities, and owner's equity on a specific date. (p. 13)

**Bank statement** a report of deposits, withdrawals, and bank balances sent to a depositor by a bank. (p. 131)

**Bill of exchange** see *draft.*

**Bill of lading** a receipt signed by the authorized agent of a transportation company for merchandise received that also serves as a contract for the delivery of the merchandise. (p. 505)

**Blank endorsement** an endorsement consisting only of the endorser's signature. (p. 127)

**Board of directors** a group of persons elected by the stockholders to manage a corporation. (p. 637)

**Book inventory** see *perpetual inventory.*

**Book value** the difference between an asset's account balance and its related contra account balance. (p. 526)

**Book value of a plant asset** the original cost of a plant asset minus accumulated depreciation. (p. 551)

**Book value of accounts receivable** the difference between the balance of Accounts Receivable and its contra account, Allowance for Uncollectible Accounts. (p. 526)

## C

**Capital** the account used to summarize the owner's equity in a business. (p. 9)

**Capital stock** total shares of ownership in a corporation. (p. 454)

**Cash discount** a deduction from the invoice amount, allowed by a vendor to encourage early payment. (p. 462)

**Cash over** a petty cash on hand amount that is more than a recorded amount. (p. 465)

**Cash payments journal** a special journal used to record only cash payment transactions. (p. 460)

**Cash receipts journal** a special journal used to record only cash receipt transactions. (p. 493)

**Cash sale** a sale in which cash is received for the total amount of the sale at the time of the transaction. (p. 254)

**Cash short** a petty cash on hand amount that is less than a recorded amount. (p. 465)

**Charge sale** see *sale on account.*

**Chart of accounts** a list of accounts used by a business. (p. 45)

**Check** a business form ordering a bank to pay cash from a bank account. (p. 67)

**Checking account** a bank account from which payments can be ordered by a depositor. (p. 126)

**Closing entries** journal entries used to prepare temporary accounts for a new fiscal period. (p. 203)

**Commercial invoice** a statement prepared by the seller of merchandise addressed to the buyer, showing a detailed listing and description of merchandise sold, including prices and terms. (p. 505)

**Component percentage** the percentage relationship between one financial statement item and the total that includes that item. (p. 184)

**Contra account** an account that reduces a related account on a financial statement. (p. 462)

**Contract of sale** a document that details all the terms agreed to by seller and buyer for a sales transaction. (p. 505)

**Controlling account** an account in a general ledger that summarizes all accounts in a subsidiary ledger. (p. 274)

**Corporation** an organization with the legal rights of a person and which may be owned by many persons. (p. 454)

**Correcting entry** a journal entry made to correct an error in the ledger. (p. 116)

**Cost of goods sold** see *cost of merchandise sold.*

**Cost of merchandise** the price a business pays for goods it purchases to sell. (p. 230)

**Cost of merchandise sold** the total original price of all merchandise sold during a fiscal period. (p. 392)

**Credit** an amount recorded on the right side of a T account. (p. 42)

**Credit card sale** a sale in which a credit card is used for the total amount of the sale at the time of the transaction. (p. 254)

**Credit memorandum** a form prepared by the vendor showing the amount deducted for returns and allowances. (p. 499)

**Creditor** a person or organization to whom a liability is owed. (p. 594)

**Current assets** cash and other assets expected to be exchanged for cash or consumed within a year. (p. 544)

**Current liabilities** liabilities due within a short time, usually within a year. (p. 598)

**Current ratio** a ratio that shows the numeric relationship of current assets to current liabilities. (p. 673)

**Customer** a person or business to whom merchandise or services are sold. (p. 252)

# D

**Date of a note** the day a note is signed. (p. 594)

**Debit** an amount recorded on the left side of a T account. (p. 42)

**Debit card** a bank card that, when making purchases, automatically deducts the amount of the purchase from the checking account of the cardholder. (p. 139)

**Debit memorandum** a form prepared by the customer showing the price deduction taken by the customer for returns and allowances. (p. 471)

**Declaring a dividend** action by a board of directors to distribute corporate earnings to stockholders. (p. 637)

**Declining-balance method of depreciation** multiplying the book value by a constant depreciation rate at the end of each fiscal period. (p. 562)

**Depreciation expense** the portion of a plant asset's cost that is transferred to an expense account in each fiscal period during a plant asset's useful life. (p. 549)

**Dishonored check** a check that a bank refuses to pay. (p. 136)

**Dishonored note** a note that is not paid when due. (p. 605)

**Distribution of net income statement** a partnership financial statement showing net income or loss distribution to partners. (p. 402)

**Dividends** earnings distributed to stockholders. (p. 636)

**Double-entry accounting** the recording of debit and credit parts of a transaction. (p. 66)

**Doubtful accounts** see *uncollectible accounts.*

**Draft** a written, signed, and dated order from one party ordering another party, usually a bank, to pay money to a third party. (p. 505)

# E

**Electronic funds transfer** a computerized cash payments system that uses electronic impulses to transfer funds. (p. 138)

**Employee earnings record** a business form used to record details affecting payments made to an employee. (p. 316)

**Endorsement** a signature or stamp on the back of a check transferring ownership. (p. 127)

**Endorsement in full** see *special endorsement.*

**Entry** information for each transaction recorded in a journal. (p. 66)

**Equities** financial rights to the assets of a business. (p. 7)

**Estimated salvage value** the amount an owner expects to receive when a plant asset is removed from use (p. 549)

**Exhibit** see *supporting schedule.*

**Expense** a decrease in owner's equity resulting from the operation of a business. (p. 27)

**Exports** goods or services shipped out of a seller's home country to a foreign country. (p. 504)

# F

**Face amount** see *principal of a note.*

**Federal unemployment tax** a federal tax used for state and federal administrative expenses of the unemployment program. (p. 338)

**Fifo** see *first-in, first-out inventory costing method.*

**File maintenance** the procedure for arranging accounts in a general ledger, assigning account numbers, and keeping records current. (p. 100)

**First-in, first-out inventory costing method** using the price of merchandise purchased first to calculate the cost of merchandise sold first. (p. 578)

**Fiscal period** the length of time for which a business summarizes and reports financial information. (p. 156)

Glossary

## G

**Gain on plant assets** revenue that results when a plant asset is sold for more than book value. (p. 559)

**General amount column** a journal amount column that is not headed with an account title. (p. 66)

**General journal** a journal with two amount columns in which all kinds of entries can be recorded. (p. 470)

**General ledger** a ledger that contains all accounts needed to prepare financial statements. (p. 99)

**Gross earnings** see *total earnings.*

**Gross pay** see *total earnings.*

**Gross profit method of estimating inventory** estimating inventory by using the previous year's percentage of gross profit on operations. (p. 583)

**Gross profit on sales** the revenue remaining after cost of merchandise sold has been deducted. (p. 394)

## I

**Imports** goods or services bought from a foreign country and brought into a buyer's home country. (p. 504)

**Income statement** a financial statement showing the revenue and expenses for a fiscal period. (p. 166)

**Interest** an amount paid for the use of money for a period of time. (p. 595)

**Interest expense** the interest accrued on money borrowed. (p. 599)

**Interest income** the interest earned on money loaned. (p. 604)

**Interest rate of a note** the percentage of the principal that is paid for use of the money. (p. 594)

**Inventory** the amount of goods on hand. (p. 368)

**Inventory record** a form used during a periodic inventory to record information about each item of merchandise on hand. (p. 575)

**Invoice** a form describing the goods or services sold, the quantity, and the price. (p. 67)

## J

**Journal** a form for recording transactions in chronological order. (p. 64)

**Journalizing** recording transactions in a journal. (p. 64)

## L

**Last-in, first-out inventory costing method** using the price of merchandise purchased last to calculate the cost of merchandise sold first. (p. 579)

**Ledger** a group of accounts. (p. 99)

**Letter of credit** a letter issued by a bank guaranteeing that a named individual or business will be paid a specified amount, provided stated conditions are met. (p. 505)

**Liability** an amount owed by a business (p. 7)

**Lifo** see *last-in, first-out inventory costing method.*

**List price** a business's printed or catalog price. (p. 461)

**Long-term liabilities** liabilities owed for more than a year. (p. 670)

**Loss on plant assets** the loss that results when a plant asset is sold for less than book value. (p. 560)

## M

**Maker of a note** the person or business who signs a note and thus promises to make payment. (p. 594)

**Markup** the amount added to the cost of merchandise to establish the selling price. (p. 230)

**Maturity date of a note** the date a note is due. (p. 594)

**Maturity value** the amount that is due on the maturity date of a note. (p. 595)

**Medicare tax** a federal tax paid for hospital insurance. (p. 312)

**Memorandum** a form on which a brief message is written describing a transaction. (p. 68)

**Merchandise** goods that a merchandising business purchases to sell. (p. 228)

**Merchandise inventory** the amount of goods on hand for sale to customers. (p. 368)

**Merchandising business** a business that purchases and sells goods. (p. 228)

## N

**Net income** the difference between total revenue and total expenses when total revenue is greater. (p. 167)

**Net loss** the difference between total revenue and total expenses when total expenses is greater. (p. 168)

**Net pay** the total earnings paid to an employee after payroll taxes and other deductions. (p. 315)

**Net purchases** total purchases less purchases discount and purchases returns and allowances. (p. 663)

**Net sales** total sales less sales discount and sales returns and allowances. (p. 663)

**Nominal account** see *temporary accounts.*

**Normal balance** the side of the account that is increased. (p. 42)

**Note** see *notes payable.*

**Notes payable** promissory notes signed by a business and given to a creditor. (p. 594)

**Notes receivable** promissory notes that a business accepts from customers. (p. 603)

**Number of a note** the number assigned to identify a specific note. (p. 594)

## O

**Opening an account** writing an account title and number on the heading of an account. (p. 101)

**Owner's equity** the amount remaining after the value of all liabilities is subtracted from the value of all assets. (p. 7)

**Owners' equity statement** a financial statement that summarizes the changes in owners' equity during a fiscal period. (p. 404)

## P

**Par value** a value assigned to a share of stock and printed on the stock certificate. (p. 666)

**Partner** each member of a partnership. (p. 226)

**Partnership** a business in which two or more persons combine their assets and skills. (p. 226)

**Pay period** the period covered by a salary payment. (p. 302)

**Payee of a note** the person or business to whom the amount of a note is payable. (p. 594)

**Payroll** the total amount earned by all employees for a pay period. (p. 302)

**Payroll register** a business form used to record payroll information. (p. 314)

**Payroll taxes** taxes based on the payroll of a business. (p. 308)

**Periodic inventory** a merchandise inventory determined by counting, weighing, or measuring items of merchandise on hand. (p. 574)

**Permanent accounts** accounts used to accumulate information from one fiscal period to the next. (p. 203)

**Perpetual inventory** a merchandise inventory determined by keeping a continuous record of increases, decreases, and balance on hand. (p. 574)

**Personal property** all property not classified as real property. (p. 547)

**Petty cash** an amount of cash kept on hand and used for making small payments. (p. 141)

**Petty cash slip** a form showing proof of a petty cash payment. (p. 142)

**Physical inventory** see *periodic inventory.*

**Plant asset record** an accounting form on which a business records information about each plant asset. (p. 553)

**Plant assets** assets that will be used for a number of years in the operation of a business. (p. 544)

**Post-closing trial balance** a trial balance prepared after the closing entries are posted. (p. 213)

**Postdated check** a check with a future date on it. (p. 128)

**Posting** transferring information from a journal entry to a ledger account. (p. 103)

**Principal of a note** the original amount of a note; sometimes referred to as face amount of a note. (p. 594)

**Promissory note** a written and signed promise to pay a sum of money at a specified time. (p. 594)

**Proprietorship** a business owned by one person. (p. 6)

**Proving cash** determining that the amount of cash agrees with the accounting records. (p. 85)

**Purchase invoice** an invoice used as a source document for recording a purchase on account transaction. (p. 233)

**Purchases allowance** credit allowed for part of the purchase price of merchandise that is not returned, resulting in a decrease in the customer's accounts payable. (p. 471)

**Purchases discount** a cash discount on purchases taken by a customer. (p. 462)

**Purchases journal** a special journal used to record only purchases of merchandise on account. (p. 455)

**Purchases return** credit allowed for the purchase price of returned merchandise, resulting in a decrease in the customer's accounts payable. (p. 471)

## R

**Ratio** a comparison between two numbers showing how many times one number exceeds the other. (p. 673)

**Real accounts** see *permanent accounts.*

**Real estate** see *real property.*

**Real property** land and anything attached to the land. (p. 547)

**Receipt** a business form giving written acknowledgement for cash received. (p. 68)

**Residual value** see *estimated salvage value.*

**Restrictive endorsement** an endorsement restricting further transfer of a check's ownership. (p. 127)

**Retail merchandising business** a merchandising business that sells to those who use or consume the goods. (p. 228)

**Retained earnings** an amount earned by a corporation and not yet distributed to stockholders. (p. 636)

**Revenue** an increase in owner's equity resulting from the operation of a business. (p. 26)

**Reversing entry** an entry made at the beginning of one fiscal period to reverse an adjusting entry made in the previous fiscal period. (p. 618)

## S

**Salary** the money paid for employee services. (p. 302)

**Sale on account** a sale for which cash will be received at a later date. (p. 26)

**Sales allowance** credit allowed a customer for part of the sales price of merchandise that is not returned, resulting in a decrease in the vendor's accounts receivable. (p. 499)

**Sales discount** a cash discount on sales. (p. 494)

**Sales invoice** an invoice used as a source document for recording a sale on account. (p. 67)

**Sales journal** a special journal used to record only sales of merchandise on account. (p. 488)

**Sales return** credit allowed a customer for the sales price of returned merchandise, resulting in a decrease in the vendor's accounts receivable. (p. 499)

**Sales slip** see *sales invoice.*

**Sales tax** a tax on a sale of merchandise or services. (p. 252)

**Salvage value** see *estimated salvage value.*

**Schedule of accounts payable** a listing of vendor accounts, account balances, and total amount due all vendors. (p. 292)

**Schedule of accounts receivable** a listing of customer accounts, account balances, and total amount due from all customers. (p. 293)

**Scrap value** see *estimated salvage value.*

**Service business** a business that performs an activity for a fee. (p. 6)

**Share of stock** each unit of ownership in a corporation. (p. 454)

**Sight draft** a draft payable on sight when the holder presents it for payment. (p. 505)

**Social security tax** a federal tax paid for old-age, survivors, and disability insurance. (p. 312)

**Sole proprietorship** see *proprietorship.*

**Source document** a business paper from which information is obtained for a journal entry. (p. 66)

**Special amount column** a journal amount column headed with an account title. (p. 66)

**Special endorsement** an endorsement indicating a new owner of a check. (p. 127)

**Special journal** a journal used to record only one kind of transaction. (p. 455)

**State unemployment tax** a state tax used to pay benefits to unemployed workers. (p. 338)

**Statement of stockholders' equity** a financial statement that shows changes in a corporation's ownership for a fiscal period. (p. 666)

**Stock ledger** a file of stock records for all merchandise on hand. (p. 576)

**Stock record** a form used to show the kind of merchandise, quantity received, quantity sold, and balance on hand. (p. 576)

**Stockholder** an owner of one or more shares of a corporation. (p. 636)

**Straight-line method of depreciation** charging an equal amount of depreciation expense for a plant asset in each year of useful life. (p. 550)

**Subsidiary ledger** a ledger that is summarized in a single general ledger account. (p. 274)

**Supplementary report** see *supporting schedule.*

**Supporting schedule** a report prepared to give details about an item on a principal financial statement. (p. 411)

## T

**T account** an accounting device used to analyze transactions. (p. 42)

**Tax base** the maximum amount of earnings on which a tax is calculated. (p. 312)

**Temporary accounts** accounts used to accumulate information until it is transferred to the owner's capital account. (p. 203)

**Terms of sale** an agreement between a buyer and a seller about payment for merchandise. (p. 233)

**Time draft** a draft that is payable at a fixed or determinable future time after it is accepted. (p. 507)

**Time of a note** the days, months, or years from the date of signing until a note is to be paid. (p. 594)

**Total earnings** the total pay due for a pay period before deductions. (p. 306)

**Trade acceptance** a form signed by a buyer at the time of a sale of merchandise in which the buyer promises to pay the seller a specified sum of money, usually at a stated time in the future. (p. 508)

**Trade discount** a reduction in the list price granted to customers. (p. 461)

**Transaction** a business activity that changes assets, liabilities, or owner's equity. (p. 9)

**Trial balance** a proof of the equality of debits and credits in a general ledger. (p. 157)

## U

**Uncollectible accounts** accounts receivable that cannot be collected. (p. 524)

## V

**Vendor** a business from which merchandise is purchased or supplies or other assets are bought. (p. 230)

## W

**Weighted-average inventory costing method** using the average cost of beginning inventory plus merchandise purchased during a fiscal period to calculate the cost of merchandise sold. (p. 580)

**Wholesale merchandising business** a business that buys and resells merchandise to retail merchandising businesses. (p. 228)

**Withdrawals** assets taken out of a business for the owner's personal use. (p. 28)

**Withholding allowance** a deduction from total earnings for each person legally supported by a taxpayer, including the employee. (p. 309)

**Work sheet** a columnar accounting form used to summarize the general ledger information needed to prepare financial statements. (p. 156)

**Working capital** the amount of total current assets less total current liabilities. (p. 673)

**Writing off an account** canceling the balance of a customer account because the customer does not pay. (p. 531)

# A


**accounts payable,** 49, 292
asset, 69–70
balance sheet, 3
cash, 10–11
chart of, 3, 45
checking, 126–130
closing entry for, 676–677
contra, 462, 526
controlling, 274
with credit balances, 676
with debit balances, 677
defined, 9
general ledger. *See* General ledger account
income summary, 204, 426. See also Income summary account
increases and decreases in, 43
on. *See* On account
opening in general ledger, 101
owner's drawing. *See* Owner's drawing account
owner's equity, 51–56
permanent, 203
posting second amount to, 104
posting to wrong, 171
reopening written off, 533–534
T. *See* T account
temporary, 203
transactions' affect on, 45–50
writing off, 531

**Accountant.** *See* Accounting at Work; Accounting in Your Career; Careers

**Account balance,** 9, 42

**Account form,** 96, 98

**Accounting**
for accrued revenue and expenses, 614–633
in ancient civilizations, 105
careers in. *See* Accounting At Work; Accounting in Your Career; Careers
for corporation, 450–690, 634
defined, 4
double-entry, 66, 76
history and, 476
for inventory, 572–591
for merchandising business, 224–449, 450–690
for notes and interest, 592–613
for partnership, 224–449
for performing artist, 77
for plant assets and depreciation, 544–571
for proprietorship, 1-223
for service business, 1–217
for uncollectible accounts receivable, 524–543

**Accounting cycle**
for corporation, 680
defined, 214
manual vs. automated, 179
for merchandising business, 438, 680
for partnership, 438
for service business, 214
*See also* Accounting period cycle

**Accounting equation,** 6–8
analyzing, 40
balance sheet and, 30–31
business activities and change in, 9–12
cash payments and, 10
defined, 7
transactions and, 26–29, 48

**Accounting estimates,** 537

**Accounting information,** 178

**Accounting period cycle,** 156, 165, 198, 214, 366, 437, 640, 660, 663, 669

**Accounting procedures**
for corporation, 450–690
for partnership, 224–449
for proprietorship, 1–223

**Accounting records**
accuracy of, 292–294
defined, 4

**Accounting system,** 452
in ancient China, 54
defined, 4
design of, 385

**Accounting at Work**
Aguirre, Pamela, 463
Chuang, John, 230
Cousins, Glenda, 376
Crawford, James W., 625
Stanhoff, Tracy, 527
Stanton, Daryl, 168
Velasquez, Arthur R., 601
Witherspoon, Mary, 74

**Accounting in Your Career**
adding a department, 41
automated accounting system, 275
business loans, 593
business opportunity, 25
business taxes, 635
cash and checking account management, 125
cash payments, 227
company benefits, 303
competitive secrets, 545
computers, 199
credit problems, 525
credit terms, 487
discounts, 453
employee costs, 331
financial reporting, 181
financial statement frequency, 421
growing the business, 253
inventory, 573
job interview, 5
journalizing standards, 65
new accounting system, 661
notes payable spreadsheet, 615
posting, 97
restaurant partnership, 391
work sheets, 155, 365

**Account number**
automated accounting, 63
defined, 99
three-digit, 99–100

**Accounts payable**
as A/P, 49
schedule of, 292

**Accounts payable ledger,** 274
completed, 284
controlling accounts, 280
opening forms, 281
posting to, 280–285
posting from cash payments journal to, 467


Index

posting credit to, 282
posting debit to, 283
posting from purchases journal to, 457
proving, 292
starting new page for vendor in, 283

**Accounts receivable**
automated accounting, 272–273
book value of, 526
posting entries for collecting written-off, 535
schedule of, 293, 502
uncollectible, 524–543, 531–536

**Accounts receivable ledger,** 274
completed, 290
controlling account, 286
opening forms, 287
posting to, 286–289
posting from cash receipts journal to, 496
posting credit to, 289
posting debit to, 288
posting from sales journal to, 490
proving, 293

**Account title,** 9

**Accrued expenses,** 621–626, 632–633

**Accrued interest expense**
adjusting entry for, 622
defined, 621
reversing entry for, 623

**Accrued interest income,** 616, 618

**Accrued revenue,** 614, 616–620
automated accounting, 632–633
reversing entry for, 618

**Accumulated depreciation,** 551

**Accuracy, importance of,** 292–294

**Adequate disclosure,** 180, 198, 390, 544, 572, 614, 622, 663

**Adjusting entry**
for accrued interest expense, 622
for accrued interest income, 617

**automated accounting,** 447, 632, 686
for corporation, 675
defined, 198
for depreciation expense, 555
general ledger accounts with posted, 210–212
for merchandise inventory, 423
for supplies inventory, 200, 424
prepaid insurance, 201, 424
recording, 200–202, 422–425
for uncollectible accounts expense, 529
on work sheet, 160–164
*See also* Adjustment

**Adjustment**
for accrued interest expense, 621
for accrued interest income, 616
analyzing and recording work sheet, 373–377
in automated accounting, 373
defined, 160
depreciation expense, 644
federal income tax expense, 646, 648
interest expense, 644
interest income, 641
merchandise inventory, 369–370, 642
partial work sheet showing, 423
planning on work sheet, 368
prepaid insurance, 162, 375–376, 643
supplies, 161, 373–374, 643
uncollectible accounts expense, 528, 641
on work sheet, 640
*See also* Adjusting entries

**Adjustments column**
errors in, 171
proving work sheet, 163

**Advising bank,** 420

**Africa**
accountancy in, 242
accounting in ancient, 105

**Allowance**
method of recording losses from uncollectible accounts, 526
purchases, 471–472

**American Business Women's Association (ABWA),** 74

**Annual report,** 627
to employees of taxes withheld, 341
letter requesting, 482

**Applied Communication**
accounting decisions, 178
accounting procedures documentation, 656
career research, 93
entrepreneur, 62
essay, 685
fax memorandum, 121
graph of sales growth, 611
income statement and balance sheet, 195
interview, 589
letter about damaged goods, 299, 517
letter of complaint, 248
letter explaining depreciation, 570
letter of first notice, 388
letter requesting annual report, 482
local business issues, 148
memo about payroll system, 327
memorandum about uncollectible account, 540
opinion memo, 630
price table, 271
public speaking, 446
report outline, 417
reports, 21
tax research, 357
resume, 37
Web page design, 220

**Asia Minor, accounting in ancient,** 105

**Assessed value,** 547

**Asset**
acquisition, 546
assessed value of, 547
on balance sheet, 13, 188, 669
categories of, 544
current, 544
defined, 7
plant, 544
record, 553

**ATM card,** 332

**Auditing,** 216, 653

**Automated Accounting**
- adjusting and closing entries for accrued revenues and expenses, 632–633
- adjusting and closing entries for proprietorships, 221
- calculating notes and interest using planning tools, 612–613
- cash control system, 149–150
- computer operation basics, 22–23
- computer safety tips, 22
- for depreciation, 571
- end-of-fiscal-period work for corporation, 518–519, 686–687
- end-of-fiscal-period work for partnership, 447
- entries for cash payments, 249–251
- entries for cash receipts, 272–273, 483–485, 518–519
- entries for purchases, 249–251, 483–485
- entries for sales, 272–273, 518–519
- error correction, 301
- financial statements, 196–197, 418–419
- general ledger accounting, 122–123
- graphs, 389
- inventory systems, 590–591
- journal entries, 358–359
- language and skills for, 38–39
- loan planner, 658–659
- manual vs. automated accounting cycle, 179
- mouse and keyboard operations, 23
- payroll accounting, 328
- payroll taxes, 358–350
- recording transactions, 94
- software database, 63
- special journals, 249–251, 272–273, 518–519
- trial balance adjustments, 373
- uncollectible accounts and write-offs, 542–543
- using special journals for corporation, 483–485

***Automated Accounting 7.0* software,** 38–39

## B

**Babylonia, early banking system in,** 105

**Bad debt,** 526. *See also* Uncollectible accounts

**Balance**
- account, 42
- column, 98
- trial. *See* Trial balance

**Balance sheet**
- accrued interest expense adjustment on, 622
- analyzing, 673
- assets section on, 188
- assets section, 669
- completed (for corporation), 672
- for corporation, 669–674
- defined, 13
- extending account balances on work sheet, 165
- heading, 187
- information on work sheet, 187–191, 408
- liabilities section on, 188, 670
- for merchandising business, 409–410
- owner's equity section of, 189–190
- for partnership, 408–412
- for proprietorship, 14, 30
- reporting changed accounting equation on, 30 31
- reporting financial information on, 13–15
- sections of, 13
- stockholders' equity section, 671
- supporting schedules for, 411

**Banking**
- bank reconciliation, 131–135, 142
- branch manager, 367
- international transactions, 420
- payroll bank account, 319
- service charge, 133–134

**Bank statement,** 131

**Batch totals,** 88

**Bill of lading,** 505

**Blank endorsement,** 127

**Board of directors,** 637

**Book value,** 526
- of accounts receivable, 526
- of plant asset, 551, 557, 559–560

**Borrowing,** 592

**Business entity,** 9

**business name,** 128
- corporation, 454, 637
- partnership, 226
- proprietorship, 6

**Business ethics,** 7
- expenses and, 663
- *See also* Professional Business Ethics

**Business plan,** 423

**Business year**
- natural, 174, 413
- *See also* Calendar year; Fiscal year; Year

## C

**Calculator tape,** 68

**Calendar year,** 174, 204. *See also* Business year; Year

**Canceled check,** 131, 134

**Capital**
- account, partners', 404
- calculating, 190
- defined, 9
- stock, 454, 666

**Careers**
- accounting assistant, 199
- accounting clerk, 25, 41, 65, 275
- accounting department assistant, 615
- accounting manager, 275, 661
- administrative assistant, 5, 125
- bank branch manager, 367
- bookkeeper, 97

Index

certified public accountant (CPA), 145, 625
credit manager, 525
financial analyst, 615
gas balancing accounting, 74
internal auditor, 453
internship program, 168
inventory specialist, 573
junior accountant, 365
office assistant, 199
office clerk, 5
office manager, 181, 227, 253
payroll department, 303
research about, 93
senior accountant, 545
staff accountant, 331
*See also* Accounting At Work; Accounting in Your Career

**Carrying totals forward,** 260–261

**Cash**
business use of, 124
buying supplies for, 235
controls, 145–150
depositing in checking account, 126
for expenses 27
for insurance, 47
journalizing purchases of merchandise for, 228–232
managing, 124
from owner as investment, 69
paid on account, 74
paid for expense, 78
paid for insurance, 72
paid to owner for personal use, 80
paid for supplies, 70
paying, 10
paying to owner for personal use, 55, 57
proving, 85, 292
purchasing merchandise for, 231
received on account, 28, 54, 79
received from owner as investment, 45
received from sales, 26, 51, 76
receiving, 9
for supplies, 46
withdrawals by partners, 241

**Cash control systems,** 124–150

**Cash credit column**
posting to general ledger, 277
posting total of, 110

**Cash debit column,** 109

**Cash discount,** 462

**Cash flows, statement of,** 682

**Cash payment,** 227
on account, 238, 462
of expense, 239
journalizing for cash purchases, 461
journalizing for expenses, 460
journalizing to replensih petty cash fund, 466
to replenish petty cash, 240

**Cash payments journal**
defined, 460
posting to accounts payable ledger from, 467
posting to general ledger from, 467
posting special amount columns to general ledger f, 468
posting separate amounts from, 467
recording expenses and purchases using, 460–464

**Cash purchases,** 461

**Cash receipts**
on account, 258, 494–495
automated accounting entries, 272–273, 518–519
journalizing from time drafts, 508
recording using cash receipts journal, 493

**Cash receipts journal**
defined, 493
posting to accounts receivable ledger from, 496
recording cash receipts using, 493
special amount columns of, 497

**Cash register tape,** 255

**Cash sale,** 254–255, 493

**Certified public accountant (CPA),** 145

**Chart of accounts**
with automated accounting, 122–123
automated accounting numbering system, 63
as COA, 49
companies with complicated, 375
defined, 45
designing, 118
Encore Music, 3, 99
Omni Import, 225
preparing, 98–121, 99
Winning Edge, Inc., 451

**Check**
canceled, 131, 134
completed, 128
computer, 484
defined, 67
dishonored, 136–137
payroll, 319–321
postdated, 128
recording voided, 129

**Checking account**
defined, 126
managing, 125

**Checking accounts,** 126–130

**Check stub**
completed, 128
deposit recorded on, 126
recording bank service charge on, 133
recording dishonored check on, 136

**Chief financial officer (CFO),** 238

**China**
accounting in ancient, 54
work day in, 281

**Chuang, John,** 230

**Closing entries**
for accounts with credit balance, 676
for accounts with debit balance, 677
for accrued expenses, 623

for accrued revenue, 618
automated accounting, 447, 632, 687
for corporation, 676
defined, 203
for dividends, 678
general ledger accounts with posted, 210–212
for income statement account, 426–430
for income statement account with credit balance, 205
for income statement account with debit balance, 206
for income summary account, 205–207, 431
for net income or loss, 431
for owner's drawing account, 208
for partners' drawing account, 432
for partnership, 433
recording, 203–209, 426–430
to record net income, 207, 678
to record net loss, 207

**COA.**
*See* Chart of accounts

**Column**
amount posted to wrong, 172
balance, 98
credit. *See* General credit column
debit. See General debit column
general amount, 66, 276
number and arrangement of journal, 229
Post. Ref. See Post. Ref. column
proving adjustments, 163
special amount, 66

**Commercial invoice,** 505

**Communication**
e-mail, 293
misspelled words in, 79
*See also* Applied Communication

**Comparative financial statements,** 192

**Component percentage,** 397–401
acceptable, 397, 664
analysis of, 184, 398
cost of merchandise sold, 398
defined, 184
gross profit on sales, 398, 400
net income, 398, 400
total expenses, 398, 400
unacceptable, 397, 400

**Computers**
components, 22–23
e-mail, 293
hand-held, 43
new accounting system with, 661
perpetual inventory using, 576
safety tips, 22
software, 38–39
*See also* Automated Accounting; Technology for Business

**Consistent reporting,** 154, 390, 581

**Contra account,** 462, 526

**Contract of sale,** 505

**Control**
business forms for, 267
cash, 145
internal categories of, 295
prenumbered documents for, 88

**Controlling accounts**
accounts payable ledger, 280
accounts receivable, 286
defined, 274
general ledger, 280

**Conversion formula,** 82

**Corporate dividends,** 636

**Corporation**
accounting for, 634
annual reports, 627
automated accounting using special journals for, 483–485, 518–519
automated financial statements for, 686–687
closing entries for, 676
defined, 454
dissolving, 564
federal income taxes, 675
financial statements for, 660
forming, 534
merchandising business organized as, 450–690
piercing the corporate veil, 470–475

**Correcting entry**
affecting customer accounts, 501
journal entry for, 116
memorandum for, 116

**Correspondent bank,** 420

**Cost, historical.** *See* Historical cost

**Costing an item,** 586

**Cost of merchandise,** 230

**Cost of merchandise sold**
calculating, 581
component percentage, 398
defined, 392

**Cousins, Glenda,** 367

**Crawford, James W.,** 625

**Credit**
analyzing credits, 45–59
defined, 42
entry, 282
letter of, 505
posting to accounts receivable ledger, 289
on T account, 98

**Credit balance**
closing entry for, 427, 676
closing income statement account with, 205
income statement account with, 427

**Credit card**
sale, 254–255, 493
slips, 256
systems, 510

**Credit column**
cash, 110
sales, 108

**Credit dividends,** 637

**Credit memorandum**
defined, 499
for sales returns and allowances, 499

**Creditor,** 594

**Credit terms,** 487. *See also* Sales terms

Index

**Credit union,** 134
**Cultural Diversity**
accounting in ancient civilizations, 105
ancient China, 54
*feng shui*, 188
professional organizations, 13
Russian business culture and accountancy, 403
U.S. cultural values, 27
valuing diversity, 551
**Current assets,** 544
**Current liabilities,** 598, 670
**Current ratio,** 673
**Customary system of measurement,** 163
**Customer**
accounts, 501
defined, 252
notes receivable from, 603
number in accounts receivable ledger, 286
under or overcharging, 288

## D

**Database,** 63
**Debit**
analyzing, 45–59
defined, 42
posting to accounts payable ledger, 283
posting to accounts receivable ledger, 288
on T account, 98
**Debit balance**
closing entry for, 428–429, 677
closing income statement account with, 206
income statement account with, 428–429
**Debit card,** 139, 332
**Debit column**
cash, 109
*See also* General debit column
**Debit dividends,** 637
**Debit entry, posting to general ledger,** 276
**Debit memorandum**
defined, 471
for purchases returns and allowances, 471–472
**Declaring a dividend,** 637
**Declining-balance method of depreciation,** 562–565
**Depreciation**
accumulated, 551
comparing methods of, 564
declining-balance method of, 562–565
partial year, 558
*See also* Depreciation expense
**Depreciation expense**
adjustment, 555, 644
calculating, 549–552, 563
defined, 549
journalizing, 553–556
journalizing annual, 554
*See also* Depreciation
***Dictionary of Occupational Titles (DOT),*** 93
**Discount**
cash, 462
cash payments on account without purchases, 463
purchases, 453, 462
sales, 494–495
trade, 461
**Dishonored check,** 136–137
**Dishonored note,** 605
**Distribution, of corporate dividends,** 636–639
**Distribution of net income statement,** 402–403
**Dividend**
closing entry for, 678
declaring, 637
defined, 636
paying, 638
**Document**
prenumbered, 88
*See also* Objective evidence; Source document
**Double declining-balance method of depreciation,** 562
**Double-entry accounting,** 66, 76
**Doubtful accounts,** 524
allowance for, 526
**Draft,** 505
sight, 505
time, 507–508
**Drawing account**
closing entry for partners', 432
partner, 404

## E

**Earnings**
retained, 636
total, 306
unequal distribution of, 403
**Earnings records, employee,** 316–317
**Electronic Federal Tax Payment System (EFTPS),** 346
**Electronic funds transfer (EFT),** 138, 320
**Electronic spreadsheet,** 584
**Employee**
cost of, 331
earnings record, 316–317
hours worked calculation, 305
income tax, 308–311, 346, 348
income tax withholding, 310–311
independent contractor vs., 322
Medicare tax, 312, 346, 348
paying, 302
payroll check, 320
salaries, 57
social security tax, 312, 346, 348
total earnings calculation, 306
withholding allowance certificate, 309
**Employer**
annual report to employees of taxes withheld, 341
annual reporting of payroll taxes, 344

IRS tax guide for, 310
Medicare tax, 336
payroll taxes, 346
quarterly federal tax return, 342–343
recording payroll taxes, 336–340
social security tax, 336
withholding taxes, 346

**Encore Music chart of accounts,** 3, 99

**Endorsement,** 127

**Entry**
adjusting. *See* Adjusting entry
correcting, 116
defined, 66
reversing, 679
to write off uncollectible account receivable, 532
*See also* Journal entry

**Equities**
defined, 7
*See also* Equity, stockholders'; Owner's equity

**Equity, stockholders',** 636, 666–668

**Errors**
calculation, 170
canceling, 109
correcting for automated accounting, 301
in journal entries, 172
overcharge or undercharge result, 288
preventing, 172
on work sheet, 170–173

**Estimated salvage value,** 549

**Estimates**
accounting, 537
inventory, 583–585

**Ethics,** 7. *See also* Professional Business Ethics

**European Community, value added tax in,** 507

**Exchange rate,** 82

**Expanded journal,** 229
at end of month, 264–265
proving, 264–265
ruling, 261, 264–265
starting new pages, 262–263

**Expense**
accrued, 621–626
cash payment of, 239
depreciation. *See* Depreciation expense
interest, 599
journalizing cash payments for, 460
matching with revenue. *See* Matching expenses with revenue
paying cash for, 27, 53, 78
section on income statement, 183
total, component percentage, 184
uncollectible accounts, 527–529

**Explore Accounting**
accounting estimates, 537
accounting and history, 476
accounting systems design, 385
alternative fiscal years, 413
annual reports, 627
audits, 653
business forms, 267
cash controls, 145
chart of accounts, 118
comparative financial statements, 192
costing an item, 586
credit card systems, 510
employee vs. independent contractor, 322
fiscal periods, 174
freight charges, 244
generally accepted accounting principles, 16
interim financial statements, 192
internal control categories, 295
leases, 566
low interest vs. cash back, 607
net income vs. taxable income, 352
owner withdrawals, 57
perpetual inventory method, 440
prenumbered documents, 88
public accounting firms, 216
revenue, 32
statement of cash flows, 682

**Exports,** 504

**Extension of time**
paying note payable issued for, 600
signing note payable for, 600

## F

**FASB.** *See* Financial Accounting Standards Board

**Fax memorandum,** 121

**Federal Deposit Insurance Corporation (FDIC),** 127

**Federal income tax**
adjustment, 648
calculating, 647
for corporation, 675
expense adjustment, 646
Federal Insurance Contributions Act (FICA), 312

**Federal Tax Deposit Coupon,** 346–347

**Federal unemployment tax,** 338, 349

***Feng shui,*** 188

**Fifo.** *See* First-in, first-out inventory costing method

**File maintenance,** 100
automated accounting, 63

**Financial Accounting Standards Board (FASB),** 16
Statement No. 13, Accounting for Leases, 566

**Financial information,** 364
in annual report, 627
on balance sheet, 13–15
recording, 452
reporting, 180

**Financial statements**
in annual report, 627
automated accounting, 418–419, 686–687
comparative, 192
for corporations, 660, 686–687
extending information on work sheet, 165–169

interim, 192
for partnership, 390–419
for proprietorship, 180–197
uses of, 390

**First-in, first-out (fifo) inventory costing method,** 578

**Fiscal period,** 156, 174
collecting note receivable issued in, 619
paying note payable signed in previous, 624

**Fiscal year**
alternative, 413
calendar year as, 204
interest at end of, 614

**Five-column journal,** 66

**FOB (free on board),** 244

**Foreign currency,** 82

**Form 8109,** 346–347

**Form 941,** 342–343, 347

**Form W-2,** 341

**Form W-3,** 344

**Form W-4,** 309

**Freight charges,** 244

## G

**GAAP.** *See* Generally accepted accounting principles

**Gain on plant assets,** 559

**GDP.** *See* Gross Domestic Product

**General amount column,** 66
posting a journal's, 276
posting amount from, 105

**General credit columns,** 107

**General debit column**
posting amount from, 103
totals of, 107

**General journal**
in automated accounting, 94–95
defined, 470
posting from, 474, 502
recording transaction using, 470–475

**General ledger**
account. *See* General ledger account
with adjusting and closing entries posted, 435–436
with automated accounting, 63, 122–123
controlling account, 280, 286
defined, 99
opening account in, 101
posting to, 96–123, 276–279
posting cash credit column total to, 277
posting from cash payments journal to, 467, 468
posting column totals from journal to, 107
with posting completed, 112–115
posting debit entry to, 276
posting from purchases journal to, 458
posting from sales journal to, 491
posting separate amounts from journal to, 103–106
posting special amount column totals of cash receipts journal to, 497
recording transactions using, 499–503
starting new page for account in, 278

**General ledger account**
after adjusting and closing entries posted, 210–212
starting new page, 278
transferring balances to work sheet, 366
transferring to work sheet, 366

**Generally accepted accounting principles (GAAP),** 16, 352, 614
on revenue, 32
rules, 216

**Ghana, unit of measurement in,** 9

**Global Perspective**
African accountancy, 242
business day, 281
business transactions, 420
foreign currency, 82
quality standards, 344
weights and measures, 163

**Going concern,** 13, 228

**Graph**
automated accounting, 389
sales growth, 611

**Greece, accounting in ancient,** 105

**Gross Domestic Product (GDP),** 239

**Gross profit**
method of estimating inventory, 583
on sales, 394, 398

## H

**Historical cost,** 230, 392, 456, 461

**History, accounting and,** 476

## I

**Imports,** 504

**Income**
interest, 604
net vs. taxable, 352

**Income statement**
affect of adjusting entry for accrued interest expense on, 622
analyzing, 664
component percentage analysis of, 184
defined, 166
distribution of net, 402–403
expenses section on, 183
extending account balances on work sheet, 166
first two sections for merchandising business, 393
heading of, 182
information on worksheet, 182
net income on, 183, 397
net loss on, 399
for partnership, 392–396
preparing, 182–186, 662–666
revenue section on, 183
with two sources of revenue and net loss, 185
uses of, 663

**Income statement account**
closing entries for, 426–430
with credit balance, 205
with debit balance, 206

**Income statement column, errors in,** 171

**Income summary account,** 426
with closing entry, 205–206
closing entry for, 207, 431
need for, 204

**Income tax, employee,** 308–311

**Independent contractor,** 322

**Insurance**
cash for, 47
paying cash for, 10, 72
prepaid. See Prepaid insurance

**Interest**
cash back vs. low, 607
collecting on note receivable, 604
defined, 595
at fiscal year end, 614
paying on note payable, 599
on promissory notes, 595

**Interest expense,** 599
accrued, 621. See also Accrued interest expense
adjustment, 644

**Interest income,** 604
accrued. *See* Accrued interest income
adjustment, 641, 616

**Interest rate,** 595
electronic calculation, 596

**Interim financial statements,** 192

**Internal control, time card system for,** 304

**Internal control categories,** 295

**Internal Revenue Service (IRS),** 174, 352
Circular E, Employer's Tax Guide, 310
Electronic Federal Tax Payment System (EFTPS), 346
Form 8109, 346–347
Form 941, 342–343
Form W-2, 341
Form W-3, 344
Form W-4, 309
independent contractor rules, 322
proprietorship rules, 57
tax rate table, 647

**International business**
business hours, 281
quality standards, 344
*See* Global Perspective

**International Chamber of Commerce,** 504

**International sale**
of goods, 420
journalizing, 506
processing, 505
recording, 504–509

**Inventory**
accounting for, 572–591
defined, 368
estimating, 583–585
merchandise, 368
most efficient quantity of, 574
periodic, 440, 574
perpetual, 440, 574
*See also* Merchandise inventory

**Inventory costing method**
comparing, 581
first-in, first-out, 578
last-in, first-out, 579
weighted-average, 580

**Inventory record,** 575

**Investment**
cash from owner as, 69
received cash from owner as, 45

**Invoice,** 67
commercial, 505
numbering, 457
purchase, 233, 471
sales, 256

**IRS.** *See* Internal Revenue Service


## J


**Job interview,** 5

**Journal**
5-column, 66
11-column, 229
automated accounting, 358–359
carrying totals forward on, 260–261
checking for errors in, 172
defined, 64
at end of fiscal period, 420
expanded, 229, 261. See also Expanded journal
not posted individually, 107
posting column totals, 278
posting column totals to general ledger from, 107
posting general amount columns on, 276
posting separate amounts to general ledger from, 103–106
posting special amount columns on, 277
proving, 82–87
purchases, 455
ruling, 82–87
sales, 488
special, 455
*See also* Entry; Journal entry

**Journal entry**
adjusting, 422
closing, 433
correcting, 116

**Journalizing,** 64
accepting note for extension of time on account receivable, 603
bank service charge, 134
buying supplies for cash, 235
buying supplies on account, 236, 473
cash paid for expense, 78
cash paid for supplies, 70
cash payment for cash purchases, 461
cash payment of expense, 239, 460
cash payment on account, 238, 462–463
cash payment for maturity value of note payable, 599
cash payment to replenish petty cash, 240
cash receipts on account, 258
cash receipts on account with sales discounts, 495

Index


cash receipts form time drafts, 508
cash received on account, 79
cash received for maturity value of note receivable, 604
cash received from owner as investment, 69
cash sales, 255, 493
cash withdrawals by partners, 241
closing entry for accounts with credit balance, 676
closing entry for dividends, 678
closing entry for net income to retained earnings, 678
correcting entries affecting customer accounts, 501
credit card sales, 255, 493
debit card transaction, 139
depreciation expense, 553–556
dishonored check, 137
dishonored note receivable, 605
electronic funds transfer, 138
employer payroll tax, 339
entry to replenish petty cash, 143
international sale, 506
paid cash for insurance, 72
payment of dividends, 638
payment of liability for employee taxes, 348
payment of liability for federal unemployment tax, 350
payment of liability for state unemployment tax, 350
payment of payroll, 334
purchase of merchandise on account, 234
purchases on account, 456
purchases and cash payments, 226–251
purchases of merchandise for cash, 228–232
purchases returns and allowances, 472
purchasing merchandise for cash, 231
receipt of cash from note payable, 598
reversing entries, 679
sale on account, 257
sales on account, 489
sales returns and allowances, 500
services sold on account, 77
signing note payable for extension of time, 600
standards for, 65
supplies bought on account, 73
time drafts, 507
transactions, 64–95
writing off an uncollectible account receivable, 531

**Journal page**
with posting completed, 112
proving, 82, 265
ruling, 83
starting new, 84


## L


**Last-in, first-out (lifo) inventory costing method,** 579

**Law**
ethics and, 7
*See also* Legal Issues in Accounting

**Leases,** 566

**Ledger**
accounts payable, 274. *See also* Accounts payable ledger
accounts receivable, 274. *See also* Accounts receivable ledger
with automated accounting, 63, 122–123
controlling accounts and 274
defined, 99
stock, 576
subsidiary, 274

**Legal Issues in Accounting**
corporation dissolution, 564
corporation formation, 534
limited liability partnerships, 364
partnership dissolution, 308
partnership formation, 254
piercing the corporate veil, 470–475
proprietorship dissolution, 80
proprietorship formation, 80

**Lending,** 592

**Letter of credit,** 420, 505

**Liabilities**
account, 74
on balance sheet, 13, 188, 670
current, 598, 670
defined, 7
long-term, 670
unlimited, 80, 254

**Lifo.** *See* Last-in, first-out (lifo) inventory costing method

**Limited liability**
of corporation, 534
partnerships (LLP), 364

**List price,** 461

**Loan, choosing,** 593

**Loan Planner (Automated Accounting),** 658–659

**Loans, Small Business Administration,** 51

**Long-term liabilities,** 670

**Loss**
net. *See* Net loss
on plant assets, 560
recording from uncollectible accounts, 526


## M


**Manual accounting, automated accounting vs.,** 38–39

**Markup,** 230

**Matching expenses with revenue,** 160–162, 182, 200, 203, 373, 375, 420, 426–428, 435, 526–527, 562, 579–580, 614, 621

**Maturity date, of promissory note,** 596

**Maturity value,** 595
of note payable, 599
of note receivable, 604

**Medicare tax,** 312
employer, 336

paying liability for, 346–347

**Memorandum,** 68
for buying supplies on account, 235
for correcting entry, 116

**Merchandise**
calculating cost of sold, 581
defined, 228
purchasing, 230
purchasing on account, 234
purchasing for cash, 231
sales of, 254
withdrawals by partners, 242

**Merchandise inventory**
adjusting entry for
adjustment for, 369, 423, 642
defined, 368
determining cost of, 578–582
determining quantity of, 574–577
importance of, 572
methods to determine quantity of, 574
recording adjustment for, 370
*See also* Inventory

**Merchandising business**
accounting cycle, 438, 680
balance sheet for, 409–410
corporation as, 450–690
defined, 228
income statement for, 393–394
partnership as, 224–449
retail, 228
wholesale, 228
work sheet for, 364–389
work sheet for (8-column), 366–372, 378–381
work sheet for (10-column), 382–383

**Metric system,** 163

**Multicultural awareness.** *See* Cultural Diversity

## N

**National Association of Black Accountants,** 13

**Natural business year,** 174, 413

**Net income**
closing entry for, 431, 678
component percentage, 184, 398
defined, 167
on income statement, 183, 397
taxable income vs., 352

**Net loss**
closing entry for, 431
income statement showing, 185, 399
owners' equity statement with, 406
recording on work sheet, 168

**Net pay,** 315

**Net purchases,** 663

**Net sales,** 663

**Normal balance,** 42

**Note payable,** 594, 598–602
paying interest on, 599
signed in previous fiscal period, 624
spreadsheet, 615

**Note receivable,** 603–606
accepting from customers, 603
collecting principal and interest on, 604
defined, 603
dishonored, 605
issued in previous fiscal period, 619

## O

**Objective evidence**
calculator tape, 68, 76
cash receipt, 258
cash register tape, 255
check, 70, 72, 74, 78, 80, 141
check stub, 128
credit memorandum, 499
debit memorandum, 471
memorandum, 73, 134, 137–138, 139
note receipt, 598
purchase invoice, 233
receipt, 79
sales invoice, 67, 77, 256, 489
source documents as, 66
*See also* Source documents

***Occupational Outlook Handbook,*** 93

**Office manager,** 227

**Omni Import chart of accounts,** 225

**On account**
buying supplies, 48, 73, 235–236, 473
cash payment, 238
cash receipts, 258, 494–495
journalizing cash payments, 462
journalizing purchases, 456
journalizing sales, 489
memorandum for buying supplies, 235
paid cash, 49, 74
purchasing merchandise, 234
received cash, 28, 54, 79
sale, 26, 32, 257
services sold, 52, 77
transactions, 11

**Opening an account,** 101

**Overtime pay,** 302

**Owner, cash paid for personal use,** 80

**Owner's drawing account,** 208. *See also* Drawing account

**Owner's equity**
accounts, 51–56
on balance sheet, 13, 189–190
changes in proprietorship affecting, 24–39
defined, 7
statement, 404–406
transactions and changes in, 28, 51–56
*See also* Equities

## P

**Parentheses, negative amounts in,** 399

**Partner**
capital account, 404
cash withdrawals by, 241
defined, 226

drawing account, 404, 432
merchandise withdrawals by, 242
*See also* Partnership

**Partnership**
accounting cycle, 438
adjusting entries for, 420–447
agreement, 254
balance sheet for, 408–412
closing entries for, 433
defined, 226
dissolving, 308
end-of-fiscal-period work (automated accounting), 447
financial statements for, 390–419
forming, 254
income division for, 406
limited liability, 364
merchandising business as, 224–449
restaurant as, 391
Revised Uniform Partnership Act, 398
*See also* Partner

**Par value,** 666

**Paying cash,** 10
on account, 11, 49
for expense, 53
to owner for personal use, 28, 55, 57

**Pay period,** 302, 348

**Payroll**
analyzing payment of, 333
automated accounting, 328
bank account, 319
checks, 319–321
defined, 302
different forms of information for, 330
journalizing payment of, 334
recording, 332–335
records, 302–328
register, 314–315, 332
time card, 304–307

**Payroll taxes,** 308
automated accounting, 358–350
employer, 336–340
employer annual reporting of, 344
employers paying, 346

**Periodic inventory,** 440, 574

**Permanent account,** 203

**Perpetual inventory,** 440, 574, 576

**Personal property,** 547

**Petty cash,** 141–144
with automated accounting, 149
cash payment to replenish, 240
replenishing, 143

**Petty cash fund,** 125
establishing, 141
journalizing cash payments to replenish, 466
making payments from, 142

**Petty cash report,** 465–466

**Petty cash slip,** 142, 149

**Philippines, value added tax,** 507

**Piercing the corporate veil,** 470

**Planning tools, automated accounting,** 612–613

**Plant asset,** 544
book value of, 551, 557, 559–560
buying, 546
depreciating, 549, 558
disposing, 557–561
gain on, 559
loss on, 560

**Plant asset record,** 553

**Point-of-sale terminals,** 576

**Post. Ref. column,** 104, 107, 265, 289

**Post-closing trial balance,** 210–215, 675, 679
defined, 213
preparing, 435–439

**Postdated check,** 128

**Posting**
to accounts payable ledger, 280–285
to accounts receivable ledger, 286
adjusting entry for accrued interest expense, 622
adjusting entry for accrued interest income, 617
adjusting entry for depreciation expense, 555
adjusting entry for uncollectible accounts expense, 529
amount from general credit column, 105
amount from general debit column, 103
cash credit column to general ledger, 277
from cash receipts journal to accounts receivable ledger, 496
cash receipts journal special amount column totals to general ledger, 497
column totals from journal to general ledger, 107
credit to accounts receivable ledger, 289
credit entry to accounts payable ledger, 282
debit to accounts payable ledger, 283
debit to accounts receivable ledger, 288
debit entry to general ledger, 276
defined, 103
entries for collecting written-off account receivable, 535
entry to write off uncollectible account receivable, 532
from general journal, 474, 502
to general ledger, 96–123, 276–279
general ledger with completed, 112–115
journal page with completed, 112
journal's column totals, 278
journal's general amount columns, 276
journal's special amount columns, 277
order from special journals, 502
proving accuracy of, 292

from purchases journal to accounts payable ledger, 457
from purchases journal to general ledger, 458
from sales journal to accounts receivable ledger, 490
from sales journal to general ledger, 491
second amount to account, 104
separate amounts from cash payments journal, 467
separate amounts from journal to general ledger, 103–106
special amount column totals to general ledger, 468
summary of, 502
total of cash credit column, 110
total of cash debit column, 109
total of sales credit column 108
to wrong account, errors in, 171

**Post Ref. column,** 112

**Prenumbered documents,** 88

**Prepaid insurance,** 10, 160
adjustment, 162, 201, 375–376, 424, 643

**Price, list,** 461

**Principal,** 595
collecting on note receivable, 604
paying on note payable, 599

**Professional Business Ethics**
business expenses, 663
discrimination vs. poor judgment, 201
fair day's work, 490
introduction, 7
privacy issues, 263
resume, 101
technology issues, 411

**Professional Organizations,** 13
American Business Women's Association (ABWA), 74
National Association of Black Accountants (NABA), 13

**Promissory note,** 594–597
defined, 594
interest on, 595
maturity date, 596

**Property tax,** 547

**Proprietorship,** 3–23
adjusting and closing entries for (automated accounting), 221
changes affecting owner's equity, 24–39
defined, 6
financial statement for, 180–197
forming and dissolving, 80
starting, 4–23

**Proving**
accounts payable ledger, 292
accounts receivable ledger, 293
accuracy of posting, 292
adjustments columns of work sheet, 163
cash, 85, 292
expanded journal at end of month, 264–265
journal at end of month, 84
journal page, 82
sales journal, 491
defined

**Public accounting firm,** 216

**Purchase invoice,** 233, 471. *See also* Invoice

**Purchases**
cash, 461
on account, 456
net, 663

**Purchases allowance,** 471–472

**Purchases discount,** 462

**Purchases journal,** 455
posting to accounts payable ledger from, 457
posting to general ledger from, 458
recording entry in, 456

**Purchases return,** 471–472

**Purchasing**
merchandise, 230
merchandise on account, 234
merchandise for cash, 231

## Q

**Quarterly federal tax return,** 342–343

## R

**Ratio,** 673

**Realization of revenue,** 26, 254, 257, 488, 524, 614

**Real property,** 547

**Receipts,** 68

**Receiving cash**
on account, 54
from sales, 51

**Reconciliation, bank,** 131–135

**Restrictive endorsement,** 127

**Retail merchandising business,** 228

**Retained earnings,** 636, 667

**Revenue**
accrued, 614
defined, 26
income statement with two sources of, 185
matching expenses with. *See* Matching expenses with revenue
section on income statement, 183
transactions, 26

**Reversing entry,** 679
for accrued interest expense, 623
for accrued interest income, 618
for accrued expenses, 623
for accrued revenue, 618
defined, 618
not using, 625

**Revised Uniform Partnership Act,** 398

**Ruled accounting paper, amounts on,** 69

**Ruling**
expanded journal to carry totals forward, 261
journal at end of month, 84, 85
journal page, 83
sales journal, 491
work sheet, 167

## S

**Safety tips, computer,** 22

**Salary**
defined, 302
employee vs. owner, 57

**Sale**
automated accounting entries, 272–273, 518–519
cash received from, 26, 51, 76
cash, 254–255
credit card, 254–255
gross profit on, 394
international, 504–509
of merchandise, 254
net, 663
on account, 32, 257, 489
of plant asset for book value, 557
of plant asset for less than book value, 560
of plant asset for more than book value, 559
terms of, 233, 462

**Sale on account,** 26

**Sales allowance**
credit memorandum for, 499
defined, 499
journalizing, 500

**Sales credit columns,** 108

**Sales discount**
cash receipts on account with, 494–495
defined, 494

**Sales invoice,** 67, 256

**Sales journal**
defined, 488
posting to accounts receivable ledger from, 490
posting to general ledger from, 491
recording sales on account using, 488–492

**Sales return**
credit memorandum for, 499
defined, 499
journalizing, 500

**Sales tax,** 252, 488, 494–495
no federal, 505

**Sales terms.** *See also* Credit terms

**Sales transaction, with automated accounting,** 272–273

**Salvage value, estimated,** 549

**Schedule of accounts payable,** 292

**Schedule of accounts receivable,** 293, 502

**Scribe,** 105

**SEC.** *See* Securities and Exchange Commission

**Securities and Exchange Commission (SEC),** 16, 192

**Service business**
accounting for, 1–217
accounting cycle for, 214
adjusting and closing entries for, 198–223
defined, 6
employment in, 73
work sheet for, 154

**Services, sold on account,** 52, 77

**Share of stock,** 454

**Sight draft,** 505

**Small Business Administration (SBA)**
advice from, 64
loans from, 51

**Small Business Spotlight,** 83, 134, 239, 286, 424, 572, 640

**Social Security Act,** 338

**Social Security Administration,** 344

**Social security number,** 308

**Social security tax,** 312
employer, 336
paying liability for, 346–347

**Software**
*Automated Accounting 7.0,* 38–39
programs for accounting, 502

**Sole proprietorship,** 6. *See* Proprietorship

**Source document**
calculator tapes, 68
debit memorandum as, 472
defined, 66
errors and, 78
memorandum, 68
receipts, 68
*See also* Objective evidence

**Special amount column,** 66, 277, 468

**Special endorsement,** 127

**Special journal,** 455
with automated accounting, 272–273, 483–485
efficiency with, 486
order of posting from, 502
recording sales and cash receipts using, 486–519

**Spreadsheet**
electronic, 142, 584
notes payable, 615

**Standard accounting practices,** 86

**Stanhoff, Tracy,** 527

**Stanton, Daryl,** 168

**Statement of cash flows,** 682

**Statement of stockholders' equity,** 666–668
retained earnings section, 667

**State unemployment tax,** 338
journalizing payment of liability for, 350

**Stock**
capital, 454, 666
share of, 454

**Stockholder,** 534
audits and, 653
defined, 636
distributing dividends to, 636
equity accounts used by corporation, 636

**Stockholders' equity**
section of balance sheet, 671
statement of, 666–668

**Stock ledger,** 576

**Stock record,** 576

**Straight-line method of depreciation,** 550, 562

**Subsidiary ledger**
defined, 274
posting to, 280–291

**Supplies**
adjusting entry for, 200, 161. See also Supplies adjustment
buying on account, 11, 48, 73, 473
paying cash for, 10, 46, 70, 235

**Supplies adjustment,** 643
analyzing, 373
recording, 374
*See also* Supplies, adjusting entry for

**Supplies inventory, adjusting entry for,** 424

**Supporting schedule,** 411

## T

**Table, price,** 271

**T account,** 40, 70
defined, 42
drawing, 55
income summary, 369, 426
merchandise inventory, 368–369
for purchases, 230
relationship to account form, 98
supplies, 369, 373
using, 42–44, 42

**Tax**
business, 635
on employer. *See* Employer
income. *See* Income tax, employee
on partnership income, 406
property, 547
rates, changing, 347
sales, 252, 488, 494
unemployment, 338
value added, 505–507

**Tax forms**
Form 8109, 346–347
Form 941, 342–343
Form W-2, 341
Form W-3, 344
Form W-4, 309

**Technology, ethics and,** 411

**Technology for Business**
bank reconciliation, 142
dining out with computers, 43
electronic spreadsheets, 142, 584
e-mail, 293
smart card, 332
software programs, 502
World Wide Web, 646

**Temporary account,** 203

**Terms of sale,** 233

**Thailand, value added tax,** 507

**Time cards, preparing payroll,** 304–307

**Time drafts,** 507–508

**Total earnings,** 306

**Totals**
batch, 88
double lines below, 261
expenses, 184, 398
work sheet, 167

**Trade acceptance,** 508

**Trade discount,** 461

**Transaction,** 24
accounting equation and, 26–29
affect on accounts, 45–50
affect on owner's equity accounts, 51–56
analyzing into debit and credit parts, 40–63
controls for cash, 145
debit card, 139
defined, 9
frequency of, 229
international business, 420
on account, 11
paid cash to owner, 28
received cash on account, 28
recording in automated accounting, 94–95
recording in general journal, 470–475, 499–503
revenue, 26

**Trial balance,** 157
automated accounting, 373, 632
errors in, 171
post-closing, 210–215, 675, 679
recording on work sheet, 367
on work sheet, 640

## U

**Uncollectible accounts**
allowance method of recording losses from, 526
defined, 524

**Uncollectible accounts expense**
adjustment, 641
analyzing and journalizing adjustment for, 528
estimating, 527
recording, 526–530
posting adjusting entry for, 529

**Uncollectible accounts receivable,** 531–536

**Unemployment tax,** 338
federal, 349. *See also* Federal unemployment tax
state. *See* Federal unemployment tax
taxable earnings, 337

**Uniform Partnership Act (UPA),** 308

**Unit of measurement**
cash, 592

Index

common, 9
currency, 82
in Ghana, 9

**Universal Product Codes (UPC),** 576

**Unlimited liability,** 80, 254

## V

**Value**
assessed, 547
cultural, 27
estimated salvage, 549
par, 666

**Value added tax,** 505–507

**Velasquez, Arthur R.,** 601

**Vendor**
defined, 230
number, 282
payments to, 238
starting new page in accounts payable ledger for, 283

**Voided check,** 129

**Voucher system,** 473

## W

**Weighted-average inventory costing method,** 580

**"What if?" questions,** 584

**Wholesale merchandising business,** 228

**Winning Edge, Inc., chart of accounts,** 451

**Withdrawals, defined,** 28

**Witherspoon, Mary,** 74

**Withholding**
allowance, 309
defined, 309
employers' taxes, 346
payroll tax, 308

**Working capital,** 673

**Work sheet**
8-column, 366–372, 378–381
10-column, 382
adjusting entries on, 160–164, 373–377
balance sheet information on, 187–191, 408
completing for income tax, 649–651
for corporation, 640–645
creating, 156–158
defined, 156
errors on, 170–173
extending balance sheet account balances on, 165
extending financial statement information on, 165–169
extending income statement account balances on, 166
general ledger account balance transfer to, 366
heading of, 156
income statement information on, 182, 392
in manual vs. automated accounting, 166
for merchandising business, 364–389
net loss on, 168
planning adjustments on, 368
prepaid insurance adjustment on, 162
proving adjustments columns, 163
recording trial balance on, 367
ruling, 167
for service business, 154
supplies adjustment on, 161
totaling, 167
trial balance on, 157
use of, 640

**World Wide Web,** 220, 646

**Writing off an account,** 531

## Y

**Year**
360- vs. 365-day, 596
calendar, 174, 204
fiscal, 413. *See* Fiscal year
natural business, 174, 413

Photo Credits

**FRONT MATTER**
p. vi: © Gibson Guitar Corp.; p. vii: West Music Company; p. viii: © Image Club Graphics; p. ix: © Image Club Graphics; p. xv: © Steve Skjold/PhotoEdit

**CHAPTER 1**
p. 5: © Greg Grosse; p. 6: © Greg Grosse; p. 10: ESP Guitar Company; p. 13: Violin made by Charles J. Rufino—Photo: Giovanni Rufino

**CHAPTER 2**
p. 25: © Greg Grosse; p. 33: Folkcraft Instruments, Winsted, CT; p. 34: West Music Company

**CHAPTER 3**
p. 41: © Greg Grosse; p. 47: West Music Company; p. 52: Photo courtesy of Gemeinhardt Co., Inc.

**CHAPTER 4**
p. 65: © Greg Grosse; p. 67: © Gibson Guitar Corp.; p. 85: West Music Company; p. 95: Copyright © 2000, Gateway 2000, Inc. Reproduced with permission. All rights reserved.

**CHAPTER 5**
p. 96: West Music Company; p. 97: © Greg Grosse; p. 98: ESP Guitar Company

**CHAPTER 6**
p. 125: © Greg Grosse/Location courtesy of CINTEL Federal Credit Union, Cincinnati, Ohio; p. 153: West Music Company

**CHAPTER 7**
p. 155: © Greg Grosse; p. 177: Oscar Schmidt, Division of Washburn International

**CHAPTER 8**
p. 181: © Greg Grosse

**CHAPTER 9**
p. 199: © Greg Grosse; p. 204: West Music Company

**CHAPTER 10**
p. 226: The Nature Company; p. 227: © Jeff Greenberg/Photo Researchers; p. 228: © Greg Grosse; p. 229: © Image Club Graphics; p. 231: The Bombay Company; p. 236: © Image Club Graphics

**CHAPTER 11**
p. 253: © Greg Grosse; p. 256: © Image Club Graphics; p. 258: The Nature Company; p. 261: © Image Club Graphics; p. 262: © Image Club Graphics; p. 265: The Nature Company

**CHAPTER 12**
p. 275: Image Copyright © PhotoDisc, Inc.; p. 277: The Nature Company; p. 280: © Image Club Graphics; p. 282: The Nature Company; p. 287: © Image Club Graphics; p. 289: © Image Club Graphics; p. 292: © Image Club Graphics; p. 300: The Nature Company

**CHAPTER 13**
p. 303: © Greg Grosse; p. 304: © P. & R. Manley/SuperStock; p. 320: © Chris Marona/Photo Researchers; p. 323: © Lois Ellen Frank/Westlight

Photo Credits

**CHAPTER 14**
p. 330: © Bruce Forster/Tony Stone Images; p. 331: © Greg Grosse/Location courtesy of Quality Central Hotel & Suites, Cincinnati, Ohio; p. 336: © John Elk/Stock, Boston; p. 338: © R. A. Clevenger/Westlight; p. 347: © Richard Pasley/Stock, Boston; p. 349: © R. Ian Lloyd/Westlight

**CHAPTER 15**
p. 365: © Greg Grosse/Location courtesy of St. Xavier High School, Cincinnati, Ohio; p. 368: © Lawrence Migdale/Stock, Boston; p. 369: Photo courtesy of Pier 1 Imports; p. 375: © John Eastcott/Yva Momatiuk/Photo Researchers; p. 376: © Fred M. Middendorf; p. 379: © Mark Adams/Westlight

**CHAPTER 16**
p. 391: © Ian O'Leary/Tony Stone Images; p. 398: © Bob Daemmrich/Stock, Boston; p. 400: The Nature Company; p. 406: The Nature Company

**CHAPTER 17**
p. 421: © Tom McCarthy/PhotoEdit; p. 423: The Bombay Company; p. 429: Photo courtesy of Pier 1 Imports; p. 433: Photo courtesy of Pier 1 Imports

**CHAPTER 18**
p. 453: Photo courtesy of Maxis, a wholly owned subsidiary of Electronic Arts; p. 454: © Greg Grosse

**CHAPTER 19**
p. 487: © Greg Grosse/Location courtesy of Ohio Valley Audio—East, Cincinnati, Ohio; p. 494: 1998 Trek Bicycle Corporation; p. 496: Photo courtesy of Golfsmith International, Inc.; p. 517: Tubbs Snowshoes, Stowe, VT, 800-882-2748

**CHAPTER 20**
p. 525: © Geoff Tompkinson/SPL/Photo Researchers; p. 540: Courtesy of K2 Snowboards

**CHAPTER 21**
p. 545: © Quest/SPL/Photo Researchers; p. 570: Black Diamond Equipment, Ltd.

**CHAPTER 22**
p. 573: © Greg Grosse/Location courtesy of King Arthur's Court Toys, Cincinnati, Ohio; p. 581: Black Diamond Equipment, Ltd.

**CHAPTER 23**
p. 593: © David Parker/SPL/Photo Researchers; p. 594: Black Diamond Equipment, Ltd.

**CHAPTER 24**
p. 615: © Greg Grosse/Location courtesy of Mariemont Theatre, Cincinnati, Ohio; p. 617: Photo courtesy of Rollerblade, Inc.; p. 631: O'Brien International, Inc.

**CHAPTER 25**
p. 635: © Billy E. Barnes/PhotoEdit; p. 636: Rossignol Ski Company, Inc.; p. 638: MIKASA SPORTS U.S.A.; p. 640: O'Brien International, Inc.

**CHAPTER 26**
p. 661: © Greg Grosse; p. 670: Black Diamond Equipment, Ltd.; p. 675: Black Diamond Equipment, Ltd.